John Ramsay's Ca

CW00348064

BRITISH DIECAST MODEL TOYS

EIGHTH EDITION

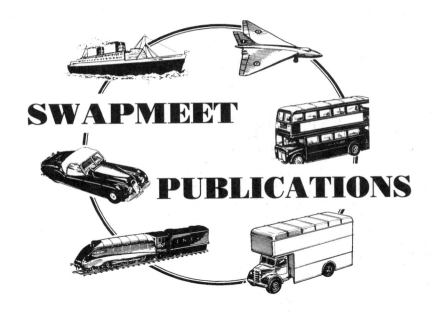

Swapmeet Publications
PO Box 47, Felixstowe, Suffolk, IP11 7LP
Phone (01394) 670700, Fax: (01394) 670730
Web site: www.swapmeet.co.uk
E-mail: info@swapmeet.co.uk

Swapmeet Toys and Models Ltd., t/a Swapmeet Publications
Reg. No. 1715966. Reg. Office: 36 Rembrandt Way, Bury St Edmunds, Suffolk. Directors: E. J. Ramsay, S. E. Ramsay, Co. Sec. M. J. Ramsay, BA

Originator and Editor
John Ramsay

Assistant Editor
John King

1st Edition published 1983
2nd Edition published 1986
3rd Edition published 1988
Update published 1989
4th Edition published 1991
5th Edition published 1993
6th Edition published 1995
7th Edition published 1997
8th Edition published 1999
(The Millennium Edition)

The contents, design and layout of this book are fully protected by copyright. Permission is hereby granted for copyright material to be quoted by publishers in newspapers, magazines and collector society publications, also by dealers in advertising matter, price lists and circulars distributed free provided that acknowledgement of the source is given. This permission does not extend to any book, catalogue or price list, album or any publication offered for sale unless prior permission has been obtained in writing in each instance from the publishers of this Catalogue: Swapmeet Toys and Models Ltd.

Copyright © 1999 by John Ramsay

ISBN 09528352 – 4 – X

Book designed by John King
Origination by Swapmeet Publications, Felixstowe
Printed by Page Bros. Ltd., Norwich
Colour sections printed by Norwich Colour Print Ltd

Front cover illustration has been taken from the Barnes Collection which was sold by Christie's of South Kensington in 1994. The pre-war models shown represent a part of the finest collection to come to the market.

CONTENTS

CONTENTS continued

Contents of 'Collectable Modern Diecasts' Section (1983 – 1999)

Dedication – to the Next Generations

Ora et labora

Mark, Caroline, Thomas, Polly, Amanda, Mark, Marianne, Alice, Debbie, Nick,

Katherine, Jim, Lisa, Benjamin and Jessica.

Also to Sally without whose patience and forbearance this Eighth Edition would not

have been published.

INTRODUCTION

Welcome to the 8th Edition of the 'British Diecast Model Toys Catalogue', now back in just one volume again.

The decision has been taken following the feedback received from many collectors and from trade sources. The process of bringing all the sections back into one volume, plus taking in a vast amount of new data, has led to some sections being reconstructed simply to save space. One big bonus for collectors is that the actual print costs have been reduced so that this single volume represents great value compared to the cost of the two 7th Edition volumes.

All the 7th Edition listings have been carefully revised and the main changes are as follows:

Dinky Toys
An exhaustive review has been instigated and collectors will find many new variations and improved listings. In particular, the 'Dinky Cars' section has been greatly enhanced by inclusion of much new information. To make the chapter more user-friendly, the 'Trains' section has been combined with the existing 'Buses, Taxis and Trams 'section to form a new 'Public Transport' section.

Corgi Toys
These listings have also been subjected to an exhaustive review. Many new variations have been included and the Corgi Junior and Husky listings have been greatly enhanced. The 'Corgi Cars' sections have been further improved by the inclusion of new variations and information, while much of the 'Miscellaneous' content has been integrated into more appropriate sections.

The 'TV and Film' Market Price Range prices reflect the strong demand for these popular models. The 'Corgi Classics' listing includes all models to the end of 1999 and these are now to be found in the new separate 'Collectable Modern Diecasts' chapter.

Matchbox Toys
These listings have been restructured and rewritten so that 1-75 'Regular Wheels' and Superfast listings now have their own separate sections. Robert Freeman has compiled a completely new Superfast section which is a great improvement over the previous listing. Horace Dunkley, the internationally renowned author of the standard 'White Book' of Models of Yesteryear has compiled a unique new 'simplified' listing to replace the previous information.

New 'Collectable Modern Diecasts' section
This section primarily includes listings of models mainly produced for adult collectors from 1980 approximately onwards. It covers Corgi Classics, Corgi 'OOC' and SuperJuniors, Matchbox Collectibles, E.F.E., Lledo 'Days Gone' and 'Vanguards', and Oxford Die-Cast. Please refer to the section introduction for details of the various factors involved in providing the Market Price guidance.

Market Prices
A pronounced feature has been the shortage of pristine boxed models coming up for sale, eg, Dinky Toys. As a result, prices achieved for the less than top quality models offered for sale have consequently often failed to reach the figures shown in the Market Price Range. This trend has led some collectors to believe that prices have fallen which we believe to be a misconception. Basically, collectors have become much more selective and models/boxes displaying faults have become priced at much lower levels than mint boxed examples. It cannot be over-emphasised that the figures provided in the 'Market Price Range' column solely relate to the likely asking prices for genuine mint models in excellent boxes. To underline this point, each section in the Catalogue now includes a specific warning to this effect.

During the past two years, the number of obsolete models sold at auction has continued to increase and the UK has experienced the emergence of online auctions. Whilst the strong pound has not helped overseas buyers, market prices for the quality boxed items have largely been maintained. Indeed, prices for the much sought after items such as the Corgi TV and Film issues have certainly increased. Prices for some of the more common issues (which were possibly overpriced) have been adjusted downwards as appropriate.

Auction Results sections
The models included have been carefully selected to provide a rich source of additional information to help support the Market Price Range figures.

New Catalogue Users Service - 'CollectorLink'
This service is aimed at bridging the gap between Catalogue editions and enables Catalogue users to keep in touch with market changes. Subscribers receive the quarterley 'CollectorLink' publication which provides an interesting combination of updating information and articles. For full details, see the 'CollectorLink' Customer Service information page at the end of the Catalogue.

Market Price Range Grading System

Based on the findings of the Market Surveys undertaken since 1983 virtually all the models have been given a 'Market Price Range'. The price gap between the lower and higher figures indicates the likely price range a collector should expect to pay for the model.

Models qualifying for a price at the top end of the range could include:

- Boxed models where both the model and the box are in pristine condition,
- A scarce or unusual colour,
- An unusual component such as special wheels
- A model with pristine decals where this is unusual
- A model in an unusual or special box,
- A model priced by a trader who disagrees with the price range quoted in the Catalogue (which is only a guide).

PRICES FOR MODELS IN LESS THAN MINT BOXED CONDITION

Many boxed models seen for sale fail to match up to the exacting standards on which the Market Price Range has been based, having slight model or box damage. In these instances models may be priced at 50% to 60% of the Market Price Range shown, and this is particularly relevant when a model is common. Boxed models with considerable damage or unboxed models will be priced at much lower level.

Note: It cannot be over-emphasised that irrespective of the price guidance provided by this Catalogue, collectors should not always expect to see prices asked within the price ranges shown. Traders will ask a price based on their trading requirements and will NOT be governed by any figures shown in this Catalogue, nor could they be reasonably expected to do so.

MODELS NOT GIVEN A 'MARKET PRICE RANGE'

It has not been possible to give every model a price range and these exceptions are as follows:

NPP   No Price Possible
This is shown alongside models never encountered in the survey and about which there is doubt as to their actual issue, even though a model may have been pictured in a catalogue. Readers will appreciate that unlike postage stamps or coins, no birth records are available in respect of all the die-cast models designed or issued.

NGPP   No Grading Possible at Present
Where a model or gift set is particularly rare and no price information whatsoever is possible, no price grading has been

shown as the Compiler believes that this is carrying rarity and value assessment into the realms of pure guesswork.
As and when information becomes available concerning these rarities it will be included in the Catalogue.

GSP   Gift Set Price

If a model forms part of a Set (and is not available separately) the price range will be shown against the entry in the relevant Gift Set section and will refer to the complete set.

NRP   Normal Retail Price

This is shown alongside models which have been recently issued or for models which have yet to attain a real collectable value. One would not expect to see asking prices for models in this grade set higher than a few pounds unless a model happens to be particulary large, e.g. a common gift set containing several models.

DESCRIPTION OF MODEL COLOURS

The descriptions of the various colours used to describe model colour variations have been derived from the following sources:-
i)   Manufacturers colour descriptions.
ii) Colours commonly used and known to refer to certain models over a period of many years.
iii) Colours which we in consultation with the trade or specialist collectors decide most closely describes a previously unrecorded genuine colour variation.
iv) Colours given a model by an bonafide auction house. If this model is a previously unrecorded colour variation we will include the variation in future catalogue listings provided that:
  a) The auction house are themselves satisfied that the model is genuine and not a repaint
  b) Specialist dealers and collectors who view the model are satisfied that the colour variation is genuine and is not a repaint.

SCARCE COLOURS AND VARIATIONS

Collectors or traders who know of other variations which they believe warrant a separate listing are invited to forward this information to the Editor together with any supporting evidence.

AUCTION PRICE REALISATIONS
Prices of common models sold are often less than the Market Price Range figures shown. In many instances, the models have been purchased by the trade who will add their own mark-up.

Classifying the condition of models and boxes

The condition of a model and its accompanying box does of course have a direct bearing on its value which makes accurate condition grading a matter of key importance.

Unlike other collecting hobbies such as stamps or coins, no one universal grading system is used to classify the condition of models and boxes. Nevertheless, whilst several versions exist, there are really two main systems of condition classification in the UK as follows:

1. The 'Specific Condition' Grading System
The following example is fairly typical of the types of descriptions and gradings seen on Mail Order lists.

M.........Mint   AM......Almost Mint
VSC ....Very Slightly Chipped   SC ....Slightly Chipped
C ....Chipped   VC.......Very Chipped

If a model is described as Mint Boxed, the condition of its box is not normally separately described. However, it is expected to be in first class and as near original condition as is possible, bearing in mind the age of the model concerned.

If a box is damaged the flaws are usually separately described. This method has always seemed to work out quite well in practice, for all reputable dealers automatically offer a 'Sale or Return if not satisfied' deal to their clients, which provides the necessary safeguard against the misrepresentation of the model's condition. The Compiler would stress that the foregoing is only an example of a mail order condition grading system and stricter box grading definitions are known to exist.

2. The 'General Condition' Grading System
This method is often used by auctioneers although it is also to be seen used on the occasional mail order list.

(M)   Mint   (E)   Excellent
(G)   Good   (F)   Fair
(P)   Poor

Usually these gradings are separately applied to describe firstly the condition of the model and secondly the condition of the box. From our observations and purely for guidance purposes, we would suggest the following descriptions approximately represent the different grades.

MODEL CONDITION GRADINGS
1. MINT (M)
The model must be complete and as fresh, new and original in appearance as when first received from the manufacturers.

2. EXCELLENT (E)
The model is almost in mint condition and is only barred from that classification by having a few slight flaws, e.g., slight paintwork chipping in unimportant areas.

3. GOOD (G)
The model is in a complete and original condition and retains an overall collectable appearance despite having a few chips or rubbed paintwork.

4. FAIR (F)
The model may not be in its original state having, for example, a broken bumper, replacement radiator or windscreen, or it may have signs of metal fatigue. The paintwork may be faded, well chipped, retouched or repainted. There may be signs of rust. Unless the model is rare it is in a barely collectable condition.

5. POOR (P)
The model may be damaged, incomplete, repainted, altered, metal fatigued, or have a rusted baseplate or heavily chipped paintwork, etc. Unless the model is rare it has little real value to a collector other than as a candidate for a complete restoration or use as spares.

BOX CONDITION GRADINGS
1. MINT (M)
The box must be complete both inside and out and contain all the original packing materials, manufacturer's leaflet and box labels. It should look as fresh, new and original in appearance as when first received from the manufacturers.

2. EXCELLENT (E)
The box is in almost mint condition but is only barred from that classification by just the odd minor blemish, e.g., there may be slight damage to the display labels caused by bad storage. The original shop price label may have been carelessly removed and caused slight damage. The cover of a bubble pack may be cracked or there may be very slight soiling etc.

3. GOOD (G)
The box is complete both inside and out, and retains an overall attractive collectable appearance. Furthermore, despite showing a few signs of wear and tear, it does not appear 'tired'.

4. FAIR (F)
The box will have a 'tired' appearance and show definite signs of wear and tear. It may be incomplete and not contain the original packing materials or leaflets. In addition it may not display all the exterior identification labels or they may be torn or soiled or a box-end flap may be missing or otherwise be slightly damaged. In this condition, unless the model is particularly rare, it will not add much to the model's value.

5. POOR (P)
The box will show considerable signs of wear and tear. It will almost certainly be badly damaged, torn, incomplete or heavily soiled and in this condition, unless it is very rare, is of little value to a collector.

Model and Box Valuation Guidelines

The research has produced the following comparative price information concerning the values of both unboxed models and separate boxes in the various condition classifications.

The guidelines have been based on the 'General Condition' grading system as described in the previous section. The percentage value ranges are designed to reflect the relatively higher values of the rarer models and boxes.

UNBOXED MODEL CLASSIFICATION	% VALUE OF MINT BOXED MODEL
Mint	50% - 60%
Excellent	40% - 50%
Good	20% - 40%
Fair	10% - 20%
Poor	0% - 10%

BOX CLASSIFICATION	%VALUE OF MINT BOXED MODEL
Mint	40% - 50%
Excellent	30% - 40%
Good	20% - 30%
Fair	10% - 20%
Poor	0% - 10%

Note: The same model may have been issued in two or more types of box (Yesteryears for example). The model in the earlier box is usually (though not always) the more valuable.

Rare Models and Sets

The exceptions to the foregoing guidelines are in respect of rare models or boxes, or models seldom found in first class condition such as some pre-war models. In these situations rarity commands a premium and the asking price or the price realised at auction will almost certainly reflect it.

Selling models to the Trade

The model value figures produced by the Price Grading system always refer to the likely *asking prices* for models.

They have been prepared solely to give collectors an idea of the amount they might reasonably expect to pay for a particular model.

The figures given are *not* intended to represent the price which will be placed on a model when it is offered for sale to a dealer. This is hardly surprising bearing in mind that the dealer is carrying all the expense of offering his customers a collecting service which costs money to maintain.

Collectors should not therefore be surprised when selling models to the trade to receive offers which may appear somewhat low in comparison with the figures shown in the Catalogue.

Dealers are always keen to replenish their stocks with quality items and will as a result normally make perfectly fair and reasonable offers for models. Indeed, depending on the particular models offered to them, the actual offer made may well at times exceed the levels indicated in the Catalogue which are only *guidelines* and not firm figures.

One last point when selling models to the trade do get quotations from two or three dealers especially if you have rare models to be sold.

How to use the Catalogue

Identifying models from their lettering

All lettering shown in CAPITAL LETTERS indicates the actual lettering on the model itself. It may appear in either the Model Type (vehicle) or Model Features (description) column. Similarly *lettering in Italics* indicates that it is shown on the actual model.

Abbreviations

In this 7th Edition dependence on abbreviations has been reduced to a minimum but where necessary they are used to include information concisely. An Abbreviations list is included (near the back of the book) and provides additional and helpful information.

Catalogue omissions

Accurate birth records do not exist in respect of all the die-cast models issued. Therefore whilst every effort has been made to provide comprehensive information it is inevitable that collectors will have knowledge of models which have not been included. Consequently the Compiler will be pleased to receive details of these models in order that they may be included in future editions. Naturally, supporting evidence regarding authenticity will be required.

This Catalogue has been prepared solely for use as a reference book and guide to the rarity and asking prices of die-cast model toys.

Whilst every care has been taken in compiling the Catalogue, neither the Compiler nor the publishers can accept any responsibility whatsoever for any financial loss which may occur as a result of its use.

BIDDLE & WEBB
of Birmingham

LADYWOOD MIDDLEWAY BIRMINGHAM B16 OPP

The Largest and Most Comprehensive Auction Rooms in the Midlands

AMPLE FREE PARKING

Catalogue subscription service

6 Toy & Juvenilia sales each year which offer vendors free insurance, free collection, advertising and photographic illustration on selected lots

An early Dinky Toys 22B closed sports Coupe sold for £350
An early Dinky Toys 28B Pickfords van sold for £640
And a similar 28K Marsh's Sausage van sold for £740

For immediate attention, further details and sales calendar please contact **Kevin Jackson**

Tel: 0121 455 8042   Fax: 0121 454 9615
E-mail: antiques@biddleandwebb.freeserve.co.uk

A. E. Dowse & Son
Sheffield

Fine Art & Antique Autioneers

Since 1915

- Full deceased estates clearance
- Single items to full houses
- Valuation for probate, insurance & family division
- Monthly antique auctions
- Monthly household auctions
- Specialist toy auctions

Cornwall Galleries
Scotland Street
Sheffield S3 7DE

Telephone: (0114) 272 5858
Fax: (0114) 249 0550

Toys & Dolls

A rare Dinky Toys *Bentalls* van sold for £3,220

Regular Auctions, each with a large and interesting die-cast section

For free valuations and advice on buying or selling, please telephone Paul Campbell on **01403 833577** Fax: 01403 833699

SOTHEBY'S SOUTH
Summers Place, Billingshurst
West Sussex RH14 9AD
www.sothebys.com

SOTHEBY'S SOUTH

Sussex

DREWEATT NEATE

FINE ART AUCTIONEERS ESTABLISHED 1759

Collectors' Sales in Central Southern England

Always strong in Dinky, Corgi, Matchbox and other diecast toys and model railways
Past results include £4,800 for a Britains Mickey Mouse set, £1,500 for a Dinky Leyland Octopus and £1,350 for a Hornby 0-gauge train set

Visit our free website for current catalogues, illustrations of major lots and a word search service:
http://www.dreweatt-neate.co.uk

For further information please contact: **Dick Henrywood** at Dreweatt Neate, Donnington Priory, Donnington, Newbury, Berkshire RG14 2JE
Telephone 01635 553553 Facsimile 01635 553599
E-mail:fineart@dreweatt-neate.co.uk

PIT STOP

Die Cast Model Specialist

Buying and Selling New and Obsolete Cars and Trains

36 High Street, Cowes, I.O.W. PO31 7RS
Tel/Fax: 01983 294173

VISA   MasterCard

World-wide Mail Order - Insurance Valuations

WANTED! Dinky, Corgi, Spot-on, Matchbox, Hornby
Trains, Victory Plastics, Minic Ships, Tinplate.

Complete collections or single items
Write, Phone or Fax your list for the best offer
Distance no object!

JOHN WORLEY OBSOLETES

'Freewaters', New Barn Lane, Gatcombe, I.O.W. PO30 3EQ
Tel: 01983 294173 (day)   01983 721439 (eve.)
Mobile: 0403 525213   john@pitstopmodels.demon.co.uk

B. & B. MILITARY
MILITARY MODELS in 1/60th and 1/55th Scale

New
Chevrolet Field Artillery Tractor
Chevrolet Field Gun Set 25-pounder
G.M.C. 6x6 Steel Cab
White Scout Car M/Gun & Tilt
Guy Ant 15 cwt G.S.
Guy Ant 5 other variations
Bedford O.B. 3-ton G.S.
Bedford O.B. 350 gal Petrol Tanker
Bedford O.B. Water Tanker
Bedford K. 3-ton G.S.
Bedford K. 350 gal Petrol Tanker
Bedford K. Water Tanker

| Trade available. |

B. & B. Commercials
5 Ex W.D. 3-ton Trucks in commercial colours
3 Bedford Petrol Tankers O.Y. O.B. and K. in
   commercial colours.   14 Dinky Transfers

Also
Karrier 3-Ton 4x4 G.S. Truck, cast canopy
90 models available and 100 figures

S.A.E for complete price list to:

LEN BULLER, 36 Cuckoo Lane, Ashford, Kent TN23 5DB.
Telephone: (01233) 632923.   Fax: (01233) 642670.

VISIT OUR WEB SITE!   http://www.bbmilitarymodels.com

MECCANO   SCHUCO   DINKY

M A T C H B O X   T R I A N G   M I N I   CORGI

'PAST PRESENT TOYS'

at 862 Green Lanes,
Winchmore Hill, London N21

For you obsolete Diecast Tinplate Toys, Trains, Dolls, Teddy Bears and related items.

MECCANO

We also have a selection of new toys, trains and teddy bears

Open: Tues, Thurs, Fri and Sat
9:30am to 4:30pm

Tel/Fax: 020 8364 1370
Sorry, no lists

 Exclusive First Editions   Gold STAR   WBritain

Y E S T E R Y E A R   H O R N B Y   W R E N

SPOT-ON

COLLECTORS

One of the best-stocked shops of old toys in Europe

*Dinky, Corgi, Matchbox, Spot-on, etc
from mint-boxed down to playworn*

Railways Hornby, Bing, Märklin, Hornby Dublo,
Tri-ang, Trix, etc.

Tin Toys Early German Lehmann, Bing, Märklin,
Money Boxes, Robots, etc.

Toys from around the world

We pay top prices for old toys

89 Northgate, Halifax HX1 1XF
01422 360434/822148/832528

Open
Mon-Sat
10:30-4:30

Closed
Thurs pm and
bank holidays

OLD TOY SHOP

When replying to advertisements, please mention 'John Ramsay's Catalogue'.

Barry Potter Auctions
The very best in collectable Toys and Trains

Each auction at The Benn Hall in Rugby includes around 250 lots of O gauge trains, 250 lots of Hornby Dublo, Wrenn and other railways and 100 lots of diecast and tinplate toys.

All lots are well described in the catalogue with estimated prices. If you have not yet seen our catalogues you will be surprised by the quality and variety of toys and trains we sell. Furthermore, you can speak to people who know the subject well and are very enthusiastic about it.

If you are interested in buying or selling, you can be in touch with no better auction company.

Our auction dates for 2000 are Saturdays: 19th February, 22nd April, 1st July, 16th September and 4th November.

Colour illustrated catalogues (only £5 post paid, or £6 overseas) can be ordered by telephone. All credit cards accepted. A six-catalogue subscription costs £24 (£27 for Europe, or rest of the world £30).

Barry Potter Auctions
13 Yew Tree Lane
Spratton
Northampton NN6 8HL

Tel: 01604 770025
Fax: 01604 771070
www.barrypotterauctions.com

SQUARE WHEELS
COLLECTABLE TOY SHOP

Holmwood Garden
High Street
Mayfield
East Sussex
TN20 6AA

Tel/Fax: 01435 873134

Offer a large selection of '00' Railway items, Hornby, Tri-ang, Wrenn, etc., plus accessories.

Obsolete Diecast: Dinky, Corgi, Spot-on, Matchbox 1-75 and Yesteryear.

Britains and other lead figures/animals.

Selection of Tinplate.

Old toys Bought, Sold and Exchanged.

Hours: 10-5 Tuesday/Thursday/Friday, 9-5 Saturday

 Mail order a pleasure

GrA's Models
New – Old – Bought – Sold

**65 Scotgate, Stamford, Lincs.
PE9 2YB**
Tel/Fax: 01780 751826
Opposite Car Park

World-Wide Mail Order Service

Stockists of: Corgi, Lledo, Dinky, Solido, Burago, Revell, EFE, Joal, Siku, Brumm, Minichamp, Vitesse, Conrad, Gama, Schabak, ERTL, etc.

Large selection of Mint & Boxed – Send SAE for 2nd-hand lists

★ CORGI GOLD STAR STOCKIST ★

Visit the lovely old town of Stamford with its ancient charms, and come to see us whilst you are here.

WANTED NOW • FOR SALE

***TOP PRICES PAID FOR:* DINKY, CORGI, MATCHBOX, SPOT-ON, YESTERYEARS, MINICS, TRAINS, TINPLATE TOYS, BRITAINS, ADVERTISING MATERIAL & CATALOGUES, ETC.**

Anything considered, will collect
Large collections, up to £100,000, a speciality
Top premiums paid for rare colours and gift sets

Just send a S.A.E. for my list of obsolete models. Over 600 items listed, mostly mint/boxed at fair prices - includes Dinky, Corgi, Matchbox, Spot-on, Tinplate, etc. with many rare items in stock. One of the best and most comprehensive sale lists available and it is FREE.

OVERSEAS TRADE VERY WELCOME, JUST SEND FAX OR PHONE FOR LIST

24 Moorland Avenue, Baildon, Nr.Bradford, W.Yorks. BD17 6RW Tel: 01274 594552   Fax: 01274 594554

INSURE Your Collection – It costs less than you think!
All Risks – No excess

Stamps and Postcards: £5,000 cover for £20 p.a.* £10,000 cover for £36 p.a.*
ALL other Collectables: £4,000 cover for £24 p.a.* £10,000 cover for £56 p.a.*
* plus Government Insurance Premium Tax

Also: Public Liability for Collector Societies; and Collectable Dealer's Scheme

C G I Services Limited trading as
Stamp Insurance Services

29 Bowhay Lane, EXETER EX4 1PE   Tel: 01392 433 949   Fax: 01392 427 632

CORGI
EXOTO
ALBEDO
DAYS G
HORNBY
ANSON
BBURAG
MAISTO
AIRFIX
REVELL
JOUEF
CARGO
GUILOY
ORIGIN
CMC CA
VANGUA
SCALEX
BRITAIN
LANSDO
BROOKL
COLLEC
UT ORIG
ITALERI
HUMBRO
MATCHB
MAJORE
AUTO A
MINICHA
ROAD
EAGL
RIO S
SOLIDO
KYOSH
VEREM
MTECH
EFE MA
SCOOP
NORSCO
CHRONO
OLD CA
MECCAN
JOAL E

PLEASE REMEMBER THAT WE ARE TRADE ONLY

If you are a trader then why not contact us and see what we can offer you?

JOHN AYREY DIE-CASTS

Bentley House, 202, Market Street
SHIPLEY, West Yorkshire, BD18 2BY
Tel: 01274 594119 or 07000 J AYREY
Fax: 01274 531505
E-mail: AYREY@msn.com

WE ARE THE UK's LEADING DIE CAST WHOLESALER STOCKING A HUGE RANGE OF MODELS, TOYS AND PLASTIC KITS, ETC

SEND FOR OUR 1999 TRADE CATALOGUE - £4.00
(including UK postage)

CUSTOMERS IN THE SOUTH!
NEW SHOWROOM OPENING IN
CHRISTCHURCH DORSET
SUMMER 1999

K.H.NORTON GROUP
Incorporating Nortons Cash & Carry

We stock the most comprehensive range of
die-cast models, plastic kits and hobby accessories available to the trade

Over 5,000 Lines Available - *Trade Buyers Only*

Massive Clearance NOW ON!

Please ring for Lists
Big Extra Discounts for Cash and Carry Purchases
Please ring or fax for terms and account details. Cash and Cary & Mail Order Service.
Full trade price lists available (Export send 2 x IRCs).
Immediate Registration and Purchase Facilities Available
Please ring or write for our die-cast or plastic kit price lists,
you will be amazed at our range and prices. Or visit our cash and carry.
Please ring if you require directions – we can post or fax them

Pingle Street, Leicester LE3 5DB Tel: (0116) 262 0601   Fax: (0116) 233 6631
E-mail: info@norton.co.uk   WWW: http://www.norton.co.uk/

International distributors & suppliers to the trade of fine scale models

New line!
Available now!
Fantastic figurines from the sporting worlds of F1, football, boxing, cricket and golf
shown at right Ian Botham and Michael Schumacher approx 10" high

starter
Featuring the Le Mans collection of every race winner since 1923 and superbly detailed rally cars not modeled elsewhere

 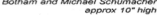 Paul's Model Art MINICHAMPS®  BRITAINS JOAL

 GATE  MIRA  ERTL EXEM

Vanguards REPLEX  QUIRALU  DetailCars COLLECTION  burago

Old Cars  Maisto. AUTOart LLEDO CORGI

PROGETTO K ORIGINAL OMNIBUS  VEM SOLIDO

Call in and choose from thousands of models at our cash and carry warehouse in the heart of England.
Open Mon - Fri 9am - 6pm.
Evenings and week-ends by appointment.
Ask for our comprehensive price list.

Pentoy Limited   The Old Garage
Priors Marston, Warks CV23 8RS England
www.e-collectable.com
e-mail: pentoy@e-collectable.com
Tel:+44(0)1327 261631 Fax: +44(0) 1327 261040

Ron's Model Rail & Diecast
THE SHOP FOR THE MODEL RAIL & DIECAST ENTHUSIAST

53 HIGH STREET, ROCHESTER, KENT ME1 1LN
Fax & Telephone: Medway (01634) 827992
Open: Mon.-Fri. 0930-1700; Sat. 0900-1700

APPOINTED 'MÄRKLIN DIGITAL' SPECIALIST
Selling: Fleischmann, Trix, Minitrix, Preiser, Kibri, Busch, Faller, Peco, Vollmer, Märklin G.1 Loco repairs
BUY, SELL, SWAP CONTINENTAL OUTLINE ITEMS (Rolling stock, Locos, etc.)
CORGI 'GOLD STAR' DEALER.
Other Diecast: Onyx, Brumm, Vitesse, Best, Bang, E.F.E., Lledo, Victoria,
Trofeu, Secondhand obsolete diecast.
WIDE RANGE OF PLASTIC KITS, GLUES, BRUSHES, PAINTS ETC.
We are successful because of you, our customers, and our good reputation.

A.B. GEE OF RIPLEY LTD.

EASTMILL, BRIDGEFOOT, BELPER, DERBYSHIRE, DE56 1XX

(15 minutes from the M1 Junctions 25, 26, 28)

Telephone (01773) 824111 (12 lines)   Fax: (01773) 828259

We are the largest model and hobby wholesaler in the country. We carry over 12,000 lines, plus a vast range of general toys and stationery.

**Opening hours between
January and September:**
Monday, Wednesday, Thursday and Friday:
8:30am - 5:00pm
Tuesday: 8:00am - 9:00pm
Saturday and Sunday: closed all day.

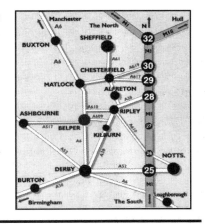

WE STOCK:

Plastic Kits	Diecast				
AIRFIX	MATTEL	ANSON	TROFEU	DAPOL(Scenics)	**Radio Control**
HELLER	BRITAINS	KYOSHO	CITY MODELS	MEHANO	
ITALERI	BBURAGO	PMA	TOP MODEL		FLY
DRAGON	CORGI	GUILOY	QUARTZO	**Slot Cars**	TYCO
ESCI	EFE	JOAL	ART MODEL		NIKKO
AMT	ERTL	MAISTO	REVIVAL	TYCO	PROSLOT
FUJIMI	LLEDO	BANG	ONYX	SCALEXTRIC	
ACADEMY	SOLIDO	BRUMM		NIKKO	
REVELL	MINICHAMPS	BEST	**Railway**	NINCO	
MATCHBOX	REVELL	OXA	RIKO (Scenics)		
		VITESSE	HORNBY		

A.B. GEE are Exclusive UK MATTEL Formula 1 and Adult Diecast Distributors. *Ferrari, Jordan, Stewart and (under non-exclusive licence) Williams and McLaren*

TRADE ONLY

PRICE LISTS AVAILABLE NOW.
Please apply in writing, enclosing a letterhead or business card.

CONTACT: Leigh, Anthony, Kev or John

The Model Shop

New Market Hall, Inverness IV1 1PJ

Corgi Collector Centre

BRITAINS, CORGI, COLIDO, VEREM, NZG,
VITESSE, E.F.E., CONRAD, TENKO

Selected Mint & Boxed Dinky when available

Postal service available

Tel: 01463 238213
Fax: 01463 223121

TOYS *Tekno* *solido* **Tri-ang** *SPOT-ON*

CORGI **DINKY TOYS**

Lesney 1-75s **MoY** *DIECAST & TINPLATE*

For Sale and Wanted Pre-1985 Models by

DAVID KERR

16 Worts Causeway, Cambridge CB1 8RL
Telephone 01223 242581

Latest sales lists now available for
Corgi, Dinky, Spot-on, etc.
Separate List for Lesney-related Toys.
S.A.E. or 3 IRCS for each list.
Best prices for pre-1985 Corgi, Dinky, Spot-on.
Lesney 1-75 all TV-related toys.
Call Now or send for list.
Visitors by appointment only please.

 UNIQUE COLLECTIONS
Established 1987
— *of Greenwich* —

Buying and selling obsolete Diecast, Dinky, Corgi,
Matchbox 1:75s, Britain's Toy Soldiers old and new
and Action Man. Triang Spot-On models/Minic Ships.

FOR SALE Diecast list available, just send in large
S.A.E. for a free comprehensive obsolete Diecast list,
or visit our website. World-wide mail order.

WANTED Obsolete Dinky, Corgi, Spot-On,
Matchbox 1:75s Diecast Toys, Britain's lead/plastic
soldiers and Action Man. Best prices paid.

Shop Opening Hours:
Monday–Friday 11 a.m. to 5.15 p.m.
Saturday and Sunday 11 a.m. to 5 p.m.

52 GREENWICH CHURCH STREET
LONDON SE10 9BL

 Tel: 0208 305 0867 *Fax:* 0208 853 1066 *Mobile:* 0410 110 760
Email: uniquecollections@compuserve.com
Website: http://WWW.Solnet.Co.uk/unique/

 # MICHAEL BOWEN
THE Specialist is in obsolete die-cast

World-wide mail order service to over 20 countries, serving the needs of the specialist collector.

For the very finest mint/boxed Dinky, Corgi, Matchbox, Lesney, Spot-on, etc.,
please send S.A.E. (1st class only) or 3 I.R.C.s for my full list of the very best in collectors' toys.

SIMPLY THE BEST!

6 Western Road, Newhaven, Sussex BN9 9JS England
Tel/Fax: 01273 513569   Mobile: 0973 308007
E-mail: dinky@mistral.co.uk   Web-site: http://www.mistral.co.uk/mbct/

David & Carole Reitsis of Quality Diecast Toys

Specialists in Mint/Boxed Dinky and Corgi Models

A first-class world-wide mail order service

See our latest stock list in Collectors Gazette and Model Collector Magazine

Tel/Fax 01443 791457   Mobile 0403 284337

www.quality-diecast-toys.co.uk   E-mail sales@quality-diecast-toys.co.uk

WANTED FOR CASH

WE ARE LOOKING TO PURCHASE COLLECTIONS OF CORGI TOYS, DINKY TOYS, MATCHBOX, EFE, CORGI CLASSICS, MINICHAMPS, ONYX, SCALEXTRIC, TINPLATE, ALL MAKES AND GAUGES OF MODEL RAILWAYS.

PLEASE CONTACT US BEFORE DISPOSING OF YOUR GOODS AS WE ARE CONFIDENT WE PAY THE BEST PRICES.

DISTANCE NO OBJECT. WE CAN COLLECT OR YOU CAN DELIVER.

FOR A QUALITY SERVICE CONTACT US NOW.

PLEASE SEND LIST OR FAX/ TELEPHONE US

SOUTHAMPTON
MODEL CENTRE

13 Junction Road, Totton, Southampton, Hampshire. SO40 9HG
Tel: (02380) 667317 (2 Lines)   Fax: (02380) 873873
E-mail: sales@southamptonmodelcentre.com

Cliff Maddock - *Vintage Toys and Collectables*

PO Box 26, Mortimer, Reading, Berks RG7 3EE
Tel: 0118 983 3062 (anytime) Mobile: 0860 786140
E-mail: cliff@maddocktoys.freeserve.co.uk
Web-site: http://www.maddocktoys.freeserve.co.uk

- Hundreds of items available on my quarterly mailing list.
- Prices to suit all pockets.
- £5 (Cheque, Stamps or IRCs) brings you four quarterly lists plus supplements as issued.
- Talk to me if selling your collection or choice items.

"BUYING OR SELLING – I OFFER A GOOD DEAL"

KERRI STANLEY
COLLECTOR OF DINKY TOYS

WANTED

FODENS, GUYS AND GIFT SETS

TELEPHONE (01245) 462694

NICK POWNER at ABBEY MODELS
42 LITTLEDOWN DRIVE, LITTLEDOWN, BOURNEMOUTH, DORSET BH7 7AQ ENGLAND
Specialists in the buying and selling of mint and boxed Dinky Toys and Corgi Toys
Personal callers welcome by appointment. Worldwide mail order service.
Tel: (9am–9pm) 01202 395999   Fax: (24hrs) 01202 395999
E-mail: npowner@bournemouth.demon.co.uk   *Internet:* http://the-internet-agency.com/abbeymodels/

DIGBYS MINIATURE AUTOMOBILES
Specialising in Model Vehicles – Worldwide

With over 15 years experience in the Model/Collectable toy car world, I am constantly looking to buy and sell any model cars, Trucks, Buses both old and new.

My stock is too diverse and numerous to list here, but callers are most welcome (by prior appointment only) to come and rummage through my stock or see me at one of the many shows that I attend. Alternatively, ring me with your specific wants.

– HONG KONG BUS MODELS –

I am now specialising in this very popular collecting Phenomenon and have over 90% of OOC models issued in stock. New models arriving all the time - why not join my mailing list and stay up to date with all that's new on the Hong Kong scene.

GEORGE HATT
16 HORSE ROAD, HILPERTON, TROWBRIDGE, WILTSHIRE BA14 7PE
TEL: 01225 768821   FAX 01225 776227

Benbros and Zebra Toys

The following history and listings of Benbros and Zebra models have been provided by Robert Newson.

Benbros was started in the late 1940s by brothers Jack and Nathan Benenson, at Walthamstow in north-east London. They first called themselves 'Benson Bros.' and made diecast toys and lead figures (some of which are marked 'Benson'). The name Benbros was adopted in 1951. One of their best known die-cast toys was a miniature coronation coach, copied from the Moko-Lesney coach. Their range of large die-cast toys was expanded during the 1950s with re-issues of

various Timpo Toys, for which Benbros had acquired the dies. The miniature 'T.V. Series' was introduced in late 1954, packed in individual boxes which resembled a 1950s television set. By 1956 there were 24 models in the T.V. Series, and soon after this the packaging was changed to red and yellow 'Mighty Midget' boxes. The Mighty Midgets were available up to 1965.

The Zebra Series was introduced in the 1960s in an attempt to update the range with better features and more accurate models. However, toy production was discontinued when Benbros was taken over in 1965.

Benbros 'T.V. Series' and 'Mighty Midgets'

Ref	Model name	Colours, features, dimensions	Market Price Range

Most models came in a very wide range of colours, so these have not been listed, but full details of colours and other variations are given in the illustrated booklet 'Benbros T.V. Series & Mighty Midgets' by Robert Newson.

Ref	Model name	Colours, features, dimensions	Market Price Range
1	Horse Drawn Hay Cart	With man and raves. Later models marked 'BENBROS'	£20-25
2	Horse Drawn Log Cart	With man and 'log', 'Made in England' under horse	£20-25
3	A.A. Motorcycle and Sidecar	With rider and separate windscreen. 'Made in England' under sidecar	£20-30
4	Stage Coach with four horses	'KANSAS STAGE' cast in, separate driver on some, 'BENBROS' on later models	£20-25
5	Horse Drawn Gipsy Caravan	No maker's name on model	£20-25
6	Horse Drawn Milk Cart	Milkman and horse, two separate or cast-in churns, 'BENBROS' on later models	£20-25
7	Three-wheeled Electric Milk Trolley	With milkman, 'EXPRESS DAIRY' cast in	£20-25
8	Foden Tractor and Log Trailer	With log (wood dowel)	£20-25
9	Dennis Fire Escape	Separate wheeled escape ladder	£20-25
10	Crawler Bulldozer	with rubber tracks	£15-20
11	Crawler Tractor with Hay Rake	Rubber tracks. Same basic casting as no. 10. No maker's name on model	£15-20
12	Army Scout Car	Separate or cast-in driver	£15-20
13	Austin Champ	Separate or cast-in driver	£15-20
14	Centurion Tank	with rubber tracks	£15-20
15	Vespa Scooter	With rider	£25-30
16	Streamlined Express Loco	('TV Series' only). Runs on four concealed wheels	£15-20
16	Chevrolet Nomad Station Wagon	('Mighty Midget' only). Most models have silver painted flash	£15-20
17	Crawler Tractor with Disc Harrow	Rubber tracks. Same tractor as no. 11. No maker's name on model	£15-20
18	Hudson Tourer	Same chassis as no. 16	£15-20
19	Crawler Tractor and Trailer	Rubber tracks. Same tractor as nos. 11 and 17. No maker's name on model	£15-20
20	Foden 8-wheel Flat Lorry	Early models in two-tone colours	£20-25
21	Foden 8-wheel Open Lorry	Early models in two-tone colours	£20-25
22	ERF Petrol Tanker	Similar to Matchbox 11a. No adverts or with 'Esso' transfer on one side	£25-30
23	AEC Box Van	No transfers. Open rear end	£20-25
23	Bedford Box Van	Without adverts or with 'Dunlop' transfers. Open rear end	£20-25
24	Field Gun	Solid wheels. No maker's name on model. Working firing mechanism	£10-15
25	Spyker	Similar to Charbens no. 2. Both models are marked with the maker's name	£10-15
26	1904 Vauxhall 5 h.p.	Same chassis as no.25	£10-15
27	1906 Rolls-Royce	Same chassis as no.25	£10-15
28	Foden 8-w Flat Lorry with Chains	'Chains' are cast with the body	£20-25
29	RAC Motorcycle and Sidecar	With rider and separate windscreen. 'Made in England' under sidecar	£20-30
30	AEC Army Box Van	Same casting as no. 23 in Military Green paint	£20-25
30	Bedford Army Box Van	Same casting as no. 23 in Military Green paint	£20-25
31	AEC Lorry with Tilt	Cast metal 'canvas' tilt, riveted in place	£20-25
31	Bedford Lorry with Tilt	Cast metal 'canvas' tilt, riveted in place	£20-25
32	AEC Compressor Lorry	Usually painted Yellow	£20-25
32	Bedford Compressor Lorry	Usually painted Yellow	£20-25
33	AEC Crane Lorry	No hook cast	£20-25
33	Bedford Crane Lorry	No hook cast	£20-25
34	A.A. Land Rover	'AA ROAD SERVICE' cast in, open rear end	£20-25
35	Army Land Rover	No lettering on sides, open rear end	£15-20
36	Royal Mail Land Rover	'ROYAL MAIL E-II-R' cast in, open rear end	£20-30
37	Wolseley Six-Eighty Police Car	A little smaller than Morestone / Budgie no. 5	£20-25
38	Daimler Ambulance	Similar to Matchbox no. 14b. Civilian or military paint	£20-25
39	Bedford Milk Float	Similar to Matchbox no. 29a	£15-20
40	American Ford Convertible	Windscreen frame and seats cast with body	£20-25
41	Army Hudson Tourer	No. 18 in Military-Green paint	£20-25

42	**Army Motorcycle and Sidecar**	Castings as nos. 3 and 29, 'Made in England' and 'AA' or 'RAC' cast on sidecar	**£20-30**
43	**Bedford Articulated Box Van**	Without adverts or with 'Dunlop' transfers, open rear end	**£20-25**
44	**Bedford Articulated Lowside Lorry**	First version has hinged tailboard, later fixed	**£20-25**
45	**Bedford Articulated Low Loader**	With log (wood dowel)	**£20-25**
46	**Bedford Articulated Petrol Tanker**	Without adverts or with 'Esso' transfer on one side	**£20-30**
47?	**Bedford Articulated Crane Lorry**	No hook cast	**£20-25**
48	**Bedford Articulated Lorry with Chains**	'Chains' are cast with the model	**£20-25**
49	**Karrier Bantam Bottle Lorry**	Similar to Matchbox 37a. 'Drink Coca-Cola' transfers. No maker's name	**£30-40**
50?	**RAC Land Rover**	'RAC ROAD SERVICE' cast in, open rear	**£20-30**

Benbros 'Zebra Toys'

Ref	Model name	Colours, features, dimensions	Market Price Range

Zebra Toys were introduced in the early 1960s and were manufactured along with the existing production of large scale Benbros vehicles. Zebra Toys were packaged in distinctive black and white striped boxes. Most of the models had jewelled headlights and some also had windows and plastic interiors.

The AA and RAC Mini Vans apparently had not been introduced when toy production by Benbros came to an end in 1965. They do not appear on a trade price list dated January 1965 but a small number of these models (probably a trial run) were sold off with the remaining toy stocks and are now in the hands of collectors.

In the following list, numbers in brackets are those shown on Zebra boxes. The other numbers are cast on the models themselves. There seems to be no connection between the two numbering systems! Original retail prices (quoted in shillings and pre-decimal pence) are those given in 1964 and 1965 trade price lists. These models are rare in today's market.

100 (16)	**Foden Concrete Mixer**	Red cab and chassis, Beige or Yellow barrel, 70 mm. (3s 1d)	**£50-60**
101 (36)	**Scammell Scarab Articulated Van 'BRITISH RAILWAYS'**	Maroon cab and trailer, Pale Orange or Mustard-Yellow tilt, 105 mm. (4s. 4d.)	**£50-60**
103 (10)	**Jaguar 'E'-type**	Metallic Light Green, Metallic Light Blue or Metallic Light Brown, 90 mm. (3s 0d)	**£75-100**
104 (30)	**Routemaster Bus**	Red, *'Fina Petrol goes a long way'* adverts, 111 mm. (4s. 11d.)	**£75-100**
106 (34)	**Heinkel Bubble Car**	Red or Blue body, 100 mm. (4s 4d)	**£75-100**
107 (27)	**Daimler Ambulance**	Cream body, 101 mm. (4s 1d)	**£75-100**
--- (20)	**Bedford Cattle Transporter**	Red cab and chassis, Light Brown body, 101 mm. (4s. 4d.)	**£50-60**
---	**Lansing Bagnall Rapide 2000**	Fork Lift Truck, Red body, 89 mm. (3s. 6d.)	**£50-60**
---	**Field Gun**	Dark Green, 'BENBROS' cast on model, 102 mm. (2s. 0d.)	**£15-20**
--- (1)	**Police Patrol Motorcycle**	(Triumph) 'Silver' plated, plastic rider, 'ENT 303' cast, 84 mm. (2s. 6d.)	**£30-40**
---	**Rally Motorcycle**	(Triumph) 'Silver' plated, plastic rider, 'ENT 303' cast, 84 mm. (2s. 6d.)	**£30-40**
--- (3)	**Army Despatch Motorcycle**	(Triumph) 'Silver' plated, plastic rider, 'ENT 303' cast, 84 mm. (2s. 6d.)	**£30-40**
--- (4)	**Telegraph Boy Motorcycle**	(Triumph) 'Silver' plated, plastic rider, 'ENT 303' cast, 84 mm. (2s. 6d.)	**£30-40**
---	**'RAC' Triumph Motorcycle and Sidecar**	Black bike, Blue sidecar, White fairing, plastic rider, 'ENT 303', 84 mm. (3s. 5d.)	**£75-100**
--- (6)	**'A.A.' Triumph Motorcycle and Sidecar**	Black bike, Yellow sidecar and fairing, plastic rider, 'ENT 303', 84 mm. (3s. 5d.)	**£75-100**
--- (60)	**Austin Mini Van**	'AA PATROL SERVICE', Yellow body. Opening side and rear doors	**£150-200**
	Austin Mini Van	'RAC', Blue body. Opening side and rear doors	**£150-200**

'Qualitoys' and other Benbros model vehicles

Model name	Colours, features, dimensions	Market Price Range

This list includes all the other vehicles in the Benbros range, mostly large scale items. Many carried the name 'Qualitoy' as well as 'Benbros', and most were individually boxed. Dating of these models is quite difficult, since there were few contemporary adverts, and the only catalogues known are trade price lists for 1964 and 1965. The Timpo re-issues were probably no earlier than 1952, and the various motorcycles were introduced in late 1955. Where a retail price is shown (in shillings and pence) the model was still available on the 1964 and 1965 price lists.

Coronation Coach with 8 horses	'ER' cast on doors, 'MADE IN ENGLAND' on drawbar. Later boxes marked 'Zebra Toys', 116 mm (3s 7d)	**£25-30**
State Landau with 4 horses	Two separate footmen. 'MADE IN ENGLAND' under coach. 105 mm. (3s 7d)	**£25-30**
Father Christmas Sleigh	With four reindeer. Metallic green or metallic blue. 110 mm. (2s 6d)	**£60-80**
Covered Wagon with 4 Bullocks	Re-issue of a model by L. Brooks (Toys) Ltd. (1958). Hollow-cast lead bullocks (diecast on the Brooks model).	**£60-80**
	'MADE IN ENGLAND' lengthwise under, Cloth canopy, Green wagon, Yellow wheels, cowboy. 186 mm	
Covered Wagon with 4 Horses	Same wagon as above. Canopy plain or with 'BUFFALO BILL'S COVERED WAGON' or	
	'CALGARY STAMPEDE COVERED WAGON' printed. Red or Green wagon (Yellow shaft) or Metallic Green or	
	Metallic Blue (Red shaft). Yellow wheels, two barrels, metal or plastic cowboy holding whip. 186 mm. (4s 8d)	**£60-80**
Rickshaw with two Passengers	Pulled by Ostrich or Zulu. Shown in the Joplin book* as Crescent, but believed to be Benbros. 150 mm	**£60-80**
Roman Chariot with two horses	With figure. Metallic Green or Yellow with Red wheels. About 135 mm	**£60-80**
Horse Drawn Farm Cart and man	Re-issue of Timpo model. Light Green or Yellow cart, Brown horse	**£50-60**
Horse Drawn Water Wagon	Re-issue of Timpo model. Light Green wagon, Brown horse	**£50-60**
Horse Drawn Log Wagon with Log	Yellow with Red wheels, or Red with Yellow wheels, or Orange with Red wheels, Brown horse. 225 mm	**£60-70**
Stephenson's Rocket		
Loco and Tender	Metallic Brown or Silver plated loco. Tender metallic Green, Metallic Blue, Orange or Red. 105 mm	**£30-40**
Caterpillar Tractor	Copy of early Lesney model. Red or Yellow or metallic Blue, rubber tracks, 97 mm. (3s 6d)	**£30-40**

Caterpillar Bulldozer ....Copy of early Lesney model. Red tractor with Black blade, or metallic Blue with Red or
....Yellow blade. Rubber tracks. 118 mm. (4s 11d) £30-40
Caterpillar Excavator with driver .....Orange (Green shovel) or metallic Blue (Red shovel), rubber tracks, Red or Green driver, 138 mm. (4s. 11d.)......£30-40
Ferguson Tractor with driver.............No name on model. Yellow or Red with unpainted wheels, metallic Green or Yellow with Red wheels, Orange with
....Black or Blue wheels. Driver Green, Brown, Blue, Metallic Blue or Grey. 73 mm. (2s 6d)................£30-35
Ferguson Tractor with
  Cab and Shovel ....No name on model. Red, Yellow or dark Green, unpainted wheels, Green or Brown driver. 100 mm £35-40
Ferguson Tractor and Log Trailer ......With driver and log. Tractor details as above. Red trailer (179mm) with yellow wheels. (4s 3d)............£40-50
Ferguson Tractor with Roller............With driver. No name on model. Former Timpo horse-drawn roller plus drawbar.
....Tractor as above, Red trailer with Yellow rollers. Trailer length 109 mm. (3s 6d)................£40-50
Ferguson Tractor with Harrow ....With driver. No name on model. Former Timpo horse-drawn harrow plus drawbar.
....Tractor as above, Red or Yellow trailer, length about 110 mm. (3s 6d) £40-50
Euclid Dumper Lorry.........................Copy of Dinky 965. Metallic Blue cab and chassis. Yellow or Orange tipper. 145mm. (5s 10d)........£50-60
Muir Hill Dumper with Driver ....Orange (Green tipper, Blue wheels), Yellow (Red or Orange tipper, Blue wheels), Metallic Green
....(Orange tipper, Blue wheels), or Red with Yellow tipper, Black wheels, 105 mm. (3s 11d)............£40-50
A101 Army Land Rover and
  Field Gun ....Open Land Rover has two figures cast, separate windscreen, metal wheels with rubber tyres.
....Field gun marked 'BENBROS', solid rubber wheels. Matt Dark Green. 111 mm. and 102 mm £60-80
A102 Lorry with Anti-Aircraft Gun..Matt dark Green, Silver gun. 117 mm................£25-30
A103 Lorry with Radar Scanner ......Matt dark Green, Silver radar dish. 117 mm £25-30
A104 Lorry with Searchlight............Matt dark Green. 117 mm £25-30
A105 Armoured Car and Field Gun..Dark Brownish-Green or matt dark Green. Field gun same as A101. 96 mm and 102 mm £30-40
A106 Army AEC Lorry with Tilt ......'SUNDERLAND' cast on cab sides. Dark Brownish-Green or matt dark Green, Green cloth tilt. 132 mm £100-125
A107 Army Closed Land Rover........Casting as A101. Matt dark Green, Black roof. Opening side and rear doors. 111 mm £40-50
A110 Army Articulated
  Low-Loader with Field Gun ....Matt Dark Green Low-loader as no. 221, Field Gun as no. A101 but with metal hubs and rubber tyres................£30-40

220 AEC Flat Lorry with chains........'SUNDERLAND' cast on cab sides. Red cab and chassis, light Green, Blue, Beige or
....Metallic Green body. 130 mm. (3s 6d)................£100-125
221 Articulated Low Loader ....Re-issue of Timpo model. Red or Green cab with Red, Yellow or metallic Green trailer.
....No name on model. 166 mm £25-30
223 Land Rover 'Royal Mail'............Red (Black roof). 'ROYAL MAIL E-II-R' cast on sides. Opening side and rear doors, 2 figures cast inside. 111mm.£100-120
224 Articulated Tanker ....Re-issue of Timpo model, no maker's name on model, 146mm (3s 6d). Red or Orange cab,
....Green or metallic Green or Yellow trailer, 'MOTOR OIL ESSO PETROL' transfer................£30-40
....Green cab, Red trailer, 'SHELL PETROL' label................£30-40
....Light Green cab, Red trailer, 'UNITED DAIRIES' transfer................£30-40
225 AEC Dropside Lorry..................'SUNDERLAND' cast on cab sides. Red cab and chassis, light Green or Blue body. 132 mm. (3s 6d) £75-100
226 Petrol Tanker ....Re-issue of Timpo model. Red cab / chassis with Red or Yellow tank, light Green
....cab / chassis with Yellow tank. 'Motor Oil Esso Petrol' or 'Fina Petrol Goes a Long Way'
....transfer. No name on model. 117 mm. (3s 1d)................£30-40

227 AEC Flat Lorry ....Re-issue of Timpo model. 'SUNDERLAND' cast on cab sides. Red cab and chassis,
....light Green, Blue or Cream body. 130 mm. (3s 1d)................£75-100
228 AEC Lorry with Tilt ....As no.225 with plain cloth tilt. 132 mm £75-100
Forward Control Box Van ....Re-issue of Timpo model, no maker's name on model. 99 mm.
....Green cab and chassis with light Green or Red body with 'Pickfords Removals' labels £30-40
....Red cab, chassis and body, plain £25-30
....Red cab and chassis, Green body, 'CHIVERS JELLIES' transfers................£30-40

Articulated Box Van ....Re-issue of Timpo model, no maker's name on model. 145 mm.
....Red or Green cab with Green, Red or Cream trailer. 'LYONS TEA' transfers.................£100-150
....Red cab with Green trailer. 'UNITED DAIRIES' transfers................£100-150
....Light Green cab with Red or Orange trailer. 'BISHOP & SONS DEPOSITORIES LTD.' transfers £100-150
A.A. Land Rover ....Casting as A107 and 223. 'AA ROAD SERVICE' cast on sides and roof sign. Opening side
....and rear doors, two figures inside. Yellow with Black roof or all Yellow. 111 mm. (5s 10d)................£100-125

310 Ruston-Bucyrus 10-RB Crane.....Maroon and Yellow body, dark Green chassis and jib, rubber tracks. 'BENBROS' cast underneath. (3s 6d)............£70-80
311 Ruston-Bucyrus
  10-RB Excavator ....Maroon and Yellow body, dark Green chassis and arms, rubber tracks. 'BENBROS' cast underneath. (3s 6d)...............£70-80
AEC Lorry and
  Ruston-Bucyrus Crane ....'SUNDERLAND' cast on cab sides. Red cab and chassis, Yellow body. Crane as
....no.310 with Maroon and Yellow body, dark green jib. 128 mm. (5s 10d) £100-125
AEC Lorry with Ruston-Bucyrus
  Excavator ....'SUNDERLAND' cast on cab sides. Red cab and chassis, Yellow body. Excavator as
....no.311 with Maroon and Yellow body, dark Green arms. 128 mm. (5s 10d) £100-125

A.A. Motorcycle and Sidecar..............Black cycle, AA badge cast on Yellow sidecar and windscreen, 'TTC147' cast on number plates. 84 mm.
....(i) Fixed front forks, windscreen with plastic glazing, dark Brownish-Green metal rider................£75-100
....(ii) Steering front forks, windscreen with curved frame cast in place of glazing, plastic rider................£75-100
RAC Motorcycle and Sidecar ....Black cycle, RAC badge cast on Blue sidecar and windscreen. 'TTC147' cast on number
....plates. Steerable front forks, windscreen with curved frame, plastic rider. 84 mm. £75-100
Solo Motorcycle with Rider ....Fixed front forks, 'TTC147' cast on number plates. 84 mm.
....(i) Police Patrol - Maroon cycle, Black metal rider................£30-40
....(ii) Telegraph Boy - Red cycle, Red metal rider................£30-40
....(iii) Army Despatch Rider - Dark Brownish-Green cycle and metal rider................£30-40
....(iv) Rally Rider - Green cycle, Blue metal rider................£30-40
Solo Motorcycle with Rider ....Steerable front forks, 'TTC147' cast on number plates. Silver plated cycles with plastic riders
....in four versions - Police Patrol, Telegraph Boy, Army Despatch Rider and Rally. 84 mm. £30-40

* Reference: 'The Great Book of Hollow-Cast Figures' by Norman Joplin (New Cavendish Books).

Britains Model Vehicles

Pre-war and early post-war

BRITAINS MOTOR VEHICLES

by Mike Richardson

Most people are aware of the military vehicles made by Britains both before the War and after in 1/32 scale to go with their soldiers, but not so many are acquainted with the contemporary civilian models. Some of these models are only colour variations of the military versions, for example the 59F 'Four-wheeled Lorry with Driver' in the farm series is the same as 1335 'Lorry, Army, Four-wheeled type' but painted in a smart duotone colour scheme instead of khaki. Other models are only available in the civilian type, usually for the good reason that the army could not possibly have a use for a militarised version. A good example of this would be 1656 'John Cobbs Railton Wonder Car' (or 'Railton Mobil Special' as we know it!).

Britains are our oldest toy company which is still in business having been started in 1860 although the first of the famous soldiers did not appear until 1890. This still means over a hundred years continuous toy manufacture, surely a record. The motor lorry models appeared in late 1932 and were based on the Albion army lorries of the time with the familiar 'square' cab design which was to be a hallmark of the Britains lorries until the end of the decade. The range of 4, 6 and 10-wheel farm lorries are still illustrated in the 1940 catalogue. After the War the cab was brought up to date by a change to a more rounded Fordson type, not nearly so attractive.

The military ambulance was also used in civilian versions, a cream 'Corporation' and a blue 'Volunteer Corps' as alternative liveries to the khaki army one. The rarest version of this model is the red and black 'Royal Mail' van which was sold for a short time towards the end of the production run.

There are three civilian cars, a 'Two-seater Coupé' and two 'Sports Model Open Tourers' in the pre-war production. The coupé and the open sports car without driver and passenger do not have military equivalents, but when the open sports car has people in it then it is either a 'Mobile Police Car with 2 Officers' (finished in green with black wings), or a 'Staff Car with 2 Officers'

as the military offering. The occupants of the car are legless and their lower regions are covered with a tartan rug - how nice for them on cold days! After the War there was a one-piece casting version of the staff car and police car without the separate grilles of the pre-war models and these were rather plain by comparison.

The final group of models consists of the superb record cars 'Bluebird' and 'Railton Special'. These came out in the late 1930s and each is over 6 inches long. The Bluebird was produced in three versions; a) with fully detailed removable chassis, b) without this part, and c) a slightly smaller one (just over 5 inches), without underside detail. The Railton Mobil Special always had the removable chassis and was available painted silver for 1s.6d. or chrome plated for 2s.6d.

After the War two new farm tractor models appeared, a couple of Fordson Majors produced with the active co-operation of the Ford Motor Company. These are excellent models both finished in the correct shade of dark blue and with the name 'Fordson' applied to the front and sides of the radiator. One version has standard wheels but the other (rarer) one had the spiked or 'spud' wheels used on heavy ground.

All these models are to the same scale as the soldiers (1/32), but there is also a similar range in '00' gauge (1/76 scale) to go with model railways. The smaller models date mainly from the post-war era although a sports car and a fastback saloon were seen pre-war. The small scale trucks have a Fordson cab similar to the later large scale farm and army lorries.

The large scale pre-war models are very collectable and prices are consequently very high for rare items in excellent condition and with original lovely boxes. Some few years ago a batch of replicas of the coupé were made here in England so exercise care when buying this model. Spare parts are, or have been available for most of these toys to enable repairs to be carried out.

Colour pictures. See the colour section following page 32.

ARMY VEHICLES

1876 Bren Gun Carrier, Carden Vickers type suspension, with Driver, Bren Gun and Gunner, and 2nd Guard.
Measures 3½" long.

1448 Staff Car, with General and Driver.
Measures 4" long.

1334 Four-wheeled Army Lorry, with Driver, Tipping body.   Measures 6" long.

1335 Six-wheeled Army Lorry, with Driver, Tipping body.   Measures 6" long.

MANUFACTURED BY  IN LONDON, ENGLAND

TRADE   MARK.

REGD. No. 459993.

An illustration from the January 1955 Britains Ltd. catalogue

Britains Motor Vehicles (pre-war issues)

The models were constructed of a lead based alloy and the main body parts were hollow cast. However, parts such as wings and running boards were die-cast individually by hand. The Market Price Range figures refer to boxed models in excellent condition.

Ref	Model name	Colours, features, dimensions	Market Price Range
59 F	Four-wheeled Lorry with Driver	Back and doors open, rubber tyres, 6"	£175-250
60 F	Six-wheeled Lorry with Driver	Two-tone Blue body, White cab roof, Silver radiator surround, back and doors open, White rubber tyres, 6"	£175-250
61 F	Ten-wheeled Lorry with Driver	Back and doors open, rubber tyres	£200-250
90 F	Builders Lorry	As 59 F plus builders name on side. 'DAVIS ESTATES LTD BUILDERS OF HOMES'	£2,000-3,000
91 F	Builders Lorry	As 60 F plus builders name on side. Never seen.	NPP
92 F	Builders Lorry	As 61 F plus builders name on side. Never seen.	NPP
1398	Sports Model Open Tourer	Cream body, Black chassis and wheels, White rubber tyres, 4.25"	£750-1,000
1399	Two-Seater Coupé (fitted bumpers)	Cream body, Tan roof, wings and running-boards, Black hubs, White tyres, 4.5". (Also in other colours)	£1,000-1,250
1413	Mobile Police Car with two Officers	2-piece casting, Green body, Black wings, White tyres, 4.75". (Also in other colours)	£500-600
1470	The Royal Household Set	Coronation State Coach, King George VI plus the Queen with twelve attendants	£300-500
1513	Volunteer Corps Ambulance with Driver, Wounded Man and Stretcher	Blue body, 'AMBULANCE', Red/White cross, White tyres	£600-700
1514	Corporation Type Motor Ambulance with Driver, Wounded Man and Stretcher	Cream body, 'AMBULANCE', Red/White cross, White tyres	£700-900
1552	'ROYAL MAIL' Van with Driver	Post-Office Red body, Black bonnet, 'GR' plus crown design, White tyres	£1,600-2,000

Military Vehicles

Early issues of lorry and truck models in the ranges 1333 - 1433 and 1641 - 1643 had 'square' cabs, (post-war issues had 'rounded' cabs).

Ref	Model name	Colours, features, dimensions	Market Price Range
1321	Armoured Car with Gun	Military Green, solid metal wheels	£100-125
1333	Lorry, Army, Caterpillar Type with Driver	Military Green finish, rubber tyres, 6"	£150-200
1334	Four-wheeled Tipper Lorry	with Driver	£150-200
1335	Lorry, Army, Six-wheeled Type with Driver	Military Green finish, rubber tyres, 6"	£150-200
1432	Tender, Army, Covered, Ten-wheeled (with Driver)	Military Green finish, White rubber tyres, 6"	£150-200
1433	Tender, Army, Covered, Ten-wheeled Caterpillar Type (with Driver)	Military Green finish, White rubber tyres, 6"	£150-200
1448	Car, Staff	Military Green car with 2 Staff Officers, White rubber tyres, 4"	£350-450
1641	Underslung Heavy Duty Lorry (18 wheels) with Driver	Military Green finish, 10"	£350-450
1641	Underslung Heavy Duty Lorry (18 wheels) with Driver	with 1749 Mounted Barrage Balloon Winch	£900-1,100
1642	Underslung Heavy Duty Lorry (18 wheels) with Driver	with Mounted Searchlight, Military Green finish, 10"	£350-450
1643	Underslung Heavy Duty Lorry (18 wheels) with Driver	with Mounted Anti-Aircraft Gun (small)	£350-450
1643	Underslung Heavy Duty Lorry (18 wheels) with Driver	with Mounted Anti-Aircraft Gun (large)	£600-800

Autogiro and Record Cars (1:43 scale)

Ref	Model name	Colours, features, dimensions	Market Price Range
1392	Autogiro	Blue body, other colours known including Military Green with pilot and three detachable rotor blades	£850-1,000
1936	Bluebird Record Car	(Napier-Campbell) Malcolm Campbell's car, lift-off body, detailed engine, White tyres	£175-200
1939	Napier Railton	John Cobb's car, '350.20 mph World Land Speed Record'	£250-300

'Circus' Series

Britains Mammoth Circus Roundabout
Six horses (Black, Brown, White) plus riders, Green, Red and Yellow Carousel canopy.
Lead and card construction. Circa 1910 .... £2,000-3,000

'Motor and Road' Series

Ref	Model name	Colours, features, dimensions	Market Price Range
1313	Volunteer Corps 'AMBULANCE'	Finished in Blue, with wounded man and stretcher	£300-400
2024	Light Goods Van with Driver	Various colours, 'BRITAINS LTD' logo	£400-500
2045	Clockwork Van (c1938)	Various colours, driver, opening rear doors. In Red box with Dark Yellow picture label	£900-1,200

NB A boxed example of 2045 with red cab and green van body, Black 'BRITAINS' logo on White background, with driver and original clockwork key sold at the Lacy, Scott & Knight 11/97 auction for £1,050

Britains Motor Vehicles (early post-war issues)

'Farm' series

59 F	**Farm Tipping Lorry** (with Driver)	Light Green or Blue, four wheels	£250-350
61F	**Farm Lorry, Ten Wheels** (with Driver)	Green, body tips, back and doors open	£350-450
127 F	**Fordson 'MAJOR' Tractor**	with Driver and spade-end wheels	£225-275
128 F	**Fordson 'MAJOR' Tractor**	with Driver and rubber-tyred wheels	£175-250

'Clockwork' series

2041	**Clockwork Unit** (2-wheeled trailer)	'Will last 1 1/2 minutes when fully wound and capable of driving any other vehicle 20-30 feet'	£45-55
2045	**Clockwork Van**	Finished in various colours with 'BRITAINS LTD' logo	£500-700

Military issues

Post-war issues of lorry and truck models in the ranges 1333 - 1433 and 1641 - 1643 had 'rounded' cabs, (pre-war issues had 'square' cabs).

1334	**Four-wheeled Tipper Lorry**	('rounded' cab) with Driver	£175-250
1335	**Six-wheeled Tipper Lorry**	('rounded' cab) with Driver	£175-250
1433	**Covered Army Truck**	('rounded' cab) Caterpillar type with Driver	£175-250
1448	**Staff Car**	with General and Driver	£350-450
1512	**Army 'AMBULANCE'**	('rounded' cab) with wounded man and stretcher	£175-250
1791	**Motorcycle Dispatch Rider**	sold unboxed	£35-50
1876	**Bren Gun Carrier with Driver, Gunner and 2nd Guard**	Carden-Vickers type suspension cast-in, separate Bren gun, 3½ "	£75-125
1877	**Beetle Lorry and Driver**		£65-85
2150	**Centurion Tank**	Military Green	£300-400
2156	**Centurion Tank**	Desert Warfare finish	£400-500
Military Set			
2048	**Military Set**	1877, 2041 and 2026 Gun	£150-200

'Lilliput' Series (1:76 scale)

LV 601	**Open Sports Car**	2.25" long	£60-70
LV 602	**Saloon Car**	2.25" long	£60-70
LV 603	**Articulated Lorry**	4" long	£60-70
LV 604	**Fordson Tractor with Driver**	1.5" long	£35-45
LV 605	**Milk Float and Horse**	with Milkman 2.25" long	£45-55
LV 606	**Tumbrel Cart and Horse**	with Hay Racks and Carter 2.75" long	£35-45
LV 607	**Austin 3-ton Covered Military Truck**		£35-45
LV 608	**Austin 3-ton Farm Truck**		£35-45
LV 609	**Austin Military Champ**		£65-75
LV 610	**Centurion Tank**		£35-45
LV 611	**Self-propelled 25-pounder Gun**		£25-35
LV 612	**Humber 1-1/2 ton Military Truck**		£35-45
LV 613	**Humber 1-1/2 ton Military Truck**	Covered version	£35-45
LV 614	**Farm Trailer**		£15-25
LV 615	**Saracen Armoured Vehicle**		£15-25
LV 616	**1½ ton Truck**		£35-45
LV 617	**Civilian Ambulance**	Cream body with 'AMBULANCE' on sides, 'BRITAINS' on rubber tyres, Red plastic hubs	£100-125
LV 618	**Army Ambulance**		NGPP
LV 619	**'ROYAL MAIL' Van**		NGPP
LV 620	**3 ton Open Truck**		NGPP

Acknowledgements

The Editor would like to express his thanks to Joe Kahn, Collectors World, 87 Portobello Road, London, W11 2QB, and to Mr E.W. Skinner of Kent and to Paul Ramsay of Croydon for kindly supplying additional information. The models listed were originally compiled for the catalogue by Mike Richardson with assistance from Norman Joplin and Steven Nagle.

Britains Auction Results

CHRISTIE'S
Britains post-war Racing Colours of Famous Owners, Lord Rosebery, Lord Astor, H.H. The Aga Khan, H.M. The King, Miss Dorothy Paget, Duke of Norfolk, Mr Winston S. Churchill and Mr H.J. Joel, in original boxes (E, boxes G, three damp staining) **£650**

A rare Britains Set 1141 The Flying Trapeze high wire act with balancing clown and suspended girl trapeze artist, twirling paper parasol, original wire and card winder, in original marbled patterned box, end label steamed open, 1936-39 (E, box G) **£2,875**

A Britains blue 59F Model Home Farm Four-wheeled Lorry (with Driver), body tips, back and doors open, in original box (F-G, box G) **£402**

A Britains green 59F Model Home Farm Four-wheeled Lorry (with Driver), body tips, back and doors open, in original box with 'Marie C. Nobel' Dutch toy retailers label (F-G, box F-G) **£345**
A Britains green 61F Model Home Farm Ten-wheeled Lorry (with Driver), body tips, back and doors open, in original box (G-E, box G) **£460**

WALLIS & WALLIS, Lewes, Sussex
A rare **Britains RHA gun team**, a late 1930s early 1940s example in khaki with troopers and officer in steel helmets, horses at the gallop, complete with the original wire traces. GC for age **£2,100**

BARRY POTTER AUCTIONS, 19th September 1998
Britains pre-war Army Co-operation Auto Giro, with pilot and all 3 rotor blades. In khaki colours with RAF roundels, Near Mint Boxed **£1,300**

Chad Valley

The Chad Valley company (makers of board games and wooden toys) produced tinplate toy vehicles from 1932 incorporating the year in the registration number on the number plates.

Their first 'Wee-Kin' diecast toy vehicles were produced around 1949 and had 'CV 1949' as the registration number. They were fitted with a key-wound clockwork motor and were designed more as toys than models having generic titles like 'Open Lorry' or 'Fire Engine'. The cars issued between 1951 and 1954 as Rootes Group promotionals are much better attempts at models and were sold at Rootes Group garages as well as normal toy shops. The tractors produced from 1952 are particularly fine and well detailed models.

The years shown below indicate the periods in which Chad Valley offered them for sale though not all the toys were available for the whole of the period and some were still in the shops well after production ceased in 1956.

Ref.	Year(s)	Model name	Colours, features, dimensions	Market Price Range

Chad Valley diecast clockwork toys and model vehicles

Ref.	Year(s)	Model name	Colours, features, dimensions	Market Price Range
220	1949-53	**Razor Edge Saloon**	Various colours, number plates 'CV 1949', approximate scale 1:43	£90-120
221	1949-53	**Traffic Control Car**	Casting as 220 plus loudspeaker, 'CV 1949', approximate scale 1:43	£90-120
222	1949-53	**Police Car**	Casting as 220 plus loudspeaker and 'POLICE' sign, 'CV 1949', scale 1:43	£90-120
223	1949-53	**Track Racer**	'CV 1949' on number plates, no other details	£90-120
224	1949-53	**Double Decker Bus**	Red body, number plates 'CV 1949', Approximate scale 1:76	£150-200
225	1949-53	**Open Lorry**	Various colours, 'CV 1949' on number plates	£100-130
226	1949-53	**Low-Loader**	Green / Red body, 'CV 1949' on number plates, three cream-coloured packing cases	£100-130
227	1949-53	**Timber Wagon**	'CV 1949', body has round bosses to fit milk churns or other 'loads'	£100-130
228	1949-53	**Cable Layer**	Red cab, Green body, silver trim, number plates 'CV 1949'	£100-130
229	1949-53	**Breakdown Lorry**	Number plates 'CV 1949', no other details	£100-130
230	1949-53	**Milk Float**	Number plates 'CV 1949', load of eight milk churns	£125-150
231	1949-53	**Fire Engine**	Red body, number plates 'CV 1949'	£100-130
232	1949-53	**Tower Repair Wagon**	Number plates 'CV 1949', no other details	£100-130
233	1949-53	**Milk Tanker**	Blue body and logo, White tank, number plates 'CV 1949'	£100-130
234	1949-53	**Petrol Tanker**	Number plates 'CV 1949', no other details	£100-130
236	1949-53	**The Hillman Minx**	Grey or Metallic Dark Blue body, Rootes Group promotional, 1:43 scale	£90-120
237	1949-53	**The Humber Super Snipe**	Metallic Dark Green body, Rootes Group promotional, 1:43 scale	£90-120
238	1949-53	**The Sunbeam-Talbot**	Light Blue or Metallic Dark Green, Rootes Group promotional, 1:43 scale. Base has the wording 'A Rootes Group Product' plus usual Chad Valley marks	£90-120
239	1949-53	**Dust Cart**	Body has tinplate sliding side panels, number plates 'CV 1949'	£100-130
240	1949-53	**Commer Avenger Coach**	Blue or Red body marked 'A Rootes Group Product', 1:76 scale, promotional	£100-150
242	1949-53	**The Commer Hands**	(6-wheel artic.), 'A Rootes Group Product', Red body with 'Commer Hands' sticker, promotional	£100-150
507	1951-54	**The Humber Hawk**	Metallic Dark Blue, Metallic Dark Green, or mid-Green body, Rootes Group promotional, 1:43 scale	£90-120
	1951-54	**Guy Van**	Dark Blue / Cream, tinplate doors, *Lyons Ice Cream Cadby Hall London W11*	£150-200
-	1951-54	**Guy Van**	Red body, Blue hubs, tinplate doors, Red 'CHAD VALLEY' logo	£150-200
-	1951-54	**Guy Van**	Green body, tinplate doors, Yellow *'Guy Motors Ltd, Commercial Vehicle Manufacturers'*	£150-200

Other issues (with or without motor)

Ref.	Year(s)	Model name	Market Price Range	Ref.	Year(s)	Model name	Market Price Range
--	1950-55	**Massey Ferguson Tractor**	£100-125	--	1950-55	**Guy Truck 'LYONS ICE CREAM'**	£100-125
--	1950-55	**Ford Tractor**	£100-125	--	1950-55	**Sunbeam-Talbot Saloon**, metallic pale brown	£75-95
--	1950-55	**Hillman Minx Saloon**	£100-125	--	1950-55	**Guy Milk Tanker**, blue /cream, 'MILK'	£75-95
--	1950-55	**Humber Super Snipe**, blue / grey body	£90-120	--	1950-55	**Guy Cable Lorry**	£75-95
--	1950-55	**Guy Truck**	£75-95	--	1950-55	**Guy Petrol Tanker 'REGENT PETROL'**	£100-125
--	1950-55	**Sunbeam Racer**	£100-125	--	1950-55	**Guy 'FIRE' Engine**	£100-125
--	1950-55	**Humber Hawk**	£75-95	--	1950-55	**Guy Container Lorry**	£75-95
--	1950-55	**Rolls-Royce Razor Edge Saloon**	£75-95		1950-55	**Guy Refuse Lorry**	£75-95
--	1950-55	**Routemaster London Bus**	£100-125				
--	1950-55	**Commer Avenger Coach**	£100-125				

Chad Valley model Tractors

--	1952	**Fordson Major E27N**	Dark Blue body, Orange wheels, rubber tyres (2 types of tread on rear), steering, towbar with pin, clockwork wound by starting handle. Scale 1:16. Illustrated box or plain box with small label	£150-200
--	1954	**Fordson Major DDN**	Mid-Blue body, Orange wheels, rubber tyres, working steering, lifting bonnet, towbar/pin, hydraulic lift at rear (detachable centre arm), clockwork wound through rear hub. Scale 1:16. Illustrated box or plain box with small label	£150-200
		Static version:	As previous model but without clockwork but without clockwork operation. Illustrated box or plain box plus small label. The word 'working' is deleted from all sides of box	£150-200
		Chrome version:	Static (non-clockwork) version in chrome plate, with or without wooden plinth. Thought to be a ploughing trophy or Ford presentation model	£250-400
--	1955	**Ford Dexta**	Mid-Blue, Orange wheels, radiator panels and 'Fordson Dexta', not steerable, rubber tyres, hook, 1:16. Illustrated box	£400-600
--	1955	**Ferguson**	Green, Red wheels, 'Ferguson' on sides, steering, hook, scale 1:16. Illustrated box inscribed 'Ferguson'. Promotional	£500-700
			Grey body, Grey wheels, hydraulic lift at rear	£600-800
--	1955	**Fordson Major E27N**	Red and Yellow with driver, clockwork, scale 1:43, boxed. Made under licence by 'Raybro & Sturdy Products S.A.', Johannesburg, South Africa (model marked 'Chad Valley GB')	£50-100

The introduction to the Chad Valley section was written by Sue Richardson who also provided the basic listing. Additional listing information came from the Cecil Gibson archives and John G. Butler of Berkhampstead, Herts.

Charbens Toys

The following history and listings have been researched by Robert Newson and Swapmeet Publications.

The firm of Charbens & Co. was started around 1928 by Charles and Benjamin Reid and was based at Hornsey Road, Holloway, London N7. They made hollow-cast lead figures, and a few lead vehicles were also produced in the 1930s. After the war zinc die-casting was introduced, and some items exist in both lead and zinc versions (the latter from new dies). Zinc castings by Charbens very often have metal failure as a result of contamination from the lead that was still used extensively in the factory.

The 'Old Crocks' series of miniature models was introduced in 1955. After 1967 all vehicle models were deleted from the catalogue except for a few items included in sets with plastic figures. Production of figures was discontinued in 1973.

Model numbers were allocated around 1954, so items which had already been withdrawn are not numbered. Dates of issue have been taken from catalogues or adverts, but inevitably are incomplete. Most pre-war items have 'RD' cast in, most post-war items have 'CHARBENS' cast underneath.
Colour pictures. See the colour section following page 32.

Ref.	Year(s)	Model name	Colours, features, dimensions	Market Price Range

Pre-war issues (part hollow-cast, part diecast construction)

-	-	Motorcycle Policeman	Solid cast machine with green petrol tank	NGPP
-	-	Police Motor Cycle and Sidecar	Solid cast machine, rider and passenger in black / white uniforms, black sidecar	NGPP
-	-	Soap Box Racer	Solid cast brown base, four red wheels (six spokes), Cub Scout pushing, Cub Scout rider	NGPP
-	-	Goat Cart with Girl	Blue cart and girl, brown goat, yellow 6-spoke wheels	NGPP
-	-	Goat Cart with Girl	Red cart and girl, white goat, 6-spoke wheels	NGPP
-	-	Road Workers Set	Contains Horse Roller (green / orange / brown), orange / black tar boiler truck with 6-spoke wheels, plus 4 workmen, a nightwatchman, hut, brazier, 'Road up' sign, pipe and 2 barriers	£150-180
-	-	Gypsy Caravan	Blue / white caravan with white horse, yellow wheels (smaller at front) plus orange / black seated Gypsy woman with baby, standing man, linen line with washing, cooking pot	£200-250
-	-	The Farm Wagon	Green / yellow four-wheel wagon with two hay racks, brown carthorse, cream / black carter figure. In red card box with cream label.	NGPP
-	-	Tumbril Cart (two wheels)	Green / yellow cart with two hay racks, brown horse, cream / black carter, cream card box	NGPP
-	-	Coster Cart with Donkey	Green / yellow cart, solid sides, grey donkey, costermonger figure (see 24 below)	NGPP
-	-	Organ Grinder's Cart (two wheels)	Brown / yellow organ, grey donkey, red monkey with mug, brown / green organ-grinder	NGPP
-	-	Governor's Cart (two wheels)	Yellow / black, cream / red or brown / black cart, 2 children, donkey, zoo-keeper figure	NGPP
-	-	Milk Float (two wheels)	Yellow / red cart with 'PURE MILK' cast in. Brown horse, milkman figure (see 25)	NGPP
-	-	Milk Float (four wheels)	Orange / white body with 'UNITED DAIRIES', 'PASTEURISED MILK' and 'CREAM' logo. 8-spoke wheels with rubber tyres, brown horse, white / blue milkman with bottle	NGPP
-	-	Cape Cart (two wheels)	Enclosed dark blue body and roof, brown horse, mid-blue figure	NGPP
-	-	Tree Wagon (four wheels)	Yellow / red log carrier, 12-spoke wheels, 4 horses, 2 white figures with poles, (see also 1)	NGPP
-	-	Dairy Float (four wheels)	Mid-blue, 'EXPRESS DAIRY', 'PURE MILK', 'BUTTER & EGGS', white shafts, brown horse, 8-spoke wheels, rubber tyres, white / blue milkman holding bottle	NGPP
-	-	Coal Cart (four wheels)	Black cart, coalman and coal sack, white / orange horse, 12-spoke wheels	NGPP
-	-	Coffee Stall (four wheels)	Orange / yellow stall, silver chimney, brown / white horse, tea urn and crockery	NGPP
-	-	Railway Wagon (four wheels)	Grey / red open wagon, 'London Midland Scottish Railway' cast in, driver, white horse	NGPP
-	-	Horse-Drawn Grass Cutter	Yellow / red cutter, brown driver and horse (see also 3)	NGPP
-	-	Horse-Drawn Roller	Green / yellow roller, brown driver and horse (see also 2)	NGPP

Pre-war Motor Vehicles (all cast in lead)

6	**Petrol Tanker**. Red, blue, yellow	
524	**Fire Engine**. Cast-in driver, separate laddes, rubber tyres	
525	**Car and Caravan**. Six-light saloon car (red, green or yellow); Caravan copied from Dinky Toys 30g, yellow with orange lower half	
526	**Motor Van**. No details	
728	**Ambulance**. Man cast on rear step. Green or brown	
864	**Racing Car**. Pale blue, green or yellow	
865	**Breakdown Lorry**. No details	
---	**Bentley Ambulance**. Copy of Dinky Toys 24a in off-white	
---	**1935 Bluebird**. Blue body	

---	**Caterpillar Tractor**. Copy of Tootsietoy but larger. 'MIMIC TOY' cast undeneath	
---	**Tank**. Copy of Tootsietoy. 'MIMIC TOY' cast undeneath. Very dark blue.	
---	**Armoured Car**. Six wheels, brown.	
---	**Mack Stake Lorry**. Copy of Tootsietoy. Green and red	
---	**Mack Lorry with AA Gun**. Copy of Tootsietoy. Light brown, black and silver	
---	**Mack Searchlight Lorry**. Copy of Tootsietoy. Light brown and black	
---	**Mack Barrage Ballon Set**. No details. Johillco made a similar set	

Post-war issues (mostly all-diecast construction)

-	late 1940s	**Packard Saloon**. 'JAVELIN' name cast underneath. Red or green	
-	late 1940s	**Petrol Tanker**. Different from the pre-war tanker. Red, Green or Blue	
-	late 1940s	**Station Wagon**. Tan with dark brown bonnet and wings, spare wheel at rear	
1	1940s-60	**Horse-Drawn Log Wagon**. Yellow, red wheels, with man, two tandem horses, wooden log, cream card box	
2	1940s-67	**Horse-Drawn Roller**. Yellow with green or red roller, with horse and man (seated)	

3	1940s-67	**Horse-drawn Grass Cutter**. Yellow, red wheels, unpainted cutter, with horse and man (seated)	
4	1940s-67	**Horse-drawn Two-wheel Farm Wagon with Raves**. Green wagon, yellow shafts and wheels	
5	1940s-67	**Horse-drawn Four-wheel Farm Wagon with Raves**. Green wagon, yellow shafts and wheels	£45-60
6	1940s-67	**Tractor with Driver**. Red or orange with metal wheels or blue with rubber wheels	
7	1940s-62	**Horse-drawn Van with Man**. Blue with cream upper half, metal wheels, 'HOVIS BREAD' or 'PURE MILK' labels. Orange with light brown upper half, rubber wheels, 'HOVIS BREAD' labels	

8	1940s-62	**Tipper Lorry**. Cab/tipper colours include: red/cream, blue/cream, dark green/yellow, orange/yellow.........................
9	1940s-62	**Motor Coach**. Yellow with red flash, dark red with cream flash, dark blue with green flash, light green with blue flash, beige with green flash......................
10 to 14		**Light Vans**. Two castings known. The first was a small boxy van with no rear windows. The second (from the early 1950s) was larger and more rounded, resembling a Ford E83W, with two rear windows.
10	1940s-60	**Royal Mail Van**. Red, second casting with black bonnet, 'ROYAL MAIL', 'G-VI-R' paper labels.................................
11	1940s-62	**'AMBULANCE'**. Cream, Red Cross on paper labels ....
12	1940s-62	**'Carter Paterson' Van**. Dark green, 'CARTER PATERSON' on paper labels...............................
13	1940s-60	**'Police' Van**. Dark blue, 'POLICE GR' on paper labels ....
14	1940s-62	**Post Office Telephones Van**. Green, 'POST OFFICE TELEPHONES' on paper labels ....
15	1940s-62	**Fire Engine and Wheeled Escape**. Red or orange-red, unpainted ladders, three firemen and hose ....
16	1940s-67	**Covered Wagon with Four Horses and Driver**. Green wagon, yellow wheels, cloth canopy, metal shaft and horses. Orange wagon, yellow wheels, cloth canopy, plastic shaft and horses ....
17	1940s-67	**Tractor and Log Trailer with Driver**. Tractor as No.6, Trailer as No.1 but with drawbar in place of shafts................
18	1940s-62	**Tractor and Grass Cutter with two Drivers**. Tractor as No.6, Trailer modified from No.3 ....
19	1940s-67	**Tractor and Reaper with two Drivers**. Tractor as No.6, green reaper with yellow metal blades or light blue reaper with red plastic blades, or all plastic.............
20	1954-67	**Mobile Crane**. Red body, green chassis, unpainted or yellow jib .... Orange body, light blue chassis, yellow jib.
21	1954-67	**Muir-Hill Dumper with Driver**. Beige or Orange with Green dumper, Orange with Yellow dumper......................... Red with Yellow plastic dumper ...
22	1954-67	**Travelling Zoo**. Elephant towing two cages with two lions, two polar bears, man. Red chassis, unpainted cages, yellow roofs, metal or plastic animals........................ Same but orange chassis, light blue cages, yellow roofs ....
23	1955-58	**Water Pistol**. no details ....
24	1954-55	**Costermonger's Cart**. Dark green cart, red or yellow wheels, donkey, man and basket ....
25	1955-?	**Horse-drawn Milk Cart**. Yellow with red wheels, 'PURE MILK' labels. With man and churn...........................
26	1954-62	**Armoured Car**. Green or beige, metal or rubber wheels ....
27	1955-67	**Large Tractor**. Cast in two halves. Red with yellow wheels or orange with light blue wheels....................
28	1954-67	**Diesel Road Roller**. Green or pale green, red wheels, unpainted flywheel......................
29	1954-62	**Mincer**. Toy kitchen equipment, Yellow ....
30	1955	**Scammell Mechanical Horse and Trailer**. Blue with 'LNER' labels, or dark brown cab with beige trailer and 'GWR' labels...................
31	1955-62	**Articulated Low-loader with Cable Drum**. Red or green cab, yellow trailer.......................
32	1955-62	**Alfa-Romeo Racing Car**. Hollow-cast lead, red with rubber wheels......................
33	1955-62	**Cooper-Bristol Racing Car**. Hollow-cast lead, green with rubber wheels ....
34	1955-62	**Ferrari Racing Car**. Hollow-cast lead, blue with yellow nose, rubber wheels........
35	1954-67	**Horse-drawn Log Wagon**. As No.1 but only one horse ....
36	1940s-55	**3-wheel Pedestrian Electric Van**. Dark blue, 'DAIRY MILK' printed on sides; milkman, crate and bottles .... Orange, 'HOVIS' printed on sides; man, tray of loaves.........
36	1957-62	**Maudslay Horse Box**. Dark red, 'HORSE TRANSPORT' printed on sides, with horse and driver ....
36	1967	**Steam Roller Large scale**. Green body, red 12-spoke wheels, unpainted roller, black chimney...................**£200-300**
37	1960-62	**Articulated Low-loader with Rocket Missile**. Dark green cab / trailer, orange / black missile launcher. No makers name on model......................
38	1955-60	**'Shoot and Save' Money Box** Savings bank, with gun to fire coin into bank ....
39	1955	**Telephone Kiosk** Red kiosk with opening door, unpainted telephone inside ......
40	1940s-55	**Fire Engine and Ladder and Firemen** Different from No.15. Red body, unpainted 2-part ladder ....
41	1955	**Fireplace** Dolls house item......................
445	c1955	**'Auto Race Set'** 'Andover series'. Made only for the Flare Import Corporation, 230 Fifth Ave., New York. Contains three racing cars (in the Dinky style) with six mechanics and a man with a chequered flag in 43mm scale, hollow-cast. Card box has colour label depicting a Formula I race scene **£300-400**

'Old Crocks', Military models and 'Miniature Lorries'

'OLD CROCKS' series

1	**1904 Darracq**. Dark Blue, Red or Orange, open 2-seater..............**£10-25**
2	**1904 Spyker**. Yellow 4-seater open car.....................**£10-25**
3	**1914 'Old Bill' Bus**. 2-piece casting, or single casting plus separate top deck, Red or Orange **£10-25**
4	**1907 Ford Model T**. 2-piece casting, tin chassis, Dark Blue ....**£10-25** Single casting, no separate chassis, Dark Blue............**£10-25**
5	**1907 Vauxhall**. Green open 2-seater.....................**£10-25**
6	**1906 De Dion Bouton**. Light Green or Violet open 2-seater **£10-25**
7	**1898 Panhard**. Light Green or Brown 2-seater **£10-25**
8	**1906 Rolls-Royce Silver Ghost**. Silver 4-seater open car **£10-25**
9	**1903 Standard 6hp**. Dark Red or Maroon with Beige roof...........**£10-25**
10	**1902 Wolseley**. Light Blue 4-seater open car.....................**£10-25**
11	**1908 Packard Runabout**. Light Green open 2-str.....................**£10-25**
12	**1905 Vauxhall Hansom Cab**, Orange / Beige **£10-25**
13	**1900 Straker Flat Steam Lorry**. Light Green, packing case........**£10-25** **1900 Straker Lowside Steam Lorry**. Light Blue, three barrels **£10-25**
14	**Stephenson's 'Rocket' Locomotive**. Yellow / Black **£10-25**
15	**Tender for 'Rocket'**, colours as 14 ....**£10-25**
16	**1909 Albion**. Dark or Light Blue open truck.....................**£10-25**
17	**1912 Rover**. Orange 2-seater open sports car.....................**£10-25**
18	**1911 Mercedes-Benz**. Dark Green open 2-seater.....................**£10-25**
19	**Bedford Horse-Box**. Brown, 'HORSE TRANSPORT' cast on sides, 'H.G. IVORY' on tailgate **£15-25**
20	**1910 Lanchester**. Light Blue 4-seater sports tourer.....................**£10-25**
21	**1922 Morris Cowley**. Beige 2-seater open car.....................**£10-25**
22	**1900 Daimler**. Maroon 2-seater.....................**£10-25**
23	**1904 Autocar**. Dark Blue, open 3-wheeler.....................**£10-25**
24	**1870/80 Grenville Steam Carriage**. Green or Light Green **£10-25**
25	**1905 Napier**. Violet or Purple 2-seater racer.....................**£10-25**
26	**Fire Engine and Escape**. Red or Orange.....................**£10-25**
27	**Articulated Breakdown Lorry**. Dark Green cab, Light Blue trailer, Orange crane.....................**£10-25**
28	**Mercer Runabout**. Dark Blue or Green 2-seater sports **£10-25**

MILITARY MODELS

30	**Searchlight on 4-wheel Trailer**. Green and Silver **£10-25**
31	**Twin Bofors Gun on Trailer**. Green and Silver.....................**£10-25**
32	**Radar Scanner on Trailer**. Green and Silver.....................**£10-25**
33	**Field Gun on Trailer**. Green and Silver.....................**£10-25**
34	**Rocket Gun on Trailer**. Green and Silver.....................**£10-25**
35	**Armoured Car**. Green.....................**£10-25**

'MINIATURE LORRIES' (not issued)

40	**Articulated Tanker**. Listed in 1960 catalogue ....**NPP**
41	**Articulated Lorry**. Listed in 1960 catalogue...................**NPP**
42	**Six-wheeled Lorry**. Listed in 1960 catalogue.....................**NPP**
43	**Six-wheeled Tanker**. Listed in 1960 catalogue.....................**NPP**

An illustration from the September 1960 UK catalogue

Mettoy
Corgi Toys

Corgi Toys were launched in 1956 by the Mettoy Company which had itself been founded in Northampton by Phillip Ullmann in 1953. The 'Mettoy' name was derived from the first three letters of 'Metal' plus 'toy' - the company's main product range being composed of lithographed metal toys. In 1948 Mettoy produced their first cast metal toys and called them 'Castoys'. The Castoys models contained a clockwork motor and when the first Corgi Toys models were introduced they also contained a mechanism. This plus the introduction of windows gave Corgi a competitive edge against their great rivals Dinky Toys.

1985 saw the company shift emphasis from the mass production of toy vehicles to the development of authentic, limited edition models aimed at adult collectors.

Since a management buyout from toy giant Mattel in August 1995, the company, now known as Corgi Classics, has moved ahead strongly. In 1996, the 40th anniversary of the Corgi brand, the company launched a new roadshow which visits exhibitions, shows and events all over the country to spread the word about diecast collecting and give enthusiasts the chance to preview forthcoming releases. New Corgi Regional Retail Centres have also been introduced which stock the widest range of models.

The Corgi Collector Club, led by Susan Pownall, continues to build on its past success and now has over 10,000 members worldwide. Members receive a regular magazine, discounts on models and many other benefits. For a unique showcase of Corgi past and present, all diecast collectors should visit the Corgi Heritage Centre in Heywood, near Rochdale.

The Corgi Classics range goes from strength to strength with four main sections. Firstly, the Corgi Classics Collectables range of classic commercial vehicles and cars. Secondly, the Original Omnibus issues for bus lovers. Incidentally, the Corgi club now has a separate section for bus model collectors - see advert on inside rear cover. Thirdly, the Aviation Archive now offers a tremendous range of model civilian and military aircraft. Finally, the Corgi Classics range now includes a superb new collection of vintage steam vehicles. Truly a comprehensive range of collectable models for the collectors of the new century. Corgi Classics listings are now included in the new 'Collectable Modern Diecasts' section of the Catalogue.

The Editor wishes to thank all who have contributed to the greatly revised listings. Similarly, many thanks to Adrienne Fuller and Paul Lumsden of Corgi Classics, Susan Pownall of the Corgi Collector Club and to Chris Brierley of the Corgi Heritage Centre for their help and co-operation.

**Market Price Range: Please note that the prices shown refer to pristine models and boxes.
Items failing to match this standard will sell for less.
Note also that boxes must contain all their original additional contents.**

Corgi Toys Identification

Often referred to as 'the ones with windows', Corgi Toys were the first manufacturer to produce models with that refinement. Some of their first models also had a mechanical motor. Spring suspension was introduced from 1959 and in 1960 the first die-cast model to have an opening bonnet. The first models were based on real cars of the period. Similarly, with the launch of the 'Corgi Major Toys' in 1959, models of real commercial vehicles were available and competed with the Dinky 'Supertoys' range.

In the 1960s Corgi produced many successful film and TV-related models. Probably the best remembered was the 'James Bond' Aston Martin which sold in huge quantities in the autumn of 1965. Indeed, such was the popularity of the model that a version was still available in 1992!

Corgi introduced many new features in the 1960s such as: jewelled headlights, opening bonnet revealing detailed engine, opening boot revealing spare, self-centering steering, ruby rear lights, etc. One particularly attractive model was the Midland Red Motorway Express Coach. The detailed interior even incorporated a toilet! Needless to say good examples of this model are highly sought after by bus collectors. Similarly the 'Chipperfields Circus' collection of models were beautifully produced and are highly prized today.

Innovations were frequent and imaginative in the 1960s. 'Golden Jacks' for instance, a built-in jacking system which enabled models to have 'Take-Off' wheels. And 'Trans-O-Lites' whereby light rays were captured and fed through prisms to illuminate the headlights. 'WhizzWheels' and the slightly larger scale of 1:42 were introduced in the 1970s.

A market strategy unique to Corgi was the launching a replica model car simultaneously with the real car. To date simultaneous launches have occurred with Austin Metro, Ford Escort, Triumph Acclaim, Ford Sierra and the MG Maestro 1600, which is a unique record. Corgi were the first die-cast manufacturers to introduce the dimensions of light, sound and movement into their models by using the micro-chip in their 'Corgitronic' range. The models 'come alive', for example by just pushing down on the rear axle or, in the case of the Road Repair Unit, by pressing the workman to activate the pneumatic drill sound. Others (like the Sonic Corgi Truck) can be operated from a remote control handset.

Mechanical. Some early Corgi Toys were produced in either the normal form or with a friction type flywheel motor. Exceptions were the sports cars and trucks which could not be converted to take the flywheel. The mechanisms were not robust and were phased out in 1959.

Boxes. July 1956 - Blue box, January 1959 - Yellow/Blue box (Two-tone cars were first to use them) December 1966 - Window box (2 square window ends) May 1973 - Angled window box (one square window end, coloured lines around box) 1980 - Yellow window box, 1987 New style Corgi logo box.

Box contents. Model boxes often contain much more than just the basic model. Prices shown in the Catalogue assume that not only is the model in pristine condition, but that it is accompanied by all the original additional contents. These can include: extra card packing, inner card or polystyrene trays, pictorial stands, plastic protectors, transit card protection intended for removal by the retailer, instruction and information leaflets, catalogues, consumables (such as unopened packets of rockets, decals, etc.). This particularly applies to some Novelty and Film/TV models, e.g., Nos. 268, 277, 497, 511, 1123, 1139, 1144 and Gift Sets 3, 10, 20 and 21. A further example relates to the early 'Blue box' models each of which should contain a concertina catalogue leaflet plus a 'Join the Corgi Club' leaflet. If original items are missing, e.g., the plastic dome protector included with 511 Chipperfields Poodle Truck or card protectors with other models, it will affect the price that a model will achieve.

Whilst every effort has been made to describe models and, where known, their accompanying contents, any further information would be welcomed.

Mettoy Diecast Toys - The 'Castoys' series

Castoys were produced by the Mettoy Company between 1948 and 1958 and were instigated by a request from Marks and Spencers for a robust, long lasting toy. The models were made of zinc alloy and were initially advertised as 'Heavy Cast Mechanical Toys'.

Generally, they had windows, a clockwork motor and brake, plus black rubber tyres on cast hubs. Of the original issues, only two models, No. 840, the 'Eight Wheel Lorry' and 870

'Delivery Van' remained in production after 1951 and these were packaged in attractive Yellow/Red boxes which displayed a picture of the model inside. The later issues of the Delivery Van with their various attractive body designs are now rare and sought after items.

The following listing contains all the information available at present. The Editor would welcome any additional information on body colours and variations.

Ref.	Year(s)	Model name	Colours, features, dimensions	Market Price Range

Large Scale Models 1:35

Ref.	Year(s)	Model name	Colours, features, dimensions	Market Price Range
810	1948-51	Limousine	Cream, Red or Green body, 'MTY 810'	NGPP
820	1948-51	Streamline Bus	Cream, Green or Red body, clockwork mechanism, Red pressed tin seating, solid rubber wheels, unpainted chassis. Registration No 'MTY 820'	£100-200
			As previous model but with opening door and registration No 'MTY 720'	£100-200
	Later issue:		Metallic Blue and Gold body with Silver raised roof section and base, Red door with Brown plastic male passenger Destination board shows 'PRIVATE' and registration 'MTY 718'	£100-200
			Metallic Brown and Pink body with Silver raised roof section and radiator, with Green female passenger	£100-200
830	1948-51	Racing Car	Light Green, 6 long approx, 'METTOY' cast in base, tinplate hollow printed wheels with motor and brake	£100-200
840	1948-58	8 Wheel Lorry	Metallic Blue cab with Grey rear body, Silver radiator and hubs	£100-200
850	1948-51	Fire Engine	Red body, Silver ladder and crank	£100-200
			Red body, Silver extending ladder, no crank	£100-200
860	1948-51	Tractor	No models seen but shown in 1951 catalogue with Yellow/Red body	£100-200
863		Ferguson TE20 Tractor and Trailer	Red/Blue tractor, Yellow trailer, Red hubs, painted plastic driver	£100-125
870	1948-51	Delivery Van	No models seen but shown in 1948 catalogue with plain Dark Blue body	£100-150
	1952-55	'EXPRESS DELIVERY'	Yellow body with Red logo and design on sides	£150-200
	1955-58	'POST OFFICE TELEPHONES'	Green body, White logo, Royal crest in Gold, Silver two part extending ladder	£200-300
	1955-58	'ROYAL MAIL'	Red body, Silver trim, Yellow logo and Royal crest, 'MTY 870'	£200-300
	1955-58	'AMBULANCE'	Cream body with Black logo on sides	£100-200
	1956-58	'BOAC'	Blue body, Silver trim, White *Fly By BOAC* on roof	£300-400

Small Scale Models 1:45

Ref.	Year(s)	Model name	Colours, features, dimensions	Market Price Range
---	1955-57	Soft Drinks Van	Dark red body, number plate 'CWS 300', Silver wheels, Logo on rear: 'CWS SOFT DRINKS - THIRST COME - THIRST SERVED'	£75-95

Special 1:18 scale issue for Marks and Spencer

Ref.	Year(s)	Model name	Colours, features, dimensions	Market Price Range
---	1958	'VANWALL' Racing Car	Diecast body, perspex screen, driver, 'VANWALL' transfers, 'push and go' motor in some. 'Vanwall the famous British Grand Prix Winner' cast in base.	
		i)	Green body, racing number '7' or '18', no Mettoy logo on base	£200-300
		ii)	French Blue body, racing number '20', no Mettoy logo on base	£200-300

The 'Miniature Numbers' series

The range of models produced between 1951 an 1954 was based on just two vehicles - the Standard Vanguard and the Rolls Royce. Models were issued in two sizes and featured a clockwork motor plus brake, adjustable steering (controlled by moving the central fog lamp sideways) and moulded grey plastic wheels. Both diecast and plastic bodies have been observed on some examples. They were packaged in attractive window boxes. The following listing has been taken from the 1951 Mettoy Catalogue and the Editor would welcome any additional information.

Ref.	Year(s)	Model name	Colours, features, dimensions	Market Price Range
502	1951	Standard Vanguard Saloon	Shown with Green body in catalogue (2 7/8 inches long)	£50-75
505	1951	Rolls-Royce Saloon	Red or Blue body, Silver trim (3 inches long)	£50-75
510	1951	Standard Vanguard Police Car	Black with White 'POLICE' logo on doors; roof siren and bell	£50-75
511	1951	Standard Vanguard Taxi	Shown in 1951 catalogue with Yellow body and Red roof rack	£50-75
512	1951	Standard Vanguard Fire Chief	Red, White 'FIRE CHIEF' on doors; single Silver ladder on roof	£50-75
602	1951	Standard Vanguard Saloon	Blue body shown in catalogue (large scale version of 502, 4¼ inches long)	£50-75
603	1951	Standard Vanguard Saloon	As 602 but with automatic to and fro bump feature	£50-75
605	1951	Rolls-Royce Saloon	Yellow body shown in catalogue (large scale version of 505, 4½ inches long)	£50-75
606	1951	Rolls-Royce Saloon	As 605 but with automatic to and fro bump feature	£50-75

CORGI TOYS
CONTINENTAL MOTOR CARS

201 Austin Cambridge — 3½ inches 90 mm — 2/9

208S Jaguar 2.4 Litre — 3¾ inches 95 mm — 3/8
With seats, steering wheel and Glidamatic spring suspension.

216 Austin A.40 — 3⅜ inches 86 mm — 3/–

226 Morris Mini-Minor — 2⅞ inches 73 mm — 3/4
With seats, steering wheel and Glidamatic spring suspension.

207 Standard Vanguard III — 3¾ inches 95 mm — 2/11

217 Fiat 1800 Saloon — 3¾ inches 95 mm — 3/6
With seats, steering wheel and Glidamatic spring suspension.

210S Citroen D.S. 19 — 3⅞ inches 97 mm — 3/10
With seats, steering wheel and Glidamatic spring suspension.

222 Renault Floride — 3⅝ inches 91 mm — 3/6
With seats, steering wheel and Glidamatic spring suspension.

An illustration from the September 1960 UK catalogue

WALLIS & WALLIS

SPECIALIST AUCTIONEERS OF DIE-CAST AND TINPLATE TOYS, TEDDY BEARS, DOLLS, MODEL RAILWAYS, TOY SOLDIERS, MODELS

*We hold sales every 6 weeks
and entries can be accepted at any time.*

If you wish to update the value of your collection our last 10 sale catalogues are available at £25 (post free) complete with prices realised.

To subscribe to our catalogues £47.50 will provide you with 9 well illustrated catalogues per year, including a colourful calendar free of charge.

Single catalogue £6.50 (including postage).

A fine selection of 1960's Corgi toys, sold in a recent auction.

TO ENTER ITEMS FOR AUCTION PLEASE ASK FOR AN ENTRY FORM

West Street Auction Galleries
Lewes, Sussex, England BN7 2NJ
Tel: 01273 480208 Fax: 01273 476562

Corgi Toys

No.868 Magic Roundabout Playground. Good overall condition.
Sold by Christie's, South Kensington (£600).

Gift Set 15 Silverstone Racing Layout Set

L-R: 309 Aston Martin, 304S Mercedes Benz 300SL Hardtop Roadster, 417S Land Rover Recovery Vehicle,
152S BRM Grand Prix Formula 1 Racing Car, 150S Vanwell Formula 1 Grand Prix Racing Car, 215S Ford
Thunderbird Open Sports, 154 Ferrari Formula 1 Grand Prix Racing Car.

All models and boxes in excellent condition.
Set sold by Christie's South Kensington, London for £1,092.
Picture reproduced by their kind permission.

Corgi Toys

Top Row: Corgi models sold: 208 Jaguar 2.4 litre (£80), 462 Commer 1 ton Van (£130), 270 James Bond Aston Martin Metallic Silver, no display card (£75).

2nd Row: 267 Batmobile 1st type, minor wear (£120), 336 James Bond Toyota 2000 GT, minor wear (£120), 270 James Bond Aston Martin Metallic Silver, 1st type with all packaging /display (£260).

Bottom Row: Co-op set 1151, 462 and 466 unsold. 1139 'Chipperfields' Menagerie Truck Model Mint Box worn overall (£180), 802 Popeye Paddle Wagon, minor wear, un-boxed (£70).

Top Row: 266 Chitty Chitty Bang Bang, Model Mint, box worn (£150), 440 Ford Consul Cortina with golfer (£100), Gift Set 47, Working Conveyor (£160).

2nd Row: 236 Austin A60 School Car (£45), 487 Land Rover Parade Vehicle, good condition (£80), 428 Smiths Softee Ice Cream Van, minor chipping, minor box wear (£90). Co-op set unsold. Two 468 Routemaster Buses, 2nd issue boxes (£60)

3rd Row: Three pairs of 468 Routemasters all sold for £60 a pair (all in 1st type boxes).

Bottom Row: 256 Volkswagon 1200 Safari, vehicle fair, box worn (£70), 448 Police Dog Van, mint (£85), 805 Hardy Boys Rolls Royce, vehicle mint, box worn (£120), 339 Monté Carlo Mini Cooper, good (£50), 485 Mini Countryman Surfing, vehicle good, box with minor wear (£75).

Models sold by Wallis & Wallis, West Street Auction Galleries, Lewes, Sussex BN7 2NJ
Pictures reproduced by their kind permission.

Britains and CharbensToys

Top Row (L-R): Set 2024 Light Goods Van VG, box VG (£460), No.1513 St John's Volunteer Corps Motor Ambulance
VG, box G (estimate £800-£1,200), Set 2045 Clockwork Van VG, box G (£690), Set 2045 Clockwork
Van VG, box F-G (£1,150).

2nd Row (L-R): Set 2042 Prairie Schooner four horse team VG (£322), Set 1399 Two-seater Coupé VG, box G-VG (£1,610),
Set 1398 Sports Model Open Tourer G (£345), Set 2024 Light Goods Van VG, box VG (£460), Britains
Royalty (part lot) (£263), Set 1441 The Flying Trapeze (Clown & trapeze artist) G, box F-G (£632).

3rd Row (L-R): Charbens Coal Cart (part lot) (£517), Charbens Set 205 Musical Trio G-VG, box F (£391), Britains
Novelties (part lot) (£207), Britains Sets 28MG Garden Shelter G, box F and Set 053 Span Roof
Greenhouse G, box F (£1,035).

4th Row (L-R): Britains Racing Colours (18 in lot) un-boxed G (£676).

5th Row (L-R): Sets 128F Fordson Tractor and Set 2041 Clockwork Trailer VG, boxes G (£172), next lot similar (£172),
but note the colour variations of the drivers, Set 61F ten wheel Farm Lorry G (£345), Set 59F four wheel
Farm Lorry E, box G (207).

All models sold by Christie's South Kensington, 85 Old Brompton Road, London SW7 3LD.
Picture reproduced by their kind permission.

Corgi Toys Cars

See also Novelty, Film and TV-related section.

Ref.	Year(s)	Model name	Colours, features, dimensions	Market Price Range
C46	1983-	**Super Kart**	Blue or Orange main body, Red/Silver racing driver	£5-10
C100	1985	**'PORSCHE' 956**	Yellow/Black body, racing number '7', 'CASTROL', 115 mm	£7-10
C100/2	1986		Yellow body, racing number '7', 'TAKA-Q'	£7-10
C100/3	1988		Black body, racing number '1', 'BLAUPUNKT'	£7-10
C101	1985	**Porsche 956**	Red/White body, racing number '14', 'CANON'	£7-10
C101/2	1985	**Porsche 956**	White body, 'Clipper' logo plus 4 Red stripes on bonnet and tail, 'ADMIRAL ENERGY GROUP Ltd' logo	£15-20
C102	1985	**Opel Manta 400**	Red body, racing number '43', 'SHELL', 105 mm	£7-10
	1988		Black body, racing number '18', 'SHELL'	£7-10
C102	1985		Yellow body, racing number '12', 'BRITISH TELECOM'	£7-10
			White body, racing number '1', 'OPEL'	£7-10
C102/4	1990	**'VAUXHALL OPEL' Manta**	White body, racing number '6', 'MOBIL' on bonnet	£7-10
C103	1985	**Opel Manta 400**	White body, racing number '15', 'CASTROL'	£7-10
C104	1985	**Toyota Corolla 1600**	White body, Red roof, Yellow racing number '16', 'LAING'	£7-10
	1986		White body, Red roof, racing number '2', 'TOTAL'	£7-10
C105	1985	**Toyota Corolla 1600**	Red body, Yellow design, racing number '8', 'DUNLOP'	£7-10
	1986		Red body, Yellow design, racing number '5', 'TOTAL'	£7-10
			Red body, Yellow/Black/Pink stripes, racing number '6', 'BRITAX WEBER'	£7-10
C106	1985	**Saab 9000 Turbo**	White body, Red/Yellow design, racing number '3'	£7-10
C106/1	1987		Red body, White design 'FLY VIRGIN'	£7-10
C106/3	1988		Black body, racing number '7', 'MOBIL'	£7-10
C106/9	1990	**Saab Turbo**	White body, Maroon roof, racing number '4', 'FEDERAL EXPRESS'	£7-10
			Red body, White stripes, racing number '7', 'DUCKHAMS', 'DUNLOP'	£7-10
C107	1985	**Saab 9000**	Red body, Yellow design, racing number '41', 'BRITAX'	£7-10
C108	1985	**Chevrolet Z-28**	Red body, Yellow design, racing number '52', 'WEBER', 115 mm	£7-10
			Red body, Black stripe, racing number '8', 'BOSCH'	£7-10
C109	1985	**Chevrolet Z-28**	White body, Black/Yellow bands, Red racing number '84'	£7-10
C110	1985	**BMW 635**	White body with Union Jacks and racing number '6'	£7-10
C110/1	1986		Red body, racing number '25', 'FERODO'	£7-10
C110/2	1987		White body, racing number '2', 'MOTUL'	£7-10
C110/3	1988		White body, racing number '46', 'WARSTEINER'	£7-10
			White body, Grey/Black stripes, racing number '41', 'GOODYEAR'	£7-10
C111	1985	**BMW 635**	White/Blue body, racing number '18', 'BRITAX'	£7-10
	1986		White body, racing number '8', 'PIRELLI'	£7-10
C113	1987	**Saab 9000**	Red body, C7PM (Swedish)	£7-10
C139/2	1987	**Porsche 911**	Orange body, racing number '24', 'JAGERMEISTER'	£7-10
C139/4	1988		Red/Blue body, racing number '91', 'DENVER'	£7-10
150	1957-61	**Vanwall Racing Car**	(Blue box) Light or Mid-Green body, Yellow seat, large 'VANWALL', Blue tinted screen, racing number '3'	£50-60
			Mid-Green body, Silver seat, 'VANWALL' logo, clear screen, RN '1'	£50-60
			Mid-Green body, Yellow seat, small 'VANWALL' logo, clear screen, RN '1'	£50-60
		Blue/Yellow box:	Red body, Yellow seat, large 'VANWALL' logo, Blue tinted screen, RN '1'	£50-60
			Red body, Silver seat, small 'VANWALL' logo, clear screen, RN '1'	£50-60
150 S	1961-65	**Vanwall Racing Car**	Light or Mid-Red body, Silver seat/driver, clear screen, '25', shaped hubs	£50-60
150	1972-74	**Surtees TS9 Formula 1**	Metallic Purple or Metallic Blue body, 'BROOKE BOND OXO' logo, 8-spoke WhizzWheels	£20-25
			Metallic Turquoise body with cast 8-stud WhizzWheels	£15-20
		Gift Set model:	Blue/Yellow body with 'DUCKHAMS', (in GS 29 only)	GSP
C150/4	1990	**Chevrolet Camaro**	Blue body, Orange/Black design, racing number '77'	£7-10
151	1958-60	**Lotus XI Racing Car**	Silver (Red seats), or Turquoise (Red seats), clear or Blue-tinted windscreen, RNs '1', '3', or none. Blue box with leaflet	£55-65
			Red body, Cream seats	£125-150
151 S	1961-63	**Lotus XI Racing Car**	Silver or Dull Blue body, maroon seats, suspension, clear or Blue-tinted windscreen, RNs '1' or '3'. Blue/Yellow box, no leaflet	£40-50
151 A	1961-63	**Lotus XI**	Blue body, Red/White design, Silver nose, Red seats, shaped hubs, clear screen, driver, racing number '1'	£50-60
			Lemon body, racing number '3', driver, spring suspension	£40-50
C151	1974-76	**Mclaren M19A**	White body, 'YARDLEY', RN '55', 8-spoke or stud WhizzWheels	£20-25
			Same but Blue stripe on White helmet, 8-stud WhizzWheels, (GS30 only)	GSP
152	1958-60	**B.R.M. Racing Car**	Dark or Mid-Green body, Yellow or Silver seat, clear or Blue windscreen, racing numbers '1', '3' or '7', smooth hubs. Blue box with leaflet	£45-55
	1959-61		Dark or Mid-Green body, Silver seat, clear or Blue windscreen, racing numbers '1', '3' or '7', cast spoked hubs Blue/Yellow box, no leaflet	£45-55
152 S	1961-65	**B.R.M. Racing Car**	Turquoise body, cast or shaped (spun) hubs, suspension, racing numbers '1', '3' or '7'. Blue/Yellow box, no leaflet	£40-45
C152	1974-76	**Ferrari 312 B2**	Red body, 'Ferrari/Shell' logo, racing number '5', White driver, Orange/Blue helmet, 8-spoke or 8-stud cast hubs	£20-25

153	1960-62	**Bluebird Record Car**	Blue body, UK and US flags on nose, metal hubs, 127 mm	£65-75
153 A	1961-65	**Bluebird Record Car**	Blue body, UK and US flags on nose, Black plastic hubs	£65-75
		variant:	Blue body with two Union Jacks on nose, Black plastic hubs	£65-75
153	1972-74	**Team Surtees TS 9B**	Red body, RN '26', Blue or Blue/White driver (Rob Walker), 8-spoke hubs	£20-25
			Red body, 'NORRIS' logo, (GS30 only)	GSP
154	1963-72	**Ferrari Formula 1**	Red/Silver body, racing number '36', driver, windscreen, 91 mm	£30-40
C154	1974-78	**'JOHN PLAYER SPECIAL' Lotus**	Black body, Gold trim, racing number '1' or '4', drivers Emerson Fittipaldi or Ronnie Petersen	
		1:	'JPS' logo, Black/Red helmet, 8-stud hubs, 'Fittipaldi' on box	£15-20
		2:	'JPS' logo, Black or Blue helmet, 'Petersen' on box	£15-20
		3:	'JPS TEXACO' logo, Red helmet	£15-20
		4:	'JPS TEXACO' logo, Black helmet, 12-spoke hubs, (GS32 only)	GSP
		5:	'JPS SHELL' logo, Black/Red helmet, (GS30 only)	GSP
		Marks & Spencers issue:	No 'Corgi' on base, 'TEXACO' logo, Orange (?) helmet	GSP
155	1965-68	**Lotus Climax Racing Car**	Green/Yellow body, racing number '1' or '4', suspension, driver, 90 mm	£45-55
C155	1974-76	**'SHADOW' Formula 1**	Black body, 'UOP', RN '17', driver (Jackie Collins) White/Maroon helmet	£20-25
156	1967-69	**Cooper-Maserati**	Blue body, racing number '7', windscreen, White driver, 90 mm	£40-50
C156	1974-76	**Graham Hill's Shadow**	White/Red body, racing number '12', driver, 'EMBASSY RACING', 132 mm	£20-25
		Special issue:	Model in box with outer sleeve as presented at the National Sporting Club showing name MENU	£25-300
158	1969-72	**Lotus Climax Racing Car**	Red/White, racing number '8', suspension, driver, windscreen, 90 mm	£20-25
C158	1975-77	**Elf Tyrrell Ford F1**	Blue body, racing number '1', 'ELF', Jackie Stewart driving, 110 mm	£25-30
159	1969-72	**Cooper-Maserati**	Yellow/White, racing number '3', driver-controlled steering, 90 mm	£20-25
C159	1974-76	**Indianapolis Racing Car**	Red body, racing number '20', Patrick Eagle driving, 130 mm	£25-30
C160	1975-78	**'HESKETH' 308 F1**	White body, 'HESKETH', Black helmet, 4-stud hubs	£20-25
		Marks & Spencers issue:	White body, no 'CORGI' on some, White driver, Orange helmet	GSP
			Yellow body, 'CORGI TEAM' logo, Orange driver (James Hunt), Black helmet, Blue belts, (GS26 only)	GSP
161	1972-75	**Santa Pod 'COMMUTER'**	Red/Silver 'Dragster' body, racing number '2', WhizzWheels, 123 mm	£20-25
161	1977	**'ELF-TYRRELL' Project 34**	Blue body, 'ELF' logo, Red or Blue helmet, 8-stud hubs, racing number '4'	£20-25
162		**Tyrell P34**	Blue/White body, 'FIRST NATIONAL BANK' logo, Red or Orange helmet	£30-35
		Marks & Spencers issue:	As previous model but no 'Corgi' on base, 8-stud hubs	GSP
162	1971-72	**'QUARTERMASTER' Dragster**	Green and White body, aerofoil, driver, plastic hubs, 146 mm	£25-30
C163	1971-76	**Santa Pod Dragster**	White/Blue lift-off body, 'GLOWORM' driver, plastic hubs, 113 mm	£25-30
164	1972-75	**Ison Bros Dragster**	Yellow/Red body, 'WILD HONEY', 'JAGUAR', WhizzWheels, 171 mm	£25-30
165	1974-76	**Adams Brothers Dragster**	Orange/Yellow body, 4 x V-8 engines, WhizzWheels	£25-30
166	1971-74	**Ford Mustang**	Yellow/Green body, 'ORGAN GRINDER', racing number '39', driver	£25-30
C167	1973-74	**USA Racing Buggy**	White/Red body, racing number '7', driver, US flag, 95 mm	£25-30
C169	1974-76	**Starfighter Jet Dragster**	Blue/Silver/Red body, 'FIRESTONE', 155 mm	£25-30
C170	1974-76	**John Woolfe's Dragster**	Blue/Yellow body, 'RADIO LUXEMBOURG', '208', 146 mm	£25-30
190	1974-76	**'JOHN PLAYER' Lotus**	1:18 scale, Black/Gold, RN '1', driver, removable wheels, tools, 270 mm	£35-40
191	1974-77	**'TEXACO MARLBORO' Mclaren**	1:18 scale, White/Red, RN '5', removable wheels, tools, 245 mm	£35-40
200	1956-61	**Ford Consul**	Cream, Dark Green, Medium Tan or Dark Tan body, no suspension, 90 mm	£90-110
			Blue, Light Greyish-Brown or Bright Green body	£90-110
			Two-tone Green, Green/Cream or Silver/Cream	£120-140
			Dark Green and Pale Green body, flat spun hubs, leaflet	£90-110
200 M	1956-59	**Ford Consul**	Blue body, flywheel motor, 90 mm	£110-130
			Dark Green or Bright Green, flywheel motor, 90 mm	£90-110
C200	1976-78	**BLMC Mini 1000**	Blue body, Silver roof with Red and White interior, 85 mm	£20-25
C200A	1978-83	**BLMC Mini 1000**	Metallic Blue body, White or Red interior, Union Jack stripe on roof, WhizzWheels	£25-35
201	1956-63	**Austin Cambridge**	Pale Blue, Turquoise or Mid-Grey body, no suspension, 90 mm	£90-110
			Light Grey body	£90-110
			Green/Cream or two-tone Green	£90-110
			Metallic Green/Silver	£100-120
201 M	1956-59	**Austin Cambridge**	Cream, Red, Slate Grey or Medium Grey body with motor, 90 mm	£90-110
			Orange body or Silver over Metallic Blue	£120-150
C201	1979-82	**BLMC Mini 1000**	Silver body, Red interior, with or without 'TEAM CORGI' and '8', 85 mm	£15-25
			As previous model but with Orange door	£15-25
			Dark Blue body without 'TEAM CORGI'	£15-25
			Dark Blue body with 'ESSO' and 'MICHELIN' labels	£15-25
202	1956-60	**Morris Cowley**	Bright Green or Grey body, smooth hubs, no suspension, 91 mm	£90-110
			Blue body, no suspension, 91 mm	£90-110
			Grey/Blue or Blue/Cream body	£100-120
			Pale Green/Blue or White/Blue body	£100-120
202 M	1956-59	**Morris Cowley**	Pale Green or Medium Green body, flywheel motor, 91 mm	£90-110
			Dark Green body or Off-White, flywheel motor	£90-110
202	1970-72	**Renault R16**	Blue/Silver body, no suspension, 91 mm	£20-25
203	1971-72	**De Tomaso Mangusta**	Metallic Dark Green, Gold stripes, racing number '1'	£20-25

Cars

203	1956-60	**Vauxhall Velox**	Red, Cream or Yellow body, no suspension, 91 mm	£90-110
			Yellow body, Red roof	£120-140
203 M	1956-59	**Vauxhall Velox**	Red or Orange body, flywheel motor, 91 mm	£130-160
203	1971-72	**De Tomaso Mangusta**	Green/Gold body, WhizzWheels, 99 mm	£20-25
204	1956-60	**Rover 90**	Off-White body, or Light or Dark Grey body, smooth hubs	£90-110
			Metallic Dark Green body, smooth hubs	£90-110
			Metallic Maroon and Grey body, smooth hubs	£120-140
			Metallic Red and White body, smooth hubs	£120-140
204 M	1956-59	**Rover 90**	Bright Mid-Green or Grey body, smooth hubs, flywheel motor	£100-125
			Metallic Mid- or Dark Green body, smooth hubs, flywheel motor	£100-125
204	1972-74	**Morris Mini-Minor**	Dark Blue body with WhizzWheels, 73 mm	£90-110
			Deep Blue body, WhizzWheels	£200-250
			Metallic Blue body, WhizzWheels	£50-60
			All-Orange body, WhizzWheels	£40-50
			Orange body, Black roof, WhizzWheels	£90-120
205	1956-61	**Riley Pathfinder**	Red or Blue body, no suspension, smooth hubs, 97 mm	£90-110
205 M	1956-59	**Riley Pathfinder**	Red body, smooth hubs, flywheel motor, 97 mm	£120-140
			Mid Blue body	£90-110
			Dark Blue body	£125-150
206	1956-60	**Hillman Husky Estate**	Tan or Greyish Light-Brown body, no suspension, 86 mm	£75-85
			Metallic Blue and Silver body	£75-85
206 M	1956-59	**Hillman Husky Estate**	Cream, Dark Blue or Grey body, flywheel motor, 86 mm	£85-100
207	1957-62	**Standard Vanguard III**	White body, Red roof, or Grey body, Red roof, smooth or shaped hubs, 95 mm	£75-85
			Pale Green up to roof line, Red roof	£75-85
			Pale Green up to windows, Red upper part and roof, shaped hubs	£100-110
207 M	1957-59	**Standard Vanguard III**	Primrose Yellow body, flywheel motor, 95 mm	£120-140
			Pale Green body, Red roof pillars	£80-100
208	1957-60	**Jaguar 2.4 litre**	White body, no suspension, 95 mm	£90-110
208 M	1957-59	**Jaguar 2.4 litre**	Metallic Dark Blue body, flywheel motor, 95 mm	£90-110
208 S	1960-62	**Jaguar 2.4 litre**	Lemon body, with spring suspension, smooth spun hubs, 95 mm	£75-85
			Pale Lemon body, shaped spun hubs	£85-95
210	1957-60	**Citroën DS19**	Yellow body, Red roof, Grey baseplate, smooth hubs, 97 mm	£75-85
			Yellow body, Red roof, Silver baseplate with detailed drive shaft	£90-110
			Metallic Dark Green body, Black roof, Grey or Silver baseplate	£75-85
			As previous but with bulge to take flywheel motor. A 210M was not produced	£120-150
210 S	1960-65	**Citroën DS19**	Red body, Grey baseplate, spring suspension, 97 mm	£60-70
211	1958-60	**Studebaker Golden Hawk**	Blue and Gold body, no suspension, smooth spun hubs, 104 mm	£60-70
			White and Gold	£75-85
211 M	1958-59	**Studebaker Golden Hawk**	White and Gold body, flywheel motor, no suspension, smooth spun hubs	£80-100
211 S	1960-65	**Studebaker Golden Hawk**	Gold ('plated') body, White flash, suspension, shaped spun hubs	£65-75
			Gold (painted) body, shaped spun hubs	£80-100
212	1958	**Road Racer**	Not released, one example known to exist	NPP
214	1959-62	**Ford Thunderbird Hardtop**	Pale Green (Cream roof) or Grey with Red roof, '1959' on rear number plate	£70-80
			Pale Green body, Cream roof, blank rear number plate	£80-90
214 M	1959-61	**Ford Thunderbird Hardtop**	Pink body, Black roof, flywheel motor	£140-170
			Pale Green body, Cream roof, flywheel motor	£170-200
214 S	1962-65	**Ford Thunderbird Hardtop**	Metallic Grey body, Red roof, or Black body, Red roof, Lemon interior, with suspension	£60-70
215	1959-62	**Thunderbird Open Sports**	White with Blue interior, smooth or shaped hubs, no suspension, 102 mm	£60-70
215 S	1962-65	**Thunderbird Open Sports**	Red body with Yellow interior and driver, with spring suspension	£60-70
216	1959-62	**Austin A40**	Two-tone Blue body, no suspension, smooth hubs, 86 mm	£90-110
			Red body, Black roof, smooth hubs	£90-110
216 M	1959	**Austin A40**	Red body, Black roof, flat spun hubs, flywheel motor, no suspension	£120-140
			All-Red body	£120-140
217	1960-63	**Fiat 1800 Saloon**	Light Blue or Two tone Blue body, smooth or shaped hubs	£30-35
			Light Tan body	£30-35
			Pale Yellow/Brown or Mustard Yellow body	£40-50
218	1960-62	**Aston Martin DB4**	Red or Yellow body, interior, suspension, smooth or shaped hubs, 95 mm	£65-75
	1961-62		Red or yellow body, interior, suspension, cast 'spoked' hubs	£75-85
219	1959-62	**Plymouth Suburban Sports**	Cream with Fawn roof, 104 mm	£40-50
220	1960-62	**Chevrolet Impala**	Blue with Red or Yellow interior, smooth or shaped hubs	£35-45
			Pink body, Yellow interior	£50-60
222	1959-60	**Renault Floride**	Dark Red, Maroon or Lime Green body, Red, White or Yellow vac-formed interior, smooth or shaped hubs, suspension, 91 mm	£35-45
			Metallic Blue body, Red interior, shaped hubs	£45-55
224	1961-66	**Bentley Continental**	Seats, opening boot with removable spare, steering, special lights, 108 mm	
			Cream/Metallic Apple Green	£70-80
			Two-tone Green, Gold, or Black/Silver body	£70-80
			Metallic Green and White body	£80-90
225	1961-66	**Austin 7 (Mini) Saloon**	Red body, windows, suspension, seats, steering wheel, 73 mm	£75-85
			Primrose-Yellow body, Red interior, smooth spun hubs	£175-225

35

No.	Year	Model	Description	Price
226	1960-71	Morris Mini Minor	Pale Blue body, Cream or Yellow interior, smooth or shaped spun hubs	£50-60
			Red body, smooth or shaped spun hubs	£50-60
			Sky Blue body, Red interior, spun hubs	£200-250
			Metallic Maroon body, suspension, detailed cast hubs, 73 mm	£50-60
			Yellow body	£200-250
			N.B. The Light Blue version of 226 was also supplied for a short time by a games manufacturer as part of table-top racing game. This version has a large drive-pin hole in the base and has 'rally' stickers on the bonnet. Not separately boxed	NGPP
227	1962-63	Mini Cooper Rally	Blue body, White roof and bonnet, spun hubs, flags, RN '1', 3' or '7'	£225-275
			Blue body and bonnet, White otherwise as above	£225-275
			Primrose Yellow body, White roof and bonnet, with flags and RN '7'	£225-275
			Primrose Yellow body and bonnet, with flags and RN '1'	£225-275
228	1962-66	Volvo P-1800	Light Brown body, (Red interior) or Dark Red (Lemon interior), spun hubs	£40-45
			Pink or Dark Pink body	£50-60
229	1961-66	Chevrolet Corvair	Blue or Gold body, smooth or shaped spun hubs, 97 mm	£45-55
230	1962-64	Mercedes-Benz 220 SE	Cream (Red interior) shaped spun hubs, spare wheel in boot	£35-45
			Maroon body, Lemon interior, shaped spun hubs, spare wheel in boot	£60-70
			Black body, Lemon interior, shaped spun hubs, spare wheel in boot	£70-80
231	1961-65	Triumph Herald	Gold top and bottom, White in centre, spun hubs, red seats, 90 mm	£65-75
			Mid Blue top and bottom, White in centre, red seats	£55-65
			All Pale Blue (other details required please)	NGPP
232	1961-65	Fiat 2100	Two-tone Mauve body, Venetian blinds, suspension, special lights, 95 mm	£35-45
233	1962-72	Heinkel Trojan	Red, Orange, 'Pink', or Lilac body, 3 smooth spun hubs or detailed cast hubs	£40-50
			Metallic Blue or Turquoise variation body, smooth spun hubs	£80-90
234	1961-64	Ford Consul Classic	Cream/Pink or Gold, opening bonnet, detailed engine, suspension, 95 mm	£50-60
235	1962-66	Oldsmobile Super 88	Black/White or Metallic Steel Blue/White, suspension, 108 mm	£40-45
			Light Blue/White body	£50-55
236	1964-69	Motor School Austin A60	Light Blue, 2 figures, steering control on roof, 'Highway Code' leaflet	£60-70
238	1962-67	Jaguar Mk10	All with spun hubs, luggage.	
			Light Blue body, Red interior, or Metallic Cerise body, Lemon interior	£50-60
			Metallic Kingfisher Blue body, Pale Lemon interior	£80-90
			Metallic issues: Deep Blue, Silver Blue, Deep Green or Sea-Green, all with Red interior	£90-110
	1966-66		Metallic Silver body, Red interior	£100-125
239	1963-68	VW 1500 Karmann Ghia	Cream (Red interior) or Red (Yellow interior) spare wheel/suitcase in boot	£40-50
			Gold body, Red or Yellow interior, spare wheel/suitcase in boot	£50-60
240	1963-65	Fiat 600 Jolly	Light Blue body, detachable roof, suspension, figures, 79 mm	£65-75
			Dark Metallic Blue body, Red seats	£75-85
241	1963-69	Chrysler Ghia L64	Shaped spun or detailed cast hubs, Corgi dog on rear shelf, 108 mm.	
			Metallic Blue/White or Metallic Green	£30-40
			Metallic Yellow, Metallic Silver Blue, or Metallic Copper	£40-50
242	1965-66	Fiat 600 Jolly	Orange-Yellow body, Red interior, two figures in swim gear, windscreen but no canopy	£200-250
245	1964-68	Buick Riviera	Metallic Gold, 'Trans-O-Lites', spoked hubs, 108 mm	£45-55
			Metallic Light Blue or Metallic Greenish Blue body, towbar	£45-55
			Pale Blue body, spun or cast hubs	£55-65
246	1965-68	Chrysler Imperial Convertible	Red or Dark Red body, Light Blue or Dull Green interior, spun-shaped or detailed cast hubs, two figures, golf trolley	£60-70
			Metallic Kingfisher Blue body, Blue or Green interior, detailed cast hubs	£150-175
247	1964-69	Mercedes-Benz Pullman	Metallic Maroon body, windscreen wipers, instruction sheet, 121 mm	£40-50
248	1965-67	Chevrolet Impala	Brown body, Cream roof/interior, Chrome side stripe, shaped spun hubs	£45-55
249	1965-68	Morris Mini-Cooper	Black/Red body, wickerwork panels, spun or cast hubs, 73 mm	£70-80
251	1963-66	Hillman Imp	Metallic Blue body, opening window, luggage, 83 mm	£40-45
			Metallic Bronze body, White side stripe	£70-80
		Dutch promotional:	Light Blue body, Yellow interior, 'JENSON'S' logo, spun hubs	£200-300
		Danish promotional:	With 'JENSEN'S' logo	NGPP
252	1963-66	Rover 2000	Metallic Kingfisher Blue or Steel Blue body, Red interior	£55-65
			Maroon body, Red or Yellow interior	£65-75
253	1964-68	Mercedes-Benz 220 SE	Metallic Maroon, or Metallic Blue, luggage, spare wheel	£40-50
255	1964-68	Motor School A60	Dark Blue body, left-hand drive, 5 language leaflet, (USA issue of 236)	£100-125
256	1971-74	'EAST AFRICAN RALLY' Volkswagen	Red body, rally number '18', steering wheel on roof, rhinoceros, 91 mm	£150-175
C257	1985	Mercedes-Benz 500 SEC	White body, 'Magic Top' (fold-away roof)	£10-15
C258	1985	Toyota Celica Supra	Brown body, Black base, opening doors and tailgate, 125 mm	£10-15
			Blue body or Blue and Cream body with Red line	£10-15
259	1966-69	Citroën 'Le Dandy'	Metallic Dark Maroon body with Yellow interior	£65-75
			Metallic Blue body, White roof and boot	£90-110
260	1969	Renault 16 TS	Metallic Maroon, opening bonnet and hatchback, adjustable seats, 91 mm	£35-45
262	1967-69	Lincoln Continental	Metallic Gold body, Black roof, with picture strip for onboard 'TV set'	£125-150
			Light Blue body, Tan roof, with picture strip for onboard 'TV set'	£150-175
263	1966-69	Marlin Rambler Sports	Red/Black (or White/Blue in No10 GS) suspension, tow-hook, 102 mm	£35-40
264	1966-69	Oldsmobile Toronado	Metallic Medium or Dark Blue body, smooth or cast spoked hubs, 108 mm	£45-55
271	1969-70	Ghia Mangusta De Tomaso	Blue/White body, Gold stripes, aerial, detailed engine	£40-45
273	1970	Rolls-Royce Silver Shadow	Metallic Silver over Blue, Golden Jacks, Take-Off wheels, spare, 120 mm	£65-75
			Metallic White over Metallic Blue	£55-65

C273	1982-83	**Honda Ballade 'BSM'**		
		Driving School Car............Yellow body and Red side stripes	£25-35
274	1970-72	**Bentley 'T' Series**................Pink body, opening doors and bonnet, special lights, WhizzWheels, 120 mm	£45-55
275	1968-70	**Rover 2000 TC** ....Metallic Olive Green body, Brown or Red interior, Golden Jacks, spare on boot (opening cover)	£50-60
		White body, Red interior, cast hubs, pictorial window box	£120-150
C275	1981-	**Mini Metro** ....Blue, Purple or Red body, Yellow interior, opening doors and hatchback	£10-15
		Gold body	£45-50
		'Royal Wedding' Metro............Mauve body with Silver 'Charles & Diana' crest, special Mauve box	£10-15
276	1968-70	**Oldsmobile Toronado** ....Metallic Blue or Red body, Golden Jacks, cast 'Take-Off wheels'	£35-40
		Gold body	£40-45
C276	1982-	**Triumph Acclaim** ....Metallic Blue, Metallic Blue or Cream body, steering control, 120 mm	£7-10
C277	1982-	**Triumph Acclaim** ....'BSM' Driving School car with Yellow and Red body, steering control, 118 mm	£15-20
C278	1982	**Triumph Acclaim**		
		Driving School Car ....Yellow body, with steering control, 'CORGI MOTOR SCHOOL' logo	£25-35
C279	1979-	**Rolls-Royce Corniche**..............Metallic Dark Red body, opening doors/bonnet/boot, tilt seats, 114 mm	£20-25
	1985	Metallic Blue, Bright Red, Off-White and Cream, Cream or Silver and Grey body	£20-25
	1987	Silver and Black body with chrome trim	£20-25
C279/3	1990	**Rolls-Royce**..........................Gold body with White seats	£5-8
		Royal Blue body with White seats	£5-8
		Light and Dark Brown body	£5-8
C280	1970-78	**Rolls-Royce Silver Shadow** .....Opening doors/bonnet/boot, special lights, WhizzWheels, 120 mm.	
		Metallic Blue/Silver (1st issue) Metallic Mid-Blue or Gold body	£20-30
281	1971-73	**Rover 2000 TC** ....Metallic Purple, Yellow interior, amber or clear roof, WhizzWheels, 95 mm	£75-85
		Metallic Purple body, Matt Black roof panel	£75-85
		Gold plated version	£100-130
C281	1982-	**'DATAPOST' Metro**................Blue/White body, rally number '77', various adverts, 94 mm	£9-12
282	1971-74	**Mini Cooper Rally** ....White/Black, rally number '177', special lights, WhizzWheels, 73 mm	£55-65
283	1971-74	**DAF 'City' Car** ....Red/Black body, White interior, opening doors/bonnet, WhizzWheels	£25-30
C284	1970-76	**Citroën SM** ....Metallic Gold or Metallic Mauve, opening doors, WhizzWheels, 112 mm	£25-30
C285	1975-81	**Mercedes-Benz 240 D** ....Silver, Blue or Copper/Beige, (all Metallic) WhizzWheels, 127 mm	£15-20
C286	1975-79	**Jaguar XJC V-12** ....Blue/Black, Red/Black, Red, Blue, Orange, (all Metallic) WhizzWheels	£15-20
C287	1975-78	**Citroën Dyane** ....Metallic Yellow/Black or Metallic Green/Black, duck decal, WhizzWheels	£15-20
C288	1975-79	**Minissima**...........................Green and Cream body, opening door and bonnet, 63 mm	£15-20
289	1976	**VW Polo 'DBP'**......................Yellow, Blue roof beacon, left-hand drive, WhizzWheels, (German issue)	NGPP
C289	1977-81	**Volkswagen Polo** ....Metallic Green body, opening doors and hatchback, 97 mm	£15-20
C289	1977-81	**VW Polo 'ADAC'** ....As previous model but Yellow body German issue	£25-35
291	1977-78	**AMC Pacer** ....Metallic Maroon body, opening doors and hatchback, 118 mm	£10-12
C291	1982	**Mercedes Benz 240 Rally** ....Muddy Cream body, RN '5', 'EAST AFRICAN RALLY' or 'E.A.R.' logos	£20-25
C293	1977	**Renault 5 TS**........................Metallic Gold body, Black trim, or Metallic Orange body, Black trim, 97 mm	£10-15
	French issue:	Light Blue body, Dark Blue roof, 'SOS MEDICINS'	£75-85
C294	1980	**Renault 5 TS Alpine** ....Black body with White stripe, opening doors and hatchback, 97 mm	£8-12
C299	1982	**Ford Sierra 23 Ghia** ....Metallic Light Brown/Black stripe, Dark Brown or Grey interior, Brown or	
		Dark Grey base. Issued in a special two-tone Blue 'Ford' box	£20-25
		As previous model but Metallic Light Brown, Metallic Blue, Red or Yellow	
		body, packed in White/Red 'Ford' box or normal Black/Yellow/Red box	£15-20
	1985	Metallic Silver or Yellow body	£15-20
	1985	Red body, White broken ground	£15-20
C299	1987	**Sierra Rally** ....Black body, rally number '7', 'TEXACO'	£10-12
C299/4	1990	**Ford Sierra** ....Pink body, 'MR TOMKINSON'S CARPETS' logo	£10-12
300	1956-63	**Austin Healey 100-4**...............Red with Cream seats or Cream with Red seats, (different shades exist)	£90-120
		Blue body with Cream seats	£175-225
300	1970-72	**Chevrolet Corvette Stingray**...Lacquered-finish Bright Green or Dark Red body, Golden Jacks, luggage	£75-85
		NB Models without box header cards contained instructions.	
C300	1979-82	**Ferrari 'DAYTONA'** ....Green, multicoloured flash, racing number '5', opening doors, 120 mm	£15-20
301	1956-59	**Triumph TR2** ....Cream body with Red seats	£80-100
		Red body with Cream seats	£80-100
		Deep Green body with Cream seats	£100-125
301	1970-73	**Iso Grifo 7 litre**....................Metallic Blue body, Black bonnet, Silver or Black roll-bar, WhizzWheels	£30-35
C301	1979-82	**Lotus Elite Racing Car**...........Yellow and Red body, racing number '7', 'FERODO', 120 mm	£10-15
302	1957-64	**MG 'MGA'** ....Red (Cream seats) smooth or shaped spun hubs, 90 mm, (paint shades exist)	£100-125
		Metallic Light or Mid-Green body (Cream or Yellow seats), smooth or shaped spun hubs	£100-125
302	1969	**Hillman Hunter Rally**.............Blue body, White roof, Matt-Black bonnet, RN '75', equipment, kangaroo,	
		'Golden Jacks', transfers, toolbox, leaflet, instructions	£100-125
C302	1979-82	**VW Polo**.............................Metallic Brown/Red body, racing number '4', various adverts, 97 mm	£9-12
303	1958-60	**Mercedes-Benz 300 SL** ....White open body, Blue seats, smooth hubs, Blue box	£65-75
		Blue open body, White seats, smooth hubs, Blue box	£65-75
		Cream open body, Blue seats, smooth hubs, Blue box	£70-80
		NB Models in rare plain overprinted box add **£20-30**.	
303	1970-72	**Roger Clark's Capri** ....White body, Black bonnet, RN '73', decal sheet, WhizzWheels, 102 mm	£40-45
		As previous model but with Gold/Red hubs	£75-85
303 S	1961-65	**Mercedes-Benz 300 SL** ....Off-White open body, Yellow seats, shaped hubs, bonnet stripe, RN '1-12'	£60-70
		Blue open body, Yellow seats, shaped hubs, bonnet stripe, RN '1-12'	£55-65
		NB As from 1963 all '303S' models included a driver in a Grey suit,	
		White shirt and red bow tie, racing numbers '3' or '7'.	
		White open body, Yellow seats, bonnet stripe, driver, shaped hubs	£55-65
		Gold 'plated' open body, Yellow and Brown seats, driver, cast hubs	£125-150

C303	1980-	Porsche 924 Racer	Orange body, racing number '2', 'PIRELLI', 118 mm	£9-12
			Yellow body with 'HELLA' logo	£35-45
304	1959-61	Mercedes-Benz 300 SL Hardtop	Yellow body, Red hardtop, smooth spun hubs, no suspension	£85-95
			All Yellow body, smooth hubs	£125-150
304	1971-73	Chevrolet Camaro	Dark Blue body, White bonnet band and detachable roof, special lights	£30-40
304 S	1961-65	Mercedes-Benz 300 SL Hardtop	Chrome body, Red roof, stripe, smooth/shaped/spoked hubs, RN '3' or '7'	£70-85
305	1960-62	Triumph TR3	Metallic Olive or Cream body, Red seats, smooth or shaped hubs, 86 mm	£75-95
305S	1962-64	Triumph TR3	Light Green or Cream body, spring suspension, shaped spun hubs, 86 mm	£90-110
305	1972-73	Mini Marcos GT 850	White and Red body, Blue and White stripes, racing number '7', 86 mm	£30-35
306	1971-73	Morris Marina 1.8 Coupé	Metallic Red (White seats), WhizzWheels, 98 mm	£40-45
			Metallic Lime Green	£35-40
C306	1980-	Fiat X1/9S	Blue with Red/Yellow bands, racing number '3' or '6', 110 mm	£10-12
307	1962-64	Jaguar 'E' type	Red or Metallic Grey body with Red removable hard-top, 95 mm	£65-75
			Plum body, Red hard-top	£70-80
307	1981-	Renault Turbo	Yellow/Red body, racing number '8', 'CIBIE', other adverts, 100 mm	£7-10
C308	1972-76	Mini Cooper 'S' 'MONTE CARLO'	Yellow body, RN '177', two spare wheels on roof-rack, WhizzWheels	£65-75
C308	1982-	BMW M1	Yellow body, racing number '25', 'GOODYEAR', detailed engine, 129 mm	£10-15
			Gold body. Only 144 thought to exist	£1000-1500
309	1962-65	Aston Martin DB4	Turquoise and White body, Yellow interior, flags, spun hubs, RN '1', '3' or '7'	£70-80
			Variation with spoked hubs	£90-110
C309	1982-	VW 'TURBO'	White and Brown body, racing number '14', various adverts, 97 mm	£10-15
310	1963-68	Corvette Stingray	Metallic Deep Pink, Yellow interior, shaped hubs, 90 mm	£30-40
			Silver body, wire wheels	£40-50
			Bronze body	£80-100
310	1984	Porsche 924 Turbo	Black body (Gold design, Red seats) or Red body with Porsche badge	£10-15
C310	1982-	'PORSCHE' 924 Turbo	Black and Gold, opening doors and hatchback, 'GOODYEAR', 124 mm	£10-15
311	1970-72	Ford Capri V6	Orange body, Gold wheels with Red hubs, Black interior, 102 mm	£80-90
			Fluorescent Orange body, WhizzWheels	£50-60
			Fluorescent Orange body, Red spot WhizzWheels	£100-150
			Red body, Black bonnet, Red spot WhizzWheels	£50-60
312	1964-68	'E' type Jaguar	Plated Gold or Silver, racing number '2', driver, suspension, spoked hubs	£70-80
312	1971-73	Marcos Mantis	Metallic Plum body with opening doors, spoked hubs, 110 mm	£20-30
C312	1983-	Ford Capri 'S'	White, racing number '6', hinged parcel shelf, various adverts, 97 mm	£10-15
313	1970-73	Ford Cortina GXL	Metallic Blue body, Black and White interior, Graham Hill figure, WhizzWheels	£60-70
			Bronze body, Black roof	£60-70
			Yellow body, Black roof	£150-175
			Metallic Pale Green body, Black roof	£100-120
		Promotional:	Tan body with 'CORTINA' number plate	£150-200
314	1965-71	Ferrari Berlinetta 250 LM	Red body, racing number '4', wire wheels, suspension, 95 mm	£45-55
C314	1976-79	Fiat X1-9	Metallic Lime Green body, Black top, or Silver body, Black top, suspension, hook, 110 mm	£25-35
C314	1982-	Supercat Jaguar XJS-HE	Black body, Red or Tan interior, opening doors, 118 mm	£10-15
315	1964-66	Simca 1000 Sports	Plated Silver, Red interior, RN '8', Red/White/Blue stripes	£35-45
			Metallic Blue body, racing number '8', Red/White/Blue stripes	£100-120
C315	1976-78	Lotus Elite	Red or Yellow with White seats, opening doors, suspension, 120 mm	£10-15
316	1963-66	NSU Sport Prinz	Metallic Red (with Yellow seats) or Maroon body, suspension, 86 mm	£40-50
316	1971-73	Ford GT 70	Green and Black body, White interior, racing number '32', flag design	£30-40
317	1964	Mini Cooper 'S' 'MONTE CARLO 1964'	Red body, White roof, Yellow interior, racing number '37', roof spotlight	£125-150
			Red body, Pink roof variation	£175-200
318	1965	Mini Cooper 'S' 'MONTE CARLO 1965'	Red body, White roof, 'AJB 44 B', racing number '52', no roof spotlight	£150-175
318	1965-67	Lotus Elan S2 Open Top	Metallic Blue, racing number '8', driver, opening bonnet, tilt seats, 'tiger' decal, 'I'VE GOT A TIGER IN MY TANK' logo on boot lid	£80-90
318	1965-68	Lotus Elan S2 Open Top	Dark Green body, Yellow stripe with Black or Red interior (GS37)	GSP
			White body, Black interior (GS40), 'tiger' label	£200-250
			Metallic Copper body	£150-200
318	1981	Jaguar XJS	Blue and Cream body with Red line	£15-20
C318	1983		Black/Red/White body, racing number '4', 'MOTUL', 'JAGUAR'	£15-20
	1985	Export issue:	Green body, racing number '12' and 'DEUTCHSLAND' logo	NGPP
C318	1985		British Racing Green body with White band, racing number '12'	£10-15
	1988		Pale Blue body, Beige seats	£10-15
318/8	1990		Blue body with White seats	£10-15
319	1967-68	Lotus Elan S2 Hardtop	Dark Green body, Yellow top, or Blue body, White top, shaped hubs	£85-95
			Red body, White top, cast hubs	£75-85
			Red body, Red top, cast hubs	£75-85
			Green and Yellow lift-off body, racing number '3', 90 mm	£80-90
			Red body with White top or Blue body with White top	£70-80
C319	1974-75	Lamborghini Miura	Silver/Purple/Yellow body, racing number '7', WhizzWheels, 95 mm	£20-25
319	1978-82	Jaguar XJS	Metallic Plum body, Black roof, opening doors, suspension, 128 mm	£15-20

320	1965-67	**Ford Mustang Fastback 2+2**	...Opening doors, suspension, Corgi dog, half-open window, 95 mm.	
			Silver (Red interior) or Metallic Deep Blue (White interior) detailed cast hubs	£70-80
			Metallic Deep Blue or Light Green body, spoked hubs	£70-80
			Metallic Lilac body, spoked hubs	£70-80
321	1965	**Mini Cooper 'S'**		
		'MONTE CARLO 1965'	...Red body, White roof, spotlight, rally number '52'.	
			317 picture box with 'No. 321' and 'MONTE CARLO WINNER' flash	£350-450
			Red body, White roof with spotlight, rally number '52'	£200-250
321	1966	**Mini Cooper 'S'**		
		'MONTE CARLO 1966'	...Red body, White roof with rally number '2' and *'TIMO MAKINEN'* and	
			'PAUL EASTER' signatures, no spotlight. Box flashed with white sticker with	
			'1966 MONTE CARLO RALLY AUTOGRAPHED MINI-COOPER 'S' in	
			Red capital letters	£250-300
	variant:		As previous issue but in 321 pictorial box with 'RALLY' text printed	
			in Red panel	**£350-400**
321	1978-82	**Porsche 924 Saloon**	...Metallic Green body with hook, 118 mm	£40-45
			Red body	£10-15
			Metallic Light Brown body, Red interior	£60-70
322	1965-66	**Rover 2000**		
		'MONTE CARLO'	...Metallic Maroon body, White roof, Red interior, rally number '136', rally plaques	£120-150
			As previous model but with Green interior	NGPP
			Model boxed in rare 252 box with 322 labels over the box ends	£175-200
	1967	**'INTERNATIONAL**		
		RALLY FINISH'	White body, Black bonnet, Red interior, White/Orange label on doors with	
			Black RN '21', cast hubs. 322 box with Red 'ROVER 2000 INTERNATIONAL	
			RALLY FINISH' and box flash. Paint shade differences are known	£175-225
323	1965-66	**Citroën DS19**		
		'MONTE CARLO 1965'	...Blue/White, rally plaques and number '75', suspension, 97 mm	£100-125
C323	1974-78	**Ferrari Daytona 365 GTB/4**	...White/Red/Blue body, racing number '81', opening doors, 122 mm	£10-15
324	1966-69	**Marcos Volvo 1800 GT**	...White body with two Green stripes	£35-40
			Blue body with two White stripes	£50-60
324	1974	**Ferrari Daytona Le Mans**	...Yellow body, racing number '33', *'A.BAMFORD'*, 122 mm	£25-35
325	1966-69	**Ford Mustang Competition**	...White body with double Red stripe (Blue interior). Shaped spun hubs,	
			detailed cast hubs, wire wheels or cast 'alloy' wheels	£50-60
			White body, double Red stripes, Gold 'alloy' wheels	£60-70
	Note:		A sheet of four racing numbers (no. '4') enclosed with each model.	
C325	1981-	**Chevrolet Caprice**	...Metallic Light Green or Dark Green body, White-wall tyres, 150 mm	£20-25
			Metallic Silver over Dark Blue (US market)	£70-80
327	1967-69	**MGB GT**	...Dark Red body, Blue or Yellow interior, spoked wheels, luggage	£70-85
328	1966-67	**Hillman Imp**		
		'MONTE CARLO 1966'	...Metallic Dark Blue/White, 'FRW 306 C', rally plaques and number '107'	£70-85
329	1973-76	**Ford Mustang**	...Green/White body, racing number '69', opening doors, suspension, 113 mm	£25-30
329	1980-	**Opel Senator**	...Dark Blue or Bronze body, opening doors, 142 mm	£15-18
			Silver body	£25-30
330	1967-69	**Porsche Carrera 6**	...White body, Red top, racing number '1' or '20', suspension, 97 mm	£35-45
			White body, Dark Blue panels, Yellow engine cover, RN '60'	£65-75
Q330/1	1989	**Mini 30th Anniversary**	...Pearlescent Cherry Red, Austin-Rover mail-order model (17,500)	£8-10
(Q24/1)	1989	**Mini 30th Anniversary**	...Q330/1 Mini specially packaged with 'MINI' book	£45-55
C330/10	1990	**Mini 'AFTER EIGHT'**	...Dark Blue with Gold stripe, French export model (5,000)	£10-15
331	1974-76	**Ford Capri GT**	...White body, Black bonnet, 'TEXACO', racing number '5' 102 mm	£45-55
332	1967-69	**Lancia Fulvia Zagato**	...Metallic Green, Metallic Blue, or Red, suspension, tilt seats	£50-60
			Yellow body, Black roof	£100-125
333	1966	**Mini Cooper S**		
		'SUN - RAC Rally'	...Red/White body, RN '21' and *'SUN RAC INTERNATIONAL RALLY'* decals, 225 box with	
			White label '1966 RAC INTERNATIONAL RALLY' in Blue, rally information leaflet	£240-280
334	1968-70	**Mini Cooper 'Magnifique'**	...Metallic Dark Blue or Green, jewelled lights, sunshine roof, 73 mm	£60-75
C334	1981-	**Ford Escort 1.3 GL**	...Blue, Green or Yellow body	£12-15
			Red body with 'AVIS' logo on roof	£25-35
335	1968-69	**Jaguar 4.2 litre 'E' type**	...Metallic Dark Red body, spoked wheels	£80-90
			Metallic Blue body, Black interior	£80-90
			Orange body, Black roof	NGPP
337	1967-69	**Chevrolet Stock Car**	...Yellow body, racing number '13', *'STINGRAY'*, suspension, 95 mm	£35-40
338	1968-71	**Chevrolet SS 350 Camaro**	...Golden Jacks and Take-Off wheels, sliding headlight cover,	
			removable hardtop, Metallic Gold/Black or Metallic Yellow body, 102 mm	£35-45
C338	1980-	**Rover 3500**	...Metallic Blue, Red/Black or Orange/Brown body, suspension	£15-20
339	1967-72	**Mini Cooper 'S'**		
		'MONTE CARLO 1967'		
	(i)		Red body, White roof, RN '177', sump guard, shaped spun hubs, Austin grille, in	
			227 box with White flash label with '1967 MONTE-CARLO WINNER B.M.C.	
			MINI-COOPER 'S' in Red capital letters, Red '339' flash on box end	£150-200
	(ii)		As (i) but with cast detailed hubs and slight Silver detail	£150-200
	(iii)		As (i) but with shaped spun hubs and slight Silver detail	£150-200
	(iv)		As (i) but with cast detailed hubs and Morris grille	£150-200
	(v)		As (i) but in 339 picture box with winner's text in Red lettering on box front.	
			Special leaflet enclosed with each model	£150-200
	(vi)		As (i) but in 339 box with the winners text in Red panel	£150-200

340	1967-68	**Sunbeam Imp** 'MONTE CARLO 1967'		
		(i)	Metallic Blue, RN '77', spun hubs, flashed 328 box with '1967 MONTE CARLO SUNBEAM IMP WINNER PRODUCTION CARS UP TO 1000cc' text in Blue capitals plus model no. '340'	**£100-125**
		(ii)	As (i) but in 340 pictorial box with 'winner' text printed in Red on the box front plus cast detailed hubs	**£100-125**
		(iii)	As (i) but Metallic Dark Blue body, cast detailed hubs, 'winner' text printed in Red panel on box front	**£150-175**
C340	1981	**Rover 'TRIPLEX'** .... White/Red/Blue, racing number '1', hinged parcel shelf, 140 mm	**£15-20**
341	1968-70	**Mini Marcos GT 850** .... Metallic Crimson (Cream seats) or Metallic Maroon body, Golden Jacks	**£30-40**
C341	1981-	**Chevrolet Caprice** .... Red/White/Blue body, racing number '43', 'STP', 150 mm	**£10-15**
342	1970-72	**Lamborghini P400 Miura** .... Red/Black, Green or Lemon Yellow, Black bull figure, WhizzWheels, spare wheel ...	**£40-50**
343	1969-73	**Pontiac Firebird** .... Metallic Silver/Black, Red seats, Gold/Red Take-Off wheels, Golden Jacks	**£25-35**
			With Red-spot WhizzWheels	**£50-60**
343	1980-	**Ford Capri 3 litre** .... Yellow or Silver body, Black designs, opening doors/hatchback, 124 mm	**£30-35**
344	1969-73	**Ferrari Dino Sports** .... Yellow (number '23') or Red (number '30') WhizzWheels, 104 mm	**£30-40**
			With Red-spot WhizzWheels	**£40-50**
345	1969	**MGC GT Competition** .... Yellow body, Black bonnet (with bulge), spoked wheels, 90 mm. 'MGB GT' on box overprinted 'NEW MGC' Self-adhesive numbers enclosed	**£80-90**
		Gift Set version:	Orange body (Car Transporter Gift Set 48)	**£150-200**
C345	1981-	**Honda Prelude** .... Metallic Blue, Cream/Green or Metallic Yellow body, sunshine roof	**£10-15**
C346	1982-84	**Citroën 2cv Charleston** .... Yellow/Black, Burgundy/Black, Red/White or Grey/Red body	**£10-15**
347	1969-74	**Chevrolet Astro Experimental** .... Metallic Dark Blue or Green body, Red-spot WhizzWheels	**£40-50**
			As previous model but with plain WhizzWheels	**£30-40**
348	1968-69	**Mustang 'Pop Art' Stock Car** .... Blue with Red/Orange 'Flower-Power' labels, racing number '20'	**£65-75**
			Blue body without labels	**£50-60**
C350	1985	**Toyota Celica Supra** .... Red/White body, racing number '14', 'HUGHES', racing tyres 112 mm	**£7-10**
C351	1985	**Ford Sierra Pace Car** .... White body, Green/Yellow tampo-print design, warning lights, flags	**£7-10**
C352	1986	**BMW 325** .... White with Black logo Swiss export model	**NGPP**
353/1	1986	**BMW 325** .... Red body, Black trim, opening features	**NRP**
353/9	1990	**BMW 325i** .... Black body with Red seats	**NRP**
C353	1987	**BMW 325i Rally** .... White body, Green logo 'CASTROL'	**£7-10**
354	1986	**BMW 325** .... White body, racing number '33', 'FAVRAUD' logo	**£7-10**
370	1982	**Ford Cobra Mustang** .... White/Black/Red/Blue, 'MUSTANG', with or without tailgate stripe, 135 mm	**£10-15**
C370	1982	**Ford Cobra Mustang** .... White body, Red interior, Blue/Red design	**£10-15**
371	1970-73	**Porsche Carrera 6** .... White/Red, racing number '60', plated Blue engine cover, WhizzWheels	**£20-25**
372	1970-72	**Lancia Fulvia Zagato** .... Red/Black body, opening doors/bonnet, suspension, WhizzWheels, 91 mm	**£30-35**
C373	1981-	**Peugeot 505** .... Red body, Silver or Black lining, opening doors, suspension, 127 mm	**£10-15**
C374	1970-73	**Jaguar 'E' type 4.2 litre** .... Red or Yellow body, WhizzWheels, 108 mm	**£30-40**
C374	1973	**Jaguar 'E' type 5.3 litre** .... Yellow or Metallic Yellow body 'New' on box label	**£40-50**
375	1970-72	**Toyota 2000 GT** .... Metallic translucent 'candy' Blue body, WhizzWheels, 102 mm	**£40-50**
			Metallic Purple body, WhizzWheels	**£45-55**
376	1970-72	**Chevrolet Corvette Stock Car** .. Silver body, racing number '13', 'GO-GO-GO', WhizzWheels, 95 mm	**£25-35**
377	1970-73	**Marcos 3 litre** .... Yellow body, Black bonnet, WhizzWheels, 91mm (324 conversion)	**£40-45**
			White body, Grey sunroof, Whizzwheels	**£70-80**
			Metallic Blue-Green body	**£30-40**
378	1970-72	**MGC GT** .... Red body, Black bonnet, opening doors/hatchback, WhizzWheels, 90 mm	**£70-85**
			Orange body, (this version in Gift Set 20)	**GSP**
C378	1982-	**Ferrari 308 GTS** .... Red or Black body, pop-up headlights, opening engine cover, 115 mm	**£20-30**
380	1970-72	**Alfa Romeo P33** .... White body, Gold roll bar, Red seats, WhizzWheels, 95 mm	**£25-30**
C380	1983-	**'BASF' BMW M1** .... Red/White, racing number '80', aerofoil, opening engine cover, 129 mm	**£7-10**
381	1970-74	**VW Beach Buggy** .... Metallic Red/White, Blue/White, Orange/White or Red/White, WhizzWheels	**£15-20**
C381	1983-	**'ELF' Renault Turbo** .... Red/White/Blue, racing number '5', 'FACOM', 100 mm	**£10-15**
			Blue/White body, racing number '13', 'ELF'	**£10-15**
382	1970-75	**Porsche Targa 911S** .... Metallic Silver-Blue body, Black roof with Gold stripe, WhizzWheels, 95 mm	**£30-40**
			Metallic Olive-Green body, Black roof with or without Gold stripe, WhizzWheels	**£30-40**
C382	1981-	**Lotus Elite 22** .... Blue body, 'Elite 22', opening doors, number plates, 120 mm	**£10-15**
383	1970-76	**Volkswagen 1200** .... Orange body	**£30-40**
			Red body with 'Flower Power' logo	**£75-85**
383	1970-73	**VW 1200 'ADAC'** .... Yellow/Black body, 'ADAC' logo (German equivalent of 'AA')	**£90-120**
		VW 1200 'PTT' .... Yellow/Black body, 'PTT' logo, Swiss issue	**£90-120**
383	1977-78	**Volkswagen 1200 Rally** .... Blue body, rally number '5', chequered roof and sides	**£10-15**
384	1978	**Volkswagen 1200 Rally** .... Blue body, rally number '5', chequered stripes	**£35-45**
			As previous model but with 'CALEDONIAN AUTOMINOLOGISTS' logo	**£80-90**
			Blue body, Cream interior, WhizzWheels, '40th Anniversary 1938 - 1978'	**£140-160**
384	1970-73	**Adams Brothers Probe** .... Metallic Maroon (Blue interior) or Metallic Gold body, WhizzWheels, 97 mm	**£15-20**
384	1983-84	**Renault 11 GTL** .... Dark Cream body, Red interior, opening doors and boot, 110 mm	**£9-12**
			Maroon or Metallic Mauve body	**£25-30**

385	1970-76	**Porsche 917**	Metallic Blue or Red body, racing number '3', cast or WhizzWheels, 108 mm	£20-25
385	1984	**Mercedes 190 E**	Silver/Black body, White seats, number plates, chrome trim	£9-12
	1985		All-Silver body	£9-12
386	1971-74	**Bertone Barchetta**	Yellow and Black 'RUNABOUT', aerofoil, WhizzWheels, 83 mm	£20-25
386	1987	**Mercedes 23/16**	White body, Black racing number '17', 'SERVIS'	£5-8
386/4	1988		As previous model but racing number '17', 'BURLINGTON AIR EXPRESS'	£5-8
386/8	1990	**Mercedes 23/16**	Red body with Beige seats	£5-8
387	1970-73	**Corvette Stingray**	Metallic Blue body, Black bonnet, roof emblem, WhizzWheels, 99 mm	£35-45
			Metallic Pink body, Black bonnet	£50-60
388	1970-74	**Mercedes-Benz C111**	Orange and Black, WhizzWheels, 104 mm	£20-25
389	1971-74	**Reliant Bond 'BUG' 700 ES**	Orange body, Orange/Black 'BUG' labels, Cream interior, WhizzWheels, 64 mm	£35-45
			Lime Green body, WhizzWheels	£65-75
392	1973-74	**Bertone Shake Buggy**	Yellow and Green or Pink and Green, detailed engine, flag, 89 mm	£25-30
C393	1972-79	**Mercedes-Benz 350 SL**	White body, Pale Blue interior with chrome, spoked wheels, 102 mm	£25-30
			Metallic Blue or Dark Blue body with chrome solid disc wheels	£25-30
			Metallic Green body	£55-65
394	1973-76	**Datsun 240 Z**	Red body, Black roof, non-rally version	£25-35
394	1973-76	**Datsun 240 Z**	Red body, Black roof, rally number '11', 'EAST AFRICAN SAFARI'	£30-40
396		**Datsun 240 Z**	Red body, White roof, rally number '46', 'JOHN MORTON', WhizzWheels	£30-40
397	1974-78	**Porsche-Audi 917-10**	Orange body, White 'L&M' logo, racing number '6', 'CORGI', racing driver	£25-30
399	1985	**Peugeot 205**	Silver body, racing number '205', multi-coloured tampo-print design	£7-10
399/5	1988	**Peugeot 205 T16**	Yellow body, racing number '2', 'VATENEN'	£7-10
C400	1974-77	**Volkswagen 1200**	Metallic Red body, 'CORGI MOTOR SCHOOL', roof steering wheel, cones	£70-80
			Metallic Blue body version	£35-45
			Metallic Blue with 'CORGI FAHR SCHULE', German issue	£100-120
C401	1975-77	**Volkswagen 1200**	Same as C400 but supplied with 24 'bollards' for miniature driving practice	£35-45
402	1985	**BMW M1**	Red and White body, racing number '101', 'CASTROL'	£7-10
403	1985	**Ford Escort**	White body, racing number '84', multicoloured print, 'TOTAL'	£7-10
404	1985	**Rover 3500**	Red body, racing number '13', 'DAILY MIRROR'	£7-10
	1986		Red body, racing number '1', 'TEXACO'	£7-10
C415	1976-78	**Mazda Camper**	Red body with drop-down tailboard, White caravan, 140 mm	£25-30
C419	1978-79	**Covered Jeep CJ5**	Green body with White plastic top, or Metallic Dark Green body	£25-35
420	1962-66	**Ford 'Airborne' Caravan**	Ford Thames in Two-tone Green, Brown interior or Blue/Pale Grey, Red interior or Blue/Green, Brown interior	£40-50
			Two-tone Lilac, Beige interior	£70-80
420	1984	**'BMW M1'**	Blue and White body, racing number '11', 'LIGIER'S'	£7-10
	1985		White body, racing number '17', 'ESSO'	£7-10
422	1984	**'RENAULT 5' TBA**	Blue body, racing number '25', 'BOSCH' and 'ELF'	£7-10
	1985		Dark Blue body, multicoloured print, racing number '18'	£7-10
423	1984	**Ford Escort**	Blue and White body, 'BROOKLYN', Red seats, racing number '69', 'SHELL'	£7-10
424	1961-65	**Ford Zephyr Estate**	Two-tone Blue, suspension, luggage, smooth or shaped spun hubs, 97 mm	£55-65
424	1984	**'FORD MUSTANG'**	Black body, Yellow/Red print, racing number '77', 'ESSO'	£8-10
426	1984	**'HEPOLITE' Rover**	Yellow and Red, racing number '4', 'FERODO'	£8-10
	1988		Yellow and Red body, 'DAILY EXPRESS'	£8-10
435	1986	**Volvo 760 Turbo**	Dark Blue or Silver body or Metallic Dark Brown body	£8-10
435/2	1987	**Volvo 760 Turbo**	White body, Blue/Yellow print, 'GILLANDERS'	£8-10
C435/12	1990	**Volvo 760 Turbo**	Green body with White seats	£8-10
440	1966-67	**Ford Cortina Estate**	Blue body, Brown panels, opening tailgate, suspension, 2 figures, golf equipment	£100-125
C440	1979-	**Mazda Custom Pick-Up**	Orange/Yellow/Red, US flag, 120 mm	£15-20
C440	1988	**Porsche 944 Saloon**	Red body	£8-10
C440	1988	**'PORSCHE 944' Rally**	White body, Red design	£8-10
C440/6	1990	**Porsche 944 Rally**	White body, Pink/Blue design, 'PIRELLI', rally number '44'	£8-10
C441	1979-82	**'GOLDEN EAGLE' Jeep**	Brown and Tan or Gold and White, detachable roof, spare wheel on some, 100 mm	£15-20
445		**Plymouth Suburban Sports Station Wagon**	Pale Blue body, Red roof, Silver stripe	£55-65
C447	1983	**'RENEGADE' 4x4 Jeep**	Yellow body, racing number '5' (As 448 but without hood). In GS 36	GSP
C448	1983	**'RENEGADE' 4x4 Jeep**	Yellow body, Red hood, racing number '5'	£8-10
C448	1985	**'RENEGADE' 4x4 Jeep**	Red and White body, roll bar, 100 mm	£5-10
C453	1984	**Ford Escort RS 1600 i**	White body, Red seats, Black design, 110 mm	£10-15
C457	1981-83	**Talbot Matra Rancho**	Red body, Black roof, or Green body, Black roof, opening doors and boot, tilt seats, 120 mm	£10-15
C457	1984	**Talbot Matra Rancho**	Orange body, Black roof, or White body, Blue roof, Brown seats, 120 mm	£20-25
485	1966-69	**Mini Countryman 'Surfing'**	Sea-Green body, 2 surfboards on roof-rack, male figure, special descriptive leaflet	£125-150
			As previous model but with unpainted grille	£140-170
491	1967-69	**Ford Cortina Estate**	Metallic Dark Grey, Brown 'wood' panels, shaped spun hubs	£50-60
			As previous model but with cast detailed hubs	£50-60
C501	1984	**Range Rover**	Beige and Dark Brown body	£5-10
C507	1987-?	**Range Rover Rally**	Navy Blue body, White roof, 'PARIS-DAKAR' logo	£20-30
C522		**Range Rover**	Red/White/Blue, 'STIMOROL'	NGPP
C567	1984	**Range Rover**	White body, 'PARIS MATCH', and 'VSD'	£7-10

Cars

600	1984	**Ford Escort**	All Red or Red/Black or Red/White body, opening doors, 110 mm	£8-10
601	1984	**Fiat N-9**	Red or Silver/Red body, opening doors, 110 mm	£8-10
602	1984	**BL Mini 1000**	Yellow body, with or without *'CITY'*, opening doors, 85 mm	£8-10
	1984		Chrome plated model, wooden plinth, in black 'Austin-Rover' box, *'Austin-Rover Mini 25th Celebration Donington Park - August 1984'*	£70-80
	1984		Metallic Dark Blue, racing number '8'	£20-25
603	1984	**Volkswagen Polo**	Green and White or White body, opening doors, 90 mm	£8-10
604	1984	**Renault 5**	Dark Blue or Black or Yellow body, with or without *'Le Car TL'*, 95 mm	£8-10
605	1984	**Austin Mini Metro**	Blue body, with or without *'TURBO'*, 90 mm	£8-10
611	1985-86	**Ford Escort**	Red body, *'DATAPOST 66'*	£8-10
612	1985-86	**Ford Escort**	Red body, *'DATAPOST 77'*	£8-10
613	1985-86	**Metro Saloon**	Red body, *'DATAPOST 66'*	£8-10
614	1985-86	**Metro Saloon**	Red, body *'DATAPOST 77'*	£8-10
C619	1986	**Range Rover**	Dark Beige body, Black ladder, roof-rack, luggage	£5-10
			Red body with 'ROYAL MAIL' logo	£10-15
			Red or Metallic Blue body, Brown 'wood' panels, shaped spun hubs	£50-60
C675/14	1990	**BMW 635**	Red and Black body, White-wall tyres	£8-10
C1009	1984	**MG Maestro**	Yellow body, White flash, *'AA SERVICE'*	£8-10
60317	1992	**F1 Racing Car**	Green and White body, 'FUJI FILM' logo, Boots promotional (35,000)	NGPP
?	?	**Jaguar XJR9**	White body, 'Martin Brundle', 'J. Nielsen' and 'R. Bosel' roof signatures	
			'CASTROL' logos, rally number '60', Petrol Co promotional	£8-10

Marks & Spencer issues

In 1978 a series of special sets and single models were produced for sale through selected M & S stores.
They were packed in attractive non-standard boxes and had unique liveries. They were not issued in great quantities.

Single models

8800	1978	Custom Van	No details available	£25-35
8801	1978	Spindrift Helicopter	Black body with Yellow chassis, floats and rotor blades	£25-35
8802	1978	Massey Ferguson Tractor	Red/Black body with White arms and Red shovel	£40-50
8803	1978	Buick 'FIRE CHIEF' Car	Red body with 'City Fire Department' logo on bonnet	£50-75

Small sets

8000	1978	F1 Racing Set	Includes 162 'ELF' Tyrrell (Dark Blue) and 160 Hesketh F1 (White)	£75-100
8001	1978	Wings Flying Team	Includes 301 Lotus Elite (Green) and Nipper aircraft (White) on Grey trailer	£100-150
8002	1978	Motorway Police Patrol	C429 'POLICE' Jaguar (Green) and Blue Fiat X1-9	£60-80
8003	1978	Spindrift Power Boat Team	301 Ferrari Daytona (Yellow) and Yellow power boat on trailer	£60-80

Medium sets

8100	1978	Racing Team	C421 Land Rover (White with 'FORMULA' logo), 338 Rover, and 301 Lotus on trailer	£150-200
8101	1978	Wings Flying School	C421 Land Rover (Grey with 'WINGS' logo) Grey helicopter and Nipper aircraft on Grey trailer	£150-200
8102	1978	Motorway Breakdown	C429 'POLICE' Jaguar, 293 Renault 5 (Yellow) plus Berliet Wrecker with 'RESCUE BREAKDOWN SERVICES'	£100-150
8103	1978	Spindrift Power Boat Team	Includes Spindrift 301 Ferrari, Helicopter and Dinghy	£150-200

Large sets

8400	1978	Grand Prix Racing	Includes 160 Hesketh (White) 162 'ELF' Tyrrell (Dark Blue) Fiat X1-9 (Blue) and Land Rover (White with 'FORMULA 1 RACING TEAM' logo)	£250-350
8401	1978	Wings Flying Club	Land Rover, Helicopter, Tipsy Nipper aircraft on trailer plus Lotus Elite	£250-300
8402	1978	Motorway Rescue	Includes 'POLICE' Jaguar, Berliet Wrecker, Renault 5 and Fiat X1-9	£250-300
8403	1978	Spindrift Power Boat Team	Includes Ferrari Daytona (Yellow) Yellow power boat on trailer, Yellow/Black helicopter, plus MF Tractor and 'RESCUE' dinghy	£250-300

Trophy Models

(Marks & Spencer special 'plated' issues)

The models were specially produced in 1961 to be sold by Marks & Spencer. The set consisted of five vacuum-plated 'gold' models taken from the existing Corgi product range, each mounted on a detachable black moulded base with a gold name label. The models were packaged in white boxes with red/grey design plus 'St Michael Trophy Models' in red. They did not sell well at the time of issue but are keenly sought after by present day collectors.

150 S	1961	**Vanwall Racing Car**	Gold vacuum-plated body, Red wheels and radiator grille	£100-200
152	1961	**BRM Racing Car**	Gold vacuum-plated body, Red wheels and radiator grille	£100-200
300	1961	**Austin-Healey Sports Car**	Gold vacuum-plated body, plastic windscreen, Red wheels and grille	£100-200
301	1961	**Triumph TR2 Sports Car**	Gold vacuum-plated body, plastic windscreen, Red wheels and grille	£100-200
302	1961	**MG 'MGA' Sports Car**	Gold vacuum-plated body, plastic windscreen, Red wheels and grille	£100-200

Land Rover models

See also Commercial Vehicles, Emergency Vehicles and Novelty sections.

406	1957-62	**Land Rover '109 WB'**	Yellow body, Black roof, smooth hubs, thin tyres	£55-65
			Metallic Dark Blue body, Cream roof, smooth or shaped hubs, thin or thick tyres	£45-55
			Green body with Tan tinplate cover, smooth hubs, thin or thick tyres	£45-55
		'ETENDARD' variant:	As previous issue but with 'ETENDARD' decals, plus Red/White/Green roundels on front wings	NGPP
406s	1963	**Land Rover '109 WB'**	Yellow body, Red seats, shaped hubs, suspension	£75-85
417	1960-62	**Land Rover Breakdown**	Red body, Yellow tinplate canopy, smooth hubs, *'BREAKDOWN SERVICE'*	£55-65
417s	1963-65	**Land Rover Breakdown**	Red body, Yellow tinplate canopy, shaped hubs, suspension, *'BREAKDOWN SERVICE'*	£45-55
C421	1977-79	**Land Rover Safari**	Orange/Black body, roof rack with ladder, spare wheel, 114 mm	£15-20
			A variant of C421 with *'FOREST FIRE WARDEN'*	£15-20
438	1963-77	**Land Rover 109**	Model has plastic canopy. Earlier issues have metal towhooks (plastic later), suspension.	
			Dark Green body Grey or Tan canopy, Yellow interior, shaped hubs	£35-45
			Dark Brown body, Light Brown canopy, Red interior, shaped hubs	£35-45
			Metallic Green body, Olive-Green canopy, Yellow interior, shaped hubs	£35-45
			Metallic Green body, Olive-Green canopy, Chrome hubs	£35-40
			Metallic Green body, Olive-Green canopy, WhizzWheels	£30-35
			Red body, Brown tilt, Red interior, shaped hubs	£35-45
		'LEPRA' variant:	Metallic Green body, Tan canopy with *'LEPRA'* logo, Yellow interior, shaped hubs, Silver steering wheel	£200-250
			Red body, Blue canopy, (in Gift Set 19)	GSP
		Promotional:	with *'10 MILLIONITH CORGI LAND ROVER'* label	£50-75
477	1966-67	**Land Rover Breakdown**	Red/Yellow/Silver, spare wheel on some, hook, WhizzWheels, 114 mm	£30-35
C522/2	1986-	**Ruby Anniversary Land Rover**	Maroon body with '40TH ANNIVERSARY' on bonnet Special box (Major Pack)	NGPP
Q619/3	1990	**'NORWEB' Land Rover**	White with 3 Black side stripes, spare wheel	£15-20

Major Pack

1126	1961-65	**Racing Car Transporter**	Metallic Dark Blue body with 'ECURIE ECOSSE' in Yellow lettering	£150-200
		later version:	with logo in Orange lettering	£90-110
			with logo in White lettering	£90-110
			with logo and raised ridges in Light Blue	£90-110
		colour variant:	Metallic Light Blue body with 'ECURIE ECOSSE' in Red lettering	£90-110

Collectors notes

Corgi Classics - Cars (original issues)

A factory fire ended production in 1969 of this original series of 'Classics' cars. Boxes are of two types: one with separate lid with coloured line-drawings printed on it and containing a separate picture of the model; and type two which has the model attached to a sliding-drawer style base in an outer box with half-flaps (similar printing to 1st type).
NB Early issues have reference number 900 and changed to 9001 etc just before release.

9001	1964-69	**1927 3-litre Bentley**	British Racing Green, racing number '3', detachable hood, driver, 102 mm	£30-40
9002	1964-68	**1927 3-litre Bentley**	Red body, civilian driver, no racing number, detachable hood	£50-60
9004	1967-69	**'WORLD OF WOOSTER'**		
		Bentley	As previous model but in Green or Red and with Jeeves and Wooster figures	£100-150
9011	1964-68	**1915 Model 'T' Ford**	Black body, driver, passenger, spoked wheels, brass radiator, 86 mm	£30-40
9012	1965-68	**Model 'T' Ford**	Version with Yellow/Black body, Black or Yellow wheels	£30-40
9013	1964-69	**1915 Model 'T' Ford**	Blue/Black body, detachable hood, spare wheel, driver cranks, 83 mm	£30-40
9014		**1915 'LYONS TEA' Van**	Appeared in 1967/68 catalogue but was not issued	NPP
9021	1964-69	**1910 38 hp Daimler**	Red body, driver and 3 passengers, folded hood, detailed chassis, 108 mm	£30-40
9022		**1910 38 hp Daimler**	Appeared in the 1966 catalogue but not issued	NPP
9031	1965-68	**1910 Renault 12/16**	Lavender/Black body with carriage lamps, spoked wheels, 102 mm	£30-40
9032	1965-69	**1910 Renault 12/16**	Same as previous model but Primrose Yellow and Black body	£30-40
9041	1966-70	**1912 Rolls-Royce Silver Ghost**	Silver and Black body, carriage lamps, spoked wheels, 118 mm	£25-35
		variant:	Maroon body, Silver roof and bonnet	NGPP

Corgi Classics - Cars (re-introduced issues)

Some of the 'Classics' were re-introduced in 1985 when original tools were discovered. These later models are distinct from the originals as they have 'SPECIAL EDITION' on their baseplates and are packed in Grey/Red boxes which do not contain a picture of the model. The model numbers are different and 13,500 of each colour were made.

C860 (9041)	1985	**1912 Rolls-Royce Silver Ghost**	Silver, Black or Ruby Red body	£8-11
C861 (9002)	1985	**1927 3-litre Bentley open top**	British Racing Green, Black or Ruby Red body	£8-11
C862 (9031)	1985	**1910 Renault 12/16**	Yellow, Pale Blue, Cream or Brown body	£8-11
C863 (9012)	1985	**1915 Model 'T' Ford**	Black, Red or Blue body	£8-11

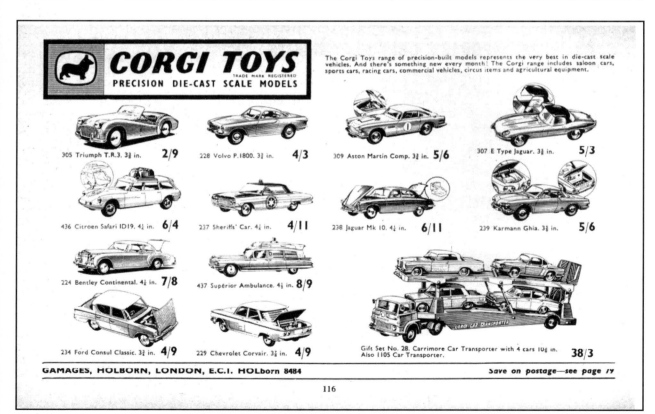

A page from Gamages 1963-64 'Model Book' catalogue

Commercial Vehicles

Excluding models issued from 1987 as 'Corgi Classics' (see 'Collectable Modern Diecasts' section).

Ref.	Year(s)	Model name	Colours, features, dimensions	Market Price Range
54	1974	Massey Ferguson Shovel	Orange/White tractor body, Silver shovel, *'Block Construction'*, 150 mm	£35-45
100	1957-61	Dropside Trailer	Cream/Red or Yellow body, drawbar, 108 mm	£10-15
101	1958-61	Platform Trailer	Grey/Yellow body, drawbar and axle swivel, 108 mm	£10-15
109	1968-69	'PENNYBURN' Trailer	Blue body, Yellow chassis, 76 mm	£30-35
403	1956-61	Bedford 12 cwt Van	'DAILY EXPRESS' on Dark Blue body, 83 mm	£80-100
			As previous model but Deep Blue body	£100-120
403 M	1956-59	Bedford 12 cwt Van	'KLG PLUGS' on Bright Red body, flywheel motor, 83 mm	£125-150
403	1974-79	Thwaites Skip Dumper	Yellow/Green tipping body, driver, WhizzWheels, 83 mm	£25-35
404	1956-62	Bedford Dormobile	Cream (Blue roof on some), Turquoise, Blue, Red or Metallic Red, smooth or ribbed roof, smooth or shaped hubs. Early issues have divided windscreen	£65-75
			Yellow body with Blue roof	£80-90
			Yellow lower half, Blue upper half	£150-200
			All-Yellow body, with suspension	£75-85
404 M	1956-59	Bedford Dormobile	Red, Metallic Red, Turquoise or Blue body, flywheel motor, 83 mm	£85-95
409	1959-63	Forward Control Jeep	Light Blue body, Red grille, smooth or shaped hubs, 91 mm	£25-35
405	1981	Ford Transit Milk Float	'DAIRY CREST' logo on cab doors, 'MILK MARKETING BOARD' logo on each side and 'MILK' on rear	£20-30
C405	1982	Ford Transit Milk Float	'LOTTA BOTTLE' on Blue/White body, opening doors, 143 mm	£10-15
406	1971-75	Mercedes-Benz Unimog	Yellow/Green or Yellow/Red body, detachable top, suspension, hook, 91 mm	£25-35
407	1957-61	Smiths Karrier Bantam	'HOME SERVICES HYGIENIC MOBILE SHOP', Pale Green/Red, 95 mm	£75-85
408	1957-59	Bedford 'AA' Service Van	Yellow/Black, divided windscreen, smooth hubs, Blue box, leaflet	£80-90
	1958-59		Yellow/Black, undivided windscreen, smooth or shaped hubs, Blue box, leaflet	£70-80
	1959-62		Yellow/Black, undivided windscreen, shaped hubs, Blue/Yellow box, no leaflet	£60-70
	late issue:		Yellow/Black, single windscreen, ridged roof, flat spun hubs	£70-80
409	1971-75	Unimog Dumper	White/Red or Blue/Yellow body, suspension, hook, 104 mm	£20-30
C409	1981	'ALLIS CHALMERS' Forklift	Yellow body, pallets/load/driver, 112 mm	£15-20
411	1958-62	Karrier Bantam Van	Yellow body, Grey plastic shutter, smooth wheels, 'LUCOZADE', Blue box	£100-120
			As previous model but with shaped wheels, Blue/Yellow box	£100-120
413	1957-62	Smiths Karrier Bantam Mobile Butchers	White/Blue van, 'FAMILY BUTCHERS', meaty decals, 93 mm. Blue box	£85-95
			As previous model but with suspension	£120-140
413	1976-78	Mazda Motorway Maintenance	Yellow/Black body, figure, road signs, bollards, decal sheet enclosed	£25-35
421	1960-62	Bedford 12 cwt Van	'EVENING STANDARD', Black body, Silver ridged roof, undivided windscreen, smooth hubs, 83 mm	£100-120
			'EVENING STANDARD', Black lower body, Silver upper body and ridged roof, undivided windscreen, smooth hubs	£100-120
			Medium Blue body, 'AVRO BODE' logo	£250-300
422	1960-62	Bedford 12 cwt Van	'CORGI TOYS', Yellow body, Blue roof, smooth or shaped hubs, 83 mm	£140-160
	reversed colours:		Blue body, 'CORGI TOYS', Yellow roof, smooth wheels	£250-350
	variation:		Blue lower half with Yellow upper body, 'CORGI TOYS'	£250-350
C423	1978-78	Chevrolet 'Rough Rider'	Yellow van, motorcycle side decals	£15-20
C424	1977-79	Security Van	Black/Yellow/White body, 'SECURITY', windows with grilles, 100 mm	£10-15
426	1962-64	Karrier Bantam Van Circus Booking Office	Red/Blue body, smooth hubs, 'Chipperfields Booking Office'	£175-200
			As previous model but with shaped hubs	£150-175
C426	1978-81	Chevrolet Booking Office Van	Yellow/Red/Blue body, 'PINDER-JEAN RICHARD', two loudspeakers	£25-35
428	1963-66	Karrier Ice-Cream Van	Blue/White body, detailed chassis, salesman swivels, 'MR SOFTEE'	£100-125
431	1964-66	Volkswagen Pick-Up	Yellow body, Red or Olive-Green canopy, Red 'VW' emblem	£55-65
			Metallic Gold body, Red 'VW' emblem	£140-160
434	1963-66	Volkswagen Kombi	Two-tone Green, Red or Yellow seats, 91 mm	£60-70
433	1962-64	Volkswagen Delivery Van	Red/White body, Red or Yellow interior, 91 mm	£60-70
	Dutch issue:		'VROOM & DREESMAN', Grey body, shaped spun wheels, promotional	£250-350
434	1962	Volkswagen Kombi	Metallic two-tone Green body, Red or Yellow 'VW' badge and seats	£65-75
435	1962-63	Karrier Bantam Van	Blue/White/Yellow body, 'DRIVE SAFELY ON MILK',	£65-75
437	1979-80	Chevrolet Van 'COCA-COLA'	Red body, White logo, tinted roof windows, crates	£20-25
441	1963-67	Volkswagen Van	Blue body with 'Trans-o-lite' headlamps, 'CHOCOLATE TOBLERONE',	£75-85
443	1963-65	Plymouth Suburban US Mail	Blue/White body, 'ADDRESS YOUR MAIL CAREFULLY', 104 mm	£65-75
447	1965-66	'WALLS ICE CREAM' Van	Ford Thames van in Blue/Cream, salesman, boy, spare transfers. Blue/Yellow card box, inner base, leaflet	£180-230
450	1964-67	Austin Mini Van	Green body with unpainted grille, 79 mm	£55-65
			Green body with painted grille	£90-110
			Green body with Austin Countryman grille	£90-110
	Promotional:		Metallic Green body, Grey base, Red interior, White 'FDR1.2009/17' logo. Housed in original 450 box with club slip. Thought to be a Dutch promotional	NGPP
452	1956-63	Commer Dropside Lorry	Red and Cream body, (raised ridge on some cab roofs), smooth or shaped hubs	£65-75
			Blue body, Cream back	£75-85
453	1956-60	Commer Refrigerated Van 'WALLS ICE CREAM'	Dark Blue cab, Cream back, smooth roof, flat spun hubs	£125-175
			Light Blue cab, Cream back, cast roof, flat spun hubs	£100-125

Commercial vehicles

454	1957-62	**Commer Platform Lorry**	Metallic Blue cab and chassis, Silver-Grey platform, 120 mm	£60-70
			Yellow cab and chassis, Silver platform	£70-80
455	1957-61	**Karrier Bantam 2-ton**	Blue, Red or Grey body, Red platform floor, smooth hubs	£60-70
		variant:	Early Mettoy issue, Red body with '*C.W.S. SOFT DRINKS*' logo on rear	£100-125
456	1960-63	**ERF 44G Dropside Lorry**	Yellow/Metallic Blue, smooth/shaped wheels, 120 mm	£65-75
457	1957-65	**ERF 44G Platform Lorry**	Two-tone Blue or Yellow/Blue body, smooth hubs	£65-75
458	1958-66	**E.R.F. Earth Dumper**	Red and Yellow body, 'ERF' cast-in, smooth or shaped hubs, 95 mm	£40-50
459	1958-60	**ERF 44G Van**	Yellow/Red, 'MOORHOUSES LEMON CHEESE', 117 mm	£150-200
459	1974-78	**Raygu Rascal Roller**	Yellow/Green body, '*Road Roller*', 125 mm	£15-20
460	1959-61	**E.R.F. Neville Cement Tipper**	Pale Yellow and Silver body, metal or plastic fillers, smooth or shaped hubs	£45-55
462	1970	**Commer Van 'CO-OP'**	White/Blue promotional model, 90 mm	£75-85
462	1971	**Commer Van 'HAMMONDS'**	Green/Blue/White promotional model, 90 mm	£100-120
465	1963-66	**Commer Pick-Up Truck**	Red/Yellow, Yellow/Red or Green/Grey, 'Trans-O-Lites', 90 mm	£50-60
466		**Commer Milk Float**	White cab, chassis and load; Blue rear roof and sides	£50-60
			As previous model but with 'CO-OP' labels	£70-80
470	1959-61	**Forward Control Jeep**	Blue/Grey or Mustard Yellow, suspension, left-hand drive, 91 mm	£30-35
471	1965-66	**Karrier Bantam Snack Bar**	Blue/White, 'JOE'S DINER' with figure and opening hatch, 95 mm	£70-85
			Blue/White, 'PATATES FRITES' Belgian issue	£160-200
474	1965-68	**Musical 'WALLS ICE CREAM' Van**	Ford Thames van in Blue/Cream, musical movement (must function), diorama but no figures.	
			Blue/Yellow card box	£175-250
478	1965-69	**Jeep Tower Wagon**	Green, Yellow and Silver body, figure, 129 mm	£25-35
479	1968-71	**Commer Mobile Camera Van**	Blue/White body, shaped hubs, 'SAMUELSON FILM COMPANY LTD', camera and operator	£80-90
			As previous model but with cast hubs	£80-90
483	1968-72	**Dodge Tipper Truck**	White cab, Blue tipper, 'KEW FARGO', cast wheels	£25-35
484	1967-71	**Dodge Livestock Transporter**	Beige/Green body, 'KEW FARGO', 5 figures, 140 mm	£30-40
C490	1967-70	**Volkswagen Breakdown**	Tan/Red, tool-box, 2 spare wheels, 102 mm	£40-50
C493	1976-78	**Mazda B 1600 Pick-Up**	Blue/White or Silver/Blue body	£10-15
494	1967-72	**Bedford Tipper**	Red cab/chassis, Yellow tipper	£40-50
			Red cab/chassis, Silver tipper	£90-110
			Yellow cab/chassis, Blue tipper	£110-130
			Blue cab/chassis, Yellow tipper	£130-150

Major Packs

1100	1958-63	**Bedford 'S' Carrimore Low Loader**	Yellow cab, Metallic Blue trailer, smooth or shaped hubs	£100-125
			Red cab, Metallic Blue trailer, winch	£100-125
1100	1971-73	**Mack Truck 'TRANS-CONTINENTAL'**	Orange cab, Black/Orange/Silver trailer, sliding doors, jockey wheel, 257 mm	£40-50
			Orange and Metallic Lime Green version	£70-80
1101	1957-63	**Bedford 'S' Carrimore Transporter**	Blue cab, Yellow transporter body, 'CORGI CAR TRANSPORTER'	£125-150
			Red cab, Blue transporter body, smooth hubs	£80-90
C1101	1976-81	**Mobile Crane**	Yellow/Blue body, '*Warner & Swasey*', 150 mm	£25-30
1102	1958-62	**'EUCLID' TC-12 Bulldozer**	Yellow body, Pale Grey tracks, 159 mm. Box has inner lining	£100-125
			As previous model but with Black tracks	£60-70
			Pale Lime-Green body	£80-100
C1102	1974-76	**'BERLIET' Bottom Dumper**	Yellow and Orange body, '*Road Construction*', 287 mm	£30-35
1103	1960-63	**'EUCLID' Crawler Tractor**	Yellow or Pale Lime-Green body, Pale Grey tracks, 111 mm	£80-90
			As previous model but with Black tracks	£60-70
1104	1957-63	**Bedford 'S' Carrimore Machinery Carrier**	Red cab, Silver trailer, smooth hubs, operable winch, 220 mm	£100-125
			Blue cab, Silver trailer, smooth hubs	£100-125
1104	1974-77	**Bedford 'TK' type Horse Transporter**	Green or Metallic Green with Orange or Yellow trailer, 'NEWMARKET', four horses and boy, 256 mm	£50-60
1105	1962-66	**Bedford 'TK' type Car Transporter**	Red cab, Blue/White trailer, collapsible decks, '*Corgi Car Transporter*'	£100-125
C1105	1977-81	**Berliet Racehorse Transporter**	Brown/White, 'NATIONAL RACING STABLES', four horses, 280 mm	£40-50
1106	1971-77	**Mack Container Truck 'ACL'**	Yellow/Black/White body, two Red containers with White logo, 290 mm	£40-50
			Promotional issue for '3M'	£120-140
1106	1984	**'CORGI' Loadlugger**	Yellow body and chassis, Red '*BIG BIN*'	£10-15
1107	1963-66	**'EUCLID' with Dozer**	Yellow body, Grey tracks, driver, 159 mm	£125-150
			Red body	£150-175
			Lime-Green body	£70-80
C1107	1979-	**Berliet Container Lorry 'UNITED STATES LINES'**	Blue cab, White chassis, 2 Grey containers	£30-40
1108	1982	**Ford Truck 'MICHELIN'**	Blue/White articulated body, two containers, 243 mm	£40-50

46

1109	1979	Ford Truck 'MICHELIN'	Blue/Black articulated body, two containers, 243 mm	£40-50
1110	1959-64	Bedford 'S' type		
		'MOBIL' Tanker	Red/White articulated body, detachable cab, 'MOBILGAS', 191 mm	£120-140
			As previous model but with shaped spun hubs	£140-160
1110	1965-67	Bedford 'TK' type		
		'SHELL' Tanker	Blue/White articulated tanker, 'SHELL BENZEEN', Dutch model	£1500-2000
1110	1976-80	'JCB' Crawler Loader	Yellow/White body, Red working bucket, Black tracks, driver	£30-40
1110	1976-80	'JCB' Crawler	Yellow and White body, driver, 115 mm	£30-40
			Light Blue/Orange with Light Blue chassis, driver	£30-40
			Yellow body, Light Blue cab, Red bucket	£30-40
			Red body, Light Blue cab and bucket	£30-40
			Orange body, 'BLOCK CONSTRUCTION' logo	£30-40
C1113	1981-86	'HYSTER' Handler	Yellow or Black/White main body, 'US Lines', hoist, 212 mm	£30-40
	1986-87		Yellow or Black/White main body, 'SEALINK', container, export model	£50-70
	1986-87		White/Dark Blue/Yellow, 'MICHELIN', container	£30-40
1116	1979	S & D Refuse Collector	Orange or Red body, 'City Sanitation', 151 mm	£15-20
1116/2	1988		Blue cab, White tipper, 'BOROUGH COUNCIL'	£5-10
1117	1980	'FAUN' Street-sweeper	Orange and Yellow or All-Yellow, with operator	£15-20
1119	1983	Mercedes Load Lugger	Yellow/Red body, 'CORGI'	£15-20
1121	1983	Ford Transit Tipper	Orange/Beige body, 'CORGI', (Corgimatic)	£15-20
1128	1963-76	'PRIESTMAN' Cub Shovel	Red/Yellow body, driver, 165 mm	£30-35
1129	1962-65	Bedford 'S' type		
		'MILK' Tanker	Blue/White articulated body, detachable cab, 191 mm	£150-175
1131	1963-66	Bedford 'TK' Carrimore		
		Machinery Low Loader	Blue cab, Silver trailer, Yellow detachable rear axle unit, spun hubs	£80-100
			Blue cab, Silver trailer, Black detachable rear axle unit, spun hubs	£70-80
1132	1963-65	Bedford 'TK' Carrimore		
		Low Loader	Yellow cab, Red trailer, spare wheels, no winch	£100-125
1137	1966-69	Ford Articulated Truck		
		'EXPRESS SERVICES'	Blue/Silver/Red body, 'H' series tilt-cab, 235 mm	£75-85
1138	1966-69	Ford Articulated Transporter		
		'CORGI CARS'	Red/Silver cab, two-tone Blue transporter body	£85-95
1140	1965-67	Bedford 'TK' Petrol Tanker	Red/Silver/White articulated body, tilting cab, 'MOBILGAS', 191 mm	£150-175
1141	1965-67	Bedford 'TK' Milk Tanker	Blue/White articulated body, tilting cab, 'MILK', 191 mm	£200-250
1145	1970-76	Unimog Goose Dumper	Yellow/Red body, '406', 171 mm	£30-35
1146	1970-73	Scammell Carrimore Mk.V		
		Tri-deck Transporter	Orange/White/Blue articulated transporter with 3 collapsible decks, 290 mm	£80-100
1147	1970-72	Scammell Truck		
		'FERRYMASTERS'	Yellow/White body, 'INTERNATIONAL HAULIERS', 235 mm	£50-60
1148	1969-72	Scammel Carrimore Mk.IV		
		Car Transporter	Red/White transporter body with Yellow chucks	£80-100
1150	1971	Mercedes Snowplough	Unimog 406 in Green/Black, 2 Red flags, Orange/Silver plough	£30-35
			Unimog 406, Yellow cab and back, Red chassis, Silver plough, 2 Red flags	£30-35
1151	1970	Scammel Truck		
		'Co-operative Society'	Blue/White body, promotional	£120-140
1151		Mack Tanker 'EXXON'	Red/White body, striped window box	£60-70
1152	1971-75	Mack Tanker 'ESSO'	White/Red/Blue articulated body, Gloster Saro Petrol Tanker (detachable)	£40-50
			As previous model but with 'EXXON' logo	£70-80
1153	1973-74	'PRIESTMAN' Crane	Red/Orange body, 'Higrab', 230 mm	£45-55
1154	1974-76	Priestman Crane Truck	Yellow/Red body, Silver boom, hook, 240 mm	£45-55
1154	1979	Giant Tower Crane	Orange/Yellow crane, White body, 'BLOCK CONSTRUCTION' logo	£35-45
C1155	1975-79	'Skyscraper' Tower Crane	Yellow/Red body, Black tracks, 340 mm	£35-40
1156	1977-80	Volvo Concrete Mixer	Yellow/Red body, 'RAPIER'	£30-35
1156	1980		Orange/White body, 'BLOCK CONSTRUCTION'	£30-35
1157	1976-81	Ford Tanker 'ESSO'	White/Red articulated body, 270 mm	£25-35
1158	1976	Ford Tanker 'EXXON'	White/Black articulated body, 270 mm German issue	£50-60
1159	1976-79	Ford Car Transporter	Blue/White or Green articulated body, 360 mm	£40-50
1160	1976	Ford Tanker 'GULF'	White/Orange articulated body, 270 mm	£30-40
1161	1979-80	Ford Tanker 'ARAL'	Blue/White/Black articulated body, 270 mm German export model	£50-60
1169	1982	Ford Tanker 'GUINNESS'	Cream/Brown/Black articulated body, 270 mm	£40-50
1170	1982	Ford Car Transporter	Red/White/Yellow articulated body, 360 mm	£50-60
1191	1985	Ford Articulated Truck		
		'FORD QUALITY'	White cab, chassis and tampo print, two Blue containers	£15-20
	1985	Ford Articulated Truck		
		'BALLANTINES SCOTCH'	Container holds 6 miniatures. Available from duty-free shops (20,000)	£65-75
	1985	Ford Truck 'KAYS'	Red/White articulated body, Cerise/Black tampo print, Mail-order model (4,000)	£10-15

CORGI MAJOR TOYS

1100 Carrimore Low-Loader No. 1   8¾ inches   220 mm   12/6
With drop-down loading ramp and haulage winch —
the articulated cab can be detached.

1102 Euclid T.C.12 Tractor with Dozer Blade   6¼ inch   159 mm   16/11
'Hydraulic' raising jacks are fitted, enabling the dozer
blade to be held in position — the model runs on heavy
rubber tracks.

1110 Mobilgas Tanker   7½ inches   191 mm   9/3
This articulated model has a detachable driving cab.

12

An illustration from the September 1960 UK catalogue

Agricultural Models

Ref.	Year(s)	Model name	Colours, features, dimensions	Market Price Range
50	1959-66	Massey-Ferguson 65 Tractor	Red bonnet, Pale Grey or Cream chassis, Red metal or plastic hubs, metal or plastic steering wheel, 79 mm	£60-70
C50	1974-77	Massey Ferguson 50B Tractor	Yellow/Black/Red body, windows, 138 mm	£25-35
51	1959-69	Massey-Ferguson Tipper Trailer	Red chassis, Yellow or Grey body, Red metal or plastic wheels, 102 mm	£15-20
53	1960-66	Massey-Ferguson 65 Tractor with Shovel	Red bonnet, Cream or Light Grey chassis, Red metal or Orange plastic hubs, operable shovel, painted or unpainted arms	£60-75
54	1974	Massey Ferguson Tractor with Shovel	Yellow/Red or White/Red body, 150 mm	£30-35
54	1958-62	Fordson Half-Track Tractor	Blue body, Orange rollers and wheels, Black rubber tracks, lights in radiator grille, 91 mm Plain 'early' box	£140-160
			Same but with Grey rubber tracks, lights at sides of grille, picture box	£120-140
55	1961-63	Fordson Major Tractor	Blue/Grey/Red body, 83 mm	£60-75
55	1977	David Brown Tractor	Black/Red/White body, steering wheel, 105 mm	£25-35
56	1961-63	Four-Furrow Plough	Red/Brown/Yellow body, 90 mm	£15-20
56	1977	Farm Tipper Trailer	Red/Yellow or Red/White body with drop-down tailboard, 130 mm	£10-15
57	1963-65	Massey Ferguson 65 Tractor with Fork	Red/Silver/Cream body, driver, steering wheel, 127 mm	£60-75
58	1965-72	Beast Carrier	Red, Cream and Blue body, four calves, 112 mm	£20-25
60	1964-66	Fordson Power Major Tractor	Blue body, plough lifts, 83 mm	£60-75
61	1964-70	Four-Furrow Plough	Blue/Silver body, 90 mm	£5-10
62	1965-70	Ford Tipper Trailer	Red/Yellow body, 144 mm	£10-15
64	1965-69	Conveyor on Jeep	Red body, Yellow/White conveyor, farmhand figure, 197 mm	£60-75
66	1966-72	Massey Ferguson 165 Tractor	Red/Blue/White body, engine sound, 76 mm	£45-55
67	1967-72	Ford Super Major Tractor	Blue/White/Silver body, 'FORD 5000', 90 mm	£45-55
69	1967-70	Massey Ferguson 165 Tractor and Shovel	Red/Blue body, Silver shovel, figure, 127 mm	£50-60
71	1967-72	Fordson Disc Harrow	Yellow/Red/Silver body, 90 mm	£5-10
72	1971-73	Ford 5000 Tractor and Towbar	As Corgi 67 but with frame, bucket and pipes, 90 mm	£70-80
73	1970-72	Massey Ferguson Tractor and Saw	As Corgi 66 plus Yellow rotating saw 90 mm	£65-75
74	1969-72	Ford 5000 Tractor and Scoop	As Corgi 67 plus Yellow/Silver scoop, 90 mm	£65-75
100	1957-61	Dropside Trailer	Yellow/Red/Grey body, 108 mm	£10-15
101	1958-61	Platform Trailer	Yellow/Grey or Blue/Grey body	£10-15
102	1958-59	Rice's Pony Trailer	Red body, Brown chassis, wire drawbar, smooth hubs, plastic pony	£50-60
			Red body, Silver chassis, wire drawbar, smooth hubs, plastic pony	£40-50
	1959-65		Red body, Black chassis, wire or cast drawbar, smooth or shaped hubs	£30-40
			Red body, Silver chassis, wire or cast drawbar, smooth or shaped hubs	£30-40
			Cream body, Red chassis, wire or cast drawbar, smooth or shaped hubs	£30-40
	1961-65		Tan/Cream body, Silver chassis, cast drawbar, shaped hubs	£30-40
112	1969-72	Rice Beaufort Horse-Box	Blue/White horse-box with mare and foal	£25-30

Major Packs (and large Agricultural Models)

Ref.	Year(s)	Model name	Colours, features, dimensions	Market Price Range
1111	1959-60	M-F Combine Harvester	Red/Yellow, Yellow metal wheels, metal tines, 172 mm	£70-80
1111	1960-61	M-F Combine Harvester	Red/Yellow, Yellow metal wheels, plastic tines	£60-70
	1961-62		Red/Yellow, Red plastic wheels, plastic tines	£90-100
C1112	1977-78	David Brown Tractor and Combine Harvester	Corgi 55 Tractor with Red/White/Black combine harvester, 220 mm	£60-70

Duo Packs

These packs combine standard models with (mainly) similar 'Junior' models.

Launched early in 1982 in France with the name 'Les Plus de Corgi', the packs later became available in the UK in Woolworths as 'Little and Large, the Little One Free'.

All NGPP except where shown.

'Les Plus de Corgi' Duo Pack range:

1352	Renault 5 (307) Metro (C275)
1353	Austin Metro
1354	Texaco Lotus (C154) Junior 53
1355	Talbot Matra Rancho (457)
1356	Fiat XI/9 (306)
1357	Golden Eagle Jeep (C441)
1358	Citroen 2cv
1359	Ford Escort (334), Junior 105

F.W. Woolworth's 'Little & Large' Promotional Duo Pack selection:

1352	Renault 5 (307) Metro (C275)
1353	Austin Metro
1355	Talbot Matra Rancho (457)
1356	Fiat XI/9 (306)
1359	Ford Escort (334), Junior 105
1363	Buck Rogers (607)
1364	Space Shuttle 'NASA' (648)
1365	469 Routemaster Bus, E71 Taxi
1371	Volkswagen Turbo (309)

Other Duo Packs (most available in UK):

1360	Batmobile (267)	
1361	James Bond Aston Martin, Silver	**£100-£125**
1362	James Bond Lotus Esprit (269)	
1363	Buck Rogers (607)	
1364	Space Shuttle 'NASA' (648)	
1365	469 Routemaster Bus, E71 Taxi	

1372	Jaguar XJS (319)
1373	Ford Capri (312) Junior 61
1376	Starsky & Hutch Ford Torino
1378	Porsche 924, Yellow
1380	Mercedes 240D, Metallic Grey
1381	Ferrari 308GTS, Red
1382	Ford Mustang (320)
1383	Mack Fire Pumper
1384	Ford Thunderbird, Cream/Orange
	Ford Thunderbird, Cream/Black
1385	Austin Metro 'DATAPOST'
1389	Ford Sierra (299) Junior 129
1390	Porsche 924, Black
1393	447 Jeep and E182 Jeep
1394	448 Jeep and E183 Jeep
1395	495 Mazda, E184 Range Rover
1396	Space Shuttle
1397	BMW M1 'BASF' (380)
1401	Lotus Elite and E10 TR7
1402	1133 Tipper plus E85 Skip Truck
1403	Mercedes Tanker, E185 Van
1405	Jaguar

49

Taxis

Ref.	Year(s)	Model name	Colours, features, dimensions	Market Price Range
221	1960-63	**Chevrolet Impala Cab**	Yellow body, '*YELLOW TAXIS*', smooth/shaped spun wheels, 108 mm	£55-65
C327	1980	**Chevrolet Caprice Taxi**	Yellow body, '*THINK TWA*', fare table on door, 90 mm	£10-15
388	1987	**Mercedes 190 Taxi**	White or Beige body, Yellow/Black '*TAXI*' logo, export model	£5-10
C411	1976-80	**Mercedes Benz 240 D**	Orange/Black or Off-White body, '*TAXI*' on roof, 127 mm	£10-15
			Cream and Black body (German issue)	NGPP
418	1960-65	**Austin FX4 Taxi**	Black body, '*TAXI*' sign, smooth or shaped hubs, no driver, 97 mm	£40-50
			Black body, '*TAXI*' sign, smooth or shaped hubs, 'younger' driver figure	£35-45
			Black body, '*TAXI*' sign, smooth or shaped hubs, 'older' driver figure	£30-40
C425	1978	**London Taxi**	FX4 type taxi with Black body, '*TAXI*', WhizzWheels, 121 mm	£10-15
425/1	1986	**London Taxi**	FX4 type taxi with Black body, '*RADIO CAB*', Yellow design on door	£5-10
430	1962-64	**Ford Bermuda 'TAXI'**	Ford Thunderbird, White body, Yellow and Red canopy, 102 mm	£60-75
			White body, Lime Green and Red canopy	£60-75
			White body, Blue and Red canopy	£60-75
			White body, Green and Pink canopy	£60-75
			Metallic Blue/Red	£150-200
434	1985	**Mercedes 'TAXI'**	Yellow body, Red taxi sign, chrome trim	£10-15
450	1983	**Peugeot Taxi**	Beige with Blue label, '*739:33:33*', (French issue)	£10-15
451		**Ford Sierra Taxi**	Cream body (No other details)	NGPP
480	1965-66	**Chevrolet Impala Taxi**	Dark Yellow and Red body, Chrome stripe, shaped spun wheels, 108 mm	£40-45
			As previous model but with detailed cast wheels	£50-55
507	1969	**Chrysler Bermuda Taxi**	Shown in catalogue but not issued	NPP
91812	1992	**Taxi**	Cream body, '*FINANCIAL TIMES*' logo	NGPP

Aircraft

Helicopters and Space Vehicles are also listed in the Emergency Vehicles, Novelty and Military Sections.

Ref.	Year(s)	Model name	Colours, features, dimensions	Market Price Range
650	1973-80	**'BOAC' Concorde**	White/Blue with Gold tail design, all-card box with 'BRITISH AIRWAYS'	£70-80
			White with Red/White/Blue tail, display stand, 'G-BBDG'	£50-60
			Version with White stripes on tail	£15-25
			Version with crown design on tail	£15-25
651	1973-81	**'AIR FRANCE' Concorde**	White/Blue with Gold tail design, all-card box	£70-80
			White body, Red/White/Blue tail, display stand	£40-50
652	1973-81	**'JAPAN AIRLINES' Concorde**	White/Red/Blue/Black, all-card box	£200-250
653	1973-81	**'AIR CANADA' Concorde**	White/Red/Blue/Black, all-card box	£200-250
1119	1960-62	**HDL Hovercraft 'SR-N1'**	Blue/Grey/White body, Yellow rudders and wheels (Major Pack)	£30-35
1301	1973-77	**Piper Cherokee Arrow**	Yellow/Black with White wings, or White/Blue, '*N 286 4 A*'	£35-45
1302	1973-77	**Piper Navajo**	Red/White or Yellow/White, '*N 9219 Y*'	£35-45
1303	1973-77	**Lockheed F104A Starfighter**	Silver or Camouflage with Black crosses	£35-45
1304	1973-77	**Mig-21 PF**	Blue or Silver, number '*57*', Red stars, retractable undercarriage	£25-35
1305	1973	**Grumman F-11a Tiger**	Blue '*NAVY*', or Silver with US stars	£25-35
1306	1973-77	**North American P51-D Mustang**	Silver or Camouflage, Black props, US stars, moveable control surfaces	£25-35
1307	1973-77	**Saab 35 X Draken**	Silver or Camouflage, retractable undercarriage, Swedish markings	£35-45
1308	1973-77	**BAC (or SEPCAT) Jaguar**	Silver or Camouflage, retractable wheels, moveable control surfaces	£35-45
1309	1973-77	**'BOAC' Concorde**	Dark Blue/White, retractable wheels	£45-55
1310	1973-77	**'AIR FRANCE' 'BOEING 707B'**	White/Blue body, Silver wings, retractable wheels	£35-45
1311	1973-77	**Messerschmitt ME410**	All Silver body, Black Iron Crosses on wings and fuselage	£35-45
1312	1973-77	**Boeing 727 'TWA'**	White body, Silver wings, retractable wheels	£35-45
1313	1973-77	**Japanese Zero-Sen A6M5**	Green or Silver with Red circles, retractable wheels	£35-45
1315	1973-77	**'PAN-AM' Boeing 747**	White body, Silver wings, hinged nose, retractable wheels	£35-45
1315/1		**'BRITISH AIRWAYS' Jumbo Boeing 747**	White/Silver, Blue logo, hinged nose, retractable wheels	£45-55
1316	1973-77	**McDonnell Douglas F-4c5**	Phantom II in Silver or Camouflage with retractable undercarriage	£35-45
1320	1978-80	**'BRITISH AIRWAYS' VC-10**	White/Silver with Red tail, Blue logo, retractable wheels	£35-45
1325	1978-80	**'SWISSAIR' DC-10**	White/Silver with Red stripe and tail, retractable wheels	£35-45

Emergency Vehicles

Ref.	Year(s)	Model name	Colours, features, dimensions	Market Price Range

See also under 'Corgi Small Commercials and Vans' and in the 'Corgi Classics' section for other references to emergency vehicle models.

Ref.	Year(s)	Model name	Colours, features, dimensions	Market Price Range
C106/13	1990	**Saab 'BRANDWEER'**	Red body, White side panels, 'ALARM', (Dutch export model)	**£15-20**
209	1958-61	**Riley Pathfinder Police Car**	Black and Silver body, bell, 'POLICE', 97 mm	**£65-75**
213	1959-61	**Jaguar Fire Chief's Car**	Red body, bell, Grey aerial, roof sign, smooth spun wheels, 95 mm	**£80-90**
213s	1961-62	**Jaguar Fire Chief's Car**	As previous model but with suspension and shaped spun wheels	**£100-120**
223	1959-61	**Chevrolet Impala 'State Patrol'**	Black body, Silver stripe, 'STATE PATROL', Grey aerial, 108 mm. Box contains internal packing	**£55-65**
237	1962-66	**Oldsmobile Sheriff's Car**	Black body, White roof, 'COUNTY SHERIFF', clear or Blue light. Box contains internal packing	**£55-65**
260	1979-81	**Buick 'POLICE' Car**	Blue/White body, 'CITY OF METROPOLIS', 2 flashing light bars	**£30-40**
284	1982-83	**Mercedes-Benz 240 D**	Red body, 'NOTRUF 112', flashing lights, German export model	**£20-25**
292	1985	**Sapeurs Pompiers**	Pale Blue or Dark Blue body	**£20-25**
			Dark Blue body, 'POLICIA'	**£25-30**
C293	1977-80	**Renault 5 TS**	Metallic Orange or Two-tone Blue body, WhizzWheels	**£15-25**
293	1980-81	**Renault 5 TS**	Two-tone Blue body, roof light, 'S.O.S. MEDICINS'	**£25-35**
295	1982-83	**Renault 5 TS Fire Chief**	Red/White 'SAPEURS POMPIERS', warning lights, French export model	**£15-20**
297	1982-86	**Ford Escort 'POLICE' Car**	Light or Dark Blue, White doors, Blue warning lights	**£15-20**
299	1985	**Ford Sierra 'POLIS' Car**	Blue/Yellow/Black body, warning lights, Swedish export model	**£15-20**
299/7	1985	**Sierra Ghia 2.3 'POLIS'**	White/Black body with White logo, (Sweden)	**£15-20**
C317	1986	**Peugeot 'POLITI'**	Black/White body, warning lights, Norwegian export model	**£15-20**
C326	1980-81	**Chevrolet Caprice Police Car**	Black/White body, 'POLICE', suspension, 150 mm	**£20-30**
C332	1980-81	**Opel Doctors Car**	White/Red body, 'NOTARTZ', opening doors	**£30-40**
C339	1980	**Rover 3500 Police Car**	White and Red body, 'POLICE', 140 mm	**£20-25**
353	1987	**BMW 'NOTARTZ'**	Red/White body, 2 Blue warning lights, German export model	**£15-20**
357	1987	**Ford Sierra 'BRANDCHEFF'**	Red body, door badge, warning lights	**£15-20**
C358/1	1987	**Ford Sierra 'POLICE'**	White body, Yellow/Black stripe, warning lights unit on roof	**£15-20**
358	1987	**Ford Sierra 'POLITI'**	White body, Red/Blue logo, warning lights, export model	**£15-20**
358	1987	**Ford Sierra 'POLICE'**	White body, Red logo, warning lights, Dutch export model	**£15-20**
C358/3	1986	**'RIJKSPOLITIE'**	White body, White/Red bonnet, crest, roof beacon, (Holland)	**£15-20**
C358/4	1986	**'LEGIBIL'**	White/Black body, 'LEGE', twin roof beacons, (West Germany)	**£15-20**
361	1987	**Volvo 'POLIS'**	White body, Black/Yellow logo, Swedish export model	**£15-20**
373	1970-76	**VW 1200 Police Car**	Black/White/Blue body, 'POLIZEI', WhizzWheels, 91 mm	**£40-50**
			Black/White body, 'POLITIE', WhizzWheels	**£80-90**
			White body, Black bonnet and boot, Blue dome light, 'POLICE' in Black on doors, WhizzWheels	**£45-55**
373	1987	**Peugeot 'POLITI'**	Black/White body, warning lights, Norwegian export model	**£15-20**
383	1970-73	**VW 1200 'ADAC'**	Yellow body, Black roof with '1341', 'ADAC STRASSENWACHT' logo on doors	**£75-85**
386	1987	**Mercedes 'POLIZEI'**	Green/White body, two Blue warning lights, German export model	**£15-20**
395	1972/73	**Fire Bug**	Orange body, Whizzwheels, Red/Black or Pink/Black stripe	**£20-30**
402	1972-77	**Ford Cortina Police Car**	White/Red body, 'POLICE' labels	**£35-45**
			White/Red body, 'POLIZEI', German issue	**£75-85**
405	1956-60	**Bedford Fire Tender**	Bright or Dark Green body, divided windscreen, Silver or Black ladder, 'A.F.S.', smooth or shaped hubs, 83 mm. (Utilicon)	**£80-100**
405 M	1956-59	**Bedford Fire Tender**	Red body, divided windscreen, Silver or Black ladder, 'FIRE DEPT', smooth or shaped hubs, friction motor, 83 mm (Utilicon)	**£120-140**
C405	1978-80	**Chevrolet Ambulance**	White/Orange, patient on stretcher and two attendants	**£20-25**
C406	1980-81	**Mercedes Bonna 'AMBULANCE'**	White body, Red/Black design, opening doors, stretcher, ambulancemen	**£30-40**
		German issue:	Cream body, 'KRANKENWAGEN'	**£30-40**
		Danish issue:	Red/White/body, 'FALCK'	**£30-40**
		Swedish issue:	White/Red/Black body, 'SDL 951'	**£30-40**
C406/2	1990	**Mercedes Bonna**	White/Red stripes, 'FALCK', (Danish export model)	**£5-10**
412	1957-60	**Bedford 'AMBULANCE'**	Cream 'Utilicon' body, divided windscreen, smooth hubs, 83 mm	**£65-75**
			As previous model but with one-piece windscreen	**£150-175**
		factory error:	A few examples of 412 were issued with 'HOME SERVICES' front labels	**NGPP**
C412	1976	**Mercedes Police Car**	White/Black body, 'POLICE' logo, Blue roof lamp	**£25-30**
			Green/White body, 'POLIZEI' logo, Blue roof lamp, German issue	**£15-20**
414	1976-77	**Jaguar XJ12-C**	White/Blue body, 'COASTGUARD'	**£10-15**
416	1959-61	**R.A.C. Land Rover**	Blue body, 'RADIO RESCUE' on cab roof sign, metal canopy, smooth hubs, Blue/Yellow box	**£85-95**
			Blue body, no cab roof sign, 'RADIO RESCUE' on canopy, shaped hubs	**£75-85**
		Belgian issue:	Yellow body, Green metal canopy, 'TS RADIO' decals on doors	**£250-300**
416s	1962-64	**R.A.C. Land Rover**	Blue body, suspension, 'RADIO RESCUE' on plastic canopy	**£65-75**
		Belgian issue:	Yellow body, Green plastic canopy, suspension, 'TS RADIO' decals on doors	**£250-300**
C416	1977-79	**Buick Police Car**	Metallic Blue body, 'POLICE', two policemen, 150 mm	**£25-30**

51

419	1960-63	**Ford Zephyr Motorway Car** ..White or Cream body, smooth or shaped hubs, *'POLICE'*, aerial, large or small roof light, 97 mm £55-65
		Export issues: with *'POLITIE'* or *'RIJKS POLITIE'* logo (Dutch) £150-200
421	1977-79	**Land Rover Station Wagon** ....Red body, White roof-rack, *'FOREST WARDEN'* £20-25
422	1977-80	**Riot Police Wagon**...................Red/White body, number '6' and *'RIOT POLICE'* on doors, water cannon £15-20
423	1960-62	**Bedford 'FIRE DEPT.'**
		12cwt. Tender ....Red body, Black ladder, undivided windscreen, smooth or shaped hubs £90-110
		Red body, unpainted ladder, undivided windscreen, shaped hubs £100-120
424	1976-79	**'SECURITY' Van** ....Black/Yellow/White body, mesh windows, WhizzWheels............£10-15
C428	1978-79	**Renault Police Car**...................Black/White body, *'POLICE'*, aerial, warning lights, 97 mm £10-15
C429	1978-80	**Police Jaguar XJ12-C**............White/Red/Blue body, *'POLICE'*, aerial, warning lights, 127 mm £25-35
C430	1978-80	**Porsche 924 'Police'** ....Black/White body, *'POLICE'*, warning light, 118 mm £15-20
C430	1978-80	**Porsche 924 'Polizei'** ....White/Black body, *'POLIZEI'*, warning light, 118 mm £15-20
C435/13	1990	**Volvo 'POLIS'** ....White with Blue panels front and rear, flashing lights bar £15-20
437	1962-65	**Cadillac Superior Ambulance** Cream over Red body, *'AMBULANCE'* on side windows £65-75
	1965-68	Light Blue over White body, *'AMBULANCE'* on sides, Red cross on bonnet £65-75
		Metallic Red over Metallic Silver body £65-75
C438	1987	**Rover Sterling 800** ....White body, Red stripe, *'POLICE'*, flashing lights bar............£15-20
439	1963-65	**Chevrolet Impala**
		'FIRE CHIEF'...................Red body, White stripe, aerial, Orange roof light, firemen, 108 mm
		with White painted door labels with *'FIRE DEPT'* £60-70
		with White rectangular label on front doors *'FIRE DEPT'* £50-60
		with round Red label on front doors *'FIRE DEPT'* £50-60
448	1964-69	**Austin Police Mini Van**...........Dark Blue body, Red interior, shaped or cast hubs, aerial, White *'POLICE'* logo,
		policeman and dog, pictorial stand and internal support packaging £125-150
454	1984	**Ford Sierra 'POLIZEI'** ....Green/White body, Swiss export model £15-20
456	1986	**Ford Sierra 'POLIZEI'** ....Green/White body, German export model £15-20
461	1972-74	**'Police' Vigilant Range Rover** White/Blue, warning lights, policemen, *'POLICE'* emergency signs £25-35
		White/Red body, *'LANGZAAM'*, policemen, emergency signs, Dutch model £50-60
463	1964-66	**Commer 'AMBULANCE'** ......Cream or White body, Red interior, Blue tinted windows and roof light, 90 mm............£55-65
464	1963-	**Commer 'POLICE' Van** ....Dark Blue, *'COUNTY POLICE'*, window bars, clear roof light, leaflet............£55-65
	1963-	As previous model but with Metallic Light Blue, with Blue roof light £50-60
		Dark Blue, window bars, Red roof light, *'CITY POLICE'*, instruction leaflet............£175-200
		Dark Blue, 'open' windows, Blue roof light, White *'POLICE'* cast into sides,
		with instructions............£45-55
		Deep Green body, *'POLICE'*, export model, opaque rear/side windows £400-500
		Metallic Green body, *'POLIZEI'*, German issue £150-175
		Metallic Blue body, *'SECOURS'*, French issue £150-175
		Metallic Blue body, window bars, *'RIJKSPOLITIE'*, Dutch issue £150-175
477	1966-67	**Land Rover Breakdown**..........Red body, Yellow canopy with spotlight and *'BREAKDOWN SERVICE'* logo
		rubber (or later plastic) 'tyre' crank, shaped or cast hubs £40-45
		As previous model but with large or small Silver crank, WhizzWheels £35-40
481	1965-69	**Chevrolet Police Car** ....White/Black body, *'POLICE PATROL'*, Red roof lights, two policemen £40-50
482	1966-69	**Chevrolet Impala**
		'FIRE CHIEF'...................Red over White body, Chrome stripe, bonnet logo, Blue light, Grey aerial.
		with rectangular *'FIRE CHIEF'* label on front doors, shaped spun wheels £45-55
		with round label on front doors *'FIRE CHIEF'*, shaped spun wheels............£65-75
		with round label on front doors *'FIRE CHIEF'*, detailed cast wheels............£55-65
482	1974-77	**Vigilant Range Rover** ....Red and White body with *'AMBULANCE'* logo............£25-30
		White body with Blue side stripe and *'AMBULANCE'* logo £25-30
483	1979	**Belgian Police Range Rover**....White body, Red stripes, warning lights, policemen, emergency signs £35-45
C484	1978-80	**AMC Pacer 'RESCUE'** ....White/Orange/Black body, number '35', *'RESCUE'*, 118 mm £10-15
		As previous issue but with *'SECOURS'* logo £25-35
C489	1980	**Volkswagen Polo** ....White/Green body, *'POLIZEI'*, opening doors and hatchback, 97 mm £20-25
C490		**Volkswagen Breakdown** ....Unpainted fittings, Chrome tools, Red 'VW' emblem, Red/Yellow stripe label, two spare wheels.
	1966-69	Tan shaped hubs, *'BREAKDOWN SERVICE'* labels............£45-55
	1968-70	As previous issue but with *'RACING CLUB'* labels (in GS 12) ....GSP
492	1966-69	**VW 1200 Car**...........................Green body, White roof, White *'POLIZEI'* on bonnet, No '18' logo £75-85
		White body with Black *'POLIZEI'* on doors and bonnet, (Germany)............£200-250
492	1966-69	**VW European Police Car** ....Dark Green body, White roof and wings, Red *'POLIZEI'*, Blue lamp, 91 mm £50-60
	NB	Box should contain 'True Scale Steering' Red/Yellow cardboard roof fitting.
		All-White body, crest on doors, *'POLITIE'*, Blue lamp, Dutch model............£140-160
		All-White body, crest on doors, *'POLITZIE'*, Blue lamp, Swiss model............£125-150
506	1968-71	**Sunbeam Imp 'Panda' Car** .....White body, Black bonnet and roof, Blue roof light £50-60
		White body, Black roof, 'luminous' door panels, Blue roof light £50-60
		Light Blue body, White roof, 'luminous' door panels, Blue roof light............£50-60

509	1970-72	Porsche Targa Police Car	White/Red body, Black roof, *'POLICE'* logo	£55-65
			White/Red body, *'POLIZEI'*, siren, warning lights	£55-65
			'RIJKSPOLITIE' export issue	£100-125
541	1986	Ford Sierra 'POLICE'	Black/White body, Norwegian/Danish export model	£10-15
541	1987	'POLITI'	White with Blue/Yellow side stripes, (Norway)	£10-15
541/2	1988	Ford Sierra 'NOTRUF'	Red body, warning lights, German export model	£10-15
542	1987	Bonna 'AMBULANCE'	Red/White body, 2 warning lights, Norwegian export model	£10-15
576	1988	Mercedes 207 D Van	Red body, White *'POMPIERS'*, French export model	£10-15
597	1986	Ford Sierra 'POLICE' Car	White body, Yellow/Black logo, two warning lights	£9-12
598	1986	Range Rover 'POLICE'	White body, Yellow/Black print, two warning lights	£9-12
619	1988	Land Rover	Red/White body, *'SAPEUR POMPIERS,* export model	£9-12
621	1986	Ford Escort 'POLICE' Van	White body, Red/Black side flash, Blue logo	£9-12
656	1987	Ford Transit Van	White/Red body, flashing lights bar, Red Cross, *'AMBULANCE'*	£9-12
656	1987	Ford Transit Van 'POLICE'	Black body, White logo, Finnish export model	£9-12
656	1987	Ford Transit Van 'FALCK'	White body, two Red stripes, warning lights, export model	£10-15
656	1987	Ford Transit Van	White/Red, *'AMBULANSE'*, flashing lights bar, Norwegian export model	£10-15
C656/28	1990	Ford Transit	White/Yellow stripe, *'NOTTINGHAM AMBULANCE SERVICE'*	£9-12
C674/1	1988	'AA' Ford Transit	Breakdown truck with Yellow body, White stripe, Black rear lifting gear	£9-12
C674/2	1988	'RAC' Ford Transit	Breakdown truck with White body, Red/Blue stripe, Black lifting gear	£9-12
C674/3	1988	'POLICE' Ford Transit	Breakdown truck with White body, Red stripe, roof lights, Black lifting gear	£9-12
C674/4	1988	'BARNINGSKAREN'	Red/Yellow Transit breakdown truck, Black lifting gear, export model	£10-12
700	1974-79	Motorway Ambulance	White/Red body, *'ACCIDENT'*, Red Cross, 98 mm	£15-20
702	1975-79	Breakdown Truck	Red/Black, single bumper, hook, *'ACCIDENT'*, 100 mm	£10-15
703	1976-78	Hi-Speed Fire Engine	Red body, Yellow ladder, warning lights, 115 mm	£10-15
911	1976-80	Air-Sea Rescue Helicopter	Blue/Yellow body, Black 'flick-spin' rotor, *'N 428'*, operable winch	£15-20
921	1975-81	Hughes OH-6A Helicopter	White/Red, *'POLICE'*, *'RESCUE'*, warning lights, 143 mm	£15-20
921/1	1975-80	'POLIZEI' Helicopter	White/Blue, *'POLIZEI'*, 'flick-spin' rotor, operable winch, German issue	£40-50
921/2	1975-80	'POLITIE' Helicopter	White/Blue, *'POLITIE'*, 'flick-spin' rotor, operable winch, Dutch issue	£40-50
921/4	1975-80	'ADAC' Helicopter	Yellow body, *'D-HFFM'*, 'flick-spin' rotor, operable winch	£40-50
921/6	1975-80	Swiss Red Cross	Red helicopter body, Black blades, 'flick-spin' rotor, operable winch	£30-40
922	1975-78	Casualty Helicopter	Sikorsky Skycrane with Red/White body	£15-20
923	1975-78	Casualty Helicopter	Army Sikorsky Skycrane with Olive/Yellow body	£15-20
924	1977-81	Air-Sea Rescue Helicopter	Orange/Yellow/Black body, *'RESCUE'*, 150 mm	£15-20
927	1978-79	Surf Rescue Helicopter	Blue/White body, *'SURF RESCUE'*, 156 mm	£15-20
931	1979-80	Jet Ranger Helicopter	White/Red body, *'POLICE RESCUE'*, 'flick-spin' rotor, operable winch	£15-20

Major Packs (Emergency Vehicles)

1103	1976-81	'PATHFINDER AIRPORT CRASH TRUCK'	Red/Silver, *'AIRPORT FIRE BRIGADE'*, operable pump and siren, orange logo	£35-45
			As previous model but non-working siren, Brick-Red logo	£35-45
			Red/Silver, operable pump and siren, *'NEW YORK AIRPORT'* logo	£35-45
C1118	1981-83	'AIRPORT FIRE SERVICE'	Red body, *'EMERGENCY UNIT'*, operable water pump	£40-50
1120	1984	Dennis Fire Engine	Red body, turntable, warning lights, Yellow plastic ladder, crest design	£10-15
1126	1977-81	'SIMON SNORKEL' Dennis Fire Engine	Red/White/Yellow, turntable, ladder, 6 firemen, 265 mm	£55-65
1127	1964-74	'SIMON SNORKEL' Bedford Fire Engine	Red/Yellow/Silver, turntable, ladder, 6 fireman, 252 mm	£50-60
1140	1982	Ford Transit Wrecker	White/Red, *'24 Hour Service'*, operable winch, hook, 131 mm	£10-15
			As previous model but logo changed to *'RELAY'*	£10-15
	1982		Red/Yellow body, *'ABSCHLEPPDEENST'*, export model	£10-15
	1987		Red body, Gold *'FALCK'* logo, Danish export model	£10-15
	1987		Red body, Yellow side panels, *'VIKING'*, export model	£10-15
1142	1967-74	'HOLMES WRECKER'	Red/White/Blue, Grey or Gold twin booms, ladder, 2 spare wheels 114 mm	£70-80
C1143	1969	'AMERICAN LA FRANCE'	Articulated Fire Engine in Red/White/Yellow, shaped spun or detailed cast wheels, 4-part extending ladder, 5 firemen, plain early box	£70-80
			As previous model but in later striped window box	£50-60
1144	1975-78	Berliet Wrecker Recovery	Red/White/Gold body, with Gold or Grey hoists, 130 mm	£40-50
2029	1979	Mack Fire Engine	Red body, warning light, detachable ladder, *'HAMMOND FIRE DEPT'*	£10-15
91822	1992	'FALKEN' Ford Transit	White body, Blue/Gold stripes, Black lifting gear, export model	£9-11

Ref.	Year(s)	Model name	Colours, features, dimensions	Market Price Range

Unless described otherwise, all models in this listing are finished in Military-Green or Olive-Drab camouflage.

Ref.	Year(s)	Model name	Colours, features, dimensions	Market Price Range
C290	1977-80	Bell Army Helicopter	Red crosses, Black rotor, 'ARMY' markings, 160 mm	£15-20
350	1958-62	Thunderbird Missile	Blue or Silver missile, Air Force Blue loading trolley, 140 mm	£40-50
351	1958-62	RAF Land Rover	Blue body, RAF roundel, spare wheel, windows, 95 mm	£65-75
			As previous model but with suspension	£90-120
352	1958-62	RAF Vanguard Staff Car	Blue bodied Standard Vanguard with RAF roundel, 95 mm	£55-65
353	1959-61	Decca Radar Scanner	Blue/Orange, scanner rotates, 83 mm	£35-45
354	1964-66	Commer Military Ambulance	Military Green body, Red cross, driver, 90 mm	£70-80
355	1964-65	Commer Van 'MILITARY POLICE'	Military Green body, driver, Blue roof light	£80-90
356	1964-66	VW Personnel Carrier	Military Green body, driver, Blue roof light	£60-70
357	1964-66	Land Rover Weapons Carrier	Military Green body, driver, White star, 95 mm	£120-140
358	1964-68	Oldsmobile Staff Car	Military Green body, White star, 'HQ STAFF', driver, 3 passengers, 108 mm	£70-80
359	1964-66	Commer Army 'FIELD KITCHEN'	Military Green, Blue interior, US star on roof, driver/attendant, 91 mm	£100-125
414	1961-64	Bedford Dormobile Military Ambulance	Olive drab body, Red crosses, smooth hubs, 83 mm	£65-75
			As previous model but with shaped hubs and suspension	£75-85
500	1963-64	US Army Land Rover	Rare version of model 357, 95 mm	£200-250
C900	1974-78	German Tiger MkI Tank	Brown/Green, Rubber tracks, fires shells (12 supplied) aerial, '144', 103 mm	£20-30
C901	1974-78	Centurion Mk.I Tank	Rubber tracks, fires shells (12 supplied) aerial, Union Jacks, 121 mm	£20-30
C902	1974-80	American M60 A1 Tank	Rubber tracks, fires shells (12 supplied) 115 mm	£20-30
C903	1974-80	British Chieftain Tank	Fires shells (12 supplied) rubber tracks, 125 mm	£20-30
C904	1974-78	German King-Tiger Tank	Rubber tracks, fires shells (12 supplied) Black crosses, 'B 34', 120 mm	£20-30
C905	1975-76	Russian SU100 Tank Destroyer	Grey, Fires shells (12 supplied) rubber tracks, Red Star, 112mm	£20-30
C906	1975-76	Saladin Armoured Car	Rubber tracks, fires shells (12 supplied) elevating gun, 108 mm	£20-30
C907	1976-80	German Rocket Launcher	Steel Blue/Red, half-track, detachable limber, fires rockets (12) 167 mm	£20-30
C908	1977-80	French AMX Recovery Tank	Crane, lifting dozer blade, equipment, 3 figures, 127 mm	£40-50
C909	1977-80	Tractor Gun and Trailer	Sand-coloured British gun and trailer, fires shells (12 supplied) 280 mm	£40-50
C920	1975-78	Bell Army Helicopter	Military-Green helicopter with Army markings, Black or Green rotor	£15-20
C922	1975-78	Casualty Helicopter	Red/White/Yellow Sikorsky helicopter, number '3', Red crosses	£15-20
C923	1975-78	Sikorsky Sky Crane	Military-Green helicopter, Red cross, 'ARMY' marking, 160 mm	£15-20

MAJOR PACKS - (Military and R.A.F. models)

Ref.	Year(s)	Model name	Colours, features, dimensions	Market Price Range
1106	1959-61	Karrier Decca Radar Van	Cream body, 4 Orange bands, rotating scanner, aerials, 134 mm	£100-125
			Cream body, 5 Orange bands, rotating scanner, aerials, 134 mm	£100-125
1108	1958-61	Bristol Bloodhound Guided Missile & Launching Ramp	Green ramp, Yellow/Red/White Guided Missile, RAF markings	£70-80
1109	1959-62	Bristol Bloodhound Guided Missile & Loading Trolley	Green ramp, Yellow/Red/White Guided Missile, RAF markings	£70-80
1112	1959-62	Corporal Guided Missile on Launching Ramp	Military-Green mechanical base, White missile, Red rubber nose cone, instruction sheet in box	£75-85
	1960-62		Same but with separately boxed 1408 Percussion head and instructions	£100-120
1113	1959-62	Corporal Guided Missile Erector Vehicle	with lifting mechanism and Guided Missile, spare wheel, 292 mm	£200-250
1115	1958-62	Bristol Ferranti Bloodhound	Yellow/Red/White Guided Missile with RAF markings	£55-65
1116	1959-62	Bloodhound Launching Ramp	Military-Green launching ramp for 1115 Rotates, has lifting mechanism	£45-55
1117	1959-62	Bloodhound Loading Trolley	for use with model 1115 Military-Green, spare wheel, drawbar pivots	£45-55
1118	1959-62	International 6x6 Army Truck	Military-Green with British markings (US markings on box picture)	£100-150
			Dutch issue with Silver grille and sidelights	£100-150
			US Army issues	£100-150
1124	1960-62	Launching Ramp for Corporal Guided Missile	Military-Green, operable mechanisms, in plain 'Temporary Pack' box	£35-45
1133	1965-66	Troop Transporter	Olive International six wheeled truck, 'US 7811332', hook, 140 mm	£125-150
1134	1965-66	'US ARMY' Fuel Tanker	Olive Bedford 'S' Type Artic, US Army star, 'NO SMOKING', 191 mm	£200-250
1135	1965	Heavy Equipment Transporter	Bedford Carrimore, Military Green, US Army star, driver, Red interior	£250-300

Novelty, Film and TV-related models

Market Price Range: Please note that the prices shown refer to pristine models and boxes. Items failing to match this standard will sell for less. Note also that boxes must contain all their original additional contents. See Corgi model identification page.

Ref.	Year(s)	Model name	Colours, features, dimensions	Market Price Range
107	1967-70	**Batboat on Trailer**	Black boat (tinplate fin cover) with Batman and Robin figures, gold trailer (suspension, cast wheels) Blue/yellow pictorial box also contains black accessory towing hook for attachment to Batmobile	**£100-125**
	1974-81	....	Black boat (plastic fin) with Batman and Robin figures, gold trailer (no suspension, Whizzwheels)	**£50-60**
201	1970-72	**The Saint's Volvo**	White body, White 'Saint' logo on red label, WhizzWheels, driver, Red/Yellow 'window' box	**£140-160**
256	1971-74	**'EAST AFRICAN RALLY' Volkswagen**	Red body, rally number '18', steering wheel on roof, rhinoceros, 91 mm	**£150-175**
258	1965-68	**The Saint's Volvo**	White body, Black 'Saint' logo (transfer), Red interior, driver, spun hubs, Blue/Yellow card box	**£130-160**
258	1968-70	**The Saint's Volvo**	White body, white 'Saint' logo on red label, Red interior, driver, cast hubs, Blue/Yellow card box ..	**£120-140**
258	1968-70	**The Saint's Volvo**	As previous version but white 'Saint' logo on blue label	NGPP
C259	1979-80	**Penguinmobile**	White car with 'Penguin' and Red/Yellow parasol, Black/Yellow 'window' box	**£35-40**
C260	1979-81	**Superman Police Car**	Blue/White body, *'CITY of METROPOLIS'*, Black/Yellow pictorial window box	**£35-40**
261	1965-69	**James Bond's Aston-Martin** ...	Gold body (metal roof) with James Bond at the wheel, passenger seat ejector (with figure). Accessories: envelope with 'secret instructions', spare passenger, self-adhesive '007' badge, (plus 'Model Car Makers to James Bond' Corgi Catalogue in earlier boxes). From the film 'Goldfinger'	**£150-200**
		variant:	As previous model but the opening roof component is made of plastic	NGPP
261	1979-81	**Spiderbuggy and Green Goblin**	Red/Blue jeep body (150 mm) with crane, Spiderman and Green Goblin figures. Black/Yellow pictorial window box	**£75-100**
262	1967-69	**Lincoln Continental**	Metallic Gold/Black body, with picture strip for onboard 'TV set'	**£125-150**
			Light Blue/Tan body, with picture strip for onboard 'TV set'	**£150-175**
262	1979-80	**Captain Marvel's Porsche**	White with flames and stars, driver, 120 mm Black/Yellow 'window' box	**£35-40**
263	1979-81	**Captain America's Jetmobile**	White/Red/Blue body (155 mm), Red wheels, Black/Yellow 'window' box	**£25-30**
264	1979-82	**Incredible Hulk Truck**	Hulk in Red cage on Mazda pick-up, 120 mm Black/Yellow 'window' box	**£45-55**
			As previous model but Hulk in Grey cage	**£55-65**
265	1979-82	**Supermobile**	Blue/Red/Silver body, (148 m), Superman at the controls, moving fists' . Black/Yellow pictorial 'window' box has 10 spare rockets / instruction leaflet	**£40-50**
266	1968-72	**Chitty Chitty Bang Bang**	Chrome, Brown and Red body (162 m), Red/Yellow retractable 'wings', figures of Caractacus Potts, Truly Scrumptious, a boy and a girl Pictorial Blue/Yellow 'window'box comes in two sizes	**£225-275**
	1992	25th Anniversary replica:	model on 'mahogany' display stand Direct mail offer from Corgi	**£60-70**
266	1979-83	**Spider Bike**	Red/Blue motorcycle, Spiderman rider, Black wheels, Black or Red handlebars forks, Black or Blue seat and fairing, amber or clear windshield, rocket launchers.	
		Box (1):	Black/Yellow pictorial 'window' box with header card, 10 spare rockets	**£50-60**
		Box (2):	Black/Yellow 'window' box without header card, 10 spare rockets	**£50-60**
		Box (3):	Black/Red/Yellow 'window' box without header card, 10 spare rockets	**£50-60**
266	1980-82	**Spider Bike**	As previous model but with White wheels	**£70-80**
267	1966-67	**Batmobile**	Gloss Black body, Red 'Bat' logo on doors and on gold cast hubs, Batman and Robin figures, 'pulsating exhaust flame', sealed secret instructions concealed in box base. 12 spare rockets (Red or Yellow), self-adhesive 'Batman' badge. Pictorial card box with diorama, earliest versions had 'features' leaflet within............................	**£400-500**
		....	As previous model but with Matt Black body...	**£400-500**
	1967-72		Same (Gloss Black body) but with brass towing hook cast into base. Blue/Yellow 'window' box..	**£160-190**
	1967-72	....	Same but with cast Silver wheels. Black/Blue/Yellow 'window' box	**£200-250**
	1973	....	As previous model but with Red WhizzWheels and without pulsating 'flame' effect. Blue/Yellow 'window' box	**£250-350**
	1974-77	....	As previous model but with Black WhizzWheels and without pulsating 'flame' effect. Copyright information cast in base Dark Blue/Yellow 'window' box (header card on some), spare rockets, no instruction sheet	**£50-60**
	1977-79	....	As previous casting but with wider WhizzWheels, no Robin figure. Black/Red/Yellow 'window' box...	NGPP
268	1978-80	**Batman's Batbike**	Black/Red rocket-firing motorcycle with Red or Grey Batman figure. Black and Yellow 'window' box (header card on some), spare rockets	**£40-50**
	1980-83	....	As previous versions but in Black/Red/Yellow 'window' box	**£30-40**
268	1967-72	**The Green Hornet's 'Black Beauty'**	Black body, Green interior, driver and Green Hornet figures, transfer on roof, spun or cast detailed hubs. Fires missile from front, radar scanner from rear. Four of each, plus 'secret instructions' are in Blue/Yellow pictorial card box which should include a greaseproof paper roof decal protector	**£350-450**

269	1977-83	James Bond Lotus Esprit	White body, Black windows, operable fins and rocket mechanism. From the film 'The Spy Who Loved Me'. Early pictorial 'window' box with plain base must contain instruction sheet and 10 spare rockets	**£80-90**
			Later pictorial 'window' box has instructions printed on base, 10 spare rockets	**£65-75**
	1977		10 gold-plated versions of 269 were presented to VIPs at the film's launch. The models had special mountings and boxes	**£3000-5000**
270	1968-76	James Bond's Aston-Martin DB5	Silver body (slightly larger than 261) Same features as 261 plus: revolving number-plates and extending tyre slashers. Box should contain innerpictorial stand, James Bond leaflet sealed 'secret instructions' packet, unused lapel '007' badge (different from 261), set of number plates and 'bandit' figure. Variations include Gold or Silver coloured bumpers, metal or plastic spoked rear wheels.	
		Box (1):	model sits on card platform under vac-formed bubble (fragile, few made)	**£250-350**
		Box (2):	Blue/Yellow 'window' box (some with card 'upstand' till 1973, few made)	**£200-250**
		Box (3):	Black/Blue/Yellow 'window' box (1973-76)	**£140-175**
270	1977-78	James Bond's Aston-Martin DB5	As previous version but with fixed number plates, 'solid' chrome WhizzWheels, no tyre-slashers, no 'secret instructions' Box has symmetrical window, ejectable passenger lodged in box inner	**£125-150**
C271	1978-83	James Bond Aston-Martin	Silver body (1:36 scale), WhizzWheels ('spoked' detail or 'alloy racing').	
			Early Black/Yellow boxes had '1:36' printed on window tag	**£60-70**
			Later Black/Yellow boxes did not have the window tag	**£50-60**
			Final boxes were Black/Red/Yellow	**£40-50**
C271	1990	'MODELAUTO'	Silver body, Red interior with 2 figures, Blue logo 'National Motor Museum Holland'	**£180-220**
?	1991-92	James Bond Aston-Martin	Reissue of C271 in clear plastic display box with plastic '007' badge	**£15-20**
C272	1981-83	James Bond Citroën 2cv	Yellow body, opening bonnet, WhizzWheels From film 'For Your Eyes Only'.	
		Box (1):	Black/Red/Yellow 'window' box with pictorial header card	**£30-40**
		Box (2):	Black/Red/Yellow 'compact' box with pictorial top flap	**£30-40**
272	1981-83	James Bond Citroën 2cv	Gold plated version (12 only produced). Strada Jewellry Certificate should be with model	**£2000-3000**
277	1968-72	'MONKEES' Monkeemobile	Red body, White roof, Yellow logo, cast detailed wheels, plus figures of Mike, Mickey, Davy and Pete. Blue/Yellow 'window' box	**£250-350**
			In Blue/Yellow 'window' box with clip-in cardboard header as used for shop display purposes	**£500-600**
			NB Pre-production model with plastic engine exists.	
278	1981-	Dan Dare's Car	Red/Yellow space vehicle. Planned but not produced	**NPP**
C290	1976-77	Kojak Buick	Bronze body (various shades, 150 mm), 4-spoke or disc type wheel hubs, 'gunfire' sound, self-adhesive 'Lieutenant' badge, figures of Kojak (no hat) and Crocker (blue jacket). Black/Yellow pictorial 'window' box	**£70-80**
	1977-80		As previous model but figure of Kojak has a hat and Crocker had a Black jacket. 'New' tag on some boxes	**£40-50**
C292	1977-82	Starsky and Hutch Ford Torino	Red/White body (150 mm), figures of Starsky, Hutch, and a suspect. Black/Yellow pictorial 'window' box	**£70-80**
	1986		Reissued as an export model (20,000)	**£10-15**
298	1982-83	Magnum P.I. Ferrari	Red Ferrari 308GTS with 4-spoke or disc wheels. Black/Red/Yellow pictorial 'window' box	**£20-30**
302	1969	Hillman Hunter Rally	Blue body, White roof, Matt-Black bonnet, RN '75', equipment, kangaroo, 'Golden Jacks', transfers, toolbox, leaflet, instructions	**£100-125**
C320	1978-81	The Saint's Jaguar XJS	White body, standard or 'dished' WhizzWheels. Black/Yellow 'window' box (yellow or black inner)	**£30-35**
336	1967-69	James Bond's Toyota 2000 GI	White body, rocket launchers in boot. From film 'You Only Live Twice'. Diorama box must have card reinforcements to protect aerial, unopened envelope with 'secret instructions', self-adhesive '007' badge, 8 spare plastic rockets on sprue	**£250-350**
C342	1980-82	'The PROFESSIONALS' Ford Capri	Silver/Black body (124 mm), tinted windows, tinted windows, dished or disc hubs, figures of Cowley, Bodie, Doyle Black/Yellow pictorial 'window' box	**£100-125**
			Version with chrome wheel hubs	**£125-150**
348	1968-69	Ford Mustang 'POP ART' Stock Car	Blue body and interior, 5 psychedelic labels '20'. Not shown in catalogues	**£70-80**
C348	1980-81	'Vegas Thunderbird	Red body with Dan Tanner figure Black/Yellow pictorial 'window' box	**£35-45**
349	1967-67	'POP ART' Morris Mini	Red body, Yellow interior, 4 psychedelic labels, *MOSTEST* logo. Model not generally released or shown in catalogues, few only produced	**£1500-2000**
391	1972-72	James Bond Ford Mustang Mach I	Red body, White interior and base, WhizzWheels (2 types known). From film 'Diamonds Are Forever'. Red/Yellow 'window' box has '007' Red sticker	**£225-285**
			As previous model but with 'CORGI TOYS' shop display stand	**£250-350**
391	1972-73	Fire Bug	Orange body, Yellow ladder, *FIREBUG*, WhizzWheels, 83 mm	**£15-25**
423	1978-78	'ROUGH RIDER'	Yellow Chevrolet van, motorcycle side labels	**£20-25**
426	1962-64	'CHIPPERFIELDS CIRCUS' Mobile Booking Office	Karrier Bantam in red and blue, with clown and circus posters, spun hubs. Blue/yellow card box	**£200-250**
C426	1978-82	Circus Booking Office	Yellow/Red Chevrolet van, 'JEAN RICHARD PINDER', WhizzWheels	**£40-60**
		NB	The 'clown's face' poster may be at the front or the rear on the nearside of the model.	
431	1978-79	'VANATIC'	White Chevrolet van, polychromatic side labels	**£15-20**
C432	1978-79	'VANTASTIC'	Black Chevrolet, Yellow/Red design	**£15-20**
C433	1978	'VANISHING POINT'	Chevrolet van shown in 1978 catalogue but not issued	**NPP**

C434	1978-80	'CHARLIE'S ANGELS'	
		Custom Van	Pink Chevrolet van, Yellow or Brown interior, 4-spoke or disc wheels.
			Black/Yellow pictorial 'window' box £20-30
C435	1979-80	'SUPERMAN' Van	Metallic Silver Chevrolet 'SuperVan'. Black/Yellow pictorial 'window'
			box (printing variations seen) £30-35
C436	1979-80	'SPIDERVAN'	Blue Chevrolet van, 'Spiderman' design, 4-spoke or disc wheels.
			Black/Yellow pictorial 'window' box £30-35
C437	1979-80	'COCA COLA'	Red Chevrolet van, White design, tinted roof windows, crates £30-35
			NB Various other labels were designed for the Chevrolet 'van' series. Some
			prototype labels were printed but not officially used. Some of these may have
			found their way on to repainted van castings - they are NOT official Corgi issues.
			Logos include: 'Apache Patrol', 'Light Vantastic', 'Vanilla Treat', 'Cosmos',
			'Columbia', 'Aquarius', 'Centaur', 'Colorama', 'Rocket Van', 'Centaur',
			plus 4 other unlettered 'psychedelic' designs.
436	1963-65	Citroën	
		'WILDLIFE SAFARI'	Yellow Citroën ID19, driver and passenger, detailed interior, roof luggage,
			'Wild Life Reservation' logo £70-80
440	1966-67	Ford Cortina Estate	Blue/Brown, opening tailgate, suspension, 2 figures, golf equipment £100-125
447	1965-66	'Walls Ice Cream' Van	Ford Thames van in Blue/Cream, salesman, boy, spare transfers.
			Blue/Yellow card box, inner base, leaflet £175-250
448	1964-69	Austin Police Mini Van	Dark Blue body, Red interior, shaped or cast hubs, aerial, White 'POLICE' logo,
			policeman and dog with lead, pictorial stand and internal support packaging £125-150
472	1964-66	'VOTE FOR CORGI'	Corgi 438 Land Rover in Green/Yellow, Blue/Yellow card box £75-85
474	1965-68	Musical	
		'Walls Ice Cream' Van	Ford Thames van in Blue/Cream, musical movement (must function), diorama but no figures.
			Blue/Yellow card box £175-250
475	1964-65	'OlympicWinter Sport'	White/Yellow Citroën Safari, '1964', roof-rack, skier, skis, 108 mm.
			Diorama 'By Special Request' box £90-110
475	1965-68	'CORGI SKI CLUB'	Citroën with Off-White body, Red roof-rack, 4 Yellow skis and 2 poles,
			bonnet transfer, Brown dashboard/rear seats, Green front seats, 108 mm £90-110
475	1965-68	'CORGI SKI CLUB'	Citroën with White body, Yellow Roof-rack, 4 Red skis and 2 poles,
			Green dashboard/rear seats, Brown front seats £90-110
479	1967-71	Mobile Camera Van	White/Blue Commer van, spun hubs, camera and operator,
			'Samuelson Film Services', equipment case box £100-125
479	1967-71		As previous model but with detailed cast hubs £80-90
485	1966-69	Mini Countryman	Sea-Green body, 2 surfboards on roof-rack, male figure, special leaflet £125-150
			As previous model but with unpainted grille £140-170
486	1967-69	'KENNEL CLUB' Truck	White/Orange Chevrolet Impala with 'Vari-View' dachshund picture, 4 dogs £50-60
487	1965-69	'CHIPPERFIELDS'	
		Parade Vehicle	472 Land Rover in Red/Blue, 'CIRCUS IS HERE', label, chimpanzee, clown,
			Blue/yellow card box £150-175
497	1966-66	The Man From UNCLE's	
		'Thrush Buster'	Oldsmobile with White body, 'UNCLE' logo, gun sound, figures of Napoleon Solo
			and Ilya Kuriakin. Blue/Yellow pictorial card box (which must include internal packaging
			and 3-D 'Waverley' ring) £350-450
497	1966-69		Same but Metallic Purplish-Blue body, 'cast or plastic spotlights £150-200
499	1967-69	'1968 Winter Olympics'	White/Blue Citroën, 'Grenoble Olympiade', Red or Yellow roof rack, Yellow or
			Red skis/poles, toboggan, guide figure and female figure, St Bernard dog in perspex bubble £125-150
503	1964-70	'CHIPPERFIELDS'	
		Giraffe Transporter	Red/Blue Bedford 'TK', cast or spun wheels, 2 giraffes, 97 mm.
			Blue/Yellow card box £100-150
	1970-71		As previous model but larger 'stepped' front wheels £130-170
			Window box variation £150-200
510	1970-72	Team Manager's Car	Red Citroën, 'Tour De France', figures, spare wheels, 'Paramount' £70-80
511	1970-71	'CHIPPERFIELDS'	
		Poodle Truck	Blue/Red Chevrolet Pick-Up, 'PERFORMING POODLES' labels, female trainer, 4 White and
			2 Black poodles, Blue/Yellow 'window' box (should include a Green plastic stand with
			dome over dogs) £350-450
513	1970-72	Citroën 'Alpine Rescue'	White/Red car, Yellow roof-rack, St Bernard, sled, skis, male figure, 108 mm,
			Blue/Yellow 'window' box £250-350
607	1963-68	'CHIPPERFIELDS'	
		Elephant Cage	A Corgi Kit with Brown plastic cage and elephant parts, instruction leaflet,
			Blue/Yellow card box £50-75
647	1980-83	Buck Rogers Starfighter	White/Blue, 150 mm, Yellow retractable wings, Wilma Dearing and
			Tweaky figures, Black/Yellow pictorial 'window' box, 10 spare rockets £40-45
648	1981-82	NASA Space Shuttle	White/Black body, 'USA Satellite', opening hatch, 156 mm £20-25
C649	1979-82	James Bond Space Shuttle	White body (C468 casting), separate satellite (early versions retained by nylon
			strap). From film 'Moonraker' Larger pictorial Black/Yellow box £50-75
681	1971	Stunt Bike	Gold body, Blue rider, Red trolley, 'window' box, (19,000 made) £125-150
700	1974-80	Motorway	
		Service Ambulance	White/Red futuristic vehicle, WhizzWheels £8-12
701	1974-80	Inter-City Mini-Bus	Orange body, Yellow labels, WhizzWheels £8-12
801	1969-69	Noddy's Car	Yellow/Red car with dickey-seat, cast hubs, chrome bumpers. Figures of Noddy,
			Big-Ears, and black-faced Golly Pictorial Blue/Yellow, 'window' box £1000-1500
			As previous model but Golly has Light Tan face £1000-1500
			As previous model but Golly has Grey face £350-500
	1969-73		As previous model but Master Tubby (light or dark brown) instead of Golly £300-400

Novelty, Film and TV-related models

802	1969-72	Popeye's Paddle-Wagon	Yellow/White body, Red wings, Blue paddle covers, White or Yellow rear wheels, anchors, moving figures of Popeye, Olive Oyl, Swee'Pea, Bluto and Wimpey. Blue/Yellow pictorial 'window' box	£400-500
803	1969-70	The Beatles Submarine	Yellow/White, psychedelic design, hatches (Yellow rear, White front) open to show John, Paul, George and Ringo, pictorial window box with Blue-Green inner lining. (Note 1997 Corgi Classics re-issue)	£350-450
	1970-71		As previous model but with Red hatch covers	£350-450
	1970-71		With one red hatch and one white hatch	£500-600
804	1975-78	Noddy's Car	Red/Yellow car, no dickey-seat, no rear bumper. Figure of Noddy only. Dark Blue/Yellow 'window' box	£175-225
805	1970-71	Hardy Boys Rolls-Royce	9041 Silver Ghost casting in Red, Blue and Yellow, plated wheels. Bubble-pack of five Hardy Boys figures also contained in the Blue/Yellow 'window' box	£175-225
806	1970-72	Lunar Bug	Red/White/Blue, 'Lunar Bug', windows, drop-down ramps, 127 mm	£65-75
807	1971-73	Dougal's Magic Roundabout Car	Yellow/Red, with Brian, Dougal and Dylan, 118 mm. Yellow/Blue 'window' box with decal sheet	£180-225
807	1973-74	Dougal's Car	As previous model but in Black/Yellow box, with decal sheet	£160-180
808	1971-73	Basil Brush's Car	Red/Yellow car with hand-painted Basil figure, 'Laugh tapes' and soundbox are in separate printed box within pictorial Blue/Yellow 'window' box	£175-200
809	1973-73	Dick Dastardly's Car	Purple/Yellow racing car with Dick and Muttley figures. Dark Blue/Yellow 'window' box	£150-175
811	1972-73	James Bond Moon Buggy	Blue/White body, Yellow WhizzWheels, Red rotating scanner, Blue/Yellow pictorial window box	£300-400
H851	1972-74	Magic Roundabout Train	Red/Blue, Mr Rusty and Basil in the locomotive (engine sound), Rosalie and Paul in the carriage and Dougal in the van, 311 mm. Blue/Yellow pictorial 'window' box with Blue nylon tow-rope	£250-300
H852	1972-74	The Magic Roundabout Carousel	Red/Yellow/Blue working roundabout with Swiss musical movement playing the TV theme Dylan, Paul, Rosalie, Florence and Basil figures 200 mm. Blue/Yellow pictorial card box	£450-550
H853	1972-74	Magic Roundabout Playground	(820 mm), contains a modified H852, H851 (with the figures), plus Zebedee, Dylan, four kids, see saw, park bench, 3 Blue and 3 Orange shrubs and 2 flowers. Operating carousel and track. Theme music plays when Dylan is wound up	£1000-1500
H859	1972-74	Mr McHenry's Trike	Red/Yellow trike and trailer, Mr McHenry and pop-up Zebedee figures, Blue and Yellow pictorial 'window' box with blue towing cord and instruction sheet	£175-225
860-868	1972-74	Magic Roundabout individual figures:	860 Dougal, 861 Florence, 862 Zebedee, 863 Mr Rusty, 864 Brian Snail, 865 Basil, 866 Ermintrude the Cow, 868 Dylan the Rabbit Each:	£20-30
C925	1976-81	Batcopter	Black body, Red 'Bat' rotors, Batman figure, operable winch, 143 mm	£65-75
C926	1978-80	Stromberg Helicopter	Black body/rotors, ten spare rockets. From the film 'The Spy Who Loved Me'. Black/Yellow 'window' box	£50-60
927	1978-80	Chopper Squad Helicopter	White/metallic Blue Jet Ranger helicopter, operating winch. Black/Yellow pictorial 'window' box	£35-45
C928	1981-82	Spidercopter	Blue/Red body, (142 mm), 'spider legs', retractable tongue, Black/Yellow pictorial 'window' box	£40-50
C929	1979-80	'DAILY PLANET' Jetcopter	Red/White body (156 mm), rocket launchers, Black/Yellow pictorial 'window' box contains 10 spare rockets	£50-60
C930	1972-80	'Drax' Helicopter	White body, 'Drax' logo, ten spare rockets. From the film 'Moonraker'. Black/Yellow 'window' box	£60-70
9004	1967-69	'The World of Wooster' Bentley	Green 9002 Bentley with figures of Jeeves and Wooster, plated wheels. Bubble-packed in display base	£70-90

The 'Exploration' Range

D2022	1980	'SCANOTRON'	Green/Black/Yellow	£15-25
D22023	1980	'ROCKETRON'	Blue/Yellow, Black tracks	£15-25
D2024	1980	'LASERTRON'	Orange/Black/Yellow	£115-25
D2025	1980	'MAGNETRON'	Red/Black	£15-25

'The Muppets Show' models

D2030	1979-80	Kermit's Car	Yellow car with a famous Green frog, bubble-packed	£40-45
	1980-82		Same model but in Red/Yellow pictorial 'window' box	£35-40
D2031	1979-80	Fozzie Bear's Truck	Red/Brown/White truck, Silver or Black hooter, bubble-packed	£35-40
	1980-82		Same model but in Red/Yellow pictorial 'window' box	£30-35
D2032	1979-80	Miss Piggy's Sport Coupé	Pink sports car, Red or Pink dress, bubble-packed	£40-45
	1980-82		Same model but in Red/Yellow pictorial 'window' box	£35-40
D2033	1979-80	Animal's Percussionmobile	Red traction-engine, Yellow or Red wheels, Yellow or Black chimney, Yellow or Silver cymbal. Bubble-packed	£35-40
	1980-82		Same model but in Red/Yellow pictorial 'window' box	£30-35

Major Packs

Original internal packaging for securing model and accessories must all be present before model can be considered complete and therefore to achieve the best price. See Corgi model identification page.

1121	1960-62	**'CHIPPERFIELDS'**	
		Crane Truck	Red body, Raised Blue log and wheels, operable grey tinplate jib and hook, instruction leaflet. Blue/Yellow lidded box with packing **£150-200**
	1963-69		Red body, raised Blue logo and wheels, operable chrome tinplate jib and hook, instruction leaflet. Blue/Yellow card box with end flaps **£150-200**
1123	1961-62	**'CHIPPERFIELDS'**	
		Circus Cage....................	Red body, Yellow chassis, smooth hubs, red diecast end and middle sliding doors, 2 plastic lions (in stapled bags), animal name decals, instruction sheet. Blue/Yellow lidded box with packing...**£75-100**
	1963-68		Red body, Yellow chassis, smooth or spun hubs, Blue plastic end and middle sliding doors, 4 animals (lions, tigers or polar bears in stapled bags), animal name decals. Blue/Yellow card box with end flaps **£75-100**
1130	1962-70	**'CHIPPERFIELDS'**	
		Horse Transporter	Bedford TK truck, Red/Blue, Green or Red 'horse-head' design at rear, cast or spun hubs, 6 Brown or Grey horses, Blue/Yellow card box with card packing around horses...........**£175-225**
	1970-72		As previous model but with larger 'truck' wheels **£150-175**
1139	1968-72	**'CHIPPERFIELDS'**	
		Menagerie Transporter......	Scammell Handyman MkIII, Blue/Red cab, Blue trailer with 3 plastic cages, 2 lions, 2 tigers and 2 bears. Blue/Yellow pictorial 'window' box with packing to hold animals, plus spare self-adhesive securing tape for animals **£350-450**
1144	1969-72	**'CHIPPERFIELDS' Crane**	
		and Cage with Rhino	Red/Blue Scammell Handyman MkIII, 'COME TO THE CIRCUS' on n/s, silver jib and hook, stepped 'truck' front wheels on some, Grey rhinoceros in plastic cage, Blue/Yellow 'window' box with pre-formed blister-pack around animals.....................**£500-600**
C1163	1978-82	**Human Cannon Truck**	Red and Blue body, 'MARVO' figure, 130 mm..**£30-40**
C1164	1980-83	**Berliet**	
		'DOLPHINARIUM'...........	Yellow cab, Blue trailer, Clear plastic tank, 2 dolphins, girl trainer. Black/Yellow 'window' box with header card on some **£100-150**
			Yellow cab, Yellow trailer, 'window' box with header card on some **£100-150**

Duo Packs (Film and TV-related models)

1360	1982-?	**Batmobile**..................................	267 plus a Corgi juniors version Black/Red/Yellow 'window' box...............................**£150-175**
1361	197?-?	**James Bond Aston-Martin**	271 plus a Corgi Juniors version Black/Red/Yellow 'window' box...............................**£125-150**
1362	197?-?	**James Bond Lotus Esprit**........	269 plus a Corgi Juniors version Black/Red/Yellow 'window' box...............................**£75-100**
1363	1982-83	**Buck Rogers**	
		'Little & Large' Set	(647) plus a smaller version Black/Yellow pictorial 'window' box...........................**£50-60**

Corgitronics and Corgimatics

These models have 'Battery-operated Micro-Chip Action'.

Ref.	Year(s)	Model name	Colours, features, dimensions	Market Price Range
C1001	1982	**HCB Angus Firestreak**	Red/Yellow/White, 'RESCUE', electronic siren, on/off switch. 165 mm........	£40-50
C1002	1981	**Sonic Corgi Truck Set**	Yellow/White/Black/Red, 'SHELL SUPER OIL', 'BP OIL', remote control............	£25-30
C1002	1981	**'YORKIE' Truck Set**	White/Yellow/Blue/Orange, 'MILK CHOCOLATE YORKIE', remote control..........	£25-30
C1003	1981	**Ford Road Hog**	Black, Yellow/White twirls, 2-tone horn, press-down start, 150 mm............	£15-20
C1004	1981	**'Beep Beep Bus'**	Red, 'BTA WELCOME TO BRITAIN', 2-tone horn, press-down start, 123 mm...........	£20-25
	1983		Red body with 'WELCOME TO HAMLEYS' logo..	£20-25
C1005	1982	**Police Land Rover**	White/Red/Blue, 'POLICE', electronic siren, press-down start, 132 mm............	£15-20
C1006	1982	**'RADIO WEST' Roadshow**	'Your Local Radio 605', AM radio, advertised but not issued......................	NPP
C1006	1982	**'RADIO LUXEMBOURG'**.....	Red/White, 'RTL 208', AM radio, 3 loudspeakers, 123 mm.........................	£25-30
C1007	1982	**Road Repair Unit**		
		Land Rover and Trailer	Yellow/Red/Silver, 'ROADWORKS', press start, road drill and sound...............	£25-35
C1008	1982	**Fire Chief's Car**	Red/White/Silver, 'FIRE DEPARTMENT', press-down start, siren...................	£15-20
C1009	1983	**MG Maestro 1600**	Yellow/Black, press start, working front and rear lights, 118 mm...........	£15-20
			Red/Black body. Sold in Austin-Rover Group box.................................	£20-25
C1024	1983	**'Beep Beep Bus'**	Red, 'BTA', supplied exclusively to Mothercare shops..........................	£20-25
1121	1983	**Ford Transit Tipper Lorry**	Orange/Black, Flashing light and working tipper..............................	£20-25

Caravans and Motorcycles

C171	1982-	**Street Bike**	Red, Silver and Black body, multicoloured swirl.....................................	£5-10
C172	1982-	**'POLICE' Bike**	White/Black/Silver body...	£5-10
C173	1982-	**Cafe Racer**	Silver and Black body racing number '26', '750 cc Class'......................	£5-10
C420	1962-66	**Ford 'Airborne' Caravan**	Two-tone Green, Brown interior, or Blue/Pale Grey, Red interior, or Blue/Green with Brown interior...	£40-50
			Two-tone Lilac, Beige interior...	£70-80
C490	1976-79	**Touring Caravan**....................	White and Blue body, opening doors, drawbar, 125 mm........................	£10-15
681	1971	**Stunt Bike**	Gold body, Blue rider, Red trolley, 'window' box, (19,000 made)...............	£125-150

Corgi Toys Major Gift Set No.1 with No.1101 Bedford 'S' type Carrimore Transporter
Picture supplied by Christie's South Kensington and reproduced by their kind permission.

Corgi Toys Major Gift Set No.28 with No.1105 Bedford 'TK' type Carrimore Transporter
Picture supplied by Christie's South Kensington and reproduced by their kind permission.

Gift Sets

Original internal packaging for securing models and accessories must all be present before sets can be considered complete and therefore to achieve the best price. See Corgi model identification page.

Ref.	Year(s)	Set name	Contents	Market Price Range
1	1957-62	Transporter and 4 Cars	1101 Blue/Yellow Bedford Carrimore Transporter plus 201 Austin Cambridge, 208 Jaguar 24, 301 Triumph TR2 and 302 MGA, plus 2 Yellow/Black 'Corgi Toys' dummy boxes	£400-500
1	1957-62	Transporter and 4 Cars	1101 Red/Two-tone Blue Transporter, 200 Ford Consul, 201 Austin Cambridge, 204 Rover 90, 205 Riley Pathfinder, 2 Yellow 'Corgi Toys' dummy boxes	£300-400
1	1959	Transporter and 4 Cars	1101 Red/Two-tone Blue Transporter, 214 Ford Thunderbird Hardtop, 215 Ford Thunderbird Convertible, 219 Plymouth Suburban Sport, 220 Chevrolet Impala. (US issue set)	£350-450
1	1961-62	Transporter and 4 Cars	1101 Red/Two-tone Blue Transporter, 210s Citroën, 219 Plymouth Suburban Sport, 226 Mini, 305 Triumph TR3. (US issue set)	£350-450
1	1969-72	Farm Set	Ford 5000 Tractor plus 58 Beast Carrier, pictorial stand	£100-120
C1	1983	Ford Sierra Set	Ford Sierra 299 with Blue body and Blue/Cream Caravan	£20-30
C1/2	1985	'London Scene'	469 'LONDON STANDARD', Sierra Police Car and 425/1 Taxi	£15-20
2	1958-66	Land Rover and Pony Trailer Set	438 Land Rover (Green, Beige tin tilt) and 102 Pony Trailer (Red/Black)	£150-175
			As previous but with All Red Land Rover	£175-200
			with Light Brown Land Rover (Cream plastic tilt), Light Brown/Cream trailer	£70-80
2	1971-73	Unimog Dumper and Shovel	1128 Mercedes Tipper and 1145 Unimog Goose Dumper	£60-70
C2		Fire Set	no details at present	£15-20
3	1959-62	Thunderbird Missile Set	Contains 350 Thunderbird Missile and 351 Land Rover	£150-175
3	1967-69	Batmobile and Batboat		
		1st issue:	267 Batmobile with 'Bat' wheels, plus 107 Batboat (cast wheels), in plain or pictorial window box with 4 figures, 12 rockets in unopened packet, sealed 'secret instructions'	£500-600
3	1979		2nd issue: 267 Batmobile (plain cast wheels), and 107 Batboat (WhizzWheels), pictorial window box, 2 figures, 12 rockets in unopened packet, sealed 'secret instructions'	£200-300
C3	1986-88	'British Gas' Set	Contains Blue/White Ford Cargo Van, Ford Escort Van (2nd), plus compressor	£20-25
4	1959-62	Bristol Ferranti Bloodhound Guided Missile Set	Contains: 351, 1115, 1116, 1117 (see 'Military Vehicles' section)	£250-350
4	1974-75	Country Farm Set	Models 50, 62 and equipment	£60-70
5	1959-60	Racing Car Set	150 (Red) 151 (Blue) 152 (Green). All have flat spun wheels. Bubble-packed on inner card tray	£150-200
5	1960-61	Racing Car Set	150 (Red) 151 (Blue) 152 (Green). All have cast spoked wheels. Bubble-packed on inner card tray	£150-200
5s	1962-63	Racing Car Set	150s (Red) 151a (Blue) 152s (Turquoise). 'Gift Set 5s' stickers on box which contains an inner polystyrene packing tray	£250-350
5	1967-72	Agricultural Set	484 Livestock Transporter and pigs, 438 Land Rover (no hood) 62, 69, accessories 1490 skip and churns, 4 calves, farmhand and dog, 6 sacks	£150-200
6	1959-62	'Rocket Age' Set	Contains: 350, 351, 352, 353, 1106, 1108, 1117 and 'Rocket Age' leaflet	£600-800
6	1967-69	Cooper Maserati Set	Contains 490 VW Breakdown Truck plus 156 on trailer	£150-175
7	1959-63	Tractor and Trailer Set	Contains 50 and 51	£75-95
7	1968-75	'DAKTARI' Set	438 Land Rover in Green with Black Zebra stripes, spun or cast hubs. 5 figures: Paula, Dr Marsh Tracy with chimp Judy on his lap, a Tiger on the bonnet, and Clarence The Short-Sighted Lion (with spectacles!)	£100-125
			Version with WhizzWheels	£55-65
8	1959-61	Combine Harvester, Tractor and Trailer Set	Contains 1111, 50 and 51	£200-250
8	1960-74	'Lions Of Longleat' Set	Land Rover, keeper, 3 lions, dens and meals (with early wheels)	£100-125
			As above but with WhizzWheels	£70-80
C8/2		Police Set	no details	£15-20
9	1959-62	Corporal Guided Missile Set	Contains: 1112, 1113, 1118 and separate instructions for Erector Vehicle and Corporal Missile	£300-400
9	1968-72	Tractor, Trailer and Shovel Set	Contains 66, 69 and 62	£100-125
9	1992	3 Racing Minis Set	Yellow, White and Blue, numbers/stripes/adverts, special Red 'Hamleys' box	£90-110
10	1968-69	Rambler Marlin & Kayaks	Blue/White 319 with Trailer and 2 Canoes	£125-150
10	1974-78	Centurion Tank and Transporter Set	Contains 901 and 1100 Mack articulated transporter	£70-80
10	1982	Jeep Set	Red 441 plus two motorcycles on trailer	£20-25
C10	1985	Sierra and Caravan Set	C299 23 Sierra plus Pale Brown caravan with Blue/Grey strip	£25-35
11	1960-64	ERF Dropside and Trailer	456 and 101 with cement and planks load	£125-150
			As above but with WhizzWheels	£60-70
11	1971-75	London Gift Set	Contains 418 Taxi with 468 'OUTSPAN' and 226 Mini	£75-95
C11	1980	London Gift Set	C425 Taxi with C469 Bus 'B.T.A.' and policeman	£30-35
12	1961-66	Circus Gift Set	1121 Circus Crane Truck and 1123 Circus Cage, plus instructions	£150-175
12	1968-70	Grand Prix Racing Set	155, 156 and 330 with Volkswagen tender, trailer and equipment	£250-300
12	1970-72	Grand Prix Racing Set	158, 159 and 330 (or 371) with Volkswagen tender, trailer and equipment. The artwork on the box and the vac-formed base are different from previous issue	£250-300
C12	1981-	Glider and Trailer Set	345 with Trailer and Glider	£40-50

13	1964-67	**Fordson Tractor and Plough Set**	Contains 60 and 61	£80-100
13	1969-72	**Renault 16 Film Unit**	White/Black, *'TOUR DE FRANCE'* , 'PARAMOUNT', cameraman with camera, cyclist/bike. Inner tray plus plain orange card backdrop	£140-160
13	1981-82	**Tour de France 'RALEIGH' Team Car**	373 Peugeot, White body, Red/Yellow 'RALEIGH' and 'TOTAL' logos, racing cycles and Manager with loudhailer	£60-70
C13	1985	**'RAC' Ford Escort and Caravan Set**	Blue and White van and caravan, 'INFORMATION CENTRE'	£45-55
14	1961-65	**Tower Wagon Set**	409 Jeep, Yellow cradle, lamp standard and electrician	£60-70
14	1969-73	**Giant 'DAKTARI' Set**	Gift Set and items plus 503 and 484 transporters, spun hubs. Pictorial card and inner tray	£250-300
			Version with WhizzWheels. Pictorial card and inner tray	£200-250
C14	1985	**'AA' Ford Escort and Caravan Set**	Yellow and White van and caravan, 'INFORMATION CENTRE'	£45-55
15	1963-64	**Silverstone Set**	Contains six model in Blue/Yellow picture boxes: 150s Vanwall, 151a Lotus XI or 152s BRM, 215s Ford Thunderbird Open Sports, 304 Mercedes Roadster (Chrome), 309 Aston-Martin DB4 Competition plus 417s Land-Rover Breakdown (tin canopy) plus Nos. 1501–1503 boxed sets of figures plus boxed kits 602, 603 (2) and 605. Six Humbrol paint phials in a sleeve plus a brush and a tube of glue. Plus a plastic layout sheet with pictorial assembly instruction sheet. First issue box had no picture on lift-up lid type of corrugated box	£1250-1500
15	1964-66	**Silverstone Set**	150s, 154, 152s, 215s, 304s, 309, 417s. Other contents as above, layout picture shown on box	£1250-1500
15	1968-76	**Land Rover and Horsebox Set**	Contains 438, 112, spun hubs, mare and foal. Box contains inner card packing	£75-95
			Version with WhizzWheels. Box contains inner card packing	£55-75
16	1961-66	**'ECURIE ECOSSE' Set**	1126 Transporter with 3 racing cars with instruction leaflet and internal packing.	
		i)	Metallic Dark Blue 1126 Transporter (with Orange lettering), 150 Vanwall (Red, no '25'), 151 Lotus Eleven (Blue, number '3'), 152 BRM (Turquoise, no '3')	£200-250
		ii)	Metallic Dark Blue 1126 Transporter (with Yellow lettering), 150s Vanwall, 151a Lotus Eleven (Blue, no '7'), 152s BRM	£250-300
	1965	iii)	Metallic Light Blue 1126 Transporter (with Red lettering), 150s Vanwall, 152s BRM, 154 Ferrari (Red, no'36')	£200-250
		iv)	Metallic Dark Blue 1126 Transporter (with Light Blue lettering and ridges), 150s Vanwall, 152s BRM, 154 Ferrari	£200-250
17	1963-67	**Ferrari Racing Set**	438 Land Rover in Red with Green top, Red 154 Ferrari F1 on Yellow trailer	£125-150
17	1976-81	**Military Set**	Contains 904, 906, 920 (see 'Military Vehicles' section)	£40-50
C17	1986	**'BRITISH TELECOM'**	Ford Cargo Box Van, Ford Escort Van and a Compressor	£15-20
18	1961-63	**Ford Tractor and Plough Set**	Contains 55 and 56	£80-100
18	1976-77	**Emergency Gift Set**	Contains 402, 481, C921 (see 'Emergency Vehicles' section)	£60-70
C18/1	?	**3 Mini Racers Set**	with *'CHELSEA'*, *'PARK LANE'* and *'PICADILLY'* logos	£20-30
C18/2	?	**Mini Special Editions Set**	with *'RED HOT'*, *'RITZ'* and *'JET BLACK'* logos	£20-30
		Note:	C18/1 and C18/2 were sold (in long 'window' boxes) exclusively by Woolworths.	
19	1962-68	**'CHIPPERFIELDS' Cage Set**	438 Land Rover (plastic tilt) and 607 Elephant and cage on trailer	£175-225
19		**'RNLI' Set**	438 Land Rover plus Orange dinghy on trailer with *Mumbles Lifeboat* logo	£60-70
C19	1972-77	**Land Rover and Nipper Aircraft**	438 Land Rover (Blue/Orange) Yellow/Red or All-Orange plane '23' on trailer	£60-70
19	1973-77	**'CORGI FLYING CLUB'**	Blue/Orange Land Rover (438) with aircraft	£60-70
C19	1979-82	**Emergency Gift Set**	Contains C339 and C921	£30-40
C19	1980-82	**Emergency Gift Set**	Contains C339 and C931 in Red/White liveries	£35-45
C19/7	1990	**'AMBULANSE' Set**	White Ford Transit Van and Saab 9000 'POLITI' (Norwegian)	£30-40
C19/8	1990	**'AMBULANS' Set**	White/Red Ford Transit & White/Blue Saab 9000 'POLIS' (Swedish)	£30-40
C19/9	1990	**Swedish Breakdown Set**	Red/Yellow Ford Transit *'Bjarnings'*, Black Saab 9000 *'BRANDCHEF'*	£30-40
20	1961	**Golden Guinea Set**	Gold-plated 224 Bentley Continental, 234 Ford Consul, 229 Chevrolet Corvair, Catalogue, 2 Accessory Packs. Inner card tray with lower card packing	£150-175
20	1973	**Tri-Deck Transporter Set**	1st issue contains 1146 Transporter with 210 'Saint's' Volvo, 311 Ford Capri, 343 Pontiac, 372 Lancia, 377 Marcos, 378 MGC GT (rare Orange version). Instruction sheet, 'Mr Retailer' transit card protector	£500-600
20		**Tri-Deck Transporter Set**	late issue with WhizzWheels (sold in Harrods): 377 Marcos (Silver Green), 382 Porsche Targa (Silver Blue), 201 Volvo (Orange 'Saint' label), 313 Ford Cortina GXL (Bronze/Black), 334 Mini (Orange).Instruction sheet, 'Mr Retailer' transit card protector	£500-600
C20	1978-80	**Emergency Gift Set**	Contains C429, C482, C921 (see 'Emergency Vehicles' section)	£30-40
C20/2	1986	**'AA' Set**	Ford Escort and Transit Vans, Ford Transit Breakdown	£15-20
C20/3	1986	**'AA' Set**	Range Rover plus caravan 'Information Centre'	£15-25
21	1962-66	**ERF Dropside and Trailer**	456 and 101 with milk churns and self-adhesive accessories	£175-225
21	1969-71	**'CHIPPERFIELDS' Circus Set**	Contains 1144 Crane and Cage, and 1139 Menagerie Transporter, internal packaging and 'Mr Dealer' box protector card	£750-1000

C21	1980-82	**Superman Set**	Contains 260, 265 and 925, plus inner tray and plastic rockets on sprue	£100-125
C21/2	1986	**RAC Set**	Range Rover, Ford Escort Van and Ford Transit Breakdown	£15-20
22	1962-66	**Farming Models Set**	111, 406, 51, 101, 53, 1487, 1490, accessories and GS18	£300-400
C22	1980-82	**James Bond Set**	Contains 269, 271 and 649, plus inner tray, rockets and bandit figures	£200-250
C22	1986	**'ROYAL MAIL' Set**	Ford Cargo and Escort Vans, Austin Mini Metro *DATAPOST*	£15-20
23	1962-66	**'CHIPPERFIELDS' Set**		
		1st issue:	1121 Crane Truck, 2 x 1123 Animal Cages (2 lions, 2 polar bears), plus Gift Set 19 and 426 Booking Office	£500-750
	1964	2nd issue:	as 1st issue but 503 'TK Giraffe Truck' replaces 426 Booking Office	£400-600
	NB		Items contained in inner polystyrene tray (both issues).	
C23	1980-82	**Spiderman Set**	Contains 261, 266 and 928	£90-110
24	1963-68	**Commer Constructor Set**	2 cab/chassis units, 4 interchangeable bodies, milkman, accessories	£80-95
24	1976-	**Mercedes and Caravan**	Contains 285 and 490 with colour change 1980	£35-45
25	1963-66	**BP or Shell Garage Set**	Contains 224, 225, 229, 234 and 419 all in Blue/Yellow boxes plus: 601 Batley Garage, 602 'AA' and 'RAC' Boxes, 606 Lamp Standards (2), 608 Filling Station, 609 accessories, 1505 Figures	£1000-1250
25	1969-71	**Racing Car and Tender**	Contains 159 and Volkswagen Tender, inner plastic tray plus 2 sets of decals in stapled bags	£140-160
25	1980	**Talbot Rancho Set**	457 plus two motorcycles on trailer	£15-20
26	1971-75	**Beach Buggy Set**	381 plus Sailing Boat	£30-40
26	1981-83	**Corgi Racing Set**	457 Talbot Matra Rancho, 160 Hesketh (Yellow), 'Corgi Racing Team' trailer	£35-45
27	1963-72	**Priestman Shovel on Machinery Carrier**	1128 and 1131 (Bedford Machinery Carrier)	£100-125
C27		**Emergency Set**	no details	£15-20
28	1963-66	**Transporter and 4 Cars**	1105 Bedford TK Transporter with 222 Renault Floride, 230 Mercedes-Benz, 232 Fiat, 234 Ford Classic, 2 dummy 'Corgi Toys' boxes, instructions. Pictorial box	£400-500
28	1963-66	**Mazda Dinghy Set**	493 Mazda plus dinghy and trailer	£40-45
C28	1987	**Post Set**	Contains 656/2, Red Sierra (racing number '63') or Brown Saab 9000	£20-25
29	1963-64	**Massey Ferguson Set**	Contains 50 Massey-Ferguson Tractor with driver and 51 Tipper Trailer	£90-110
C29	1981	**'CORGI' Pony Club**	Contains 441 Jeep, 112 trailer, girl on pony, 3 jumps, 3 hay bales	£55-65
29	1975-76	**Ferrari Racing Set**	Contains 323 and 150, *'DUCKHAMS'*	£60-75
30	1973-73	**Grand Prix Gift Set**	'Kit' versions of 151 Yardley (1501), 154 JPS (1504), 152 Surtees (1502) plus 153 Surtees (1503)? in unique Norris livery. Mail order only	£150-200
C30	1978-80	**Circus Gift Set**	Land Rover and Trailer	£60-75
31	1965-68	**Buick Riviera Boat Set**	245 Buick, Red boat trailer, and Dolphin Cabin Cruiser towing water skier. Pictorial sleeve box with internal packing around models	£125-150
C31	1977-80	**Safari Land Rover Set**	C341 Land Rover with animal trailer, Warden and Lion	£55-65
32	1965-68	**Tractor, Shovel and Trailer Set**	Contains 54 and 62	£100-125
C32	1976-79	**Lotus Racing Set**	Black/Gold C301 Lotus Elite, and C154 JPS Lotus on trailer	£50-75
C32	1979-83	**Lotus Racing Set**	Black/Gold C301 Lotus Elite, and C154 Texaco Lotus on trailer	£50-75
C32	1989-90	**3 Model Set**	Contains Concorde, Taxi and Routemaster Bus 'STANDARD'	£20-30
33	1965-68	**Tractor and Beast Carrier**	Contains 55 and 58	£100-125
	1968-72		Contains 67 and 58	£70-80
C33	1980	**'DLRG' Rescue Set**	White/Red 421 Land Rover and boat on trailer	£25-30
34	1977-79	**Tractor & Tipping Trailer**	Contains 55 and 56	£55-65
35	1965-68	**London Gift Set**	418 Taxi with 468 *'Corgi Toys'* or *'Outspan'* Bus and policeman	£140-160
C35	1978-79	**'CHOPPER SQUAD' Surf Boat**	Contains 927, 419, trailer, rescue boat	£30-40
36	1967-70	**Marlin Rambler Set**	Contains 263 and Boat	£45-65
36	1967-70	**Oldsmobile Toronado Set**	Contains 276 (Greenish-Blue) Chrome trailer, Yellow/Blue boat, 3 figures	£120-140
36	1983	**Off-Road Set**	447 (Dark Blue/Cream, racing number '5') plus power-boat on trailer	£25-35
C36	1976-78	**Tarzan Set**	Light Green 421 Land Rover and trailer, paler Green 'zebra' stripes, Tarzan, Jane, Cheetah (chimp), boy, dinghy with hunter, elephant, snake, vines, etc. Box should also contain printed card, '3-D' jungle panorama	£140-160
37	1966-69	**'Lotus Racing Team'**	490 VW Breakdown Truck, Red trailer with cars 318, 319, 155, plus 2 sets of unused racing numbers ('5' and '9' or '4' and '8'), a 1966 illustrated checklist and an unopened pack of cones	£200-250
37	1979-82	**Fiat X-19 Set**	Fiat X-19 and Boat 'Carlsberg'	£30-40
38	1977-78	**Mini Camping Set**	Mini with 2 figures, tent, barbecue in perspex bubble	£45-55
38	1965-67	**'1965 Monte Carlo Rally'**	318 Mini Cooper 'S', 322 Rover 2000, and 326 Citroën DS19. Monte Carlo Rally emblem on each bonnet. Box contains pictorial stand and inner card packing	£400-500
C38	1980-	**Jaguar XJS Set**	319 with Powerboat on Trailer	£20-30
40	1967-69	**The Avengers Set**	John Steed's Bentley: Green body, Red wire wheels and figure, plus Emma Peel figure, Lotus Elan with Black/White body, 3 Black umbrellas. Inner pictorial stand	£500-600
			As previous set but Bentley in Red/Black livery with Silver wire wheels	£400-500
C40	1977-80	**Batman Gift Set**	Contains 107, 267, 925, plus inner tray with card packing	£200-300
41	1966-68	**Ford 'H' Series Transporter and six Cars**	1138 Transporter (Red/Two-tone Blue), 252 Rover 2000 (Metallic Plum), 251 Hillman Imp (Metallic Bronze), 440 Ford Cortina Estate (Metallic Blue), 204 Morris Mini-Minor (Light Blue), 321 Austin Mini Cooper 'S' (Red, RN '2', '1966 Monte Carlo Rally', with roof signatures), 180 Morris Mini Cooper 'S' (Black/Red, 'wickerwork' panels). Box also contains 16 cones in unopened packet plus instructions. Only sold by mail order	£500-750

Tinplate & Diecast Toys

*A fine selection
of '0' Gauge
Trains and
Dinky Toys.*

Our quarterly specialist sales include a wide range of lots for both new and established
collectors alike. Our auctions regularly feature famous manufacturers such as:
Dinky, Corgi, Matchbox, Spot-on, Marklin, Hornby, Bing, Meccano and others.

If you are considering selling either indiviual items of merit or an entire collection,
please contact us for free auction valuations and competitive proposals of sale.

Catalogue & Subscription Enquiries:
01666 502 200

Specialist Enquiries:
Leigh Gotch ~ 0171 393 3951

 65-69 Lots Road, London SW10 0RN Tel: 0171 393 3900
Fax: 0171 393 3906 Internet:www.bonhams.com

AUCTIONEERS & VALUERS SINCE 1793

Corgi cars in early 'Blue boxes'. Top Row: 202, 207m, 211m, 303.
Bottom Row: 210, 208m, 205, 204.

'CHIPPERFIELDS' Circus Models - main items sold:-

Top Row: Gift Set 21 Models (E), Box(G) (£550).
2nd Row: 1139 Menagerie Transporter Model (E), Box(G) (£180).
3rd Row: 1144 Circus Crane with Rhino cage Model (E), Box (G) (£220),
    511 Performing Poodles, lacking dome otherwise (G) (£140).

Models sold by Bonhams, Chelsea, 65-69 Lots Road, London SW10 0RN.
Picture reproduced by their kind permission.

No.267 Batmobile with rare Red Whizz wheels, B+ condition (£420)

No.277 Monkeymobile, B+ cond.
with rare pictorial header (£600)

No.349 Pop art Morris Mini Minor
Mostest Model A, Box B (£1,400)

GS 40 Avengers Gift Set
Mostly B+ condition (£550)

Budgie Toys, No.196 Supercar
Model B+, Box C (£400)

No.1402 Husky Batmobile Trade Pack of 12
(£1,200)

Shackleton Toys, Foden FG 6-Wheeled Flatbed
Model B+, Box C (£320)

Models sold by Vectis Auctions Ltd, Fleck Way, Thornaby, Stockton-on-Tees TS17 9JZ.
Picture reproduced by their kind permission.

Spot-on Model Archive

The 109 E.R.F. Truck usually appeared in yellow, light blue or aqua. The above colours are all rare.

Picture kindly supplied by Bruce Sterling of New York City, USA.

Miniatures Set No.6 (with 'Royal Mail' van)

L-R: 145 Roadmaster Bus, Gift Set 702, 109 E.R.F. Truck, 156 Mulliner Coach, 116 Caterpillar D9 Bulldozer, 158A Bedford 'S' type, 10 tonner 2000 gal Shell/BP Tanker, 109/3B E.R.F. G89, Flat Float with sides with barrel load, 137 Massey Ferguson 65 Tractor, 2 x 229 Lambretta, 807 'Pit Stop' Tommy Spot Set, 4 x New Zealand issues in yellow boxes:- 115 Volkswagon Variant, 102 Austin Healey Sprite, 112 Land Rover, 103 MG Midget, 213 Ford, 154 Un-boxed Austin A40 'Maggi' promotional.

All models sold by Christie's South Kensington, 85 Old Brompton Road, London SW7 3LD.
Picture reproduced by their kind permission.

C41	1977-81	**Silver Jubilee Set**	The State Landau with HRH Queen Elizabeth and Prince Phillip (and a Corgi!)	£15-20
C42	1979-80	**Agricultural Set**	Contains C34, C43, Silo/Elevator	£45-55
C43	1979-80	**Silo and Conveyor Set**	Silo and Conveyor *'CORGI HARVESTING COMPANY LTD'*	£40-50
C43	1985	**'TOYMASTER' Transport Set**	C496 *'ROYAL MAIL'*, C515 'BMX' and Volvo 'TOYMASTER' truck	£20-25
C44	1978-80	**Metropolitan Police Set**	421 Land Rover, 112 Horsebox plus Policeman on horse	£55-65
45	1966	**'All Winners' Set**	261 James Bond's Aston-Martin, 310 Chevrolet Stingray, 324 Marcos Volvo, 325 Ford Mustang Competition, 314 Ferrari Berlinetta 9,000 sets sold	£300-400
C45	1978-80	**Royal Canadian Police Set**	RCMP Land Rover (421), Trailer (102) and 'Mountie' on horse	£85-95
46	1966-69	**'All Winners' Set**	264 Oldsmobile Toronado (Metallic Blue), 307 Jaguar 'E'-type (Chrome finish, RN '2', driver), 314 Ferrari Berlinetta (Red, RN '4'), 337 Chevrolet Stingray (Yellow, RN '13'), 327 MGB GT (Red/Black, suitcase). Box should contain unopened bag of cones and unused decal sheets	£225-275
47	1966-69	**Ford Tractor and Conveyor Set**	Contains 67, trailer with conveyor belt, figure, accessories plus inner display card	£140-160
C47	1978-80	**Pony Club Set**	421 Land Rover and Horsebox in Metallic Bronze, girl on pony figure	£25-30
48	1967-68	**Ford 'H' series Transporter and six Cars**	1159 Transporter (Orange/Silver/Two-tone Blue) with 252 Rover 2000 (Metallic Maroon), 251 Hillman Imp, 440 Ford Cortina Estate, 180 Morris Mini Cooper 'S' (with 'wickerwork' panels), 204 Morris Mini-Minor (Metallic Maroon), 321 Mini Cooper 'S' ('1966 Monte Carlo Rally'), Red/White, RN '2'	£250-300
	1968	**'SUN/RAC' variation**	As previous set but 321 Mini Cooper is replaced by 333 SUN/RAC Rally Mini. Also 251 Hillman Imp is changed to Metallic Gold with White stripe and the 204 Mini Minor is now Metallic Blue with RN '21'	£350-450
48	1969	**Scammell Transporter and six Cars**	1148 Transporter (Red/White) with 378 MGB (Yellow/Black), 340 Sunbeam Imp (1967 Monte Carlo, Metallic Blue, RN '77'), 201 Saint's Volvo P1800 (White with Orange label), 180 Morris Mini Cooper 'S' (with 'wickerwork' panels), 339 Mini Cooper 'S' ('1967 Monte Carlo Rally', RN '177'), 204 Morris Mini-Minor (Metallic Maroon), plus sealed bag of cones and leaflet	£500-600
C48	1978-81	**'PINDER' Circus Set**	Contains C426, C1163, C30, ringmaster, artistes, animals, seating, and cardboard cut-out 'Big-Top' circus tent	£100-125
C48/1	1986	**Racing Set**	C100/2 plus 576/2	£20-25
C49	1978-80	**'CORGI FLYING CLUB'**	Green/White Jeep (419) with Blue/White Nipper Aircraft	£50-60
C51		**'100 Years of the Car' Set**	3 Mercedes: C805 (White) C806 (Black) C811 (Red) (Originally for Germany)	£20-25
?	1978-80	**'The Jaguar Collection'**	C804 (Cream), C816 (Red), C318 (Mobil Green/White). ('UNIPART' stores)	£30-35
C54	1978-80	**Swiss Rega Set**	Bonna Ambulance and Helicopter	£30-35
C55	1978-80	**Norway Emergency Set**	Police Car, Breakdown Truck, Ford Transit Ambulance	£12-18
C56	1978-80	**Swedish Set**	Ford Sierra 'POLIS', Bonna Ambulance	£12-18
C57	1978-80	**Swedish Set**	Contains Volvo and Caravan	£12-18
C57	1978-80	**Volvo 740 and Caravan**	Red/White, White/Red/Blue Caravan Swedish export set	£15-20
C61	1978-80	**Swiss Fire Set**	1120 Dennis Fire Engine, Sierra 'POLITZEI', Escort Van 'NOTRUF'	£30-35
C62	1986	**Swiss Services Set**	C564 *'PTT'*, Box Van *'DOMICILE'*, VW Polo *'PTT'* Export Set	£20-25
C63	1986	**French Set**	Bonna Ambulance, Peugeot 505, Renault 5 'POLICE'	£30-35
C63	1986	**Emergency Set**	Mercedes Ambulance (White body, Blue designs and roof lights, Fire Chief Car (*'Sapeurs Pompiers'*) 'POLICE' Car (White body, Black doors, Blue roof light)	NGPP
64	1965-69	**FC Jeep 150 and Conveyor Belt**	Jeep (409) Yellow/White Conveyor	£40-45
C65	1978-80	**Norway Set**	Ford Transit Ambulance plus Helicopter	£12-18
C67/1/2/3	1978-80	**Cyclists Sets**	Sold in France, 2 Cars, 2 Bicycles	£15-20
C70	1978-80	**Danish 'FALCK' Set**	Bonna Ambulance and Ford Breakdown Truck	£15-20
C72	1978-80	**Norway Set**	Contains C542 plus Helicopter *'LN OSH'*	£12-18
C73/1	1990	**Swedish 'POLIS' Set**	White/Blue Volvo 740 and Red/White Jet Ranger Helicopter	£12-18
C330/2-5		**Mini 30th Anniversary**	4 Minis (*'ROSE'*, *'SKY'*, *'FLAME'* and *'RACING'*), interior colours vary	£40-50
?		**Mini 30th Anniversary**	Model of a Mini with Anniversary Book	£35-45
C330/6-9		**Four Mini Set**	Silver (*'CITY'*), Blue (*'MAYFAIR'*), Maroon (*'MAYFAIR'*), Yellow (*'CITY'*)	£20-30
448	1964-69	**Austin Police Mini Van**	Dark Blue body, Red interior, shaped or cast hubs, aerial, White 'POLICE' logo, policeman and dog, pictorial stand and internal support packaging	£125-150
1151	1970	**Scammell 'Co-op' Set**	Contains 1147, 466 & 462 in Blue/White livery Promotional in brown box	£150-175
C1412	?	**Swiss Police Set**	Range Rover and Helicopter *'POLITZEI'*	£18-22
?	1967	**Monte Carlo Game**	Fernel Developments game with two Lavender 226 Minis, '1967 Rallye Monte Carlo' bonnet labels, RNs 1 and 4, plastic/paper winding roads, cards, dice shakers, Blue/White/Red box. Set made for the Scandinavian market	£250-350
?	1985	**Wiltshire Fire Brigade**	Dennis Fire Escape plus Escort Van both in red (650)	£45-55
?	1985	**Race Team Set**	'ADMIRAL ENERGY GROUP Ltd' logos on 501 Range Rover (White), Porsche 956 (White) on trailer	£35-45
?	1980	**Construction Site Set**	Contains 54 with 440 (Mazda Pick-Up)	£30-35
?	1988	**'ROYAL MAIL' Set**	Post Office Display Set not sold to the public includes 611, 612 and 496 Escort Vans, 613, 614 and 615 Metro Vans, 616 General Motors (Chevrolet) Van, 617/ Leyland Artic and 618 Mercedes Benz Artic, plus Juniors 39, 90/1/2/3/4	£500-750
?	1992	**Set of 4 Minis**	Black (*'Check'*), White (*'Designer'*), Red (*'Cooper'*), Metallic Blue (*'Neon'*)	£12-14

NB See also Marks & Spencers Gift Set issues at the end of the Cars section.

Buses, Minibuses and Coaches

(Excluding models issued as 'CORGI CLASSICS')
Only models thought to have been 100% produced by Corgi have been included in the listings.

Identification of Routemaster
Double-Decker Bus models

1ST CASTING, 1964 - 1975
MODEL No. 468 ONLY – CLOSED TOP MODEL

Length 114 mm, die-cast body comprised of two separate castings which make up the lower and upper decks. The castings are separated by a white plastic joint.

The baseplate is die-cast, painted grey and stamped 'Corgi Toys', 'LONDON TRANSPORT', 'ROUTEMASTER', 'MADE IN ENGLAND' plus the Patent No. 904525. The early issues had turned metal wheels with rubber tyres. These lasted until 1973 when cast metal wheels were introduced with plastic tyres and in 1974/75 WhizzWheels were seen.

Early issues also had jewelled headlights which were replaced in 1973 by the cast-in type painted silver. The decals are of the transfer printed variety and there is a board at the front only. The model has spring suspension, windows, a metal platform handrail and a driver and clippie. The interior seats are white or cream.

2ND CASTING, 1975 ONWARDS
CLOSED TOP AND OPEN TOP MODELS

MODEL Nos: C460, C463, C464, C467, C469, C470, C471, C473, C475, C476, C477, C479, C480, 1004 and all the numbers allocated to the 'Specials'. Length 123 mm, die-cast body comprised of two separate castings which make up the lower and upper decks. The castings are separated by a cream plastic joint for normal issues and very often by a coloured joint for 'Specials'. Until Model No. 480 was issued as an AEC Renown in 1983 the plastic baseplates were stamped 'CORGI', 'LONDON TRANSPORT', 'ROUTEMASTER' and 'MADE IN ENGLAND'. However 'LONDON TRANSPORT' and 'ROUTEMASTER' were removed from this time onwards.

The logos were originally stick-on labels followed by tampo printing in the mid-eighties. The seats were normally white or cream but other colours are used for the 'Specials' (eg. Red in the 'BRITISH DIE-CAST MODEL TOYS CATALOGUE' Special). The model has silver painted cast-in headlights, spring suspension, windows, a metal platform handrail but apart from the very early issues does not have a driver or clippie.

The wheels are of the WhizzWheel type. The early issues were of a close fitting type e.g. 'BTA', 'SWAN & EDGAR', 'DISNEYLAND'. However by the time the model was issued they had become protruding. The wheel hubs are either chrome (earlier models) or painted with plastic tyres.

Ref.	Year(s)	Model name	Colours, fleetname, features, etc.	Market Price Range

Routemaster Buses, 1964-1975, (1st casting)

Ref.	Year(s)	Model name	Colours, fleetname, features, etc.	Market Price Range
468	1964-66	'NATURALLY CORGI'	Red, London Transport, *CORGI CLASSICS*	£60-70
468	1964	'NATURALLY CORGI'	Green/Cream/Brown, (Australian) 'NEW SOUTH WALES', *CORGI CLASSICS*	£500-750
468	1966	'RED ROSE TEA'	Red body, driver and clippie, 1st type box, Australian promotional	£150-200
468	1967	'OUTSPAN ORANGES'	Green/Cream/Brown body, Australian issue	£150-200
468	1967-75	'OUTSPAN ORANGES'	Red, London Transport, 10, (diecast or WhizzWheels)	£40-50
468	1968	'GAMAGES'	Red, London Transport, '10'	£150-175
468	1969	'CHURCH'S SHOES'	Red, London Transport, '10', Union Jacks	£110-130
468	1970	'MADAME TUSSAUDS'	Red, London Transport, '10'	£90-110
468	1975	'THE DESIGN CENTRE'	Red, London Transport, '10'	£50-60
468	?	'cokerchu', '2d'	Red, London Transport, Promotional	£110-130

Routemaster Buses, 1975 onwards, (2nd casting)

Ref.	Year(s)	Model name	Colours, fleetname, features, etc.	Market Price Range
C467	1977	'SELFRIDGES'	Red, London Transport, '12'	£15-20
C469	1975-76	'BTA WELCOME TO BRITAIN'	Red, London Transport, '11', driver, clippie	£15-20
C469	1976	'THE DESIGN CENTRE'	Red, London Transport, '11', driver, clippie, *Visit The Design Centre* in black or red	£110-130
C469	1977	'CADBURYS'	Orange, *Cadburys Double Decker*, on-pack offer, special box	£12-18
C469	1979	'SELFRIDGES'	Red, London Transport, '12'	£15-20
C469	1979	'LEEDS PERMANENT BUILDING SOCIETY'	Leeds '22'	£15-20
C469	1979	'SWAN & EDGAR'	Red, London Transport, '11'	£25-35
C469	1979	'HAMLEYS'	Red, London Transport, '11'	£15-20
C469	1980	'HAMLEYS'	Five clowns advert., '6'	£10-15
C469	1978-80	'BTA'	Red, London Transport, ('7', '11' or '12')	£10-15
C469	1982	'BLACKPOOL'	Cream/Green, 'Blackpool Illuminations', '21'	£30-40
C469	1983	'GAMLEYS'	Red, *Toyshop Of The South*	£10-15
C469	1983	'EAGLE STAR'	White/Black, '1 Threadneedle Street'	£10-15
C469	1983	'REDGATES'	Cream/Brown (Red seats) '25'	£30-40
C469	1983	'L. T. GOLDEN JUBILEE'	Red/White/Silver, 21, *1933-1983 *, (1,000)	£30-40
C469	1983	'BLACKPOOL PLEASURE BEACH'	Cream/Green, Blackpool Transport, '23', *Britain's No.1 Tourist Attraction*	£35-45
C469	1983	Open-top version:	As previous model but with open top	£50-55
C469	1983	'NORBROOK MOTORS'	Dark Blue (White seats) route '57'	£12-18
C469	1983	colour change:	As previous model but Red version	£12-18
C469	1983	'DION DION'	Dark Blue, *Saves You More* in Orange	£10-15
C469		South African issue:	has incorrect label *Saves You Money*	£15-20
C469	1983	'THORNTONS'	Brown/Cream, route '14'	£10-15
C469	1983	'MANCHESTER LIONS'	Cream, route '105BN Manchester'	£15-20
C469	1984	'NEW CORGI COMPANY'	Red, '29th March 1984', *South Wales - De Cymru*, (2,000)	£15-20
C469	?	'COBHAM BUS MUSEUM'	no details	£25-35
C470	1977	'DISNEYLAND'	Yellow Open Top, Disney characters.	£10-15
C471	1977	'SEE MORE LONDON'	Silver, '25', *The Queens Silver Jubilee London Celebrations 1977*	£10-15
C471	1977	'WOOLWORTHS'	Silver, '25', *Woolworths Welcome The World* & *Queens Silver Jubilee 1977*	£20-30
C638	1989	'Great Book of CORGI'	Yellow/Blue, '1956-1983'. Originally only available with book	£25-35

Other 2nd casting Routemaster Buses, (1975 onwards)

Market Price Range £5-8

C460 'BOLTON EVENING NEWS' ....
C463 'BRITISH MEAT' ....
C464 'BRITISH MOTOR SHOW' ....
C469 'DIECAST and TINPLATE' ....
C469 'JOLLY GIANT' ....
C469 'GLOUCESTER TOY SALE' ....
C469 'ARMY AND NAVY' ....
C469 'MANCHESTER UNITED' ....
C469 'LLANDINDROD' ....
C469 'TROWBRIDGE TOYS' ....
C469 'MANCHESTER EVE. NEWS' ....
C469 'ROUND LONDON' ....
C469 'BTA WELCOME' ....
C469 'BRITISH TOY' ....
C469 'JOHN WEBB' ....
C469 'TWINNINGS' ....
C469 'STRETTON SPRING WATER' ....
C469 'READING EXPRESS' ....
C469 'LIVERPOOL GARDEN FESTIVAL' ....
C469 'HAMLEYS' ....
C469 'GEMINI DIECAST' ....
C469 'BTA' ....
C469 'MIDLAND BUS MUSEUM' ....
C469 'GREAT WESTERN RAILWAY' ....
C469 'ESSEX ORGAN STUDIOS' ....
C469 'FAREWELL TO ROE' ....
C469 'HAMLEYS' ....
C469 'HAMLEYS' (Open Top) ....
C469 'UNDERWOODS' ....
C469 'JUST A SECOND' ....

C469 'COWES STAMP and MODEL SHOP' ......
C469 'OLD SMUGGLER' ....
C469 'BTA' ....
C469 'LONDON STANDARD' ....
C469 'ANDREX' ....
C469 'TAYLOR & McKINNA' ....
C469 'TDK CASSETTES' ....
C469 'WORLD AIRWAYS' ....
C469 'LINCOLN CITY' ....
C473 'GAMLEYS' ....
C475 'TAKE OFF FROM BRISTOL' ....
C476 'BRITISH TELECOM' ....
C476 'CULTURE BUS' ....
C476 'WHITE LABEL WHISKY' ....
C477 'THE BUZBY BUS' ....
C478 'SUNDECKER' ....
C479 'LONDON CRUSADER' ....
C480 'WHITE LABEL WHISKY' ....
C481 'BEA' ....
C482 'LEEDS BUILDING SOCIETY' ....
C483 'HMV SHOP' ....
C485 'I. O. W. COUNTY PRESS' ....
C485 'ML ELECTRICS' ....
C486 'THE CULTURE BUS' ....
C488 'NEW CORGI COMPANY' ....
C488 'BEATTIES' ....
C492 'GLOBAL SALES' ....
C521 'HAIG WHISKY' ....
C523 'BRITISH DIE-CAST
          MODEL TOYS CATALOGUE' ....

C524 'STEVENSONS' ....
C527 'TIMBERCRAFT CABINETS' ....
C529 '1985 CALENDAR BUS' ....
C530 'YORKSHIRE POST' ....
C558 'RADIO VICTORY' ....
C566 'GELCO EXPRESS' ....
C567 'LINCOLN CITY' ....
C567 'SEE MORE LONDON' ....
C570 'BUS COLLECTORS Soc.' ....
C571 'The TIMES' ....
C572 'The TIMES' ....
C574 'BLACKPOOL CENTENARY' ....
C580 'GUIDE DOGS' ....
C583 'MANCHESTER EVE. NEWS' ....
C589 'AUTOSPARES' ....
C590 'MEDIC ALERT' ....
C591 'MEDIC ALERT' ....
C591 'ROLAND FRIDAY' ....
C596 'HARRODS' ....
C625 'CITYRAMA' ....
C627 'MODEL MOTORING' ....
C628 'POLCO PLUS' ....
C633 'HOSPITAL RADIO' ....
C638 'WEETABIX' ....
32401 ....
32402 ....
32403 ....
32705 ....
91765 'CROSVILLE' ....
91766 ....

Routemasters difficult to catalogue

Shortly before and after Mettoy ceased trading during the period 1982-84 the following models were all given a '469' number and were issued in rapid succession in many different colour variations

The models were normally issued as a closed-top version but some will also be found as open-tops as well. These (open-tops) were issued in either an orange or yellow livery with often a 'BOURNEMOUTH' fleetname. The Route numbers seen were usually '14' or '24'. Corgi have referred to this period as the 'oddball patch'.

The models are: 'OLD HOLBORN', 'OXO', 'AERO', 'TDK', 'LION BAR', 'BARRATT', 'WORLD AIRWAYS', 'PENTEL', 'BUY BEFORE YOU FLY - DUTY FREE'. **The colours seen:** Brown/Cream, Blue/Cream, Green/Yellow, Blue, Green, Black, Cream, White.

Fleetnames were not used on the majority of these issues with the following exceptions:
'TAYSIDE' ('Barratt', 'Oxo', 'Aero')
'TRANSCLYDE' ('World Airways', 'Buy Before You Fly')
'SOUTH YORKS' ('TDK', 'World Airways')
'LONDON TRANSPORT' ('Lion Bar', 'Oxo', 'Aero').

Model No 470 was issued bearing the 'LONDON COUNTRY' fleetname in respect of 'Barratt', 'Pentel', 'Buy Before You Fly', 'TDK', and no doubt others. It is known that at the time of Mettoy going into receivership batches of labels were sold off to the trade which no doubt accounts for many of the different variations to be found. Therefore with this background it is not possible to provide meaningful price and rarity guidance.

Customer-Exclusive models

Market Price Range NGPP

These models are listed for the sake of completeness but there is little real opportunity of collectors obtaining them as very few were issued (usually 50 or less).

C468 'RED ROSE COFFEE' ....
C469 'METTOY SALES CONFERENCE' ....
C469 'MGMW DINNER' ....
C469 'QUALITOYS VISIT' ....
C469 'VEDES VISIT TO SWANSEA' ....

C469 'MARKS & SPENCER
          VISIT SWANSEA' ....
C469 'HAROLD LYCHES VISIT' ....
C469 'METTOY WELCOMES SWISS
          BUYERS to SWANSEA' (Sold for
          £450 by Vectis, 10/96) ....
C469 'FINNISH VISIT TO SWANSEA' ....
C469 'MGMW DINNER' ....
C469 'OCTOPUSSY' ....
C469 'MARRIOT HOTELS' ....

C469 'CHARLIE'S ANGELS' ....
C469 'CORGI COLLECTORS Visit' ....
C469 'REDDITCH' ....
C469 'SKYRIDER BUS
          COLLECTORS SOCIETY' ....
C469 'WHATMAN PAPER' ....
C469 'COLT 45 CONFERENCE' ....
C469 'SKYRIDER' ....
C461 'MANNHEIM VISIT 1986' ....

Electronic issues

1004   1981   'CORGITRONICS' ....'FIRST in ELECTRONIC DIE-CAST', Red, London Transport, '11' **£15-20**
Other issues will be found combining 'BTA', 'HAMLEYS', 'OXO', etc with the 'CORGITRONICS' logo. See that section for details.

Major Models – Coaches

1120   1961-62   'MIDLAND RED COACH' ......Mid-Red body, Black roof, Lemon interior, flat spun hubs **£55-65**
                                                      Dark Red body, Black roof, Lemon interior, spun hubs...**£65-75**

Miscellaneous

508   1968-69   Commer 2500 Minibus..............Orange/White/Green body, 'HOLIDAY CAMP' logo **£45-55**

A fine selection of Corgi Military Vehicles
Picture supplied by Christie's South Kensington and reproduced by their kind permission.

Corgi 1100 Carrimore Low-Loader, 1101 Carrimore Car Transporter, and Gift Set No.16 Ecurie Ecosse Racing Car Transporter
and Three Cars. Picture supplied by Christie's South Kensington and reproduced by their kind permission.

Accessories

Corgi Kits

601	1961-68	Batley 'LEOFRIC' Garage	£20-25
602	1961-66	'A.A.' and 'RAC' Telephone Boxes	£50-60
603	1961-66	Silverstone Pits	£30-40
604	1961-66	Silverstone Press Box	£50-60
605	1963-67	Silverstone Club House and Timekeepers Box	£60-70
606	1961-66	Lamp Standards (2)	£5-10
607	1963-67	Circus Elephant and Cage	£45-55
608	1963-66	'SHELL' Filling Station Building	£35-45
609	1963-66	'SHELL' Filling Station Forecourt Accessories	£25-35
610	1963-66	Metropolitan Police Box and Public Telephone Kiosk	£60-70
611	1963-66	Motel Chalet	£25-35

Spare wheels

(for 'Take-off Wheels' models)

Nos 1341 - 1361 were bubble-packed on card.

1341	1970	for 344 Ferrari Dino Sport. Shown in 1969 catalogue but model issued with WhizzWheels	£10-15
1342	1968	for 300 Chevrolet Corvette	£10-15
1351	1968	for 275 Rover 2000 TC	£10-15
1352	1968	for 276 Oldsmobile Toronado	£10-15
		for 338 Chevrolet Camaro	£10-15
		for 343 Pontiac Firebird. Shown in 1969 catalogue but not issued with 'Take-off Wheels'	£10-15
1353	1970	for 342 Lamborghini P400	£10-15
		for 302 Hillman Hunter Rally	£10-15
1354	1970	for 273 Rolls Royce Silver Shadow	£10-15
1361	1968	for 341 Mini Marcos GT 850. (This was the first 'Take-Off Wheels' model)	£10-15

Spare tyre packs

1449	1970-71	New Standard 15 mm	£10-15
1450	1958-70	Standard 15 mm	£10-15
1451	1961-70	Utility Vehicles 17 mm	£10-15
1452	1961-70	Major Models 19 mm	£10-15
1453	1965-70	Mini Cars 13 mm	£10-15
1454	1967-70	Tractor wheels (Rear) 33 mm	£10-15
1455	1967-70	Tractor wheels (Front) 19 mm	£10-15
1456	1967-70	Racing wheels (Rear) 16 mm	£10-15
1457	1967-70	Racing wheels (Front) 14 mm	£10-15
1458	1967-70	Commercial (Large) 24 mm	£10-15
1459	1967-70	Commercial (Medium) 19 mm	£10-15

Self-adhesive accessories

1460	1959	'A' Pack (66 items) including Tax Discs, Number Plates, 'GB' and 'Running-In' labels, etc	£10-15
1461	1959	'B' Pack (36 items) including White-wall tyre trim, 'Styla Sportsdiscs', Number Plates, etc	£10-15
1462	1959	'C' Pack (69 items) including Number Plates, Commercial & Road Fund Licences (A, B and C), 20mph and 30mph Speed Limit and Trailer Plates, etc	£10-15
1463	1959	'D' Pack (100 items) including Number Plates, Corps Diplomatique and 'L' Plates, Touring Pennants, etc	£10-15
1464	1961	'E' Pack (86 items) including Assorted Badges, Take-Off Wheels, Trade and Licence Plates, etc	£10-15

Corgi 'Cargoes'

Bubble-packed on card.

1485	1960	Lorry Load - Planks	£10-15
1486	1960	Lorry Load - Bricks	£10-15
1487	1960	Lorry Load - Milk Churns	£10-15
1488	1960	Lorry Load - Cement	£10-15
1490	1960	Skip and 3 Churns	£10-15

Figures

1501	1963-69	Racing Drivers and Pit Mechanics (6)	£10-15
1502	1963-69	Silverstone Spectators (6)	£10-15
1503	1963-69	Race Track Officials (6)	£10-15
1504	1963-69	Press Officials (6)	£10-15
1505	1963-69	Garage Attendants (6)	£10-15

Miscellaneous

1401	1958-60	Service Ramp (operable)	£15-20
1445	1962	Spare Red bulb for 437 Ambulance	£2-3
1441	1963	Spare Blue bulb for 464 Police Van	£2-3
1443	1967	Red flashing bulb for 437 Ambulance	£2-3
1444	1967	Blue flashing bulb for 464 Police Van	£2-3
1445	1967	Spare bulb for 'TV' in 262 Lincoln	£2-3
1446	1970	Spare tyres for 1150 Snowplough	£2-3
1480	1959	Spare nose cone for Corporal Missile	£2-3
1497	1967	James Bond Spares (2 Bandits and lapel badge for 261)	£15-25
1498	1967	James Bond Spares (Pack of missiles for 336 Toyota)	£10-15
1499	1967	Green Hornet Spares (Pack of missiles and scanners for 268)	£10-15
	1960s	Corgi Club Badge. Gold Corgi dog on Red background	£20-25

'Husky' models and 'Corgi Juniors' 1965 - 1969

'Husky' models were introduced by Mettoy Playcraft in 1965 to compete with the Matchbox 1-75 range. These small-scale models have plenty of detail and action-features and the range includes cars, commercials, military and Film/TV specials.

The models have either a plastic or die-cast chassis together with various types of regular wheels and WhizzWheels. Models could only be obtained from 'Woolworths' stores and were only sold in blister packs. Production under the 'Husky' trade name ceased in 1969 and the range was reissued in 1970 as 'Corgi Juniors'. To facilitate this change, 'HUSKY' was removed from the baseplates which were then re-engraved 'CORGI JUNIORS'.

The models were mostly fitted with 'WhizzWheels' to enable them to be used on the 'Rocket Track' and to compete against the new Matchbox 'Superfast' range. Corgi Juniors were blister packed on blue/white card for the 'regular' issues and red/white card for the 'specials'. Each pack incorporated a 'Collectors Card' picture of the real vehicle and these could be cut out and pasted into a special collectors album.

Whilst 'Husky' and 'Corgi Juniors' in mint condition blister packs are no longer cheap, plenty of low priced unboxed models are available hence this range offers the younger collector plenty of scope.

Ref.	Year(s)	Model name	Colours, features, dimensions	Market Price Range

Husky models issued 1965-1969

Ref.	Year(s)	Model name	Colours, features, dimensions	Market Price Range
1-a1	1965-66	**Jaguar Mk.10** (small casting)	Metallic Blue, Yellow interior, Grey plastic wheels	£20-25
1-a2	1966	**Jaguar Mk.10** (small casting)	Red, Yellow interior, Grey plastic wheels	£40-45
1-b1	1967	**Jaguar Mk.10**	Light Metallic Blue, Yellow interior, Grey plastic wheels	£20-25
1-b2	1967	**Jaguar Mk.10**	Blue, Yellow interior, Grey plastic wheels	£25-30
1-b3	1968	**Jaguar Mk.10**	Light Metallic Blue, Yellow interior, tyres	£25-30
1-b4	1968	**Jaguar Mk.10**	Cream, Yellow interior, tyres	£45-55
1-b5	1969	**Jaguar Mk.10**	Dark Blue, Yellow interior, tyres	£25-30
1-b6	1969	**Jaguar Mk.10**	Dark Maroon, Yellow interior, tyres	£30-35
2-a1	1965-66	**Citroën Safari with Boat** (small casting)	Pale Yellow, Tan boat, Grey plastic wheels	£20-25
2-b1	1967	**Citroën Safari with Boat**	Metallic Green, Brown boat, Yellow interior, Grey plastic wheels	£45-50
2-b2	1967	**Citroën Safari with Boat**	Metallic Gold, Blue boat, Yellow interior, Grey plastic wheels	£40-45
2-b3	1968-69	**Citroën Safari with Boat**	Metallic Gold, Blue boat, Yellow interior, tyres	£20-25
3-a1	1965-67	**Mercedes 220**	Pale Blue, Yellow interior, Grey plastic wheels	£15-20
3-bt	1967-68	**Volkswagen Police Car**	White/Black doors, smooth hubs with tyres	£25-30
3-b2	1969	**Volkswagen Police Car**	White/Black doors, detailed hubs with tyres	£25-30
4-a1	1965-66	**Jaguar Fire Chief** (small casting)	Red, chrome siren, 'Fire' labels on doors, Yellow interior, Grey plastic wheels	£25-30
4-bl	1967	**Jaguar Fire Chief**	Red, chrome siren, 'Fire' labels on doors, Yellow interior, Grey plastic wheels	£25-30
4-b2	1968-69	**Jaguar Fire Chief**	Red, chrome siren, 'Fire' labels on doors, Yellow interior, tyres	£30-35
5-a1	1965	**Lancia Flaminia**	Red, Yellow interior, Grey plastic wheels	£40-45
5-a2	1965-66	**Lancia Flaminia**	Blue, Yellow interior, Grey plastic wheels	£15-20
5-b1	1967-69	**Willys Jeep**	Metallic Green, Grey windshield, tyres	£15-20
5-b2	1967-69	**Willys Jeep**	Metallic Green, Yellow windshield, tyres	£25-30
6-a1	1965-67	**Citroën Safari Ambulance**	White, Red Cross, Blue warning lights, Grey plastic wheels	£20-25
6-b1	1968-69	**Ferrari Berlinetta**	Red, Red interior, chrome engine, tyres	£25-30
6-b2	1968-69	**Ferrari Berlinetta**	Maroon, Red interior, chrome engine, tyres	£25-30
7-a1	1965-66	**Buick Electra**	Orange-Red, Yellow interior, Grey plastic wheels	£15-20
7-b1	1967	**Duple Vista 25 Coach**	Green/White, tinted windows, Yellow interior, Grey plastic wheels	£20-25
7-b2	1968-69	**Duple Vista 25 Coach**	Green/White, tinted windows, Yellow interior, tyres	£20-25
8-a1	1965-66	**Ford Thunderbird**	Pink, Black open body, Yellow interior, Grey plastic wheels	£20-25
8-b1	1967	**Ford Thunderbird Hardtop**	Yellow, Blue detachabte hard top, Yellow interior, Grey plastic wheels	£30-35
8-c1	1967-69	**Tipping Farm Trailer**	Yellow, Red back, tyres	£10-15
9-a1	1965-67	**Buick Police Patrol**	Dark Blue, Yellow interior, Red warning light, 'Police' on doors, Grey plastic wheels	£20-25
9-b1	1968-69	**Cadillac Eldorado**	Light Blue, Red interior, tyres	£20-25
10-a1	1965-67	**Guy Warrior Coal Truck**	Red, tinted windows, Grey plastic wheels	£15-20
10-a2	1968-69	**Guy Warrior Coal Truck**	Red, tinted windows, tyres	£20-25
11-a1	1965-67	**Forward Control Land Rover**	Green, Brown removable tilt, rear corner windows, Grey plastic wheels	£15-20
11-a2	1968-69	**Forward Control Land Rover**	Metallic Green, Brown removable tilt, no rear corner windows, Grey plastic wheels	£15-20
12-a1	1965-66	**Volkswagen Tower Wagon**	Yellow, Red tower, Grey plastic wheels	£20-25
12-b1	1967	**Ford Tower Wagon**	Yellow, Red tower, Grey plastic wheels	£30-35
12-b2	1967	**Ford Tower Wagon**	White, Red tower, Grey plastic wheels	£15-20
12-b3	1968-69	**Ford Tower Wagon**	White, Red tower, tyres	£20-25
13-a1	1965-66	**Guy Warrior Sand Truck**	Yellow, tinted windows, Grey plastic wheels	£15-20
13-a2	1967-68	**Guy Warrior Sand Truck**	Blue, tinted windows, Grey plastic wheels	£15-20
13-a3	1969	**Guy Warrior Sand Truck**	Blue, tinted windows, tyres	£20-25
14-a1	1965-66	**Guy Warrior Tanker** (round tank)	Yellow, 'Shell' decals, Grey plastic wheels	£20-25
14-b1	1967	**Guy Warrior Tanker** (square tank)	Yellow, 'Shell' decaIs, Grey plastic wheels	£20-25
14-b2	1967	**Guy Warrior Tanker** (square tank)	White, 'Esso' decals, Grey plastic wheels	£20-25
14-b3	1968-69	**Guy Warrior Tanker** (square tank)	White, 'Esso' decaIs, tyres	£20-25
15-a1	1965-66	**Volkswagen Pick Up**	Turquoise, Brown removable canopy, Grey plastic wheels	£15-20
15-b1	1967-68	**Studebaker Wagonaire TV Car**	Yellow, tinted windows, Grey plastic wheels	£20-25
15-b2	1968	**Studebaker Wagonaire TV Car**	Metallic Blue, Blue tinted windows, Grey plastic wheels	£25-30
15-b3	1969	**Studebaker Wagonaire TV Car**	Metallic Blue, Blue tinted windows, tyres	£25-30
16-a1	1965-66	**Dump Truck/Dozer**	Yellow, Red back, chrome dozer, Grey plastic wheels	£15-20
16-a2	1966	**Dump Truck/Dozer**	Red, Grey back, chrome dozer, Grey plastic wheels	£20-25

17-a1	1965-66	**Guy Warrior Milk Tanker**	White, 'Milk' decals, round tank, Grey plastic wheels	£20-25
17-b1	1967	**Guy Warrior Milk Tanker**	White, 'Milk' decals, square tank, Grey plastic wheels	£20-25
17-b2	1968	**Guy Warrior Milk Tanker**	Cream, 'Milk' decals, round tank, Grey plastic wheels	£20-25
17-b3	1969	**Guy Warrior Milk Tanker**	Cream, 'Milk' decals, round tank, tyres	£20-25
18-a1	1965-66	**Plated Jaguar** (small casting)	Chrome, Yellow interior, Grey plastic wheels	£20-25
18-bi	1967-68	**Plated Jaguar**	Chrome, Yellow interior, Grey plastic wheels	£20-25
18-b2	1969	**Plated Jaguar**	Chrome, Yellow interior, tyres	£30-35
19-a1	1966	**Commer Walk Thro' Van**	Red, sliding Red door, Grey plastic wheels	£40-45
19-a2	1966-67	**Commer Walk Thro' Van**	Green, sliding Red door, Grey plastic wheels	£25-30
19-b1	1968-69	**Speedboat on Trailer**	Gold trailer, Red, White and Blue boat, tyres	£15-20
20-a1	1965-66	**Ford Thames Van**	Red, Yellow interior, Yellow ladder and aerial, Grey plastic wheels	£20-25
20-b1	1967	**Volkswagen 1300 with Luggage**	Tan, Yellow interior, tyres	£30-35
20-b2	1967-69	**Volkswagen 1300 with Luggage**	Blue, Yellow interior, tyres	£20-25
21-a1	1966-67	**Military Land Rover**	Military Green, 'star' decal on roof, Grey plastic windows	£15-20
21-b1	1968-69	**Jaguar 'E'-type 2+2**	Maroon, Yellow interior, tyres	£20-25
22-a1	1965-66	**Citroën Safari Military Ambulance**	Khaki, Red Cross on roof, Blue roof lights, Grey plastic wheels	NGPP
22-b1	1967-68	**Aston-Martin DB6**	Metallic Gold, Yellow interior, Grey plastic wheels	£25-30
22-b2	1968-69	**Aston-Martin DB6**	Purple, Yellow interior, tyres	£30-35
23-a1	1966-67	**Guy Army Tanker**	Khaki, US Army decals on tank, Grey plastic wheels	£15-20
23-b1	1968	**Loadmaster Shovel**	Orange, chrome shovel, Black plastic wheels	£25-30
23-b2	1968-69	**Loadmaster Shovel**	Yellow, chrome shovel, Black plastic wheels	£15-20
24-a1	1966-67	**Ford Zephyr Estate**	Blue, Yellow interior, Grey plastic wheels	£20-25
24-a2	1968-69	**Ford Zephyr Estate**	Red, Yellow interior, Grey plastic wheels	£25-30
25-a1	1966-67	**SD Refuse Van**	Light Blue, chrome back, Grey plastic wheels	£15-20
25-a2	1968	**SD Refuse Van**	Red, chrome back, Grey plastic wheels	£30-35
25-a3	1968-69	**SD Refuse Van**	Red, chrome back, tyres	£40-45
26-a1	1966-67	**Sunbeam Alpine**	Metallic Bronze, Blue removable hard top, Yellow interior, Grey plastic wheels	£25-30
26-a2	1967	**Sunbeam Alpine**	Red, Blue removable hard top, Yellow interior, Grey plastic wheels	£40-45
26-a3	1968-69	**Sunbeam Alpine**	Red, Blue removable hard top, Yellow interior, tyres	£50-55
27-a1	1966-67	**Bedford Skip Lorry**	Maroon, Grey plastic wheels	£20-25
27-a2	1967	**Bedford Skip Lorry**	Dark Green, Grey plastic wheels	£50-60
27-a3	1967	**Bedford Skip Lorry**	Orange, Grey plastic wheels	£20-25
27-a4	1968-69	**Bedford Skip Lorry**	Orange, tyres	£20-25
28-a1	1966-67	**Ford Breakdown Truck**	Blue, chrome hoist, metal jib, Grey plastic wheels	£15-20
28-a2	1968-69	**Ford Breakdown Truck**	Blue, chrome hoist, Gold jib, tyres	£20-25
29-a1	1966-67	**ERF Cement Mixer**	Yellow, Red barrel, metal chute, Grey plastic wheels	£15-20
29-a2	1968-69	**ERF Cement Mixer**	Yellow, Red barrel, metal chute, tyres	£20-25
30-a1	1966-67	**Studebaker Wagonaire Ambulance**	White, Red Cross decals, stretcher, Grey plastic Wheels	£25-30
30-a2	1968-69	**Studebaker Wagonaire Ambulance**	White, Red Cross decals, stretcher, tyres	£25-30
30-a3	1969	**Studebaker Wagonaire**	Pale Green, Green tinted windows, tyres	£35-40
31-a1	1966-67	**Oldsmobile Starfire Coupé**	Olive Green, Yellow interior, Grey plastic wheels	£15-20
31-a2	1968-69	**Oldsmobile Starfire Coupé**	Olive Green, Yellow interior, tyres	£20-25
32-a1	1966-67	**Volkswagen Luggage Elevator**	White, Yellow conveyor, Grey plastic wheels	£25-30
32-a2	1967	**Volkswagen Luggage Elevator**	White, Blue conveyor, Red belt, Grey plastic wheels	£30-35
32-a3	1968-69	**Volkswagen Luggage Elevator**	Red, Blue conveyor, Red belt, Grey plastic wheels	£35-40
33-a1	1967	**Farm Trailer and Calves**	Olive Green, tyres	£10-15
33-a2	1968-69	**Farm Trailer and Calves**	Turquoise, tyres	£10-15
34-a1	1967	**Tractor**	Red, Red exhaust, tyres	£20-25
34-a2	1968-69	**Tractor**	Red, Black exhaust, tyres	£20-25
35-a1	1967	**Ford Camper**	Yellow, chrome back, Grey plastic wheels	£20-25
35-a2	1967	**Ford Camper**	Metallic Blue, chrome back, Grey plastic wheels	£25-30
35-a3	1968-69	**Ford Camper**	Metallic Blue, chrome back, tyres	£25-30
36-a1	1967	**Simon Snorkel Fire Engine**	Red, chrome snorkel, Grey plastic wheels	£20-25
36-a2	1968-69	**Simon Snorkel Fire Engine**	Red, chrome snorkel, tyres	£20-25
37-a1	1968-69	**NSU RO80**	Metallic Blue, tyres	£25-30
38-a1	1968	**Rices Beaufort Single Horse Box**	Turquoise, tyres	£10-15
38-a2	1969	**Rices Beaufort Single Horse Box**	Metallic Green, tyres	£20-25
39-a1	1969	**Jaguar XJ6 4.2**	Yellow, Red interior, tyres	£45-55
40-a1	1969	**Ford Transit Caravan**	Red, Cream interior, White rear door, tyres	£25-35
40-a2	1969	**Ford Transit Caravan**	Lime green, Cream interior, White rear door, tyres	£25-35
41-a1	?	**Porsche Carrera 6**	Shown in catalogue but not issued	NPP

Novelty, Film and TV-related models

See also following section and 'Corgi Rockets'.

1001-a1	1967	**James Bond Aston Martin DB6**	Silver, Red interior, 2 ejector figures, Grey plastic wheels	£180-200
1001-a2	1968-69	**James Bond Aston Martin DB6**	Silver, Red interior, 2 ejector figures, tyres	£180-200
1002-a1	1967-69	**Batmobile**	Black, Batman and Robin figures, tow hook, Grey plastic wheels	£150-160
1003-a1	1967-69	**Batboat**	Black boat, Red fin, Batman and Robin figures, Grey plastic wheels	£150-160
1004-a1	1968-69	**Monkeemobile**	Red, White roof, 4 figures, 'Monkees' on doors, tyres	£160-180
1005-a1	1968-69	**Man From UNCLE Car**	Blue, 3 Missiles on sprue, 2 figures, tyres	£160-175
1006-a1	1969	**Chitty Chitty Bang Bang**	Chrome, Dark Grey base, Red wings, Yellow fins, 4 figures, tyres	£120-140

Ref.	Year(s)	Model name	Colours, features, dimensions	Market Price Range

Note: The models in this list were each accompanied by a colourful Picture Card, the lack of which could adversely affect the model's potential price.

Ref.	Year(s)	Model name	Colours, features, dimensions	Market Price Range
1-a1	1970	Reliant TW9 Pick Up	Beige, Green tinted windows, removabte plastic front bumper, Black WhizzWheels	£20-25
1-a2	1970-72	Reliant TW9 Pick Up	Orange, Green tinted windows, removable plastic front bumper, Black WhizzWheels	£15-20
2-a1	1970	Citroën Safari with Boat	Blue, White boat, Yellow interior, tyres	£25-30
2-a2	1970	Citroën Safari with Boat	Blue, White boat, Yellow interior, Black WhizzWheels	£20-25
2-a3	1971-2	Citroën Safari with Boat	Yellow, White boat, Yellow interior, Black WhizzWheels	£15-20
2-a4	1971-2	Citroën Safari with Boat	Purple, White boat, Yellow interior, Black WhizzWheels	£15-20
3-a1	1970	Volkswagen 1300 Police Car	White, Black 'Police' sign on doors, Red interior, Blue light, tyres	£30-35
3-a2	1970	Volkswagen 1300 Police Car	White, Black 'Police' sign on doors, Red interior, Blue light, Black WhizzWheels	£20-25
3-a3	1971-72	Volkswagen 1300 Police Car	White, Black 'Police' sign on doors, Red interior, Blue light, chrome WhizzWheels	£15-20
3-a4	1971-72	Volkswagen 1300 Police Car	White, Black 'Police' sign on doors, Yellow interior, Blue tinted windows, chrome WhizzWheels	£15-20
4-a1	1970-72	Zeteor 5511 Tractor	Orange, Red base, Black chimney, Black plastic wheels	£10-15
5-a1	1970	Willys Jeep	Tan, Brown interior, Grey windshield, tyres	£15-20
5-a2	1970	Willys Jeep	Tan, Brown interior, Grey windshield, Black WhizzWheels	£10-15
5-a3	1971	Willys Jeep	Tan, Brown interior, Grey windshield, chrome WhizzWheels	£10-15
5-a4	1970	Willys Jeep	Orange, Brown interior, Grey windshield, Black WhizzWheels	£10-15
5-a5	1971	Willys Jeep	Orange, Brown interior, Grey windshield, chrome Whizzwheels	£10-15
5-a6	1971-72	Willys Jeep	Red, Yellow interior, Grey windshield, chrome WhizzWheels	£10-15
6-a1	1970	De Tomaso Mangusta	Lime Green, Green tinted windows, Black WhizzWheels	£10-15
6-a2	1970	De Tomaso Mangusta	Metallic Purple, Green tinted windows, Black WhizzWheels	£10-15
6-a3	1971-2	De Tomaso Mangusta	Metallic Purple, Green tinted windows, chrome WhizzWheels	£10-15
7-a1	1970	Duple Vista 25 Coach	Red, White, Yellow interior, Green tinted windows, tyres	£20-25
7-a2	1970	Duple Vista 25 Coach	Yellow, White, Yellow interior, Green tinted windows, Black WhizzWheels	£12-15
7-a3	1971-2	Duple Vista 25 Coach	Purple, White, Yellow interior, Green tinted windows, chrome WhizzWheels	£12-15
7-a4	1971-2	Duple Vista 25 Coach	Orange, White, Yellow interior, Green tinted windows, chrome WhizzWheels	£12-15
8-a1	1970	Tipping Farm Trailer	Blue, Orange back, tyres	£10-15
9-a1	1970	Cadillac Eldorado	Metallic Green, Red interior, Red tow hook, tyres	£25-30
9-a2	1970	Cadillac Eldorado	Metallic Green, Red interior, Red tow hook, Black WhizzWheels	£15-20
9-a3	1970	Cadillac Eldorado	White, Black bonnet, Red interior, Red tow hook, Black WhizzWheels	£15-20
9-a4	1971	Cadillac Eldorado	White, Black bonnet, Red interior, Red tow hook, chrome WhizzWheels	£15-20
9-b1	1971-72	Vigilant Range Rover	White, 'Police' decals on doors, Blue tinted windows, chrome WhizzWheels	£12-15
10-a1	1970	Guy Warrior Coal Truck	Orange, Green tinted windows, tyres	£15-20
10-b1	1971-2	Ford GT70	Orange, Green tinted windows, Silver engine cover, chrome WhizzWheels	£10-12
11-af	1970	Austin Healey Sprite Le Mans	Red, Blue interior, Amber windows, Grey base, RN '50', sticker pack, Black WhizzWheels	£30-35
11-a2	1971	Austin Healey Sprite Le Mans	Red, Yellow interior, Amber windows, Grey base, RN '50', sticker pack, chrome WhizzWheels	£30-35
11-a3	1971-2	Austin Healey Sprite Le Mans	Red, Yellow interior, Amber windows, Black base, RN '50', sticker pack, chrome Whizzwheels	£30-35
12-a1	1970	Reliant-Ogle Scimitar GTE	White, Amber tinted windows, Yellow interior, Black WhizzWheels	£20-25
12-a2	1970	Reliant-Ogle Scimitar GTE	Metallic Blue, Amber tinted windows, Yellow interior, chrome WhizzWheels	£20-25
12-a3	1971-2	Reliant-Ogle Scimitar GTE	Matt Blue, Amber tinted windows, Yellow interior, chrome WhizzWheels	£20-25
13-a1	1970	Guy Warrior Sand Truck	Blue, Green tinted windows, tyres	£15-20
13-a2	1971-72	Guy Warrior Sand Truck	Red, Green tinted windows, chrome WhizzWheels	£12-15
14-a1	1970	Guy Warrior Tanker (square tank)	White, Green tinted windows, 'Esso' decals, tyres	£15-20
14-a2	1971-2	Guy Warrior Tanker (square tank)	White, Green tinted windows, 'Esso' decals, Black plastic base, chrome WhizzWheels	£12-15
15-a1	1970	Studebaker Wagonaire TV Car	Metallic Turquoise, Blue tinted windows, tyres	£35-40
15-a2	1970	Studebaker Wagonaire TV Car	Yellow, Blue tinted windows, Black WhizzWheels	£25-30
15-a3	1970	Studebaker Wagonaire TV Car	Metallic Lime Green, Blue tinted windows, Black WhizzWheels	£25-30
15-a4	1971-2	Studebaker Wagonaire TV Car	Metallic Lime Green, Blue tinted windows, chrome WhizzWheels	£25-30
16-a	1970-2	Land Rover Pick Up	Metallic Green, Orange tinted windows, chrome WhizzWheels	£10-12
17-af	1970	Volkswagen 1300 Beetle	Metallic Blue, Yellow interior, 'flower' decals	£45-50
17-a2	1970-72	Volkswagen 1300 Beetle	Metallic Green, Yellow interior, 'flower' decals	£20-25
18-a1			nothing issued	
19-a1	1970	Speedboat on Trailer	Blue trailer, Red,White and Blue boat, tyres	£15-20
19-a2	1970	Speedboat on Trailer	Blue trailer, Red,White and Blue boat, Black WhizzWheels	£10-15
19-a3	1971-2	Speedboat on Trailer	Blue trailer, Red,White and Blue boat, chrome WhizzWheels	£10-15
20-a1	1967	Volkswagen 1300 with Luggage	Mustard Yellow, Yellow interior, tyres	£25-30
20-a2	1967-69	Volkswagen 1300 with Luggage	Red, Yellow interior, Black WhizzWheels	£20-25
21-a1	1971-72	BVRT Vita-Min Mini Cooper S	Metallic Purple, chrome interior, Blue tinted windows, chrome WhizzWheels	£25-30
22-a1	1970	Aston-Martin DB6	Purple, Yellow interior, tyres	£45-50
22-a2	1970	Aston-Martin DB6	Metallic Olive, Yellow interior, tyres	£45-50

22-b1	1971-72	**Formula 1 Grand Prix Racing Car**	Yellow, Union Jack on front, White driver, chrome WhizzWheels	£12-15
23-a1	1970-2	**Loadmaster Shovel**	Yellow, chrome shovel, Black plastic wheels	£10-12
24-a1	1971-2	**Aston-Martin DBS**	Green, Black bonnet, Cream interior, chrome WhizzWheels	£20-25
25-a1	1970-72	**SD Refuse Van**	Orange, chrome back, Green tinted windows, tyres	£15-20
26-a1	1971-72	**ERF Fire Engine Water Tender**	Red, Green tinted windows and roof lights, Yellow ladder, chrome WhizzWheels	£12-15
27-a1	1970	**Bedford Skip Lorry**	Orange, Silver skip, tyres	£20-25
28-a1	1970	**Ford Breakdown Truck**	Blue, chrome hoist, Gold jib, Green tinted windows, tyres	£20-25
28-a2	1970	**Ford Breakdown Truck**	Blue, chrome hoist, Gold jib, Green tinted windows, Black WhizzWheels	£15-20
28-a3	1970	**Ford Breakdown Truck**	Turquoise, chrome hoist, Gold jib, Green tinted windows, Black WhizzWheels	£15-20
29-a1	1971-72	**Simon Snorkel Fire Engine**	Red, Yellow snorkel, Green tinted windows, chrome WhizzWheels	£12-15
30-a1	1970	**Studebaker Wagonaire Ambulance**	White, Red Cross decals, Blue windows, removable stretcher, tyres	£25-30
30-a2	1970	**Studebaker Wagonaire Ambulance**	White, Red Cross decals, Blue windows, removable stretcher, Black WhizzWheels	£20-25
30-a3	1970	**Studebaker Wagonaire Ambulance**	White, Red Cross decals, Blue windows, non-removable stretcher, Black WhizzWheels	£15-20
30-a4	1971	**Studebaker Wagonaire Ambulance**	White, Red Cross decals, Blue windows, non-removable stretcher, small chrome WhizzWheels	£15-20
30-a5	1971-72	**Studebaker Wagonaire Ambulance**	White, Red Cross decals, Blue windows, non-removable stretcher, chrome WhizzWheels	£15-20
31-a1	1970-71	**Land Rover Breakdown**	Purple, 'Wrecker Truck' labels, Gold hook, Amber windows	£12-15
31-a2	1972	**Land Rover Breakdown**	Red, 'Wrecker Truck' labels, Gold hook, Amber windows	£12-15
32-a1	1970-71	**Lotus Europa**	Metallic Green, Yellow interior and engine cover, chrome WhizzWheels	£15-20
32-a2	1972	**Lotus Europa**	Green, Yellow interior and engine cover, chrome WhizzWheels	£15-20
33-a1	1970	**Farm Trailer and Calves**	Orange, tyres	£10-15
33-b1	1970-72	**Jaguar 'E'-type Series 2**	Yellow, Red interior, chrome WhizzWheels	£12-15
34-a1	1970-72	**B.M. Volvo 400 Tractor**	Red, Yellow plastic Wheels, tyres	£15-20
35-a1	1970	**Ford Camper**	Turquoise, chrome back, Green tinted windows, tyres	£25-30
35-a2	1970-2	**Ford Camper**	Turquoise, chrome back, Green tinted windows, Black WhizzWheels	£25-30
35-a3	1970-2	**Ford Camper**	Red, Cream back, Green tinted windows, Black WhizzWheels	£20-25
36-a1	1970	**Simon Snorkel Fire Engine**	Red, chrome Snorkel, tyres	£20-25
37-a1	1970	**NSU RO80**	Metallic Blue, Silver interior, Green tinted windows, tyres	£25-30
37-a2	1970	**NSU RO80**	Metallic Mauve, Silver interior, Green tinted windows, Black WhizzWheels	£15-20
37-a3	1970	**NSU RO80**	Purple, Black bonnet, Silver interior, Green tinted windows, Black WhizzWheels	£15-20
37-a4	1971-2	**NSU RO80**	Purple, Black bonnet, Silver interior, Green tinted windows, chrome WhizzWheels	£15-20
37-a5	1971-2	**NSU RO80**	Metallic Copper, Black bonnet, Silver interior, Amber tinted windows, chrome WhizzWheels	£15-20
38-a1	1970	**Rices Beaufort Single Horse Box**	Metallic Green, horse, tyres	£15-20
38-a2	1970	**Rices Beaufort Single Horse Box**	Red, White horse, tyres	£15-20
38-a3	1970	**Rices Beaufort Single Horse Box**	Red, White horse, Black WhizzWheels	£10-15
38-a4	1971-72	**Rices Beaufort Single Horse Box**	Metallic Copper, White horse, chrome WhizzWheels	£10-15
39-a1	1970	**Jaguar XJ6 4.2**	Yellow, Red interior, tyres	£30-35
39-a2	1970	**Jaguar XJ6 4.2**	Silver, Red interior, Black Whizzwheels	£20-25
39-a3	1971-72	**Jaguar XJ6 4.2**	Silver, Red interior, chrome Whizzwheels	£20-25
39-a4	1971-72	**Jaguar XJ6 4.2**	Metallic Red, Yellow interior, chrome WhizzWheels	£20-25
39-a5	1971-72	**Jaguar XJ6 4.2**	Red, Yellow interior, chrome WhizzWheels	NGPP
4d-a1	1970	**Ford Transit Caravan**	Yellow, Blue interior, Silver rear door, tyres	£25-30
40-a2	1970	**Ford Transit Caravan**	Yellow, Cream interior, Silver rear door, Black WhizzWheels	£20-25
40-a3	1970	**Ford Transit Caravan**	Blue, Cream interior, Silver rear door, Black WhizzWheels	£20-25
40-a4	1971-72	**Ford Transit Caravan**	Blue, Cream interior, Silver rear door, chrome WhizzWheels	£20-25
40-a5	1971-72	**Ford Transit Caravan**	Metallic Pale Blue, Cream interior, Silver rear door, chrome WhizzWheels	£15-20
40-a6	1972	**Ford Transit Caravan**	Metallic Pale Blue, Cream interior, Silver rear door, Black plastic base, chrome WhizzWheels	£15-20
41-a1	1970	**Porsche Carrera 6**	White, clear canopy, RN '19', tyres	£20-25
41-a2	1970	**Porsche Carrera 6**	White, Blue tinted canopy, RN '19', Black WhizzWheels	£15-20
41-a3	1971-72	**Porsche Carrera 6**	White, Blue tinted canopy, RN '19', chrome WhizzWheels	£15-20
42-a1	1970	**Euclid Dumper**	Yellow cab, Red back, Dark Grey base, Black wheels	£15-20
42-a2	1970	**Euclid Dumper**	Red cab, Yellow back, unpainted Base, chrome WhizzWheels	£10-15
42-a3	1971-72	**Euclid Dumper**	Yellow cab, Red back, Dark Grey base, Black WhizzWheels	£10-15
42-a4	1971-72	**Euclid Dumper**	Blue cab, Silver back, Dark Grey base, chrome WhizzWheels	£10-15
42-a5	1971-72	**Euclid Dumper**	Blue Cab, Yellow back, Dark Grey base, chrome WhizzWheels	£10-15
43-a1	1970	**Massey Ferguson Tractor Shovel**	Yellow, Red interior, Black plastic wheels	£12-15
43-a2	1971-72	**Massey Ferguson Tractor Shovel**	Yellow, Red shovel and interior, Black plastic wheels	£10-15
44-a1	1970-72	**Raygo Rascal Road Roller**	Blue, Orange front, Grey roller, Grey seat and engine, Black plastic wheels	£10-12
45-a1	1970	**Mercedes 280SL**	Metallic Silver, Red interior, tyres	£30-35
45-a2	1970	**Mercedes 280SL**	Metallic Blue, Red interior, Black Whizzwheels	£20-25
45-a3	1970	**Mercedes 280SL**	Yellow, Red interior, unpainted base, Black Whizzwheels	£15-20
45-a4	1970	**Mercedes 280SL**	Yellow, Red interior, White base, Black Whizzwheels	£15-20
45-a5	1970	**Mercedes 280SL**	Red, Cream interior, Black WhizzWheels	£25-30
45-a6	1971-72	**Mercedes 280SL**	Red, Cream interior, chrome WhizzWheels	£25-30
45-a7	1971-72	**Mercedes 280SL**	Blue, Cream interior, unpainted base, chrome WhizzWheels	£20-25

46-a1	1970	**Jensen Interceptor**	Maroon, Yellow interior, Green tinted windows, unpainted base, tyres	**£35-40**
46-a2	1970	**Jensen Interceptor**	Maroon, Yellow interior, Green tinted windows, unpainted base, Black WhizzWheels	**£25-30**
46-a3	1971	**Jensen Interceptor**	Orange, Yellow interior, Green tinted windows, unpainted base, chrome WhizzWheels	**£25-30**
46-a4	1972	**Jensen Interceptor**	Metallic Green, Yellow interior, Green tinted windows, unpainted base, chrome WhizzWheels	**£25-30**
47-a1	1971-72	**Scammell Concrete Mixer**	White cab, Blue base, Red mixer, Amber windows, chrome WhizzWheels	**£10-15**
48-a1	1971-72	**ERF Tipper Truck**	Red cab, Silver back, unpainted base, Amber windows, chrome WhizzWheels	**£10-15**
48-a1	1971-72	**ERF Tipper Truck**	Blue cab, Orange back, unpaintsd base, Amber windows, chrome Whizzwheels	**£10-15**
48-a1	1971-72	**ERF Tipper Truck**	Blue cab, Orange back, Dark Grey base, Amber windows, chrome WhizzWheels	**£10-15**
48-a1	1971-72	**ERF Tipper Truck**	Blue cab, Yellow back, Dark Grey base, Amber windows, chrome WhizzWheels	**£10-15**
49-a1	1971-72	**Pininfarina Modulo**	Yellow, Red stripe, Red interior, chrome WhizzWheels	**£10-12**
50-a1	1971-72	**Ferrari 512s**	Mettalic Red, Cream interior, unpainted base, chrome WhizzWheels	**£10-12**
51-a1	1971-72	**Porsche 917**	Gold, RN '23', chrome interior, Red base, chrome WhizzWheels	**£10-12**
52-a1	1971-72	**Adams Probe 16**	Metallic Pink,White interior, Green tinted windows, Black plastic base, chrome WhizzWheels	**£10-12**
54-a1	1971-72	**Ford Container Wagon**	Red, Yellow skip, Yellow plastic base, chrome WhizzWheels	**£10-12**
55-a1	1970-72	**Daimler Fleetline Bus**	Red, Yellow interior, 'Uniflo' adverts, chrome WhizzWheels	**£10-12**
56-a1	1970-72	**Ford Capri Fire Chief**	Red, White bonnet, 'Fire' decal on door, White interior, Blue windows, chrome WhizzWheels	**£25-30**
56-a2	1970-72	**Ford Capri Fire Chief**	As previous model but with 'Fire Chief' decal on door	**£25-30**
56-a3	1970-72	**Ford Capri Fire Chief**	All-Red, 'Fire Chief' decal on door, Yellow interior, Blue windows, chrome WhizzWheels	**£25-30**
57-a1	1970-72	**Caddy Hot Rodder**	Metallic Blue, Red interior, 'Caddy Hot Roddy' on doors, sticker pack, chrome WhizzWheels	**£12-15**
57-a2	1970-72	**Caddy Hot Rodder**	Metallic Pink, Red interior, 'Caddy Hot Roddy' on doors, sticker pack, chrome WhizzWheels	**£12-15**
58-a1	1971-72	**G.P. Beach Buggy**	Metallic Red, Cream interior, chrome WhizzWheels	**£10-12**
58-a2	1971-72	**G.P. Beach Buggy**	Metallic Red, Yellow interior, chrome WhizzWheels	**£10-12**
59-a1	1971-72	**The Futura**	Orange, Blue windows, 'Futura' on sides, Black base, sheet of stickers, chrome WhizzWheels	**£10-12**
60-a1	1971-72	**VW Double Trouble Hot Rod**	Metallic Pink, chrome interior, Green tinted windows, chrome WhizzWheels	**£12-15**
61-a1	1970-72	**Mercury Cougar Police Car**	White, Black roof, 'Sheriff', Yellow interior, Blue windows and lights, chrome WhizzWheels	**£12-15**
62-a1	1970	**Volvo P1800**	Red, Black bonnet, Yellow interior, chrome WhizzWheels	**£35-40**
62-a2	1971-72	**Volvo P1800**	Red, Black Bonnet, Blue interior, chrome WhizzWheels	**£25-30**
62-a3	1972	**Volvo P1800**	Red, Black Bonnet, Cream interior, chrome WhizzWheels	**£45-50**
63-a1	1970-72	**Ford Escort Monte Carlo Rally Car**	Metallic Blue, RN '32', Red interior, sheet of stickers, chrome WhizzWheels	**£35-40**
63-a2	1972	**Ford Escort Monte Carlo Rally Car**	Metallic Blue, RN '32', Yellow interior, sheet of stickers, chrome WhizzWheels	**£45-50**
63-a3	1972	**Ford Escort Monte Carlo Rally Car**	Metallic Blue, RN '32', Cream interior, , sheet of stickers, chrome WhizzWheels	**£45-50**
64-a1	1971-72	**Morgan Plus 8**	Yellow, Black interior, chrome WhizzWheels	**£20-25**
64-a2	1971-72	**Morgan Plus 8**	Red, RN '20' on doors, Black interior, chrome WhizzWheels	**£20-25**
65-a1	1971-72	**Bertone Carabo**	Metallic Purple, Pale Green base, White interior, Amber tinted windows, chrome WhizzWheels	**£12-15**
65-a2	1971-72	**Bertone Carabo**	Metallic Purple, Pale Green base, Orange interior, Amber tinted windows, chrome WhizzWheels	**£10-12**
67-a1	1971-72	**Ford Capri Hot Pants Dragster**	Yellow, 'Hot Pants' decal on roof, opening body, Red interior, chrome WhizzWheels	**£35-40**
70-a1	1971-72	**US Racing Buggy**	Blue, 'Stars and Stripes' on roof, White driver, chrome WhizzWheels	**£10-12**
71-a1	1971-72	**Marcos XP**	Orange, chrome interior, Amber tinted windows, chrome WhizzWheels	**£12-15**
72-a1	1971-72	**Mercedes-Benz C111**	Red, Amber tinted windows, chrome Intsrior, Black plastic base, chrome WhizzWheels	**£10-12**
73-a1	1971-72	**Pininfarina Alfa Romeo P33**	Blue, White interior and base, chrome WhizzWheels	**£10-12**
74-a1	1971-72	**Bertone Barchetta**	Orange, Red interior, White base, chrome WhizzWheels	**£10-12**
75-a1	1971-72	**Superstock Car**	Silver, Blue base, Union Jack on bonnet, Red interior, sticker pack, chrome WhizzWheels	**£20-25**
76-a1	1971-72	**Chevrolet Astro**	Metallic Red,Cream interior, chrome WhizzWheels	**£12-15**
77-a1	1971-72	**Bizzarrini Manta**	Pink, Cream interior, Black base, chrome WhizzWheels	**£10-12**
78-a1	1971-72	**Old MacDonalds Truck**	Red, Brown back, chrome WhizzWheels	**£25-30**
1017-a1	1971-72	**Holmes Wrecker & Towing Cradle**	Yellow cab, Red back, Amber glass, 'Auto Rescue' decals, Gold booms, Red cradle and hooks	**£100-120**

Collectors notes

Novelty, Film and TV-related models

See also preceding section and 'Corgi Rockets'.

1001-a1	1970	**James Bond Aston-Martin DB6**	Silver, Red interior, 2 ejector figures, tyres	£180-200
1001-a2	1970	**James Bond Aston-Martin DB6**	Silver, Red interior, 2 ejector figures, Black WhizzWheels	£160-180
1001-a3	1971-72	**James Bond Aston-Martin DB6**	Silver, Red interior, 2 ejector figures, chrome WhizzWheels	£160-180
1002-a1	1970	**Batmobile**	Black, Batman and Robin figures, tow hook, Grey plastic wheels, 'Corgi Junior' label on base	£150-160
1002-a2	1970	**Batmobile**	Black, Batman and Robin figures, tow hook, Black WhizzWheels	£150-160
1002-a3	1971-72	**Batmobile**	Black, Batman and Robin figures, tow hook, chrome WhizzWheels	£150-160
1003-a1	1970	**Batboat**	Black boat, Red fin, Batman and Robin figures, GPW, 'Corgi Junior' label on base	£140-150
1003-a2	1970	**Batboat**	Black boat, Red fin, Batman and Robin figures, Black WhizzWheels	£130-140
1003-a3	1971-72	**Batboat**	Black boat, Red fin, Batman and Robin figures, chrome WhizzWheels	£140-150
1004-a1	1970	**Monkeemobile**	Red, White roof, 4 figures, 'Monkees' on doors, tyres, 'Corgi Junior' label on base	£160-180
1004-a2	1970	**Monkeemobile**	Red, White roof, 4 figures, 'Monkees' on doors, tyres, 'Corgi Junior' base	£160-180
1004-a3	1971	**Monkeemobile**	Red, White roof, 4 figures, 'Monkees' on doors, tyres, Black WhizzWheels	£150-160
1005-a1	1970	**Man From UNCLE Car**	Blue, 3 missiles on sprue, 2 figures, tyres, 'Corgi Junior' label on base	£160-175
1006-a1	1970	**Chitty Chitty Bang Bang**	Chrome, Dark Grey base, Red wings, Yellow fins, 4 figures, tyres	£130-140
1006-a2	1971	**Chitty Chitty Bang Bang**	Chrome, Dark Grey base, Red wings, Yellow fins, 4 figures, Black WhizzWheels	£120-130
1007-a1	1971-72	**Ironsides Police Van**	Blue, 'San Francisco' logo, Ironside in back, chrome WhizzWheels	£160-180
1008-a1	1971-72	**Popeye's Paddle Wagon**	Yellow, Blue, Popeye with Olive and Sweet Pea, chrome WhizzWheels	£120-130
1010-a1	1972	**James Bond Volkswagen**	Orange, Green stripe and 'Corgi Toys' on roof, RN '5', Yellow interior, chrome WhizzWheels	£600-800
1011-a1	1971-72	**James Bond Bobsleigh**	Yellow, '007' decal, Grey plastic bumper, George Lazenby figure, Black WhizzWheels	£400-450
1012-a1	1971-72	**S.P.E.C.T.R.E. Bobsleigh**	Orange, 'Boars Head' decal, Grey plastic bumper, Blofield figure, Black WhizzWheels	£400-450
1013-a1	1971-72	**Tom's Go Cart**	Yellow, Tom figure, chrome WhizzWheels	£50-60
1014-a1	1971-72	**Jerry's Banger**	Red, Jerry figure, chrome WhizzWheels	£50-60

Major Models

2001	1968-69	**'HUSKY' Multi Garage**	A set of four garages, (no cars) 'Husky' on base	£15-20
	1970-75	Corgi Juniors issue:	As previous model but with 'CORGI' logo, 'Juniors' on base	£10-15
2002	1967-69	**'HUSKY' Car Transporter**	Hoynor MkII, White/Blue/Orange, detachable cab, 'Husky' on base	£30-40
	1970-72	Corgi Juniors issue:	As previous model but with 'CORGI' logo, 'Juniors' on base	£25-35
2003a	1968-69	**Machinery Low-Loader**	Red/Blue/Yellow, detachable cab, drop-down ramp, 'Husky' on base	£25-35
2003b	1970-73	Corgi Juniors issue:	As previous model with metal wheels or WhizzWheels, 'Juniors' base	£25-35
2004a	1968-69	**Removals Delivery Van**	Red or Blue cab, plated box, 'HUSKY REMOVALS', metal wheels, 'Husky' on base	£45-55
2004b	1970-72	Corgi Juniors issue:	As previous model but 'CORGI REMOVALS', WhizzWheels, 'Juniors' base	£20-30
2006	1970-79	**Mack 'ESSO' Tanker**	White body and tank, WhizzWheels, 'Juniors' on base	£10-15

Husky and Corgi Juniors Gift Sets 1968 - 1970

3001	1968-69	**4 Garage Set**	Contains 23, 27, 29, or 9, 30 or 36	£75-100
3002	1968-69	**Batmobile Set**	1002 Batmobile and 1003 Batboat on trailer	£150-200
3002	1970	**'Club Racing' Set**	Juniors set of 8 racing cars inc Mini Cooper 'S' (Metallic Mauve), Ford Capri, Morgan, etc	£150-250
3003	1968-69	**Car Transporter Set**	2002 Husky Car Transporter plus 16, 26, 6-2, 21-2, 22-2, 26	£150-200
3004	1968-69	**4 Garage Set**	Contains 23-2, 29	£60-80
3004		**James Bond 'OHMSS' Set**	Contains 1004, 1001, 1011, 1012 plus un-numbered VW Beetle in Red with Black No'5' on White circle on sides. (From film 'On Her Majesty's Secret Service')	£2000-2500
3005	1968-69	**Holiday Time / Leisure Time**	Contains 2-2, 5-2, 7-2, 15-2, 19-2, 20-2, 21-2, 35-1	£150-200
3006	1968-69	**Service Station**	Contains 14-c, 22-2, 28	£60-80
3007	1968-69	**'HUSKY MULTIPARK'**	In 1968 catalogue but not issued	NPP
3008	1968-69	**Crime Busters Set**	Contains 1001, 1002, 1003, 1005	£450-550
	1970	Corgi Juniors issue:	As previous set	£350-450
3011		**Road Construction Set**	Gift Set containing seven models	£120-140

Husky Accessories

1561/2	1968-69	**Traffic Signs**	£20-30
1571	1968-69	**Pedestrians**	£10-15
1572	1968-69	**Workmen**	£10-15
1573	1968-69	**Garage Personnel**	£10-15
1574	1968-69	**Public Servants**	£10-15
1580	1968-69	**Husky Collector Case** storage for 48 models	£15-25
1585	1968-69	**Husky Traveller Case** opens to form Service Station (this item never seen)	NPP
2001	1968-69	**'HUSKY' Multi Garage** A set of four garages, (no cars) 'Husky' on base	£20-25
	1970-75	Corgi Juniors issue: As previous model but with 'CORGI' logo, 'Juniors' on base	£10-15

Husky and Corgi Juniors Catalogues and listings

HUSKY CATALOGUES
Mettoy Playcraft (Sales) Ltd 1966

	1966	**Leaflet (single fold)**	Red, illustrating No.1 Jaguar Mk.10 on cover and Nos.1-29 inside. '1/9 each'	£20-25
same ref.	1966	**Leaflet (Belgian issue)**	As previous leaflet but Nos.1-32 shown, printed in French	£20-25
same ref.	1966	**Booklet (10 pages)**	Front/rear covers feature a row of garages and cars. Good pictures of 1002 Batmobile and 1001 James Bond's Aston-Martin, plus Nos.1-36	NGPP
no ref.	1967	**Catalogue (24 pages)**	Cover features boy with Husky vehicles and sets. Good pictures of all the rare models and Gift Sets plus accessories and models 1-41	£30-40

CORGI JUNIORS CATALOGUES
Mettoy Playcraft 1970

	Catalogue (16 pages)	Blue cover with 10 models featured. Contains excellent pictures of all the rare early models including GS 3004 James Bond 'O.H.M.S.S.' Set etc. £30-40

Qualitoys

A range of sturdy toys made up from the same basic parts. First issued in 1969, they were aimed at the pre school age group.

They were publicized as being from the 'makers of Corgi Toys' and did not form part of the Corgi range as such. They have little collectable value at the present time.

Q701 **Pick Up Truck** ....
Q702 **Side Tipper** ....
Q703 **Breakdown Truck** ....

Q704 **Tower Wagon** ....
Q705 **Horse Box** ....
Q706 **Giraffe Transporter** ....
Q707 **Fire Engine** ....
Q708 **Pick Up Trailer** ....

A Corgi Juniors page from the Mettoy Playcraft 1970 catalogue.

The following listing represents the best information available to us.
The listing is in no way complete and the Editor would welcome further details on other variations/issues and price levels.
Market Price Range - Scarcer items as shown, otherwise under £15
These models are fitted with WhizzWheels.

E1	1977-83	Mercedes 220D Ambulance, White or Cream...........
E2	1980-81	Blake's Seven Liberator £75-100
E3	1977-81	Stromberg's Helicopter £25-35
E4	1975-79	Zetor Farm Tractor £15-20
E5	1980-82	NASA Space Shuttle ....
E6	1979-80	'Daily Planet' Helicopter £15-20
E7	1976-80	Dumper Truck, Red/Yellow or Blue/Yellow.............
E7	1976-80	Dumper Truck, Yellow/Red or Yellow/Black............
E8	1979-83	Rover 3500 ....
E9	1975-80	'POLICE' Range Rover ....
E10	1977-81	Triumph TR7, White/Blue £20-25
		Triumph TR7, Silver/Red body £20-25
		Triumph TR7, Orange body £15-20
E11	1979-85	Supermobile £20-30
E12	1980-82	Jeep ....
E13-1	1976-78	Rough Terrain Truck, Red or Blue body ....
E13-2	1980-81	Buck Rogers Starfighter £30-40
E14	1975-76	(14d) 'ESSO' Tanker £20-25
E14-2	1977-80	Buick Royal 'TAXI' ....
E15	1975-84	(15-3) Mercedes 'SCHOOL BUS',
		Yellow or Red body ....
E16-1	1975-77	Land Rover Pick-Up ....
E16-2	1980-82	Rover 3500 'POLICE' Car ....
E17-1	1975-77	(17-2) Volkswagen 1300 Beetle....................£15-20
E17-2	1979-81	Metropolis 3500 'POLICE' Car £25-35
E18	1977	'AMF' 'Ski-Daddler' Snowmobile, (see Twin-Packs)
E19	1980-82	Pink Panther Motorcycle £15-20
E20-1	1976-78	Site Cement Mixer ....
E20-2	1979-81	Penguinmobile £20-30
E21	1977-80	Charlie's Angels Chevrolet Van...................£15-20
E22-1	1975-77	(22-3) Formula 1 Racer ....
E22-2	1981-82	'PARAMEDIC' Van ....
E23	1979-81	Batbike £75-100
E24	1979-80	'SHAZAM' Thunderbolt £40-50
E25	1979-80	'CAPTAIN AMERICA' Porsche £40-50
E26	1977-90	ERF Fire Tender, Yellow body ....
E27	1976-80	(27/2) Formula 5000 Racing Car ....
E28-1	1975-76	Hot Rodder ....
E28-2	1977-80	Buick Regal 'POLICE' Car,
		White or Black body ....
E29	1975-80	Simon Snorkel Fire Engine ....
E30	1976-83	Mobile Cement Mixer, Green/Yellow,
		Blue/White or Red/Silver..........
E31	1975-79	Land Rover Breakdown, Red body,
		'WRECKER TRUCK'...............
		Land Rover Breakdown, Blue body,
		'CRASH SERVICE'.................
E32	1970-74	The Saint's Jaguar XJS £65-85
E33	1979-80	'WONDERWOMAN's Car..........................£30-40
E34-1	1975-78	Sting Army Helicopter ....
E34-2	1980	'HERTZ' Chevrolet Van ....
E35-1	1975-79	Air Bus Helicopter ....
E35-2	1983-87	Tipper Truck, Silver/Blue or Red/Brown ....
E36-1	1975-77	Healer-Wheeler 'AMBULANCE'....................
E36-2	1979-80	'COCA-COLA' Chevrolet Van ....
E37	1976-79	Porsche Carrera 'POLICE' Car.....................
E38	1980-83	Jerry's Banger £15-20
E39	1975-77	Jaguar 'E' Type £35-45
E40-1	1977-80	Army Red Cross Helicopter ....
E40-2	1979-81	James Bond's Aston-Martin £75-125
E41	1979-81	James Bond Space Shuttle £15-20
E42	1977-81	'RESCUE' Range Rover ....
E43	1976-80	Massey-Ferguson 3303 Farm Tractor
		with Blade, Orange/Black,
		Yellow/Red or all Yellow.............£20-30
E44-1	1976-78	Raygo Rascal 600 Road Roller ....
E44-2	1979-80	Starship Liberator £50-75
E45	1977-81	Starsky and Hutch Ford Gran Torino £15-20
E46	1976-80	'POLICE' Helicopter,
		White or Metallic Blue body ....
E47	1978-80	'SUPERVAN' (Chevrolet).............................
E48	1975-79	Shovel Loader, red ....
E49-1	1977-79	Tipping Lorry ....
E49-2	1981-83	Woody Woodpecker's Car ....

E50	1979-80	'Daily Planet' (Leyland) Van,
		Red or Silver...........................£15-20
E51	1976-78	Volvo 245 Estate Car, Metallic green,
		White or Blue tailgate ....
E52-1	1976-79	Mercedes Benz 240D 'TAXI'.......................
E52-2	1982-83	Scooby Doo's Vehicle £20-25
E53	1977-79	'FIRE' Launch ....
E54-1	1980-82	'CORGI' Formula 1 Racer, Black car,
		Yellow or White driver.................
E54-2	1976-78	(54) Ford D1000 Container Truck,
		Red/Yellow or Red/Orange ....
E55	1976-80	Refuse Truck, Blue/Yellow,
		Bronze/Blue or Green/White ....
E56	1979-80	Chevrolet 'SPIDERVAN' £20-25
E57-1	1975-77	Ferrari 312s, Blue body, number '6' ....
E57-2	1979-80	Spiderbike £20-25
E58	1976-78	Beach Buggy..
E59-1	1980-83	Tom's Cart £15-20
E59-2	1977-79	Mercedes 240D 'POLIZEI' Car £15-20
E59-3	1982-84	Mercedes 240D, Blue, Red or White ....
E60	1977-79	James Bond Lotus Esprit £50-75
E61-1	1979-81	Buick Regal 'SHERIFF' Car £15-20
E61-2	1980-82	Ford Capri 3-litre £15-20
E62	1977-80	AMC Pacer, Metallic Blue or Red ....
E63	1977-80	'SURF RESCUE' Helicopter ....
E64	1980-82	'The Professionals' Ford Capri £15-20
E65	1976-81	Caravan Trailer..
E66-1	1976-79	Centurion Tank..
E66-2	1980	Ice Cream Van ....
E67-1	1976-80	Road Roller ....
E67-2	1980-83	Popeye's Tugboat £15-20
E68	1977-79	Kojak's Buick Regal £20-25
E69	1976-80	Batmobile £50-75
E70-1	1975-77	Cougar 'FIRE CHIEF' ....
E70-2	1977-81	Ford Torino 'FIRE CHIEF' ....
E71	1980-85	London Austin 'TAXI' ....
E72-1	1975-77	(72) Mercedes C111 ....
E72-2	1979-83	Jaguar XJS, Blue or Red body ....
		Jaguar XJS, Red body,
		White 'MOTOR SHOW' logo £20-30
E73	1980	'DRAX' Helicopter £20-25
E74	1978-80	'RYDER TRUCK RENTAL' Leyland Van.......
E75	1977-80	Spidercopter £20-30
E76	1976-78	(76) Military Jeep ....
E77	1977-80	Poclain Digger, Yellow/Red or White/Red.......
E78	1976-81	Batcopter £30-40
E79-1	1975-76	Land Rover Military Ambulance ....
E79-2	1980-83	Olive Oyl's Aeroplane £15-20
E80	1979-80	'MARVEL COMICS' Van £20-25
E81	1975-83	Daimler Fleetline London Bus,
		various logos, with or without faces
		at windows ....
E82-1	1975-78	Can-Am Racer, Metallic Blue ....
E82-2	1981-82	Yogi Bear's Jeep £20-30
E83-1	1975-77	'COMMANDO' Armoured Car ....
E83-2	1980-81	'GOODYEAR' Blimp ....
E84-1	1975-78	Daimler Scout Car ....
E84-2	1980-83	Bugs Bunny Vehicle £15-20
E85	1975-78	Skip Truck ....
E86	1974-80	Fiat X1-9, Green body £25-35
		Fiat X1-9, Gold body, RN '4' £15-20
		Fiat X1-9, Gold body, RN '9', 'FIAT' ....
E87	1975-80	Leyland Truck, 'COCA-COLA' ....
		Leyland Truck, 'PEPSI-COLA' ....
		Leyland Truck, 'WEETABIX' ....
		Leyland Truck, 'W.H. SMITH'......................
E88	1975-80	Mobile Crane ....
E89	1975-82	Citroen Dyane, dark Yellow, Gold or Purple.....
E90	1977-79	'FIREBALL' Chevrolet Van ....
E91a	1977-79	'GOLDEN EAGLE' Chevrolet Van ....
E91b	1980-81	'VANTASTIC' Chevrolet Van
		(new casting) ....
E92	1977-81	Volkswagen Polo, Metallic Lime or
		darker Green body.......................

E93-1	1977-78	Tugboat	
E93-2	1980-81	Dodge Magnum	£15-20
E94-1	1975-77	Porsche 917	
E94-2	1978-80	'ADIDAS' Chevrolet Van	
95	1977-82	'COCA-COLA' Leyland Van	
96-1	1975-78	Field Gun, military Green	
96-2	1980-83	Ford Thunderbird, Red, Cream or Green	
97-1	1977-78	'EXXON' Petrol Tanker	£25-35
97-2	1977-80	'TEXACO' Petrol Tanker	
		'SHELL' Petrol Tanker	
		'BP OIL' Petrol Tanker	
98-1	1975-77	Marcos	
98-2	1977-79	Mercedes-Benz Mobile Shop	
98-3	1980-81	'POLICE' Helicopter	
99	1979-81	Jokermobile	£30-40
100	1981-83	Hulk Cycle	£30-40
102	1981-83	Renault 5 Turbo	
103	1981-83	Ford Transit Wrecker	
104	1981-83	Ford Mustang Cobra	
105	1981-83	Ford Escort 1.3GL, Metallic Green or Blue	
E107	1981-83	Austin Metro, Metallic Dark Mid Blue	
E108	1981-83	Locomotive	
E111	1981-83	Passenger Coach	
E112	1981-83	Goods Wagon	
E113	1982-83	Paddle Steamer	
E114	1981-83	Stage Coach	
E115	1981-83	James Bond 2cv Citroën	£40-50
E116	1982	Mercedes-Benz 'ESPANA 82'	
J89	1988	Mercedes 23/16 Racer, White, 'Servis'	
J90	1988	Mercedes 23/16 Saloon, Red	
J91	1988	Jaguar XJ40, White, 'Police'	
J93	1988	Jaguar XJ40, White, 'Jaguar'	
J94	1988	Mercedes 300E Estate, Red	
J95	1988	Mercedes 300E Estate Taxi, Yellow	
J97	1988	Land-Rover 110, Red, 'Fire Salvage'	
J98	1988	Porsche Targa, Red	
J99	1988	Porsche Targa, White, 'Turbo'	
E117	1982	Chevrolet 'ESPANA 82' Custom Van	
E119	1983	'FLUGHAFEN-FEURWEHR' Fire Engine (German Issue)	£15-20
120	?	Leyland Van, 'Eiszeit' (German Issue)	£15-20
120	1983	Ice Cream Van, 'FRESHLICHE' (German Issue)	£15-20
121	1983	Chevrolet Van, 'TECHNISCHER' (German Issue)	£15-20
E123	1982-83	'AIRPORT RESCUE' Tender	
124	1982-83	Mercedes-Benz 500SL	
125	1982-83	Ford Transit Lorry	
E125	1983	Ford Dropside Truck	
126	1982-83	Ford Transit Breakdown, 'ABSCHIEPPDIENST', (German Issue)	£15-20
127	1982-83	'ADAC' Car, (German Issue)	£20-25
128	1982-83	Fred's Flyer	£25-35
129	1982-83	Ford Sierra 2.3 Ghia, Blue, Red or Silver body	
131	1982-83	Ferrari 308GTS, 'Magnum PI'	£25-35
133	1982-83	Buick Regal 'POLICE' Car, 'Magnum PI'	£25-35
134	1982-83	Barney's Buggy, Red/Orange, (The Flintstones')	£25-35
135	1982-83	Austin Metro 'DATAPOST'	
E136	1982-82	Ferrari 308GTS, Red or Black	
E137	1982-84	VW Turbo	
E138	1982-84	Rover 3500	
E139	1982-84	Porsche 911 Turbo	
E140	1982-84	Ford Mustang Cobra	
E141	1982-84	Ford Capri S 'ALITALIA'	
E143	1983-84	Leyland 'ROYAL MAIL' Van	
E144	1983-84	'BRITISH GAS' Van	
E145	1983-84	'BRITISH TELECOM' Van	
E146	1983-84	Ford Transit Pick-Up, 'Wimpey' ...	
E147	1983-84	Leyland 'ROADLINE' Lorry	
E148	1983-84	USS Enterprise	£15-20
E149	1983	Klingon Warship	£15-20
E150	1983	'Simon and Simon' Police Car	
E151	1983	Wilma's Coupé	£25-35
E152	1983	'Simon and Simon' 1957 Chevy	
E156	1983	1957 Chevy	
E160	1983	VW Hot Rod	
E161	1983	Opel Corsa 13SR	
E170	?	Vauxhall Nova	
E174	1983	Quarry Truck	
175	?	Ford Escort	
E175	1983	Pipe Truck	
176	?	Ford Capri 'S'	
E177	1983	'Corgi Chemco' Tanker	
E178	1983	'Corgi' Container Truck	
E179	1983	Chevy Corvette, Yellow or Aqua Blue	
E180	1983	Pontiac Firebird SE	
181	?	Mercedes 300sl	
E182	1983	4x4 Renegade Jeep	
E183	1983	Renegade Jeep with Hood	
E184	1983	Range Rover	
E185	1983	Baja Off Road Van	
190	1983	Austin Metro	
190	1983	Buick Regal	
191	1983	Rover 3500	
192	1983	Triumph TR7, 'British Airways'	
192	1983	Mercedes 'Arabic' Ambulance	
193	1983	Chubb 'Arabic' Fire Truck	
195	1983	Leyland Van 'Arabic Miranda'	£15-25
E196	1983	'Police Tactical Force' Van	
198	1983	James Bond Citroen 2cv	£25-35
201	1983	Chevrolet Van 'Arabic Team'	£15-25
E203	1983	Fiat X19, Orange/Red or Yellow	£30-40
E204	1983	Renault 5 Turbo	
E205	1983	Porsche 911	
E206	1983	Buick Regal	
208	1983	Ford Sierra 'Notartz'	£15-25
209	1983	Leyland Van 'DBP'	
210	1983	Matra Rancho 'Safari Park'	
211	1983	Ford Escort 'Fahrschule'	£15-25
212	1983	VW Polo 'Siemens'	
219	1983	Ford Sierra 'Polizei'	£15-25
222	1983	Chevrolet Van 'Swissair'	
223	1983	Matra Rancho 'Safari Park'	
224	1983	Chevrolet Van 'Rivella'	£15-25
226	1983	Ford Wrecker 'Abschleppdienst' ...	£15-25
228	1983	Leyland Van 'Waser Papeterie'	£15-25
250	1983	Simon Snorkel 'Brandbil'	£15-25
251	1983	ERF Fire Tender	£15-20
252	1983	Ford Transit Wrecker 'Falck'	£15-25
253	1983	Mercedes Ambulance 'Falck'	£15-25
254	1983	Mercedes 240D 'Falck'	£15-25
?	?	Leyland Van 'Geest', special card ...	£20-30
?	?	Chevrolet Van 'Unichem'	£15-25

Corgi Juniors Sets

2601	Batman Triple-Pack	£140-180
E3001	Multi Garage and three cars	£35-45
E3005	Leisure Time Set	£100-125
E3013	Emergency Rescue Set (Rescue Station + 3 models)	£70-85
3019/1	James Bond 'Octopussy' Set, 1983-84	£150-200
E3021	Crimefighters Gift Set (E45, E60, E68, E69, E75, E78)	£200-300
E3023	Mercedes Transporter plus 4 cars	£75-100
E3024	Construction Gift Set (6 vehicles)	£75-100
E3026	Emergency Gift Set (6 vehicles)	£75-100
E3030	James Bond 'The Spy Who Loved Me' Gift Set, 1976-77 (E3, E60, 'Jaws' Van, Mercedes, Speedboat)	£200-300

E3080	Batman Gift Set, 1980-82 (E20, E23, E69, E78, E99)	£200-300
E3081	Superman Gift Set (E6, E11, E17, E47, E50)	£125-150
E3082	James Bond 'Goldfinger' Gift Set, 1980-82, (E40, E41, E60, E73, plus 'Jaws' van)	£200-300
E3084	Cartoon Characters Set (E19, E38, E58, E67, E79)	£100-125
E3100	Construction Gift Set (7 items)	£75-100
E3101	Fire Gift Set (6 items)	£75-100
E3103	Emergency Gift Set (6 items)	£75-100
E3105	Transporter Gift Set (Mercedes Transporter + 4 cars)	£75-100

'J' Series

J1	1984	NASA Space Shuttle ....
J1	1988	Ford Capri, 'Duckhams'..
J2	1984-85	Dump Truck ....
J2	1988	Iveco Tanker, 'Esso'..
J3	1984-85	Triumph TR7, Black or Red/Blue..............................
J4	1984	Starfighter, (Buck Rogers) ....
J4	1988	Ford Transit Van, 'Kremer Racing' ....
J5	1984-85	'Holiday Inn' Bus, Green or White ....
J6	1984	Rover 'Police' Car...
J7	1984	ERF Fire Engine..
J8	1984-85	Simon Snorkel Fire Engine...
J9	1984-85	Mobile Cement Mixer..
J9	1988	Iveco Container, 'Mars' ....
J10	1984	Aston-Martin DB5, Red..
J10	1985	Aston-Martin DB5, Yellow, 'DB6'................................
J11	1984	Volvo Estate Car, White..
J11	1985	Volvo Support Car, White, 'Castrol' ....
J12	1984	Skip Truck, Red/White..
J12	1988	Iveco Tanker, 'BP Oil'..
J13	1984	Refuse Truck, Yellow/Grey...
J13	1988	Iveco Truck, 'Pepsi'..
J14	1984	Mercedes 240D ....
J14	1985	Mercedes 240D Rally Car..
J15	1984	Lotus Esprit ....
J15	1988	Ford Transit Van, 'Police' ....

J16	1984	Ford Capri, White, Silver or Blue..............................
J16	1988	BMW 3251 Saloon, Red..
J17	1984	London FX4 Taxi..
J18	1984-85	Jaguar XJS, White, Silver or Green............................
J19	1984	Matra Rancho, Green/Black or Blue...........................
J20	1984-88	London Bus, Red...
J39	1988	Chevrolet 'ROYAL MAIL' Van....................................
J62	1985	Mobile Shop ....
J63	1988	Ford Transit Van, 'Royal Mail' ....
J64	1988	Land-Rover 110, Yellow, 'AA'.....................................
J66	1988	Land-Rover 110, White, 'Police'.................................
J73	1988	Ford Escort XR3i...
J74	1988	Land-Rover 110, White, 'Safari Rally'.......................
J77	1988	Ferrari Testarossa, White..
J79	1988	Mercedes 300E Ambulance ....
J81	1988	Buick, Blue, 'Police NYPD'...
J85	1988	Porsche 935 Racer..
J86	1988	Porsche 935 Racer..
J87	1988	Porsche 935, Red, no markings....................................
J90	1988	Escort 'DATAPOST', '66' ....
J91	1989	Escort 'DATAPOST', '77' ....
J92	1988	Metro 'DATAPOST', '66'...
J93	1989	Metro 'DATAPOST', '77'...
J94	1989	Metor Van 'ROYAL MAIL'...

900 Series Issues

90010	1991	Ford Transit Van 'Kremer Racing' ....
90013	1991	Ford Transit Van 'Police', Dark Blue ....
90015	1991	Ford Transit Van 'RAC', White ....
90030	1991	ERF Fire Engine, Red/Silver.......................................
90035	1991	Simon Snorkel Fire Engine, Red/White......................
90040	1991	Iveco Container Truck 'Wispa'....................................
90065	1991	Iveco Tanker 'Shell'..
90076	1991	BMW 325i, Metallic Silver-Blue..................................
90100	1991	Matra Rancho, Yellow, 'M'..
90125	1991	Ford Transit Wrecker 'Police'.....................................
90126	1991	Ford Transit Wrecker 'Kremer Racing' ....
90145	1991	BMW M3, Black/White..
90160	1991	Ford Sierra, Metallic Blue...
90190	1991	Ferrari Testarossa, Red, 'Ferrari'...............................
90200	1991	Corvette, Black/Red, 'Flame' design ....
90201	1991	Corvette, Red/White, 'Vette'.......................................
90300	1991	Pontiac Firebird, Silver, Red bodyline.......................
90301	1991	Pontiac Firebird, Yellow/Black, 'Fire Bird'...............
90310	1991	Military Jeep, Olive body, Brown top..........................
90360	1991	US Custom Van, Black/Red, 'Team Racing' ....
90371	91	Land-Rover, 'Coastguard', Blue/Yellow.....................
90374	1991	Land-Rover, 'Emergency - Fire', Red ....

90390	1991	Mercedes Ambulance, White, red crosses ....
90420	1991	Buick 'Police' Car, Black/White..................................
90421	1991	Buick 'Fire Chief' Car, Red/White..............................
90430	1991	Volvo 760 Saloon, Metallic Grey..................................
90440	1991	Porsche 935 Racer, Red, '33'.......................................
90460	1991	Mercedes 23/16, Blue, 'Mobil', 'Koni' ....
90461	1991	Mercedes 23, Red..
90470	1991	Jaguar XJ40, 'Police', White ....
90471	1991	Jaguar XJ40, Metallic Bronze......................................
90500	1991	Helicopter, 'Police', White/Black ....
90520	1991	Ford Thunderbird, Black..
90540	1991	Ford Mustang, Blue, 'Goodyear', '77' ....
90541	1991	Ford Mustang, White, Red stripes, '7'........................
90550	1991	BMW 850i, Black...
90560	1991	Ferrari 348 TB, Red...
90570	1991	Mercedes 500sl, Red...
90580	1991	Jaguar XJR9, White/Purple, 'Jaguar'.........................
91000	1991	MAN Container Truck 'Perrier', Green.......................
91020	1991	MAN Tanker 'Texaco', White.......................................
91040	1991	MAN Open Back Tipper, Yellow...................................

Corgi Juniors Twin-Packs

Corgi Juniors bubble-packed in pairs from 1977 approximately.
The market price range is NGPP except where shown otherwise.

2501	London Bus and Taxi ....
2502	Land Rover Breakdown and Jaguar XJS ....
2503	Land Rover and Horse Box...
2504	Land Rover Breakdown and AMC Pace Car....................
2505	'DAILY PLANET' Van and Helicopter **£20-30**
2506	Supermobile and Superman Van......................................
2507	Tom's Cart and Jerry's Banger **£20-30**
2508	Popeye's Tugboat and Olive Oyl's Aeroplane......**£20-30**
2510	Formula 1 and Formula 5000 Racing Cars ....
2511	Sting Helicopter and Scout Car.......................................
2512	Space Shuttle and Star Ship 'Liberator' ....
2513	Fire Tender and Ambulance ....
2514	Building Set ....
2515	Citroen and Speedboat ....
2516	Tractor and Tipping Trailer ....

2518	Mercedes and Caravan ....
2519	Batmobile and Batboat.....................................**£100-150**
2520	Rescue Set ....
2521	James Bond Space Shuttle, Drax Helicopter......**£35-45**
2522	Army Attack Set...
2523	Police Car and Helicopter...
2524	Custom Van Twin ....
2525	Triumph TR7 and Dinghy on Trailer ....
2526	Dumper Truck and Shovel Loader...................................
2527	'Kojak' and New York Police Helicopter............**£20-30**
2528	Starsky and Hutch Twin Pack............................**£20-30**
2529	James Bond Lotus and Helicopter......................**£60-80**
2530	Rescue Range Rover and Helicopter ....
?	AMF 'Ski-daddler' Snowmobile and trailer.....**£100-150**

Corgi Super Juniors and Super Haulers

Corgi Super Juniors and Super Haulers were introduced in 1970.
See page 269 in the 'Modern Diecasts' section.

Corgi Rockets

This model range was issued between 1970 and 1972 to compete against Mattel 'Hot Wheels' and similar products. The models had 'WhizzWheels' and featured a special 'Tune-Up' system which increased the play value and speed of the virtually frictionless wheels. In addition they were very robust, being advertised as 'four times stronger' than most other diecast racers. To begin with seven Corgi Juniors were adapted as Rockets and five of those received a superb vacuum metallised finish. A range of accessories was also issued in the form of 'Speed Circuits' etc, and each car was issued with a special 'Golden Tune-Up Key' which released the base. The bubble-packed models are difficult to find in top condition and the prices reflect their scarcity.

Ref.	Year(s)	Model name	Colours, features, dimensions	Market Price Range
D 901	1970-72	**Aston-Martin DB-6**	Metallic Deep Gold body, Green interior	£60-70
D 902	1970-72	**Jaguar XJ-6**	Metallic Green body, Cream interior	£60-70
D 903	1970-72	**Mercedes-Benz 280 SL**	Metallic Orange body, White interior	£60-70
D 904	1970-72	**Porsche Carrera 6**	Orange-Yellow body, Black number '19'	£60-70
D 905	1970-72	**'The Saint's Volvo P1800**	White body, Blue/White 'Saint' label on bonnet	£70-85
D 906	1970-72	**Jensen Interceptor**	Metallic Red body, Yellow interior	£60-70
D 907	1970-72	**Cadillac Eldorado**	Metallic Copper body, White interior	£60-70
D 908	1970-72	**Chevrolet Astro**	Metallic Red/Black body	£40-50
D 909	1970-72	**Mercedes-Benz C111**	Red or Blue body, White interior	£30-40
D 910	1970-72	**Beach Buggy**	Orange body, Black interior	£30-40
D 911	1970-72	**Marcos XP**	Gold body, Chrome interior	£30-40
?	1970-72	**Ford Capri**	Purple body	£40-50
D 913	1970-72	**Aston-Martin DBS**	Metallic Blue, Yellow interior	£60-70
D 916	1970-72	**Carabo Bertone**	Metallic Green/Blue, Orange interior	£20-30
D 917	1970-72	**Pininfarina Alfa-Romeo**	Metallic Purple/White	£20-30
D 918	1970-72	**Bitzzarini Manta**	Metallic Dark Blue, White interior	£20-30
D 919	1970-72	**'Todd Sweeney' Stock Car**	Red/Purple, Yellow/Black front, RN '531'	£75-100
D 920	1970-72	**'Derek Fiske' Stock Car**	White/Red, Silver bonnet, Red logo, RN '304'	£75-100
D 921	1970-72	**Morgan Open Sports**	Metallic Red body, Black seats	£60-75
D 922	1970-72	**Rally Ford Capri**	Yellow body, Orange/Black stripe, RN '8'	£60-75
			Green body, Black bonnet, (GS 2 model)	£60-75
D 923	1970-72	**'James Bond' Ford Escort**	White body, Pale Blue stripes, 'JAMES BOND', White '007' and 'SPECIAL AGENT' logos (From film 'On Her Majesty's Secret Service')	£200-300
D 924	1970-72	**Mercury Cougar XR7**	Red body with Black roof, Yellow interior	£30-40
		'James Bond' issue:	Red/Black with Yellow side flash, interior and skis on roof rack (From film 'On Her Majesty's Secret Service').	£200-300
D 925	1970-72	**'James Bond' Ford Capri**	White body with Black/White check design, 2 bonnet stripes and RN '6' (From film 'On Her Majesty's Secret Service').	£200-300
D 926	1970-72	**Jaguar 'Control Car'**	Metallic Brown body, Red roof blade, Blue/White figures	£100-150
D 927	1970-72	**Ford Escort Rally**	White body, Red RN '18', 'DAILY MIRROR' labels on doors, '1970 Mexico World Cup Rally Winner'	£200-300
D 928	1970-72	**Mercedes 280 SL 'SPECTRE'**	Black body with Red 'SPECTRE' logo, plus boars head design	£200-300
D 930	1970-72	**Bertone Barchetta**	Metallic Green over White body, Red interior	£40-50
D 931	1970-72	**'Old MacDonalds Truck'**	Yellow cab, Brown rear, Silver engine	£100-125
D 933	1970-72	**'Holmes Wrecker'**	White or Blue cab, White back, *'AUTO RESCUE'*	£100-125
D 937	1970-72	**Mercury Cougar**	Metallic Dark Green body, Yellow interior and spoiler	£20-30

Corgi Rockets Gift Sets

D 975	1970	**Super Stock Gift Set 1**	Contains D 905, D 919, Trailer and 3 figures	£250-350
D 976	1970	**Super Stock Gift Set 2**	Contains Green/Black D 922, D 920, Trailer and 3 figures	£250-350
D 977	1970	**Super Stock Gift Set 3**	Contains D 926, D 919, D 920 and 5 figures	£250-350

The listing above has been prepared from a Corgi Rockets 1970 catalogue. The sets themselves have not been seen and further information is required.

D 978		**'OHMSS' Gift Set**	Models of cars in the James Bond film 'On Her Majesty's Secret Service': D 923 and D 925 (as driven in the ice-racing scene), D 924 (as driven by 'Tracey'), D 928 (as driven by the Chief of 'SPECTRE')	£2,000-2,500

Corgi Rockets Accessories

D 2051	1970	**Action Speedset**	One car, 'Autostart', 12 ft of track	NGPP
D 2052	1970	**Super Autobatics Speedset**	One car, 'Autostart', 16 ft of track plus 'leaps' etc	NGPP
D 2058	1970	**Race-Abatic Speedset**	Two cars, 'Autostart', 2 x 16 ft of track plus 'leaps' etc	NGPP
D 2071	1970	**Jetspeed Circuit**	One car, 'Superbooster', 16 ft of track plus 'leaps' etc	NGPP
D 2074	1970	**Triple-Leap Speed Circuit**	One car, 19 ft, 6 in of track plus 'leaps' etc	NGPP
D 2075	1970	**Grand Canyon Speed Circuit**	One car, 12 ft of track	NGPP
D 2079	1970	**World Champion Speedset**	Two cars, 2 x 16 ft of track, 2 Boosters	NGPP

D 1931 **Superleap**	D 1937 **Autostart**	D 1970 **Super Booster**	D 1978 **Pitstop**
D 1934 **Autofinish**	D 1938 **Super Crossover**	D 1971 **Hairpin Tunnel**	D 1979 **Spacehanger Bend**
D 1935 **Connections** (3)	D 1945 **Adaptors** (3)	D 1976 **Quickfire Start**	
D 1936 **Space Leap**	D 1963 **Track** (16ft)	D 1977 **Lap Counter**	

Corgi Rockets Catalogues

no ref	1969	**8-page booklet**	listing the first 7 issues, Green model on cover	£20-25
no ref	1970	**16-page booklet**	listing most issues, good pictures of rare models, sets and accessories	£30-35

Information taken from the Cecil Gibson Archives and this Catalogue compiler's own collection of reference material.
Note: 'Concertina' leaflets were issued with models sold in the early Blue boxes.

Ref.	Year(s)	Publication	Cover features and details	Market Price Range
no ref.	1956	**Concertina leaflet**............	Blue cover, famous Corgi dog, shows first 14 models, no prices	**£15-20**
no ref	1956	**Concertina leaflet**............	Blue cover with Red/Gold Corgi dog Depicts first 14 models and shows prices of both normal and mechanical models	**£20-25**
50/157/K1	1957	**Concertina leaflet**............	Blue cover with Red/Gold Corgi dog Depicts ten models and lists the mechanical models in red	**£5-10**
40/257/K1	1957	**Concertina leaflet**............	Blue cover with Red/Gold Corgi dog Depicts ten models but does not list mechanical models	**£5-10**
40/257/K2	1957	**Concertina leaflet**............	As previous leaflet but with the addition of 208	**£5-10**
50/557/K3	1957	**Concertina leaflet**............	As 40/257/K2 plus 100,150, 408, 454, 'WOW! CORGI TOYS' logo	**£5-10**
100/1057/K3	1957	**Concertina leaflet**............	Blue cover showing 100, 150, 207, 208, 302, 405, 408, 453, 455	**£5-10**
50/1057/K4	1958	**Concertina leaflet**............	Blue cover, 'WOW! CORGI TOYS' logo. Listings include models 102, 406/7, and first 'MAJOR' toy (1101)	**£15-20**
50/1157/K4	1957	**Concertina leaflet**............	Cover shows 102, 210, 406, 407, 412, 1101, 'WOW! CORGI TOYS' logo.	**£5-10**
52/258/K5	1958	**Concertina leaflet**............	Cover shows GS 1 and 2, 101, 211, 302, 457, 459, 1100, 1401, 1450	**£5-10**
52/258/K6	1958	**Concertina leaflet**............	As previous leaflet plus 350, 351	**£5-10**
300/658/K7	1958	**Concertina leaflet**............	Shows GS 3, 151, 209, 458, 'NEW CORGI TOYS' logo and prices	**£5-10**
25/257/C1/UK	1957	**Four-fold leaflet**	'Blue box' 208 Jaguar on cover, 15 model pictures inside	**£50-75**
25/257/C2/UK	1957	**Four-fold leaflet**	As previous leaflet but with 24 model pictures inside	**£50-75**
50/1057/C3/UK	1957	**Four-fold leaflet**	Shows GS 1 Bedford Transporter and 6 cars on Blue/Yellow cover with details of 100, 150, 200-8, 210, 300-2, 403-8, 412, 452-5, 1101	**£25-30**
25/1157/C4/UK	1957	**Four-fold leaflet**	As previous leaflet plus 101 and 102	**£25-30**
no ref	1958	**Four-fold leaflet**	As previous leaflet plus 211 No prices, car listing or ref no	**NGPP**
650/858/C8	1958	**Catalogue**	First 'book' catalogue Cover depicts boy playing with Bloodhound Missile, many other vehicles	**NGPP**
no ref	1959	**Four-fold leaflet**	Blue cover with 'THE ROCKET AGE WITH CORGI TOYS' (This leaflet was issued with Rocket Age models)	**£15-20**
no ref	9/59	**Interim leaflet**.................	Lists 152, 50 Tractor, 350 Thunderbird, new TT van and accessories	**NGPP**
UK 9/59	1959	**16 page Catalogue**............	Cover features Massey Ferguson Tractor No. 50 and BRM Racer No. 152. Agricultural and 'MAJOR' issues (No.1100 etc) are listed	**£30-40**
no ref	1959	**Single page leaflet**.........	Features Renault Floride plus 'STRAIGHT FROM THE MOTOR SHOW' logo	**£10-15**
no ref	1959	**Two fold leaflet**................	Features 'AUTHENTIC ROCKET AGE MODELS' logo and models plus 1102 Tractor Dozer	**£10-15**
no ref	1960	**Interim leaflet**............	Depicts M1 Motorway scene	**£5-10**
UK 9/60	1960	**20 page Catalogue**...........	Cover has motorway bridge scene and Corgi models. This catalogue was the first with listings of 'CHIPPERFIELDS' issues	**£30-40**
UK 9/61	1961	**24 page Catalogue**...........	Racetrack scene on cover. Listings and pictures include new Sports Cars, Express Coach and Kits	**£20-25**
no ref	1962	**Two-fold Checklist**..........	Leaflet front cover depicts Blue/Yellow 'CORGI TOYS' plus seven models and their features Red/Grey interior plus first check list	**£15-20**
C/100/62	1963	**32 page Catalogue**...........	Cover depicts schoolboy (in red cap and blazer) crossing road with Corgi dog. No catalogue date is shown on front cover	**£50-75**
no ref	1963	**32 page Catalogue**...........	Same cover as C/100/62 but boy's cap and blazer are Blue. The date '1963-64' is shown on front cover	**£15-20**
Playcraft Toys Ltd 1964	1964	**Two-fold Checklist**..........	Leaflet with Blue/Yellow 'Corgi Toys' design on cover featuring 241 Ghia	**£15-20**
Playcraft Toys Ltd 1964	1965	**40 page Catalogue**...........	Cover logos: 'CORGI TOYS', 'CORGI CLASSICS', '1965'. Contains Classics and first Routemaster in the listings	**£15-20**
Mettoy Playcraft (Sales) Ltd 1965	1965	**Two-fold Checklist**..........	Leaflet with six model cars from six different nations featured on the cover	**£5-10**
Playcraft Toys Ltd 1965	1966	**40 page Catalogue**...........	Cover depicts model 261 James Bond's Aston Martin DB5. Contents give details of special Rallye Monte Carlo issues. 'Price 3d'	**£15-20**
C2038/66	1966	**Leaflet**	Cover proudly states 'MODEL CAR MAKERS TO JAMES BOND'	**£8-12**
C2039/4/66	1966	**Four-fold Checklist**........	Leaflet similar to previous with 'MODEL CAR MAKERS TO JAMES BOND'. The contents feature 1127 Simon Snorkel etc	**£10-15**
C2017/9/66	1967	**48 page Catalogue**...........	The cover and contents are dominated by Film and TV-related models of 'BATMAN' and 'THE AVENGERS' etc. Also contains details of a model never issued - 498 Mini Countryman	**£15-20**
Mettoy Playcraft (Sales) 1967	1967	**Three-fold Checklist**.......	Leaflet cover shows 'NEW' in 5 languages plus 1142 Holmes Wrecker. Listings include 1967 Monte Carlo Rally winners	**£15-20**
C/2017/7/67	67-68	**48 page Catalogue**...........	Model 262 Lincoln Continental makes up the covers. 'Price 6d'. 2 models shown but not issued : 9022 Daimler 38 with Hood, and 9014 Model 'T' Van 'Lyons Tea' (eventually issued as Corgi Classic C865 in Feb 1986)	**£10-15**
C2017/9/68	1968	**48 page Catalogue**...........	Cover features 268 'Chitty Chitty Bang Bang'. Listings include 803 'Yellow Submarine' and 'Take-off Wheels' issues	**£15-20**

Corgi Toys UK Catalogues

Mettoy Playcraft (Sales) Ltd 1969	1969	**Seven-fold Checklist**	Leaflet has 'Concorde' model on cover plus 302 Hillman Hunter. Listings include 'Corgi Comics', 'CHIPPERFIELD' and Scammell Transporter Set No.48	£5-10
The Mettoy Co Ltd 1970	1970	**48 page Catalogue**	Cover depicts 388 Mercedes-Benz C111, first 'WhizzWheels' models listed	£5-10
1970 Mettoy Co Ltd	1971	**Two-fold Checklist**	Leaflet with 6 WhizzWheels models on the cover. The final 'Take-Off Wheels' issues are listed	£5-10
C2017 Petty 7/71/LOI7b	1972	**48 page Catalogue**	Cover shows 1972 Car models. Excellent 'CORGI COMICS' pictures inside	£5-10
C2017 Petty 7/71/LOI7B (2nd)	1972	**48 page Catalogue**	Cars across both covers	£5-10
1973 Mettoy Co Ltd	1973	**40 page Catalogue**	F1 Racing Cars featured on the cover. Good Racing/Rally pictures within	£5-10
1974 Mettoy Co Ltd	1974	**40 page Catalogue**	'John Player' Lotus on cover, good Military and Aircraft pictures	£5-10
1975 Mettoy Co Ltd	1975	**Three-fold leaflet**	Helicopters, Noddy's Car, etc on the cover. Numbers given 'C' prefix	£5-10
1976 Mettoy Co Ltd	1976	**Three-fold leaflet**	First page features 'KOJAK'. Good Roadmaking and Public Services listings	£5-10
C2210	1977	**48 page Catalogue**	Silver Jubilee Coach on cover. Large section listing Corgi 'Juniors'	£5-10
The Mettoy Co Ltd	1978	**48 page Catalogue**	James Bond's Lotus on cover, 'JEAN RICHARD PINDER' models within	£5-10
C2250	1979	**48 page Catalogue**	James Bond's Space Shuttle C649 'MOONRAKER' is featured on the cover, and 'SUPERMAN' and 'THE MUPPETS' are listed inside	£5-10
C2270	1980	**48 page Catalogue**	Rover 3500 'POLICE' C339 and C1001 HCB ANGUS are the cover features. Good listings of Emergency vehicles includes foreign 'POLICE' issues	£5-10
C2285	1981	**32 page Catalogue**	'CORGI' container on cover. Listings feature Film/TV models	£5-10
C2337	1982	**32 page Catalogue**	Cover features 'Gull-wing' Mercedes (C802), 'Corgitronics' within	£5-10
The Mettoy Co PLC	1983	**36 page Catalogue**	Boxed models on cover, new Mercedes and Scania trucks inside	£5-10
no ref	1984	**32 page Catalogue**	'CORGI `84' and boxed models on cover. Large scale '800' series cars listed. This was the last catalogue to display Corgi Dog emblem	£3-5
no ref	1985	**48 page Catalogue**	Cover shows new 'CORGI' trade name logo. The new 'CLASSICS' Commercials range is listed	£3-5

Trade Catalogues

Catalogues for trade purposes have been produced for some years and occasionally are offered for sale to collectors. No information is available on catalogues issued before 1980 but those from the 1980-90 decade tend to be in the £5 to £15 range.

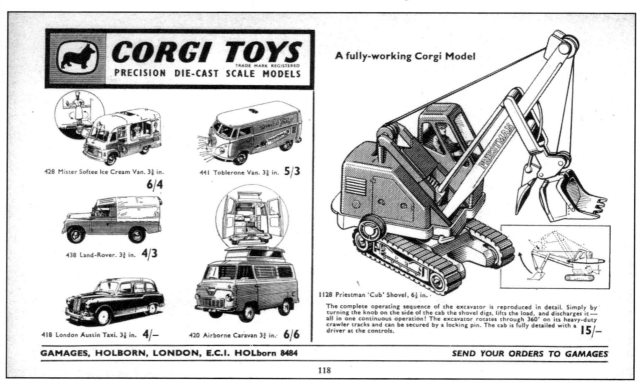

A page from Gamages 1963-64 'Model Book' catalogue

Overseas Editions of Corgi Catalogues, Leaflets and Box Inserts

The overseas editions are comprised of specially amended U.K. editions and there are many versions. They may be identified by:

- All the text being in the relevant language.
- A special reference number (but not always) e.g. 52/258/K5 AUSTRALIA.
- An adapted checklist/pricelist in the language/currency of the country concerned.
- The name of the country either on the cover, on page two, or on the checklist.
- Some complete catalogues were issued with all the text being in the language concerned, e.g. French, German, etc.
- Normally overseas editions, unlike U.K. editions, do not display the catalogue price on the cover. The exception to this rule being those issued with all the text in the language concerned.

Identifying Overseas Catalogues/Leaflets/Box Inserts

As stated in the introduction, the overseas editions are the same as the U.K. editions. Similarly the catalogues, leaflets and box inserts issued in any one particular year were the same for all overseas countries. The only basic differences being the reference numbers, the type of language and currency shown.

The following listing of overseas editions correspond with the country by country listings and will assist collectors identify the various editions. The reference codes shown, e.g. 52/258/K5 are common to all countries with a country reference being added as required, e.g. 52/258/K5 EAST AFRICA. The '258' refers to the month and year of issue, i.e. Feb. 1958.

Types of Catalogues Listed

Box Inserts - These were inserted in the early blue box issues circa 1957-1959. They have a single fold and contain a checklist with prices in the local currency, plus a few pictures of the latest models.

Catalogue Leaflets - These are large, full colour leaflets, usually listing the full range available, together with pictures plus a checklist with prices.

Catalogues - These may contain 16, 20, 32, 40 or 48 pages and are full colour booklets containing the complete current range.

Interim Leaflets - Usually a double folded leaflet issued to supplement the main catalogues. These contain six pages, plus a checklist of the latest issues.

The information contained in these listings has been obtained from Corgi archive material. Whilst many issues have been listed, we believe others exist and we would welcome any such information.

Overseas catalogues were produced in much smaller numbers than were the U.K. editions. Consequently as they seldom appear for sale, it is not possible to give their individual market prices. For guidance purposes however, some have been known to sell for prices in excess of **£100**. As a result the extremely rare issues such as British East Africa, West Africa, Malta, Hong Kong, etc. may be expected to attract a premium. In the circumstances all the editions have been categorised **NGPP**.

Ref.	Date of Issue	Publication	Identification

Leaflets, Box Inserts and Catalogues 1957 - 1982

Ref.	Date of Issue	Publication	Identification
20/657/C2	1957	**Catalogue Leaflet**	Unfolded size (11" x 8 3/4"). Cover shows 1st type blue box for 208 Jaguar.
15/158/C4	1958	**Catalogue Leaflet**	Unfolded size (1' x 11"). 1101 Car Transporter on cover.
10/258/C5	1958	**Catalogue Leaflet**	Unfolded size (1' x 11"). 1101 Car Transporter on cover.
40/258/C5	1958	**Catalogue Leaflet**	Same as previous.
52/258/K5	1958	**Box Insert**	1401 Corgi Service Ramp on cover.
52/258/K6	1958	**Box Insert**	350 'Thunderbird' Guided Missile on cover.
3.350/658/K7	1958	**Box Insert**	1401 Corgi Service Ramp on cover.
5/658/K7	1958	**Box Insert**	458 E.R.F. Truck & 209 Police Car on cover.
10/658/K7	1958	**Box Insert**	Same cover as previous issue.
120/1058/K8	1958	**Box Insert**	Same cover as previous issue.
40/1058/C8	1958	**16 page Catalogue**	Boy with large collection on cover.
---	1959	**20 page Catalogue**	Racing Car and Tractor design on cover.
---	1960	**20 page Catalogue**	Motorway picture on cover.
---	1960/61	**Interim Leaflet**	1119 H.D.L. Hovercraft, etc. on cover.
---	1961	**24 page Catalogue**	Formula 1 Racing Cars on cover.
---	1961/62	**Interim Leaflet**	231 Triumph Herald, etc. on cover.
C/100/62	1962/63	**32 page Catalogue**	Red boy with Corgi dog on cover.
---	1962/63	**Interim Leaflet**	224 Bentley and 304s Mercedes, etc. on cover.
C/100/62	1963/64	**32 page Catalogue**	Red boy with Corgi dog on cover.
---	1962/63	**Interim Leaflet**	224 Bentley & 304s Mercedes, etc. on cover.
---	1963/64	**40 page Catalogue**	Blue boy with Corgi on cover.
---	1964	**Interim Leaflet**	251 Hillman Imp, etc. on cover. 'Playcraft Toys Ltd. 1964' on checklist.
---	1964/65	**40 page Catalogue**	9001 1927 Bentley, etc. on cover. 'Playcraft Toys Ltd. 1964' on rear cover.
---	1965	**Interim Leaflet**	155 Lotus Climax Racing Car, etc. Mettoy playcraft (Sales) Ltd. 1965 on cover.
---	1965/66	**40 page Catalogue**	261 Aston Martin and with or without '1966' and 'Playcraft Toys Ltd. 1965' on cover.
C2017/9/66	1966	**48 page Catalogue**	Batman, Avengers, 007, Man from U.N.C.L.E. on cover.
C2017/7/67	1967/68	**48 page Catalogue**	262 Lincoln continental on cover. 'Mettoy Playcraft (Sales) Ltd. 1967' rear cover.
---	1967	**Interim Leaflet**	1142 'Holmes' Wrecker Recovery Vehicle on cover.
C2017/9/68	1969	**48 page Catalogue**	266 Chitty Chitty Bang Bang on cover.
---	1969	**Catalogue Leaflet**	Unfolded size 2'6" x 83/4" Concorde on cover. 'Mettoy Playcraft (Sales) Ltd. 1969' on rear cover.
---	1970	**48 page Catalogue**	388 Mercedes Benz C111 on cover.
---	1973	**40 page Catalogue**	152 Ferrari 312 B2 Racing Car, etc. on cover.
C2107	1974	**40 page Catalogue**	'Corgi '74' on cover.
C2111	1974	**40 page Catalogue**	'Corgi '74' on cover.
---	1975	**Catalogue Leaflet**	Unfolded. Size 2' x 8½", 'Corgi 75' on cover.
C2211	1977	**48 page Catalogue**	'Corgi 77' on cover.
C2222	1977	**32 page Catalogue**	'Corgi 77' on cover.

C2275	1980/81	**48 page Catalogue**	Fire 'RESCUE' Vehicle plus 1980/81 on cover.
C2282	1980/81	**32 page Catalogue**	Same as previous, but no Juniors included.
C2283	1980/81	**32 page Catalogue**	Same as previous.
C2290	1981/82	**32 page Catalogue**	'Corgi' Container on cover.
C2292	1981/82	**32 page Catalogue**	'Corgi' Container on cover.

African issues
English text - local currency

BRITISH EAST AFRICA

---	1960	**20 page Catalogue**	'British East Africa 9/60' on cover.
---	1962/63	**Interim Leaflet**	'British East Africa' on checklist.
---	1961/62	**Interim Leaflet**	'British East Africa' on top of page two.

EAST AFRICA

52/258/K5 East Africa	Feb. 1958	**Box Insert**	'East Africa' on checklist.
---	1965	**Interim Leaflet**	'East Africa' plus 'Mettoy 1965' on checklist.
---	1964/65	**40 page Catalogue**	'East Africa 8/64' on checklist.

KENYA, UGANDA & TANGANYIKA

| 15/158/C3 KUT | Jan. 1958 | **Catalogue Leaflet** | 'Kenya, Uganda and Tanganyika' on checklist. |
| 3.350/658/K7/KEN.-UG.-TAN | June 1958 | **Box Insert** | 'Ken.-Ug.-Tan' on checklist. |

RHODESIA   Early Distributors: Coombe & Dewar Pty Ltd. P.O. Box 1572, Bulawayo and P.O. Box 663, Salisbury.

---	1961/2	**Interim Leaflet**	'Rhodesia' top of page two.
---	1962/3	**Interim Leaflet**	'Rhodesia' on checklist.
C/100/62	1962	**32 page Catalogue**	'Rhodesia 1/63' on checklist. Red boy on cover.
---	1964	**Interim Leaflet**	'Rhodesia' and 'Playcraft 1964' on checklist.
---	1965	**Interim Leaflet**	'Rhodesia' and 'Mettoy 1965' on checklist.

RHODESIA, ZAMBIA & MALAWI

| --- | 1965/66 | **40 page Catalogue** | 'Rhodesia/Zambia/Malawi 8/65' on checklist, plus '1965' on cover. |

SOUTH AFRICA & RHODESIA

| 52/258/K5 South Africa/Rhodesia | Feb 1958 | **Box Insert** | 'South Africa/Rhodesia' on checklist. |
| 52/258/K6 South Africa/Rhodesia | Feb 1958 | **Box Insert** | 'South Africa/Rhodesia' on checklist. |

SOUTH AFRICA

10/658/K7/S. Africa	June 1958	**Box Insert**	'S. Africa' on checklist page.
40/1058/C8/S. Africa	1958/59	**16 page Catalogue**	'S. Africa' on rear page.
---	1961/62	**Interim Leaflet**	'South Africa on page two.
---	1962/63	**Interim Leaflet**	'South Africa' on checklist.
---	1964	**Interim Leaflet**	'S. Africa' and 'Playcraft Toys Ltd. 1964' on checklist.
---	1965	**Interim Leaflet**	'South Africa' and 'Mettoy 1965' on checklist.
C/2017/9/66	1966	**48 page Catalogue**	'South Africa' on checklist and cover.
---	1967	**Interim Leaflet**	'South Africa' on cover, plus 'Mettoy, etc. 1967' on last page.

NB As listed under CANADA a catalogue was issued in 1970 with a combined CANADA and SOUTH AFRICAN checklist.

Australia
Address of Corgi Club in 1959: The Secretary, Corgi Model Club (Australian Section),
P.O. Box 1607, M. Melbourne C1.

20/657/C2/AUS	June 1957	**Catalogue Leaflet**	Checklist dated 1.6.57. Cover shows early 'Blue Box' with Model 208.
52/258/K5/Australia	1958	**Box Insert**	Cover shows Model 350.
52/258/K6/Australia	1958	**Box Insert**	Cover shows 1401 Corgi Service Ramp.
10/658/K7/Aus	1958	**Box Insert**	Cover shows Models 209 & 458.
---	1959	**16 page Catalogue**	Australia 8/59 on cover.
---	1961/62	**Leaflet**	'Australia' on top of page two.
---	1962/63	**Leaflet**	'Australia' on checklist.
---	1967	**Leaflet**	'Australia' on cover. Page two.

Austria
German Text. "Kontrolliste fur den sammler"

20/657/C2/A	June 1957	**Leaflet**	'Austria' on checklist.
---	1964	**Interim Leaflet**	'Austria' on checklist.
---	1961/62	**Interim Leaflet**	'Austria' on top of page two.
---	1964/65	**40 page Catalogue**	'Austria 9/64' on checklist.
---	1965	**Interim Leaflet**	'Austria' on checklist.

Belgium

Early distribution: Joets Eisenmann, S.A., 111/113 Rui Masui, Bruxelles, Teleph: (02) 15.48.50.

English Text - (French Checklist). "Liste de Contrôlle pour le Collectionneur"

Ref	Year	Type	Description
52/258/K6/Belgium	1958	**Box Insert**	'Belgium' on checklist.
5/658/K7/Belg.	1958	**Box Insert**	'Belg' on checklist.
---	1967	**Leaflet**	'Belgium' on cover.

English Text (Flemish Checklist). "Kontroleer zo de Verzameling"

Ref	Year	Type	Description
C/2017/9/66	1966	**48 page Catalogue**	'Belgium' on cover and on checklist.
---	1967	**Leaflet**	Belgium (Flemish) on cover.

English Text (separate French and Flemish checklists)

Ref	Year	Type	Description
---	1974	**40 page Catalogue**	'C2103 Belgium' on Flemish checklist plus 2107 on French checklist.
C2017/7/67	1967/68	**48 page Catalogue**	'Belgium 8/67' on Flemish checklist and 'Belgium' (French) '8/67' on French checklist.
---	1961/62	**Interim Leaflet**	'Belgium' on top of page two.
---	1962/63	**Interim Leaflet**	'Belgium' on checklist.
---	1963/4	**40 page Catalogue**	'Belgium 8/63' on checklist.
---	1964	**Interim Leaflet**	'Belgium' and 'Playcraft 1964' on checklist.
---	1965	**Interim Leaflet**	'Belgium' and 'Mettoy 1965' on checklist.
---	1967	**Leaflet**	'Belgium' on cover.
C/2017/7/67	1967/68	**48 page Catalogue**	'Belgium (French) 1967' on checklist.

English Text (French/Flemish combined checklist)

Ref	Year	Type	Description
20/657/C2/B	1957	**Catalogue Leaflet**	'Belgium' on checklist.
20/258/C5/B	1958	**Catalogue Leaflet**	'Belgium' on checklist.

French Text - French checklist

Ref	Year	Type	Description
120/1058/K8/Belg	1958	**Box Insert**	No. 458 E.R.F. on cover.
---	1960	**20 page Catalogue**	'Belgium 9/60' and Frs.3. - on cover.
---	1961	**24 page Catalogue**	'Belgium 9/61' and Frs.3. - on cover.
---	1965/66	**40 page Catalogue**	'Belgium 8/65' on checklist.

1958 Belgian Corgi Club: M. Le Secretaire du Club Corgi, Jouets Eisenmann, 20 BD M. Lemonnier, Bruxelles.

Canada

English Text - Local Currency Issues

Ref	Year	Type	Description
40/258/C5/CA	1958	**Catalogue Leaflet**	'Canada' on checklist.
52/258/K5/Canada	1958	**Box Insert**	'Canada' on checklist.
52/258/K6/Canada	1958	**Box Insert**	'Canada' on checklist.
5/658/K7/CAN	1958	**Box Insert**	'CAN' on checklist.
---	1960	**20 page Catalogue**	'Canada 9/60' on cover.
---	1960/61	**Interim Leaflet**	'Canada' on checklist.
---	1961/62	**24 page Catalogue**	'Canada 9/61' on cover.
---	1961/62	**Interim Leaflet**	'Canada' on checklist.
C/100/62	1963	**32 page Catalogue**	'Canada 1/63' on checklist.
---	1964	**Interim Leaflet**	'Canada' and 'Playcraft Toys Ltd. 1964' on checklist.
---	1965	**Interim Leaflet**	'Canada' and 'Mettoy etc. 1965' on checklist.
---	1964/65	**40 page Catalogue**	'Canada 9/64' on checklist plus '1965' on cover.
---	1965/66	**40 page Catalogue**	'Canada 8/65' on checklist plus '1966' on cover.
C2017/9/60	1966	**48 page Catalogue**	'Canada' on cover and checklist.
---	1967	**Interim Leaflet**	'Canada' on cover plus 'Mettoy 1967' on last page.

French Text Issue

Ref	Year	Type	Description
C/2017/9/66	1966	**48 page Catalogue**	'Canadian (French)' on cover.

Combined Canadian and South African checklist

Ref	Year	Type	Description
---	1970	**48 page Catalogue**	'Canada, South Africa' on checklist. 'The Mettoy Co. Ltd. 1970' on rear cover.

Denmark

All the text in Danish language

Ref	Year	Type	Description
---	1960	**20 page Catalogue**	'Denmark 9/60' and '25 re' on cover.
---	1961/62	**24 page Catalogue**	'Denmark 9/61' and '25 re' on cover.
C2214	1977	**48 page Catalogue**	'Katalog' and 'Corgi '77' on cover.

English Text - Danish checklist. 'Samlerers Kontrolliste'

Ref	Year	Type	Description
---	1960/61	**Interim Leaflet**	'Denmark' on checklist.
---	1961/62	**Interim Leaflet**	'Denmark' on page two.
---	1963/64	**40 page Catalogue**	'Denmark 8/63' on checklist plus '1963-64' on cover.
---	1964	**Interim Leaflet**	'Denmark' and 'Playcraft 1964' on checklist.
---	1964/65	**40 page Catalogue**	'Denmark 9/64' on checklist plus 1965 on cover.
---	1965/66	**40 page Catalogue**	'Denmark 8/65' on checklist plus 1966 on cover.
C2017/9/66	1966	**48 page Catalogue**	'Denmark' on cover and checklist.
C2105 1974	1974	**40 page Catalogue**	Danish checklist plus 'Corgi '74' on cover.
C2271	1980/81	**48 page Catalogue**	Danish checklist plus 1980/81 on cover.
C2292	1981/82	**30 page Catalogue**	Danish checklist plus 1981-82 on cover.

Corgi Toys Overseas Catalogues

Eire

52/258/K6/EIRE	1958	**Box Insert**	'Eire' on checklist.
5/658/K7/EIRE	1958	**Box Insert**	'Eire' on checklist.
---	1960/61	**Interim Leaflet**	'Eire' on checklist.
---	1962/63	**Interim Leaflet**	'Eire' on checklist.
---	1964/65	**Interim Leaflet**	'Eire' plus 'Playcraft 1964' on checklist.

Finland

English Text - local currency

---	1963/64	**40 page Catalogue**	'Finland 8/63' on checklist plus '1963-64' on cover.
---	1965	**Interim Leaflet**	'Finland 6/65' and 'Mettoy 1965' on checklist.

France

English Text - French checklist

---	1961/62	**Interim Leaflet**	'France' on page two.
---	1962/63	**Interim Leaflet**	'France' on checklist.
---	1963/64	**40 page Catalogue**	'France 8/63' on checklist plus 1963-64 on cover.
---	1964/65	**Interim Leaflet**	'France' & 'Playcraft 1964' on checklist.
---	1965	**Interim Leaflet**	'France' and 'Mettoy 1965' on checklist.

French Text and checklist   "Liste de Controle pour le Collectioneur".

---	1965	**40 page Catalogue**	'France 8/65' on checklist plus 'Playcraft Toys Ltd. 1965' on rear cover.
C2017/8/67	1968	**48 page Catalogue**	French text - 1968 on cover.
C2017/9/68	1969	**48 page Catalogue**	French text - 1969 on cover.
---	1973	**40 page Catalogue**	French text - 1973 on cover.
C2107 1974	1974	**40 page Catalogue**	French text - 1974 on cover.
---	1975	**Catalogue Leaflet**	French text - 'Corgi '75' on cover.
C2222	1977	**16 page Catalogue**	French text plus 'Corgi '77' on cover.
C2275	1980/81	**48 page Catalogue**	French text plus 1980/81 on cover (includes Juniors).
C2282	1980/81	**32 page Catalogue**	French text plus 1980/81 on cover.
C2290	1981/82	**32 page Catalogue**	French text plus '1981 Mettoy' on rear cover.

Holland / Netherlands

Agent for Holland: N.V.S/O, Herengracht 25, Amsterdam.

Dutch Text throughout

---	1959	**20 page Catalogue**	'Holland 8/59' plus 'FL.O.10' on cover plus Dutch text.
---	1961	**24 page Catalogue**	'Holland 9/61' plus 'F.O.10' on cover plus Dutch text.

French Text - Dutch checklist. "Kontroleer zo de Verzameling".

C2281	1980/81	**48 page Catalogue**	French text, Dutch checklist, plus '1980 Mettoy' on rear cover.
C2291	1981/82	**30 page Catalogue**	French text, Dutch checklist, plus '1981 Mettoy' on rear cover.

English Text with French and Dutch checklists

---	1974	**40 page Catalogue**	'C2107 1974' on French checklist. 'C2103 1974' on Dutch checklist.

English text - Dutch checklist

20/657C2/NL	1957	**Catalogue Leaflet**	'Holland' on checklist.
15/158/C4/H	1958	**Catalogue Leaflet**	'Holland' on checklist.
52/258/K5/HOLLAND	1958	**Box Insert**	'Holland' on checklist.
52/258/K6/HOLLAND	1958	**Box Insert**	'Holland' on checklist.
5/658/K7/HOL	1958	**Box Insert**	'HOL' on checklist.
---	1960/61	**Interim Leaflet**	'Holland' on checklist.
---	1961/62	**Interim Leaflet**	'Holland' top of page two.
---	1962/63	**Interim Leaflet**	'Holland' on checklist.
---	1963/64	**40 page Catalogue**	'Holland 8/63' on checklist.
---	1964	**Interim Leaflet**	'Holland' on checklist.
---	1964/65	**40 page Catalogue**	'Holland 9/64' on checklist.
---	1965	**Interim Leaflet**	'Holland' on checklist
C2017/9/66	1966	**48 page Catalogue**	'Holland' on cover and checklist.
---	1967	**Interim Leaflet**	'Holland' on cover.
C2017/7/67	1967/68	**48 page Catalogue**	'Holland 8/67' on checklist.
C2017/9/68	1969	**48 page Catalogue**	'Holland 10/68' on checklist
C2211 1974	1974	**40 page Catalogue**	Dutch text in checklist.
---	1974	**40 page Catalogue**	C2107 on French checklist plus C2103 on Dutch checklist.

Hong Kong

---	1961	**24 pages**	'Hong Kong 9/61' on cover.
---	1961/62	**Interim Leaflet**	'Hong Kong' on page two.
C/100/62	1963	**24 pages**	'Hong Kong 3/63' on checklist.
---	1963	**Interim Leaflet**	'Hong Kong' on checklist.
---	1964	**Interim Leaflet**	'Hong Kong' on checklist
---	1965/66	**40 pages**	'Hong Kong 8/65' on checklist.
C2017/9/66	1966	**48 pages**	'Hong Kong' on cover and checklist.

Italy

1963 Concessionairia per l'Italia: Ditta "Guimar" via Disciplini 7, Milano (303).
'Distinta di Controllo per l'Collezzionisti".

Ref	Year	Type	Note
52/258/K5 ITALY	1958	**Box Insert**	'Italy' on checklist.
52/258/K6 ITALY	1958	**Box Insert**	'Italy' on checklist.
5/658/K7 ITALY	1958	**Box Insert**	'Italy' on checklist.
---	1959	**20 pages**	'Italy 8/59' on cover.
---	1960/61	**Interim Leaflet**	'Italy' on checklist.
---	1961	**24 pages**	'Italy 9/61' on cover.
---	1961/62	**Interim Leaflet**	'Italy' on page two.
---	1962/63	**Interim Leaflet**	'Italy' on checklist.
---	1963/64	**40 pages**	'Italy 8/63' on checklist.
---	1964	**Interim Leaflet**	'Italy' on checklist.
---	1964/65	**40 pages**	'Italy 9/64' on checklist.
---	1965	**Interim Leaflet**	'Italy' on checklist.
---	1967	**Interim Leaflet**	'Italy' on cover. 'ATTENDETE OGNIMESE LE NOVITA 'CORGI'

1974 concessionaria per l'Italia: Toyuro s.n.c., Via S. Vittore 45, Milano (20123).

Ref	Year	Type	Note
C2112 1974	1974	**40 pages**	'Italia' reference on checklist.
C2278	1980/81	**48 pages**	Italian text throughout.
C2293	1981/82	**32 pages**	Italian text throughout.

Japan

Ref	Year	Type	Note
---	1973	**40 pages**	Japanese text throughout.

Malta

Ref	Year	Type	Note
---	1964	**Leaflet**	'Malta' on checklist.
---	1964/65	**40 pages**	'Malta 8/64' on checklist.
---	1965	**Leaflet**	'Malta' in checklist.

New Zealand

Ref	Year	Type	Note
---	1964/65	**40 pages**	'New Zealand 8/64' on checklist.
---	1965	**Leaflet**	'New Zealand' on checklist.
---	1965/66	**40 pages**	'New Zealand 8/65' on checklist.

Sweden

'Kontrollista för Samlaren'.

English text - Swedish checklist

Ref	Year	Type	Note
52/258/K5/SWEDEN	1958	**Box Insert**	'Sweden' on checklist.
52/258/K6/SWEDEN	1958	**Box Insert**	'Sweden' on checklist.
5/658/K7/SWEDEN	1958	**Box Insert**	'Sweden' on checklist.
---	1959	**16 pages**	'Sweden 8/59' on cover.
---	1960/61	**Leaflet**	'Sweden' on checklist.
---	1961	**24 pages**	'Sweden 9/61' on cover.
---	1961/62	**Leaflet**	'Sweden' on page two.
---	1962/63	**Leaflet**	'Sweden' on checklist.
---	1963/64	**40 pages**	'Sweden 8/63' on checklist.
---	1964/65	**40 pages**	'Sweden 9/64' on checklist.
---	1965	**Leaflet**	'Sweden' on checklist.
---	1966	**40 pages**	'Sweden 6/65' on checklist.
C2017/9/66	1966	**40 pages**	'Sweden' on cover and checklist.
---	1967	**Leaflet**	'Sweden' on cover.
C2106 1974	1974	**40 pages**	Swedish text on checklist.
---	1975	**Leaflet**	Swedish text throughout.
C2277	1980/81	**48 pages**	Swedish text throughout.

Swedish text - Norwegian checklist

Ref	Year	Type	Note
C2287	1981/82	**32 pages**	Swedish text with Norwegian checklist.

Switzerland

English Text - English/Swiss checklist

Ref	Year	Type	Note
20/657/C2/CH	1957	**Catalogue Leaflet**	'Switzerland' on checklist.
52/258/K5/Switzerland	1958	**Box Insert**	Reference on checklist.
52/258/K6/Switzerland	1958	**Box Insert**	Reference on checklist.
5/658/K7/SWITZ	1958	**Box Insert**	Reference on checklist.
25/1058/C8/SWITZ	1958	**16 pages**	'Switz' on checklist. New issues in French.
5/658/C5/CH	1958	**Catalogue Leaflet**	'Switzerland' on checklist.
---	1960/61	**Leaflet**	'Switzerland' on checklist.
---	1961	**24 pages**	'Switzerland 9/61' on cover.
---	1961/62	**Leaflet**	'Switzerland' on page two.
C100/62	1962/63	**32 pages**	'Switzerland 1/63' on checklist.
---	1962/63	**Leaflet**	'Switzerland' on checklist.
---	1964	**Leaflet**	'Switzerland' on checklist.
---	1964/65	**40 pages**	'Switzerland?' on checklist.
---	1965	**Leaflet**	'Switzerland' on checklist.
---	1966	**40 pages**	'Switzerland 8/65' on checklist.
C/2017/9/66	1966	**48 pages**	'Switzerland' on cover and checklist.
---	1967	**Leaflet**	'Switzerland' on cover.
C2017/9/68	1969	**48 pages**	'Switzerland 10/68' on checklist.

Corgi Toys Overseas Catalogues

Norway

'Se dem alle 1 den nye Katalogen, Samlers Liste'

English Text - Norwegian checklist

---	1961/62	**Leaflet**	'Norway' on page two.
---	1962/63	**Leaflet**	'Norway' on checklist.
---	1964	**Leaflet**	'Norway' on checklist.
---	1964/65	**40 pages**	'Norway 9/64' on checklist.
---	1965	**Leaflet**	'Norway' on checklist.
---	1966	**40 pages**	'Norway 8/65' on checklist.
C2017/9/66	1966	**48 pages**	'Norway' on cover and checklist.
C2017/7/67	1967/68	**48 pages**	'Norway 8/67' on checklist.
---	1970	**48 pages**	'Norway' on checklist.
C2113	1974	**40 pages**	Norwegian checklist.
C2272	1980/81	**48 pages**	Norwegian checklist.

Norwegian text throughout

---	1975	**Catalogue Leaflet**	Text plus '1975 Mettoy'.

Portugal

'Lista de controle para o colecionador'

English Text - Portuguese checklist.

25/257/C2/P	1957	**Catalogue Leaflet**	'Portugal' on checklist.
---	1960	**Leaflet**	'Portugal' on checklist.
---	1961/62	**Leaflet**	'Portugal' on page two.
---	1962/63	**Leaflet**	'Portugal' on checklist.
---	1963/64	**40 pages**	'Portugal 8/63' on checklist.
---	1964	**Leaflet**	'Portugal' on checklist.
C2017/7/67	1967/68	**48 pages**	'Portugal 8/67' on checklist.

Singapore and Malaya

52/258/K5 SINGAPORE/MALAYA	1958	**Box Insert**	'Singapore/Malaya' on checklist.
10/258/C5/SM	1958	**Catalogue Leaflet**	'Singapore/Malaya' on checklist.
3.350/658/K7 SING.-MAL	1958	**Box Insert**	'Sing.-Mal' on checklist.
---	1960	**20 pages**	'Singapore Malaya 9/60' on cover.
---	1960	**Leaflet**	'Singapore/Malaya' on checklist.
---	1961	**24 pages**	'Singapore/Malaya 9/61' on checklist.
---	1962/63	**Leaflet**	'Singapore/Malaya' on checklist.
C/100/62	1962/63	**32 pages**	'Singapore/Malaya 2/63' on checklist
---	1965	**Leaflet**	'Singapore/Malaya' on checklist.

Spain

"Lista de Coleccionistas"

Spanish Text and checklist

---	1961	**24 pages**	'Spanish 9/61' on cover.

English Text - Spanish checklist "Lista de Precios para Coleccionistas"

C/100/62	1962	**Checklist**	'Spanish' on checklist.
C2273	1980/81	**Checklist**	Spanish text in checklist.

United States of America

1958 Sole Distributor for U.S.A.: Reeves International Incorp., 1107 Broadway, New York 10, N.Y.

20/458/C5/U.S.A.	1958	**Catalogue Leaflet**	'U.S.A.' on checklist.
20/658/K7/U.S.A.	1958	**Box Insert**	'U.S.A.' on checklist.
---	1961	**24 pages**	'U.S.A. 9/61' on cover.
---	1961/62	**Leaflet**	'U.S.A.' on page two.
---	1962/63	**Leaflet**	'U.S.A.' on checklist.
---	1965/66	**40 pages**	'U.S.A. 8/65' on checklist.
---	1967	**Leaflet**	'U.S.A.' on cover.

International Issues 1981 - 1985

The catalogue listings are printed in English, French and German. Catalogue C2293 was issued as a miniature booklet.

1965 Corgi Club addresses

Canada: Kleinberg Agencies 1085 St. Alexander St., Montreal'Can, Quebec, Canada.
South Africa: PO Box 6024, Johannesburg,
U..S.A.: 1107 Broadway, New York 10, N.Y.

Shop display and 'point-of-sale' items

Ref.	Year(s)	Item	Details	Market Price Range
no ref	1957-59	**Display stand, wooden**	Ten cream 'corrugated' hardboard shelves, pale blue display background with yellow/blue plastic 'CORGI TOYS' sign screwed to top of display, (30 x 29 x 12 inches)	£200-300
no ref	1957-59	**Display card/sign**	Tin/cardboard, yellow/blue with gold 'dog' logo, 'Wow! Corgi Toys - The Ones With Windows'	£50-60
no ref	1957-59	**Display card/sign**	As previous item but with 'new Corgi Major Toys - The Ones With Windows'	£50-60
no ref	1957-59	**Counter display unit**	Two shelf stand with Blue backing logo 'CORGI TOYS', 'THE ONES WITH WINDOWS', 'MODEL PERFECTION' and 'NEW' plus the early gold Corgi dog on red background	£300-400
no ref	1957-59	**Counter display unit**	Cardboard, single model display card, 'new - CORGI TOYS' logo	£50-60
no ref	1957-59	**Counter display unit**	Cardboard, 2 tier unit with 'new - CORGI MAJOR TOYS' yellow/blue design	£200-300
no ref	1957-59	**Counter display unit**	Cardboard, 2 tier unit, 'COLLECT CORGI TOYS' and 'new MODELS EVERY MONTH' logos in yellow/blue design	£200-300
no ref	1957-59	**Counter display unit**	Cardboard, Renault Floride (222) pictorial display card with '1959 MOTOR SHOW' and 'EARLS COURT' logos	£75-100
no ref	1957-59	**Counter display unit**	Cardboard, Citroen (475) pictorial display card with 'new - THE CITROEN' and 'OLYMPIC WINTER SPORTS' logos	£75-100
no ref	1957-67	**Metal display stand**	Tiered stand 75cm x 3 cm x 45cm high, three 'CORGI TOYS' and Black logos, plus three early gold Corgi dog emblems	£175-200
no ref	1960-61	**Window sticker**	'new MODELS EVERY MONTH'	£15-20
no ref	1966-69	**Window sticker**	Window bills advertising new releases	£15-20
no ref	1960-69	**Oblong window sign**	Glass or plastic with 'CORGI TOYS' and 'PRECISION DIE-CAST SCALE MODELS' logos plus gold Corgi 'dog' logo in blue/yellow/red design	£100-125
no ref	1960s	**Tinplate stand**	5 Grey tiers topped by 'CORGI TOYS'/Gold dog header	£200-300
no ref.	1960-69	**Glass display sign**	Square sign, gold corgi dog on Red panel within Blue lined glass surround	£75-100
no ref	1961	**Corgi Dog**	Moulded dog standing on hind feet holding a 'CORGI CHRISTMAS CARD'	£200-300
no ref	1968-83	**Metal display stand**	Tiered stand 75 cm x 3.5 cm c 45 cm high, with three 'CORGI TOYS' Black/Yellow logos, plus three White/Red late Corgi dog emblems	£145-175
no ref	1971-73	**Oblong sign**	Plastic, with 'CORGI' and 'TESTED BY THE CORGI TECHNOCRATS' logos plus white Corgi 'dog' logo on red square, yellow background plus 3 'Technocrats' faces	£50-75
C2001/2	1963-65	**Display stand, rotary**	For self-selection, 7 tray unit, large 'CORGI TOYS' header sign	£200-300
C2003	1963-65	**Display stand, rotary**	Self-selection, 4 columns, 4 compartments (45 x 30 in.), large 'CORGI TOYS' header boards	£200-300
C2004	1963-65	**Display stand, rotary**	Self-selection, 4 column, 72 compartments (72 x 30 in.)	£200-300
C2005	1963-65	**Display stand, rotary**	Self-selection, 2 column, 36 compartments (72 x 30 in.)	£150-200
C2006	1963-65	**Display stand, rotary**	Self-selection, 2 column, 36 compartments (55 x 30 in.)	£100-150
C2007	1963-65	**Display stand, plastic**	Large moulded plastic counter display to house up to 50 models, large black header display board with 'NATURALLY CORGI TOYS' on yellow/blue background, and 'JOIN THE CORGI MODEL CLUB' on display front	£200-300
C2008	1960s	**Display stand, revolving**	Glass fronted large electric display to house 100-120 models with light and dark simulated wood panels with four 'CORGI' logos, (38 x 24 x 24 in.)	£400-600
C2009	1957-66	**Showcase, glass**	Three glass shelves, three 'CORGI TOYS' logos (black/blue) plus gold Corgi 'dog' logo on red background, (20 x 15 x 9 in.)	£200-300
E9051	1970s	**Corgi Juniors unit**	Yellow plastic (21.75 x 21.75 in.), displays 48 models, logo 'LOOK FOR WHIZZWHEELS MODELS'	£100-150
---	1975	**Army diorama**	Plastic unit for dispalying tank models	£140-160
---	1976	**Kojak's Buick**	Card counter-diplay unit	£80-90

NB The Editor would welcome any further information on Corgi display material.

Acknowledgements

The Editor would like to express appreciation to the following collectors, traders and manufacturers, who very kindly took the time and trouble to provide information about new entries and colour variations.

Chris Brierley, The Corgi Heritage Centre, 53 York Street, Heywood, Rochdale, Lancs., OL10 4NR
Susan Pownall, Corgi Collectors Club (see back cover advertisement)
Adrienne Fuller, Corgi Classics Ltd., Leicester
Gerry Savage, Collectors Gazette and Diecast Collector Magazine
George Hatt, Trowbridge, Wiltshire
Dick Henrywood, Dreweatt Neate Auctioneers, Donnington, Berkshire
Brian Goodall and David Nathan, Vectis Auctions Ltd, Stockton-on-Tees
Hugo Marsh and Nigel Mynheer of Christie's Model Auctions
George Beevis of Lacy Scott & Knight Model Auctions
Paul Campbell of Sotheby's Model Auctions

Glen Butler of Wallis & Wallis Auctioneers
Barry Potter of Barry Potter Auctions
Kevin Sweeney, Ballarat, West Victoria, Australia
Keith Harbour, Middlesex
C.J.T. Sawday, Leicester
John C. Robertson, Whiteness, Shetland, Scotland
Joyce Peterzell, Los Angeles, California, USA
Mr R.J. Scott, Newcastle Upon Tyne
Michele Lomolino, Palermo, Italy
Simon Cole, Dartford, Kent
Mike Ennis, Toyman Fairs
Norm Porter of British Columbia, Canada
Mark Jones, Halesworth, Suffolk
John Baker of Swanley
Yves Reynaert, Brussels, Belgium

Corgi Toys Numerical Index

Refer first to the Contents List (page 3) for quick guidance to main sections. Sets, for example, are not listed here since that section is easily found and items in it are listed numerically. Corgi Classics are not included in this index (see the 'Modern Diecasts' section of the book).

A quick check through this general (alphabetical) list may also prove helpful.

Collectors notes

Corgi Toys Auction Results

Wallis and Wallis

West Street Auction Galleries, Lewes, Sussex

Condition grading used in Wallis and Wallis catalogue:
Mint - Virtually original state
VGC - Very Good Condition, a fine item
GC - Good Condition, a sound item
QGC - Quite good condition, some wear and/or damage

1998-1999 RESULTS

Gift Set 17 Land Rover with Ferrari racing car on trailer, vehicles in red, trailer in yellow. Complete boxed, with insert. Vehicles VGC minor wear.**£170**
Scarce James Bond Aston Martin DB5 (270) in metallic silver, 1st type with spoked wheels and rear tyre slashers. In original display box with paperwork and men **£380**
Volkswagen 1200, East African Safari (256). In original display box **£170**
Gift Set 40 The Avengers, comprising 4.5 litre Bentley in red...................**£390**
Scarce James Bond Toyota 2000 GT (336). VGC to Mint **£200**
Batmobile (267) 1st type, in black, with Batwheels. Boxed with insert and packing ring. Mint...**£310**
Corgi Major Ford Tilt Cab H Series, with detachable trailer (1137) in metallic blue and red with aluminium sliding doors, Express Service to sides. In original box, with display insert figure, minor wear, vehicle Mint **£100**
Commer Milk Float (466), in white and light blue Co-Op livery, boxed, minor wear, van VGC minor chips...**£80**
Monte Carlo (1966) Hillman Imp (328). Boxed. Vehicle Mint **£70**
Monte Carlo BMC Mini Cooper S (321) in red with white roof, RN52, AJB 44B numberplates. Boxed. Mint **£115**
BMC Mini Countryman Surfing, (485). Boxed. Vehicle VGC to Mint.....**£95**
Chevrolet Impala Kennel Service Wagon (486) complete with all 4 dogs. Boxed. Mint..**£80**
Citroen Safari Corgi Ski Club (475) in white. Boxed. Mint.....................**£95**
Volkswagen European police car (492) in dark green and white, Polizei livery, boxed, with small packing ring. Mint..**£90**
Commer Van with Samuelson Film Services. Boxed. Mint......................**£90**
A Rare Corgi Musical Walls Ice Cream Van on Ford Thames (474). Boxed. Mint..**£160**
A scarce Corgi Gift Set 37 Lotus Racing Team. In original display box. VGC Mint **£310**
A rare original 1960s rubber toy in the form of **the Corgi dog,** sitting up on its hind legs holding a reproduction card "A Merry Christmas from Corgi Toys" **£190**
Rare Corgi Batmobile (267) rare 1970s example in black with red plastic 'tyres'. Minor wear. Vehicle Mint..**£280**
Monte Carlo Autographed BMC Mini Cooper S (321), red with white roof, RN", autographs to roof, boxed, minor wear. Vehicle minor chipping........**£240**
A rare "10 Millionth Corgi Land Rover" in white with red interior, based on the current issue Land Rover **£100**
An original 1960s Chitty Chitty Bang Bang (266). Vehicle Mint...........**£210**
Black Beauty Green Hornet Crime Fighting Car (268). Boxed, with display insert. Vehicle Mint..**£360**
Corgi Major 1139 Chipperfields Menagerie. Mint. Boxed.....................**£180**

Vectis Auctions Ltd.

Royal National Hotel, Bedford Way, Russell Square, London

Grading system used by Vectis Auctions:
A+   As near mint or pristine condition as at time of issue
A   Virtually mint boxed - any faults of a most minor nature
B   Model is near mint - box has slight faults
B   Slight model or box faults - e.g. some chips or box rubs but model and box complete
C   More obvious model chips and box faults inc. tears but still complete
D   Same as C but box has one or more end flaps missing and model may have faded paint as well as chips
E   Model and box have considerable faults

16th DECEMBER 1998

No.201 Austin Cambridge - Light Blue/FSP - B+ in B+ BB with FL; and
No.301 Triumph TR2 - Cream/Red Seats/FSP - B+ in B BB with FL......**£140**
No.216M Austin A40 - Red/Black Roof/FSP - B+ in B to B+ BY **£170**
No.1110 Bedford S-Type Tanker "Mobilgas" - Red/FSP - lovely B+ to A (minor box rubs only) in B+ "lift-off lid" BY with card packing **£105**

No.1137 Ford Articulated Truck & Trailer "Express Service" - Figure/SP - superb A to A+ in B to B+ BY - inner pictorial stand is A to A+ with card packing **£120**
No.1140 Bedford TK Tanker "Mobilgas" - B+ in B "end flap" BY with card packing **£105**
No.1141 Bedford TK Milk Tanker - B+ to A in very good B to C BY with card packing **£180**
No.468 Routemaster Bus "Church's Shoes" - Red/Driver & Clippie/SP - B+ to A in B+ to A BY **£180**
No.54 Fordson Power Major Half Track Tractor - Blue/Orange Hubs/Grey Rear Tracks - superb A+ in A BY with card packing **£150**
GS11 ERF Dropside Lorry & Platform Trailer with Load - Yellow/Met Blue/FSP - A to A+ (loads are only B+) in C BY - inner card stand is B to B+ **£240**
GS11 London Gift Set - A to A+ in very good C STB (some minor tears) - inner polystyrene tray is A+ **£90**
GS27 Bedford TK Machinery Carrier & Priestman Excavator - Machinery Carrier is A - Excavator is B+ in B+ BY (graffitti to one end) - polystyrene tray is B+ **£140**
GS41 Car Transporter Gift Set - containing (1) Ford H Series Car Transporter - A (some minor paint chips caused during assembly); (2) Ford Cortina Estate - Met Graphite Grey/CW - A+; (3) Hillman Imp - Met Bronze/White Int & Stripe/Jewelled Headlights/SP - B+ (rear suspension collapsed); (4) Rover 2000 - Maroon/Cream Int/SP - A; (5) Mini Cooper Wicker Work - Black/Red Roof/Lemon Int/CW - A to A+; (6) Mini Cooper '1966 MCR' - Red/White Roof Signatures/Red Int/2/SP - B to B+; and (7) Morris Mini Minor - Light Blue/Red Int/CW - A+ - in B+ box - polystyrene tray is C complete with instructions and 16 cones - very rare set produced for mail order through Kays catalogue and containing rare variations on some of the cars **£400**

No. 333 Mini Cooper "1966 RAC/Sun International Rally" - Red/White Roof/21/Red Int/SP - B in B BY for No.225 Austin 17 with "RAC International Rally" box flash...**£160**
No.246 Chrysler Imperial - Met Kingfisher Blue/figures/Pale Blue Int/golf trolley/CW - good B+ to A unboxed (slight discolouration to front seats) .**£180**
No.321 Mini Cooper "1966 MCR" - good B to B+ - unboxed...............**£105**
Group of Four Corgi Rockets - all A+ in A blister packs (apart from each header card has 5 overlapping card holepunch holes to top area of card) - No.910 Beach Buggy; No.916 Alfa Carabo; No.921 Morgan; and No.904 Porsche Carrrera...**£130**

10th MARCH 1999

C271/1 Aston Martin DB5 "Modelauto" - 1990 Promotional for Classic Car Museum in Holland - A to A+ in B+ to A WB...**£200**
No.96445 Aston Martin DB5 "30th Anniversary of Goldfinger" - A complete with Certificate No. 0007 of only 7,500 produced - in B+ P WB - desirable with this certificate number **£270**
GS22 James Bond 007 Gift Set - contents B+ to A - in B to B SWB......**£275**
Corgi Junior No.3082 James Bond 007 Gift Set - contents are A to A+ in B to C WB - "Jaws" Van with Silver paper label instead of the usual clear plastic label **£210**
No.3030 James Bond "Spy Who Loved Me" Gift Set - superb A+ in A WB - inner card tray and protective bubble are A+ **£220**
Corgi Junior No.3021 Crime Fighters Gift Set - contents A to A+ **£300**
Corgi Rockets No.923 James Bond Ford Escort - A+ in B+ blister pack - rare and desirable **£600**
No.925 James Bond Ford Capri - A+ in B+ blister pack - rare and desirable **£78**
Corgi Junior E3019 Octopussy Gift Set - A+ in A+ blister pack............**£110**
No.336 James Bond Toyota 2000GT - A in A WB **£160**
No.391 James Bond Ford Mustang Mach 1 - Red/Black bonnet - A in B+ WB complete with "Diamonds are Forever" box flash...............................**£180**
No.267 Batmobile - Black/figures/aerial/Red WW - B+ to A in B WB - rare issue with these red wheels **£420**
No.277 Monkeemobile - B+ in A WB this example is rare detachable pictorial header card **£600**
No.1402 Husky Batmobile with tow hook - factory trade pack of 12 - all A+ in A+ to A+ blister packs..**£1,200**
No.349 Pop Art Morris Mini Minor "Mostest" - Orange-Red/Lemon Int/CW - A - in correct good B BY **£1,400**

7th APRIL 1999

Large Perspex Fronted Wooden Electrically Operated **Shop Window Display Unit** plus 10 common models - condition B - condition of display unit is B+ **£700**

94

Barry Potter Auctions

13 Yew Tree Lane, Spratton, Northampton, NN6 8HL

19th SEPTEMBER 1998
Corgi Toys Shop Display glass Cabinet with sloping front. 50cm high, 38cm wide, 24cm deep, with 3 shelves and 'Corgi Toys' along each shelf, Excellent Plus **£230**
Corgi Toys metal 76cm long **Shelf Display Stand**. Slots on top to display vehicles, 'Corgi Toys' & dog printed 3 times along the front. Colourful, Near Mint **£190**

21st NOVEMBER 1998
Chipperfields Circus - Crane Truck No.1121, Near Mint Boxed. Giraffe Transporter with giraffes No.503, Animal Cage with polar bears No.1123, Both Mint Boxed **£180**
Ecurie Ecosse Gift Set No.16 (car transporter and individually boxed Lotus, BRM and Vanwall racing cars). Excellent Plus Boxed **£140**

Lacy Scott and Knight

10 Risbygate Street, Bury St Edmunds, Suffolk, IP33 3AA

Condition grading used by Lacy Scott and Knight:
B = BOXED; in the manufacturer's original box or container, in
    appropriate condition.
D = DAMAGED; refers to box only.
M = MINT; in perfect or near perfect condition.
NM = NEAR MINT; excellent overall condition
G = GOOD general condition with some chips or scratches of a minor nature.
F = FAIR condition with an average proportion of chips and marks for age.
P = POOR; in only moderate condition, perhaps incomplete.

7th AUGUST 1998 (Corgi Rockets)
933 Holmes Wrecker, unboxed, (M) **£155**
978 James Bond 'OHMSS' Set, models (M), window box (F-G).........**£2,100**
927 Ford Escort Rally, (M), box (F) **£100**
921 Morgan Open Sports, (MB) **£52**
1011 James Bond's Bobsleigh, (MB) **£330**
1012 James Bond SPECTRE Boblseigh, (MB) **£380**

13th FEBRARUY 1999
Car Transporter with 6 cars (48) (BDM-NM, some tyres missing).........**£170**
Chitty Chitty Bang Bang (266) (BDNM) **£95**
ERF Flatbed Eddie Stobart (97940) (BM) **£70**
Ford Thunderbird open sports (2155) (BNM) **£65**
Fiat 2100 (232) (BNM)...**£45**
Ford Consul Classic (234) (cream and pink) (BNM)...............................**£50**
Chevrolet Impala (248) (BNM)...**£45**
Public address vehicle (472) (BM) **£90**
Commer Police van with flashing light (464) (BNM) **£58**
Bentley Continental sports saloon (224) (black & silver) (BNM)............**£65**
Bentley Continental sports saloon (224) (cream & green) (BNM)............**£65**
Mack Truck with trans-continental trailer (1100) (BDM) **£55**
Club racing gift set (3020) (BM) **£140**
Leisure Time gift set (3026) (BM) **£85**
The World of Wooster (9004) (BDM) **£60**
Juniors road construction gift set (3011) (BDM) **£48**
Ecurie Ecosse racing car transporter (1126) (BDNM) **£50**
Commer mobile camera van (479) (BNM) **£55**
Austin Seven (225) (BNM) **£42**
Massey Ferguson 165 tractor (66) (BNM) **£42**

15th MAY 1999
James Bond's Volkswagen 1300 (1010) (BM)......................................**£560**
'Ironside' Police Van (1007) (BM) **£140**
'The Avengers' Gift Set (40) (BDM) **£380**
James Bond DB5 with gold bumpers **£200**
James Bond Aston Martin DB5 with instructions & leaflet (261) (BM)..**£180**
Wings Flying School 2096/8101 (BM) **£110**
Carrimore detachable axle machinery carrier (1131) (BM)....................**£60**
Spindrift power boat racing 2096/8103 (BM) **£100**
Chitty Chitty Bang Bang, 1 figure missing (266) (BDNM) **£130**
Foden G & C Moore Ltd (97955) (BM) **£58**
Foden Flatbed 'Pickfords' (97956) (BM) **£55**
ERF tanker 'Blue Circle' (97930) (BM) **£35**
ERF flatbed 'Eddie Stobart' (97940) (BM) **£65**
Noddy's car (804) (G)...**£50**

Christie's

85 Old Brompton Road, South Kensington, London, SW7 3LD

Descriptions of paintwork as used in Christie's catalogue:
M= Toys apparently never taken out of mint original boxes.
E = Excellent Toys with no or very few apparent paint chips or defects.
G = Good Toys with minor scratches to the paint.
F = Fair Toys with an acceptable amount of paint damage.
P = Poor Toys probably suitable for repainting or restoration.
SD = Some damage.

Where referring to boxes:
E = Excellent original box with very little or no damage, complete with
    all interior fittings.
G = Good box with normal use wear only, but fittings not necessarily complete.
F = Fair box, possibly slightly torn or split, but with label intact.
P = Poor box, likely to be split or torn, and in need of repair.

1998 and 1999 RESULTS
858 Magic Roundabout Playground with 851 Train, figures and accessories, card packing, in original box (E-M, box E) **£600**
Chipperfields Circus, Gift Set 23 Circus Models, 1st issue with Mobile Booking Office 1962 to 1966, with two combination Crane, cord, instructions and Model Club slips in original box with corrugated protective sheet, 1130 Circus Horse Transporter with inner display case and packing pieces and 503 Circus Giraffe Transporter with Giraffes with Model Club slip, in original boxes, (E-M, boxes G)...**£850**
858 Magic Roundabout Playground with train, figures and accessories, in original box and Mr McHenry's Trike 1972-1974 (G, box F) **£240**
A Rare 858 Magic Roundabout Playground with 851 train, figures and accessories in original plastic bag, card packing, in original box (E-M, figures bloomed, seems to eash off, box E)..**£747**
Grey **433 'Vroom and Dreesman' Volkswagen Van** and 443 Plymouth Suburban US Mail, in original boxes (E, boxes G-E)...............................**£345**
28 Carrimore Car Transporter Set, Bedford TK, cream 230, red 222, pale lilac 232, cream 234, original boxes, (G-E, boxes G-E), 222 Set box F-G)**£200**
1st type Bedford Light Vans green 405 Utilicon AFS Tender with concertina catalogue and Model Club slip, 405M Utilicon Fire Tender, light blue 404M Dormobile Personnel Carrier, cream 412 Utilicon Ambulance and 408 AA Road Service Van, in original boxes, (E, boxes G) **£340**
GS 38 Monte-Carlo Rally comprising BMC Mini-Cooper-S, Rover 2000 and Citroen DS19, in original box, packing card (E, box G)............................**£437**

Lloyd Ralston Toys

109 Glover Avenue, Norwalk, CT06850, USA

Condition Grading: C1Poor to C10 Mint
Boxed '3D' effect **Shop Display** (1970s), C8-9...................................**$950**
Set 23 (2nd issue), C9..**$1,900**
268 Green Hornet, boxed, C7-8 ....**$150**
267 Batmobile, red WhizzWheels, boxed, C9.......................................**$525**
270 James Bond Aston-Martin, boxed, C8-9 ....**$140**
1139 Menagerie Truck, boxed, C8-9 ....**$400**
2 x Gift Sets 19, both boxed, C9...**$325**
Revolving 1960s **Shop Display**, C8-9 ....**$750**

Dreweatt Neate Auctions

Donnington Priory, Donnington, Newbury, Berkshire, RG14 2JE

10th FEBRUARY 1999
853 Magic Roundabout Playground, near mint condition, box excellent **£350**
A Corgi Brass Prototype Car c.1969, made for an unreleased model of the DAF city car...**£20**

22nd APRIL 1999
267. Rocket Firing Batmobile with gloss black body, instruction and seven spare rockets, in pictorial card box with diorama; very good condition......**£180**
339. Monte Carlo 1967 Mini Cooper S, good condition, unboxed............**£85**
497. The Man from Uncle Thrushbuster in metallic purple, mint condition complete with Waverley ring, box excellent with all inner packaging **£140**
Chevrolet Cars. 229 Chevrolet Corvair with blue body, near mint boxed and 480 Chevrolet Impala Taxi Cab, very good condition, box good **£50**

Crescent Toys

The Crescent Toy Company was founded in July 1922 by Henry G. Eagles and Arthur A. Schneider in a workshop 30 feet square at the rear of a private house at 67 De Beauvoir Crescent, Kingsland Road, London N1.

They manufactured model soldiers, cowboys, kitchen sets, etc. from lead alloy. These were hollow castings, hand painted, packed one dozen to a box, and sold to wholesalers at six shillings per dozen boxes. The small firm prospered and eventually opened up a factory in Tottenham. With the second World War came a ban on metal toys and production was changed to munitions. After the War the firm resumed making metal hollow-cast toys and in addition marketed the diecast products of a firm called DCMT (Die Casting Machine Tools Ltd).

As a consequence early post-war models had 'DCMT' cast into the underside of the body. In 1948 the firm opened a modern factory on a four-acre site at Cymcarn, a Welsh mining village near Newport, Monmouth (now Gwent) and two years later transferred all production there, maintaining only an office in London. From this time Crescent toys made their own diecast products without 'DCMT' on them. Hence it is possible to find the same models with or without 'DCMT' cast in. Die Casting Machine Tools went their own way and from 1950 produced models under the name of 'Lone Star'.

Crescent Toys will be best remembered for their excellent ranges of military models and farm equipment but probably most of all for their superb reproductions of the racing cars of the 1950s.

The following post-war model listings have been extracted from a unique collection of original trade catalogues (1947-80) most kindly provided by Mr. J. D. Schneider, the former Managing Director of Crescent Toys Ltd. All of the original research and actual compiling of the lists was undertaken by Ray Strutt.

The Editor would also like to thank Les Perry of Rochdale for additional information.

Ref.	Year(s)	Model	Market Price Range

EARLY POST-WAR MODELS (various colours)

Ref.	Year(s)	Model	Market Price Range
223	1948	**Racing Car**	£25-35
422	1949	**Sports Car**	£30-40
423	1949	**Oil Lorry**	£30-40
424	1949	**Truck Lorry**	£30-40
425	1949	**Saloon Car**	£30-40
800	1947-49	**Jaguar**	£35-45
802	1947-49	**Locomotive**	£25-35
803	1947-48	**Locomotive**, Silver	£25-35
804	1948-49	**Police Car**, Black	£35-45
1221	1949	**Fire Engine**, Red body	£40-50
-		**Garages**, retailing at 1/-, 1/6, 2/6 and 4/-. Complete with Modern Pumps, Motor Cars and Garage Attendants, 'CRESCENT GARAGES' logo	NGPP
FC 330		**Domestic Iron and Stand**	£10-15

FARM EQUIPMENT (various colours)

Ref.	Year(s)	Model	Market Price Range
1802	1949-60	**Tractor and Hayrake**	£65-75
1803	1967-74	**Dexta Tractor and Trailer**	£45-55
1804	1950-59	**Tractor and Disc Harrow**	£55-65
1805	1950-61	**Tractor**	£55-65
1806	1950-60	**Hayrake**	£5-10
1807	1950	**Disc Harrow**	£5-10
1808	1950-56	**Platform Trailer**	£5-10
1809	1950-56	**Ricklift Trailer**	£5-10
1809	1962-80	**Dexta Tractor**	£25-35
1810	1950-80	**Box Trailer / Farm Trailer**, (No.148 1968-74)	£15-20
1811	1950-67	**Animal Trailer / Cattle Trailer**, (No.148 1968-71)	£10-15
1811	1975-81	**Dexta Tractor and Trailer**	£15-20
1813	1950	**Timber Wagon** (Horse Drawn)	£75-95
1814	1950-60	**Plough Trailer**, (No.150 1968-71)	£10-15
1815	1950	**Hayloader**	£10-15
1816	1950	**Roller Harrow**	£5-10
1817	1950-56	**Timber Trailer**	£10-15
1818	1954-60	**Tipping Farm Wagon**	£10-15
1819	1954-55	**Large Farm Wagon**	£25-35

DIECAST ACTION TOYS (various colours)

Ref.	Year(s)	Model	Market Price Range
1222	1954-59	**Builders & Decorators Truck** (red handcart), unpainted ladder and bucket, beige builder figure on green base	NGPP
1268	1954-59	**Mobile Space Rocket**	NGPP
1269	1954-59	**Mobile Crane**	£30-40
1272	1954-59	**Scammell Scarab and Box Trailer**	£70-80
1274	1954-59	**Scammell Scarab and Low Loader**	£70-80
1276	1955-59	**Scammell Scarab and Oil Tanker**	£70-80
2700	1956-60	**Western Stage Coach**	£70-80
2705	1955	**Western Stage Coach**	NGPP
-		**Scammell Scarab Set**, Mechanical Horse, Box Trailer and Low Loader	NGPP

MILITARY MODELS (All in military colours)

Ref.	Year(s)	Model	Market Price Range
155	1960-68	**'Long Tom' Artillery Gun**	£15-20
235	1946	**Cannon**, operable	NGPP
F 355	1938	**Tank and Cannon Set**	NGPP
650	1954-59	**Military Set**: two 696 British Tanks, 698 Scout Car, one 699 Russian Tank	NGPP
NN656/2	1938-40	**Field Gun and Gunner**	NGPP
NN692	1938-40	**Deep Sea Diver**, with equipment	NGPP
NN693	1938-40	**A.R.P. Searchlight Unit**, 3 personnel, boxed	£60-80
NN694	1938-40	**A.R.P. Rangefinder Unit**, 2 personnel, boxed	£60-80
695	1938-40	**A.R.P. First Aid Post**: a tent, two stretcher bearers and patient, Red Cross nurse	£100-125
F 695	1946	**Howitzer**, unpainted, with spring and plunger, 'CRESCENT' cast-in	£10-12
696	1954-59	**British Tank**	£30-40
698	1954-56	**Scout Car**	£20-30
699	1954-56	**Russian Tank**	£30-40
NN700	1938-40	**Royal Engineers Field Set**: Engineers (2 standing, 2 kneeling), telegraph pole, transmitter, aerial	£100-125
701	-	**GPO Telephone Engineers Set**: 4 men, telegraph pole, hut, cart, accessories, boxed	£120-150
702	-	**Sound Locator Unit**, operator figure, boxed	£60-80
K 703	1938-40	**Field Wireless Unit** with two Soldiers	NGPP
K 704	1938-40	**R.A.M.C. Stretcher Party**, 2 Soldiers and Patient	NGPP
1248	1957	**Field Gun**	£5-10
1249	1958-79	**18-pounder Quick-Firing Gun**	£10-15
1250	1958-80	**25-pounder Light Artillery Gun**	£10-15
1251	1958-80	**5.5" Medium Heavy Howitzer**	£10-15
1260	1976-79	**Supply Truck**	£30-40
1263	1962-80	**Saladin Armoured Scout Car**	£20-30
1264	1975-80	**Scorpion Tank**	£12-16
1265	1977-80	**M109 Self-Propelled Gun**	£12-15
1266	1978-79	**Recovery Vehicle**	£12-15
1267	1958-63	**'Corporal' Rocket and Lorry**	£50-60
1270	1958-60	**Heavy Rescue Crane**	£40-50
1271	1958-60	**Long Range Mobile Gun**	£20-30
1271	1976-80	**Artillery Force**	£15-20
2154	1962-74	**Saladin Armoured Patrol** (No.1270 1975-80)	£10-15

HISTORICAL MODELS (in Regal colours)

1300	1975-76	**Royal State Coach**	£20-30
1301	1977-79	**Royal State Coach**, (Commemorative box)	£20-30
1302	1977	**Royal State Coach and Figures**	£20-30
1450	1956-60	**Medieval Catapult**	£20-30
1953	1954-60	**Coronation State Coach**	£30-40

Miniature 'WILD WEST' Transport

906	1956	**Stage Coach**, various colours	£30-40
907	1956	**Covered Wagon**, various colours	£30-40

GRAND PRIX RACING and SPORTS CARS

1284	1956-60	**Mercedes-Benz**, all-enveloping silver body	£80-100
1285	1956-60	**B.R.M. Mk.II**, bright green	£80-100
1286	1956-60	**Ferrari**, orange-red	£80-100
1287	1956-60	**Connaught**, dark green	£80-100
1288	1956-60	**Cooper-Bristol**, light blue	£80-100
1289	1956-60	**Gordini**, French blue	£80-100
1290	1956-60	**Maserati**, cherry red	£80-100
1291	1957-60	**Aston-Martin DB3s**, white/light blue	£80-100
1292	1957-60	**Jaguar 'D' type**, dark green	£80-100
1293	1958-60	**Vanwall**, dark green	£80-100
6300	1957	**Racing Cars Set**, 1284 - 1289 in display box	NGPP
	1958-60	Same set but 1290 replaces 1284	NGPP

LONG VEHICLES (various colours)

1350	1975-80	**Container Truck**	£20-25
1351	1975-80	**Petrol Tanker**	£20-25
1352	1975-80	**Girder Carrying Truck**	£20-25
1353	1975-80	**Flat Platform Truck**	£20-25

'TRUKKERS' (various colours)

1360	1976-81	**Cement Mixer**	£5-20
1361	1976-81	**Covered Truck**	£5-20
1362	1976-81	**Tipper Truck**	£5-20
1363	1976-81	**Recovery Vehicle**	£5-20
1364	1976-81	**Super Karrier**	£5-20

CRESCENT AIRCRAFT

O 2	1940	**Spitfire Set**. Two Spitfires with two Pilots and two Mechanics	£50-75
Q 2	1940	**Spitfire Set**. As O 2 but new ref. no.	£50-75
U 2	1940	**Aircraft Set**. Five Aircraft plus three Pilots and six Groundcrew	£75-100
FC 38	1946	**Aeroplane**, Spitfire	£5-10
FC 89	1946	**Aeroplane**, Mosquito	£5-10
FC 90	1946	**Aeroplane**, Lightning, 3" x 2", US markings	£5-10
FC 179	1946	**Khaki Bomber**	£5-10
FC 372	1946	**Aeroplane**, Lightning, 4.75" x 3", US markings	£5-10
FC 663	1946	**North Sea Patrol**. Aeroplane with pilot and one other crew member	£20-25

CRESCENT AUCTION RESULT

Sold by CHRISTIE'S:

A **Crescent Dan Dare Set** complete with five figures and rocket launcher, in original box (F-G, rocket launcher damaged, lacks tie-card, box F-G), extra Dan Dare figure marching (F, repaired head) and a Dan Dare child's belt with plastic buckle (F) **£368**

CRESCENT SHIPS

BATTLESHIPS

---		HMS **'King George V'**. Grey hollow-cast, with main armament only, boxed	£15-20
---		Same but additional separately cast secondary armament	£15-20
---		HMS **'Vanguard'**. Grey / black / white, solid, *'CRESCENT'* cast-in	£5-7
Q 3	1940	**Battleship Set**, Battleship plus four Sailors	NGPP
S 3	1940	**Warships Set**, Battleship and Destroyer plus eight Sailors	NGPP
NN 691		HMS **'Malaya'**, grey hollow-cast, black funnels, boxed	£15-20

AIRCRAFT CARRIERS

-		HMS **'Victorious'**, grey hollow-cast body, separate unpainted aircraft, boxed	£20-25
NN 667		HMS **'Eagle'**, grey hollow-cast body, unpainted aircraft, Union Jack sticker attached to box	£10-15

OTHER WARSHIPS

---		**'H' or 'I' Class Destroyer**. Unpainted solid cast body, *'CRESCENT'* cast into bow	£15-20
---		**'H' or 'I' Class Destroyer**. As previous model plus three lead figures of naval personnel	£20-25
---		**'V' and 'W' Class Destroyer**. Grey hollow-cast body	£2-3
A 34		**Gunboat**. Grey hollow cast body	£2-3
234		**Submarine**. Unpainted, conning tower and deck gun, 4"	£10-15
C 310		**'County' Class Cruiser, 'Cumberland'**, grey hollow-cast	£7-9
K 664		**'County' Class Cruiser**, grey hollow-cast body	£7-9
K 665		**War Transport Ship**, grey hollow-cast body, boxed	£15-20

PASSENGER SHIPS

---		**'Queen Mary'**. Black / white / red, hollow-cast body, boxed	£15-20
---		**'Dunnottar Castle'**. Mauve / white / red, hollow-cast, boxed	£25-30
---		**'Athlone Castle'**. Mauve / white / red, hollow-cast, boxed	£25-30

'Dunnottar Castle' and 'Athlone Castle' were part of the 'Union Castle' fleet and the models were sold in souvenir boxes, probably on board.

SHIP MODEL IDENTIFICATION. Crescent Ships are of rather crude manufacture and have virtually no identifying features. Only the HMS 'Vanguard' and the 'H' or 'I' Class Destroyer are known to have *'CRESCENT'* cast in. A few of the early models had a little paper 'Crescent' half-moon label. Ship models were packed in cream cardboard boxes of varying quality.

MISCELLANEOUS

'Tower Bridge'	Solid cast model of the famous landmark, in various colours	£5-10

'Dial 999' Police and Robbers Set. Contains black police car with loudhailer on roof and four semi-flat action figures (policeman running, policeman and dog, two fleeing villains, one with swag).
Packed in card box with black and white label £150-175

xx

THE MECCANO MAGAZINE

TOYS OF QUALITY MADE BY MECCANO LTD.

DINKY *200 VARIETIES* TOYS

A FASCINATING COLLECTING HOBBY

TRAM CAR
Dinky Toys No. 27
Assorted colours. Price 3d. each

MOTOR BUS
Dinky Toys No. 29
Assorted colours. Price 4d. each

24E 24G
24F 24C
24D 24A
24H 24B

MOTOR CARS
Dinky Toys No. 24
Fitted with detachable rubber tyres and silver-plated radiators
No. 24a Ambulance ... ... each 9d.
No. 24b Limousine ... ... „ 9d.
No. 24c Town Sedan ... ... „ 9d.
No. 24d Vogue Saloon ... ... „ 9d.
No. 24e Super Streamline Saloon ... „ 9d.
No. 24f Sportsman's Coupé ... ... „ 9d.
No. 24g Sports Tourer (4 seater) ... „ 9d.
No. 24h Sports Tourer (2 seater) ... „ 9d.
Price of complete set 6/-

47e 47n 47s 47h 47g 47f
47r 47m 47k 47p 47t 47q

ROAD SIGNS
Dinky Toys No. 47
No. 47e "30 Mile Limit" Sign ... 2 for 3d.
No. 47f "De-restriction" Sign ... „ 3d.
No. 47g "School" Sign ... ... „ 3d.
No. 47h "Steep Hill" Sign ... ... „ 3d.
No. 47k "Bend" Sign ... ... „ 3d.
No. 47m Left-hand "Corner" Sign ... „ 3d.
No. 47n Right-hand "Corner" Sign ... „ 3d.
No. 47p "Road Junction" Sign ... „ 3d.
No. 47q "No Entry" Sign ... ... „ 3d.
No. 47r "Major Road Ahead" Sign ... „ 3d.
No. 47s "Crossing, No Gates" Sign ... „ 3d.
No. 47t "Round-About" Sign ... „ 3d.
Price of complete set of twelve 1/6

25F 25B
25D 25C
25E 25A

COMMERCIAL MOTOR VEHICLES
Dinky Toys No. 25
Fitted with detachable rubber tyres and silver-plated radiators
No. 25a Wagon ... ... each 9d.
No. 25b Covered Van ... ... „ 9d.
No. 25c Flat Truck ... ... „ 9d.
No. 25d Petrol Tank Wagon ... „ 9d.
No. 25e Tipping Wagon ... ... „ 9d.
No. 25f Market Gardener's Van ... „ 9d.
Price of complete set 4/6

GARAGE
Dinky Toys No. 45
Fitted with opening double doors. Will accommodate any two Dinky Toy Motor Cars.
Price 1/6 each

60E 60A 60C
60D 60F 60B

AEROPLANES
Dinky Toys No. 60
No. 60a Imperial Airways Liner each 9d.
No. 60b D.H. "Leopard Moth" „ 6d.
No. 60c Percival "Gull" ... „ 6d.
No. 60d Low Wing Monoplane „ 6d.
No. 60e General "Monospar" „ 6d.
No. 60f Cierva "Autogiro" „ 6d.
Price of complete set 3/-

FILLING AND SERVICE STATION

PETROL STATION
Dinky Toys No. 48
Accurate reproduction of a filling station.
Tastefully printed in appropriate colours.
Price 1/6 each

PASSENGER TRAIN SET
Dinky Toys No. 17
No. 17a Locomotive ... ... each 9d.
No. 17b Tender ... ... „ 5d.
No. 20a Coach ... ... „ 7d.
No. 20b Guard's Van ... ... „ 7d.
Price of complete set 2/3

MIXED GOODS TRAIN SET
Dinky Toys No. 19
No. 21a Tank Locomotive ... ... each 9d.
No. 21b Wagon ... ... „ 4d.
No. 21d Petrol Tank Wagon ... ... „ 6d.
No. 21e Lumber Wagon ... ... „ 5d.
Price of complete set 1/11

GOODS TRAIN SET
Dinky Toys No. 18
No. 21a Tank Locomotive ... ... each 9d.
No. 21b Wagons (3) ... ... „ 4d.
Price of complete set 1/9

G.W.R. RAIL CAR
Dinky Toys No. 26
Assorted colours. Price 4d. each

PASSENGER TRAIN SET
Dinky Toys No. 20
No. 21a Tank Locomotive ... ... each 9d.
No. 20a Coaches (2) ... ... „ 7d.
No. 20b Guard's Van ... ... „ 7d.
Price of complete set 2/6

Ask your dealer for a complete illustrated list of Dinky Toys

MECCANO LIMITED — BINNS ROAD — LIVERPOOL 13

A page from the December 1935 'Meccano Magazine'

Meccano
Dinky Toys

During the course of the period 1997-99 some fine collections have been sold at auction and the amounts realised have been included in the Auction Results section. These have included collections containing examples of almost every pre-war motor vehicle, set and accessory produced. In addition the post-war model auctions have been very comprehensive and have included previously unrecorded variants as well as rare colours and export issues. The impact of all this information on the catalogue listings has been considerable, particularly in respect of the pre-war and early post-war car listings which have been greatly enhanced.

All pre-war issues must be considered rare and market prices have reflected this. Similarly the prices paid for the early post-war issues have also increased considerably. One of the benefits of the large volume and quality of items sold, has been the amount of new model identification information which has emerged, particularly in respect of the early post-war car issues. Overall the demand for top quality Dinky Toys remains very strong.

The 7th Edition listings have been completely revised and enhanced. The 'Trains' section has been combined with the 'Buses, Taxis and Trams' section to form a more user-friendly new 'Public Transport' section.

HISTORY OF DINKY TOYS

In 1931 Meccano Ltd introduced a series of railway station and trackside accessories to accompany their famous 'HORNBY' train sets. These 'Modelled Miniatures' were in sets numbered 1 - 22 and included railwaymen, station staff, passengers and trains. Set number 22 was comprised of six vehicles which were representative rather than replicas of actual vehicles. It was first advertised in the Meccano Magazine of December 1933.

At about this time 'Tootsie Toys' of America were introducing model vehicles into the United Kingdom and they were proving to be very popular. Consequently Meccano Ltd decided to widen their range of products and issue a comprehensive series of models to include vehicles, ships and aircraft. 'Modelled Miniatures' therefore became 'Meccano Dinky Toys' and set number 22 the first set of 'Dinky Cars'. The first 'Dinky Toys' advertisement appeared in the April 1934 edition of the Meccano Magazine. The first Dinky car produced after the change of name was 23a in April 1934. It was probably based on an early MG but was again generally representative rather than an accurate model. Set 22 cost 4/- and consisted of: 22a Sports Car, 22b Sports Coupé, 22c Motor Truck, 22d Delivery Van, 22e Tractor and 22f Tank and is today highly sought after.

The range of models produced grew quickly so that the Meccano Magazine of December 1935 was claiming that there were 200 varieties to choose from! Although the phrase 'Dinky Toys' became a household name, the actual range was of course far greater and was not limited to cars; it even included dolls house furniture. Indeed, by the time the famous Binns Road factory in Liverpool finally closed its doors in November 1979 over 1000 different designs had been produced. Pre-war models are rare today and fetch high prices, which reflects how difficult it is to find a model in really good condition. This is because so many 1930s models were made from an unstable alloy which has tended to crystallise and disintegrate. Fortunately the post-war models do not suffer from the same problem and much of today's collecting interest is centred around the delightful models produced in the fifties and sixties with Gift Sets being particularly sought after.

In 1987 the Dinky trade name was bought by Matchbox who were at the time part of the Universal International Co. of Hong Kong. They introduced the 'Dinky Collection' in 1988 with some very fine models in a constant scale of 1:43. On the 7th May 1992 it was announced in the 'New York Times' that 'Tyco Toys Inc.' had acquired by merger the 'Universal Matchbox Group' and with it the famous 'Dinky Toys' brand name. In 1998, Mattel bought the Matchbox brand and in 1999 disclosed that all new car models will be classified as 'Dinky Toys', including those previously included in their Matchbox Models of Yesteryear range. These issues will now found in the new 'Collectable Modern Diecasts' section of the Catalogue. It will be interesting to see the model range of 21st century Dinky Toys.

Market Price Range: Please note that the prices shown refer to pristine models and boxes.
Items failing to match this standard will sell for less.
Note also that boxes must contain all their original additional contents.

Dinky Toys Model Identification

Common Features. There are several features common to various groups of models and to avoid unnecessary repetition in the listings they are shown below. Exceptions to these general indications are noted in the listings.

'Dinky Toys', 'Meccano Ltd', or 'Meccano Dinky Toys'.
These wordings are to be found cast or stamped on the base-plate or chassis or in the case of early models without a base they are cast into the model itself. Some very early models have 'HORNBY SERIES' cast-in (e,g, those in the 22 series).

Wheel hubs. Solid one-piece wheel/tyre castings were fitted to the 'Modelled Miniatures' and first pre-war 'Dinky Toys'. They had 'Hornby' or 'Meccano' cast onto their rims and were covered in a thin colour wash or silver-plated. This casting was soon replaced with more realistic cast hubs (having a smooth convex face) fitted with white (sometimes coloured) rubber tyres. Pre-war hubs may be black, coloured or sometimes silver-plated. Post-war hubs were of the 'ridged' type having a discernible ridge simulating a hub cap. They were painted and usually fitted with black rubber tyres.

Supertoys hubs and tyres. When Supertoys were introduced in 1947 the ridged type of hub was used on the Fodens with black 'herringbone pattern' tyres, and on the Guys with smooth black tyres. Fodens graduated to the use of 'fine radial-tread' tyres first in black, later in grey, then to black again but with a more chunky 'block' tread. Supertoys later acquired plastic hubs and plastic tyres.

Hub materials. Lead was used originally for a short time, the majority of models from the mid-1930s to the early 1960s having diecast mazak hubs. Small models like motor-cycles or the 35b Racer were fitted with solid one-piece wheel/tyre moulding (white or black rubber pre-war, black post-war). In 1958/9 aluminium hubs were introduced and some models (such as 131, 178, 179, 180, 181, 182 and 290 Bus) appeared fitted with either type. Plastic hubs replaced the diecast versions on racing cars numbered 230-235 while the Austin A30 and Fiat 600 were given solid one-piece wheel/tyre plastic injection mouldings. **Speedwheels** were introduced in the 1970s and some model can be found fitted with metal wheels or Speedwheels. The former are more collectable.

Baseplates are tinplate or diecast unless described otherwise. Plastic moulded baseplates are generally restricted to a few models made after 1970. **Model Numbers** appear on many Dinky Toys baseplates but not all. The **Model Name** however appears on virtually every post-war Dinky Toy. Pre-war models usually had neither (the 38 and 39 series are exceptions having the model name on their baseplates).

Construction Materials. All models assumed to be constructed at least in part of a diecast alloy. Some pre-war models were made of a lead alloy like the 22 and 28 series plus the few odd models such as 23 a Racing Car and 23m Thunderbolt. The Blaw-Knox Bulldozer was one of the very few produced (right at the end of its production) in plastic.

Windows. Pre-war and early post-war models had tinplate or celluloid windscreens. Moulded plastic windscreens appeared in the 1950s on open car models. The first Dinky to be fitted with all-round plastic window glazing was the Austin A105 Saloon. Some models in production at the time were fitted with glazing later and may therefore be found with or without it.

Hooks were not fitted to the first Supertoys Foden models (1947). Small hooks were fitted in early 1948, the usual (larger) hook appearing in mid-1948.

Axles were all 'crimped' pre-war and on these series of models post-war: 23, 25, 29, 30, 34, 35, 36, 37, 38, 39, 40 and 280. Otherwise models had rivet-ended axles until the advent of Speedwheels. Early Guy models had tinplate clips to retain the front axles. Pre-war axles are generally thinner than post-war at 0.062mm diameter while post-war axles are 0.078mm in diameter.

Size of models (wher shown) is in millimetres and refers to the longest overall measurement (usually the length). In the case of pre-war models slight inaccuracies may occur from expansion of the casting as it ages in the course of time.

The Scale of Dinky Toys was originally 1:43 (with a few exceptions). Supertoys Foden and Guy vehicles (introduced in 1947) were in a scale of 1:48 while military models issued from 1953 were smaller at 1:60. Most aircraft models before 1965 were around 1:200 and ships 1:1800. In the late 1960s and early 1970s the 1:36 scale was introduced, mostly for cars.

Dinky Numbering System. The dual/triple reference numbers used on some Dinky Toys and Supertoys (for example 409 / 521 / 921 Bedford Articulated Lorry) refers to the basic model type and casting and not to model colours. The renumbering by Meccano was an administration process to re-catalogue production of existing lines and introduce new models. New colours on existing castings which arise at about the time of renumbering are therefore coincidental with it rather than a consequence of it.

Identification of early post-war Dinky Toys cars.
Note that pre-war wheel hubs may be smooth diecast or the rare chrome ('Tootsie-Toy') type hubs which attract a premium.

Post-war 30 Series
Circa 1946.........Open chassis with smooth black wheel hubs.
Circa 1948.........Plain chassis with ridged black wheel hubs.

36 Series
Circa 1946.........Moulded chassis with smooth black wheel hubs.
Circa 1948.........Moulded chassis with ridged black wheel hubs.

38 Series
Circa 1946........With pre-war lacquered metal base, silvered sidelights, smooth black hubs, spread spigots not rivets.
Circa 1946.........Solid steering wheels, smooth black hubs, silvered sidelights, black painted baseplate.
Circa 1947.........As above but with silver-edged windscreen.
Circa 1948-49....Open or solid steering wheel, ridged hubs, black painted baseplate.
Circa 1950.........As above but with coloured wheel hubs.

39 Series
Circa 1946.........'Gold' pre-war baseplate, smooth black wheel hubs, silver door handles.
Circa 1948.........Black painted baseplate, ridged black wheel hubs.
Circa 1950.........As above but with coloured wheel hubs.

Dinky Toys Cars Box Types

Box Types Introduction

A mint condition model car without its correct box is worth but a fraction of its mint boxed equivalent. Furthermore, as model boxes made from card do not survive as well as their die-cast contents, pristine box examples are scarce and becoming scarcer. The condition of a box is of paramount importance and attention is drawn to the section in the catalogue introduction, namely: 'Classifying the Condition of Models and Boxes'.

The following listing provides collectors with a working knowledge of the range of box types issued. In addition details are given of their dates of issue, their design and of the models which used them.

Whilst every care has been taken in preparing the listing, other variations may exist and information on them is welcomed. Similarly, with no 'dates of birth' available the dates of issues shown are approximate and again any further information is welcomed.

Box Identification

Model colour identification marks - colour spots

These are shown on the box lid end flap and take the form of a circular colour spot. This may be either a single colour or, in the case of the later two-tone car issues, a two-tone colour spot. Colour spots were used until the early 1960s.

NB The dual numbered 234/23H box displays the **Ferrari** model name against a blue panel which matches the main body colour.

Dual numbered boxes 1953 - 1954

A new numbering system was introduced which resulted in models being issued displaying both the old and new reference numbers. The information was shown on the box end flaps as follows:

Old model number shown in red letters on either side of a larger white number set on a black oval background, e.g. 40J **161** 40J. Dual numbered boxes were only issued for a short period and may attract a premium. The numbers may be large or small.

Pre-war issues

Apart from special issues such as 23m Thunderbolt Speed Car and 23p Gardner's M.G. Record Car, individual models were sold unboxed. They were usually packaged in half-dozen retailers trade packs (see the section on Trade Packs). Models were also sold in boxed sets (see the Gift Set Section).

Post-war After the second world war models continued to be sold unboxed from trade boxes until 1953/54 when the first individual boxes were introduced.
The boxes have been catalogued into three types as follows:

Type 1: Card boxes with tuck-in flaps
Type 2: Display boxes -Blister packs, rigid plastic packs, vacuform packs and card window boxes.
Type 3: Export Issue boxes.

Type 1 1953 - 1975 All card box with tuck-in end flaps

(i) 1953- 1954 Deep yellow box with 'DINKY TOYS' in red plus the model's name and type in black. A white reference number on a black oval background is on the box end flaps but no reference number is shown on the box face. The model is pictured on the box sides but without a white shaded background. Colour spots shown on box-end flaps as applicable.

Foreign language information is shown on one of the end flaps of the early issue boxes. See picture on page 32. Box in general use during the model renumbering period. Consequently, dual numbered boxes will be found. It would appear that only models 23F, G, H, J, K and N were housed in individual boxes prior to renumbering. Please supply details of any other models housed in boxes displaying just their old type of reference number.

(ii) 1955 - 1956 Same as (i) but a white reference number on a black oval background is shown on the face of the box to the left of the model picture. Also as (i) but with a white reference number on a red oval background and placed either to the left or the right of the model picture. Box in general use for all issues.

(iii) 1956 - 1960 Same as (ii) but model pictures are displayed against a white shadow background. In some instances only one picture. had a shadow, e.g. 171 Hudson Commodore and in others both pictures were given a shadow; e.g. 152 Austin Devon. Box in general use for all issues. Later issues display 'WITH WINDOWS', caption in a red line features box.

(iv) c1960 Deep yellow plain box with no model picture, 'DINKY TOYS' and text in red; rarely used. Colour spots shown as applicable. We believe these boxes may have been used for mail-order or possibly export purposes. The Editor would welcome any new information. Known examples: 103, 108, l09, 163 and 191.

(v) 1959 - 1961 Plain lighter yellow box with no model picture. It has two yellow and two red sides. `DINKY TOYS' is shown in yellow on red sides. Colour spots shown as applicable. Models recorded: 105, 109, 150, 165, 169, 173. 174, 178, 187, 189, 191 and 230 to 235. The special issue 189 Triumph Heralds used this box. (vi) 1960 - 1966 Yellow box with a separate red line features box placed to the right of the model picture. Colour spots still in use on early 1960s issues. Foreign language text on one box end flap and 'WITH WINDOWS' captions on box face. Models recorded: 105, 112, 113, 131, 144,

148, 157, 164-167, 176, 178, 181/2, 191-195, 199, 230-235, 237, 239 and 449. Later issues without colour spots. Boxes used for some South African issues display both English and Afrikaans text.

(vii) c.1962 - 1963 Lighter yellow box similar to (v) but colour spots not in use. A scarce issue box which may attract a premium. Model recorded: 166.
(viii) 1962 - 1963 Yellow box with a red end features panel around the left side of the box. Recorded models-: 113, 147 and 198.

(ix) 1963-70 Yellow box with a red end features panel around the right side of the box. The panel is bisected by the model picture and is with or without a large or small white arrow design. Models recorded: 112-114. 120, 127-130, 133-139, 140-148 and 240-243. Some South African issues used this box, e.g. 141 Vauxhall Victor Estate Car. They display both English and Afrikaans text. The rare Triumph 2000 Saloon promotional issues will be found in this box. Some of these have an applied white label on the box face which shows the colour of the model, e.g. Olive-Cactus.

(x) 1966 - 1969 Detailed full colour picture box with pictorial scene on two sides with 'DINKY TOYS' in red letters. Recorded issues: 133, 136, 183, 212, 214, 225 plus Hong Kong issues 57/001-57/006.
(xi) 1968 -1974 White-fronted box with a thin yellow band across the box face. A yellow laurel leaf design on a black background is a main box feature. The white face of the box may contain features information such as '1st AGAIN' and 'SPEEDWHEELS'. Variation exists with a semi-pictorial box face (probably an export special) e.g. 176 NSU R80. Models recorded: 157, 159 165/6 174/5, 179, 192 and 205. NB. A variation of this box exists with a large red 'DINKY TOYS' and number to the left of the picture and no yellow band across the face, e.g. 138 Hillman Imp.

Type 2 1962 - 1980 Display boxes, Blister packs, Rigid plastic and Vacuform packs, Window boxes

A 1962 - 1964 Blister Card Packs used for racing cars nos. 205210. Red/yellow display card with chequered flag design.
B 1967 - 1971 Rigid plastic 'see-through' case with lift-off lid. models displayed on a card base with a black `roadway' surface. The base sides are yellow with 'DINKY TOYS' in red. Recorded issues: 110, 116, 127, 129, 131/2, 142, 152-154, 158, 161, 163/4, 168, 175, 187-189, 190, 208, 210, 213, 215, 216, 220/1 and 223/4.
C 1972 - 1976 Vacuform Packs. Models displayed on a black base with a blue surface with 'DINKY TOYS' in red/white letters. The model is covered by a close fitting plastic cover. Known issues: 129, 131, 149, 168, 178 and 192 plus 1:25 issues 2214, 3162 and 2253.
D 1976 - 1979 Window Box with 'see-through' cellophane front and blue and red header card with a 'DINKY DIECAST TOYS' in yellow letters. Variations exist with a model picture on the header card e.g. 112 'Purdey's TR7'. Known issues: 113, 120, 122/3/4, 128. 180, 192, 207/8, 211, 221/2/3 and 226/7.
E 1968 - 1969 Plastic see-through red boxes made in a garage shape to house 'Mini Dinky' issues.
F 1979 Bubble Pack 219 'Big Cat' Jaguar.

Type 3 1966 - 1980 Export issue boxes

A 1966 - 1980 An all yellow card and cellophane 'see-through' display box with outward-folding ends. 'DINKY TOYS' and four diagonal stripes plus 'A MECCANO PRODUCT MADE IN ENGLAND' are in red on the box face. The box display base may be either yellow or have a black `roadway' design. Whilst generally used for export issues it was specifically used for the U.S. export series `MARVELS IN MINIATURE - which appeared in red letters on the box front. Later issues listed the models on the base of the box.
A box variation exists with just 'DINKY' and 'A MECCANO PRODUCT' on the face of the box plus the model name and number. The base of the box is yellow. The box was issued with a card protection strip which stated: 'Mr DEALER PLEASE REMOVE THIS STRIP'. Models known to have been issued in this box include: 110-115, 120, 127/8, 133-138, l41/2. 151, 161, 170-172, 190, 192, 196, 215, 237, 240-243, 258, 57/006. NB We believe this box was probably used in the UK but would be grateful for confirmation.
B 1966- 1968 All gold card and cellophane 'see-through' display box with just 'DINKY' in gold letters set in a red panel on the box front plus red and black diagonal stripes. 'A MECCANO PRODUCT MADE IN ENGLAND' is shown in black also on the front of the box. Only used for a short time so models in these boxes often sell at a premium. The known issues are: 112, 113, 148, 238, 242, 340 and 448.
C 1979 - 1980 A flat yellow box with blue end flaps. Used to house the Swiss promotional issue No. 223 Hesketh F1 Racing Car 'OLYMPUS CAMERAS'.
Export issue: 449 has been observed in an 'all gold' box.

Identification of casting types

Dinky Toys Cars chassis types 1934 - 1950

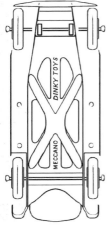 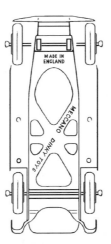  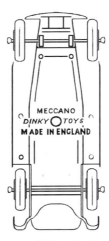 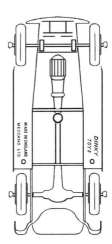

1934 - 1935	**1935 - 1936**	**1936 - 1940**	**1946 - 1947**	**1948 - 1950**
'Criss-cross' chassis 1st type with or without slot for spare wheel	'Criss-cross' chassis 2nd type with or without slot for spare wheel	Open chassis with or without slots for figures	Plain chassis no slots for figures	'Moulded' (detailed) chassis

24 series radiator grille types 1934 - 1940

1st type **1934 - 1938**	**2nd type** **1934 - 1938**	**3rd type** **1938 - 1940**
With diamond shape in centre of bumper No radiator badge No over-riders	No diamond shape in centre of bumper No radiator badge No over-riders	'Bentley' style with radiator badge and over-riders

The first and second type grilles will be found on the both the first and second type chassis.
The later third type grille will be found with the second type chassis.

Ref.	Year(s)	Model name	Colours, features, dimensions	Market Price Range

Note: Pre-war wheel hubs may be smooth diecast or the rare chrome (Tootsie Toy type) hubs which attract a premium.

22a	1933-35	**Open Sports Car**	'Modelled Miniature' with 'HORNBY SERIES' cast into lead body, solid metal wheel/tyre castings (thinly painted in metallic blue, purple, green, yellow or red, or not painted at all) lead windscreen surround, tinplate radiator (grille may be same colour as body, or overpainted with the colour of the mudguards), 82 mm.	
			Blue body, Yellow seats and mudguards	£250-350
			Blue body, Red seats and mudguards	£250-350
			Cream body, Red seats and mudguards	£250-350
			Cream body, Green seats and mudguards	£250-350
			Cream body, Blue seats and mudguards	£250-350
			Red body, Cream seats and mudguards	£250-350
			Yellow body, Green seats and mudguards	£250-350
			Orange-Brown body, Cream seats and mudguards	£250-350
22b	1933-35	**Closed Sports Coupé**	'Modelled Miniature' with 'HORNBY SERIES' cast into lead body, solid metal wheel/tyre castings (coloured or plain, as 22a) tinplate radiator (painted in main body colour) 82 mm.	
			Cream body, Red roof and mudguards or Green roof and mudguards	£250-350
			Red body, Blue roof and mudguards	£250-350
			Red body, Cream roof and mudguards	£250-350
			Yellow body, Green roof and mudguards	£250-350
22g	1935-41	**Streamline Tourer**	Model has cast steering wheel and windscreen, smooth diecast hubs which may be painted as body colour or a contrasting colour. Some have chrome hubs. 85 mm.	
			Body colours: Green, Red, Light or Dark Blue, Cream, Buff or Black	£175-225
22h	1935-41	**Streamlined Saloon**	Red, Blue or Cream saloon version of 22g (no steering wheel) 85 mm	£175-225
23	1934 -35	**Racing Car** 1st casting:	Lead body, no racing number or driver, coloured tyres on some, 0, 2, 3 or 4 exhausts stubs, 94 mm.	
		variations:	Cream or White body with either Blue, Cream, Green, Orange or Red top flash	£200-300
			Yellow body with Blue upper body flash, 3 exhaust stubs	£200-300
23a	1935-41	**Racing Car** (23 re-issued)	As 1st casting but diecast body, no driver, no racing number, Black or White tyres, 4 exhausts, 94 mm.	
		variations:	White body and hubs, Blue top flash and circle on nose	£100-150
			Cream body and hubs, Red top flash and circle on nose	£100-150
			Blue body, White top flash and circle on nose	£100-150
			Orange body, Green top flash and circle on nose	£100-150
			Yellow body, Dark Blue top flash and circle on nose	£100-150
			Brown body, Cream top flash	£100-150
23a		**Racing Car** 2nd casting:	With driver plus raised circles for racing numbers, 6 exhausts in fishtail, 94 mm.	
		colour type 1:	With minor colour sidestripes and perhaps coloured tyres,	
		colour type 2:	Broad nose flash, even width top rear flash,	
		colour type 3:	Broad flash at cockpit and pointed ends top flash, cast circle on nose.	
		variations:	(type 1) Cream body, Red stripes, number '9', ('Humbug' version)	£300-400
			(type 2) Blue with White 'humbug' stripes and driver, racing number '11'	£300-400
			(type 2) Yellow body, Dark Blue top flash, racing number '7'	£100-150
			(type 2) Blue body, White top flash, racing number '11'	£100-150
			(type 3) White body, Blue nose/circle/top flash, number '2'	£100-150
			(type 3) Cream body, Red nose/circle/top flash, number '3'	£100-150
			(type 3) Red body, Cream nose/top flash, no number, no transverse ribs	£100-150
			(type 3) White body, Green nose/circle/top flash, number '6'	£100-150
			(type 3) Orange body, Green nose/circle/top flash, number '4'	£100-150
		casting variation:	With driver, raised racing number circle on nearside only, no detailed exhaust,	
			Orange body, Green nose circle, Green racing number '4'	£100-150
			Orange body, long Green upper body flash, 3 exhaust stubs, Green RN '4' or '10'	£100-150
			Yellow body, long Dark Blue upper body flash, chrome hubs	£100-150
23a (220)	1946-52	**Racing Car** 3rd casting:	With transverse body ribs, no raised circle for racing numbers, and only issued in colour type 3, with or without racing numbers	
			Red body, Silver nose circle, top flash and side circle (Red RN '4'), Red hubs	£40-50
			Silver body, Red nose circle, top flash and side circle (Silver RN '4'), Red hubs	£40-50
		note:	Details of any other 23a colour are welcomed.	
23b	1935-41	**Hotchkiss Racing Car**	Blue body, Dark Blue, Red or Silver flash and racing number '2' or '5', 96 mm	£200-300
	1935-41		Yellow (Blue flash and RN), Orange (Green flash and RN), or Green (Yellow flash and RN)	£200-300
	1946-48		Red with Silver flash and RN '5', or Silver with Red flash and RN '5'	£50-60
23c	1936-38	**Mercedes Benz Racing Car**	Red, Light Blue, Yellow or Green, plain clipped-in base, with or without racing numbers, driver cast-in, Black hubs, treaded tyres, 92 mm	£100-150
	1938-40		As previous model but with rivetted baseplate bearing information	£100-150
	1946-50	('Large Open Racing Car')	Re-issued 23c in Blue or Silver, various racing numbers, 92 mm	£40-50
23d	1936-38	**Auto-Union Racing Car**	Early pre-war issues without driver: Red, Blue, Pale Green, Yellow or Silver body, Black racing numbers, clipped-in tinplate base, 100 mm	£100-125
	1938-41		Later pre-war issue with driver, rivetted baseplate	£90-100
	1946-50		Early post-war issue with driver: Red or Silver body	£90-100
			Later post-war issue without driver	£50-60

103

23e	1936-38	**'Speed Of The Wind'**		
		Racing Car............................	Red, Blue, Light Blue, Green, Yellow or Silver body, plain clipped-in tinplate base, driver, various racing numbers, Black hubs and herringbone tyres, lead versions exist, 104 mm	**£75-95**
	1938-41	....	As previous model but with rivetted baseplate bearing information	**£40-50**
	1946-49	....	Red or Silver, rivetted informative baseplate	**£40-45**
23f (221)	1950-54	....	Silver body and hubs, plain base	**£40-45**
23f (232)	1952-54	**Alfa-Romeo Racing Car**........	Red body, White racing number '8', Red diecast hubs, 100 mm	**£85-95**
23g (233)	1952-54	**Cooper-Bristol Racing Car**...	Green body, White racing number '6', Green diecast hubs, 89 mm	**£75-85**
23h (234)	1953-54	**Ferrari Racing Car**................	Blue body, Yellow nose, racing number '5' and diecast hubs, 101 mm	**£85-95**
23j (235)	1953-54	**H.W.M. Racing Car**..............	Light Green body, Yellow racing number '7', Green diecast hubs, 99 mm	**£85-95**
23k (230)	1953-54	**Talbot-Lago Racing Car**........	Blue body, Yellow racing number '4', Blue diecast hubs, 103 mm	**£85-95**
23m	1938-41	**'Thunderbolt' Speed Car**.....	Silver body (Black detailing), Union Jacks on tail, Silver baseplate. In original Blue box dated '2-38', code: 'A2247', 126 mm	**£150-175**
23n (231)	1953-54	**Maserati Racing Car**.............	Red, White flash and racing number '9', Red diecast hubs, 94 mm	**£85-95**
23p	1939-40	**Gardner's MG Record Car**...	Dark Green, White flash and 'MG' logo, Union Jacks, 'MG Magnette' on lacquered unpainted tinplate baseplate, Yellow box, dated '9-39', 104 mm	**£150-200**
	1946-47	....	Dark Green, Union Jacks, no flash, 'MG Record Car' on base, not boxed	**£80-100**
23s	1938-40	**Streamlined Racing Car**........	Light Green (Dark Green detailing), lead, 126 mm	**£100-125**
			Light Blue (Dark Blue or Silver detailing), lead	**£100-125**
			Orange body, lead	**£100-125**
			Light Green, Light Blue or Orange body, mazak	**£75-100**
23s (222)	1948-54	....	Light, Mid or Dark Green, or Dark Blue, Silver flashes	**£60-70**
			Silver body with Red, Green or Blue flashes	**£60-70**
			Red body with Silver or Black flashes, Black base	**£100-125**
24a	1934-40	**Ambulance**............................	See 'Fire, Police and Ambulance Vehicles' Section.	
24b	1934-38	**Limousine**.............................	Types 1 or 2: criss-cross chassis. Types 1, 2 or 3: grille, no sidelights, no spare wheel, 3 side windows, 3 'stacked' parallel horizontal bonnet louvres. Plated, Blue or Black hubs, 98 mm.	
		body/chassis colours:	Maroon/Dark Maroon, Maroon/Grey, Maroon/Black, Blue/Yellow, Dark Blue/Black, Yellow/Brown	**£750-1000**
	1937-40	.................casting change:	Same colours but no spare wheel slot, 3 parallel bonnet louvres, open chassis, 'Bentley' grille and bumper	**£300-400**
24c	1934-38	**Town Sedan**...........................	Types 1 or 2: criss-cross chassis. Types 1, 2 or 3: grille, spare wheel, no sidelights, separate windscreen/steering wheel casting, Blue, Black or plated hubs, 97mm.	
		body/chassis colours:	Green/Black, Green/Yellow, Pale Green/Red, Dark Blue/Dark Blue, Cream/Dark Blue, Cream/Black, Dark Blue/Black	**£750-1000**
	1937-40	.................casting change:	Same colours but open chassis, no spare wheel slot, narrower boot, shorter door handles	**£400-600**
24d	1934-38	**Vogue Saloon**.........................	Types 1 or 2: criss-cross chassis. Types 1, 2 or 3: grille, with spare wheel, no sidelights. Blue, Black or plated hubs, 97 mm.	
		body/chassis colours:	Blue/Dark Blue, Blue/Black, Blue/Maroon, Cream/Blue, Brown/Green, Pink/Green, Green/Blue, Red/Grey	**£750-1000**
	1937-40	.................casting change:	Same colours but open chassis, higher 'domed' roofline	**£400-600**
24e	1934-38	**Super Streamlined Saloon**.....	Types 1 or 2: criss-cross chassis. Types 1, 2 or 3: grille, no spare or sidelights, 12 bonnet louvres. Blue, Black or plated hubs, 97 mm.	
		body/chassis colours:	Maroon/Black, Red/Dark Red, Red/Black, Green/Red, Green/Blue, Red/Brown	**£300-400**
	1937-40	.................casting change:	As previous model but with 13 bonnet louvres	**£300-400**
24f	1934-38	**Sportsmans Coupé**................	Criss-cross chassis, with spare wheel, no sidelights, 97 mm.	
			Blue/Blue, Blue/Black, Yellow/Brown, Cream/Dark Blue, Brown/Buff	**£300-400**
	1937-40	.................casting change:	Open chassis, higher 'domed' roofline, no spare wheel	**£300-400**
24g	1934-38	**Sports Tourer Four-seater**....	Types 1 or 2: criss-cross chassis. Types 1, 2 or 3: grille, spare wheel hub cast-in, no sidelights, open tinplate windscreen, separate dashboard/steering wheel casting. Plated, Blue or Black hubs, 100 mm.	
		body/chassis colours:	Yellow/Black, Yellow/Blue, Blue/Brown, Cream/Green, Cream/Brown, Black/Cream, Blue/Maroon	**£300-400**
	1937-40	.................casting change:	Open chassis, filled-in windscreen, cast impression of spare	**£300-400**
24h	1934-38	**Sports Tourer Two-seater**......	Types 1 or 2: criss-cross chassis. Types 1, 2 or 3: grille, spare wheel hub cast-in, no sidelights, open tinplate windscreen, separate dashboard/steering wheel casting. Plated, Blue or Black hubs, 98 mm.	
		body/chassis colours:	Red/Red, Green/Green, Yellow/Green, Yellow/Blue, Yellow/Black, Black/Cream, Cream/Green, Red/Green	**£300-400**
	1937-40	.................casting change:	Open chassis, filled-in windscreen, cast impression of spare	**£300-400**

Note: The rarest of the 24 Series have coloured tyres matching the body colour and a higher value can be expected.

25j	1947-48	**Jeep**	Red body, Red or Blue hubs, 68 mm	**£80-100**
			Green body, Black or Red hubs	**£80-100**
			Aqua Blue or Sky Blue body, Black or Yellow hubs	**£100-150**
25y (405)	1952-54	**Universal Jeep**.....................	Green or Red body with hook, Maroon hubs, spare wheel on side. 83 mm	**£80-90**
			Red body with hook, Blue hubs, spare wheel on side. 83 mm	**£80-90**
27d (340)	1950-54	**Land Rover**...........................	Green, Dark Blue or Orange body, tinplate windscreen frame, driver, 90 mm	**£55-65**
			As previous model but with Red body	**£65-75**
	1952-53	.................Gift Set model: ...	Dark Brown body. Only in Gift Set No.2, Commercial Vehicles Set.	**GSP**
27f (344)	1950-54	**Estate Car**............................	Pale Brown body with Dark Brown panels, rear axle pillars, Fawn hubs, 105 mm	**£70-80**
			Grey body with Red side panels	**£100-125**
27m (341)	1950-54	**Land-Rover Trailer**...............	Orange body (Beige hubs), Green body (Green hubs), Blue (Blue hubs), Red (Red hubs)	**£25-35**

30a (32)	1935-40	**Chrysler 'Airflow' Saloon**	No chassis, separate bumper units, lead versions exist, 103 mm.	
			Turquoise, Maroon, Cream, Green, Blue, Red, (hubs may be any colour)	**£300-400**
			Rare issues with plated chrome hubs	**£400-500**
	1946		Cream or Green body, smooth hubs, White tyres	**£150-200**
	1946-48		As previous model but Blue, Cream or Green body (hubs usually Black)	**£100-125**
30b	1935-40	**Rolls-Royce**	Open chassis, no sidelights, authentic radiator, 101 mm.	
	1935-40		Cream/Black, Red and Dark Red, Blue/Black, Dark Blue/Black, Fawn/Black,	
			Red/Black, All Black	**£200-300**
			Yellow/Brown, Red/Red, Grey/Grey, Green/Green, Pale Green/Black	**£200-300**
			Light Blue body, smooth black wheel hubs, open chassis	**£200-300**
	1946		Fawn body, smooth hubs, open chassis	**£100-125**
	1946-50		Plain (closed) chassis, Violet-Blue/Black, Mid-Blue/Black, Dark Blue/Black, Light Blue/Black,	
			Fawn/Black or Greyish-Brown/Black	**£100-150**
30c	1935-40	**Daimler**	Open chassis, no sidelights, authentic radiator, 98 mm.	
	1935-40		Cream/Black, Blue/Black, Dark Blue/Black, Yellow/Black, Fawn/Black	**£200-300**
			Turquoise/Black, Fawn/Black, Light Green/Black	**£200-300**
			Pink/Maroon, Red/Red	**£175-250**
			Two-tone Grey or two-tone Green	**£300-500**
	1946		Sand body, smooth black wheel hubs, open chassis	**£300-400**
			Green or Fawn body, open chassis, smooth or ridged hubs	**£100-125**
	1946-50	**Daimler**	Plain (closed) chassis, Dark Green/Black, Cream/Black, Greyish-Brown/Black,	
			Grey/Black, Light Green/Black	**£100-125**
			Medium Green body with Pale Green hubs	**£125-150**
30d	1935-40	**Vauxhall**	Open chassis, no sidelights, spare wheel, 'egg box' or 'shield' grille, 98 mm.	
	1935-38		Green/Black, Blue/Black, Grey/Black, Yellow/Black, Brown/Black	**£200-300**
			Yellow/Brown, Cream/Brown, Tan/Brown	**£200-300**
			Two-tone Grey or two-tone Green	**£300-500**
	1938-40	radiator change:	As previous model but with 'shield' grille, Black chassis	**£200-300**
			With 'shield' radiator and coloured chassis	**£200-300**
	1946		Dark Olive Green body, open chassis, smooth black hubs, White tyres	**£100-125**
	1946-50		Plain (closed) chassis, no spare wheel, 'shield' radiator,	
			Green/Black, Brown/Black, Maroon/Black, Yellow/Black,	
			Grey/Black, Olive-Green/Black, Blue/Black	**£100-125**
		Variation:	with Silver cast ridged hubs, thick axles, with Dark Olive Green body, black chassis	**£200-250**
30e	1935-48	**Breakdown Car**	See 'Commercial vehicles and Vans' section.	
30f	1936-41	**Ambulance**	See 'Fire, Police and Ambulance' vehicles section.	
30g	1936-50	**Caravan**	See Caravan section.	
32 (30a)	1934-35	**Chrysler 'Airflow' Saloon**	Maroon (lead) body, no chassis, separate bumper units, 103 mm	**£200-250**
			Maroon (diecast) body, no chassis, separate bumper units, 103 mm	**£200-250**
34a	1935-40	**'Royal Air Mail' Service Car**	See 'Commercial Vehicles and Vans' section.	
35a	1936-40	**Saloon Car**	Some versions may have spare wheel cover in darker shade of main colour.	
			Blue, Maroon, Grey, Yellow, Red, Turquoise, Black or White solid rubber wheels, 51 mm	**£90-120**
	1946-48		Grey or Blue body (spare wheel cover not enhanced), Black rubber wheels	**£60-70**
35az	1939-40	**Fiat 2-seater Saloon**	Red, Blue or Green, White rubber wheels, 'Simca 5' cast inside. French issue	**£80-100**
35b	1936-39	**Racer**	Red, Silver, Yellow or Blue body, with or without driver, White solid rubber wheels,	
			Red grille and steering wheel, 57 mm	**£65-75**
35b (200)	1939-54	**Midget Racer**	Silver body, Red grille, Brown driver, solid Black rubber wheels only	**£65-75**
			Silver body, Red grille, Silver driver, solid Black rubber wheels only	**£65-75**
			Green body, Black tyres	**£150-175**
35c	1936-40	**MG Sports Car**	Red, Pale or Dark Green, Turquoise, Blue or Maroon, Silver detailing,	
			White solid rubber wheels, 52 mm	**£100-125**
	1946-48		Red or Green body, Silver on radiator only, Black rubber wheels only	**£70-80**
35d	1938-40	**Austin 7 Car (open tourer)**	Wire windscreen frame, Black or White rubber wheels, Silver radiator and steering wheel,	
			hole for driver, 50 mm. Blue, Turquoise, Grey, Lime Green, Maroon or Yellow,	
			(Yellow may have Orange spare wheel cover)	**£100-125**
	1946-48		Blue, Grey or Yellow body, Silver on radiator only, Black rubber wheels only	**£50-70**
			Fawn body, Silver on radiator only, Black rubber wheels only	**£70-90**
36a	1937-41	**Armstrong-Siddeley Limousine**		
		with Driver and Footman	Detailed chassis with slots, tinplate figures, sidelights, 97 mm.	
			Red/Dark Red, Grey/Dark Grey, Maroon/Dark Maroon	**£300-400**
	1946		Grey body, Black smooth wheel hubs, Moulded chassis with or without slots	**£100-150**
36a	1947-50	**Armstrong-Siddeley**	(no slots or figures), moulded chassis, ridged hubs.	
			Mid-Blue/Black, Grey/Black, Maroon/Black, Red/Maroon, Sky Blue/Black,	
			Powder Blue/Black, Saxe-Blue/Black, Olive-Green/Black	**£90-120**
			Turquoise body, moulded chassis, ridged hubs	**£140-170**
36b	1937-41	**Bentley 2 seat Sports Coupé**		
		with Driver and Footman	Detailed chassis with slots, tinplate figures, sidelights, 94 mm.	
			Cream/Black, Yellow/Maroon, Grey/Grey	**£300-400**
	1946		Light Green or Saxe Blue body, smooth black hubs, moulded chassis (slots on some)	**£200-300**
36b	1947-50	**Bentley**	(no slots/figures). Moulded chassis, ridged hubs.	
			Green/Black, Blue/Black, Grey/Black, Fawn/Black, Light Fawn/Black	**£90-120**
			Light Blue, moulded chassis, ridged hubs	**£125-150**
36c	1937-41	**Humber Vogue Saloon**		
		with Driver and Footman	Detailed chassis with slots, tinplate figures, sidelights, 91 mm.	
			Green/Dark Green, Blue/Dark Blue, all Royal Blue	**£300-400**
	1946		Early post war issues with smooth Black hubs, moulded chassis with or without slots	**£100-150**

36c	1947-50	**Humber Vogue**........................Brown/Black, Blue/Black, Grey/Black, Maroon/Black, (no slots/figures)...£90-120		
		Light Blue and Black, moulded chassis, ridged hubs £175-225		
36d	1937-41	**Rover Streamlined Saloon**		
		with Driver and Footman......Detailed cast chassis with slots, tinplate figures, sidelights, Black hubs, 94 mm.		
		Green/Dark Green, Red/Maroon...£300-400		
	1946	....Early post war issues with smooth Black hubs and moulded chassis with or without slots £100-150		
36d	1947-50	**Rover** ....(no slots/figures). Dark, Mid or Bright Blue/Black, Light or Mid-Green/Black.......................£90-120		
		Green body with Light Green hubs £125-150		
		Blue body, Black wings, Light Blue hubs..£100-125		
		Navy Blue body, Black wings, Black hubs £750-1,000		
36e	1937-41	**British Salmson Two-seater**		
		Sports Car with Driver..........Detailed chassis, hole in seat for driver, cast driver, Black hubs, solid windscreen,		
		sidelights, 93 mm. (spare wheel on some, 96 mm.)		
		Royal Blue/Black, Blue/Dark Blue, Red/Black, Grey/Dark Grey £300-400		
	1946	**British Salmson** ....Early post war issues with smooth Black hubs, moulded chassis £100-125		
		Rare Brown issues £100-125		
36e	1947-50	**British Salmson Two-seater**		
		Sports Car.............................Red/Black, Light or Mid-Green/Black, Fawn/Black,		
		Mid-Blue/Black, Sky-Blue/Black or Saxe-Blue/Black, No hole in seat.................................£90-120		
		Red or Brown body, moulded chassis, ridged hubs £250-300		
36f	1937-41	**British Salmson Four-seater**		
		Sports Car with Driver........Detailed chassis, hole in seat for driver, cast driver, sidelights, Black hubs and		
		solid windscreen, cast-in spare wheel, 96 mm. Red/Maroon, Green/Dark Green.............................£300-400		
36f	1947-50	**British Salmson Four-seater**		
		Sports Car............................Light or Mid-Green/Black, Brown/Black, Grey/Black, Fawn/Black, (no hole).......................£90-120		
		Brownish-Grey/Black or Light Grey/Black...£90-120		

N.B. Early Post War Issues 38 and 39 Series - see the Model Identification section for details.

38a	1940-41	**Frazer Nash BMW Sports**.....Red (Maroon seats), Dark Blue (Fawn seats), lacquered metal base, 82 mm. £150-175		
	1946	.......................Special Issue: ...Dark Blue body, Light Blue seats, spread spigot not rivet, 'Hornby Series' tinplate sheet £200-300		
	1946-50	...................Regular Issues: ...with Black base, smooth hubs:		
		Light or Dark Blue (Fawn or Grey seats)...£90-120		
		Grey (Fawn, Khaki or Blue seats), or Grey (Red seats and hubs) £90-120		
		Light Grey (Blue seats, Black hubs), Blue with Putty seats..£90-120		
38a (100)	1950-55	....Same as previous models but made for export only (renumbered in 1954) ....NGPP		
38b	1940-41	**Sunbeam Talbot Sports** ....Red (Maroon tonneau), Red or Black hubs, lacquered metal base, 92 mm. £150-200		
	1946	....Grey body, Fawn seats or Green with Dark Green seats...£300-400		
	1947-49	....Red/Maroon or Maroon/Grey, Black baseplate...£90-120		
		Light Green/Green, Brown/Blue, Black baseplate £90-120		
		Light Grey (Grey or Dark Blue tonneau), Black hubs, Black baseplate £90-120		
		Dark Grey (Grey or Light Blue tonneau), Black hubs, Black baseplate £90-120		
		Yellow body and ridged hubs with matt Fawn tonneau, Black painted baseplate £150-175		
		Deep Yellow body and hubs with Dark Green tonneau, Black base, Silver edged screen......................£150-175		
		Dark Blue body, Light Grey tonneau, Black hubs and baseplate £90-120		
		Light Blue body, Dark Grey tonneau, Black hubs and baseplate..£90-120		
		Brown body, Blue tonneau, Silver edged screen £150-175		
	1950	....Late post war issues with coloured hubs, e.g. Yellow body, Green tonneau, Yellow hubs or		
		Red body, Maroon tonneau, Red hubs, plain screen £150-175		
		Red body, Dark Green tonneau, Red hubs, Black baseplate £150-175		
38b (101)	1950-55	....As previous models but made for export only (renumbered in 1954). ....NGPP		
38c	1946	**Lagonda Sports Coupé** ....Early post war issues with Black wheel hubs £200-300		
	1947-50	....Green (Black seats), or Green (Dark Green seats), Black baseplate, 102mm. £90-120		
		Grey (Fawn seats), or Grey (Maroon seats)..£90-120		
		Maroon (Dark Blue seats or Grey seats), Black baseplate..£90-120		
		Light Grey (Dark Grey seats), or Mid-Grey (Grey seats)..£90-120		
38c (102)	1950-55	....As previous models but made for export only (renumbered in 1954) ....NGPP		
	1950	....Late post war issues with coloured hubs, eg. Maroon body with Green hubs..........................£200-250		
38d	1940-41	**Alvis Sports Tourer** ....Green body, Black seats and hubs or Maroon body, Red seats, lacquered base, 95 mm. £150-175		
	1946	....Early post war issues £200-300		
	1947-50	....Green/Dark Green, Green/Brown, Black painted baseplate...£90-120		
		Green body, Black seats and hubs, Black painted baseplate £90-120		
		Green body, Black seats, Green hubs, Black painted baseplate £90-120		
		Maroon/Grey, Red hubs, Maroon/Red, Light Blue/Dark Blue, Black base............................£100-150		
		Blue/Grey, Grey/Blue, Black painted base £80-100		
	1950	....Late post war issues with coloured hubs, eg. Maroon body with Grey hubs.........................£200-250		
38d (103)	1950-55	....As previous models but made for export only (renumbered in 1954) ....NGPP		
38e	1940 ?	**Triumph Dolomite**................Planned and catalogued but not issued..NPP		
38e	1946	**Armstrong Siddeley Coupé** ...Early post war issues with Black wheel hubs £200-300		
	1947-50	....Grey/Blue, Light Grey/Blue, Black painted baseplate, 96 mm..£90-120		
		Light Grey/Green, Light Green/Grey or Grey/Dark Green..£90-120		
		Bright Green/Grey, Red/Maroon, Cream/Blue, Black painted baseplate..............................£90-120		
	1950	....Late post war issues with coloured hubs, e.g. Light Green (Apple Green hubs) or Mid or		
		Light Green and Grey (Mid-Green hubs) or Light Grey and Dark Green (Grey hubs) £200-250		
38e (104)	1950-55	....As previous models but made for export only (renumbered in 1954) ....NGPP		

38f	1940-41	**Jaguar (SS100) Sports Car**....Khaki/Blue, Blue/Grey, Light Blue/Grey, Grey/Blue, Grey/Black, Red/Maroon, Dark Brown/Black, 2 windscreens, clear lacquered baseplate, 80 mm	£150-175
	1946	....Early post-war issues with Black wheel hubs	£90-120
	1947-50	....Light, Mid- or Dark Blue body, Grey or Putty seats, Black painted baseplate	£90-120
		Light Brown body, Blue seats, Black painted baseplate or Red body	£90-120
		Brownish-Grey body, Black seats and hubsc	£150-200
	1950	....Late post-war issues with coloured hubs, e.g. Light Blue body, Putty seats (Blue hubs) or Red body, Maroon seats and tonneau (Red hubs)	£150-180
38f (105)	1950-55	....As previous models but made for export only (renumbered in 1954)	NGPP
39a	1939-41	**Packard Super 8 Tourer**.......Light Green, Grey, Black, Yellow, Blue, lacquered baseplate, 107 mm	£200-300
	1946	....Early post-war issues with Black smooth wheel hubs	£125-175
	1947-50	....Brown, Green or Olive-Green body, Black painted baseplate	£90-120
	1950	....Late post-war issues with coloured ridged hubs	£200-250
39b	1939-41	**Oldsmobile 6 Sedan**.................Black, Maroon, Yellow, Mid Blue, Light or Mid-Grey or Green, lacquered base, 100 mm	£200-300
	1946	....Early post-war issues with Black smooth wheel hubs	£100-150
	1947-50	....Grey, Brown, Green or Fawn body, oval baseplate supports, Black painted baseplate open at rear, ridged hubs	£90-120
		Cream body	£125-150
		Violet-Blue, Black chassis	£150-200
	1947-50	.................US issue: ....Light Blue body, Black ridged hubs, oval baseplate support, open rear baseplate	£200-300
	1950	....Late post-war issues with coloured hubs	£200-250
	1952	...................Export issue: ....Sand body and hubs, oval front supports, closed rear baseplate	£200-300
39bu	1950-52	**Oldsmobile Sedan** (US issue).Cream with Dark Blue wings or two-tone Blue, Black painted baseplate	£800-1,000
		Cream body, Tan wings, Black painted baseplate (closed at rear), blued axles, oval studs	£500-700
		Tan body and hubs, oval studs, baseplate closed at rear	£600-800
39c	1939-41	**Lincoln Zephyr Coupé**..........Grey, Yellow Red or Green body, lacquered baseplate, 106 mm	£150-175
	1946	....Early post-war issues with Black smooth wheel hubs	£100-150
	1947-50	....Grey, Brown, Maroon or Red body, Black painted baseplate, ridged hubs	£90-120
	1950	....Late post-war issues with coloured ridged hubs e.g. Light 'Riley' Green with darker Green hubs or Red body with Red hubs	£200-250
39cu	1950-52	.................US issue: ....Red body and ridged hubs, Maroon wings, Black painted baseplate	£500-700
39cu	1950-52	.................US issue: ....Cream body and ridged hubs, Brown wings, Black painted baseplate	£500-700
39cu	1950-52	.................US issue: ....Tan with Brown wings, Black painted baseplate	£500-700
39d	1939-41	**Buick Viceroy Saloon**...........Grey, Green, Maroon, Cream or Blue, lacquered baseplate, 103 mm	£200-250
	1946	....Early post-war issues with Black smooth wheel hubs	£100-150
	1946	Olive body, smooth hubs	£100-150
	1947-50	....Light or Dark Green, Maroon, Fawn, Blue, Beige or Grey body, Black base, ridged hubs	£90-120
		Mustard body, Black painted baseplate	£150-200
		Greyish-Brown body, Light Brown hubs, Black painted baseplate	£140-160
		Apple Green body and hubs	£300-400
	1950	....Late post-war issues with coloured hubs, eg. Light 'Riley' Green body with darker green hubs or Brown body with Green hubs	£200-250
39e	1939-41	**Chrysler Royal**......................Yellow, Green, Royal Blue or Grey body, lacquered baseplate, 106 mm	£200-250
	1946	....Early post-war issues with Black smooth wheel hubs	£100-150
	1947-50	....Light Blue, Mid-Blue, Dark Blue, Light Green, Mid-Green, Dark Green or Dark Grey body, Black ridged hubs and baseplate	£110-140
		As previous models but with Silvered baseplate	£250-350
		Cream body, Green hubs, Black painted baseplate	£100-150
	1950	....Late post-war issues with coloured hubs, eg. Light 'Triumph 1800' Blue with blue hubs	£200-250
39eu	1950-52	**Chrysler Royal** (US issue)......Yellow with Red wings, Yellow hubs or two-tone Green body with Light Green hubs, Black baseplate, Blued axles	£500-700
39f	1939-41	**Studebaker State Commander** Yellow, Green or Dark Grey body, lacquered baseplate, 103 mm	£200-250
	1946	....Early post-war issues with Black smooth wheel hubs	£100-150
	1947-50	....Yellow body, Black smooth hubs	£250-350
		Green, Olive or Maroon body, Black baseplate, ridged hubs	£90-120
		Grey or Light Grey body, Black ridged hubs	£90-120
		Dark Maroon body, Black ridged hubs	£90-120
		Very Dark Blue or Navy Blue body, Black ridged hubs	£90-120
		Tan body, Black ridged hubs	£120-150
		Mid-Blue body, Black baseplate, Mid-Blue ridged hubs	£200-250
		Dark Breen body, Black baseplate, ridged hubs	£120-140
	1950	....Late post-war issues with coloured ridged hubs	£200-250
40a (158)	1947-55	**Riley Saloon** ....Pale or Dark Grey body, Black or Grey hubs, small lettering on baseplate	£90-120
		Dark Blue body, Black baseplate	£150-200
		Mid-Blue body, Black hubs, small lettering on baseplate	£140-170
		Dark Green body, Black hubs, small lettering on baseplate	£90-120
		Mid-Green body and hubs, large lettering on baseplate	£120-140
40b	1948-49	**Triumph 1800** (Renown) ....Light Blue, Fawn, Grey, rear axle held by pillars, Black baseplate, 91 mm	£90-120
		Gloss Black body, Black hubs, rear axle held by pillars, Black baseplate	£750-1,000
40b (151)	1949-55	....Fawn body, Green hubs	£90-120
		Grey body and hubs	£90-120
		Dark Blue body and hubs	£90-120
		Black body and hubs	£1,000-1,500

NB Early 1948-1950 issues have the rear axle held by pillars.
All issues have small lettering on their baseplates.

| 40c | 1940 | **Jowett Javelin** .... Factory drawing exists, but model not issued .... NPP |

40d (152)	1949-54	**Austin (A40) Devon** .... Maroon body and hubs, small lettering on baseplate	£90-120
		Blue body, Mid-Blue hubs, small lettering on baseplate	£90-120
		Dark Green body, Cream hubs, small lettering on baseplate	£80-90
		Red body, Maroon hubs, small lettering on baseplate	£400-500
		Light Grey-Green body and hubs, Black baseplate, large lettering on baseplate	£90-120
		Grey-Green body, Beige hubs, Black baseplate, large lettering on baseplate	£90-120
40e	1948-50	**Standard Vanguard** .... Tan body and hubs, 'open' rear wheel arches, small lettering on base, rear axle clip, name inside roof, 91mm	£90-120
		As previous version but with no name inside roof	£140-180
40e (153)	1950-54	.... Tan body, Red hubs, 'open' rear wheel arches, small lettering on base, rear axle clip	£160-200
		Tan body and hubs, 'closed' rear wheel arches, small lettering on base, no axle clip	£90-120
		Light Blue body and hubs, 'closed' rear wheel arches, small lettering on base, no axle clip	£90-120
		Dark Blue body, Beige hubs, 'closed' rear arches, small lettering on base, no axle clip	£90-120
		Maroon body and hubs, 'closed' rear wheel arches, no name under roof, large lettering on base	£1,000-1,500
		Light Green body, Green hubs, 'closed' rear wheel arches, large lettering on base	£1,000-1,500
40f (154)	1951-54	**Hillman Minx** .... Light Tan body, Cream hubs, small lettering on baseplate, 88 mm	£80-110
		Green body, Light Green hubs, small lettering on baseplate	£80-110
		Dark Tan body, Grey hubs, large lettering on baseplate, 88 mm	£80-110
40g (159)	1950-54	**Morris Oxford** .... Light Grey body and hubs, 93 mm	£90-120
		Light Tan body and hubs, Black baseplate, small print on baseplate (Export issue)	£400-600
		Mid-Green body and hubs	£90-120
40j (161)	1953-54	**Austin (A40) Somerset** .... Pale Blue body and hubs, 89 mm	£90-120
101	1957-60	**Sunbeam Alpine** (touring) ...... Pink body, Cream interior, Beige diecast hubs, Grey driver, 94 mm	£90-120
		Light Turquoise body, Dark Blue interior, Light Blue diecast hubs, Grey driver	£90-120
		Light Turquoise body, Dark Blue interior, spun hubs, Grey driver	£90-120
102	1957-60	**MG Midget** (touring finish) .... Orange body, Red seats and diecast hubs, Grey driver, 83 mm	£175-225
		Light Green body, Cream seats, Cream diecast hubs, Grey driver	£175-225
		Late issues with spun aluminium hubs	£200-250
103	1957-60	**Austin Healey 100** (touring) ... Red body, Grey seats, diecast hubs and driver, 85 mm	£175-200
		Cream body, Red seats and diecast hubs, Grey driver	£175-200
104	1957-60	**Aston-Martin DB3S** (touring) Light Blue body, Dark Blue interior, Mid-Blue hubs, Grey driver, 87 mm	£145-175
		Salmon-Pink body, Red seats and diecast hubs, Grey driver	£145-175
105	1957-60	**Triumph TR2** (touring finish) Grey body, Red seats and diecast hubs, 84 mm	£115-135
		As previous issue but with spun hubs in 'plain' printed box	£200-300
		Lemon body, Green seats and diecast hubs, Grey driver	£150-175
	1959-60	.... As previous models but with spun hubs, in 'plain' printed box with Yellow spot	£200-250
106 (140a)	1954-58	**Austin A90 Atlantic** .... Light Blue body, Cream seats, Cream hubs, 95 mm	£90-120
		Light Blue body, Red seats, Red hubs	£90-120
		Light Blue body, Dark Blue seats, Cream hubs	£90-120
		Light Blue body, Dark Blue seats, Dark Blue hubs	£90-120
		Black body, Red seats and hubs, White tyres	£90-120
		Pink body, Cream interior, Cream hubs, '106' on baseplate	£90-120
		NB Interiors may have a gloss or matt finish.
107	1955-59	**Sunbeam Alpine** (competition finish) .... Light Blue, Tan or Cream seats, Beige hubs, '26', racing driver, 94 mm	£100-130
		Deep Pink body, Grey seats, Beige hubs, RN '34', racing driver	£100-130
108	1955-59	**MG Midget** (competition) ...... Red body, Tan seats, Red hubs, RN '24', racing driver, 83 mm	£120-140
		White body, Maroon seats, Red hubs, RN '28', racing driver	£120-140
		Note: The version of 108 issued in the US is numbered 129.
109	1955-59	**Austin-Healey 100** (competition finish) .... Cream body, Red seats and hubs, racing driver and racing number '23', 85 mm	£90-110
		Yellow body, Blue seats and hubs, racing driver and racing number '21' or '28'	£90-110
110	1956-59	**Aston-Martin DB3S** (competition finish) .... Grey body, Blue seats and hubs, racing driver and number '20', 87 mm	£100-130
		Light Green body, Red interior, Red ridged hubs, RN '22'	£100-130
110	1966-67	**Aston-Martin DB5** .... Metallic Red, Cream or Black seats, '110' on base, spoked wheels, 111 mm	£70-85
	1967-71	Metallic Red or Blue, Cream or Black seats, plain base, spoked wheels	£70-85
111	1956-59	**Triumph TR2 Sports Car** (competition finish) .... Salmon-Pink body, Blue seats and hubs, racing driver and RN '29', 84 mm	£115-135
		Turquoise body, Red seats and hubs, racing driver and racing number '25'	£115-135
112	1961-66	**Austin-Healey Sprite Mk.II** .. Red body, Cream interior, spun hubs, 78 mm	£80-100
		South African issues: Turquoise, Pink, Light Blue or Dark Blue body, spun hubs	£500-750
113	1962-69	**MG 'MGB'** .... Ivory body, Red seats, Grey plastic driver, 85 mm	£70-90
	1966	South African issue: Mid-Blue body (Red interior), or Red body, spun hubs	£500-750
114	1963-71	**Triumph Spitfire** .... Sports car with Blue lady driver (plastic), spun hubs, 87 mm.
	1963-66	Metallic Silver-Grey body (Red seats), or Red body (Cream seats)	£75-90
	1966-70	Metallic Gold body with Red seats and 'Tiger In Tank' on bootlid	£75-90
	1966-70	Metallic Gold body, without bootlid logo	£75-90
	1970-71	Metallic Purple body	£100-125
115	1965-69	**Plymouth Fury Sports** .... White open body, Red interior, cast wheels, driver and passenger	£70-80

116	1966-71	**Volvo P 1800 S**	Red body, White interior, wire wheels, 105 mm	£60-75
			Metallic Red body, Light Blue interior, wire wheels	£80-100
120	1962-67	**Jaguar 'E' type**	Red, detachable Black or Grey hardtop/optional Cream or Grey folded soft-top, 92 mm	£50-60
			Metallic Blue and White, Black, Grey or Cream body	£50-60
			Metallic Light Blue and Black body, Cream seats	£600-800
122	1977-78	**Volvo 265 DL Estate**	Metallic Blue (Brown interior), or Cream with '265DL' wing badges, cast hubs, 141 mm	£30-35
	1979-80		Orange version without '265 DL' (made in Italy by Polistil), Brown box	£40-50
123	1977-80	**Princess 2200 HL**	Metallic Bronze with black roof side panels, plastic wheels	£30-35
			All White	£30-35
			White body, Blue roof	£30-35
			White body, Blue side panels	£30-35
124	1977-79	**Rolls-Royce Phantom V**	Metallic Light Blue, boot opens - bonnet does not (see 152), 141 mm	£35-45
127	1964-66	**Rolls-Royce**		
		Silver Cloud Mk.3	Metallic Blue or Metallic Green, suspension and steering, 125 mm	£65-75
	1966-69		Metallic Gold, Light Blue interior, cast wheels	£55-65
	1969-72		Metallic Red	£55-65
128	1964-67	**Mercedes-Benz 600**	Metallic Red body, white interior, spun hubs, three figures/luggage, 147 mm	£45-55
	1967-75		Metallic Red body, White interior, spun hubs or Speedwheels, driver only	£30-40
	1975-79		Metallic Blue body, White interior, driver, Speedwheels	£30-35
129	? - ?	**MG Midget** (US issue)	White body, Maroon or Red interior and tonneau, Red hubs, no driver or racing number (see 108), Yellow box with '129'	£300-400
			Red body, Tan interior and tonneau, Red hubs, no driver or racing number (see 108), Yellow box with '129'	£300-400
129	1965 -72	**Volkswagen 1300 Sedan**	Metallic Blue body, White interior, spun hubs	£35-45
	1972-76		Metallic Blue body, plastic Speedwheels	£30-35
130	1964-66	**Ford Consul Corsair**	Red or Metallic Wine Red body, Off-White interior, spun hubs, 106 mm	£55-65
	1966-69		Light Blue, Metallic Dark Grey base, Off-White interior, spun hubs	£45-55
			N.B. Baseplates on 130 may have rounded or dimpled rivets.	
131	1956-61	**Cadillac Eldorado**	Yellow body, Red interior, Grey driver, Cream diecast hubs, 118 mm	£85-100
			Salmon-Pink body, Grey interior, Grey driver, Cream diecast hubs	£85-100
	1962-63		As previous models but with spun aluminium hubs	£90-120
131	1968-70	**Jaguar 'E'-type 2+2**	White body, suspension, tilting seats, cast spoked wheels, 112 mm	£80-90
	1970-75		Metallic Bronze body, Blue interior, cast spoked wheels or plastic wheels	£65-75
	1975-76		Metallic Purple, cast spoked wheels or Speedwheels	£100-125
	1976-77		Bronze body, Speedwheels	£65-75
	1977-77		Metallic Red or Post Office Red body, Blue interior, Speedwheels	£70-80
132	1955-61	**Packard Convertible**	Light Green body, Red interior and hubs, Grey driver, 112 mm	£85-100
			Light Brown body, Red interior and hubs, Grey driver	£85-100
	1962-63		As previous models but with spun aluminium hubs	£90-120
132	1967-74	**Ford 40 RV**	Metallic Silver or Blue body, wire wheels	£30-40
			Red/Yellow body, White interior, wire wheels	£30-40
			N.B. Early models have red headlight recesses.	
133	1955-60	**Cunningham C5R**	White body, Dark Blue stripes, Brown interior, RN '31', Blue hubs, Light Blue driver	£65-75
			Off-White body, Blue interior and driver	£65-75
			As previous models but with spun aluminium hubs	£70-80
133	1964-66	**Ford Cortina**	Metallic Gold/White, spun hubs, 101 mm, (issued to replace 139)	£55-65
	1966-68		Pale Lime body, Red interior, spun hubs	£65-75
134	1964-68	**Triumph Vitesse**	Metallic Aqua Blue body, White side stripe, Red interior	£70-85
135	1963-69	**Triumph 2000 Saloon**	Red interior, Grey base, spun hubs, wipers, luggage, 105 mm.	
		normal colours:	Metallic Green with White roof or Metallic Blue with White roof	£60-70
		Gift Set 118 colour:	White body, Blue roof	GSP
		promotional colours:	Each promotional issue was packed in a standard Yellow/Red card picture box.	
			Black body, Cactus-Green or White roof	NGPP
			Blue Grey body, Black roof	NGPP
			Light Green body, Lilac roof	NGPP
			Brown body, Light Green roof	NGPP
			British Racing Green, White roof	NGPP
			Cherry Red body, White roof, Blue interior	NGPP
			White body, Black or Light Green or Light Grey roof, Blue interior	NGPP
			Dark Green body, Cactus-Green roof	NGPP
			Gunmetal body, Black roof, with 'Gunmetal/WD' label on box	NGPP
		NB	The above 'NGPP' issues have sold for prices in excess of £250 in the mid-1990s at Vectis Auctions Ltd.	
136	1964-65	**Vauxhall Viva**	White body, suspension and fingertip steering, 93 mm	£45-55
	1965-68		Metallic Bright Blue body, Red interior	£40-50
	1969-73		Pale Metallic Blue body, Red interior	£50-60
137	1963-66	**Plymouth Fury Convertible**	Green, Pink, Blue or Metallic Grey body, Cream hood, spun hubs	£70-80

138	1963-66	**Hillman Imp** .... Metallic Silver-Green body, luggage, spun hubs, cast headlamps, 85 mm.....................	£70-80
	1966-68	.... Metallic Red body, luggage, spun hubs, jewelled or plastic headlamps...................	£70-80
	1968-73	.... Metallic Blue body, Red interior, luggage, spun hubs, jewelled headlamps.................	£40-50
		As previous issue but with Blue interior, in picture box with white background...................	£100-125
	Late issue:	Metallic Deep Blue body, Red interior, bare metal baseplate, spun hubs...................	£140-160
139	1963-64	**Ford Cortina** .... Pale Blue body, Off-White interior, spun hubs, cast headlamps, 101 mm...................	£55-65
	1964-65	.... Metallic Blue body, Off-White interior, spun hubs...................................	£65-75
	1966	.... South African issue: ....Green body, spun hubs, Fawn interior...................................	£500-600

NOTE: South African Dinky Toys - The boxes are printed in both English and Afrikaans, and with the distributors name.

139a (170)	1949-54	**Ford Fordor Sedan** .... All have small lettering on the baseplates.	
		Yellow, Red, Green or Tan body, (all with matching hubs), 102 mm...................	£90-110
		Brown body, Red hubs...	£90-110
		Tan body, Red hubs...	£90-110
		Red body, Maroon hubs...	£90-110
139am	1950-54	**US Army Staff Car** .... (170m) Ford Fordor in Olive drab with White stars on roof and doors...................	£175-250
	Canadian issue:	As previous model but without stars...................................	NGPP
139b (171)	1950-54	**Hudson Commodore** .... Dark Blue body, Stone roof and hubs, 111 mm...................	£90-110
		Dark Blue body, Fawn roof and hubs...................................	£90-110
		Cream body, Maroon roof and hubs....................................	£90-110
		Royal Blue body, Stone roof and hubs.................................	£125-150
		Fawn lower body, Light Blue roof, as per 151 (40b) Triumph Renown Blue...................	NGPP
140a (106)	1951-53	**Austin A90 Atlantic** .... Mid-Blue body, Red seats, Cream hubs...................	£90-120
		Mid-Blue body, Dark Blue seats, Mid-Blue hubs...................	£500-750
		Deep Blue body, Red seats and hubs...................................	£100-150
		Red body, Brown seats and hubs.......................................	£100-150
		Light Blue body, Red seats, Cream hubs...............................	£90-120
		Red body, Cream seats and hubs.......................................	£100-150
		NB Interiors may have a gloss or matt finish.	
140b (156)	1951-54	**Rover 75 Saloon** .... Maroon (Maroon hubs), or Cream (Cream hubs), 101 mm...................	£90-110
140	1963-69	**Morris 1100** .... Light Blue or Dark Blue, spun hubs...................	£40-50
	1966	.... South African issue: ....White body, Blue roof or Light Caramel, Red interior...................	£500-750
141	1963-67	**Vauxhall Victor Estate Car** ...Yellow or Maroon body, suspension and steering, spun hubs, 92 mm...................	£45-55
	1966	.... South African issue: ....Pink body with Blue interior, spun hubs...................	£500-750
142	1962-68	**Jaguar Mk.10** .... Metallic Blue or Light Blue, suspension, spun aluminium hubs, 107 mm...................	£40-50
	1966	.... South African issue: ....Green body with White roof, spun hubs...................	£500-750
	NB	Gold, US export issue 'see-through' window boxes. Model nos. 134, 138 and 142 housed in these boxes may attract a premium of 50%. See 'Cars - Box Types' for a complete listing.	
143	1962-67	**Ford Capri** .... Turquoise body, White roof, Red interior, spun hubs, 90 mm...................	£50-60
144	1963-67	**Volkswagen 1500** .... Off-White body, luggage, spun hubs, 93 mm...................	£45-55
		Gold body, Blue interior, luggage, spun hubs...................	£45-55
		Gold body, Red interior, luggage, spun hubs...................	£100-150
		Metallic Green body, spun hubs...................	£400-600
145	1962-67	**Singer Vogue** .... Metallic Light Green body, Red interior, spun hubs, 93 mm...................	£55-65
		Yellow body, Red interior, spun hubs...................	£1,500-2,000
146	1963-67	**Daimler 2.5 litre V8** .... Metallic Pale Green body, Red interior, spun hubs, 95 mm...................	£60-70
147	1962-69	**Cadillac '62** .... Metallic Green body, Red or White interior, spun hubs, 113 mm...................	£55-65
148	1962-65	**Ford Fairlane** .... (Non-metallic) Pea Green body, Cream interior, open or closed windows, spun hubs...................	£65-75
		As previous issue but with Red interior...................	NGPP
	1965-67	.... Light Metallic Green, Off-White interior, open or closed windows, spun hubs...................	£125-150
		US issue:	Metallic Emerald Green body, spun hubs, US issue Gold 'see-through' window box...................	£500-600
	1966	.... South African issue: ....Bright Blue body, open windows, spun hubs, White tyres...................	£500-750
	1966	.... South African issue: ....Greyish-Lilac, spun hubs, no base number, White tyres...................	£500-750
149	1971-75	**Citroën Dyane** .... Metallic Bronze body, Black roof and interior, Speedwheels, 91 mm...................	£30-35
	1971-75	.... Light Grey body, Dark Grey or Black roof, suspension, Speedwheels...................	£25-30
150	1959-64	**Rolls-Royce Silver Wraith** ..... Two-tone Grey body, suspension, spun hubs, Chromed metal bumpers, 117 mm...................	£60-75
		Later issues with plastic bumpers...................	£50-60
		N.B. The French version of 150 (French reference 551) was cast from English-made dies, was assembled in France, and has 'Made in France' on the baseplate.	
151 (40b)	1954-59	**Triumph 1800** (Renown) .... Blue body and hubs, 91 mm...................	£90-120
		Fawn body, Blue hubs...................	£90-120
		NB Large lettering on baseplate. Rear axles are held in by the baseplate. However, models are known with rear axle pillars.	
151	1965-69	**Vauxhall Victor 101** .... Yellow, Metallic Red or Lime Green, suspension, spun hubs, 105 mm...................	£65-75
152 (40d)	1954-56	**Austin A40 Devon** .... Tan body, Green hubs, 86 mm...................	£400-500
		Light Green body, Green or Maroon hubs...................	£90-120
		Dark Blue body, Light Blue hubs...................	£200-225
		Mid-Blue body and hubs...................	£400-500
		Maroon body, Red hubs...................	£200-225
	1956-60	.... Yellow lower body, Blue upper body and hubs...................	£170-190
		Pink lower body, Lime Green upper body, Beige hubs...................	£170-190
		NB All issues have large lettering on their baseplates.	

152	1965-67	**Rolls-Royce Phantom V**	Navy Blue body, Beige interior, chauffeur and two passengers, spun hubs or cast wheels	£40-50
	1967-77	design change:	Dark Blue or Black body with Chauffeur but no passengers	£30-40
153 (40e)	1954-59	**Standard Vanguard**	Blue body, Beige hubs, large lettering on baseplate, 'ridge' on boot lid of some	£90-120
			Cream body and hubs, large lettering on baseplate, 'ridge' on boot lid of some	£90-120
153	1967-71	**Aston-Martin DB6**	Metallic Silver Blue body, Red interior, wire wheels, 111 mm	£60-70
			Metallic Green body	£70-80
154 (40f)	1954-56	**Hillman Minx**	Tan body, Cream hubs, 87 mm	£80-110
			Tan body, Blue hubs	£80-110
			Tan body, Green hubs	£200-250
			Light Green body, Mid-Green hubs	£80-110
	1956-59		Light Blue lower body, Deep Pink upper body, Mid-Blue hubs	£175-225
	1956-59		Bright Green lower body, Cream upper body	£175-225
	1956-59		Olive-Green lower body, Cream upper body	£175-225
			Lime Green lower body, Cream upper body	£175-225
			NB All issues have large baseplate lettering.	
154	1966-69	**Ford Taunus 17M**	Yellow body, White roof, Red interior, rounded spun hubs or cast wheels, 110 mm	£25-35
155	1961-66	**Ford Anglia 105E**	Turquoise or Green body, Red interior, suspension, windows, spun hubs, 81 mm	£70-80
			Turquoise body, Pale Blue interior, spun hubs	£100-150
			Very Pale Green body, Red interior, spun hubs. In mail-order box with correct spot	£350-450
			NB Meccano issued a batch to Ford to mark the first Ford made on Merseyside on	
			8th March 1963. Some were fixed on plinths and given as souvenirs.	
	1966	South African issue:	Deep Cream body, Red interior, spun hubs	£500-750
156 (140b)	1954-56	**Rover 75**	Cream body, Ivory or Light Blue hubs, 101 mm	£80-100
			Red (Red hubs), or Maroon (Red hubs), '156' and '40b' shown on box	£80-100
	1956-59		Dark Green lower, Light Green upper body, Light Green hubs	£150-200
			Cream lower, Light Blue upper body, Ivory hubs	£150-200
			Cream lower, Dark Blue upper body, Ivory hubs	£250-300
			Cream lower body and hubs, Violet-Blue upper body	£300-400
156	1968-71	**Saab 96**	Metallic Red or Metallic Blue body, suspension, spun hubs, 98 mm	£65-75
157	1954-57	**Jaguar XK120**	Greyish-Green (Cream hubs), or Red (Red hubs), 97 mm	£150-200
			Yellow (Yellow hubs), or White (Fawn or Brown hubs)	£150-200
	1957-59		Turquoise lower body, Deep Pink upper body and hubs	£200-250
	1957-59		Yellow lower body, Grey upper body, Grey hubs	£200-250
	1959-62		Greyish-Green body, spun aluminium hubs, lighter Yellow box	£200-250
			Red body, spun aluminium hubs	£200-250
157	1968-73	**BMW 2000 Tilux**	Blue/White, Red interior, cast hubs, 121 mm, box has inner pictorial stand	£55-65
			Metallic Blue with Gold upper half, pictorial box inner	£90-120
			Pale Blue body, Red interior, spun hubs	NGPP
158 (40a)	1954-60	**Riley Saloon**	Mid-Green body and hubs	£90-120
			Cream body and Green hubs	£90-120
			Pale Green body and hubs	£90-120
			N.B. All the 158 Riley issues have large lettering on their baseplates.	
158	1967-70	**Rolls-Royce Silver Shadow**	Metallic Red, suspension, spun hubs, 125 mm	£45-55
	1970-73		Metallic Blue, suspension, opening doors/bonnet/boot	£55-65
159 (40g)	1954-56	**Morris Oxford**	Dark Green body, Light Green hubs, 93 mm	£90-120
			Mid-Blue body, Grey hubs. (Body colour is shade of blue similar to 481 'Ovaltine' Van)	£1,000-1,500
			Light Brown (Sand) body with matching hubs	£1,000-1,500
	1956-59		Cream lower body, Green upper body and hubs	£200-250
			Dark Pink lower body, Cream upper body and hubs	£200-250
159	1967-70	**Ford Cortina Mk.II**	White body, suspension, tilting seats, spun aluminium hubs, 105 mm	£60-70
160	1958-62	**Austin A30**	Turquoise body, smooth or treaded solid grey plastic wheels, 77 mm	£80-100
			Light Brown body, smooth or treaded solid grey plastic wheels	£80-100
			N.B. A version of the Austin A30 has been reported with spun hubs, but is not confirmed.	
160	1967-74	**Mercedes-Benz 250 SE**	Metallic Blue body, suspension, steering, working stop-lights, 117 mm	£25-35
161 (40j)	1954-56	**Austin A40 Somerset**	Pale Blue body, Dark Blue hubs, 89 mm	£90-120
			Dark Blue body, Light Blue hubs	£90-120
			Red body and hubs	£90-120
	1956-59		Red lower body and hubs, Yellow upper body including boot and inner edge of rear wings	£200-250
			As previous issue but Red extends over rear wings to boot edges	£200-250
			Black lower body, Cream roof and hubs	£200-250
161	1965-69	**Ford Mustang Fastback**	White (Red seats), 'MUSTANG' badge on wings, cast wheels	£50-60
	1969-73		Yellow body, Blue seats, cast-in logo replaces decal badge	£60-70
			Orange body (without decal), Speedwheels	£30-40
162	1956-60	**Ford Zephyr Mk.I**	Cream and Dark Green body, Cream hubs, 96 mm	£100-125
			Two-tone Blue body, Grey hubs	£100-125
			Lime-Green and Cream body, Deep Cream hubs	£100-125
162	1966-70	**Triumph 1300**	Light Blue body, Red interior, fingertip steering, spun aluminium hubs, 93 mm	£55-65
163	1956-60	**Bristol 450 Coupé**	British Racing Green body, Light Green hubs, RN '27', 98 mm	£65-75

163	1966-71	**Volkswagen 1600 TL**	Red or Dark Metallic Red, suspension, cast detailed hubs, 102 mm	£40-50
			Metallic Blue body, Speedwheels	£60-70
164	1957-60	**Vauxhall Cresta**	Maroon lower body, Beige upper body, Cream hubs, 96 mm	£100-125
	1957-60		Green lower body, Grey upper body, Grey hubs	£100-125
164	1967-71	**Ford Zodiac Mk.IV**	Metallic Silver body, Red interior, Yellow or Black chassis, cast wheels, 114 mm	£50-60
			Pale Metallic Blue body, Yellow chassis, cast wheels	£75-85
			Metallic Bronze body, Red interior, Yellow chassis, cast wheels	£120-150
165	1959-60	**Humber Hawk**	Black and Green lower body, Black roof, spun hubs, 102 mm	£90-120
			Maroon and Cream lower body, Maroon roof, spun hubs	£90-120
			N.B. Both versions available with or without a front number plate casting.	
	1959-63		Black lower body, all Green upper body, spun hubs, with front number plate casting, in late issue lighter Yellow box with Green spot	£125-175
165	1969-76	**Ford Capri**	Metallic Green, Purple (Yellow interior) or Blue body, Speedwheels, 102 mm	£60-70
166	1958-63	**Sunbeam Rapier**	Orange lower body, Deep Cream upper body and hubs, 89 mm	£80-100
			Orange lower body, Deep Cream upper body, spun hubs	£90-120
			Mid-Blue lower body and hubs, Light Blue upper body	£90-120
166	1967-70	**Renault R16**	Metallic Blue, suspension and fingertip steering, spun hubs, 99 mm	£40-50
167	1958-63	**A.C. Aceca Sports Coupé**	Grey body, Red roof, Red hubs, 89 mm	£80-100
			Cream body, Reddish-Maroon roof, Silver cast hubs	£160-190
			Deep Cream body, Dark Brown roof, Cream hubs	£80-100
			All Cream body, spun aluminium hubs. (Lighter Yellow box with Cream spot)	£160-190
			Cream body, Maroon roof, spun aluminium hubs	£160-190
168	1959-63	**Singer Gazelle Saloon**	Deep Brown lower, Cream upper body, spun aluminium hubs, 92 mm	£80-100
			Dark Green lower, Grey upper body, spun aluminium hubs	£80-100
168	1968-70	**Ford Escort**	Pale Blue or White, cast detailed hubs, 97 mm	£40-50
	1970-74		Metallic Red body, spun aluminium hubs	£67-75
	1974-75		Metallic Blue body, Speedwheels	£67-75
169	1958-63	**Studebaker Golden Hawk**	Light Brown body, Red rear side panel and hubs, White tyres, plain Yellow/Red box	£80-100
			As previous issue but with spun aluminium hubs, White tyres	£90-120
			Light Green body, Cream rear side panel and hubs, White tyres	£80-100
			As previous issue but with spun aluminium hubs, White tyres	£90-120
169	1967-69	**Ford Corsair 2000 E**	Silver body, Black textured roof, suspension and steering, 108 mm	£60-70

Two paint schemes exist for two-colour issues on models 170, 171 and 172:
1: Lower colour covers wing tops and doors up to windows (generally known as 'Highline')
2: Lower colour extends only up to ridge on wings/doors ('Lowline').

170 (139a)	1954-56	**Ford Fordor Sedan**	Brown body, Red hubs, 102 mm	£90-110
			Yellow body, Red hubs	£90-110
			Green body, Red hubs	£90-110
			Red body, Red hubs	£90-110
	1956-58	('Highline')	Red lower body, Cream upper body, Red hubs	£175-225
	1956-58	('Highline')	Blue lower body, Pink upper body, Blue hubs	£175-225
	1958-59	('Lowline')	Red lower body, Cream upper body, Red hubs	£175-225
	1958-59	('Lowline')	Blue lower body, Pink upper body, Blue hubs	£175-225
170m	1954-54	**Ford US Army Staff Car**	(139am) Military Green, US issue, renumbered 675	£200-250
170	1964-70	**Lincoln Continental**	Metallic Bronze body, White roof, Blue interior, cast wheels	£75-85
			Light Blue body, White roof, Mid-Blue interior, cast wheels	£75-85
170	1979	**Granada Ghia**	Not issued	NPP
171 (139b)	1954-56	**Hudson Commodore Sedan**	Dark Blue body, Stone roof and hubs, small lettering on baseplate, 111 mm	£90-110
			Royal Blue body, Stone roof and hubs, small lettering on baseplate	£150-200
			Cream body, Dark Maroon roof and hubs, small lettering on baseplate	£90-110
			Cream body, Dark Maroon roof and hubs, large lettering on baseplate	£90-110
	1956-58	('Highline')	Turquoise lower body with Red upper body, Red hubs	£175-225
		('Highline')	Blue lower body, Red upper body, Red hubs	£175-225
		('Highline')	Grey lower body with Blue upper body, Blue hubs	£175-225
	1958-59	('Lowline')	Turquoise lower body with Red upper body, Red hubs	£175-225
		('Lowline')	Grey lower body with Blue upper body, Blue hubs	£175-225
171	1965-68	**Austin 1800**	Pale Blue or Metallic Blue, suspension, steering, spun hubs, 101 mm	£50-60
172	1954-56	**Studebaker Land Cruiser**	Light Green body, Mid-Green or Mid-Blue hubs, 107 mm	£90-120
			Blue body, Brown or Beige hubs	£90-120
	1956-58	('Highline')	Cream lower body, Maroon upper body, Beige hubs	£150-200
		('Highline')	Cream lower body, Tan upper body, Beige hubs	£150-200
	1958-59	('Lowline')	Cream lower body, Maroon upper body, Beige hubs	£150-200
		('Lowline')	Cream lower body, Tan upper body, Beige hubs	£150-200
172	1965-69	**Fiat 2300 Station Wagon**	Blue, TT Blue or White/Blue, suspension, steering, spun hubs, 108 mm	£50-60
173	1958-62	**Nash Rambler Station Wagon**	Turquoise body with Cerise flash, Grey hubs, no number on later baseplates, 101 mm	£60-70
			Pink body with Blue flash, Cream hubs, no number on later baseplates	£60-70
			As previous issues but with spun hubs, in plain Yellow/Red box without picture	£70-80
173	1969-73	**Pontiac Parisienne**	Metallic Maroon body, Lemon interior, retractable aerials, cast wheels, 132 mm	£55-65
			Metallic Blue body	£55-65
174	1958-63	**Hudson Hornet**	Red/Cream body, Beige hubs, 111 mm	£80-95
			Red/Cream body, spun aluminium hubs	£90-120
			Yellow/Grey body, Light Grey hubs	£80-95
			Yellow/Grey body, spun aluminium hubs	£90-120

174	1969-73	**Ford Mercury Cougar**	Red body, cast or Speedwheels, retractable aerial, 122 mm	£35-45
			Blue or Metallic Dark Blue body, cast or Speedwheels	£35-45
175	1958-61	**Hillman Minx**	Grey lower body, Mid-Blue upper body and hubs, 88 mm	£80-100
			Light Brown body, Green roof and boot, Beige hubs	£80-100
			Light Brown body, Green roof and boot, spun hubs	£90-120
175	1969-73	**Cadillac Eldorado**	Metallic Purple body, Black roof, Yellow interior, cast or Speedwheels, 133 mm	£50-60
			Metallic Blue body, Black roof, Yellow interior, cast or Speedwheels	£50-60
176	1958-63	**Austin A105 Saloon**	First Dinky Toys car to have full window glazing. Body sides have a contrasting side flash. Treaded tyres may be Black or White. 102 mm.	
	1958-59		Cream body, Dark Blue side flash, Cream hubs	£80-95
			Grey body, Red side flash, Red hubs	£80-95
	1959-63		Cream body, Dark Blue roof and side flash, Cream hubs or spun hubs	£150-175
			Cream body, Mid-Blue roof and side flash, Cream hubs	£150-175
	1959-63		Cream body, Mid-Blue roof and side flash, spun aluminium hubs	£150-175
			Grey body, Red roof and side flash, Red hubs or spun hubs	£150-175
176	1969-74	**N.S.U. Ro80**	Metallic Red body, spun hubs, luminous seats, working lights, 114 mm	£40-50
			Metallic Blue body	£100-150
177	1961-66	**Opel Kapitan**	Light Greyish-Blue body, Red interior, spun hubs, 100 mm	£50-60
	1966	...........South African issue:	...Dark Blue body	£500-750
	1966	...........South African issue:	....Pale Yellow body, Red interior	£500-750
178	1959-63	**Plymouth Plaza**	Light Blue body, Dark Blue roof and side stripe, spun hubs, 108 mm	£80-95
			Pink body, Green roof and side stripe, spun hubs	£80-95
			Light Tan body, Light Green roof and side stripe, matt-Black base, spun hubs	£175-200
			Light Blue body, White roof and stripe, spun hubs, 'plain' box	£200-250
			Pale Blue body, White roof and flash, spun hubs, late issue - no number on baseplate	£150-200
178	1975-79	**Mini Clubman**	Bronze body, opening doors, jewelled headlights on some, 82 mm	£40-50
			Red body version	£100-125
179	1958-63	**Studebaker President**	Pale Blue body, Blue stripe, Beige or aluminium hubs, 108 mm	£80-95
			Yellow body, Blue stripe, Mid-Blue or aluminium hubs	£80-95
179	1971-75	**Opel Commodore**	Metallic Blue body, Black roof, suspension, Speedwheels, 107 mm	£45-55
180	1958-63	**Packard Clipper**	Cerise upper body, Cream lower body and hubs, 108 mm	£80-95
			Orange/Grey body, Grey hubs, White tyres	£80-95
			Orange/Grey body, spun hubs, White tyres	£90-120
			All Green body, White tyres	£80-95
180	1979-80	**Rover 3500**	White body, plastic chassis and wheels, 131 mm. Made in Hong Kong	£15-20
181	1956-70	**Volkswagen Saloon**	Grey, Airforce Blue or Lime Green, Dark Blue or Green hubs, 90 mm	£55-65
			Light Blue or Airforce Blue, spun aluminium hubs	£55-65
			Light Blue body, unpainted baseplate (no model number), spun hubs. Lighter Yellow box	£100-150
			Light Blue body, Blue plastic hubs, Lighter Yellow late issue box	£150-200
	1966	...........South African issue:	...Light Green body, spun hubs	£500-750
	1966	...........South African issue:	....Mid-Green body and interior, spun hubs	£500-750
	1966	...........South African issue:	...Cream body, spun hubs	£500-750
	1966	...........South African issue:	...Light Blue body, spun hubs	£500-750
182	1958-66	**Porsche 356a Coupé**	Light Blue or Cerise body, Cream hubs, 87 mm	£80-100
			Light Blue or Cerise body, spun hubs	£90-120
			Red body and diecast hubs, in lighter Yellow box with Red spot	£160-190
			Cream body, Blue hubs	£80-100
			Red body, diecast or spun hubs. In standard Yellow box	£125-150
	1966	...........South African issue:	....Plum body, spun aluminium hubs	£500-750
183	1958-60	**Fiat 600**	Red body, smooth or treaded solid Grey plastic wheels, 71 mm	£55-65
			Light Green body, smooth or treaded solid Grey plastic wheels	£55-65
183	1966-72	**Morris Mini Minor Saloon**	Metallic Red (gloss Black roof) or Metallic Red or Blue (matt Black roof), White interior, spun hubs, 75mm. Box contains 'Meccano Automatic Transmission' leaflet	£70-80
			Metallic Red body and roof, Speedwheels	NGPP
			Metallic Blue body, White interior, spun hubs, registration no. 'MTB 21 G'	£150-175
	Note:		Model number plates were updated along with the real cars (e.g., 'UVR 733', 'UVR 576D', 'HTB 21H').	
	1966	...........South African issue:	....Red body and roof or Mid Blue body, spun hubs	£500-750
184	1961-65	**Volvo 122 S**	Red body, Off-White interior, spun hubs, 97 mm	£70-80
			White body, Off-White interior, spun hubs	£175-200
			Cream body, Cream interior	£200-225
	1966	...........South African issue:	....Greyish Lilac with White interior	£500-650
	1966	...........South African issue:	....Greyish Green with White interior or Pale Green, Fawn interior	£500-650
185	1961-63	**Alfa Romeo 1900 Sprint**	Red or Yellow body, Red interior, spun hubs, 102 mm	£65-75
186	1961-67	**Mercedes-Benz 220 SE**	Light Blue or RAF Blue, Pale Grey interior, spun hubs, 102 mm	£35-45
	1966	...........South African issue:	....Greyish Light Blue with Cream interior, spun hubs	£500-750
187	1959-64	**VW Karmann Ghia Coupé**	Red body, Black roof, spun hubs, 96 mm, 'plain' box	£55-65
			Green body, Cream roof, spun hubs, 'plain' box	£55-65
			As previous issue but in rare late issue picture box	£150-200
187	1968-77	**De Tomaso Mangusta 5000**	Red body, White panels front/rear, Black interior, cast wheels, racing number '7'	£35-40
188	1968-74	**Jensen FF**	Yellow or Green body, Black interior, cast wheels, 121 mm	£45-55

189	1959-64	**Triumph Herald Saloon**........Green/White, spun aluminium hubs, 86 mm, standard box..£65-75
		Blue/White, spun aluminium hubs, standard box..£65-75
	special issue:	Lilac body, spun hubs, standard box...NGPP
	special issue:	Magenta body, spun hubs, standard box..NGPP
	special issue:	Red lower, White upper body, plain printed box with Red spot..NGPP
	special issue:	Greyish-Green, Pale Whitish-Green roof, plain box with correct colour spot........................NGPP
	special issue:	Pinkish-Brown body with Pale Grey roof, standard box...NGPP
	special issue:	Dark Grey body and roof, Pale Grey bonnet and boot, standard box.....................................NGPP
	special issue:	All Red body in plain box with red spot, standard box..NGPP
	special issue:	Very Dark Blue body, Pale Blue hubs, standard box...NGPP
	special issue:	Very Dark Blue lower body and roof, Pale Blue mid-section, spun hubs.................................NGPP
	special issue:	Deep Grey and White body...NGPP
	special issue:	Pale Lilac body, Bluish White roof in box with Blue and White spot.......................................NGPP
	special issue:	Black and Pale Grey body, spun hubs...NGPP
	NB	The above 'NGPP' issues have sold for prices in excess of £250 in the mid-1990s at Vectis Auctions Ltd.
189	1969-76	**Lamborghini Marzal**...............Green/White or Red/White, cast detailed hubs, 137 mm...£25-45
		Yellow/White body, cast detailed hubs...£40-45
	1976-78	............................Metallic Blue/White or Dark Metallic Green/White, Speedwheels................................£35-45
190	1970-74	**Monteverdi 375 L**..................Metallic Red body, White interior, cast wheels or Speedwheels, 116 mm..................£35-45
191	1959-64	**Dodge Royal Sedan**..............Cream body with Brown flash, spun hubs, 111 mm..£90-110
		Cream body, Blue flash, spun hubs, lighter Yellow box, late issue - no number on base.......£150-200
		Light Green body with Black flash, spun hubs..£90-110
192	1959-64	**De Soto Fireflite**....................Grey body, Red roof and flash, spun aluminium hubs, 114 mm..............................£90-110
		Turquoise body, Light Tan roof and flash, spun aluminium hubs...£90-110
192	1970-80	**Range Rover**..........................Metallic Bronze (Pale Blue interior), Yellow body (Red interior), or Black body (? interior),
		cast detailed or Speedwheels...£25-35
193	1961-69	**Rambler Station Wagon**.......Lemon Yellow body, White roof, Black plastic roof-rack, spun hubs, standard box........£70-80
		As previous issue but in Gold 'see-through' export window-box..£150-175
	1966	...........South African issue: ...Pink/Mauve, All Mauve, or Lime-Green body...£500-750
	1966	...........South African issue: ...Pale Lilac body, Black roof or Pale Blue, Cream roof...................................£600-800
	1966	...........South African issue: ...Light Greyish-Green body, Black roof, Red interior.......................................£600-800
194	1961-67	**Bentley 'S' Coupé**..................Grey body, Maroon seats, Tan tonneau, driver, spun hubs, 113 mm......................£65-75
		Metallic Bronze body, Ivory interior, Dark Blue tonneau, driver, spun hubs............................£120-140
		N.B. Late issues have plated plastic parts.
	1966	...........South African issue: ...Avocado Green body, Dark Red seats, spun hubs...£600-800
	1966	...........South African issue: ...Cream body, Red interior, spun hubs..£500-750
195	1960-66	**Jaguar 3.4 Mk.II**...................Maroon, Cream or Grey body, suspension. First with fingertip steering, 95 mm...........£70-90
		South African issue: ...Pale Bluish-Grey body, White interior or Red interior, White interior...........£600-800
196	1963-70	**Holden Special Sedan**..........Bronze body, White roof , 108 mm...£55-65
		Turquoise body, White roof..£80-90
		N.B. First Dinky Toys model to be fitted with jewelled headlights.
	1966	...........South African issue: ...White body, Turquoise roof..£500-750
197	1961-71	**Morris Mini Traveller**...........Ivory body, Yellow interior...£800-1,000
		Ivory body, Red interior...£70-80
		Almond Green body, Yellow interior...£600-800
		Fluorescent Green body with front number plate...£155-175
		Fluorescent Green body without front number plate..£175-195
		Fluorescent Green body with front number plate...£155-175
		NB No 'colour change' label on box.
		Fluorescent Pink body..£175-195
		NB Unlike 199, there is no 'colour change' label on the 197 box.
198	1962-69	**Rolls-Royce Phantom V**.........Cream lower body, Metallic Light Green upper body, Light Blue interior,
		chauffeur, spun hubs. (First Dinky Toys model with metallic paint and opening windows)........£70-80
		Cream upper body, Grey lower body, Red interior, chauffeur, spun hubs...............................£70-80
		Two tone Grey body, Red interior, chauffeur, spun hubs...£75-85
	1966	...........South African issue: ...Dark Grey over Metallic Cream body, Red interior...£500-750
		Green or Two-Tone Grey...£500-750
		Pale Grey body, Ivory roof, Red interior...£500-750
199	1961-71	**Austin 7 Countryman**............Blue body with Yellow interior..£100-150
		Electric Blue, Blue or Blue-Grey body with Red interior and 'wood' trim..................................£70-80
		Fluorescent Orange body, Box must have affixed a small oblong label stating:
		'COLOUR OF MODEL MAY DIFFER FROM ILLUSTRATION'..£150-175
		Deep Grey body, Red interior, Brown 'woodwork', spun hubs..£150-200
200 (35b)	1954-57	**Midget Racer**.........................Silver body, Red grille, Brown driver, solid Black rubber wheels, 57 mm.................£65-75
200	1971-78	**Matra 630 Le Mans**...............Blue body, racing number '5', '9' or '36', Speedwheels..£25-30
201	1979-80	**Plymouth Stock Car**..............Blue body, racing number '34', wide plastic wheels, 135 mm..................................£35-45
202	1971-75	**Fiat Abarth 2000**...................Fluorescent Red/White body, opening doors, Speedwheels, 91 mm........................£20-30
202/2	1979-80	**Customised Land Rover**.......Yellow body with white crash guard. White or Black rails/aerials (344 casting)............£25-35
203	1979-80	**Customised Range Rover**.....Black body, Yellow/Red design, White plastic chassis/crash guard, 115 mm...............£20-25
204	1971-74	**Ferrari 312 P**.........................Metallic Red body and opening doors, Speedwheels, RN '60', 99 mm......................£25-30
		Metallic Red body, White opening doors, Speedwheels, RN '60'..£25-30

Ref	Years	Model	Description	Price
205 (230)	1962-64	Talbot Lago Racing Car	Blue, Red or Yellow plastic hubs, RN '4', bubble-packed ('230' on base)	£175-225
205	1968-73	Lotus Cortina Rally	White body, Red bonnet and side stripe, 'Monte Carlo' logo, RN '7', 2 aerials/spotlamps	£70-80
206 (231)	1962-64	Maserati Racing Car	Red/White, Red or Yellow plastic hubs, bubble-packed, ('231' on base)	£175-225
206	1978-80	Customised Corvette	Red/Yellow or White/Black, plastic chassis and wide wheels, 113 mm	£20-30
207 (232)	1962-64	Alfa-Romeo Racing Car	Red, Red plastic hubs, bubble-packed, ('232' on base), 100 mm	£175-225
207	1977-80	Triumph TR7 Rally	White/Red/Blue, RN '8', plastic chassis and wheels, 'Leyland', 98 mm	£25-35
208 (233)	1962-64	Cooper-Bristol Racing Car	Dark Green, Red plastic wheel hubs, bubble-packed, ('233' on base), 89 mm	£175-225
		variant:	As previous model but with Green metal hubs	£150-200
208	1971-75	VW Porsche 914	Yellow body, Black interior, cast detailed wheel hubs, 89 mm	£25-30
	1976-80		Metallic Blue/Black body, Speedwheels	£25-30
209 (234)	1962-64	Ferrari Racing Car	Blue, Yellow triangle, Yellow plastic hubs, bubble-packed, ('234' on base)	£175-225
210 (239)	1962-65	Vanwall Racing Car	Green, Yellow plastic hubs, bubble-packed, ('239' on base), 95 mm	£175-225
210	1971-73	Alfa-Romeo 33 Tipo	Red body, Black doors, White interior, racing number '36', cast wheels, leaflet in box	£30-35
211	1975	Triumph TR7 Sports Car	Metallic Blue body, Union Jack badge	£90-100
			Yellow body, Black bumpers and interior	£90-100
			Yellow body, Grey bumpers and interior	£90-100
			Red body, Black bumpers and interior	£50-60
			Red body, Grey bumpers and interior	£50-60
212	1965-70	Ford Cortina Rally	White body, Black bonnet, 'EAST AFRICAN SAFARI' and 'CASTROL' logos, RN '8', spotlight, Red interior	£65-75
213	1970-73	Ford Capri Rally	Metallic Red body, Black bonnet, Yellow interior, racing number '20'	£45-55
	1973-75		Bronze body, Black bonnet, spotlights, wing mirrors, Speedwheels	£40-50
214	1966-69	Hillman Imp Rally	Dark Blue body, Red interior, 'MONTE CARLO RALLY' logo, RN '35', spun hubs	£55-65
215	1965-66	Ford GT Racing Car	White body with racing number '7', spun hubs, 96 mm	£40-50
	1966-70		White body with racing number '7', Silver spoked wheels	£35-40
	1970-74		Metallic Green body, Orange/Black stripe, Yellow interior, RN '7', Silver spoked wheels	£60-70
			Metallic Green body, Dark Blue/White stripe, White interior	£60-70
			Yellow or Metallic Blue, removable bonnet, Silver or Gold spoked wheels	£35-45
216	1967-69	Dino Ferrari	Red body, Light Blue interior	£40-50
	1969-75		Metallic Blue/Black, Silver or brass spoked wheels or Speedwheels	£30-40
217	1968-70	Alfa Romeo Scarabeo OSI	Pink body, cast spoked wheels, 132 mm	£30-35
	1969-74		Red, Orange or Green body, Speedwheels	£25-30
218	1969-73	Lotus Europa	Yellow body, Blue panels/roof, chequered flags, Gold engine, 96 mm	£35-45
	1973-75		Yellow/Black body or Metallic Blue body, Silver engine, Speedwheels	£30-35
219	1977-79	Leyland Jaguar XJ-5.3	White body, 'Leyland' decal, 137 mm. (Made in Hong Kong)	£35-45
219	1978-79	'Big Cat' Jaguar	White/Red, Black 'Big Cat' decal. (Bubble-packed)	£35-45
220 (23a)	1954-56	Small Open Racing Car	Silver (Red hubs), or Red (Silver hubs), RN '4', 94 mm	£40-50
220	1970-73	Ferrari P5	Metallic Red body, Yellow interior, cast hubs, 96 mm	£25-30
	1973-75		Metallic Red body, Yellow interior, Speedwheels	£25-30
221 (23e)	1954-56	'Speed Of The Wind' Racing Car	Silver diecast body with plain baseplate, 104 mm	£40-45
221	1969-76	Corvette Stingray	Metallic Gold body, Silver or Gold spoked wheels, 113 mm	£25-35
	1976-78		Red or White body, Black bonnet, opening doors, Speedwheels	£25-35
222 (23s)	1954-56	Streamlined Racing Car	Silver body with Red, Blue or Green trim, 126 mm	£60-70
222	1978-80	Hesketh 308 E	Dark Blue or Bronze, RN '2', cast-detailed or Speedwheels, 132 mm	£20-30
	promotional issue:		As previous model but in 'OLYMPUS CAMERAS' box, (Swiss)	£50-75
223	1970-75	McLaren M8A Can-Am	White body, Metallic Blue engine cover, cast detailed wheels, 94 mm	£20-25
	1976-78		Metallic Green body, Black engine cover, White interior, Speedwheels	£20-25
224	1970-74	Mercedes-Benz C111	White or Metallic Dark Red, White interior, cast wheels	£20-25
225	1971-76	Lotus F1 Racing Car	Metallic Red body with racing number '7', 127 mm, inner pictorial box and stand	£20-25
	1976-77		Lime-Green or Metallic Blue body with racing number '7'	£20-25
226	1972-75	Ferrari 312 B2	Red body with racing number '5', 121 mm	£20-25
	1976-78		Bronze or Gold body, Black, White or Yellow rear wing, racing number '5'	£20-25
227	1975-77	Beach Buggy	Yellow/Grey, Yellow/White, Green/Grey or Pink/Black body, 105 mm	£20-25
228	1970-72	Super Sprinter	Blue/Silver or Blue/Orange body, suspension, Speedwheels, 115 mm	£20-25
230 (23k)	1954-60	Talbot Lago Racing Car	Blue body, Yellow racing number '4', Blue diecast hubs, 103 mm	£85-95
	1960-62		Blue body, Yellow racing number '4', spun aluminium hubs	£85-95
	1962-64	late issue:	Blue body, RN '4', Red or Yellow plastic hubs, lighter Yellow box (see 205)	£100-125
231 (23n)	1954-60	Maserati Racing Car	Red body, White flash and RN '9', Red diecast hubs, 94 mm	£85-95
	1960-62		Red body, White flash and racing number '9', spun aluminium hubs	£85-95
	1962-64	late issue:	Red body and plastic hubs, White flash and RN '9', lighter Yellow box, (see 206)	£100-125
	1962-64	late issue:	Red, Yellow plastic hubs, White flash and RN '9', lighter Yellow box, (see 206)	£100-125
232 (23f)	1954-60	Alfa-Romeo Racing Car	Red body, White racing number '8', Red diecast hubs, White racing driver, 100 mm	£85-95
	1960-62		Red body, White racing number '8', spun aluminium hubs, White racing driver	£85-95
	1962-64	late issue:	Red body, White RN '8', Red plastic hubs, , White driver, lighter Yellow box (see 207)	£100-125
233 (23g)	1954-60	Cooper-Bristol Racing Car	Green body, White flash and RN '6', Green diecast hubs, 89 mm	£85-95
	1960-62		Green body, White flash and racing number '6', spun aluminium hubs	£85-95
	1962-64	late issue:	Green body and plastic hubs, White flash and RN '6', lighter Yellow box, (see 208)	£85-95
234 (23h)	1954-60	Ferrari Racing Car	Blue body, Yellow nose, diecast hubs and RN '5', 101 mm	£85-95
	1960-62		Blue body, Yellow nose and racing number '5', spun aluminium hubs	£85-95
	1962-62		Blue body, Yellow triangle on nose, RN '5', spun hubs, boxed	£175-225
	1962-64	late issue:	Blue, Yellow triangle on nose, Yellow plastic hubs, lighter Yellow box (see 209)	£175-225
	South African issue:		Red body, RN '36', spun hubs (as UK issue but with dimpled rivets). South African box	£175-225

235 (23j)	1954-60	**H.W.M. Racing Car**	Light Green body, Yellow RN '7', Green diecast hubs, 99 mm	**£85-95**
236	1956-59	**Connaught Racing Car**	Pale Green body, Red seats, Mid-Green hubs, RN '32', White driver, 96 mm	**£75-85**
237	1957-60	**Mercedes-Benz Racing Car** ...	Gloss White body, Red interior, Red hubs or spun hubs, Red RN '30', Blue driver, 98 mm	**£75-85**
	1960-62	....	Matt Cream body, Red hubs or spun hubs, RN '30', Blue driver	**£75-85**
	1962-64		Matt Cream body, plastic hubs, RN '30', Tan driver	**£50-60**
		late issue:	Matt White body, Red plastic hubs, RN '36', Blue driver, lighter Yellow box	**£70-80**
			As previous issue but with Yellow driver	**£70-80**
238	1957-60	**Jaguar 'D' type**	Turquoise body, Blue interior, White driver, RN '4', Blue diecast hubs, 87 mm	**£90-120**
	1960-62		Turquoise body, Blue interior, White driver, RN '4', spun aluminium hubs	**£80-100**
	1962-65		Turquoise body, Blue interior or Turquoise interior, White or Yellow driver, RN '4',	
			Blue or Yellow plastic hubs, in lighter Yellow box	**£110-140**
239	1958-60	**Vanwall Racing Car**	Green body, Green hubs, White driver, racing number '35', 95 mm	**£85-95**
	1960-62		Green body, White driver, RN '35', spun aluminium hubs	**£85-95**
	1962-65		Green body, White or Tan driver, RN '35', Yellow plastic hubs	**£100-125**
	1962-65		Green body, Yellow driver, RN '35', Yellow plastic hubs	**£100-125**
240	1963-70	**Cooper Racing Car**	Blue/White, RN '20', spun aluminium hubs, suspension, 80 mm	**£50-60**
241	1963-70	**Lotus Racing Car**	Green body with racing number '36', suspension, spun hubs	**£50-60**
			Green body with racing number '24', spun hubs	**£45-55**
242	1963-71	**Ferrari Racing Car**	Red body, RN '36', suspension, opening engine cover, spun hubs, 89 mm	**£50-60**
243	1963-71	**B.R.M. Racing Car**	Green, Yellow opening engine cover, RN '7', suspension, spun hubs, 82 mm	**£50-60**
	1963-71		Metallic Green, Yellow opening engine cover, racing number '7'	**£50-60**
		NB	Gold, US export issue 'see-through' window boxes. Model nos. 237 - 243 housed in these boxes may attract a premium of 50%.	
260	1971-72	**VW 'Deutsche Bundespost'** ...	Yellow body (129 casting, 100mm), German export model	**£100-150**
262	1959-60	**Volkswagen 'PTT' Car**	(181 casting, 90mm, fixed doors), Yellow/Black, 'PTT', cast hubs, Swiss export model	**£500-750**
	1960-62		As previous issue but with spun aluminium hubs, Swiss export	**£500-750**
	1962-66		As previous issue but with plastic hubs, Swiss export	**£500-750**
			NOTE 262 models listed above should be in the correct French / German box with 'Auto Suisse VW' and 'Schweizer Postauto VW' on the end flap.	
	1966-68	.... 129 casting:	Yellow/Black, opening doors, spun aluminium hubs, hard plastic case	**£150-200**
	1968-72		Yellow/Black, opening doors, plastic hubs, 100 mm., Swiss export	**£100-125**
	1972-76		Yellow/Black, opening doors, Speedwheels, Swiss export	**£100-125**
340 (27d)	1954-66	**Land Rover**	Green body, Brown interior and metal hubs, Tan cast driver, 92 mm	**£55-65**
	1966-69		Orange body, Green interior and plastic hubs, Blue, cast or plastic driver	**£55-65**
	1969-71		Red body and plastic hubs, Yellow interior, Blue plastic driver	**£55-65**
	1971		Red body, Blue plastic driver, Green or Yellow plastic hubs	**£80-100**
341 (27m)	1954-66	**Land-Rover Trailer**	Orange body (Red hubs), or Green body (Green hubs)	**£20-30**
			Olive-Drab body	**£150-200**
342	1966-72	**Austin Mini-Moke**	Metallic Green, Grey canopy with 1 or 2 windows, bubble-packed or boxed, 73mm	**£35-45**
	1972-75		Metallic Greenish-Blue, 1 canopy window, bubble-packed or boxed, 76mm	**£35-45**
344 (27f)	1954-61	**Estate Car**	Brown/Fawn body, Beige hubs, rear axle pillars, 104 mm	**£60-80**
			Grey body with Red panels	**NGPP**
344	1970-72	**Land Rover Pick-Up**	Metallic Blue or Metallic Red body, bubble-packed, 108 mm	**£15-20**
	1973-78		Metallic Blue or Metallic Red body, bubble-packed	**£15-20**
370	1969-76	**Dragster Set**	Yellow/Red, driver, 'FIREBALL', 'INCH-PINCHER', starter unit, 113 mm	**£40-50**
405 (25y)	1954-66	**Universal Jeep**	Red or Green body, diecast hubs, tinplate windscreen frame, 83 mm	**£80-90**
	1966-67		Orange body, red plastic hubs, boxed in late lighter yellow box	**£200-300**
448	1963-68	**Chevrolet El Camino Pick-Up with Trailers**	Turquoise/Cream/Red Pick-up and 2 trailers, 'Acme Trailer Hire', 256 mm	**£200-250**
449	1961-69	**Chevrolet El Camino Pick-up**	Turquoise body, White roof, Red interior, spun hubs, 111 mm	**£80-90**
			Turquoise body, White roof, Pale Turquoise interior, spun hubs	**£150-200**
			Turquoise body, White roof, Lemon interior, spun hubs	**£150-200**
			NB Various shades of Turquoise are known to exist.	
		South African issue:	All-Turquoise body, spun hubs	**£500-750**
		South African issue:	Cream over Chocolate Brown lower body, spun hubs	**£500-750**
		South African issue:	Turquoise over Cream lower body, spun hubs	**£500-750**
475	1964-66	**Model 'T' Ford**	Blue body, Yellow panels and wheels, driver/female passenger, 79 mm	**£45-55**
476	1967-69	**Morris Oxford** ('Bullnose')	Yellow body, Blue chassis, Fawn hood, driver, 92 mm	**£45-55**
516	1965-66	**Mercedes-Benz 230 SL**	Metallic Red, Cream roof, windows, 85 mm. (French issue)	**£75-95**
675 (170m)	1954-?	**Ford US Army Staff Car**	Olive-Drab body, White star, export-only (to US) in 'plain' printed box	**£175-250**
2162	1973-76	**Ford Capri**	Metallic Blue, Black roof, Black or Blue interior, 175 mm (1:25 scale, vacuform packed on card base).....	**£70-90**
2214	1974-76	**Ford Capri Rally Car**	Red, Black roof and bonnet, RN '12', Black or Blue interior, 175 mm (1:25 scale, vacuform packed)	**£80-100**
2253	1974-76	**Ford Capri Police Car**	White/Orange, 'POLICE', Blue light, suspension, windows, 175 mm (1:25 scale, vacuform packed)......	**£80-100**

Dinky Toys cars made by Meccano, Paris, France and sold in Britain

24kz	1939-40	**Peugeot Car**	Red or Blue, tinplate front bumper, rubber tyres for UK	NGPP
516		**Mercedes-Benz 230sl**	Bronze body, Cream interior	£70-80
518	1962-65	**Renault 4L**	Brown or Grey body, suspension, steering, windows, 85 mm. (Renault issue)	£65-85
524	1965-67	**Panhard 24c**	Dark Metallic Grey body, (French issue)	£65-85
532		**Lincoln Premiere**	Metallic Light Green body, Dark Green roof	£70-80
530	1965-66	**Citroën DS19**	Light Green body, Light Grey roof. (French issue)	£65-85
535	1962-65	**Citroën 2cv**	Blue body, suspension, steering, windows, 88 mm. (French issue)	£65-85
550	1962-65	**Chrysler Saratoga**	Pink/White body, windows, suspension, steering, 129 mm. (French issue)	£65-75
551	1959-64	**Rolls-Royce Silver Wraith**	Same as UK issue 150 'Made in France'	£75-85
553	1962-65	**Peugeot 404**	Green or White, suspension, steering, windows, 102 mm. (French issue)	£65-75
555	1962-65	**Ford Thunderbird**	White, driver, windscreen, suspension, steering, 121 mm. (French issue)	£65-75

Dinky Toys cars made in Hong Kong

Hong Kong made models were issued in tab-ended alternative pictorial card boxes or rare yellow 'see-through' cellophane window boxes.

57-001	1965-67	**Buick Riviera**	Light Blue body with White roof and Red interior, opening bonnet and tailgate	£80-100
57-002	1965-67	**Chevrolet Corvair Monza**	Red body, Black roof, opening bonnet and rear engine cover, 107 mm	£100-125
57-003	1965-67	**Chevrolet Impala**	Yellow body with White roof and Red interior, opening bonnet and tailgate	£100-125
		US / Canadian issue:	Yellow body with Yellow roof	£100-125
57-004	1965-67	**Oldsmobile Dynamic '88'**	White body, Blue roof, Red interior	£125-150
57-005	1965-67	**Ford Thunderbird**	Blue body with White roof, Red interior	£140-160
57-006	1965-67	**Nash Rambler Classic**	Light Green body with Silver roof trim, Cream interior	£125-150
180	1979-80	**Rover 3500**	White body with opening doors, plastic wheels, 131 mm	£20-25
219	1978-79	**'Big Cat' Jaguar**	White/Red, Black 'Big Cat' decal. (This model was not boxed)	£35-45

NB Models 57-001 to 57-006 all have spun hubs, detailed end-flap picture boxes, and are in a scale of 1:42.

Dinky Toys made in Italy by Polistil under licence to Dinky Tri-ang

122	1979-80	**Volvo Estate Car**	Orange body, Brown interior, plastic wheels, Brown card box	£20-30
			Cream body, Red interior, cast wheels	£20-30
243	1979-80	**Volvo 'Police' Car**	White body, Brown card box	£15-20

'Mini-Dinky' models

These were issued in 1968 and were made in Hong Kong and Holland. Each model was sold with a free red plastic garage. The cars are fitted with Flexomatic Independent Suspension. Racing cars 60 and 61 were made by Best Box of Holland (now EFSI). The models listed are illustrated in the 1968 US issued 3-page fold-out leaflet which advertised them as 'Swinging Value' at 59 cents and 69 cents. Models 94-99 Construction Vehicles are illustrated in a US issued 'Mini-Dinky' fold-out launch leaflet '1'. The Market Price Range is **£30-40** each.

10 **Ford Corsair**, Yellow or Metallic Gold
11 **Jaguar 'E' type**, Red or Metallic Maroon
12 **Corvette Stingray**, Blue or Metallic Dark Blue
13 **Ferrari 250 LM**, Red or Metallic Maroon
14 **Chevrolet Chevy II**, Yellow or Met. Maroon
15 **Rolls-Royce Silver Shadow**, Blue
16 **Ford Mustang**, White, Cream or Metallic Blue
17 **Aston Martin DB6**, White
18 **Mercedes Benz 230 SL**, White/Black
19 **MGB Roadster**, Blue
20 **Cadillac Coupé de Ville**, Silver or White
21 **Fiat 2300 Station Wagon**, Blue or Yellow/White

22 **Oldsmobile Toronado**, Metallic Pale Blue
23 **Rover 2000**, Blue
24 **Ferrari Superfast**, Red
25 **Ford Zephyr 6**, Silver
26 **Mercedes 250 SE**, White or Bronze
27 **Buick Riviera**, Blue
28 **Ferrari F 1**, Red, '7'
29 **Ford F 1**, White
30 **Volvo 1800s**, Blue
31 **Volkswagen 1600TC**, Blue or Metallic Green
32 **Vauxhall Cresta**, Silver or Dark Green
33 **Jaguar**, Red

57 **Chevrolet Corvair Monza Club Coupé**, Red/Black
60 **Cooper**, Blue '10'
61 **Lotus Racing Car**, Green, '4'
94 **International Bulldozer**, Yellow
95 **International Skid Shovel**, Yellow
96 **Payloader Shovel**, White
97 **Euclid R40**, Yellow, 10 wheels
98 **Michigan Scraper**, Yellow
99 **Caterpillar Grader**, Orange
- **'Mini-Dinky' 12-Car Collector Case**, with models £400-600

'Matchbox Dinky' - 'The Collection' 1988 onwards

See under Matchbox Collectibles in the 'Modern Diecasts' section.

DINKY TOYS

A FASCINATING COLLECTING HOBBY

Dinky Toys are the most realistic and the most attractive models in miniature ever produced. These wonderful toys are unique in their perfection of finish, and their range is so wide as to appeal to all tastes. A selection is illustrated on these pages. As will be seen, trains, motor vehicles, aeroplanes, famous liners, etc., are already included in the range. Many other models of equal interest are in preparation.

ASK YOUR DEALER FOR A COPY OF THE DINKY TOYS FOLDER, which gives illustrations and prices of the complete range.

STREAMLINE FIRE ENGINE
Dinky Toys No. 25h
Fitted with detachable rubber
tyres   Price 9d. each

MOTOR VEHICLES   Dinky Toys No. 30
Fitted with detachable rubber tyres and silver-
plated radiators
No. 30a Chrysler Airflow Saloon   each 9d.
No. 30b Rolls-Royce Car ...   ...   „ 9d.
No. 30c Daimler Car ...   ...   „ 9d.
No. 30d Vauxhall Car ...   ...   „ 9d.
No. 30e Breakdown Car ...   ...   „ 9d.
No. 30f Ambulance ...   ...   „ 9d.
          Price of complete set 4/6

TRAM CAR
Dinky Toys No. 27
Assorted colours
Price 3d. each

MOTOR BUS
Dinky Toys No. 29a
Assorted colours
Price 4d. each

PILLAR LETTER BOX AIR MAIL
Dinky Toys No. 12b
Price 3d. each

RAILWAY MECHANICAL HORSE AND TRAILER VAN
Dinky Toys No. 33R
Fitted with detachable rubber tyres
No. 33Ra Railway Mechanical
          Horse ...   .   each 8d.
No. 33Rd Trailer Van...   ...   „ 10d.
Price, complete, L.M.S.R., L.N.E.R., G.W.R.
          or S.R., 1/6

CUNARD WHITE STAR LINER "QUEEN MARY"
Dinky Toys No. 52a
Fitted with rollers and supplied in presentation box.   Price 1/- each
          Dinky Toys No. 52m
Similar to No. 52a but not fitted with rollers, nor supplied in presentation box.   Price 9d. each

COMMERCIAL MOTOR VEHICLES
Dinky Toys No. 25
Fitted with detachable rubber tyres and silver-plated radiators
No. 25a Wagon ...   ...   each 9d.
No. 25b Covered Van ...   ...   „ 9d.
No. 25c Flat Truck ...   ...   „ 9d.
No. 25d Petrol Tank Wagon ...   „ 9d.
No. 25e Tipping Wagon ...   ...   „ 9d.
No. 25f Market Gardener's Van ...   „ 9d.
          Price of complete set 4/6

STRONGLY MADE
UNBREAKABLE
MODELS

TANK
Dinky Toys No. 22f
Price 9d. each

DELIVERY VANS
Dinky Toys No. 28/1
Fitted with detachable rubber tyres
No. 28a Golden Shred Van ...   each 6d.
No. 28b Seccotine Van ...   ...   „ 6d.
No. 28c Manchester Guardian Van ...   „ 6d.
No. 28e Firestone's Tyres Van ...   „ 6d.
No. 28f Palethorpe's Sausage Van ...   „ 6d.
No. 28n Atco Lawn Mowers Van ...   „ 6d.
          Price of complete set 3/-

A realistic model of the latest type of streamline train

"SILVER JUBILEE" TRAIN SET
Dinky Toys No. 16
Price 1/6 each

TRACTOR
Dinky Toys No. 22e
Price 9d. each

STREAMLINE SALOON
Dinky Toys No. 22h
Assorted colours. Fitted with detachable rubber tyres and silver-plated radiator. Price 6d. each

G.W.R. RAIL CAR
Dinky Toys No. 26
Assorted colours   Price 4d. each

R.A.C. BOX, MOTOR CYCLE PATROL AND GUIDES
Dinky Toys No. 43
This set is representative of the familiar road hut and personnel of the R.A.C. Each item is finished in correct colours.
No. 43a R.A.C. Box ...   ...   each 6d.
No. 43b R.A.C. Motor Cycle Patrol ...   „ 9d.
No. 43c R.A.C. Guide directing traffic „ 3d.
No. 43d R.A.C. Guide at the salute ...   „ 3d.
          Price of complete set 1/9

GARAGE
Dinky Toys No. 45
Fitted with opening double doors. Will accommodate any two Dinky Toys Motor Cars.   Price 1/6 each

ROBOT TRAFFIC SIGNAL
Dinky Toys No.
47a (Four face)
Price 3d. each
No. 47b (Three face)
Price 3d. each
No. 47c (Two face)
Price 3d. each

POLICE BOX, MOTOR CYCLE PATROL AND POLICEMEN
Dinky Toys No. 42
No. 42a Police Box ...   ...   each 6d.
No. 42b Motor Cycle Patrol ...   „ 10d.
No. 42c Point Duty Policeman (in White Coat) „ 3d.
No. 42d Point Duty Policeman ...   ...   „ 4d.
          Price of complete set 1/11

MECCANO LTD.   —   BINNS ROAD   —   LIVERPOOL 13

A page from the December 1936 'Meccano Magazine'

A page from the December 1936 'Meccano Magazine'

Identification of casting types

The 25 series Lorries 1934 - 1950

Type 1: **(1934-36)**, 'open' chassis (usually black), tinplate radiator, no headlamps,
   no front bumper, 'smooth' cast hubs (various colours) with large white tyres. 105 mm.
Type 2: **(1936-46)**, 'open' chassis (usually black), diecast radiator with headlamps but
   no front bumper, 'smooth' cast hubs (various colours), with large white tyres. 105 mm.
Type 3: **(1947-48)**, 'closed' chassis (only in black), diecast radiator with headlamps but
   no front bumper, 'smooth' or 'ridged' wheel hubs (only in black) ,with black tyres. 105 mm.
Type 4: **(1948-50)**, detailed moulded chassis (only in black), diecast radiator with headlamps and
   with bumper, 'ridged' coloured wheel hubs with black tyres. 110 mm.

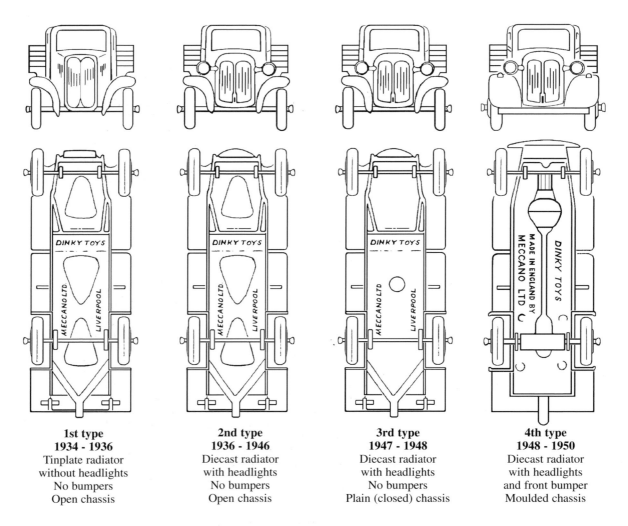

| **1st type**
1934 - 1936
Tinplate radiator
without headlights
No bumpers
Open chassis | **2nd type**
1936 - 1946
Diecast radiator
with headlights
No bumpers
Open chassis | **3rd type**
1947 - 1948
Diecast radiator
with headlights
No bumpers
Plain (closed) chassis | **4th type**
1948 - 1950
Diecast radiator
with headlights
and front bumper
Moulded chassis |

25 Series Trucks 1934-50 Wheel types The first pre-war issues have cast metal wheels followed by chrome (rare) or diecast hubs with large white tyres. The early post-war issues c.1946 have smooth hubs and large black tyres. **1947-48** issues have ridged black hubs with large black tyres. The last issues **c.1949-50** have coloured ridged hubs and attract a premium. Similarly early cast or chrome hubs also attract a premium.

Foden cab types

1947 - 1952
Foden 'DG'
(1st type) cab
Exposed radiator
Colour flashes on sides

1952 - 1964
Foden 'FG'
(2nd type) cab
Radiator behind grille
No colour flashes on sides

Guy cab types

Guy 1st type cab 1947 - 1954
Exposed radiator
No gusset at either
side of number plate

Guy 2nd type cab 1954 - 1958
Exposed radiator
With gusset at each
side of number plate

Guy Warrior cab 1958 - 1964
Radiator behind grille
Restyled front with
sidelights in wings

28 and 280 series Delivery Vans

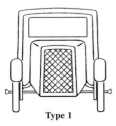 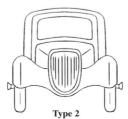 

Type 1   Type 2   Type 3

Type 1: **(1933-35)**, two-piece lead body with *'HORNBY SERIES'* (early issues) or *'DINKY TOYS'* cast-in under cab roof, tinplate radiator, no headlamps, thinly-painted coloured solid wheel/tyre castings (some silver plated), 84 mm. (Coloured wheels tend to attract a premium to the price of the model.)

Type 2: **(1935-39)**, one-piece diecast body, cast-in shield-shaped radiator, rear wheel spats, cast smooth wheel hubs with rubber tyres (usually white), 81 mm. All carried advertising.

Type 3: **(1939-41)**, one-piece diecast body with rear wheel spats, cast smooth wheel hubs (various colours) with black tyres, open rear windows, 83 mm. All carried advertising.

Type 3: **(1947-54)**, one-piece diecast body with rear wheel spats, cast ridged wheel hubs (usually black) with black tyres, filled-in rear windows, cast boss under roof , 83 mm. No advertising.

Identification of Ford Transit Van castings (not illustrated)

Type 1: **(1966-74)**, has sliding driver's door, opening hinged side door, and twin rear doors.
Type 2: **(1974-78)**, non-sliding driver's door, one side-hinged door, one top-hinged rear door.
Type 3: **(1978-80)**, as Type 2 but with a slightly longer bonnet (18 mm.)

Commercial Vehicles Box Types Introduction

A mint condition commercial vehicle without its correct box is worth a fraction of the value of its boxed equivalent. Furthermore, as model boxes made from card do not survive as well as their die-cast contents, pristine box examples are scarce and becoming scarcer. The condition of a box is of paramount importance and attention is drawn to the section in the main catalogue introduction, namely: 'Classifying the Condition of Models and Boxes'.

The following listing provides collectors with a working knowledge of the range of box types issued. In addition details are given of their dates of issue, their design and of the models which used them.
Whilst every care has been taken in preparing the listing other variations no doubt exist and information on these is welcomed.
Similarly with no 'dates of birth' available the dates of issue shown are approximate and again any further information is welcomed.

Commercial Vehicles Box Identification

Box Pictures
To assist identification, pictures of the various box types were shown in the 7th edition. See also the many examples in this edition.

Model Colour Identification Marks
These are shown on the box lid and label and take the form of either a circular colour spot or a capital letter, e.g. 'R' for red. A colour spot may be a single colour or in the case of the later two-tone colours models a two-tone colour spot.

'Lead-free' labels 'LF'
In the 1950s the government introduced new regulations concerning the lead content of die-cast models. Consequently, to indicate that a model complied with the new regulations, a round white label with 'LF' in blue was added to box end labels for a short time. Alternatively, an 'LF' coloured ink stamp was used.

Model Reference Numbers
These are always shown on the box lid and label.

Dual numbered boxes c. 1953 – 1954
A new numbering system was introduced which resulted in models being issued displaying both the old and new reference numbers. The information was shown in one of two ways:
(a) A black new number stamped alongside the old number
(b) A small old model number shown in red on either side of a larger black new number, e.g. '511', '911', '511'. Dual numbered boxes (issued for a relatively short period) may attract a premium.

Quality Control Box Markings. 1947 – 1957
(a) **Factory Checkers Marks**
A quality control mark may be found on the base of the buff coloured boxes. This takes the form of a coloured ink stamp of a reference number within a circle, e.g. 'M42' or 'M19'. Stamped on the underside of the blue covered box lid may be found a similar ink stamp e.g. 'ZQ Z8'.
(b) **Date Stamps**
Ink stamped on the base of boxes or box lids may be found a purple date stamp relating to the date of the model's issue. Recorded examples include: 'GR950' on a (25x) orange coloured box; '10 KR 55' on a (933) blue/white stripe box; 'H656' on a (902) blue/white stripe box; 'KB956' on a (433) yellow covered box lid; '01057' on a (689) military blue/white box.
The Editor would welcome any further information on this subject.

Pre-war issues 1933 – 1939
Apart from sets (see the Gift Sets listing) commercial vehicles were sold unboxed. They were usually packaged in half-dozen retailers trade packs such as Nos. 28/1, 28/2 and 28/3 Delivery Vans.

Post-war Issues 1947 – 1979
In 1947 the first individual boxes were introduced to house the exciting new range of 'Supertoys' models. However, the small commercial vehicles continued to be sold unboxed from trade packs until 1953/54.
The boxes have been catalogued into four types as follows:
Type 1 1947-75 - Boxes with lift-off lids
Type 2 1953-75 - All card boxes with tuck-in end flaps
Type 3 1963-79 - Display boxes
Type 4 1964-64 - Export only boxes

A   1947-50
Buff coloured box with separate labels on the box top and one box end. The half red and white box labels show 'DINKY SUPERTOYS' plus the model number. In addition the main label displays an illustration of the model and whilst the main design of the label remains constant, the position of the model does vary as follows:

i) Facing inwards on the right side of the label.
 Models recorded using this box: 501 (1st type) and 521.

ii) Facing outwards on the left side of the label.
Models recorded using this box: 502, 503, 511, 512, 513 (all 1st types). The small separate label attached to the right side of the box lid is white with red model information text. Some labels include a line drawing of the model eg. 503 and 513.

iii) Buff coloured box with a single 'wrap round' red and white label which covers the box lid from end to end with 'DINKY SUPERTOYS' in red on the larger Foden type box, one end of the label contains information about the model in German, French and Spanish. In addition, the model number on the top and ends is now white on a circular black background. The model picture is facing inwards from the right and the models recorded in this box to date are: 504 Tanker 1st type and 531.

iv) As previous issue but the model picture is facing outwards from the left. Models recorded: 511, 512 and 533.

B   c.1950
Green covered box with red and white wrap-around label. Models recorded in this box: 501, 504 (1st and 2nd types), 511, 521 and 504 'MOBILGAS'. Model picture facing inwards from the right. 'DINKY SUPERTOYS' in red letters.

C   c.1950
(i) Pale or dark blue covered box with wrap-around red and white label. Model picture facing inwards from the right with 'DINKY SUPERTOYS' logo. Models recorded: 504 (1st and 2nd types), 531, 532 and 533.

(ii) Pale or dark blue box with wrap-around orange and white label with 'DINKY SUPERTOYS'. Model picture facing inwards from the right front. Beneath the model picture is a black factory code, e.g. on the 522 Big Bedford lorry issue the code is '50522'. Models recorded: 504 (1st / 2nd), 511, 514 'LYONS' and 'SLUMBERLAND' and 531.

(iii) Same as C(ii) but with model picture facing outwards from the left. Models recorded: 502(1st), 503 (2nd) and 512.

(iv) Same as C(ii) but with model picture facing inwards from the right front but with 'DINKY TOYS'. Models recorded: 504 'MOBILGAS', 514 'WEETABIX' 514 'SLUMBERLAND', 514'SPRATTS', 522, 591, 501(1st type), 504 Tanker (1st and 2nd types).

(v) Same as C (iv) but with model picture facing outwards from the left front. Models recorded: 502, 503 (1st types), 512, 513 (1st types).

(vi) Same as C (iv) but with model picture facing inwards from the left front. Models 505 (1st type), 532 and 581 US issue.

D   (i) Blue and white striped box lid with dark blue bottom section. Box lid is white with dark blue parallel stripes. 'DINKY TOYS' logo is shown in red plus a colour picture of the model facing inwards from the right. The model number is on the left of the picture. Colour identification spots shown as appropriate on box ends. Models recorded: 901/2/3(2nd type), 409, 418, 582, 511/12/13, 911/12/13. 917, 923 ('ketchup bottle'), 923 ('baked beans can'), 930, 932/33, 941/42, 963, 980, 982, 991.
NB The 417 Leyland Comet Lorry yellow/green issue was housed in a box with a blue/yellow picture.

(ii) As D (i), but with 'DINKY SUPERTOYS' logo and with the model picture facing inwards from the right. Models recorded: 901/2/3, 905, 913, 918/9, 923, 930, 934/5/6, 942/3, 948, 954, 958, 960, 963/4, 966/7/8/9, 973, 977, 982/3/4, 986, 991.
On the box side is a note stating the colour of the model which may vary from the one illustrated on the box front. This only happened when a model was issued for a short time and hence some of the rarest models were issued in this manner (e.g. 902 Foden Flat Truck in yellow/green livery was issued in box

with red/green model picture; 913 Guy Flat Truck with tailboard in yellow/green livery issued in box with all-green model picture; 934 Leyland Octopus Wagon in blue and yellow livery was issued on the standard box with a yellow/green model picture but displaying a dark blue colour spot).
The Editor would welcome any further examples.

(iii) As D (ii), but with model picture facing outwards from the left. 'DINKY SUPERTOYS' logo. Model recorded No.982.

(iv) As D (ii), but with model picture facing inwards from the left. 'DINKY SUPERTOYS' logo. Model recorded No. 979.

(v) Plain blue and white striped box with no model picture on lid. A white end label 'DINKY SUPERTOYS' and the model details in blue letters. Models recorded: 920 and 923.

E Yellow covered box lid with blue bottom section.
(i) c.1956 - 1959
On two of the box sides is a picture of the model set against a white shadow background. The top of the box lid has a 'DINKY TOYS' logo in red. Colour spots shown as appropriate. In addition white circular 'LF' (lead free) labels may be found. Models recorded: 408/9, 417, 419, 430/1/2/3.
NB. The rare 408 Big Bedford Lorry in pink and cream livery was issued in this box but with the standard maroon and fawn model box picture.

(ii) Yellow covered box lid but with red side panels with pictorial scene with 'DINKY TOYS' logo in red. The box lid shows the model picture facing inwards from the right with a pictorial scene in an end panel on the left. Models recorded: 401, 408, 417, 425, 430, 434, 448, 450, 925, 960, 972 and 978.

(iii) Same as previous issue but with 'DINKY SUPERTOYS' logo. Models recorded: 908, 934, 935, 944, 958/9, 962, 964, 972 and 978.
NB. No. 935 Leyland Octopus with chains in the rare dark blue and grey livery was issued in the standard box with the green and grey version illustrated but with a dark blue spot displayed.

(iv) All yellow covered lid with a pictorial scene in the middle of the box lid top. 'DINKY SUPERTOYS' in red. Models recorded: 959, 987/8/9.

F 'One off' box issues with lift-off lids.

(i) Plain dark blue covered box with no picture. White label on box lid end with dark blue text. Model recorded: 982 Pullman Car Transporter in rare mid-blue livery with brownish-grey decks.

(ii) Orange covered box (c.1952) with white/orange wrap-around lid label. Models recorded: 25x Breakdown Truck and 14c Coventry Climax Fork Lift Truck.

TYPE 2   1953 - 1975
ALL CARD BOXES WITH TUCK-IN END FLAPS

A 1953 - 1964
(i) Deep yellow box with 'DINKY TOYS' in red plus the model's name and type in black. A white reference number on a black or red oval background is on the box end flaps but no reference is shown on the box face. The model is pictured on the box sides with or without a white shadow background. Colour spots shown as applicable. Foreign language information is shown on one of the box end flaps. Box used for small and medium size models, e.g., 431/432. Box in general use during the model renumbering period. Consequently dual numbered boxes will be found.
Very few boxes were issued displaying just the old type of reference number. Recorded models to date: 25d, e, f, g and 30e. In addition, 29c Bus and 29e Coach have been identified. Please send details if you have any other examples. Later issues display 'WITH WINDOWS' captions.

(ii) Plain light yellow box with two red sides and no model picture. The 'DINKY TOYS' logo, the model type and its reference number are shown in yellow and white. Colour spots are shown as appropriate. Models recorded: 252, 413, 414 and 428 plus 070 and 071 Dublo Dinky.

(iii) 1963 - 1970
Yellow box with red end features panel around the front right side, with or without an upward pointing white arrow. Models recorded: 273, 274, 435.

(iv) 1966 - 1969
A detailed full colour picture box with 'DINKY TOYS' in red plus a pictorial

scene on two sides. A yellow laurel leaf design on a black background incorporates the model number Models recorded: 280, 402, 407 'KENWOOD', 914, 923, 944/5, 959/60, 965, 970, 972 and 978.

(v) 1968 - 1974
White fronted box with a narrow yellow band across the face. The box front displays 'DINKY TOYS' in red plus the model number and type in black and white letters. A colour picture of the model is shown on two sides. Models recorded: 407, 438/9/40, 91, 917, 974, 978 and 980.

(vi) 1966 - 1970
Picture box used for large commercials with two full pictorial sides with 'DINKY TOYS' in red. The other sides are yellow and red. Models recorded: 434 'AUTO SERVICES', 914 and 945.

(vii) 1970 - 1975
Heavy card box used for heavy models e.g. 924 Centaur Dump Truck. Box has white face with a colour picture of model combined with a black band across the face and sides.

(viii) Promotional Box Types
(a) No. 274 'JOSEPH MASON PAINTS' Minivan. Dark red box with white letters plus an enclosed leaflet.
(b) No. 491 Plain yellow box with red letters. 'JOBS DAIRY'.
(c) No. 940 Mercedes-Benz LP1920 Truck with 'HENRY JOHNSON' logo. Plain white card box with no lettering
(d) No. 940 Mercedes-Benz, 'FISONS', plain white box

TYPE 3   1963 - 1979   DISPLAY BOXES

A 1970 - 1976 Vacuform packs
Models displayed on a black card base with a blue surface with 'DINKY TOYS' in red and white. The model is covered by a close-fitting see-through protective plastic cover. Known examples include: 407,416, 438/9, 915, 944, 945 'ESSO' and 'LUCAS' issues.

B 1976 - 1979 Window boxes
Cellophane fronted window boxes with a dark blue and red header card giving the model's name and 'DINKY DIECAST TOYS' in yellow and white letters. Known examples include: 275, 432, 440, 451, 940, 950 and 980.
C   1963 - 1966 Fold-back lid display box
224 Commer Convertible Truck and 975 Ruston Bucyrus Excavator which also had a coloured outer box display wrapper issued for a while.

TYPE 4   1964 - 1966   EXPORT ONLY BOXES

A 1964 - 1966
An all-yellow card and cellophane 'see-through' display box.
'DINKY' plus the model type and number is shown across the box front in red letters plus 'A MECCANO PRODUCT MADE IN ENGLAND'. Box issued with a card protection strip. Known models include: 275, 434, 492, 914. A version of this box was used for the 944 'SHELL BP' tanker - see picture in the colour section, Also used for the U.S. Export Series: 'MARVELS IN MINIATURE' which is shown on the sides of the box front in red capital letters, e.g. 275, 434, 437, 448 and 965. Later issues display the range on the base of the box.

B c.1965
Same as previous issue but all-gold box with two black and red diagonal stripes. A rare box type. Known issues include 434 and 989.

INNER BOX LININGS and MODEL SUPPORTS

To be complete a box should contain all its original model supports. The following issues all had supports or linings. In some instances top and bottom linings are included (2).
14c, 400, 561, 581, 908(2), 924, 930(2), 958, 964, 965, 967, 968, 969(2), 972, 974, 976, 977(2), 979(2), 980, 982, 983(2), 984(2), 985(2), 986, 989(2).

Ref.	Year(s)	Model name	Colours, features, dimensions	Market Price Range
14a (400)	1948-54	B.E.V. Truck	Mid-Blue body with Blue hubs, Fawn driver, hook, 85 mm	£30-35
			Grey body (with Blue, Grey or Red hubs), Fawn driver, hook	£30-35
14c (401)	1949-54	Coventry Climax Fork Lift	Orange, Brown or Dark Red body, Green forks, Fawn driver, 108 mm	£25-30
14z	1938-40	Three-wheel Delivery Van	'Triporteur' with Green, Red, Grey, Blue or Yellow body, Black hubs,	
			White tyres, driver is always a different colour from van, French model	NGPP
22c	1933-35	Motor Truck	Two-piece lead body with 'HORNBY SERIES' cast-in, tinplate radiator,	
			diecast coloured wheels, 90mm.	
			Blue cab, Red or Yellow truck body	£300-400
			Red cab, Green, Blue or Cream truck body	£300-400
			Yellow cab, Blue truck body	£900-1000
22c	1935-40	Motor Truck	Orange-Red, Maroon, Green or Blue (diecast one-piece) body, open rear window,	
			coloured diecast hubs, 84 mm	£100-125
			Dark Blue body, chrome hubs	£125-150
			Off-white body, Mid-Blue hubs	£125-150
	1945-47		Red, Green or Brown body, open rear window, Black diecast hubs	£60-70
	1948-50		Red, Green or Brown body, closed rear window, Black diecast hubs	£60-70
22d	1933-34	Delivery Van	Lead body, tinplate radiator, 'HORNBY SERIES' cast-in, 84 mm.	
			Orange/Blue body or Blue/Yellow body, no advertising, Type 1	£900-1200
	1934-34		As previous models but with 'DINKY TOYS' cast-in	£400-500
	1934	Delivery Van 'MECCANO'	Orange cab and chassis, Blue van with Red/Black 'Meccano Engineering For Boys'	£2000-2500
22d (28n)	1934-35		Yellow body (lead), 'Meccano Engineering For Boys' in Red and Black,	
			Type 1, 84 mm. 22d till April 1935, renumbered 28n	£900-1200
25a	1934-36	Wagon	Maroon, Green, Red or Blue body, Black chassis, Type 1	£300-400
	1936-40		Maroon, Green, Red or Blue body, Black or Red chassis, Type 2	£100-125
	1936-40		Blue body with Orange chassis, Type 2	£150-200
	1946		Grey, Green or Blue, Type 2, smooth hubs	£60-70
	1947-48		Grey, Green, Red, Orange or Blue body, Black chassis, Type 3	£60-70
	1948-50		Grey, Green, Light Blue or Orange body, Black chassis, Type 4	£60-70
			Cream or Red body, Black chassis, Type 4	£60-70
25b	1934-36	Covered Wagon	Blue body, Cream tilt, Black chassis, Type 1	£300-400
	1936-40		Green body, Green, Cream or Yellow tilt, Black chassis, Type 2	£100-150
			Cream/Yellow or Fawn/Cream, Black chassis, Type 2	£100-150
			Orange body, Cream tilt, Green chassis, Type 2	£150-200
	1936-40	Covered Wagon		
		'CARTER PATERSON'	Green body, Blue hubs, Green tilt, Black chassis, Type 2, 'Express Carriers London'	£300-350
		'CARTER PATERSON'	Green body, Blue hubs, Type 2, 'Special Service To The Seaside'	£400-500
		'MECCANO'	Green body, Cream tilt, Black chassis, Type 2, 'Engineering For Boys'	£250-300
			Variation with chrome hubs	£500-600
		'HORNBY TRAINS'	Fawn body, Cream tilt, Black chassis, Gold lettering, Type 2	£250-300
	1945-47	Covered Wagon	Green/Green, Grey/Light or Dark Grey, Blue/Grey, Black chassis, Type 3	£70-100
	1947-50		Green/Green, Grey/Grey, Cream/Red, Yellow/Blue, Black chassis, Type 4	£70-100
25c	1934-36	Flat Truck	Dark Blue body, Black chassis, Type 1	£150-200
	1936-40		Green or Stone body, Black chassis, Type 2	£100-125
	1946		Fawn, Green or Grey body, smooth hubs, Type 2	£60-70
	1947-48		Green, Blue or Grey body, Black chassis, Type 3	£60-70
	1948-50		Green, Blue, Orange or Stone body, Type 4	£60-70
		NB	Some pre-war (1934-40) Truck issues will be found with a '20 mph' disc on the rear.	
25d	1934-35	Petrol Tank Wagon	Same chassis casting as other 25 series lorries but with hook removed.	
		(plain)	Red body, no advertising, Black chassis, Type 1	£200-250
		'SHELL BP'	Red body, Black chassis, Type 1	£400-500
		'ESSO'	Green body, Black chassis, Type 1	£400-500
		'POWER'	Green body, Black chassis, Type 1	£400-500
		'PRATTS'	Green body, Black chassis, Type 1	£400-500
		'CASTROL'	Green body, Black chassis, Blue hubs, Red logo, Type 1	£400-500
		'TEXACO'	Red body, Black chassis/hubs, White logo 'PETROLEUM & PRODUCTS', Type 1	£400-500
	1936-46	'PETROL'	Red body, Black chassis, Black or White lettering, Type 2	£150-200
		'SHELL BP'	Red body, Black chassis, Blue or chrome hubs, Type 2	£250-300
		'MOBILOIL'	Red body, Black chassis, Type 2	£250-300
		'TEXACO'	Red body, Black chassis, Type 2	£250-300
		'PETROL'	Green body, Black chassis, Type 2	£250-300
		'ESSO'	Green body, Black chassis, Black or Blue hubs, Gold lettering, Type 2	£250-300
		'POWER'	Green body, Black chassis, Type 2	£250-300
		'CASTROL'	Green body, Black chassis, Black or Blue hubs, Red lettering, Type 2	£250-300
		'REDLINE GLICO'	Blue body, Black chassis, Red panel, Gold lettering, Type 2	£250-300
	1945	'POOL' (Wartime)	Grey body, White chassis, Black hubs, Black lettering, Type 2	£400-500
	1945-46	'POOL' (Wartime)	Grey body, Black chassis, Type 2	£300-400
	1945-46	'PETROL' (Wartime)	Grey body, Type 2	£300-400
	1946-47	'PETROL'	Red or Green body, Black chassis, Type 3	£100-150
	1947-48	'PETROL'	Orange body, Type 4	£300-400
	1948-50	'PETROL'	Red, Light Green or Mid-Green body, Black chassis, Type 4	£70-100
	1948-?	'PETROL'	Yellow body, Black chassis, Type 4	£200-300

25e	1934-35	**Tipping Wagon**	Maroon/Yellow body, Black chassis, Type 1	**£150-200**
	1936-40		Maroon/Yellow, Brown/Turquoise or Fawn/Fawn body, Black chassis, Type 2	**£100-125**
			Fawn/Fawn body, Black chassis, Type 2	**£100-125**
	1946		Grey, Green or Fawn, Type 2	**£60-70**
	1947-48		Grey, Stone, Green or Yellow body, Black chassis, Type 3	**£60-70**
	1948-50		Grey, Stone or Brown body, Black chassis, Type 4	**£60-70**
	1948-50		Blue/Pink body, Black chassis, Type 4	**£60-70**
		NB	Some early post-war 25 series Trucks variations exist with smooth hubs.	

25f	1934-35	**Market Gardeners Lorry**	Green body, Black chassis or Yellow body, Green chassis, Type 1	**£150-200**
	1936-40		Green or Yellow body, Black chassis, Type 2	**£100-125**
			Green body, Yellow chassis, Type 2	**£150-200**
	1945-47		Green, Grey or Yellow body, Black chassis and hubs, Type 3	**£100-120**
	1947-50		Green, Grey, Yellow or Red body, Black chassis and hubs, Type 4	**£100-120**
			Orange body, Black chassis and hubs, Type 4	**£150-200**
			Green or Yellow body, Black chassis, Yellow hubs, Type 4	**£100-125**

25g	1935-40	**Trailer**	Dark Blue or Green body with cast-in hook, tinplate drawbar, 69 mm	**£35-40**
	1946-47		Green, Stone, Pale Blue or Orange body, cast-in hook, tinplate drawbar	**£15-20**
	1947-48		Green, Stone, Pale Blue or Orange body, cast-in hook, wire drawbar	**£15-20**
	1948-49		Green, Stone, Pale Blue or Orange body, tinplate hook, wire drawbar	**£15-20**
25g (429)	1950-54		Green or Red body with tinplate hook and wire drawbar	**£15-20**

25m (410)	1948-52	**Bedford End Tipper Truck**	Green cab and body, Green hubs, crank-handle operates tipper, 100 mm	**£100-130**
	1948-52		Green cab and truck body, Black hubs	**£100-130**
	1948-52		Orange cab and truck body, Black hubs	**£80-90**
	1948-52		Orange cab and truck body, Green hubs	**£80-90**
	1952-52		Orange cab and truck body, Pale Green hubs	**£100-130**
	1952-52		Cream cab and truck body, Red hubs	**£300-400**
	1952-52		Green cab and truck body, Pale Green hubs	**£300-400**
	1952-54		Red cab with window glazing, Cream body, Red hubs	**£300-400**
	1952-54		Yellow cab, Mid-Blue truck body, Yellow hubs	**£250-350**
	1953-53		Yellow cab, Dark Blue body, Yellow hubs	**£300-400**
		NB	All 25m models were sold from trade packs of six.	

| 25p (251) | 1948-54 | **Aveling Barford Road Roller.** | Mid or Pale Green body with driver and hook, Red wheels, 110 mm | **£30-40** |

25r (420)	1948-54	**Forward Control Lorry**	Red, Green, Grey, Cream, Light Blue or Orange body, Black hubs, 107 mm	**£60-70**
			Cream body, Blue hubs	**£90-120**
			Dark Brown body, Green hubs	**£90-120**

25s	1937-40	**Six-wheeled Wagon**	Reddish-Brown body, Cream, Brown or Grey tilt, holes in seat (but no figures)	**£100-125**
			Royal Blue body	**£200-250**
	1945-48		Brown (various shades), Green or Dark Blue body, Grey or Light Blue tilt, with or without holes for figures (but no figures)	**£100-125**

| 25t | 1945-47 | **Flat Truck and Trailer** | (25c Flat Truck (Type 3), and matching 25g Trailer), Green, Blue, Orange or Stone | **£140-160** |
| | 1947-50 | | (25c Flat Truck (Type 4), and matching 25g Trailer), Green or Orange | **£120-140** |

25v (252)	1948-54	**Bedford Refuse Wagon**	Fawn body, Green opening hatches and rear door, 106 mm	**£80-90**
25w (411)	1949-54	**Bedford Truck**	Green cab and truck body, Green hubs, 100 mm	**£125-150**
			Dark Green cab, Light Green truck body, Light Green hubs	NGPP
25x (430)	1949-54	**Commer Breakdown Lorry**	'DINKY SERVICE', operable crane, 123 mm.	
			Dark Grey cab with Ocean Blue back, (packed in Orange box)	**£100-120**
			Dark Grey cab with Royal Blue back, (in Orange box)	**£100-120**
			Dark Brown cab with Mid or Dark Green back, (in Orange box)	**£100-120**
			Mid Tan cab with Mid or Dark Green back, (in striped box)	**£100-120**

Note: Models housed in boxes with the correct picture and end colour spot and displaying dual numbers (e.g. '30J/412') attract a premium.

28 series **DELIVERY VANS** Note that coloured metal cast wheels on 1st type vans tend to attract a price premium.

28a	1934	'HORNBY TRAINS'	Orange body, 'Hornby Trains' logo, 1st Type	**£700-900**
28a		'HORNBY TRAINS'	Yellow body, 'Hornby Trains British & Guaranteed' in Gold,	
	1934-35		Type 1, 84 mm	**£500-600**
	1935-36		Type 2, 81 mm	**£250-350**
28a		'GOLDEN SHRED'	Cream body, 'Golden Shred Marmalade' on right hand side, 'Silver Shred Marmalade' on left hand side,	
	1936-39		Type 2, 81 mm	**£600-800**
	1939-41		Type 3, 83 mm	**£300-400**
28b		'PICKFORDS'	Dark Blue, 'Pickfords Removals & Storage, Over 100 Branches' in Gold,	
	1934-35		Type 1, 84 mm	**£500-600**
	1935	'PICKFORDS'	Dark Blue. Late version with diecast hubs, White tyres, Type 1	**£700-900**
	1935-35		Type 2, 81 mm	**£300-400**
28b		'SECCOTINE'	Blue body, 'Seccotine Sticks Everything' in Gold,	
	1935-39		Type 2, 81 mm	**£300-400**
	1939-41		Type 3, 83 mm	**£300-400**
28c		'MANCHESTER GUARDIAN'	'The Manchester Guardian' in Gold,	
	1934-35		Black/Red body, Type 1, 84 mm	**£500-600**
	1935-39		Red body, Type 2, 81 mm	**£300-400**

	1939-41		Red body, Type 3, 83 mm	£300-400
28d		'OXO'	Blue body, 'Beef In Brief' and 'Beef At Its Best' in Gold,	
	1934-35		Type 1, 84 mm	£500-600
	1935-39		Type 2, 81 mm	£300-400
	1939-41		Type 3, 83 mm	£500-700
28e		'ENSIGN LUKOS'	Orange body, 'Ensign Cameras' and 'Ensign Lukos Films' in Gold,	
	1934-35		Type 1, 84 mm	£500-600
28e		'FIRESTONE'	'Firestone Tyres' in Gold,	
	1934-35		White body, Type 1, 84 mm	£500-600
	1935-39		Blue or White body, Type 2, 81 mm	£300-400
	1939-41		Blue or White body, Type 3, 83 mm	£200-300
28f		'PALETHORPES'	Pale Grey-Blue body, Pink sausage decal, 'Palethorpes Royal Cambridge' on van sides, 'Palethorpes Model Factory' on rear,	
	1934-35		Type 1, 84 mm	£500-700
	1935-38		Type 2, 81 mm	£400-500
28f		'VIROL'	Yellow body, 'Give Your Child A Virol Constitution' in Black,	
	1938-39		Type 2, 81 mm	£600-800
	1939-41		Type 3, 83 mm	£300-400
28g		'KODAK'	Yellow body, 'Use Kodak Film To Be Sure' in Red,	
	1934-35		Type 1, 84 mm	£500-600
	1935-39		Type 2, 81 mm	£300-400
	1939-41		Type 3, 83 mm	£600-800
28h		'SHARPS TOFFEES'	'Sharps Toffee, Maidstone' in Gold,	
	1934-35		Black/Red body, Type 1, 84 mm	£500-600
	1935-35		Red body, Type 2, 81 mm	£400-500
28h		'DUNLOP'	Red body, 'Dunlop Tyres' in Gold,	
	1935-39		Type 2, 81 mm	£300-400
	1939-41		Type 3, 83 mm	£300-400
28k		'MARSH & BAXTER'	Dark Green body, 'Marsh's Sausages' and pig logo in Gold,	
	1934-35		Type 1, 84 mm	£500-600
	1935-39		Type 2, 81 mm	£300-400
	1939-41		Type 3, 83 mm	£500-600
28L		'CRAWFORDS'	Red body, 'Crawfords Biscuits' in Gold,	
	1934-35		Type 1, 84 mm	£500-600
28m		'WAKEFIELD'S CASTROL'	Green body, 'Wakefleld Castrol Motor Oil' in Red,	
	1934-35		Type 1, 84 mm	£500-600
	1935-39		Type 2, 81 mm	£300-400
	1939-41		Type 3, 83 mm	£800-1000
28n		'MECCANO'	Yellow body, 'Meccano Engineering For Boys' in Red and Black,	
	1934-35		Type 1, 84 mm. Was 22d	£500-600
	1935-35		Type 2, 81 mm	£300-400
28n		'ATCO'	Green body, 'Atco Lawn Mowers Sales and Service' in Gold/Red,	
	1935-39		Type 2, 81 mm	£300-500
	1939-41		Type 3, 83 mm	£500-600
28p		'CRAWFORDS'	Red body, 'Crawfords Biscuits' in Gold,	
	1935-39		Type 2, 81 mm	£300-400
	1939-41		Type 3, 83 mm	£800-1000
28r		'SWAN'	Black body, 'Swan Pens' and logo in Gold,	
	1936-39		Type 2, 81 mm	£300-500
	1939-41		Type 3, 83 mm	£200-300
28s		'FRYS'	Brown or Cream body, 'Frys Chocolate' in Gold,	
	1936-39		Type 2, 81 mm	£300-500
	1939-41		Type 3, 83 mm	£300-400
28t		'OVALTINE'	Red body, 'Drink Ovaltine For Health' in Gold/Black,	
	1936-39		Type 2, 81 mm	£300-400
	1939-41		Type 3, 83 mm	£300-400
28w		'OSRAM'	Yellow body, 'Osram Lamps - a G.E.C. Product' in Gold/Black,	
	1936-39		Type 2, 81 mm	£300-400
	1940-41		Type 3, 83 mm	£300-500
28x		'HOVIS'	White body, 'Hovis For Tea' in Gold/Black,	
	1936-39		Type 2, 81 mm	£400-600
	1939-41		Type 3, 83 mm	£300-400
28y		'EXIDE'	Red body, 'Exide Batteries' and 'Drydex Batteries' in Gold/Black,	
	1936-39		Type 2, 81 mm	£300-400
	1939-41		Type 3, 83 mm	£300-400
		NB Further issues in this series were numbered 280a - 280f.		
30e	1935-40	**Breakdown Car / Crane Lorry**	Red, Yellow, Green, Brown or Grey body, Black wings, Black or Blue hubs, rear window, 92 mm	£70-80
			Blue body, Dark Blue wings, Blue hubs, rear window	£100-120
	1946-46		Red or Grey body, Black wings, rear window	£60-70
	1947-48		Red, Grey or Green body and wings, no rear window	£40-50
30j (412)	1950-54	**Austin Wagon**	Mid-Blue body with hook, Light Blue hubs, 104 mm	£100-120
			Light, Medium or Dark Maroon body, Maroon or Red hubs	£100-150
			Brown body, Tan hubs	£400-500
			Dark Blue body, Light Blue hubs	NGPP
			Red body, Red hubs	NGPP
30m (414)	1950-54	**Rear Tipping Wagon**	Maroon or Orange cab, Pale Green rear, 'Dodge' on baseplate, 100 mm	£60-70
			Blue or Dark Blue cab, Grey rear	£60-70

30n (343)	1950-54	**Farm Produce Wagon**	Green/Yellow, Yellow/Green or Blue/Red body, hook, 104 mm	£60-70
30p	1950-54	**Petrol Tanker**	Based on a Studebaker vehicle, 112 mm	
30p	1950-51	**'PETROL'**	Red or Green body, cast in aluminium	£70-80
	1951-52	**'PETROL'**	Red or Green body, cast in mazak	£70-80
30p (440)	1952-54	**'MOBILGAS'**	Red body, Blue lettering on White background	£100-120
30pa (441)	1952-54	**'CASTROL'**	Green body and hubs, some cast in aluminium, most in mazak	£100-120
30pb (442)	1952-54	**'ESSO'**	Red body and hubs, 'MOTOR OIL - ESSO - PETROL'	£100-120
30r (422)	1951-54	**Fordson Thames Flat Truck**	Red or Green body with hook, 112 mm	£60-70
			Brown body, Brown hubs	£60-70
			Brown body, Maroon hubs	NGPP
30s (413)	1950-54	**Austin Covered Wagon**	Maroon body, Cream cover, Cream hubs, 104 mm	£100-150
			Dark Blue body, Light Blue cover, Light Blue hubs	£400-500
			Mid-Blue body, Light Blue cover, Light Blue hubs	£100-150
			Red body, Tan cover, Red hubs	£400-500
			Dark Blue body, Cream cover	£400-500
		Electric Dairy Van		
30v (491)	1949-54	**'N.C.B.'**	Cream body, Red chassis, hubs and logo, 85 mm	£75-90
			Grey body, Blue chassis, hubs and logo	£75-90
30v (490)	1949-54	**'EXPRESS DAIRY'**	Cream body, Red chassis, hubs and logo	£75-90
			Grey body, Blue chassis, hubs and logo	£75-90
30w (421)	1952-54	**Hindle-Smart Helecs**	Maroon body, 'British Railways', hook, trailer uncouples, 135 mm	£60-70
31	1935-35	**Holland Coachcraft Van**	Red, Green, Blue or Orange, 'Holland Coachcraft Registered Design', lead body, 88 mm	£300-350
	1935-36		Red, Blue or Orange, 'Holland Coachcraft Registered Design', diecast body	£250-300
	1935		Mid-Green body, Gold stripe, Silver advert., Chrome hubs	£750-1000
	1935		Cream body with Red coachline	£800-1000
		NB	The model owned by Frank Holland, founder of Holland Coachcraft was sold by Christie's in 1994 for £1,200 (with provenance).	
31a (450)	1951-54	**Trojan 15 cwt Van 'ESSO'**	Red body and hubs, 85 mm	£100-130
31b (451)	1952-54	**'DUNLOP'**	Red body and hubs, 'The Worlds Master Tyre'	£100-130
31c (452)	1953-54	**'CHIVERS'**	Green body and hubs, 'CHIVERS JELLIES' and design	£100-130
31d (453)	1953-54	**'OXO'**	Dark or Mid-Blue body, Blue hubs, 'Beefy OXO' (not boxed)	£200-250
33a	1935-36	**Mechanical Horse**	Red, Green, Blue or Yellow body, 2.5 mm. trailer step, 65 mm	£150-175
			N.B. 1st type have long slot and chrome hubs.	
	1936-40		As previous model but trailer step is 9.5 mm. long	£125-150
	1946-?		As previous model but also in Brown, Grey or Khaki	£125-150
33b	1935-40	**Flat Truck Trailer**	Red, Green, Blue or Yellow body, no sides, 61 mm	£45-55
33c	1935-40	**Open Truck Trailer**	Red, Green, Blue or Yellow body with sides, 61 mm	£45-55
33d	1935-40	**Box Van Trailer**	Green tinplate body on cast chassis, no advertising, 70 mm	£100-125
		'HORNBY TRAINS'	Dark Blue body, 'Hornby Trains British and Guaranteed' in Gold	£125-175
		'HORNBY TRAINS'	Green body, 'Hornby Trains British and Guaranteed' in Gold	£125-175
		'MECCANO'	Green body, 'Meccano Engineering For Boys' in Red and Black	£125-175
		NB	Models 33a and 33d combined and given Ref No 33r	£200-300
33e	1935-40	**Dust Wagon Trailer**	Blue or Yellow 33c (Open Trailer) with Blue tinplate top, 61 mm	£70-90
			Grey or Green 33c (Open Trailer) with Green or Blue tinplate top	£70-90
	1946-47		Grey or Red body with Blue tinplate top	£70-90
33f	1935-40	**Petrol Tank Trailer**	Green (33b) chassis/Red tank, or Red chassis/Green tank, no logo, 61 mm	£70-90
		'ESSO'	Green chassis/Red tank with 'ESSO' in Gold	£70-90
		'CASTROL'	Red chassis/Green tank, 'Wakefield Castrol'	£70-90
33r	1935-40	**Railway Mechanical Horse and Trailer Van**	33a Mechanical Horse and 33d Box Van Trailer in railway liveries. 112 mm. These were also available separately as 33ra and 33rd (see below).	
33r		**'L.N.E.R.'**	Blue and Black, 'L.N.E.R. Express Parcels Traffic'	£200-300
33r		**'L.M.S.'**	Maroon and Black, 'L.M.S. Express Parcels Traffic'	£200-300
33r		**'G.W.R'**	Brown and Cream, 'G.W.R. Express Cartage Services'	£200-300
33r		**'S.R.'**	Green (Cream cab roof) and Black, 'Southern Railway'	£200-300
33ra	1935-40	**Mechanical Horse 'L.N.E.R.'**	Blue and Black, 'L.N.E.R. 901', 65 mm	£200-300
33ra		**'L.M.S.'**	Maroon and Black, 'L.M.S. 2246'	£200-300
33ra		**'G.W.R.'**	Brown and Cream, 'G.W.R. 2742'	£200-300
33ra		**'S.R.'**	Green (Cream roof) and Black, '3016 M'	£200-300
33rd		**Railway Trailer 'L.N.E.R.'**	Blue and Black, 'L.N.E.R. Express Parcels Traffic'	£200-300
33rd		**'L.M.S.'**	Maroon and Black, 'L.M.S. Express Parcels Traffic'	£200-300
33rd		**'G.W.R.'**	Brown and Cream, 'G.W.R. Express Cartage Services'	£200-300
33rd		**'S.R.'**	Green and Black, 'Southern Railway'	£200-300
33w (415)	1947-54	**Mechanical Horse and Open Wagon**	Grey, Fawn, Dark or Mid-Green, Olive, Red, Brown, Blue or Yellow cab, with Maroon, Brown, Light or Mid-Green, Olive or Cream trailer, 102 mm	£75-95
34a	1935-40	**'ROYAL AIR MAIL SERVICE'**	Blue car body with Silver lettering and Gold crest, 83 mm	£200-250
34b	1938-47	**'ROYAL MAIL' Van**	Red body, Black bonnet/wings/roof/hubs, open rear windows, 83 mm	£100-150
	1948-51		Red body, Black bonnet/wings/roof, Black or Red hubs, filled-in rear windows	£80-100
	1952-52		Red body/roof/hubs, Black bonnet/front wings, filled-in rear windows	£100-125
34c (492)	1948-54	**Loudspeaker Van**	Fawn, Green, Brown or Blue body (280 casting) Black loudspeakers, 81 mm	£60-70
			Brown, Blue or Green body (280 casting) Silver loudspeakers	£60-70
60y	1938-40	**Thompson Aircraft Tender**	Red with 'Shell Aviation Services' in Gold; Black or White solid rubber wheels	£250-350

Commercial vehicles

151b (25s)	1937-40	**6-wheel Covered Wagon**	Gloss Green body, tinplate canopy, seat holes, spare wheel, 99 mm	£125-150
151b (620)	1947-54	**6-wheel Covered Wagon**	Matt-Green or Greenish-Brown body, (export only from 1950)	£60-70
251 (25p)	1954-63	**Aveling Barford Road Roller**	Green body with driver and hook, Red wheels, 110 mm.	£30-40
252 (25v)	1954-60	**Bedford Refuse Wagon**	Fawn body, Green tinplate shutters, Red hubs	£80-100
	1960-63		Lime Green body, Black tinplate shutters, Cream hubs, with or without window glazing	£200-250
	1963 only		Orange cab, Light Grey body, Green tinplate shutters and diecast hubs, window glazing, Black grille	£300-350
	1964		Orange cab, Light Grey body and diecast hubs, Green plastic shutters, window glazing	£200-350
	1964-65		Orange cab, Light Grey body, Green plastic shutters, Red plastic hubs, window glazing	£200-250
260	1955-61	**'ROYAL MAIL' Van**	(Morris 'J') Red body, Black roof, Gold 'E II R' crest, 78 mm	£80-100
260	1971-72	**VW 'DEUTSCHE BUNDESPOST'**	Yellow body (129 casting, 100mm), made for German Market	£100-150
261	1955-61	**Telephone Service Van**	(Morris 'Z') Olive-Green/Black, 'POST OFFICE TELEPHONES', ladder, 73 mm	£80-110
273	1965-70	**Mini Minor Van 'R.A.C.'**	Blue body, White roof, Black base, Red interior, 'ROAD SERVICES', 78 mm	£100-125
			As previous model but with Blue interior	£75-95
			With Red interior, Silver baseplate and redesigned rear doors	£75-95
	NB		Factory errors have resulted in rear door logos reading 'ROAD ROAD' instead of 'ROAD SERVICES' as normal.	NGPP
274	1964-73	**Mini Minor Van 'A.A.'**	Yellow body, White roof, 'PATROL SERVICE', original 'entwined' logo	£100-125
			Same, but with Yellow roof	£100-125
			Yellow body, White roof, Red interior, 'AA SERVICE', modern 'simple' logo, Silver or Black base	£60-70
			As previous model but with Blue interior	£60-70
			With Yellow roof and Blue interior	£60-70

Note: 'AA' logo designs a) Embossed paint 'AA'
b) Waterslide transfer into recessed square
c) Waterslide transfer onto raised panel

Rear door casting variations: a) Rear door hinge pins extend directly into chassis holes
b) Rear door hinge pins located into slots

Van body central base colour variations: a) Red, b) Blue, c) White

274	1970-70	**'JOSEPH MASON PAINTS'**	(Mini Minor Van). Promotional in special Red box with advert card. 650 issued. Maroon body, Red seats and rear van body base, roof sign, 'PAINTS' labels, spun hubs.	£250-300
275	1964-66	**Brinks Armoured Car**	Grey/Blue, 'Brinks Security Since 1859', 2 figures, 2 crates, plastic hubs	£90-110
	1966-70		Same as previous model but no driver or crates, US packaging	£40-50
			Grey body White roof, Blue base, metal hubs, assembled in USA	NGPP
	Mexican issue:		Blue body with Grey doors and Red/White/Blue crests, plastic hubs	£1000-1500
279	1965-71	**Aveling Barford Diesel Roller**	Orange body, Grey engine covers, Blue rollers, 116 mm	£45-55
	1971-80		Yellow cab, Black roof, Silver rollers	£40-50
			Yellow cab, Black roof, Black rollers	£35-45
			Yellow cab, Blue roof, Yellow square engine covers, Silver rollers	£25-35
			Yellow cab, Black roof, Yellow square engine covers, Silver rollers	£25-35
			Yellow cab, Grey Roof, Yellow square engine covers, Silver rollers	£25-35
280	1945-47	**Delivery Van**	Red or Blue body, Type 3, open rear windows	£50-60
	1948-54		Red or Blue body, Type 3, filled-in rear windows, no advertising	£50-60
280	1966-68	**Mobile 'MIDLAND BANK'**	White/Silver, Blue stripe, Gold crest, opening doors, figure, 124 mm	£70-80

280 series DELIVERY VANS
Delivery Vans numbered 280a - 280k are an extension of the 28 series.

280a		**'VIYELLA'**	Blue body,'Viyella for the Nursery' in White and Black,	
	1937-39		Type 2, 81 mm	£250-350
	1939-41		Type 3, 83 mm	£175-225
280b		**'LYONS TEA'**	Dark Blue body, 'Lyons Tea Always the Best' in Red and White,	
	1937-39		Only issued as Type 2, 81mm	£350-450
280b		**'HARTLEYS JAM'**	Cream body, 'Hartleys is Real Jam' in Red/Green,	
	1939-39		Type 2, 81 mm	£800-1000
	1939-40		Type 3, 83 mm	£300-400
280c		**'SHREDDED WHEAT'**	Cream body, Red stripe, 'Welwyn Garden City, Herts' in Black,	
	1937-39		Type 2, 81 mm	£250-350
	1939-40		Type 3, 83 mm	£175-225
280d	1937-40	**'BISTO'**	Yellow body, 'Ah! Bisto' with logo, Type 2, 81 mm	£300-500
280d	1940	**'BISTO'**	Yellow body, wording altered to 'Bisto' with logo,	
	1938-39		Type 2, with large Bisto Kids transfer, 81 mm	£300-400
			Type 2, small Bisto Kids transfer, with pie on table	£600-800
	1939-40		Type 3, small Bisto Kids transfer with pie on table, 83 mm	£300-400
280e	1937-39	**'ECKO'**	Dark Green body, 'ECKO Radio' in Gold, Type 2, 81 mm	£250-350
280e		**'YORKSHIRE EVENING POST'**	Cream body, 'Yorkshire Evening Post - The Original Buff'	
	1938-39		Type 2, 81 mm	£300-350
	1939-39		Type 3, 83 mm	£600-800
280f		**'MACKINTOSHS'**	Red body, 'Mackintosh's Toffee' in Gold,	
	1937-39		Type 2, 81 mm	£600-800
	1939-40		Type 3, 83 mm	£300-400
280 g	1939 ?	**'BENTALLS'**	Green body, Yellow upper side panels, White roof, 'Bentalls Kingston on Thames' and 'Phone Kin: 1001' in Yellow, promotional, Type 2. Two examples known	£5000-8000

280 h	1939 ?	'BONNETERIE'	Dark Red, 'Maison de Bonneterie, Leverancier', promotional, Type 2	£2000-3000
280 i	1939 ?	'LIVERPOOL ECHO'	Promotional, Type 2, no other details available.	£2000-3000
280 j	1939	'FENWICK'	Apple Green body, White roof, 'Newcastle on Tyne', promotional, Type 2 Two examples known	£2000-3000
280 k	1939	'H. G. LOOSE'	Dark Green body, 'H. G. LOOSE' on Cream panel, 'Looe' and 'Phone 123', promotional, Type 2. One example known	£2000-3000
343 (30n)	1954-64	Dodge Farm Produce Wagon	Green cab with Yellow rear, or Yellow cab with Green rear, 104 mm	£60-70
			Red cab with Blue rear	£100-125
			Late issues with plastic hubs and boxed in the late lighter Yellow box	£125-150

'CONVOY' Series (380-387). Budget-priced models, having the same generic cab but with different rear body types.

380	1977-79	Skip Truck	Yellow and Orange body, 112 mm	£10-15
381	1977-80	Farm Wagon	Yellow and Brown body, 110 mm	£10-15
382	1978-80	Dumper Truck	Red body/Grey back, Red body/Black back or Yellow body/Grey back, 118 mm	£10-15
383	1978-80	'N.C.L.' Truck	Yellow body, 'NATIONAL CARRIERS Ltd', 110 mm	£10-15
384	1977-79	Fire Rescue Wagon	Red body, White fire escape, 126 mm	£10-15
385	1977-79	'ROYAL MAIL' Truck	Red body, 110 mm	£10-15
386	1979	'AVIS' Truck	Red body. Catalogued but not issued	NPP
387	1979	'PICKFORDS' Truck	Red and Blue body. Catalogued but not issued	NPP
?	1979	'HARRODS' Truck	Khaki body	NGPP
?	1979	'POST OFFICE TELEPHONES'	Khaki body	NGPP
?	1979	'A.A.' Truck	Yellow body	NGPP
?	1979	'AMERICAN FIRE BRIGADE'	No details	NGPP

NB See also 687 Convoy Army Truck in the Military Vehicles section.

390	1978	Customised Transit Van	Metallic Blue body with 'VAMPIRE' and 'flame' design, Type 3	NGPP
400 (14a)	1954-60	B.E.V. Truck	Dark Blue or Mid-Blue or Grey with Blue, Grey or Red hubs	£30-35
401 (14c)	1954-64	Coventry Climax Fork Lift	Orange body, Green forks, Tan driver, 108 mm	£25-30
			Red body, Green forks	£300-400
402	1966-69	Bedford TK Lorry	Red and White body, 'COCA-COLA', six trays of crates, 121 mm	£125-150
404	1967-72	Climax Fork Lift	Red/Yellow body with 'CG4' rear logo	£25-35
			Red/Yellow front with all Red rear, plus stick-on 'CG4' label.	£20-25
	1978		Yellow body with 'Climax' on fork guide and 'TC4' on engine cover	£20-25
406	1963-66	Commer Articulated Truck	Yellow/Grey, Blue plastic hubs, Supertoy, (424 without accessories), 175 mm	£80-100
407		**Ford Transit Vans**		
	1966-69	'KENWOOD'	Blue/White, 'KENWOOD', promotional, 122 mm. Type I	£50-60
	1970-71	'TELEFUSION'	White body, 'Colour TV, Telefusion'. A promotional never issued	NPP
	1970-75	'HERTZ'	Yellow body, 'Hertz Truck Rentals', promotional, 122 mm. Type I	£50-60
	1970-73	'AVIS'	Red body, 'Avis Truck Rentals'. Kit only but not issued	NPP
		'PELTZ BADKEREI'	Blue lower body, Yellow upper half, promotional	£50-60
408 (922)	1956-63	Big Bedford Lorry	Maroon cab, Fawn truck body, Fawn or Cream hubs, 146 mm	£125-150
			Blue cab, Yellow truck body, Yellow or Cream hubs	£200-300
			Pink cab, Cream truck body, Cream hubs	£1500-2000
			Blue cab, Orange truck body, Pale Yellow or Cream hubs	£250-350
409 (921)	1956-63	Bedford Articulated Lorry	Yellow or Yellowish-Orange body, Black or Silver radiator, Black wings, Red hubs, 'Dinky Toys' on base. Yellow box 'DINKY TOYS'	£80-100
			As previous model but with window glazing. Lighter Yellow box	£150-200
410 (25m)	1954-61	Bedford Tipper Truck	Red cab and diecast hubs, Cream truck body	£100-150
			Yellow cab and diecast hubs, Mid-Blue truck body	£100-150
	1962-63		Red cab and plastic hubs, Cream body, window glazing, Black or Silver grille, matt Black baseplate	£125-165
			Yellow cab and plastic hubs, Mid-Blue body, window glazing, Black grille, matt Black baseplate	£125-165
410		Bedford CF Vans	All are 90mm long.	
	1972-72	'SIMPSONS'	Red/Black, 'Simpsons' and logos, Canadian promotional	£35-45
	1974	'DANISH POST'	Yellow body, 'Danish Post' emblem, Danish promotional	£35-45
	1974-75	'JOHN MENZIES'	Dark Blue body with 'John Menzies' logo, promotional	£25-30
	1974-74	'BELACO'	Brown/Black, 'Belaco Brake and Clutch Parts', promotional	£35-45
	1975-76	'M.J. HIRE'	White body, 'M.J. Hire Service', promotional	£25-30
	1975-77	'MODELLERS WORLD'	White body, 'Modellers World'. This is a Code 2 model	£25-30
	1975-75	'MARLEY TILES'	Red body with 'Marley Building' logo, 90 mm	£25-30
	1979	'COLLECTORS GAZETTE'	White body, 'Collectors Gazette' logo, 90 mm. A Code 2 model	£25-30
	1972-74	'ROYAL MAIL'	Red body with 'ROYAL MAIL' and 'E II R' crest, 90 mm.	£15-20
	1974-80	'ROYAL MAIL'	As previous model but with raised rectangle on roof	£15-20

NB Many Code-2 issues exist (produced by John Gay) and include the following liveries: 'MOBIL', 'BN', 'HERTZ TRUCK RENTAL', 'JIMMY CARTER', 'MATRA', 'ELF', 'SILVER JUBILEE 1952-1977', 'KLG', 'PORTAKABIN', 'WIMPEY',.

411 (25w)	1954-59	Bedford Truck	Pale Green body and hubs, matt base, 104 mm	£125-150
	1954-56		Same, but with Black front mudguards	£125-150

	1959-60		Mid-Green cab and body, Pale Green hubs, gloss base, block-tread tyres	£125-150
412 (30j)	1954-60	**Austin Wagon**	Powder Blue body, Pale Yellow or Dark Blue hubs, 104 mm	£350-450
			Dark Red body, Pale Red hubs	£150-200
			Dark Blue body, Blue hubs	£250-350
			Lemon Yellow body, Green or Blue hubs	£350-450
412	1974-80	**Bedford CF Van 'AA'**	Yellow body, 'AA SERVICE', headboard, plastic hubs, 90 mm	£15-20
413 (30s)	1954-60	**Austin Covered Wagon**	Maroon body, Cream cover, Cream hubs, 104 mm	£100-150
			Dark Blue body, Light Blue cover, Light Blue hubs	£300-400
			Mid-Blue body, Light Blue cover, Light Blue hubs	£100-150
			Red body, Grey cover, Cream or Grey hubs	£300-400
			Red body, Tan cover, Red hubs	£300-400
			Light or Mid-Blue body, Cream cover, Lemon-Yellow hubs. Plain box	£275-325
			Red body, Grey, Grey hubs	£275-325
			Light Maroon body, Tan cover, Red hubs	£300-400
414 (30m)	1954-61	**Dodge Rear Tipping Wagon**	Red or Orange cab (with bonnet louvres), Green tipper body, 99 mm	£60-70
	1961-64		Red or Orange cab (no bonnet louvres), Green tipper body	£60-70
	1961-64		Blue cab, Grey tipper body	£60-70
			Royal Blue cab, Grey tipper and hubs	£125-150
415 (33w)	1954-59	**Mechanical Horse and Wagon**	(Models 33a + 33d), Blue horse/Cream trailer or Red horse/Brown trailer	£125-175
416, 417		**Ford Transit Vans**		
416	1975-78	**'FORD'**	Orange-Yellow body, cast hubs, '1,000,000 TRANSITS', Type 2, promotional	NGPP
416	1975-78	**'MOTORWAY'**	Yellow body, 'Motorway Services', special lights, Type 2	£25-35
417	1978-79	**'MOTORWAY'**	As previous model but Type 3 casting	£20-30
417 (931)	1956-58	**Leyland Comet Lorry with Stake Body**	Dark Blue cab and chassis, Dark Yellow stake body with rivet fitting, Pale Blue hubs, 'DINKY TOYS' on chassis. Yellow box	£150-175
	1958-59		Yellow cab and chassis, Light Green stake body with rivet fitting, Mid-Green hubs, 'DINKY TOYS' on chassis. Yellow box	£300-350
418 (932)	1956-59	**Leyland Comet with Hinged Tailboard**	Green cab, Orange truck body, Cream or Green hubs. Yellow picture box 'DINKY TOYS'	£90-110
			Dark Blue cab and chassis, Mid-Blue truck body, Blue, Cream or Red hubs. Yellow picture box 'DINKY TOYS'	£100-150
			Red cab and chassis, Mid-Blue truck body secured by rivet, Mid-Blue, hubs. Yellow box	£300-400
419 (933)	1956-59	**Leyland Comet Cement Lorry**	Yellow body, 'Portland Blue-Circle Cement', 144 mm	£100-125
420 (25r)	1954-61	**Forward Control Lorry**	(Leyland) Red, Grey, Orange, Green or Blue body, hook, 107 mm	£60-70
421 (30w)	1955-59	**Electric Articulated Vehicle**	(Hindle-Smart), Maroon body, 'British Railways', hook, 135 mm	£60-70
422 (30r)	1954-60	**Fordson Thames Flat Truck**	Dark Green or Red body, window glazing, hook, 112 mm	£60-70
			Bright Green body and hubs	£100-130
424	1963-66	**Commer Convertible Articulated Vehicle**	Yellow or Grey cab, 406 plus Blue trailer canopy and 'stake' body fittings, 175 mm	£130-150
425	1964-69	**Bedford TK Coal Wagon**	Red body, 'HALL & Co.', window glazing, 6 coal bags, scales, 121 mm	£100-125
428 (951)	1955-64	**Large Trailer**	Grey body, hook, Red hubs, Black front axle mount, Supertoy, 111 mm	£20-25
	1967-71		Red body with hook, Silver hubs, Silver front axle mount	£20-25
			Yellow body, Red hubs	£20-25
429 (25g)	1954-64	**Trailer**	Dark Green or Red, hook, axle pivot is part of main casting, 69 mm	£20-25
430 (25x)	1954-64	**Commer Breakdown Truck**	'DINKY SERVICE' logo, operable crane, late issues have window glazing, 123 mm.	
			Light Tan cab, Green back, Red hubs. Yellow or Blue/White striped box	£100-120
			Mid-Tan cab, Green back. Striped box	£100-120
			Cream cab, Pale Blue back, Red hubs. Yellow box	£300-400
			Dark Stone cab, Blue back, Red hubs. Yellow box	£300-400
			Red cab, Pale Grey back, Blue or Red metal hubs. Yellow box	£300-400
			Red cab with glazing, Pale Grey back, Blue plastic hubs. Yellow box	£300-400
			Red cab with glazing, Pale Grey back, Red plastic hubs. Yellow box	£500-750
430	1977-80	**Johnson 2 ton Dumper**	Orange/Red body with Blue driver, Black or Orange engine, 106 mm..	£20-25
431 (911)	1956-57	**Guy 4 ton Lorry**	Red 2nd type cab/chassis, Grey body, Red hubs, unpainted hook.	£350-450
			Dark Blue 2nd type cab/chassis, Light Blue body, Green hubs	£200-300
431	1958-60	**Guy Warrior 4 ton Lorry**	Light Tan cab (no window glazing), Dark Green truck body, Green hubs	£350-450
			Red cab and chassis, Dark Green truck body, Red hubs	£350-450
	1960-64		Light Tan cab (with window glazing), Dark Green truck body, Green hubs	£350-450
432 (912)	1956-57	**Guy Flat Truck**	Pale Blue 2nd type cab/chassis/hook, Red flatbed, Pale Blue hubs	£200-300
	1956-57		Red 2nd type cab/chassis/hook, Pale Blue flatbed and hubs	£400-500
432	1958-60	**Guy Warrior Flat Truck**	Green cab (no window glazing), Red flatbed, Red hubs 136 mm	£300-400
	1960-64		Green cab (with window glazing), Red flatbed, Red hubs	£300-400
432	1976-79	**Foden Tipping Lorry**	White cab, Red chassis, Yellow rear body, 175 mm.	£30-35
433 (913)	1956-57	**Guy Flat Truck with Tailboard**	Dark Green 2nd type cab/chassis/hook, Mid-Green flatbed and hubs	£200-300
			Deep Blue 2nd type cab/chassis/hook, Orange body, Light Blue hubs	£200-300

434	1964-66	Bedford TK Crash Truck	White body with Green flash, 'TOP RANK Motorway Services', Blue or Red interior	£55-65
	1966-70		Red or Metallic Red cab, Pale Grey back, 'AUTO SERVICES'	£55-65
435	1964-66	Bedford TK Tipper	Grey cab with Blue roof, Red rear body, 121 mm	£35-40
	1966-68		Yellow cab with Yellow or Black roof, Silver rear body	£35-40
	1968-71		White cab and roof, Silver and Blue rear body	£35-40
			Blue body, Orange and Grey rear body	£75-100
436	1963-69	'ATLAS COPCO' Lorry	Yellow body, Pale Grey interior, matt baseplate	£50-60
			Yellow body, Dark Blue interior, gloss baseplate	£50-60
437	1962-70	Muir Hill 2WL Loader	Red body with hook, no grille detail, 121 mm	£20-25
			Yellow body with Red or Silver hubs	£20-25
	1970-78		Yellow with Red arms with hook, with or without grille detail	£20-25
			Orange body with Orange or Black arms	£30-40
438	1970-77	Ford D800 Tipper Truck	Metallic Red cab, Yellow tipper, Yellow or Silver hubs	£25-35
			Metallic Red cab, Dark Metallic Blue tipper, Yellow hubs	£25-35
			Orange cab, Orange or Yellow tipper, Silver hubs, opening cab doors	£25-35
			Bright Red cab, Orange tipper, Silver hubs, opening cab doors	£25-35
			Bright Red cab, Bright Red tipper, Silver hubs, opening cab doors	£25-35
	promotional issue:		White cab, Blue back, Silver chassis, with cardboard load 'POLCARB'.	
			Packed in plain White box with folded leaflet	£200-250
439	1970-76	Ford D800 Snow Plough	Dark Metallic Blue cab, Orange tipper, Yellow plough, White hubs	£40-50
	1976-78		Dark Metallic Blue cab, Pale Blue tipper, Yellow plough, Silver hubs	£40-50
			Light Metallic Blue cab, Orange tipper, Dark Yellow plough, Silver hubs	£40-50
			Medium Blue cab, Yellow plough, Powder Blue tipper, Silver hubs	£40-50
			Orange cab and tipper, Dark Yellow plough, Silver hubs	£40-50
			Orange cab, Dark Yellow tipper and plough, Silver hubs	£40-50
			All-Orange body, cast Silver hubs	£40-50
440	1977-78	Ford D800 Tipper Truck	Orange cab, Yellow tipper, Silver or Black chassis	£35-40
			Orange cab, Orange tipper, Black chassis	£35-40
			Orange cab, Light Blue tipper, Black chassis	£35-40
			Red cab, Red Tipper, Black chassis, Silver hubs	£35-40
			Red cab, Orange Tipper, Silver chassis, Silver hubs	£35-40
			Red cab, Light Blue Tipper, Black chassis, Silver hubs	£35-40
			Red cab with Black roof, Red Tipper, Red hubs	£35-40
440 (30p)	1954-58	Petrol Tanker 'MOBILGAS'	Red body, 'MOBILGAS' in White letters with Blue borders, 112 mm	£110-140
	1958-61		Red body, 'MOBILGAS' in Blue letters on White background	£110-140
441 (30pa)	1954-60	Petrol Tanker 'CASTROL'	Green body, 112 mm	£110-140
442 (30pb)	1954-60	Petrol Tanker 'ESSO'	Red body, 'ESSO MOTOR OIL - PETROL', 112 mm	£110-140
442	1973-79	Land Rover Breakdown Crane	White and Red body, 'Motorway Rescue', operable winch, 121 mm	£15-20
	1974-		White/Red or All-Red body, 'FALCK', export model for Denmark	£25-30
443	1957-58	Petrol Tanker 'NATIONAL'	Yellow body, 'NATIONAL BENZOLE MIXTURE', 112 mm	£150-175
448	1963-68	Chevrolet El Camino Pick-Up with Trailers	Turquoise/Cream/Red Pick-up and 2 trailers, 'Acme Trailer Hire', 256 mm	£200-250
449	1961-69	Chevrolet El Camino Pick-up	Turquoise body, White roof, Red interior, spun hubs, 111 mm	£80-90
			Turquoise body, White roof, Pale Turquoise interior, spun hubs	£150-200
			Turquoise body, White roof, Lemon interior, spun hubs	£150-200
	NB		Various shades of Turquoise are known to exist.	
	South African issue:		All-Turquoise body, spun hubs	£500-750
	South African issue:		Cream over Chocolate Brown lower body, spun hubs	£500-750
	South African issue:		Turquoise over Cream lower body, spun hubs	£500-750
449	1977-79	Johnston Road Sweeper	Yellow or Lime-Green body, (non-opening doors), 142 mm	£30-35
			All Yellow body, promotional with 'JOHNSTON' stickers, normal box	£40-50
			All Yellow body, promotional with 'JOHNSTON' stickers, special box	£70-80
			Orange cab, Metallic Green rear	£40-50
450 (31a)	1954-57	Trojan Van 'ESSO'	Red body, White stripe, Red or Maroon hubs, 'Esso' logo, 85 mm	£110-140
			Maroon hub version issued in U.S.A. trade packs	NGPP
450	1965-70	Bedford TK Van 'CASTROL'	Green/White body, 'CASTROL - The Masterpiece In Oils', 143 mm	£100-125
451 (31b)	1954-57	Trojan Van 'DUNLOP'	Red body and hubs, 'Dunlop The Worlds Master Tyre', 85 mm	£110-140
451	1971-77	Johnston Road Sweeper	Orange cab (449 with opening doors), Metallic Green tank, 142 mm	£30-35
	1971-77		Metallic Green cab (449 with opening doors), Orange tank, 142 mm	£30-35
452 (31c)	1954-57	Trojan Van 'CHIVERS'	Green body, Mid-Green hubs, 'CHIVERS JELLIES' logo, 85 mm	£100-130
453 (31d)	1954-54	Trojan Van 'OXO'	Blue body and hubs, White 'Beefy OXO', Silver trim, (not boxed)	£200-250
454	1957-59	Trojan Van 'CYDRAX'	Light Green body and hubs, 'DRINK CYDRAX' logo	£125-150
455	1957-60	Trojan Van 'BROOKE BOND'	Dark Red body, Red hubs, 'BROOKE BOND TEA' logo	£125-150
	promotional issue:		As previous issue with White label on roof. The Red logo states: 'Since 1924 more than 5,700 Trojan 'Little Red Vans' supplied. Replaced on a long life basis'. A similar label is attached to its (normal) box	£400-600
465	1959-59	Morris 10 cwt Van 'CAPSTAN'	Light Blue and Dark Blue body with cigarette design 'Have A Capstan'	£150-200
470	1954-56	Austin A40 Van 'SHELL-BP'	Red and Green body with 'SHELL' and 'BP' decals, 89 mm	£125-150
471	1955-60	Austin A40 Van 'NESTLES'	Red body, Yellow wheel hubs, 'Nestles' logo, 89 mm	£100-125
472	1956-60	Austin A40 Van 'RALEIGH'	Dark Green body with 'Raleigh Cycles' decals, 89 mm	£150-175
480	1954-56	Bedford CA Van 'KODAK'	Yellow body, 'Kodak Cameras and Films' in Red and Black, 83 mm	£80-100

481	1955-60	**Bedford Van 'OVALTINE'**	Blue body with 'Ovaltine' on Cream panel, 83 mm	£70-90
482	1956-60	**Bedford Van 'DINKY TOYS'**	Cream and Light Orange body, 'Dinky Toys' logo in Red, 83 mm	£100-125
490 (30v)	1954-60	**Electric Dairy Van 'EXPRESS DAIRY'**	Cream body with Red chassis, hubs and logo, 85 mm	£65-75
			Grey body with Blue chassis, hubs and logo	£65-75
491 (30v)	1954-60	**Electric Dairy Van 'N.C.B.'**	Cream body with Red chassis, hubs and logo, export model	£65-75
			Grey body, Blue chassis, hubs and logo, export model	£65-75
491	1960	**Electric Dairy Van 'JOB'S DAIRY'**	Cream/Red. 1176 made for promotional purposes (Code-2)	£90-110
492 (34c)	1954-57	**Loudspeaker Van**	Blue body, Silver loudspeakers, (280 casting, Type 3), 83 mm	£60-70
492 (34c)	1954-?	**Loudspeaker Van**	Fawn or Blue body (280 casting), Black loudspeakers, 81 mm	£60-70
			Blue or Green body (280 casting), Silver loudspeakers	£60-70
492	1964-64	**Election Mini-Van**	White body, Orange loudspeakers, 'Vote for Somebody', figure, 78 mm.	
			Yellow 'see-through' box	£60-70
501	1947-48	**Foden Diesel 8-Wheel Wagon**	1st type cab with flash, spare wheel, hook on some, no tank slits in chassis, no chain-post bosses, Black 'herringbone' tyres, Supertoy, 185 mm.	
			Pale Grey cab and body, Red flash and hubs, Black chassis, no hook	£750-1000
			Dark Blue cab and body, Silver flash, Blue hubs, Black chassis, no hook	£600-700
			Brown cab and body, Silver flash, Brown hubs, Black chassis, no hook	£250-350
			Red cab and body, Silver flash, Red hubs, Black chassis, no hook, (US only issue)	£4000-5000
			Dark Grey cab and body, Red flash, chassis and hubs, small unpainted hook on some	£400-500
501	1948-52	**Foden Diesel 8-Wheel Wagon**	Hook and tank-slits in chassis (introduced 1948), Black 'radial' tyres.	
			Dark Blue cab/chassis, Light Blue flash/body/hubs, small unpainted hook	£1000-1200
			Red cab/chassis/hubs, Silver flash, Fawn body, unpainted hook, slits on some	£400-500
501 (901)	1952-54	**Foden Diesel 8-Wheel Wagon**	2nd cab, no flash, large painted hook, Supertoy hubs, 188 mm.	
			Dark Blue cab/chassis, Light Blue body and hubs, Grey tyres	£600-700
			Red cab/chassis, Fawn body, Red hubs, Grey tyres	£250-350
502	1947-48	**Foden Flat Truck**	1st type cab with flash, spare wheel, hook on some, no tank slits in chassis, no chain-post bosses, Black 'herringbone' tyres, Supertoy, 185 mm.	
			Green cab and body, Silver flash, Black chassis, Green hubs, no hook	£350-450
			Pale Blue cab and body, Dark Blue flash/chassis/hubs, no hook	£650-750
502	1948-52	**Foden Flat Truck**	Hook and tank-slits in chassis introduced in 1948, Black 'radial' tyres.	
			Dark Blue cab/wings/chassis, Red flash and body, Blue hubs, slits on some	£700-800
			Brownish-Orange cab/chassis, Green flash and body, Green hubs, slits on some.	
			In Dark Blue box showing 2nd cab model	£600-700
502	1952-52	**Foden Flat Truck**	2nd cab, no flash, large painted hook, Supertoy hubs, 188 mm.	
			Blue cab/chassis, Red body, Pale Blue hubs, chain-post bosses	£2000-2500
502 (902)	1952-54	**Foden Flat Truck**	Dull Orange cab/chassis, Green body and hubs, chain-post bosses	£350-450
			Yellow cab/chassis, Green body and hubs, Black or Grey tyres, bosses	£600-700
503	1947-48	**Foden Flat Truck with Tailboard**	1st type cab with flash, spare wheel, hook on some, no tank slits in chassis, no chain-post bosses, Black 'herringbone' tyres, Supertoy, 185 mm.	
			Red cab and flatbed, Black flash and chassis, Red hubs, no hook	£650-750
			Pale Grey cab and flatbed, Blue flash and chassis, Blue hubs, no hook	£700-800
503	1948-52	**Foden Flat Truck with Tailboard**	Hook and tank-slits in chassis introduced in 1948, Black 'radial' tyres.	
			Dark Green cab/chassis, Light Green flash/flatbed/hubs, small hook	£600-700
			Deep Blue cab/chassis, Dull Orange flatbed, Light Blue hubs, hook, slits	£600-700
503	1952-52	**Foden Flat Truck with Tailboard**	2nd cab, no flash, large painted hook, Supertoy hubs, 188 mm.	
			Dark Green cab/chassis, Light Green flatbed and hubs, Grey tyres, bosses	£1500-2000
503 (903)	1952-56		Dark Blue cab/chassis, Orange flatbed, Light Blue hubs, chain-post bosses	£250-350
503	1952-53		Dark Orange cab/chassis, Yellow flatbed and hubs, Grey tyres, bosses	£1700-2000
503 (903)	1953-54		Dark Blue cab/chassis, Yellow body, Light Blue hubs, chain-post bosses	£600-700
504	1948-52	**Foden 14 ton Tanker**	1st type cab with flash, spare wheel, tinplate tank, hook, no advertising, Black 'fine radial tread' tyres, Supertoy, 185 mm.	
			Dark Blue cab/chassis, Silver flash, Light Blue tank and hubs	£250-350
			Dark Blue cab/chassis, Light Blue flash, tank and hubs	£250-350
504	1948-52		Red cab/chassis, Silver flash, Fawn tank, Red hubs	£450-550
504	1952-57	**Foden 14 ton Tanker**	2nd cab, no flash, large painted hook, Supertoy hubs, 188 mm.	
504	1952-52		Dark Blue cab/chassis, rivetted back, Light Blue tank and hubs, Grey tyres.	
			Model housed in 2nd type picture box	£2000-3000
504	1952-53		Red cab/chassis, Fawn tank, Red hubs, Grey tyres	£450-550
504 (941)	1953-54	**Foden 14 ton Tanker 'MOBILGAS'**	Red cab/chassis/tank/hubs, 'MOBILGAS', Grey tyres.	
			With Red 'Pegasus' logo at cab end of tank facing the cab	£250-350
			Same, but with Red 'Pegasus' logo at rear of tank facing away from cab	£1,500-2,000
505	1952-52	**Foden Flat Truck with Chains**	1st type cab with flash, spare wheel, hook, slits in chassis, 'dimpled' post bosses, Black 'fine radial tread' tyres, Supertoy, 185mm. Blue covered box showing 1st type cab.	
			Green cab/chassis/flatbed, Light Green flash and hubs	£1500-2000
			Maroon cab/chassis, Silver flash, Maroon flatbed and hubs	£2000-2500
505	1952-54	**Foden Flat Truck with Chains**	2nd cab, no flash, large painted hook, Supertoy hubs, 188 mm.	
			Green cab/chassis/flatbed, Light Green hubs, 'dimpled' chain-post bosses	£200-300
			Maroon cab/chassis/flatbed/hubs, 'dimpled' chain-post bosses	£250-350
505 (905)	1954-56		Green cab/chassis/body, Light Green hubs, 'rounded' chain-post bosses	£200-300
			Maroon cab/chassis/body/hubs, 'rounded' chain-post bosses	£250-350

511	1947-48	**Guy 4 ton Lorry**	1st cab casting, Supertoy, spare wheel, small unpainted hook, 129 mm.	
			Green cab, truck body and hubs, Black chassis and wings	£200-300
			Brown cab, truck body and hubs, Black chassis and wings	£250-350
			Grey cab, truck body and hubs, Red chassis and wings	£200-300
511 (911)	1948-52	**Guy 4 ton Lorry**	1st cab casting, Supertoy, large painted or unpainted hook, 132 mm.	
			Red cab/chassis/wings/ 'ridged' hubs, Fawn truck body	£250-350
			Dark Blue cab/chassis/wings, Light Blue truck body and 'ridged' hubs	£200-300
	1952-54		Red cab/chassis/wings/ 'grooved' hubs, Fawn truck body	£250-350
			Dark Blue cab/chassis/wings, Light Blue truck body and 'grooved' hubs	£200-300
512	1947-48	**Guy Flat Truck**	1st cab casting, Supertoy, spare wheel, small unpainted hook, 129 mm.	
			Maroon cab, flatbed and hubs, Black chassis and wings	£300-400
			Dark Brown cab, flatbed and hubs, Black chassis and wings	£400-500
			Yellow cab and flatbed, Black chassis and wings, Red hubs	£350-450
			Khaki cab and flatbed, Black chassis and wings, Green hubs	£550-650
			Grey cab and flatbed, Red chassis and wings, Red hubs	£550-650
			Grey cab and flatbed, Black chassis, Black hubs	£500-600
			Red cab and flatbed, Black chassis, Black hubs	£700-800
	1948-48		Brown cab/chassis/wings, Green flatbed, Green 'ridged' hubs	£400-500
512 (912)	1948-54	**Guy Flat Truck**	1st cab casting, Supertoy, small or large unpainted hook, 129/132 mm.	
			Blue cab/chassis/wings, Red flatbed, Light Blue 'ridged' hubs	£200-300
	1949-54		Orange cab/chassis/wings, Green flatbed, Green 'ridged' hubs	£400-500
	1952-54		Blue cab/chassis/wings, Red flatbed, Light Blue 'grooved' hubs	£200-300
513	1947-48	**Guy Flat Truck with Tailboard**	1st cab casting, Supertoy, spare wheel, small unpainted hook, 129 mm.	
			Dark Yellow cab/flatbed, Black chassis, wings and hubs	£400-500
			Dark Yellow cab/flatbed, Dark Blue chassis, wings and hubs	£450-550
			Grey cab and flatbed, Black chassis, wings and hubs	£300-400
			Grey cab and flatbed, Dark Blue chassis, wings and hubs	£750-1000
513	1948-52	**Guy Flat Truck with Tailboard**	1st cab, 'ridged' hubs, Supertoy, small or large unpainted hook, 129/132 mm.	
			Dark Green cab/chassis/wings, Green body and hubs, small hook	£200-300
			Deep Blue cab/chassis/wings, Orange body, Light Blue hubs, large hook	£250-350
513 (913)	1952-54	**Guy Flat Truck with Tailboard**	1st cab, Supertoy, 'grooved' hubs, large unpainted hook, 132 mm.	
			Dark Green cab/chassis/wings, Green body and hubs	£200-300
			Deep Blue cab/chassis/wings, Orange body, Light Blue hubs	£250-350
			Yellow cab/chassis/wings, Green hubs	£1000-1200
514	1950-52	**Guy Van 'SLUMBERLAND'**	Red 1st type cab/chassis/body and 'ridged' hubs, 'Slumberland Spring Interior Mattresses', spare wheel, Supertoy, 134 mm	£250-350
514	1952-52	**Guy Van 'LYONS'**	Dark Blue 1st type cab/body, Light Blue 'ridged' hubs, 'Lyons Swiss Rolls', spare wheel, Supertoy, 134 mm	£700-900
			Same model but rear axle in cast mounts	£700-900
514	1952-52	**Guy Van 'WEETABIX'**	Yellow 1st type cab/body, Yellow 'ridged' hubs, 'More Than a Breakfast Food', spare wheel, Supertoy, 134 mm	£1250-1500
514	1952-54	**Guy Van 'WEETABIX'**	Yellow 1st type cab/body, Yellow 'grooved' hubs, 'More Than a Breakfast Food', spare wheel, Supertoy, 134 mm	£1250-1500
514 (917)	1953-54	**Guy Van 'SPRATTS'**	Red/Cream 1st type cab/body, Red 'grooved' hubs, 'Bonio Ovals & Dog Cakes', spare wheel, Supertoy, 134 mm	£300-400
521 (921)	1948-48	**Bedford Articulated Lorry**	Red body, Black wings, Black or Red hubs, '20' transfer, 'Supertoys' on base, 166 mm. Brown box	£150-200
	1949-50		Yellow body, Black wings, Black hubs, '20' transfer, 'Supertoys' on base. Brown box with Red/White label	£200-250
	1950-54		Yellow or Yellowish-Orange body, Black wings, Red hubs, '20' transfer, 'Supertoys' or 'Dinky Toys' on base. Blue box, Orange or White label	£80-100
522 (922)	1952-54	**Big Bedford Lorry**	Maroon cab, Fawn truck body, Fawn hubs, Supertoy, 146 mm	£125-150
			Blue cab, Yellow truck body, Yellow hubs, Supertoy, 146 mm	£200-300
531 (931)	1949-54	**Leyland Comet Lorry with Stake Body**	Red cab and chassis, Yellow stake body with screw fitting, Yellow hubs, 'SUPERTOYS' on chassis	£200-300
			Mid-Blue cab and chassis, Brown stake body with screw fitting, Red hubs, 'SUPERTOYS' on chassis	£200-300
			Light Blue cab and chassis, Brown stake body with screw fitting, Blue hubs, 'SUPERTOYS' on chassis	£200-300
	NB Odd colours:		Be wary of colour combinations not listed. The screw fitting makes it easy to interchange the chassis and body components.	
532 (932)	1952-54	**Leyland Comet Lorry with Hinged Tailboard**	Green cab and chassis, Orange truck body with screw fitting, Yellow hubs. Blue box with Orange label	£120-150
			As previous model but with Green hubs. Blue/White box	£120-150
			Dark Blue cab and chassis, Light (Powder) Blue truck body with screw fitting, Yellow hubs. Blue/White box	£300-400
			Dark Blue cab and chassis, Mid-Blue truck body with screw fitting, Red hubs. Blue/White box	£100-130
533 (933)	1953-54	**Leyland Comet Cement Wagon**	Yellow body, 'Portland Blue-Circle Cement', Supertoy, 142 mm	£100-125
551 (951)	1948-54	**Trailer**	Grey body, Black hubs, hook, Supertoy, 105 mm	£20-30
			Yellow body, Black hubs, hook, Supertoy	£100-125
			Green body, Black hubs, hook, Supertoy	£100-125
	1969-73	Gift Set issue	Red body, Grey front chassis, protruding chromed hubs. Only in GS 339	GSP

Commercial vehicles

561 (961)	1949-54	**Blaw Knox Bulldozer**	Red body, Green or Black rubber tracks, driver, lifting blade, Supertoy.	
			Blue box with Orange/White label, or 'natural' card box with Red/White label	**£40-50**
561	1962-64	**Citroën Delivery Van**	Light Blue body, Red/Yellow 'CIBIE' logo, sliding door, 90 mm. French issue	**£60-70**
562 (962)	1948-54	**Muir Hill Dump Truck**	Yellow body, metal wheels/tyres, hook, 105 mm	**£15-20**
563 (963)	1948-54	**Blaw Knox Heavy Tractor**	Red, Orange or Blue 561 without the dozer blade, 116 mm.	
			Brown cardboard box has Red/White label	**£60-70**
			Dark Blue body, Mid-Blue rollers, Green rubber tracks, driver.	
			Brown box with Black/White picture label	**£175-200**
564 (964)	1952-54	**Elevator Loader**	See 964 for details.	
571 (971)	1949-54	**Coles Mobile Crane**	Yellow and Black, operable crane, Supertoy, 160 mm.	**£30-40**
579	1961-63	**Simca Glaziers Lorry**	UK issue: Yellow and Green body, mirror/glass load, 'MIROITIER'	**£70-80**
		French issue:	Grey and Green body, mirror/glass load, 'SAINT GOBAIN'	**£80-90**
581 (981)	1953-54	**Horsebox**	Maroon body (cast in aluminium) 'British Railways', 175 mm.	**£70-80**
581 (980)	1953-54	US issue:	Maroon, 'Hire Service', 'Express Horse Van', 'Express'. Blue box has Orange/White	
			labels with picture of US model	**£500-700**
581	1962-64	**Berliet Flat Truck**	Red and Grey body, 6 wheels plus spare, hook, 130 mm. French issue	**£70-80**
	NB		The French issues listed above have been included because they were sold in the U.K.	
582 (982)	1953-54	**Pullmore Car Transporter**	Bedford cab/chassis, aluminium trailer with 'DINKY TOYS DELIVERY SERVICE' logo on sides. Same logo on rear ramp plus '20' sign. No window glazing, 'DINKY TOYS' on baseplate, Black grille/bumper, Silver trim.	
	1953 only		Light Blue cab, trailer and hubs, Fawn decks, six lower deck retaining rivets. Model only issued for very short period	NGPP
	1953-54		As previous model but decks may be Fawn or Grey. Four lower deck retaining rivets	**£90-120**
	1954 only		Dark Blue cab, trailer and hubs, Fawn decks, four lower deck retaining rivets.	
			Model supplied in 582/982 all Dark Blue box with White end label	**£500-750**
			Model supplied in 582/982 Blue/White striped box	**£300-400**
591 (991)	1952-54	**A.E.C. Tanker**	Red/Yellow, 'SHELL CHEMICALS LIMITED', Supertoy, 151 mm	**£140-175**
620 (151b)	1950-54	**6-wheel Covered Wagon**	Matt-Green or Greenish-Brown body, 'Export only' (to USA)	**£60-70**
752 (973)	1953-54	**Goods Yard Crane**	Yellow operable crane on Blue (or Dark Blue) base (steps in some). Dark Blue box	**£30-40**
893	1962-64	**Unic Pipe Line Transporter**	Beige articulated body, spare wheel, 6 pipes, 215 mm. French issue	**£90-110**
894	1962-64	**Unic Boilot Car Transporter**	Grey body, 'Dinky Toys Service Livraison', 325 mm. French issue	**£100-120**
901 (501)	1954-57	**Foden 8-wheel Diesel Wagon**	2nd type cab, Supertoy, spare wheel, large hook, 188 mm.	
			Red cab and chassis, Fawn truck body, Red hubs	**£230-350**
902 (502)	1954-56	**Foden Flat Truck**	2nd type cab, Supertoy, spare wheel, large hook, 188 mm.	
			Yellow cab and chassis, Green flatbed body, Green hubs	**£600-700**
	1954-57		Orange cab and chassis, Green flatbed body, Green hubs	**£250-350**
	1957-59		Dark Red cab and chassis, rivetted back, Green flatbed, Green hubs	
			(NB Red similar to colour of 919 Guy 'GOLDEN SHRED' van)	**£2000-3000**
			Cherry-Red cab, wings and chassis, Green flatbed body	**£600-700**
			Orange cab and chassis, Fawn flatbed body, Mid-Green hubs	**£500-600**
903 (503)	1954-55	**Foden Flat Truck with Tailboard**	2nd type cab, Supertoy, spare wheel, large hook, 188 mm.	
			Dark Blue cab and chassis, Yellow flatbed, Light Blue hubs	**£600-700**
	1954-57		Dark Blue cab and chassis, Orange flatbed, Light Blue hubs	**£250-350**
	1957-60		Mid Blue cab and chassis, rivetted back, Fawn flatbed, Pale Blue hubs	**£600-700**
905 (505)	1954-56	**Foden Flat Truck with Chains**	2nd type cab, Supertoy, spare wheel, large hook, 188 mm.	
			Maroon cab, chassis and flatbed, Maroon hubs, rounded chain-post bosses	**£250-350**
	1954-58		Green cab, chassis and flatbed, Light Green hubs, rounded chain-post bosses	**£200-300**
	1956-57		Maroon cab, chassis and flatbed, Maroon hubs, rounded chain-post bosses	**£250-350**
			As previous issue but with Red hubs	**£300-350**
	1957-64		Red cab and chassis, Grey flatbed, Red hubs, rounded chain-post bosses	**£250-350**
	19??-64		Red cab and chassis, rivetted back, Grey flatbed, Red plastic hubs	**£450-550**
908	1962-66	**Mighty Antar and Transformer**	Yellow cab, Red/Grey trailer, Supertoy, plastic transformer, 335 mm	**£400-500**
911 (431)	1954-56	**Guy 4 ton Lorry**	2nd type cab casting, Supertoy, 'grooved' hubs, large hook, 132 mm.	
			Red cab and chassis, Grey truck body, Red hubs	**£300-400**
			Dark Blue cab and chassis, Light Blue truck body and hubs	**£200-300**
912 (432)	1954-56	**Guy Flat Truck**	2nd type cab casting, Supertoy, 'grooved' hubs, large hook, 132 mm.	
			Orange cab and chassis, Green flatbed body and hubs	**£400-500**
			Blue cab and chassis, Red flatbed body, Light Blue hubs	**£150-250**
913 (433)	1954-54	**Guy Flat Truck with Tailboard**	2nd type cab casting, Supertoy, 'grooved' hubs, large hook, 132 mm.	
			Yellow cab and chassis, Green body, Green hubs	**£1000-1200**
	1954-56		Dark Green cab and chassis, Green flatbed body and hubs.	**£200-300**
			Deep Blue cab and chassis, Orange flatbed body, Light Blue hubs.	
			Usually in Blue/White striped box with picture of Green lorry	**£200-300**
			Deep Blue/Orange model in box with correct colours	**£1000-1200**
914	1965-70	**A.E.C. Articulated Lorry**	Red cab, Grey trailer, Green tilt 'British Road Services', 210 mm	**£110-130**

915	1973-74	A.E.C. with Flat Trailer....................	Orange cab, White trailer, 'Truck Hire Co Liverpool', 210 mm....................	£45-55
			Orange cab, White trailer, 'Thames Board Mills', bubble-packed. Truck carries load of four Brown card tubes with 'UNILEVER' logos in Black....................	NGPP
917 (514)	1954-56	Guy Van 'SPRATTS'....................	Red 2nd type cab, chassis and Supertoy hubs, Cream/Red van body with 'Bonio Ovals & Dog Cakes' design.	£300-400
917	1968-74	Mercedes Truck and Trailer.............	Blue cab/chassis (White roof), Yellow trailers, White tilts, 397 mm....................	£45-55
			Blue cab/chassis (White roof), Yellow trailers, Yellow tilts....................	£55-65
			Dark Blue cab/chassis, Yellow trailers, Dark Blue tilts....................	£65-75
		'MUNSTERLAND'....................	Dark Green cab and trailers, White tilts, Green logo, promotional....................	£250-350
	NB	A pictorial inner stand was included with each issue.		
918	1955-58	Guy Van 'EVER READY'.................	Blue 1st type cab with small square sides to front number plate (never seen)....................	NGPP
			Blue 2nd type cab/body, Red 'grooved' hubs, 'Ever Ready Batteries For Life', spare wheel, Supertoy, 134 mm....................	£250-300
919	1957-58	Guy Van 'GOLDEN SHRED'..........	All Red 2nd type cab and body, Yellow Supertoy hubs, 'Robertsons Golden Shred' and 'golly' design, spare wheel, 134 mm....................	£500-750
920	1960-60	Guy Warrior Van 'HEINZ'.............	Red cab and chassis, window glazing, Yellow van body and Supertoy hubs, spare wheel, 'HEINZ 57 VARIETIES' and 'Tomato Ketchup' bottle design....................	£1,250-1,500
921 (409)	1954-56	Bedford Articulated Vehicle..............	Yellowish-Orange body, Black wings, Black hubs, Supertoy (521 / 921 / 409)....................	£80-100
922 (408)	1954-56	Big Bedford Lorry..........................	Maroon cab, Fawn truck body, Fawn hubs, Supertoy (522 / 922 / 408)....................	£90-110
			Blue cab, Yellow truck body, Yellow hubs....................	£200-300
923	1955-58	Big Bedford Van 'HEINZ'..............	Red/Yellow, 'Heinz 57 Varieties' plus Baked Beans can, Supertoy, 146 mm....................	£300-400
923	1958-59	Big Bedford Van 'HEINZ'..............	As previous model but with 'Tomato Ketchup' bottle advertising....................	£500-750
924	1972-76	Aveling Barford 'CENTAUR'..........	Red/Yellow body, tipping dump truck, 180 mm....................	£30-40
925	1965-69	Leyland Dump Truck.......................	8-wheeled Supertoy with 'SAND BALLAST GRAVEL' on tailgate. White (tilting) cab and chassis, Blue cab roof, Orange diecast tipper....................	£150-190
			As previous model but with tinplate tipper in Orange, Pale Grey or Red....................	£150-190
930	1960-64	Bedford Pallet-Jekta Van..................	Orange and Yellow body, 'Dinky Toys' and 'Meccano', Supertoy, 177 mm....................	£250-300
931 (417)	1954-56	Leyland Comet Lorry with Stake Body..........................	Dark Blue cab and chassis, Deep Yellow stake body with screw fitting, Red hubs. 'SUPERTOYS' on chassis. Blue/White 'DINKY TOYS' box....................	£200-300
932 (418)	1954-56	Leyland Comet with Hinged Tailboard....................	Green cab and chassis, Orange truck body with screw fitting, Green hubs. Blue/White box....................	£130-150
			Dark Blue cab and chassis, Light Blue truck body with screw fitting, Yellow or Light Blue hubs. Blue/White box....................	£100-130
			Dark Blue cab, chassis and truck body with screw fitting, Red hubs. Blue/White box....................	£100-130
933 (419)	1954-56	Leyland Comet Cement Wagon........	Yellow body, 'Portland Blue-Circle Cement', Supertoy (533 / 933 / 419)....................	£100-125
934	1956-58	Leyland Octopus Wagon..................	Yellow cab and chassis, Green truck body secured to chassis by a screw, Green band around cab (but without Yellow band above radiator), Red diecast Supertoy hubs....................	£175-225
	1958-59		As previous model but with Green diecast hubs. Body secured by rivet....................	£175-225
	1958-63		As previous model but with Yellow band immediately above radiator, Red diecast hubs, body secured by rivet....................	£300-350
	1963-64		Dark Blue cab/chassis, Yellow truck body, Red diecast hubs....................	£1500-2000
	1963-64		Dark Blue cab/chassis, Yellow truck body, Grey plastic hubs....................	£1500-2000
	1964-64		Dark Blue cab/chassis, Yellow truck body, Red plastic hubs....................	£1500-2000
935	1964-66	Leyland Octopus Flat Truck with Chains..........................	6 chain-posts, 8 wheels, flatbed held by rivet, Supertoy, 194 mm. Green cab/chassis, Pale Grey flatbed body, Red plastic hubs....................	£1000-1200
			Green cab/chassis, Pale Grey flatbed body, Grey plastic hubs....................	£1200-1400
			Blue cab/chassis, Yellow cab flash, Pale Grey flatbed and hubs....................	£3000-4000
936	1964-69	Leyland 8-wheel Chassis.................	Red/Silver, 'Another Leyland on Test', three '5-ton' weights, 197 mm....................	£70-80
940	1977-80	Mercedes-Benz LP.1920 Truck........	White cab, Pale Grey cover, Red chassis, hubs and interior, 200 mm....................	£30-40
			As above but with Black interior and White hubs....................	£35-45
		'HENRY JOHNSON'....................	Dark Green cab, White cover, Green logo. Promotional in plain White box....................	£250-300
		'HALB UND HALB'....................	'MAMPE' & 'BOSCH' on Blue cab, Elephant design. Promotional....................	£75-100
		'FISON'S'....................	White body, Red interior, chassis and hubs, Grey plastic cover, 'FISON'S THE GARDEN PEOPLE' labels, 2 peat samples. Promotional....................	£75-100
941 (504)	1956-56	Foden 14 ton Tanker 'MOBILGAS'	Red body and hubs, Black filler caps (see 504), Black or Grey tyres, Supertoy....................	£400-500
942	1955-57	Foden 14 ton Tanker 'REGENT'......	Dark Blue cab/chassis, Red/White/Blue tank, Black tyres, Supertoy, 188 mm....................	£350-450
943	1958-64	Leyland Octopus Tanker 'ESSO'......	Red body and tinplate tank with waterslide transfers, 'ESSO PETROLEUM', diecast hubs, spare wheel, hook, Supertoy, 192 mm....................	£300-400
			As previous model but with plastic hubs....................	£300-400
			With plastic hubs, logos on self-adhesive labels....................	£350-450
944	1963-70	Leyland Octopus Tanker 'SHELL-BP'....................	White/Yellow cab and body, Grey chassis and plastic hubs....................	£250-300
			White/Yellow cab and body, Grey chassis, Black plastic hubs....................	£500-750
			White/Yellow cab and body, Grey chassis, Red plastic hubs....................	£500-750
			White/Yellow cab and body, White chassis, Grey or Black hubs....................	£250-300
	Export issue:		Yellow cab, White chassis, White plastic tank, Red plastic hubs. 'See-through' export box....................	NGPP
		NB	Each issue has 'SHELL' and 'BP' sticky labels on the front half of the plastic tank.	

Commercial vehicles

---	1963-64	Leyland Octopus Tanker 'CORN PRODUCTS'	White body and plastic tank, 'Sweeteners For Industry' in White on Black labels. Only 500 of these promotionals issued	£1500-2000
945	1966-75	A.E.C. Fuel Tanker 'ESSO'	'ESSO PETROLUEUM' on White body, 'Tiger in Your Tank' logo on rear, 266 mm	£70-80
	1975-77		As previous model but without logo at rear, card boxed or bubble-packed	£60-70
	1977-77	'LUCAS OIL' Tanker	Green cab and tank, White design on labels, promotional, bubble-packed	£100-125
948	1961-67	Tractor-Trailer 'McLEAN'	Red cab, Light Grey trailer, Red plastic hubs, Supertoy, 290 mm	£180-230
			As previous model but with Black plastic hubs	£175-225
950	1978-79	Foden S20 Tanker 'BURMAH'	Red cab, Red/White trailer, Black or Grey hatches, Red or Cream hubs, 266 mm	£40-50
950	1978	Foden Tanker 'SHELL'	Red cab, Red/White trailer, Cream hubs, 266 mm	£60-70
951 (428)	1954-56	Trailer	Grey body with hook, Red hubs, (551 / 951 / 428), 105 mm	£20-25
			Dark Grey body with hook, Lemon Yellow hubs	£50-70
958	1961-66	Guy Warrior Snow Plough	Yellow/Black body and plough blade, spare wheel, Supertoy, 195 mm	£150-200
			Yellow/Black body, Silver plough blade	£150-200
			Silver blade version in box with picture showing Silver blade	£250-300
959	1961-68	Foden Dump Truck and Bulldozer	Red body, Orange back, model number badge, driver, windows, Supertoy, 165 mm	£50-60
			Red body, Silver back	£150-175
			All-Red body	£150-175
960	1960-68	Albion Lorry Concrete Mixer	Orange body, Yellow/Blue rotating drum, spare wheel, Supertoy, 130 mm	£40-50
			Orange body, Grey rotating drum	£40-50
961 (561)	1954-62	Blaw-Knox Bulldozer	Red or Yellow body, rubber tracks, Tan driver, Supertoy	£40-50
	1962-64		Blue body, rubber tracks, Tan driver	£40-50
	1963-64		Red or Yellow body, rubber tracks, Blue driver	£40-50
	1964-64		Orange plastic body with Silver engine detail, Black diecast lifting gear, Green plastic blade and exhaust pipe, Blue driver, Light Green or Olive-Green roller wheels	£200-250
962 (562)	1954-66	Muir Hill Dumper	Yellow body, hook, Supertoy, 105 mm. Fitted with rubber tyres from 1962	£15-20
963 (563)	1954-58	Blaw Knox Heavy Tractor	Red or Orange body, Green or Black tracks, 116 mm. Blue/White striped box	£40-50
	1958-59		Yellow body, Green or Black tracks. Blue/White striped box	£40-50
963	1973-75	Road Grader	Yellow/Red articulated body, Silver blade, Red lower arm, 238 mm.	£20-30
			White or Yellow lower arm.	£30-40
964 (564)	1954-68	Elevator Loader	Blue/Yellow chutes or Yellow/Blue chutes	£40-50
965	1955-61	'EUCLID' Dump Truck	Yellow, 'STONE - ORE - EARTH', no windows, operable tipper, 142 mm	£45-55
		NB	1955-56 Grey backed logo, 1959-61 Red backed logo.	
	1961-69		As previous model but with window glazing.	£45-55
965	1969-70	'TEREX' Rear Dump Truck	Yellow body (as previous model but 'TEREX' cast under cab) 142 mm	£75-100
966	1960-64	Marrel Multi-Bucket Unit	(Albion) Pale Yellow body, Grey skip, Black hubs, Supertoy, 115 mm.	£50-60
967	1959-64	BBC TV Control Room	Dark Green, 'BBC Television Service', Supertoy, 149 mm	£125-150
967	1973-78	Muir-Hill Loader/Trencher	Yellow/Red or Orange/Black body, with driver, 163 mm.	£25-35
968	1959-64	BBC TV Roving-Eye Vehicle	Dark Green body, BBC crest, camera, Supertoy, 110 mm	£125-150
969	1959-64	BBC TV Extending Mast	Dark Green body, BBC crest, dish aerial, mast, Supertoy, 195 mm	£125-150
970	1967-71	Jones Fleetmaster Crane	(Bedford TK) Red and Black body, White folding crane, 178 mm	£50-60
	1971-77		Metallic Red and Black with White folding crane	£60-70
	1971-77		Yellow and Black with White folding crane	£60-70
971 (571)	1954-64	Coles Mobile Crane	Yellow/Black body; Yellow crane, diecast hubs and driver, Supertoy, 160 mm	£30-40
	1964-66		Yellow/Black body; Silver crane, plastic hubs and driver, Supertoy	£30-40
972	1955-62	Coles 20 ton Lorry-Mounted Crane	Yellow/Orange (no 'Long Vehicle' signs), 2 drivers, Supertoy, 240 mm	£40-50
	1962-69		Yellow/Orange (with 'Long Vehicle' signs), 2 drivers, Supertoy	£40-50
	1967-69		Yellow/Black, Blue metal driver in lorry cab only, Yellow plastic hubs, Black tyres, Black/White diagonal stripes around jib, Yellow 'COLES CRANE' at rear	£100-150
973 (752)	1954-59	Goods Yard Crane	Yellow operable crane on Blue base. Blue/White striped box	£30-40
973	1971-75	Eaton 'YALE' Tractor Shovel	Red/Yellow body with Yellow or Silver bucket exterior, 178 mm	£20-30
			Yellow/Red body, Silver wheels, no engine covers	£25-35
			All Yellow body, Blue wheels, engine covers	£25-35
974	1968-75	A.E.C. Hoynor Car Transporter	Blue/Yellow/Orange body, 'Silcock & Colling Ltd', 322 mm	£60-70
975	1963-67	Ruston-Bucyrus Excavator	Yellow/Red/Grey plastic body, rubber tracks, operable digger, 190 mm	£175-250
976	1968-76	'MICHIGAN' Tractor Dozer	Yellow/Red body, driver, engine covers, Red hubs, 147 mm.	£20-25
977	1960-64	Servicing Platform Vehicle	Red and Cream body, operable platform, spare wheel, 197 mm	£150-200
		NB	Version seen using 667 Missile Servicing Platform Vehicle chassis in the Red/Cream 977 livery	NGPP
977	1973-78	Shovel Dozer	Yellow/Red/Silver, Black or Silver plastic tracks, bubble-packed, 151 mm.	£20-25
978	1964-72	Bedford TK Refuse Wagon	Diecast cab, plastic tipping body, 2 plastic bins, 152 mm.	
			Green cab, Grey tipping body, Red hubs, White (later Grey) plastic roof rack	£50-60
	1973-74		Dark Metallic Green cab, Grey tipping body, White (later Grey) plastic roof rack	£35-45
	1975-77		Lime-Green cab, Black or Brown chassis, plastic or cast roof rack	£35-40
	1978-80		Yellow cab with Brown chassis, cast roof rack	£35-40
		NB	Over its 16-year production run, 978 came in five different types of packaging: lidded box, pictorial and non-pictorial end-flap boxes, bubble-pack, and window box.	
979	1961-64	Racehorse Transport	Grey/Yellow, 2 horses, 'Newmarket Racehorse Transport Service Ltd', Supertoy	£200-250

980 (581)	1954-60	**Horsebox (US issue)**	Maroon body (cast in aluminium), 'Hire Service', 'Express Horse Van', 'Express'.
			In Blue/White striped box with picture of model and 'Hudson Dobson'	**£400-500**
980	1972-79	**Coles Hydra Truck 150T**	Lemon-Yellow body, triple extension crane, handle at side and rear	**£30-40**
			Yellow or Orange body, 2 side handles, no rear handle, 210 mm	**£50-60**
		'SPARROWS'	Red body, 'SPARROWS CRANE HIRE', (promotional model)	**£200-300**
981 (581)	1954-60	**Horsebox**	Maroon body (cast in aluminium), 'British Railways', 175 mm	**£70-80**
982 (582)	1955-63	**Pullmore Car Transporter**	Bedford 'O' series cab and chassis plus aluminium trailer with 'DINKY TOYS DELIVERY SERVICE' on sides. Same logo on rear ramp but without '20' sign (see 582). Black grille/bumper, Silver trim.
	1955-61		Dark Blue cab and hubs, Light Blue trailer and decks, no window glazing
			Blue/White striped box has picture of 994 Loading Ramp introduced in 1955	**£90-110**
	1961-63		As previous issue but cab has window glazing	**£120-140**
983	1958-63	**Car Carrier and Trailer**	Red/Grey, 'Dinky Auto Service', (Supertoys 984 and 985)	**£150-200**
984	1958-63	**Car Carrier**	Red/Grey body, 'Dinky Auto Service', Supertoy, 240 mm	**£100-150**
984	1974-79	**Atlas Digger**	Red/Yellow body, Yellow arm/cylinders, Silver or Yellow bucket	**£30-40**
			Red/Yellow body, Black plastic arm, Black or Yellow cylinders, Silver bucket.	**£30-40**
985	1958-63	**Trailer for Car Carrier**	Red/Grey body, 'Dinky Auto Service', Supertoy, 196 mm	**£50-60**
986	1959-61	**Mighty Antar with Propeller**	Red cab (window glazing on some), Grey low-loader, Bronze propeller, 295 mm	**£300-400**
987	1962-69	**'ABC TV' Control Room**	Blue/Grey/Red, 'ABC TELEVISION', camera/operator/cable	**£120-140**
988	1962-69	**TV Transmitter Van 'ABC-TV'**	Blue/Grey body, Red stripe, revolving aerial dish, Supertoy, 110 mm	**£150-200**
989	1963-65	**Car Transporter**	'AUTO TRANSPORTERS', Yellow/Light Grey/Blue, Supertoy boxed in all-card picture box or export-only Gold 'see through' window box	**£2000-2500**
991 (551)	1954-70	**Large Trailer**	See 551 for details.
991 (591)	1954-55	**A.E.C. Tanker**	Red/Yellow 'SHELL CHEMICALS LIMITED', Supertoy, 150 mm	**£90-120**
	1955-58		Red/Yellow, 'SHELL CHEMICALS', Supertoy, 150 mm	**£90-120**

Dinky Supertoys 983 Car Carrier with Trailer,
943 Leyland Octopus 'Esso' Tanker and 942 Foden 14-ton 'Regent' Tanker

Dinky Toys Emergency Vehicles

NB Ford Transit casting types are described at the beginning of the Commercial Vehicles section.

Ref.	Year(s)	Model name	Colours, features, dimensions	Market Price Range
24a	1934-38	Ambulance	Types 1 or 2 criss-cross chassis, types 1, 2 or 3 grille, plated chrome or Black hubs, open windows.	
			Cream body (Red chassis), Cream body (Grey chassis)	£250-350
			Grey body (Dark Grey chassis), Grey body (Maroon chassis)	£200-250
	1938-40	Ambulance	Type 2 criss-cross chassis, open windows, type 3 grille, 102 mm. See 30f.	
			Cream body (Red chassis), Cream body (Grey chassis)	£200-250
			Grey body (Dark Grey chassis), Grey body (Maroon chassis)	£250-300
			Black body, Black chassis (thought to be for export only)	£500-750
25h	1936-37	Streamlined Fire Engine	Red body, no tinplate chassis, tinplate ladder and bell, White tyres	£175-225
	1937-40		Red body, tinplate baseplate, ladder and bell, Black or White tyres	£125-150
25h (250)	1948-54		Red body and ladder, tinplate baseplate, brass bell, Black tyres	£80-90
25k	1937-39	Streamline Fire Engine	Red body, tinplate base, 6 firemen, ladder, bell, White tyres, 101 mm	£400-500
30f	1935-38	Ambulance	Grey body, Red wings/criss-cross chassis, plain radiator, open windows	£150-200
	1938-40		Grey body, Black moulded chassis, radiator badge, open windows	£90-110
	1938-40	South-African issue:	Grey body, Red cross, 'Bentley type' radiator	£750-950
	1946-47		Grey body, Black moulded chassis, open windows	£90-110
	1947-48		Cream body, Black moulded chassis, filled-in or open windows	£90-110
30h (253)	1950-54	Daimler Ambulance	Cream body, Red crosses and wheels, no window glazing, 96 mm	£80-90
30hm (624)	1950-54	Daimler Military Ambulance	Military-Green body, Red crosses on White backgrounds, (US issue)	£200-300
123-P	1977	Austin Princess 'POLICE' Car	All-White, Bronze/Blue or White/Blue. (Model has not yet been seen)	NPP
195	1971-78	Fire-Chief's Range Rover	Red or Metallic Red, 'Fire Service', Speedwheels, bubble-packed	£35-40
243	1978-79	Volvo 'POLICE' Car	White body, plastic chassis, 141 mm. (Some made in Italy by Polistil)	£35-40
244	1978-79	Plymouth Fury Police Car	Black/White, 'POLICE', warning lights, plastic chassis & wheels	£25-30
250 (25h)	1954-62	Fire Engine	Red/Silver body, tinplate ladder and bell, 99 mm	£70-80
250	1968-71	Police Mini Cooper 'S'	White or Off-White, rubber tyres, boot detail on transfer, 75 mm	£45-55
	1971-73		As previous model but cast boot detail, no aerial	£45-55
	1973-75		As previous model but with Speedwheels	£35-45
		NB...Boot casting variations: (1) 'Morris Mini-Minor' cast-in, (2) 'Austin Mini-Cooper S' cast-in.		
251	1970-73	U.S.A. 'POLICE' Car	(Pontiac Parisienne), White/Black, siren, 2 aerials, driver	£45-55
252	1971-74	R.C.M.P. Police Car	(Pontiac Parisienne), Blue/White, driver, Blue light, Speedwheels	£45-55
253 (30h)	1954-58	Daimler Ambulance	Cream body, Red crosses and cast hubs, no window glazing, 96 mm	£80-90
	1958-60		White body, Red crosses and cast hubs, no window glazing	£80-90
	1960-62		White body, Red crosses and cast hubs, with window glazing	£80-90
	1962-64		White body, Red plastic hubs, with window glazing	£80-90
254	1977-79	Police Range Rover	White body, 'Police', opening doors, aerial on some, Speedwheels	£35-45
255	1955-61	Mersey Tunnel Police Van	(Land Rover), Red body, 'Mersey Tunnel' and 'Police', hook, 77 mm	£60-70
255	1967-71	Ford Zodiac 'POLICE' Car	White body, driver, suspension, steering, aerial, warning lights, 114 mm	£55-65
255	1977-79	Police Mini Clubman	Blue/White body, 'POLICE', opening doors and bonnet, plastic wheels	£30-35
256	1960-64	Humber Hawk 'POLICE' Car	Black body, Cream interior, White 'POLICE' sign on roof, 'PC 49' licence plates, driver and observer, spun hubs	£80-90
257	1960-68	Canadian 'FIRE CHIEF' Car	(Nash Rambler), flashing light, suspension, windows, 102 mm	£55-65
258		**U.S.A. POLICE CAR**		
258	1960-61	DeSoto Fireflite	(192), Black/White body, beacon, windows, 114 mm	£80-90
258	1961-62	Dodge Royal Sedan	(191), Black body, aerial, windows, 111 mm	£80-90
258	1962-66	Ford Fairlane 'RCMP'	(149), Mid-Blue/White, aerial, rooflight, open front window, 2 Mounties	£80-90
			Same but Dark Blue/White, with closed windows	£80-90
258	1966-68	Cadillac 62	(147), Black/White, suspension/steering, 113 mm	£80-90
259	1961-69	Fire Engine (Bedford Miles)	Red body, 'FIRE BRIGADE' and crest, tinplate ladder and bell, 115 mm	£70-85
			As previous model but with 'AIRPORT FIRE TENDER' (from 276)	£70-85
			Red body, Silver cast wheels	£100-125
261	1967-77	Ford Taunus 'POLIZEI'	White and Green body, (German issue), 110 mm. with label	
			'Special contract run for Meccano Agent in W. Germany'	£150-200
263	1962-68	Superior Criterion Ambulance	Cream, 'AMBULANCE' on windows, stretcher, no beacon, 127 mm	£50-60
263	1978-80	E.R.F. Fire Tender	Yellow body, 'Airport Rescue', flashing light, 177 mm	£40-50
264	1962-66	R.C.M.P. Ford Fairlane	Dark Blue body, White doors, aerial, red beacon	£75-85
264	1966-68	R.C.M.P. Cadillac	Dark Blue body, White doors, aerial, red beacon	£85-95
264	1978-80	Rover 3500	White/Yellow, 'POLICE', beacon, opening doors and bonnet, 131 mm	£20-30
266	1976-79	E.R.F. Fire Tender	Red body, 'Fire Service', White wheeled escape ladder, 223 mm	£50-60
	1979-80		As previous model but with Metallic Red body	£50-60
	1976-79	Danish issue:	Red body, 'FALCK'	£70-85
267	1967-71	Superior Cadillac Ambulance	White/Red body, 'AMBULANCE' on roof, flashing light, 152 mm	£50-65
267	1978-79	Paramedic Truck	Red, Yellow cylinders, 2 figures, lapel badge, (TV Series 'Emergency')	£20-30
268	1973-77	Range Rover Ambulance	White, 'AMBULANCE', stretcher, bubble-packed, 109 mm	£20-30
269	1962-66	Motorway 'POLICE' Car	(Jaguar) White body, suspension/steering, 2 policemen, 95 mm	£85-100
269	1978-79	Ford Transit 'POLICE' Van	White/Red/Blue, figures/lights/signs/cones, Type 3 casting, 129 mm	£35-45
270	1969-72	Ford 'POLICE' Panda Car	Turquoise body, White doors, Blue/White roof sign, cast hubs, 97 mm	£45-55
	1972-77		As previous model but fitted with Speedwheels	£40-50
271	1975-76	Ford Transit 'FIRE'	Red body, hose/axe/bells/plastic ladder, bubble-packed, Type 2, 129 mm	£55-65
		Danish issue:	As previous model but with 'FALCK' logo	£65-75
272	1975-77	'POLICE' Accident Unit	White, radar gun/beacon/aerial/cones/signs, Type 2 casting, 129 mm	£35-45
274	1978-79	Ford Transit Ambulance	White, 'AMBULANCE', Red crosses, beacon, Type 3 casting, 129 mm	£35-45

276	1962-69	**Airport Fire Tender** ....Red body, 'AIRPORT FIRE CONTROL', bell, 115 mm **£50-65**
		As previous model but 'FIRE BRIGADE' logo (from 259), no crest **£50-65**
276	1976-78	**Ford Transit Ambulance** ....White body, 'AMBULANCE', Type 2 casting...**£30-40**
277	1962-68	**Superior Criterion Ambulance**........Metallic Blue, White roof and tyres, driver, roof light, 127 mm.............**£55-70**
277	1977-80	**'POLICE' Land Rover** ....Blue body, White tilt, flashing light, 110 mm **£20-30**
278	1964-69	**Vauxhall Victor Ambulance** ....White, 'AMBULANCE', suspension/steering, stretcher, 91 mm...............**£60-75**
282	1973-79	**Land Rover Fire Appliance** ....Red, 'Fire Service', metal ladder, bubble-packed, 119 mm **£30-40**
	1974-78	Danish issue: As previous model but with 'FALCK' logo **£35-45**
285	1969-79	**Merryweather Marquis** ....Metallic Dark Red body, escape ladder, working pump, 'FIRE SERVICE' ...**£55-65**
		As previous model but (non-Metallic), Red body **£55-65**
		Danish issue: As previous model but Red or Metallic Dark Red body, 'FALCK' logo..........**£85-95**
286	1968-74	**Ford Transit 'FIRE'** ....Red, 'Fire Service', hose Type 1 casting, bubble-packed, 122 mm **£75-90**
		As previous model but with Metallic Red body **£75-90**
		Danish issue: As previous model but with 'FALCK ZONEN' logo **£85-95**
287	1967-71	**Police Accident Unit**........................Cream/Orange body, roof sign, aerial, Type 1 casting, 122 mm **£50-65**
	1971-74	White/Red body, radar gun, roof rack, Type 1 casting **£50-65**
288	1971-79	**Superior Cadillac** ....White/Red, 'AMBULANCE', stretcher, no flashing light, 152 mm **£40-45**
		Danish issue: White body with Red mid-section and roof bar, 'FALCK' **£85-95**
		Danish issue: Black body/White roof, Blue interior and roof bar, 'FALCK' **£85-95**
555 (955)	1952-54	**Fire Engine (Commer)**......................Red body with Silver trim and ladder, no windows **£75-85**
624(30hm)	1954-?	**Daimler Military Ambulance**.............Military-Green body, Red crosses on White backgrounds, (US issue) **£200-300**
954	1961-64	**Fire Station** ....Red, Yellow and 'brick' plastic, base 252 mm. x 203 mm......................**£175-225**
955 (555)	1954-60	**Fire Engine (Commer)**......................Red body and diecast hubs, Silver trim and ladder, no window glazing **£75-85**
	1960-64	Red body and diecast hubs, Silver trim and ladder, with window glazing **£75-85**
	1964-70	Red body and diecast or plastic hubs, window glazing, 'picture' box **£125-150**
956	1958-60	**Turntable Fire Escape Lorry** ....(Bedford cab). Red body and diecast hubs, no windows, Silver deck and ladder, 200 mm.........**£85-100**
	1960-68	Red body and diecast hubs, with window glazing **£85-100**
	1968-70	Red body and plastic hubs, with window glazing **£60-70**
	NB	A version of 956 has been discovered (in Norway) that has 3 ladders instead of 2.
956	1970-74	**Turntable Fire Escape Lorry** ....(Berliet). Metallic Red body and hubs, windows, 'ECHELLE INCENDIE', Silver platform **£175-225**
		As previous model but with Black platform **£150-200**
	1974-?	Danish issue:..Metallic Red body and hubs, windows, 'FALCK' **£175-225**
2253	1974-76	**Ford Capri Police Car** ....White/Orange, 'POLICE', Blue light, suspension, 175 mm. (1/25 scale) **£80-100**

'Dublo Dinky' models

All the 'Dublo Dinky' wheels are made of plastic. Smooth wheels are fairly soft and treaded wheels are hard.

Ref.	Year(s)	Model name	Colours, features, dimensions	Market Price Range
061	1958-59	**Ford Prefect** ....Fawn or Grey body, Silver trim, Grey smooth wheels, 59 mm.......................**£50-60**
		As previous but with treaded Grey wheels **£65-75**
062	1958-60	**Singer Roadster** ....Orange or Fawn body, Red interior, Grey smooth or treaded wheels **£65-75**
		Yellow body, Grey treaded wheels...**£125-150**
063	1958-60	**Commer Van**.............Blue body, Silver trim, Grey smooth or treaded wheels, 54 mm.................**£45-55**
064	1957-62	**Austin Lorry** ....Green body, Black treaded or Grey smooth or treaded wheels, 64 mm.......**£45-55**
065	1957-60	**Morris Pick-up** ....Red body, Silver trim, Grey treaded wheels, 54 mm................................**£45-55**
066	1959-66	**Bedford Flat Truck** ....Grey body, Silver trim, Grey smooth wheels, with hook, 116 mm.............**£45-55**
		Grey body, Silver trim, Grey smooth or treaded wheels, without hook.......**£45-55**
067	1959-64	**Austin 'TAXI'** ....Blue lower body, Cream upper body, Black or Grey treaded wheels..........**£65-75**
068	1959-64	**'ROYAL MAIL' Morris Van** ....Red body, 'E II R' crest, Grey or Black treaded wheels, 47 mm.................**£60-75**
069	1959-64	**Massey Harris Tractor** ....Blue body, Silver trim, Grey treaded wheels, hole for driver, 36 mm **£45-55**
		With Grey treaded wheels on front and very Light Tan rear wheels............**£75-85**
070	1959-64	**A.E.C. Mercury Tanker** ....Green cab, Red tank, Black or Grey treaded wheels, 'SHELL-BP'............**£85-95**
071	1960-64	**Volkswagen Delivery Van** ....Yellow body with Red 'HORNBY DUBLO' logo, Black treaded wheels........**£60-70**
072	1959-64	**Bedford Articulated Truck**...............Yellow cab, Red semi-trailer, Black or Grey smooth wheels, 117 mm.......**£50-60**
073	1960-64	**Land Rover/Trailer/Horse**.................Green car (Grey or Black treaded wheels), Tan or White horse. Trailers:
		with Bright Green trailer (Green ramp, smooth Grey wheels)....................**£100-125**
		with Green trailer (Brown ramp, treaded Grey wheels)............................**£100-125**
		with Bright Green trailer (Black ramp, treaded Black wheels) **£100-125**
		with Orange trailer (Black wheels and ramp)..**£100-125**
076	1960-64	**Lansing Bagnall Tractor & Trailer** ...Maroon tractor/trailer, Blue driver/seat, Black smooth or treaded wheels.....**£50-60**
078	1960-64	**Lansing Bagnall Trailer** ....Maroon body, Black smooth or treaded wheels, hook, wire drawbar **£30-35**

Dinky Toys Farm and Garden models

Ref.	Year(s)	Model name	Colours, features, dimensions	Market Price Range
22e	1933-40	Farm Tractor	'Modelled Miniature' with 'HORNBY SERIES' cast-in, no hook, 70 mm.	
			Yellow/Dark Blue (lead) body, Red or Yellow (lead) wheels	£175-200
			'DINKY TOYS' cast-in, with hook, Red or Yellow diecast wheels arelead, diecast or both,	
			Green/Yellow, Yellow/Blue, Red/Blue, Red/Red	£150-175
			Cream/Blue, Cream/Red, Blue/Cream	£150-175
27a (300)	1948-54	Massey-Harris Tractor	Red body, Yellow cast wheels, driver, steering wheel, hook, 89 mm	£70-80
27ak (310)	1952-54	Tractor and Hay Rake	27a Tractor and 27k Hay Rake, 157 mm	£125-150
27b (320)	1949-54	Halesowen Harvest Trailer	Brown body, Red racks, Yellow metal wheels, 133 mm	£25-35
27d (340)	1950-54	Land Rover	Green or Orange body, tinplate windscreen frame, driver, 90 mm	£60-70
			As previous model but with Red body	£65-75
	1952-53	Gift Set model:	Dark Brown body. Only in Gift Set No.2, Commercial Vehicles Set	GSP
27c (321)	1949-54	M.H. Manure Spreader	Red body with drawbar, hook, working shredders, 121 mm	£30-40
27f (344)	1950-53	Estate Car	Pale Brown body, Brown side panels and hubs	£70-80
			Grey body with Red side panels	£100-125
27g (342)	1949-54	Moto-Cart	Brown and Green body, driver, 3 metal wheels/tyres, body tips, 110 mm	£40-50
27h (322)	1951-54	Disc Harrow	Red/Yellow body, Silver disc blades, tinplate hook, 86 mm	£20-25
27j (323)	1952-54	Triple Gang Mower	Red frame, Yellow blades, Green wheels, cast-in hook, 114 mm	£20-25
27k (324)	1953-54	Hay Rake	Red frame, Yellow wheels, wire tines, operating lever, 77 mm	£20-25
27m (341)	1952-54	Land Rover Trailer	Orange or Green body and diecast hubs, drawbar and hook, 79 mm	£20-25
27n (301)	1953-54	'FIELD MARSHALL' Tractor	Orange body, Silver metal wheels, Tan driver, hook, 76 mm	£85-95
			As previous model but with Green metal wheels	£140-160
30n (343)	1950-54	Farm Produce Wagon	Model has stake sides to rear body, Black metal base and hook. 104 mm.	
			Yellow cab and chassis, Green stake body and hubs	£70-80
			Green cab and chassis, Yellow stake body and hubs	£70-80
			Red cab and chassis, Blue stake body and hubs	£70-80
105a (381)	1948-54	Garden Roller	Green handle and Red roller sides, 67 mm	£15-25
105b (382)	1948-54	Wheelbarrow	Brown and Red body, single metal wheel, 82 mm	£15-25
105c (383)	1948-54	4 wheeled Hand Truck	Green/Yellow or Blue/Yellow, 126 mm	£10-15
105e (384)	1948-54	Grass Cutter	Yellow body, Green metal wheels, Red blades, 73 mm	£15-20
107a (385)	1948-54	Sack Truck	Blue or Pale Green body with two small Black metal wheels, 65 mm	£10-15
192	1970-74	Range Rover	Bronze body, various interior colours, cast detailed or Speedwheels	£25-35
	1973-79		Black or Yellow body, Speedwheels	£25-35
300 (27a)	1954-62	Massey-Harris Tractor	Red body, Yellow cast wheels, 'MASSEY-HARRIS', Tan cast driver	£70-80
	1962-64		Red, Yellow wheels (cast rear, plastic front, rubber tyres), cast driver	£70-80
	1964-66		Red, Yellow wheels (all plastic), cast-in seat, plastic driver	£75-85
300	1966-71	Massey Ferguson Tractor	As previous model but name changed to 'MASSEY-FERGUSON'	£70-80
301 (27n)	1954-61	'FIELD MARSHALL' Tractor	Orange body, Green metal wheels, Tan driver, hook, 76 mm	£140-160
			Orange body, Yellow or unpainted wheels, Tan driver, hook	£150-200
	1962-66		Orange body, Green wheels (plastic front, cast rear, rubber tyres)	£150-180
			Orange body, Green plastic hubs (front and rear), Black plastic exhaust	£150-200
	1964-66		Red body, Green plastic hubs, rubber tyres	£80-90
305	1965-67	David Brown 900 Tractor	Red cowl, Grey engine, Yellow cab/wheels, 'David Brown 990', in detailed picture box	£150-200
	1967-74		White cowl/cab/wheels, Grey engine, 'David Brown Selectamatic 990'	£60-70
	1974-75		White cowl/cab, Red engine/wheels, '995 David Brown Case, bubble-packed	£60-70
308	1971-72	Leyland 384 Tractor	Metallic Red body, Cream hubs, 'LEYLAND', 86 mm, bubble-packed	£50-75
	1972-77		Blue body, unpainted or Black steering wheel	£40-50
	1977-79		Orange body, unpainted steering wheel	£50-60
310 (27ak)	1954-60	Tractor and Hay Rake	300 Tractor and 324 Hay Rake, 157 mm	£125-150
319	1961-71	Weeks Tipping Trailer	Red/Yellow body, cast or plastic wheels, plain or planked trailer bed	£25-30
320 (27b)	1954-60	Halesowen Harvest Trailer	Red/Brown body, Red racks, drawbar, hook, cast or plastic wheels	£25-35
			Red body, Yellow racks, drawbar, hook, cast or plastic wheels, 133 mm	£25-35
321 (27c)	1954-62	M.H. Manure Spreader	Red body, Yellow cast wheels, 'MASSEY-HARRIS', shredders	£25-35
321	1962-73		Red body, Red or Yellow plastic hubs, no logo	£25-35
322 (27h)	1954-67	Disc Harrow	Red/Yellow body, Silver disc blades, tinplate hook, 86 mm	£25-35
322	1967-73		White/Red body, Silver disc blades, no hook, 79 mm	£25-35
			All White version	NGPP
323	1954-63	Triple Gang Mower	Red frame, Yellow blades, Green wheels, cast-in hook, 114 mm	£25-35
324 (27k)	1954-64	Hayrake	Red frame, Yellow wheels, wire tines, Black or Silver operating lever,	£20-30
325	1967-73	David Brown Tractor and		
		Disc Harrow	305 and 322 in White and Red, 152 mm	£80-90
			305 and 322 in Yellow and Red, 152 mm	£120-140
340 (27d)	1954-66	Land Rover	Green body, Brown interior and metal wheels, Tan cast driver, 92 mm	£60-70
340	1966-69		Orange body, Green interior and plastic hubs, Blue cast or plastic driver	£60-70
	1969-71		Red body and plastic hubs, Yellow interior, Blue plastic driver	£60-70
	1971		Red body and Green plastic hubs	£80-90
341 (27m)	1954-73	Land Rover Trailer	Orange, Green or Red, drawbar and hook, cast or plastic hubs, 79 mm	£20-25
342 (27g)	1954-61	Moto-Cart	Tan and Green body, driver, 3 metal wheels/tyres, body tips, 110 mm	£25-35
343 (30n)	1954-61	Farm Produce Wagon	Red cab and chassis, Blue stake body and cast hubs, 107 mm	£70-80
			Green cab and chassis, Yellow stake body and cast hubs, 107 mm	£70-80
343	1961-64		As previous models but no bonnet louvres, cast or plastic hubs	£80-100
344 (27f)	1950-53	Estate Car	Pale Brown body, Brown side panels and hubs	£70-80
344	1970-72	Land Rover Pick-Up	Metallic Blue or Red, cast wheels	£20-25
	1972-78		Metallic Blue or Red, Speedwheels	£20-25
381 (105a)	1954-58	Garden Roller	Green and Red, 67 mm	£15-25
381	1977-80	Convoy Farm Truck	Yellow cab, Brown plastic high-sided truck body, 110 mm	£15-20
382 (105b)	1954-58	Wheelbarrow	Brown and Red body, single metal wheel, 82 mm	£15-25
383 (105c)	1954-58	4 wheeled Hand Truck	Green or Blue body, 126 mm	£10-15
384 (105e)	1954-58	Grass Cutter	Yellow body, Green metal wheels, Red or Green blades, 73 mm	£15-20

385 (107a)	1954-58	**Sack Truck**	Blue with two small metal wheels, 65 mm	**£10-15**
386 (751)	1954-58	**Lawn Mower**	Green/Red, separate grassbox, 'Dinky Toys' cast-in, 140 mm	**£80-90**
399	1969-75	**Tractor and Trailer**	300 combined with 428	NGPP
564 (964)	1952-54	**Elevator Loader**	Yellow body with Blue or Dark Blue hubs, hopper and chute	**£60-70**
			Blue or Dark Blue body and hubs with Yellow chutes	**£80-90**
751 (386)	1949-54	**Lawn Mower**	Green/Red, separate grassbox, 'Dinky Supertoys' cast-in, 140 mm	**£80-90**
964 (564)	1954-58	**Elevator Loader**	See 564 above.	

Dinky Toys Motor Cycles

See also Accessories and Gift Sets sections.
SWRW = solid White rubber wheels, SBRW = solid Black rubber wheels (both are of a larger diameter than those used on the small cars).

14z	1938-40	**'Triporteur'**	Three-wheel delivery van with Green, Red, Grey, Blue or Yellow body, Black hubs, White tyres, rider is always a different colour from van, French model	**£200-300**
37a	1937-40	**Civilian Motor Cyclist**	Black motor cycle with Silver engine/exhaust detail, Blue, Maroon, Green or Black rider, SWRW or thick SBRW, 45 mm	**£40-50**
	1946-49		Black motor cycle without Silver detail, Green or Grey rider, thin SBRW	**£30-35**
37a (041)	1950-54		Black motor cycle, without Silver detail, Green or Grey rider, thin SBRW, export only	**£30-35**
37b	1937-40	**Police Motor Cyclist**	Black motor cycle with Silver engine/exhaust detail, Dark Blue rider, SWRW or thick SBRW	**£75-85**
	1946-49		Black motor cycle without Silver engine/exhaust detail, Dark Blue rider, thick SBRW	**£40-50**
37b (042)	1950-54		As previous model, export only	**£40-50**
37c	1937-39	**Signals Despatch Rider**	Green motor cycle, Silver engine/exhaust detail, Khaki rider, SWRW or thick SBRW	**£125-175**
42b	1935-40	**Police Motorcycle Patrol**	Dark Blue motor cycle, Silver engine/exhaust detail, Dark Green/Black sidecar, Black figures, SWRW or thick SBRW, 47 mm	**£75-95**
	1946-49		As previous model but without Silver detailing and with thin SBRW	**£45-55**
42b (043)	1950-55		Blue/Green, Blue figures, little detailing, SBRW, export only	**£40-50**
43b	1935-40	**R.A.C. Motorcycle Patrol**	Blue/Black motor cycle/sidecar, Silver engine/exhaust detail, Blue/Black rider with Red sash, SWRW or thick SBRW, 46 mm	**£75-95**
	1946-49		As previous model but no Silver detailing, thin SBRW. **NB** - two shades of Blue used post-war	**£45-55**
44b	1935-40	**A.A. Motorcycle Patrol**	Black/Yellow, Brown rider, more detailing, 5mm 'AA' badge, SWRW	**£100-125**
44b (270)	1946-50		Black/Yellow, Tan rider, little detailing, 7mm 'AA' badge, SBRW	**£50-60**
44b (045)	1950-55		As previous model but made for export only	**£50-60**
270 (44b)	1959-62	**A.A. Motorcycle Patrol**	Black/Yellow, Tan rider, 'AA' sign, solid Grey plastic wheels, 46 mm	**£40-50**
271	1959-62	**T.S. Motorcycle Patrol**	Yellow motorcycle combination, Belgian equivalent of the A.A.	**£150-200**
272	1959-62	**A.N.W.B. Motorcycle Patrol**	Yellow motorcycle combination, Dutch equivalent of the A.A.	**£250-300**

Dinky Toys Military models

See also Action Kits, Aircraft, Ships, Gift Sets

Identification
Models issued **1933 - 1940**: Gloss or Matt Green or Camouflage finish with smooth diecast wheel hubs on thin axles.
Models issued **circa 1946**: Matt Green finish with smooth hubs and early tyres (black smooth, or thick black ribbed, or thin white tyres).
Models issued **1947 - 1949**: Matt Green finish with ridged hubs.
Models issued **circa 1950**: Finished in a glossy Olive Drab with ridged diecast hubs and black thin ribbed tyres.

Ref.	Year(s)	Model name	Colours, features, dimensions	Market Price Range
22f	1933-34	**Army Tank**	'Modelled Miniature' with 'HORNBY SERIES' cast-in, 87 mm.	
			Green lead body, Orange revolving turret, Red rubber tracks	**£200-250**
			Green lead body, Orange revolving turret, Green rubber tracks	**£200-250**
	1935-40		Green/Orange lead body, 'DINKY TOYS' cast-in, Red or Green tracks	**£150-200**
			Khaki lead body, 'DINKY TOYS' cast-in, Green tracks	**£150-200**
			Grey drab lead body, 'DINKY TOYS' cast-in, Green tracks	**£150-200**
22s	1939-40	**Searchlight Lorry**	Green body, (22c casting), 84 mm	**£200-300**
25b	19??-??	**Army Covered Wagon**	Military-Green body and hubs. South-African issue	**£1,200-1,500**
25wm (640)	1952-54	**Bedford Military Truck**	Olive-Drab body, (made for export to the USA only)	**£200-250**
27m (341)	1952-54	**Land Rover Trailer**	Olive-Drab body, (to fit 25wm)	**£300-400**
28	19??-??	**Army Delivery Van**	Military-Green body and hubs, Type 3. South-African issue	**£750-1,000**
30hm (624)	1950-54	**Daimler Military Ambulance**	Olive-Drab body, Red crosses on White backgrounds, (US issue)	**£200-250**
30sm (625)	1952-54	**Austin Covered Wagon**	Olive-Drab body, made for export to USA only), 112 mm	**£200-250**
37c	1937-40	**Signal Dispatch Rider**	Green body, Khaki rider, White or Black rubber wheels, 45 mm	**£150-175**
139am	1950-54	**US Army Staff Car**	(170m) Ford Fordor in Olive drab with White stars on roof and doors	**£200-250**
150a (600)	1937-40	**Royal Tank Corps Officer**	Khaki uniformed figure with Black beret, and binoculars in hand	**£25-30**
150b (604)	1938-54	**Royal Tank Corps Private**	Die-cast figure in Khaki uniform, sitting, 22 mm. Box of 12	**£50-70**
150c	1937-40	**Royal Tank Corps Private**	Die-cast figure in Khaki uniform, standing, 30 mm	**£25-30**
150d	1937-40	**Royal Tank Corps Driver**	Die-cast figure in Khaki uniform, sitting, 25 mm	**£25-30**
150e	1937-40	**Royal Tank Corps NCO**	Die-cast figure in Khaki uniform, walking, 30 mm	**£10-15**
151a	1937-40	**Medium Tank**	Gloss or Matt-Green body/base, White markings, chain tracks, aerial	**£125-150**
			As previous model but with Black rubber wheels instead of tracks	NGPP
	1947-49		(Matt) Green body, Black base, no markings, made for export only	**£150-200**

151b	1937-40	**6-wheel Covered Wagon** ......Gloss Green body, tinplate canopy, seat holes, spare wheel, 99 mm	£125-150
	1937-40	............Lead issue:..Gloss Green body, Black ribbed tyres	£125-150
	1940	............................Camouflage body	£150-200
151b	1946	............................Matt-Green with smooth hubs and early tyres	£150-200
151b	1947-49	............................Matt-Green with ridged hubs	£125-175
151b	1950-54	............................Gloss Olive-Green, no seat holes, smooth tyres	£125-175
151b (620)	1950-54	............................Matt-Green or Greenish-Brown body, 'Export only' from 1950	£200-250
151c	1937-48	**Cooker Trailer** ......Gloss or Matt-Green trailer, wire stand, hole in seat but no figure	£50-70
		............Note:..Two styles of baseplate lettering are known for 151c.	
151d	1937-48	**Water Tank Trailer** ......Gloss Green, 52 mm	£50-70
152a	1937-40	**Light Tank** ......Gloss or Matt-Green body/base, White markings, chain tracks, aerial	£100-125
		............As previous model but with Black rubber wheels instead of tracks	NGPP
	1947-50	............................(Matt) Green body, Black base, no markings, chain tracks, aerial	£150-200
152a (650)	1950-54	............................(Gloss) Green body, Black base, no markings, made for export only	£150-200
152b	1937-40	**Reconnaissance Car** ......(Gloss) Green body/base, six wheels, 89 mm	£100-125
	1946	............................Matt Green with smooth hubs and early tyres	£150-200
	1947-49	............................Matt Green with ridged hubs	£125-175
152b (671)	1950-54	............................Glossy Olive-Green body, Black base, made for export only	£125-175
152c	1937-40	**Austin Seven** ......Matt Green body, wire windscreen frame, hole in seat, 50 mm	£125-150
	1937-40	............Camouflage issue:..Matt Green body	£100-125
	1940-41	............Lead issue:..Matt Green body	£100-150
153a	1946-47	**Jeep** ......Gloss Dark Green, US White star on flat bonnet and left rear side, smooth hubs,	
		............................solid steering wheel, no round hole in base	£150-200
	1947	............................As previous model but with open spoked steering wheel	£60-75
		............................As previous model but with Brown body	£150-200
	1948-52	............................Matt or Gloss Green body, raised 'domed' bonnet, round hole in base	£60-75
153a (672)	1952-54	............................Matt Olive-Green body, some have rounded axle ends, US export only	£150-200
160a	1939-40	**Royal Artillery NCO** ......Khaki uniform, 28 mm	£10-15
160b (608)	1939-54	**Royal Artillery Gunner** ......Khaki uniform, seated, hands on knees, 24 mm	£10-15
160c	1939-40	**Royal Artillery Gunlayer** ......Khaki uniform, seated, hands held out, 24 mm	£10-15
160d	1939-40	**Royal Artillery Gunner** ......Khaki uniform, standing, 28 mm	£10-15
161a	1939-40	**Searchlight on Lorry** ......Gloss Green body, 151b casting plus diecast or lead searchlight	£200-250
161b	1939-40	**Anti-Aircraft Gun on Trailer** ......Gloss Green, gun elevates, figure holes, cast drawbar and hook	£40-50
	1946-50	............................Matt Green or Dark Brown	£80-100
161b (690)	1950-54	............................Glossy Olive-Green, US export issue	£125-175
162a	1939-40	**Light Dragon Tractor** ......Gloss Green body, holes in seats, chain tracks, 65 mm	£100-125
		............As previous model but with Black rubber wheels instead of tracks	£200-250
	1946-55	............................Matt Green body (holes in some), chain tracks	£100-150
162b	1939-40	**Ammunition Trailer** ......Gloss Green body and baseplate, drawbar and hook, 54 mm	£20-25
	1946-55	............................Matt Green body, Black baseplate	£20-25
162c	1939-40	**18 pounder Gun** ......Gloss Green body, drawbar cast-in, tinplate shield, 78 mm	£20-25
	1946-55	**18 pounder Gun** ......Matt Green body and shield	£20-25
170m	1954-54	**Ford US Army Staff Car** ......(139am) Olive-Drab, US issue, renumbered 675	£200-250
281	1973-76	**Military Hovercraft** ......Olive-Drab body, Gunner, aerial, 'Army', 139 mm	£25-35
341 (27m)	1960	**Land Rover Trailer** ......Olive-Drab body with drawbar and hook, 79 mm	£300-400
600 (150)	194?-4?	**Royal Tank Corps Officer** ......US only re-issue	£8-12
601	1974-76	**Austin Paramoke** ......Olive-Drab, Tan hood, spun hubs, parachute, 76 mm	£40-50
	1976-78	............................Olive-Drab, Tan hood, Speedwheels	£30-40
603	1950-68	**Army Private (seated)** ......Diecast figure in Khaki uniform, Black beret, seated, 20 mm, box of 12	£40-50
	1968-71	............................Plastic figure in Khaki uniform, Black beret, seated, 20 mm, box of 12	£40-50
603a	1950-68	**Army Personnel Set** ......Six diecast figures (Khaki uniforms, Black berets, seated)	£20-30
	1968-71	............................Six plastic figures (Khaki uniforms, Black berets, seated)	£20-30
604 (150b)	1954-60	**Royal Tank Corps Private** ......Die-cast, Khaki uniform, sitting, export only (to USA), box of 12	£50-70
604	1960-72	**Army Personnel** ......Six army driver figures (Khaki uniforms)	£20-30
604	1976-79	**Land Rover Bomb Disposal** ......Olive-Drab/Orange, 'Explosive Disposal', robot de-fuser, 110 mm	£55-65
608 (160b)	1954-55	**Royal Artillery Gunner** ......Khaki uniform, seated, hands on knees, 24 mm. (Export only)	£10-15
609	1974-78	**105 mm. Howitzer and Crew** ......Olive-Drab body, three soldiers, bubble-packed, 199 mm	£30-40
612	1973-79	**Commando Jeep** ......Army-Green or Camouflage, driver, two guns, jerricans, aerial	£25-35
615	1968-74	**US Jeep and 105 mm. Gun** ......Olive-Drab body with US Army markings, driver, 108/199 mm	£35-45
616	1968-78	**AEC with Chieftain Tank** ......AEC articulated Transporter 'ARMY' with 683 Tank, 318 mm	£55-65
617	1967-78	**VW KDF and 50 mm. Gun** ......Grey, German markings, operable anti-tank gun, 115/159 mm	£55-65
618	1976-79	**AEC with Helicopter** ......AEC articulated Transporter 'RESCUE', 724 Helicopter and net	£55-70
619	1976-78	**Bren Gun Carrier and AT Gun** ......Khaki, plastic tracks, figures, gun/shells, White '57' on red shield	£35-40
		NB Two variations exist (i) 2035703 4 (ii) T2272616 plus star.	
620 (151b)	1954-55	**6-wheel Covered Wagon** ......Matt-Green or Greenish-Brown body, blued axles, export only (to USA)	£200-250
620	1971-73	**Berliet Missile Launcher** ......Military-Green launcher body with White/Red missile, 150 mm	£100-120
621	1954-60	**3 ton Army Wagon** ......(Bedford 'S') tin tilt, no windows, driver in some, 113 mm	£60-70
	1960-63	............late issue:..(Bedford 'S') tin tilt, with window glazing, driver in some	£60-70
622	1954-63	**10 ton Army Truck** ......(Foden) Olive-Drab, driver, tin tilt, 137 mm. Supertoys box	£70-80
	1954-63	............................(Foden) Olive-Drab, driver, tin tilt, Dinky Toys striped box	£70-80
		............late issue: As previous model but in a Yellow lidded picture box	£200-300

622	1975-78	Bren Gun Carrier	Green body, White star, driver, passenger, plastic tracks, 125 mm	£20-30
623	1954-63	Army Covered Wagon	(Bedford 'QL') Military-Green body with or without driver, 105 mm	£35-45
624 (30hm)	1954-?	Daimler Military Ambulance	Olive-Drab body, Red crosses on White backgrounds, (US issue)	£250-350
625 (30sm)	1952-54	Austin Covered Wagon	Olive-Drab body, made for export only (to USA) 112 mm	£250-350
625	1975-78	Six-pounder Gun	Green anti-tank gun, 159 mm	£15-20
626	1956-61	Military Ambulance	Olive-Drab, Red crosses cast-in, driver on some, no windows	£40-50
	1961-62		Olive-Drab, Red crosses cast-in, driver on some, with window glazing	£60-70
630	1973-78	Ferret Armoured Car	Olive-Drab body, plastic wheels, spare wheel, 80 mm	£15-20
640 (25wm)	1954-?	Bedford Military Truck	Olive-Drab body, made for export only (to the USA)	£250-350
641	1954-61	Army 1 ton Cargo Truck	Olive-Drab, tin tilt, with or without driver, no windows, 79 mm	£35-40
	1961-62		As previous model but with window glazing, with or without driver	£40-50
642	1957-62	R.A.F. Pressure Refueller	RAF Blue, French roundel, with or without driver, Supertoys box	£80-90
	1957-62		RAF Blue, French roundel, with or without driver, Dinky Toys box	£90-110
643	1958-61	Army Water Tanker	Olive-Drab body, no windows, with or without driver, 89 mm	£30-35
	1961-64		Olive-Drab body with window glazing, with or without driver	£30-35
650 (152a)	1954-55	Light Tank	Matt Green body, Black base, no markings, export only (to USA)	£100-125
651	1954-70	Centurion Tank	Olive-Drab (may be glossy or matt) or Matt-Green body, metal or plastic rollers, rubber tracks, Supertoy. Yellow or Blue/White box	£40-50
		Export issue:	Version housed in U.S. Gold 'see through' box	£75-100
		late issue:	As previous model but in a Yellow lidded or endflap picture box	£60-70
654	1973-79	155 mm. Mobile Gun	Olive-Drab body with star, operable gun, plastic shells, 151 mm	£15-20
656	1975-79	88 mm. Gun	German Grey, fires plastic shells, 218 mm	£15-20
660	1956-61	Tank Transporter	Thorneycroft Mighty Antar, Army Green, no windows, driver in some	£60-70
	1961-64		As previous model but with window glazing, with or without driver	£60-70
660a	1978-80	Anti-Aircraft Gun with Crew	Olive-Drab, 3 soldiers, 218 mm. (Bubble-packed model)	£15-20
661	1957-65	Recovery Tractor	Army Green, six diecast wheels, driver, operable crane, Supertoy	£60-70
			As previous model but with plastic wheels, in Yellow 'picture' box	£150-200
662	1975-77	88 mm. Gun with Crew	German Grey gun (656 without wheels), 3 crew, shells, bubble-packed	£15-20
665	1964-75	Honest John Missile Erector	Olive-Drab, Black/White missile, 10 wheels plus spare, 188 mm	£90-100
666	1959-64	Missile Erector Vehicle and		
		Corporal Missile Launcher	Olive-Drab body, metal erector gears, White missile with Black fins	£250-350
			Olive-Drab body, Black plastic erector gears, all-White missile	£125-150
667	1960-64	Missile Servicing Platform	Olive-Drab, windows, spare wheel, platform lifts, Supertoy	£100-125
667	1976-78	Armoured Patrol Car	Olive-Drab body, aerial, spare wheel, 80 mm	£15-20
668	1976-79	Foden Army Truck	Olive-Drab body, windows, plastic tilt and wheels, 197 mm	£25-35
669	1956-58	U.S.A. Army Jeep	Olive-Drab body with White star, (US issue in 'plain' box)	£300-400
670	1954-70	Armoured Car	Olive-Drab body, turret rotates, diecast wheels, 73 mm	£20-25
	1964-70		Olive-Drab body, turret rotates, plastic hubs, 73 mm	£20-25
671 (152b)	1954-55	Reconnaissance Car	(Matt) Green body, Black base, made for export only	£125-175
672 (153a)	1954-55	US Army Jeep	Matt Olive-Green body, some have rounded axle-ends, US export only	£150-200
673	1953-61	Scout Car	Olive-Drab body, squadron markings, holes for personnel, 68 mm	£15-20
674	1954-66	Austin Champ	Olive-Drab body, driver, tinplate windscreen, diecast hubs, 69 mm	£35-45
	1966-71		Military-Green body, driver, tinplate windscreen, plastic hubs	£20-25
674	1958-70	'U.N.' Austin Champ	White body, driver, tinplate windscreen. Made for export only	£250-300
675 (170m)	1954-59	Ford US Army Staff Car	Olive-Drab body, White star, export only (to US), 'plain' printed box	£200-250
676	1955-62	Armoured Personnel Carrier	Olive-Drab, squadron markings, 6 wheels, revolving turret, 82 mm	£25-30
676a	1973-76	Daimler Armoured Car	Army-Green body, Speedwheels, 73 mm. (new version of 670)	£15-20
676a	1973-74	Daimler Armoured Car	French made version with camouflage net ('Made in England' on base)	NGPP
677	1957-62	Armoured Command Vehicle	Olive-Drab body, 6 wheels, (based on an A.E.C. vehicle), 133 mm	£60-70
680	1972-78	Ferret Armoured Car	Sand or Army-Green, Speedwheels, spare wheel, bubble-packed	£10-15
681	1972-78	DUKW Amphibious Vehicle	RAF Blue or Army-Green body, Speedwheels, bubble-packed, 127 mm	£10-15
682	1972-78	Stalwart Load Carrier	Olive-Drab body, 6 Speedwheels, bubble-packed, 103 mm	£10-15
683	1972-79	Chieftain Tank	Olive-Drab body, plastic tracks, fires shells, bubble-packed, 217 mm	£25-35
686	1957-71	25-pounder Field Gun	Olive-Drab, cast drawbar, (cast hubs, plastic from 1968) 90 mm	£10-15
687	1957-67	25-pounder Trailer	Olive-Drab, cast drawbar, (cast hubs, plastic from 1968) 58 mm	£10-15
687	1978-79	Convoy Army Truck	Green/Black body, 110 mm	£10-15
688	1957-61	Field Artillery Tractor	Olive-Drab, driver in some, no windows, cast hubs, 81 mm	£30-40
	1961-70		Olive-Drab, driver in some, windows, (plastic hubs from 1968)	£30-40
689	1957-66	Medium Artillery Tractor	Olive-Drab, driver in some, holes, 6 wheels, tin tilt, Supertoy	£30-40
690 (161b)	1954-55	Anti-Aircraft Gun on Trailer	Matt Green, 115 mm., made for export only	£80-100
690	1974-79	Scorpion Tank	Olive-Drab, camouflage net, working gun, bubble-packed, 120 mm	£15-20
691	1974-79	Striker Anti-Tank	Olive-Drab, plastic tracks, aerials, 5 firing rockets, 122 mm	£15-20
692	1955-62	5.5 Medium Gun	Olive-Drab body, twin cast drawbar, elevating barrel, 131 mm	£15-20
692	1974-79	Leopard Tank	Grey with German markings, plastic tracks, bubble-packed, 198 mm	£40-50
693	1958-67	7.2 inch Howitzer Gun	Olive-Drab body, cast drawbar, elevating barrel, 130 mm	£30-40
694	1974-80	Hanomag Tank Destroyer	Grey, German markings, plastic tracks/wheels, bubble-packed, 171 mm	£40-50
696	1975-79	Leopard Anti-Aircraft Tank	Grey-Green, German markings, plastic tracks, bubble-packed, 152 mm	£40-50
699	1975-78	Leopard Recovery Tank	Grey-Green, German markings, dozer blade/jib, aerial, bubble-packed	£40-50
815	1962-64	Panhard Armoured Tank	Military-Green with French flag, 104 mm. (French issue)	£75-100
816	1969-71	Berliet Missile Launcher	Military-Green body, (French issue)	£150-200
817	1962-64	AMX 13-ton Tank	Green body with French flag, 107 mm. (French issue)	£75-100
822	1962-64	Half-Track M3	Green body, rubber tracks, 121 mm. (French issue)	£75-100
884	1962-64	Brockway Bridge Truck	Military-Green, 10 wheels, bridge parts, inflatables. French issue	£150-200

Ref.	Year(s)	Model name	Colours, markings, features, dimensions	Market Price Range
60a	1934-36	**Imperial Airways Liner**	(Armstrong-Whitworth Atalanta) cast body, tinplate wings, 4 x 2 PB, Plain or 'Sunray' effect, Silver/Blue, Gold/Blue, Yellow/Blue, Red/Cream, White/Blue/Green, White/Blue, Blue/Yellow, Cream/Green, Cream/Red with no markings	£200-250
	1936-39		Blue, Cream, Gold, Red, Silver or White. Black 'G-ABTI' marking	£200-250
60a (66a)	1939-41		Gold, Green or Silver, 'G-ABTI', 'Imperial Airways Liner' under wing	£200-250
60b	1934-36	**De Havilland 'Leopard Moth'**	Cast fuselage, tinplate wings, single 2-blade propeller, 76 mm. Green/Yellow or Dark Blue/Orange, Silver/Green, Blue/Yellow, Blue/Red, Gold/Red, no markings, open windows	£100-150
	1936-39		All-over Green, Gold or Silver, 'Beige, Mid or Pale Blue, Red, 'G-ACPT', open windows	£100-150
60b (66b)	1939-41		As previous but blank side windows, 'DH Leopard Moth' under wing	£200-250
60c	1934-36	**Percival 'Gull' Monoplane**	Cast fuselage, tinplate wings, large 2-blade propeller, 76 mm. Blue/Red, Buff/White, Buff/Blue, Buff/Red, Gold/Green, Red/White, Silver/Green, White/Green, open windows with no markings	£100-150
60c (60k)	1936-39		White, Red, Yellow or Light Blue, 'G-ADZO' in Black, open windows	£100-150
60c	1936	**'Lewis's' 'Amy Mollison'** Souvenir Issue	Mid-Blue with Silver wings and a Blue 'G-ADZO' marking. Sold at Lewis's of Liverpool department store in yellow box	NGPP
60c (66c)	1939-41		Same but blank or open side windows, 'Percival Gull' under wing	£200-250
60d	1934-36	**Low Wing Monoplane**	(Vickers Jockey) Cast body, tinplate wings, 2-blade propeller, 76 mm. Red/Cream, Orange/Cream Blue/Yellow, Silver/Red or Gold/Blue, no markings, no pilot	£100-150
60d (66d)	1936-41		Red, Orange, Blue, Gold or Silver, Black 'G-AVYP', pilot's head cast-in	£100-150
	1936-41		Red with cream tail and wingtips, no pilot, with 'G-AVPY' marking	NGPP
			As previous but with pilot	NGPP
60e	1934-36	**General 'Monospar'**	Two-piece diecasting, 2 x 2-blade propellers, 80 mm. Blue/White, Cream/Red, Gold/Red, Red/Cream, Salmon Blue or Silver/Blue, no markings	£100-150
60e (66e)	1936-41		Silver, Lilac or Gold, 'G-ABVP' in Black	£100-150
			Same but with 'General Monospar', Cream, Gold, Lilac, Silver or Blue	£100-150
60f	1934-36	**Cierva 'Autogiro'**	Gold body (49 mm.) Blue rotor/propeller, no pilot	£200-300
60f (66f)	1936-40		Gold/Blue body, unpainted rotors, pilot cast-in	£100-150
	1936-40		Red/Cream body, Silver rotors, pilot cast-in	£100-150
60g	1935-36	**De Havilland 'Comet'**	Cast fuselage and wings, enclosed wheels, 2 x 2-blade propellers, 86 mm. Red/Gold, Gold/Red or Silver/Blue, no markings	£100-125
			Silver body with black 'G-ACSR' with no 'DH Comet' shown	NGPP
	1936-41		Red, Silver or Gold, 'G-ACSR', 'DH Comet' under wing	£100-125
60g	1945-49	**Light Racer (DH 'Comet')**	Yellow, Red or Silver, 'G-RACE', 'Light Racer' under wing, 2 x 3 PB	£175-225
60h	1936-36	**'Singapore' Flying Boat**	Cast fuselage (126 mm.), tinplate wings, 4 x 2-blade propellers Silver with stencilled RAF roundels, no roller or 'gliding' hole	£250-300
60h (60m)	1936-39		As previous model but with plastic or wooden roller and 'gliding' hole	£250-300
60h	1939-40		Silver or Grey with accurate RAF roundel (waterslide transfers)	£250-300
	1940-41		As previous with gun seat, cutaway bow, no hole, name under wing	£250-300
60k	1936-41	**Percival 'Gull' (Amy Mollison)**	Blue/Silver version of 60c, 'G-ADZO' in Blue, special box	£150-200
60k	1936-41	**Percival 'Gull' (H. L. Brook)**	Blue/Silver version of 60c, 'G-ADZO' in Black, special box	£150-200
60k (60c)	1945-48	**Light Tourer (Percival 'Gull')**	Red, Silver or Dark or Light Green, 'Light Tourer' or 'Percival Tourer' under wing, no markings, small or large 2-blade propeller, 76 mm.	£150-200
60m	1936-40	**Four Engined Flying Boat**	Red, Light Blue, Light Green, Dark Green, Gold, Cream or Silver, 'civilian' version of 60h with 'G-EUTG', 'G-EVCU', 'G-EXGF', 'G-EYCE' or 'G-EYTV'. N.B. With or without bow hollow, wood or plastic roller or gliding hole.	£175-225
60n	1937-40	**Fairey 'Battle' Bomber**	Silver or Grey, RAF roundels, 1 x 3 PB, undercarriage, 75 mm.	£90-120
60n (60s)	1938-41		Silver or Grey, RAF roundels, 1 x 3 PB, without undercarriage. N.B. Early issues did not have name of plane cast in.	£120-150
60p	1936-39	**Gloster 'Gladiator'**	Silver, stencilled roundels, Red 1 x 2 PB, no name under wing, 38 mm.	£100-140
	1939-41		Silver or Grey, transfer roundels, 'Gloster Gladiator' under wing	£100-140
60r	1937-40	**Empire Flying Boat**	Silver, 4 x 3 PB, plastic roller, hole, own box, 156 mm. Liveries: 'CALEDONIA', ('G-ADHM'), 'CANOPUS', ('G-ADHL'), 'CORSAIR', ('G-ADVB'), 'CHALLENGER', ('G-ADVI'), 'CLIO', ('G-AETY'), 'CALYPSO', ('G-AEUA'), 'CENTURION', ('G-ADVE'), 'CAPELLA', ('G-ADUY'), 'CERES', ('G-AETX'), 'CALPURNIA', ('G-AETW'), 'CAMILLA', ('G-AEUB'), 'CORINNA', ('G-AEUC'), 'CAMBRIA', ('G-ADUV'), 'CHEVIOT', ('G-AEUG'), 'CORDELIA', ('G-AEUD')	£150-175
60r (60x)	1940-49	**Empire Flying Boat**	As previous models but plastic, wood or brass roller, no hole. 'CALEDONIA', ('G-ADHM'), or 'CAMBRIA', ('G-ADUV'). N.B. Camouflage issues: Early issues have Red/White/Blue with a Yellow outer ring. The later (rarer) issues have a darker camouflage with just Blue/Red roundels.	£150-175
60s (60n)	1938-40	**Medium Bomber**	Camouflaged 60n with undercarriage, single roundel has Yellow ring	£100-150
60s	1940-41	**Fairy 'Battle' Bomber**	Camouflaged body, two Blue/Red roundels, no undercarriage, 1 x 3 PB. N.B. Early issues did not have name of plane cast in.	£150-200
60t	1938-41	**Douglas DC3 Air Liner**	Silver, 'PH-ALI' 2 x 3 PB, hole, tail wheel on some, own box, 132 mm	£150-175
60v (62t)	1937-41	**Armstrong Whitworth Bomber**	Silver body, 'gliding' hole in some, RAF roundels, 2 x 3 Red PB	£150-200
60w	1938-40	**Flying Boat 'Clipper III'**	Silver body, 'USA NC16736', 4 x 3 PB/SBX, plastic roller, 'gliding' hole, 164 mm. (Sikorsky S32)	£140-160
	US issue:		Silver body, 'NC 16736' markings, 'gliding' hole, Red plastic roller, leaflet	£150-200

60w	1945-48	**Flying Boat**	Silver, Blue or Green, no markings, 4 x 3 PB, brass roller, 164 mm	£100-130
60x	1937-41	**Atlantic Flying Boat**	Blue/Cream, 'DAUNTLESS', 'G-AZBP', 4 x 3 PB, name under wing	£175-200
			Green/Cream, 'WHIRLWIND', 'G-AZBT'	£175-200
			Black/White, 'DREADNOUGHT', 'G-AZBV'	£175-200
			Orange/Cream 'SWIFTSURE', 'G-AZBU' and Blue/Cream 'ENTERPRISE', 'G-AZBR' and Black/Cream 'ENDEAVOUR', 'G-AZBQ', Red/Cream 'VALORIUS', 'G-AZBS'	£175-200
62a	1939-40	**Vickers-Supermarine 'Spitfire'**	Silver body (short nose), RAF roundels, 1 x 3 PB. 52 mm	£100-130
	1940-41	**'Meccano Spitfire Fund'**	Model 62a in special souvenir box (at 2/6 each). Brass ring through fin allows use as badge or pendant. Proceeds went to Spitfire Fund.	
			Blue, Green, Grey, Magenta, Red, Yellow, or Camouflage	£450-500
			Chromium plated version (originally 10/6)	£1000-1200
62a	1945-49	**'Spitfire'**	Silver, (long nose, bubble cockpit) RAF roundels, 1 x 3 PB. 54 mm	£100-130
62b	1939-40	**Bristol 'Blenheim' Bomber**	Silver body, RAF roundels, Red 2 x 3 PB, name under wing, 78 mm	£100-130
62b	1945-49	**Medium Bomber**	Silver body, RAF roundels, Red 2 x 3 PB, name under wing, 78 mm	£60-80
62d	1940-41	**Bristol 'Blenheim' Bomber**	62b in Camouflage/Black/White, RAF roundels, 2 x 3 PB. 78 mm	£100-130
62e	1940-41	**Vickers-Supermarine 'Spitfire'**	62a in Camouflage/Black/White, RAF roundels, 1 x 3 PB. 52 mm	£100-130
62f	1939-40	**D.H. Flamingo Airliner**	Not issued	NPP
62g	1939-41	**Boeing 'Flying Fortress'**	Silver, 4 x 3 PB, 'gliding' hole, name under wing, with 'U.S.A.A.C.' markings/stars, own box, 144 mm	£140-160
			Pale Grey version	NGPP
62g	1945-48	**Long Range Bomber**	Silver body, Red 4 x 3 PB, no hole, not boxed	£90-120
62h	1938-40	**Hawker Hurricane Fighter**	Camouflaged body, RAF roundels, 1 x 2 PB, undercarriage on some	£100-130
62k	1938-41	**The King's Aeroplane**	Airspeed 'Envoy', Silver/Red/Blue, 'G-AEXX', 2 x 2 PB, own box	£150-175
62m	1938-41	**Airspeed 'Envoy' Monoplane**	Red ('G-ACVJ'), Silver ('G-ADCB'), Blue ('G-ADAZ'), Green ('G-AENA'), or Yellow ('G-ACVJ')	£120-150
62m	1945-48	**Light Transport Plane**	Red, Yellow, Silver or Blue body, 'G-ATMH', 2 x 2 PB, name under wing, 91 mm	£85-115
62n	1938-41	**Junkers 'Ju90' Air Liner**	Silver body, ('D-AALU', 'D-AIVI', 'D-AURE', or 'D-ADLH'), 4 x 3 PB, own box	£200-250
62p	1938-41	**'Ensign' Air Liner**	Silver body, Red 4 x 3 PB, gliding hole in some, own box. Liveries: 'ENSIGN' ('G-ADSR'), 'ELSINORE' ('G-ADST'), 'EXPLORER' ('G-ADSV'), 'ECHO' ('G-ADTB'), 'ETTRICK' ('G-ADSX'), 'ELYSIAN' ('G-ADSZ')	£150-200
62p	1945-49	**Armstrong Whitworth Air Liner**	As previous casting but no hole, name under wing, 4 x 3 PB, no box, Silver, Blue, Green, with Silver or Grey/Green trim, 'EXPLORER' or 'ECHO' markings	£100-125
62r	1939-41	**D.H. 'Albatross' Mail Liner**	Silver, 'G-AEVV', Red 4 x 3 PB, hole, name under wing, own box	£150-175
62r	1945-49	**Four Engined Liner**	Grey, Light Blue or Silver, no markings, no hole, not boxed, 145 mm	£100-130
			Grey, Fawn, Light Blue or Silver, 'G-ATPV', Red 4 x 3 PB, 145 mm	£100-130
62s	1939-41	**Hawker 'Hurricane' Fighter**	Silver body, RAF roundels, with or without undercarriage, 1 x 2 or 3 PB, 55 mm	£90-120
	1945-49		Silver body, RAF roundels, no undercarriage, 1 x 3 PB, 55 mm	£60-70
62t	1939-41	**Armstrong Whitley Bomber**	Light Green/Brown camouflage, Yellow ring roundels, 2 x 3 PB, box	£125-160
			Dark camouflage version, Yellow roundels	£200-300
			Dark camouflage, Red and Blue roundels	£125-160
62w (68b)	1939-41	**'Frobisher' Class Air Liner**	Silver body (casting as 62r), 4 x 3 PB, hole, own box, 3 liveries: 'FROBISHER' ('G-AFDI'), 'FALCON' ('G-AFDJ'), 'FORTUNA' ('G-AFDK')	£150-175
62x (68a)	1939-41	**British 40 Seat Airliner**	Grey/Green, Red/Maroon, TT-Green, Yellow/Maroon, Two-tone Blue, 'G-AZCA', not boxed, with or without gliding hole	£125-150
62y	1939-40	**Giant High Speed Monoplane**	Blue/Brown, Blue/Silver, Olive/Green, Yellow/Maroon, Red/Maroon, TT-Blue or TT-Green, 'D-AZBK', hole, not boxed	£100-125
	1945-49		Light/Dark Green, Grey/Green or Silver, no hole or box, 'G-ZBK'	£100-125
63	1939-41	**Mayo Composite Aircraft**	Models 63a and 63b together in special box (see below)	£200-300
63a	1939-41	**Flying Boat 'MAIA'**	Silver body, 'G-ADHK', 'Mayo Composite', own box	£100-150
63b	1939-41	**Seaplane 'MERCURY'**	Silver, 'G-ADHJ', 'Mercury Seaplane' under wing, 'hole' in some	£75-100
63b (700)	1945-49	**Seaplane**	Silver body, 'G-AVKW', no 'gliding' hole, 'Seaplane' under wing	£90-120
66a	1940-41	**Heavy Bomber**	Camouflaged body, RAF roundels, 4 x 2 PB, no name under wing	£250-300
66b	1940-41	**Dive Bomber Fighter**	Camouflaged body, RAF roundels, 1 x 2 PB, 76 mm	£150-200
66c	1940-41	**Two Seater Fighter**	Camouflaged body, RAF roundels, 1 x 2 PB, 76 mm	£150-200
66d	1940-41	**Torpedo Dive Bomber**	Camouflaged body, RAF roundels, 1 x 2 PB, 76 mm	£150-200
66e	1940-41	**Medium Bomber**	Camouflaged body, RAF roundels, 2 x 2 PB, 'General Monospar' under	£150-200
66f	1940-41	**Army Co-operation Autogiro**	Silver body and blades, Red/White/Blue roundels, (60f casting) 49 mm	£150-200
67a	1940-41	**Junkers Ju89 Heavy Bomber**	Black/Pale Blue body, German markings, no hole, own box, 160 mm	£250-300
68a	1940-41	**'Ensign' Air Liner**	Camouflaged body, RAF roundels, no 'gliding' hole, 4 x 3 PB, 173 mm	£150-200
68b	1940-41	**'Frobisher' Class Air Liner**	Light or Dark Camouflage, RAF roundels, 4 x 3 PB, 'hole' in some	£150-200
70a (704)	1946-49	**Avro 'York' Airliner**	Silver body, 'G-AGJC', Red 4 x 3 PB, 160 mm. Early version has Silver propeller pins, tinplate base and blued cockpit.	£80-100
70b (730)	1946-49	**Tempest II Fighter**	Silver body, RAF roundels, Red 4 blade prop with large spinner, 63 mm	£35-45
70c (705)	1947-49	**Viking Air Liner**	Silver or Grey body, 'G-AGOL', Red 2 x 4 PB, large spinners, 140 mm	£55-65
70d (731)	1946-49	**Twin-Engined Fighter**	Silver body, no markings, 2 x Red 3-blade propellers, pointed spinners	£25-35
			As previous model but 'N' in 'MECCANO' is reversed	NGPP
70e (732)	1946-49	**Gloster 'Meteor'**	Silver body, RAF roundels (with or without Yellow rings), 67 mm	£25-35
70f (733)	1947-49	**Lockheed 'Shooting Star'**	Silver body, US markings on wings (star on port wing only), with 'Made in England by MECCANO Ltd' under wing, 61 mm	£25-35
700 (63b)	1954-57	**Seaplane**	Silver body with 'G-AVKW' marking	£75-100
			Silver body, 'G-AVKW', no 'gliding' hole, 'Seaplane' under wing	£75-100
700	1979	**Spitfire Mark II ('Jubilee')**	Plated model on plinth, 1 x 3 PB, 'Diamond Jubilee of the RAF', special Blue card display box	£100-125

701	1947-49	Short 'Shetland' Flying Boat	Silver, 'G-AGVD', Black 4 x 4 PB, first Supertoys aircraft, own box	£300-400
702 (999)	1954-55	DH 'Comet' Jet Airliner	White/Blue body, Silver wings, 'B.O.A.'C livery, 183 mm	£100-130
704 (70a)	1954-59	Avro 'York' Airliner	Silver body, 'G-AGJC', Red 4 x 3 PB, 160 mm. ('704' beneath wing)	£70-90
705 (70c)	1952-62	'Viking' Air Liner	Silver body with 'G-AGOL' marking, flat head spinners	£60-75
			Silver or Grey body, 'G-AGOL', Red 2 x 4 PB, 140 mm	£60-75
706	1956-57	Vickers 'Viscount' Airliner	Silver/Blue/White, 'AIR FRANCE', 'F-BGNL', Red 4 x 4 PB, 149 mm	£100-120
708	1957-65	Vickers 'Viscount' Airliner	Silver/White or Metallic Grey/White, 'B.E.A.', 'G-AOJA'	£100-120
710	1965-76	Beechcraft S35 'Bonanza'	Red/White, Bronze/Yellow, or Red/Blue/White body, 1 x 2 PB, 133 mm	£40-50
		German Promotional:	Green/White, 'GLUCK MIT WICKULER' on towing pennant and box	£400-500
712	1972-77	US Army T.42A	Military Green (715), Beechcraft plus wing-tip tanks, 2 x 2 PB. 153 mm	£60-75
715	1956-62	Bristol 173 Helicopter	Turquoise body with Red rotors and stripes, 'G-AUXR', 53 mm	£40-50
715	1968-76	Beechcraft C55 'Baron'	White/Yellow or Red/Yellow body, Yellow 2 x 2 PB, 150 mm	£40-50
716	1957-62	Westland Sikorsky S-51	Red and Cream helicopter body, 2 x 3-blade rotors 66 mm	£40-50
717	1970-75	Boeing '737'	White/Blue body, White or Blue engine pods, 'LUFTHANSA', 152 mm	£55-65
718	1972-75	Hawker 'Hurricane' Mk IIc	Camouflaged body, RAF roundels, Black 1 x 3 PB, guns, 188 mm	£65-75
719 (741)	1969-77	Spitfire Mk.II	Camouflaged, RAF roundels, Black 1 x 3 PB (battery-operated), 173 mm	£55-70
			Early issues in 'Battle of Britain' pictorial card box	£50-60
721	1969-80	Junkers Ju87b Stuka	Camouflage/Yellow, German markings, 1 x 3 PB, cap-firing bomb	£55-70
			Early issues in 'Battle of Britain' pictorial card box	£50-60
722	1970-80	Hawker 'Harrier'	Metallic Blue/Olive Camouflage, RAF markings, pilot, aerial, 125 mm	£65-80
723	1970-73	Hawker Siddeley HS 125	Yellow/White/Blue or Metallic Blue/White, drop-down door/steps	£35-45
724	1971-79	'Sea King' Helicopter	Metallic Blue/White, 5-blade rotors, with 'Apollo' space capsule	£50-60
			Early issues in card picture box with pictorial inner stand	£40-50
725	1972-77	Royal Navy 'Phantom II'	Dark Blue body, Black nose, roundels, decals in bubble-pack, 132 mm	£80-90
726	1972-74	Messerschmitt Bf-109E	Desert camouflage, 1 x 3 PB, decals in bubble-pack, 165 mm	£90-110
	1974-76		Grey/Green camouflage, Yellow wing-tips/nose, decals in bubble-pack	£100-130
727	1974-?	U.S.A.F. Phantom F4 Mark II	Brown/Olive camouflage, 2 missiles, 2 figures, (no transfers issued)	£500-750
728	1972-75	R.A.F. 'Dominie'	Metallic Blue and camouflage, roundels, retractable wheels, bubble-pack	£40-50
729	1974-76	Multi-Role Combat Aircraft	Grey/Camouflage, swing-wings, decals in bubble-pack, 164 mm	£40-50
730 (70b)	1952-57	Tempest II Fighter	Same as 70b with flat head spinners	£35-45
730	1972-76	US Navy 'Phantom II'	Grey/Red, 'NAVY', 'USS Saratoga', fires missiles, retractable wheels	£80-90
731 (70d)	1954-55	Twin-Engined Fighter	Silver body, no markings, two Red 3-blade propellers, 76 mm	£40-50
731	1973-76	S.E.P.E.C.A.T. 'Jaguar'	Metallic Blue and camouflage body, Orange pilot, opening cockpit	£40-50
732 (70e)	1952-62	Gloster 'Meteor'	Same as 70e with '732' beneath wing	£25-35
732	1974-80	Bell 'POLICE' Helicopter	Orange/Blue/White or Red body, sign boards and cones, 211 mm	£35-45
733 (70f)	1954-62	Lockheed 'Shooting Star'	Silver body, US markings on wings (star on port wing only), 61 mm	£25-35
			Variant with 'in' of 'Made in England by Meccano Ltd' missing	NGPP
733	1973-76	German 'Phantom II'	Grey/Green camouflage body, 'Bundesluftwaffe', two white missiles, instructions and transfers, (German/Austrian market)	£200-300
733	1976-77	US F-4K 'Phantom II'	Brown camouflage, retractable wheels, fires missiles, (US market only)	£80-90
734	1955-62	Supermarine 'Swift'	Grey/Green camouflaged body, RAF markings, 51 mm	£30-40
734	1975-78	P47 'Thunderbolt'	Metallic Silver/Black, Red 1 x 4 PB, retractable wheels, 'U.S.A.A.F.'	£125-150
735	1956-66	Gloster 'Javelin'	Camouflaged 'delta-wing' body, RAF markings. 83 mm	£35-45
736	1955-63	Hawker 'Hunter'	Camouflaged body, RAF markings, 54 mm	£30-40
736	1973-78	Bundesmarine 'Sea King'	Grey/Orange helicopter, German markings, decals in bubble-pack	£25-35
737	1959-68	P.1B 'Lightning' Fighter	Silver (metal wheels) or Metallic Grey (Black plastic wheels) 55 mm	£60-70
738	1960-65	DH 110 'Sea Vixen' Fighter	Grey/White body, Black nose, RAF roundels, 'ROYAL NAVY', 80 mm	£50-60
739	1975-78	A6M5 'Zero Sen'	Metallic Green/Black, Japanese markings, decals in bubble-pack	£60-70
741	1978-80	Spitfire Mk II	Camouflaged body, (non-motorised version of 719), 173 mm	£60-70
749 (992)	1955-56	RAF Avro 'Vulcan' Bomber	Silver body (aluminium), only 500 models were made (for Canadian market) 992 is the catalogue (and box) number, '749' is cast into the model. Two castings exist; one has pointed wingtips, the other more rounded	£2000-2500
997	1962-65	Caravelle SE 210 Airliner	Silver/White/Blue, 'AIR FRANCE', metal or plastic wheels, 126 mm, Yellow lidded picture box with card support	£100-150
998	1959-64	Bristol 'Britannia'	Silver/White body, Red or Blue lines, 'CANADIAN PACIFIC', 'CF-CZA', striped picture box with card support	£175-200
	1964-65		Metallic Grey/White body, Red lines, 'CANADIAN PACIFIC', 'CF-CZA', Yellow lidded picture box with card support	£200-250
999 (702)	1955-65	DH 'Comet' Jet Airliner	White/Blue body, White tailfin, 'G-ALYV' or 'G-ALYX' registration	£100-125
			White/Blue body, Blue tailfin, 'G-ALYX' registration	£100-125
			As previous model but with Silver/Grey wings	£100-125

BOX TYPES: Many 1970-79 issues were 'vacuform' packed and these include model nos: 710,712, 715, 717, 718, 721 to 734 inc., plus 736 and 739.
Recommended reading:
'**Dinky Toys Aeroplanes - A Collectors Guide and Checklist**'. Contact D.C. Barratt, 230 Earlham Road, Norwich, Norfolk, NR2 23RH. (Tel: 01630-453650).

67a Junkers JU89
Heavy Bomber
with its individual box.

Dinky Toys Public Transport Vehicles

Buses, Taxis, Trams and Trains

Ref.	Year(s)	Model name	Colours, features, dimensions	Market Price Range
16	1936-37	Silver Jubilee Set	Locomotive and two interlocking coaches, 'LNER' and '2590' cast-in, open windows, smooth hubs with White tyres, special box, 300 mm.	
			Silver loco and coaches, Grey, Mid-Blue, Dark Blue, Red or Orange trim	£200-250
			Silver loco and coaches with Dark Blue trim	£200-250
			Cream loco and coaches with Red trim	£250-275
			Blue loco and coaches with Dark Blue trim	£250-275
			Green loco and coaches with Dark Green trim	£250-275
16	1937-40	Streamlined Train Set	As previous models but with a change of name and box	£200-250
16	1946-52	Streamlined Train Set	Blue/Black loco, 'LNER', Brown/Grey coaches, closed windows, Black tyres	£125-150
16 (798)	1952-54	Streamlined Train Set	As previous model but with 'BR' crest on tender	£100-125
16z	1935-40	Articulated Train	Two-tone Blue, or Gold/Red, or Cream with Red, Blue or Orange.	
			French issue sold in UK	£200-250
17	1935-40	Passenger Train Set	Black/Maroon loco 17a, Maroon tender 17b,	
			Maroon/Cream coaches 20a/20b	£300-400
			Black/Green loco 17a, Green tender 17b, 2 Green/Cream coaches 20a/20b	£300-400
			Lead and Mazak set in 2nd type box with correct colour spot	£400-500
17a	1934-40	Locomotive	Black/Maroon or Black/Green, diecast cab/boiler, lead chassis, 82 mm	£100-125
17b	1934-40	Tender	Maroon or Green diecast body, 62 mm	£40-50
18	1935-40	Tank Goods Train Set	Green/Black loco (21a), and 3 Green/Black open wagons (21b)	£300-400
19	1935-40	Mixed Goods Train	Maroon/Black loco (21a), Green/Red open wagon (21b), Red/Blue 'SHELL' tanker wagon (21d), Yellow/Red/Green lumber wagon (21e)	£400-500
	rare box version:		Set in 3rd type pictorial landscape box	£800-1000
20	1935-40	Tank Passenger Set	Green/Black loco (21a), 2 Brown/Green coaches (20a), Guard's van (20b)	£300-400
20a	1935-40	Coach	Brown/Cream or Green/White roof, diecast body, lead chassis, 81 mm	£40-60
20b	1935-40	Guard's Van	Brown/Cream or Green/White roof, diecast body, lead chassis, 81 mm	£40-60
21	1933-35	Modelled Miniatures Train Set	Blue/Red loco (21a), Green open wagon (21b), Green/Blue crane wagon (21c), Red/Blue 'SHELL' tank wagon (21d), Yellow/Red/Green lumber wagon (21e), 'HORNBY SERIES' cast into lead body	£500-600
21a	1932-34	Tank Locomotive	Red/Blue 0-6-0 tank loco, 'HORNBY SERIES' cast into lead body, 82 mm	£50-75
	1934-41		Maroon/Black or Green/Black, 'DINKY TOYS' cast into lead body, 82 mm	£50-75
21b	1932-34	Open Wagon	Green/Red, Green/Blue, Green/Black, Maroon/Black, 'HORNBY SERIES' cast into lead body	£40-50
	1934-41		Colours as previous model, 'DINKY TOYS' cast into lead body, 58 mm	£40-50
21c	1932-34	Crane Wagon	Green body, Blue chassis, 'HORNBY SERIES' cast-in, lead, 62 mm	NGPP
21d	1932-34	Tanker Wagon	Red tank, Blue or Black chassis, 'HORNBY SERIES' cast-in, lead, 58 mm	£35-45
	1934-41		Red tank, Blue or Black chassis, 'DINKY TOYS' cast-in, lead, 58 mm	£35-45
21e	1932-34	Lumber Wagon	Brown/Blue, Yellow/Red or Yellow/Black, 'HORNBY SERIES' in lead	£35-45
	1934-41		Brown/Blue, Yellow/Red or Yellow/Black, 'DINKY TOYS', lead, 58 mm	£35-45
26	1934-40	G.W.R. Rail Car	Early issues are lead, later issues are mazak, plastic rollers, 106 mm.	
			Cream roof, Brown, Green, Yellow or Red body	£100-125
			Green body with Red roof	£125-150
26z	1937-40	Diesel Road Car	Cream roof, Red, Green, Orange, Yellow or Blue body, 99 mm. (French)	£100-125
27	1934-38	Tram Car	Plastic or metal wheels, no logo 'OVALTINE' or 'LIPTONS TEA' or no logo, 77 mm.	
			Red, Orange, Green, Yellow or Light or Dark Blue body, Cream upper windows and roof	£200-250
			Light Blue or Dark Blue body, Cream lower/upper windows and roof	£200-250
29 (29a)	1934-38	Motor Bus	Plastic or metal wheels, no logo, or Silver or Red 'MARMITE', 70 mm.	
			Blue, Green, Maroon, Yellow or Red body, Cream or Silver roof	£200-250
29b	1936-46	Streamlined Bus	Green/Cream, Orange/Cream, Red/Cream, Black or White tyres, smooth hubs	£150-200
			Two-tone Blue, Yellow/Orange, Red/Maroon, Turquoise/Red, all with smooth Black hubs, open rear window, 88 mm	£150-200
	1946-47		Cream and Dark Blue, smooth hubs, open windows	£130-160
	1947-50		Grass Green/Light Green or Grey/Blue body, Black tyres, filled-in rear window	£150-200
29c		Double Decker Bus	The different casting types are shown in the diagrams above.	
	1938-40	'DUNLOP TYRES'	1st Type AEC/STL, cutaway wings, stairs cast-in, smooth hubs, White tyres, crimped axle ends. Advert in Black on Yellow rectangle, 100 mm.	
	regular issues:		Cream upper deck and roof with Red, Light Blue, Maroon, Green or Orange lower deck	£200-300
	1938	early Grey roof issues:	As previous but with Grey roof	£300-400
	late issue:		Dark Blue lower deck, Cream upper deck and roof	£300-400
	1938-40	without advertisments:	As above but without advertisements	£200-300
			N.B. Baseplates: 1st issue 'Made in England', 29 mm x 2 mm	
			2nd issue 'Made in England', 28 mm x 1.5 mm	
	1946	without advertisments:	1st type AEC/STL grille, cutaway wings, no staircase, six vertical inside body ribs, smooth Black hubs.	
	colours:		Green lower deck with Cream or Grey upper-deck	£100-150
			Red lower deck with Cream or Grey upper deck	£100-150
	1947-48	without advertisments:	As previous model but with post-war Black ridged hubs	£85-95
			As previous model but with Two-tone Green body	£130-160
	1948-49	without advertisments:	3rd type, Leyland or AEC grille, straight-across wings, Black ridged hubs. Early issues had 6 vertical inside body ribs, later issues had 5 (3 on n/s, 2 on o/s)	
	colours:		Red or Green lower deck, Cream upper deck	£90-110

147

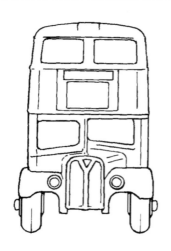  

1st Type 1938-47
AEC/STL grille, large 'V' shape
Cutaway wings, smooth hubs
No model number on base

2nd Type 1949-53 and 1957-59
AEC/Regent grille, small 'V' shape
Straight across wings, ridged hubs
No model number or
'29c' cast into base

3rd Type 1948-49 and 1954-63
Leyland grille, undivided shape
Straight across wings, ridged hubs
'29c', '290' or '291' on base

29c	1949-53	......................without advertisments:	...2nd type, AEC/Regent grille, straight-across wings, lengthwise chassis strengthener with hole in chassis centre, or (1952) eight vertical inside body ribs, ridged hubs, plus in (1953) '29c' cast in chassis.	
		colours:	Red or Green lower deck, Cream or White upper deck, hubs match the lower deck colour	£90-110
29c (290)	1954-54	'DUNLOP'	...3rd type Leyland Titan grille and straight across wings, early issues have recessed stop lights, late issues (1959) protrude. Logo 'DUNLOP -The World's Master Tyre' in Black and Red. Sloping and upright designs exist.	
		colours:	Red or Green lower deck, Cream upper deck, hubs match lower deck colour	£80-100
29dz	1939-40	Autobus	Green or White body, metal wheels, (French issue sold in UK)	£80-90
29e	1948-52	Single Deck Bus	Blue/Dark Blue or Light Green/Dark Green, 113 mm.	£75-85
29f (280)	1950-54	Observation Coach...........	Grey body and hubs, Red flashes	£70-80
			Cream body and hubs, Red flashes	£80-90
29g(281)	1951-54	Luxury Coach	Maroon body with Cream flashes	£80-100
			Orange body with Cream flashes	£150-200
			Fawn body with Orange flashes	£100-125
			Blue body with Cream flashes	£150-175
			Cream body with Blue flashes	£150-175
			Cream body with Red flashes	£175-225
			Cream body with Orange flashes, Green hubs	£200-250
		NB	Model based on the Maudsley Marathon III Coach.	
29h(282)	1952-54	Duple Roadmaster Coach	Dark Blue body, Light Blue hubs, Silver coachlines	£80-100
			Red body and hubs, Silver coachlines	£80-100
			Green lower body, Cream upper body and hubs	£150-200
		NB	Early issue had a flat roof underside. Later issues have a rib front to back.	
36g		Taxi with Driver	'TAXI' cast into Black roof, driver cast into chassis, 72 mm.	
	1936-46		Grey, Dark Blue or Red body, Black roof, open rear window	£150-200
			Green body, Black roof	£80-90
			Yellow body, Black roof, open rear window	£400-500
	1947-50		Dark Blue, Green, Light Green, Red, Maroon or Brown body, Black roof on all, some open rear windows (usually filled-in)	£80-100
40h(254)	1951-54	Austin Taxi (FX3)...............	Yellow body and hubs, Black interior and chassis	£80-100
			Dark Blue body and hubs, Black interior and chassis	£80-100
		NB	White 'TAXI' sign on roof, driver cast into chassis.	
067	1959-64	......................'Dublo Dinky' version:	Blue/Cream body, driver and 'TAXI' cast-in, Grey plastic wheels, 59 mm	£40-50
115	1979-79	United Biscuits Taxi	Yellow/Blue/Black, casting as 120, promotional, 86 mm	£45-55
120	1979-80	Happy Cab	White/Yellow/Blue, solid wheels, 'flower-power' stickers, 86 mm	£45-55
241	1977-77	'SILVER JUBILEE TAXI'	Silver body and hubs, Union Jack on bootlid, 284 casting, 112 mm	£30-35
254(40h)	1954-56	Austin Taxi (FX3)...........	Yellow body and hubs, Brown interior	£100-125
			Mid Blue body, Light Blue hubs, Black interior	£200-250
	1956-59		Dark Green lower body, Yellow upper body and hubs, Black interior	£100-125
	1959-62		Black body, Grey interior, spun aluminium hubs	£100-125

265	1960-64	**Plymouth U.S.A. Taxi**	Yellow/Red, '25c First 1/5 Mile, 5c Additional', windows, aerial, 108 mm	£80-90
266	1960-66	**Plymouth Canadian Taxi**	Yellow/Red body with 'Taxi' and '450 Metro Cab', 108 mm	£125-150
268	1962-67	**Renault Dauphine Mini Cab**	Red body with 'Meccano', 'Kenwood', and various other adverts, 92 mm	£90-110
278	1978-80	**Plymouth Yellow Cab**	Yellow body, 'Yellow Cab Co', plastic chassis, wheels and aerial, 135 mm	£20-30
280 (29f)	1954-60	**Observation Coach**	Grey (Red flashes) or Cream (Red flashes), 112 mm	£65-75
281 (29g)	1954-59	**Luxury Coach**	Fawn/Orange, Cream/Orange, Fawn/Cream or Maroon/Cream, 113 mm	£100-125
			Blue body, Cream flash, Lemon wheels	£200-250
282 (29h)	1954-60	**Duple Roadmaster Coach**	Dark Blue body, Light Blue hubs, Silver coachlines	£80-100
			Red body and hubs, Silver coachlines	£80-100
			Light Blue body and hubs, Silver coachlines	£80-100
			Yellow body, Red coachlines and hubs	£150-200
		US issue:	Dark Green lower body, Cream upper body and hubs	£200-250
		US issue:	As previous model but with Red hubs	£200-250
282	1967-69	**Austin 1800 Taxi**	Blue/White body, Red/White 'TAXI' labels on doors and roof, 101 mm	£65-75
283	1956-63	**B.O.A.C. Coach**	Dark Blue/White, *'British Overseas Airways Corporation'*, 120 mm	£80-90
		NB	Model based on Commer Harrington Contender Coach.	
283	1971-77	**Single Deck Bus**	Red body with White band, operable doors and bell, 'RED ARROW'	£40-50
			As previous model but Metallic Red finish	£50-60
284	1972-79	**London Taxi (FX4)**	Black (or very Dark Blue) body, detailed boot on some, Speedwheels, driver, 'TAXI', 112 mm	£30-40
289		**Routemaster Bus**	'London Transport', Route '221', 'KINGS CROSS', driver/conductor, cast hubs, spun hubs or Speedwheels, 121 mm.	
	1964-65	'TERN SHIRTS'	Red body, *'FOR 8am CRISPNESS'* transfers	£80-100
	1966-69	'SSSCHWEPPES'	Red body, Blue-Green logo on White transfers, spun hubs	£80-100
	1969-80	'ESSO'	Red body, White label, *'ESSO SAFETY-GRIP TYRES'*	£50-60
			Same as previous issue but with transfers	£100-150
		'ESSO' variant:	Deep Purple body, *'London Transport'* and *'ESSO SAFETY-GRIP TYRES'* logos, Blue driver and clippie	£400-600
	1968-68	'LONDON STORES'	Red body, Black/Gold logo 'Festival of London Stores', promotional	£100-150
	1970	'INGERSOLL RAND'	Red body, promotional	£100-125
	1974-74	'MECCANO'	Gold body, 'MECCANO - DINKY TOYS'. (Very few issued to Press only)	NGPP
	1977-79	'MADAME TUSSAUDS'	Red body, driver/conductor, White lower deck seating, Blue on White advert., cast wheels	£80-100
			Red body, driver/conductor, Dark Blue lower deck seating, White on Blue ad., plastic wheels	£80-100
			Red body, with figures, packed in 'SCHWEPPES' picture box	£100-120
	1977-77	'WOOLWORTHS'	Silver body, (Silver Jubilee limited issue) figures in some	£25-30
	1977-77	'EVER READY'	Silver body, (New Zealand Silver Jubilee issue) no figures	NGPP
	1979	'THOLLENBEEK'	Gold body, *'Thollenbeek 1929-79'*, Belgian promotional	£90-110
		'FORDATH'	Red body, Light Blue upper deck seating, Deep Blue lower deck seating. Issued in plain White box with 'WITH THE COMPLIMENTS OF FORDATH LIMITED' labels to box ends. Promotional	£175-225
290 (29c)		**Double Decker Bus**	Type 2 (AEC grille), *'DUNLOP - The World's Master Tyre'* advert may be upright or sloping, '290' cast on base, diecast hubs match lower deck.	
	1954-59	'DUNLOP'	Green lower deck, Cream upper deck	£80-100
			Red lower deck, Cream upper deck	£80-100
	1959-61	'DUNLOP'	Type 3 (Leyland grille), diecast hubs match lower deck colour, roof route box added, Mid Green or Dark Green lower deck, Cream upper deck	£80-100
			Red lower deck, Cream upper deck	£80-100
	1961-63		Same colours as previous with sloping lettering but with spun hubs	£100-150
	1963		Same body colours but with Green or Red plastic hubs	£125-175
	1963	'EXIDE BATTERIES'	Red or Green lower deck, Cream upper deck with '290' cast into base	NGPP
291		**Double Decker Bus**	Type 3 (Leyland grille) with route '73' on roof route box.	
	1961-62	'EXIDE BATTERIES'	Red body with Red diecast hubs, logo in Black and Yellow	£100-120
	1962-63		Same body colours as previous model but with spun aluminium hubs	£125-150
	1963		Same body colours as previous but with Red plastic hubs	£125-175
291 - 293		**Atlantean City Bus**	A Leyland double-decker bus (123 mm. long) available in several versions:	
291	1974-77	'KENNINGS'	Orange body, White engine cover and interior, *'VAN & TRUCK HIRE'*	£40-45
			As previous model but with Pale Blue engine cover and interior	£40-45
			As previous model but seen with 'Yellow Pages' stickers	NGPP
	1977	'LONDON & MANCHESTER ASSURANCE'	White model on plinth. *'Your Best Man For Life'*. (500 issued to agents)	£400-500
292	1962-65	'RIBBLE'	Red and White body with or without 'REGENT' advertisement	£90-110
			Red and Cream body with *'CORPORATION TRANSPORT'* fleetname	£90-110
			As previous model but no fleetname or logo	£90-110
292	1977	'LONDON COUNTRY'	Green body, shown in 1977 catalogue but never issued.	
293	1963-65	'BP'	Green/Cream body, Yellow logo and smooth roof, *'BP IS THE KEY'*	£90-110
			As previous model but with ribbed roof	£110-130
293	1973-78	**Swiss Postal Bus 'PTT'**	Yellow body with Cream roof, clear or tinted windows, (296 casting)	£25-35
295	1963-69	**Atlas Kenebrake Bus**	Light Blue/Grey body, suspension, windows, 86 mm	£45-55
			As previous model but all Blue body, Red interior	£80-100
295	1973-74	**Atlantean Bus 'YELLOW PAGES'**	Yellow body, *'Let Your Fingers Do The Walking'*, 123 mm	£40-50
295	1974-76		As previous model but deeper shade of Yellow	£40-50
			As previous model but finished in Silver, no front or rear destination blinds	NGPP
296	1972-75	**Duple Viceroy 37 Coach**	Metallic Blue body, clear or tinted windows, bubble-packed, 119 mm	£20-25
			As previous model but Yellow and Cream body (see also 293)	£25-30

Public Transport Vehicles

297	1977-77	**Silver Jubilee Bus**	Leyland Atlantean (291) Silver/Black body, 'National', 123 mm	£25-30
	1977-77	**'WOOLWORTHS'**	Silver Jubilee Bus (Leyland Atlantean) Silver body, promotional	£25-30
949	1961-66	**Wayne 'SCHOOL BUS'**	Deep Yellow body, Red body lines and interior, windows, Supertoy	£175-225
			As previous model but with Black lines on sides	£175-225
952	1964-71	**Vega Major Luxury Coach**	Pale Grey with Maroon flash, with electric lights, Supertoy	£70-85
			As previous model but White body with Maroon flash	£70-85
			Late issues with Red interior, clear indicators, cast hubs	£100-125
953	1963-65	**Continental Touring Coach**	Pale Blue body, White roof, 'Dinky Continental Tours', Supertoy	£250-350
954	1972-77	**Vega Major Luxury Coach**	As 952 but without electric lights	£70-80
961	1973-77	**Vega Major Coach 'PTT'**	Orange/Cream body, 'P.T.T.' and emblem, Swiss model (in normal box)	£150-175
		box variant:	961 in Swiss box (Red/White/Yellow, 'Autocar Postal', 'Postauto', etc), plus label 'Special contract run 1973 Swiss Post Office Bus - also specially boxed for Swiss Meccano Agent for sale under their name'	£200-250
784	1972-74	**Dinky Goods Train Set**	Blue loco 'GER', one Red Truck, one Yellow Truck	£30-40
798 (16)	1954-59	**Express Passenger Train Set**	Green/Black loco, BR crest, Cream coaches (Grey roofs), Black hubs/tyres	£100-125
			Green/Black loco, BR crest, Cream coaches/roofs/hubs, Black tyres	£80-100
			Green/Black loco, BR crest, Cream coaches/roofs, Red hubs, White tyres	£100-125

Dinky Toys Ships, Boats and Hovercraft

Ref.	Year(s)	Model name	Colours, features, dimensions	Market Price Range
50a	1934-41	**Battle Cruiser 'HMS Hood'**	Battleship Grey, (without name cast underneath 1939-41) 146 mm	£30-35
50b	1934-41	**Battleship 'Nelson' Class**	Battleship Grey, 'HMS Nelson' underneath (no name 1939-41) 117 mm	£30-35
50b	1934-41	**Battleship 'Nelson' Class**	Battleship Grey, 'HMS Rodney' underneath (no name 1939-41) 117 mm	£30-35
50c	1934-41	**Cruiser 'HMS Effingham'**	Battleship Grey, (without name cast underneath 1939-41) 100 mm	£30-35
50d	1934-41	**Cruiser 'HMS York'**	Battleship Grey, (without name cast underneath 1939-41) 98 mm	£30-35
50e	1934-41	**Cruiser 'HMS Delhi'**	Battleship Grey, (without name cast underneath 1939-41) 81 mm	£30-35
50f	1934-41	**Destroyer 'Broke' Class**	Battleship Grey, no wording underneath, 57 mm	£15-20
50g	1935-41	**Submarine 'K' Class**	Battleship Grey, wire mast, no wording underneath, 57 mm	£15-20
50h	1935-41	**Destroyer 'Amazon' Class**	Battleship Grey, no wording underneath, 52 mm	£15-20
50x	1935-41	**Submarine 'X' Class**	Battleship Grey, wire mast, no wording underneath, 61 mm	£15-20
51b	1934-40	**Norddeutscher-Lloyd 'Europa'**	Black hull, White superstructure, Brown funnels, name under, 165 mm	£35-45
51c	1934-40	**Italia Line 'Rex'**	Black hull, White decks, Red/White/Green funnels, name under, 152 mm	£35-45
51d	1934-40	**CPR 'Empress of Britain'**	Canadian Pacific Railway colours – White hull, Cream funnels, 130 mm	£30-35
51e	1935-40	**P & O 'Strathaird'**	White hull, Cream funnels, name underneath, 114 mm	£30-35
51f	1934-40	**'Queen of Bermuda'**	Furness-Withy Line, Grey/White hull, Red/Black funnels, 99 mm	£30-35
51g	1934-40	**Cunard 'Britannic'**	'White-Star' Liner, Black/White/Brown hull, Black/Tan funnels, 121 mm	£30-35
52	1934-35	**Cunard White-Star Liner 'No. 534'**	Black/White/Red, '534' cast underneath, boxed, no rollers, 175 mm	£70-80
			Same model but '534 Queen Mary' cast underneath	£50-60
52 (52b)	1935-35		As previous model with 'Queen Mary' cast underneath, but without '534'	£50-60
52a	1935-41	**Cunard White-Star Liner 'Queen Mary'**	Black/White/Red, boxed, with plastic rollers, 175 mm	£60-80
	1946-49		Black/White/Red, boxed, with brass rollers	£50-60
52b (52)	1935-36	**Cunard 'Queen Mary'**	Black/White/Red, boxed, without rollers, (renumbered from 52)	£60-80
52c	1935-40	**'La Normandie'**	Black/White, Red/Black funnels, boxed, made in France, pictorial insert	£60-80
52c	1939	**Cunard 'Queen Elizabeth'**	Announced in 1939 catalogue but never produced	NPP
52m	1936-40	**Cunard 'Queen Mary'**	Renumbered from 52b, without rollers, supplied unboxed	£20-30
53az	1938-39	**Battleship 'Dunkerque'**	Battleship Grey, with or without plastic rollers, boxed French issue	£40-60
281	1973-76	**Military Hovercraft**	Olive Drab body, Gunner, aerial, 'ARMY', 139 mm	£25-30
290	1970-76	**SRN-6 Hovercraft**	Red or Metallic Red body, Blue or Black skirt	£15-20
671	1976-78	**Mk.1 Corvette**	White/Grey/Brown/Black plastic body, fires missiles, 260 mm	£15-20
672	1976-77	**OSA-2 Missile Boat**	Grey/Whit/Black, fires missiles, 206 mm	£15-20
673	1977-78	**Submarine Chaser**	Grey/White/Black, fires depth charges, 197 mm	£15-20
674	1977-78	**Coastguard Missile Launch**	White/Blue/Red/Yellow, 'Coastguard', fires missiles, 155 mm	£15-20
675	1973-77	**Motor Patrol Boat**	Grey hull with Cream/Black/Red, 170 mm	£15-20
678	1974-77	**Air-Sea Rescue Launch**	Grey/Black/Yellow, Orange dinghy, pilot/launch, 170 mm	£15-20
796	1960-62	**Healey Sports Boat on Trailer**	Cream hull with Green, Red or Yellow deck (plastic), Orange cast trailer	£25-30
797	1966	**Healey Sports Boat**	Sold without trailer from trade box of 6	£15-20

Dinky Toys Novelty, Space, Film and TV-related models

100	1967-75	**Lady Penelope's 'FAB 1'**	Pink body, clear or tinted sliding roof (Pink stripes on early issues), rockets/harpoons, Lady Penelope and Parker figures (TV series 'Thunderbirds').	
			Card picture box with pictorial inner stand	£150-200
			As previous model but with Luminous Pink body	£250-300
101	1967-73	**Thunderbirds II and IV**	Gloss Green body with Yellow legs, plastic Thunderbird IV inside	
			Card picture box with pictorial inner stand	£200-250
	1973-73		Metallic Dark Green, Yellow legs, Thunderbird IV inside. Bubble-packed	£200-250
			Turquoise body	NGPP
102	1969-75	**Joe's Car**	Metallic Green, driver, battery powered, 139 mm. (TV series 'Joe 90')	
			Card picture box with pictorial inner stand	£100-125

103	1968-75	**Spectrum Patrol Car**	TV series 'Captain Scarlet', shaped hubs, 'screaming motor', Red body with Yellow base, Yellow or Cream plastic interior. Card picture box with pictorial inner stand	£100-125
			Metallic Red body with White base, Yellow or Cream plastic interior	£75-100
			Metallic Gold body, Blue tinted windows, Yellow or Cream interior	£75-100
104	1968-72	**Spectrum Pursuit Vehicle**	Metallic Blue, 'SPV', separate seat/figure, 160 mm. ('Captain Scarlet')	£100-125
	1973-75		As previous model but seat and figure attached to door	£75-100
105	1968-75	**Maximum Security Vehicle**	White body, Red or Blue interior, 'RADIOACTIVE' crate, ('Cpt. Scarlet')	£75-100
			Late issue without Red body stripe	£75-100
106	1967-70	**'The Prisoner' Mini-Moke**	White body, Red/White canopy, 'bicycle' decal on bonnet, 73 mm	£150-200
			With axles penetrating spun hubs	£300-350
			With cast hubs and painted or unpainted side sills	£280-320
			NB Windscreen: Silver or Black metal, add	£30-40
106	1974-77	**Thunderbirds II and IV**	Metallic Blue body, Black metal base, Yellow legs, 153 mm. Vacuum-packed	£80-100
			Metallic Blue body, White plastic base, Yellow legs, 153 mm	£80-100
	1977-79		Metallic Blue body, Black plastic base, Red legs, 153 mm	£70-80
107	1967-68	**'Stripey the Magic Mini'**	White/Red/Yellow/Blue stripes, with Candy, Andy and the Bearandas. Card picture box with pictorial inner stand	£175-225
108	1969-75	**Sam's Car**	Keyless motor, 111 mm., separate 'WIN' badge, (TV series 'Joe 90'), Silver plated body, Red or Silver trim, Yellow interior. Card picture box with pictorial inner stand	£75-95
			Gold body, Red or Silver trim, Yellow interior	£100-120
			Pale Blue body, Red or Silver trim, Yellow interior	£120-140
			Metallic Red body, Red or Silver trim, Yellow interior	£90-120
			Wine Red body	£120-140
109	1969-71	**Gabriel's Model 'T' Ford**	Yellow/Black, (TV series 'The Secret Service'). Card picture box with pictorial inner stand	£75-85
111	1976-78	**Cinderella's Coach**	Pink/Gold, plastic figures and horses. ('The Slipper & The Rose')	£20-25
112	1978-80	**Purdey's TR7**	Yellow body, Black 'P' logo, Speedwheels. ('The New Avengers')	£45-55
			As previous model but with Yellow 'P' in Black logo on bonnet	£100-125
			As previous model but with Silver 'P' logo on bonnet	£35-45
113		**John Steed's Jaguar XJC**	Metallic Dark Blue, Gold pinstripes, rubbery 'Steed' inside. Officially not issued	NGPP
115	1979-79	**United Biscuits Taxi**	Yellow/Blue/Black, casting as 120, promotional, 86 mm	£50-60
120	1979-80	**Happy Cab**	White/Yellow/Blue, solid wheels, 'flower-power' stickers, 86 mm	£40-45
281	1968-70	**'PATHE NEWS' Camera Car**	Black body, Camera and operator, opening doors, (Fiat 2300), 108 mm	£90-120
350	1970-71	**Tiny's Mini Moke**	Red body, White/Yellow striped top, 73 mm. ('The Enchanted House')	£90-120
351	1971-79	**U.F.O. Interceptor**	From Gerry Anderson's TV series 'U.F.O', 'S.H.A.D.O.' labels on Light Metallic Green body. Initially packed in card box with pictorial inner mount (prices 20% higher), later bubble-packed.	
			with Black nose, White missile, clear canopy, Red or Orange skids	£120-140
			with Black nose, White missile, Blue canopy, Red or Orange skids	£90-120
			with Red nose, Yellow missile, clear canopy, Red or Orange skids	£65-85
			with Red nose, Yellow missile, Blue canopy, Red or Orange skids	£65-85
			NB The above 'Red nose' issues are housed in bubble packs.	
352	1971-75	**Ed Straker's Car**	Gold plated body, Blue interior, keyless motor, (TV series 'U.F.O.')	£80-90
			Yellow body, Blue or White interior, Silver trim	£80-90
			Red body, Silver trim	£60-70
353	1971-79	**'SHADO 2 Mobile'**	Military Green body, operable rocket, 145 mm. (TV series 'U.F.O.')	£60-70
			As previous model but later version with Metallic Blue body	£120-140
354	1972-77	**Pink Panther**	Pink car and Panther, flywheel drive, card endflap box, 175 mm	£35-45
	1977-79	**Pink Panther**	Similar to previous model but without flywheel, bubble-packed	£35-45
			N.B. A single experimental Green diecast version exists (Christies sale 4/95).	
355	1972-75	**Lunar Roving Vehicle**	Metallic Blue, White astronauts, front/rear steering, 114 mm	£35-45
357	1977-80	**Klingon Battle Cruiser**	Metallic Blue, fires 'photon torpedoes', 220 mm. (from 'Star Trek')	£35-45
358	1976-80	**'USS Enterprise'('NCC 1701')**	White body, Yellow or White 'photon torpedoes', shuttlecraft, 234 mm	£50-60
359	1975-79	**Eagle Transporter**	White/Green body, Red cones/landing gear, (from 'Space 1999')	£55-65
360	1975-79	**Eagle Freighter**	White, Red cargo pod, 'RADIOACTIVE' drums, (from 'Space 1999')	£55-65
			As previous model but with White cargo pod	£55-65
361	1978-80	**Zygon War Chariot**	Mid-Green body, two Red spacemen and rocket motor	£25-35
361	1978-80	**Galactic War Chariot**	Metallic Green body, two White/Green spacemen, Silver rocket motor	£25-35
361	1978-80	**Missile-firing War Chariot**	Metallic Blue body, two Red spacemen/rocket motor, blister card	£25-35
362	1978-79	**Trident Star Fighter**	Black/Orange, fires rockets, drop-down stairway, 170 mm	£30-35
			Metallic Gold body. 500 only issued to guests at a special Meccano Dinner in 1979	£100-150
363	1979-79	**Cosmic Interceptor**	Metallic Silver/Blue, 2 pilots, Marks & Spencer model ('St.Michael' box)	£35-45
363	1979-80	**Zygon Patroller**	Metallic Silver/Blue, 2 pilots, ('368' in some catalogues, '363' on box)	£30-35
			Yellow/Red/Blue version in 'U.S.S. Enterprise' box	NGPP
364	1979	**NASA Space Shuttle**	White booster and shuttle, decals, instructions, plastic Orange satellite. Pictorial window box	£75-85
366	1979	**Space Shuttle**	unboxed version of 364 without booster, with plastic or carboard load	£20-30
367	1979-80	**Space Battle Cruiser**	White/Red body, pilot, plastic weapons, 187 mm	£35-45
368	1979-79	**Cosmic Cruiser**	Blue body, Marks & Spencer model (in 'St.Michael' box)	£35-45
368	1979-80	**Zygon Marauder**	Red/White, 4 spacemen, ('363' in some catalogues, '368' on box)	£30-35
371 (801)	1980	**Pocket-size 'USS Enterprise'**	Small version of 358, bubble-packed, released after factory closure	£45-55
372 (802)	1980	**Pocket-size Klingon Cruiser**	Small version of 357, bubble-packed, released after factory closure	£45-55
477	1970-72	**Parsley's Car**	Green/Black/Yellow, head swivels, ('The Adventures of Parsley'). Card picture box with pictorial inner stand	£80-90
485	1964-67	**Santa Special Model T Ford**	Red/White body, Santa Claus, Xmas tree/toys/decals, 79 mm	£75-95
486	1965-69	**'Dinky Beats' Morris Oxford**	Pink/Green, 'Da gear', 3 beat-group figures, 92 mm	£75-95
602	1976-77	**Armoured Command Car**	Blue-Green or Green body, White star, driver, scanner, 8 plastic wheels, fires sparks	£35-45
801 (371)	1980	**Pocket-size 'USS Enterprise'**	Small version of 358, bubble-packed, released after factory closure	£35-45
802 (372)	1980	**Pocket-size Klingon Cruiser**	Small version of 357, bubble-packed, released after factory closure	£35-45

Dinky Toys 'Action Kits'

These Action Kits were issued in the 1970s. Screws were usually included to attach their bases (which have no model numbers).
Paint supplied with the kit is not always the same colour or shade as on the relative model when supplied built and finished.

1001	1971-77	**Rolls-Royce Phantom V**	Various colours (usually Blue), casting as 152	£20-30
1002	1971-75	**Volvo 1800s Coupé**	Yellow paint, casting as 116	£20-30
1003	1971-75	**Volkswagen 1300**	Red and White paint supplied, casting as 129	£20-30
1004	1971-77	**Ford Escort Police Car**	Blue and White paint with 'POLICE' transfers, casting as model 270	£20-30
1006	1973-77	**Ford Escort Mexico**	Red paint and 'MEXICO' transfers supplied, casting as model 168	£20-30
1007	1971-75	**Jensen FF**	Various colours of paint (usually Blue), casting as 188	£20-30
1008	1973-77	**Mercedes-Benz 600**	Red, Yellow or Green paint supplied, casting as model 128	£20-30
1009	1971-75	**Lotus F1 Racing Car**	Green paint and ``Gold leaf'' transfers supplied, casting as 225	£20-30
1012	1973-75	**Ferrari 312-B2**	Red paint and 'SHELL' transfers supplied, casting as 226	£20-30
1013		**Matra Sports M530**	This item was considered for possible production but was never issued	NPP
1014	1975-77	**Beach Buggy**	Blue paint supplied, casting as 227	£20-30
1017	1971-77	**Routemaster Bus**	Red paint and 'ESSO Safety-Grip Tyres' transfers in kit, casting as 289	£20-30
1018	1974-77	**Leyland Atlantean Bus**	Various (mostly White), usually 'NATIONAL' transfers, as model 295	£30-40
		Leyland Atlantean Bus	'YELLOW PAGES'. There are three variations of this:	
			1) With Mid-Blue interior, reversed front 'Yellow Pages' sign	NGPP
			2) With White interior and reversed front 'Yellow Pages' sign	NGPP
			3) With White interior, correct reading front 'Yellow Pages' sign	NGPP
1023	1972-77	**A.E.C. Single Decker Bus**	Green paint and 'GREEN LINE' transfers supplied, casting as 283	£30-40
1025	1971-75	**Ford Transit Van**	Red paint and 'Avis Truck Rental' transfers supplied, casting as 407	£20-30
1027	1972-77	**Lunar Roving Vehicle**	Blue/White paint, casting as model 355	£20-30
1029	1971-77	**Ford D800 Tipper Truck**	Green or Yellow paint supplied, casting as model 438	£20-30
1030	1974-77	**Land Rover Breakdown Truck**	Red or White paint in kit, casting as 442	£20-30
1032	1975-77	**Army Land Rover**	Military-Green paint and various 'ARMY' transfers in kit, casting as 344	£20-30
1033	1971-77	**U.S.A. Army Jeep**	Military-Green paint and military transfers supplied, casting as 615	£20-30
1034	1975-77	**Mobile Gun**	Military-Green paint in kit, casting as 654	£20-30
1035	1975-77	**Striker Anti-Tank Vehicle**	Military-Green paint and transfer supplied, casting as 691	£20-30
1036	1975-77	**Leopard Tank**	Military-Green paint and transfers supplied, casting as 692	£20-30
1037	1974-77	**Chieftain Tank**	Military-Green paint and transfers, casting as 683	£20-30
1038	1975-77	**Scorpion Tank**	Military-Green paint and transfers, casting as 690	£20-30
1039		**Leopard Recovery Tank**	This item was considered for production but was never issued	NPP
1040	1971-77	**Sea King Helicopter**	White with Blue or Orange paint plus 'USAF' transfers, casting as 724	£20-30
1041	1973-76	**Hawker Hurricane Mk.IIc**	Camouflage paints and RAF roundels in kit, casting as 718	£30-35
1042	1971-77	**Spitfire Mk.II**	Camouflage paints and RAF roundels in kit, casting as 719	£25-35
1043	1974-76	**S.E.P.E.C.A.T. Plane**	Blue and Green paints and transfers supplied, casting as 731	£20-30
1044	1972-75	**Messerschmitt BF-109e**	Brown paint and Luftwaffe transfers in kit, casting as 726	£20-30
1045	1975-76	**Multi-Role Combat Aircraft**	Camouflage paints and transfers supplied, casting as 729	£20-30
1050	1975-77	**Motor Patrol Boat**	Black/Blue/White paints/stickers, as model 675	£20-30

No. 68 'Set of Camouflaged Aeroplanes' and French-made No. 64 'Avions' Set.

Dinky Toys Gift Sets

BOX TYPES

Sets 001-006: Housed in Green card boxes with plain Yellow inserts.
Sets 1, 2, 3, 4, 5, 6:
c 1934   Purple marbled 'Modelled Miniatures' box
c 1936   Blue patterned 'MECCANO DINKY TOYS' box
c 1939   Green box with pictorial insert
Post-war - Green box with plain insert

Sets 24, 25 and 30 series:
c 1934   Purple marbled 'Modelled Miniatures' box.
c 1935   Purple marbled 'MECCANO DINKY TOYS' box with
Yellow/Red label picturing eight assorted cars and lorries.
Purple insert with Gold script on two central lines
'MECCANO DINKY TOYS No '24', '25' or '30'.
NB The 24 Series and 30 series sets also contained a purple packing
card stating 'PLEASE REMOVE THIS PACKING CARD
TO DISPLAY CONTENTS'.

c 1936   Blue patterned box lid with Yellow/Red label picturing eight
assorted cars and lorries. Purple insert with no Gold Script on
25 series (no details available on 24 and 30 series).

Sets 12, 42, 43, 44 and 49 (Pre-war issue):
Blue landscape boxes with inner Blue/Green pictorial inserts.
Sets 151, 152, 156, 161, 162:
Grey/Blue or Blue (152) display boxes with inner pictorial
scenic backdrop and packing boards.

Early Post-war USA Special Sets: Sets for the US market were distributed by
H. Hudson Dobson of New York. They are housed in flat boxes with a mottled
greenish-blue lid. The picture label on the lid depicts a boy's face plus line
drawings of various models. The lid often still retains a red 'H. Hudson Dobson'
label. The Set number and type are shown on the main label, e.g. 'No. 6
Commercial Vehicles'. Sets 1, 2, 3 and 6 are listed – the Editor would welcome
any new information on the contents of these, and of Sets 4 and 5.

Ref.	Year(s)	Set name	Contents	Market Price Range

Pre-war sets without 'fatigue' and with pristine boxes attract a premium, as do early Accessory Sets in 'Modelled Miniatures' boxes.

Ref.	Year(s)	Set name	Contents	Price
001 (1)	1954-56	**Station Staff ('0' gauge)**	(35mm). 1b Guard (flag in right hand), 1c Ticket Collector (right arm extended), 1d Driver, 1e Porter (with oblong bags), 1f Porter (standing).	£90-120
002 (2)	1954-56	**Farmyard Animals (6)**	2 x 2a horses, 2 x 2b cows, 1 x 2c pig, 1 x 2d sheep, simplified painting	£200-300
003 (3)	1954-56	**Passengers ('0' gauge)**	(35mm). 3a Woman (with child on left), 3b Businessman (Brown suit and case), 3c Male hiker (no stick), 3d Female hiker (Blue shirt), 3e Newsboy (Grey tray), 3f Woman (Light Red coat, round case)	£90-120
004 (4)	1946-54	**Engineering Staff ('0' gauge)**	(35mm). 2 x 4b Fitter (all-Blue and all-Brown), 4c Storekeeper (all-Brown), 4d Greaser, 4e Engine-Room attendant	£80-100
005 (5)	1954-56	**Train and Hotel Staff ('0' gauge)**	(35mm). 5a Conductor, 2 x 5b waiters, 2 x 5c Porter (both Brown or Blue).	£90-120
006 (6)	1954-56	**Shepherd Set**	6a Shepherd (Green hat), 6b sheepdog (all-Black), 4 x 2b sheep	£200-300
007	1960-67	**Petrol Pump Attendants**	1 male (White overalls), 1 female (White coat), plastic, 35 mm. tall	£30-40
008	1961-67	**Fire Station Personnel**	Set of 6 fire-fighters in Blue uniforms plus hose, plastic, 35 mm. tall	£30-40
009	1962-66	**Service Station Personnel**	Set of 8 plastic figures in various colours and stances, 35 mm. tall	£30-40
010	1962-66	**Road Maintenance Personnel**	Set of 6 workmen using pick, barrow, shovels, drill etc, plus hut, brazier, barrier, and 4 lamps. Plastic, figures are 35 mm. tall	£60-70
050	1961-68	**Railway Staff ('00' gauge)**	Set of 12 Blue plastic figures	£40-50
051 (1001)	1954-59	**Station Staff ('00' gauge)**	Set of 6 Blue figures (re-issue of pre-war Hornby-Dublo Set D1)	£45-55
052	1961-69	**Railway Passengers ('00')**	Set of 12 plastic figures	£40-50
053 (1003)	1954-59	**Passengers ('00' gauge)**	Set of 6 Blue figures (re-issue of pre-war Hornby-Dublo Set D2)	£45-55
054	1962-70	**Railway Station Personnel**	Set of 12 mostly Blue plastic figures	£40-50
1	1932-39	**Station Staff (6) (large)**	(40mm). 1a Station Master, 1b Guard (flag in left hand), 1c Ticket Collector (with open arms), 1d Driver, 1e Porter (round/oblong bags), 1f Porter (walking). 'HORNBY SERIES' (early issues), 'DINKY TOYS' (later)	£225-275
1	1932-39	**Station Staff (6) (small)**	(35mm). As previous set but smaller figures.	£100-125
1	1939-41	**Station Staff (6)**	(35mm). 1a and 1d as above, 1b Guard (flag in right hand), 1c Ticket Collector (right arm extended), 1e Porter (oblong bags), 1f Porter (standing)	£150-200
1 (001)	1946-54	**Station Staff (5)**	(35mm). 1b Guard (flag in right hand), 1c Ticket Collector (right arm extended), 1d Driver, 1e Porter (with oblong bags), 1f Porter (standing).	£90-120
No.1	1934-39	**Railway Accessories Set**	'Miniature Luggage and Truck'. A Porter's truck and 4 pieces of luggage (tinplate and cast), items not available separately	£100-125
No.1	1946-48	**Commercial Vehicles Set**	29c Bus, 25b Wagon, 25d Tanker, 25e Tipper and 25f Market Gardeners Lorry, in mottled Green, Blue and Fawn box with inner Green card base. Box lid has Light Green and Blue label	£2,500-3,000
No.1 (398)	1952-54	**Farm Gear Gift Set**	27a Massey-Harris Tractor, 27b Harvest Trailer, 27c Manure Spreader, 27h Disc Harrow, 27k Hay Rake. Blue and White striped box	£1,000-1,500
No.1 (699)	1954-55	**Military Vehicles Set**	621 3-ton Wagon, 641 1-ton Truck, 674 Austin Champ, 676 Armoured Car. Blue/White box	£300-400
2	1934-35	**Farmyard Animals**	2 x 2a horses, 2 x 2b cows, 1 x 2c pig, 1 x 2d sheep, in 'Modelled Miniatures' box	£750-1,000
2	1935-40	**Farmyard Animals**	Six items as previous set but displayed in 'Dinky Toys' box.	£500-600
2 (002)	1946-54	**Farmyard Animals**	Six items as previous set but simplified (less detailed) painting.	£200-300
No.2	1934-?	**Railway Accessories Set**	'Milk Cans and Truck'. A 4-wheel barrow and 6 milk churns, not available separately	NGPP
No.2	1946-48	**Private Automobiles Set**	39a Packard, 39b Oldsmobile, 39c Lincoln, 39d Buick, 39e Chrysler. Inner Green card base in Green, Blue and Orange mottled box, Green and Blue lid label	£2,500-3,000
No.2	1952-53	**Commercials Vehicles Set**	25m Bedford End Tipper, 27d Land Rover (Dark Brown), 30n Farm Produce Wagon, 30p 'Mobilgas' Tanker, 30s Austin Covered Wagon	£2,500-3,000
3	1932-39	**Passengers (large)**	(40mm). 3a Woman (with child on right), 3b Businessman (left hand on chest), 3c Male hiker (with stick), 3d Female hiker (White shirt), 3e Newsboy (running), 3f Woman (Red jacket, oblong case) 'HORNBY SERIES' (early issues), 'DINKY TOYS' (later)	£225-275
3	1932-39	**Passengers (small)**	(35mm). As previous set but smaller figures.	£150-175
3	1939-41	**Passengers**	3a Woman (with child on left), 3b Businessman (case in left hand), 3c Male hiker (no stick), 3d Female hiker (White shirt), 3e Newsboy (standing), 3f Woman (Red coat, round case)	£125-175
3 (003)	1946-54	**Passengers**	3a Woman (with child on left), 3b Businessman (Brown suit and case), 3c Male hiker (no stick), 3d Female hiker (with Blue shirt), 3e Newsboy (Grey tray), 3f Woman (Light Red coat, round case)	£90-120

No.3	1934-?	**Railway Accessories Set**	'Platform Machines Etc'. A posting box, ticket machine, label machine and two benches, not available separately	NGPP
No.3	1947-52	**Private Automobiles Set** (i)	30d Vauxhall, 36a Armstrong, 36b Bentley, 38a Frazer-Nash, 39b Oldsmobile. Inner Green card base in Green, Blue and Orange mottled box, Green and Blue lid label	£1,250-1,500
No.3	1947-52	**Private Automobiles Set** (ii)	30d Vauxhall, 36b Bentley, 36d Rover, 38a Fraser Nash, 38c Lagonda. Inner Green card base in Green, Blue and Orange mottled box, Green and Blue lid label	£2,500-3,000
No.3	1952-54	**Passenger Cars Set**	27f Estate Car, 30h Daimler Ambulance, 40e Standard Vanguard, 40g Morris Oxford, 40h Austin Taxi, 140b Rover 75. Blue and White striped box	£3,000-4,000
4	1932-41	**Engineering Staff (6) (large)**	(40mm). 4a Electrician, 2 x 4b Fitter (Blue/White and Brown/White), 4c Storekeeper (Brown/Black), 4d Greaser, 4e Engine-Room attendant 'HORNBY SERIES' (early issues), 'DINKY TOYS' (later)	£200-250
4	1932-41	**Engineering Staff (6) (small)**	As previous set but smaller figures	£150-175
4 (004)	1946-54	**Engineering Staff (5)**	2 x 4b Fitter (all-Blue and all-Brown), 4c Storekeeper (all-Brown), 4d Greaser, 4e Engine-Room attendant	£125-175
No.4	1934-?	**Railway Accessories Set**	A combination of No.1 ('Miniature Luggage & Truck'), No.2 ('Milk Cans & Truck'), and No.3 ('Platform Machines Etc'). Individual items were not available separately	NGPP
No.4 (249)	1953-54	**Racing Cars Set**	23f Alfa-Romeo, 23g Cooper-Bristol, 23h Ferrari, 23j HWM, 23k Talbot-Lago and 23n Maserati. Blue and White striped box	£750-1,000
5	1932-39	**Train and Hotel Staff (large)**	(40mm). 5a Conductor, 2 x 5b waiters, 2 x 5c Porter (1 Red, 1 Green), 'HORNBY SERIES' (early issues), 'DINKY TOYS' (later)	£300-350
		NB	Also sold in USA - boxes often display 'H. Hudson Dobson' label.	
5	1932-39	**Train and Hotel Staff (small)**	As previous set but smaller figures	£150-175
5	1939-41	**Train and Hotel Staff**	5a Conductor, 2 x 5b waiters, 2 x 5c Porter (both Brown or Blue)	£125-175
5 (005)	1946-54	**Train and Hotel Staff**	5a Conductor, 2 x 5b Waiter, 2 x 5c Porter (Brown or Blue) less detail	£90-120
5	c1950	**Military Vehicles Set**	153a (672) US Army Jeep, 161b (690) Mobile AA Gun, 151a Medium Tank, 151b (620) Transport Wagon, and 152b (671) Reconnaisance Car. Inner Green card base and card cut-out packing piece, in Green box. Blue, Light Green and Red mottled lid has applied Purple and Yellow label	£2,250-2,500
6	1934-36	**Shepherd Set**	6a Shepherd (Dark Brown smock, hat and leggings, Black boots, lamb under arm), 6b Collie dog (Black/White), 4 x 2b sheep (Beige, 'Hornby Series' cast-in), set presented in 'Modelled Miniatures' box	£500-750
6	1936-40	**Shepherd Set**	As previous set but in 'Dinky Toys' box	£250-350
6 (006)	1946-54	**Shepherd Set**	6a Shepherd (all Brown below neck, Green hat), 6b Collie dog (all Black), 4 x 2b sheep (without 'Hornby Series')	£150-200
No.6	1946-48	**Commercial Vehicles Set**	29c Bus, 29b Streamline Bus, 25h Fire Engine, 30e Breakdown Car, and 30f Ambulance. Mottled Greenish-Blue box with Beige/Blue label	£2,000-2,500
12	1938-40	**Postal Set**	12a GPO Pillar Box, 12b Air Mail Pillar Box, 12c Telephone Call Box, 12d Telegraph Messenger, 12e Postman, 34b Royal Mail Van	£500-750
15	1937-41	**Railway Signals Set**	1 x 15a 'Home' and 1 x 15a 'Distant' (single-arm signals), 2 x 15b 'Home/Distant' (double-arm signals), 1 x 15c 'Home' and 1 x 15c 'Distant' (double-arm signals)	£150-175
16	1936-37	**Silver Jubilee Train Set**	Locomotive and two interlocking coaches, 'LNER' and '2590' cast-in, open windows, smooth hubs with White tyres, special box, 300 mm.	
			1: Silver loco / coaches, Grey, Mid-Blue, Dark Blue, Red or Orange trim	£200-250
			2: Silver loco and coaches with Dark Blue trim	£200-250
			3: Cream loco and coaches with Red trim	£250-275
			4: Blue loco and coaches with Dark Blue trim	£250-275
			5: Green loco and coaches with Dark Green trim	£250-275
16	1937-40	**Streamlined Train Set**	As previous models but with a change of name and box	£200-250
16	1946-52	**Streamlined Train Set**	Blue/Black loco, 'LNER', Brown/Grey coaches, solid windows, Black tyres	£125-150
16 (798)	1952-54	**Streamlined Train Set**	As previous model but with 'BR' crest on tender	£125-145
17	1935-40	**Passenger Train Set**	Black/Maroon loco 17a, Maroon tender 17b, Maroon/Cream coaches 20a/20b	£300-400
			Black/Green loco 17a, Green tender 17b, two Green/Cream coaches 20a/20b	£300-400
			Lead and Mazak set in 2nd type box with correct colour spot	£400-500
18	1935-40	**Tank Goods Train Set**	Green/Black loco (21a) and 3 Green/Black open wagons (21b)	£300-400
19	1935-40	**Mixed Goods Train**	Maroon/Black loco (21a), Green/Red open wagon (21b), Red/Blue 'SHELL' tanker wagon (21d), Yellow/Red/Green lumber wagon (21e)	£400-500
		rare box version:	Set in 3rd type pictorial landscape box	£800-1,000
20	1935-40	**Tank Passenger Set**	Green/Black loco (21a), 2 Brown/Green coaches (20a), Guard's van (20b)	£300-400
21	1933-35	**Modelled Miniatures Train Set**	Blue/Red loco (21a), Green open wagon (21b), Green/Blue crane wagon (21c), Red/Blue 'SHELL' tank wagon (21d), Yellow/Red/Green lumber wagon (21e)	£500-600
22	1933-35	**Motor Vehicles Set**	22a and 22b Cars, 22c Motor Truck, 22d Delivery Van, 22e Tractor, 22f Tank, with 'Hornby Series' or 'Dinky Toys' cast-in. 'Modelled Miniatures' box, Purple lid, full-size full-colour label	£2,000-2,500
23	1936-40	**Racing Cars Set**	23c Mercedes-Benz, 23d Auto-Union, 23e 'Speed of the Wind'. Blue box	£500-600
24	1934-40	**Motor Cars Set** 1st issue:	24a Ambulance, 24b Limousine, 24c Town Sedan, 24d Vogue Saloon, 24e Super Streamlined Saloon, 24f Sportsman's Coupé, 24g Sports Tourer (2 seater), 24h Sports Tourer (4 seater). Purple and Gold marbled box, lid has colour top label and Yellow/Red end label with code 'DT24'	£6,000-8,000
		later issue:	Blue box lid (with colour label), Purple inner (A2205)	£5,000-6,000
25	1934-37	**Commercial Motor Vehicles**	25a Wagon, 25b Covered Wagon, 25c Flat Truck, 25d Tank Wagon, 25e Tipper, 25f Market Gardener's Lorry. Mauve 'grained' box lid (colour label) (A1052)	£2,000-2,500
		revised set:	Contains 25b, d, e, f, g and h	£1,700-1,900

28/1	1934-40	**Delivery Vans Set in Trade Box**	(1st type) 28a Hornby, 28b Pickfords, 28c Manchester Guardian, 28d Oxo, 28e Ensign Lukos, 28f Palethorpes Sausages (A1008)	**£6,000-8,000**
28/1		revised set:	28a Hornby, 28b Pickfords, 28c Manchester Guardian, 28e Firestone, 28f Palethorpes, 28n Atco Mowers	**£6,000-8,000**
28/2	1934-40	**Delivery Vans Set in Trade Box**	(1st type) 28g Kodak, 28h Sharps Toffees, 28k Marsh's, 28L Crawfords Biscuits, 28m Wakefield Castrol, 28n Meccano (A1008)	**£6,000-8,000**
28/2		revised set:	28d Oxo, 28g Kodak, 28h Dunlop Tyres, 28k Marsh's, 28m Wakefield Castrol, 28h Crawfords	**£6,000-8,000**
28/3	1936-40	**Delivery Vans Set in Trade Box**	(2nd type) 28r Swan Pens, 28s Frys Chocolate, 28t Ovaltine, 28w Osram Lamps, 28x Hovis, 28y Exide Batteries	**£3,000-5,000**
30	1935-37	**Motor Vehicles**	30a Chrysler 'Airflow', 30b Rolls-Royce, 30c Daimler, 30d Vauxhall, 30e Breakdown Car (22c 2nd casting), 30f Ambulance	**£3,000-4,000**
30	1937-41	**Motor Vehicles**	As previous set but 30g Caravan replaces 30f Ambulance	**£2,500-3,500**
33/1	1935-37	**Mechanical Horse and Five Assorted Trailers**	33a Mechanical Horse, 33b Flat Truck, 33c Open Wagon, 33d Box Van, 33e Dust Wagon, 33f Petrol Tank with 'WAKEFIELD CASTROL' logo. Blue 'grained' box lid, large colour label	**£750-1,000**
33/2	1935-37	**Mechanical Horse and Four Assorted Trailers**	with 33a, 33b, 33c and 33e in Green box (A2036). (Rarer than 5 trailer set 33/1). In Green display box with Yellow inner tray, Box code A2036	**£600-800**
35	1935-40	**Small Cars Set**	35a Saloon Car, 35b Racer and 35c MG Sports Car. In display type box (A2222) with tuck in flap and scenic backdrop	**£500-600**
36	1936-40	**Motor Cars with Drivers, Passengers and Footmen**	36a Armstrong-Siddeley, 36b Bentley, 36c Humber, 36d Rover, 36e British Salmson 2-seater, 36f British Salmson 4-seater, all with figures. Set housed in Blue landscape box with Yellow tray with Purple inner and Brown board top packing piece. Box code A2205, dated 6-38	**£5,000-7,500**
37a	1937-40	**Motor Cycles Set**	Six of 37a civilian Motor Cyclists in various colours, hand-painted detail, solid White rubber tyres. Blue box with Green and White pictorial inner	**£400-600**
37	1938-40	**Motor Cycles Set**	Contains 37a (civilian), 37b (Police), 37c (Signals Despatch)	**£400-600**
39	1939-41	**USA Saloon Cars Set**	39a Packard, 39b Oldsmobile, 39c Lincoln, 39d Buick, 39e Chrysler, 39f Studebaker. Mauve box with full colour label on lid	**£1,250-1,750**
42	1935-40	**Police Set**	42a Police Box, 42b Motor Cycle Patrol, 42c Point-Duty Policeman (White coat), 42d Point-Duty Policeman (Blue uniform), in Blue box with pictorial inner (A2114)	**£300-400**
43	1935-40	**'R.A.C.' Set**	43a RAC Box, 43b RAC Motor Cycle Patrol, 43c RAC Guide directing traffic, 43d RAC Guide saluting. Blue box, pictorial inner part, (A2064)	**£400-600**
44	1935-40	**'A.A.' Set**	44a AA Box, 44b AA Motor Cycle Patrol, 44c AA Guide directing traffic, 44d AA Guide saluting. Blue box, pictorial inner part, (2065)	**£400-600**
46	1937-40	**Pavement Set**	Dark Grey 'stone' effect (cardboard) pavement pieces in a box	**£100-150**
47	1935-40	**Road Signs Set**	12 road signs, 47e to 47t, (White under base, triangles usually filled-in) Yellow box and inner, box code A2073	**£175-225**
47 (770)	1946-50	**Road Signs Set**	12 road signs, 47e to 47t, (Black under base, open triangles)	**£90-120**
49	1935-40	**Petrol Pumps Set**	'Pratts': 49a, 49b, 49c, 49d, 49e. White rubber hoses, Blue box	**£150-200**
49 (780)	1946-50	**Petrol Pumps Set**	plain: 49a, 49b, 49c, 49d, 49e. Yellow plastic hoses, Yellow box	**£90-110**
			'Pratts': 49, 49b, 49c, 49d, 49e. White rubber hoses, Yellow box	**£150-200**
			plain: 49, 49b, 49c, 49d, 49e. White plastic hoses, Yellow box	**£100-140**
50	1934-42	**Ships of the British Navy**	50a 'Hood', 50b 'Nelson', 50b 'Rodney', 50c 'Effingham', 50d 'York', 50e 'Delhi', 3 x 50f 'Broke', 50g 'X'-class Submarine, 3 x 50h 'Amazon', 50k 'K'-class Submarine. Blue box with Green/Blue label on lid	**£200-300**
51	1934-40	**Great Liners Set**	51b 'Europa', 51c 'Rex', 51d 'Empress of Britain', 51e 'Strathaird', 51f 'Queen of Bermuda', 51g 'Britannic'	**£200-250**
60	1934-35	**Aeroplanes Set**	1st issue: 60a Imperial Airways, 60b Leopard Moth, 60c Percival Gull, 60d Low-Wing Monoplane, 60e General Monospar, 60f Autogiro, no registration letters. Dark Blue box with Green, Blue and White 'Atlanta' airliner on lid label, Yellow/Green side label dated '5-34'	**£1,200-1,500**
60	1936-41	**British Aeroplanes Set**	2nd issue: 60a Imperial Airways, 60b Leopard Moth, 60c Percival Gull, 60d Low-Wing Monoplane, 60e General Monospar, 60f Autogiro. All the planes in this set (except 60f) have 'GA-' markings	**£1,000-1,250**
		Box Type i)	Blue box with multicoloured label plus '150 varieties' slogan	
		Box Types ii) and iii)	Same as previous but with '200' or '300 varieties' slogans	
60p	1938-40	**Gloster Gladiator Set**	Six planes in Silver livery with RAF roundels	**£400-600**
60s	1938-40	**'Medium Bomber' Set**	Two renumbered 62n Fairey 'Battle' Bombers in Stone-colour box	**£150-200**
60z	1937-40	**'Avions' Set**	French Aeroplanes Set with 60az 'Arc-en-Ciel', Potez 58, Hanriot 180t, 61az DeWetoine 500, Breguet Corsair, 60f Cierva Autogiro. Blue box	**£900-1,200**
61	1937-41	**R.A.F. Aeroplanes Set**	60h 'Singapore' Flying Boat, 2 x 60n Fairey 'Battle' Bombers, 2 x 60p Gloster 'Gladiator' Biplanes. Contained in Blue box with full colour label on lid	**£500-700**
61z	1937-40	**'Avions' Set**	French Aeroplanes Set with DeWoitine D338, Potez 56, Potez 58, 61az DeWetoine 500d, Farman F360, 60f Cierva Autogiro. Blue box	**£900-1,200**
62h	1939	**Hawker Hurricane Set**	Six planes, camouflaged tops, Black undersides, mounted on card base with 'DINKY TOYS No.62h HAWKER HURRICANE SINGLE SEATER FIGHTER'. Green box dated 7-39	**£400-600**
62d	1939	**Bristol Blenheim Bomber Set**	Six planes, camouflaged, mounted on card base with 'BRISTOL BLENHEIM BOMBER MARK IV - DINKY TOYS 62d'. Green box	**£400-600**
62s	19??-??	**Hurricane Fighters Set**	Six Fighters, Silver fuselages, RAF roundels, undercarriages, Blue box	**£300-400**

No.	Years	Name	Contents	Price
64	1939-41	**Aeroplane Set**	60g Light Racer, 62h 'Hurricane' (Camouflaged), 62k 'Kings Aeroplane', 62m Light Transport, 62s 'Hurricane' (Silver), 63b Seaplane 'Mercury'. (In 1940 either 62a 'Spitfire' or 62s were substituted for 62h and 62s)	£750-1,000
64z	193?-4?	**'Avions' Set**	French Aeroplanes Set with 61az Dewoitine 'F-ADBF', 64a Amiot 370, 64b Bloch 220 'F-AOHJ', 64c Potez 63, 64d Potez 662 'F-ARAY'. Blue box, Yellow inner	£2,000-2,500
65	1939-41	**Aeroplane Set**	60r Flying Boat, 60t 'DC3', 60v 'Whitely' Bomber, 60w 'Clipper III', 62n Junkers, 62p 'Ensign', 62r 'Albatross', 62w 'Frobisher'. Blue box, illustrated leaflet enclosed	£1,750-2,000
66	1940-41	**Camouflaged Aeroplanes Set**	66a Heavy Bomber, 66b Dive Bomber Fighter, 66c Fighter, 66d Torpedo, 66e Medium Bomber, 66f Army Autogiro (Silver). Yellow-Brown box	£2,000-3,000
68	1940-41	**Camouflaged Aeroplanes Set**	2 x 60s 'Battle' Bombers, 2 x 62d 'Blenheim', 3 x 62h 'Hurricane' (Camouflage), 3 x 62s 'Hurricane' (Silver), 62t 'Whitely', 68a 'Ensign', 68b 'Frobisher'. Blue or Yellow box, light or dark camouflage	£2,500-3,500
	19?-?	US issue	Camouflaged version of 60s, 62d, 62e, 62h, 62t, 68a and 68b. Box picture shows civilian aircraft. Red box label states 'Sold by Meccano Company of America Inc., 200 5th Avenue, New York'	NGPP
101	1936-40	**Dining-Room Furniture**	101a Table, 101b Sideboard, 2 x 101c Carver Chair, 4 x 101d Chair	£250-350
102	1936-40	**Bedroom Furniture**	102a Bed, 102b Wardrobe, 102c Dressing Table, 102d Dressing Chest, 102e Dressing Table Stool, 102f Chair. Brown or Pink. Green box	£250-350
103	1936-40	**Kitchen Furniture**	103a Refrigerator, 103b Kitchen Cabinet, 103c Electric Cooker, 103d Table, 103e Chair. Light Blue/White or Light Green/Cream	£250-350
104	1936-40	**Bathroom Furniture**	104a Bath, 104b Bath Mat, 104c Pedestal Basin, 104d Stool, 104e Linen Basket, 104f Toilet. Brown or Pink	£250-350
118	1965-69	**Towaway Glider Set**	135 Triumph 2000 (Cream/Blue), Cream/Red trailer, Yellow glider	£150-200
121	1963-66	**Goodwood Racing Set**	112 Austin-Healey Sprite, 113 MGB, 120 Jaguar, 182 Porsche, 9 figures	£1,000-1,250
122	1963-65	**Touring Gift Set**	188 Caravan, 193 Station Wagon, 270 'AA' Patrol, 295 Atlas Kenebrake, 796 Healey Sports Boat on Trailer	£750-1,000
123	1963-65	**Mayfair Gift Set**	142 Jaguar, 150 Rolls-Royce, 186 Mercedes-Benz, 194 Bentley, 198 Rolls-Royce, 199 Austin Mini Countryman, and 4 figures	£1,500-2,000
124	1964-66	**Holiday Gift Set**	952 Vega Luxury Coach, 137 Plymouth, 142 Jaguar, 796 Healey Sports Boat	£500-600
125	1964-66	**Fun Ahoy! Set**	130 Ford Corsair with driver, 796 Healey Sports Boat with pilot	£200-250
126	1967-68	**Motor Show Set**	127 Rolls-Royce, 133 Cortina, 151 Vauxhall Victor, 171 Austin 1800	£1,000-1,250
126	1968-69	**Motor Show Set**	127 Rolls-Royce, 159 Cortina, 151 Vauxhall Victor, 171 Austin 1800	£1,000-1,250
149	1958-61	**Sports Cars Set**	107 Sunbeam Alpine, 108 MG Midget, 109 Austin-Healey, 110 Aston-Martin, 111 Triumph TR2, all in 'competition finish'. Blue/White striped box	£1,000-1,200
150	1937-41	**Royal Tank Corps Personnel**	150a Officer, 2 x 150b Private, 2 x 150c Private, 150e N.C.O. Grey/Blue box with Yellow inner, code A2187	£200-300
	1946-50	**U.S. Export only Set**	Post-war issue of pre-war figures in original Green box with 'H. Hudson Dobson' label	£200-300
151	1937-41	**Medium Tank Set**	151a Tank, 151b 6-wheel Wagon, 151c Cooker Trailer, 151d Water Tank Trailer, 150d Royal Tank Corps Driver. Blue box with pictorial inner	£250-350
152	1937-41	**Light Tank Set**	152a Tank, 152b Reconnaissance Car, 152c Austin 7 Car with 150d Royal Tank Corps Driver. Blue box with pictorial inner	£250-350
156	1939-41	**Mechanised Army Set**	151a Tank, 151b 6-wheel Wagon, 151c Cooker Trailer, 151d Water Tank Trailer, 152a Tank, 152b Reconnaissance Car, 152c Austin 7 Car with 150d Royal Tank Corps Driver, 161a Lorry with Searchlight, 161b AA Gun on Trailer, 162a Light Dragon Tractor, 162b Ammunition Trailer, and 162c 18-ponder Gun. Grey-Blue box with code '11-39' and four packing pieces	£1,750-2,250
160 (606)	1939-53	**Royal Artillery Personnel**	160a N.C.O., 2 x 160b Gunner, 160c Gunlayer, 2 x 160d Gunner (standing). Grey-Blue box (code: A2308) dated 11-39, Yellow box (code: A2303) and inner box dated 12-39. Production of this set continued post-war but only for export (to USA)	£150-200
161	1939-41	**Mobile Anti-Aircraft Unit**	161a Lorry with Searchlight and 161b A.A. Gun on Trailer, in Blue box	£400-500
162	1939-54	**18-pounder Field Gun Unit**	162a Light Dragon Tractor, 162b Trailer, 162c Gun. Blue box	£150-200
201	1965-68	**Racing Cars Set**	240 Cooper, 241 Lotus, 242 Ferrari, 243 B.R.M.	£300-400
237	1978-79	**Dinky Way Set**	Contains: 178 Mini Clubman, 211 Triumph TR7, 382 Convoy Truck, 412 Bedford 'AA' Van. **N.B.** Export only version of Set 240.	£80-100
240	1978-80	**Dinky Way Set**	211 Triumph TR7, 255 Police Mini, 382 Dump Truck, 412 Bedford Van, 20ft of 'roadway', 20 road signs, decal sheet	£60-80
245	1969-73	**Superfast Gift Set**	131 Jaguar 'E'-type, 153 Aston-Martin DB6, 188 Jensen FF	£100-125
246	1969-73	**International Gift Set**	187 De Tomaso Mangusta, 215 Ford GT, 216 Ferrari Dino	£100-125
249	1962-63	**World Famous Racing Cars**	230 Talbot-Lago, 231 Maserati, 232 Alfa-Romeo, 233 Cooper-Bristol, 234 Ferrari, 239 Vanwall. Bubble-packed onto large display card	£1,000-1,500
249 (4)	1955-58	**Racing Cars Set**	Contains 231, 232, 233, 234, 235	£700-900
294	1973-77	**Police Vehicles Gift Set**	250 Mini-Cooper, 254 Range-Rover, 287 Accident Unit. (Replaces Set 297)	£100-125
297	1963-73	**Police Vehicles Gift Set**	250 Mini-Cooper, 255 Ford Zodiac, 287 Accident Unit. (Replaced by Set 294)	£150-175
298	1963-66	**Emergency Services Set**	258 Ford Fairlane, 263 Ambulance, 276 Fire Tender, 277 Ambulance, with Ambulance-man, Ambulance-woman and Policeman	£600-800
299	1957-59	**Post Office Services**	260 'Royal Mail' Morris Van, 261 'GPO Telephones' Van, 750 Call Box, 011 Messenger, 012 Postman (but no Pillar Box!). Blue and White striped box	£350-450
299	1963-66	**Motorway Services Set**	434 Bedford Crash Truck, 269 Motorway Police Car, 257 Fire Chief's Car, 276 Airport Fire Tender, 263 (later 277) Criterion Ambulance	£800-1,100
299	1978-79	**'Crash Squad' Action Set**	244 Plymouth Police Car and 732 Bell Helicopter	£45-55
300	1973-77	**London Scene Set**	Contains 289 Routemaster Bus 'ESSO' and 284 London Taxi	£65-75
302	1979-?	**Emergency Squad Gift Pack**	Paramedic Truck and Plymouth Fire Chief Car plus figures of Gage and DeSoto. Not issued	NPP
303	1978-80	**Commando Squad Gift Set**	687 Convoy Army Truck, 667 Armoured Car, 732 Army helicopter	£75-100
304	1978-79	**Fire Rescue Gift Set**	195 Fire Chief Range Rover, 282 Land Rover, 384 Convoy Fire Truck	£70-90
306	1979-?	**'Space' Gift Pack**	358 'USS Enterprise', 357 Klingon Battle Cruiser, plus Galactic War Chariot. Not issued	NPP
307	1979-?	**'New Avengers' Gift Pack**	Purdey's TR7, John Steed's Special Leyland Jaguar, plus a 'fly-off' assailant!. Not issued	NPP
309	1978-80	**Star Trek Gift Set**	357 Klingon Battle Cruiser and 358 'USS Enterprise'	£80-100
398 (No.1)	1954-64	**Farm Equipment Gift Set**	300 Massey-Harris Tractor, 320 Harvest Trailer, 321 Manure Spreader, 322 Disc Harrow, 324 Hay Rake. Grey box with Red and Yellow overprinting	£900-1,200

399	1969-73	Farm Tractor and Trailer	300 Massey-Harris Tractor and 428 Large Trailer (Red/Silver)	£120-140
399	1977-79	'Convoy' Gift Set	380 Skip Truck, 381 Farm Truck, 382 Dumper Truck. 'Window' box	£35-45
606 (160)	1954-55	Royal Artillery Personnel	1 x 160a, 2 x 160b, 1 x 160c, 2 x 160d. Export only (to USA)	£150-200
616	1976-78	AEC Transporter and Tank	Militarised version of 974 with 683 Chieftain Tank and camouflage net	£65-80
618	1976-79	Transporter and Helicopter	Militarised versions of 974 and 724 with camouflage netting	£70-80
619	1976-78	Bren-Gun Carrier Set	622 Bren-Gun Carrier and 625 6-pounder Anti-Tank Gun	£35-45
677	1972-75	Task Force Set	680 Ferret Armoured Car, 681 D.U.K.W., 682 Stalwart Load Carrier	£35-45
695	1962-66	Howitzer and Tractor	689 Medium Artillery Tractor and 693 7.2in. Howitzer	£250-350
697	1957-71	Field Gun Set	688 Field Artillery Tractor, 687 Trailer, 686 25-pounder Field Gun	£80-100
698	1957-65	Tank Transporter Set	660 Mighty Antar Tank Transporter and 651 Centurion Tank	£120-150
699 (No.1)	1955-58	Military Vehicles Set	621 3-ton Wagon, 641 1-ton Truck, 674 Austin Champ, 676 Armoured Car. Striped box with inner lining and stand	£250-350
754	1958-62	Pavement Set	Twenty various Grey cardboard pieces representing paving	£30-40
766	1959-64	British Road Signs	Country Set 'A'. Six signs of the times, mostly 55 mm high. Yellow box	£55-65
767	1959-64	British Road Signs	Country Set 'B'. Six signs of the times, mostly 55 mm high. Yellow box	£55-65
768	1959-64	British Road Signs	Town Set 'A'. Six signs of the times, mostly 55 mm high. Yellow box	£55-65
769	1959-64	British Road Signs	Town Set 'B'. Six signs of the times, mostly 55 mm high. Yellow box	£55-65
770 (47)	1950-54	Road Signs Set	12 road signs, 47e to 47t, (Black under base, open triangles) US export only	£125-175
771	1953-65	International Road Signs	Set of 12 various road signs with Silver posts and bases, in Yellow box	£100-125
772	1959-63	British Road Signs	(Sets 766, 767, 768 and 769). 24 various road signs in a Red/Yellow box	£150-200
780 (49)	1950-54	Petrol Pumps Set	49a, 49b, 49c, 49d, 49e (plain). Yellow plastic hoses, export only	£90-110
			Version issued in picture box	£100-150
784	1972-74	Dinky Goods Train Set	Blue loco 'GER', one Red Truck, one Yellow Truck	£30-40
798 (16)	1954-59	Express Passenger Train Set	Green/Black loco, 'BR' crest, Cream coaches (Grey roofs), Black tyres	£100-125
			Green/Black loco, 'BR' crest, Cream coaches/roofs/hubs, Black tyres	£100-125
			Green/Black loco, 'BR', Cream coaches/roofs, Red hubs, White tyres	£100-125
851	1961-	Sets of vehicle 'Loads'	2 each of 846 Oil Drums, 847 Barrels, 849 Packing Cases and 850 Crates	£30-40
900	1964-70	'Building Site' Gift Set	437 Muir-Hill Loader, 960 Albion Concrete Mixer, 961 Blaw-Knox Bulldozer, 962 Muir-Hill Dumper, 965 Euclid Rear Dump Truck. Grey/Red/Yellow box	£700-900
950	1969-70	Car Transporter Set	974 AEC Car Transporter with 136 Vauxhall Viva, 138 Hillman Imp, 162 Triumph 1300, 168 Ford Escort, 342 Austin Mini-Moke. Not issued	NPP
957	1959-65	Fire Services Gift Set	257 Fire Chief's Car, 955 Fire Engine, 956 Turntable Fire Escape	£350-450
990	1956-58	Car Transporter Set	Contains 982 Pullmore Car Transporter and these cars: 154 Hillman Minx (Light Green/Cream), 156 Rover 75 (Cream/Blue), 161 Austin Somerset (Red/Yellow), 162 Ford Zephyr (Green/White)	£750-950
1001 (051)	1952-54	Station Staff ('00' gauge)	Set of 6 figures (re-issue of pre-war Hornby-Dublo Set D1)	£45-55
1003 (053)	1952-54	Passengers ('00' gauge)	Set of 6 Blue figures (re-issue of pre-war Hornby-Dublo Set D2)	£45-55
49N2269	1965	Road Racers Set	Contains: 113 MGB, 114 Triumph Spitfire, 120 Jaguar E-type, 237 Mercedes-Benz, 238 Jaguar D-type, 242 Ferrari Racing Car, 243 BRM Racing Car. Special set for US Mail-order company Sears-Roebuck	NGPP

This Dinky Toys No. 299 Post Office Services Set was produced between 1957 and 1959.

See also: Public Transport Models, Ships, Motor Cycles and Gift Sets sections.
Approximate size of figures: large 40mm; small 35mm.

Ref.	Year(s)	Accessory	Details	Market Price Range
1a	1932-41	**Station Master (large)**	Dark Blue uniform with Gold or Silver buttons on long coat	£30-35
1a	1932-41	**Station Master (small)**	As previous version but smaller	£20-25
1b	1932-39	**Guard (large)**	Dark Blue coat (Gold or Silver buttons), blowing whistle, flag in left hand	£30-35
1b	1932-39	**Guard (small)**	As previous version but smaller	£20-25
1b	1939-41	**Guard (large)**	Dark Blue coat (Gold or Silver buttons), blowing whistle, flag in right hand	£30-35
1b	1939-41	**Guard (small)**	As previous version but smaller	£20-25
1c	1932-41	**Ticket Collector (large)**	Dark Blue uniform (Gold or Silver buttons), slightly open arms	£30-35
1c	1932-41	**Ticket Collector (large)**	As previous model but with only right arm extended	£30-35
1c	1932-41	**Ticket Collector (small)**	As previous version but smaller	£20-25
1d	1932-39	**Driver (large)**	Mid-Blue uniform (Gold or Silver buttons), holding oil-can	£30-35
1d	1932-39	**Driver (small)**	As previous version but smaller	£20-25
1e	1932-39	**Porter with Bags (large)**	Dark Blue uniform, oblong case in right hand, round hat-box in left	£30-35
1e	1939-41	**Porter with Bags (small)**	Dark Blue, oblong case in each hand. (Smaller than previous model)	£20-25
1f	1932-39	**Porter (large)**	Dark Blue uniform, walking, no luggage.	£30-35
1f	1939-41	**Porter (small)**	Dark Blue, standing, no luggage. (Smaller than previous model)	£20-25
2a	1932-41	**Horses**	One Light Brown or Dark Brown horse, one White horse	£20-30
2b	1932-41	**Cow**	3 versions were available; Light Brown, Dark Brown, or Black and White	£20-25
2c	1932-41	**Pig**	A Pink porker	£15-20
2d	1932-41	**Sheep**	White sheep with Black hand-painted detail	£15-20
3a	1932-39	**Woman and Child (large)**	Woman in Green coat, child (in Red) is on woman's right	£30-35
3a	1939-41	**Woman and Child (small)**	Woman in Green suit with Grey scarf and Red hat, child on woman's left	£20-25

A pre-war illustrated list of Dinky Toys Accessories and other models.

3b	1932-39	**Business Man (large)**	Dark Blue suit/hat, walking stick in right hand, left hand holds lapels	£30-35
3b	1939-41	**Business Man (small)**	Grey suit, left hand holds attach case	£20-25
3c	1932-39	**Male Hiker (large)**	Brown clothing, Khaki rucksack, walking stick in right hand	£30-35
3c	1939-41	**Male Hiker (small)**	Brown clothing, Khaki rucksack, no walking stick	£20-25
3d	1932-41	**Female Hiker (large)**	Blue skirt, White blouse, walking stick in right hand	£30-35
3d	1932-41	**Female Hiker (small)**	All Blue clothing, or Dark Blue skirt, White blouse	£20-25
3e	1932-41	**Newsboy (large)**	Brown or Blue clothing, running, papers in right hand and under left arm	£30-35
3e	1939-41	**Newsboy (small)**	Dark Blue clothing, standing, papers in Cream tray	£20-25
3f	1932-39	**Woman**	Red jacket, White skirt, coat over left arm, oblong case in right hand	£25-30
3f	1939-41	**Woman**	Dark Red coat, Black collar, coat over left arm, round case in right hand	£25-30
4a	1932-41	**Electrician (large)**	Blue overalls, White sleeves, carrying equipment	£30-35
4a	1932-41	**Electrician (small)**	Blue overalls, White sleeves, carrying equipment	£20-25
4b	1932-41	**Fitter (large)**	All-Blue overalls, or Brown overalls /White sleeves, carrying equipment	£30-35
4b	1932-41	**Fitter (small)**	As previous model but smaller	£20-25
4c	1932-41	**Storekeeper (large)**	Brown coat, Black trousers, holding forms in right hand, casting as 1a	£30-35
4c	1932-41	**Storekeeper (small)**	Brown coat, Black trousers, holding forms in right hand, casting as 1a	£20-25
4d	1932-41	**Greaser (large)**	Brown overalls, holding oil-can in right hand, casting based on 1d	£30-35
4d	1932-41	**Greaser (small)**	Brown overalls, holding oil-can in right hand, casting based on 1d	£20-25
4e	1932-41	**Engine-Room Attendant**	(large), Blue overalls, with or without White sleeves	£30-35
4e	1932-41	**Engine-Room Attendant**	(small), Blue overalls, with or without White sleeves	£20-25
5a	1932-41	**Pullman Car Conductor**	(large), White jacket, Blue trousers, slightly open arms, casting as 1c	£30-35
5a	1932-41	**Pullman Car Conductor**	(small), White jacket, Blue trousers, slightly open arms, casting as 1c	£20-25
5b	1932-41	**Pullman Car Waiter (large)**	White jacket, Blue trousers, two slightly different poses were available	£30-35
5b	1932-41	**Pullman Car Waiter (small)**	White jacket, Blue trousers, two slightly different poses were available	£20-25
5c	1932-41	**Hotel Porter (large)**	Red jacket/Brown trousers, or Green jacket/Blue trousers, casting as 1e	£30-35
5c	1932-41	**Hotel Porter (small)**	Red jacket/Brown trousers, or Green jacket/Blue trousers, casting as 1e	£20-25
6a	1932-41	**Shepherd**	Brown with Dark Brown hat	£50-75
6b	1932-41	**Sheep-dog**	Black and White sheep-dog	£20-30
12a	1935-40	**GPO Pillar Box 'GR'**	Red, with or without Red/Yellow 'Post Office' sign on top, White panel	£25-30
12b	1935-40	**Air Mail Pillar Box**	Blue body, 'Air Mail', White panel, casting as 12a, 50 mm	£35-40
12c	1936-40	**Telephone Box**	Cream with Silver windows, 58 mm	£20-30
12d	1938-40	**Telegraph Messenger**	Dark Blue body, picked out detail in darker Blue, Brown pouch, 35 mm	£20-25
12e	1938-40	**Postman**	Dark Blue body, darker Blue detail, Brown post bag and badge, 35 mm	£20-25
13	1931-40	**'HALLS DISTEMPER'**	Figures (lead) usually White, Cream (cardboard) panel, Red lettering	£250-300
15a	1937-41	**Single Arm Signal**	One Red 'Home' signal, or Yellow 'Distant' signal, 65 mm high	£30-40
15b	1937-41	**Double Arm Signal**	One Red 'Home' signal and one Yellow 'Distant' signal on single pole	£40-50
15c	1937-41	**Junction Signal**	Two Red 'Home' signals, OR two Yellow 'Distant' signals on single pole	£65-75
30g	1936-39	**Caravan Trailer**	2 wheels, drawbar, body length 81 mm. open roof windows, Blue/Cream, Red/Cream, Green/Cream, Orange/Cream, Two tone-Green	£90-120
			Chocolate and Beige, Blue hubs	£150-175
30g	1939-40		As previous models but with filled-in roof windows	£80-110
42a	1936-40	**Police Box**	Dark Blue box, 'POLICE' in Silver, 66 mm high	£25-35
42c	1936-40	**Point Duty Policeman**	(cast in lead), White coat, Black helmet, 42 mm high	£25-35
42d	1936-40	**Point Duty Policeman**	(cast in lead), Dark Blue uniform, White gauntlets, 40 mm tall	£25-35
43a	1935-40	**'RAC' Box**	Blue and White (tinplate) call-box with 'RAC' emblem, 51 mm	£100-125
43c	1935-40	**'RAC' Guide**	(cast in lead), Blue uniform, Red sash, directing traffic, 37 mm tall	£25-35
43d	1935-40	**'RAC' Guide (saluting)**	(cast in lead), Blue uniform with Red sash, 36 mm tall	£25-35
44a	1935-40	**'AA' Box**	Black/Yellow tinplate box with 'AA' badge and 3 signs, 81 mm	£100-125
44c	1935-40	**'AA' Guide**	(cast in lead), Tan uniform, Blue sash, directing traffic, 37 mm tall	£20-25
44d	1935-40	**'AA' Guide (saluting)**	(cast in lead), Tan uniform, Blue sash, 36 mm tall	£20-25
45	1935-40	**Garage**	Cream/Orange (tinplate), Green opening doors, boxed, 127 x 90 mm	£250-350
46	1937-40	**Pavement Set**	Dark Grey 'stone' effect (cardboard) pavement pieces in a box	£100-150
47a	1935-40	**4-face Traffic Lights**	Black on White post, Yellow beacon, White base, 62 mm high	£15-20
47b	1935-40	**3-face Traffic Lights**	Black on White post, Yellow beacon, White base, 62 mm high	£15-20
47c	1935-40	**2-face Traffic Lights**	Back-to-back lights, Black on White post, Yellow beacon, White base	£15-20
47c	1935-40	**2-face Traffic Lights**	Lights at 90 degrees, Black on White post, Yellow beacon, White base	£15-20
47d	1935-40	**Belisha Beacon**	Black on White post, Orange globe, White base, 51 mm high	£15-20
47e	1935-40	**'30 MPH' Limit Sign**	Black on White post, Red top '30', 52 mm high	£15-20
47f	1935-40	**De-restriction Sign**	Black on White post, diagonal Black bar on White circle, 52 mm high	£15-20
47g	1935-40	**'School' Sign**	Black on White post, Red top, Black 'beacon' design, 51 mm high	£15-20
47h	1935-40	**'Steep Hill' Sign**	Black on White post, Red top, Black 'incline' design, 51 mm high	£15-20
47k	1935-40	**'S-Bend' Sign**	Black on White post, Red top, Black 'S-Bend' design, 51 mm high	£15-20
47m	1935-40	**'Left-Hand Bend' Sign**	Black on White post, Red top, Black 'curve' design, 51 mm high	£15-20
47n	1935-40	**'Right-Hand Bend' Sign**	Black on White post, Red top, Black 'curve' design, 51 mm high	£15-20
47p	1935-40	**'T-Junction' Sign**	Black on White post, Red top, Black 'T' design, 51 mm high	£15-20
47q	1935-40	**'No Entry' Sign**	Black on White post, Red 'bar' design, 48 mm high	£15-20
47r	1935-40	**'Major Road Ahead' Sign**	Black on White post, Red top, Black lettering, 54 mm high	£15-20
47s	1935-40	**'Crossing No Gates' Sign**	Black on White post, Red top, Black 'loco' design, 51 mm high	£15-20
47t	1935-40	**'Roundabout' Sign**	Black on White post, Red top, Black 'arrows' design, 51 mm high	£15-20

NB Pre-war issues have filled in triangles.

48	1935-40	**Filling/Service Station**	Yellow with Blue, Orange or Green base, Green, Brown or Yellow roof, tinplate. Orange box	£300-400
49a	1935-53	**Bowser Petrol Pump**	Green pump body, White rubber hose, (Yellow plastic post-war), 46 mm	£25-35
49b	1935-53	**Wayne Petrol Pump**	Pale Blue pump, White rubber hose, (Yellow plastic post-war), 39 mm	£25-35
49c	1935-53	**Theo Petrol Pump**	Blue or Red pump, White rubber hose, (Yellow plastic post-war), 58 mm	£25-35
49d	1935-53	**'SHELL' Petrol Pump**	Red pump body, White rubber hose, (Yellow plastic post-war), 53 mm	£25-35
49e	1935-40	**'Pratts' Oil Bin**	Yellow bin body and opening tinplate lid, 'Pratts Motor Oil', 32 mm	£40-50
			49e was only available post-war in Set 49 and without 'Pratts' logo	£25-35

101a	1935-40	**Dining Table**	'Wood' effect dining-room table, 64 mm	£30-35
101b	1935-40	**Sideboard**	'Wood' effect sideboard with opening doors, tinplate back, 63 mm	£30-35
101c	1935-40	**Carver Chair**	'Wood' effect chair with armrests, 33 mm high	£15-20
101d	1935-40	**Dining Chair**	'Wood' effect chair without armrests, raised 'leather' cushion	£10-15
102a	1935-40	**Bed**	Brown or Pink double bed, 74 mm	£30-35
102b	1935-40	**Wardrobe**	Brown or Pink wardrobe with opening door, tinplate back, 63 mm	£30-35
102c	1935-40	**Dressing Table**	Brown or Pink, opening drawers, tinplate mirror, 51 mm	£30-35
102d	1935-40	**Dressing Chest**	Brown or Pink, opening drawer, tinplate back, 40 mm high	£30-35
102e	1935-40	**Dressing Table Stool**	Brown or Pink stool, 13 mm high	£15-20
102f	1935-40	**Chair**	Brown or Pink	£10-15
103a	1935-40	**Refrigerator**	Light Blue/White or Light Green/Cream, door, tinplate back and food tray	£35-45
103b	1935-40	**Kitchen Cabinet**	Light Blue/White or Light Green/Cream, opening doors/drawer, tin back	£35-45
103c	1935-40	**Electric Cooker**	Light Blue/White or Light Green/Cream, opening door, tinplate back	£35-45
103d	1935-40	**Kitchen Table**	Light Blue/White or Light Green/Cream, 34 mm high	£30-35
103e	1935-40	**Kitchen Chair**	Light Blue/White or Light Green/Cream, casting as 102f	£10-15
104a	1935-40	**Bath**	Pink/White or Light Green/White, Gold taps, 69 mm	£35-45
104b	1935-40	**Bath Mat**	Mottled Green (rubber) mat, 50 x 37 mm	£10-15
104c	1935-40	**Pedestal Hand Basin**	Pink/White or Light Green/White, Gold taps, tinplate mirror, 63 mm	£30-35
104d	1935-40	**Bathroom Stool**	Pink/White or Light Green/White, 15 mm high	£15-20
104e	1935-40	**Linen Basket**	Pink/White or Light Green/White, hinged lid, 22 mm high	£15-20
104f	1935-40	**Toilet**	Pink/White or Light Green/White, hinged lid, 34 mm high	£35-45
	1935-40	**'Dolly Varden' Dolls House**	Not given a reference number, made of 'leather board' (heavy reinforced cardboard), and supplied packed flat. Cream/Brown upper storey, Red brick ground floor, Red roof, 476 x 260 mm base, 476 mm high	£500-750

Dinky Toys Accessories (Post-War)

See also: Public Transport Models, Ships, Motor Cycles and Gift Sets sections.

001 (1)	1954-56	**Station Staff ('0' gauge)**	1b Guard (flag in right hand), 1c Ticket Collector (right arm extended), 1d Driver, 1e Porter (with oblong bags), 1f Porter (standing)	£90-120
002 (2)	1954-56	**Farmyard Animals (6)**	2 x 2a horses, 2 x 2b cows, 1 x 2c pig, 1 x 2d sheep, simplified painting	£200-300
003 (3)	1954-56	**Passengers ('0' gauge)**	3a Woman (with child on left), 3b Businessman (Brown suit and case), 3c Male hiker (no stick), 3d Female hiker (Blue blouse), 3e Newsboy (Grey tray), 3f Woman (Light Red coat, round case)	£90-120
004 (4)	1946-54	**Engineering Staff ('0' gauge)**	2 x 4b Fitter (all-Blue and all-Brown), 4c Storekeeper (all-Brown), 4d Greaser, 4e Engine-Room attendant	£90-120
005 (5)	1954-56	**Train and Hotel Staff**	('0' gauge), 5a Conductor, 2 x 5b waiters, 2 x 5c Porter (Brown or Blue)	£90-120
006 (6)	1954-56	**Shepherd Set**	6a Shepherd (Green hat), 6b sheepdog (all-Black), 4 x 2b sheep	£150-200
007	1960-67	**Petrol Pump Attendants**	1 male (White overalls), 1 female (White coat), plastic, 35 mm tall	£15-20
008	1961-67	**Fire Station Personnel**	Set of 6 fire-fighters in Blue uniforms plus hose, plastic, 35 mm tall	£65-75
009	1962-66	**Service Station Personnel**	Set of 8 plastic figures in various colours and stances	£65-75
010	1962-66	**Road Maintenance Personnel**	Set of 6 workmen using pick, barrow, shovels, drill etc, plus hut, brazier, barrier, and 4 lamps Plastic, figures are 35 mm tall	£65-75
011(12d)	1954-56	**Telegraph Messenger**	Mid-Blue uniform, detailing in darker Blue, Brown pouch, 35 mm	£10-15
012(12e)	1954-56	**Postman**	Mid-Blue body, darker Blue detail, Brown post bag and badge, 35 mm	£15-20
013(13a)	1954-56	**Cook's Man**	(Agent for the Thomas Cook travel company), Dark Blue coat, 40 mm high	£20-30
036		**Battery**	15 volt battery for use with models 276 and 277	NGPP
037		**Lamp**	Red light-bulb for use with model 277	NGPP
038		**Lamp**	Blue (or Orange) light-bulb for use with model 276	NGPP
039		**Lamp**	Clear light-bulb for use with model 952	NGPP
050 - 054		**Sets of Figures**	See the Gift Sets section.	
081		**Spare tyre**	White fine tread tyre, 14 mm in diameter	NGPP
082		**Spare tyre**	Black narrow tread tyre, 20 mm in diameter	NGPP
083		**Spare tyre**	Grey tyre, 20 mm in diameter, (also catalogued as 099)	NGPP
084		**Spare tyre**	Black 'recessed' tyre, 18 mm in diameter	NGPP
085		**Spare tyre**	White tyre, 15 mm in diameter, (also catalogued as 092 and 14095)	NGPP
086		**Spare tyre**	Black fine tread tyre, 16 mm in diameter	NGPP
087		**Spare tyre**	Black big 'tractor' tyre, 35 mm in dia, (also catalogued as 60687)	NGPP
089		**Spare tyre**	Black 'tractor front tyre', 19 mm in dia, (also catalogued as 60689)	NGPP
090		**Spare tyre**	Black fine tread tyre, 14 mm in diameter, (also catalogued as 60790)	NGPP
090		**Spare tyre**	White fine tread tyre, 14 mm in diameter, (also catalogued as 60791)	NGPP
091		**Spare tyre**	Black block tread tyre, 13 mm in diameter, (also catalogued as 60036)	NGPP
092		**Spare tyre**	Black block tread tyre, 15 mm in diameter, (also catalogued as 14094)	NGPP
092		**Spare tyre**	White block tread tyre, 15 mm in diameter, (also catalogued as 14095)	NGPP
093		**Spare tyre**	Black medium tractor tyre, 27 mm in dia, (also catalogued as 13978)	NGPP
094		**Spare tyre**	Black smooth tyre, 18 mm in diameter, (also catalogued as 6676)	NGPP
095		**Spare tyre**	Black block tread tyre, 18 mm in diameter, (also catalogued as 6677)	NGPP
096		**Spare tyre**	Tyre, 19/32, (15 mm) in diameter, (also catalogued as 7067)	NGPP
097		**Spare wheel**	Solid rubber wheel, 12 mm in diameter, (also catalogued as 7383)	NGPP
098		**Spare wheel**	Solid rubber wheel, 12 mm in diameter, (also catalogued as 10118)	NGPP
099		**Spare tyre**	Black block tread tyre, 20 mm in diameter, (also catalogued as 10253)	NGPP
099		**Spare tyre**	Grey block tread tyre, 20 mm in diameter, (also catalogued as 10253)	NGPP
1a	1946-54	**Station Master**	Dark Blue uniform (cap, long coat), (in Set 001 till 1956)	£20-25
1b	1946-54	**Guard**	Dark Blue uniform, blowing whistle, flag in right hand (see Set 001)	£15-20
1c	1946-54	**Ticket Collector**	Blue uniform, only right arm is extended (in Set 001 till 1956)	£15-20
1e	1946-54	**Porter with Bags**	Blue uniform, oblong case in each hand (in Set 001 till 1956)	£15-20

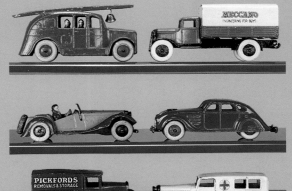

Christie's holds up to twelve auctions annually; no other auction house offers either such a large variety of material from numerous makers or such expertise in so many fields.

Christie's offers a comprehensive service to buyers and sellers with catalogues detailing the condition of each lot.

ENQUIRIES:
Hugo Marsh on (020) 7321 3274, Daniel Agnew (020) 7321 3335
Nigel Mynheer (020) 7321 3410 or e-mail hmarsh@christies.com

Consultants:
James Opie (Toy Soldiers and Figures)
Chris Littledale (Railways)

CATALOGUES:
(020) 7321 3152 / (020) 7389 2820

CHRISTIE'S
SOUTH KENSINGTON
85 Old Brompton Road, London SW7 3LD
Tel: (020) 7581 7611 Fax: (020) 7321 3321
www.christies.com

More fine Dinky Toys at Christie's South Kensington

Dinky Toys

Top Set: No.2 Private automobiles, circa 1946-48 (£2,600).

Bottom Set: No.3 Private automobiles circa 1947-52 (£3,200)

Set No.5 Military Vehicles circa 1950 (£2,600).
Set No.1 Commercial Vehicles circa 1946-48 (£3,200).

Models sold by Christie's of South Kensington, London.

Pictures reproduced by their kind permission.

No.60 Aeroplanes Set. L-R: 60a Imperial Airways Gold/Blue "Sunburst" (B+), 60b DH Leopard Moth Green/Yellow (C-B), 60c Percival Gull White/Blue (C), 60d Low Wing Monoplane Red/Cream (C), 60e General Monospar Silver/Deep Blue (B), 60f Cierva Autogyro Gold/Deep Blue Rotor (B-B+), Outer Box B, inner card stand A. Sold for £1000.

Retailers shop display card "WORLD FAMOUS RACING CARS" with models. No.'s 230, 231, 232, 233, 234, & 239 strung onto card. Display card in good (B) condition, models mostly B+. Sold for £1,000.

Models sold by Vectis Auctions Ltd, Fleck Way, Thornaby, Stockton-on-Tees TS17 9JZ.
Picture reproduced by their kind permission.

A fine selection of rare post-war models - note the colours of the scarce commercial vehicles and the rare two colour cars such as the US Market issues in the foreground.

e.g. the red and yellow 39en Chrysler Royal Sedan, the cream and tan 39bu Oldsmobile 6 Sedan and another two tone blue 39bu Oldsmobile 6 Sedan. The 40 Series colour variations should also be noted.

All the models sold by Christie's of South Kensington, London.
Picture has been reproduced by their kind permission.

LACY SCOTT AND KNIGHT

10, RISBYGATE ST., BURY ST EDMUNDS, SUFFOLK. ON THE A14.
TEL: (01284) 763531 FAX: (01284) 704713
CATALOGUE WEBSITE: http//www.thesaurus.co.uk/lacy-scott&knight

THE LARGEST REGULAR DIECAST, TINPLATE, LEAD & STEAM MODEL AUCTIONS IN THE COUNTRY

Rare and collectable Die Cast Models
in Mint condition always wanted

"O" & "OO" Model Railways are much
sought after and fetch high prices

Strong Interest from home & abroad, for rare
Lead Models has brought some Record Prices

Craftsman built Live Steam
Models are a Speciality

We provide the following services

- Refreshments on Sale Days
- Free On-site Parking
- Individual Descriptions
- Printed Sales Results within 5 Days

- Payment to Vendors within 10 working days
- 4 Major Sales per Year of 1500 Lots
- 7000 sq ft of Salerooms
- Free Valuations for Vendors

We make no charge to Vendors for: Lotting, Storage, Insurance, Photography & Unsold Lots

BUYER'S PREMIUM 12% INC V.A.T.

For details of all the above Services contact the Collectors Model Department.

Dinky Toys

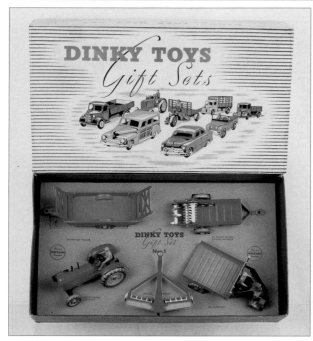

No.1 Farm Gear Gift Set (estimate £700-£1,000),
B+ condition overall

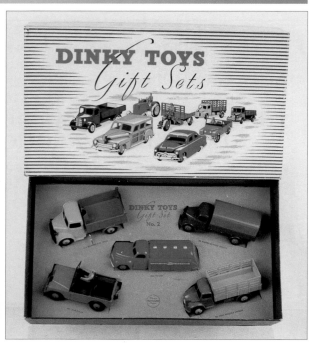

No.2 Commercial Vehicles Gift Set (£2,100),
B-B+ condition overall

No.3 Passenger Cars Gift Set (£1,800),
B-B+ condition overall

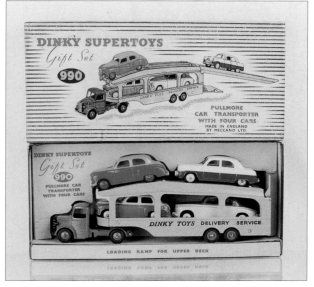

No.990 Pullmore Cars Transporter Set (estimate £800-
£900), models B-B+ condition, Box C.

Models sold by Vectis Auctions Ltd, Fleck Way, Thornaby, Stockton-on-Tees TS17 9JZ.
Picture reproduced by their kind permission.

No.504 Foden 14 ton Tanker, rare 2nd type cab. Two tone blue livery with rivetted back, sold for £5,000.

No.504 Foden 14 ton Tanker 2nd type in red and fawn livery (£1,400).

No.902 Foden Flat Truck 2nd Type cab with rivetted back. Rare red/green livery (£2,300).

No.903/503 Foden Flat Truck with Tailboard (2nd type), violet blue cab with yellow back and mid blue hubs with grey tyres (£1,500)

No.503 Foden Flat Truck with Tailboard (1st type), rare grey and dark blue livery (£1,600).

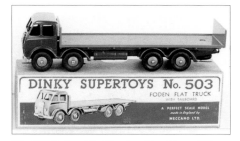

No.503 Foden Flat Truck with tailboard (1st type) in two tone green livery (£1,000).

No.501 Diesel Wagon (2nd type), violet blue and mid blue livery (£2,000).

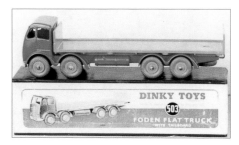

No.503 Foden Flat Truck with tailboard (2nd type),burnt orange and yellow livery (£2,100).

Models sold by Vectis Auctions Ltd, Fleck Way, Thornaby, Stockton-on-Tees TS17 9JZ.
Picture reproduced by their kind permission.

Dinky Toys

Top Row: Five Dublo Dinky Models, models and boxes all excellent (£270).
Middle Row: No.100 Lady Penelope's Fab 1 plus the Corgi Batmobile No.267, both (E) £340.
Bottom Row: No.923 Big Bedford 'Heinz' Van, both model and box (E) £860.

N.B. Prices not available for the models unlisted.

Timpo Models
Lead Station Figures (circa 1950) in excellent condition, sold for £450.

Models sold by Barry Potter Auctions of 13 Yew Tree Lane, Spratton, Northampton NN6 8HL. (Saleroom The Benn Hall, Rugby).
Pictures reproduced by their kind permission.

ADD TO YOUR COLLECTION EVERY MONTH

With Britain's Newest Collecting Monthly

If you are a collector who likes to be in the know with all the latest information of new releases OR if you enjoy a nostalgic approach to model collecting -

YOU NEED

On sale 2nd of every month

You can also visit our Website
www.diecast-collector.com

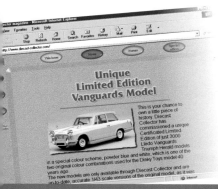

► Toyfair times ◄
► News ◄
► Bid for a Bargain ◄
► Swapshop ◄
► Subscriptions ◄
► Back Issues ◄
► Special Offers ◄

ALL ON LINE

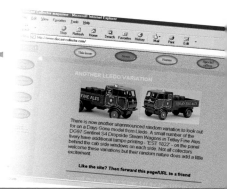

Don't forget to leave a message in our guestbook!

Dinky Toys

Top Row: No.62n (£200), No.60w (£100), No.998 Bristol Britannia 'Canadian Pacific' (£160), No.62w 'G-A FDK' (£390), No.62w 'G-A FDJ' (£360).

Middle Row: No.62t Whitley Bomber (£100), No.62w 'G-A FDI' (£280), No.60t 'PH-ALI' (£160), Skybirds Set (£230).

Bottom Row: No.72i (£120), No.62t Set 1 Spitfire and 3 Hurricanes (£350).

N.B. No details are available for the models unlisted.

Top Row: No.982 (£100), No.908 Mighty Antar (£460)

Middle Row: No.450 Bedford (£110), No. 450 Leyland Octopus (£170), No.925 Leyland Truck (£80),

Bottom Row: No.411 Bedford (£170), No.281 'Pathe TV' car (£125), No.110 Aston Martin DB3 (£110).

Models sold by Wallis & Wallis, West Street Auction Galleries, Lewes, Sussex BN7 2NJ

Pictures reproduced by their kind permission.

No.903 Foden Flat Truck with Tailboard (2nd type) in rare mid blue and fawn with rivetted back, model and box in excellent condition (£725).

No.934 Leyland Octopus Wagon in rare blue and yellow livery, model and box in excellent condition (£1,058).

No.935 Leyland Octopus Flat Truck with chains in rare dark blue and grey livery, model and box in excellent condition (£1,725).

Models sold by Dreweatt Neate, Donington Priory, Donington, Berkshire RG14 2JE.
Pictures reproduced by their kind permission.

No.915 A.E.C. Articulated Flat Truck promotional 'THAMES BOARD' issue. Sold for £1,700.

Model sold by Vectis Auctions Ltd, Fleck Way, Thornaby, Stockton-on-Tees TS17 9JZ.
Picture reproduced by their kind permission.

SELLING OR BUYING?

check out the UK's biggest

Browse the catalogue and bid against the world. Or list your items in the auction for as little as 20p.

online

Part of
auction universe
*biggest online
auction network*

Why not log on for a viewing with no obligation. New items every day —watch the bids mount!

From Typewriters to Teapots, from Dinky Cars to Dolls. We auction all collectables.

www.auctionuniverse.co.uk

1f	1946-54	**Porter**	Dark Blue uniform, standing, no luggage (in Set 001 till 1956)	**£15-20**
2a	1946-54	**Horses**	3 versions; Dark Brown horse (Black tail and mane), Light Brown horse (Light Brown tail and mane), White horse (2 in Set 002 till 1956)	**£20-25**
2b	1946-54	**Cows**	Light Brown, Dark Brown, or Black/White (2 in Set 002 till 1956)	**£20-25**
2c	1946-54	**Pig**	Cream body (in Set 002 till 1956)	**£15-20**
2d	1946-54	**Sheep**	White body with Black hand-painted detail (in Set 002 till 1956)	**£15-20**
3a	1946-54	**Woman and Child**	Woman in Green suit and hat (Brown scarf), child on left (see Set 003)	**£20-25**
3b	1946-54	**Business Man**	Brown suit, left hand holds attaché case (in Set 003 till 1956)	**£20-25**
3c	1946-54	**Male Hiker**	Brown clothing, Khaki rucksack, no stick (in Set 003 till 1956)	**£20-25**
3d	1946-54	**Female Hiker**	Blue or Dark Blue skirt and shirt, stick in right hand (see Set 003)	**£20-25**
3e	1946-54	**Newsboy**	Dark Blue clothing, standing, papers in Grey tray (in Set 003 till 1956)	**£20-25**
3f	1946-54	**Woman**	Light Red coat, round case in right hand (in Set 003 till 1956)	**£20-25**
4a	1946-54	**Electrician**	Blue overalls, White sleeves, carrying equipment (in Set 004 till 1956)	**£15-20**
4b	1946-56	**Fitters**	2 versions; one in Blue, the other Brown, carrying equipment (Set 004)	**£15-20**
4c	1946-56	**Storekeeper**	Brown coat, Black trousers, holding forms in right hand	**£15-20**
4d	1946-56	**Greaser**	Brown overalls, holding oil-can in right hand	**£15-20**
4e	1946-56	**Engine-Room Attendant**	Blue overalls, Blue sleeves	**£10-15**
5a	1946-56	**Pullman Car Conductor**	White jacket, Blue trousers, slightly open arms, casting as 1c	**£20-25**
5b	1946-56	**Pullman Car Waiter**	White jacket, Blue trousers, two slightly different poses are known	**£20-25**
5c	1946-56	**Hotel Porter**	Red jacket/Brown trousers, or Green jacket/Blue trousers, casting as 1e	**£20-25**
6a	1946-56	**Shepherd**	Brown with Green hat	**£40-50**
6b	1946-56	**Sheep-dog**	All-Black sheep-dog	**£20-30**
12c(750)	1946-54	**Telephone Box**	Red call-box with Black window frames, 58 mm high	**£20-30**
12d(011)	1946-54	**Telegraph Messenger**	Dark Blue body, picked out detail in darker Blue, Brown pouch, 35 mm	**£15-20**
12e(012)	1946-54	**Postman**	Mid-Blue body, darker Blue detail, Brown post bag and badge, 35 mm	**£15-20**
13a(013)	1952-54	**Cook's Man**	(An Agent for the Thomas Cook travel company), Blue coat, 40 mm high	**£20-30**
30g	1948-50	**Caravan**	Orange/Cream body, 'Caravan Club', drawbar, body length 81 mm	**£45-55**
42a(751)	1954-60	**Police Hut**	Dark Blue hut, 'POLICE' in Silver, 66 mm high	**£25-35**
49e	194?-?	**Oil Bin**	As pre-war 'Pratt's' Oil Bin but only available post-war in Set 49 and without 'Pratts' logo	**£25-35**
107a(385)	1948-54	**Sack Truck**	Blue or Pale Green body, two small Black metal wheels, 65mm	**£10-15**
117	1963-69	**Four Berth Caravan**	Blue/Cream, clear roof, suspension, detailed interior, 117 mm	**£25-35**
			Yellow/Cream, clear roof, suspension, detailed interior, 117 mm	**£25-35**
188	1961-63	**Four Berth Caravan**	Green/Cream or Blue/Cream, windows, detailed interior, 132 mm	**£25-35**
	1963-63		As previous model but larger windows, (this model replaced by 117)	**£25-35**
190	1956-62	**Caravan**	Orange/Cream, or Blue/Cream, drawbar, metal jockey wheel, 118 mm	**£25-35**
	1962-64		Orange/Cream, or Blue/Cream, drawbar, plastic jockey wheel, 118 mm	**£25-35**
502	1961-63	**Garage**	Blue/Grey plastic garage, opening door, 272 mm (French issue)	**£90-110**
750(12c)	1954-62	**Telephone Box**	Red call-box with Black window frames, 58 mm high	**£25-35**
751(42a)	1954-60	**Police Hut**	Dark Blue hut, 'POLICE' in Silver, 66 mm high	**£25-35**
752(973)	1953-54	**Goods Yard Crane**	Yellow with Blue or Dark Blue, mazak or cast-iron base (100 x 100 mm)	**£40-50**
753	1962-67	**Police Crossing**	Black/White box on traffic island with policeman directing traffic	**£80-100**
754	1958-62	**Pavement Set**	Grey cardboard paving slabs (20 items in box)	**£50-60**
755	1960-64	**Lamp Standard (Single)**	Grey/Fawn/Orange, plastic single-arm lamp on metal base, 145 mm high	**£20-30**
756	1960-64	**Lamp Standard (Double)**	Grey/Fawn/Orange, plastic double-arm lamp on metal base, 145 mm high	**£30-40**
760	1954-60	**Pillar Box**	Red and Black pillar box with 'E II R' cast-in, 42 mm high	**£25-35**
763	1959-64	**Posters for Hoarding**	Six different coloured poster advertisements (on paper)	**£25-35**
764	1959-64	**Posters for Hoarding**	Six different coloured poster advertisements (on paper)	**£25-35**
765	1959-64	**Road Hoardings (6 Posters)**	Green plastic hoarding, 'David Allen and Sons Ltd', 205 mm	**£50-60**

NB For Road Sign sets 766-772 see Gift Sets

773	1958-63	**4 face Traffic Lights**	Black/White, Black base, similar to 47a but without beacon, 62 mm	**£15-20**
777	1958-63	**Belisha Beacon**	Black/White post on Black base, Orange globe, casting as 47d, 51 mm	**£10-15**
778	1962-66	**Road Repair Boards**	Green and Red plastic warning signs, 6 different, 30-40 mm	**£30-40**
781	1955-62	**'ESSO' Petrol Station**	'ESSO' sign, no kiosk, 2 pumps ('ESSO' and 'ESSO EXTRA'), 114 mm	**£60-75**
782	1960-70	**'SHELL' Petrol Station**	'SHELL' sign, Green/Cream kiosk, 4 Red/Yellow 'SHELL' pumps, 203 mm	**£60-75**
783	1960-70	**'BP' Petrol Station**	'BP' sign, Green/Cream kiosk, 4 Green/White 'BP' pumps, 203 mm	**£60-75**
785	1960-64	**'SERVICE STATION'**	Fawn and Red plastic, with 'BP' sign, 335 x 185 mm (unbuilt kit, boxed)	**£175-225**
786	1960-66	**Tyre Rack with tyres**	Green tyre rack with 21 assorted tyres and 'DUNLOP' on board, 52 mm	**£35-45**
787	1960-64	**Lighting Kit**	Bulb and wire lighting kit for model buildings	**£20-25**
788	1960-68	**Spare Bucket for 966**	Grey bucket for use with 966 Marrel Multi-Bucket Unit	**£10-15**
790	1960-64	**Granite Chippings**	Plastic bag of imitation granite chippings (50790)	**£15-20**
791	1960-64	**Imitation Coal**	in a plastic bag	**£15-20**
792	1960-64	**Packing Cases (3)**	White/Cream plastic packing cases, 'Hornby Dublo', 38 x 28 x 19 mm	**£15-20**
793	1960-64	**Pallets**	Orange pallets for 930 Bedford Pallet-Jekta Van and 404 Conveyancer	**£15-20**
794(994)	1954-64	**Loading Ramp**	Blue loading ramp for use with 582/982 Carrimore Transporter, 233 mm	**£15-20**
846	1961-	**Oil Drums**	Pack of 6 oil drums French issue	**£15-20**
847	1961-	**Barrels**	Pack of 6 barrels French issue	**£15-20**
849	1961-	**Packing Cases**	Pack of 6 packing cases French issue	**£15-20**
850	1961-	**Crates of Bottles**	Pack of 6 crates French issue	**£15-20**
851	1961-	**Sets of vehicle 'Loads'**	Two each of 846 Oil Drums, 847 Barrels, 849 Packing Cases and 850 Crates	**£50-60**
954		**Fire Station Plastic Kit**	Red doors, Cream roof, Grey floor, clear roof, 'FIRE STATION'. 'DINKY TOYS' in Red	**£200-250**
994(794)	1954-55	**Loading Ramp**	Renumbered from 794 to 994 then back to 794 after only a year!	**£15-20**
973(752)	1954-59	**Goods Yard Crane**	Yellow with Blue or Dark Blue base, early issues have steps, mazak or cast-iron base	**£40-50**

Ref.	Year(s)	Publication	Cover features and details	Market Price Range

Pre-War Catalogues, leaflets and listings

Hornby 'Modelled Miniatures' were introduced in 1931 as model railway accessories. The first catalogue listings appeared in Hornby Train catalogues, Meccano catalogues and in the 'Meccano Magazine'.

Ref.	Year(s)	Publication	Cover features and details	Market Price Range
-	1932-33	Hornby 'Book of Trains'	First 'Modelled Miniatures' listed as 'Railway Accessories'	£40-50
-	1932	Meccano trade catalogue	First 'Modelled Miniatures' listed as 'Railway Accessories'	£40-50
-	1933	'Meccano Magazine'	42 Hornby 'Modelled Miniatures' listed in December issue	£20-25
-	1933-34	Hornby 'Book of Trains'	Accessories are depicted in full colour	£40-50
-	1934	Meccano trade catalogue	'Modelled Miniatures' briefly renamed 'Meccano Miniatures'	NGPP
-	1934	'Meccano Magazine'	February issue contained the last published 'Modelled Miniatures' listing	£30-40
-	1934	'Meccano Magazine'	April issue contained the first 'Meccano Dinky Toys' listing	£30-40
-	1934	'Meccano Magazine'	The May, June, July, August, September and November issues each reflected the increasing number of varieties of 'Dinky Toys'	£15-20
-	1934	'Meccano Magazine'	'150 varieties of Dinky Toys' on double pages in October and December issues	£15-20
-	1934-35	Hornby 'Book of Trains'	Catalogue shows 150 'Dinky Toys' in full colour on a double page	£50-75
13/834/900	1934-35	Meccano Catalogue	Boat plane and model plus boy on cover, 3 pages of Dinky Toys	NGPP
16/934/100	1934-35	'Hornby Trains/Meccano' Catalogue	Blue cover, full colour design of 'The World', lists 150 models of Dinky Toys	£70-90
-	1934-35	Meccano Book	Cover depicts viaduct over river, complete Dinky Toys range is listed	NGPP
-	1935	Meccano Magazine	January to November issues have various Dinky Toys listings	£15-20
-	1935	Meccano Magazine	December issue shows 200 varieties of Dinky Toys in Black and White	£15-20
7/835/65	1935-36	Hornby 'Book of Trains'	Catalogue features 200 varieties of Dinky Toys in full colour	£40-50
-	1935-36	Hornby/Meccano	Catalogue with the same cover as the 1934-35 issue	£70-90
-	1936	Meccano Magazines	The February and August issues featured a road layout and a competition; the May issue introduced the 'Queen Mary' model	£15-20
-	1936-37	Hornby 'Book of Trains'	The catalogue features full colour pictures of the Dinky Toys range	£40-50
-	1937	Hornby/Meccano	Catalogue with 1934-35 'World' cover again. Seven pages of listings	£50-70
-	1937	Meccano Magazines	Details given in the monthly listings of the superb new 'Army' range	£15-20
13/638/1150	1938	Hornby/Meccano	74 page Catalogue, full Dinky Toys listings. Numerous b/w pictures	£30-40
13/638/1150/UK	1938	'Wonder Book of Toys'	Two boys with Meccano models plus 11 pages with Dinky Toys	NGPP
8/1238/25	1938	'DINKY TOYS' Catalogue	(Booklet). Cover shows boy and 6 models including 29c Bus, 151a Tank, and 63 Mayo Composite Aircraft. Brown print on pale-yellow paper	£75-100
-	1938	Meccano Magazine	Details of the full range (with pictures) are published each month	£15-20
1/439/10	1939	'DINKY TOYS' leaflet	'New Products' leaflet detailing items such as the Presentation Aeroplane Sets Nos 64 and 65. Black printing on pinkish paper	£20-30
-	1939	MECCANO booklets	with complete Dinky Toys listings, various	NGPP
13/639/1	1939	Hornby/Meccano	74 page Catalogue, full Dinky Toys listings and Black/White pictures	£30-40
13/639/ 11500 UK	1939	'A Wonder Book Of Toys'	Green and Yellow cover depicts two boys with their Meccano models. The booklet includes 13 pages of Dinky Toys information	£30-40
2/739/10 (1P)	1939	'DINKY TOYS' Catalogue	Famous Red/Yellow cover picture of schoolboy with outstretched arm and 17 models. Contains 14 black and white pages	£200-250
-		'Toys Of Quality'	Maroon Express train features on cover plus 'The Hornby Railway Co' logo. 13 pages of Dinky Toys listings are included	£30-40
-	1939	Trade catalogue	Cover depicts boy with Dinky Toys and Hornby pictures with 'MECCANO TOYS OF QUALITY' logo	£30-40
2/1139/20(3P) UK	1939	'DINKY TOYS' Catalogue	Superb Red and Yellow cover picture of schoolboy with outstretched arm and 17 models. Contains 10 Black/White pages of listings and pictures	£100-150
-	1939	Meccano Magazine	Each month contained Dinky Toys listings	£15-20
16/1040 /100	1940	Meccano Price List	All products listed but no pictures	NGPP
16/1040 /200	1940	'DINKY TOYS' leaflet	Listing of models with pictures	£15-20
-	1940	Meccano Magazine	Wartime Dinky aircraft and the Meccano 'Spitfire Fund' are featured	£15-20
16/541/25 UK	1941	'DINKY TOYS' leaflet	Wartime camouflaged aircraft feature in this leaflet	£15-20
16/641/20 UK	1941	'DINKY TOYS' leaflet	Similar to previous leaflet, military models listed	£15-20
16/1141 /20 UK	1941	'DINKY TOYS' leaflet	Listing of models and retail prices	£15-20

Full Dinky Toys listings also appeared in the toy catalogues of major retailers such as Gamages and Bentalls. These catalogues are difficult to find. Each: £30-40

Post-War Catalogues, leaflets and listings
Early Post-War period, 1945 – 1954

There were at least two editions per annum so the following listings are not complete. The 'leaflet' approach reflects the shortage of paper in early post-war years.

Ref.	Year(s)	Publication	Cover features and details	Market Price Range
16/1145/75 UK	1945	Meccano leaflet	leaflet lists the models to be reintroduced after the War and features pictures of 23e, 29c, 39a, 62s, 62p. Sepia print on cream paper	£10-15
16/546/30 UK	1946	Meccano leaflet	Sepia printed listing on cream paper featuring pictures of models 70a, 38c, 29c, 23e	£10-15
16/1146 /65 UK	1946	Meccano leaflet	Blue/Black print on cream paper, featuring models 70a, 38c, 70b, 38e	£10-15
16/347/50 UK	1947	Meccano leaflet	Brown print on light cream paper. Models depicted are 70a, 70b, 70c, 70e, 38c, 38e, 38f, and 153a Jeep	£10-15
16/448/30	1948	Meccano General Products	booklet with green printing on light cream paper	£10-15
16/948/200	1948		Same as previous issue but with mauve print on light cream paper	£10-15
16/1248 /5	1948	'Dinky Toys Tyre Sizes'	Simple Leaflet giving information on Dinky Toys spare tyres	£10-15
16/449/100	1949	Meccano General Products	booklet with brown printing on light cream paper	£10-15
	1949	Independent shop listings	Full Dinky Toys listings and pictures featured in the catalogues published by the larger toy shops such as Bentalls, Gamages, etc	£15-20
16/450/150	1950	Meccano General Products	booklet with pale Blue/Black printing on light cream paper	£10-15
-	1950	Independent shop listings	Full Dinky Toys listings and pictures featured in the catalogues of larger toy shops such as Gamages, Bentalls, etc	£15-20

16/251/33 1951	**Meccano General Products** ......booklet with brown printing on light cream paper..**£10-15**
- 1951	**Independent shop listings** ....Full Dinky Toys listings and pictures featured in the catalogues of larger
	toy shops such as Bentalls, Gamages, etc **£15-20**
13/952/250 1952	**Price List** ....Beige leaflet with pictures and prices..**£10-15**
13/953/678 1953	**Meccano Catalogue** ....Includes Dinky Toys, Meccano and Hornby Dublo **£15-20**
16/85/25 1953	**Price List** ....Beige leaflet with pictures and prices..**£15-20**
16/854/25 1954	**Price List** ....Beige leaflet with pictures and prices..**£10-15**

Meccano Magazines, 1942 - 1952

During the latter part of the war and especially during the early post-war years when Dinky Toys catalogues were not issued, the Meccano Magazine was the main source of new information for collectors. It advised on the reintroduction of models after the war and of the forthcoming new releases. Consequently the Magazines of this period are highly collectable in their own right.

1942 - September 1943. No Dinky Toys adverts or listings appeared.
September 1943 - December 1944. Back page adverts for Meccano incorporated listing and pictures of De Havilland Flamingo Aircraft and Buick 'Viceroy' Saloon.
January - November 1945. Back page adverts said 'Sorry, not available but will be ready after the war'.
December 1945. Advert on back page announced 'Ready during December'.

1946. Virtually every month a new model was added to the listing printed on the inside front cover. A picture of each model was shown.
January - September 1947. New models added regularly each month.
October 1947. First advert appears of Dinky Supertoys with pictures of 501 Foden Diesel Wagon, 502 Foden Flat Truck, 503 Foden Flat Truck with Tailboard, 511 Guy 4 ton Lorry, 512 Guy Flat Truck, 513 Guy Flat Truck with Tailboard, and 701 Short 'Shetland' Flying Boat.
1948. Single page advert every month, new models continually introduced.
1949, 1950, 1951. Double page advert each month listing new models.
1952. Double page adverts each month. The December issue shows Gift Sets No1 Farm Gear and No2 Commercial Vehicles.
Prices for Meccano Magazines of this period range between **£10-15** each.

UK Catalogue editions, 1952 – 1965

The series included fourteen editions although not all issues were given an edition number. More than one catalogue was issued in some years. It was common for catalogues to be overprinted with the name and address of the toy retailer. In addition to issuing Dinky Toys catalogues, Meccano Ltd continued to issue 'Meccano Toys Of Quality' leaflets which provided a full listing of Dinky Toys with their retail prices plus details of their 'Hornby', 'Hornby-Dublo' and 'Meccano' products. As many as five printings per annum were produced using green, pink, blue or buff paper. When in perfect condition these leaflets sell for **£5-8** each.

16/152/50 1952	**(February) 16 pages** ....Cover features unknown 'C6321' **£40-50**
15/852/165 1952	**(September) 16 pages** ....Cover shows hands holding 27f Estate Car, 'Dinky Toys' logo...........**£40-50**
1953	**24 page catalogue** ....Cover shows boy wearing green sweater, 'Dinky Toys' and 'Price 3d'....**£40-50**
7/953/150 1953	**24 page catalogue** ....As next item: 7/953/360.
7/953/360 1953	**(1st October) 24 pages**...............(1) Cover features 555 Fire Engine, 522 Big Bedford Lorry and
	....25x Breakdown Lorry, price '2d' **£40-50**
13/953/678 1953	**(1st October)** ....(2) Cover shows 'Meccano Magic Carpet', two boys plus globe with flag **£40-50**
7/754/600 1954	**(1st September) 24 pages** ....Cover features 157 Jaguar, 480 'Kodak' Van, 641 Army Truck,
	....'Dinky Toys' logo, price '2d' **£30-40**
7/455/250 1955	**(May) 8 page leaflet**.................251, 641, 170 and 401 on cover, 'Dinky Toys' and 'Dinky Supertoys' **£15-20**
7/755/945 1955	**24 page catalogue** ....'Dinky Toys', 'Supertoys', 481 'Ovaltine' Van on cover, ('2d') **£30-40**
7/456/800 1956	**(June) 32 pages** ....Cover has 942 'REGENT' Tanker, 255 Mersey Tunnel 'Police' Land
	....Rover, 157 Jaguar XK120, 'Dinky Toys' & 'Dinky Supertoys', '2d' **£30-40**
7/657/820 1957	**(August) 28 pages** ....Cover shows 290 'DUNLOP' Double Decker Bus etc, 'Dinky Toys',
	....and 'Dinky Supertoys', price '2d UK' **£30-40**
7/458/856 1958	**28 page catalogue** ....Houses of Parliament shown on front cover with 'Dinky Toys' and
	....'Dinky Supertoys', price '2d UK' **£30-40**
7/559/900 1959	**28 page catalogue** ....Red Jaguar XK120 Coupe (157) on front cover with 'Dinky Toys' and
	....'UK Seventh Edition', price '3d' **£20-25**
7/3/800 1960	**32 page catalogue** ....Motorway bridge on cover, 'Dinky Toys' and 'UK Eighth Edition' **£20-25**
7/561/700 1961	**32 page catalogue** ....Black/Yellow cover with 6 models, 'Dinky Toys', 'UK 9th Edition' **£20-25**
72537/02 1962	**32 page catalogue** ....Cover features 120 Jaguar 'E' type, 'Dinky Toys', price '2d' **£15-20**
7/263/400 1963	**?** ....No details available for this reference number ....NGPP
13/163/200 1963	**32 page catalogue** ....Motor Show stands featured on cover, '11th Edition', 'UK', '2d' **£15-20**
13/763/400 1963	**32 page catalogue**.....................11th Edition, 2nd impression ....NGPP
7/164/450 1964	**8 page catalogue** ....'Widest Range & Best Value In The World' and 'Dinky Toys' logos Price '3d' ...**£15-20**
7/64/45 1964	**8 page catalogue** (2nd printing).As 7/164/450 except that page 8 shows Bedford TK instead of accessories **£15-20**
7/265/200 1965	**16 page catalogue** ....Rolls-Royce (127) on cover with 'Dinky Toys by Meccano' Price '3d' **£15-20**
72557/02 1965	**16 page catalogue** ....Cover features cars 127, 128, 133, 151 and 178...................................**£15-20**

UK Catalogue editions, 1966 – 1978

72561/2 1966	**106 page catalogue** ....'1st Edition', '6d', 'Always Something New From Dinky' on the
	....cover. Accompanied by separate (pink) price list **£25-30**
72561/2 1966	**(after 21st July)** ....2nd edition, same cover as 1st, 104 pages plus (buff) price list **£20-25**
72571 1967	**104 page catalogue** ....'No.3', '6d' 12 models on cover, same logo as 72561/2. Price list (green paper) included ..**£20-25**
72580 1968	**104 page catalogue** ....'No.4', '6d', Spectrum Pursuit Vehicle (104) on cover. Logo as 72561/2. Buff price list.....**£20-25**
72585 1969	**(1st Sept) 24 pages** ....'No.5', '3d', (2nd printing). Cover features 102 'Joe's Car', has same logo as 72561/2 ......**£15-20**
165000 1970	**24 page catalogue** ....'No.6', '3d', many models on cover. Same logo as 72561/2.................**£15-20**
100103 1971	**24 page catalogue** ....'No.7', '2p', '1971 Meccano Tri-ang Ltd' on rear cover. Same logo
	....as on 72561/2. (Note the change to Decimal Currency in 1971)...........**£10-15**
100107 1972	**(1st November) 28 pages** ....'No.8', '2p', 2nd printing, shows 683 Chieftain Tank, 'Dinky Toys' **£10-15**
100108 1972	**28 pages**.......................................'No.8', 725 Phantom, 784 Goods Train etc. on cover **£10-15**
100109 1973	**(October) 40 pages** ....'No.9', '3p', 2nd printing, shows 924 'Centaur', 'Dinky Toys' **£10-15**
100113 1974	**(May) 48 pages** ....'No.10', '4p', cover shows 731 S.E.P.E.C.A.T. 'Dinky Toys' **£10-15**
100115 UK.....................1975	**(June) 48 pages** ....'No.11', '5p', 'Dinky Toys' and 675 Motor Patrol Boat on cover **£10-15**
100118 UK.....................1976	**48 page catalogue** ....'No.12', '5p', 'Dinky Toys' and 358 'USS Enterprise' on cover............**£10-15**
100122 (UK)..................1977	**44 page catalogue** ....'No.13' and '5p'. Cover features 357 Klingon Battle Cruiser **£5-10**
100100 1978	**44 page catalogue** ....'No.14', '5p', 'AIRFIX GROUP' and 180 Rover 3500 on cover **£5-10**

Leaflets and Price Lists, 1954 – 1978

Further information. It is known that other leaflets, literature and price lists were published. The Editor would welcome more information to add to these listings.

no ref.....................................1957	**Booklet**.......................................Yellow cover, 'A NEW SERIES' and 'DUBLO DINKY TOYS' in red £20-30
DT/CF/5 16/159/100 1959	**Illustrated price list** ....Colour cover showing 983 Transporter and cars, etc....................................£10-15
DT/CF/7 16/160/100 (3P) .1960	**Illustrated price list** ....Colour cover with 666 Missile Vehicle and 785 Service Station, etc..................£10-15
DT/CF/8 16/160/100 (4P) .1960	**Illustrated price list** ....Colour cover with 930 Pallet-Jekta plus GS 951 Fire Service, etc......................£10-15
DT/CF/11 8/561/100..........1961	**Illustrated price list** ....(72535/02) Colour cover with 4 cars and 'Purchase Tax Surcharges 26th July 1961' £10-15
72557/02 1965	**Leaflet**......................................Cover with 133, 127, 128, 151 and 171, with price list.........................£10-15
72579 1967	**Leaflet**......................................Trade Fair leaflet, 'THUNDERBIRDS'..£10-15
72569 1968	**Leaflet**......................................Features 103-105 'Captain Scarlet' vehicles.......................................£10-15
100217 1971	**Leaflet**......................................Four page 'Action Kits' leaflet...£10-15
100482 1971	**Adhesive poster**.......................Shop poster advertising 'No 451 Road Sweeper' £20-25
100362 1972	**Single sheet**............................'All Action Fighting Vehicles' £10-15
100367 1973	**Singe Sheet** ....'Highway Action Models'..£10-15
....1979	**Trade Catalogue 1979** ....'Fifty New Models', 11½ x 8¼ inches..£20-30
DT/CF/3 16/257/250 (1P) .1957	**Leaflet and Price List**..............Yellow front leaflet '1st January 1957', pictures of 716, 162, 626, and 250 Fire Engine, 'Dinky Toys' and 'Dinky Supertoys' in Red £25-35
DT/CL/20 16/1157/100uk .1957	**Two-sided Leaflet** ....Headed 'Dublo Dinky Toys' in Red on Yellow. Pictures of first 3 issues: 064, 065, 066 .....£10-15
DT/CF/6 16/759/1002ndP .1959	**Price List with colour pictures**.Leaflet cover shows nos. 998, 967, 968 and 986. Dated '1959/UK' on front.....................£10-15

Meccano Trade Catalogues listing Dinky Toys

These were issued for many years but little information has been recorded (please send any information that you may have). For example:
Ref. 100126 – **1978 Trade Catalogue** with 'Todays World', 'Todays

Meccano', Todays Dinky Toys' on the cover plus colour design of late 1970s models on Motorway with 'Meccano' buildings in background.
Ref. 100102 – **1979 Trade Catalogue** 'Today's Meccano & Dinky'.

Overseas Catalogues

Catalogues were often adapted so that they could be switched for use in most countries in the world irrespective of the language or the currency used. An example of this is the 1965 catalogue:

72257/02UK 1965	**UK catalogue**.............................16 pages. Cover depicts 5 cars namely Nos.127, 128, 133 and 171 plus a ....description of various model features £15-20
72557 1965	**Overseas edition**.......................16 pages. The cover is the same but replacing the features listing is a panel with 'Precision ....Diecast Scale Models' printed in English, German, French, Spanish, Italian and Swedish. ....The catalogue pages contain only the basic English model name and number - all the ....English text having been removed. The models are the same as 72257/02 ....£20-25
72559 1965	**Overseas edition**.......................24 pages. Whilst the cover is the same as 72557, the listings are entirely different for they ....feature both English and French Dinky Toys, including the French issues sold in the UK...£40-50

Price lists. Prior to the overseas editions being despatched, price lists in the correct language and currency would be inserted.
The Editor would like to express his thanks to the many collectors around the world who have contributed to this listing. New information would be welcomed.

Dinky Toys Overseas Catalogue editions recorded to date

Africa

KENYA 1961	**Illustrated List**...£50-75
RHODESIA 1953	**Illustrated Price List**..£75-100
....1954	**Illustrated Price List**..£75-100
SOUTH AFRICA		
7/655/20 1955	**Catalogue**...................................Ovaltine Van + 7 others, prices in shillings/pence, 24 pages...............................£50-75
TANGANYIKA and UGANDA	**Combined Catalogue**..£75-100

Australia

Agents (in 1952): E. G. Page & Co. (Sales) Pty., Ltd., Danks Building, 324 Pitt Street, Sydney, Australia.

13/852/12 1952	**Catalogue**...................................Cover shows boy with green sweater........................An example sold at auction in 1998 for **£250**
7/757/30 1957	**Catalogue**...................................Piccadilly Circus, colour, vertical, no prices, 28 pages £75-100

Belgium and Luxembourg (French printing)

Agents: P FREMINEUR et Fils, Rue des Bogards 1, Bruxelles 1

Pre-War Edition

13/736/265 1936	**Meccano Catalogue**...£75-100

Post-War Editions - Mostly same covers as equivalent UK issues

16/1053 /10 1954	**Catalogue**...................................Same cover as 1953 UK issue...£30-40
16/1054 /2 1954	**Catalogue**...................................Same cover as 1954 UK issue...£30-40
16/656/156 1956	**Catalogue**...................................(DT/CL/5) Same cover as 1956 UK issue £30-40
7/539/- 1959	**Catalogue**...................................with Red Jaguar XK140 on cover..£30-40
no ref............................1960	**48 page Catalogue** ....English and French models in one catalogue. Printed and issued only in Belgium and/Luxembourg. Cover depicts Land Rover plus two French Dinky Toys cars. Frs 3-. £75-100

Belgium (Flemish printing)

16/1054 /2 1954	**Illustrated price list**...£40-50
72551 1966	**1st Edition price list** ....in French and Flemish, 164 pages..£40-50

Canada

Agents: Meccano Limited, 675 King Street West, Toronto and 187 - 189 Church Street, Toronto.

Pre-War Editions

10/34	1934	**Leaflet**	Yellow leaflet with 'LOCKE BROS. OF MONTREAL' stamp	£50-60
7/38	1938	**Leaflet**	Ten page fold-out leaflet showing the full range	£50-60
13/840/5	1940	**Leaflet**	Twelve pages in black and white, size 8.75 x 5.875 inches. Cover shows boy with outstretched arms plus 62h, 151a, 36g, 43a, and 33r. 'The Fascinating Collecting Hobby'.	£50-60
6/41	1941	**Leaflet**	Twelve page fold-out leaflet showing the full range.	£50-60

Post-War Editions

16/351/25	1951	**Catalogue**	Boy with 3 models, pictures in blue, 16 pages	£50-60
7/953/150	1953	**Catalogue**	555 Fire Engine, 522 Big Bedford, 25x Breakdown Truck, 28 pages	£40-50
16/355/90	1955	**Illustrated price list**	Printed on Off-White leaflet	£30-35
7/655/90	1955	**Catalogue**	Illustration of Bedford 'Ovaltine' Van plus seven other models	£40-50
7/556/90	1956	**Catalogue**	Regent Tanker/Tunnel, 1st June 1956 in colour, 32 pages	£40-50
16/656/18c	1956	**Illustrated price leaflet**	(DT/CL/4) in colour, featuring 131 Cadillac and 660 Tank Transporter	£15-20
16/756/18	1956	**Illustrated price leaflet**	in colour, featuring 706 Vickers 'Air France' Airliner	£15-20
7/757/90	1957	**Catalogue**	Piccadilly Circus, vertical, in colour, with prices, 28 pages	£40-50
7/559/90	1959	**Catalogue**	Red Jaguar + 6 models on cover, in colour, 28 pages	£40-50
3/41/25 7252 3/42	1961	**Catalogue**	Black with 7 models, Cover 9th Canada/English, 32 pages	£30-40
13/163/100 7254 2/42	1963	**Catalogue**	Motor Show 11th, Canada/English, 32 pages	£30-40
13/1063 /50 7254 8/42	1963	**Catalogue**	Flyer 8in x 10¼in Cover, 10 models, Canada 1963, 8 pages	£10-15
7/464/150 72550/42	1964	**Catalogue**	12th 8in x 11in, Canada/English, 8 pages	£10-15
None	1964	**Catalogue**	Flyer, 5½ x 3½, shows 6 Hong Kong models, 12 pages	£10-15
None	1965	**Catalogue**	1st Edn 8½ x 5½, 5 models on cover, 16 pages	£20-25
72561	1966	**Catalogue**	1st Edition, 108 pages	£30-40
72561	1966	**Catalogue**	2nd Edition, 106 pages	£30-40
72571	1967	**Catalogue**	3rd edition, 106 pages	£30-40
72580	1968	**Catalogue**	4th Edition, 106 pages	£30-40
72585	1969	**Catalogue**	5th Edition, 24 pages	£20-30

Cyprus

(Distributor unknown)

No Ref	1969	**Catalogue**	Same as UK issue	£20-25

Egypt

(Distributor unknown)

5/652/2	1952	**Catalogue**	Different page nine from UK issue with pictures of US 39 Series cars and British cars	£20-25

Eire and Channel Islands

Agents: S.J. Gearey, 1 St Stephens Green, Dublin. (Ceased trading 1968).
Agents from 1969: Kilroy Bros Ltd, Shanowen Road, Whitehall, Dublin 9.

7/755/20	1955	**Catalogue**	'Eire' and 'C.I.' on cover	£20-25
7/659/75	1959	**Catalogue**	'Eire' on cover	£20-25
7/364/7	1964	**Catalogue**	'Eire' on cover	£20-25
No.5	1969	**Catalogue**	'Irish' on cover Distributed by Kilroy Bros Ltd.	£20-25

Hong Kong

Representatives: W.R.Loxley & Co. Ltd., Jardine House, 11th Floor, 20 Pedder Street, Hong Kong.

DT/CF/5	1959	**Illustrated price list**	Same cover as 1959 UK issue DT/CF/5	£20-25

Italy

Agents: Alfredo Parodi, Piazza 8, Marcellino 6, Genova

Post-War Editions

16/657/5	1957	**Leaflet**	with 101-105	£10-15
16/3/57/5	1957	**Leaflet**	677 and 472 'Raleigh'	£10-15
16/357/5	1957	**Leaflet**	642 and 455 Brooke Bond Tea	£10-15
16/857/5	1957	**Leaflet**	237 Mercedes front, 136, 236, 238 back	£10-15
16/457/5	1957	**Leaflet**	697 Military Set	£10-15
16/457/5	1957	**Leaflet**	661 and 919 'Golden Shred'	£10-15
no ref	1957	**Leaflet**	with 163, 236 and 238 on racing circuit	£20-25
no ref	1957	**Leaflet**	with 237, 661, and 919 'Golden Shred'	£20-25
16/357/5	1957	**Illustrated price list**	with 'Italy' printed after the reference number	£20-25
12/757/50	1957	**Leaflet**	(DT/CL/15) 642 and 455 'Brooke Bond' shown	£20-25
7/857/50	1957	**Catalogue**	Same cover as UK issue 7/657/820	£30-40
DT/CL/12	1957	**Leaflet**	with 677 and 472 on cover	£20-25
7/758/50	1958	**Catalogue**	Same cover as UK issue 7/458/856	£30-40
7/364/40 7225 0/37	1964	**Catalogue**	12th 8in x 11in, includes 4 pages of French Dinky, 12 pages	£20-30

Malaya and Singapore

Agents: King & Co, Singapore.

16/557/25 (IP)	1957	**Catalogue (8 pages)**	Cover depicts 170, 626, 716, 955, includes other pictures and price list in $ (DT/CF/3)	£40-50
7/958/10	1958	**Catalogue**	Same cover as UK, 4 pages with prices in $	£40-50

Catalogues

Netherlands/Holland

Agents: Hausemann & Hotte NV, Kromboomsloot 57-61, Amsterdam

Pre-War Editions

1/736/5 1936		Yellow paper with Black ink	£75-100
13/637/75 1937		Yellow paper with Black ink	£75-100
13/738/22 1938		Yellow paper with Black ink	£75-100

Post-War Editions - Some black/white, later coloured as per UK issues

16/954/108 1954	**Illustrated price list**	Printed in French	£15-20
8/1255/50 (DT/L/7) 1955		no details	£30-35
16/256/30n (DT/CL/2)..1956		no details	£20-25
16/256/30n (DT/L/9) ...1956		no details	£20-25
16/1158 /20 1958		'Nederland Frs 3-'. Cover same as 1958 UK issue.	£30-35
16/256/30 (72538/29) ...1962		no details	£20-25
72571 1967	**Catalogue**	3rd Edition, price list in Dutch, florins, 162 pages	£40-50
no ref...........................1970	**Catalogue**	6th Edition includes 8 pages of French Dinky, 32 pages	£20-30

Portugal

1956	**Illustrated Catalogue**	no details	£40-50
1959	**Illustrated Catalogue**	no details	£40-50
1963	**Illustrated Catalogue**	no details	£30-40

Spain

DT/CL15 SP 16/457/5 ..1957	**Ilustrated Leaflet**	Similar to Italian leaflet with 697 on colur front of single sheet, unpriced list on reverse	£10-15

Sweden

Agents: Ludvig Wigart & Cos, AB Helsingborg.

7/654/14 1954	**4 pages**	3 pages colour pictures plus price list in Kroner with Swedish text	£30-40
16/357/15 1957	**Leaflet**	Leaflet depicts 455 'Brooke Bond' Trojan plus 642 RAF Tanker and	
....		price list in Kroner with Swedish text	£15-20
14/561/60 1961	**Catalogue**	Same as 1961 UK issue, text in Swedish	£20-30
72580 1968	**162 page Catalogue**	Same as UK 1968 edition, but in Swedish	£20-30

Switzerland

Agents: Riva & Kunzmann SA Basel 2, Switzerland. From 1965 address changed to Prattela, Switzerland.

7/356/20 1956	**Catalogue**	Ovaltine Van + 7 others, prices in francs, 24 pages	£40-50
72537/25 1962	**Catalogue**	10th Edition, 48 pages, same as UK issue 72537/02 plus French Dinky	£40-50
13/163/175 1963	**Catalogue**	11th Edition, 48 pages, same as UK issue 13/163/20 plus French Dinky	£40-50
72559 1965	**Catalogue**	24 pages, same cover as UK issue 72557 plus French Dinky	£40-50

United States of America

Agents: H. Hudson Dobson, PO Box 254, 26th St and Jefferson Avenue, Kenilworth, NJ.
In 1952 the address was: PO Box 254, 906 Westfield Avenue, Elizabeth, NJ.
From 1957 the address changed to 627 Boulevard, Kenilworth. New York showroom: 200, Fifth Avenue, PO Box 255.
Models sold by this distributor will often be found with an 'H.Hudson Dobson' label
From 1963: Lines Bros Inc, 1107 Broadway, New York. From ?: AVA International, Box 7611, Waco, Texas 76710.

War-Time Issue

no ref...........................1941	**Large leaflet**	No details available	NGPP

Post-War Editions

no ref...........................1951	**Catalogue**	Boy's side face, 5 models, black and white, green printing, 16 pages	£50-75
no ref...........................1952	**Catalogue**	Hands holding 27f (139b and 25x in picture). Unlike the UK edition,	
		39b, 39c and 39e are shown in two-tone colours	£50-75
7/753/150 1953	**Catalogue**	Same cover as 1953 UK issue 7/953/360	£50-75
7/954/150 1954	**Catalogue**	Same cover as 1954 UK issue 7/754/600	£50-75
7/753/150 1954	**Catalogue**	157 Jaguar, 480 Kodak, 641 Army, Separate price list, 28 pages	£50-75
no ref...........................1955	**Catalogue**	20 models on cover, 5 French, black and white, prices in $, 32 pages	£50-75
no ref...........................1956	**Catalogue**	'Ever-Ready' + 11 others, Feb 57, black/white, prices in $, 32 pages	£50-75
no ref...........................1957	**Catalogue**	Yellow/Red cover shows model 697 plus Red lined sections displaying	
		English and French models. Red panel with US address of H.Hudson Dobson.	
		36 black/white pages of English and French models	£75-100
no ref...........................1957	**Catalogue**	Yellow, Red lines, black/white, 9-30-57, prices in $, 36 pages	£50-75
7/958/250 1958	**Catalogue**	House of Parliament in colour, prices in $, 32 pages	£50-75
7/7/125 1959	**Leaflet**	Colour, English and French, prices in $	£20-30
7/559/250 1959	**USA Catalogue**	Cover depicts Red Jaguar XK140 etc. 26 pages English models, 6 pages French	£50-75
7/8/125 1959	**Leaflet**	3 pages of colour pictures plus price list Cover shows English and	
....		French models, eg 195 Jaguar 3.4, 265 Plymouth Taxi	NGPP
no ref...........................1960	**Leaflet**	6 pages introducing 'Mini-Dinky', plus pictures of complete range	£40-45
7/3/30 NP 1960	**Catalogue**	No details	NGPP
16/161/100 72529/22...1961	**Leaflet**	4 pages. Page 1 features 798 Healey Sports Boat, 258 Police Car and 265 Taxi.	
		Page 2 lists models and prices, page 3 lists Supertoys	£20-30
14/561/200 1961	**Catalogue**	Black with 7 models, USA 1961, 16 pages, French & UK, 48 pages	£50-75
9/762/50 1962	**Leaflet**	72542/22 and D.T./CL 14	£10-15
725377/22 1962	**Catalogue**	10th Edition, 48 pages, same as UK 7253702 plus French Dinky	£20-30
72537/22 1962	**Catalogue**	120 Jaguar 'E'-type, 10th Edn. 5c, 16 pages of French Dinky, 48 pages	£50-75
13/763/60 1963	**Catalogue**	11th Edition, 48 pages, same as UK 13/763/400 plus French Dinky	NGPP
16/163/50 7254 7/22...1963	**Leaflet**	Illustrated Flyer price list, black and white	£20-30
13/763/10 7254 5/22.....1963	**Catalogue**	Motor Show 11th USA, 16 pages French Dinky, 48 pages	£25-35

no ref.............................1965	Leaflet..Lines Bros Flyer 8½in x 11in, Hong Kong on cover...	**£20-30**
no ref.............................1965	'Lines Bros' leaflet ....4 pages, Yellow/Red cover with 113 MGB...	**£30-35**
72577/3 1967	Leaflet..10in x 12³/₄in includes 5 Hong Kong Dinky...	**£15-20**
100103 1971	Catalogue..................................7th Edition, same as UK, 24 pages	**£10-15**
100108 1972	Catalogue..................................8th Edition, same as UK, 28 pages	**£10-15**
100110 1973	Catalogue..................................9th Edition, same as UK, 40 pages	**£10-15**
100265 1973	Leaflet..4 pages Dinky Kits Catalogue	**£10-15**
100114 1974	Catalogue..................................10th Edition, same as UK, 48 pages	**£10-15**
100/117 1975	Catalogue..................................11th Edition, 40 pages, same as UK 100115	**£10-15**
100/120 1976	Catalogue..................................12th Edition, 40 pages, same as UK 100118	**£10-15**
100/135 1977	Catalogue..................................13th Edition, 40 pages, same as UK 100122 but background on cover is Blue not Red......**£10-15**
100/101 1978	Catalogue..................................14th Edition, 64 pages, same as UK 100/100	**£10-15**

West Germany

Agents: Biengngraeber of Hamburg.

72585 1969   Catalogue ....32 pages, No.5 features 'Joe's Car' on cover, Catalogue in English, price list in German ...**£20-25**

Meccano Catalogues 1954 - 1958   with colour 'Dinky Toys' and 'Hornby-Dublo' listing.

These contained sections with listings and pictures of 'Dinky Toys' and 'Hornby-Dublo' products. Details known to the compiler relate solely to issues in the mid-1950's period. 'MECCANO TOYS OF QUALITY' logo on each cover.

13/654/995UK	1954-55	**24 pages, price '2d'**.................Cover depicts 4 boys on a desert island. Black/White pictures..............................	**£20-25**
13/655/797UK	1955-56	**28 pages, price '2d'**.................Cover shows boys looking in toyshop window Black/White pictures	**£20-25**
13/756/525UK	1956	**32 pages, price '4d'**.................Cover depicts Dinky Toys, Hornby-Dublo, and a Meccano helicopter. This is a large catalogue with colour printing..............................	**£30-35**
13/757/500UK	1957	**32 pages, price '4d'**.................Famous cover showing Meccano Tower, Hornby-Dublo train crossing a viaduct and Dinky Toys passing beneath. Large, with colour pictures	**£50-75**
13/758/450UK	1958	**20 pages, price '4d'**.................Cover depicts boy, Hornby-Dublo train, 8 Dinky Toys and a Meccano model. Includes some superb engine pictures	**£30-35**

Factory drawings

A number of models were planned but not actually produced by Meccano. This is list of known factory drawings and plans for such models.
Austin A40 Van 'OMNISPORT' drawing dated 31-8-57. **Guy Warrior Van** 'GOLDEN SHRED' drawing dated 26-3-57, Job No. 14794. **Leyland Fuel Tanker** drawing dated 30-9-65, Job No. 62520. **Single-Deck Bus** drawing dated 14-5-34, Job No. 6763. **Jowett Javelin Saloon** drawing dated 10-10-47, Job No. 12886. **Renault Fregate** drawing dated 4-7-57, Job No. 20106. **Triumph Dolomite** (intended 38e) drawing dated 1939. **Vampire Jet** drawing dated 27-11-45, Job No. 12157. **Firebrand Aircraft** drawing dated 18-12-45, Job No. 12159.

Meccano Magazines 1952 - 1975

With the introduction of yearly Dinky Toys catalogues from 1952 the Meccano Magazine lost its somewhat unique role as a combined magazine/catalogue. However, with the help of 'The Toyman' and his monthly articles plus superb colour advertising of new models, the Magazine continued to provide a valuable service for collectors.
Meccano Magazines of this period are in the price range of **£5-10**.

The Dinky Drivers Diary

1972-75   6 model pictured on the cover, plus descriptions and diagrams of 1970s models inside ....NGPP

Dinky Toys Club Literature

DTC/L/1	1958-59	**Collector's Licence**, Brown cover, 16 pages.......**£50-75**
DTC/L/2	1959-60	**Collector's Licence**, Red cover, 16 pages **£50-75**
DTC/L/3	1960-61	**Collector's Licence**, Green cover, 16 pages.......**£50-75**
DTC/L/4	1961-62	**Collector's Licence**, Yellow cover, 16 pages.......**£50-75**
19/759/35	1959-?	**Dinky Toys Club Newsletter**, '3d'. Stirling Moss on cover, 150 Rolls-Royce featured in centre-fold, b/w pictures ....NGPP

Dinky Toys Trade Boxes

Virtually all Dinky Toys models were supplied in their own individual boxes from around 1954. Before then most small models were supplied to shopkeepers in 'Trade Boxes' containing 3, 4, 6 or 12 identical models separated by strips of card. (Some aircraft and ship models were an exception to this general rule). A single item would be sold without further packaging except perhaps for a paper bag.

These Trade Boxes have become collectors items in their own right whether full or empty (the latter selling for between £20 and £50 depending on its rarity and that of its original contents. Most of these boxes that come to auction are full and the listing below derives from a recent survey of such items. It is known that others exist and the Editor would welcome any information regarding Trade Boxes.

YB = Yellow box, YBS = Yellow box with sleeve, GB = Green box, GRB = Grey box, CB = Cream box, BB = Blue box, BF = Buff box. Early post-war boxes are Buff, Cream or Grey with either printed model details, or a with Yellow label on the end of the box lid.

078	**Lansing Bagnall Trailers**, Box of 6	**£140-170**
12c	**Telephone Box**, YB x 6	**£150-200**
12d	**Telegraph Messenger** (post-war) GB x 6	**£60-70**
12e	**Postman** (post-war) GB x 6	**£80-90**
13a	**Cook's Man**, box of 6 (50174)	**£30-40**
22g	**Streamline Tourer**, YB x 6 Code A2018	**£1,500-1,750**
23b	**Small Closed Racing Car**, YB x 6	**£200-300**
23c	**Racing Car**, YB x 6	**£200-300**
23e	**Speed of the Wind**, YB x 6	**£200-300**
23f	**Alfa Romeo**, YB x 6	**£250-300**
23s	**Streamlined Racing Car**, YB x 4	**£200-225**
24g	**Sports Tourer**, A1017, YB x 6	**£1,500-2,000**
25d	**Petrol Wagon**, (common colours) YB x 6	**£200-300**
25e	**Tipping Wagon**, YB x 6	**£250-350**
25f	**Market Gardeners Lorry**, YB x 6	**£200-300**
25g(405)	**Jeep**, YB x 3	**£150-200**
25h	**Fire Engine**, YB x 6	**£300-400**
25j	**Jeep**, 6 models, various colours	**£250-350**
25m	**Bedford Truck** (common colours), YB x 6	**£200-300**
25p	**Aveling Barford**, YB x 6	**£150-200**
25p	**Aveling Barford Diesel Roller**, YB x 3	**£150-200**
25r	**Forward Control Lorry**, YB x 6	**£200-250**
25t	**Flat Truck and Trailer**, YB x 3	**£300-325**
25v	**Refuse Truck** (common colours), YB x 4	**£200-300**
25w	**Bedford Truck** (common colours), YB x 6	**£200-300**
25y	**Universal Jeep**, YB x 6	**£150-225**
27	**Tram Car** (pre-war) YB x 6	**£900-1,200**
27a	**Massey-Harris Tractor**, YB x 3	**£150-200**
27b	**Harvest Trailer**, YB x 6	**£75-85**
27c	**MH Manure Spreader**, YB x 3	**£85-100**
27d	**Land Rover**, GRB x 6	**£225-275**
27e	**Estate Car**, YB x 6	**£200-300**
27g	**Motocart**, YB x 3	**£100-140**
27h	**Disc Harrow**, YB x 4	**£60-80**
27j	**Triple-Gang Mower**, YB x 6	**£150-200**
27m	**Land Rover Trailer**, YB x 3	**£70-90**
28/1	**Delivery Vans**, 1st Type, A1008, YB x 6	**£5,000-7,500**
29a	**'Q' type Bus**, YB x 6	**£1,000-1,200**
29c	**AEC Bus** (post-war) YB x 6	**£200-300**
29f	**Observation Coach**, YB x 6	**£300-400**
29g	**Luxury Coach**, YB x 6	**£400-500**
29h	**Duple Roadmaster**, YB x 6	**£300-400**
30b	**Rolls Royce**, YB x 6	**£300-400**
30d	**Vauxhall**, YB x 6	**£300-400**
30e	**Breakdown Lorry**, YB x 6	**£150-200**
30f	**Ambulance**, YB x 6	**£300-400**
30h	**Daimler Ambulance**, YB x 4	**£200-300**
30m	**Rear Tipping Wagon**, YB x 6	**£150-200**
30p	**'Mobilgas' Tankers**, YB x 6	**£500-600**
30pa	**'Castrol' Tanker**, YB x 6	**£500-700**
30pb	**'Esso' Tanker**, YB x 6	**£500-700**
30j	**Austin Wagon**, YB x 6	**£250-300**
30m	**Dodge Tipping Wagon**, YB x 6	**£150-180**
30r	**Thames Flat Truck**, YB x 6	**£130-160**
30s	**Austin Covered Wagon**, YB x 6	**£150-200**
30v(490)	**Electric Milk Float**, YB x 6	**£250-300**
30v(491)	**NCB Milk Float**, YB x	**£250-300**
30w	**Electric Articulated Vehicle**, YB x 6	**£300-400**
31a	**Trojan 'Esso' Van**, YB x 6	**£500-600**
31b	**Trojan 'Dunlop' Van**, YB x 6	**£500-600**

31c	**Trojan 'Chivers' Van**, YB x 6	**£600-800**
33w	**Horse and Wagon**, Grey box x 3	**£110-150**
34b	**Royal Mail Van**, YB x 6	**£300-400**
34c	**Loudspeaker Van**, YB x 6	**£150-180**
35a	**Saloon Car**, YB x 6	**£290-330**
35b	**Racer** (Silver/Red) YBS x 6	**£280-330**
35c	**MG Sports Car**, YBS x 6	**£250-300**
36a	**Armstrong-Siddeley**, YB x 6	**£400-500**
37b	**Police Motor Cyclist** (6)	**£150-200**
37c	**Signals Despatch Rider**, YB x 6	**£150-200**
38b	**Sunbeam-Talbot**, YB x 6	**£400-500**
38e	**Armstrong-Siddeley**, YB x 6	**£450-550**
40a	**Riley**, YB x 6	**£350-450**
40b	**Triumph 1800**, GRB x 6	**£350-450**
40e	**Standard Vanguard**, YB x 6	**£350-450**
40d	**Austin Devon**, YB x 6	**£350-450**
40f	**Hillman Minx**, YB x 6	**£250-350**
40g	**Morris Oxford**, YB x 6	**£350-450**
40h	**Austin Taxi**, YB x 6	**£350-450**
40j	**Austin Somerset**, YB x 6	**£350-450**
42a	**Police Box**, YB x 6	**£140-170**
43b	**'RAC' Motorcycle Patrol**, CB x 6	**£200-300**
44b	**'AA' Motorcycle Patrol**, CB x 6	**£200-300**
47c	**Two-face Traffic Lights**, YB x 12	**£40-70**
62s	**Hurricane Fighters**, BB x 6	**£300-400**
70d	**Twin Engined Fighter**, YB x 6	**£110-130**
70e	**Gloster Meteor**, YB x 6	**£40-60**
70f	**Shooting Star**, YB x 6	**£100-150**
105a	**Garden Roller**, YB x 6	**£80-90**
105b	**Wheelbarrow**, YB x 6	**£80-90**
105c	**Hand Truck**, YB x 6	**£40-60**
105e	**Grass Cutter**, YB x 6	**£90-110**
106	**Austin A90 Atlantic**, YB x 6	**NGPP**
107a	**Sack Truck**, YB x 6	**£90-110**
139a	**Ford Fordor**, YB x 6	**£350-450**
139b	**Hudson Commodore**, YB x 6	**£500-700**
140a	**Austin Atlantic**, YB x 6	**£500-700**
140b	**Rover 75**, YB x 6	**£350-450**
152b	**Reconnaisance Car**, YB x 6	**£400-500**
152c	**RTC Austin 7**, YB x 6	**£400-500**
160b	**Royal Artillery Gunners**, YB x 12	**£200-250**
161b	**Mobile AA Gun**, YB x 6	**£300-400**
253	**Daimler Ambulance**, YB x 4	**£150-200**
270	**'AA' Motor Cycle** (post-war), YB x 6	**£200-300**
432	**Foden Tipping Lorry**, factory shrink-wrapped trade pack of 6	**£80-100**
551	**Trailer** (Grey/Red), YB x 3	**£45-65**
551	**Trailer** (various colours), Blue box x 3	**£65-85**
603a	**Army Personnel** (metal), YB x 12	**£80-110**
	NB Early YB long, later issues square.	
603a	**Army Personnel** (plastic), YB x 12	**£40-50**
687	**Field Gun Trailer**, YB x 6	**£65-85**
705	**Viking Airliner**, YB x 6	**£200-300**
750	**Telephone Call Box**, YB x 6	**£200-300**
751	**Police Hut**, YB x 6	**£150-180**
755	**Lamp Standard, single-arm**, YB x 6	**£30-40**
756	**Lamp Standard, double-arm**, YB x 6	**£30-40**
760	**Pillar Box**, YB x 6	**£150-200**
768	**Racks with Tyres**, YB x 6	**£75-100**
773	**Traffic Lights**, YB x 12	**£150-175**

777	**Belisha Beacon**, YB x 12	**£65-90**
786	**Tyre Rack**, YB x 6	**£120-160**
788	**Spare Bucket** for 966, YB x 6	**£175-225**
797	**Healey Raceboats**, YB x 6	**£150-200**
994	**Loading Ramp**, Plain box x 3	**£55-80**
14095	**Tyres**, YB x 12	**£5-10**

Trade Packs of BOXED models
106	**'The Prisoner' Mini-Moke**, (6)	**£600-800**
159	**Morris Oxford** (3 Green, 3 Tan)	**£250-350**

161	**(40j) Austin Somerset**, (6)	**£600-800**
190	**Caravan**, later type GRB x 6	**£175-200**
195	**Jaguar 3.4 Saloon**, (6)	**£400-500**
471	**Austin Vans 'NESTLE'**, (6)	**£300-400**
491	**Electric Dairy Van 'NCB'** (6)	**£300-400**

NB Expect Trade Boxes containing rare colour variations to attract a corresponding premium.
NB See also Gift Sets for 62h and 62d Pre-War Aeroplane Trade Box items.

Dinky Toys Trade Accessories

Trade Display Unit packed in plain cardboard box. Black wooden case with 'Property of Meccano Ltd Liverpool' in black on gold; three shelves in light blue/white/yellow; four gold supports with two yellow and two red supports; four red tin flags 'DINKY TOYS'; three tin flags 'ASK FOR BOOKLET', 'OVER 200 MODELS', and 'ALWAYS SOMETHING NEW'; plus two red and two yellow balls **£400-500**

Glass Display Case. Oak frame with three glass shelves. Size approximately 32" (80 cm.) wide, 24" (60 cm.) high, 9" (22 cm.) deep. With 'DINKY TOYS' in green lettering on glass front **£300-400**

Trade Display Stand Large yellow folding cardboard stand which non-erected measures approximately 28" (70 cm.) x 14" (35 cm.); three display levels with 'DINKY TOYS' logo in green plus 'MECCANO PRODUCT' in red on top header board. Outer corrugated cardboard packing has green printed instruction leaflet........**£200-300**

Trade Display Stand Small yellow and red folding cardboard stand which non-erected measures approximately 12" (31 cm.) x 7" (15 cm.); with one 'DINKY TOYS' and two 'DINKY SUPERTOYS' logos in red plus yellow 'MASTERPIECES IN MINIATURE' logo on red background. **£75-100**

Display Stand (circa 1950 - 1960) Large metal stand which measures approximately 36" x 21" x 22" (91.5 x 53 x 56 cm.); with nine display shelves covered in black plastic track. Metal advertisement affixed to top states in yellow/white/red/black 'A MOTOR SHOW FOR GIRLS AND BOYS', 'PRECISION DIE-CAST MODELS BY MECCANO', 'BEST RANGE', and 'BEST VALUE IN THE WORLD'. Lower large transfer also in yellow/red/black repeats the message. **£400-500**

Window Sign (plastic), Top half is dark blue with white 'MECCANO' logo, bottom half is yellow with red 'Dinky Toys' logo. Approximately 18" x 6". **£70-80**

Counter Display (cardboard), Small display stand suitable for a single new model, 'ALWAYS NEW MODELS' logo in white on red background, header states 'DINKY TOYS' in red on yellow. **£70-80**

Counter Display (cardboard) 'BATTLE OF BRITAIN' Blue/yellow displaying 719 Spitfire MkII and 721 Junkens JU 87b Stuka........**£100-150**

Illuminated Shop Display Sign with 'DINKY TOYS' in large wooden letters above a glass panel lettered either 'Made by Meccano Ltd' or 'British and Guaranteed'........**£300-400**

Shop Display Carousel with tripod base supporting four stacks of clear plastic. **£200-300**

Illuminated Counter or Window display unit 13" x 9" with perspex front 'DINKY TOYS' and 'NEW MODELS EVERY MONTH' logo........**£100-1500**

Counter Carousel Unit with 'Always Something New from Dinky' around its edge. Red/Yellow 'DINKY TOYS BY MECCANO' sign on top, 26" high overall. **£200-250**

Metal Counter Display Sign, triangular in shape with red 'DINKY TOYS' on yellow background, approximately 8" x 1" x 1"........**£30-40**

Electric Revolving 'Meccano' Wooden Display Stand 'DINKY TOYS - LOOK FOR THE NAME ON THE BASE' logo, (28" square and 10" high) **£250-350**

Pre-War 'Meccano Dinky Toys' Advertising Sign. An example of this double-sided hanging sign was sold by Christies', South Kensington for £632. It shows pictures and details of 22, 24, 25 and 28 series models available in 'Season 1934'. Date code: '16/734/1'. Size: 11in x 9in (28cm x 23cm). **£500-600**

Note: This section is far from complete and the Editor would welcome details of other trade stands, posters, display cards, promotional material and advertising signs.

Acknowledgements

The Editor would like to express his thanks to the following collectors and dealers for new Dinky Toys information received:

John Clark of Cambridgeshire; John Kinchen, Hampshire; Dick Henrywood, Dreweatt Neate Auctioneers, Newbury, Berks., Bruce D. Hoy, Queensland, Australia; Hugo Marsh and Nigel Mynheer of Christie's; Brian Goodall and David Nathan of Vectis Auctions; George Beevis, Lacy Scott and Knight, Bury St Edmunds; Barry Potter, Barry Potter Auctions, Northampton; Rob Butler, Wallis and Wallis Auctions, Lewes; Leigh Gotch, Bonhams Auctioneers; Paul Campbell, Sotheby's Auctions; Kegan Harrison, Phillips Auctioneers, Tim Arthurs, Lloyd Ralston Auctions, Norwalk, USA, Mary Beth Christie, QXL Online Auctions, Mrs Joyce Peterzell, Los Angeles, USA; José F. Heraud, Glenshaw, Pa, USA; R Hoeksema, The Hague; Filippo Zama, Bracciano, Italy;

Daniel Hostettler, Allschwil, Switzerland; Gerry Savage, Diecast Collector and Collectors Gazette; Michael Batsford of Essex; Bob Burnett, North London; Mark Jones, Halesworth, Suffolk; David Bartley and Norm Porter of British Columbia; Peter Jenkins of Dorking; Par-Olof Danielsson, Uppsala, Sweden; Barry Thompson, Leek, Staffs.; Peter Jenkins, Dorking; Tim Walker, Grimsby; Jarle Moldekleiv, Bergen, Norway.

The Editor would also like to express his appreciation to the many other collectors who took the time and trouble to contact us with updating information. Do please keep it coming!

Dinky Toys Auction Results

Vectis Auctions Ltd.

Royal National Hotel, Bedford Way, Russell Square, London

Grading system used by Vectis Auctions:
A+ As near mint or pristine condition as at time of issue
A Virtually mint boxed - any faults of a most minor nature
B Model is near mint - box has slight faults
B Slight model or box faults - e.g. some chips or box rubs but model and box complete
C More obvious model chips and box faults inc. tears but still complete
D Same as C but box has one or more end flaps missing and model may have faded paint as well as chips
E Model and box have considerable faults

Abbreviations used in Vectis Auctions catalogues:
BPW Smooth Wheels   YB   Yellow Card Box
RW   Ridged Wheels   STB   Blue and White Striped Supertoy Box
SP   Spun Wheels   DPB   Detailed Picture Box
WIR Wire Wheels   RPC   Rigid Perspex Case
CW   Cast Wheels   BP   Bubble Pack
PW   Plastic Wheels   WB   Window Box
ST   Supertoy Wheels
N.B. All boxes have the correct colour spot, unless otherwise stated

16th SEPTEMBER 1998
ENGLISH DINKY TOYS COMMERCIAL VEHICLES
No. 274 Mini Minor Van 'Joseph Mason Paints' - Maroon/roof sign/SP - lovely A in B+ special promotional box, complete with promotional leaflet and card packing £430
No. 252 Bedford Refuse Wagon - Orange cab/chassis/Light Grey back, Green plastic shutters/Silver grille/windows/Red PW - B to A in C YB....£280
No. 491 Electric Dairy Van 'Job's Dairy' - Cream/Red loadbed and RW - A to A+ in B+ 'plain' YB £140
No. 430 Commer Breakdown Lorry - Cream cab and chassis/Blue back/Red RW - B+ to A (some minor paint chips to bumper and string replaced) in good C - YB £440
No. 501 Foden Diesel Wagon - 2nd Type cab - Red cab and chassis/Fawn back/Red ST - cab/chassis are B - back is B+ to A in good 'blue' box........£170
No. 514 Guy Van 'Lyons Swiss Rolls' - 1st cab - Dark Blue/Mid Blue RW - B to C (paint chips touched in) - adverts are B- in B ' blue' box..............£400
No. 581 Horse Box 'Express Horse Van' - B+ (apart from paint chips to ramps which are only B) - in B 'blue' box £350
No. 917/514 Guy Van 'Spratts' - 1st cab - Red/Cream/Red ST - B to B+ - adverts are B+ in B to C scarce dual numbered STB (non-matching box base) £400
No. 918 Guy Van 'Ever Ready' - 2nd cab - Blue/Red ST - B+ to A (a few minor paint chips) - adverts are A to A+ - in A STB................................£230
No. 935 Leyland Octopus Flat Truck with Chains - Green cab and chassis/Light Grey bumper cab band and riveted back/Red PW - B to B+ (scratch to roof) - in B box £900
No. 958 Guy Warrior Snow Plough - Yellow/Black/Yellow ST - A (apart from paint chip to tailboard) - in lovely A to A+ STB................................£130
No. 989 Car Transporter 'Auto Transporters' - Lemon Yellow/Light Grey/Silver-Blue ramps/Red PW - B (although leading edge of top deck is C) in C YB with damaged card packing £950
No. 915 AEC Articulated Flat Truck ' Thames Board' - White/four card tubes with 'Unilever' Logos/CW - A to A+ (some minor paint chips caused during assembly at factory) - in B+ BP £1,700

CONSTRUCTION VEHICLES
No. 975 Ruston Bucyrus Excavator - B to C (exhaust glue repaired and one track perished) - in B box with card packing £150

EMERGENCY VEHICLES
No. 261 Ford Tannus Police Car 'Polizei' - White/Dark Green/Blue roof light/aerial - A to A+ in good C RPC with card packing ring £260
No. 956 Bedford Turntable Fire Escape - Red/Silver platform/windows/Red ST - B+ in A STB - with all card packing and tested tag £130
No. 954 Fire Station Kit - A to A+ - complete and having had very light use only - in B+ STB (slight crush to one corner)..£190

FARM VEHICLES
No. 325 David Brown Tractor and Disc Harrow - All White/Red exhaust/All White Disc Harrow - B+ in B to B+ box - with part card packing..............£90

BUSES and COACHES
No. 289 Routemaster Bus 'Schweppes' - Factory shrinkwrapped trade pack of six - all obviously A+ - condition of boxes varies from B+ to A+.........£210
No. 949 Wayne School Bus - Orange/Red body stripes/Red Int and PW -

good B in B+ to A STB £190
No. 953 Continental Touring Coach - Turquoise/White roof/Fawn Int/Red PW - good B to B+ in B to B+ box £250
No. 961 Vega Major Coach 'PTT' - Orange-Yellow/Cream roof/Dark Blue INT/CW - nice B+ in C special box £120

MILITARY VEHICLES
No. 661 Recovery Tractor - Green/driver/windows/Green PW - A (apart from bare metals parts tarnished) - in B+ YB with detailed picture panel and card packing £155
No. 666 Missile Erector Vehicle with Corporal Missile and Launching Platform - Green/metal erector gears/White missile with Black tail fins - A (a few minor marks) - in A to A+ STB with slightly damaged all card packing and instructions £400
No. 666 Missile Erector Vehicle with Corporal Missile and Launching Platform - Green/Black plastic erector gears/All White missile - B+ in B STB - with damaged card packing £110

ACCESSORIES
No. 6 Shepherd Set - B to A+ (some minor paint chips) tied onto original backing card in B to B+ box £180
No. 772 British Road Signs Set - A in B box - inner card plinth is A to A+ £150
No. 45 Pre-War Garage - B to C (some tarnishing and rusting, although this is by no means severe) - in C box £320

TRADE PACKS
No. 270 Motorcycle Patrol 'AA' - Trade Pack of Six - containing 5 x smooth Grey plastic wheels - A to A+; and 1 x treaded Grey plastic wheels - B+ in good B YB with card dividers £180
No. 272 Motorcycle Patrol 'ANWB' - Trade Pack for Six - containing 4 x 'ANWB' Patrols - 1 x B+; 2 x B; and 1 x C; plus 2 x 'TS/TW' Patrols - 1 x B+; 1 x B to B+ - all have Black rubber wheels - yellow trade box is slightly grubby B to B+ with card dividers £850
No. 30V Electric Dairy Van ' Express Dairy' - Trade Pack for six - containing five examples - all are Cream/Red load bed and RW - 3 x B+; 2 x B - cream trade box is C (missing dividers)..£180
No. 440/30P Studebaker Tanker 'Mobilgas' - Trade Pack for six - containing four examples - all are Red Body and RW/small base plate print - 3 x A (very minor paint chips, probably caused by the factory); 1 x B - yellow trade box is slyghtly grubby B to B+ complete with all card dividers £320
No. 29C Double Deck Bus - Trade Pack for six - containing three examples - all are type 1 castings - (1) Dark Green/Grey/Black RW - good B to B+; (2) Dark Green/Cream/Black RW - C; (3) Red/Cream/Black RW - B to C - buff trade box is good B with card dividers £220

GIFT SETS, PRE-WAR
No. 42 Police Set - C - apart from Police Box which is B to B+ in C box - printed card inlay is B to B+..£250
No. 151 Medium Tank Unit - containing No. 151A Medium Tank - B+; No.151B Transport Wagon - C to D; No.151C Cooker Trailer - C to D; and No. 151D Water Tank - D (wheel hubs fatigued although body castings are not showing visible signs of fatigue) in C box - printed card inlay is B to B+ £250
No. 152 Light Tank Unit - containing No. 152A Light Tank - B (turret and wheels fatigued); No. 152C Austin 7 with driver - B+ (severely fatigued however); and No.152B Reconnaissance Car - D (hubs fatigued) in B box with repro card packing £150
No. 162 18 lb Quick Firing Field Gun Unit - B+ in good C box (surface tear to lid) inner card plinth is B+ complete with card packing........................£360

POST WAR
No. 2 Commercial Vehicles Gift Set - containing No.25M Bedford Tipper - Yellow/Mid Blue back/Yellow RW - B; No.27D Land Rover - Burnt Orange, Dark Blue Int/Driver/Red RW - B; No.30N Dodge Farm Produce Wagon - Mid Green cab and chassis/Yellow Back and RW - B to B+; No.30PB Studebaker Tanker 'Esso' - B; and No. 30S Austin covered Wagon - Dark Blue cab and chassis/Mid Blue back and RW - B to B+ in C STB £2,100
No.3 Passenger Cars Gift Set - containing No.27F Estate Car - T/T Brown/small baseplate print/Brown RW - C; No.30H Daimler Ambulance - Cream/large baseplate print/Red RW - B+ to A; No.40E Standard Vanguard - Mid Blue/large baseplate print/Brown RW - B to C; No.40G Morris Oxford - Dark Green/Mid Green RW - B+ to A; No.40H Austin Taxi - Yellow Body and RW - B (some paint chips touched in); and No.140B Rover 75 - Dark Red/Maroon RW -C (surface rust to base plate) in C STB with repro inner card plinth..£1,800
No.3 Private Automobiles Gift Set - containing No. 30D Vauxhall - Dark Brown/Black open chassis and RW - C; No.36B Bentley - Dark Blue/Black chassis and RW - C; No.36D Rover - Mid Green/Black chassis/Mid Green RW - B+; No.38A Frazer-Nash - Mid Blue/Grey Seats/Black RW - B; and No.38C Lagonda - Grey/Dark Grey seats/Black SW - B to B+ in C box

complete with 'H Hudson Dobson' US Distributors label (lid illustration is A) £1,500
No.123 Mayfair Gift Set - containing Rolls Royce Silver Wraith - A (some minor marks to roof); Rolls Royce Phantom V - Met Silver-Green/Cream, driver/SP - A; Bentley S2 - Bronze/Blue tonneau/Ivory Int/driver/SP - B+ (slightly faded on one side and crack to windscreen); Jaguar MKX - Met Silver Blue/Red Int/luggage/SP - A+; Mercedes 220SE - Light Blue - B; and Austin 7 Countryman - Light Blue/Red Int/SP - A to A+ - complete with figures, good C box - inner card plinth is B+ complete with tested tag ..£1,600
No.124 'Holidays' Gift Set - containing Vega Major Luxury Coach with flashing indicators - A; Plymouth Fury - Met Silver Green/Very Pale Grey Roof - B+; Jaguar MKX - Deep Silver Blue/Red Int/SP - B to B+ (box rub to roof); and Healey Sports Boat on Trailer - BPW - B+ - in C box with C inner card plinth....................£600
No.149 Sports Car Gift Set - containing No.107 Sunbeam Alpine - Cerise/Grey Int/driver/34/Cream RW - overall B although front and rear bumpers are badly chipped and only C; No. 108 MG Midget - White/Maroon Int/driver/28/Red RW - B (some paint chips lightly touched in); No. 109 Austin Healey - Yellow/driver/21/Mid Blue Int and RW - B to C; No. 110 Aston Martin - Green/driver/22/Red Int and RW - good B; and No. 110 Triumph TR2 - Salmon Pink/Driver/29/Mid BLue Int and RW - C - in very good C STB (sellotape repair to one box corner) complete with inner card plinth which is A £1,400
No. 299 Post Office Services Gift Set - B+ apart from telephone box which is only C in C STB - inner pictorial card plinth is C £175
No. 695 - 7.2 Howitzer and Tractor Gift Set - B+ apart from tow hook of Howitzer is only C - in good C box - complete with inner card packing and plinth which are C....................£250
No. 698 Mighty Antar Tank Transporter and Centurion Tank Gift Set - B+ in B STB - complete with all inner card packing and card plinth.........£130
No. 699 Military Vehicles Gift Set - containing Austin Champ with Driver - B+; Army Cargo Truck - B - (some discoloration to paintwork due to damp damage); Armoured Personnel Carrier - B; and Bedford covered Army Wagon - B+ in good B to C STB with inner card plinth....................£230

SHOP DISPLAY
Wooden Four Tier Shop Display Stand - A to A+ unassembled in original C plain cardboard transit box - highly desirable and complete with extra tinplate advertising signs....................£390
Cardboard Counter Display Stand - designed to display No. 719 Spitfire and No. 721 JU87B Stuka from the film 'Battle of Britain' - B+ to A £250

STANDARD PRODUCTION ISSUES
No. 148 Ford Fairlane - Green/Red Int/SP - B+ in B YB....................£200
No. 161 Austin Somerset - Cream/Black/Cream RW - B+ (marks to roof) in good B to B+ YB £160

UNBOXED
No. 22F Pre-War Army Tank - Grey - B....................£160
No. 25WM Bedford Military Truck - Military Green Body, Grille and RW - B to B+....................£280
No. 30HM Daimler Military Ambulance - Small Base Plate Print - B+.£200
No. 139AM US Army Staff Car - Green Body and RW/small base plate print/star to roof and doors - A £190

PRE-WAR
No. 36F Salmson - Red/Maroon chassis/Black SW - very presentable C - complete with repro driver £260
No. 25D Petrol Tank Wagon 'Shell-BP' - Red Body/Yellow Type 1 chassis/tinplate radiator/Violet-Blue SW - overall C....................£400
No. 22D Delivery Van - Orange/Blue back/'Hornby Series' cast under roof/Light Purple cast wheels - very nice B £950

POST-WAR, UNBOXED
No. 38B Sunbeam Talbot - Yellow body and RW/Dark Green tonneau - B+ £300
No. 39E Chrysler Royal - Mid-Blue body and RW - presentable B £170
No. 39E Chrysler Royal - T/T Green/Mid-Green RW - D....................£230
No. 262 VW Beetle 'PTT' - Yellow/Black wings/Yellow RW - B (paint chips carefully touched in) £120
No. 155 Ford Anglia - Deep Cream/Red Int/SP - B £290
No. 30B Rolls Royce - Dark Grey/Black chassis and RW - good B to B+£130
No. 39B Oldsmobile - Dark Brown/Black RW - B to B+....................£140
No. 152 Austin Devon - Yellow/Mid-Blue upper body and RW - A (rather thin factory paint finish)....................£140
No. 156 Rover 75 - T/T Green/Mid-Green RW - lovely A to A+.............£115
No. 157 Jaguar XK120 - White/Brown RW - B+ to A £150
No. 157 Jaguar XK120 - Yellow/Light Grey upper body and RW - A.....£140
No. 231 Maserati Racing Car - Red/9/Yellow PW - A; plus No. 232 Alfa Romeo Racing Car - Red/8/SP - B+ £130
No. 412 Austin Wagon - Powder Blue/Lemon RW - lovely B+ to A £180

No. 413 Austin Covered Wagon - Mid-Blue/Cream Canopy/Lemon RW - B+ to A....................£190
No. 413 Austin Covered Wagon - Red/Light Grey Canopy and RW - B+ to A (very minor paint chips only)....................£240

POST-WAR, BOXED
No. 159 Morris Oxford - Mid-Green/Cream/Mid-Green RW - A - in B YB £180
No. 178 Plymouth Plaza - T/T Blue/SP - B+ - in B+ lighter YB - very rare issue without model number on base plate....................£150
No. 172 Studebaker Land Cruiser - "Lowline" - Cerise upper body/White lower body/Cream RW - B+ to A (minor box rubs to sides) - in A to A+ YB £250
No. 455 Trojan Van "Brooke Bond Tea" - Dark Red/Red RW - B+ in B to B+ YB....................£110
No. 465 Morris Van "Capstan" - T/T Blue/Mid-Blue RW - B+ to A in B+ to A YB £130
No. 482 Bedford Van "Dinky Toys" - A to A+ in slightly grubby B+ YB £140
No. 152 Austin Devon - Grey-Green/Large Baseplate Print/Cream RW - A to A+ in B+ YB £210
No. 413 Austin Covered Wagon - Mid-Blue/Cream canopy/Lemon RW - A in A YB £430
No. 157 Jaguar XK120 - Grey-Green/Brown RW - A to A+ in A............£240
No. 252 Bedford Refuse Wagon - Orange cab and chassis/Light Grey/Green plastic shutters/windows/Silver grille/Red PW - B+ to A in C YB £200
No. 943 Leyland Octopus Tanker "Esso" - Dark Red body and ST - superb A to A+ - apart from minor wear to tow hook - in B+ STB £320
No. 532 Leyland Comet Wagon - Violet Blue cab and chassis/Mid Blue back/Yellow ST - C in C box....................£300
No. 261 Ford Taunus Police Car "Polizei" - White/Dark Green/Red Int/Blue roof light/aerial - A (minor mark to roof) in B+ RPC....................£270

GIFT SETS
No. 1 Commercial Vehicles Gift Set - containing No. 25B Covered Wagon - Green/Dark Green canopy/Black Type 3 chassis and RW - B to B+; No. 25D Petrol Tanker - Dark Green/Black - Type 3 chassis and RW - B+; No. 25E Tipping Wagon - Grey-Brown/Black Type 3 chassis and RW- B; No. 25F Market Gardeners Wagon - Fawn/Black Type 3 chassis and RW - C (paint chips touched in); and No. 29C Double Deck Bus - Red/Cream/Type 1 Grille with cutaway wings/Black ..SW - B+ apart from wing edges which are only B - in good C box (illustrated label ...is B+) with repro card packing - complete with Harrods retailers label to base of box £1,800

SHOP DISPLAY
Wooden Dealers Display Cabinet - "Dinky Toys" in Green/four glass shelves, plain glass sliding door panels - 75cms x 60cms x 22cms - B to B+ £360

CATALOGUES
"H Hudson Dobson 200 5th Avenue New York" 1950 US Distributors Catalogue - very good B to C £110
Belgium/French Issue 1951 Catalogue - B - contents are A £50
Rhodesia 1954 - B+; Rhodesia 1953 - B to B+; and Kenya 1961, Tanganyika and Uganda Combined Catalogue - B+ to A....................£330

25th NOVEMBER 1998, BOXED
No. 501 Foden Diesel Wagon - Dark Grey cab and back/Red chassis cab flash and RW/early axle clips/small hook/no tank slits - B (paint chip to edge of back only, both of which are very minor) in B "buff" box £680
No. 501 Foden Diesel Wagon - Voilet Blue cab and chassis/Mid Blue back cab flash and RW/early axle clips/small hook/no tank slits - B (paint chips to wing edges, sides of back and cab touched in) in B+ "buff" box complete with colour spot £900
No. 502 Foden Flat Truck - First cab - Dark Green cab Back and RW/Silver cab flash/Black chassis/early axle clips/no tank slits or hook/HB - A to A+ in B+ to A "buff" box with "G" colour stamp (rusting to staples) £500
No. 502 Foden Flat Truck - Mid Blue cab and back/Dark Blue cab flash chassis and .RW/early axle clips/no tank clips or hook/HB - lovely A to A+ in B+ "buff" box (picture label is A to A+)....................£720
No. 502 Foden Flat Truck - First cab - Burnt Orange cab and chassis/Mid Green back cab flash and RW/early axle clips/tank slits/large hook - B+ (some minor paint chips to front bumper and headlamps and some minor paint chips lightly touched in) in B+ to a "buff" box £660
No. 502 Foden Flat Truck - First cab - Dark Blue cab and chassis/Red Back and cab flash/early axle clips/no tank slits/small hook/Mid Blue RW - B+ to A (paint chips to cab roof and box rubs to corners of back) in slightly sun faded B+ blue covered box with second type label....................£770
No. 503 Foden Flat Truck- Grey cab and back/Dark Blue cab flash chassis and RW/early axle clips/no tank slits or hook/HB - B+ (edge of tailboard repainted) - in A "buff" box with grey colour spot £1,600
No. 503 Foden Flat Truck - First cab - T/T Green/early axle clips/no tank

slits/small hook/Mid Green RW - B+ (apart from cab roof colour wash and cab winged edges touched in) in A "buff" box with green colour spot.........**£1,000**
No. 503 Foden Flat Truck - First cab - Violet Blue cab and chassis/Burnt Orange Back and cab flash/Mid Blue RW/early axle clips/tank slits/large hook - B+ to a (cab wing edges lightly touched in) in A "buff" box (very slight rub to lid label and staples somewhat rusty) complete with card packing piece...**£900**
No. 504 Foden 14T Tanker - First cab - T/T Blue Silver flash/early axle clips/small unpainted hook/Mid Blue RW - A (box rubs to filler caps) in B+ "buff" box with "B" colour stamp **£500**
No. 504 Foden 14T Tanker - First cab - T/T/Blue/Mid Blue cab flash/early axle clips/large painted hook/Mid Blue RW - lovely A to A+ (slight factory blemishes to cab roof) in B+ blue covered box with orange and white label and "B" colour stamp **£650**
No. 501 Foden Diesel Wagon - Second cab - Violet Blue cab and chassis/Mid Blue back and ST - lovely A to A+ in B+ box complete with correct "B" colour stamp **£2,000**
No. 503 Foden Flat Truck with Tailboard - Burnt Orange cab and chassis/Yellow back and ST - B+ in B+ box with card packing **£2,100**
No. 504 Foden 14T Tanker - T/T Blue/riveted back/Mid Blue ST - A (wear to tow hook) in A box **£5,000**
No. 504 Foden 14T Tanker - Red cab and chassis/Fawn tank/riveted back/Red St - B+ to A (some very minor paint chip to wing edges lightly touched in and paint cracked around one filler cap) in B+ box **£1,400**
No.902/502 Foden Flat Truck - Orange cab and chassis - Mid Green back and St - B+ to A (some very minor paint chips to radiator, headlight surrounds and edges of back) in C scarce dual numbered STB **£325**
No. 902 Foden Flat Truck - Deep Red cab and chassis/Mid Green back and ST/riveted back - B to B+ (paint chips to rear edge of back and paint chips to cab roof and wing edges lightly touched in) in good B to B+ STB complete with "H HUDSON DOBSON" US Distributors label.......................**£2,300**
No. 903/503 Foden Flat Truck with Tailboard - Violet Blue cab and chassis/Yellow back/Mid Blue ST/Grey tyres - superb A to A+ in A - scarce dual numbered STB **£1,500**
No.903 Foden Flat Truck with Tailboard - Violet Blue cab and chassis/Burnt Orange back/Mid Blue ST - superb A to A+ complete with card packing in B+ to A STB **£460**
No. 903 Foden Flat Truck with Tailboard - Mid Blue cab and chassis/Fawn riveted back/Mid Blue ST - superb A to A+ in B+ to A STB showing correct colour illustration of model...**£1,100**
No. 905 Foden Flat Truck with Chains - Maroon Body and ST - rounded chain post bosses - excellent A to A+ in B+ to A STB **£440**
No. 905 Foden Flat Truck with Chains - Red cab and chassis/Light Grey riveted back/Red St - B+ (minor paint chips to wing edges and side of cab very lightly touched in) in absolutely superb A to A+ STB..........................**£550**
No. 941 Foden 14T Tanker "Mobilgas" - Black filler cap - A (3 almost imperceptible paint chips to cab and very minor wear to rear decal) in B STB with "H HUDSON DOBSON" US Distributors label to box side **£430**
No. 935 Leyland Octopus Flat Truck with Chains - Green cab and chassis/Red Radiator/Pale Grey cab band, bumper and back/riveted back/Grey plastic wheels B+ to A, Box B+ **£900**

COMMERCIAL VEHICLES
No. 961 Blaw Knox Bulldozer - Plastic Construction - Orange body/Green bulldozer blade and exhaust stacks/Black hydraulic rams and tracks/Blue plastic driver/Olive Green PW - superb A+ in somewhat grubby B STB with all card packing - very rare issue particularly with these olive green wheels instead of the usual mid green colour...**£180**

7th APRIL 1999, PRE-WAR
No.23A Racing Car - 2nd Type casting with six exhausts in fishtail - C to B - no fatigue **£380**
No.23B Hoskiss Racing Car - B - but body showing fatigue **£170**
No.22C Motor Truck - Turquoise/Black SW - B+.................................**£180**

BOXED
No.60 Aeroplane Set - including No.60A Imperial Airways - Gold/Blue, "Sunburst" - B+ in B box - inner card stand is A **£1,000**

BOXED MODELS
Retailer's Shop Display Card "World Famous Racing Cars" - with 230/231/232/233/234/239 - display card is good B - rare and desirable .**£1,100**
No.491 Electric Dairy Van "Jobs Dairy" - Cream/Red base and RW - B+ in A to A+ "plain" YB - scarce...**£160**

12th MAY 1999
No.22D Delivery Van "Hornby Series" - Orange cab and chassis/Mid Blue back/solid unpainted wheels - C to B **£450**
No.28P Delivery Van "Crawfords Biscuits" - Second Type/Red/Black SW - C - no fatigue **£450**
No.60Y Thompson Refueller - Red/"Shell Aviation Service" in gold/small White solid rubber tyres - C **£230**

Wallis and Wallis
West Street Auction Galleries, Lewes, Sussex

Condition grading used in Wallis and Wallis catalogue:
Mint - Virtually original state
VGC - Very Good Condition, a fine item
GC - Good Condition, a sound item
QGC - Quite good condition, some wear and/or damage

1998-99 AUCTION RESULTS
Scarce **Dinky Election Mini Van** (492). Boxed. Vehicle VGC to Mint **£140**
Scarce **Dinky Atlas Bus** (295), all light blue example with red interiors. Boxed, minor wear, vehicle Mint **£100**
Rare **Dinky Humber Hawk** (165) in light green and black, example with light green not black roof, boxed, minor wear. Vehicle VGC to Mint **£170**
Rare **Dinky Volvo 122S** (184) in cream with cream seats. Boxed, vehicle VGC to Mint, minor wear **£240**
A rare pre war **Dinky Double Deck Motor Bus** (29C) in light blue and cream with Dunlop Tyres adverts to sides, dark grey roof. GC to VGC for age...**£360**
A rare pre war **Dinky 30 series Vauxhall** (30d) body in fawn with dark brown base and black wheel hubs. Complete with original white tyres and spare. GC to VGC for age, some fatigue patches to nearside. Tyres flat....................**£660**
A rare pre war **Dinky 30 series Rolls Royce Car** (30b), body in deep blue with black open chassis, black smooth hubs with original tyres. VGC very minor wear, a fine example **£660**
A rare pre war **Dinky 36 series Streamlined Saloon** (36d) Rover body, but with rarer style grille, mid green body, black open criss cross chassis, black smooth hubs, with original white rubber tyres. A fine example **£720**
Rare **Dinky Swiss PTT Volkswagen** (262) in yellow and black livery, with yellow wheel hubs. Boxed, 1 end flap replaced, GC to VGC some chipping to roof **£200**
Rare pre war **Dinky Junkers JU90 Air Liner** (62N). Boxed. Aircraft GC to VGC **£240**
Scarce pre war **Dinky Flying Boat Clipper III** (60w). Boxed. Aircraft GC to VGC **£160**
Dinky Bristol Britannia Airliner (998), Canadian Pacific livery, boxed. Aircraft VGC...**£160**
Scarce Pre War **Dinky Imperial Airways Liner** Frobisher Class (62w). Fortuna to fuselage. Boxed, dated 1-39. Aircraft GC to VGC.............................**£390**
Scarce Pre War **Dinky Imperial Airways Liner** Frobisher Class (62w) in silver, G-A FDJ to wing tops, Falcon to fuselage, VGC to Mint, Boxed ...**£360**
Scarce Pre War **Dinky Imperial Airways Liner** Frobisher Class (62W) in silver, G-A FDI to wing tops, Frobisher to fuselage, aircraft GC for age ..**£280**
Scarce Pre War **Dinky Douglas DC3 air liner** (60t), in silver, PH-ALI to wing tops. Boxed, aircraft VGC **£160**
Rare WWII period **Dinky Armstrong Whitworth Whitley Bomber** (62t), camouflaged. Boxed, dated 11-39. Aircraft fatigued but complete...........**£100**
A rare pre war **Dinky set No. 62t**, containing Hawker Hurricane Single seater fighter (shadow shaded), box contains 3 original Hurricane and a Spitfire, complete with insert, lid dated 1-39. VGC forage. Aircraft-2 Hurricanes VGC, the other example and Spitfire fatigued and props missing **£350**
A rare pre war **Dinky 30 series Vauxhall** (30d) body in fawn with dark brown base, complete original tyres and spare. VGC for age, minor fatigue **£700**
A rare pre war **Dinky 28 series Delivery Van** (28c) in the Manchester Guardian red livery. GC to VGC body has fatigued. Paintwork is in VGC **£800**
A rare pre war **Dinky Covered Wagon** (25b), in green "Carter Paterson Express Carriers London", white rubber tyres on plated wheel hubs. QGC to GC. Tin rear tilt with decals in VGC **£300**
A rare Pre War **Dinky Royal Air Mail Service Car** (34a) in blue RMAS livery, black smooth hubs, with original white rubber tyres. VGC minor fatigue, a nice example...**£350**
Dinky Lady Penelope's Fab 1 (100), in pink, with 1st type wheels, with both seated figures. Rocket missing, boxed, with display insert. Vehicle VGC a few minor chips **£320**
A scarce **Dinky Diamond Jubilee RAF Spitfire Mk II** (700), silver plated model with detachable alabaster stand. VGC...**£380**
Scarce Pre War **Dinky Chrysler Royal Sedan** (39e) in dark blue with lacquered tinplate base, smooth black hubs. QGC to GC for age. Body complete, minor fatigue to front...**£310**
Scarce Pre War **Dinky Buick Viceroy Saloon** (39d) in maroon, with lacquered tinplate base, smooth black hubs. QGC to GC...**£280**
A Scarce **Dinky Austin Seven Countryman**, (199) in fluorescent orange with red interior, boxed, vehicle mint **£260**
A **Dinky Ford Fordor Sedan** (170) scarce, hard to find low line example in cream and red, with deep red wheelhubs. Boxed, vehicle VGC to Mint minor chips to bumpers **£150**
A Rare Pre War **Dinky Hornby Series Delivery Van** (22d) orange cab and chassis, blue rear box, solid metal wheels, with maroon pinkish finish. Complete. GC to VGC for age **£210**

Dinky Supertoys Mighty Antar with Transformer (908), yellow tractor unit, light grey trailer with red ramps, complete with grey plastic kit transformer. Boxed with paperwork. Vehicle Mint...**£460**
Dinky Leyland Octopus Wagon (934) in yellow and green livery with red hubs. Boxed, minor wear, damage, vehicle VGC to Mint minor chips **£170**
Dinky Bedford End Tipper (410) red cab, chassis and wheel hubs, cream tipping loadbed. Boxed, vehicle mint...**£170**
Dinky Pathe News Car. Vehicle Mint..**£125**
Dinky Guy Van (917) Spratts in red and cream livery, complete with rear doors boxed, vehicle VGC to Mint for type **£220**
Rare **Dinky Big Bedford Van Heinz** (923) Ketchup bottle example. Boxed, Vehicle GC to VGC **£500**
Dinky Guy 4 ton Lorry (511) dark blue cab, wings and chassis, mid blue loadbed, sides and ridged wheel hubs. Boxed, vehicle VGC to Mint.........**£150**

Lloyd Ralston Toys

109 Glover Avenue, Norwalk, CT06850, USA

Condition Grading: C1Poor to C10 Mint
Trade Pack, 6 x 37b Motorcyclists, C7-8 ....**$320**
Trade Pack, 6 x 105e Lawn Mowers, C8-9 ....**$200**
150 Royal Armoured Corps Personnel, boxed, C9 ....**$220**
Dinky plastic Service Station, C7-8 ....**$275**
923 'Heinz' Van, boxed, C8 ....**$310**
161 Mobile Anti-Aircraft Unit, boxed, C8 ....**$625**
Boxed Light Dragon Set, C9 ....**$575**
151 Medium Tank Set, boxed, C8 ....**$675**
152 Light Tank Set, boxed, C8 ....**$800**
156 Mechanized Army Set, boxed, restored, C7-9 ....**$2,500**

Barry Potter Auctions

13 Yew Tree Lane, Spratton, Northampton, NN6 8HL

1998-1999 RESULTS
Dinky Toys coloured 1950's Shop Display Showcard (36cm x 23cm) showing 27 different models. Striking and unusual showcard.Near Mint ..**£400**
Dublo Dinky Toys - AEC Mercury 'Shell BP' Tanker, Land Rover and Trailer (with horse), Ford Perfect, Singer Roadster, Bedford Flat Truck, 'Royal Mail' Van, Austin Lorry, Morris Pickup. All Near Mint Boxed **£290**
Dinky Newmarket Racehorse Transport No. 979, with both horses, Near Mint Boxed **£250**
Dinky Ruston Bucyrus Excavator No. 975, with instructions, slight wear to box, model is Mint Boxed **£150**
Dinky Big Bedford 'Heinz' Van No. 923 with sauce bottle and picture box. Lovely condition, Near Mint Boxed **£860**

19th SEPTEMBER 1998
Dublo Dinky Toys. VW 'Hornby Dublo' Van, 'Royal Mail' Van, both Mint Boxed. Austin Taxi, near Mint Boxed **£180**
Dinky Foden 'Regent' Tanker No.942, near Mint Boxed **£190**
Dinky Big Bedford Van 'Heinz' No.923, near Mint Boxed **£160**
Dinky pre-war AA Box Motorcycle Patrol and Guides Set No.44. All complete with very nice box and picture insert, Excellent plus Boxed **£270**
Dublo Dinky Toys - 5 Volkswagen 'Hornby Dublo' Vans, individually boxed, within printed trade box for six, all Excellent plus - near Mint Boxed.........**£390**
Dinky Mighty Antar with Grey Propeller No.986, near Mint Boxed **£110**
Dinky Shop Display wood and glass **Cabinet.** 'Dinky Toys' in green letters. 81cm wide, 61cm high, 23cm deep, 3 glass shelves, Excellent.................**£260**
Dinky 1st Series Foden Flat Truck No.502 (t/t blue), Mint Boxed **£390**

21st NOVEMBER 1998
Dinky Newmarket Racehorse Transport No. 979, with both horses, near Mint Boxed **£250**
Dinky Ruston Bucyrus Excavator No.975, with instructions, slight wear to box, model is Mint Boxed...**£150**
Dinky Big Bedford 'Heinz' Van No.923 with sauce bottle and picture box. Near Mint Boxed...**£860**
Dinky ABC TV Transmitter Van No.988, near Mint Boxed. Jones Fleetmaster Crane No.970 (with instructions) Mint Boxed **£170**

13th FEBRUARY 1999
Dinky 'Lyons' Guy Van No.514, superb transfers, Excellent Boxed........**£300**
Dublo Dinky VW 'Hornby Dublo' Van, Austin Taxi, 'Royal Mail' Van, Commer Van, Ford Prefect, Morris Pickup, all near Mint - Mint Boxed ...**£220**

10th APRIL 1999
Dinky - British Road Signs Set No.772 (24 signs). International Road Signs Set No.771 (12 signs, with leaflet), Both Near Mint Boxed **£260**

Dinky - Road Maintenance Personnel Set No.010, box of 6 Cook's Men (box is worn), both near Mint Boxed. Box of 6 Sheep, Mint Boxed **£100**
Dinky Pre-War Silver Jubilee Train Set No.16 (loco, tender and 2 articulated coaches). In lovely blue and silver picture box with coloured picture insert, Excellent Plus Boxed **£290**
Dinky Foden 'Regent' Tanker No.942, superb, near Mint Boxed **£310**

Lacy Scott and Knight

10 Risbygate Street, Bury St Edmunds, Suffolk, IP33 3AA

Condition grading used by Lacy Scott and Knight:
B = BOXED; in the manufacturer's original box or container, in appropriate condition.
D = DAMAGED; refers to box only.
M = MINT;in perfect or near perfect condition.
G = GOOD general condition with some chips or scratches of a minor nature.
F = FAIR condition with an average proportion of chips and marks for age.
P = POOR; in only moderate condition, perhaps incomplete.

15th MAY 1999
Thunderbirds 2+4 (101), metallic green (BM)..............................**£250**
Lady Penelope's Fab 1 (BDNM) **£110**

13th FEBRUARY 1999
Big Bedford Van Heinz (923) (BDG) **£75**
Foden Flat Truck with Chains (905) (BDG)...................................**£70**
Foden Flat Truck with Tailboard (503) (G)....................................**£40**
Tinys Mini Moke (350) (BM)...**£140**
MG Midget Sports (108) (BNM)...**£70**
Austin Healey 100 Sports (109) (BM)..**£65**
Aston Martin DB3 Sports (110) (BNM)..**£50**
Triumph TR2 Sports (111) (BNM)..**£45**
Cadillac Tourer (131) (BDNM)...**£28**
Cunningham C.5R Road Racer (135) (BNM)..................................**£50**
Jaguar XK120 Coupe (157) (BNM)...**£110**
Bristol 450 Sports Coupe (163) (BM)..**£45**
Porsche 356A Coupe (182) (BD)..**£45**
Jaguar D type racing car (yellow plastic hubs) (238) (BDNM) **£70**
Plymouth Plaza (178) (BDNM)...**£42**
Plymouth U.S.A. Taxi (265) (BDNM)..**£45**
Packard Clipper Sedan (180) (BNM)..**£45**
Joe's Car (102) (BNM)..**£60**
Spectrum Pursuit Vehicle (104) (BDM)...**£42**
Shado 2 Mobile (353) (BM)..**£40**
Express Horse Box BR (981) (NM)..**£38**
BBC TV extending mast vehicle (BNM)...**£70**
Guy van Slumberland (514) (BDNM)..**£70**

15th MAY 1999
Vega Major luxury coach (954) (BDM)...**£38**
Porsche 356A coupe (182) (BNM)...**£55**
Triumph Herald (189) (BDNM)...**£32**
Comet Wagon (532) (BDG)...**£45**
Honest John missile launcher (665) (BDM)..................................**£70**

Dreweatt Neate Auctions

Donnington Priory, Donnington, Newbury, Berkshire, RG14 2JE

10th FEBRUARY 1999
Three Dinky Motorcyclists, two 37a Civilian Motorcyclists, and one 37b Police Motorcyclist with white wheels, all good condition, unboxed...........**£80**
Three Dinky Motorcycle Patrols, 42b Police Motorcycle Patrol, 43b RAC Motorcycle Patrol, 44b AA Motorcycle Patrol, very good condition, unboxed **£190**
Dinky 16 Express Passenger Train Set, excellent condition in plain cardboard trade box **£190**
Dinky 47 Road Signs Set, white tray-type box **£140**
Dinky 49 Petrol Pumps and Oil Bin Set, with plain oil bin and brown, blue, green and red pumps with yellow hoses; near mint condition in excellent original white tray-type box **£110**
Dinky 103 Austin-Healey 100, in red with grey seats; excellent condition, box good..**£130**
Dinky 104 Aston Martin DB3S, in salmon pink with red hubs; excellent condition, box good **£110**
Dinky 106 Austin Atlantic Convertible, in light blue with red seats and hubs; excellent condition, box very good...**£80**
Dinky 107 Sunbeam Alpine Sports, in light blue with cream seats; excellent condition, box good..**£90**
Dinky 109 Austin-Healey 100 Sports, in cream; excellent, box good........**£90**

Auction results

Dinky 111 Triumph TR2 Sports, in turquoise with red seats, and hubs; mint condition, box excellent £90
Dinky 171 Hudson Commodore Sedan, in turquoise with red upper body and hubs; good condition, box good £100
Dinky 408 Big Bedford Lorry, in blue with orange truck body and yellow hubs; near mint condition, yellow box excellent £140

Dinky Supertoy 502 Foden Flat Truck, with 1st-type cab in green and black, with silver flash; excellent condition, blue box with orange label good (base not stapled) £210
Dinky Supertoy 504 Foden 14-Ton Tanker, with 1st-type cab in dark blue with light blue flash and tank; good condition, green box with red label very good £190
Dinky Supertoy 511 Guy 4-Ton Lorry, in grey with red chassis and wings; very good condition, brown box with red label good (rusty staples) £170
Dinky 511 Guy 4-Ton Lorry, in two-tone blue with light blue ridged hubs; excellent condition, blue-striped box excellent £135
Rare colour variant Dinky Supertoy 903 Foden Flat Truck with Tailboard, in light blue with fawn rivetted flatbed; near mint condition, blue-striped box excellent to mint £630
Dinky Supertoy 905 Foden Flat Truck with Chains, in green with lighter green ridged hubs; excellent condition, blue-striped box very good £170
Rare Colour Variant Dinky Supertoy 934 Leyland Octopus Wagon, in dark blue with light yellow riveted truck body and red hubs; some minor paint retouching on edges of truck body otherwise excellent, box near mint £920
Rare Colour Variant Dinky Supertoy 935 Leyland Octopus Flat Truck with Chains, in dark blue with yellow bands, grey riveted flatbed, and grey plastic hubs; near mint, yellow picture box, correct blue spot very good £1,500
Dinky 942 Foden 14-Ton Tanker "Regent", excellent condition, blue-striped box near mint £300
Dinky Supertoy 986 Mighty Antar Low-Loader with Propeller, no window glazing, otherwise mint boxed with internal packing £220
Dinky Trade Box Outer 320 Halesowen Farm Trailer, containing full set of six boxed trailers; virtually mint boxed as new £100

Bonhams Auctions

65-69, Lots Road, Chelsea, London, SW10 0RN

6th OCTOBER 1998
SINGLE OWNER COLLECTION OF BOXED DINKY TOYS
A **Dinky 108 M.G. Midget Sports,** Body and hubs finished in red, tan seats (E, box E) £110
A **Dinky 102 M.G. Midget Sports,** Finished in Orange (E, box VG) £140
A **Dinky 102 M.G. Midget Sports,** Light Green Body (E, box G) £130
A **Dinky 110 Aston Martin DB3 Sports,** Grey Body (E, box VG) £90
A rare **Dinky 110 Aston Martin DB3 Sports,** 1956-59, Light Green body (E, box VG) £180
104 **Aston Martin DB3S,** 1957-60, Light Blue (E, box E-M) £120
105 **Triumph TR2 Sports,** Grey, Red Seats (E-M, box E-M) £150
238 **Jaguar Type D,** Racing Car, Light Turquoise (VG-E,box E) £70
A **Dinky 231 Maserati Racing Car,** English 1960-62 (VG, box VG-E)...£60
A **Dinky 157 Jaguar XK120 Coupe,** Two Tone Finish with lower body in yellow and grey upper (E-M, box E) £140
A **Dinky 157 Jaguar XK120 Coupe,** All-Red (E-M, box VG-E) £90
A **Dinky 157 Jaguar XK120 Coupe,** Finished in Dark Green/Grey, with rare light brown hubs (E-M, box E) £110
A **Dinky 131 Cadillac Tourer,** Finished in Yellow with a Dark Pink interior (E, Box G) £70
Dinky 170 Ford Sedan, Red lower body and Cream upper (E, box G) £130
A **Dinky 481 Bedford 'Ovaltine' Van,** (E, box E) £80
A **Dinky 482 Bedford 'Dinky Toys' Van** (VG, box E) £80
A **Dinky 260 'Royal Mail' Van** - (E-M, box E) £60
A **Dinky 472 Austin 'Raleigh Cycles' Van,** English 1956-60 (G, box F) ..£50
A **Dinky 441 'Castrol' Tanker,** English 1954-60 (E, box E) £70
A **Dinky 533 Leyland Cement Wagon** (VG, box E) £100
A **Dinky 923 'Heinz' Big Bedford Van** (E, box E) £220
A **Dinky 942 'Regent' Foden 14-Ton Tanker** (E, box E).....................£220
A **Dinky 504 Foden Tanker,** Dark Blue cab, chassis, light blue tank (E-M, box E) £220
A **Dinky 908 Mighty Antar with Transformer** (E-M, box E) £320
A **Dinky 505 Foden Flat Truck with Chains,** Totally finished in maroon with 'dimpled' chain-post chromes (E, box E) £190
A **Dinky 903 2nd Type Foden Flat-Truck,** Dark Blue chassis, cab, orange flatbed and light blue 'grooved' hubs (E, box VG)............................£180
A **Dinky 502 Foden Flat Truck,** Dark Green cab. flatbed and hubs, silver flash to cab, black chassis and wings (E, box VG-E) £220
A **Dinky 25R Forward Control Lorry Trade Box,** Five finished in cream with blue hubs, one in cream, with black hubs (G-VG, box G) £150
A **Dinky 25R Forward Control Lorry Trade Box,** All finished in orange, three with black hubs and three with light green (G, box VG) £150

Trade Box of 23F Alfa Romeo Racing Cars, Six in total (VG-E, box G-VG) £160
Dinky 29E Single Deck Bus Trade Box, Six in box (G-VG, box VG) £300
A **Dinky 35A Saloon Car Trade Box,** 1936-40, the Trade box complete with six cars (G-VG, box E) £140

Christie's

85 Old Brompton Road, South Kensington, London, SW7 3LD

Descriptions of paintwork as used in Christie's catalogue:
M= Toys apparently never taken out of mint original boxes.
E = Excellent Toys with no or very few apparent paint chips or defects.
G = Good Toys with minor scratches to the paint.
F = Fair Toys with an acceptable amount of paint damage.
P = Poor Toys probably suitable for repainting or restoration.
SD = Some damage.

Where referring to boxes:
E = Excellent original box with very little or no damage, complete with all interior fittings.
G = Good box with normal use wear only, but fittings not necessarily complete.
F = Fair box, possibly slightly torn or split, but with label intact.
P = Poor box, likely to be split or torn, and in need of repair.

A **Dinky 983 Car Carrier with Trailer** with four packing pieces, tested tag and instructions dated 5.58, original box (G-E, minor chips to ramps, box G).£207
A Rare Yellow **Dinky 145 Singer Vogue** in original box (E, box F-G).....£805
Dinky No.4 Racing Cars Set, original box, base dated 9.53 (E, box F-G)£460
A **Dinky 514 Guy 'Slumberland' Van** in original box (E, box E) £437
Dinky 432 Guy 'Warrior' Flat Truck pale green cab, red flat bed and wheels, windows, in original box (E, box G, slight paper tears) ..est.£300-400 (unsold)
A **Dinky 918 Guy 'Ever Ready' Van** in original box (E-M, box G-E) £322
Dinky 125 'Fun A'Hoy Set' Red Ford Consul Consair, Healey Sports Boat and Trailer, original box with replacement cellophane shrink wrap (E, box G)£230
Dinky Pre-War six silver **60n Fairey Battle Bombers** two with blue shaded windows, four with tail-skids, original box 1936-1937 (G-E, box F)........£276
A **Dinky Pre-War No.60 Aeroplanes Set** in original box, lid dated 12.34 (G-E, Imperial Airways Airliner fuselage restored and overpainted, General Monospar overpainted, box E) £1,150
Dinky ABC TV Vehicles 987 Mobile Control Room and 988 Transmitter Van, in original boxes (E, boxes G) £380
Dinky Commericals 986 Mighty Antar Low Loader with Propellor and beige and red 977 Commercial Servicing Platform Vehicle, in original boxes (G, boxes G) £299
Dinky Coach and Bus turquoise and white 953 Continental Touring Coach and orange 949 Wayne School Bus with black detailing, in original boxes (G-E, boxes G) £276
Dinky Castrol Tanker Trade Box six green 30pa Tankers , in original yellow Half-Dozen Trade Box (G, box F-G) £276
Dinky Gift Set 299 Post Office Services comprising Royal Mail Van, Telephone Service Van, Call Box, Postman and Telegraph Messenger, in original box (E, box G) £280
Dinky Guy 919 'Golden Shred' Van in original box (G, box G) £300
Dinky Red 983 Car Carrier with Trailer in original box, packing card and instructions (G, box F-G) £240
Dinky Pre-War 67a Junkers JU89 Heavy Bomber matt black with pale matt blue underside, in original box dated 4.40 (E, box G) £552
Dinky Tan and Green 431 Guy Warrior 4-Ton Lorry green hubs and windows, in original box (E, box G) £368
Rare **Dinky 934 Leyland Octopus Wagon** dark blue cab and chassis, yellow truck body, front two hubs red plastic and rear six red metal, in original box with green and yellow version illustrated on lid, date stamp 10.61 (G, box G) .£690
Dinky 930 Bedford Pallet Jekta Van with windows, packing card, instruction, original box (E, missing pallets, slight corrosion to crank handle, box F) .£299
Dinky 919 Guy 'Golden Shred' Van, in original box (E, box G) £667
Dinky Yellow and Green **934 Leyland Octopus Wagon,** packing piece, in original box (E, box G) £218
Dinky 943 Leyland Octopus 'Esso' Tanker in original box (E, box G).£460
Dinky 942 'Regent' Foden 14-Ton Tanker, packing card, in original box (E, box G) £345
A Rare Red **Dinky 189 Triumph Herald** 1959-1964 (G-E).....................£517
A Pre-War **Dinky Red 25b 'Meccano' Covered Wagon** with Cream Tilt, cast radiator, Tootsie Toy-type chrome hubs, 'Meccano Engineering for Boys' transfers on tilt, circa 1935 (G)..£977
Rare Pre-War **Dinky Toy Modelled Miniatures, 22a Sports Car,** marked Meccano Dinky Toys (missing windshield frame), 22b Sports Coupe, 22c Motor Truck metallic yellow wheels and 22d Delivery Van, all finished in blue and yellow, tinplate grilles, 22a, 22b and 22d with metallic blue wheels, circa 1934 (F-G, some slight chipping); Pre-war Dinky 23 Racing Car, lead body, no driver, cream with blue top flash (missing one tyre and slightly distorted), silver 23e Speed of the Wind Racing Car (F); Tootsie Toy dark green 0616 Town Car

(missing windshield); Johillco Golden Arrow (F) and Hill Fire Ladder (P) **£4,600**

Dinky Rare Set No.1 Commercial Vehicles comprising red and cream 29c Double Deck Bus, green 25b Covered Wagon, green 25d Tank Wagon, grey 25e Tipping Wagon and yellow 25f Market Gardeners Lorry with inner green card base, in original green, blue and fawn mottled box with light green and blue lid label 1946-1948 (E-M, box G-E).....................................**£3,200**

Dinky rare Set No.5 Military Vehicles U.S. and Home Market, comprising 153a (672) US Army Jeep, 161b (690) Mobile AA Gun, 151a Medium Tank, 151b (620) Transport Wagon and 152b (671) Reconnaisance Car, with inner green card base and card cut-out packing piece, in original green box with blue, light green and red mottled lid with applied purple and yellow lid label and a paper 9/6 retailers label to lid side circa 1950 (E-M, box G-E)..............**£2,600**

Dinky rare Set No.2 Private Automobiles American Motor Cars comprising olive green 39a Packard, grey 39b Oldsmobile, brown 39c Lincoln Zephyr, fawn 39d Buick and blue 39e Chrysler with inner green card base in original green, blue and orange mottled box with applied green and blue lid label 1946-1948 (E-M, box E)..**£2,600**

Dinky Rare Set No.3 Private Automobiles Second Type comprising brown 30d Vauxhall, green 36b Bentley Cuope, blue 36d Rover, grey 38a Frazer-Nash with brown interior and green 38c Lagonda with dark green interior, with inner green card base, in original green, blue and orange mottled box with applied green and blue lid label 1947-1952 (E-M, box E)...................................**£3,200**

A rare black **Pre-War Dinky 24a Ambulance** with chromed hubs (F-G) **£550**

A Rare **Empty 24 Series Motor Cars Box** purple and gold marbled ground with colour lid label and yellow and red end label code DT24 1935 (G)...**£380**

A Rare **Pre-War Dinky No.156 Mechanised Army Set** comprising 151a Medium Tank, 151b Transport Wagon, dark gloss green 151c Cooker Trailer, 151d Water Tank, 152a Light Tank, 152b Reconnaisance Car, 152c Austin 7 Car, 161a Searchlight Lorry, 161b AA Gun, 162a Light Dragon, 162b Trailer and 162c 18-Pounder Gun, in original grey-blue display box with insert and four packing pieces, code no.A2308 dated 11.39 (G-E, box F).......................**£1,000**

Dinky Pre-War Set 60 Aeroplanes comprising gold and blue Imperial Airways Airliner, blue and silver Percival Gull, gold and blue Cierva Autogiro, silver Monospar, green and yellow Leopard Moth and red and cream Low Wing Monoplane, in original rare blue box with green, blue and white lid label and yellow and green side label dated 5.34 (P-G, box F-G)..............................**£850**

A **Dinky Pre-War 60t Douglas D.C.3 Airliner** with instructions dated 11.37, in original box (E, box G, lid grubby) **£260**

Pre War Dinky No.17 Passenger Train: green and red tank locomotive and three coaches, one red, one green and one blue, all with 'Hornby Series' cast on underside, in original purple marbled 'ladder' box (G-E, box G) **£400**

Dinky Pre-War No.42 Police Set in original box (F, box F) and blue 37a Motor Cycle Civilan half-dozen trade box with one Cycle (Cycle P, box F, no internal packing)..**£400**

A Rare **Dinky Pre-War No.48 Petrol Station** lithographed tinplate with orange base and yellow roof, in original orange box (G-E, box F-G) **£400**

Dinky early post war 30 and 39 Series Cars blue 30b Rolls-Royce with smooth hubs, one green and one fawn 30c Daimler, green 30d Vauxhall, brown 39a Packard and grey 39c Lincoln Zephyr with silver base plate and smooth hubs (overall G, one minute chipping, 39a roof grazed) **£500**

Dinky early post war 36 Series Cars blue 36b Bentley, grey 36c Humber Vogue and blue 36d Rover, all with smooth hubs and blue 36e British Salmson Two-Seater (G-E) **£420**

JOB.13984 - **Sunbeam Alpine - Competition Model** (107), side, cut-away side and top rear section elevations, signed F.T.R, dated 3.12.53, and additional dates up to 4.7.60, framed and glazed (F)..**£518**

JOB.12140 - **Jeep** (153A), side, aerial and rear elevations, signed H.M. dated 29.10.45 and JOB.12142 **Jeep** windscreen, signed H.M. dated 26.10.45, framed and glazed as one (F-G)..**£322**

JOB.10896 - **Double Deck Omnibus**, (29c-. side, front and upper deck 'Dunlop' transfer elevations, signed (indistinct), dated 22.7.37, and additional dates to 3.11.61, framed and glazed (G) **£633**

JOB.14794 **Unissued Guy Warrior Golden Shred Van**, side and front elevations, signed H.R.B., dated 26.3.57, additional job dates up to 14.1.60, framed and glazed (F-G) **£1,035**

Dinky Toys 'ABC-TV' vans – 987 Mobile Control Room and 988 Transmitter Van.

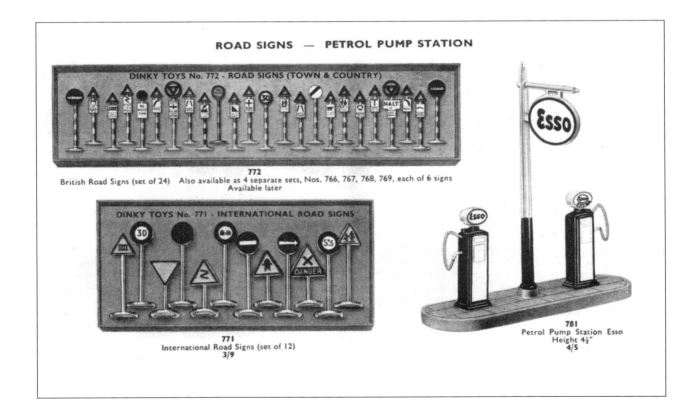

Dinky Toys Accessories as shown in the May 1959 UK Catalogue 7/559/900

Lone Star

Robert Newson has provided the following information on Lone Star models.

'Lone Star' was the trade name of Die Casting Machine Tools Ltd (DCMT) who started in 1939 as manufacturers of diecasting machines. They were based at Palmers Green in North London. After the war they started making diecast toys which were distributed by The Crescent Toy Co Ltd. In the Crescent Toys section of this catalogue, the items listed as 'early post-war models' were all made by DCMT with the exception of the Locomotive and the Racing Car. From 1950 DCMT arranged their own distribution direct to wholesalers. Over the next four decades DCMT Lone Star made several ranges of diecast vehicles including

'Slikka Toys' (early 1950s), 'Modern Army Series' (mainly 1960s), 'Roadmaster Majors' (1960s and 1970s), 'Farmer's Boy' (1980s) and the well known 'Lone Star Locos' miniature railway system (later called 'Treble-O-Lectric' or 'Treble-O-Trains'). The four ranges of most interest to collectors are listed here - the original DCMT 'Roadmasters' of 1956, the 1:50 scale 'Roadmasters' (1960s), the 'Impy' and 'Flyers' series made in various forms from 1966 to the mid 1980s, and the miniature 'Tuf-Tots' (1970s).

The Editor would also like to thank Bryan Holden of Wakefield and Tim Mackintosh of City Models, Perth, Western Australia for additional information on Lone Star Tuf-Tots.

DCMT Lone Star Roadmasters

This was a short-lived series introduced in 1956, consisting of three sports cars and four veteran cars, all around 1:35 to 1:40 scale. The models had diecast bodies but all other components were plastic. Plastic drivers and passengers were included with the models. Nowadays the models are hard to find hence all are **NGPP**.

-	-	**1904 Darracq 'Genevieve'**	Black or Red body, Yellow plastic chassis; Metallic Blue or Silver body, Black plastic chassis
-	-	**1904 Daimler 'Windsor' Phaeton**	Red body, Yellow plastic chassis
-	-	**1912 Ford Model 'T'**	Silver body, Black plastic chassis
-	-	**1912 Morris Oxford 'Bullnose'**	Metallic Blue body, Black plastic chassis
-	-	**Daimler Conquest Roadster**	Red, Metallic Light Blue, Pale Yellow, Pale Green or Pale Blue
-	-	**Ford Thunderbird**	Red, Metallic Light Blue, Pale Yellow, Pale Green or Pale Blue
-	-	**MG Midget TF**	Metallic Light Blue or Red

Lone Star Roadmasters - 1:50 scale

In 1960 Lone Star produced four American cars on behalf of the US firm of Tootsietoy. These were the first four models listed below and they had 'Tootsietoy Classic Series' cast underneath. This arrangement only lasted for a couple of years, as by 1962 there were eight models available, all now marked 'Lone Star Roadmasters'. The models featured plated grilles, bumpers and wheels, and glazed windows but no interior detail. Around 1964 the plated parts were replaced by less attractive painted or self-coloured plastic, and vacuum-formed interiors were fitted. Five further numbers were added to the range before they were withdrawn around 1966. **All NGPP.**

1258	-	**Farm King Tractor and Trailer**	Red tractor, 'Farm King' paper label, Blue trailer, 'Farm Estates Co.' paper label. (Road Master Major)
1470	-	**Chevrolet Corvair**	Red or Orange-Red
1471	-	**Rambler Rebel Station Wagon**	Sea-Green, Metallic Blue-Green or Green with Cream roof, Metallic Brown with White roof or all Green
1472	-	**Cadillac 62**	Pale Blue, Blue with Cream roof or all Blue
1473	-	**Ford Sunliner Convertible**	White or Light Blue; Red interior
1474	-	**Chevrolet El Camino Pick-Up**	Yellow or Orange
1475	-	**Dodge Dart Phoenix**	Metallic Dark Blue or Mid Blue
1476	-	**Rolls-Royce Silver Cloud II**	Grey with Black upper half or Metallic Blue
1477	-	**Dodge Dart Police Car**	Black, 'POLICE PATROL' or 'POLIZEI'
1478	-	**Rambler Ambulance**	White, Red Cross transfer on bonnet
1479	-	**Chevrolet Corvair**	Red body, 'FIRE CHIEF', 'FEUERWEHR' or 'BRANDWEER'
1480	-	**Chevrolet Corvair**	Army Staff Car (continued after 1966 as no.1273 in ``Modern Army'' series), Olive Green
1481	-	**Rambler Military Ambulance**	(continued after 1966 as no.1274 in 'Modern Army' series), Olive Green
1482	-	**Citroën DS19**	Turquoise
-	-	**Rambler Police Car**	White body, 'POLIZEI' on bonnet

Lone Star 'Tuf-Tots'

The first thirteen Tuf-Tots were introduced in 1969, and the next five followed in 1970. The remainder had appeared by 1972. They were available boxed or bubble-packed, and when bubble-packed there was an additional '2' in front of the model number to give a four-digit reference. Later, models were sold in open counter-top trays.

The trucks were based on a common US Ford chassis. Most models exist in numerous colour variations. The series was discontinued after 1980. Market Price Range is **£5 to £10**.

601	**Ford Petrol Tanker**	'ESSO' labels
		'ESSO' cast into sides
602	**Citroën DS Convertible with Driver**	
603	**Chevrolet Corvette Stingray Convertible with Driver**	
604	**Dodge Dart Convertible with Driver**	
605	**Mercedes-Benz 280SL Convertible with Driver**	
606	**Ford 'TT' Tow Truck**	
607	**Ford 'Big L' Dumper Lorry**	
608	**Jeep and Trailer**	'Herts. Farm', scale 85:1
609	**Ford 'Autos' Flat Truck** with metal petrol pump island	
		with palstic petrol pump island
610	**Ford Tipper Lorry**	'LS Construction Co.' labels
		with ribs cast onto body instead of labels
611	**Ford Luton Van**	with 'Express Freight' labels
		with ribs cast onto body instead of labels
612	**Ford Articulated Low-Loader** 'Apache'	
613	**Chris Craft Capri Speedboat** (plastic) **on Trailer**, scale 86:1	
614	**Ford Refuse Lorry**	with 'City Refuse' labels
		with 'City Refuse' cast lettering

615	**Ford Cement Mixer**	
616	**Ford Milk Float**	'Milk, Milk, Milk' cast on each side
617	**Ford Cattle Transporter**	
618	**Ford Skip Lorry**	
619	**Citroën DS Coupé**	
620	**Chevrolet Corvette Stingray Coupé**	
621	**Dodge Dart Coupé**	
622	**Mercedes-Benz 280SL Coupé**, scale 86:1	
623	**Routemaster Bus**	with 'London Bus' advertisements
624	**ERF Fire Engine**	with ladder, 'Fire Brigade' labels
625	**Caravan**	
626	**Ford Circus Cage Lorry** with plastic lion, 'Circus' cast-in	
627	**Tractor Shovel**	

Gift Sets

2570	**Building Site Playset**	4 models plus sand hopper
2571	**Garage Playset**	4 models plus car ramp
2572	**Highway Playset**	4 models plus street and traffic lights
2573	**Travel Playset**	4 models plus 'Stop' barrier
2574	**Dutch Farm Playset**	4 models plus windmill
2575	**Bridge Playset**	4 models plus girder bridge
579	**Commercial Vehicle Set** 6 models	
580	**Car and Trailer Set** 6 models	
581	**12 Vehicle Set** 12 models	
582	**Highway Set**	
	3 models plus sand hopper, car ramp, street and traffic lights	
583	**Travel Set**	
	3 models plus girder bridge, windmill and 'Stop' barrier	

In the following listing the year shown is the date of introduction. Most models remained in production until 1976. **IW** = Impy wheels, **FW** = Flyers wheels, **HSW** = Hi-Speed wheels, **BPW** = black plastic wheels.

7	1971	**Vauxhall Firenza**, IW / FW, RHD and LHD	£15-25
8	-	**Ford Capri**, not issued	NPP
9	1970	**Maserati Mistral**, IW or FW	£10-20
10	1966	**Jaguar Mk.X**, IW or FW	£10-20
11	1966	**Chevrolet Corvette Stingray GT**, IW or FW	£10-20
12	1966	**Chysler Imperial**, IW or FW	£10-20
13	-	**Ford Thunderbird**, not issued	NPP
13	1971	**Toyota 2000 GT**, Flyers wheels	£10-20
14	1966	**Ford Zodiac Mk.III Estate**, IW or FW	£10-20
15	1966	**Volkswagen Microbus**, IW or FW	£10-20
16	1966	**Ford Zodiac Mk.III Estate 'POLICE' Car**, IW or FW	£10-20
16	-	**Chrysler Imperia 'POLICE' Car**, IW or FW	£10-20
16m	-	**Mercedes-Benz 220 SE 'POLIZEI' Car**, Impy wheels	£10-20
17	1966	**Mercedes-Benz 220 SE**, IW or FW	£10-20
18	1966	**Ford Corsair**, IW or FW	£10-20
19	1967	**Volvo 1800 S**, IW or FW	£10-20
20	1967	**Volkswagen Ambulance**, IW or FW	£10-20
21	1967	**Fiat 2300 S Coupé**, IW or FW	£10-20
22	1967	**Rolls-Royce Silver Cloud III Convertible**, IW or FW	£10-20
23	1967	**Alfa Romeo Giulia 1600 Spider**, IW or FW	£10-20
24	1967	**Foden Tilt-cab 8w Tipper**, black plastic or HSW	£10-20
25	1967	**International Harvester Tractor Shovel**	£10-20
26	1967	**Foden Tilt-cab Petrol Tanker**, 'MOBIL', BPW or HSW	£10-20
27	1967	**Ford Taunus 12M**, IW or FW	£10-20
28	1967	**Peugeot 404 Saloon**, IW or FW	£10-20
29	-	**Cement Mixer Lorry**, not issued	NPP
29	1971	**Foden Tilt-cab Box Van**, 'LUCAS', BPW or HSW	£15-25
29	1972	**Foden Tilt-cab Box Van**, 'EXPRESS FREIGHT' labels, black plastic wheels	£15-25
30	1967	**AEC Merryweather Fire Engine**, black plastic or HSW	£10-20
31	1967	**Ford Transit Breakdown Lorry**, 'ESSO', BPW or HSW	£10-20
32	1968	**'FIRE CHIEF' Car**, Ford Corsair, red, IW or FW	£10-20
32		**'FEUERWEHR' Car**, Ford Corsair, red, Impy wheels	£10-20
33	1968	**Austin-Western Mobile Crane**, elevating jib	£10-20
34	1968	**Euclid Crawler Tractor**, rubber tracks	£10-20
35	-	**Articulated Flat Truck**, not issued	NPP
36	1969	**Lotus Europa**, Flyers wheels	£10-20
37		**Ford GT**, not issued	NPP
38	1971	**Chevrolet Corvette Stingray**, Flyers wheels	£15-25
39	1971	**Ford Mustang**, Flyers wheels	£15-25
40	1973	**Cadillac Eldorado**, Flyers wheels	£10-20
41	1972	**Leyland Builders Supply Lorry**, 4 girders, 8 HSW	£10-20
41	1973	**Leyland Builders Supply Lorry**, 6 girders, 6 HSW	£10-20
41	1973	**Foden Half-cab Builders Supply Lorry**, 4 girders,6 HSW	£10-20
42	1972	**Foden Half-cab Tipper**, 'TILCON' labels, 8 HSW	£15-25
43	1973	**Leyland Flat Lorry with Pipes**, 6 HSW	£10-20
43	1973	**Foden Half-cab Flat Lorry with Pipes**, 6 HSW	£10-20
44	1972	**Leyland Marine Transport Lorry**, Speedboat, 8 HSW	£10-20
44	1973	**Leyland Marine Transport Lorry**, Speedboat, 6 HSW	£10-20
44	1973	**Foden Half-cab Marine Transport Lorry**, Speedboat, 6 HSW	£10-20
46	1973	**Leyland Dropside Lorry**, 6 Hi-Speed wheels	£10-20
47	1973	**Leyland High-Side Lorry**, 6 Hi-Speed wheels	£10-20
47	1973	**Foden High-Side Lorry**, Half-cab, 6 HSW	£10-20
48	1973	**Leyland Hopper Lorry**, 6 HSW	£10-20
48	1973	**Foden Half-cab Hopper Lorry**, 6 HSW	£10-20
49	1973	**Foden Half-cab Tipper**, 6 HSW	£10-20

GIFT SETS All are scarce, hence NGPP

301	1967	**Six-piece Gift Set**	NGPP
302	1967	**Six-piece Gift Set**	NGPP
303	1968	**'MOBIL' Gift Set**	NGPP
304	1968	**Five-piece Commercial Vehicle Gift Set**	NGPP
309	1968	**Twelve-piece Gift Set**	NGPP

IMPY ACCESSORIES

401	1967	**Car Lifting Ramp**	£5-10
402	1967	**Lock-Up Garage** (plastic)	£5-10
403	-	**Service Station** (not issued)	
404	1968	**'MOBIL' Petrol Pump Island**, Canopy, Forecourt Sign	£5-10
406	-	**Fire House** (not issued)	NPP

IMPY TWO-PACKS

422	**VW Ambulance** (20) and **Mercedes-Benz 'Polizei'** (16M)		£20-30
423	**Fiat 2300S** (21) and **Breakdown Lorry** (31)		£20-30
424	**Foden Tanker** (26) and **Ford Taunus** (27)		£20-30
425	**Ford Zodiac** (14) and **Tractor** (25)		£20-30
427	**Alfa Romeo** (23) and **'MOBIL' Petrol Pumps** (404)		£20-30
431	**Chevrolet Corvette** (11) and **Fiat 2300S** (21)		£20-30
432	**Fire Engine** (30) and **Ford Corsair 'FEUERWEHR'** (32)		£20-30

IMPY series, post-1976

The Market Price Range is shown as £5 - £10 but as yet there is little collectors' interest in these recent models.

50	**Six-wheel Tipper**	£5-10
51	**Six-wheel High Side Lorry**	£5-10
52	**Six-wheel Flat Lorry with Crane**	£5-10
53	**Six-wheel Flat Lorry with Speedboat**	£5-10
54	**Six-wheel Cement Mixer**	£5-10
55	**Six-wheel Luton Van**	£5-10
56	**Six-wheel Dropside Lorry**	£5-10
57	**Six-wheel Flat Lorry with Water Tank**	£5-10
58	**Six-wheel Hopper Lorry**	£5-10
59	**Six-wheel Flat Lorry with Pipes**	£5-10
60	**Six-wheel Flat Lorry with Planks**	£5-10
61	**Six-wheel Petrol Tanker**	£5-10
71	**Range Rover**	£5-10
72	**Cadillac Eldorado**	£5-10
73	**Chevrolet Corvette Stingray**	£5-10
74	**Toyota 2000 GT**	£5-10
75	**Range Rover Police Car**	£5-10
76	**Chevrolet Corvette Stingray 'GT Rally'**	£5-10
77	**Jaguar Mk.X**	£5-10
78	**Maserati Mistral**	£5-10
79	**Ford Mustang**	£5-10
80	**Lotus Europa**	£5-10
81	**Volvo Coupé**	£5-10
82	**Mercedes-Benz**	£5-10
181	**Articulated Flat Lorry with Crane**	£5-10
182	**Articulated Petrol Tanker**	£5-10
183	**Articulated Low Loader with Tuf-Tots car**	£5-10
184	**Articulated Flat Lorry with Pipes and water tank**	£5-10
185	**Cadillac Eldorado with Tuf-Tots car on trailer**	£5-10
185	**Range Rover with Tuf-Tots Speedboat on trailer**	£5-10
185	**Range Rover 'RNLI' with boat on trailer**	£5-10
185	**Jaguar Mk.X with Cabin Cruiser on trailer**	£5-10
186	**Crane Lorry (no.52) with Impy car**	£5-10
187	**Luton Van (no.55) with Trailer**	£5-10
188	**Articulated Low Loader with Cabin Cruiser**	£5-10
189	**Articulated Flat Lorry with Planks**	£5-10
190	**Petrol Tanker (no.61) with Trailer**	£5-10
191	**High Side Lorry (no.51) with Trailer**	£5-10
192	**Cement Mixer (no.54) with Flat Trailer**	£5-10
1251	**Articulated Car Transporter**	£5-10
1252	**AEC Merryweather HTTL Fire Engine** (re-packed no.30)	£5-10
1256	**Car Transporter (no.1251) with four Impy cars**	£30-40

Lone Star Set

International Peace Force Vehicles Set (made 1974) contains: 1271 Small Tank, 1272 Searchlight on Trailer, 1273 Mortar Launcher, 1274 Radar Detector Unit, 1275 Ack-Ack Gun, 1276 Silver Small Canon, 1277 All Blue Military Jeep ....NGPP

Lone Star Routemaster Bus (made 1972 - 1989)

Made from two castings which include seats and stair details. Red body with Silver trim, paper adverts on sides 'SEE LONDON BY BUS' and 'BUY LONE STAR'. Route is '29 VICTORIA', Black plastic tyres. Cast into base: 'LONE STAR' and 'MADE IN ENGLAND', No. 1259 ....**£5-10**

Lone Star 'Aircraft of the World' Series (1:250 scale)

'Scandinavian Airlines' Caravelle £40-50
'Pan American' Boeing 707 ....£50-60

Miscellaneous

RAC Land Rover and Caravan ....no details..NGPP

TREVOR BANNISTER Matchbox Toy Specialist

- • MOKO LESNEY 1-75 GIFT SETS • • KINGSIZE •
- • SERVICE STATION SETS • • MAJOR SERIES • • SUPERFAST •

STOCKIST OF OBSOLETE AND RARE MODELS OF THE FINEST QUALITY.
WORLD WIDE MAIL ORDER SERVICE. Visa. Mastercard. Eurocard.
We pay top cash price for your models. If you wish to sell, call us now.
22 Lansdown Road, Seaford BN25 3LR
Phone: 01323 898302 Fax: 01323 490662 E-mail: trevorb@mistral.co.uk

Internet web site: http://www3.mistral.co.uk/trevorb

THE MODEL STORE

Matchbox Toy Specialists
Moko Lesney/1-75's/Superfast
Majors/King Size
Models of Yesteryear

Large selection of obsolete models always available,
send for a list or visit our web site

We are always looking for models so give us a call if
you are thinking of selling

Worldwide Mail Order

Boundary Elms, Burchetts Green Lane,
nr Maidenhead, Berks SL6 3QP

Tel: 01628 822992
Fax: 01628 823823

www.modelstore.co.uk
enquiries@modelstore.co.uk

Cars & Boxes
The Leading German Matchbox Shop

We are looking for Matchbox!

1-75 Series, Superfast, Models of Yesteryear, displays,
gift sets, empty boxes

Best prices
paid for rare items and mint boxed collections

Cars & Boxes, Brückenstr. 14, 10179 Berlin
Tel: 0049 30 275 51 63
Fax: 0049 30 279 50 72

CLARK'S COLLECTABLES

Matchbox ■ Corgi ■ Dinky ■ etc

Yesteryears 1956 to Latest Releases
Moko Lesney – 1-75 Kingsize
Major Series – Early Lesney Toys
Corgi – Corgi Classics – Dinky

LOCATING ■ SEARCHING ■ BUYING ■ SELLING WORLDWIDE
WANTED: Rare, scarce, obsolete, colour trials, pre-production models in Yesteryear, Early Lesney,
Moko, TP Series, 1 to 75, Regular Wheels, Major, King Size, Accessories, Dinky, Corgi, Budgie, etc.
Enquiries invited for any model of the above makes.
We also supply all new releases in Yesteryear, Dinky, Corgi, etc.
Oak Acres, Park Hall Road, Somersham, Cambs. PE17 3HQ
Tel: 0468 357693 or 01487 840540 Fax: 01487 840540

Visitors Welcome
by Appointment

Matchbox Toys

Introduction

The company was founded in 1947 by the unrelated Leslie and Rodney Smith who combined their names to form 'Lesney' Products Ltd. They were soon joined by Jack Odell – a recognised diecasting expert.

The most famous of the various early products was the 'Coronation Coach'. During the 1950s the company developed the highly successful Matchbox '1-75' and 'Models of Yesteryear' ranges.

Lesney Products Ltd was bought in 1982 by the Universal Toy Co. of Hong Kong. In May 1992 it was announced in the 'New York Times' that 'Tyco Toys Inc.' had acquired by merger the Universal Matchbox Group. Matchbox then became known as 'Tyco-Matchbox' although the products are still marketed under the famous Matchbox brand name. Late in 1992 Tyco Toys announced the formation of a new division called Matchbox Collectibles which became responsible for the sales and marketing of Matchbox 'Models of Yesteryear'. In 1996 Mattel Inc., the world's largest toymakers agreed to merge with Tyco Toys Inc. and plans to use its powers to boost overseas sales.

Mattel have set out their brand name strategy for the future as follows: All cars, irrespective of whether they have previously been part of the Models of Yesteryear or Dinky ranges will be classified as Dinky Toys. All commercial vehicles, i.e., lorries and vans, will be classified as Models of Yesteryear.

The new 8th Edition Matchbox chapter shows many changes over previous editions. The 1-75 Series now has separate Regular Wheels and Superfast sections. The Editor would like to express his thanks to Robert Freeman for compiling the generally enhabced Superfast listing. Thanks are also due to Horace Dunkley who has compiled a unique new 'simplified' Models of Yesteryear section and John Clark has brought the quite unique Matchbox Dinky section up to date. Finally, a 'thank you' to the Matchbox Collectibles staff for kindly supplying the catalogue pictures.

Collectors of the more recent issues should note that models produced by Tyco and Mattel Matchbox Collectibles are now listed in the new 'Collectable Modern Diecasts' section betwen pages 293 and 296.

Market Price Range: Please note that the prices shown refer to pristine models and boxes.
Items failing to match this standard will sell for less. Note also that boxes must contain all their original additional contents.

'Moko' Products

'Moko' Products was a toy distribution firm founded by Moses Kohnstam who came to Britain from Nuremburg, Germany at the turn of the century.

Moko provided the distribution and storage facilities and, irrespective of the supplier, all toys were marketed as Moko products. The early issues after the Second World War were housed in plain cardboard boxes with 'tuck in' ends. These usually had only single colour printing that did not include a picture of the model. During the early 1950s the packaging became much more attractive with

brightly coloured boxes displaying a picture of the model inside. Moko will best be remembered for their distribution of the early Matchbox '1-75' toys under the name of 'MoKo-Lesney'. Moses Kohnstam was succeeded by Richard Kohnstam in 1953.

The following listing of Moko items constitutes all the information available to publish at present. Additional information would be welcomed by the Editor.

c1948-53	**Mechanical Tractor** Probably early Lesney. Orange body, Green rubber tracks, Black wheels, Green/Black driver, (early issue in plain box)	**£125-150**	
1950-55	**Mechanical Tractor** As previous model but with Orange wheels, (later issue in picture box)	**£125-150**	
1947-50	**Excavator (with open cab)** Orange body and jib, Black digger and chassis, Green rubber tracks, Orange crank handle. Early card box has 'Moko TOYS OF DISTINCTION' logo	**£160-200**	
1950-55	**'RUSTON BUCYRUS' Excavator** Yellow over Red body with Black '10 RB' logo. Black or Dark Grey chassis, jib, digger, crank wheel and rubber tracks. Later box with full colour picture	**£160-200**	
1950-55	**Builders Crane** All Blue crane base and jib with unpainted metal hook. Later card box with full colour picture	**£160-200**	

1950-55	**Drummer Boy (Mechanical)** Red body, Gold trim, Black busby. Cream/Yellow drum, Gold drumsticks	**£500-750**
1947-50	**Crawler Bulldozer** Red body and dozer blade (possibly early Lesney). Early plain card box	**£125-150**
1947-50	**Hayrick** Yellow/Green body	**£160-200**
1947-50	**Fairground Carousel** Blue/Red base and centre column, Maroon/Blue roof, 2 Red and 2 Blue seated figures. Plain card box	**£160-200**
1947-50	**Mechanical Mouse** Grey body with Red eyes plus curling tail. Early plain card box	**£100-150**
1950-55	**Model Motor Scooter** Dark Red scooter with Black seat. Female figure has blonde hair, blue sweater, red trousers. Later box with full colour picture	**£250-350**

Moko 'Farmette' Series

Miniature size models packed in end-flap type boxes with colour picture of the model. The die-cast horses have dark brown bodies and white feet.

No.1	1950-53	**Timber Trailer with two Horses**	Green body, four Red wheels, timber load	**£125-150**
No.2	1950-53	**Farm Cart with two Horses**	Mid or Dark Blue cart body, Red raves, four Red 12-spoke wheels	**£125-150**
No.3	1950-53	**Bull Wagon with two Horses**	Green wagon body, two horses in tandem, Brown metal bull, four Red 12-spoke wheels.	**£125-150**

'Treasure Chest' Series

Packed in Brown 'Chests' with Yellow 'Strapping'.

No.10	1950-53	**Hay Cart**	Orange body, two Green raves, two Green wheels, one horse	**£50-75**
No.11	1950-53	**Millers Cart**	Blue body, two Red wheels, three White sacks, one horse	**£50-75**
No.12	1950-53	**Water Cart**	Green/Red cart, two Red wheels, one horse	**£50-75**

The early 'Lesney' toys

Lesney Products issued their first diecast toys in 1948. Whilst production ceased during the Korean war period (1950-52), the models produced formed the basis from which the 1-75 series was launched in 1953. They were sold in boxes under the name of 'MoKo' who were ultimately to also market all the early 1-75 series models.

Road Roller ....All Green body and flywheel, unpainted wheels................................**£250-300**
As previous model but with Red roller wheels and Yellow flywheel.........................**£250-300**
With a driver but without a flywheel............**£175-200**
Without a driver and without flywheel.........**£150-175**

Cement Mixer..............All Green or All-Blue body, Red wheels......**£150-175**
Pale Green body, Red mixer and wheels......**£125-150**
Dark Green body, Red mixer and wheels......**£100-150**
Red body, Green mixer and wheels..............**£125-150**

Caterpillar Tractor .....Orange or Yellow body, Red roller wheels, Black rubber tracks, driver **£125-150**

Caterpillar Bulldozer..Green, Orange or Red body, driver, Black rubber tracks **£125-150**
Yellow body, Red dozer blade and wheels **£125-150**

Prime Mover...............Orange tractor (Green engine on some), Beige or Blue trailer, Red/Yellow dozer, 'BRITISH ROAD SERVICES' **£800-1000**
As previous model but with Beige trailer......**£500-600**

'MASSEY-HARRIS' Tractor ....Red body, Cream hubs, Black rubber tyres ...**£300-400**

Milk Cart ....Orange body, White driver and six crates, Black or Brown horse, Black or Grey wheels, 'PASTEURISED MILK' cast into cart..........**£400-500**
As previous model but with Blue body **£600-700**

Breadbait Press ....1st type: Red body, unpainted 'butterfly' press...................................**£40-50**
2nd type: As 1st type but with Green press.......**£50-60**
3rd type: As 2nd type but with 'MILBRO' cast onto Red body **£60-70**

Quarry Truck ....Yellow body, Black tyres, 'LAING'. Only one example known to exist ....NPP

Covered Wagon with Barrels.............Green body, White cover, two Red barrels, six Mid-Brown horses (with White tails), with postilion rider and wagon driver **£200-250**

Covered Wagon without Barrels ....As previous model but with Chocolate Brown horses and no barrels **£200-250**

'RAG & BONE MERCHANTS' Cart.Yellow body, Red wheels, Black horse, Brown driver, with seven pieces of 'junk': mangle-wheel, bike frame, bedhead, bath, bucket, box, cistern **£750-1000**
Same but Green body, Red wheels ....NGPP

Soap-Box Racer..........Brown box, Grey spoked wheels (16 and 9), Dark Blue boy with Pink face............................NGPP

Coronation Coach (large).......................Gold coach with King and Queen, eight White horses, Gold/Red trappings, four Red riders. 200 issued...**£750-850**

Coronation Coach (large).......................Gold, Silver or Gilt coach with just the Queen inside. Horses and riders as for previous model...**£150-200**

Coronation Coach (small) ....Silver or Gold coach, eight White horses, Red/Gold trappings, four Red riders, 'A MOKO TOY BY LESNEY' cast into horsebar (1,000,000 sold) **£85-100**

'Muffin The Mule' ......White body, Red/Gold harness, Black trim ...**£175-200**

Excavator ....Digger and chassis are Dark Brown **£100-125**

Motor Scooter.............Blue Scooter ....NGPP

Other early Lesney toys. Collectors should be aware that in addition to die-cast models some tin-plate items were also produced, namely: a clockwork 'JUMBO' Elephant, 'PEREGRINE' Puppet, and a red Drummer-Boy.

Colour pictures. See the colour section following page 192.

Illustration from 1958 advertising literature showing MB44a Rolls-Royce Silver Cloud

Matchbox Model Identification

Model Number is always cast into the base, chassis or body. Obvious exceptions are the early models which were not numbered. 'Lesney' is cast into the base, chassis or body of all issues between 1953 and 1982.

'Matchbox' or **'Matchbox Series'** is shown on the base or chassis of all issues after 1965. All issues after 1957 had the model name on the base or chassis. Exceptions include those without a base (No.24 Excavator for example).

Suspension and **windows**. All car models were fitted with window glazing after 1961 and with suspension after 1965.

Baseplates are metal castings until the late 1970s when plastic bases introduced. From 1983 they are marked 'Made in Macau' and from 1986 'Made in China'.

Wheels were metal castings on early models and were gradually changed to grey, silver or black plastic. **Superfast wheels** introduced in late 1960s and issues from 1968-69 may be found with either type. Novelties such as **'Laser Wheels'** introduced in the late 1980s. **'Rolamatics'** were introduced in the 1970s having working parts that were operated by pushing. See the Superfast section for models with these features.

Model descriptions. This Catalogue tries to give original makers description of model names and colours but early Matchbox listings are known to be inaccurate graphically. Photographs in maker's catalogues are often taken of mock-ups months before production starts while model designs become changed before release. Because of space limitations, it has been necessary to include a number of descriptive abbreviations (refer to list at the foot of this page).

Dimensions refer to the greatest overall measurement (usually the length).

MB 1

1a	53	**Diesel Road Roller** (Aveling Barford) Red metal roller wheels, Tan driver cast-in, no number, crimped axles, 49mm. **Type 1**: curved lower canopy ends and thin braces above canopy supports, Type 2: straight ends and thick braces above supports, brace extension.	
		Dark Green body, Type 1 ....**£100-125**	
		Dark Green body, Type 2 ....**£40-50**	
		Light Green body, Type 2..........**£100-120**	
1b	56	**Diesel Road Roller** (Aveling Barford) Light Green body, Red metal roller wheels, Light or Dark Tan driver, high peaked canopy, no number, crimped axles, hook, 57 mm **£35-45**	
1c	58	**Diesel Road Roller** (Aveling Barford) Light Green body and driver, Red metal roller wheels, number cast-in, high peaked canopy, hook, 62 mm.........**£60-80**	
		Dark Green body **£30-40**	
1d	62	**Diesel Road Roller** (Aveling Barford) Green body and driver, Red plastic rollers, 67 mm **£15-20**	
1e	67	**Mercedes Truck** Turquoise body, Orange canopy, Black plastic wheels, 75 mm............**£8-12**	

See Superfast section for subsequent issues.

MB 2

2a	53	**Muir Hill Site Dumper** Dark Green body, Red dumper, Green painted MW, 42 mm....................................**£65-85**	
		Same but with unpainted MW........**£30-40**	
2b	57	**Muir Hill Site Dumper** Same but Tan driver, metal wheels, 46 mm ...**£30-40**	
		Same but GPW, crimped axles.......**£40-50**	
		Same but GPW, rounded axles.......**£30-40**	
2c	62	**Muir Hill Dumper Truck** Red body, Green dumper, 'LAING', Black plastic wheels, 54 mm..........**£15-25**	
		Same but 'MUIR HILL' logo and picture-box (72 only known)..........**£60-80**	
2d	67	**Mercedes Trailer** Turquoise body, Orange top, BPW .**£8-10**	

See Superfast section for subsequent issues.

Abbreviations used in this listing:

BPT = Black plastic tyres
BPW = Black plastic wheels
GPW = Grey plastic wheels
MPR = Market Price Range
MW = metal wheels
RN = Racing or rally number
SPW = Silver plastic wheels

MB 3

3a	53	**Cement Mixer**	
		Orange MW, Blue main body.........**£25-35**	
		GPW, crimped axles **£80-90**	
		GPW, rounded axles **£40-50**	
3b	61	**Bedford Tipper Truck** (All have Grey body and chassis)	
		Maroon dump, GPW, 24 treads ..**£150-200**	
		Maroon dump, GPW, 45 treads ..**£200-250**	
		Maroon dump, BPW.......................**£20-30**	
		Red dump, GPW.........................**£80-100**	
		Red dump, BPW............................**£25-35**	
3c	67	**Mercedes Ambulance** Cream or Off-White body **£10-15**	

See Superfast section for subsequent issues.

MB 4

4a	54	**Massey Harris Tractor** (with mudguards over rear wheels), Red body, Tan driver **£40-50**	
4b	57	**Massey Harris Tractor** (without mudguards over rear wheels), metal wheels **£30-35**	
		Grey plastic wheels **£45-55**	
4c	60	**Triumph T110 Motor Cycle** Steel Blue bike/sidecar, Silver wheels, Black plastic tyres **£35-45**	
		Same but with Copper body ...**£1500-2000**	
4d	66	**Stake Truck** Blue stake body **£50-60**	
		Green stake body **£8-12**	

See Superfast section for subsequent issues.

MB 5

5a	54	**London Bus** (52 mm) 'Buy Matchbox Series' on paper label **£45-55**	
5b	57	**1957 London Bus** (57 mm) 'Buy Matchbox Series' decal, metal wheels **£40-50**	
		'Buy Matchbox Series' decal, Grey plastic wheels **£60-70**	
		'Players Please' decal, GPW **£90-110**	
		'BP Visco-Static' decal, GPW ...**£200-220**	
5c	60	**Routemaster** (66 mm) 'Players Please' decal, GPW **£75-90**	
		'Peardrax', GPW or BPW **£1500-2000**	
		'BP Visco-Static' decal, Grey or Black plastic wheels **£25-35**	
		'Baron of Beef' decal, Grey or Black plastic wheels **£350-400**	
5d	65	**Routemaster** (70 mm) 'BP Longlife' decal **£15-20**	
		'BP Visco-Static' decal or label ..**£12-16**	
		'Baron of Beef' decal.................**£250-300**	
		'Pegram' label **£300-350**	

See Superfast section for subsequent issues.

MB 6

6a	54	**Quarry Truck** 55mm. Orange body, Grey tipper with six ribs, metal wheels **£25-30**	
		Same but with Grey plastic wheels, domed/crimped axles..................**£450-750**	
6b	59	**Euclid Quarry Truck** Yellow body, four ribs, decals, six BPW, 'Euclid'..........................**£20-30**	
		Knobbly GPW, domed axles ..**£1200-1600**	
6c	63	**Euclid Dump Truck** Six Black wheels (rear double wheels are one piece) **£15-18**	
		Ten Black wheels (rear wheels are normal double wheels) **£12-15**	
6d	68	**Ford Pick Up** Red body, White canopy, chrome grille **£8-12**	
		Same but White grille....................**£12-15**	

See Superfast section for subsequent issues.

MB 7

7a	54	**Horse Drawn Milk Float** Dark Orange body, White driver, crates and logo, metal wheels.........**£45-60**	
		As previous but with GPW **£75-95**	
		Pale Orange body, metal wheels **£50-60**	
		Pale Orange body, White hat and crates only, Grey plastic wheels **£70-85**	
		Pale Orange body, Silver driver and crates, Grey plastic wheels ..**£400-600**	
7b	61	**Ford Anglia** Light Blue, Green windows, Grey plastic wheels, 67 mm...........**£50-60**	
		With Silver plastic wheels.............**£35-50**	
		With Black plastic wheels **£25-35**	
7c	67	**Refuse Truck** Orange-Red body, Grey and Silver dumper...**£8-12**	

See Superfast section for subsequent issues.

MB 8

8a	55	**Caterpillar Tractor** (42 mm) Yellow body and rollers, Red driver, Green tracks............**£200-250**	
		Same but with unpainted rollers.....**£40-45**	
		Orange body and driver, Gold or Silver grille, Green tracks.**£55-65**	
		Yellow body, four ribs, Silver or Yellow grille, Green or Grey tracks.....**£30-35**	
8b	58	**Caterpillar Tractor** (42 mm) Yellow body and driver, no.'8' cast-in, Green rubber tracks **£50-60**	
8c	61	**Caterpillar Tractor** (48 mm) Yellow body, metal rollers, Green tracks **£20-30**	

Same but with Silver rollers..........£55-70
Same but with Black rollers..........£25-35

8d 64 Caterpillar Tractor (51 mm)
Yellow body, no driver,
Green rubber tracks, Black rollers .£12-15

8e 66 Ford Mustang
White body, Black wheels with
Silver hubcaps £15-20
White body, Silver wheels with
Black tyres £12-15
Orange body, Silver wheels........£180-220
See Superfast section for subsequent issues.

MB 9

9a 55 Dennis Fire Escape (57mm)
Red body, no front bumper,
metal wheels, crimped axles..........£45-55

9b 58 Dennis Fire Escape (58mm)
Red body, with front bumper,
MW, number cast underneath........£40-50
Same but with GPW £250-300

**9c 59 Merryweather Marquis
Series III Fire Engine**
Red body with Tan ladder,
GPW, crimped axles, 64 mm..........£45-55
Same but with rounded axles £30-40
Same but with Gold ladder............£35-45
With Gold ladder and BPW............£20-25
With Silver ladder, BPW £60-70
With Tan ladder, BPW...................£50-60

9d 66 Boat and Trailer (76mm, 77mm)
Blue/White boat, Blue trailer,
Black plastic wheels.......................£10-15
See Superfast section for subsequent issues.

MB 10

10a 57 Scammell Mechanical Horse
Red cab, Gold trim, Grey trailer,
crimped axles, MW, 56 mm £35-45

10b 57 Scammell Mechanical Horse
Red Cab, Brown trailer, crimped
axles, metal wheels, 75 mm £35-45
Red cab, Gold trim, Light Brown
trailer, Grey plastic wheels...........£80-90
Red cab, Silver trim, Light Brown
trailer, Grey plastic wheels............£55-70

10c 60 Foden 8-wheel Sugar Container
Dark Blue body, with crown on
rear decal, Grey wheels £65-75
Without crown, Grey wheels..........£60-70
Without crown, Silver wheels........£80-90
Without crown, Black wheels........£35-45

10d 66 Leyland Pipe Truck
Red body, 6 or 7 Grey pipes,
Silver base and grille £10-15
Same but White base and grille......£40-50
See Superfast section for subsequent issues.

MB 11

11a 55 E.R.F. Road Tanker
All models with metal wheels.
Green body, Gold trim..........£1500-1750
Dark Yellow body, Silver trim ...£120-140
Light Yellow body, Silver trim....£75-100
Red body, Gold trim, small
'ESSO' decal on rear of tank.......£90-110
Same but large 'ESSO' decal £55-65
Same but two small 'ESSO'
decals on tank sides £250-350
Same but two large 'ESSO'
decals on sides £175-200

11b 58 'ESSO' Petrol Tanker (E.R.F.)
All models with red body and
'ESSO' decal at rear.
Metal wheels, Gold trim.............£250-300
Metal wheels, Silver trim £40-50
Grey plastic wheels £40-50
Silver plastic wheels.................£600-700

Black plastic wheels £60-70

11c 65 Jumbo Crane
Yellow body and weight box..........£12-15
Yellow body, Red weight box £8-12

11d 69 Mercedes Scaffolding Truck
Silver body, Yellow plastic
scaffolds...£8-12
See Superfast section for subsequent issues.

MB 12

12a 55 Land Rover
Green body, Silver trim on some,
Tan driver, metal wheels, 43 mm ...£25-35

12b 59 Land Rover Series II
Green body, Black plastic wheels,
crimped axles £35-45
BPW, rounded axles £25-35
Grey plastic wheels £230-270

12c 65 Land Rover Safari
Green body, Brown luggage, BPW £12-15
Blue body, Brown or Red-Brown
luggage, Black plastic wheels £10-14
Metallic Gold body, Red-Brown
luggage, Black plastic wheels £500-700
See Superfast section for subsequent issues.

MB 13

13a 55 Wreck Truck (51mm)
Tan body, Red crane and hook,
metal wheels on crimped axles £30-40

13b 58 Wreck Truck (54mm)
Light Brown body, Red crane and
hook, '13' cast-in, metal wheels £35-45
Same but with GPW £60-80

13c 60 Thames Trader Wreck Truck
All models with Red body and crane.
Yellow side decals, knobbly tread
wheels (24 treads), Red hook.........£40-50
Fine tread Grey wheels (45 treads),
Grey hook £65-80
BPW, Silver or Grey hook.............£30-40

13d 65 Dodge Wreck Truck
Green cab, Yellow body, Grey hook,
'BP' decal £1000-1500
note: Fakes from 1970 have red
hooks, 'BP' labels, crimped axles and
the thick crane casting. Only the original
Green cab version has a thin crane.
But these fakes (only 24 were produced)
are now sought after by many collectors
and are also very valuable (£400-500)!
Yellow cab, Green body,
Grey hook £15-20
Same but with Red hook £10-15
See Superfast section for subsequent issues.

MB 14

14a 55 Ambulance (Daimler) (49mm.)
Cream body, Silver trim, Red cross
on roof, metal wheels on crimped or
domed/crimped axles, no number,
'Ambulance' cast on sides..............£30-35

14b 58 Daimler Ambulance (59 mm.)
All models with 'Red Cross' on roof.
Cream body, metal wheels.............£35-45
Cream body, Grey plastic wheels ...£50-60
Off-White body, metal wheels....£100-125
Off-White body, GPW £35-45
Off-White body, SPW £150-200

14c 62 Bedford Lomas Ambulance
All models with 'Red Cross' and
'LCC Ambulance' on sides.
White body, Black wheels £80-120
White body, Silver wheels.........£200-250
Off-White body, Silver wheels......£75-85
Off-White body, locating marks for
Red Cross cast into roof, Silver
grille, Silver wheels..................£300-400

Off-White body, Grey wheels £150-180
Off-White body, Black wheels.......£25-30

14d 68 Iso Grifo
Metallic Blue body, Blue interior...£25-30
Dark Metallic Blue, Blue interior.....£8-12
See Superfast section for subsequent issues.

MB 15

15a 55 Diamond T Prime Mover
Yellow body, six metal wheels,
hook, no number, 55 mm.......£1200-1600
Orange body, six metal wheels.......£25-30
Same but with ten GPW £300-400

15b 59 Super Atlantic Tractor
Orange body, Black base, hook,
Black plastic wheels, 67 mm.........£20-30
Orange body, knobbly GPW £500-750

15c 63 Tippax Refuse Collector
All models with Blue body,
Grey container and Black wheels.
With knobbly tread wheels
(24 treads), decal £60-70
With fine tread wheels,
'Cleansing Service' decal or label..£12-16

15d 64 Volkswagen 1500 Saloon
Off-White or Cream body,
'137' decals on doors £25-35
Same but '137' labels on doors.....£15-20
See Superfast section for subsequent issues.

MB 16

16a 55 Transporter Trailer
Tan body, 6 MW (crimped axles
or domed and crimped axles)........£25-30

16b 60 Super Atlantic Trailer
Tan body, Grey plastic wheels.....£60-75
Orange body, GPW....................£500-750
Orange, BPW, Black drawbar £25-30
Orange, BPW, Orange drawbar.....£30-40

16c 63 Scammell Snow Plough
Grey body, Orange tipper, Red/White
or Orange/White decal, GPW........£80-90
With Black plastic wheels £12-16

16d 69 Case Bulldozer Tractor
Red/Yellow body, Green rubber
tracks, hook, 64 mm £8-10
See Superfast section for subsequent issues.

MB 17

17a 55 Bedford Removals Van
All models with 'MATCHBOX
REMOVALS SERVICE' decals
and metal wheels.
Light Blue body, Silver trim.......£200-250
Maroon body, Silver trim £250-300
Maroon body, Gold trim.............£200-250
Green body, Silver trim £40-50

17b 58 Bedford Removals Van
Green body, metal wheels, decal
with or without Black outline £35-45
Green body, Grey plastic wheels,
decal with outline £60-75
Dark Green body, GPW,
decal with outline £150-200

17c 60 Austin FX3 Taxi
Maroon body, Mid-Grey interior,
Tan driver, Grey plastic wheels £45-55
Same but with SPW,
Mid-Grey interior £75-90
US issue: With Pale Grey interior
and Silver plastic wheels ....NGPP

17d 64 Foden Tipper
Red chassis, Orange tipper,
'HOVERINGHAM', Black base £15-20
Same but with Red base £10-15
See Superfast section for subsequent issues.

MB 18

18a 55 **Caterpillar Bulldozer** (46 mm)
Yellow body, Red blade,
Green tracks.....................................**£30-35**

18b 58 **Caterpillar Bulldozer** (50 mm)
Yellow body and blade,
Green tracks.....................................**£50-60**
Same but with Grey tracks **£80-100**

18c 61 **Caterpillar Bulldozer** (58 mm)
Yellow body and blade,
Green tracks, metal rollers **£15-20**
Same but Silver plastic rollers.......**£70-80**
Same but Black plastic rollers.......**£15-20**

18d 64 **Caterpillar Bulldozer** (62 mm)
Yellow body and blade, no driver,
Green tracks, Silver plastic
rollers...**£100-125**
Black plastic rollers **£10-15**

18e 69 **Field Car**
Yellow body, Red-Brown roof,
Red hubs **£10-15**
Same but unpainted base **£7-10**
Same but with Green hubs **£220-250**

See Superfast section for subsequent issues.

MB 19

19a 56 **MG Midget TD**
Cream body, Brown driver, Red
seats, MW, no number, 51 mm......**£65-75**
Off-White body, metal wheels......**£90-130**

19b 58 **MG 'MGA' Sports Car**
All models with Off-White body,
Red seats and Tan driver.
Metal wheels, Gold trim.............**£200-250**
Metal wheels, Silver trim **£55-75**
Grey plastic wheels, Silver trim....**£60-75**
Silver plastic wheels..................**£100-120**

19c 62 **Aston Martin DBR5**
All models with Metallic Green body,
Yellow wheels, White driver,
Number '19' **£25-35**
Number '41' or '52' **£75-90**
Number '3' or '5' **£55-70**

19d 65 **Lotus Racing Car**
Dark Green body, Yellow wheels,
White driver, racing number '3' as
decal or label **£9-12**
Orange body, RN '3' **£30-40**

See Superfast section for subsequent issues.

MB 20

20a 56 **E.R.F. Stake Truck**
Light Green body, Silver trim,
metal wheels **£1500-1750**
Maroon body, Gold trim, MW ...**£180-220**
Maroon body, Silver trim, MW......**£25-35**
Maroon body, Silver trim,
Grey plastic wheels **£250-300**
Dark Red body, metal wheels.........**£40-50**
Dark Red body, GPW................**£250-300**

20b 59 **E.R.F. 68G Truck**
All models with Dark Blue body and
'EVER READY' decals on sides.
Early decals are with Orange outline,
later with Red outline.
GPW, crimped axles **£65-75**
GPW, rounded axles **£45-65**
Silver plastic wheels..................**£100-150**
Black plastic wheels **£55-75**

20c 65 **Chevrolet Impala Taxi**
Orange-Yellow body, Cream interior,
Grey wheels, Taxi decal **£300-400**
Orange-Yellow body, Cream interior,
BPW, Silver base, Taxi decal **£30-40**
Same but with unpainted base........**£10-12**

Same but with red interior..............**£12-18**

Yellow body, Cream interior,
Taxi label **£80-100**
Same but with Red interior **£18-22**

See Superfast section for subsequent issues.

MB 21

21a 56 **Bedford Coach** (57 mm)
Green body and base,
'LONDON-GLASGOW', MW **£35-45**

21b 58 **Bedford Coach** (68 mm)
All models with Black base and
'LONDON TO GLASGOW' decals.
Green body, metal wheels **£45-55**
Green body, Grey plastic wheels....**£70-80**
Dark Green body, GPW...............**£80-100**

21c 61 **Commer Bottle Float**
All models with Pale Green body
and Black base. On early models the
bottles are Cream, later are White.
Bottle on door, SPW,
clear windows............................**£100-130**
Bottle on door, SPW,
Green windows **£50-60**
Cow on door, SPW **£40-50**
Cow on door, GPW **£100-130**
Cow on door, BPW.........................**£20-25**

21d 68 **Foden Concrete Truck**
Yellow body, Red chassis,
Black wheels **£8-12**

See Superfast section for subsequent issues.

MB 22

22a 56 **Vauxhall Cresta**
Body colours and shades from Dark
Red to Maroon, roof from White to
Cream..**£35-40**

22b 58 **Vauxhall Cresta**
Pale Pink or Cream body,
without windows, metal wheels .**£400-500**
Same but Grey plastic wheels **£65-85**
Same but with windows **£100-130**
Pale Pink body,
Blue-Green side panels...........**£1200-1500**
Light Metallic Brown body,
Blue-Green side panels, GPW....**£100-130**
Light Grey body, Lilac side panels,
Grey or Silver plastic wheels.....**£80-110**
Light Gold body, Grey or SPW...**£90-120**
Dark Gold body, Silver wheels **£90-120**
Metallic Copper body,
Grey, Silver or Black wheels......**£120-140**

22c 65 **Pontiac GP Sports Coupé**
Red body, Grey interior, BPW **£10-15**

See Superfast section for subsequent issues.

MB 23

23a 56 **Berkeley Cavalier Caravan**
Pale Blue, 'On Tow MBS 23',
metal wheels, 65 mm.......................**£30-40**

23b 57 **Berkeley Cavalier Caravan**
All models with 'ON TOW' rear decal.
Pale Blue, metal wheels **£25-35**
Lime-Green, metal wheels **£75-90**
Lime-Green, GPW..........................**£55-70**
Metallic Lime-Green, GPW ...**£1000-1250**

23c 60 **Bluebird Dauphine Caravan**
All models without windows and
with 'ON TOW' rear decal.
Metallic Lime-Green body,
Grey plastic wheels **£500-600**
Metallic Mauve body,
Maroon base **£500-600**
Metallic Mauve body and base,
Grey plastic wheels **£25-35**

Metallic Mauve body and base,
Silver wheels **£30-40**
Metallic Mauve body and base,
Black wheels **£300-400**

note: A few issues of 23c are known
to exist fitted with plastic
windows..................................**£800-1000**

23d 65 **Trailer Caravan**
Yellow body,
knobbly-tread wheels....................**£10-15**
Yellow body, fine-tread wheels **£30-40**
Pink body, knobbly-tread wheels ...**£30-40**
Yellow body, fine-tread wheels.......**£8-12**

See Superfast section for subsequent issues.

MB 24

24a 56 **'Hydraulic' Excavator**
Orange-Yellow body, metal wheels,
'WEATHERILL', 58 mm **£25-35**
Same but Yellow body, metal
wheels, 'WEATHERILL'................**£35-50**

24b 59 **'Hydraulic' Excavator**
Yellow body, Grey plastic wheels,
crimped axles..................................**£35-40**
Yellow body, Grey plastic wheels,
rounded axles **£25-30**
Yellow body, Black palstic wheels.**£15-20**

24c 67 **Rolls-Royce Silver Shadow**
All models with Metallic Red body
and Black base.
Black wheels with Silver hubcaps..**£12-18**
Silver wheels with Black tyres.......**£10-15**

See Superfast section for subsequent issues.

MB 25

25a 56 **Bedford 12 cwt Van**
Dark Blue body, Black base,
'DUNLOP' decals, metal wheels ...**£25-35**
Grey plastic wheels **£30-40**
Black plastic wheels **£300-400**

25b 60 **Volkswagen 1200**
Silver-Blue body, Grey plastic
wheels, clear windows, 62 mm **£40-50**
As previous model but with
Green tinted windows.....................**£25-35**
Same but with SPW.......................**£35-45**

25c 64 **Bedford Petrol Tanker**
Yellow cab, Green chassis,
White tank, 'BP', BPW **£12-18**
Same but Grey plastic wheels **£350-450**

64 German issue: Dark Blue cab
and chassis, White tank, 'ARAL',
Black plastic wheels **£175-200**

25d 68 **Ford Cortina Mk.II**
Metallic Light Brown body,
Black plastic wheels **£10-15**
Gift Set issue:
Same but with Yellow roof rack.....**£35-45**

See Superfast section for subsequent issues.

MB 26

26a 56 **E.R.F. Cement Mixer**
Orange body, Gold trim, MW,
crimped axles, 45 mm **£220-250**
Same but with Silver trim **£30-35**
With GPW, Silver trim **£70-80**
With SPW, Silver trim **£300-400**

26b 61 **Foden Cement Mixer** (66mm)
Orange body, Light or Dark Grey
barrel, small knobbly GPW **£500-600**
Orange body, Orange barrel,
Grey or Black plastic wheels.........**£18-25**
Orange body, Orange barrel,
Silver plastic wheels..................**£400-500**

26c 68 **G.M.C. Tipper Truck**
Red cab, Green chassis, Silver tipper,
Black plastic wheels, 67 mm...........**£6-10**

See Superfast section for subsequent issues.

MB 27

27a 56 **Bedford Low Loader** (78mm)
Pale Blue cab, Dark Blue trailer,
six MW, crimped axles **£500-600**
Pale Green cab, Tan trailer **£60-75**
27b 58 **Bedford Low Loader** (95mm)
Pale Green cab, Tan trailer,
metal wheels **£80-90**
Same but with GPW **£95-110**
Dark Green cab, Light Brown trailer,
Grey plastic wheels **£100-130**
27c 60 **Cadillac Sixty Special**
Metallic Pale Green/White,
Crimson base, SPW **£275-300**
Silver-Grey body,
Off-White roof, SPW **£90-110**
Metallic Lilac body, Pink roof,
Crimson base, GPW or SPW **£70-80**
Same model but with Black base ... **£70-80**
Same but Black base and BPW **£90-110**
27d 66 **Mercedes 230 SL**
White body, Red interior **£10-15**
See Superfast section for subsequent issues.

MB 28

28a 56 **Bedford Compressor**
Orange/Yellow body, Silver trim,
metal wheels, 47 mm **£20-30**
Yellow body, Silver trim,
MW, domed/crimped axles **£40-50**
28b 59 **Ford Thames Compressor Truck**
Yellow body, Black wheels,
crimped axles **£40-50**
Yellow body, Black wheels,
rounded axles **£20-25**
Yellow body, Grey wheels **£300-400**
28c 64 **Jaguar Mk.10**
Pale Metallic Brown, Cream seats,
Black plastic wheels, 74 mm **£20-25**
With 'Matchbox' lapel badge **£50-60**
With GPW and without
'Matchbox Series' on base **£400-500**
28d 68 **Mack Dump Truck**
Orange body, Red wheels **£10-12**
Orange body, Yellow wheels **£12-15**
See Superfast section for subsequent issues.

MB 29

29a 56 **Bedford Milk Delivery Van**
Light Brown body, White bottle
load, metal wheels, 57 mm **£25-30**
Same but GPW, White or
Cream bottles **£30-35**
29b 61 **Austin A55 Cambridge**
Two-tone Green body,
Green tinted windows, GPW **£30-35**
Same but SPW, clear or
tinted windows **£20-25**
Same but with BPW **£20-25**
29c 66 **Fire Pumper Truck**
Red body, with or without
'Denver' decal **£8-12**
See Superfast section for subsequent issues.

MB 30

30a 56 **Ford Prefect**
Grey-Brown body, Red and Silver
trim, metal wheels, 58 mm **£25-35**
Same but with GPW **£30-40**
Same but Light Blue body,
Grey plastic wheels, 58 mm **£150-180**
30b 61 **Magirus-Deutz Crane Lorry**
Light Brown body,

Red or Orange crane **£1750-2000**
Silver body, Orange jib and hook,
Grey or Silver wheels **£45-55**
Silver body, Orange jib, Grey or
Silver hook, Grey or Black wheels **£25-30**
30c 65 **8 Wheel Crane Truck** ....
Green body, Orange jib **£10-12**
Turquoise body, Orange jib **£300-400**
See Superfast section for subsequent issues.

MB 31

31a 57 **Ford Station Wagon**
Yellow body, metal wheels,
hook, 66 mm **£30-35**
Yellow body, Grey plastic wheels .. **£40-50**
31b 60 **Ford Station Wagon**
Yellow body, Black base,
Grey wheels **£220-250**
Yellow body, Black base,
Silver wheels **£200-230**
Yellow body, Crimson base,
clear or Green windows **£180-210**
Metallic Green body, Pink roof,
Crimson base, GPW or SPW **£25-35**
Same but with Black base, SPW ... **£60-70**
Same but with Black base, GPW ... **£60-70**
Same but with Black base, BPW ... **£70-90**
31c 64 **Lincoln Continental**
Metallic Blue body, BPW **£12-15**
Sea Green body **£10-12**
Metallic Lime Green body **£1200-1500**
See Superfast section for subsequent issues.

MB 32

32a 57 **Jaguar XK-140**
Off-White body, Black base,
metal wheels, 60 mm **£25-35**
Same but with GPW **£40-50**
Bright Orange-Red body, GPW .. **£130-160**
Dark Red, Black base, GPW **£130-160**
32b 62 **Jaguar 'E'-type**
Metallic Red body, Green windows,
Grey tyres, 66 mm **£80-100**
Metallic Red body,
clear windows, grey tyres **£34-45**
Metallic Red body,
clear windows, Black tyres **£30-35**
32c 68 **Leyland Tanker**
Green chassis, White tank,
Silver base and grille, 'BP' decal ... **£30-40**
Green chassis, White tank,
Silver base and grille, 'BP' label **£8-12**
Green chassis, White tank,
White base and grille, 'BP' label ... **£40-50**
Blue chassis, White tank, Silver
base and grille, 'ARAL' label..... **£100-125**
See Superfast section for subsequent issues.

MB 33

33a 57 **Ford Zodiac**
Dark Green body, hook,
no windows, MW, 68 mm **£30-40**
58 Dark Blue body, hook,
no windows, metal wheels **£400-500**
58 Sea-Green body, hook,
no windows, metal wheels **£80-90**
Samw but with GPW **£60-75**
59 Metallic Mauve body, Orange
panels, no windows, GPW **£80-100**
60 Same but with Green tinted
windows, GPW or SPW **£60-80**
33b 63 **Ford Zephyr 6**
Sea-Green body, GPW, 67 mm **£30-35**
same but with SPW **£20-30**
same but with BPW **£15-20**

33c 68 **Lamborghini Miura**
Yellow body, Red interior, 71 mm.
Black plastic wheels **£12-15**
Yellow body, White interior,
Chrome hubs........................... **£220-250**
Metallic Gold body, White interior,
Chrome hubs (US issue)............. **£250-300**
See Superfast section for subsequent issues.

MB 34

34a 57 **Volkswagen 15cwt Van**
All models with Blue body and
'MATCHBOX' side decals.
Metal wheels........................... **£30-35**
Grey plastic wheels **£30-40**
Silver plastic wheels **£120-150**
34b 62 **Volkswagen Caravette**
All models with Pale Green body
and Green interior.
Silver wheels **£180-220**
Knobbly-tread Grey wheels
(24 treads)............................ **£25-35**
Fine-tread Grey wheels (45 treads) **£50-60**
Black wheels........................... **£20-30**
34c 67 **Volkswagen Camper**
Silver body,
with high roof (7 windows)........... **£20-25**
same but lower roof (1 window).... **£15-20**
See Superfast section for subsequent issues.

MB 35

35a 57 **E.R.F. Marshall Horse Box**
Red cab, Light Brown box,
metal wheels, 52 mm **£25-35**
Same but with GPW..................... **£30-40**
With Silver plastic wheels **£125-150**
With Black plastic wheels **£75-90**
35b 64 **Snow-Trac**
Red body, Silver base, White tracks,
'Snow Trac' on sides **£20-25**
same but with 'Snow Trac' decals
on sides **£15-20**
same but without 'Snow Trac'........ **£12-15**
See Superfast section for subsequent issues.

MB 36

36a 57 **Austin A50 Cambridge**
Blue-Green body, Black base,
metal wheels, 60 mm **£20-25**
Samw but with GPW **£25-35**
Pale Blue body **£30-40**
36b 61 **Lambretta and Sidecar**
Pale Metallic Green Scooter and
side-car, BPW, 49 mm **£35-50**
36c 66 **Opel Diplomat**
Metallic Gold body, Silver engine.. **£10-15**
Metallic Gold body, Grey engine ... **£35-45**
See Superfast section for subsequent issues.

MB 37

37a 57 **Karrier Bantam Lorry**
All models with 'COCA-COLA' side
and rear decals.
Orange-Yellow body, uneven load,
metal wheels **£140-160**
Yellow body, uneven load,
metal wheels........................... **£140-160**
Orange-Yellow body, even load,
metal wheels **£45-55**
Orange-Yellow body, even load,
grey plastic wheels **£180-220**
Yellow body, even load,
metal wheels **£40-50**
Yellow body, even load,
Grey plastic wheels **£200-230**

37b 60 **Karrier Bantam Lorry**
All models with *'COCA-COLA'*
side and rear decals.
GPW, crimped axles **£75-85**
GPW, rounded axles **£35-45**
Silver plastic wheels **£400-500**
Black plastic wheels **£75-85**
37c 66 **(Dodge) Cattle Truck**
Yellow body, Grey cattle box,
2 White bulls, Silver plastic base ...**£15-20**
Unpainted metal base **£8-12**
See Superfast section for subsequent issues.

MB 38

38a 57 **Karrier Refuse Collector**
All models with
'Cleansing Department' side decals.
Grey-Brown body, MW **£280-320**
Grey body, metal wheels..............**£25-30**
Grey body, GPW, crimped axles **£35-50**
Grey body, GPW, rounded axles ...**£25-35**
Silver body, GPW **£40-50**
Silver body, SPW **£300-350**
38b 63 **Vauxhall Victor Estate**
Yellow body, Red interior,
Grey wheels **£150-200**
same but with Silver wheels...........**£18-25**
same but with Black wheels **£15-20**
Yellow body, Green interior, GPW **£40-50**
same but with Silver wheels...........**£20-30**
same but with Black wheels **£15-20**
See Superfast section for subsequent issues.

MB 39

39a 57 **Zodiac Convertible**
Pale Peach body, Light Brown
base/interior/driver, MW **£250-300**
Same but with Light Green base
and interior, metal wheels............**£30-40**
Same but with Light Green base,
Grey plastic wheels **£35-45**
Dark Peach body, Blue-Green base
and interior, Grey plastic wheels....**£35-45**
Same but with SPW.......................**£75-90**
Dark Peach body with Sea-Green
base, Grey plastic wheels **£50-60**
39b 62 **Pontiac Convertible**
Metallic Purple body, Crimson base,
Red steering wheel, SPW **£70-80**
same but with Grey wheels **£250-300**
Lemon body, Crimson base,
Red steering wheel, SPW or GPW.**£50-75**
Same but Cream steering wheel.....**£25-35**
Lemon body, Black base, SPW **£50-75**
Same but with Grey wheels...........**£35-45**
Same but with Black wheels **£15-20**
39c 67 **Ford Tractor**
Blue body, Yellow engine cover,
Black plastic tyres, 55 mm..............**£8-12**
Blue body and engine cover..........**£12-15**
All-Orange body, Yellow hubs.......**£40-50**

MB 40

40a 57 **Bedford 7 Ton Tipper**
Red body, Brown tipper,
metal wheels, 53 mm.....................**£35-45**
Same but with Grey plastic wheels,
domed crimped axles.....................**£30-35**
Same but with Grey plastic
wheels on rivetted axles **£30-35**
40b 61 **Leyland Tiger Coach**
Steel Blue body, GPW....................**£75-85**
Silver plastic wheels......................**£25-35**
Black plastic wheels **£20-25**

40c 67 **Hay Trailer**
Blue body, Yellow plastic hay racks
and wheels, Black plastic tyres **£6-10**
note: Model 40c deleted in 1972 but
appeared in Two-Packs between 1976-1981.

MB 41

41a 57 **Jaguar 'D'-Type** (55 mm)
Green body, MW, No '41' **£30-40**
Green body, MW, No '52'.............**£70-80**
Green body, GPS, No '41' **£90-120**
41b 60 **Jaguar 'D'-Type** (62 mm)
All models with Green body
and Black base.
GPS, crimped axles, No '41' **£50-60**
same but with rounded axles **£40-50**
Wire hubs with Black tyres,
No '41'..**£35-40**
same but with No '5' or '6'...........**£75-90**
Red hubs with Black tyres.........**£280-320**
41c 65 **Ford GT Racer**
All models with racing number '6'.
White body, Red hubs, BPT......**£150-175**
White body, Yellow hubs,
Black tyres **£10-15**
Yellow body, Yellow hubs,
black tyres (Italian 5 Pack set) ...**£120-150**
See Superfast section for subsequent issues.

MB 42

42a 57 **Evening News Van**
Yellow body, *'EVENING NEWS'*
decals, metal wheels, 57 mm.........**£35-40**
GPW with 24 treads **£45-55**
GPW with 45 treads **£120-150**
BPW with 24 treads...................**£100-125**
BPW with 45 treads....................**£120-150**
42b 65 **Studebaker Lark Wagonaire**
(With hunter and dog figures),
Blue body, sliding rear roof
painted as body **£40-50**
same but rear roof
painted Light Blue **£12-15**
42c 69 **Iron Fairy Crane**
Red body, Yellow boom, BPS **£10-15**
See Superfast section for subsequent issues.

MB 43

43a 58 **Hillman Minx**
Light Green body, Silver/Red
trim, metal wheels, hook **£300-350**
Blue/Grey body, Pale Grey roof,
metal wheels **£30-35**
Same but with GPS **£60-70**
Turquoise body, Cream roof,
Grey plastic wheels **£35-50**
43b 62 **A.B. Tractor Shovel**
Yellow body, driver and shovel **£90-110**
Yellow body and shovel,
Red driver and base **£15-20**
Yellow body, driver and base,
Red shovel **£20-30**
Yellow body, Red driver,
base and shovel..........................**£200-250**
43c 68 **Pony Trailer**
Yellow body, Grey ramp,
Light Brown base, BPS **£12-18**
same but with Dark Green base **£8-12**
See Superfast section for subsequent issues.

MB 44

44a 58 **Rolls-Royce Silver Cloud**
Metallic Silver-Blue body,
Red trim, metal wheels, 67 mm **£25-35**
60 As previous but with GPS.............**£30-40**
Same but with SPW......................**£50-60**

44b 64 **Rolls-Royce Phantom V**
Metallic Mauve body,
Black wheels.................................**£20-25**
Same but with Grey wheels...........**£60-80**
Same but with Silver wheels........**£90-120**
Meatallic Silver-Grey body, BPW.**£80-90**
Same but with Silver wheels **£300-350**

44c 67 **GMC Refrigerator Truck**
Red body, Sea-Green container,
Black wheels, 76 mm **£8-12**
See Superfast section for subsequent issues.

MB 45

45a 58 **Vauxhall Victor**
Red body, MW, 61 mm **£2000-3000**
Yellow or Lemon body, MW....**£35-45**
Yellow body, metal wheels,
no dashboard casting bar....**£250-300**
Yellow or Lemon body, GPW,
no window glazing **£35-45**
same but with clear windows **£70-80**
same but with Green windows **£70-80**
Lemon, Green windows, SPW **£45-55**
Yellow body, SPW **£60-70**
Yellow body, BPW.......................**£60-70**
45b 65 **Ford Corsair with Boat**
Cream body, Red interior,
Black wheels, Silver painted base ..**£25-30**
Same but with unpainted base.......**£10-15**
Same but with Grey wheels...........**£50-60**
Models with white interior are
pre-productions **£500-600**
See Superfast section for subsequent issues.

MB 46

46a 58 **Morris Minor 1000**
Pale Brown body, no windows,
metal wheels, 53 mm.............**£1500-1750**
Dark Green body, Black base,
MW, domed crimped axles.............**£60-70**
Dark Blue/Green body, MW **£70-80**
Same but with GPW **£100-125**
Blue body, GPW........................**£125-150**
46b 60 **'PICKFORDS' Removals Van**
Dark Blue body, Grey wheels,
three line decal............................**£90-120**
Dark Blue body, Silver wheels,
three line decal............................**£90-120**
Dark Blue body, Grey wheels,
two line decal............................**£100-130**
Dark Blue body, Silver wheels,
two line decal............................**£180-220**
Green body, Grey wheels **£55-65**
Green body, Silver wheels **£60-80**
Green body, Black wheels **£35-45**
'BEALES BEALESONS' Van
Light Brown body,
'Beales Bealesons' decal,
without box **£300-400**
Same but in special White box
with *'Sun'* and *'It's A Pleasure'*
decal..**£400-450**
46c 68 **Mercedes-Benz 300 SE**
Green body **£12-15**
69 Metallic Blue body **£9-12**
See Superfast section for subsequent issues.

MB 47

47a 58 **Trojan Van**
Red body,
'BROOKE BOND TEA' decals,
metal wheels, 58 mm.....................**£30-40**
Same but with GPS **£35-45**
47b 63 **Commer Ice Cream Van**
'LYONS MAID',
Metallic Blue body, BPW.............**£75-100**
Same but with Blue body **£25-35**

Blue body, Grey wheels.............**£175-200**
Blue body, Black wheels,
White side decals.....................**£35-45**
Cream body, *'LYONS MAID'*.....**£180-220**
Cream body, White side decals **£50-60**
'LORD NIELSENS ICE CREAM',
Cream body, Red/White labels.....**£50-60**
Blue body, Black plastic wheels.**£125-150**

47c 68 DAF Container Truck
Sea Green body, Grey roof,
Yellow container, BPW **£55-65**
Silver body, Grey or Silver roof,
Yellow container, BPW **£8-12**
See Superfast section for subsequent issues.

MB 48

48a 58 Meteor Sports Boat and Trailer
Black trailer, Light Brown boat,
Blue hull, metal wheels **£25-30**
With Grey plastic wheels............**£30-35**
With Silver plastic wheels..........**£130-160**

48b 61 Sports Boat and Trailer
Boat with Cream or White deck
and Red hull or with Red deck and
Cream or white hull,
Dark Blue trailer, Black wheels **£15-20**
Dark Blue trailer, Grey wheels.....**£75-100**
Light Blue trailer, Black wheels....**£20-30**

48c 66 (Dodge) Dumper Truck
Red body, Silver trim, wide or
narrow BPW, 76 mm **£8-12**
See Superfast section for subsequent issues.

MB 49

49a 58 M3 Personnel Carrier
Military Green, White *'Star'* decal
on bonnet, MW and rollers..**£20-30**
Grey plastic wheels, metal rollers..**£20-30**
Grey plastic wheels and rollers ..**£350-400**
Grey plastic wheels, Silver rollers..**£60-80**
BPW and rollers, Grey tracks........**£25-35**
BPW and rollers, Green tracks......**£35-45**

49b 67 (Mercedes) Unimog
Light Brown body,
Sea-Green base, 61 mm................**£12-15**
Light Brown body, Red base **£700-800**
Light Blue body, Red base **£8-12**
See Superfast section for subsequent issues.

MB 50

50a 58 Commer Pick-Up
Pale Brown body, MW, 64 mm......**£25-35**
Pale or Light Brown body, GPW ...**£35-45**
Light Brown body, SPW **£100-130**
Red and White body, SPW........**£400-500**
Red and Grey body, SPW.........**£120-150**
Red and Grey body, GPW **£60-70**
Red and Grey body, BPW **£60-70**

50b 64 John Deere Lanz Tractor
Green body, Yellow hubs,
Grey tyres, 50 mm........................**£15-20**
Same but Black tyres **£10-15**
With Green hubs, Black tyres.....**£500-600**

50c 69 Ford Kennel Truck
Metallic Green body, White grille,
smooth kennel floor, 71 mm **£15-20**
Same but textured kennel floor **£8-12**
Same but with Silver grill **£12-15**
See Superfast section for subsequent issues.

MB 51

51a 58 Albion Chieftain
All models with Yellow body, Tan or
Light Beige load, *'PORTLAND
CEMENT'* decals, metal wheels **£40-50**
*'BLUE CIRCLE PORTLAND
CEMENT'* decals, metal wheels **£30-40**

Same but with GPW **£35-45**
Same but with SPW....................**£100-130**
Same but with knobbly BPW **£200-250**

51b 64 Tipping Trailer
Green body, three Yellow barrels,
Yellow hubs, Grey tyres **£10-15**
With Yellow hubs, Black tyres........**£6-10**
With Green hubs, black tyres **£250-300**

51c 69 AEC Mammoth Major 8 Wheel Tipper
Orange body, Silver tipper,
'DOUGLAS', White base grille.....**£50-60**
Same but chrome base...................**£20-25**
Yellow body, Silver tipper,
'DOUGLAS' **£40-50**
Yellow body, Silver tipper,
'POINTER' **£12-18**
See Superfast section for subsequent issues.

MB 52

52a 58 1948 Maserati 4 CLT
Red body, Cream driver, no decal,
Black plastic wheels, 61 mm.......**£30-40**
Same with racing number '52' **£35-45**
Red body, racing number '52',
wire wheels, Black plastic tyres.**£200-250**
Lemon body, wire wheels, '52' **£35-45**
Same but number '3' or '5'.........**£70-100**

52b 65 B.R.M. Racing Car
Blue body, Yellow hubs, BPT, '5' **£8-12**
Same but with racing number '3' **£60-75**
Dark Blue (Ultramarine) body,
racing number '5' **£60-80**
Gift Set model: Red body, Yellow
hubs with Black tyres **£60-80**
Dark Cherry Red body, Yellow hubs,
racing number '5' **£100-120**
See Superfast section for subsequent issues.

MB 53

53a 58 Aston Martin DB2-4 Mk.I
Metallic Green body, MW, 65 mm.**£30-40**
Same but with GPW **£35-45**
Metallic Red, knobbly GPW **£150-220**
Metallic Red, knobbly BPW **£150-200**

53b 63 Mercedes-Benz 220SE
Maroon body, Silver wheels...........**£15-25**
Maroon body, Grey wheels **£30-40**
Maroon body, Black wheels..........**£60-75**
Dark Red body, Grey wheels.........**£35-45**
Dark Red body, Black wheels **£12-18**

53c 68 Ford Zodiac Mk.IV
Light Metallic Blue body, BPW **£8-12**
Light Metallic Green body,
Black plastic wheels **£400-500**
See Superfast section for subsequent issues.

MB 54

54a 58 Saracen Personnel Carrier
Olive Green body, six Black plastic
wheels, crimped axles, 57 mm **£25-35**
Same but with rounded axles **£20-25**

54b 65 Cadillac Ambulance
White, Red cross label or decal and
roof lights, Black plastic wheels **£8-12**
See Superfast section for subsequent issues.

MB 55

55a 58 DUKW Amphibian
Olive Green body, MW, 71 mm **£15-20**
Same but GPW or BPW **£20-30**
In box with Green model picture
(normally Red picture) **£100-150**

55b 63 Ford Fairlane 'POLICE' Car
Non-metallic Dark Blue, BPW.....**£180-220**
Metallic Blue, knobbly BPW **£80-100**
Metallic Blue, BPW **£20-30**
Metallic Blue, GPW **£900-1200**

Metallic Blue, SPW **£180-220**

55c 66 Ford Galaxy 'POLICE' Car
White body, *'Police & Shield'* decal,
Blue roof light **£80-100**
same but with Red roof light..........**£12-15**

55d 68 Mercury 'POLICE' Car
White body, *'Police & Shield'*
labels, Red roof light **£250-300**
Same but with Blue roof light **£12-15**

MB 56

56a 58 London Trolley Bus. All models
with Red body, *'DRINK PEARDRAX'*
and destination decals.
Black poles, metal wheels **£130-150**
Black poles, GPW **£250-300**
Red poles, metal wheels **£40-50**
Red poles, GPW or BPW **£35-45**
Red poles, SPW **£140-160**

56b 65 Fiat 1500 (all have BPW)
Sea-Green body, Brown luggage .**£12-18**
Same but with Red-Brown luggage .**£8-12**
Gift Set version:
Red body, Red-Brown luggage **£60-80**
See Superfast section for subsequent issues.

MB 57

57a 58 Wolseley 1500
Pale Green body, GPW,
Gold trim, 55 mm **£180-200**
Same but with Silver trim **£30-40**

57b 61 Chevrolet Impala
All models with Metallic Blue body
and pale Blue roof.
Clear windows, Black base, SPW ..**£60-75**
Clear windows, Dark Blue base,
SPW **£30-40**
Green windows, Dark Blue base,
SPW **£20-25**
Same but with GPW **£30-40**
Green windows, Pale or Light
Blue base, SPW **£75-90**
Black base, GPW **£45-55**
Black base, SPW **£35-45**
Black base, BPW **£25-35**

57c 66 Land Rover Fire Truck
Red body, *'KENT FIRE BRIGADE'*,
Black plastic wheels, 64 mm **£12-16**
Same but with GPW **£350-450**
See Superfast section for subsequent issues.

MB 58

58a 58 AEC 'BEA' Coach
Dark Blue body, White letters,
Grey wheels, 65 mm.....................**£40-50**
Dark Blue body, Black letters on
White ground, Grey wheels **£35-45**
Same but with Silver wheels **£100-130**
Same but with Black wheels **£120-150**

58b 62 Drott Excavator
Red body, Silver base,
Black rollers, Green tracks **£12-18**
Same but with Silver rollers..........**£70-90**
Orange body, Silver base,
Black rollers...............................**£20-25**
Orange body and base,
Black rollers...............................**£15-20**

58c 68 DAF Girder Truck
White body, Red base and 12 girders,
6 Black plastic wheels, 75 mm.........**£8-12**
See Superfast section for subsequent issues.

MB 59

59a 58 Ford Thames Van 'SINGER'
Pale Green body, Red seats, GPW .**£40-50**
Same but SPW, rivetted axles.....**£175-225**
Dark Green body and Grey
plastic wheels, rivetted axles **£140-160**

Dark Green body, Silver
plastic wheels, rivetted axles **£150-200**
59b 63 **Ford Fairlane Fire Chief**
All models with Red body and
'FIRE CHIEF' decals on doors
and bonnet, Black wheels..............**£20-25**
With Grey wheels **£75-90**
With Silver wheels **£190-220**
With *'SHIELD'* decals on doors.**£200-250**
59c 66 **Ford Galaxie Fire Chief**
Red body, Blue dome light,
'FIRE CHIEF & SHIELD'............**£10-15**
Same but with Red dome light...**£220-250**
See Superfast section for subsequent issues.

MB 60

60a 58 **Morris J2 Pick Up**
All with Light Blue body and
'BUILDERS SUPPLY COMPANY' decals.
'Supply Company' in Black,
Grey plastic wheels **£50-60**
'SUPPLY COMPANY' in White,
with rear window, GPW or BPW...**£25-35**
Same but with SPW.......................**£40-50**
Without rear window, GPW **£90-120**
Without rear window, BPW **£35-45**
60b 66 **Site Hut Truck**
Blue body, Yellow and Green plastic
building, Black wheels **£8-12**
See Superfast section for subsequent issues.

MB 61

61a 59 **Ferret Scout Car**
Olive Green body, Tan driver,
Black plastic wheels, 57 mm..........**£20-25**
61b 66 **Alvis Stalwart 'BP'**
White body, Green wheels with
Black tyres, smooth carrier bed......**£25-30**
Same but with ribbed carrier bed ...**£10-15**
White body, Yellow wheels with
Black tyres **£35-45**
Two-Pack version: Military Olive
Green body, Black wheels.............**£15-25**
See Superfast section for subsequent issues.

MB 62

62a 59 **AEC General Service Lorry**
Olive Green body, tow hook,
six Black plastic wheels, 68 mm....**£25-30**
62b 63 **Commer TV Service Van**
All models with Cream body and Red
plastic ladder, aerial and three TVs.
'RENTASET', knobbly
Grey wheels (24 treads)..............**£120-150**
'RENTASET', Black wheels **£40-50**
'RENTASET', fine-tread
Grey wheels (45 treads)..............**£220-250**
'RADIO RENTALS', BPW.............**£50-60**
'RADIO RENTALS', fine-tread
Grey wheels **£350-400**
62c 68 **Mercury Cougar**
Cream body, White interior,
Chrome hubs..........................**£1500-1750**
Metallic Lime Green body,
Red interior **£10-15**
See Superfast section for subsequent issues.

MB 63

63a 59 **Service Ambulance (Ford)**
Olive Green body, Red crosses,
BPW, crimped axles **£30-35**
Same but with rounded axles **£25-30**
63b 63 **Alvis Foamite Crash Tender**
Red body, Silver hose nozzle,
six Black plastic wheels, 63 mm....**£60-70**

With Gold hose nozzle **£20-30**
63c 68 **Dodge Crane Truck**
Yellow body, Red hook, 76 mm.......**£8-12**
Yellow body, Yellow hook **£10-15**
See Superfast section for subsequent issues.

MB 64

64a 59 **Scammell Breakdown Truck**
Olive Green body, metal or plastic
hook, BPW, 64 mm **£25-35**
64b 66 **MG 1100**
Green body, White seats, driver,
dog, Black plastic wheels, 67 mm....**£8-12**
See Superfast section for subsequent issues.

MB 65

65a 59 **Jaguar 3.4 litre**
Dark Blue body, Silver rear
number-plate, GPW, 62 mm...........**£45-55**
As previous but with Blue rear
number plate...............................**£35-45**
Metallic Blue body and number
plate, Grey plastic wheels...........**£100-130**
65b 62 **Jaguar 3.8 Sedan**
Metallic Red body, Silver base,
Silver plastic wheels, 68 mm **£70-80**
Red body, Silver plastic wheels......**£30-40**
Red body, Grey plastic wheels **£35-45**
Red body, Black plastic wheels......**£20-25**
65c 67 **Claas Combine Harvester**
Red body, Yellow blades and
front hubs, no hole in base **£80-100**
As previous but with hole in base **£6-10**
See Superfast section for subsequent issues.

MB 66

66a 59 **Citroën DS 19**
Yellow body, Silver trim, GPW......**£35-45**
Same but with SPW **£80-95**
66b 62 **Harley-Davidson Motor Cycle**
Metallic Bronze bike and sidecar,
spoked wheels, Black plastic tyres.**£70-80**
66c 66 **'GREYHOUND' Coach**
Silver-Grey body, clear windows,
Black plastic wheels **£60-70**
Silver-Grey body, Amber windows,
Black plastic wheels **£10-12**
See Superfast section for subsequent issues.

MB 67

67a 59 **Saladin Armoured Car**
Olive Green body, six Black plastic
wheels, crimped axles, 61 mm **£25-35**
Same but with rounded axles **£25-30**
67b 67 **Volkswagen 1600 TL**
Red body, Black wheels with
Silver hubcaps **£15-20**
Red body, Silver wheels with
black tyres......................................**£10-15**
Gift Set version: Red body with
Maroon plastic roof rack **£50-60**
Metallic Purple body,
Silver wheels with Black tyres...**£250-300**
See Superfast section for subsequent issues.

MB 68

68a 59 **Austin Radio Truck Mk.II**
Olive Green body and base,
BPW, crimped axles **£30-35**
Same but with rounded axles **£25-30**
68b 65 **Mercedes Coach** (all have BPW)
Turquoise/White body,US issue .**£100-150**
Orange/White body, BPW **£8-12**
See Superfast section for subsequent issues.

MB 69

69a 59 **Commer Van 'NESTLES'**
Maroon body, driver, Yellow logo,
Grey plastic wheels, 56 mm **£35-45**
Red body, GPW with 20 treads......**£55-70**
Red body, GPW with 36 treads......**£75-85**
69b 65 **Hatra Tractor Shovel**
Orange body, Orange wheels,
Grey tyres, 78 mm **£60-75**
With Red hubs, Grey tyres **£25-35**
With Red hubs, Black tyres...........**£15-20**
With Yellow hubs, Black tyres **£10-15**
Yellow body, Yellow hubs.............**£10-15**
Yellow body, Red hubs...................**£70-90**
Orange body, Yellow shovel......**£250-300**
See Superfast section for subsequent issues.

MB 70

70a 59 **Ford Thames Estate Car**
Turquoise and Yellow body,
Grey wheels, no windows **£30-35**
Grey wheels, clear windows..........**£35-40**
Grey wheels, Green windows **£25-30**
Silver wheels, clear windows **£35-40**
Silver or Black wheels,
Green windows **£25-30**
70b 66 **Ford Grit Spreader**
Red body, Pale Lemon container,
Black plastic wheels, 68 mm...........**£8-12**
Red body, Dark Yellow container,
Black or Grey slide, Black wheels.**£25-35**
See Superfast section for subsequent issues.

MB 71

71a 59 **200 gallon Water Truck**
Olive Green body, BPW **£25-30**
Same model with first
'Matchbox Collectors' badge **£55-65**
71b 64 **Jeep Gladiator Pick-Up**
Red body, Green interior,
Black plastic wheels, 66 mm..........**£50-60**
Red body, White interior **£10-15**
71c 69 **Ford Heavy Wreck Truck** (all BPW)
Red and White body, Amber
windows, smooth loadbed **£200-250**
Same but with ribbed loadbed **£100-150**
Same but with Green windows **£8-12**
Military Green body **£8-12**
See Superfast section for subsequent issues.

MB 72

72a 59 **Fordson Major Tractor**
All models with Blue body.
Grey front wheels, Orange rear
hubs with Grey tyres, 50 mm **£35-40**
Black front wheels, Orange rear
hubs with Black tyres **£35-40**
Orange hubs front and rear,
Grey tyres **£35-40**
Orange hubs front and rear, BPT ...**£30-35**
Yellow hubs front and rear,
Grey or Black tyres **£300-400**
72b 66 **Jeep CJ5**
Orange-Yellow body,
Yellow hubs, White interior **£600-700**
Yellow body, Yellow hubs,
Red interior **£8-12**
See Superfast section for subsequent issues.

MB 73

73a 59 **Leyland R.A.F. 10 ton Refueller**
Airforce-Blue body, roundel,
six Grey plastic wheels, 66 mm **£35-45**
Same but with BPW **£800-1100**

73b 62 Ferrari F1 Racing Car
Red body, Grey or White driver,
RN '73', 'spoked' metal hubs,
Black plastic tyres **£20-25**

73c 68 Mercury Commuter Station Wagon
Metallic Lime Green body,
Silver hubs, Black plastic tyres **£8-12**
See Superfast section for subsequent issues.

MB 74

74a 59 Mobile 'REFRESHMENTS' Bar
White body, Pale Blue base,
Blue interior, GPW **£100-130**
Cream body, Light Blue base,
Grey plastic wheels **£110-140**
Pink body, Light Blue base,
Grey plastic wheels **£300-400**
Silver body, Light Blue base,

Grey plastic wheels **£30-40**
Silver body, Light Blue base,
Silver plastic wheels **£35-45**
Silver body, Light Blue base,
Black plastic wheels **£300-350**
Silver body, Sea Green or
Dark Blue base **£60-75**

74b 66 Daimler Fleetline Bus
Cream body, 'ESSO' decals............**£12-18**
Cream body, 'ESSO' labels **£25-35**
Green body, 'ESSO' labels **£15-20**
Red body, 'ESSO' labels **£25-35**
See Superfast section for subsequent issues.

MB 75

75a 60 Ford Thunderbird
All models have Cream body and
Peach side panels.

Blue base, Silver wheels................**£30-35**
Blue-Green base, Silver wheels ...**£90-120**
Black base, Silver wheels.............**£70-80**
Black base, Grey wheels................**£55-75**
Black base, Black wheels **£180-220**

75b 65 Ferrari Berlinetta
Metallic Green body, wire wheels,
Silver painted base.......................**£50-60**
Metallic Green body, wire wheels,
unpainted base **£10-15**
Metallic Green body, Silver wheels
with Black tyres **£12-18**
Red body, Silver wheels with
Black tyres **£250-300**
Red body, wire wheels..............**£400-500**
See Superfast section for subsequent issues.

Early Accessory Packs

A1a 1957 **'ESSO' Petrol Pump Set** ....Red pumps, White figure...**£25-35**

A1b 1963 **'BP' Petrol Pump Set** ....White pumps, Yellow/White decal **£20-25**

A2 1957 **Car Transporter**...............................Box type 1: Dark Blue/Yellow front and back 'MOKO - LESNEY' line-drawing box.
Box type 2: Yellow front/back, Blue end tabs, 'LESNEY MATCHBOX SERIES' logo.
1: Pale blue body, Dark Blue logo 'MATCHBOX CAR TRANSPORTER', metal wheels on tractor and trailer, 1st type box **£35-45**
2: Pale Blue body, Red 'CAR COLLECTION Ltd CAR TRANSPORTER', GPW (tractor), BPW (trailer), 1st box **£150-200**
3: Pale Blue body, Red 'CAR COLLECTION Ltd CAR TRANSPORTER', Black plastic wheels on tractor and trailer, 1st type box **£35-45**
4: Pale Blue body, Red 'CAR COLLECTION Ltd CAR TRANSPORTER', Grey plastic wheels on tractor and trailer, 1st type box **£35-45**
5: Red cab and lower deck, Grey upper deck and sides, BPW, Red logo: 'CAR COLLECTION Ltd' on Pale Yellow background, 2nd box ...**£150-200**

A3 1957 **Garage** ....Yellow/Green/Red, opening doors, all metal **£20-30**
A4 1960 **Road Signs Set**...............................Eight Red/White/Black signs 'Lesney' on base **£20-25**
A5 1960 **'HOME STORES' Shop**................Food shop with window display and opening door...**£20-25**
? c1958 **Service Station and Showroom**......'MATCHBOX GARAGE', Red plastic building with Yellow base and roof sign **£50-75**
Same but Yellow plastic building with Red base and roof sign **£50-75**
MG1 1960-63 **Service Station and Showroom**......'MATCHBOX', Yellow plastic building and ramp, Red sign 'MATCHBOX' **£150-200**
Same but White plastic building with Green base and Yellow sign 'BP' **£150-200**
MG1 c1968 **Service Station** ....Green and Yellow plastic building and card forecourt 'BP' **£75-100**
MF1 1963-67 **Fire Station** ....White building with Red roof, 'MATCHBOX FIRE STATION' on a Brown or Red background..............**£50-75**
Same but Green roof, wood effect decal background **£125-175**

Major Packs Series

M1 58 Caterpillar Earthmover
Yellow body, MW, crimped or rounded axles, 99mm............**£35-45**

M1 63 'BP' Petrol Tanker
Green/Yellow/White body, knobbly or fine tread BPW **£25-35**

M2 58 Bedford Articulated Truck 'WALLS ICE CREAM'
All versions have a Light Blue tractor cab, 101mm.
Cream trailer, metal wheels **£50-60**
59 Cream trailer, Grey plastic wheels **£45-55**
59-61 White trailer, Grey plastic wheels **£60-80**

M2 61 Bedford Tractor and York Trailer 'DAVIES TYRES'
Orange cab, Silver trailer, clear windows, knobbly BPW **£60-75**
With Green tinted windows, knobbly BPW **£45-60**
With Grey knobbly tread wheels **£75-90**
With Black fine tread wheels (45 treads) **£60-80**
With Green fine tread wheels (45 treads)........................**£100-140**
Silver cab, Dark Red trailer, Black base **£180-220**

M2 64 Bedford Tractor and York Trailer 'LEP INTERNATIONAL'
Silver cab, Dark Red trailer, Dark Red base..................**£100-120**
Silver cab, Dark Red trailer, Black base **£55-70**

M3 59 Mighty Antar Tank Transporter and Centurion Tank
Both models in Military Olive Green, Transporter always
has Black wheels. Tank with metal rollers **£30-40**
Tank with Grey plastic rollers **£220-250**
Tank with Black plastic rollers **£30-40**

M4 59 Ruston Bucyrus Excavator
Maroon cab, Yellow shovel arms, Black base, Green tracks .**£50-70**

M4 65 'FREUHOF' Hopper Train
Maroon tractor, two Silver trailers, Red wheels, BPT..........**£35-45**

M5 59 'MASSEY FERGUSON 780' Combine Harvester
Red body, Yellow blades, Silver front wheels, Black rear **£35-45**
Orange front wheels, Black rear wheels **£55-65**
Yellow front wheels, Black rear wheels **£70-80**

Orange front and rear wheels with Black tyres **£60-70**
Yellow front and rear wheels with Black tyres **£75-90**

M6 60 Scammell Transporter 'PICKFORDS'
Dark Blue tractor, Maroon low-loader, BPW, 279mm...........**£60-75**
Blue tractor, Bright Red low-loader, Black plastic wheels ..**£80-100**

M6 66 Racing Car Transporter 'BP'
Green body, Silver ramp/rear door, Red hubs with BPT,
'Monza/Le Mans/Sebring/Nurburgring' on sides.............**£220-250**
With 'Le Mans/Sebring/Silverstone/Nurburgring' on sides ...**£40-50**

M7 60 Thames Trader Cattle Truck 'JENNINGS', Dark Red cab,
Light Tan box trailer, knobbly GPW **£35-45**
With Dark Tan trailer, Red rear lamp, knobbly GPW **£40-50**
As previous model but with knobbly BPW **£60-70**
Same but with Grey fine-tread wheels (45 treads) **£80-100**
Same but with Black fine-tread wheels (45 treads)..............**£70-80**

M8 61 'MOBILGAS' Petrol Tanker
Red body, White 'MOBILGAS' logo, knobbly GPW **£60-80**
With Black knobbly-tread wheels (24 treads) **£125-150**
With Black fine-tread wheels (45 treads) **£150-180**

M8 64 Guy Warrior Car Transporter Blue-Green cab, Orange trailer,
Orange wheels with Grey tyres, 209 mm.
'FARNBOROUGH-MEASHAM' in Black, White outline .**£80-100**
'FARNBOROUGH-MEASHAM' in White, Black outline ...**£35-50**

M9 62 Inter-State Double Freighter 'COOPER-JARRETT'.
All versions have a Dark Blue cab.
Silver trailers, one-piece double wheels, Yellow lettering **£75-90**
Same but double wheels are two separate wheels.................**£60-80**
Same but Orange lettering **£95-120**
Grey trailers, Yellow lettering **£80-110**

M10 62 Whitlock Dinkum Dumper
Yellow body, 'DD-70', unpainted metal wheels, 108 mm **£45-65**
Same but Red plastic hubs with Black tyres **£50-70**

"Absolutely the best UK auction site around. QXL has pages of advice to reassure and encourage the uncertain."
The Evening Standard

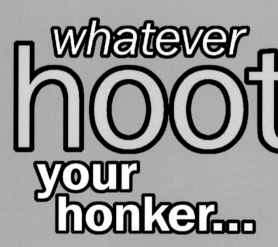

whatever
hoots
your
honker...

You'll find it on www.qxl.com - the UK's premiere site for trading Matchbox, Corgi, and more.

qxl

Two No.42 Bedford 'Evening News' Vans one with metal wheels and one with black plastic wheels, note the different box types.
Two No.37 Karrier Bantam Lorries one orange-yellow with uneven load and one in yellow with even load.

N.B. Models formed part of a larger lot so no individual prices are available.

No.57 Land Rover Fire Trucks, 1-75 series, one with slide on 'Kent Fire Brigade' transfer and rare grey plastic wheels and one with paper label and black plastic wheels. Sold for £483.

Top Row: Two silver 74 Mobile Canteens, one with silver plastic and one with grey wheels, plus a pink 74 and an off-white 74.

2nd Row: Lesney issues - i) Lesney Milk Cart

ii) Rag and Bone Merchants Cart (£1,035)

Moko issue - Model Motor Scooter (£437), plus Moko Jumbo Elephant

3rd Row: Moko - Tractor and Trailer, Excavator plus Lesney green Cement Mixer.

4th Row: Model of Yesteryear Y9 Showmans Engine, plus Y6 A.E.C. 'Osram Lamps'.
1-75 series in yellow, 31 Ford 1960 Station Wagon with maroon base plus 25 'ARAL' Tanker and yellow 11 Tanker.

5th Row: Land Rover Fire Truck 57 with grey plastic wheels, green 11 Petrol Tanker sold for (£1,380).
Two No.17 Removal Vans, one light blue and one maroon with one box sold for (£207), plus green 43 Hillman Minx sold for (£207).

6th Row: No.53 Two Aston Martins metallic red, one with grey and one with black plastic wheels. No.17 Morris Minor in blue livery plus No.14 Bedford Lomas Ambulance with cast in roof locating marks.

Bottom Row: Six No.22 Vauxhall Cresta PB's which sold for £690.

N.B. Where sale price figures not shown, individual price details are not available.

Models sold by Christie's of South Kensington, London.
Pictures reproduced by their kind permission.

Shop display stands from the mid sixties. Similar items (without models) today sell for hundreds of pounds.

Matchbox Presentation and Gift Sets

Presentation Sets

The first presentation set was sold in the USA in 1957 and consisted of an enlarged normal 'Matchbox' containing eight of the sixty-four models that Lesney manufactured at that time. The first sets were not sold in the UK until 1959.

Ref.	Year	Set name	Contents	Market Price Range
PS 1	1957	**Matchbox Presentation Set**......Contains models 1 - 8 (only available in USA)		**£1500-2500**
PS 2	1957	**Matchbox Presentation Set**......Contains models 9 - 16 (only available in USA)		**£1500-2500**
PS 3	1957	**Matchbox Presentation Set**......Contains models 17 - 24 (only available in USA)		**£1500-2500**
PS 4	1957	**Matchbox Presentation Set**......Contains models 25 - 32 (only available in USA)		**£1500-2500**
PS 5	1957	**Matchbox Presentation Set**......Contains models 33 - 40 (only available in USA)		**£1500-2500**
PS 6	1957	**Matchbox Presentation Set**......Contains models 41 - 48 (only available in USA)		**£1500-2500**
PS 7	1957	**Matchbox Presentation Set**......Contains models 49 - 56 (only available in USA)		**£1500-2500**
PS 8	1957	**Matchbox Presentation Set**......Contains models 57 - 64 (only available in USA)		**£1500-2500**
PS 1	1959	**Private Owner Set** .....Contains 19 MGA, 43 Hillman Minx, 45 Vauxhall Victor, A-3 Garage		**£150-175**
PS 2	1959	**Transporter and 4 Cars Set**.....Contains 30 Ford, 31 Ford Station Wagon, 33 Ford Zodiac, 36 Austin A50, and an A-2 Transporter		**£150-175**
PS 3	1959	**Transporter and 6 Cars Set**.....Contains 22 Vauxhall Cresta, 32 Jaguar XK, 33 Ford Zodiac, 43 Hillman Minx, 44 Rolls-Royce Silver Cloud, 45 Vauxhall Victor and an A-2 Transporter		**£200-250**
PS 4	1959	**Commercial Vehicle Set** ....Contains No.5 Bus, 11 Petrol Tanker, 21 Long Distance Coach, 25 'Dunlop' Van, 35 Horse Box, 40 Bedford Tipper, 47 'Brooke Bond' Van and 60 Morris Pickup		**£400-450**
PS 5	1959	**Army Personnel Carrier Set** ....Contains M3 Personnel Carrier, 54 Saracen, 55 DUKW, 61 Ferret, 62 General Service Lorry, 63 Ambulance, M-3 Tank Transporter		**£150-175**

Gift Sets

The packaging for the first UK issued sets consisted of a frail blue box with a yellow lid panel on which were displayed (in red) the models making up the set. Sets in similar packaging were issued for the German market. Note however that contents may vary within the same type of box (the G4 Farm set listed below is an example). Please advise us of any other different model combinations you may have.

Ref.	Year	Set name	Contents	Market Price Range
G 1	1960-61	**Commercial Motor Set**.............Contains: 5b 'Players Please', 20a, 37a (even load), 47a, 51a, 59a, 60a and 69a. (All models in G 1 had Grey plastic wheels)		**£300-400**
G 1	1962-63	**Commercial Vehicle Set** ....Contains 5c 'Visco-Static', 10c, 12b, 13c, 14c, 21c, 46b, 74a		**£250-300**
G 1	1965	**Motorway Set**.....Contains 6, 10, 13, 33, 34, 38, 48, 55, 71 and R-1 layout		**£200-250**
G 1	1967	**Service Station Set**...Contains A1 Service Station, 31c or 32c, 13d and 64b in pictorial display case		**£125-150**
G 2	1960-61	**Car Transporter Set**................A-2 Transporter (metal wheels) and cars 22b, 25b, 33b, 39a, 57b and 75a		**£500-600**
G 2	1960-61	2nd issue: ....A-2 Transporter (with Grey plastic wheels to tractor and Black plastic wheels to trailer), plus cars 7b, 22b, 25c, 27c, 57b and 75a		**£500-600**
G 2	1962-63	**Car Transporter Set**.....Contains models 25b, 30b, 31b, 39b, 48b, 65b and Accessory Pack No.2.		**£700-900**
G 2	1965	**Car Transporter Set**.....Contains 22c, 28c, 36c, 75b and Major Pack 8b		**£300-400**
G 2	1967	**Transporter Set**.....Contains M86 Transporter, 14d, 24c, 31c and 53c		**£100-125**
G 3	1960-61	**Building Constructors Set** ....Contains 2, 6, 15, 16, 18, 24, 28 and M-1		**£150-175**
G 3	1962-63	**Constructional Plant Set**.....Contains 2, 6, 15, 16, 18, 24, 28 and M-1		**£200-250**
G 3	1963-64	**Farm and Agricultural Set** ......Contains K3, K11, M5 and M7		**£100-140**
G 3	1965	**Vacation Set**..........Contains 12c, 23c, 27d, 42b, 45b, 56b, 68b, and Sports Boat on Trailer		**£200-300**
G 3	1968	**Farm Set**.....Contains 12c, 37d, 40c, 43c, 65c, 72b, 47c and 39c		**£75-95**
G 4	1960-61	**Farm Set** (1st issue) ....M-7 Cattle Truck (GPW), 12b Land Rover (BPW), 23b Berkeley Caravan (Lime Green, BPW), 31b Ford (Met.Green/Pink/Maroon, SPW), 35a Horse Box (MW), 50a Commer (Lt.Brown, SPW), 72a Fordson (Orange rear hubs, GPW)		**£200-250**
		(2nd issue)................M-7 Cattle Truck (GPW), 12b Land Rover (BPW), 23c Bluebird Dauphine Caravan (Metallic Mauve, SPW), 31b Ford (Yellow, Maroon base, clear windows, SPW), 35a Horse Box (SPW), 50a Commer (SPW), 72a Fordson (Orange rear hubs, GPW)		**£175-225**
G 4	1963	**Agricultural Implements Set** ....Contains 12, 23, 31, 35, 50, 72 and M-7		**£175-225**
G 4	1963	**Grand Prix Set** ....Contains 13c, 14b, 19c, 41b, 47b, 52a, 32b, 73b and Major Pack No.1, R-4 Racetrack, instructions		**£400-500**
G 4	1965	**Racetrack Set** .....13d, 19d Green, 19d Orange, 41c White, 41c Yellow, 52b Blue, 52b Red, 54b, Major Pack M-6 29c		**£200-250**
G 4	1968	**Race 'n' Rally Set** .....19d Orange, 19d Green, 52b Blue, 52b Red, 29d, 3c, 41c, 67b, 25d, 8e		**£125-150**
G 5	1960-61	**Military Vehicles** .....Contains 54, 62, 63, 64, 67, 68 and M-3		**£150-200**
G 5	1963	**Army Gift Set** .....Contains 54a, 62a, 63a, 67a, 68a, 64a and Major Pack No.3		**£150-200**
G 5	1965	**Army Gift Set** .....Contains 12, 49, 54, 61, 64, 67 and M-3 (picture box)		**£140-160**
G 5	1965	**Fire Station Set** .....Contains Fire Station, 29c, 54b and 59c		**£150-200**
G 6	1965	**Commercial Trucks Set** ....Contains 6, 15, 16, 17, 26, 30, 58 and 62		**£100-150**
G 6	1966	**Truck Set** .....Contains 16c, 17d, 25c, 26b, 30c, 69b, 70b, 71b		**£100-150**
G 9	1963	**Major Series Set** .....Contains Major Packs 1, 2, 4 and 6		**£250-350**
G 9	1965	**Service Station Set** .....Contains 13, 33, 71, A-1, MG-1		**£100-125**
G 10	1963	**Service Station Set** .....Contains Service Station, 13c, 25b, 31b, and Accessory Pack No.1		**£100-125**
G 10	1965	**Fire Station Set** .....Contains MF-1, 14, 59, 2 of No.9		**£100-125**
	c1960	**Garage Set 'C'** .....'MATCHBOX' Sales and Service Station (Red/Yellow), Roadway Layout, Accessories Pack No.1 (Esso petrol pumps), Accessory Pack No.2 (Car Transporter, Blue/Red lettering), Major Pack No.6 ('Pickfords' Transporter), 1-75 series models (5c, 29b, 31b, 42a, 45a, 46b, 57b, 74a). All models are individually boxed and housed in larger display box printed with 'MATCHBOX SERIES' and pictures of the garage and models, etc.		**£750-1000**
?	?	**Matchbox Traffic Game**...........Contains two cars plus game board, etc		**£150-175**
?	?	**'GAF' Racing Car Game** ....Belgian game set contains four 24d 'TEAM MATCHBOX' racing cars including the rare Metallic Blue and Yellow variants. Set issued by 'GAF', not by Matchbox.		**£300-400**

Matchbox 'King-Size' Series

Following successful sales of Major Models, Lesney Products decided to further develop the range by
introducing a larger scale toy. The name chosen was 'King-Size'. In 1966 the popular Major Models
were discontinued in name but were themselves built into the King-Size range.

K1-1 60 **Hydraulic Shovel**
All Yellow body, Grey plastic wheels, 'WEATHERILL' ...**£25-30**

K1-2 63 **Tipper Truck**
Red cab and chassis, Orange tipper, 'HOVERINGHAM' ..**£30-35**
NB 'HOVERINGHAM GRAVELS LTD' issued models in
their own outer box to their customers.

K1-3 70 **'O & K' Excavator**
Red body, Silver shovel, tinted windows, BPT.................**£20-25**

K2-1 60 **Dumper Truck**
Red body, 'MUIR HILL 14B', Black or Green MW.........**£25-30**

K2-2 64 **Dumper Truck**
Yellow body, 'KW DART' logo, 6 Red wheels, BPT........**£25-30**

K2-3 68 **Scammell Wreck Truck**
White body, Red jib and wheels, Grey hook, 'ESSO' **£30-35**
Gold body version **£30-35**

K3-1 60 **Caterpillar Bulldozer**
Yellow body, Red engine, Grey metal rollers...................**£25-30**
As previous model but with Red metal rollers.................**£25-30**
As previous model but with Yellow metal rollers.............**£25-30**

K3-2 65 **'HATRA' Tractor Shovel** Orange body, Red wheels......**£25-30**

K3-3 70 **'MASSEY FERGUSON' Tractor and Trailer**
Red body, Yellow trim..**£25-30**

K4-1 60 **'McCORMICK INTERNATIONAL' Tractor**
Red body, Green wheels...**£30-35**
As previous model with Orange or Red wheel hubs.........**£25-30**

K4-2 67 **GMC Tractor and Hoppers**
Dark Red cab, 2 Silver hoppers, 'FREUHOF' logo..........**£50-55**

K4-3 69 **Leyland Tipper**
Dark Red cab and chassis, Silver tipper 'W. WATES'.......**£25-30**
As previous model but with Yellow/Green body colours ...**£25-30**
With Red cab and chassis, Green tipper...........................**£25-30**
With Blue cab and chassis, Silver tipper 'Miner' label **£25-30**
With Silver tipper and 'LE TRANSPORT' logo................**£30-35**

K5-1 61 **Tipper Truck**
Yellow body and tipper, Red wheels, 'FODEN' logo........**£25-30**

K5-2 67 **Racing Car Transporter**
Green body, Silver drop down rear door, Red wheels **£35-40**

K5-3 70 **Tractor and Trailer**
Yellow body, Red chassis, 'MUIR HILL' **£25-30**

K6-1 61 **Earth Scraper**
Orange body, Red engine, 'ALLIS CHALMERS'..............**£30-35**

K6-2 67 **Mercedes Ambulance**
White body, Red badge, ambulance-man, stretcher...........**£25-30**

K7-1 61 **Rear Dumper**
Yellow body, Red engine, 'CURTISS-WRIGHT'..............**£25-30**

K7-2 67 **Refuse Truck**
Red body and wheels 'CLEANSING DEPARTMENT' **£25-30**
Blue body version..**£25-30**

K8-1 62 **Prime Mover and Transporter with Crawler Tractor**
Orange bodies, Yellow tractor, 'LAING', (6 x 6 wheels) ...**£75-80**

K8-2 67 **Guy Warrior Transporter** 'FARNBOROUGH - MEASHAM'
Blue cab, Yellow car transporter **£50-60**
Orange cab, Orange or Yellow transporter........................**£50-60**

K8-3 70 **'CATERPILLAR TRAXCAVATOR'**
Yellow body and shovel, Blue or White driver..................**£30-35**

K9-1 **'AVELING BARFORD' Diesel Road Roller**
Green body, Red wheels and driver....................................**£25-30**

K9-2 67 **'CLAAS' Combine Harvester**
Red body, Yellow blades and wheels, ...**£25-30**
Green body, Red blades and wheels...................................**£25-30**

K10-1 63 **'AVELING BARFORD' Tractor Shovel**
Blue-Green body, Red seat and wheels **£30-35**

K10-2 66 **Pipe Truck**
Yellow body, Red wheels, 6 Grey pipes..............................**£30-35**
('Super-Kings' issue) Purple body, Grey or Yellow pipes..**£25-30**

K11-1 63 **'FORDSON SUPER MAJOR' Tractor and Trailer**
Blue tractor, Grey/Blue trailer..**£35-45**

K11-2 69 **DAF Car Transporter** Yellow body, Yellow/Red decks..**£25-30**
Metallic Blue body, Gold trailer decks..............................**£25-30**

K12-1 63 **Breakdown Truck** 'MATCHBOX SERVICE STATION',
Green body, Yellow jib, ...**£50-60**

K12-2 69 **Scammell Crane Truck**
Yellow body and chassis, 'LAING' on crane.......................**£30-35**

K13-1 63 **Concrete Truck**
Orange body and barrel, 'READYMIX' logo......................**£35-45**
As previous model but with 'RMC' logo.............................**£35-45**

K14-1 64 **Jumbo Crane**
Yellow body and crane, 'TAYLOR JUMBO CRANE'.......**£30-35**

K15-1 64 **Merryweather Fire Engine**
Red body, Silver ladder, 'KENT FIRE BRIGADE'...........**£40-45**

K16-1 66 **Tractor and Twin Tippers**
Green cab, Yellow tippers, 'DODGE TRUCKS' in Red .....NGPP
Yellow cab, Blue tippers same logo (22w).........................**£45-55**

K17-1 67 **Low Loader and Bulldozer**
Green cab and loader, Red/Yellow Bulldozer.....................**£35-45**

K18-1 66 **Articulated Horse Box** 'ASCOT STABLES',
Red cab, Brown box, 4 White horses...................................**£35-45**

K19-1 67 **Scammell Tipper** Red body, Yellow tipper, Silver trim ...**£25-30**

K20-1 68 **Tractor Transporter**
Red body, Yellow rack, 3 Blue tractors (39c)....................**£40-50**
As previous model but with Orange tractors.......................**£70-75**

K21-1 69 **Mercury Cougar** Gold body, Cream or Red seats.........**£40-50**

K22-1 69 **Dodge Charger** Blue body, Yellow or Pale Blue seats....**£40-50**

K23-1 69 **Mercury 'POLICE' Car**
White body with 'HIGHWAY PATROL' logo **£40-50**

K24-1 69 **Lamborghini Miura** Red body, Cream seats..................**£25-30**

For 'Super-Kings', Speed-Kings' and 'Sea-Kings' models, please refer to
the end of the Superfast section.

'King-Size' Gift Sets

---	1963	King-Size Set..........................Contains K1-1, K2-1, K3-1, K5-1, K6-1..	**£60-65**
---	1965	Construction Set ....Contains K16-1, K7-1, K10-1, K13-1, K14-1...	**£75-80**
---	1966	King-Size Set..........................Contains K16-1, K11-1, K12-1, K15-1	**£40-45**

'Matchbox' Series Painting Books

Four different types of cover and contents numbered 1 to 4. Mint unused set of book...**£2,000-3,000**

Lincoln Industries 'Matchbox Series'

Collectors should be aware that a range of models exists which were made in New Zealand and which at first sight appear to be Matchbox Miniatures. The packaging in particular is strikingly similar to early Lesney Matchbox boxes, even to the extent of having 'MATCHBOX SERIES' printed in a banner as on the Lesney boxes.
It seems that the makers, Lincoln Industries, were so taken with the Lesney idea of 'a model in a matchbox' that they were tempted to capitalise on it by adopting it themselves. 'Lincoln Industries Ltd' and 'Made in New Zealand' are also clearly marked on the boxes so confusion should be avoidable. The models are a little cruder than genuine Matchbox products and all seem to have metal wheels. They are nevertheless collectable and include: a Utility Truck, Breakdown Truck, Large Parcels Van, Ambulance, and a sports car resembling a Jaguar XK120.
The Editor would welcome more details of these products.

Matchbox Catalogues

1957 **Folded Leaflet** .... Yellow cover has Blue edging and depicts No.1 Diesel Roller. Colour pictures of nos. 1 - 42 of '1-75'series...........................**£50-75**

1957 **Folded Leaflet** .... Blue/Yellow cover featuring MOY No.1 Allchin 7nhp Traction Engine 1st series box. Contents list first nine Yesteryears...........**£75-100**

1958 **16-page catalogue** .Cover shows Rolls-Royce (44), emerging from box. Models 1 - 60 in colour inside, early 'Major Packs' and Accessory Packs ..**£50-75**

Reprints .... Catalogue reprinted for DTE in 1982 ....**£15-20**

1959 **Folded Leaflet** .... Features first 14 Yesteryears in colour **£75-100**

1959 **16-page catalogue** .Same cover as 1958 catalogue with '1959 Edition'. Lists 1-75's, Major Packs and accessories. Colour pictures **£50-75**

1959 **24-page catalogue** .'UK' and '2d' on cover with MOY No.9, 1-75 series, No.'43', and Accessory No.'2'. Colour contents show MB 1 - 72 and MOY 1 - 14 plus Accessories and Major Packs. ..**£50-75**

1960 **32-page catalogue** .'UK' and '3d' on cover featuring logo *'ALL THE MATCHBOX POCKET TOYS BY LESNEY'* plus semi-circle picture of MOY and 1-75's. Contents illustrate all ranges **£50-75**

1961 **32-page catalogue** .'*International Pocket Catalogue*' on cover with picture of 1-75 model No.5 Bus. New style smaller catalogue listing all issues in colour plus International price list.............**£50-75**

1962 **20-page catalogue** .'2d', '*International Pocket Catalogue*' and '*1962 Edition*' on cover. All issues listed, European price list included......................**£35-45**

1963 **20-page catalogue** .No.53 Mercedes-Benz printed on cover with '2d' and '*1963 Edition*'. Contents include good Gift Set pictures and listings .**£10-14**

1964 **32-page catalogue** .'3d' on cover depicting Blue Mk.10 Jaguar (No.28). '*1964 Matchbox Prices*' on back cover. Contents include superb Gift Set pictures and listings **£8-11**

1965 **32-page catalogue** .Cover features Motor Racing Cars. '*1965 Matchbox Prices*' on back cover. Excellent full colour Gift Set pictures (Price 3d).........**£8-11**

1966 **40-page catalogue** .London scene and '*Price 3d*' on cover. Excellent pictures of mid-sixties Gift Sets plus history of Matchbox..........................**£8-11**

1967 **40-page catalogue** .Cover shows flags and 1-75 issues, '*Price 3d*'. Contents list and depict Veteran Car Gifts. ...**£8-11**

1968 **40-page catalogue** .1968 car picture and '*Price 3d*' on cover. Includes details of manufacturing processes .**£8-11**

1969 **48-page catalogue** .Cover features Motorway scene. Contents include detailed history of the real cars making up the MOY range...........................**£8-11**

2nd edition: ....The 2nd edition of the 1969 catalogue includes first reference to '*Superfast*' issues.**£8-11**

1970 **64-page catalogue** .Only drawings of models (no photographs) throughout. Superfast track featured. '6d', '*MATCHBOX SUPERFAST*' and a collage of models on cover **£5-8**

1971 **64-page catalogue** .'24p' on Blue/Red cover with scorpion design. 'Speed Kings' listed plus pictures of first Superfast Gift Sets.........................**£5-8**

1972 **72-page catalogue** .Yellow '*MATCHBOX*' and '3p' on cover. Contents feature launch of 'Scream'n Demon' bikes and excellent Gift Set pictures...............**£5-8**

1973 **80-page catalogue** .'5p' and '1973' on cover of the largest Matchbox catalogue produced. Contents include good 'Super Kings' and Aircraft Kit listing ...**£5-8**

1974 **64-page catalogue** .'2p' and '1974' on cover. Includes first 'SKYBUSTERS' listing.................................**£5-8**

1975 **64-page catalogue** .'2p' and '1975' on cover. Contents feature 'Rolamatics' and 'Battle Kings'................**£5-8**

1976 **64-page catalogue** .'1976' on cover. Contents feature 'Sea Kings' plus 'Baby Dolls' and 'Disco Girl Dolls' **£5-8**

1977 **80-page catalogue** .'1977' on cover. Contents list the 'Two Pack' (TP) range of 1-75's. Good Gift Set pictures and listings of 1-75's **£5-8**

1978 **64-page catalogue** .'1978' on cover. Includes good 'SKYBUSTERS' and 1-75 Gift Set pictures ..**£5-8**

79-80 **80-page catalogue** .'5p' and '1979-80' on cover. The contents feature good pictures of Gift Sets G1 - G8. '900' TP series introduced **£4-6**

80-81 **80-page catalogue** .'5p' on cover. All ranges listed including 'Walt Disney' and 'Power Track' equipment .**£3-4**

81-82 **64-page catalogue** .'5p' and '1981-82' on cover. 'Adventure 2000' space models pictured. 'Playtrack', 'Popeye' and 'Streak Sets' listed.................................**£2-3**

82-83 **64-page catalogue** .'1982-83' on cover. 'Convoy' series introduced, good MOY pictures....................**£2-3**

1984 **64-page catalogue** .'1984' on cover. 'MATCHBOX SPECIALS' introduced, good Gift Set pictures, 'Burnin' Key Cars', 'Rough Riders' and 'Lock Ups' ...**£2-3**

1985 **48-page catalogue** .'1985' and 'chequered flag' design on cover. All ranges listed plus introduction of 'Trickshifters', 'Power Blasters', 'Matchmates' and 'Carry Cases'. (Printed in Italy).............**£1-2**

1986 **48-page catalogue** .'1986' on cover. 'High Riders', 'Twin-Pack', 'Action Packs' listed inside. 'Motor City' **£1-2**

1987 **72-page catalogue** .'1987' on cover. Listing includes 'Superfast Lasers', 'Pocket Rockets', 'Speed Riders', 'Streak Racing', 'Hot Rod Racers', 'Turbo 2', 'Turbo Specials' and 'Demolition Cars'. **£1-2**

1988 **88-page catalogue** .'1988' on cover. Listing includes Miniatures Gift Sets pictures, 'Lasers', 'Super GT Sport' and 'Super Miniatures', 'Team Convoy', 'Road Blasters', 'Motor City' and 'Action Matchbox'. Also includes 'MICA' and 'Junior Matchbox Club' membership details **£1-2**

1989 **80-page catalogue** .'1989' on cover. Listings include 'Miniatures', 'Twin-Pack', 'Motor City' Gift Sets, 'Dinky Collection', 'World Class', 'Conn-Nect-Ables', 'Flashbacks', 'Super ColourChangers' and 'Skybusters ColourChangers' **50p**

1990 **48-page catalogue** .'1990' on cover. Contents include 'Superfast Minis' listing plus normal range of products ...**50p**

1991 **56-page catalogue** .'1991' on cover. Includes 'Graffic Traffic', 'Action Series', 'Lightning Sets', 'Matchbox 2000' range and Matchbox 'Railways' **£1-3**

1991 **A4 leaflet** .... Full-colour sheet with MOY on one side and the 'Dinky Collection' on the other **50p**

Overseas Catalogue Editions

During the 1960s there were normally six editions of each catalogue: British, International, U.S.A., German, French and French-Canadian.

The catalogues were usually of the same format as the UK editions but with the appropriate language and currency. 'INTERNATIONAL CATALOGUE' was shown on the front cover together with the edition, e.g. 'EDITION FRANCAISE', 'INTERNATIONAL' or 'U.S.A. EDITION'.

The 1960 'International Pocket Catalogue' listed the national prices for every product in Australia, Austria, Belgium, Spain, Denmark, Eire, France, Germany, Great Britain, Holland, Hong Kong, Italy, Kenya and East Africa, Singapore and Malaysia, South Africa, Sweden and Switzerland. From 1972 the country-specific editions only listed the model range available in that country.

Market Price Range
Prices are equivalent to those asked for UK editions.

Other Matchbox literature

'**Mike and The Modelman**' (1st edition 1970), was a childrens' book issued by Lesney telling the Matchbox story.
A copy in perfect condition should cost between £10 - £15.

Trade Catalogues have been published for many years and occasionally become available for sale. Those before 1970 are scarce and no price information is possible at present. Those from the 1970-80 period tend to be in the region of £10-15 while post-1980 editions sell for £2-5 depending on content and condition.

The Matchbox Collectors Passport (introduced in 1987), also served as a catalogue providing a full colour listing of the MOY range available in the years in which it was current. In 1991 the Dinky Collection then available was also pictured with the Special Editions and the Passport scheme model offer.

Matchbox - Moko - 1:75 - Models of YesterYear - Major & King Size - Lesney
Buying & Selling World-Wide

With over 35 years of experience in Matchbox models, we **BUY & SELL** anything made by **MOKO-LESNEY-MATCHBOX** in the last 50 years. Our world-wide **MAIL ORDER** service is efficient and 100% reliable, and we can communicate in English, French, German, Russian & Czech. Our Sophisticated database helps us in either meeting your requirements immediately from our stock, or in keeping track of your wanted rarer items until we locate them, double-check with you and buy them for you. We specialise in **RARITIES**, pre-pros & colour trials. 100% GUARANTEE. We also **BUY** entire collections or individual models. FREE ESTIMATES.

Payment by cheque (to Romantic Robots), PO, cash, Access, Mastercard or VISA. Please send a SAE or 2 IRC for a full catalogue. COLLECTIONS required NOW!

ROMANTIC ROBOT ☎ +44 020 8200 8870
54 Deanscroft Ave, London NW9 8EN FAX +44 020 8200 4075

MATCHBOX MINIATURES

Nigel Cooper
46 Thyme Close
Chineham
Basingstoke
RG24 8XG
Tel/Fax: 01256 841418

COOPERTOYS

Latest US miniature range
Latest German miniatures
Rarer models a speciality
Twenty years experience

World Promotionals
Latest UK models available
Latest Australian releases
Wants lists welcome
12-page bi-monthly list

The Collectors Toy and Model Shop

Always over 5,000 models in stock at reasonable prices.
We BUY, SELL and EXCHANGE and give FREE VALUATIONS
All DIECAST, TINPLATE, TOYS, DOLLS, TRAINS,
MECCANO, FIGURES, SCI-FI, TEDDIES, STEAM, etc.
We specialise in Scalextric.

We guarantee the highest prices paid - ON THE SPOT !

52 Canterbury Road, Margate, Kent, CT9 5BG
24 hour telephone service: (01843) 232301

Bob May 25 Oakwood Way, Hamble le Rice, Hampshire, UK SO31 4HJ
● 1/75 REGULAR WHEELS ● 1/75 SUPERFAST ●
● KING SIZE ● MAJOR PACKS ● GIFT SETS ●
ALL MATCHBOX TOYS WANTED

Your Sales Lists Invited
Please send 2 x 1st class
stamps or 2 x IRCs for my
latest sales list

MATCHBOX TOYS
By Mail Order
WORLDWIDE
(Callers by appointment please)
Tel/Fax: 02380 453318

"MATCHBOX" SERIES Nº 15 VOLKSWAGON 1500

"MATCHBOX"
LESNEY PRODUCTS & CO LTD. LEE CONSERVANCY ROAD. LONDON. E 9
01·985 5533

An illustration from 'Matchbox News', Lesney's Press Office advertising literature, showing MB15 'Monte Carlo Rally' VW 1500

When replying to advertisements, please mention 'John Ramsay's Catalogue'.

Matchbox Superfast 1969 - 1983

This listing refers to Superfast models produced between 1969 and 1983. In this period, most models in the range were presented in picture boxes with some variations being sold in Twin Packs and carded 'bubble packs'. The 'cut-off point' for many collectors of these Matchbox Miniatures is 1983 when picture boxes ceased. 'See-through' window boxes sealed at both ends were then introduced.

All the models listed have 'Made in England' bases. Those with 'Macau', 'China', 'Thailand' or elswhere are too numerous to mention and are outside the scope of this listing. There are also many wheel variations for the models listed, such as 5-spoke, 4-spoke, 'dot-dash' etc., but again, only specific wheel variations such as hub colour are noted.

Due to limitations of space, it has been necessary to introduce the use of the following abbreviations into the listing. These have been mainly restricted to indicate colour of bases and window glazing.

Windows
AG = amber glass
BG = blue glass
CG = clear glass
GG = green glass
OG = orange glass
PG = purple glass

Base colour
BB = black base
GB = grey base
SB = silver base
UB = unpainted base
WB = white base
YB = yellow base

Wheels
BW = black wheels
NW = narrow wheels
UW = unpainted
WW = wide wheels

General
BE = black engine
CE = chrome engine
LE = limited edition
SE = silver engine
TP = Twin Pack

MB 1e   Mercedes Truck

70-70	Metallic gold body, yellow or orange canopy, green glass, narrow wheels...**£8-12**
76	Military olive drab green body, tan canopy, purple glass, WW, '4TS702K' decals (TP) **£20-25**
76-80	Same but military olive green **£6-9**
76-80	Red body, yellow or orange canopy, purple glass, wide wheels, 'Transcontinental' (TP) **£5-8**
80-82	Light blue body, light orange canopy, purple glass, WW, 'IMS' (TP) **£8-10**

MB 1f   Mod Rod

71	Yellow body, OG, SE, red wheels, UB or SB, 'spotted cat's head' label **£20-30**
71-75	Same but with black wheels...........**£7-12**
	Black wheels and silver base **£12-15**
71-75	Same but with 'Wildcat' label **£7-12**
73	Same but with 'Flower' label **£18-25**
74	Same but with 'Scorpion' label **£20-30**
78	Striped silver body, black wheels, glass and engine, UB. (U.S.A. 'Roman Numeral' LE) **£10-15**

MB 1g   Dodge Challenger

76-79	Red body, white roof, silver interior **£4-6**
76-79	Same but with white interior.............**£8-10**
76-79	Same but with red interior **£10-12**
80-82	Blue body, white roof, red interior.......**£4-6**
82-83	Orange body, blue roof, black interior, UB or SB, 'Revin Rebel' **£4-6**
82	Same but with white roof.................**£7-10**

MB 2d   Mercedes Trailer

70	Metallic gold body, yellow or orange canopy, green glass, narrow wheels...**£8-12**
76	Military olive drab green body, tan

canopy, WW, '4TS702K' (TP)' **£20-25**
76-80	Same but military olive green **£6-9**
76-80	Red body, WW, yellow or orange canopy, 'Transcontinental' (TP)..........**£5-8**
80-82	Light blue body, light orange canopy, WW 'IMS' (TP)..................**£8-10**

MB 2e   Jeep Hot Rod

71-75	Pink body, white or cream seats, light or dark green base....................**£10-15**
	Same but white base........................**£40-50**
75-76	Red body, white or cream seats, white base....................................**£10-15**
	Same but green base........................**£40-50**

MB 2f   Rescue Hovercraft

76-78	Light or dark lime green body, fawn or light brown skirt, red or silver air intakes, amber or red windows, 'Rescue' **£4-7**
76-79	Same but metallic light or dark green body **£4-6**
	Same but with red windows................**£6-8**
78	Same but black skirt.........................**£6-9**
	Same but red or purple windows.........**£7-10**
78-80	Pale green body, black skirt, purple or AG, '2000' or 'Rescue' **£10-15**

MB 2g   S-2 Jet

81-82	Black/yellow, yellow or red glass........**£3-6**
82-83	Metallic light blue and white or grey, clear glass, 'Viper' on some............**£3-6**

MB 3c   Mercedes 'Binz' Ambulance

70-73	Cream or off-white body, light blue glass, red cross on doors and bonnet, NW, opening rear door **£15-18**
	Same but with dark blue glass............**£15-18**
77-80	Cream body, dark blue glass, red cross on doors, rear door cast shut (TP)......**£8-12**
78-80	Military olive-green body, WW with silver hubs, rear door cast shut (TP)**£15-25**
	Same but with black hubs **£10-15**

MB 3d   Montiverdi Hai

73-78	Orange body, pale yellow interior, black or UB, '3' on bonnet **£5-8**
	Same but with '6' on bonnet............**£12-15**
	Orange body, pale yellow interior, black base, '3' or '6' on bonnet......**£12-15**

MB 3e   Porsche Turbo

78-79	Metallic brown body, cream interior, clear glass, black base .**£5-8**
79-80	Metallic brown body, UB..................**£7-10**
	Silver body, CG, cream or red interior, black or dark grey base **£3-6**
	Tan interior, black base **£10-15**
	Tan interior, dark grey base.............**£10-15**
	Tan interior, brown base **£15-20**
	Red interior, brown base **£7-10**
80-82	Metallic green body, cream interior, clear glass, black or dark grey base **£4-6**
	With light or dark yellow interior **£3-5**
	Same but with unpainted base **£6-9**
	Red interior, dark GB or BB **£10-15**
	Red body, tan interior, opaque glass, black base, 'Porsche Turbo 90'..........**£9-12**
82-83	Red body, tan or white interior, CG, black or dark grey base, 'Porsche Turbo 90' on some..............................**£3-6**

MB 4d   Stake Truck

70-72	Orange-yellow cab, green stake body, green glass **£12-15**
	Same but bright yellow cab **£50-60**

MB 4e   Gruesome Twosome

71-75	Gold body, SB or UB, cream interior, purple glass.......................................**£6-10**

	With white or yellow interior..........**£10-15**
	Gold body, SB, cream interior, AG..**£60-75**
75	Red body, SB or UB, yellow interior, purple glass.....................................**£10-12**
	Same but with cream interior **£12-15**
	Orange-red body, SB or UB, cream interior, purple glass **£20-25**

MB 4f   Pontiac Firebird

75-77	Metallic light blue body, UB, AG........**£5-8**
78-80	Same but metallic dark blue...........**£12-15**

MB 4g   '57 Chevy

80-81	Purple body, silver interior, UB, CG....**£4-6**
82-83	Red body, silver interior, SB or UB, CG, 'Cherry bomb' **£6-8**
	Same but with black base..............**£15-25**

MB 5e   Lotus Europa

69-70	Dark metallic blue body, ivory interior, UB, NW **£12-15**
	As previous model but without 'Superfast' cast on base **£120-150**
	Dark metallic blue body, ivory interior, UB, NW, '20' and stripe labels from G5 racing set **£15-18**
70-75	Pink body, ivory interior, silver base, NW or WW **£20-30**
	Same but with unpainted base **£10-12**
	Same but UB, NW, '20' and stripe decals from G5 set **£15-18**
77-78	Black body, ivory interior, UB, NW, 'JPS' (Japanese issue).............**£20-25**
	Same but without 'JPS' (TP) **£12-15**

MB 5f   Seafire

75-79	White deck, blue hull, orange-yellow, blue or lemon man, black or red exhausts **£3-5**
79-82	Red deck, white hull, orange-yellow or lemon man, red exhausts, black trailer (TP) **£7-10**
81	Red deck, blue hull, lemon man, red exhausts, black trailer (TP)........**£55-65**
81	White deck, brown hull, orange -yellow man, red exhausts...............**£65-80**
	White deck, brown hull, lemon man, red exhausts **£65-80**
82	Black deck, yellow hull, red man, red exhausts, black trailer (TP) **£25-35**
83	Red deck, yellow hull, red man, red exhausts, black trailer (TP).......**£35-45**

MB 5g   US Mail Truck

78-82	Dark or light blue body, matt or gloss white roof (small or large windows), white base, black wheels, black or silver hubs, 'US Mail' and red stripe on some........**£5-7**
	Same but with black base...................**£6-8**
78	Pale blue body, white roof, 'sleet and snow' base, 'US Mail' and red stripe, U.S.A. Ltd edition **£9-12**

MB 5h   4x4 Jeep Off-Road

82-83	Metallic light or dark bronze body, black base, 'Golden eagle' **£3-5**

MB 6d   Ford Pick-up

70-71	Red body, white roof, white or chrome grille, NW or WW, black base........**£10-15**
	Metallic green or UB **£25-35**
	Green or Grey base **£10-15**

MB 6e   Mercedes 350sl

74-75	Orange body, black roof, UB, ivory or pale yellow interior, amber or CG **£7-10**
75-79	Yellow body, black roof, UB, pale yellow interior, amber or CG **£6-9**

77 Silver body, black roof, UB, pale yellow interior, CG, 'Rennservice' (German issue) **£35-45**
Same but without 'Rennservice' **£25-35**
79 Metallic bronze body, black roof, UB, pale yellow interior, amber glass **£10-15**
79-81 Metallic bronze, white roof, AG, UB, pale yellow or cream interior **£5-8**
81-82 Metallic red body, white roof, UB, pale yellow interior, AG or CG **£4-7**

MB 6f   Mercedes Convertible

82-83 Metallic blue body, white interior, UB or SB, silver side stripe on some **£4-6**
83-84 Maroon body, white interior, black base, SB or UB **£5-8**

MB 7c   Ford Refuse Truck

70-72 Orange or orange-red cab, grey tipper, narrow or wide wheels **£10-15**

MB 7d   Hairy Hustler

71-74 Metallic bronze body, AG, yellow side stripe '5', bonnet square '5', grey or black base **£8-10**
Same but purple glass **£30-40**
Metallic bronze body, AG, blue side stripe '5', bonnet square '5', unpainted or black base **£8-10**
Same but green base...................**£12-15**
Same but green base, plain sides **£12-15**
Same but black base, plain sides **£10-12**
Metallic bronze body, AG, round '3' side labels, bonnet square '5', BB ...**£20-25**
Metallic bronze body, AG, round '3' or square '137 side labels, bonnet 'Scorpion' label, green or black base.................**£35-45**
75-77 White body, AG, red stripes with black/white check pattern, grey base, ('Streakers' version)..........................**£7-10**
Same but with black base..............**£7-10**
78 White body, AG, grey base.............**£20-25**
78-79 Yellow body, AG, 'flames', BB, US 'Roman Numeral' Ltd Edition...**£10-15**

MB 7e   Volkswagen Golf

76-77 Metallic green body, yellow interior, AG, BB, roof-rack, black surfboards..**£6-8**
77-81 Same but metallic light green body **£6-8**
77-81 Metallic dark green body, yellow or lemon interior, AG, black or grey base, roof rack and black surfboards.............**£6-8**
Same but with orange glass **£6-8**
Red interior, grey base **£20-25**
77 Yellow body and interior, matt black base, 'ADAC', (German issue).......**£20-25**
79-80 Red body, yellow interior, CG or AG, BB, roof rack, surfboards, (TP)......**£12-15**
Red body, red interior, CG, BB, roof rack and black surfboards (TP)......**£30-40**
81-82 Yellow body, red interior, CG, BB or GB, roof rack and black surfboards **£4-6**
82-83 Silver body, red interior, CG, BB, Green stripes and 'Golf'...............**£3-5**
Same but with tan interior...............**£15-20**
Same but red interior, grey base **£3-5**

MB 8e   Ford Mustang

70 White body, red interior, BB, CG **£70-80**
70-71 Red body, red interior, BB, CG...**£200-250**
Same but with ivory interior......**£80-120**
Orange-red body, red interior..........**£60-70**
Same but with ivory interior **£40-50**

MB 8f   Wildcat Dragster

71 Pink body, yellow interior, black and orange 'Wild cat' labels, BB **£12-15**
71-75 Orange body, yellow interior, BB, black/orange 'Wild cat' labels **£10-12**
Same but with UB or orange base ...**£20-25**
With dark or bright yellow base **£20-25**

Same but with grey base **£10-12**
Orange body, yellow interior, BB, yellow/orange 'Wild cat' labels **£10-12**
Same but without labels **£12-15**
Same but grey base **£10-12**
Same but with UB or green base **£20-25**
Orange, yellow interior, black base, 'Rat Rod' labels **£30-40**
Same but with 'Sailboat' labels **£40-50**

MB 8g   De Tomaso Pantera

75-81 White body, red interior, blue base, '8' and 'Pantera' bonnet and side labels on some **£9-12**
Same but orange interior....................**£4-6**
With UB **£6-8**
White body, orange interior, yellow 'Sun' in black or green circle bonnet label, no side labels, blue base.............**£7-9**
White body, orange interior, blue base, '9' bonnet label, no side labels **£12-15**
81-82 Blue body, black interior, '8' and 'Pantera' bonnet and side labels on some, black base, US issue............**£4-6**
NB MB8g can be found with the larger rear wheels swapped with the smaller front.

MB 8h   Rover 3500

81 Yellow body, red interior, sunroof, black base, (G1 Gift set) **£225-250**
Metallic bronze body, white interior, sunroof, black base.......................**£10-12**
Same but dark or light tan interior......**£5-8**

MB 9d   Boat and Trailer

70-72 White hull, light turquoise deck, dark blue trailer **£10-12**
76-83 White hull, light blue deck, light blue trailer (TP) **£10-12**
82 White hull, black deck, light or dark blue trailer (TP)..........**£40-50**
Same but with black trailer **£20-25**

MB 9e   AMX Javelin

72-78 Metallic lime green body with opening doors, yellow interior, AG, black air intake, UB or SB **£6-8**
Same but with silver air intake **£20-25**
Metallic lime green body, orange interior, AG, black air intake, UB or SB **£8-10**
Same but white interior, UB **£25-30**
Same but with blue interior..........**£35-40**
76-78 Metallic light blue body, yellow or orange-yellow interior, AG, black air intake, UB or SB...............**£4-6**
78-81 Metallic dark blue body with cast-in doors, orange-yellow interior, AG, UB or SB, black air intake (TP)........**£4-6**
80-81 Blue body with cast-in doors, UB or SB, orange-yellow interior, AG, black air intake, white '1', (US Ltd.Ed.).....**£8-10**
81-83 Metallic dark green body, cast-in doors, orange-yellow interior, AG, UB or SB, black air intake, (TP) **£4-6**
82 Red body, cast-in doors, UB or SB, orangey-yellow interior, AG, black air intake, (TP)..............................**£20-25**

MB 9f   Ford Escort RS2000

78-82 White body, tan interior, BB, CG, '9', 'Ford', 'Shell', and 'Dunlop' decals..**£8-10**
Same but with grey base **£10-12**
Same but red interior, black base....**£70-80**
White body, tan interior, BB, CG, 'Phantom' decals, (TP)..................**£18-20**
80-82 Blue body, tan interior, BB, CG, 'Phantom' decals (TP)..................**£8-10**
Same but with grey base **£10-12**
Same but with blue-grey base.........**£15-18**
82-84 Green body, tan interior, BB, CG, 'Phantom' decals (TP) **£8-10**

Same but with grey base **£10-12**
Green body, white interior, BB, CG, 'Phantom' decals, (TP) **£20-25**
Same but with red interior **£70-80**

MB 10d   Pipe Truck

70 Red body, silver base and grille, 6 grey pipes on sprue **£40-50**
70-73 Same but orange-red body **£18-20**
Orange body, silver base and grille, 6 Grey or yellow pipes on sprue.....**£12-15**
Same but grey base and grille.........**£20-25**

MB 10e   Piston Popper

73-80 Metallic blue body, yellow interior, AG, 'Superfast' on UB **£80-100**
Metallic blue body, yellow interior, AG, 'Rola-Matic' on UB **£6-8**
Same but with silver base **£12-15**
Metallic blue body, yellow interior, CG, 'Rola-Matic' on UB or SB **£12-15**
80 White body, yellow interior, AG, 'Rola-Matic' on UB (German multi-pack issue)..........................**£200-225**
80-81 Yellow body (with red flames), AG, yellow interior, 'Rola-Matic' on UB, US Ltd. Ed. **£8-10**

MB 10f   Plymouth Gran Fury Police Car

79-81 White body, black panels, blue or pale or dark yellow glass, UB, 'Police'......**£4-6**
82-83 Same but with 'Metro Police Traffic Control', shield and '012', UB or SB..**£4-6**
Same but 'Mercury' base from no 55..**£6-8**

MB 11d   Scaffolding Truck

70-72 Silver body, red base and grille, green glass, yellow scaffolding, NW, 'Builders Supply Company'............**£12-15**

MB 11e   Flying Bug

72-77 Red body, SB, grey glass, yellow exhausts, silver helmet, square cut or heart-shape bonnet decal...............**£8-10**
Same but UB, square cut decal **£12-15**
Same but heart shape bonnet decal....**£8-10**
Heart-shape decal, UB, blue glass ...**£20-30**
78 Orange body, UB, black glass and exhausts, flying beetle bonnet decal, US Ltd. Ed.....................................**£12-15**

MB 11f   Car Transporter

NB MB11f usually comes with 3 cars: 1 red, 1 blue and 1 yellow. Other combinations are common (e.g., 1 blue and 2 yellow) but this does not affect the price.
77-80 Orange cab, white or beige back, BB or UB, blue, purple or green glass.......**£5-8**
80-83 Red cab, beige or grey back, BB, SB or UB, blue or purple glass **£5-8**
83 Dark orange cab, beige or grey back, black base, blue glass..........................**£5-8**

MB 12c   Safari Land-Rover

70 Metallic blue body, white interior, UB, NW, brown luggage...............**£450-500**
70-71 Metallic gold body, white interior, UB, NW, brown luggage...............**£12-15**

MB 12d   Setra Coach

71 Metallic gold body, grey roof, unpainted base, clear glass................................**£20-25**
Same but with white roof..................**£18-20**
72-73 Yellow body, white roof, UB, CG...**£15-18**
Same but with green glass **£150-200**
73-74 Metallic crimson body, white roof, unpainted base, clear glass **£10-12**
Same but with green glass **£12-15**
74-75 Metallic purple body, white roof, unpainted base, clear glass **£10-12**
Same but with green glass **£12-15**

MB 12e   Big Bull

75-79	Orange body, green shovel, black tracks and rollers £30-40
	Same but with yellow rollers £12-15
	Same but with orange rollers £5-7

MB 12f   Citroën CX

79-82	Light or dark metallic blue body, pale yellow or cream or ivory interior, SB or GB or BB or UB, clear or blue glass ...£5-8
	Light metallic blue, tan interior £8-10
	Dark metallic blue, red interior........£80-90
82-83	Yellow body, red interior, black base, dark blue glass, (TP) £8-10
	With clear glass, BB, GB or SB, (TP) ...£5-7
	Yellow, red interior, BB, CG, 'Team Matchbox' in black or blue, (TP) £8-10
83	White body, red interior, BB or UB, blue glass/lights, 'Ambulance', (TP) ...£5-7
	Same but 'Police', 'Marine Division' and '8' prints, blue stripes, (TP) £5-7

MB 13d   Dodge Wreck Truck

70-71	Yellow (or lighter yellow) cab, green back, yellow crane, red hook 'B.P.' .£18-20

MB 13e   Baja Buggy

71-78	Metallic light green body, orange interior, UB, SE, black or red exhausts, red or orange bonnet flower label................£6-8
	With red exhausts, no bonnet label...£8-10
	With red exhausts, 'Police' bonnet label from 55d £15-18
	Same but with red interior £18-20
	Metallic light green body, orange interior from 47c, UB, SE, red exhausts, orange bonnet flower label..........£150-200
78	Metallic dark green body, orange interior, UB, SE, red exhausts, orange flower bonnet label, ...£6-8
	Same but 'Sun' label from 47c £10-12

MB 13f   Simon Snorkel

78-80	Light red body, SB or UB, blue glass, blue lights, yellow crane and man £3-5
	Same but amber glass and lights......£20-30
80-82	Dark red body, SB or UB, blue glass, blue lights, Yellow crane and man £3-5
82	Same but white crane and man £8-10

MB 14d   Iso Grifo

69-71	Metallic dark blue body, pale or dark blue interior, UB, NW....................£18-20
	Same but with white interior........£200-225
71-75	Lighter metallic blue body, white interior, UB or SB, NW £12-15
	Sky blue, white interior, UB, NW ...£15-18
77-78	Lighter powder blue, white interior, UB, WW, (Japanese issue)..............£18-20

MB 14e   Mini Ha Ha

75-82	Red body, dark blue glass, UB, 'flesh' coloured man, brown helmet, 4 circle side labels..........................£15-20
	Same but with purple man £20-25
	'Flesh' man, light blue glass £6-8
	Purple man, light blue glass.............£12-15
	Pink man, light blue glass...............£8-10
	Red body, light blue glass, 'flesh' or pink man, 2 circle side labels..........£10-12

MB 14f   Leyland Petrol Tanker

82-83	Red cab, white tank, 'ELF' with red/blue stripes or orange/turquoise stripes £4-6

MB 15d   Volkswagen 1500

69-70	Off white or cream body, cream interior, '137', 'Monte Carlo' £20-25
70-72	Metallic red body, cream interior, '137', 'Monte Carlo' on some £15-18

77-78	Off white body, cream interior, '137', no bumper decal (Japanese issue)....£18-20

MB 15e   Forklift Truck

72-77	Red body, yellow hoist, grey forks, UB, black steering wheel, 'horse' and 'Lansing Bagnall' labels £4-6
	Same but with green or black base £6-8
77-82	Red body, unpainted hoist, yellow forks, UB, black steering wheel, 'horse' and 'Lansing Bagnall' labels.....................£4-6
	Same but with green or black base £6-8
	Same but no steering wheel £4-6
	Same but with black or grey forks.......£4-6
	Red body, unpainted hoist, red forks, UB, no steering wheel, 'horse' and 'Lansing Bagnall' labels.....................£8-10
82-83	Orange body, unpainted hoist, black forks and roof, UB or SB or BB, no steering wheel, 'Hi-Lift' labels............£6-8
NB	Models can be found with 'horse' label facing forwards or backwards and before or after 'Lansing Bagnall'.

MB 16d   Case Bulldozer

69-74	Red body, yellow cab, shovel, engine and base, green rubber tracks....................£6-8
	Same but with black tracks £10-12
77	Military olive drab green body, black shovel, black tracks (TP) £35-40
	Same but olive green body (TP) £15-18

MB 16e   Badger

74-80	Metallic bronze body, SB, silver radar, green glass (Rola-Matic) £10-12
	Same but BB, cream radar £6-8
	Same but with light or dark grey base ..£6-8
	Dark grey or black base, black radar ...£6-8
	Same but with purple glass £10-12
	Black base, white radar, green glass ...£6-8
	Same but with dark grey base £6-8
76	Military olive drab green body, light grey base, cream radar, green glass(TP) ..£25-30
76-78	Same but olive green body (TP) £12-15

MB 16f   Pontiac Firebird

80-81	Metallic light brown body, red interior, UB, 'Eagle' bonnet label on most........£4-6
81-82	Same but metallic light gold body £3-5
	Same but metallic dark gold body £3-5
82-83	White body, red interior, UB or SB, 'Eagle' bonnet label with stripe and 'Firebird' labels on most £2-4

MB 17e   Horse box

70	Red cab, dark green box, grey door, chrome base and grille, two white horses on sprue................................£35-40
70-71	Same but orange-red cab................£20-25
	Orange-red cab, light grey-white box, mustard door..................................£18-20
	Same but orange cab £15-18
	Yellow-mustard cab, dark green box, grey door £15-18

MB 17f   'Londoner' Buses

Unless otherwise stated all buses have red bodies and white interiors. Most have metal bases in gloss or matt black, grey, brown or unpainted. Before changing to the Titan bus some were fitted with plastic bases. Factory issued models are listed first, then Lesney issued promotional models.

72-74	'Swinging London' 'Carnaby Street'...£4-6
73	Silver plated Gift Ware version........£70-80
73	Gold plated Gift Ware version.........£70-80
73-80	'Berger Paints'. (Brushes may be at front or rear of label)..........................£4-6
73	Same but silver body £70-80
73	Same but gold body £70-80
73	Same but orange body.....................£45-50
73	Same but cream body, brown roof £60-65

75	'Esso Extra Petrol' £65-70
77	'Silver Jubilee 1952-77'. Silver body with red interior, special issue box ..£12-15
	Same but red body, white interior....£65-70
78	'Matchbox 1953-78'............................£4-6
	Same but orange body.....................£65-70
	Same but blue body........................£35-40
72	'Preston Guild Merchant'................£75-80
73	'Impel 73' Trade Fair......................£35-40
	'London and Kensington Hilton' £75-80
	'The Baron of Beef'.........................£80-85
	'Sellotape Selbstklebebander' £200-250
	'Sellotape Packaging Systems' ...£125-150
	'Sellotape Electrical Tapes' £125-150
	'Barclays Bank'...............................£55-60
	'Chambourcy Yogurt' £65-70
	'Interchemicals and Plastics'......£200-250
74	'Typhoo puts the 'T' in Britain'.......£65-70
76	'Impel 76' Trade Fair. Cream body with brown roof, white interior........£25-30
	'British Airways Busch Gardens' £55-60
	'Ilford HP5 Film' £90-100
	'A.I.M. Building Fund 1976' £35-40
	'Selfridges'.....................................£8-10
	'Santa Claus, Aviemore Centre' £35-40
	'Amcel takes you places' £65-70
	'Eduscho Kaffee' £100-125
77	'New! The Museum of London' £15-20
	'Army and Navy' £15-20
	'Jacob's the Biscuit Makers' Red body with white interior £25-30
	Orange body with white interior......£12-15
78	'Aral-Deutschlands Autopartner' Blue body with white interior £45-50
	Same but red body £85-90
79	'Impel 79' Trade Fair......................£25-30
80	'You can't kid a Bisto kid'................£8-10
	'Borregaard Paper'..........................£70-90

MB 17g   Leyland Titan Bus

82	'Berger Paints' £2-4
	'Laker Skytrain' £2-4
82	'Chesterfield Transport Centenary'....£3-5
	'Matchbox No.1, Montepna' Pale blue/white (Greek issue) £10-12
	Same but red body £15-18
	'I.C.P. Interchemicals'....................£50-60

MB 18e   Field Car

70-75	Light yellow body, light brown roof, white interior, SB, NW or WW £15-18
	Same but WW, UB £12-15
	Black roof, UB, WW £25-30
76	Military olive drab green body, tan roof, black interior, BB, 'A' square door labels, black wide wheels (TP) £25-30
76-80	Same but olive green body (TP) £12-15
	Same but 'RA391' bonnet label.......£10-12
	With circled star bonnet label (TP)...£20-25
77-78	White body, black roof, black interior, BB, Black/white checked bonnet label, black wide wheels (TP)................£200-225
	Same but silver wheel hubs (TP) ...£200-225
	Orange body, black roof, black interior, BB, black/white checked bonnet label, black wide wheels (TP) £12-15
	Same but silver wheel hubs (TP) £12-15
	Orange body, black roof, black interior, SB, black/white checked bonnet label, black wide wheels (TP)......................£20-25
78-80	Metallic ruby-red body, tan roof, black interior, SB or BB, '44', 'Champion' and 'Goodyear' bonnet label (TP) £6-8
80	Dark orange body, black roof, black interior, BB or SB, 'AC Filters' and '179 Scout Racing' labels, US Ltd. Ed...£20-25
	Same but no labels, US Ltd. Ed.......£20-25
82-83	Dark yellow body, black or tan roof, black interior, SB, black/white checked bonnet label, (TP) £25-30
	Orange, black roof and interior, BB, black/white checked bonnet, (TP)....£18-20

Orange body, black or tan roof, white interior, BB, '44', 'Champion' and 'Goodyear' bonnet label, (TP).........**£18-20**

MB 1f   Hondarora

74-75   Red body, chrome forks etc., SE, black seat, 'Honda' tank labels, WW **£12-15**
75-80   Same but no labels **£8-10**
        Same but black wheels......................**£8-10**
        Red body, black forks etc., SE, white seat, 'Honda' tank labels, WW **£65-70**
        Same but with black seat **£10-12**
76   Orange body, black forks etc., SE, black seat, WW, 'Honda' labels, (King Size set 6)...........................**£18-20**
76   Military olive drab green body, black forks etc., BE, black seat, no labels, WW (TP)....................................**£25-30**
76-78   Same but military olive green (TP) .**£12-15**
81-82   Metallic green body, black forks etc., BE or SE, black seat, no labels, black wheels **£6-8**
82-83   Yellow body, black forks etc., SE, black seat, no tank labels, black wheels ..**£4-6**
        Same but with brown or tan rider **£4-6**

MB 19d   Lotus Racing Car

70   Metallic purple body, UB, SE, white driver, round No.'3' side labels **£20-25**

MB 19e   Road Dragster

70-75   Light red body, UB or SB, off-white interior, '8' labels normal or sideways **£6-8**
        Same but with 'Scorpion' labels.......**£35-40**
72   Metallic pink body, UB, off -white interior, large 'Wynns' labels, (Promotional issue) **£45-50**
        Same but small 'Wynns' labels.......**£55-60**
75   Metallic purple body, UB, off-white interior, 'Scorpion' labels.................**£40-45**
        Same but with '8' labels or no labels **£8-10**
        Metallic red body, UB, off-white interior, '8' labels as normal **£200-250**

MB 19f   Cement Truck

76-81   Red body, yellow barrel with red stripes, unpainted base, green glass.................**£3-5**
        Same but black stripes or no stripes **£3-5**
79   Red body, grey barrel with red stripes unpainted base, green glass................**£5-7**
        Same but with purple glass **£8-10**
81-82   Red body, lemon barrel with red stripes unpainted base, green glass................**£3-5**
        Same but black stripes or no stripes ...**£3-5**
        Same but with purple glass **£6-8**

MB 19g   Peterbilt Cement Truck

82-83   Metallic green body, orange barrel, yellow or white 'Big Pete' **£2-5**

MB 20d   Lamborghini Marzal

69   Metallic red body, white interior, unpainted base.................................**£15-18**
70   Same but with 'Avon' and '2' labels from G3 Racing Specials set...........**£18-20**
71   Bright pink body, white interior, unpainted base..................................**£10-12**
        Bright pink, silver base **£20-30**
        Same but with 'Avon' and '2' labels from G3 Racing Specials set...........**£12-15**
71-75   Orange or orange-pink body, white interior, unpainted base **£10-12**
72   Yellow body, white interior, UB, ('Brroom Stick' blister pack issue) ..**£30-35**

MB 20e   Police Patrol

75-80   White body, UB, orange 'Police' stripe, orange light and interior (Rola-Matic).**£4-6**
        Same but with red 'Police' stripe.......**£6-8**
        White body, UB or SB, orange 'Police' stripe, blue or yellow light & interior ..**£5-8**
        Same but with black base..................**£8-10**

White body, UB, 'Ambulance' and Red Cross, orange light and interior........**£12-15**
76-78   White body, UB, orange 'Site Engineer' stripes, orange light and interior, (G3 Construction Set) **£30-35**
        Same but with orange body **£25-30**
        Orange body, UB, orange 'Police' stripe, orange light and interior, (G3 Construction Set) **£25-30**
76   Military olive drab green body, UB, yellow and red 'Police' arrow, orange light and interior (TP) **£30-35**
        Same but 'Ambulance' labels **£30-35**
76-77   Military olive green body, UB, yellow and red 'Police' arrow, orange light and interior (TP)...............................**£15-20**
        Same but with 'Ambulance' labels..**£15-20**
80   Blue body, UB, yellow 'Paris-Dakar 81' stripe, orange or yellow light and interior, (French issue blister pack) **£25-30**
81   White body, UB, blue 'County Sheriff' labels, blue light and interior **£8-10**
        Same but with '017', 'Sheriff' and blue roof **£12-15**
81-83   White body, UB, yellow 'Police' and 'shield' stripe above chequered stripe .**£4-6**
        Same but with black base..................**£6-8**
        White body, black 'Police' on sides, yellow light and interior.......**£12-15**
83   Light brown or beige body, UB, yellow 'Securite-Rallye Paris-Dakar 83'.......**£8-10**

MB 21d   Foden Concrete Truck

70-73   Dark yellow cab, yellow barrel, red body and shute, green base **£12-15**
        Same but bright yellow cab, green or dark green base **£15-20**

MB 21e   Rod Roller

73-78   Yellow body, black wheels with metallic red hubs, GB, 'flame' label from 40d on bonnet **£18-20**
        Same but with matt red hubs **£15-18**
        Yellow or darker yellow body, black wheels, GB or BB, 'flame' or no label**£6-9**

MB 21f   Renault 5TL

78-79   Metallic blue body, red interior, black or silver base....................**£12-15**
        Metallic blue body, tan interior, black, dark grey or silver base **£4-7**
        Yellow body, red interior, BB or SB, 'Le Car' and stripe prints..............**£12-15**
        Yellow body, tan interior, BB or SB or dark grey base, 'Le Car' prints........**£4-7**
79-81   Silver body, red interior, BB or SB, 'A5' and stripe prints **£12-15**
        Same but no tampo prints **£4-6**
        Silver body, tan interior, SB **£15-20**
81-82   Silver body, red interior, dark grey or BB or SB, 'Le Car' and stripe prints....**£4-7**
82-83   White body, tan interior, BB, 'Renault' and '4' on green prints.....................**£4-6**
        Same but 'Renault' roof prints............**£4-6**
        White body, white interior, BB, 'Renault' and '4' on green prints **£6-8**
        White body, tan interior, BB, 'Roloil' and '21' on yellow prints **£4-6**
        Same but with orange base **£15-20**
        White body, white interior, BB, 'Roloil' and '21' on yellow prints....................**£6-8**

MB 22c   Pontiac GP Sports Coupé

70   Red body, grey interior, BB **£500-600**
        Light purple, grey interior, BB **£25-30**
        Dark purple, grey interior, BB **£25-30**

MB 22d   Freeman Intercity

70-71   Metallic purple body, off-white interior, UB, yellow arrow labels on some......**£8-10**
71-72   Metallic gold body, off-white interior, UB, yellow arrow labels **£12-15**

72-75   Metallic red body, off-white interior, UB or SB, arrow labels on some **£6-8**

MB 22e   Blaze Buster

75-80   Red body, silver interior, UB, yellow ladder, 'Fire' labels **£2-4**
        Same but with black ladder..............**£20-25**
        Same but with white ladder **£125-150**
        Red body, silver or white interior, BB, yellow ladder, 'Fire' labels..........**£2-4**
        Same but dark grey base **£3-5**
80-82   Dark red body, white interior, grey or BB, yellow ladder, 'Fire' labels............**£2-4**
83   Light red body, white interior, BB, dark yellow ladder, 'Fire' labels **£2-4**
        Same but 'No.32' on yellow labels....**£8-10**

MB 23e   Volkswagen Camper

70-72   Blue body, orange interior and hinged roof, UB, CG, rear sailboat side labels on some, petrol filler cap, NW........**£30-40**
        Same but no filler cap **£15-18**
72-75   Orange body, orange interior and hinged roof, UB, CG, sailboat labels, NW ..**£80-90**
        Light or dark orange body, white interior, orange hinged roof, UB, CG, sailboat labels on some, NW **£12-15**
77-80   Military olive green body, no interior, cast roof, BB, dark blue glass, Red Cross labels, wide wheels (TP).......**£15-19**
80   White body, no interior, cast roof, BB, light or dark green glass, 'PizzaVan', wide wheels (USA Ltd edition) **£20-25**

MB 23f   Atlas Truck

75-81   Metallic blue body, orange tipper with yellow and red arrow labels, chrome interior, AG, UB...............................**£10-12**
        Same but without tipper labels............**£6-8**
        Metallic blue body, orange tipper, grey interior, CG, SB **£4-6**
        Same but with AG **£6-8**
        Metallic blue body, orange tipper, grey interior, CG, UB **£4-6**
        Same but with AG **£6-8**
        With CG and SB **£8-10**
81   Metallic blue body, silver tipper, grey interior, CG, SB **£8-10**
81-82   Same but red body, black interior **£10-12**

MB 24c Rolls-Royce Silver Shadow

70-73   Light metallic red body, cream interior, black base **£12-15**
        Dark metallic red body, cream interior, black base **£10-12**
        Same but with pink base **£18-20**
        Same but SB or grey base **£15-18**
        Same but with metallic green base ..**£20-30**
77-78   Light metallic gold body, cream interior, UB, (Japanese issue) **£80-120**
        Same but BB (Japanese issue) **£18-20**

MB 24c Team Matchbox

73   Bright yellow body, white man, '4' (or '8') and 'Team Matchbox' bonnet label **£180-200**
        Metallic blue body, white man, '1' and 'Team Matchbox' label ...**£225-250**
        Same but '5' and 'Team Matchbox' bonnet label **£200-225**
73-75   Metallic green body, white man, '5' (or '8') and 'Team Matchbox' label, (G4 'Team Matchbox' set).....**£25-30**
73-78   Metallic red body, white man, '8' and 'Team Matchbox' label **£3-5**
78-80   Metallic ruby-red body, white man, '44', 'Champion', 'Goodyear', black trailer (TP) **£6-8**
82-83   Same but orange body, yellow man.**£40-50**

MB 24e   Diesel Shunter

78   Metallic dark green body, light brown
control panel, red base 'Railfreight' **£6-8**
Same but with 'D1496-RF' labels **£4-6**

78-83 Light or dark yellow body, light brown
control panel (or none), red base,
'D1496-RF' **£3-5**

MB 25d   Ford Cortina GT

70   Metallic light brown body, off white
interior, unpainted base **£50-60**

70-72 Same but metallic light blue body ...**£15-18**
Same but metallic dark blue body ...**£18-20**

MB 25e   Mod Tractor

72-78 Metallic purple body, BB, yellow seat,
headlights cast on rear mudguards..**£25-30**
Without lights on rear mudguards.......**£6-8**
Metallic purple body, BB, red seat ..**£80-90**
Metallic purple, UB, yellow seat **£8-10**

76-79 Red body, BB, yellow seat (TP) **£8-10**

MB 25f   Flat Car Container

78-80 Light beige container red roof, black flat
car, 'United States Lines' labels **£8-10**
Same but with 'N.Y.K.' labels **£2-4**
Same but with 'Sealand' labels...........**£4-6**
Dark beige container, red roof, black
flat car, 'N.Y.K.' or 'Sealand' labels ...**£2-4**
Same but with 'OCL' labels.............**£10-12**
Dark brown container, red roof, black
flat car, 'N.Y.K.' labels **£12-15**

MB 25g   Audi Quattro

82-83 White and black, 'Audi' and '20' **£3-5**

MB 26c   GMC Tipper Truck

70-72 Red tipping cab, silver tipper, green
chassis, green glass, wide wheels **£10-12**

MB 26d   Big Banger

72-76 Red body, UB, 'Big Banger',
dark blue glass..................................**£6-8**
Same but with amber glass **£8-10**

78   Dark brown, 'Brown Sugar', WB,
amber, black or blue glass (USA)....**£12-15**

81-83 White body, BB, 'Cosmic Blues'
clear or blue glass, (US issue)..........**£10-12**

MB 26e   Site Dumper

76-78 Yellow body, yellow dumper,
black seats, black base **£4-6**

78-81 Same but with red dumper **£2-4**
Same but dark grey base **£8-12**
Same but brown base **£12-15**

81-82 Orange-red body, silver dumper, white
seats, black base **£2-4**
Same but wheels have yellow hubs **£6-8**
Orange-red body, silver dumper, white
seats, dark grey base **£2-4**
Same but wheels have yellow hubs **£6-8**

MB 26f   Cable Truck

82-83 Orange-yellow body, red base, blue
glass, two light grey cable drums ..**£10-15**
Same but dark grey or BB **£3-5**

83   Bright yellow body, BB, blue glass,
two dark grey cable drums..............**£40-50**
Same but dark red body **£10-12**

MB 27d   Mercedes 230sl

70-71 White body, red interior, clear glass,
unpainted base, narrow wheels **£25-30**

71   Same but yellow body...................**£20-25**

71-73 Yellow body, black interior,
CG, UB, NW or WW **£12-15**

MB 27e   Lamborghini Countach

73-75 Yellow body, BB, red glass, '3' **£4-6**
Same but with amber glass **£6-8**
Same but with purple glass **£8-10**

Yellow body, UB, red glass, '3' **£6-8**
Same but with purple glass **£8-10**

75   Orange body, UB, red glass, '3' **£20-30**
Same but with amber glass **£20-30**

75-81 **Lamborghini 'Streakers'.** All have
green/black 'Streaker' prints and a red
'8' on the bonnet.
Orange body, chrome interior, BB **£6-8**
Same but with amber or green glass ..**£8-10**
Orange body, grey interior, BB, GG **£6-8**
Same but with purple glass **£8-10**
Orange body, grey interior, UB, green
glass, red '8' on bonnet......................**£6-8**
Same but with brown base **£8-10**
Orange body, yellow interior, BB or
dark grey base, green glass **£6-8**
Orange, chrome interior, UB, green
or amber glass, red '8' on bonnet **£8-10**
Orange body, grey interior, dark grey
base, green glass..................................**£6-8**
Same but with purple glass **£8-10**
Orange body, beige interior,
dark grey base, green glass **£6-8**
Same but with purple glass **£8-10**
Orange body, beige interior, BB, GG ..**£6-8**

MB 27f   Swing Wing

81-83 Red/white, red glass **£2-4**
Red/white, dark yellow-orange glass....**£3-5**
Red/white, red or black 'Jet Set'.........**£3-6**

MB 28d   Mack Dump Truck

70-73 Metallic lime green body and dumper,
UB, cab steps cast closed.................**£12-15**
Same but with steps cast open **£15-18**

77-79 Military olive drab green body/dumper,
BB, cab steps cast closed (TP)........**£35-40**
Military olive green (TP) **£15-18**

MB 28e   Stoat

73-76 Metallic gold body, UB or BB, dark
brown man, (Rola-Matic issue)...........**£3-6**

77   Military olive drab green body, BB,
dark brown man, (TP) **£35-40**

77-79 Military olive green body, BB, dark
brown man, (TP) **£15-18**

MB 28f   Lincoln Continental

79   Light red body, white roof,
beige interior, clear glass, UB **£4-6**

79-81 Dark red body, beige, dark brown
or grey interior, clear glass, UB **£4-6**

MB 28g   Formula Racing Car

81-83 Metallic brown-grey body, BB or UB,
white driver, 'Exxon' and '8' prints **£3-5**

MB 29c   Fire Pumper Truck

70   Red body, white back and ladders,
UB, blue glass, narrow wheels........**£35-40**

81   Same but 'P1' and 'Los Angeles Fire
Dept.', wide wheels ('Code Red') ...**£12-15**

MB 29d   Racing Mini

70-72 Metallic bronze body, SB or UB,
off-white interior, '29' on yellow
labels (orange edges)......................**£15-18**

72-76 Orange body, SB or UB, cream or
off-white interior, '29' on yellow
labels (orange edges)......................**£12-15**
Same but with green label edges **£10-12**

76-81 Red body, SB or UB, off-white or
cream interior, '29' on yellow
labels (green edges) (TP)..................**£8-10**
Red body, SB, cream interior, '3' on
white circle door labels (TP)...........**£35-40**
Same but with no labels **£10-12**

MB 29e   Tractor Shovel

76-78 Light yellow body, red shovel, silver
engine and seat, yellow base................**£4-6**

77   Lime green body, yellow shovel, silver
engine and seat, yellow base
(German PS1000 set issue) **£60-70**

78-81 Yellow body, red shovel, silver or
black engine and seat, yellow base **£2-4**
Same but with cream base **£8-10**
Same but with black base **£6-8**
Yellow body, red shovel, black engine
and seat, yellow base, yellow hubs.....**£6-8**
Yellow body, black shovel, black engine
and seat, yellow base...........................**£2-4**
Same but with cream base **£8-10**
Same but with black base **£6-8**

79   Yellow body, black shovel, black engine
and seat, BB, black stripes, ('C' prints
on some), (G5 Construction Set) **£6-8**

81   Orange-red body, red shovel, dark grey
engine and seat, black base, ...**£20-25**

82-83 Same but with black shovel **£10-12**

MB 30c   8-wheel Crane

70   Red body, dark orange crane arm with
yellow hook, UB **£225-250**
Same but with gold crane arm **£18-20**

MB 30d   Beach Buggy

70-76 Light metallic purple body, yellow
spots, UB, white interior **£15-18**
Same but with yellow interior.............**£6-8**
Same but dark metallic purple body **£6-8**

NB   The yellow spots on this model can
vary from only a few spots to almost
an entire body covering.

MB 30e   Swamp Rat

76-81 Military green deck, light brown hull,
'Swamp Rat' labels on some **£2-4**

MB 30f   Articulated Truck

81-83 Metallic steel-blue cab, WB,
red glass, silver trailer **£4-6**
Blue cab, WB or YB, silver trailer **£2-4**

83   Blue cab, pale yellow or WB, blue
trailer with 'Pauls' white labels,
(Ltd. blister-pack issue of 900)........**£25-30**
Blue cab, WB or YB, yellow
trailer, 'International' labels **£8-10**
Red cab, YB, yellow trailer with
'International' labels **£8-10**
Red cab, YB, silver trailer **£10-12**

MB 31e   Lincoln Continental

70   Sea-green body, white interior,
unpainted base, CG, NW ....**£1,000+**
Metallic lime-green body, white
interior, UB, CG, NW **£10-12**
Same but with wide wheels **£20-25**

MB 31d   Volksdragon

71-77 Red body, purple glass, UB or SB,
yellow or cream interior,
'eyes' label on some...........................**£8-10**
Red body, purple glass, UB or SB,
yellow interior, 'flower' label **£15-18**

78   Black body, purple glass, UB, yellow
interior, 'bug'/ 'flames' (US issue) ..**£12-15**

MB 31e   Caravan

77-83 White body, off-white or light brown
interior, UB, AG, orange or yellow door,
orange stripe with white bird labels.....**£4-6**
White body, light yellow interior, light
blue, orange or yellow door, orange
stripe with white bird labels on some ..**£2-4**
Same but dark blue door, blue stripe
with white bird labels on some **£4-6**

MB 32c   Leyland Petrol Tanker

70-73 Dark green cab and body, white tank,
SB, blue glass, 'B.P.' labels in centre
or front of tank, NW **£12-15**

Dark green cab and body, white tank,
GB, 'B.P.' labels in centre of tank ...**£30-40**
Blue cab and body, white tanker, SB,
'Aral' labels in centre of tank, (German
issue in Aral Tankwagen box) **£80-100**
Metallic purple cab and body,
silver tank, SB, no labels **£100-125**
Same but with 'N.A.M.C.' labels **£150-175**
Red cab and body, white tank,
SB, 'N.A.M.C.' labels..................**£300-400**

MB 32d   Maserati Bora
73-78   Metallic crimson body, lime green base,
yellow interior, stripe and '8' label......**£5-7**
Same but with dark green or UB **£6-9**
Same but dark green base, '3' label.**£12-15**
Same but with no label.......................**£6-8**
79   Metallic gold, SB, yellow interior,
no bonnet label, tow hook, (TP) **£35-40**

MB 32e   Field Gun
77-81   Military green body, light or dark brown
base, 2 soldiers and 4 shells on sprue,
black wide wheels..............................**£3-5**
Same but black wheels, silver hubs.**£30-40**
78   Military olive green body, no base,
soldiers or shells, black wheels (TP) ...**£3-5**

MB 32f   Excavator
81-82   Orange-red body, dark grey or black
swivel base, silver-grey tracks............**£6-8**
82-83   Yellow body, black swivel base, black
tracks, black stripes & 'CAT' prints ..**£8-10**
Same but with no 'CAT' print **£6-8**

MB 33c   Lamborghini Miura P400
69   Yellow body, red interior, UB, NW .**£80-90**
70   Light metallic bronze body,
red interior, UB, NW.....................**£20-30**
Dark metallic bronze body,
red interior, UB, NW.....................**£75-100**
70 -73   Light metallic gold body, off-white
interior, UB, NW...........................**£12-15**
Same but dark metallic gold body ...**£12-15**
Dark metallic gold body, red interior,
UB, NW **£20-30**
Light metallic gold body, off-white
interior, red or pink-red base, NW..**£18-20**
77-78   Light gold body, off-white interior,
UB or BB, WW (Japanese issue).....**£18-20**

MB 33d   Datsun 126X
73-75   Yellow body, orange base, AG...........**£4-6**
Same but with unpainted base **£30-40**
75-77   Yellow body, orange base, AG,
red/orange or red/black flame prints,
('Streakers' issue)..........................**£7-10**
78   Yellow body, BB, AG, red/black flame
prints, (US Roman Numeral)..**£18-20**
Gold plated body, BB, black glass,
green prints, (US Roman Numeral) .**£12-15**

MB 33e   Police Motorcycle
77-79   White frame, chrome or black engine,
white bars, UW, blue man, white or
black seat and panniers, 'Police'.........**£4-6**
79   White frame, chrome engine, white bars,
UW, green man, seat and panniers,
'Polizei' (German) **£12-15**
79   Same but cream frame, man has white
helmet and gloves (King Size 71
German Polizei Patrol set) **£15-18**
79   All black bike and wheels, dark blue
man, white helmet, 3 stripes and shield,
white seat and panniers, 'Police',
gold star tank labels (KS 66 set).....**£18-20**
79   White frame, black engine and wheels,
white bars, blue man, white helmet
and gloves, white seat and panniers,
'Police' labels.................................**£8-10**

79-81   White frame, black engine, white bars,
black wheels, green man, seat and
panniers, 'Polizei' labels (German) **£6-8**
79   Same but white helmet and gloves **£8-10**
79-81   Same but white helmet and gloves,
UW, (KS 66 Police Patrol set) **£15-18**
81   White frame, black engine white bars,
black wheels, green man, white
seat and panniers, 'LAPD' labels ...**£15-18**
81   White frame, chrome engine, black
bars, black wheels, no man, white
seat and panniers, 'Police' labels.....**£10-12**
81-82   Black frame, chrome engine, white
bars, black wheels, blue man, white
seat/panniers, 'LAPD' (Code Red)..**£12-15**

MB 34d   Formula I Racing Car
71-72   Metallic purple body, UB, CG, yellow
or blue stripe, '16' label, 4 NW **£12-15**
71   Same but yellow stripe, 'Wynns'
labels (Promotional issue)................**£45-50**
72-75   Yellow body, UB, CG, blue bonnet
stripe, '16' label, 4 NW or NW........**£6-8**
Same but front NW, rear WW **£8-10**
Yellow body, UB, CG, yellow stripe,
'16' label, 4 NW.............................**£8-10**
Yellow body, UB, AG, blue or yellow
stripe, '16' label, 4 WW..................**£12-15**
73-75   Metallic blue body, UB, CG, yellow
or blue stripe, '15' label, 4 WW (or
front NW, rear WW) (G4 set)..........**£25-30**
Orange body, UB, CG, blue or
yellow stripe, '16', 4 WW (or front
NW, rear WW) (G4 set)..................**£20-25**
Orange-yellow body, UB, CG, blue
stripe, '16' label, 2 NW, 2 WW **£15-18**

MB 34e   Vantastic
75-78   Orange body, WB, GG, white interior,
rear stripes labels...............................**£6-8**
Same but motif instead of stripes.......**£8-10**
Same but with stripes and UB **£100-150**
78   Orange body, WB, GG, white interior,
'Jaffa Mobile', (Promotional) **£200-250**
78   Orange body, WB, GG or CG, white
interior, bonnet 'Sun' label **£20-30**
78-81   Orange body, WB, GG, white interior,
'34', rear stripes labels on some **£4-6**

MB 34f   Chevy Pro-Stocker
81-83   White body, UB, blue '34' prints..........**£2-4**
Same but with no tampo prints **£4-6**
White body, red base, blue '34' **£8-10**

MB 35c   Merryweather Fire Engine
69-71   Metallic red body, GB, white ladder,
'London Fire Service', NW **£18-20**
71-75   Red body, GB, white ladder, 'London
Fire Service', NW or WW **£12-15**
Red, GB, 'Flame-Proof Wool' **£50-80**
Same but in promotional box........**£100-150**
Red body, BB, ladder, 'London
Fire Service', wide wheels..............**£20-25**
Same but with tan base **£25-30**
Red body, GB, different style ladder,
'London Fire Service', WW, (TP) ...**£12-15**
81   Red body, GB, white ladder and man
from 13f, 'Los Angeles City Fire
Dept.' prints, WW, (Code Red) **£12-15**

MB 35d   Fandango
75-77   White body, red interior, red base,
red or silver rear disc, arrow and '35'
bonnet label (Rola-Matic)...................**£4-6**
White body, red interior, UB, red rear
disc, arrow and '35' bonnet label **£20-30**
White body, red interior and base,
silver rear disc, stripe and '6' bonnet
label from 41c **£15-18**
77-82   Red body, red interior, red base,
blue arrow and '35' bonnet label,
blue or silver rear disc **£80-100**

Red body, off-white interior, WB,
blue arrow and '35' label, blue, silver
or red rear disc **£4-6**
Red body, off-white or white interior,
UB, blue rear disc, arrow and '35' **£6-8**
Red body, white interior, UB, blue rear
disc, 'Sun' bonnet label from 47d..**£12-15**

MB 35e   Zoo Truck
82   Red body, blue cage, light brown lions,
blue glass, black base..........................**£2-4**
Same but with red base **£20-25**
Same but with grey base **£8-10**
83   Red body, silver cage, light or dark
brown lions, blue glass, black base......**£2-4**

MB 36c   Opel Diplomat
70   Metallic light or dark gold body,
silver grille, white interior, BB **£15-20**
Same but without silver grille..........£12-15

MB 36d   Hot Rod Draguar
70-73   Metallic dark red body, off-white or
light yellow interior, silver 'Draguar'
label **£10-12**
Same but with orange interior.........**£12-15**
Same but lemon or white interior **£6-8**
73-75   Metallic pink body, light yellow
interior, silver 'Draguar' label **£12-15**
Metallic pink body, cream interior,
no boot label.....................................**£8-10**
Metallic pink body, light or dark
yellow interior, no boot label **£6-8**
Same but with amber glass **£8-10**

MB 36e   Formula 5000
75-77   Orange body, blue or yellow man,
'Formula 5000' and orange or yellow
'3', '5000' on rear spoiler **£3-5**
77   Same but red body, yellow man **£4-6**
77-78   Red body, yellow man, 'Texaco 11' on
bonnet, no spoiler label or 'Marlboro'.**£5-8**
78-80   Same but 'Champion' on rear spoiler..**£6-8**

MB 36f   Refuse Truck
80-82   Metallic red cab, all-yellow container,
red load, no labels **£3-5**
Same but without 'Collectomatic'
on container **£50-75**
82-83   Blue cab, all-yellow or all-orange
container, black or red load,
'Metro DPW66' on side labels **£2-4**
Same but orange container with
yellow opening back, red load **£4-6**

MB 37c   Cattle Truck
70-71   Orange-yellow cab and body, grey
back and 2 white cattle.......................**£8-10**
71   Same but orange cab and body **£20-25**
Orange cab and body, silver back **£80-90**
72   Bright-yellow cab/body, grey back ..**£60-70**

MB 37d   Soopa Coopa
72-75   Metallic light blue body, yellow interior,
AG, unpainted or silver base...............**£4-6**
75-76   Metallic light purple body, yellow
interior, AG, UB, 'flower' label **£8-10**
Same but with red base **£150-200**
77   Orange body, yellow interior, AG,
SB, 'Jaffa Mobile' (Promotional) ..**£90-100**

MB 37e   Skip Truck
76-81   Red cab/body, yellow skip, chrome
interior, AG, BB **£6-8**
Same but grey interior, clear glass.......**£3-5**
Same but with brown base **£5-7**
Red cab/body, yellow skip,
orange interior, CG, BB **£6-8**

Red cab/body, blue skip, grey interior, CG, BB **£90-100**
77 Orange cab/body, yellow skip, grey interior, CG, BB (German issue) **£60-70**
Red skip (German PS1000 set)........**£60-70**
81-82 Metallic blue cab/body, yellow skip, grey interior, CG, gloss or matt BB **£6-8**
Same but with silver base **£8-10**

MB 37f Matra Rancho

82 Blue body, blue base, black interior.....**£2-4**
83 Yellow body, yellow base, black interior, red side stripe prints **£8-10**

MB 38c Honda Motorcycle and Trailer

70-71 Metallic blue-green bike, yellow trailer, 'Honda' labels...........**£15-18**
71 Same but metallic pink bike.............**£25-30**
72-73 Same but metallic purple bike **£25-30**
77 Metallic green bike, orange trailer with 'Honda' labels on some (TP)...**£12-15**
82 Same but yellow trailer (TP)............**£10-12**

MB 38d Stingeroo

73-76 Metallic purple body, purple forks white horse's head............................**£8-10**
Same but with pale blue forks **£35-40**
Same but with chrome forks **£250-300**

MB 38e Jeep

76-80 Military green body, gun, BB/seats, '21*11' or 'star' label **£4-6**
77 Military olive drab green body, no gun, BB/seats, 'star' label, (TP) .**£45-50**
Same but military olive green body.**£25-30**
Same but with '21*11' label (TP)....**£18-20**
Yellow body, BB/seats, 'Gliding Club', (TP with yellow glider trailer) **£8-10**
Same but with white base, (TP with yellow glider trailer) **£30-40**
Red body, BB/seats, 'Gliding Club', (TP with red glider trailer) ....**£500+**

MB 38f Ford Camper

80-82 Orange-red body, green glass, cream back with AG, UB with no.'35'.......**£50-70**
Same but camper back with no glass...**£2-4**

MB 38g Ford Model 'A' Van

82 'CHAMPION SPARK PLUGS'...........**£2-4**
84 'KELLOGGS' **£2-4**
84 'TOY FAIR 84' (US), roof label ...**£80-100**
Same but without roof label.............**£50-70**
84 'PEPSI COLA', 'Come Alive'...........**£7-10**
Same but without 'COME ALIVE'.**£10-15**
'PEPSI COLA', 'Matchmates'...........**£8-12**
84 'BEN FRANKLIN'.....................**£300-400**
84 'MATCHBOX USA'.......................**£20-25**
84 'ARNOTTS'..**£6-8**
84 'LARK LANE'.......................................**£2-4**
84 'TITTENSOR FIRST SCHOOL'.........**£2-4**
85 'BASS MUSEUM' **£2-4**
85 'COLLECTORS GUIDE'.....................**£2-4**
85 'The AUSTRALIAN' **£2-4**
86 'BBC 1925'..**£7-9**
86 'WEET-BIX'/'SANITARIUM' **£6-9**
86 'H.H. BRAIN'.....................................**£7-10**
86 'MATCHBOX SPEED SHOP'............**£2-4**
86 'ISLE of MAN TT 86'.........................**£2-4**
86 'SMITHS POTATO CRISPS'..............**£2-4**
87 'W.H.SMITH & SON Ltd', Red........**£8-12**
87 'MICA' 2nd CONVENTION.......**£125-175**
87 'JUNIOR MATCHBOX CLUB'..........**£2-4**
87 'ISLE of MAN TT 87'.........................**£2-4**
87 'SILVO 1912-1987 ` **£10-12**
87 'CHESTY BONDS' **£2-4**
87 'DEWHURST'.......................................**£2-4**
87 'ISLE of MAN POST OFFICE'..........**£2-4**
87 'JOHN WEST SALMON' **£2-4**
87 'This Van Delivers', with phone no.**£10-12**
without phone no..........................**£300-400**
87 'RICE KRISPIES', Mid-Blue (UK) **£2-4**
87 'RICE KRISPIES', Dark Blue, (US) .**£9-11**
88 'MICA 3rd CONVENTION' **£8-10**
88 'MICA 1st N.A. CONVENTION'......**£6-9**
88 'JAMES NEALE & Sons' **£2-4**
88 'ISLE of MAN TT 88'.........................**£2-4**
88 'ISLE of MAN POST OFFICE' **£2-4**
88 'ROYAL MAIL'....................................**£2-4**
88 'MANX CATTERY' **£2-4**
88 'MERVYN WYNN', gold 'island' **£2-4**
with black 'island'...........................**£20-25**
88 'P.M.G. 252' (Australia) **£2-4**
88 'ALEX MUNRO'...................................**£2-4**
88 'CHESTER HERALDRY CENTRE' ..**£2-4**
88 'W.H. SMITH & SON Ltd', Yellow..**£8-12**
88 'TOY MUSEUM, CHESTER' **£2-4**
88 'COBB of KNIGHTSBRIDGE' **£2-4**
88 'ROWNTREES JELLY' **£2-4**
88 'SHERBERT FOUNTAIN'..................**£2-4**
88 'GUERNSEY POST OFFICE' **£2-4**
88 'RAYNERS CRUSHA' **£2-4**
88 'HISTORICAL COLLECTION' **£2-4**
88 'BIG SISTER' (Australia) **£2-4**
88 'UNIROYAL' (Canada) **£10-12**
88 'NATWEST BANK' **£2-4**
88 'GREENS SPONGE MIXTURE'........**£2-4**
89 'MATCHBOX SERIES' **£2-4**
89 'MICA 4th CONVENTION' **£7-9**
89 'MICA 2nd N.A. CONVENTION' **£7-9**
89 'SOUVENIR of CHESTER'...............**£2-4**
89 'CHEESES'..**£2-4**
89 'ISLE of MAN TT 89'.........................**£2-4**
89 'JORDANS'..**£2-4**
89 'JUNIOR MATCHBOX CLUB'..........**£2-4**
89 'RIBENA'...**£2-4**
89 'SHERBET FOUNTAIN',
Black base, normal box.......................**£2-4**
Red base, Woolworths box...................**£6-9**
89 'MOORLAND CENTRE' **£2-4**
89 'LIGHTWATER VALLEY' **£2-4**
89 'TANDY ELECTRONICS' **£2-4**
89 'YORK FAIR' (US)............................**£2-4**
89 'BALTIMORE ORIOLES' (US) **£2-4**
89 'ASDA BAKED BEANS' **£2-4**
89 'LION WHOLESALERS'....................**£2-4**
89 'MB US COLLECTORS CLUB' **£20-25**
89 'JACKY MAEDER' (Swiss) **£6-9**
89 'JOHNSONS SEEDS' **£2-4**
89 'SWARFEGA'...................................**£10-12**
89 'CAMPERDOWN' (Australia)..........NGPP
90 'PAVA RUSTPROOFING' (Danish). ..**£2-4**
90 'MATCHBOX 40th' (US)...............**£10-15**
90 'CARMELLE' (Saudi-Arabia).........**£10-12**
90 'FRESH DAIRY CREAM' **£2-4**
90 'LYCEUM THEATRE'........................**£2-4**
90 'RICE KRISPIES', Dark Blue (US). .**£7-10**
90 'COCA-COLA'......................................**£2-4**
90 'ISLE of MAN TT 90'.........................**£2-4**
90 'MB USA 9th CONVENTION' **£8-10**
90 'CANADA DRY'...............................**£12-15**
90 'YORK FAIR 1990'.............................**£2-4**
90 'PENN STATE' (US)...........................**£6-9**
90 'COLLECTORS CLUB 90' (US)....**£35-45**
90 'JOHNNY WALKER' **£18-22**
90 'TYNE BRAND' **£8-12**
90 'LYONS TEA'.....................................**£7-10**
90 'PG TIPS'...**£10-12**
90 'MITRE 10'..**£2-4**
90 'WILLIAM LUSTY' **£2-4**
90 'RUTTER Bros.' (US) **£6-8**
90 'USA BASEBALL TEAMS', each **£2-4**
Set of 26 ....**£100-130**
91 'DAIRYLEA CHEESE' **£7-10**
91 'COLLECTORS CLUB 91' (US)....**£45-55**
91 NAT. F'BALL LEAGUE (US) each....**£2-4**
Set of 28 ....**£100-130**
'MATCHBOX USA CLUB 15th'....**£45-55**
'MB Collectors Club', silver..........**£75-100**
Green/orange **£35-45**
92 'COLLECTORS CLUB 92 (US).....**£25-30**
92 'Nat Hockey League' set of 6 pairs.**£50-60**
92 'Nat Hockey League 92' set of 6.....**£25-30**
92 'Flavours of Australia' set of 6........**£20-25**
93 'Wines of Australia' set of 6............**£25-30**
93 'USA COLLECTORS CLUB '93' ..**£30-40**
94 'Pills, Potions and Powders' (6)........NGPP
95 'The Circus Comes to Town (6) ....NGPP
95 'International Postal Trucks' (6), ea...**£8-11**
MICA European Conventions 1993, 1994, or 1995 ....NGPP

MB 39c Ford Tractor

67-71 Blue body, yellow engine cover.........**£8-10**
68-71 Same but with all blue body, (from K20 Tractor Transporter set)..**£15-18**
72 All orange body, (Big-MX Tractor Transporter set)....**£45-50**

MB 39d Clipper

73-79 Metallic crimson body, yellow interior, AG, unpainted base, chrome or white exhausts, (Rola-Matic) **£10-15**
With green base and amber glass........**£6-8**
With green base and clear glass.........**£8-10**

MB 39e Rolls-Royce Silver Shadow

79-81 Silver body, Red interior, SB or UB **£4-6**
81-82 Metallic red body, off-white or yellow interior, silver or unpainted base..........**£3-5**
82-83 Metallic gold-brown body, white interior, silver or unpainted base..........**£4-6**
83 Ruby red body, white interior, matt black or matt silver base **£3-5**

MB 40c Hay Trailer

67-70 Dark blue body, yellow sides, BW with yellow hubs..........................**£6-8**
79-79 Light yellow body, no sides, BW (TP)**£4-6**
Same but with black fixed sides (TP)..**£4-6**
Orange-yellow body, black fixed sides, black wheels (TP)...............................**£6-8**
79 Same but with light blue body, (TP)....**£7-9**
80 Same but with red body, (TP)............**£8-10**
81 Same but with beige body, (TP) **£45-50**

MB 40d Vauxhall Guildsman

71-74 Pink body, GG, cream interior, UB, blue circle flame bonnet label.............**£6-8**
Same but with silver base **£15-20**
With UB, black circle flame label......**£8-10**
Same but with silver base **£15-20**
75 Pink body, GG, cream interior, UB, blue '40' print (Streakers issue).....**£80-120**
75-76 Red body, AG or GG, cream interior, UB or SB, blue '40' (Streakers) **£8-12**
76 Red body, GG or AG, cream interior, unpainted base, Blue circle flame bonnet label, (TP)...**£10-15**
Red body, AG, UB, cream interior, no bonnet label, (TP)......................**£10-12**

MB 40e Horse Box

77-80 Orange cab, cream box, light or dark brown door, BB, SB, GB or UB **£7-10**
80-83 Light metallic green cab, cream box, dark brown door, unpainted base **£4-6**
Same but with white door **£6-8**
Dark metallic green cab, cream box, dark brown door, UB, SB or BB..........**£4-6**
Same but lime green door, SB or BB **£8-10**
83 Dark metallic green cab, dark brown box, white door, unpainted base **£12-15**
Yellow cab, dark brown box, lime green door, black base......................**£15-18**
Same but with white door **£12-15**
Orange cab, dark brown box, lime green door, BB, SB or UB **£8-10**
Same but with white door **£4-6**

MB 41c Ford GT

69-70 White body, light or dark green or BB, red interior, '6' on bonnet, NW **£15-18**
71-72 Metallic bronze body, dark green or BB, red interior, '6', NW or WW....**£10-15**

Same but WW, cream base £20-25
Same but WW, grey base £12-15
WW, light or dark yellow base £20-25
977 White body, red interior, 'Wildcat'
or '6' label, BB, (Japanese issue) £18-20
79 Yellow body, red interior, BB, no
bonnet label, MP1 Italian issue......£1,000+

MB 41d   Siva Spyder

72-75 Metallic red body, cream interior, black
band, unpainted base, clear glass £6-8
Same but with chrome band............£15-18
Metallic red body, white interior, black
band, unpainted base, clear glass £6-8
75-78 Metallic dark blue body, white or cream
interior, black band, UB, CG, stars &
stripes, '8', (Streakers issue)............£8-10
77 Light blue body, off-white interior, black
band, UB, black glass or CG, 'Spider'
print, (US Roman Numeral issue)....£12-15

MB 41e   Ambulance

78-81 White body, grey interior, side stripe
with 'Ambulance', red cross labels......£3-5
Same but with yellow interior..............£6-8
White body, grey interior, side stripe
with 'Emergency Medical Services' £4-6
Same but with yellow interior..............£6-8
White body, grey interior, no stripe -
only 'Ambulance' in grey letters £12-15
80 Silver body, grey interior, 'Paris-Dakar
81' (French blistercard issue)..........£25-30
Same but with white rear doors ....£30 -35
81 Red body, grey interior, 'Notarzt' and
red cross prints, (German issue) £18-20
White body, grey interior, side stripe
with 'Ambulance', Blue Cross labels ..£3-5
Same but with 'Pacific Ambulance,
Emergency, 101' prints (Code Red).£12-15

MB 42c   Iron Fairy Crane

70 Red body, yellow boom/hook/base...£80-90
Light or dark orange-red body, lime
boom, yellow hook, yellow base £20-25

MB 42d   Tyre Fryer

72-77 Metallic light blue body,
yellow interior, unpainted base £20-25
Same but with black base....................£4-6
Metallic dark blue body,
orange-yellow interior, black base ...£10-15
77 Orange body, yellow interior, BB,
'Jaffa Mobile' (Promotional) £90-100

MB 42e Mercedes Container Truck

77 All-yellow body, BG, BB, 'Deutsche
Bundespost' labels (German issue)..£20-25
77-80 Red cab/body, cream container with
red doors and roof, BG, UB,
'Sealand' or 'NYK' labels £4-6
Same but with black base...................£6-8
Same but with UB, 'OCL' labels.......£8-10
81 Same but with 'Confern Mobeltransport-
betriebe' labels, PG (German issue) £18-20
Dark blue cab and body, blue container
BG, UB, 'Karstadt'(German issue)...£20-25
81-82 Red/white, 'Matchbox', BG or PG £4-6
Metallic green/yellow, BG or PG,
'Mayflower' and ship labels £4-6
Same but with red glass £8-10
Same but red/white body, BG or PG £4-6

MB 42   '57 Thunderbird

82-83 Red body, white interior, UB or SB £2-4

MB 43c   Pony Trailer

70-71 Yellow body, grey door, light green
base, 2 white horses, NW..................£20-25
Same but with dark green base £15-18
76-79 Orange body, brown door, BB or GB,
2 horses, 'horse head' labels (TP)....£10-15
79-83 Same but light brown body.............£10-15

83 Light brown body, brown door, BB,
2 horses, 'Silver Shoes' or
no labels (TP) £10-12

MB 43d   Dragon Wheels

72-77 Dark green, BB, 'Dragon Wheels'....£8-10
Same but with unpainted base £15-18
Light green, BB, 'Dragon Wheels'..£12-15

MB 43e   Steam Locomotive

78-82 Red cab/sides, black engine, '4345' £2-4
Same but with 'NP' labels £5-7
81 Green cab/sides, black engine,'4345' £8-10
81-83 Same but with side 'NP' labels (TP) ...£6-8

MB 44c   Refrigerator Truck

70 Red cab and body, breen back, grey
rear door, green glass, UB, NW.....£90-100
70-71 Yellow cab and body, red back, grey
rear door, green glass, UB, WW......£10-12

MB 44d   Boss Mustang

72 Yellow body, black bonnet, UB, WW...£5-7
Same but with silver base £20-30
80 Green, UB, 'Cobra', (US Ltd. Ed.)...£10-12
82-83 Dark or light orange body, off-white
interior, UB, 'The Boss' and '5' £6-8

MB 44e Passenger Coach / Caboose

78-83 Red/black, off-white roof, green glass,
red '431 432' side labels....................£6-8
Same but with clear glass.................£8-10
Same but with no glass £4-6
Red/black, off-white roof, no glass,
red '5810 6102' side labels £4-6
Same but with cream or tan roof £6-8
Red/black, off-white roof, no glass,
green '5810 6102' side labels £6-8
Red/black, off-white or cream roof,
no glass, green 'GWR' side labels....£8-10
81-83 Green/black, off-white raised roof, no
glass, green '5810 6102' labels (TP) ...£6-8
Red/black, off-white raised roof, no
glass, red '431 432' labels (TP)..........£4-6
Same but red '5810 6102' labels (TP).£4-6

MB 45c   Ford Group 6

70 Non-metallic green body, white interior
CE, CG, UB, '7' label, NW....£250-300
70-71 Dark metallic green body, CE,
CG, UB or BB, '7' label, NW £25-30
Same but 'Burmah' labels (G3 set) .£20-25
Dark metallic green body, CE,
CG, BB or GB,'45' label, NW £12-15
Same but with pink base £18-20
71-73 Metallic lime green body, CE,
AG, BB, '45' label, WW £10-12
Same + 'Burmah' labels, (G3 set) ..£12-15
Metallic lime green body,
grey engine, AG, BB, '45', NW £10-12
Same but grey or CE, GB, WW......£10-12
73-76 Metallic dark or light purple body,
grey or CE, AG, BB, '45', WW £8-10
Metallic dark purple body, CE, AG,
BB, 'eyes' label from 31d, WW £25-30

MB 45d   BMW 3.0 CSL

76-81 Light or dark orange body, cream
interior, GG, 'BMW' label on some £6-8
Same but with clear glass.................£10-12
77 White body, cream interior, GG,
'BMW' and 'Manhalter' signature
label, (Austrian 50,000 issue) £25-30
White body, GG, 'Polizei 123', blue
or yellow light, (German issue) £45-50
Same but no light or 'Polizei 123'...£45-50
82 Red body, GG, 'BMW' (G15) £70-80

MB 45e   Kenworth Cabover

82-83 White body, AG, blue/brown stripes £2-4

MB 46c   Mercedes 300se Coupé

70 Metallic blue body, white interior, UB,
opening doors and boot, NW £80-90
70-71 Metallic light or dark gold body,
opening doors and boot, NW £45-50
Metallic light gold body, opening boot
but doors cast shut, NW...................£20-25
77 Military olive green body, boot and
doors cast shut, 'Staff' labels (TP) ..£12-15
81 Silver body, WW, (Multi Pack)....£125-150

MB 46d   Stretcha Fetcha

72-77 All-white body, red base, BG,
'Ambulance', large Red Cross labels...£6-8
Same but no 'Amulance', small RC £15-18
All-white body, UB, BG, 'Ambulance'
and large Red Cross labels.................£8-10
All-white body, red base, 'Ambulance',
large Red Cross labels, AG................£15-18
Same but no 'Amulance', small RC ...£18-20
77 All-red body, red base, BG, 'Unfall
Rettung' labels (German issue).......£30-35
80 Lime green/white, WB or BB, AG,
'Viper Van' prints (US Ltd. Ed.)......£12-15

MB 46e   Ford Tractor and Harrow

78-81 Blue body, yellow interior, UB, black
wheels, yellow plastic harrow.............£2-4
Same but black wheels, yellow hubs ...£4-6
Blue body, white interior, UB, black
wheels, yellow hubs, yellow harrow....£4-6
79 Blue body, yellow interior, UB, black
wheels, no harrow (TP).......................£2-4
81 Metallic lime green, yellow interior,
BW, yellow hubs, no harrow (TP) £4-6
81-83 Metallic green body, yellow interior,
BW, yellow hubs, yellow harrow........£2-4
83 Blue body, white interior, GB, BW
with gold hubs, no harrow (TP).........£6-8

MB 47c   DAF Container Truck

70-72 Silver cab/body, yellow tipper £12-15

MB 47d   Beach Hopper

73-78 Blue body with paint spots, light or
dark pink base, orange interior, light
brown man, clear or no windscreen,
'Sun' label, wide WW (Rola-Matic)....£5-8
Same but UB, no windscreen............£15-18
With light pink base, yellow interior,
no windscreen, dark brown man £20-25

MB 47e   Pannier Locomotive

79-82 Dark green and black, BB, 'G.W.R.' ...£3-5
Same but with unpainted base £8-10
Same but with brown or grey base ..£10-12

MB 47f   Jaguar SS100

82-83 Red body, light brown interior, BB......£2-4
Same but with grey base £3-5

MB 48c   Dodge Dumper Truck

69-71 Blue cab and body, yellow tipper,
chrome base, NW or WW...............£12-15

MB 48d   Pie-Eyed Piper

72-77 Metallic blue body, silver engine and
exhausts, BG, UB, '8' and stars..........£6-8
Same but with amber glass £10-12
Red body, 'Big Banger', CE and
exhausts, BB........................£150-200
78 White body, silver/black engine, black
exhausts, glass and base, orange
prints, (US Roman Numeral issue) ..£12-15
81-83 Red body, SE, black exhausts, AG,
BB, 'Red Rider' prints (USA) £10-12

MB 48e   Sambron Jack Lift

77-81 Yellow body, BB, red 'Sambron'...£80-120
Same but with no tampo prints £2-4
Yellow body, BB, yellow hubs............£4-6

Same but with grey or brown base **£7-10**
81-83 Yellow body, black forks, BB or GB ...**£3-6**

MB 49b Unimog

70 Blue body, red base, green glass, silver or plain grille **£20-30**
70-71 Same but metallic steel-blue body ...**£20-25**
71-72 Same but sky blue body, plain grille **£15-18**
78 Military olive green body, BB, GG, tan load, 'A' label in square (TP).....**£18-20**
Same but 'star' circle label, tan load on some, (TP) **£35-40**

MB 49c Chop Suey

73-76 Metallic red-purple frame, chrome forks, CE, 'bull's head' **£250-300**
Same but with red forks **£8-10**
With black or orange forks **£35-40**

MB 49d Crane Truck

76-79 Yellow body and crane arm, red hook, black base, green glass **£4-6**
77 Red body, yellow crane arm, red hook, BB, CG (German PS1000 set) **£70-80**
Same but GG (German PS1000 set) **£60-70**
80-82 Yellow body, black crane arm, red hook, black base, purple or red glass .**£8-10**
Same but green glass....**£4-6**
82-83 Same but 'A1 Crane Service' on arm + 'Safety First', 'C', 'Cat' on some...**£8-10**

MB 50c Kennel Truck

70-71 Dark or light metallic green body, BB, silver grille, 4 white dogs, NW........**£12-15**
Dark Metallic Green body, Grey base, silver grille, 4 white dogs, NW........**£15-18**
Same but with yellow base **£20-25**
72-73 Lime Green body, BB or GB, silver grille, 4 white dogs, WW.......**£10-15**
Same but white grille, BB or GB.....**£25-30**
Same but with unpainted base **£35-40**

MB 50d Articulated Truck

73-79 Yellow cab/body, BB, light blue trailer with yellow chevron side labels, yellow or orange trailer body, red or PG **£7-10**
Same but no labels **£4-6**
80 Red cab/body, BB, light blue trailer, no labels, red trailer body, PG...............**£35-40**
Yellow cab/ body, light blue trailer, no labels, yellow trailer body, white tow hook, purple glass (TP) **£4-6**
Red cab/body, silver trailer (red body), white hook on some, PG (TP)..........**£35-40**
80 **Articulated Trailer** Light blue trailer (yellow body) (TP) **£4-6**
Silver trailer, red trailer body (TP) ..**£35-40**

MB 50e Harley-Davidson

80-82 Light gold frame, black handlebars **£6-8**
82-83 Dark bronze frame, black bars.........**£10-12**

MB 51c 8-wheel Tipper

70-71 Yellow cab and body, silver tipper, BG, SB, 'POINTER' labels on some **£20-25**
Same but with grey base **£50-60**

MB 51d Citroën SM

72-74 Metallic bronze body, cream interior, unpainted base, NW **£12-15**
Same but with orange interior..........**£55-60**
Same but with yellow interior..........**£15-18**
With cream interior, silver base **£12-15**
75 Metallic blue body, yellow interior, unpainted base, WW **£25-30**
75-78 Same plus '8', UB (Streakers issue) ..**£8-10**
With '8', UB and off-white or orange interior (Streakers issue) **£10-15**
79 Metallic blue body, orange interior, UB, roof rack, 'Yamaha Shell STP' (TP)**£15-18**

MB 51e Combine Harvester

78-81 Red body, yellow blades/arm, BB, black 'regular wheels' **£6-8**
Same but with black Superfast wheels **£4-6**
Same but with yellow hubs **£8-10**
Red body, yellow blades/arm, no base, black Superfast wheels **£6-8**
Same but with yellow hubs **£10-12**
Yellow body, red blades/arm, no base, '2' print, Superfast wheels (Gift Set).**£8-10**

MB 51f Pontiac Firebird SE

82-83 Red body, tan interior, silver base........**£2-4**

MB 51i Motorcycle Trailer

79-82 Metallic blue body, 3 orange-yellow or yellow bikes (TP) **£6-8**
Same but with 3 red bikes (TP) **£10-12**
82-83 Red body, 3 yellow bikes (TP) **£12-15**

MB 52c Dodge Charger Mk.III

70-71 Metallic light or dark red body, black interior **£8-10**
Same but with '5' labels (G3 set) **£20-25**
71 Metallic purple body, black interior...**£8-10**
71-75 Metallic lime green, black interior.....**£8-10**
Same but with '5' labels (G3 set) **£20-25**
Same but with UB (G3 set)....**£20-30**

MB 52d Police Launch

76-80 White deck, light blue hull, dark BG, orange stripes, 'Police', 2 light blue men, 2 horns **£8-10**
81 Same but with no roof horns....**£2-4**
Same but light blue glass, no horns **£2-4**
Same but frosted BG, no horns **£6-8**
White deck, red hull, roof and rear, BG, 'Los Angeles Fire Department', 2 light blue men (Code Red issue)...**£45-50**
Same but 2 yellow men (Code Red) **£12-15**

MB 52e BMW M1

81-83 Silver body, red interior, BB, CG, black stripes and '52' tampo prints **£2-4**
Same but blue-grey base **£8-10**
With BB, amber glass **£25-30**
With BB, CG, no tampo prints **£4-6**

MB 53c Ford Zodiac Mk.IV

70 Metallic light blue body, NW **£300-400**
70-71 Metallic light green body, NW **£15-18**
Metallic dark green body, NW........**£15-18**
Metallic emerald green body **£20-25**
72 Lime green body, wide wheels **£35-40**

MB 53d Tanzara

72-74 Orange body, SE, silver interior, UB, AG **£5-7**
Same but with green glass **£10-12**
75-76 White body, SE, silver interior, UB, AG, blue/orange stripes/stars, '53' print, (Streakers)....**£12-15**
Same but with no tampo prints **£18-20**
With blue/red stripes/stars, '53' **£10-12**
Same but with green glass **£12-15**
White body, red engine, red interior, UB, AG, blue/red stripes/stars, '53' tampo print, (Streakers)....**£80-90**

MB 53e CJ6 Jeep

77-80 Red body, yellow interior, light brown roof, UB, WW **£3-5**
Same but with black interior....**£6-8**
With yellow interior, silver base **£4-6**
81-82 Metallic green body, yellow interior, light brown roof, UB, WW **£3-5**
Same but with black interior....**£6-8**
With yellow interior, silver base **£4-6**
Pale yellow body, dark brown roof, black interior, BB or GB, 'CJ6' print..........**£8-10**

MB 53f Flareside Pick-up

82-83 Blue body, '326' and 'Baja Bouncer' ..**£2-4**
Same but with some or prints or none .**£3-5**

MB 54b Cadillac Ambulance

70 White body, silver grille, red roof lights, BB, small Red Cross door labels **£20-25**
Off-white body, plain grille, red roof lights, BlB, large Red Cross labels ..**£18-20**

MB 54c Ford Capri

71 Pink or orange body, black bonnet, UB, wide wheels **£12-15**
72-75 Metallic crimson body UB or SB **£8-10**
76 Orange body, UB, (TP) **£12-15**

MB 54d Personnel Carrier

76-79 Military green body, black base, green glass, light brown soldiers on some **£4-7**

MB 54e Mobile Home

80-82 Cream or white body, brown door, side stripes on some, BB **£2-4**
Same but with grey or brown base **£3-6**

MB 54f NASA Tracking Vehicle

82-83 White/red/black, BB, 'US Space Shuttle Command Centre', 'NASA' **£5-8**
Same but with grey base **£8-10**

MB 55d Mercury Police Car

70 White body, 2 men, blue roof light, shields and 'Police' label **£30-35**
Same but with red roof light **£25-30**

MB 55e Mercury Estate Police Car

71-74 White body, off-white interior, no men, UB, 2 red roof lights, bonnet shield and 'Police' label and side shield labels.**£20-25**
Same but UB or SB, bonnet and side 'Police' arrow labels **£12-15**
Same but UB or SB, bonnet 'Police' arrow label, plain sides **£15-18**

MB 55f Hellraiser

75-76 White body, red interior, UB, 'Stars and Stripes' bonnet label **£4-6**
77-78 Metallic blue body, red interior, SB, 'Stars and Stripes' bonnet label **£10-12**
Metallic blue body, off-white interior, UB or SB, 'Stars and Stripes' **£3-6**
Metallic blue body, off-white interior, SB, bonnet stripe and '3' label **£20-25**
Same but with no label....**£3-5**

MB 55g Ford Cortina

79-80 Metallic green body, red interior, UB, clear glass, opening doors **£6-8**
Same but with light yellow interior ...**£8-10**
81 Metallic red body, light yellow interior, UB, opening doors **£6-8**
82-83 Metallic light brown body, white interior, UB or SB, opening doors, black stripe **£6-8**
Light red body, white interior, UB or SB, doors cast shut....**£6-8**
Same but with gloss black base **£18-20**
Bright red body, white interior, UB or SB, opaque glass, doors cast shut (Gift Set issue) **£15-18**
83 Light red body, light brown interior, UB or SB, doors cast shut, black side stripe prints (TP)....**£15-18**
Same but white interior (TP) **£6-8**

MB 56c BMC 1800 Pinifarina

69-70 Metallic gold body, UB, NW **£12-15**
Same, with '17', 'Gulf' (G3 set) **£20-25**
71-73 Peach body, UB, NW **£25-30**
Orange body, UB, NW or WW..........**£8-12**
With '17' and 'Gulf' (G3 set)..........**£18-20**

MB 56d   Hi-Tailer

74-78	White body, orange/blue stripes, UB, 'MB5 Team Matchbox', yellow man..**£4-6**	
	Same but with silver or red base.........**£6-8**	
	Same but with blue man......................**£4-6**	
79	Red base, 'Martini 7' (Gift Set)......**£10-12**	

MB 56e   Mercedes 450 SEL

79-80	Metallic blue body, red interior.........**£8-10**
	Same but with light brown interior......**£5-7**
81-83	Light brown body, light or dark brown interior, red 'Taxi' sign, UB or SB **£4-6**

MB 57c   Land-Rover Fire Truck

70	Red body, white ladder, 'Kent Fire Brigade' labels **£50-60**
	Same but with 'Kent Fire Brigade' labels cut around words **£60-70**

MB 57d   Eccles Trailer Caravan

70-71	Cream body, orange roof, green interior, maroon side stripe labels ..**£12-15**
	Same but brown side stripe labels ..**£15-18**
	With brown stripe and flower labels**£12-15**
72	Pale Yellow body, orange roof, green interior, brown stripe, flower labels.**£15-18**
76-78	Yellow body, red-orange roof, white interior, black stripe, flowers (TP)..**£10-12**
	Same but with side red dots label from K-27 Camping Cruiser set (TP)......**£25-30**
79-81	Light brown, red-orange roof, white interior, black stripe, flowers (TP)..**£8-10**
	Same but 'white bird' label (TP) **£20-25**
82	White body, red-orange roof, white interior, 'Sunset', palm tree **£15-18**

MB 57e   Wildlife Truck

73-80	Yellow body, clear back, red glass, orange or light brown lion, 'Ranger' (Rola-Matic version) **£6-8**
	Same but with amber back.............**£10-12**
81	White body, clear back, red glass, light brown lion, black/white camouflage prints, (Rola-Matic version)..............**£8-10**
	Same but with amber glass **£10-12**
	Same but with purple glass **£12-15**
	Same but tinted detachable back.....**£12-15**

MB 57f   Carmichael Rescue Vehicle

82	White body, 'Police Rescue' **£8-10**
83	Red body, 'Fire' **£10-15**

MB 58c   DAF Girder Truck

70	Cream or off-white cab and body, red base (with 'Pat App' on some) ..**£70-80**
70-71	Metallic lime green cab and body....**£15-18**

MB 58d   Woosh 'n' Push

72-75	Yellow body, red interior, '2' label **£4-6**
	Same but pale yellow interior.........**£25-30**
	With red interior, 'flower' label......**£12-15**
76	Metallic red body, pale yellow interior, '2' label on roof **£6-8**
	Same but '8' and stars label............**£12-15**

MB 58e   Faun Dump Truck

76-81	Yellow body, yellow tipper **£2-4**
79	Yellow body, red tipper (G5 set).....**£25-30**
82-83	Yellow body, yellow tipper, 'CAT' **£6-8**

MB 59e   Ford Galaxie Fire Chief

70	Red body, white interior, 'Fire Chief' and side shield labels **£25-30**

MB 59d   Mercury Fire Chief

71-74	Red body, '59' or '73', 2 men, yellow 'Fire Chief' on bonnet, 'shield' labels on sides.................................**£15-18**
	Same but 'helmet & axes' on sides ..**£12-15**
	Same but yellow bonnet 'helmet and axes' label, plain sides..................**£10-12**
	Same but yellow 'helmet and axes'

	labels on bonnet and sides **£10-12**
	Same but with only '59' on base **£10-12**
78	Same but with no men (TP) **£8-10**
	Red body, CG, 'Fire', shield (TP).....**£8-10**
	Same but with purple glass (TP).....**£12-15**
79	White, CG, 'Police', shield (TP)......**£18-20**
81	Red body, 'Los Angeles Fire Dept' tampo prints (Code Red)................**£12-15**
	White body, CG or BG, 'Los Angeles Police' tampo prints, (Code Red) ...**£12-15**
82	White body, CG, PG or BG, 'Police' and shield, black wing panel prints..**£10-15**
	White body, CG or BG, 'Metro Police', black wing tampo prints as 10f.........**£8-10**
	Same but with white wing panels **£10-12**

MB 59e   Planet Scout

75-77	Metallic green and lime green **£3-5**
78-80	Metallic red and light brown.............**£8-10**
77	Avocado/black, PG or AG (Adventure 2000 K2005 Command Force set)...**£20-30**
80	Metallic blue/black, PG, (Adventure 2000 set) **£50-60**

MB 59f   Porsche 928

80-81	Light metallic brown body, brown interior, black base, clear glass **£4-6**
	Same but cream or off-white interior...**£6-8**
	With brown interior, amber glass.......**£8-10**
	Dark metallic brown body, brown interior, black base **£4-6**
	Same but with amber glass **£8-10**
	Same but with brown glass **£10-12**
	With clear glass, brown or grey base.**£8-10**
	With AG, brown or grey base **£10-12**
81-82	Metallic blue body, brown interior, clear glass, black base **£4-6**
	Same but with grey or silver base......**£6-8**
82-83	Black body, brown interior, 'Porsche' ..**£4-6**
	Same but with red interior **£6-8**

MB 60b   Truck with Site Office

70	Blue truck, yellow/green office.......**£18-20**

MB 60c   Lotus Super 7

71-75	Orange body, black interior and boot, bonnet 'flame' label **£8-10**
	Same but with Yellow body **£12-15**
75-76	Same but blue stripe and check design + bonnet '60' prints, (Streakers)......**£12-15**

MB 60d   Holden Pick-up

77	Metallic ruby red body, yellow interior, AG, yellow bikes, '500' label **£10-12**
77-80	Bright red body, yellow interior, AG, yellow bikes, '500' label **£4-6**
	Same but with orange glass **£6-8**
	Bright red body, red interior, orange or AG, olive green bikes, '500' label.....**£8-10**
	Bright red body, red interior, orange or AG, olive green bikes, 'Sun' label.....**£15-18**
	Bright red body, yellow interior, AG, yellow bikes, 'striped' bonnet label.**£15-18**
80	Metallic blue body, yellow interior, orange or amber glass, yellow bikes, 'Paris-Dakar 81' (French issue).......**£12-15**
81-83	Cream body, red interior, orange or AG, red bikes, stripes and Superbike' .**£5-7**
	Same but with yellow bikes **£8-10**
	Cream body, red interior, AG, red bikes, 'Honda' labels **£18-20**

MB 61b   Alvis Stalwart

66-71	White body, yellow detachable top, clear glass, 'BP Exploration' labels, regular black wheels, black hubs...**£30-40**
78	Metallic olive green body, fixed top, GG, black wide wheels (TP)...........**£20-25**

MB 61c   Blue Shark

71-77	Metallic blue, UB or SB, CG, '86' **£4-6**

	Same but with '69' label from 69d....**£8-10**
	Metallic blue body, SB, CG or AG, 'Scorpion' label on bonnet...............**£25-30**
	Metallic blue body, UB or SB, AG, bonnet arrows and '86' label **£8-10**
	Same but with '69' label from 69d..**£10-12**

MB 61d   Wreck Truck

78-80	Red body, white arms, red hooks, BB or GB, AG and 2 roof lights.........**£3-6**
	With red or white arms, black hooks ...**£3-5**
	Red body, red arms, red hooks **£8-10**
	Red body, white arms, red hooks, BB, blue glass and 2 roof lights **£25-30**
81	Red body, off-white arms, red hooks, BB, AG, 'Radio Despatches 24 Hour Towing' tampo prints (TP) **£8-10**
81-82	Light yellow body, red arms, black hooks, AG, black or grey base.............**£3-5**
	Same but with brown base **£6-8**
	Same but with silver base **£8-10**
	With red arms & hooks, BB or GB......**£3-5**
	Light yellow body, white arms, red hooks, BB or GB, AG and lights **£20-25**
	Light yellow body, green arms, red or black hooks, BB or GB, AG lights..**£6-8**
	Dark yellow body, red arms, black hooks, BB, AG **£3-5**
	Same but with brown base **£6-8**
	Dark yellow body, red arms, red hooks, BB or GB, AG and lights **£3-5**
	Dark yellow body, white arms, red hooks, BB, AG and lights **£20-25**
	Dark yellow body, green arms, red or black hooks, BB, AG and lights ...**£12-15**
	Same but with grey base **£15-20**

MB 61e   Peterbilt Wreck Truck

82-83	Red-orange, white 'Eddies Wrecker'...**£2-4**
	Same but with black tampo prints **£6-8**
	Blue body, no tampo print, from 'Highway Express' Gift Set)............**£20-25**

MB 62c   Mercury Cougar

70	Light metallic gold or gold-green body red interior....................................**£20-25**

MB 62d   Mercury Cougar Dragster

70	Light green body, red interior, UB, 'Rat Rod' labels **£15-18**
70-73	Same but lime green body **£10-12**
	Same but with silver base **£25-35**
	Same but UB, 'Wild Cat' labels **£25-30**

MB 62e   Renault 17TL

74-78	Red body, white interior, '9' label **£6-8**
	Red-orange body, white interior, '9'...**£6-8**
	Same but label reversed to read '6' ...**£8-10**
76	Red body, white interior, 'Fire' labels, (from G12 Rescue set).........**£15-18**

MB 62f   Chevrolet Corvette

79-81	Metallic ruby red body, grey interior, UB, CG, white bonnet prints **£4-6**
	Same but with black interior **£6-8**
	Same but white interior....................**£12-15**
	Same but with black interior **£6-8**
	Same but with grey interior **£4-6**
81-83	Black body, grey interior, UB, CG, orange/yellow bonnet stripes **£3-5**
	Same but with white base **£5-7**
83	Same but UB, opaque glass, (from Streak Racing set) **£10-12**

MB 63c   Dodge Crane Truck

70-72	Yellow body, yellow crane, arm and hook (orange hook on some).....**£12-15**

MB 63d   Freeway Gas Tanker

73	Red/black/white, 'Castrol' labels.....**£60-70**
73-77	Red/black/white, 'Burmah' labels......**£4-6**
	Same but with tow hook hole in rear....**£6-8**

76	Military olive drab green and black, 'Canadian' flag labels (TP).........**£300-400**
	Same but with 'French' flag (TP)....**£70-80**
76-77	Military olive green cab black base, '95 High Octane' labels (TP)...........**£18-20**
77	Light blue/black/white, 'Aral' labels (German issue)......................**£20-25**
78-79	Red/black/white, 'Chevron' labels, tow hook hole in rear of tanker........**£6-8**
	Same but with white tow hook (TP)..**£8-10**
	Red/black/white, 'Burmah' labels, cream tow hook (TP) **£8-10**
79-80	White/yellow, 'Shell' labels, PG.......**£6-8**
	Same but with red glass **£10-12**
	Yellow/black/white, 'Shell', PG **£15-18**
80-81	White/yellow, 'Exxon' labels...........**£15-18**
	White/black, 'Exxon' labels............**£15-18**
	White/yellow, 'Shell' labels, cream tow hook (TP) **£6-8**
	White/yellow, 'Exxon' labels, cream tow hook (TP) **£15-18**
81-82	White/black/green, 'BP Super' **£8-10**
	White/yellow, 'BP Super' (TP).......**£20-25**

MB 63dx Freeway Gas Trailer

78-79	White/red, 'Chevron' labels (TP) **£8-10**
	Same but with 'Burmah' labels (TP) .**£8-10**
80-81	White/yellow, 'Shell' labels (TP) **£6-8**
	White/yellow, 'Exxon' labels (TP) ..**£15-18**
81-82	White/yellow, 'BP Super' (TP).......**£20-25**

MB 63e 4x4 Open Back Truck

82-83	Orange or light orange body, '24' and 'FWD' or '4x4' prints.........................**£4-6**

MB 64b MG 1100

70	Green body, white interior with man and dog, unpainted base, clear glass..**£200-225**
70-71	Same but metallic light blue body ...**£18-20**
	Same but metallic dark blue body ...**£20-30**

MB 64c Slingshot Dragster

71-72	Metallic pink body, BB, black exhausts, bonnet flame and '9' labels...........**£10-12**
73	Orange body, BB, black exhausts, bonnet flame and '9' label.........**£90-100**
	Same but red exhausts.................**£150-200**
73-75	Metallic blue-green body, red exhausts, bonnet flame, '9' label **£15-18**
	Same but BB, front NW or WW.........**£6-8**
	Same but with '3' **£18-20**

MB 64d Fire Chief Car

76-79	Red body, 'Fire', some yellow shield labels have black edging **£4-6**
	Same but with orange body **£6-8**

MB 64e Caterpillar D-9 Tractor

79-81	Yellow body, brown roof, yellow shovel, black tracks, orange or yellow rollers..**£4-6**
82	Yellow body, black roof, yellow shovel, 'C'on cab, black tracks, yellow rollers **£6-8**
82-83	Same but black shovel, black or silver tow hook, 'C' on cab....................**£4-6**
	Same plus 'CAT' print, (black hook)...**£6-8**

MB 65c Claas Combine Harvester

67-72	Red body, yellow cutters, black base, black wheels with yellow hubs **£8-10**

MB 65d Saab Sonnet III

73-76	Metallic blue body, yellow interior, UB, AG, grey rear door **£6-8**
79	White body, yellow interior, UB, AG, grey rear door, (Multi Pack).........**£200-225**

MB 65e Airport Coach

NB All Airport Coach models have white roofs

77-81	Metallic blue body, off-white or pale yellow interior, AG or CG, UB, 'British Airways' **£6-9**
	Same but with labels reversed **£10-12**

	Metallic blue body, off-white interior, UB, AG, 'American Airlines' labels ..**£8-10**
	Same but with clear glass................**£8-10**
	Same but pale yellow interior, AG **£8-10**
	Same but with clear glass...............**£10-12**
	Metallic blue body, off-white or pale yellow interior, AG, 'Lufthansa' (German)..**£8-10**
	Same but with clear glass...............**£10-12**
81	Orange body, pale yellow interior, UB, AG, 'Schulbus' (German issue)......**£20-25**
81-83	Red body, 'TWA' **£6-8**
	Red body, 'Qantas'.........................**£6-8**
82	Red body, 'Fly Braniff' **£18-20**
	White body, 'Stork SB'(Australian) **£12-15**
	Metallic Blue body, 'Girobank' (Promotional issue) **£10-12**
83	Metallic Blue body, UB or SB, AG, 'British' labels.............................**£6-8**
	Metallic Blue body, UB or SB, AG, 'Australian' labels **£8-10**
	White body, UB or SB, 'Alitalia' **£10-12**
	White body, UB or SB, 'Lufthansa' **£18-20**

MB 66c Greyhound Coach

70	Silver body, yellow interior, AG, matt or gloss BB, 'Greyhound'..........**£15-18**
	Same but with yellow or pink base..**£25-30**

MB 66d Mazda RX500

71-74	Orange body, SE, white base, PG **£6-8**
	Same but with unpainted base **£15-20**
	Orange body, SE, white base, AG **£10-12**
75-76	Red body, SE, WB, AG, white/green '77' and stripes(Streakers version) **£6-8**
	Same but with PG (Streakers)..........**£10-12**
	Same but UB, AG (Streakers).........**£10-12**
	Red body, light brown engine, WB, AG, '77' and stripes (Streakers) **£12-15**
	Same but with PG (Streakers)..........**£15-18**

MB 66e Ford Transit

77-80	Orange body, green glass, UB, brown load, green interior...............**£15-20**
	Same but light brown interior **£12-15**
	Same but light yellow interior **£4-6**
	Orange body, amber glass, UB, beige load, green interior **£15-20**
	Light brown or light yellow interior **£12-15**
81-82	Yellow-orange body, off-white or green interior, UB, brown load, green glass ..**£6-8**
	Same but with beige load **£4-6**
	Yellow-orange body, green interior, GB, brown or beige load, green glass **£6-8**
	Same but with black base.................**£15-20**

MB 66f Tyrone Malone Superboss

82-83	White body, blue/red stripes on 'Tyrone Malone' on white aerofoil......**£4-6**
	With plain white or cream aerofoil......**£2-4**

MB 67b Volkswagen 1600TL

70	Dark or light red body, white interior, UB, CG, NW **£60-70**
70-71	Metallic purple body (may be dark, mid or light), white interior, UB, CG, narrow or wide wheels....................**£18-20**
71-72	Metallic pink body, white interior, UB, CG, NW or WW.....................**£15-18**

MB 67c Hot Rocker

73-74	Metallic green-gold body, white interior, UB, CG (Rola-Matic version)..........**£10-12**
	Same but with silver base **£20-30**
	Same but metallic green body, UB ...**£8-10**
	Same but with silver base **£20-30**
75-77	Red body, UB, (Rola-Matic version) ...**£6-8**
	Same but with silver base **£20-30**

MB 67d Datsun 260Z 2+2

78-80	Metallic crimson body, white interior, clear glass, black base **£6-8**
	Same but with grey base **£8-10**

79	Metallic blue body, pale yellow interior, matt yellow base (TP)...........**£15-20**
	Same but with red interior (TP).......**£30-40**
	Metallic blue body, red interior, brown base (TP) **£40-50**
80	Metallic red body, pale yellow interior, black base **£8-10**
81-83	Silver body, red interior, black base.....**£4-6**
	Same but grey or blue-grey base **£6-8**
	Same but with brown base **£8-10**
	Silver body, white interior, GB or BB, red stripes, black 'Datsun 2+2' (TP)..**£6-8**
	Silver body, black interior, BB, blue stripes, black 'Datsun 2+2' (TP).......**£8-10**
83	Black body and interior, BB (TP)....**£20-30**

MB 68c Porsche 910

70-74	Metallic red body, pale yellow interior, UB, AG, '68' label on bonnet, NW ...**£8-10**
	Same + '68' side labels (G3 set)......**£20-25**
	Metallic red body, pale yellow interior, UB, AG, bonnet '68' label, WW **£8-10**
	Same but with '45' label from 45c .**£25-30**
72	White body, pale yellow interior, UB, AG, WW ('Brroom Stick' issue) **£30-35**

MB 68d Cosmobile

75-78	Metallic light blue body, yellow under, white or silver interior, AG.................**£4-6**
77	Avocado body, black under, white interior, AG, (Adventure 2000 set)..**£18-20**
	Same but with purple glass (set).....**£15-18**
	Same but with silver interior (set) ...**£20-30**
78-79	Metallic red body, beige under, white or silver interior, AG................**£8-10**
80	Metallic dark blue, black under, silver interior, PG (Adventure 2000 set)....**£50-80**

MB 68e Chevy Van

79-80	Orange body, UB, BG, blue/red or blue/white stripes **£4-6**
	Same but CG, blue/red stripes **£10-12**
	Same but BG, red/black stripes...........**£4-6**
	Same but with green or red glass **£6-8**
80-81	Orange body, 'Matchbox Collectors Club' labels, BG (Ltd. Edition) **£15-18**
81-82	White body, 'Adidas' (German) **£18-20**
	White body, 'USA-1' (US issue) **£10-12**
	Green body, 'Chevy' with brown or yellow segmented stripes **£4-6**
82-83	Yellow body, 'Collect Exciting Matchbox' (Australian issue)...........**£18-20**
	Silver body, blue glass, 'Vanpire' **£4-6**

MB 69c Rolls-Royce Silver Shadow

69-70	Metallic blue body, brown interior, tan folded top, BB, AG, NW **£12-15**
	Same but dark or light yellow base .**£20-25**
71-72	Metallic light gold body, brown interior, tan folded top, BB, AG, WW **£10-12**
	Same but dark or light yellow base .**£20-25**
	Same but with silver base **£12-15**
	With black folded top, BB **£10-12**
	Same but with light yellow base **£20-25**
	Same but with silver or grey base ...**£12-15**
	With off-white interior, black folded top, black base, AG, WW **£10-12**
	Same but with grey base **£12-15**
	Metallic dark gold, AG, off-white interior, black folded top, BB, WW .**£10-12**
	Same but with grey or silver base....**£12-15**
	Metallic dark gold body, brown interior, black folded top, BB, AG, WW.......**£10-12**
	Same but with grey or silver base ...**£12-15**
72-73	Metallic lime gold body, off-white or brown interior, black folded top, BB, AG, WW **£10-12**
	Same but with grey or silver base.....**£12-15**

MB 69d Turbo Fury

73-77	Metallic red body, CG, '69' and arrows label, (Rola-Matic version) **£8-10**

Same but AG (Rola-Matic version) .**£10-12**
Metallic red body, '86' and arrows
label, (Rola-Matic version) **£12-15**
Same but 'Scorpion' (Rola-Matic)...**£35-40**

MB 69e Security Truck

78-83 Dark red body, cream roof, UB or SB,
BG, '732 2031', 'Wells Fargo' **£8-10**
Light red body, white roof, SB, CG,
'732 2031' and 'Wells Fargo' **£12-15**
Same but BG, UB or SB **£4-6**
Light red body, white roof, SB, BG,
'QZ 2031' and 'Wells Fargo'............**£8-10**
81 Metallic dark green body, SB, BG,
'Dresdner Bank' (German promo)...**£15-18**

MB 70b Grit Spreading Truck

70 Red cab and body, dark or pale yellow
grit spreader, UB, GG, NW **£10-12**

MB 70c Dodge Dragster

71-75 Dark pink body, BB, 'snake' labels ...**£8-10**
With purple, cream, light green, light
yellow, dark yellow or grey base **£25-30**
With brown or unpainted base **£35-40**
Dark pink body, BB, 'Wild Cat' **£40-50**
Dark pink body, 'Rat Rod' labels ...**£40-50**
Light pink body, BB, 'snake' labels **£15-18**
Bright pink body,BB, 'snake' labels **£15-18**
78 Yellow body, red glass, GB or BB,
side prints, (US Roman Numeral)....**£12-15**

MB 70d S.P. Gun

76-80 Military green body, black or brown
tracks, (Rola-Matic version) **£3-6**

MB 70e Ferrari 308 GTB

81-83 Red body and base, black stripe, CG ...**£4-6**
Red body and base, CG, 'Ferrari' **£3-5**
Same but with AG **£6-8**
83 Red body, silver base, no 'Ferrari' **£8-10**

MB 71c Ford Heavy Wreck Truck

70-72 Red cab, white body, red crane and
hook, BB, GG, 'Esso' **£15-18**
Same but with yellow hook **£18-20**
79 Military olive green, black hook,
BB, GG, '3LGS64' labels (TP) **£18-20**
81 Dark blue, blue crane, black hook,
BB, GG, no labels (Multi Pack).......**£80-90**

MB 71d Jumbo Jet

73-75 Metallic blue frame, red elephant head,
dark blue handlebars, black wheels **£6-8**
Same but light blue handlebars **£20-25**

MB 71e Cattle Truck

76-81 Metallic orange-red cab, dark yellow
back, UB, GG or BG, 2 black cattle ..**£8-10**
With GG or BB, SB **£6-8**
With AG, PG or orange glass, SB **£8-10**
79-83 Dark red cab, off-white back,
SB, BG, 2 black cattle (TP) **£6-8**
Same but with red or PG (TP) **£8-10**
Dark red cab, dark or light yellow back,
SB, PG, 2 black cattle (TP)...............**£8-10**
81-83 Metallic light green cab, off-white back,
SB, OG, 2 brown cattle **£6-8**
Metallic light or dark green cab, yellow

back, SB, red or OG, 2 brown cattle....**£4-6**
Metallic dark green cab, dark brown
back, SB, red or AG, 2 brown cattle....**£4-6**
83 Yellow cab, dark brown back, BB or SB,
red or AG, 2 light brown cattle..........**£4-6**
With dark or light brown back, UB **£4-6**
With light brown back, BB, red or AG,
2 light brown cattle **£4-6**
Yellow cab, dark brown back, BB, UB
or SB, red or AG, black tow hook,
2 light brown cattle (TP).....................**£4-6**

MB 71ex Cattle Truck Trailer

79-83 Dark red body, off-white or light or dark
yellow back, SB, 2 black cattle (TP) ...**£4-6**
83 Yellow body, dark yellow back, SB,
2 light brown cattle (TP)......................**£4-6**

MB 72b Standard Jeep

70-71 Dull yellow body, red interior, UB ..**£12-15**
Bright yellow body, red interior.......**£50-60**
Orange body **£15-20**

MB 72c SRN Hovercraft

72-78 White body, BB, BG, 'R.N.L.I.' **£6-8**

MB 72d Bomag Road Roller

79-82 Yellow/red, black roller, 2 wheels........**£4-6**
Same but 2 wheels have yellow hubs **£6-8**

MB 72e Dodge Delivery Truck

82-83 Red cab, white back, 'Pepsi'..............**£2-4**
Red cab, white back, 'Kelloggs' **£2-4**
Either of the above with gold hubs **£4-6**
Red cab, white back, 'Smiths Crisps'
(Promotional offer)..............................**£2-4**
Same but with gold hubs (Promo) **£4-6**

MB 73c Mercury Commuter

70-71 Metallic lime green body, UB with '59',
'55' or '73', NW or WW **£25-30**
71-73 Red body, UB, 'Bull head' label on
bonnet of some, wide wheels..........**£10-12**

MB 73d Weasel

74-76 Metallic green body, metallic green and
green base, (Rola-Matic)......................**£6-8**
76 Military olive drab green body,
metallic green and green base,
(Rola-Matic) (TP)............................**£35-40**
76-79 Same but with military olive green
body (Rola-Matic) (TP) **£12-15**
Military olive green body, olive green
and green base, (Rola-Matic) ..**£12-15**
Same but olive green and black base,
(Rola-Matic) (TP)............................**£12-15**

MB 73e Ford Model 'A' Car

79-80 Cream body, dark green wings, GG...**£8-10**
Same but no spare wheel or glass........**£6-8**
80 White body, dark green wings, GG ...**£8-10**
80-82 Metallic green body, dark green wings,
GG or no glass **£3-5**
82-83 Light brown body, dark brown wings,
amber glass **£4-6**
Same but with clear glass....................**£6-8**

MB 74b Daimler Bus

70-72 Red body, white interior, 'Esso' **£12-15**

72 Same but 'dayglo' pink body..........**£18-20**
Red body, 'Inn on the Park' labels ..**£70-80**
Red body, 'The Baron of Beef' **£80-90**
Red body, 'Big T Scotch Whiskey'
labels (Promotional) **£70-80**
Red body, 'NAMC', 'The Miniature
Vehicle' labels (Promotional)........**£90-100**
Red body, 'Swinging London' **£70-90**
Red body, 'Beefeater Gin' **£70-90**
Red body, 'Fly Cyprus Airways' **£70-90**
Red body, 'Barclays Bank' **£70-90**
Red body, 'Kensington Hilton' **£70-90**
Red body, 'I.C.P. Interchemicals' **£70-90**

MB 74e Tow Joe

72-77 Metallic green-gold body, UB, AG and
roof light, green arms, Red hooks....**£10-12**
Same but with BB or SB.................**£10-12**
With UB and black hooks................**£12-15**
Metallic green body, BB, AG and
roof light, green arms, red hooks **£6-8**
76-81 Yellow body, BB, SB or UB, AG, red
arms, black hooks (TP)......................**£8-10**
With matt base, red or black hooks**£75-100**
Metallic green body, BB, AG,
red arms, black hooks (TP)..............**£25-30**
Same, BB or SB, white arms (TP).**£90-100**
Red body, BB, AG, red or green arms,
red or black hooks (TP) **£150-175**
82 Yellow body, UB, AG, red arms, black
hooks, 'Hitch Hiker' labels (TP) .**£100-125**

MB 74d Cougar Villager

78-81 Metallic light or dark green body,
yellow interior, UB, AG.......................**£6-8**
81-82 Metallic blue body, yellow or orange-
yellow interior, UB, AG..................**£15-18**

MB 74e Fiat Arbath

82-83 White body, red interior, 'Matchbox' ...**£4-6**
Same but with black interior **£40-60**

MB 75b Ferrari Berlinetta

70 Metallic green body, off-white interior,
unpainted base, clear glass...........**£100-125**
70-71 Red body, off-white interior, UB,
CG, silver grille on some **£40-50**

MB 75c Alfa Carabo

71-75 Metallic Purple body, YB, NW..........**£8-10**
Same but with unpainted base **£10-12**
75 Metallic light pink body, YB, WW...**£15-18**
75-76 Metallic light pink or red body,
yellow/black/green prints, WW,
(Streakers version) **£10-12**

MB 75d Seasprite Helicopter

77-81 White body, Red underside, BG or GG,
black rotors, blue 'Rescue' labels **£8-10**
Same but with red glass **£12-15**
Same but with purple glass **£15-18**

MB 75e Helicopter

82-83 White/orange, black interior, black skids,
AG, 'MBTV News' tampo prints **£6-8**
White/black, black or grey interior, black
skids, AG or CG, 'Police' and '36' **£4-6**
White/black, black or grey interior,
black or grey skids, AG, 'Rescue' **£6-8**

We regret that it has not been possible to continue listing the Miniatures models produced
from 1983 (with the exception of the important 'Londoner Bus' issues.
We would suggest that collectors requiring more information should
contact Bob May, 25 Oakwood Way, Hamble le Rice, Hampshire, SO31 4HJ (see Catalogue advertisement) or
Carr Collectables, Central House, High Street, Ongar, Essex, CM5 9AA (tel. 01277-366144).
The Matchbox Collectors Club provides full details of all new issues (see membership details on facing page).

Matchbox Superfast and Miscellaneous Sets

G 1	1970	**Service Station Set**	
		Contains 13e, 32d, 15e and 'BP' Service Station......**£100-125**
G 1	1981	**Transporter Set**	
		Contains Transporter and 5 Superfast Cars **£15-20**
G 1	1984	**Transporter Set** Contains K10 plus 4 cars....................**£8-11**
G 2	1970	**Transporter Set**	
		Contains Transporter and 5 Superfast models **£75-95**
G 2	1973	**Transporter Set**	
		Contains Transporter and 5 Superfast models **£75-95**
G 2	1981	**Railway Set** Contains 43e, 2 x 44e, 25f.....................**£10-15**
G 2	1987	**Car Transporter Set**	
		Contains K120 Transporter plus MB25 Audi Quattro,
		MB33 Renault 11, MB55 Ford Sierra 4x4, MB74 Toyota,
		MB75 Ferrari Testarossa ....**NGPP**
G 3	1970	**Racing Specials Set**	
		Contains 5e, 20d, 45c, 56c, 52c and 68c **£75-95**
G 3	1973	**'WILD ONES' Set** ....Contains 5 Superfast Cars...**£55-65**
G 3	1981	**Racing Car Set** Transporter and 4 Racing Cars........**£10-15**
G 3	1987	**JCB Gift Set** No details ....**NGPP**
G 4	1970	**Truck SuperSet**	
		Contains 47c, 63c, 58c, 49b, 16d, 21d, 11d and 51c.....**£55-65**
G 4	1973	**Team Matchbox Set**	
		Contains Racing Car Transporter and 4 Racing Cars....**£55-65**
G 4	1981	**Military Assault** Landing Craft + 6 military models ..**£10-15**
G 5	1981	**Construction Set** Contains 5 construction models.....**£25-30**
G 6	1970	**Truck Set**	
		Contains 1e, 10d, 21d, 26c, 30c, 60b, 70b and 49b.......**£75-85**
G 6	1973	**Drag Race Set** Contains 6 Superfast Cars **£40-50**
G 6	1981	**Farm Set** Contains 6 farming models.........................**£10-15**
G 7	1973	**Ferry Boat** With Plastic Boat and 4 Superfast Cars..**£15-20**
G 7	1978	**Car Ferry Set** Contains 3 Cars and Sports Boat.........**£15-20**
G 7	1981	**Emergency Set** Contains 5 Rescue models..................**£10-15**
G 7	1984	**Emergency Set** With models 8, 12, 22, 57 and 75 ......**£10-15**
G 8	1984	**Turbo Charged Set**	
		Contains Turbo Charger plus 7, 9, 52, 60 and 68..........**£10-15**
G 10	1986	**'PAN-AM' Set**	
		Contains 10, 54, 64, 65 and 'Sky-Buster' Boeing.........**£25-30**
G 11	1978	**Strike Force Set** Contains 6 Army Vehicles **£45-50**
G 11	1986	**'LUFTHANSA' Set**	
		Contains 30, 54, 59, 65 and 'Sky-Buster' Airbus **£30-40**

G 12	1978	**Rescue Set** Contains 6 Rescue Vehicles **£30-40**
G 13	1978	**Construction Set** Contains 6 Construction Vehicles..**£30-40**
G 14	1978	**Grand Prix Set** Transporter and 4 Racing Cars.........**£25-35**
G 15	1978	**Transporter Set** Transporter and 5 Superfast Cars **£25-35**
G 40	1988	**40 years Set**	
		Aveling Barford Road Roller, London Bus, Horse Drawn
		Milk Float Massey Harris Tractor, Dennis Fire Engine.
		(Models may be distinguished from the original issues
		as they have 'Made in China' cast underneath)............**£20-25**
C 6		**Emergency Gift Set** All Japanese Set **£15-20**
C 11		**Airport Gift Set**	
		Japanese Foam Pump, Ikarus Coach and Aircraft........**£20-25**
		Cars Gift Set Japanese set:	
		JPS Lotus, VW, Gold Rolls-Royce and Mercedes **£30-35**
		Las Vegas Dodge Set Car and Van **£120-140**
MG 9		**Gear Shift Garage**	
		Gear lever operates car lift and four other functions ....**NRP**
MP804	1990	**Porsche Set**	
		Contains MB3 (911), MB7 (959), MB59 (944)................**NRP**
---	1971	**Matchbox Crash Game**	
		With 4 assorted cars, racetrack, dice and instructions ....**NGPP**
SS 100		**Smash 'n' Crash** Action Playset with two vehicles ......**NRP**
		Multi-Pack Gift Set Contains 5 Superfast models......**£15-20**
		'Days Of Thunder'	
		Film-related sets issued in the US only:
		i) Modified MB10 Buick Le Sabre in 5 liveries............**NGPP**
		ii) Modified MB54f Chevrolet Lumina in 5 liveries ......**NGPP**
A1	70-73	**Service Ramp** 'CASTROL' **£25-35**
A2	1970	**'Superfast Auto Sales'**	
		Plastic kit includes 'MATCHBOX SALES OFFICE',
		'STAR VALUE' stand, 3 'M' flagpoles and 4 lamp
		posts, plus pink card base, signs and advert. stickers.
		25 items in total...**£75-100**
A2	71-73	**'Matchbox' Sales Park**	
		Pink card sales park with four lamp posts ....**NGPP**
A3	c1971	**'Brrooom Stick'**	
		Blister-packed car with steering control. Contains
		No.20 Lamborghini Marzal in Yellow and
		No.68 Porsche in White ....**NGPP**

MICA – The Matchbox International Collectors Association

MICA was founded in 1985 and provides its members with a bi-monthly magazine which is full of useful information about past, present and future issues across the whole Matchbox and 'Dinky Collection' range of products.

All aspects of collecting are included and cover such topics as new releases, variations, past issues and a members advertisement section.

Every year social conventions are held where talks on Matchbox are held and Matchbox auctions take place. A special 'members model' is issued to commemorate the event.

HOW TO JOIN
MICA NORTH AMERICA:
President Joe Recchia. Rita Schneider, Membership Secretary, PO Box 28072, Waterloo, Ontario, Canada N2L 6JB.
Telephone: 519 885- 0529, Fax: 519 885-1902.

MICA AUSTRALIA, NEW ZEALAND and SOUTH PACIFIC:
President Tom Mathieson. Elaine Winkworth, Membership Secretary, PO Box 26, Winston Hills, NSW 2153, Australia. Telephone and Fax: (02) 9686-6685

MICA UK and EUROPE:
Maureen Quayle, Membership Secretary, 13a, Lower Bridge Street, Chester, UK, CH1 1RS.
Telephone (01244) 346297, Fax (01244) 340437.

Recommended reading

'The Yesteryear Book 1956 - 1996'. Kevin McGimpsey and Stewart Orr, joint editors of the MICA magazine, assisted by several club members have produced the ultimate book for MOY collectors. It contains 250 pages packed with details of every variation issued plus diagrams and superb colour photos. Contact: Major Publications, 13a Lower Bridge Street Row, Chester, CH1 1RS (Tel. 01244-346297). A new edition is anticipated in 2000.

'Collecting Matchbox Diecast Toys - The First Forty Years'.
This important book was published in 1989 and contains chapters on every aspect of Matchbox production since 1947. MICA members provided much of the technical input to this well-illustrated book which is now out of print.

Matchbox Models of Yesteryear

Many variants of Yesteryears have resulted from long production runs which often required renewal or modification of worn dies. Considerable numbers of model variations have thus been issued over the years, some of them quite minor. The objective of this listing is to identify for the Yesteryear collector all those price-significant variations which really do matter. Collectors requiring details of the all the variations issued should contact:
The Matchbox International Collectors Association (M.I.C.A.)
13a, Lower Bridge Street
Chester
Cheshire CH1 1RS England
Telephone: (01244) 346297

This new listing has been produced by the well known Models of Yesteryear authority Horace Dunkley, assisted by John Clark the experienced model trader.

Identification

Common features. Many models have common identifying features and these are shown below to avoid unnecessary repetition in the Features column.
Model name and number. Both 'Models of Yesteryear' and 'Made in England by Lesney' are cast underneath all models issued up to the end of 1982. With the change of ownership this was replaced by 'Matchbox Intl Ltd.' From 1987 'Made in Macau' appears on the base. All models have their 'Y' number shown underneath.

Wheels. All the wheels prior to 1970 were of metal construction. From 1972 (approximately), plastic wheels were used on all models. Nevertheless the models issued at this changeover period are to be found with either metal or plastic wheels. The varieties of wheels are:
Metal Spoked Wheels
Metal or Plastic Spoked Wheels
Plastic Bolt Head Wheels
Plastic Spoked Wheels
Solid Spoked Wheels

Scale of models ranges from 1:34 to 1:130. The scale of each model is usually shown on its box.

Logos and designs. The early models had waterslide transfers. Labels have also been used and currently models are tampo printed. The abbreviation 'RN' means 'racing (or rally) number'.
Catalogue listings. Do not place too much reliance on the model colours shown in catalogues. Very often the pictures shown are from mock-ups in colours never actually issued. For example, the 1969 catalogue showed a picture of a blue Y-5 Peugeot that was issued in yellow. Similarly the 1973 catalogue showed a silver Hispano Suiza which was then issued in red.
Bumpers, dashboards, headlights, radiator shells and windscreens. All assumed to be of metal construction prior to 1974 (approx.), after which plastic was increasingly used.
Base plate and chassis are usually of metal construction. Exceptions include the Y30 Mack Truck.
Tyres are of treaded black plastic unless otherwise indicated.
Seats are all made of plastic unless otherwise indicated.

Boxes

1956-57	All card box with just a plain black number shown on box ends. Line drawing of model on the front of box.
1957-60	All card box with line drawing used for first 15 models issued, blue number shown on white circle on endflap
1960-61	As first box but with a red number. All card box with coloured picture of the model (3 varieties of this box exist). All card box with model pictures on the box endflaps.
1968-69	Pink and yellow box with clear window.
1968-70	As previous box with hanging display card (developed in the US market and led to blister-pack design).
1969-70	Mauve and yellow box with window.
1974-78	'Woodgrain' window box in various colours
1979-83	'Straw' (light cream), window box.
1984-90	'Red' (maroon), window box.
1990	'New-style red'. Bigger, folded clear plastic
1993-94	New style direct mail high quality card boxes with full colour box model picture designs.
From 1995	Matchbox 'direct-mail' boxes have become more pictorial and specialised.

Market Price Range
NGPP = no price grading possible at present.
GSP = Gift Set price

Intro	Details	MPR		Intro	Details	MPR

Y1-1 Allchin Traction Engine

Scale 1:80. Early issues have rear wheel treads with a straight-across pattern, second type are diagonal; third type has a smooth tread.

1956	Green body, full gold trim, straight across treads on rear wheels. Copper boiler door	£150-200
	Green body, full gold trim, straight across treads on rear wheels. Green boiler door	£200-300
	Green body, full gold trim, angled treads on rear wheels. Copper boiler door	£70-90
	Green body, full gold trim. Red angled treads on rear wheels. Copper boiler door	£100-125
	Green body, full gold trim, angled treads on rear wheels. Gold boiler door	£70-90
	Green body, full gold trim. Red angled treads on rear wheels. Gold boiler door	£100-125
1960	Green body, full gold trim, angled treads on rear wheels. Green boiler door	£175-250
	Green body, partial gold trim, angled treads on rear wheels. Green boiler door	£175-250
	Green body, partial gold trim, angled treads on rear wheels. Gold boiler door	£70-90
1963	Green body, partial gold trim. Red angled treads on rear wheels. Gold boiler door	£100-125
	Green body, partial gold trim, angled treads on rear wheels. Silver boiler door	£90-110
	Green body, partial gold trim. Red angled treads on rear wheels. Silver boiler door	£120-145
1965	Green body, partial gold trim. Smooth rear wheels. Gold boiler door	£750-1000
	Green body, partial gold trim. Smooth rear wheels. Silver boiler door	£750-1000

Y1-3 1911 Ford Model 'T'

Scale 1:42.
All Y1-3 models have 'brass effect' finish wheels.

1964	Red body and chassis, 2 holes in base, Black smooth roof, twin brake lever	£90-120
	Red body and chassis, 2 holes in base, Black smooth roof, single brake lever	£10-20
	Red body and chassis, no holes in base, Black smooth roof, single brake lever	£10-20
	Red body and chassis, no holes in base, Black smooth roof, small wheels, single brake lever	£70-85
	Red body and chassis, no holes in base, Black textured roof, single brake lever	£80-100
1964	All models produced from this date had no base holes, only single brake levers and chrome effect finish wheels. Milky White body, Red chassis, Black textured roof, Bright Red seats, 12-spoke wheels	£80-100
	Milky White body, Red chassis, Black textured roof, Dark Red or Black seats, 12-spoke wheels	£80-100
	Milky White body, Red chassis, Dark Red textured roof, Dark Red or Black seats, 12-spoke wheels	£5-10
	Milky White body, Red chassis, Dark Red textured roof, Dark Red or Black seats, 24-spoke wheels	£5-10
	Milky White body, Red chassis, Dark Red textured roof, Bright Red seats, 12-spoke wheels	£15-25
	Black body and chassis, Black textured roof, Black seats, 12-spoke wheels	£300-350
1975	Cream body, Red chassis, Dark Red textured roof, Dark Red or Black seats, 12-spoke wheels	£5-10
	Cream body, Red chassis, Dark Red textured roof, Dark Red or Black seats, 24-spoke wheels	£5-10

Cream body, Red chassis, Dark Red textured roof,
Bright Red seats, 12-spoke wheels **£15-25**
1984 Black body and chassis, Black textured roof, Fawn seats,
Brass 12-spoke wheels (in 'Connoisseur Collection').......................GSP

Y1-3 1936 Jaguar SS100

Scale 1:38. All have Black seats and Chrome wheels with 12 or 24 spokes.

1977 Off-White body, small side lights, 24-spoke wheels **£165-175**
Light Cream body, large side lights, 24-spoke wheels **£5-10**
1978 Steel Grey body, large side lights, 24-spoke wheels **£125-150**
1979 Steel Blue body, large side lights, 12 or 24-spoke or solid wheels..**£5-10**
1981 Dark Green body, large side lights, 24-spoke wheels **£5-8**
1986 Pale Yellow body, large side lights, 24-spoke wheels **£50-60**
Yellow over sprayed Dark Green body, large side lights,
24-spoke wheels **£20-40**
NB   The above have 'Lesney' bases.
The following models all have large side lights and 24-spoke wheels.
1987 Dark Yellow body, 'Made in Macau' base **£8-12**
1991 Bright Red body, 'Made in China' base **£10-15**
1992 Model made entirely in pewter, mounted on wooden plinth........**£20-25**
1994 Bright Red body, Tan steering wheel, 'Made in China' base........**£15-20**

Y2-1 1911 'B'-type London Bus

Scale 1:100. The diecast driver may be found in any shade of mid or dark
blue, sometimes black.

1956 Red body, Grey wheels, 4 over 4 windows **£100-150**
The following models all have 8 over 4 windows.
1956 Red body, Grey wheels, bare metal ceiling **£65-85**
1958 Red body, Grey wheels, Tan ceiling **£65-85**
1959 Red body, Grey wheels, Tan ceiling, riveted axles.........................**£65-85**
1961 Red body, Black wheels, Tan ceiling, riveted axles **£75-95**

Y2-2 1911 Renault Two-Seater

Scale 1:40. Note that the red pigment used in the plastic seats is prone to
fading in bright light.

1963 Green body, 4-prong spare tyre carrier, gap at sides
between bonnet and radiator **£60-80**
1964 Green body, 4-prong spare tyre carrier, no bonnet/radiator gap.....**£20-30**
Green body, 3-prong spare tyre carrier, no bonnet/radiator gap.....**£15-25**
1968 Green body, Black plastic steering wheel **£10-20**

Y2-3 1914 'Prince Henry' Vauxhall

Scale 1:47. The model usually has 24-spoke wheels.

1970 Red body and chassis, Brass petrol tank.................................**£5-15**
Red body and chassis, Copper petrol tank................................**£250-300**
1975 Blue body and chassis, Copper petrol tank, Bright Red seats....**£450-650**
Blue body and chassis, Brass petrol tank, Cream seats................**£5-10**
Blue body and chassis, Copper petrol tank, Cream seats..............**£10-20**
1978 Blue body and chassis, 12-spoke Chrome wheels, Cream seats **£25-30**
1979 Bright Red body, Black chassis **£5-10**

Y2-4 1930 4½ litre Bentley

Scale 1:40.

1985 Dark Green body and chassis, 'Made in England' base...................**£5-7**
1988 Dark Green body and chassis, 'Made in Macau' base **£15-20**
1989 Dark Blue body and chassis, 'Made in Macau', plain White box..**£30-35**
1990 Dark Blue body and chassis, 'Made in Macau', window box.........**£8-12**
1991 Dark Blue body and chassis, 'Made in China' base....................**£20-30**
1991 Burgundy body and chassis, 'Made in China' base......................**£10-15**

Y3-1 1907 'E'-class Tramcar

Scale 1:130. All versions have a bright Red body with Yellow 'LONDON
TRANSPORT' fleetname and 'NEWS OF THE WORLD' decals.

1956 Cream roof, Silver lights, metal wheels, thin 'cowcatcher'
guards, gap under stairs, hole to top deck, Black base...............**£90-125**
Same but with Grey base **£150-250**
1957 Cream roof, Silver lights, metal wheels, thick 'cowcatcher'
guards, gap under stairs, hole to top deck, Black base...............**£80-100**
Cream roof, Gold lights, metal wheels, thick guards,
gap under Stairs, hole to top deck, Grey base **£150-250**

1958 Cream or White roof, Silver or Gold lights, metal wheels,
thick guards, partial gap or no gap under stairs, hole to
top deck, Black base **£50-65**
1962 White or Cream roof, Gold lights, Black plastic wheels.............**£60-70**
1965 White roof, Gold lights, Black plastic wheels,White guards **£90-120**

Y3-2 1910 Benz Limousine

Scale 1:54. The model usually has Dark Green or Dark Red seats and radiator
grille (exceptions noted).

1965 Cream body and chassis, Dark Green roof,
open rear mudguard struts..**£15-25**
Cream body and chassis, Dark Green roof,
closed rear mudguard struts...**£10-20**
1969 Cream body and chassis, Light Yellow roof.........................**£175-225**
Light Green body, Dark Green roof..............................**£175-225**
Light Green body, Light Yellow roof, open rear struts **£175-225**
Light Green body, Light Yellow roof, closed rear struts **£10-20**
Light Green body, Light Yellow roof, Black plastic
steering wheel **£10-20**
1970 Light Green body, Black roof, Light Green metal or
Black plastic steering wheel...**£90-125**
Dark Green body, Light Yellow roof, 2 holes in base **£250-300**
Dark Green body, Light Yellow roof, no holes in base **£350-400**
Dark Green body, Black roof, 2 holes in base or no holes...........**£20-25**
1984 Black body and chassis, Matt Black roof, Tan seats, Brown grille.
In Connoiseur Set ....GSP

Y3-3 1934 Riley MPH

Scale 1:35. Except where noted, models have Chrome 12 or 24-spoke wheels.

1974 Purple body and chassis, Black seats and grille **£175-225**
Purple body and chassis, Off-White seats and grille **£30-50**
1975 Ruby Red body and chassis, Black seats and grille,
Chrome 24-spoke wheels **£175-225**
Ruby Red body and chassis, Off-White seats............................**£10-15**
1976 Same but Bright Red body and chassis **£10-15**
1977 Light Red body and chassis, Off-White seats, Chrome 12 or
24-spoke or Red 12-spoke wheels....................................**£5-20**
1979 Blue body and chassis, RN '6', Chrome 12 or 24-spoke or
Red 12-spoke wheels **£5-20**
Blue body and chassis, RN '3', Chrome 24-spoke wheels **£30-35**

Y3-4 1912 Ford Model 'T' Tanker

Scale 1:35. **Except where noted**, wheels have 12 spokes; chassis and seats
are Black.

'BP'
1981 Green body, Red tank, 'No. Y12' cast on base,
'B.P.' with shadow effect **£90-120**
Same but without 'No. Y12' cast on base **£10-15**
Green body, Red tank, 'B.P.' without shadow effect.....................**£5-10**
Green body, Red tank, Black tank filler caps **£50-60**
Green body, Red tank, Gold or Chrome wheels **£15-25**

'ZEROLENE'
1981 Green body and tank, Gold or Red wheels...........................**£30-60**

'EXPRESS DAIRY'
1983 Blue body and tank, Gold, Red or Chrome wheels **£5-20**
Blue body and tank, Tan seat, Gold wheels............................**£20-25**

'CARNATION'
1984 Cream body, Plum Red tank and chassis, Bright Red
12 or 24-spoke or Gold 12-spoke wheels, 'Lesney' base........**£5-10**
Cream body, Plum Red tank and chassis, Pinkish Tan seat,
Bright Red 12-spoke wheels, 'Lesney' base.......................**£30-35**
Cream body, Plum Red tank and chassis, Bright Red
or Plum Red 12 spoke wheels, 'Matchbox Int'l' base **£5-15**

'MOBILOIL'
1985 Bright Red cab, Dark Blue tank, Red wheels...............................**£15-20**
Bright Red cab, Dark Blue tank, Pinkish Tan seat,
Red 12 or 24-spoke wheels **£5-15**

Matchbox 'Models of Yesteryear'

'CASTROL'
1986 Dark Green body and tank, Dark Tan, Pinkish Tan or
    Black seat, Maroon wheels, 'Lesney' base.....................**£10-20**
    Dark Green body and tank, Pinkish Tan seats,
    Gold wheels, 'Lesney' base....................................**£10-15**
    Dark Green body and tank, Dull Red, Maroon,
    Gold or Chrome wheels, 'Matchbox Int'l' base **£5-15**

'RED CROWN'
1986 Bright Red body and tank, 'Lesney' base.................**£15-20**
    Bright Red body and tank, Matchbox 'Limited Edition' base **£10-15**
    Bright Red body and tank, 'Matchbox © 1985' base.................**£25-30**
    Same but 'Matchbox ©1986' base **£10-15**

'SHELL'
1989 Yellow body and tank, Black chassis, 'Matchbox Macau' base **£5-10**

Y4-1 1928 Sentinel Steam Wagon

Scale 1:100. **'SAND & GRAVEL SUPPLIES'**. All have Black chassis.

1956 Blue cab and body, Grey metal wheels, crimped axles **£50-70**
    Blue cab and body, Grey metal wheels, riveted axles **£80-110**
    Blue cab and body, Black plastic wheels, riveted axles **£100-130**

Y4-2 1905 Shand-Mason Fire Engine

Scale 1:63. All have Red metal body, two horses, three plastic firemen, and metal wheels (13 spokes front, 15 rear).

1960 'Kent' Fire Brigade, Grey Horses, Dark Grey or
    White manes and tails **£450-600**
    'Kent' Fire Brigade, White horses...................**£125-150**
1963 'London' Fire Brigade, White horses, hose locker horizontal ...**£175-225**
    'London' Fire Brigade, White horses, no hose locker ribs **£100-125**
1965 'London' Fire Brigade, Bronze horses **£250-300**
    'London' Fire Brigade, Black horses...........................**£100-150**

Y4-3 1909 Opel Coupé

Scale 1:38.

1967 White body and chassis, roof to body pins,
    Maroon grille and seats.............................**£100-125**
    Same but with Red grille, Maroon seats...............**£20-30**
1968 White body and chassis, roof to body pins, Red grille and seats...**£10-15**
1970 White body and chassis, roof to seat pins, Red grille and seats.....**£10-15**
    Same but with Maroon seats.........................**£10-20**
1971 White body and chassis, Tan textured roof with rear window,
    Red seats...**£300-350**
    Same but with Maroon seats.........................**£325-375**
1975 Orange body, gloss Black chassis, Black textured roof,
    Maroon seats......................................**£25-30**
    Same but with matt Black chassis **£5-10**
1984 Bright Red body, Dark Red chassis, Tan textured roof,
    Ruby Red seats, in Connoisseur Set ....GSP

Y4-4 1930 Duesenberg 'J' Town Car

Scale 1:43. **Except where noted**, hood colour is the same as the seat colour.

1976 White body, Orange-Red or Red chassis, Yellow seats........**£1750-2000**
    White body, Orange-Red or Red chassis, Black seats...........**£1750-2000**
1976 Dark Red body and chassis, Black seats, hollow air horns............**£15-20**
    Dark Red body and chassis, Black seats, solid air horns **£10-15**
    Dark Red body and chassis, Black seats,
    Chrome 12-spoke wheels..............................**£20-25**
    Dark Red body and chassis, Maroon seats...........**£200-250**
    Dark Red body and chassis, Dark Green seats................**£90-120**
1979 Light Green body and chassis, Lime Green side and rear panels,
    Dark Green seats, solid or 24-spoke Chrome wheels..............**£75-85**
    Light Green body and chassis, Lime Green rear panel only,
    Dark Green hood seats, solid or 24-spoke Chrome wheels............**£5-10**
    Light Green body and chassis, Lime Green side panels,
    Black seats...**£15-20**
1983 Brown body and chassis, Dark Cream side panels, Light Cream,
    Beige or Rust Brown seats, Chrome 24-spoke or
    solid wheels, 'Lesney' or 'Matchbox Int'l' base **£5-10**
1986 Silver body, Blue chassis and side panels, Black seats,
    Blue 24-spoke wheels, 'Matchbox Int'l England' base...............**£5-10**
    Same but with 'Matchbox Int'l Macau' base **£25-30**
    Same but with 'Matchbox Int'l China' base.....................**£15-20**

1989 Powder Blue body, Dark Blue chassis, Off White hood, Tan seats,
    Chrome 24-spoke wheels, 'Matchbox Int'l Macau' base................**£5-10**
    Same but with 'Matchbox Int'l China' base....................**£10-15**
1997 Maroon body, Dark Tan chassis and seats, Black hood,
    'Matchbox Int'l China' base **£20-25**

Y5-1 1929 Le Mans Bentley

Scale 1:55. All are finished in British Racing Green

1958 British Racing Green body, Grey folded hood, Silver radiator ..**£120-130**
    Same but with Gold radiator.......................**£130-150**
1959 British Racing Green body and folded hood, Gold radiator..........**£50-75**
    Same but with Green radiator.......................**£70-80**
1960 British Racing Green body and folded hood,
    Gold radiator, riveted axles...........................**£50-75**
1961 Same but steering wheel is also in British Racing Green **£80-100**

Y5-2 1929 4½ litre Bentley

Scale 1:52. Model has Union Jacks and racing numbers on its sides, folded windscreen and silver 24-spoke wheels, (spare on nearside).

1962 Apple Green body, Black RN '5', Green or
    Dark Red seats and tonneau........................**£250-300**
1963 British Racing Green body, Black RN '5', Green seats **£35-45**
    Same but with Dark Red seats.......................**£50-60**
    Same but with Bright Red seats.......................**£20-25**
1968 British Racing Green body, Bright Red seats, Black RN '3' **£45-60**
    Same but with Red RN '6'...........................**£85-100**

Y5-3 1907 Peugeot

Scale 1:43. Except where noted, the model has 12-spoke wheels.

1969 Yellow body and chassis, Black roof, no rib on rear edge of
    front seat side panels...................................**£75-85**
    Yellow body and chassis, Black roof, cast rib on rear edge of
    front seat side panels, Dark Orange windows...................**£10-20**
    Same but with Pale Amber windows...................**£10-20**
    Same but with Clear windows.......................**£130-150**
1975 Yellow body and chassis, Gold roof, Pale Amber windows **£130-150**
    Orange-Gold body, Matt Black roof, Pale Amber windows **£100-125**
    Orange-Gold body and roof, Pale Amber windows **£10-15**
    Orange-Gold body and roof, Dark Orange windows **£10-15**
1976 Light Gold body, matt Black roof, Pale Amber windows **£100-125**
    Same but with Light Gold roof.......................**£10-15**
1977 Light Gold body and roof, Clear windows,
    Chrome 12 or 24-spoke wheels **£130-150**

Y5-4 1927 Talbot Van

Scale 1:47.

'LIPTONS TEA' (with royal crest)
1978 Dark Green body, matt Black chassis and roof,
    shadow effect to Light Yellow 'Liptons Tea' **£40-50**
    Dark Green body, gloss Black chassis, matt Black roof,
    shadow effect to Light Yellow 'Liptons Tea' **£7-12**
    Same but without shadow effect to 'Liptons Tea' **£35-40**
    Dark Green body, gloss Black chassis, matt Black roof, shadow
    effect to 'Liptons Tea', Chrome 12 or 24-spoke wheels **£20-25**

'LIPTONS TEA' (with City Road address)
1978 Dark Green body, matt Black roof, 'Liptons Tea' with
    shadow effect, Dark Green or Olive Green 12-spoke wheels **£50-60**
    Dark Green body, matt Black roof, no shadow effect to
    'Liptons Tea, Dark Green 12-spoke wheels **£5-10**
    Same but with Olive Green 12-spoke wheels................**£10-15**
    Same but with Chrome 12-spoke wheels.....................**£15-25**
    Same but with Chrome 24-spoke wheels.....................**£15-25**
    Dark Green body, gloss Black roof,
    Olive Green 12-spoke wheels.......................**£30-35**
    Dark Green body, Olive Green 12-spoke wheels,
    Lime Green tampo printing, gloss or matt Black roof **£40-50**

'CHOCOLAT MENIER'
1978-79 Royal Blue body, gloss Black chassis, Off-White
    tampo printing, Chrome 12-spoke wheels **£15-20**
    Royal Blue body, gloss Black chassis, Light Yellow
    tampo printing, Chrome 12-spoke wheels **£5-8**
    Same but with Chrome 24-spoke wheels................**£15-20**

Same but with Red 12-spoke wheels..£15-25
Same but with solid Red wheels...£20-30
Same but with Dark Green 12-spoke wheels............................£20-30

'TAYSTEE BREAD'
1980 Bright Yellow body and chassis, Bright Red or
     Dark Red 12-spoke wheels..£5-8
     Same but with Black chassis..£5-10
     Same but with solid Red wheels....................................£15-20

'NESTLES'
1981 Blue body and Black chassis, matt Black roof..........................£230-250
     Same but with gloss Black roof....................................£330-350
     Same but with Dark Grey roof...£5-10
     Same but with Light Grey roof......................................£30-45

'CHIVERS'
1982 Cream body, Dark Green chassis, Black seat, Brass trim,
     Dark Red or Bright Red 12-spoke wheels..........................£5-8
     Same but with Tan seat, Bright Red 12-spoke wheels.............£10-15
     With Black seat, Chrome trim, Bright Red 12-spoke wheels.......£10-15

'WRIGHTS'
1982 Dark Brown body and roof, Beige chassis, Gold trim and
     12-spoke wheels...£250-280
     Same but with Beige roof and chassis................................£5-8
     Same but with Chrome trim and 12-spoke wheels...................£15-20
     Same but with or Chrome trim and Gold 12-spoke wheels..........£15-20

'EVER READY'
1983 Dark Blue body, Gloss Black chassis, Tan or Black seats............£5-8
     Same but with Pinkish Tan seats...................................£10-15

'DUNLOP'
1984 Black body and chassis, Dark Yellow 12-spoke wheels,
     Tan or Black seats...£5-15
     Same but with Light Yellow 12-spoke wheels.......................£35-45

'ROSES'
1985 Light Cream body, Bright Green chassis and roof,
     Black or Tan seats...£5-25
1986 Light Cream body, Dark Green chassis, Bright Green roof,
     Black or Tan seats...£5-25
1987 Light Cream body, Bright Green chassis and roof,
     Red 12-spoke wheels...£10-25
1988 Light Green body, Bright Green chassis and roof,
     'Matchbox Int'l Macau' base.......................................£25-30

'LYLES'
     Bright Green body, Black chassis, Gold 12-spoke wheels..........£5-10
     Same but with Black 12-spoke wheels..............................£20-25

Y5-5 1929 Leyland Titan Bus
Scale 1:76.

'SOUTHDOWN'
1989 Light Green body, Mid-Green chassis, 'Robin Starch' adverts........£8-15

'ASHTON-under-LYNE'
1990 Blue body, Black chassis, 'Swan Fountpens' adverts.
     Passport Scheme model available in framed cabinet only...........£60-70

'CITY of COVENTRY'
1991 Maroon body, Black chassis, 'Newcastle Brown Ale' adverts.......£8-12

Y6-1 1916 AEC 'Y' type Lorry
Scale 1:100. 'OSRAM LAMPS'

1957 Pale Blue cab, body and chassis, Grey metal wheels,
     crimped axles, Gold or Siver radiator............................£1800-2000
     Mid Blue cab, body and chassis, Grey metal wheels,
     crimped axles, Silver radiator...................................£1800-2000
     Light Grey cab, body and chassis, Grey metal wheels,
     crimped axles, Gold radiator......................................£100-120
     Same but with Silver radiator.....................................£80-100

1958 Dark Grey cab, body and chassis, Grey metal wheels,
     crimped axles, Silver radiator....................................£140-160
     Same but with riveted axles.......................................£120-140
1961 Dark Grey cab, body and chassis, Black plastic wheels,
     riveted axles, Silver radiator...................................£1400-1500

Y6-2 1935 Type 35 Bugatti
Scale 1:48. Model has a black baseplate and gold 8-spoke wheels with a spare on the nearside. Racing number '6' may be upside-down and appear as '9'.

1961 French Blue body, Gold radiator grille, Red dashboard,
     Grey knobbly tyres..£100-120
     Same but with Black knobbly tyres..................................£30-40
     Same but with smooth Black tyres...................................£20-30
     With French Blue body and grille, Black knobbly tyres.............£150-175
     Same but with smooth Black tyres..................................£150-175
1965 French Blue body, Gold radiator grille, White dashboard.........£350-400
     Italian Racing Red body, Gold radiator grille, White dashboard...£20-30
     Same but with Italian Racing Red radiator grille.................£150-175
     Italian Racing Red body, Gold grille, Black dashboard............£400-450

Y6-3 1913 Cadillac
Scale 1:48. Except where noted, the model has 12-spoke wheels.

1968 Light Gold body, smooth Dark Red roof, no lug on windscreen,
     no seat pin cut outs, no pips on hood............................£100-120
     Same but with pips on hood...£40-50
     Same but with lug on windscreen....................................£30-40
     Same but with seat pin cut outs....................................£20-25
     Light Gold body, smooth Dark Red roof, lug on windscreen,
     seat pin cut outs, pips on hood, smaller (11mm dia.) wheels.......£50-60
1970 Dark Gold body, textured Dark Red roof...........................£80-100
     Same but with smooth Dark Red roof.................................£15-25
1975 Dark Gold body, Chrome 12-spoke wheels,
     thick spare tyre carrier..£80-100
     Green body, textured Black roof, thin spare tyre carrier..........£80-100
     Same but with thick spare tyre carrier, Chrome 12-spoke wheels....£5-10
     Same but with Chrome 24-spoke wheels..............................£10-15
     Same but with Red or Yellow 12-spoke wheels.......................£10-15

Y6-4 1920 Rolls-Royce Fire Engine
Scale 1:48. Except where noted, the chassis is the same colour as the body.

1977 Bright Red body, White ladder with small lugs,
     no lugs on body for label..£130-150
     Same but with Brown or Orange ladder with small lugs.............£100-120
     Same but with 12-spoke Gold wheels................................£80-100
     Bright Red body, Brown or Orange ladder with small lugs,.....lugs
     on body for label, Gold 12-spoke or Chrome 24-spoke wheels.....£15-25
1978 Bright Red body, White, Brown or Orange ladder with large lugs,
     Gold 12-spoke wheels...£7-15
     Same but with Chrome 24-spoke or Red 12-spoke wheels.............£15-20
1983 Red body, Red seats, White, Brown or Orange ladder,
     bronzed metal side seats or Black plastic side seats............£250-300
1984 Darker Red body, Black chassis, Black seats, White ladder,
     Gold 12-spoke or Chrome 12-spoke wheels............................£5-15

Y6-5 1932 Mercedes-Benz L5 Lorry
Scale 1:69.

'STUTTGARTER HOFBRAU'
1988 Cream body and cab, Black steps and mudguards, Grey chassis,
     deep body planking...£5-10
1989 Same but with shallow body planking...............................£5-10

Y7-1 1918 Leyland 4-ton Van
Scale 1:100. 'W. & R. Jacob & Co. Ltd.'

1957 Dark Brown body, bare metal wheels, White roof..................£100-120
     Same but with Cream roof...£80-110
     Lighter Brown body, bare metal wheels, Cream roof,
     middle line of body transfers missing............................£550-600
     Same but with complete transfer...................................£75-100
1959 Reddish Brown body, bare metal wheels, Cream roof................£75-100
1960 Same but with Black plastic wheels, 24-tread pattern on
     front wheels, 32-tread pattern on rear wheels....................£800-900

Y7-2 1913 Mercer Raceabout type 35J

Scale 1:46.

1961 Pale Lilac body and chassis, Black knobbly tread tyres £25-65
1963 Light Lilac body and chassis, Black fine tread tyres £25-30
1965 Yellow body and chassis, Gold radiator £25-30
      Same but with Yellow radiator £30-50
NB On 1961-1963 issues, colour can vary from almost
      Silver (early issues) to Light Lilac (late issues).

Y7-3 1912 Rolls-Royce

Scale 1:48.

1968 Silver body and bonnet, Dark Red chassis and smooth roof,
      Brass 12-spoke wheels, Dark Red seats £15-20
      Same but with Yellow seats £850-900
1969 Silver body and bonnet, Dark Red chassis, Grey ribbed roof,
      Brass 12-spoke wheels, Dark Red seats £75-125
      Same but with Dark Red ribbed roof £10-20
1974 Silver body and bonnet, Dark Red chassis and ribbed roof,
      Dark Red seats, Chrome 12-spoke wheels £75-125
      Gold body, Silver bonnet, Red chassis and ribbed roof,
      Dark Red or Black seats, Brass 12-spoke wheels £75-125
      Gold body and bonnet, Red chassis and ribbed roof,
      Dark Red or Black seats, Chrome 12-spoke wheels £5-10
      Same but with Chrome 24-spoke wheels £10-20
      Gold body and bonnet, Red chassis and ribbed roof,
      Green seats and grille, Chrome 12-spoke wheels £250-300
1979 Yellow body and bonnet, Red chassis, Black ribbed roof
      and seats, Gold 12-spoke wheels £300-350
      Yellow body and bonnet, Black chassis, roof and seats,
      Gold or Chrome 12-spoke wheels £8-12
      Same but with Red 12-spoke or Chrome 24-spoke wheels £12-18

Y7-4 1930 Ford Model 'A' Breakdown Truck

Scale 1:40.

'BARLOW MOTOR SALES'
1985 Orange body, Black chassis and roof, Green crane,
      'Made in England' base £5-10
      Same but with 'Made in Macau' base £25-30

'SHELL'
1988 Yellow body, Black chassis and roof, Light Green crane £5-10
      Same but with Grey crane £15-20

Y8-1 1926 Morris Cowley

Scale 1:50.

1958 Tan body, Dark Brown chassis, Silver or Light Copper wheels £60-90

Y8-2 1914 Sunbeam Motorcycle and Sidecar

Scale 1:34

1962 Chrome plated motorcycle and sidecar, bare metal wheels,
      Black motorcycle seat, Dark Green sidecar seat £35-60
      Same but Pale Gold plated motorcycle and sidecar £600-650
1967 Chrome plated motorcycle and sidecar, bare metal wheels,
      Black motorcycle seat, Emerald Green sidecar seat £250-300
      or Black sidecar seat £250-300

Y8-3 1914 Stutz Roadster

Scale 1:48.
1969 Dark Red body and chassis, smooth Tan roof £10-20
      Same but with textured Tan roof £30-35
1973 Blue body and chassis, Black textured roof,
      White seats and grille £10-20
      Same but with Bright Red seats and grille £35-45

Y8-4 1945 MG 'TC'

Scale 1:35

1978 Dark Green body and chassis, Tan roof, Chrome 24-spoke wheels,
      Red seats £10-15
      Same but with Tan seats £30-35

      Same but with Red seats, Green 12-spoke wheels £15-20
      Same but with Red seats, Red 12-spoke wheels £25-35
1981 Bright Red body and chassis, Chrome 24-spoke wheels,
      Tan or Rust Brown top, Black seats £5-10
      Same but with Tan top, Red seats £20-25
      With Tan roof, solid wheels £10-15
1982 Darker Red body and chassis, Chrome 24-spoke wheels,
      Tan or Rust Brown top, Black seats £5-10
      Same but with Tan top, Red seats £20-25
1983 Blue body and chassis, Chrome 24-spoke wheels,
      Tan or Rust Brown top, Tan seats £5-10
      Same but with Rust Brown top and Black seats £10-15
1984 Cream body and Dark Brown chassis, Chrome 24-spoke wheels,
      Tan or Rust Brown top, Tan or Black seats £5-10

Y8-5 1917 Yorkshire Steam Wagon

Scale 1:61.

'JOHNNIE WALKER'
1987 Strawberry Red cab and body, Black chassis, Bright Red
      lettering on truck canopy, 2 rivets in cab roof £110-120
      Same but with 3 rivets in cab roof £45-50
      Same but Maroon lettering on canopy, 3 rivets in cab roof ... £8-12

'SAMUEL SMITH'
1989 Green cab and body, Black chassis. Passport Scheme model,
      available in framed cabinet with nickle-plated components ... £60-70

'WILLIAM PRITCHARD'
1989 Dark Blue cab and body, Black chassis £8-12

'FYFFES'
Yellow cab and bonnet, Navy Blue chassis £8-10

Y9-1 1924 Fowler Showman's Engine

Scale 1:80. **'Lesney's Modern Amusements'**.

1958 Dark Maroon body, Cream roof, Yellow wheels,
      Gold cylinder block £150-200
      Same but with Dark Maroon cylinder block £80-140
      Light Purple body, Cream roof, Yellow wheels,
      Gold cylinder block £250-300
      Same but with Light Purple cylinder block £250-300
1960 Maroon body and cylinder block, Yellow wheels, Cream roof £65-85
      Same but with White roof £100-120
1965 Bright Red body and cylinder block, Yellow wheels,
      Cream roof £100-120
      Same but with White roof £80-100

Y9-2 1912 Simplex

Scale 1:48. Except where noted, the model is fitted with 12-spoke wheels.

1968 Lime Green body and chassis £30-45
1969 Mid Green body, Bright Red seats, smooth Tan roof £10-15
      Same but with Light Yellow seats £300-350
      Same but with Bright Red seats, textured Tan roof £25-40
1970 Gold body, Dark Red chassis, Black textured roof, Brass wheels .. £20-35
      Same but with Chrome 12-spoke wheels £30-45
      Same but with Brass 12-spoke wheels and Bright Red chassis .. £85-110
1975 Red body & chassis, Black textured roof, Chrome or Red wheels .. £8-20
1979 Dark Red body, Black chassis, Black textured roof,
      Bright Yellow seats, Red or Chrome 12-spoke wheels
      or Chrome 24-spoke wheels £8-12
1983 Dark Red body, Black chassis, Yellow textured roof,
      Yellow seats, Red 12-spoke wheels £8-12
      Same but with Orange-Yellow textured roof £10-15
      Same but with Orange-Yellow textured roof and seats £10-20
1986 Yellow body and bonnet, gloss Black chassis, plastic diorama
      in box, 'Made in England', Yellow or Black textured roof ... £8-10
1988 Darker Yellow body and bonnet, gloss Black chassis, diorama in
      box, 'Made in Macau', Yellow or Black textured roof £275-300

Y9-3 1920 Leyland 3-ton Lorry

Scale 1:62

1985 Dark Green cab and truck body, Bright Red chassis £15-20

Y9-4 1936 Leyland Cub Fire Engine FK-7

Scale 1:49. 'Special Limited Edition' model, 1989.

1989 Bright Red cab and body, Black roof, Red escape ladders,
'Made in Macau' **£55-60**

Y10-1 1908 'Grand Prix' Mercedes

Scale 1:54.

1958 Cream body, Black baseplate, Light Green seats **£60-95**
Same but with White body..**£150-220**
1959 Cream body, Black baseplate, Dark Green seats **£60-95**
Same but with White body..**£130-180**

Y10-2 1928 Mercedes-Benz 36-220

Scale 1:52

1963 White body and chassis, twin spare wheels, 2 holes in base,
Black seats and folded top...............................**£1500-1800**
Same but with Red seats and folded top..........................**£40-50**
White body and chassis, single spare wheel, 2 holes in base,
Red seats and folded top **£30-35**
Same but with twin spare wheels, no holes in base **£55-60**
Same but with single spare wheel, no holes in base.......**£20-30**

Y10-3 1906 Rolls-Royce Silver Ghost

Scale 1:51.

1969 Lime Green body, Bronze chassis, Dark Red seats and grille.......**£15-25**
1974 White body, Purple or Ruby Red chassis, Black seats and grille,
Chrome 12-spoke wheels...**£8-12**
With Chrome 24-spoke wheels or Red 12-spoke wheels **£15-18**
1979 Silver body, Purple chassis, Black seats and grille,
Chrome 12-spoke wheels...**£350-400**
Silver body and chassis, Black seats and grille,
Chrome 12-spoke wheels or Red 12-spoke wheels **£5-10**
1980 Silver body and chassis, Dark Reddish Brown seats and grille,
Red 12-spoke wheels or Chrome 12-spoke wheels...........**£5-10**
1981 Silver body and chassis, Yellow seats, Black grille,
Red 12-spoke wheels **£15-30**
Same but with Chrome 12 or 24-spoke wheels **£35-50**
1983 Silver body and chassis, Off-White seats, Black grille,
Red 12-spoke wheels **£350-400**

Y10-4 1957 Maserati 250F

Scale 1:35.

1986 Red body and chassis, no copyright date on base,
Chrome 24-spoke wheels or Aluminium 24-spoke wheels **£10-15**
Same but with copyright date cast on base.......................**£5-10**

Y10-5 1931 'Diddler' Trolley-Bus

Scale 1:76. **'London Transport'**. 'Special Limited Edition' model, 1988.

1988 Red body and Black chassis, 'Ronuk' adverts **£15-25**

Y11-1 1920 Aveling & Porter Steam Roller

Scale 1:80.

1958 Mid-Green body, boiler and roof, Black roof supports **£70-90**
Same but with Mid-Green roof supports **£70-90**
Mid Green body, boiler, roof and roof supports,
Gold makers plate (on front of cylinder housing) **£300-350**

Y11-2 1912 Packard Landaulet

Scale 1:50.

1964 Dark Red body and chassis, Black bonnet,
4-prong spare tyre carrier **£15-40**
Same but with 3-prong spare tyre carrier **£15-20**
1971 Orange-Red body and chassis, Black bonnet,
3-prong spare tyre carrier..**£20-30**

1984 Cream body and bonnet, Black roof, very Dark Brown chassis.
Only available in 'Connoisseur Collection'......................................GSP

Y11-3 1938 Lagonda Drophead Coupé

Scale 1:43. Except where noted, this model is fitted with 24-spoke wheels.

1972 Gold body, Black seats, floor etc, with Purple chassis.............**£700-750**
With Dark Red chassis..**£250-300**
With Strawberry Red chassis......................................**£230-280**
With Light Maroon chassis...**£130-180**
With Dark Maroon chassis..**£20-30**
1974 Orange body, Gold chassis, Black seats,
Brass (narrow section) 24-spoke wheels........................**£125-150**
Same but with Chrome (wide section) 24-spoke wheels.................**£7-15**
1975 Copper body, Gold chassis, Black seats, Chrome wheels **£7-15**
Same but with Red or Chrome 12-spoke wheels.............**£12-20**
1978 Copper body, Gold chassis, Maroon seats, Chrome wheels...........**£7-15**
Same but with Red 12-spoke wheels................................**£12-20**
Copper body, Gold chassis, Bright Red seats,
Chrome 24-spoke wheels **£300-350**
1979 Copper body, Black chassis, Maroon seats,
Chrome solid wheels...**£200-250**
Dark Cream body, Gold chassis, Maroon seats,
Chrome 24-spoke wheels **£200-250**
Dark Cream body, Black chassis, Maroon seats,
Chrome 12 or 24-spoke wheels or Red 12-spoke wheels **£7-15**
Same but with Chrome solid wheels.................................**£5-10**
1983 Dark Cream body, Black chassis, Black seats,
Chrome solid wheels or Chrome 24-spoke wheels **£25-35**
1985 Maroon body and chassis, Gold 24-spoke wheels,
Black or Maroon seats. In 1985 'Fathers Day' Set ....GSP

Y11-4 1932 Bugatti type 51

Scale 1:35.
1986 Blue body, Brown seats, Aluminium wheels, Black RN '4' **£5-10**

Y11-5 1927 Bugatti type 35

Scale 1:35
1990 Light Blue body, Black seats, Chrome wheels, White RN '6' **£5-10**

Y12-1 1899 Horse-drawn Bus

Scale 1:100.

1959 Red body and chassis, Brown horses, drawbar fixed to body
with single rivet (narrow end)......................................**£70-90**
Red body and chassis, Dark Brown horses, drawbar fixed to
body with double rivets (square end)..........................**£60-70**

Y12-2 1909 Thomas Flyabout

Scale 1:48.
1967 Blue body and chassis, smooth Tan roof, Yellow seats and
grille, roof - to - body pins..**£800-900**
Same but with Dark Red seats and grille..........................**£15-25**
Blue body and chassis, Dark Red seats and grille,
roof - to - seat pins, smooth Tan roof **£10-20**
Same but with textured Tan roof......................................**£20-30**
1975 Purple-Red body and chassis, Off-White seats, Black grille,
textured Black roof, Chrome 12-spoke wheels..............**£10-20**
Same but with Chrome 24-spoke wheels...........................**£15-25**
Ruby Red body and chassis, Off-White seats, Black grille,
textured Black roof, Chrome 12-spoke wheels..............**£10-20**
Same but with Chrome 24-spoke wheels...........................**£15-25**

Y12-3 1912 Ford Model 'T' Van

Scale 1:35.

'COCA COLA'
1979 Off-White body, Black chassis, 5 vertical Red printed lines,
Chrome trim **£350-400**
Same but with Gold trim...**£350-400**
Off-White body, Black chassis, 4 vertical Red printed lines,
Black seats, Red 12-spoke wheels **£25-30**
Same but with Tan seat...**£50-60**
Same but with Black seats, Chrome 12 or 24-spoke wheels.........**£50-60**
With Black seats and Light Gold 24-spoke wheels.......................**£60-70**

'COLMANS MUSTARD'
1979 Yellow body, Black chassis, matt Black roof, Red single line
rear doors, 'No, Y12' cast on base, Red 12-spoke wheels..............**£5-10**
Same but with Chrome 12 or 24-spoke wheels............................**£20-25**
1981 Yellow body, Black chassis, matt Black roof, Red double lines
on rear doors, 'No,Y12' not cast on base, Red 12-spoke wheels....**£5-15**
Same but with Gold 12-spoke wheels **£20-25**
Same but with Red 12-spoke wheels and gloss Black roof...........**£35-45**

'TAYSTEE'
1980 Yellow body, Black chassis, matt Black roof, Red single line
rear doors, 'No. Y12' cast on base, Red 12-spoke wheels.........**£375-400**
NB There are known to be fakes which have the smaller labels as
used on the Y5-4 Talbot Van. Genuine 'Taystee' labels for the
Ford Model 'T' Van measure 29mm end to end of 'Taystee' oval
and 11mm top to bottom of the oval.

'SUZE'
1980 Yellow body, Black chassis, matt Black roof, Black single line
on rear doors, 'No. Y12' cast on base, Red 12-spoke wheels..........**£5-10**
Same but with Chrome 12 or 24-spoke wheels............................**£20-25**
1981 Yellow body, Black chassis, matt Black roof, Black double lines
on rear doors, 'No. Y12' not cast on base, Red 12-spoke wheels ..**£5-10**
Same but with Gloss Black roof, Black double lines rear doors....**£35-40**
Same but with Gloss Black roof, Red double lines rear doors...**£135-150**

'SMITHS CRISPS'
1981 Blue body, Black chassis, White roof, single line White rear doors,
'No. Y12' cast on base, Tan seats....................**£5-10**
Same but with Black seats.......................................**£15-20**
Blue body, Black chassis, White roof, 'No. Y12' cast on base,
Tan seats, double lines White rear doors **£15-20**
Same but with 'No. Y12' not cast on base.....................**£5-10**
Blue body, Black chassis, White roof, 'No. Y12' not cast on base,
Black seats, double lines White rear doors.................**£15-25**

'25 YEARS SILVER JUBILEE'
1981 Light Green body, Dark Green chassis, Grey roof, Yellow
12-spoke wheels, 'No. Y12' cast on base,
Silver single line rear doors...........................**£350-400**
Same but with Silver double lines rear doors.................**£15-20**
Light Green body, Dark Green chassis, Grey roof, 'No. Y12' not
cast on base, Silver double lines rear doors,
Yellow 12-spoke wheels **£5-10**
Same but with Chrome or Red 12-spoke wheels...............**£10-15**
Same but with Yellow 24-spoke wheels.......................**£70-75**

'BIRDS CUSTARD'
1982 Blue body, Black chassis, Yellow roof, Red 12-spoke wheels,
Yellow double lines rear doors, Black or Tan seats........................**£5-12**
Metallic Blue body, Black chassis, Yellow roof, Red 12-spoke
wheels, Yellow double lines rear doors, Black seats.................**£80-120**
Blue body, Black chassis, Yellow roof, Yellow 12-spoke wheels,
Yellow double lines rear doors, Back seats..........................**£25-35**
Blue body, Black chassis, Yellow roof, cast rear doors outline,
Black or Tan seats, Red 12-spoke wheels..............................**£5-12**
Same but with Chrome 12-spoke wheels...............................**£25-30**

'CEREBOS'
1982 Light Blue body, Black chassis, Yellow roof, Gold components,
Red 12-spoke wheels **£200-250**
With Chrome components, Red or Gold 12-spoke wheels **£200-250**
Light Blue body, Black chassis, White roof, Gold components,
Black seat, Gold 12-spoke wheels **£5-12**
Same but with Tan seat **£65-75**
With Black seat and Red or Chrome 12-spoke wheels **£5-12**

'ARNOTTS'
1982 Bright Red body, Black chassis, gloss Black roof....................**£125-145**
Same but with matt Black roof **£110-120**
NB This model can have double labels applied on one or both
sides. Such examples usually attract a premium of **£5-10**

'HARRODS'
1982 Dark Green body, Black chassis, Khaki roof, Black seats,
Cream double lines rear doors **£5-10**
Same but cast rear doors outline, Black or Tan seats **£5-10**
Same but with Pale Cream seats **£10-15**

'SUNLIGHT SEIFE'
1983 Yellow body, Black chassis, matt Black roof, Black seats,
Red 12-spoke wheels, Red double lines rear doors......................**£80-85**

NB 'Sunlight' models exist with fake labels. Genuine labels have a clothes
line post to the right of the woman hanging out the washing.

'ROYAL MAIL'
1983 Bright Red body, Black chassis and roof, Yellow double lines
rear doors, Red or Gold 12-spoke wheels...................................**£210-250**
Post Office Red body, Black chassis and roof, cast rear
doors outline Red or Gold 12-spoke wheels.................**£5-10**
Same but with Chrome 12 or 24-spoke wheels **£10-15**

'CAPTAIN MORGAN'
1983 Black body and chassis, White roof, one piece label covering
cab doors and body sides, Tan seats, Gold 12-spoke wheels **£5-10**
Same but with Black seats **£45-50**
With Red 12-spoke wheels and Black seats **£50-55**
1984 Black body and chassis, White roof, two piece labels, one for
cab doors, one for body sides, Tan seats, Gold 12-spoke wheels **£5-10**
Same but with Black seats **£45-50**
Same but with Tan seats, cast hole in rear base of body **£60-70**
Same but with Black seats, cast hole in rear base of body..........**£90-100**

'HOOVER'
1983 Blue body, Black chassis, White roof, Black seats,
with certificate **£600-650**
Same but without certificate **£400-450**
Orange body, Black chassis and roof, Black seats,
Black 12-spoke wheels **£5-10**
Same but with Tan seats **£40-50**
With Black seats, cast hole in rear base of body **£5-10**
With Black seats, Black 24-spoke wheels **£10-15**

'PEPSI COLA'
1984 White body, Blue chassis, Red roof, Chrome 12 or 24-spoke
wheels or with Red 12-spoke wheels....................**£5-10**
NB This model can have either 'Lesney' Products or 'Matchbox
International' cast on their bases.

'MOTOR 100'
1985 Bronze body, Dark Brown chassis, Dull Red 12-spoke wheels,
world globe with White land, Blue oceans, with certificate **£35-45**
Same but without certificate **£5-10**
Same but with Red or Gold 12-spoke wheels **£5-10**
With Dull-Red 12-spoke wheels, Blue land, White oceans **£480-530**

'IMBACH' (Truck)
1985 Blue body, Black chassis, Tan seat, Gold 12-spoke wheels **£5-12**
Same but with Red 12-spoke wheels **£15-25**

'HEINZ'
1986 Light Greenish-Grey body and roof, Dark Green chassis,
'Lesney Products' base **£250-300**
Very Pale Greenish-Grey body and roof, Dark Green chassis,
'Matchbox International' base **£5-15**
NB Many variations of this model are known to exist with different
wheels. All are 12-spoke design finished in Maroon, Dark Red,
Bright Red, Dull Red or Gold. Base plates can be © 1985 or © 1986.

'ROSELLA'
Dark Blue body, Black chassis, Yellow roof **£5-40**
NB Many variations are known to exist with different wheels.
All are 12-spoke design finished in Maroon, Dark Red, Bright Red,
Gold or Chrome. Base plates can be 'Lesney Products' or
'Matchbox International Limited Edition', © 1985 or © 1986

Y12-4 1829 Stephenson's 'Rocket'

Scale 1:64 ('S' gauge).

1987 Yellow body and tender, Black chassis, 'Made in Macau'............**£8-12**

Y12-5 1937 GMC Van

Scale 1:45.

'GOBLIN'
1988 Black body and chassis, Grey roof **£10-20**
Same but with Black roof **£5-10**

'BAXTERS'
1989 Cream body and roof, Dark Green chassis **£5-10**

'GOANNA'
1991 Dark Blue body and roof, Black chassis **£5-8**

Y13-1 'Santa Fe' Locomotive (1862)

Scale 1:112.
1959 Dark Green cab and boiler, Dark Red chassis and smokebox........**£75-95**
NB The level of Gold trim was reduced over the years thus it is
possible to find models with Gold chimney rim and condenser
tops through various combinations to Dark Red chimney rim and
Dark Green condenser tops.
Mid Green cab and boiler, Dark Red chassis and smokebox,
Gold chimney rim and condenser tops **£700-800**

Y13-2 1911 Daimler

Scale 1:45.

1966 Yellow body and bonnet, Black chassis, 5-spoke steering wheel,
Black seats..**£25-35**
Same but with Dark Red seats..**£15-25**
1967 Yellow body and bonnet, Black chassis, 4-spoke steering wheel,
Black seats..**£25-35**
Same but with Dark Red seats..**£10-18**
1984 Blue body, Powder Blue chassis, 4-spoke steering wheel,
Brown seats. In 'Connoisseur Collection' ....GSP

Y13-3 1918 Crossley Lorry

Scale 1:47. 'RAF' Tender

1975 RAF Blue cab, body and chassis, Tan canopy and tilt,
no brake between front mudguards and chassis,
Dull Dark Red seats **£250-400**
Same but with Milky White seats **£300-350**
1976 RAF Blue cab, body and chassis, Tan canopy and tilt, brace
between front mudguards and chassis, Milky White seats............**£10-30**
Same but with Dull Dark Red seats..**£150-200**
Same but with Green seats..**£150-200**
RAF Blue cab, body and chassis, Tan canopy and tilt,
Milky White seats and grille **£100-110**
Same but with Olive Green canopy and grille............................**£45-70**
Same but with Dark Charcoal Grey canopy and grille.............**£250-300**
NB Almost all above variations can have Chrome 12 or 24-spoke wheels.

Y13-4 1918 Crossley Lorry

Scale 1:47.

'EVANS Bros.'
1979 Dark Red cab and body, Black chassis, 'RAF Tender' base,
Red 12-spoke wheels or Chrome 12 or 24-spoke wheels **£10-15**
1980 Same but without 'RAF Tender' on base **£10-15**
1982 Bright Red cab and body, Black chassis, Red 12-spoke wheels **£5-10**

'CARLSBERG'
1983 Cream cab and body, Black chassis, Light Green canopy and tilt,
'Lesney Products' base, Chrome or Gold 12-spoke wheels......**£45-55**
'Matchbox Toys Ltd' base, Chrome or Gold 12-spoke wheels..........**£5-8**
1984 'Matchbox Toys Ltd' base, Darker Green canopy and tilt **£5-8**

'WARING and GILLOW'
1985 Dark Green body, Black chassis, White or Cream canopy and tilt ..**£5-10**

'KOHLE and KOKS'
1988 Lemon cab and body, Black chassis, Black 12-spoke wheels..........**£5-10**
Same but with Dark Green 12-spoke wheels................................**£45-50**

Y14-1 Duke of Connaught' Locomotive (1903)

Scale 1:130.

1959 Dark Green cab and boiler, Dark Brown chassis,
with Gold boiler door **£75-130**
With Silver boiler door **£100-120**

Y14-2 1911 Maxwell Roadster

Scale 1:49.

1965 Turquoise body and chassis, Brass petrol tank..........................**£120-150**
Same but with Copper petrol tank **£15-20**
1984 Dark Cream body, Dark Green chassis, Copper petrol tank.
In 'Connoisseur Collection' ....GSP

Y14-3 1931 Stutz Bearcat

Scale 1:44.

1974 Lime Green body, Dark Green chassis, Bright Red seats **£8-12**
Same but with Dark Red seats..**£50-75**
1979 Cream body, Bright Red top panels, Darker Red chassis,
Bright Red seats **£30-45**
Same but with Black seats..**£5-10**
1981 Cream body and top panels, Emerald Green chassis,
Chrome 24-spoke wheels..**£5-10**
Same but with Red 12-spoke wheels..**£20-25**
1985 French Blue body, Dark Grey chassis..**£5-8**
1990 Dark Blue body and chassis, Cream panels, Dark Blue chassis **£8-12**
1995 Bright Red body, Black chassis **£8-10**

Y14-4 1936 ERA type R1-B

Scale 1:35.

1986 Gloss Black body and chassis..**£10-15**
1988 Blue body, Yellow chassis, 'Made in Macau' **£8-10**
1991 Blue body, Yellow chassis, 'Made in China' **£10-15**

Y15-1 1907 Rolls-Royce Silver Ghost

Scale 1:55.

1960 Light Green body and chassis, Black seats,
Silver 12-spoke wheels, Grey knobbly tyres **£45-55**
Same but with Black knobbly tyres..**£25-30**
Same but with Brass 12-spoke wheels, Black knobbly tyres......**£15-30**
Same but with Silver 12-spoke wheels, Black smooth tyres........**£15-30**
Light Green body and chassis, Brass 12-spoke wheels,
Black smooth tyres, Dark Green seats......................................**£60-70**

Y15-2 1930 Packard Victoria

Scale 1:46.

1969 Brownish-Gold body, Dark Brown chassis,
Dark Red seats and roof..**£10-20**
1974 Lime Gold body, Dark Brown chassis, Dark Red seats and roof,
or Black roof, narrow cast coachline to rear side panels...............**£10-15**
With Black roof and wide cast coachline to rear side panels........**£40-60**
1979 Gloss Black body and chassis, Dark Red side panels,
Black or White roof..**£5-10**
1984 Dark Sand body, Dark Brown chassis, Brown or White roof **£5-8**
Same but with Orange-Brown roof..**£90-110**

Y15-3 1920 'Preston type' Tram Car

Scale 1:87.

'LONDON TRANSPORT'
1987 Red body, White window frames, 'Swan Vestas' side adverts **£5-10**
'Passport Scheme' version in cabinet plus extra components....**£60-70**

'DARLINGTON CORPORATION'
1988 Blue body, Off-White window frames, 'Swan Soap' side adverts...**£5-10**

'PAISLEY DISTRICT'
1989 Orange body, Cream window frames, 'Golden Shred' side adverts **£5-12**

'NEWCASTLE CORPORATION'
1991 Dark Brown body, Pale Cream window frames,
'Zebra Grate Polish' side adverts..**£5-10**

Y16-1 1904 Spyker

Scale 1:45.

1961 Pale Cream body and chassis, Grey knobbly tyres...................**£300-350**
Pale Lemon body and chassis, Grey knobbly tyres....................**£50-70**
Same but with Black knobbly tyres **£30-40**
Same but with smooth tyres **£20-30**
Pale Lemon body and chassis, 2 cast holes in base **£110-130**
Maroon body and chassis, Black knobbly or smooth tyres....**£1750-2000**
1968 Pale or Mustard Yellow body and chassis **£15-25**

Matchbox 'Models of Yesteryear'

Y16-2 1928 Mercedes-Benz SS Coupé

Scale 1:45.

1972 Silver body, Red chassis, cast rear axle differential casing.......**£100-125**
    Same but rear axle differential not cast **£15-25**
1974 Lime Green body and chassis, separate cast exhaust underneath,
    Black roof and seats...**£15-30**
    Same but with Dark Green roof and seats **£30-45**

    Lime Green body, Dark Green chassis (as Y14-3 Stutz),
    Black roof and seats **£175-225**
    Lime Green body and chassis, exhaust cast as ridge
    on baseplate, Dark Green roof and seats **£25-35**
    Same but with Black roof and seats.........................**£10-20**
1979 White body and chassis, Black roof and seats.................**£10-15**
    White body, Black chassis, Black roof and seats **£370-420**
1981 Blue body and chassis, Mid-Grey side panels.................**£5-15**
    Same but with Duck Egg Blue side panels **£45-60**
    With Milky White side panels **£75-90**
    With Beige side panels **£5-15**
1985 Red body, Silver chassis, top in folded position...............**£5-10**
1990 Pinkish-Grey body, Black chassis, Black roof (closed) and seats..**£12-15**

Y16-3 1960 Ferrari Dino 246 V12

Scale 1:35.

1986 Red body and chassis, Chrome 24-spoke wheels **£5-10**
    Same but with Aluminium spoked wheels **£10-18**

Y16-4 1923 Scania-Vabis Post Bus

Scale 1:49. 'Special Limited Edition' model, 1988.

1988 Yellow body, gloss Black chassis, Grey roof, Brown interior.......**£10-20**
    Same but with Black interior **£150-200**

Y16-5 Scammell 100-ton Truck and Trailer

Scale 1:64. 'PICKFORDS'. 'Special Limited Edition' model, 1989.

1989 Blue prime mover and trailer, White cab roofs and 'PICKFORDS'
    logo, Red chassis and wheels. Very dark Blue E4 Class 2-4-0
    locomotive in G.E.R. livery, Gold trim and number '490' **£80-100**

Y17-1 1938 Hispano-Suiza

Scale 1:48.

1975 Dark Red body, Black chassis, Chrome 24-spoke wheels...............**£7-15**
    Same but with Chrome 12-spoke wheels......................**£15-25**
1980 Pale Blue body and chassis, Powder Blue side panels,
    Chrome 24-spoke or solid wheels.............................**£7-12**
    Pale Blue body, Black chassis, Powder Blue side panels,
    Chrome 24-spoke wheels **£15-25**
    Same but with Chrome solid wheels **£7-12**
1981 Silver body, Silver or Black chassis, Powder Blue side panels,
    Chrome solid wheels **£110-125**
1986 Mid-Green body, Dark Green chassis, Gold 24-spoke wheels,
    'Lesney Products' base **£5-15**
    Same but with 'Matchbox Int'l England' base................**£40-60**
    Same but with 'Matchbox Int'l Macau' base **£7-10**
1990 Light Green body and chassis, Lime Green side panels.................**£10-15**
1995 Navy Blue body and chassis, Gold 24-spoke wheels **£12-15**

Y18-1 1937 Cord 812

Scale 1:48.

1979 Red body and chassis, White roof and seats,
    Chrome 24-spoke wheels or Red or Chrome solid wheels **£5-10**
1981 Darker Red body and chassis, White roof and seats,
    Chrome solid wheels...**£10-15**
1983 Plum Red body and chassis, White roof and seats,
    Chrome solid wheels...**£10-15**
    Same but with Chrome 24-spoke wheels......................**£15-20**

1990 Pale Yellow body and chassis (Black baseplate),
    Brown roof and seats **£15-20**
    Same but with in plain White box **£20-25**
1995 Rich Cream body, chassis and base, Tan hood,
    Dark Brown seats **£15-20**

Y18-2 1918 Atkinson 'D' type Steam Wagon

Scale 1:60.

'LAKE GOLDSMITH'
1985 Green body, Red chassis, Green and-spoke wheels......................**£12-20**

'BLUE CIRCLE CEMENT'
1986 Yellow body, Black chassis, Yellow 8-spoke wheels **£7-10**

'BASS & Co.'
1987 Dark Blue body, Black chassis, Red 8-spoke wheels,
    7 barrel load, posts and chains to truck body **£15-20**

'BURGHFIELD MILLS'
1988 Red body, Black chassis, Red 8-spoke wheels, sacks load **£5-8**

Y19-1 1936 Auburn Speedster

Scale 1:42.

1979 Beige body and bonnet sides, Light Brown top panels,
    Dark Brown chassis, solid Red, Cherry Red or Chrome wheels **£5-10**
1983 Creamy White body and bonnet sides and tops, Black chassis,
    Red solid or 12-spoke wheels................................**£8-15**
1985 White body, bonnet and chassis, Blue side panels,
    Blue 24-spoke wheels **£5-10**
1990 Dark Tan body, bonnet and chassis, Cream side panels,
    Chrome 24-spoke wheels **£12-18**
    Same but in plain White box **£20-25**

Y19-2 Fowler B6 Showman's Engine

Scale 1:68. 'Heigh-Ho, Come to the Fair'. 'Special Limited Edition', 1986.

1986 Blue body and boiler, Black smokebox, Off -White roof **£25-35**

Y19-3 1929 Morris Cowley Van

Scale 1:39. All Y19-3 models have 12-spoke wheels.

'BRASSO'
1987 Dark Blue body, White roof, Black chassis, 'Macau'
    baseplate, Red 12-spoke wheels **£5-10**
    Same but with Chrome wheels **£15-25**
    Same but with Red wheels, 'China' baseplate **£10-15**

'MICHELIN'
1988 Dark Blue body, Yellow roof, Black chassis, Chrome wheels **£5-10**

'SAINSBURY'
1990 Dark Brown body, White roof, Black chassis, Chrome wheels **£5-10**

Y20-1 1937 Mercedes-Benz 540K

Scale 1:45.

1981 Silver body, Black chassis, seats ranging in colour from
    Amber to Red, Chrome 24-spoke wheels **£5-15**
    Same but with Red 12-spoke wheels **£15-20**
1985 White body and chassis, Red seats, Red 24-spoke wheels.................**£5-8**
1987 Red body and chassis, Brown seats, Chrome 24-spoke wheels **£5-10**
1990 Black body and chassis, Maroon seats, Tan steering wheel,
    Chrome 24-spoke wheels **£5-8**
1995 Black body and chassis, Bright Red seats, Black steering wheel,
    Chrome 24-spoke wheels **£10-15**

Y21-1 1930 Ford Model 'A' Woody Wagon

Scale 1:40.

1981 Yellow bonnet, Dark Brown chassis, Red seats,
    Chrome 24-spoke wheels, 'Lesney' base......................**£5-30**
    Same but with 'Matchbox Int'l' base **£20-30**

218

1983 Copper bonnet, Dark Brown chassis, Red seats,
Chrome 12-spoke wheels, 'Lesney' or 'Matchbox Int'l' base **£5-10**
1985 Orange bonnet, Dark Brown chassis, Red seats,
Chrome 12-spoke wheels, 'Lesney' or 'Matchbox' base **£10-15**

Y21-2 1930 Ford Model 'A' Woody Wagon

Scale 1:40

'A. & J. BOX'
1983 Copper bonnet, Dark Brown chassis, Off-White seats,
Chrome 12-spoke wheels, 'Lesney' base **£5-15**
Same but with 'Matchbox Int'l' base **£5-10**
1984 Orange bonnet, Dark Brown chassis, Off-White seats,
Chrome 12-spoke wheels, 'Lesney' or 'Matchbox Int'l' base **£5-10**
Yellow bonnet, Black chassis, Off-White or Red seats,
Chrome 24-spoke wheels, 'Lesney' base **£40-50**

'CARTERS SEEDS'
1985 Blue bonnet, Black chassis, Off-White seats,
Chrome 12-spoke wheels, 'Lesney' base **£15-25**
Same but with 'Matchbox Int'l' base **£5-10**

Y21-3 Aveling and Porter Road Roller

Scale 1:60. **'James Young & Sons, Edinburgh'**. 'Special Ltd. Edition' 1987.

1987 Green body and Boiler, Black firebox and smokebox, no cast
lettering on underside of roof, very Pale Grey rear 'tyres' **£550-600**
Same but with Mid-Grey rear 'tyres' **£150-200**
Same but with cast lettering on underside of roof and
with Mid-Grey rear 'tyres' **£20-25**

Y21-4 1955 BMW 507

Scale 1:38.

1988 Blue body, Black roof, Red seats **£8-12**

Y21-5 1926 Ford Model 'TT' Van

Scale 1:41.

'OSRAM'
1989 Dark Green body, Black chassis, Red roof, Chrome grille **£10-15**
Same but with Black radiator grille **£5-10**

'MY BREAD'
1990 Sandy Beige body and roof, Black chassis, riveted axle ends **£5-10**
Same but with wheels press-fitted onto axles **£10-15**

'DRAMBUIE'
1992 Black body, roof and chassis, Brass 12-spoke wheels..................**£10-20**

Y22-1 1930 Ford Model 'A' Van

Scale 1:41.

'OXO'
1982 Red body, Black chassis, Red seats and interior, 'Lesney' base **£130-150**
Red body, Black chassis, Fawn seats and interior, 'Lesney' base,
matt Black van roof...**£5-10**
Same but with gloss Black van roof **£15-20**
Same but with matt Black van roof, 'Matchbox Int'l' base **£20-25**

'MAGGI SOUPS'
1984 Yellow body, Black chassis, Red roof, Chrome 24-spoke wheels,
'Lesney' base **£25-40**
Same but with Red 12-spoke wheels **£40-50**
1985 Yellow body, Black chassis, Red roof, Chrome 24-spoke wheels,
'Matchbox Int'l' base **£5-8**
Same but with Chrome 12-spoke wheels **£5-15**

'TOBLERONE'
1984 Beige body, Dark Brown chassis, Red roof, 'Matchbox Int'l' base...**£5-8**

'PALM TOFFEE'
1984 Light Cream body, Red chassis and roof, Dark Green colour in
logo, Gold 24-spoke wheels.......................................**£5-8**
Same but with Chrome 24-spoke wheels.............................**£10-15**
Same but Gold 24-spoke wheels, Light Green Colour in logo **£8-12**

'CANADA POST'
1984 Red body, Black chassis and roof, Black 24-spoke wheels,
'Postes Canada Post' on box......................................**£10-15**
Same but with regular box (no 'Postes Canada Post' printed).........**£5-8**
Same but with Chrome 24-spoke wheels (regular box) **£10-15**

'SPRATTS'
1986 Brown body, Dark Brown chassis, Off-White roof,
Chrome 24-spoke wheels **£5-12**
Same but with Gold 12-spoke wheels **£15-20**

'LYONS TEA'
1987 Blue body, Black chassis, White roof, 'Matchbox Int'l',
'Made in Macau' base, Chrome or Red 12-spoke wheels...............**£5-10**
Same but with Light Gold 12-spoke wheels.........................**£8-12**
1991 Blue body, Black chassis, White roof, Chrome 12-spoke wheels,
'Matchbox Int'l, Made in China' base.............................**£15-20**

'CHERRY BLOSSOM'
1989 White body, Black chassis and roof, riveted axle ends,
'Matchbox Int'l, Made in Macau' base **£5-10**
1991 White body, Black chassis and roof, wheels press-fitted on axles,
'Matchbox Int'l, Made in China' base.............................**£15-20**

'PRATTS'
1991 White body, Black chassis and roof, Orange solid wheels.............**£5-10**

Y23-1 1922 AEC Omnibus

Scale 1:72.

'SCHWEPPES'
1983 Red body, gloss Black chassis, side adverts in White with
Red printing, Light Tan, Fawn or Dark Brown seats and panels ...**£65-80**
Same but with side adverts in White with Black printing..............**£5-15**
1984 Red body, gloss Black chassis, Fawn seats and side rails,
side adverts in Yellow with Black and White printing....................**£5-15**

'R.A.C.'
1985 Red body, gloss Black chassis, Fawn seats and side rails, 'RAC' ...**£5-10**

'MAPLES'
1985 Red body, Gloss Black chassis, Fawn seats and side rails, 'Maples'.
This model was only available in 'Fathers Day' Set........................**GSP**

'HAIG'
1986 Dark Brown body, gloss Black chassis, Cream upper deck,
Dark Brown seats, Dark or Bright Red 12-spoke wheels...............**£5-10**

'RICE KRISPIES'
1988 Red body, gloss Black chassis, Pinkish-Tan seats **£5-10**

'LIFEBUOY'
1989 Blue body, Light Cream upper deck, Dark Brown seats **£5-10**

Y23-2 Mack Bulldog Tanker

Scale 1:60.

'TEXACO'
1989 Red cab and tank, Black chassis, Red wheels **£5-12**
Same but with Gold wheels **£50-60**

'CONOCO'
1991 Red cab, White tank, Black chassis, 'Made in Macau' base..........**£65-75**
Same but with 'Made in China' base...............................**£5-10**

Y24-1 1928 Bugatti T44

Scale 1:72.

1983 Black body and chassis, Bright Yellow side panels, Beige seats **£5-10**
Same but with Brown, Green or White seats **£200-250**
1984 Black body and chassis, Lemon side panels with Black stripe below
door windows, Chrome 24-spoke wheels, Beige seats....................**£5-10**
Same but with White seats **£75-100**
Same but with Black seats **£15-20**
With Black seats and Chrome 12-spoke wheels **£75-100**
1987 Light Grey body, Red chassis, Dull Red side panels, Beige seats,
Chrome solid wheels...**£5-10**

1990 Black body and chassis, Red side panels, Light Brown seats,
Chrome 24-spoke wheels **£5-10**
1995 Black body and chassis, Khaki wicker-work printed side panels,
Light Tan seats, Chrome 24-spoke wheels **£8-12**

Y25-1 1910 Renault 'AG' Van

Scale 1:38.

'PERRIER'
1983 Green body, Dark Green chassis, White seats, roof rack with
only 3 side struts, right hand sidelight with protruding lens,
Gold 12-spoke wheels **£220-250**
NB The following models have roofs with rack with 4 side struts.
1983 Green body, Dark Green chassis, White or Dark Red seats,
right hand sidelight with protruding lens, Gold 12-spoke wheels....**£5-10**
Same but with Red 12-spoke wheels **£10-15**
With flat lens to right hand sidelight **£5-10**
With Chrome 12-spoke wheels **£5-10**

'JAMES NEALE'
1985 The basic model has a Yellow cab and body with a White roof.
Mounted on Royal Blue chassis with closed grab handles **£15-20**
Same but with cast hole in cab floor **£25-30**
With cast hole in cab floor, open grab handles.....................**£25-45**
Mounted on Navy Blue chassis with closed grab handles **£60-80**
Same but with cast hole in cab floor **£35-50**
With cast hole in cab floor, open grab handles.....................**£30-45**
NB The 12-spoke wheels can be Light or Dark Yellow or Orange-Yellow,
but these differences do not usually attract further premiums.

'DUCKHAMS'
1985 Silver body, Navy Blue chassis, open grab handles **£10-15**
Same but with closed grab handles....................................**£50-60**
NB Although sometimes for sale as individual models, the Duckhams
Van was only issued as part of the 1985 'Fathers Day' Set ....**GSP**

'EAGLE PENCILS'
1985 Blue body, Navy Blue chassis, Gold 12-spoke wheels,
open grab handles, 'Matchbox © 1983' base **£5-10**
Same but with closed grab handles....................................**£50-60**
Open grab handles, Chrome 12-spoke wheels.......................**£5-10**
Open grab handles, 'Matchbox © 1986' base **£5-10**
Open grab handles, 'Matchbox © 1986 Limited Edition' base......**£15-20**

'BRITISH RED CROSS'
1986 Army Green body, Black chassis, 'Matchbox © 1986' base **£12-18**
Same but with 'Matchbox © 1986 Limited Edition' base **£12-18**

'TUNNOCKS'
1987 Bright Red body, Black chassis, Black 12-spoke wheels,
'Matchbox Int'l © 1983' or 'Matchbox Int'l © 1986' base.............**£5-10**
Same but with Gold 12-spoke wheels **£10-15**
With closed grab handles **£25-35**
With 'Matchbox © 1986 Limited Edition' base **£10-15**

'DELHAIZE'
1987 Dark Green body, Black chassis, Gold 12-spoke wheels,
'Matchbox © 1986' base **£5-10**

'SUCHARD'
1989 Pale Lilac body, Black chassis, Gold 12-spoke wheels,
'Matchbox © 1986' base **£5-10**

Y26-1 Crossley Delivery Truck

Scale 1:47.

'LOWENBRAU'
1984 Powder Blue body, Black chassis, Red solid wheels, Tan roof,
Brown barrels, 'Renault Y25' base..**£225-250**
Same but with 'Crossley Y13' base....................................**£40-50**
Same but with 'Crossley Y13/Y26' base..............................**£5-10**
1985 Powder Blue body, Black chassis, Red solid wheels, Light Tan
roof, Brown barrels, 'Crossley Y13/Y26' base **£5-10**
Same but with Red 12-spoke wheels **£20-25**
1986 Powder Blue body, Black chassis, Red solid wheels, Cream roof,
Dark Brown barrels, 'Crossley Y13/Y26' base **£5-10**
Same but with Light Olive Green roof **£20-25**

'ROMFORD BREWERY'
1986 Black body, Mid Brown chassis, Light Brown seats, Black grille...**£5-10**

Same but with Ruby Red seats **£10-20**
Same but with Ruby Red seats and radiator grille **£10-20**

'GONZALEZ BYASS'
1987 White body, Ruby Red chassis, Gold 12-spoke wheels,
with or without tampo print on barrels **£5-10**
Same but with Chrome 12-spoke wheels..............................**£15-20**

Y27-1 1922 Foden Steam Lorry

Scale 1:72.

'PICKFORDS'
1984 Blue body, Red chassis, Light Grey cab roof and canopy,
'© 1984' base, truck body butts up to cab sides **£15-25**
Same but truck body overlaps cab sides **£70-80**
Same but truck body overlaps cab sides with full-length bearer......**£5-10**
NB The following issues have truck body overlapping cab sides with
full-length bearer.
1985 Blue body, Red chassis, Dark Grey cab roof and canopy,
'© 1984' or '© 1986' base **£10-15**
Same but with Light Grey cab roof and canopy, '© 1986' base......**£5-10**
1986 Blue body, Red chassis, Light or Dark Grey cab roof and canopy,
'© 1986' base, with tow hook **£10-15**
Blue body, Red chassis, Light or Dark Grey cab roof and canopy,
'© 1986' base, with rivet only (no hook) **£150-200**

'HOVIS'
1985 Dark Brown body, Black chassis, Yellowish-Cream or
Light Yellowish-Cream cab roof, canopy and wheels.................**£10-15**

'TATE and LYLE'S'
1986 Brown body, Black chassis, body side panel cast relief as the 'Hovis',
'© 1984' base, Jet Black cab roof and canopy **£25-35**
Same but with Charcoal Grey cab roof and canopy **£50-60**
Brown body, Black chassis, shallower side panel cast relief,
Jet Black cab roof and canopy, '© 1984' or '© 1986' base..........**£10-15**

'FRASERS' (Lorry and Trailer)
1986 Dark Green bodies, Black chassis, White cab roof and canopies ..**£20-25**

'SPILLERS'
1987 Pale Cream body, Green chassis, Dark Cream sacks load,
with tow hook rivet **£15-20**
Same but without tow hook rivet **£10-15**
NB The colour of the truck body side panels can range from very
Dark Green to Emerald Green, all with or without tow hook rivets.

'GUINNESS'
1989 Dark Blue body, Black chassis, Dark Brown barrels **£15-25**

'JOSEPH RANK'
1990 Dark Green body, Light Brown chassis, Off-White sacks,
2 cast holes in bed of truck body **£15-25**
Same but without cast holes in bed of truck body....................**£10-15**
NB The wheels can have open ended or closed ended hub centres.

'McMULLEN'
1992 Black body, Red chassis, 5 Dark Brown barrels **£15-25**

Y28-1 1907 Unic Taxi

Scale 1:42.

1984 Dark Red body, Black chassis, Black hood and roof,
Brown seats, Red, Maroon or Gold 12-spoke wheels **£5-12**
1987 Dark Blue body, Black chassis, Black hood and roof,
Brown seats, Red, Maroon or Chrome 12-spoke wheels **£5-10**
1991 White body, Black chassis, Black hood, roof and seats **£10-15**

Y29-1 1919 Walker Electric Van

Scale 1:51.

'HARRODS'
1985 Khaki Green body, Black chassis, Cream canopy and tilt...............**£5-10**

'JOSEPH LUCAS'
1986 Bright Green body, Black chassis, Bright Green canopy and tilt.....**£5-10**
NB The surface of the canopy/tilt can vary from fine texture to
eggshell effect.

'HIS MASTERS VOICE'
1988 Dark Blue body, Black chassis, Pinkish-Beige canopy and tilt........£8-12

'HARRODS BREAD'
1989 Khaki Green body, Black chassis, Dark Green canopy and tilt £8-12

Y30-1 1920 Mack Truck

Scale 1:60.

'ACORN STORAGE'
1985 Cambridge Blue body, Dark Blue chassis and cab steps,
Dark Grey cab and van body roof, 'Made in England' base...........£8-15
1986 Same but with Dark Grey cab steps.....................................£10-15
1987 Aqua Blue body, Dark Blue chassis and cab steps, Pale Grey cab,
Charcoal Grey van body roof, 'Made in Macau' £350-400

'CONSOLIDATED'
1985 Yellow body, Dark Brown chassis, Yellow cab and roof,
Dark Tan truck body cover £5-10
Same but with very Pale Olive Truck body cover.......................£80-100

'ARCTIC ICE CREAM'
1987 Cream body, Dark Green chassis, Beige Van body roof £5-8

'KIWI'
1988 Red body, Black chassis, Beige van body roof £5-10
NB The Kiwi bird etc., can be Light, Mid or Dark Brown.

Y31-1 1931 Morris Courier Van

Scale 1:59.

'KEMPS'
1990 Red body, Black chassis, Off-White roof, full-length van body cast
horizontal lines £70-75
Same but cast horizontal lines are 2mm short of full-length..........£5-10

'WEETABIX'
1992 Yellow body and roof, Black chassis £5-10

Y32-1 Yorkshire Steam Wagon

Scale 1:54.

'SAMUEL SMITH'
1990 Maroon cab and body, Black chassis, 'Y8' cast on base.................£5-10
Same but with 'Y32' cast on base £10-15

Y33-1 1920 Mack 'AC' Truck

Scale 1:60.

'GOODYEAR'
1990 Cambridge Blue body, Dark Blue chassis, Dark Grey roof £5-10

Y34-1 1933 Cadillac V16

Scale 1:48.

1990 Navy Blue body and chassis, White hood, 'Macau Y34' base £5-10
1992 White body, Navy Blue chassis, Black hood,
'China YY46, Y34' base...£8-12

Y35-1 1930 Ford Model 'A' Pick-up Truck

Scale 1:40.

'W. CLIFFORD & SONS'
1990 Cream cab and body, Black chassis, Black roof.............................£5-10

'AMBROSIA'
1992 Blue cab and body, Cream chassis and roof £5-15

Y36-1 1936 Rolls-Royce Phantom I

Scale 1:46.

1990 Dark Red body, Black chassis and roof, Dark Red seats £5-15

1992 Blue body, Black chassis and roof, Maroon seats £5-10
1994 Dull Dark Red body, Black chassis, Dark Brown seats £5-10

Y37-1 1931 Garrett Steam Wagon

Scale 1:59.

'CHUBB'S SAFE DEPOSITS'
1990 Pale Blue cab and body, Navy Blue chassis, White/Cream roof,
'Garrtt' cast on base £80-90
'Garrett' cast on base £10-15

'MILKMAID MILK'
1992 Cream body, Navy Blue cab and chassis and cab roof,
White Van body roof, Pale Blue wheels......................................£70-75
Same but with Red wheels..£10-15

Y38-1 1920 Rolls-Royce Armoured Car

Scale 1:48. 'HMAC Ajax'.

1990 Sand body, turret and chassis...£15-20

Y39-1 1820 Passenger Coach

Scale 1:43. 'York to London'.

1990 Black body, Red chassis, Black roof, 4 horses, 6 figures..............£35-40

Y40-1 1931 Mercedes-Benz 770

Scale 1:48.

1991 Grey body and chassis, Dark Blue roof, Maroon seats £10-15

Y41-1 1932 Mercedes-Benz 'L5' Lorry

Scale 1:69. 'HOWALDTSWERKE A.G.'

1991 Dark Green cab and body, Dark Grey chassis, Black mudguards and
steps, Dull Silver radiator £10-15
Same but with Bright Chrome radiator...£5-10

Y42-1 1939 Albion 'CX7' 10-ton Lorry

Scale 1:60. 'LIBBYS'

1991 White cab, Blue body, Navy Blue chassis, Dull Silver radiator.....£10-15
Same but with Bright Chrome radiator..£5-10

Y43-1 1905 Busch Steam Fire Engine

Scale 1:43. 'Special Edition', 1991 model

1991 Dark Green body and crew area, 5 figures/crew,
Copper boiler pipes etc. £80-100
Same but with Brass boiler pipes...£40-45

Y44-1 1910 Renault 'T45' Bus

Scale 1:38.

1991 Yellow body, Black chassis and Black roof....................................£5-15
Same but with Red roof £80-90

Y45-1 1930 Bugatti Royale 'Napoleon'

Scale 1:46.

1991 Black body, bonnet and chassis, Dark Blue side panels,
Dark Blue seats £10-15
1994 Same but with Lilac-Blue seats £10-15

Y46-1 1868 Merryweather Fire Engine

Scale 1:43. 'Special Edition', 1991 model.

1991 Red body, Brass boiler etc, 2 White horses, 4 figures/crew..........£35-60

Y47-A 1929 Morris Cowley Van

Scale 1:39. 'CHOCOLAT LINDT'

1991 Black body and chassis, Yellow roof...£5-10

Y61 1933 Cadillac Fire Engine

Scale 1:46. 'FEUEWEHR AARU'

1992 Red body and chassis, Light Brown ladder £10-20

Y62 1932 Ford Model 'AA' Truck

Scale 1:46. 'PEACOCK'

1992 Light Green cab and body, Black chassis, Light Grey roof,
       Light Brown sacks £10-15

Y63 1939 Bedford 'KD' Truck

Scale 1:46. 'G. FARRAR'

1992 Red cab, Light Brown body, Black chassis, loose stones.............£25-35

Y64 1938 Lincoln Zephyr

Scale 1:43.

1992 Cream body and mudguards, Black running boards, Brown seats,
       Dark Cream folded top...£15-20
1995 Maroon body and mudguards, Silver running boards,
       Light Brown seats, Off-White folded top £15-20

Y65 1928 Austin 7 (Set)

Scale 1:43. 'Special Limited Edition' Set.

1992 Austin 7 Van; Red body, Black chassis, 'Castrol' logo,
       Rosengart Saloon; Blue body, Black chassis, textured Black plastic roof,
       BMW Dixie open tourer; White body, Black chassis, Black folded top
       ....£40-50

Y66 State Coach

Scale 1:100. 'Special Limited Edition', 1992.

1992 Gold coach and wheels, 8 horses (in pairs) with 4 riders.................£4-7
       Same but with Brass coach and wheels £4-7

Models of Yesteryear Gift Sets

G 6	1960	**Gift Set**	Contains Nos. 1, 2, 5, 10 and 13. Lesney line-drawing box		£325-375
G 7	1960	**Gift Set**	Contains Nos 3, 8, 9, 12 and 14. Lesney line-drawing box		£325-375
G 6	1962	**Veteran & Vintage Car Set**	Contains Nos 5, 6, 7, 15 and 16. Lesney picture box		£325-375
G 7	1962	**Gift Set**	Contains Nos 3, 4, 11, 12 and 13. Lesney picture box		£325-375
G 7	1965	**Veteran & Vintage Set**	Contains Y2, Y5, Y10, Y15 and Y16. Picture box		£100-125
G 7	1966	**Gift Set**	Y1-2 Model T Ford, Y3-2 Benz, Y11-2 Packard, Y14-2 Maxwell. Picture box		£75-100
G 5	1968	**Gift Set**	Y4-3 Opel, Y6-3 Cadillac, Y9-2 Simplex, Y9-2 Simplex		£55-65
G 5	1970-72	**Gift** Set	Contains Y8-3 Stutz Red, Y14 Maxwell, Y16-1 Spyker (Dark Yellow), Y7-3 Rolls-Royce Silver and Red. Picture box		£45-55
Y-50	1982	**Gift Set**	Contains Y3-4 'BP' Tanker, Y5-4 Talbot Van 'Chivers', Y10-3 Rolls Royce, Y12-3 Model 'T' Van, Y13-3 Crossley Coal Lorry		£35-40
	1984	**'Connoisseur Collection'**	Contains Y1-2 Black 1911 Model 'T' Ford, Y4-3 Red/Beige 1909 Opel, Y3-2 Blue/Black 1910 Benz Limousine, Y11-2 White/Black 1912 Packard Landaulet, Y13-2 Blue 1911 Daimler, Y14-2 Beige/Black 1911 Maxwell. 30,000 certificated and numbered sets issued in beechwood display case		£80-100
	1985	**'Fathers Day' Set**	Y11-3 Lagonda, Y23-1 'MAPLES' Bus, Y25-1 Renault Van 'DUCKHAMS'		£20-30
	1987	**30 years Set** (A)	Y6-4 Rolls-Royce Fire Engine, Y25-1 'Eagle Pencils', Y29-1 'Harrods'		£15-20
	1987	**30 years Set** (B)	Y4-4 Blue Duesenberg, Y28-1 Red Unic Taxi, Y29-1 'Harrods' Van		£15-20
	1987	**Starter Kit**	(5 for 4 Set) Australian Gift Set		£25-30
Y65	1992	**1928 Austin 7** (Set)	A Special Limited Edition Set comprising Austin 7 Van (Red body, 'CASTROL'), BMW Dixi 3/15 (Blue body, Black roof) ROSENGART 3-seater Tourer (White body). All three have Black chassis, Tan seats and Chrome wheels Scale 1:43		£25-30

Models of Yesteryear plated souvenir and giftware models

Models specially plated to adorn giftware (e.g., cigarette boxes, ashtrays, penstands, boxes and pipestands. Non-plated versions of the models listed will also be found with the two baseplate holes used for fixing the plated models to the various items.

SILVER PLATED MODELS

Y1-2	1911	Model 'T' Ford	**£20-30**
Y2-2	1911	Renault 2 seater	**£20-30**
Y2-3	1914	Prince Henry Vauxhall	**£20-30**
Y3-3	1934	Riley MPH	**£20-30**
Y4-3	1909	Opel Coupé	**£20-30**
Y5-2	1929	4½ Litre Bentley	**£30-40**
Y6-2	1926	Type 35 Bugatti	**£75-95**
Y7-2	1913	Mercer Raceabout	**£45-65**
Y7-3	1912	Rolls-Royce	**£20-30**

Y10-2	1928	Mercedes-Benz 36-220	**£30-40**
Y10-3	1906	Rolls-Royce	**£20-30**
Y12-2	1909	Thomas Flyabout	**£20-30**
Y13-2	1911	Daimler	**£20-30**
Y13-3	1918	Crossley	**£175-225**
Y14-2	1911	Maxwell Roadster	**£15-20**
Y15-1	1907	Rolls-Royce Silver Ghost	**£15-20**
Y16-1	1904	Spyker	**£20-30**

GOLD PLATED MODELS

Y1-2	1911	Model 'T' Ford	**£30-40**
Y2-3	1914	Prince Henry Vauxhall	**£15-20**
Y4-3	1909	Opel Coupé	**£15-20**
Y5-2	1929	4½ Litre Bentley	**£35-40**
Y7-2	1913	Mercer Raceabout	**£100-120**
Y7-3	1912	Rolls-Royce	**£15-20**

Y10-2	1928	Mercedes-Benz 36-220	**£75-95**
Y10-3	1906	Rolls-Royce	**£20-30**
Y12-2	1909	Thomas Flyabout	**£20-30**
Y13-2	1911	Daimler	**£20-30**
Y13-3	1918	Crossley	**£200-250**
Y14-2	1911	Maxwell Roadster	**£15-20**
Y15-1	1907	Rolls-Royce Silver Ghost	**£40-50**

GOLD PLATED SETS
Golden Veteran Set with 3 models:
Y7-3, Y13-2, Y14-2 ......£50-65
Heritage Gifts, 2 models: Y7-3, Y10-3 ......£35-50

Lesney 'Pub Signs'

A series of plated figurines made for attachment to giftware. The base of each is marked 'Lesney Co. Ltd. 1975'. They have 'spurs' underneath to aid fixing to such items as ashtrays, etc. The Editor would be pleased to receive more details. Market Price Range £10-15.

'The Cock'	'The Swan'	'The Bull'	'Pig & Whistle'	'Dick Turpin'	'The Volunteer'
'The Lion'	'The Unicorn'	'Rose & Crown'	'George & Dragon'	'Sherlock Holmes'	'Britannia'

Matchbox Models of Yesteryear 'Code 2' models 1976-1997

A system of categorising models has evolved among collectors to distinguish between authentic manufacturers output and acceptable but unauthorised alteration of their models for later resale. The explanation which follows refers to a coding system adopted generally (but not officially) throughout the model collecting fraternity in the UK and elsewhere, and may be applied to models produced by any manufacturer.

CODE 1 Applies to models which have been originated and totally produced by an established manufacturer.

CODE 2 As CODE 1 but labelled or finished outside the factory WITH the manufacturer's permission.

CODE 3 Same as CODE 2 but model re-labelled, altered or re-worked WITHOUT authorisation or permission from the manufacturer.

Y1-2 1911 Ford Model 'T' Car Black body, textured roof, grille
76 and seats, Chrome 12-spoke wheels, brass trim, bare windscreen frame. 900 models made for the USA.......**£300-400**

Y5-4 1927 Talbot Van with 12-spoke wheels and Chrome trim.
78 '2nd AIM CONVENTION', Dark Green body and wheels, 'Toy Show, Harrisburgh PA May 27, 28 1978'..............**£80-100**
81 'CRAWLEY SWAPMEET 1981', Royal Blue body, Black roof and chassis, 'Follow Us To Crawley'.........**£140-150**
81 'VARIETY CLUB'
1: Yellow body and chassis, Black roof, Red wheels, 'Sunshine Coach Appeal'......................................**£180-200**
2: As 1 but with Black chassis.............................**£180-200**
80 'MERITA BREAD', Yellow body, Black roof, Red wheels, 'Old Fashioned Enriched Bread'......................................**£40-45**
80 'LANGENDORF', Yellow body, Black roof, Red wheels, 'Old Fashioned Enriched Bread'......................................**£40-45**
80 'TAYSTEE BREAD', Yellow body, Black roof, Red wheels and Pale Yellow 'Taystee' on Red oval..............**£70-80**
81 'IRONBRIDGE'
1: Yellow body, matt Black roof, Red wheels, 'The World's First Iron Bridge'...................................**£160-180**
2: As 1 with gloss Black chassis and mudguards.........**£160-180**
81 'BEES'
1: Yellow body, Black roof, Red wheels, plain or White-wall tyres, 'Bees Art & Model Service'.........**£90-110**
2: As 1 but Black chassis and mudguards.....................**£90-110**
81 'DUTCH MATCHBOX MEET'. 1st Matchbox meeting in Holland on 4th October 1981.
1: Blue and Grey body, Black roof and chassis, 'Stoevclaar', with Certificate..................................**£250-300**
2: Yellow and Red body, Black roof and chassis, 'Stoevclaar', 72 only presented to stallholders.......**£500-600**
81 'LAWRENCE FRASER TOYS', Blue body.................**£300-350**
95 'AIM COLLECTORS EXCHANGE CLUB'. 25th Anniv. model in Black and Yellow. 600 only..........................**£70-80**

Y5-5 92 **Leyland Titan Bus**. 'MICA', 'City of Chester'. 5,000 ...**£35-40**
Y7-3 82 **1912 Rolls-Royce** Wedding of Prince Charles and Princess Diana. Bright Yellow and Black, Red wheels, 600 ...**£160-180**

Y12-3 Ford Model 'T' Van
81 'BANG & OLUFSEN', White/Red/Black, certificate...**£350-400**
81 'RAYLEIGH SWAPMEET', Yellow body, Black roof.....**£60-90**
82 'CADA TOYS Have Moved', Yellow/Black, 600........**£180-200**
82 'DEANS of LEEDS', Yellow body, Black roof, Red 'Deans for Toys', telephone no. on some, 800.....**£120-130**
80 'CAMBERLEY NEWS', Yellow/Black, '75th', 750....**£120-140**
83 'HOOVER', Blue body, White roof, Black chassis,
1: With certificate, 500...**£700-800**
2: Without certificate, 50...**£400-450**
98 'HAINES GAS SERVICES', White cab roof, 600...........**£40-50**
Same but with Dark Blue cab roof, 50.....................**£100-150**
YGB19 97 'MICA MEMBERS MEET AT HERSHEY', PA, June 28th/29th 1997, Chocolate Brown, 464.................**£30-40**
36 exist with a Y12 base and much smaller decals.......**£80-100**
YGB14 97 'Dueschland Matchbox Club', Cream roof, 2,000.........**£30-35**
Same but with Dark Blue roof, 20............................**£200-250**

Y12-5 94 **GMC Van** 'MSS SECURITY', White/Black, 2,000......**£40-50**
95 'MICA 2nd European Convention' '10 Sept 1995'. Bright Yellow body, Blue chassis. 600..........................**£40-50**
YGB08 Same but with Pale Yellow body, Blue chassis. 600........**£40-50**

Y13-3 1918 Crossley
79 'UK M'BOX CLUB', Red/Yellow, '800 Members'.....**£180-200**
81 'ASPECTS and IMAGES', Red/Light Brown.............**£160-180**

81 'SURREY MODEL FAIR', Red body, 'Tangley Model Workshop' on rear of Grey canopy only, 500............**£150-180**

Y19 Morris Cowley Van
95 'CHURTON'S WHISKEY', 1,200.................................**£40-50**
97 'VITACRAFT'. Multicoloured body.
1,000 with windows rear of cab, 1,000 without...............**£40-50**
Same but with body side window and White roof, 50..**£200-250**
97 '12th MICA CONVENTION, ALDERSHOT, 15th March. 1997'. (see M3 Set),
White body, Maroon roof, 'Macau' base. 1,000..............**£40-50**

Y21-5 1926 Ford Model 'TT' Van
92 'BBC ANTIQUES ROADSHOW', Black body, Gold 12-spoke wheels, 'The Next Generation', 24........**£1000-1200**
92 'MODELS of AUSTRALIA ART SET'. 2 models:
1: Royal Blue body, 'Jenny Kee' and face logos (multicoloured one side, Gold outline other side)
2: Dark Green body, 'Pro Hart' and insect design (multicoloured one side, Gold outline other side)
1,000 numbered sets, special box...........................**£600-800**
95 'CLASSIC TOYS MAGAZINE'. Green body, Cream roof, Gold wheels, magazine pictured on sides, 1,500...........**£40-50**
YGB14 96 '3rd MICA CONVENTION, SYDNEY 1996'.
Dark Blue body, Cream roof. 1,100..........................**£40-50**
Same but PaleBlue body, 100..................................**£60-80**
96 'BARCLAY'S PROPERTY HOLDINGS Ltd'.
120 certificated models..**£600-700**
Same but approximately 20 uncertificated models.......**£400-500**
YGB13 97 'ROYAL AUTOMOBILE CLUB of VICTORIA', Dark Blue, Cream roof, Copper wheels, 200.............**£250-300**
Dark Blue, Cream roof, Gold wheels, 100.................**£300-400**
YCH2-1 97 'RONALD McDONALD HOUSE CHARITIES', 'Magical Million 11th Annual Ball', 300....................**£250-300**

Y22 Ford Model 'A' Van
95 'BRAVO - COLONEL GOLF BALLS'.
Orange body, Blue chassis, Black roof. 2,000.................**£45-50**
95 'MATCHBOX and LESNEY TOY MUSEUM', USA.
Brown body, White roof. 2,000..................................**£45-50**
98 'MICA at HERSHEY', Black or Brown chassis, 24........**£40-50**
YPP08 97 'MATCHBOX USA 16th Annual Convention, 250.........**£50-60**

Y23 Mack AC Tanker.
97 'SUPERTEST PETROLEUM' in White...................100 **£60-80**
'SUPERTEST PETROLEUM' in Black...................400 **£40-50**
98 Canadian Military, Desert Brown, 400........................**£40-50**
Same but with Grey land colour, 100......................**£80-100**

Y26 Crossley Lorry.
95 'De BORTOLI WINE', White body, Maroon chassis. 2,000..**£45-50**
96 '11th MICA CONVENTION 13th April 1996 TELFORD'.
1: Maroon/Cream, Maroon seats. 1,500....................**£35-40**
2: Same model but in Gift Set with MB38g Van. 26 have Brown seats. 250 sets...................................**£90-100**

Y27 Foden Steam Lorry
98 YGB11 Foden (red chassis) 'MICA 13th Conv.', 1000....**£50-60**

Y37-1 Garrett Steam Wagon.
94 'MICA'.
1: Grey and Yellow body, 'Year Ten 1984-1994' on n/s. 3,000...**£60-70**
2: Blue and Silver body, 'Year Ten 1984-1994' on o/s. Presented to each of the members who had attended ten MICA Conventions. 52 only...............**£300-400**

Y47-A 1929 Morris Van
91 'ANTIQUES ROADSHOW', Black body, Yellow roof, 'Going Live - BBC Television', 24.........................**£1000-1200**
95 'CHURTONS WINE IMPORTERS'.
Black body, Yellow roof. 1,200.....................................**£40-45**

Y65 Austin 7 Van.
96 'The YESTERYEAR BOOK'. Dark Green base, Light Green top (4 shades), White or Cream print, White or Dark Blue seats. 1,500..........................**£45-55**
YSC01 97 '1st GERMAN COLLECTOR CLUB MEETING', 'Erlangen 23-03-1997', 2,000................................**£25-30**

YCC02 98 'MICA 13th Convention', (white seat), 1000..................**£50-60**
YCC02 98 'MICA 6th European Convention', (white seat), 600 ......**£30-40**
YCC02 98 'MICA 14th Convention', (white seat), 1000..................**£30-40**

YHN10 Holden FJ Van.
YHN01SA 'Australian Collectors Club' '98, no wing mirrors, 500 ...**£50-60**
Same but with wing mirrors, 50 ....**£70-80**
YHN01SC 'Ronald McDonald' 'Love Boat', 12th Annual Ball,
with date on rear doors, 300 ....**£200-250**
Same but with date on body side, few only..................**£300-350**
YHN01SC 'DEPENDABLE PLUMBING', 500 ....**£40-50**

YTF5 Citroën 'H' Van.
96 'BRISBANE INT'L MOTOR SHOW 1996'.
Silver/Cream/Maroon. 2,000.....................................**£35-40**
Same but with larger decals extending over door, 50...**£100-150**
96 'MATCHBOX 15th USA CONVENTION,
June 15-16 1996', Cream body, Red roof.
Blue or Red wording and decals. 500 of each.................**£60-80**
Same but in Silver/Maroon/Cream. Rear doors have
11 names of attendees of all 15 events. 15 only........**£200-300**

YPP03 Mercedes L5 Lorry.
98 '2nd German Matchbox Conv.', Black cab roof, 750 ....**£40-60**
Same but with Grey cab roof, in wooden box, 80........**£130-150**

YPP04 Dodge Route Van.
MSM01 96 'The HERSHEY HERALD', MICA Meet at Hershey,
1: Black body, Silver grille, 300 ....**£50-60**
2: Black body, Black grille, 50 ....**£80-90**
3: Red body, Silver grille, 150 ....**£140-150**
4: Silver body, Silver grille, 10 ....**£400-500**
98 'COCA-COLA', Bright Red, 300 ....**£80-100**

YY048SB Garrett Steam Wagon
98 Grey roof, 'MICA 6th European Convention', 1000 ....**£40-50**
98 Dark Blue cab, 'MICA 14th Convention', 1000 ....**£40-50**

CODE-2 SETS
M1 Set 96 Y26 **Crossley** (Maroon seats) and **MB38 Ford A Van**
'MICA 11th Convention, Telford', 250 ....**£90-100**
Same but Crossley Lorry packed in separate box, 1000 ...**£40-50**
Same but Crossley Lorry has Brown seats, 40 ....**£60-80**
M3 Set 97 Y19 **Morris Cowley Van** ('China' base) and YCC02
Austin 7 Van '12th MICA CONVENTION', 250........**£90-100**
M5 Set 98 YGB11 **Foden** (black chassis) and YCC02 **Austin 7 Van**
(blue seat), 'MICA 13th Convention', 200....................**£90-110**
M6 Set 98 YY048SB **Garrett** (grey roof) and YCC02 **Austin 7 Van**
(blue seat), 'MICA 6th European Convention', 200 ......**£90-110**
M7 Set 98 YY048SB **Garrett** (grey cab) and YCC02 **Austin 7 Van**
(blue seat), 'MICA 14th Convention', 200....................**£90-110**

Collectors notes

Vectis Auctions Ltd.

Royal National Hotel, Bedford Way, Russell Square, London

Grading system used by Vectis Auctions:

A+   As near mint or pristine condition as at time of issue
A   Virtually mint boxed - any faults of a most minor nature
B   Model is near mint - box has slight faults
B   Slight model or box faults - e.g. some chips or box rubs but
        model and box complete
C   More obvious model chips and box faults inc. tears but still complete
D   Same as C but box has one or more end flaps missing and
        model may have faded paint as well as chips
E   Model and box have considerable faults

20th JANUARY 1999
1-75 SERIES, REGULAR WHEELS
No.2C Muir Hill Site Dumper "Muir Hill" - B+ to A in B to B+ MB......£50
No.3B Bedford TK Tipper Truck - Light Grey/Red/ No Silver Trim/GPW - B+ in B to B+ MB £130
No.12C Safari Land Rover - Met Gold/BPW - superb A to A+ in C 1969 last issue MB (sellotape repair to one end flap) - very rare issue produced during the change over to Superfast wheels............£800
No.12C Safari Land Rover - Blue/SF - superb A to A+ in B to B+ correct 1969 first issue Superfast box - extremely rare model produced during the change over to Superfast wheels............£550
No.15A Prime Mover - Yellow/Silver Trim/MW - C (some paint chips touched in) in good B to C MK without model numbers on end flaps........£460
No.20B ERF Truck "Ever Ready" - Dark Blue/Orange Outline Decals/GPW/Crimped Axles - B+ to A in B MK £70
No.22B Vauxhall Cresta PA - Light Brown/Sea Green Lower Body/Green Windows/GPW - B+ (3 paint chips) in B MK £100
No.22B - a further pair - (1) Met Light Gold/Green Windows/SPW - A in A MB; (2) Met Copper/Green Windows/BPW - B+ in good C MB £160
No.26B Foden Cement Truck - Orange/Grey Barrel/Small GPW - B+ in B first issue LB............£430

No.27 Bedford Low Loader - T/T Blue/MW - B in C MK £310
No.27B Bedford Low Loader - a pair - (1) Light Green/Light Brown trailer, MW - A to A+ in B MK; (2) as (1) but GPW - overall B in B to C MK....£100
No.39B Pontiac Convertible - Met Purple/Red steering wheel/Crimson base/SPW - B+ in slightly grubby B+ MB............£55
No.45A Vauxhall Victor - Yellow/MW - presentable B in B MK - this example has NO DASHBOARD CASTING BAR, a feature normally only found on the very rare red coloured versions, as the dashboard bar was added to the casting when full production commenced and the colour changed to yellow............£330
No.45B Ford Corsair - GPW - superb A+ - in A to A+ MB £75
No.47B Commer Ice Cream Van - Blue/knobbly GPW - B+ (paint chip to roof) in slightly grubby B to B+ MB............£220
No.53A Aston Martin DB2/4 - Met Rose Red/knobbly BPW - superb A+ in A MB showing correct colour illustration of model £350
No.56A London Trolley Bus "PEARDRAX" - Red/Black trolley poles, GPW, crimped axles - A in B+ to A correct later issue MK £300

No.59A Ford Thames Van "SINGER" - Dark Green/GPW - B in B MK with model details on end flaps............£95
No.65A Jaguar 3.4 - Met Blue/GPW - lovely A to A+ in B+ MK (one end flap is however only C............£95
No.67B VW 1600 TL - Met Purple/Silver Plastic hubs with Black tyres - B+ in B correct last issue 1969 MB - very rare issue produced during the change over to Superfast wheels............£240
No.74A Mobile Canteen - Cream/Light Blue Base/knobbly GPW - B+ to A (one paint chip to roof touched in) in A MB............£95
No.75B Ferrari Berlinetta - Red/Chrome hubs with Black plastic tyres - B+ to A in A correct 1969 last issue MB - rare issue produced during the change over to Superfast Wheels £300

UNBOXED
No.11A ERF Tanker - Green/Gold trim/MW - good B to C............£260
No.46A Morris Minor - Light Tan/MW - C............£500

BOXED MODELS
No.8A Caterpillar Tractor - Orange/Silver grille/Black hat to driver/MW - B+ (wear to driver's hat) in B MK............£65
No.17B Bedford Removals Van - Dark Green/Decal with Black outline/GPW - A to A+ in good C MK............£140
No.22B Vauxhall Cresta - Met Copper/Green windows/GPW - B+ in B to C MB - rare issue with grey wheels............£160

No.25C Bedford TK Petrol Tanker "Aral" - Dark Blue/White/BPW - A to A+ in B+ to A MB showing correct colour illustration of model............£210
No.26B Foden Cement Truck - Orange/Dark Grey barrel/small knobbly GPW - B+ - in C correct first issue LB............£350
No.27A Bedford Low Loader - T/T Blue/MW - cab is B (paint chips touched in) - trailer would be A apart from coupling lugs snapped off - in good MK without model numbers on end flaps............£370

No.43A Hillman Minx - Green/MW - A to A+ in C MK............£390
No.46A Morris Minor - Blue/GPW/crimped axles - A in B+ MK............£140
No.47B Ice Cream Van - Met Blue/knobbly BPW - A in B+ MB............£80
No.53A Aston Martin - Met Rose Red/knobbly GPW - B+ (slight corrosion to edge of body) in B MK with model details on end flaps............£130
No.53A Aston Martin - Met Pale Rose Red/knobbly BPW - A to A+ in B MK with model details on end flaps............£150

No.56A London Trolley Bus "Peardrax" - Red/Black trolley poles/MW - A in good C MK............£170
No.59A Ford Thames Van "Singer" - Dark Green/GPW/rounded axles - B+ to A in B to C MK with model details on end flaps............£110
No.75A Ferrari Berlineta - Red/Chrome hubs - A in B+ blister pack - rare issue produced during the factory change over to Superfast wheels........Unsold
No.8C Caterpillar Tractor - Yellow/SPW - A+ in A MB............£95
No.10C Foden Container Truck "Tate & Lyle" - Dark Blue/Silver trim/no rear crown/BPW - A to A+ in B+ to A MB............£55
No.11B ERF Tanker "Esso" - Red/Silver grille/revised body casting with sealed rear rectangle and small open circular casting vent to base/BPW - A in B+ MB............£100
No.22B Vauxhall Cresta - Met Copper/Green windows/GPW - A in A MB............£150

No.37B Karrier Bantam Delivery Lorry "Coca Cola" - Yellow-Orange/small knobbly BPW - A to A+ in MB............£80
No.42A Bedford Van "Evening News" - Yellow/45 tread GPW - lovely A to A+ in A to A+ MB............£170
No.45A Vauxhall Victor - Yellow/Green windows/SPW - A (one very minor paint chip to roof) in A to A+ MB............£60

No.50B Drott Excavator - Red/Silver Grey base/SPW - A in B+ MB........£85
No.59A Ford Thames Van "Singer" - Dark Green/SPW - superb A+ in slightly crushed B to B+ MK with model details on end flaps............£210
No.66B Harley Davidson Motor Cycle & Sidecar - Met Bronze/Wir - A to A+ in A to A+ MB............£90
No.69B Hatra Tractor Shovel - Orange body and plastic hubs/Grey tyres - B+ in A correct first issue MB............£60
No.75A Ford Thunderbird - Cream/Salmon Pink/Black base/SPW - B+ in A+ MB............£80
No.30A Ford Prefect - Light Blue/GPW - A+ in A+ MK............£160
No.31C Lincoln Continental - Met Lime Green/BPW - B+ to A (scratch to roof) in B to B+ correct 1969 issue MB - very rare issue produced during the factory change over to Superfast wheels............£1,600
No.52A Maserati Racing Car - Red/Cream driver/52/Wir - A in B+ showing correct colour illustration of model £210

No.5C Routemaster Bus "Peardrax" - Red/GPW - A (minor wear to raised edge of radiator) in B+ LB illustrating the "Players Please" version £2,200
No.6B Euclid Quarry Truck - Yellow/knobbly GPW - B+ to A (minor paint chips to front bumper) in B MK with model details on end flaps £1,820
No.26B Foden Cement Mixer - Orange/Silver grille/Dark Grey barrel/small knobbly GPW - superb A to A+ in C correct issue LB - superb example which needs box upgrading............£850
No.51A Albion Cement Lorry "Blue Circle Portland Cement" - Yellow/Light Tan Load/Small knobbly BPW - A in good B MB £230
No.68B Mercedes Coach - Turquoise/White/BPW - B+ in A+ MB - scarce US export issue............£105
No.2C Muir Hill Dumper "Muir Hill" - Red/Green/BPW - A to A+ in A+ MB £100

No.37A Karrier Bantam Delivery Lorry "Coca Cola" - Orange-Yellow/even load/small knobbly GPW/crimped axles - B+ to A (wear to rear decal) in good C LB with model details on end flaps............£120
No.39C Ford Tractor - Orange/Yellow hubs - B+ to A in B+ correct issue "Superfast" style box £65
No.33C Lamborghini Miura - Met Gold/White Int/Chrome hubs - A+ in B to B+ US issue blister pack............£255
No.56A London Trolley Bus "Peardrax" - Red/SPW - A in good B+ MK............£170

No.27D Mercedes 230 SL - Green/Maroon-Red Int (not the usual red colour) BPW - A (very slight paint chip to front wheel arch), A+ MB - exceptionally rare pre-production colour trial. **WORLD RECORD** £4,100
No.41C Ford GT40 - White/bonnet decal/Red Int/Wir - B+ (very minor paint chips only) in C MB - extremely rare factory error, possibly unique £1,450

No.14C Bedford Lomas Ambulance - Off-White/locating marks for Red Cross cast into roof/Silver grille/SPW - A (rear doors are B+) in correct B issue LB - very rare indeed as the body casting was quickly revised to omit the roof locating marks £550
No.19A MG Midget - Off-White/Tan driver/Red seats/MW - B+ to A in B MK £65
No.8A Caterpillar Tractor - Yellow/Red driver with Black hat/Yellow MW/Grey tracks - good B in C MK...£150
No.39A Ford Zodiac Convertible - Peach/Tan Int and driver/MW - B to B+ in C MK...£130
No.41C Ford GT 40 - White/Red hubs - B in B+ first issue MB - rare model with red hubs £130

UNBOXED
No.25C Bedford TK Tanker "Aral" - Dark Blue/White/BPW - B+ £50
No.45A Vauxhall Victor - Red/MW - good B to B+ - genuine factory produced item with model having no dashboard casting bar....................£3,200

MODELS OF YESTERYEARS
PRE-PRODUCTION and COLOUR TRIALS
Y1 Jaguar SS100 - Black/Red chassis/Maroon seats/plastic 24 spoke Chrome wheels/incomplete Y number and copyright date to base/small side lights - B+ to A (a couple of very minor paint chips only) in A "Woodgrain" WB - very rare pre-production colour trial casting £650
Y4 Duesenberg Model J - White/Orange-Red chassis Yellow seats and roof with small rear window/cross braced roof support/Chrome 24 spoke wheels - A (one small paint chip to rear wheel arch) in A "Woodgrain" WB - exceptionally rare issue £2,000

STANDARD PRODUCTION ISSUES
Y2 Prince Henry Vauxhall - a pair - (1) Red/Silver Bonnet/White seats/Red grille/Copper fuel tank - B+ in A to A+ Pink/Yellow WB rare model with copper petrol tank; (2) as (1) but standard issue gold fuel tank included for comparison purposes - A unboxed £100
Y2 Prince Henry Vauxhall - Violet Blue/Silver bonnet/Red seats/Copper Pptrol tank/Chrome 24 spoke wheels - A to A+ in A to A+ woodgrain box - exceptionally rare with red seats £550
Y12 Ford Model T Van "Coca Cola" - White/5 line body/Black chassis and roof/Type 1 doors/Red 12 spoke wheels - B+ to A in A to A+ straw box - very rare first issue with the body style quickly being changed to 4 vertical line tampo print £310
Y12 "Coca Cola" - "Hoover" - Blue/White roof/Black chassis/Pale Tan seat/Type 3 doors/Gold 12 spoke wheels - A in A straw box (missing certificate) - rare promotional issue..£360
Y12 Ford Model T Van "Sunlight" - Yellow/Black roof and chassis/Type 2 doors/Red 12 spoke wheels - A in A to A+ straw box..........................Unsold
Y12 Ford Model T Van "Arnotts" - Orange-Red/Black roof and chassis, Type 2 doors/Gold 12 spoke wheels - A in A to A+ straw box £65
Y12 Ford Model T Van "Royal Mail" - "Arnotts" Red Body/Black roof and chassis/Type 2 doors/Chrome 12 spoke wheels - A to A+ apart from factory assembly error to windscreen - in A to A+ straw box - rare first issue £180
Y12 Model T Van - a pair (1) "Sunlight" - B+ in A to A+ straw box; (2) "Arnotts" - A to A+ in A to A+ straw box....................................£110
Y13 Crossley Delivery Lorry "UK Matchbox" - Red/Yellow roof and Canopy/Black seats and grille/Black chassis/Maroon 12 spoke wheels - A in B+ straw box - rare code 2 issue £75

Y8 Sunbeam Motor Cycle and Sidecar - Chrome plated/Emerald Green seat - A unboxed £340
Y8 Sunbeam Motor Cycle and Sidecar - Chrome plated/Bright Red side car seat - B+ unboxed..Unsold
Y8 Sunbeam Motor Cycle and Sidecar - Chrome plated/Maroon side car seat/Red motor cycle seat - A - unboxed..£380

Y4 Opel Coupe - White/Bright Red seat and grille/Tan textured roof with rear window - A (a couple of minor marks) in B+ pink/yellow WB - very hard to find with this roof £190
Y21 Ford Model TT Van "Barclay's Property Holdings Limited" - White/Blue/Black chassis - A+ in A to A+ box - complete with certificate of authenticity showing this to be No.106 of only 120 produced - promotional model authorised by Matchbox Collectibles £340
Y12 Ford Model T Van "Bang and Olufsen" - Red/White/Black roof and chassis/Maroon 12 spoke wheels - A+ in A box - complete with certificate, dated Sept. 1981, showing this to be number 491 - rare code 2 model......£460
Y7 Rolls Royce - Charles and Diana "Duchy of Cornwall" - A to A+ in A to A+ box - rare code 2 ....£220
Y5 Talbot Van "Iron Bridge" - A in A+ box - rare code 2 ....£140
Y12 Ford Model T Van "Cerebos Table Salt" - Yellow roof/Gold plated parts/Gold 12 spoke wheels - A (2 very small paint chips to wing edges) in B+ to A box - rare...£150

Y16 Mercedes - White/Black plastics/Black chassis - A+ in B box - very rare indeed with black chassis...£410
Y1 Ford Model T - Red/Black plastic seats and steering wheel/Maroon grille/Black textured roof - superb A+ in B+ to A MB................................£110
Y1 - Ford Model T - Cream/Met Red chassis/Black seats and grille/Black textured roof/Chrome 12 spoke wheels - A to A+ in B+ to A woodgrain box - rare £90
Y7 Rolls Royce - Silver/Red/Met Grey ribbed roof - B+ in A Pink/Yellow WB £50
Y4 Sentinal Steam Wagon "Sand and Gravel" - knobbly BPW - superb A+ in B LB...£140
Y2 London Bus - Red/Dark Blue driver/four on four windows - B+ to A in B+ LB - rare early issue...£190
Y7 Leyland Van "Jacobs" - two line/two piece decal - B+ to A in C LB - very rare issue..£520
Y5 1929 4.5 Litre Bentley - Met Apple Green/Dark Red seats/RN5 - A in good B colour LB..Unsold
Y1 Allchin Traction Engine - Green/Silver boiler door/unpainted diagonal treads - lovely A to A+ in A colour LB - rare issue.................................£110
Y5 1929 4.5 Litre Bentley - Met Apple Green/Dark Green seats/RN5 - B+ (wear to decals) in C MB...£130

ACCESSORY PACKS, MAJORS and KINGSIZE
M2 Bedford TK Articulted Truck and Trailer "Davies Tyres" - Orange Cab, Trailer chassis and rear doors/Silver Back/knobbly BPW - superb A+ (slight surface rusting axles) in A+ LB - exceptional example....................£75
MF1 Fire Station - A to A+ in B+ to A MB (minor wear to box corners)£290
MG1 Service Station "BP Matchbox Sales and Service Station" - Green/White/Yellow - A to A+ in B to B+ MB - complete with A to A+ forecourt sign..£190

EARLY LESNEY TOYS
Lesney Soapbox Racer - Met Copper Bronze/unpainted base and wheels - C (missing figure)...£250
Large Scale Horse Drawn Milk Float - Orange float/Black horse and wheels/5 White crates/White driver - C in E box....................................£230
Moko Builder's Crane - Blue/original unpainted hook - B+ in E box £120
Rag and Bone Merchant's Cart - Mustard Yellow/Met Graphite horse/Tan driver/unpainted bedstead, toilet cistern and bath tub - C.......................£290
Coronation Coach - Large Scale - 1st issue with figures of King George and The Queen - Silver linked tracers/White horse drawbar - B+ in good B to C box - very hard to find with both figures and the white drawbar £500

1-75 GIFT SETS
Commercial Motor Set - 1st issue - A (some paint to wheels) - in C sellotape repaired LB - complete with all card packing - rare set............................£300
G1 Commercial Vehicles Set - 2nd issue - A to A+ in C MB complete with slightly damaged all card packing £300
G3 Vacation Set - A to A+ in highly unusual C plain cardboard box - inner clear vacformed tray is C - highly unusual packing for this set believed to have been produced for MACEYS DEPARTMENT STORE to be used for mail order purposes..£300
G8 Kingsize Set - containing K1 Foden Tipper - A to A+; K11 Fordson Tractor and Trailer - A to A+ apart from coupling hook broken; K12 Foden Recovery Truck - A to A+; and K15 Merryweather Fire Engine - B (plastic ladder broken in two) - in highly unusual B plain yellow card box - inner blue vac formed tray is C - again believed to have been produced for MACEYS DEPARTMENT STORE for mail order purposes......................................£260
G7 Models of Yesteryear Gift Set - in C LB with card packing £310
G4 Grand Prix Set - B+ to A - in good C MB - complete with B+ yellow card plinths, A+ card packing piece - B+ in B late issue colour printed paper sleeve..£440
G6 Superfast Drag Race Set - excellent example..................................£60
G1 Service Station Set - all A to A+ in A box..£140

SHOP DISPLAY
The London to Brighton Veteran Car Game - contains Y15 Rolls Royce Silver Ghost and Y16 Spyker - both A to A+ game is complete with Roadways/wheels and Axles/23 Fuel Cards/Shakers and Dice - in very good C box - inner polystyrene tray is B+ complete with instructions £170
005 Austin A40 Van "Fourth Mica European Convention" - Mid-Grey/Black wheels - A+ in A box - rare pre-production colour (production issues are all pale grey)..£85

SUPERFAST
PRODUCTION ISSUES
No.30C Crane Truck - Red/Orange - B+ to A (Some minor paint chips only) - very rare colour £180
No.32C Leyland Tanker - Red/White tank/no labels - A - rare colour £250
No.38 Stingeroo - Met Purple/Chrome forks - superb A to A+ - very rare issue..£170

No.49C Chop-Suey - Met Red/Chrome forks - A - very rare issue...........£170
No.17F London Bus - Group of Three - (1) "Barclays Bank" - Yellow - B+ to A; (2) Borregaard Paper - A; (3) Eduscho Kaffee - B+ to A (front axle slightly bent) - rare group £280
No.17F Further Group of Four - all A to A+ - (1) "Preston Guild Merchant" - forward facing labels; (2) "Sellotape Packaging System"; (3) "Chambourcy Yogurts"; (4) "Typhoo"...£140
No.74B - Daimler Bus - "Fly Cyprus Airways" - Cherry Red/Maroon Superfast wheel covers - A to A+ £85
No.74B - Daimler Bus - "Barclays Bank" - A to A+ - rare.................£60
No.74B - Daimler Bus - "Stay at the Kensington Hilton" - A to A+ - rare .£60
No.74B - Daimler Bus pair - (1) "Inn on the Park" - B+ (rather poor factory paint finish); (2) "The Baron of Beef" - B+ to A - rare pair.......................£85
No.74B - Daimler Bus - "ICP Interchemicals and plastics" - A to A+ in A box - rare issue £85
No.74B - Daimler Bus - "The Baron of Beef" - B+ to A (slight scratch to roof) in A to A+ box - rare £50

No.17 London Bus - a pair (1) "Stay at the London Hilton" - Red/Bare Metal base - A to A+ in A box; (2) "Museum of London" - Red/Unpainted base - A to A+ in A to A+ box - scarce pair £45
No.17 Londoner Bus - a further pair - (1) "Chambourcy Yogurts" - A to A+ in A to A+ box; (2) "Charbonnier Wine" - A in A to A+ box - scarce pair..£65
No.17 Londoner Bus - Group of Three - (1) "1972 Preston Guild Merchant" - foward facing labels; (2) "Aviemore Centre"; (3) Busch Gardens - Fly British Airways" - all A to A+ in A to A+ boxes - scarce group £100

"Walt Disney Holiday Special" Christmas Stocking containing WD1 Mickey's Fire Engine; WD8 Jiminy Cricket's Old Timer; and WD9 Goofy's Sports Car - all A+ blister packed (slight crush to one blister) - outer card shaped display is good C (would have been B+ but for 4cm tear to header card) - rare; plus WD3 Goofy's Beetle - A+ in A to A+ blister pack; and CS15 Olive Oyl's Convertible - A+ in A to A+ blister pack £190
No.25D Ford Cortina - Met Bronze - A (slight mark to roof) in B+ 1st issue Superfast box showing correct colour illustration of model - rare.................£35
No.33 Lambourghini Miura - Yellow/Red Int - A to A+ in B+ to A 1st issue Superfast box showing correct colour illustration of model - rare.................£55
No.64 MG1100 - Green - B+ to A in A 1st issue Superfast box showing correct colour illustration of model - rare...£100
No.23 VW Camper - Blue/Yellow Int/Orange roof/cast fuel filler cap - A to A+ in B+ to A box - scarce £60

7th APRIL 1999
No.46B Removal Van "Pickfords" - Dark Blue/2 Line Decal/knobbly GPW - A..£140
Y8 Sunbeam Motor Cycle and Sidecar - Chrome plated/Black seat to both Motor Cycle and Sidecar - B+ in B pink/yellow WB £550

Christie's

85 Old Brompton Road, South Kensington, London, SW7 3LD

Descriptions of paintwork as used in Christie's catalogue:
M= Toys apparently never taken out of mint original boxes.
E = Excellent toys with no or very few apparent paint chips or defects.
G = Good toys with minor scratches to the paint.
F = Fair toys with an acceptable amount of paint damage.
P = Poor toys probably suitable for repainting or restoration.
SD = Some damage.

20th AND 27th MAY 1999
A Lesney Green Rag and Bone Merchants Cart, original Red and Blue Box (G-E, lacks box from junk pile, box F-G)...............................£1,035
A Lesney Prime Mover, Trailer and Bulldozer in original box 1948-1950 (G, box P-F)...£402
A Moko 'Pop-Up' Series Dark Red Model Motor Scooter in original blue, red and yellow box (G, box F-G)..£437
A Green Lesney Matchbox 43 Hillman Minx (E, box G)......................£207
14 Bedford Lomas Ambulance with silver plastic wheels and cast-in locating marks for cross on roof, in original box (E, box G)............................£747
Lesney Matchbox 1-75 Series 17 Removals Vans one light blue, one maroon and one green, with an original box £207
Lesney Matchbox 1-75 Series 53 Aston Martins metallic red with grey plastic wheels, metallic red with black plastic wheels and pale metallic green with metal wheels, in original boxes G-E, boxes G-E £253
Lesney Matchbox 11 Petrol Tank Lorries one green with gold radiator and one red, with an original box (VG - E, box) £1,380
Lesney Matchbox 1-75 Series 57 Landrover Fire Trucks one with slide-on 'Kent Fire Brigade' transfer and grey plastic wheels and one with paper label

and black plastic wheels with an original box (G-E, box F-G)....................£483
A rare Lesney German-market Matchbox P.S-4. 'Lastwagen and Omnibuse' Gift Set in original box 1959 (G-E)...............................£575
A rare Lesney Massey-Harris Tractor red scale model, steering and rubber tyres, in original box, circa 1954 (G, lacks exhaust, box P-F, lacks one end flap)...£207
Model of Yesteryear 1st type Y6 'Osram Lamps' Lorries rare dark grey with black plastic wheels (G, front wheels scuffed) pale blue (F) and mid-grey (F)...£345
A Lesney Matchbox King Size G-8 Civil Engineering Gift Set, Building Construction Vehicles K1, K2, K3, K5 and K6, with packing piece, in original box 1963 (E) £368
A Rare Lesney Y6 AEC 'Osram Lamps' Lorry dark grey with black plastic wheels, in original box (E, box F-G)...£920

Lloyd Ralston Toys

109 Glover Avenue, Norwalk, CT06850, USA

Condition Grading: C1Poor to C10 Mint
Lesney Massey-Harris Tractor $660
Moko Mechanical Drummer Boy, C7-8...$375
Moko Tractor Dozer, C9...$500
G6 Construction Set (1-75's), C9-10..$145
G1 Commercial Motors Set, C8-9..$200
MG1 BP Service Station, C9...$170
MF1 Fire Station, green roof, boxed, C9...$370
1-75's, 37 BPW, 25 GPW, 34 GPW, all 3 boxed C9...........................$310
Yesteryears, Y6, Y3, Y11 boxed in Fred Branner packaging, C10 ....$220

Barry Potter Auctions

13 Yew Tree Lane, Spratton, Northampton, NN6 8HL

13th FEBRUARY 1999
Lesney Coronation Coach. The rare version with both King and Queen figures inside, Near Mint Boxed. 2 further Coronation Coaches including miniature Lesney. Both Near Mint £330

Lacy Scott and Knight

10 Risbygate Street, Bury St Edmunds, Suffolk, IP33 3AA

Condition grading used by Lacy Scott and Knight:
B = BOXED; in the manufacturer's original box or container, in appropriate condition.
D = DAMAGED; refers to box only.
M = MINT;in perfect or near perfect condition.
NM = Excellent overall condition
G = GOOD general condition with some chips or scratches of a minor nature.
F = FAIR condition with an average proportion of chips and marks for age.
P = POOR; in only moderate condition, perhaps incomplete.

15th MAY 1999
Moko Muffin the Mule (BDNM) £140
1912 Ford Model T van Sunlight Seife (Y12-3) (BM) £50
Similar Model Arnotts Biscuits (Y12-3) (BM) £60

Dreweatt Neate Auctions

Donnington Priory, Donnington, Newbury, Berkshire, RG14 2JE

22nd APRIL 1999
Matchbox Miniature 17a, Removals Van in maroon with gold trim, near mint condition, box good..£100
Matchbox Miniature 22b, Vauxhall Cresta in metallic brown with blue-green side panels, near mint condition, box fair.....................................£90
Matchbox Miniature 37a, Karrier Bantam 2-ton 'Coca-Cola' Lorry in orange-yellow with uneven load, mint condition, box good.........................£40
Matchbox Miniature 46b, 'Pickfords' Van in blue with 3-line decal, mint boxed..£55
Matchbox Miniature 55c, Ford Galaxie Police Car with blue roof light, good condition, box good £48
Matchbox Miniature 56a, London Trolley Bus with black poles and metal wheels, mint condition, box excellent £110
Matchbox Miniature 74a, Mobile Canteen in cream, mint condition, box very good £80

Matchbox Skybusters

This listing has been researched and compiled by specialist collector Tony Martin of Farnham. Only individual known production models are listed.

Casting variations. The main differences between castings came about when dies were altered for use in other countries and when Matchbox International took over from Lesney. Where 'Made in Macau' or 'Made in Thailand' have been substituted for 'Made in England' for instance, this information appears on raised blocks usually cast on the underside of the model. Some are marked 'SP' instead of 'SB' in the casting. Different factory reference numbers can be found cast on the inside of otherwise identical components. These minor differences help to make collecting more interesting but they are not to be considered as variations which warrant a different price level.

Wheel mountings and retainers vary in thickness or extent depending on the country or year of manufacture. Some models were fitted with a wire undercarriage; this is shown in the listing where appropriate. SB 1 models made in England have wheel retainers 4mm wide and 1mm deep. Those made in Macau have wheel retainers 2mm wide and 1mm deep. SB 1 models from Thailand have wheel retainers 2mm wide and 2mm deep.

Printed detail. Some models have logos, printed detail or artwork applied as self-adhesive labels, most is applied by tampo-printing. There is much variation to be found here. Labels in particular are liable to be inaccurately cut, crooked, variable in size, shape or printing, wrongly applied or missing altogether.

Tampo-printing can also vary enormously in depth of colour or shade. But remember that these are toys made in the tens of thousands and odd items like these are bound to slip through the net. They have no greater significance than that and consequently no greater value.

Colours. Variations of shade and depth will inevitably be found particularly where metallic colours are used. Models described as being 'silver plated' or 'gold plated' (which also can vary in shade) are just 'vacuum-metallized'. Military models have a camouflage finish which, by its very nature, is likely to vary considerably.

Plastic parts originally specified as white can be found translucent, pure white, cream or ivory. Canopies are usually clear plastic but a variety of colours exists. It is quite possible that alternative colours will be found on models not normally thought to have them - please let us know if you discover any.

Country of manufacture:
E = England, M = Macau, C = China, T = Thailand

Price information:
NGPP = no guide price at present
NRP = normal retail price. In this Skybusters listing it indicates a price range **under £5**.

Country	Details	Market Price Range

SB 1 Lear Jet

Country	Details	Market Price Range
E	Lemon/white, 'D-ILDE', wire undercarriage	£8-10
E	Lemon/white, 'D-ILDE',	£9-12
E	Yellow/white, 'D-ILDE', wire undercarriage	£8-10
E, M	Yellow/white, 'D-ILDE', 'Gates Lear Jet' on tanks	£8-10
M	Lemon/white, 'Gates Lear Jet' on tanks	£6-8
M	Red, 'Datapost', yellow lettering	£5-8
M	Purple/white, 'Federal Express' orange/white lettering	£5-8
M, T, C	White/orange, 'QXpress', pale orange stripes/band	£5-8
M, T	White, 'USAF'	£8-11
M	Color-Changer, 'USAF'	£8-11
M	White, 'JCB', 'G-JCB' markings (issued in set only)	£12-15
T, C	White, 'DHL' in red	NRP

SB 2 Corsair A7D

Country	Details	Market Price Range
E	Green/white, 'Stars and Stripes' on wings, 'LA282' on fin, wire undercarriage	£10-12
E	Green/white, 'Stars and Stripes' on wings, 'LA282' on fin	£10-12
E	Metallic light blue/white, 'Stars and Bars' on wings, 'LA282' on fin	£10-12
E	Metallic light blue/white, red/white/blue/yellow roundels on wings	£40-50
E, M	Metallic blue/white, 'Stars and Bars' on wings, 'LA282' on fin	£8-10
M, T	Camouflage, 'Stars and Bars' on wings, 'LA282' on fin	£5-7
M	Color-Changer, 'Stars and Bars' on wings, 'LA282' on fin	£8-11

SB 3-A A300B Airbus

This model was later renumbered SB28.

Country	Details	Market Price Range
E	White/silver, 'Air France' labels or tampo print, wire undercarriage	NRP
E	White/silver, 'Air France'	NRP
E	White/silver, 'Lufthansa', 'D-AXJI'	NRP
E	White/silver, 'Delta', 'N601DA'	NGPP

SB 3-B Space Shuttle

Country	Details	Market Price Range
E	White/grey, 'NASA UNITED STATES' label	£5-8
M	White/silver, 'NASA UNITED STATES' labels	NRP
T, C	White/black, 'NASA UNITED STATES' labels	NRP
T	White, no markings. (From 'Graffic Traffic' set)	£6-8

SB 4 Mirage F-1

Earlier issues have a slimmer nose section and are without a hole in the fuselage under the canopy.

Country	Details	Market Price Range
E	Metallic red, yellow/blue/white/red roundels, wire undercarriage	£5-7
E	Metallic red, yellow/blue/white/red roundels	£6-9
E	Red, clear canopy, yellow/blue/white/red roundels	£10-12
M	Metallic maroon, yellow/blue/white/red roundels	£8-10
M, T, C	Yellow/red/blue, 'VAQ132'	NRP
M	Color-Changer, 'VAQ132'	£6-8
M, T	White/blue, 'Marines ZE-146'	NRP
T	Red/blue/white, Patrouille de France colours	NRP
C	Olive/cream camouflage, French roundels on wings	NRP

SB 5 Starfighter F105

Country	Details	Market Price Range
E	White/silver, 'RCAF', blue canopy	£6-8
E	White/silver, 'RCAF', blue canopy, wire undercarriage	£10-12
E	Red/silver, 'RCAF', blue or clear canopy	£12-15

SB 6 MIG-21

Country	Details	Market Price Range
E	Turquoise/white, round star-shaped labels	£5-8
E	Turquoise/white, star-shaped labels, wire undercarriage	£10-12
E	Blue/white, star-shaped labels, wire undercarriage	£25-30
M, T	Metallic silver, '23', red stars	NRP
M, T	Black/yellow, '23 988'	NRP
M	Color-Changer, '25 988'	£6-8
C	Camouflaged, red stars on wings	NRP

SB 7 Junkers JU87-E Stuka

Country	Details	Market Price Range
E	Black/silver, swastika on fin, wire undercarriage	£40-50
E	Green, swastika on fin, wire undercarriage	£10-12
E	Green, cross or no label on fin	£8-10
E	Gold-plated souvenir issue	£60-70
E	Black/beige/brown, plain fin	£9-12
E	Black/cream, plain fin	£20-25
M	Black/beige/brown, cross on fin	£9-12

SB 8 Spitfire

Country	Details	Market Price Range
E	Dark brown/bronze, fin stripes, wire undercarriage	£30-40
E	Green/gold, fin stripes, wire undercarriage	£8-10
E	Green/gold, plain fin	£7-8
E	Plum/khaki camouflage, plain fin	£12-15
M	Tan/khaki camouflage, plain fin	£5-8

T	Gold/green/camouflage. Intended Kellogg's promotional, not issued, no box	NRP

SB 9 Cessna 402

E	Metallic green/white, brown/orange labels, wire undercarriage	£8-10
E	Metallic light green/white, 'N7873Q'	£5-8
M	Light brown/light beige, 'N402CW'	NRP
M, T, C	Blue/yellow, 'S7-402'	NRP
M, T	White/red, 'DHL' in light brown	NRP
C	Black, yellow 'S7-402' on wings, yellow shield on nose	£25-35
C	Olive, white stars on wings, flaming torch on nose	£25-35
C	White, 'Delivery Service' in red on wings	NRP

SB 10 Boeing 747

E	'B.O.A.C.', wire undercarriage	£20-25
E	White/gold-plate, 'B.O.A.C.', mounted on pen-stand	£20-30
E	'British Airways', wire undercarriage	£8-10
E	'British Airways' tampo-printed	£8-10
E	White/gold-plate, 'British Airways', mounted on ash-tray	£15-20
E	'MEA' (Middle East Airlines)	£50-60
E	White/dark blue, 'Qantas' in red	£20-25
E	White/silver, 'Qantas' in red	£15-20
E	White/silver, 'United States of America'. 'Airforce One'	£30-40
E	White/blue, 'United States of America'. 'Airforce One'	£60-70
E, M	White with metallic blue or dark blue, 'British'	£25-30
M	'British Caledonian'	£9-12
M, T	'Pan Am'	£5-8
M	'All Nippon Airways', (in set only)	£70-80
M	'Cathay Pacific'	£6-8
M, T	'Lufthansa'	NRP
M, T	'Virgin'	NRP
M, T	'Aer Lingus'	NRP
M, T	'KLM'	NRP
M	'Japan Airlines'	£70-80
M	'Air France'	£70-80
T	'El Al'	£15-20
T	'South African Airlines'	£15-20
T	'Olympic'	NRP
T	'Saudi Arabian Airlines'	NRP
T	'Swissair'	£70-80

SB 11 Alpha Jet

E	Orange-red/white, 'Luftwaffe', wire undercarriage	£12-15
E	Red/white, 'Luftwaffe'	£8-10
E	Blue/red, no markings	£15-20
E, M	White/red, RAF markings, 'AT39'	£10-15
M	Blue/red, red/white/blue stripes on wings, Patrouille de France livery	£5-8
M, T	Blue, '162' on wings	NRP
C	Black with green/black/yellow roundels, 'AT39'	£25-35
C	Olive, star and 'T30' in white on wings, flaming torch behind canopy	£25-35

SB 12 Mission Helicopter

Issued as a Skybuster in the USA, 'MB57' but no SB number on model ....NRP

SB 12-A Skyhawk

E	Metallic blue/white, 'Navy' on fin, wire undercarriage	£10-12
E	Metallic blue/white, 'Navy' on fin	£15-20
E	Metallic blue/white, 'US Marines'	£8-10

SB 12-B Pitts Special

SB 12/b can be found with different propeller bosses.

E	Maroon/white, check pattern on wings	£12-15
E	Maroon/white, red/white flares on wings	£15-20
E	Maroon/white, red/white check pattern on top wing, red/white flares on bottom wing	£20-25
E, M	Green/white, red/white flares on wings	£12-15
M	Blue/white, 'Matchbox'	£7-10

M	Red, 'Red Rebels Aerobatics'	NGPP
M, T	Red, 'Virgin', '0293-38222'	£6-8
T	White, red pilot. From 'Graffic Traffic' set	£6-8

SB 13 DC10

E	Red/white, 'Swissair' label, wire undercarriage	£6-8
E	Red/white, 'Swissair' label	£6-8
E	White/silver, 'Swissair'	£6-8
M	White/grey, 'Swissair'	NRP
E, M	White/silver, 'United'	£6-8
M	White, 'Japan Air Lines'	£70-80
M	White, 'UTA' in blue	£30-35
M, T	'Aeromexico' in red	NRP
M, T	'Thai', pink/purple/gold stripe	NRP
M, T	Silver, 'American' in red	NRP
T	White, 'Scandinavian' in mauve, 'SAS' on fin	£12-15
T, C	White/blue/silver, 'KLM' in blue	NRP
T	White/silver, 'SABENA' in turquoise	NRP

SB 14 Cessna 210G

E	Orange/white, black/orange wing stripes, wire undercarriage	£10-12
E	Orange/white, black/orange wing stripes	£7-9
E	Orange/white, 'N94209' on wing	£7-9
E	Red/white, float plane (became SB 26, black floats)	NRP

SB 15 Phantom F-4E

E	Metallic red/white, RAF markings, large or small fin labels	£8-10
E	Red/white, RAF markings	£15-20
M, T	Grey/orange, 'MARINES', 'AJ135' on fin	NRP
C	White, '5000 Navy' in black	NRP

SB 16 Corsair F4U-5N

E	Blue, 'NAVY' on one wing, star on other wing	£10-15
E	Dark orange, 'NAVY' and star	£15-20
M	Orange, 'NAVY' and star	NRP

SB 17 Ramrod

E	Red/white, lightning labels on wings	£8-10

SB 18 Wild Wind

E	Lime green/white, yellow/orange labels, '7' on fin	£6-8
E	Lime green/white, yellow/orange labels, blue star on fin	£25-30
E	Green/white, orange labels, '7' on fin	£20-25
M	Green/white, orange labels, '7' on fin	NRP

SB 19 Commanche

E	Red/yellow, 'N246P' yellow labels on wings	£6-8
M	Red/yellow, 'N246P' tampo-printed	NRP
M	White, 'XP' in black, yellow and green stripes on wings	£5-7
M, T, C	Tan/dark blue, 'Piper' on fuselage, 'Comanche' on wings	NRP

SB 20 Helicopter

Either 'SB 20' or 'SB 25' may be found on the tail rotor of this issue. Some of those with 'SB 20' have been issued in 'SB 25' boxes.

E	Olive, 'Army', white or cream seats	£8-10
E, M	White/red, 'Police', white or cream seats	£8-10
E	White/light blue, 'Coast Guard'	£8-10
E	Yellow/white, no markings	£18-22
M	Metallic dark blue, 'Gendarmerie', 'JAB'	£25-30

SB 21 Lightning

E	Olive/grey or dark olive/grey, 'RAF' markings	£10-12
E	Silver/grey, 'RAF' markings	£10-12
E	Silver, 'RAF' markings	£12-15
E	Silver, 'USAF' markings	£40-50
M	Silver/grey, 'RAF' markings	£12-15

SB 22 Tornado

E, M	Grey/light grey/white, Luftwaffe markings	NRP
M	Red/white, 'RAF 06' on fin	£5-7
T	Grey/white, 'RAF 06' on fin	£10-12
M, T, C	Grey/white, 'RAF J' on fin	NRP
M	ColorChanger, 'RAF J' on fin	£5-7
C	Grey and olive camouflage, RAF roundels on wings and tailplanes.	NRP

SB 23 Supersonic Airliner

E	White, 'Air France F-BVFA', 'Concorde' on fuselage	£100-150
E, M	White, 'Air France L-EJDA', no 'Concorde' markings	NRP
T, C	White, 'Air France F-BVFA', no 'Concorde' markings	NRP
E	White, 'Singapore Airlines'	£75-100
M, T	White, 'Supersonic Airlines', 'G-BSAA'	NRP
T, C	White, 'British Airways', grey lining on wings	NRP
T	White, 'British Airways', no lining on wings	£15-20
T	White, no markings (Graffic Traffic)	£6-8
T	White, 'Heinz' logo in red on wings, '57' in red on tail fin	£75-100

SB 24 F16A Fighter

E, M	White/red, 'USAF' markings	£6-8
E, M	White/red, no markings	£10-15
M, T	Red/white, 'USAF', United States Airforce	£8-10
M	White/black, 'Thunderbird' markings	£8-10
M, T, C	Camouflage, 'USAF', '13316' on fin	NRP
M	Color-Changer, 'USAF', '13316' on fin	£6-8
T	White, no markings, red canopy, (Graffic Traffic)	£6-8
C	Camouflage, Israeli Airforce markings	NRP

SB 25 Helicopter

SB 20 casting with 'SB 20' removed. Most have two rotor blades and skids.
Sometimes issued in SB 20 boxes.

E	Yellow, 'Rescue'	£12-15
E	White/red, 'LA Fire Dept'	£20-25
M	White/red, '007' in black, only issued in a set	£15-18
M	Blue, 'RAF Rescue', yellow rotors	NRP
C	Blue, 'RAF Rescue', black rotors	£5-8
C	Bluish grey, 'RAF Rescue', black rotors	NRP
M	Dark blue, 'Air Aid', four wheels	£5-7
M, T	White, 'Shell'	NRP

SB 26 Cessna Float Plane

E, M	Red/white, 'N246H', (numbered SB14 or SB 26)	NRP
M	Black/white, 'C210F'	NRP
M	White, '007 James Bond' in black, only issued in a set	£15-18
M, T	Red, 'Fire', '36' on nose and tail fin	NRP
C	White, 'National Park Service' in green on wing, green prop.	NRP
C	White, 'Forest Service' in green on wing, 'FS' on fin, green prop.	NRP

SB 27 Harrier

E	White/red/blue, 'US Marines'	£8-10
M	White/red/blue, 'US Marines'	£5-8
E	White/red, no markings	£10-12
M	Blue/white or metallic blue/white, 'Royal Navy 100'	£5-8
T	Blue/white, 'Royal Navy'	NRP
M, T	Light grey/white, 'RAF XZ131'	NRP
M, T	Camouflage/white, 'US Marines'	NRP
M	Color-Changer, 'US Marines'	£6-8

SB 28 A300B Airbus

Casting as SB 3.

M	White/silver, 'Lufthansa'	NRP
M, T	White, 'Alitalia'	NRP
M, T	Blue/silver, 'Korean Air'	NRP
M	White/silver, 'Swissair'	NRP
M	White, 'Iberia'	NRP
M	White, 'Air Inter'	£25-30
M	Silver, 'Eastern'	£70-80
M, T	'Air France'	NRP

T	White, 'Air Malta'	£10-12
T	White/silver, 'Delta'	NGPP

SB 29 SR71 Blackbird

M, T	Matt black, 'USAF'	NRP
C	Silver/black, 'USAF'	NRP

SB 30 Grumman Tomcat

M, T, C	Grey/white, 'Navy', '610'	NRP
C	White, star and bars with '15' on wing	NRP

SB 31 Boeing 747-400

There is no 'SB' on this model.

M, T	White/grey, 'Cathay Pacific' in red	£8-10
T	White/silver, 'Lufthansa'	NRP
T, C	Grey/dark blue, 'British Airways'	NRP
T	White/silver, 'Singapore Airlines'	£5-8

SB 32 A10 Thunderbolt

M, T	Camouflage	£5-8
C	Brown/sand, 'Desert Storm' livery	NRP
C	Cream, orange and green 'blobs' over top of aircraft	NRP

SB 33 Bell Jet Ranger

M, T	White/blue/orange	NRP

SB 34 Hercules

M, T	White, 'USCG', orange wing tips	NRP

SB 35 MIL HIND MI-24 Helicopter

T	Brown/beige, 'USSR', military markings	NRP
C	Camouflage/grey, '0709' on side	NRP

SB 36 Stealth Fighter

M, T, C	Dark grey, 'USAF' markings	NRP
M	White, no markings, (Graffic Traffic)	£12-15
C	Black, 'USAF' markings	NRP

SB 37 BAe Hawk T Mk.I

There is no 'SB' number marked on this model.

T	Red, 'Red Arrow' livery, white arrow on underside	NRP
T	Red, 'Red Arrow' livery, no white arrow	NRP

SB 38 BAe 146

T	White/grey, 'Dan Air'	£5-8
T	White/grey, 'Dan Air-London'	£25-30
C	White, 'Continental', blue/red cheat line	NRP
C	White, 'Continental', blue/gold cheat line	£5-8

SB 39 Stearman PT17

T, C	Yellow, 'Crunchie'	NRP
T	Silver, 'Australian National Airways', 'Royal Mail in black	£10-15
T	White, 'Circus Circus', issued in set only	£12-15
C	Blue or yellow, or blue/yellow, or yellow/blue, 'Ditec'	£30-35

SB 40 Boeing 737

T	White/blue/silver, 'Britannia'	NRP
T	Blue/silver, 'KLM'	NRP
T	White, 'Lufthansa'	£15-20

SB 41 Boeing 777

C	White, in prototype aircraft colours, in double pack only	pack: £30-35
C	Unpainted, in double pack only	pack: £30-35

Morestone, Modern Products, Budgie Toys and Seerol

The following history and listings have been provided by Robert Newson.

The history of these makes is a fascinating story of inter-linked companies, take-overs and bankruptcies reflecting the ups and downs of the toy trade. In the late 1940s Morris & Stone was a toy wholesaler selling the products of many small toy manufacturers including those from Modern Products who had started as die-casters. Morris and Stone decided to have their own exclusive 'Morestone' branded lines and some were made by Modern Products, who increasingly relied on Morestone for the sole marketing and distribution of their toys. Morestone continued to use several suppliers but in 1954 set up a die-casting company jointly with Rodney Smith (one of the founders of Lesney Products).

From the mid-1950s to 1966 the Morestone and Budgie ranges contained models that came either from the in-house factory or from Modern Products. Morestone's production expanded with new ranges of models, such as the 'Noddy' and 'Big-Ears' vehicles in 1956 and the Esso Petrol Pump Series of miniatures, launched at Christmas of that year. In 1958, the 'Trucks of the World International Series' was introduced, but only ran to three models.

Some of the earlier Morestone and Modern Products models were re-issued as part of the Budgie range which was introduced in 1959. Model numbers were allocated in 1960 and new additions to the range continued every year up to 1966. During 1961, Morris & Stone was taken over by S. Guiterman & Co. Ltd., who changed the name of their new subsidiary to Budgie Models Ltd. Although the range included many interesting and unusual subjects, they failed to compete with Corgi, Dinky and Matchbox, and losses in Budgie Models Ltd. contributed to losses in the Guiterman group. In March 1966 these companies went into voluntary liquidation.

Modern Products was badly hit by this but eventually were able to set up a new company called Budgie Models (Continuation) Ltd and purchase the Budgie trade mark from the receiver. They wanted the Budgie dies as well, but these were destroyed in a fire while negotiations were in progress. The only dies to survive were those in their own factory. Thus the main range of Budgie commercial vehicles came to an end in 1966.

Modern Products continued to produce the Budgie miniatures, mainly for the USA, until 1969 when the stronger competition this time was from Mattel's 'Hot Wheels'. Modern Products direction for the 1970s was to produce models for H. Seener Ltd., distributors of toys and souvenirs to London's tourist shops. The old Budgie Routemaster bus was reintroduced for Seener, followed by a new FX4 Taxi and Rolls-Royce Silver Cloud.

In 1983, following the death of one of the partners in Modern Products, the business was sold to a neighbouring engineering company called Starcourt Ltd (some boxes say Merracroft Ltd - an associated company of Starcourt). The new owners reintroduced several models from the original moulds, starting with the Aveling Barford Road Roller. However, a disagreement developed with Seener who withdrew the dies for the Taxi and Rolls-Royce (which he had paid for), and arranged for these to be made by Corgi together with a completely new Routemaster bus. These 'Seerol' models appeared in 1985 and are still available. Starcourt ceased toy production in 1985.

Some unpainted castings for no.204 Volkswagen Pick-Up and some empty boxes were sold to a Dutch firm and have since appeared in various liveries. These are classed as 'Code 3' models and have not been listed. The die-casting moulds were sold to Autocraft (Dave Gilbert) in 1988, and these include most of the 1950s Modern Products and part of the 1960s Budgie range. Autocraft are now in the process of adapting dies for a range of some 35 various models. Only one model has so far been reintroduced - a run of 1000 of no.258 Daimler Ambulance in kit form.

A complete history of these companies and their products is contained in the book 'Budgie Models' by Robert Newson. This hardback book also has full descriptions of all the models, 58 pages of colour photographs illustrating over 180 models, and reproductions of Budgie leaflets.

Morestone and Modern Products

Ref.	Year(s)	Model name	Colours, features, dimensions	Market Price Range
-	c.1946	**Racing Car**	Red, Dark Blue, Dark Green or Light Brown. One piece casting including driver. No identification on model. 135 mm	£30-40
-	c.1947	**Stage Coach with Four Horses**	English mail coach with driver and trunk, Yellow body, Red wheels, 173 mm. 'Ye Olde Coach and Four' on box	£100-150
-	c.1948-56	**Fire Escape** (large)	Brass bell and wheel hubs. Base consists of sump and prop shaft only. Extending wheeled escape ladder. 108 mm. (excluding ladder)	£60-80
-	c.1950	**Fire Escape** (smaller)	Plain flat base, wheeled escape ladder, 66 mm. (excluding ladder)	£60-80
-	c.1948	**Fire Engine**	Clockwork motor and bell underneath, 'Morestone Series' cast-in, 135 mm	£80-90
-	c.1948-58	**0-6-0 Tank Locomotive**	Green or Red, 'British Railways' cast in, re-issued as Budgie 224, 119 mm	£25-35
-	1949-51	**Horse Drawn Snack Bar**	'SAM'S' cast on side below counter, removable roof, separate man, tea urn and two mugs, 117mm. Wide range of colours	£65-85
-	1949-59	**Horse Drawn Hansom Cab**	Black / Yellow, driver, elastic band for reins, 118 mm. (re-issued as Budgie 100)	£50-70
-	c.1948-61	**Horse Drawn Covered Wagon with Four Horses**	Green, Red or Orange, driver, cloth canopy plain or printed with 'Thundering Hooves and Blazing Guns on the Western Trail', or 'Walt Disney's Davy Crockett Frontier Wagon' or 'Last of the Mohicans Chingachgook Hawkeye', later with two barrels, 'Made in England' cast transversely under, 190 mm. (Budgie 404).	£70-90
-	1949	**'Wells Fargo' Stage Coach with two 'Galloping' Horses**	Brown / Yellow, driver and guard, eccentric wheel for 'galloping' effect, some with 'Copyright F.W. Birch & Co.' cast inside, 164 mm	£70-90
-	c.1950	**'Wells Fargo' Stage Coach**	Various colours, four horses, driver, 172 mm	£70-90
-	1952-58	**Stage Coach with Two Horses**	Red or Orange (no lettering), Black plastic horses, wheels and figures,165 mm	£70-90
-	1954-59	**Horse Drawn Covered Wagon with Six Horses**	Red, Yellow wheels, printed cloth canopy 'The Wild West Land of Buffalo and Covered Wagon', driver, two barrels, 'Made in England' cast transversely underneath, 265mm	£70-90
-	1950-51	**Road Sweeper**	'City Cleansing Dept.' cast-in, clockwork motor in some, 91 mm	£80-100
-	c.1950	**Compressor**	With man and pneumatic drill. No identification cast on model. 76 mm	£40-50
-	1953	**State Landau with Six Horses**	Coronation souvenir, three figures cast-in. No identification on model. 111 mm	£30-40
-	1953	**Prime Mover with Trailer**	Red prime mover, 'British Road Services', 'NO 311' and 'MAX 20 MPH' cast-in, Black plastic wheels, 83 mm. Orange plastic trailer, 136 mm	£100-125
-	1953	**Sleigh with Father Xmas**	One reindeer. No identification on model. About 140 mm	£65-85

Morestone and Modern Products

-	1953-55	**RAC Motorcycle and Sidecar**	Cast wheels / tyres and rider, no windscreen, hinged lid on sidecar, 70 mm	**£75-100**
-	1954-55	**A.A. Motorcycle and Sidecar**	Cast wheels / tyres and rider, windscreen, non-opening sidecar, separate rails	**£75-100**
-	1956-57	**RAC Motorcycle and Sidecar**	Cast rider, windscreen, separate rails and hinged lid on sidecar, steering front forks, rubber tyres, plain number plates, 82 mm	**£75-100**
-	1956-57	**A.A. Motorcycle and Sidecar**	Cast rider, windscreen, separate rails and hinged lid on sidecar, steering front forks, rubber tyres, plain number plates, 82 mm	**£75-100**
-	1956-57	**Solo Motorcycle**	Cast rider, steering front forks, rubber tyres, plain number plates, 82 mm. There are four versions: Police Patrol, Despatch Rider, GPO Messenger and TT Rider. Each	**£50-75**
-	?	**Police Motorcycle and Sidecar**	Black machine, Dark Blue sidecar, Black uniformed figures, cast wheels	**£50-75**
-	1954-55	**Horse Drawn Gipsy Caravan**	Yellow / Green, tinplate roof and base, separate driver and rear steps, 190 mm	**£200-250**
-	1954-56	**Bedford Dormobile**	Red or Green body. 90 mm	**£100-125**
-	1955-58	**Leyland Double Deck Bus**	'Finest Petrol - ESSO - in the World', Red or Green, route '7', 103 mm	**£70-80**
			'ESSO - for Happy Motoring - ESSO', Red body, route '7', 103 mm	**£70-80**
			'Motor Oil - ESSO - Petrol', Red body, route '7', 103 mm	**£70-80**
-	1955-56	**Aveling-Barford Road Roller**	Green, Yellow or Red, with driver, 117 mm. Re-issued as Budgie 701	**£40-50**
-	1955-59	**Wolseley 6/80 Police Car**	Black, loudspeaker, aerial, 113 mm. No maker's name. (Budgie 246)	**£50-60**
1	1955-57	**Foden 8-wheel Petrol Tanker**	Red body, 'Motor Oil Esso Petrol' transfers, 136 mm	**£175-200**
2	1955-56	**Foden 8-wheel Open Lorry**	Light brown cab and chassis, Red truck body, 138 mm	**£125-150**
3	1955-56	**Foden Flat Lorry with Chains**	Green cab and 8-wheel chassis, Beige flatbed, brass chain, 138 mm	**£125-150**
4	1955-57	**Foden 8-wheel Flat Lorry**	Yellow or Orange cab and chassis, Grey flatbed, 138 mm	**£125-150**
-	1956-57	**Bedford Car Transporter**	Orange cab, Grey trailer, collapsible top deck, two loading ramps, 243 mm	**£75-90**
-	1956	**Daimler Ambulance**	White or Cream body (no transfers), Silver base, opening rear doors, no maker's name, 110 mm. Re-issued as Budgie 258	**£75-90**
-	1955-57	**A.A. Land Rover** (large)	Yellow / Black, 'AA ROAD SERVICE' cast-in, opening rear doors, driver, passenger, 108 mm	**£100-125**
-	1957-58	**A.A. Land Rover** (medium)	Yellow / Black, driver, 79 mm. 'AA ROAD SERVICE' transfers, no rear windows	**£100-125**
			Same but 'AA ROAD SERVICE' cast-in, two rear windows	**£100-125**
-	1958	**Military Police Land Rover**	Olive Green, driver, 'MP Military Police' cast on sides, 79 mm	**£150-200**
-	1958	**Breakdown Service Land Rover**	Red body, driver, 'Breakdown Service Unit' cast on sides, 79 mm	**£75-100**
-	1958	**Foden Dumper**	Orange cab and chassis, Grey dumper, 108 mm. Re-issued as Budgie 226	**£40-50**

Morestone 'Trucks of the World International' Series

-	1958	**Klöckner Side Tipper**	Red cab, Black chassis, Cream tipper, 81 mm. (with 'Driving Licence')	**£40-50**
-	1958	**Scammell Articulated Tanker**	Orange cab, Cream tank. 'LIQUID IN BULK' cast on sides, 114 mm	**£35-45**
-	1958	**International Articulated Refrigerator Lorry**	Red / Blue cab, Silver trailer, 'COAST to COAST REFRIGERATION' transfers, 153 mm. Re-issued as Budgie 202	**£40-50**

'Noddy' items by Morestone and Budgie

The 'Noddy' items were given numbers when incorporated in the Budgie range around 1960.

301	1956-61	**Noddy and his Car** (large)	Yellow / Red, windscreen, solid rubber wheels, metal or plastic 'Noddy', 98 mm	**£100-150**
-	1957-58	**Big Ears on Bicycle** (large)	Red bicycle (64 mm.), metal 'Big Ears' with legs that move as the model is pushed along. No maker's name on model	**£125-175**
-	c.1959	**Clown on Bicycle** (large)	Metallic Light Brown bicycle (64 mm. as previous model), metal clown figure with moving legs. No maker's name on model	**£100-125**
-	1958	**Noddy's Garage Set**	331 Noddy's Car and 'Esso' series nos. 7, 13, 16 and 20. Box folds into garage	**£150-175**
303	c.1961	**Noddy and his Car** (large) with Big Ears	As 301 but with additional metal Big Ears Figure	**£125-175**
305	1959-61	**Noddy's Gift Box**	Contains numbers 331, 333 and plastic Mr. Plod the Policeman	**£150-200**
307	1959-61	**Locomotive and Wagon with Noddy and Big Ears**	Yellow loco with red cab. Red wagon. Plastic figures, 104 mm	**£100-125**
309	c.1961	**Noddy and Locomotive**	As no.307 but without wagon, 57 mm	**£60-80**
311	1960-61	**Noddy on Bicycle with Trailer**	Yellow bicycle, red trailer, plastic figure, 81 mm	**£80-100**
331	1958-61	**Noddy and his Car** (small)	Yellow car, red base and wheels, plastic figure, 52 mm	**£80-100**
333	1958-61	**Big Ears on Bicycle** (small)	Red. No maker's name on model. Plastic figure, 48 mm	**£80-100**

Morestone and Budgie Miniatures

Packed in 'Esso' Petrol Pump boxes from 1956 to around 1959, then in Budgie bubble packs (yellow backing card) till 1964, and from 1965 in bubble packs with blue backing card. In early 1960s conventional boxes marked 'Mobile Vehicle Series' or 'Modern Vehicle Series' were also used.

1	1956-58	**A.A. Motorcycle and Sidecar**	Rider, separate windscreen, 'MADE IN ENGLAND' under lid, 46 mm	£30-40
2	1956-58	**RAC Motorcycle and Sidecar**	Rider, separate windscreen. 'MADE IN ENGLAND' under lid, 46 mm	£30-40
3	1956-58	**A.A. Land Rover**	'AA ROAD SERVICE' cast-in, spare wheel (on bonnet) on some, 54 mm	£25-35
4	1956-58	**A.A. Bedford Van**	AA badge and 'ROAD SERVICE' cast-in, 57 mm	£25-35
5	1956-70	**Wolseley 6/80 Police Car**	Black or green body, 65 mm	£15-20
6	1956-58	**Cooper-Bristol Racing Car**	Blue or Dark Blue body, Off-White base and driver, 58 mm	£15-20
7	1956-65	**Mercedes-Benz Racing Car**	Silver body, Red base and driver, 60 mm	£15-20
8	1956-70	**Volkswagen 1200 Saloon**	Metallic Light Blue body, 58 mm	£15-20
9	1956-58	**Maudslay Horse Box**	Red body, 'HORSE BOX SERVICE' cast-in, 57 mm	£20-30
10	1956-58	**Karrier GPO Telephones Van**	Dark green body, 57 mm	£20-30
11	1957-65	**Morris Commercial Van**	Red body, 'ROYAL MAIL' and 'E-II-R' cast-in, 58 mm	£15-20
12	1957-70	**Volkswagen Microbus**	Light Brown, Pale Blue or Metallic Dark Blue, 61 mm	£15-20
13	1957-64	**Austin FX3 Taxi**	Black body, Silver base and driver, 58 mm	£15-20
14	1957-70	**Packard Convertible**	Beige or Metallic Lt.Blue body, Red base/seats, Lt. Brown or Gold driver	£15-20
15	1957-70	**Austin A95 Westminster Countryman**	Blue or Orange, (Silver flash on some); or Metallic Mauve, 66 mm	£15-20
16	1957-64	**Austin-Healey 100**	Red body, Off-White base and driver, 57 mm	£20-25
17	1957-58	**Ford Thames 5 cwt. Van**	Blue body, 60 mm	£40-50
18	1957-66	**Foden Dumper**	Red cab and chassis, Lemon-Yellow or Grey dumper, 60 mm	£15-20
19	1957-70	**Rover 105R**	Green or Gold body, 65 mm	£15-20
20	1957-64	**Plymouth Belvedere Convertible**	Pale Pink or White body, Red base and driver, 64 mm	£20-30
20	1968-70	**Austin A95 Emergency Vehicle**	As 15 but White with Orange beacon, 'EMERGENCY' transfer, Red base	£35-45
21	1963-66.	**Bedford TK Tipper Lorry**	Dark Green tipper. Yellow, Off-White or Orange cab, 58 mm	£15-20
21	1968-70	**Oldsmobile Town Sedan**	Gold body, 66 mm	£20-25
22	1963-66	**Bedford TK Crane Lorry**	Dark Green cab, Orange crane, Orange or Dark Green platform, 56 mm	£15-20
22	1968-70	**Cattle Transporter**	Adapted from no.58. Light Brown body, Dark Brown rear door, 61 mm	£20-25
23	1963-66	**Bedford TK Cement Mixer**	Off-White mixer. Green, Yellow, Red or Orange cab and chassis, 59 mm	£15-20
24	1963-66	**Bedford TK Refuse Lorry**	Green, Orange, Red or Yellow cab, Silver back, 59 mm	£15-20
25	1963-66	**Bedford TK Cattle Lorry**	Light brown body. Off-White, Orange or Yellow cab, 58 mm	£15-20
26	1963-66	**Aveling-Barford Road Roller**	Similar to Lesney Matchbox no.1c. Green body, Red wheels, 55 mm	£15-20
27	1963-70	**Wolseley 6/80 Fire Chief Car**	Same as no.5 with altered base lettering. Red body, 65 mm	£20-25

Models 50 - 55 were designated the 'Road Tanker Series'.

50	1963-66	**'BP Racing Service' Tanker**	Green with White tank, 61 mm	£15-20
51	1963-66	**'Shell' Tanker**	Yellow, 61 mm	£15-20
52	1963-64	**'Shell BP' Tanker**	Green or Yellow; White tank, 61 mm	£15-20
53	1963-66	**'National' Tanker**	Blue with Yellow tank, 61 mm	£15-20
54	1963-66	**'BP' Tanker**	Green with White tank, 61 mm	£15-20
55	1963-66	**'Mobil' Tanker**	Red body, 61 mm	£15-20
56	1966-70	**GMC Box Van**	'HERTZ TRUCK RENTAL' transfers and 'TRUCK RENTAL' cast-in. Light Green or Pale Blue body, 61 mm	£15-20
57	1966-70	**International Parcels Van**	Green body, sliding door. 'REA EXPRESS' transfers, 67 mm	£15-20
58	1966-70	**'Modern Removals' Van**	'MODERN REMOVALS' transfers. Light Brown or Metallic Green, 61 mm	£15-20
59	1967-70	**AEC Merryweather Fire Engine**	Copied from Lesney Matchbox no.9c. Red body, Gold ladder, 65 mm	£15-20
60	1966-70	**Rover 105R Squad Car**	As no.19 but with altered base lettering. Black or Red body, 65 mm	£15-20
61	1966-70	**Austin A95 'Q Car'**	As no.15 but with altered base lettering. Black or Metallic Dark Blue body	£15-20

Sets of three vehicles (bubble-packed)

94	1966	**Interpol Set**	Intended to contain no.5 Police Car, 60 Squad Car, 61 'Q' Car. Not issued	NPP
95	1966	**Road Haulage Set**	Intended to contain 56 Hertz Van, 57 REA Van, 58 Removals Van. Not issued	NPP
96	1965-66	**Road Construction Set**	Contains no.18 Dumper, 23 Cement Mixer, 26 Road Roller	£50-75
97	1965-66	**Truck Set**	Contains no.21 Tipper, 22 Crane, 25 Cattle Lorry	£50-75
98	1965-66	**Utility Vehicle Set**	Contains no.12 VW Microbus, 24 Refuse Lorry, 55 Mobil Tanker	£50-75
99	1965-66	**Traffic Set**	Contains no.8 Volkswagen, 15 Austin, 27 Fire Chief	£50-75
95	1968-70	**Town Set**	Contains no.20 Emergency Vehicle, 21 Oldsmobile, 56 Hertz Van	£50-75
96	1967-70	**Service Set**	Contains no.5 Police Car, 19 Rover, 59 Fire Engine	£50-75
97	1967-70	**Truck Set**	Contains no.12 VW Microbus, 57 REA Van, 58 Removals Van	£50-75
98	1967-70	**Utility Vehicle Set**	Contains no.27 Fire Chief, 60 Squad Car, 61 Q Car	£50-75
99	1967-70	**Traffic Set**	Contains no.8 Volkswagen, 14 Packard, 15 Austin	£50-75

Gift Sets

	1962	**Gift Set No.8**	Contains numbers 5, 8, 11, 12, 13, 15, 18 and 19	£100-130
	1962	**Gift Set No.12**	Contains 5, 7, 8, 11, 12, 13, 14, 15, 16, 18, 19 and 20 (Plymouth)	£120-150

Ref.	Year(s)	Model name	Colours, features, dimensions	Market Price Range
100	1972-84	**Horse Drawn Hansom Cab**	With driver, elastic band for reins. Re-issue of a Morestone/Modern Products model. 'Gold' plated or Metallic Light Brown, 118 mm	£10-15
101	1977-84	**Austin FX4 Taxi**	Also issued as no.703. Re-issued by Seerol. Black or Maroon. 106 mm	£10-15
101	1984	**Austin FX4 Taxi**	Silver body, 'LONDON VINTAGE TAXI ASSOCIATION'. Limited (1,000) commemorative marking 25 years of the FX4. Normal box	£20-25
102	1981-84	**Rolls-Royce Silver Cloud**	Re-issued by Seerol. Gold (painted or 'plated'), Black, Silver, Cream, Red, Blue, Metallic Lt.Blue, Metallic Turquoise or Metallic Dark Pink, 107 mm	£15-20
202	1959-66	**International Articulated Refrigerator Lorry**	Re-issued 'Trucks of the World' model. Red / Blue or Red cab (windows later). Silver trailer, 'COAST TO COAST REFRIGERATION', 153 mm.	£40-50
204	1959-64	**Volkswagen Pick-Up**	Blue body, Cream base, cloth tilt 'EXPRESS DELIVERY', 92 mm	£35-45
206	1959-64	**Leyland Hippo Coal Lorry**	Green or Orange cab, Light Brown body, 'COAL AND COKE' cast-in, coal load, 92 mm	£45-55
208	1959-61	**RAF Personnel Carrier**	RAF blue, roundels, White tilt. 'A MORESTONE PRODUCT', 104 mm	£90-120
210	1959-61	**US Army Personnel Carrier**	As 208 but Army brown body with star, Light Brown tilt, 104 mm	£90-120
212	1959-61	**British Army Personnel Carrier**	As 208 but Dark Green with Red / Yellow square, Light Brown tilt	£90-120
214	1959-64	**Thornycroft Mobile Crane**	Red cab and chassis, Yellow crane engine, Light Blue crane, 100 mm	£50-60
216	1959-64	**Renault Truck**	Yellow cab, Red body. Cloth tilt, 'FRESH FRUIT DAILY', 103 mm	£35-45
218	1959-63	**Seddon 'Jumbo' Mobile Traffic Control Unit**	Yellow cab and trailer with Black flash and catwalk. 'AUTOMOBILE ASSOCIATION' and AA badge transfers, 168 mm	£100-120
220	1959-66	**Leyland Hippo Cattle Transporter**	Orange cab, Light Brown body, Dark Brown base and ramp, 97 mm	£35-45
222	1959-65	**International Tank Transporter with Centurion Tank**	Army brown with star transfers. Cab as no.202. 155 mm. (with ramps up)	£45-55
224	1959-66	**0-6-0 Tank Locomotive**	As Modern Products model. Red, 'BRITISH RAILWAYS' cast-in, 119 mm	£25-35
224	1971-84	**0-6-0 Tank Locomotive**	Red, Metallic Brown, Black or Dark Green, 'BRITISH RAILWAYS' on transfers or labels.	£10-15
226	1959-66	**Foden Dumper**	Re-issue of a Morestone model. Orange cab and chassis, Grey dumper. 'BUD 123' number plate transfers, 108 mm	£30-40
228	1959-64	**Karrier Bantam Bottle Lorry**	Orange-Yellow, 12 maroon plastic crates. 'DRINK COCA-COLA' transfers, 'COMMER LOW LOADER' cast underneath, 134 mm.	£120-140
230	1959-66	**Seddon Timber Transporter**	Orange cab (no windows), or Green cab (with windows), Yellow trailer, five 'logs', 178 mm.	£45-55
232	1960-66	**Seddon Low Loader**	Red cab (windows later), Orange trailer, 3 wooden cable drums. 167 mm	£60-70
234	1960-65	**International Low Loader with Caterpillar Tractor**	Orange cab, Light Brown trailer, Orange tractor, 155 mm. (with ramps up)	£40-50
236	1960-66 and 1969-84	**AEC Routemaster Bus**	Also issued as nos.704, 705 and 706. All models have destination transfers for route '9' and and 'LONDON TRANSPORT' transfers or labels. They were available with or without windows. 108 mm.	
			Red, 'Esso GOLDEN Esso'	£10-20
			Red, 'Esso UNIFLO - the tuned motor oil'	£10-20
			Red, 'GO ESSO - BUY ESSO - DRIVE ESSO'.	£10-20
			Red, 'UNIFLO sae 10W/50 Motor Oil'	£10-20
			Red, Green or Gold, 'Houses of Parliament Tower Bridge'.	£10-20
236	1973	Promotional issue:	Red body (with windows), 'Sheraton-Heathrow Hotel' on sides, 'OPENING 1st FEBRUARY 1973' on roof, Special box.	£60-70
238	1960-63	**Scammell Scarab Van**	Crimson / Cream body. 'BRITISH RAILWAYS' and 'CADBURYS', 150mm. Note: Chocolate Bar picture may be vertical or horizontal.	£75-85
238	1964-66	....	Yellow cab, Black chassis, Yellow trailer. 'Railfreight', 'CADBURYS'	£65-75
238	1985	....	Maroon cab, Maroon / Cream trailer. 'BRITISH RAILWAYS' and 'CADBURYS'.	£15-20
			Yellow cab and trailer. 'Railfreight' and 'CADBURYS' transfers. Most of these were issued in original 1960s boxes. 150 mm.	£15-20
240	1960-64	**Scammell Scarab Wagon**	Red / Cream cab, Yellow chassis, Red trailer, Green cloth tilt, 150 mm	£55-65
242	1960-66	**Euclid Dumper**	Red cab, Orange chassis and dumper. 114 mm	£35-45
244	1961-65	**Morris Breakdown Lorry**	Blue body, Yellow base, tool box and jib. 'BUDGIE SERVICE', 120 mm	£45-55
246	1960-63	**Wolseley 6/80 Police Car**	Re-issued Modern Products model. Black, loudspeaker, aerial, 'BUDGIE TOYS' cast under, 'POLICE' transfers on grille and boot, 113 mm	£35-45
246	1983	**Wolseley 6/80 Police Car**	Light Blue, 'POLICE' labels, spotlights and roof sign replace the loudspeaker and aerial. Trial run only - did not go into full production	£45-55
248	1961	**Stage Coach with Four Horses**	Listed on this number as 'available later', but issued as no. 434.	
250	------	Pack reference	This number was used for packs of one dozen of the Budgie miniatures.	
252	1961-63	**Austin Articulated Lorry with Railway Container**	Crimson / Cream cab, windows, Crimson trailer / container, 'BRITISH RAILWAYS' transfers	£65-75
252	1964	....	Crimson cab / trailer, windows, Blue container, 'Door to Door' transfers	£75-85
254	1961-64	**AEC Merryweather Fire Escape**	Red, windows, Silver extending turntable ladder. 97 mm. (excl. ladder)	£65-75
256	1961-64	**Foden Aircraft Refuelling Tanker 'Pluto'**	Red, with windows. 'ESSO AVIATION PRODUCTS' transfers, 149 mm	£100-125
258	1961-63	**Daimler Ambulance**	Re-issued Modern Products model. Cream with Red base ('BUDGIE TOYS' cast-in), 'AMBULANCE' and 'EMERGENCY' transfers, 110 mm	£65-75

258	1991	**Daimler Ambulance Kit**	Re-issued as a kit of unpainted castings (by Autocraft)	**£10-20**
260	1962	**Ruston-Bucyrus Excavator**	Yellow / Red cab, '10-RB', Beige or Olive-Green base and jib, 73 mm	**£100-125**
262	1962-64	**Racing Motorcycle**	No maker's name. Unpainted cycle, tinplate fairing in Metallic Blue, Metallic Lilac, Metallic Brown or Lime Green, Black plastic rider, 104 mm	**£75-100**
264	1962-64	**Racing Motorcycle and Sidecar**	Cycle as 262, sidecar and fairing in Metallic Blue, Metallic Pinkish-Red, Metallic Green, Metallic Lilac, Metallic Brown or Lime Green. Black plastic rider / passenger, no maker's name, 104 mm	**£75-100**
266	1962-64	**Motorcycle and Delivery Sidecar**	Blue cycle as 262, Red sidecar, 'EXPRESS DELIVERY' cast-in, no maker's name, Black plastic rider. 108 mm	**£75-100**
268	1962-64	**A.A. Land Rover**	Different from Morestone AA Land Rovers. Yellow body, Black roof, windows, opening rear doors, 'AA ROAD SERVICE' transfers, 97 mm	**£125-150**
270	1962-66	**Leyland Articulated Tanker**	Red, windows, 'ESSO PETROLEUM COMPANY LTD' labels, 132 mm	**£50-60**
272	1962-64	**Supercar**	From TV series. Red / Silver body, Red wings (or colours reversed), clear plastic canopy, 'SUPERCAR' transfers, 122 mm	**£175-225**
274	1962-66	**Ford Thames Refuse Lorry**	Blue cab / Silver body, or Yellow cab / Metallic blue body, windows	**£45-55**
276	1962-66	**Bedford LWB Tipper**	Red cab with windows, Yellow tipper, 'HAM RIVER GRIT', 128 mm	**£40-80**
278	1963-64	**RAC Land Rover**	Casting as 268, Blue, windows, 'RAC RADIO RESCUE' transfers, 97 mm	**£125-150**
280	1963-64	**AEC Super Fueller Tanker**	White cab and trailer, windows, Green base and canopy, 'AIR BP', 219 mm	**£300-400**
282	1963-66	**Euclid Scraper**	Yellow or Lime Green, windscreen, 'EUCLID', Black plastic wheels, 163 mm	**£35-45**
284	1962	**Euclid Crawler Tractor**	Not issued	**NPP**
286	1962	**Euclid Bulldozer**	Not issued	**NPP**
288	1963-66	**Leyland Bulk Flour Tanker**	Red cab, windows, Off-White silos, Yellow hopppers, 'BULK FLOUR', 107 mm	**£45-55**
290	1963-64	**Bedford Ice Cream Van**	No maker's name on model. Blue body and base, windows, 'Tonibell' transfers, Pink plastic cow on roof, 103 mm	**£85-110**
292	1963-66	**Leyland Bulk Milk Tanker**	Blue or Red cab, windows, White tank, 'MILK', 107 mm	**£45-55**
294	1963-66	**Bedford TK Horse Box**	Off-White cab, windows, Brown body, Light Brown doors. two Brown plastic horses. 'EPSOM STABLE' transfer, 109 mm	**£45-55**
296	1963-66	**Motorway Express Coach**	Midland Red livery: Red body, Black roof, 'BIRMINGHAM-LONDON MOTORWAY EXPRESS' transfers, windows, 121 mm	**£70-85**
		USA livery:	Light Blue body, Cream roof, 'WASHINGTON D.C.' and 'BLUE LINE SIGHTSEEING CO.' transfers, phone number 'LA9-7755' at rear	**£300-400**
298	1963-66	**Alvis Salamander Crash Tender**	Red body, windows, Silver plastic ladder, Yellow engine cover at rear, Black plastic wheels. 'FIRE SERVICE' transfers, 92 mm	**£100-125**
300	1963-65	**Lewin Sweepmaster**	Blue / Silver, windows, Black plastic wheels, Black sweeping brush	**£45-55**
302	1963-66	**Commer Cabin Service Lift Truck**	Blue cab, windows, Silver body, 'BOAC CABIN SERVICES', 104 mm	**£45-55**
304	1964-66	**Bedford TK Glass Transporter**	Off-white cab and chassis, windows, Green body. 'TOWER GLASS CO.' transfers. Four clear plastic 'glass' sheets, 108 mm	**£45-55**
306	1964-66	**Fiat Tractor with Shovel**	Orange tractor, Metallic Blue shovel, 108 mm	**£75-100**
308	1964-66	**Seddon Pitt Alligator Low Loader**	Green cab, windows, Yellow trailer with Black ramp, 163 mm	**£45-55**
310	1964-66	**Leyland Cement Mixer**	Orange cab, windows, Silver mixer, 'INVICTA Construction Co.', 98 mm	**£45-55**
312	1964-66	**Bedford Super Tipmaster**	Dark Green cab, windows, Silver tipper. 'SUPER TIP-MASTER', 127 mm	**£45-55**
314	1965-66	**Fiat Tractor with Dozer Blade**	As 306 but enclosed cab, Orange tractor, Metallic Blue blade, 81 mm	**£45-55**
316	1965-66	**Albion Overhead Maintenance Vehicle**	Green body, windows, Silver / Black boom assembly, 107 mm	**£40-50**
318	1965-66	**Euclid Mammoth Articulated Dumper**	Modified from no.242. Green cab, Yellow chassis, Orange tipper, 201 mm	**£75-95**
322	1965-66	**Scammell Routeman Pneumajector Transporter**	Light Blue cab, Cream or White tank, 'THE ATLAS CARRIER CO.', 111 mm	**£50-60**
324	1965-66	**Douglas Prospector Duomatic Tipper**	Tips in two directions. Blue cab and chassis, windows, Grey tipper, 112 mm	**£55-65**
326	1965-66	**Scammell Highwayman Gas Transporter**	Green cab, windows, Dark Green trailer, 6 White / Red gas cylinders, 146 mm	**£125-150**
328	1966	**Scammell Handyman Artic**	Planned but not issued	**NPP**
330	1966	**Land Rover**	Modified 268, planned but not issued	**NPP**
332	1966	**'Kenning' Breakdown Lorry**	Planned but not issued	**NPP**
334	1966	**Austin Gipsy Fire Tender**	Planned but not issued	**NPP**
404	1960-61	**Horse Drawn Covered Wagon**	with Four Horses. For details see Morestone and Modern Products entry.	
410	1961	**Stage Coach with Four Horses**	Blue or 'Gold' plated coach, no lettering cast on sides but 'WELLS FARGO STAGE COACH' and 'A BUDGIE TOY' cast underneath, plastic horses and driver, bubble-packed, 118 mm	**£70-90**
430	1960-61	**Wagon Train Set**	Contains 3 of no. 432 plus two more horses with riders, bubble-packed	**£100-150**
432	1960-61	**Horse Drawn Covered Wagon with Two Horses**	Red wagon, ('A BUDGIE TOY' on floor), Grey, White or Lemon metal canopy, 2 barrels, plastic horses, driver, passenger, bubble packed, 82 mm	**£35-45**
434	1961	**Stage Coach with Four Horses**	'WELLS FARGO' above windows, 'STAGE LINES' on doors, luggage cast on roof, Red or Blue, plastic horses and driver, 189 mm	**£70-90**
452	1958-63	**A.A. Motorcycle and Sidecar**	Initially in Morestone box. Windscreen, plastic rider, integral rails and hinged lid on sidecar, steerable, rubber tyres, plain number plates, 82 mm	**£75-100**
452	1964-66	**A.A. Motorcycle and Sidecar**	New design. Sidecar with transfers and 'BUDGIE' underneath, plastic rider, windscreen and leg guards, plain number plates, 84 mm	**£75-100**
454	1958-63	**RAC Motorcycle and Sidecar**	Initially in Morestone box. Windscreen, plastic rider, integral rails and hinged lid on sidecar, steerable, rubber tyres, plain number plates, 82 mm	**£75-100**
454	1964-66	**RAC Motorcycle and Sidecar**	New design. Sidecar with transfers and 'BUDGIE' underneath, plastic rider, windscreen and leg guards, plain number plates, 84 mm	**£75-100**

Budgie Toys and Models

456	1958-66	**Solo Motorcycle**	Initially in Morestone boxes. Two casting versions as 452 and 454 but 'Silver plated'. Plastic riders:	
			Police Patrol (Blue uniform)	**£40-50**
			Despatch Rider (Light Brown uniform)	**£40-50**
			GPO Messenger (Light Blue uniform)	**£40-50**
			'Tourist Trophy' Rider (White racing overalls)	**£40-50**
701	1983	**Aveling-Barford Road Roller**	Re-issued Modern Products model. Dark Green body, Silver / Red wheels, Dark Blue driver.	**£10-15**
702	1984-85	**Scammell Scarab Vans**	Re-issue of 238. Very Dark Blue cab and trailer, White 'RN' on doors, 'ROYAL NAVY' on tilt	**£15-20**
			Very Dark Blue cab and trailer, 'HALLS MENTHO-LYPTUS' labels	**£15-20**
			Maroon cab and trailer, 'LMS LIVERPOOL ROAD' transfers	**£15-20**
			Maroon cab and trailer, 'SPRATTS BONIO' transfers	**£15-20**
			Maroon cab and trailer, 'REA EXPRESS' transfers	**£15-20**
703	1984	**Austin FX4 Taxi**	As no.101 but in window box. Black, Silver, Met.Dk.Pink, Gold, Dark Green, Grey or White.	**£15-20**
704	1984	**AEC Routemaster Bus**	Yellow / Red body with windows, 'SHOP LINKER' labels, casting as 236	**£10-15**
705	1984	**AEC Routemaster Bus**	Silver body with windows, '25 FAITHFUL YEARS' labels, casting as 236	**£10-15**
706	1984	**AEC Routemaster Bus**	Yellow / Red with windows, 'Watford FA Cup Final 84' labels, 236 casting	**£10-15**

Budgie Gift Sets

No. 4	1961	**Gift Set No.4**	Contains four models. Price depends on contents which vary	**£125-165**
No. 5	1961	**Gift Set No.5**	Contains five models. Price depends on contents which vary	**£150-200**

Seerol Models

-	1985	**Austin FX4 Taxi**	Re-issue of Budgie no.101 with amended base lettering and low friction wheels. Black body, 106mm. Still available.	**£3-5**
-	1985	**Rolls-Royce Silver Cloud**	Re-issued Budgie 102, amended lettering, low friction wheels. Black, Silver, White, Yellow, Dark Blue, Pink or Maroon, 107 mm. Still available	**£3-5**
-	1985	**AEC Routemaster Bus**	New design, 1:76 scale, 108 mm., still available.	
-			Red, Light Green or Dark Green, 'Houses of Parliament Tower Bridge' labels	**£8-11**
-			Red, 'The Original London Transport Sightseeing Tour' labels	**£8-11**
-			Red, 'Greetings from London' tampo print	**£3-5**
-			Red, 'Tower of London' tampo print	**£3-5**
-			Red, 'Petticoat Lane' tampo print	**£3-5**
-			Red, 'Buckingham Palace' tampo print	**£3-5**

Budgie Leaflets and Catalogues

A leaflet was included in the box with most Budgie Toys. Dates are not shown on any except the 1963 and 1964 catalogues.

-	1959	**Leaflet**	Printed on one side only. 'Budgie Toys Speak for Themselves' at top.	
		1st version:	Includes the Six-horse Covered Wagon.	**£10-20**
		2nd version:	Timber Transporter replaces the Covered Wagon	**£10-20**
-	1960	**Leaflet**	'Budgie Toys Speak for Themselves' on front, 'Budgie Toys for Girls and Boys' on reverse	**£10-20**
-	1961	**Leaflet**	'Budgie Toys Speak for Themselves' on Black background	**£5-10**
	1961	**Trade catalogue**	Fold-out leaflet showing Noddy items, Wagon Train and Budgie miniatures as well as the main Budgie range. Separate price list marked 'Price List 1961' showing wholesale and retail prices.	**£30-40**
-	1962	**Leaflet**	'Die-Cast Models by Budgie They Speak for Themselves' on Black background.	
		1st version:	268 AA Land Rover on front, 258 Daimler Ambulance on reverse	**£5-10**
		2nd version:	214 Mobile Crane on front, 266 Express Delivery Motorcycle on reverse	**£5-10**
-	1963	**Leaflet**	'Die-Cast Models by Budgie They Speak for Themselves' on Black background.	
		1st version:	278 RAC Land Rover on front, 258 Daimler Ambulance on reverse	**£5-10**
		2nd version:	278 RAC Land Rover on front, 266 Express Delivery Motorcycle on reverse ...	**£5-10**
-	1963	**Trade Catalogue** (8 pages)	Landscape format, includes retail price list	**£30-40**
-	1964	**Trade Catalogue** (8 pages)	'Budgie Models' on cover (portrait format). Includes retail price list	**£30-40**

Budgie Auction Result

VECTIS AUCTIONS Ltd.
10th March 1999

Budgie No.272 Supercar - B+ (usual paint chips to retractable wings associated with this model) in C box - nice example without any fatigue .. **£400**

(See picture of actual model in colour section following page 64).

Shackleton Models

The company was formed by Maurice Shackleton and traded as James Shackleton & Sons Ltd. from 1939 to 1952. They had premises in Cheshire and originally produced wooden toys such as lorries and dolls houses. The toy lorries were only made pre-war and had four wheels, a simple wooden chassis and body with a green name badge on the rear of the cab, and were fitted with a highly detailed aluminium radiator grille. Known models are a Chain Lorry, Breakdown Lorry and a Sided Wagon. Their price today is around £100 each.

In 1948 having expanded its staff to nearly 40 people, the company started to produce diecast constructional models based on the Foden FG six-wheel platform lorry. The models consisted of separate parts all of which were, incredibly, made 'in house', including the clockwork motor, its key, and the

wheels and tyres. The models were advertised in the 'Meccano Magazine' with the slogan 'You can dismantle it - Just like the real thing', and they were originally priced at £2/19/6. Eventually the range was extended to include a Dyson Drawbar Trailer and a Foden Tipper. Each model was packed in its own distinctive box which displayed a black and white picture of the model inside.

In 1952, whilst in the midst of producing the David Brown Trackmaster 30 Tractor, a shortage of materials coupled with difficult trading conditions brought about the end of the company. Some remaining models from this period were acquired and distributed by Chad Valley. The unique models produced by the Shackleton company are now highly collectable and difficult to find.

---	1948-52	**Foden FG 6-wheelPlatform Lorry**	........Yellow, Blue, Grey or Green body with Red wings, Grey chassis and Red or Grey fuel tanks, 12½ inches (305 mm.) long, initially in Blue/Yellow box, later in mottled Green box, (20,000 made)	**£200-300**
			Same colours as above but with Grey or Black wings and Red chassis	**£300-400**
			Same casting but with Red, Orange or Brown cab	**£300-400**
		NB Box difficult to find:	...........................Blue box with paper label having picture of chassis.	
---	1949-52	**Dyson 8-ton Drawbar Trailer**	................Yellow, Blue, Grey or Green body, packed in Red and Yellow box, (15,000)	**£100-150**
---	1950-52	**Foden FG 6-wheelTipper Lorry**	............Yellow, Blue, Grey or Green body with Red wings, Grey chassis and Red or Grey fuel tanks, Silver wheels, (5,000)	**£300-400**
			As previous models but with Grey wings and Red chassis	**£300-400**
			As previous models but with Blue wings, Grey chassis, Grey wheels	**£300-400**
			Orange or Red body	**£300-400**
---	1952	**David Brown Trackmaster 30 Tractor**	..Red body, Black rubber tracks, 10 inches long, boxed. Only 50 models thought to exist	**£750-950**
		Note: It is known that some prototype models were made of Ploughs and Harrows, though it is not known if any were produced for sale.		
---	1958-60	**Foden S21 8-wheel Platform Lorry**	.......Dark Blue, Dark Green or Light Turquoise fibreglass cab with Red metal chassis and wheels, wooden flatbed, length overall 18½ inches (470 mm), plastic injection moulded springs and axle parts, powered by 'Minimax' electric motor. (250 made as a promotional for Foden)	**£750-950**

The information in this listing has been taken from an original article written by John Ormandy in the 'Modellers World' magazine, Volumes 12 and 13, and is used by kind permission of the Editors, Mike and Sue Richardson. Robert Taylor provided additional information. Thanks also to Gary Irwin of Canada who contributed new information on the DB Trackmaster.
Colour picture: see colour section following page 64.

Scamold Racing Cars

Manufactured between 1939 and 1950 by Scale Models Ltd from whose title the model name was obtained. The models are extremely accurate 1/35 diecast scale models, with their original measurements being taken from the real racing cars at the famous Brooklands race track. Pre-war boxes state 'MANUFACTURED BY SCALE MODELS LTD, BROOKLANDS TRACK, WEYBRIDGE, ENG.'. This was dropped after the war.

The model detail and castings are outstanding, with features such as removeable exhausts, spring suspension, steering wheels and dashboards. In addition the back axle could be exchanged for one containing a clockwork motor which was wound up by a long starting handle. The wheel axles were crimped and the hubs were either brass (early) or aluminium (later) with black treaded rubber tyres.

101	1939-50	**ERA Racing Car**	...................Blue (Light or Dark), Green (Light or Dark), Yellow, White or Black body	**£90-120**
103	1939-50	**Maserati Racing Car**	............Red, Blue, Green (Mid or Dark), Silver body	**£90-100**
105	1939-50	**Alfa Racing Car**	....................Green (Mid or Dark), Silver, White or Blue	**£90-120**

Mobil Midget Fun-Ho! Series

Manufactured and distributed by the Underwood Engineering Co. Ltd, Mamaku Street, Inglewood, New Zealand.

Market Price Range. Most small cars and trucks etc. **£20-30**. Exceptions: No.7 BOAC Observation Coach **£40-50**, No.9 VW Beetle **£40-50**, No.11 Morris Mini Minor **£80-90**, No.2 Vauxhall Velox **£30-40**, No.? Morris 1100 **£40-50**, No.17 Austin Mini **£80-90**, No.23 Mark 10 Jaguar **£80-90**, No.25 MG Sports **£80-100**; No.43 E Type Jaguar **£80-90**.
Larger Commercials/Emergency vehicles etc.:
Nos.18, 21, 22, 27, 31, 35, 36, 40 **£30-40**.

Technical Information. Models from No.10 are 1:80 scale. Early models 1-32 1963-66 were all either chrome or copper plated. Painted finishes were introduced in 1966. Boxed models 1-18 include a folded leaflet in black and white giving details of the first 18 models and all have Black plastic wheels. Similarly the later issues contained leaflets showing the complete 1-46 model range as per the above leaflet.

'Fun Ho!' Mighty Mover Sets
1 Army Construction Battalion Kit Set: Contains six Military models, Bulldozer, Cement Mixer, Road Roller, Earth Mover, JCB, Land Rover, Brown display box **£50-60**
2 Civilian Road Construction Set: Yellow/Silver Bulldozer, Red/Silver Bedford Lorry, Green Aveling Road Roller, Blue Earth Mover, Red/Blue Ford Sand Dumper, Yellow JCB, Red window display box **£50-60**
3 Fire Service Kit Set: Contains six Red models, 21 Fire Engine, Jeep, Pick Up, Artic Lorry, Rescue Truck, Fire Van with Blue light, Red window display box **£50-60**

Later issues (c.1965?) Window Boxes
48 Ford, Brown/Green, Two-tone Green or Maroon White body **£10-15**, 49 Ford Sand Dumper, Red/Blue body **£10-15**, 50 Ford Dumper **£10-15**, 51 Ford Articulated Truck **£15-20**, 52 Sand Dumper Trailer **£5-10**

Taylor and Barrett

Taylor and Barrett Lead Vehicles and the Postwar Re-issues

by Mike Richardson

The firm of Taylor and Barrett dates from the early 1920s when they started producing mainly figures but with a few odd carts. The vehicles themselves were only introduced in about 1935. These were rather crude by comparison with the Dinky Toys of the day as the lead gravity casting process was incapable of working to the fine limits possible with pressure diecasting as used by Meccano Ltd. The majority of the vehicles use a basic chassis incorporating the bonnet and wings. Different bodies are attached to this base unit by tabs and a radiator is plugged into the front. Some versions have the grille cast integrally with the bonnet, and most of these use plain metal wheels instead of having rubber tyres. These vehicles have a tremendous amount of charm as toys while they are only a generic representation of the types of vans and small trucks of the time.

A wide variety of types were made including petrol tankers, a pick-up truck and a couple of mail vans. The breakdown truck is particularly attractive with a working crane on the rear. These toys were made until the production was halted in 1940 when the factory was bombed out of existence. All salvageable tools, moulds and stock was moved to a new location in North Finchley but production stopped very soon after because of the munitions requirements of the war effort.

During the war the tools were split between the Taylors and the Barretts for safe keeping but they did not join up again afterwards and two separate companies, F.G.Taylor & Sons and A.Barrett & Sons, started up in 1945. The main part of the range, the small commercial vehicles and the cars, does not seem to have survived the War, only the trolley buses, which became Barretts, and the Leyland coach which appeared in one-piece casting form as a Taylor. It is interesting to note that the trolleybus carries a route board '621 Finchley' which probably means that they went past the factory.

A range of very nice fire engines came along in the late 1930s with a super turntable ladder appliance as the top of the range. These were longer than the main range and had many parts. To mark the advent of the Home Office Fire Precautions scheme (where fire appliances were made available to local areas by central government), Taylor and Barrett painted their range in grey as well as the more traditional red. These grey models are highly sought after now.

Personnel were also available to go with these fire engines. A 'Decontamination Squad' being a particular favourite with their gas masks and chemical-proof overalls. There is also a fire engine in the short chassis range but it is not very impressive. The trolley buses came in two sizes. The large one has a separate driver figure (and conductor as well in the T & B version but not the later Barrett), and the body is in two pieces, upper and lower decks. The small one is in one piece and has no driver. Needless to say there is a vast difference in the values of the two sizes.

There are generic cars, roadster, coupé, saloon, on the short base but there is also quite a good model of the 1935 Singer Airstream saloon. This is also the poor man's Chrysler Airflow but never really caught on, the styling made the car look too tall to be appealing. A rather crude one-piece Austin Seven racer was the final car but this was to a larger scale.

Dinky Toys were not the only factory to make a model of the Air Mail Service Car based on the Morris Commercial chassis. T & B also made one and a nice chunky toy it is too. A couple of aeroplanes, a De Havilland Comet and an air liner, completed the range of powered vehicles. A modified version of the Comet seems to have been made by Barrett later but it differs a lot from the T & B, which is a much better model.

Some of the moulds were still around a few years ago and some attempts were made to make models again. These were fairly unsuccessful as casting techniques had changed and the new metals did not have the same flow characteristics as the early lead. Some models are definitely known to have been re-made as they have been seen at a swapmeet some time back, so collectors are advised to be wary.

Editor's notes: All the models are rare - any new auction prices that become available will be published in a subsequent edition of 'CollerctorLink'. The following listing has been compiled from original manufacturer's records by Mr Norman Joplin to whom the Editor would like to express his gratitude. Models listed are those issued by Taylor and Barrett between 1920 and 1939. Post war production was split between F. G. Taylor & Sons and A. Barrett & Sons, each firm inheriting some moulds and continuing to make some but not all of the models until about 1952.

(FGT) = produced by F. G. Taylor after 1945, (AB) = produced by A. Barrett after 1945, (-) = date and company not known for certain,
Where no price grading shown, no grading is possible at present (NGPP).

14	**Trotting Pony Racer** (FGT)	
15	**Turntable Fire Escape** (AB)	
16	**Fire Engine and Escape** (FGT)	
17	**Fire Engine and Men** (FGT)	£200-300
20	**Horse Drawn Water Cart** (FGT)	£300-400
21	**Horse Drawn Brewer's Cart** (FGT)	£100-200
22	**Horse Drawn Window Cleaner's Cart** (FGT)	£100-200
23	**Horse Drawn Baker's Cart** (FGT)	
26	**Roman Chariot** (FGT)	
27	**Donkey Drawn Coster Cart with Dog and Boy** (FGT)	
28	**Donkey Drawn Coster Cart, Plants load, Walking Coster** (FGT)	
28a	**Donkey Drawn Coster Cart, Vegetable load, Walking Coster** (FGT)	
29	**Ice Cream Bicycle**, 'ICE BRICKS' logo (FGT)	£200-300
36	**Milk Float and Milkman** (AB)	
42	**Fire Escape and Team of Firemen** (FGT)	
43	**Air and Land Postal Service Set** (-)	
49	**Street Cleaning Barrow with two Bins** (FGT)	
92	**Llama Cart** (FGT)	
92a	**Donkey Cart** (FGT)	
109	**Pony Drawn Governor's Cart** (AB)	
109a	**Pony Drawn Cart** (AB)	
111	**Saloon Car** (-)	
112	**Transport Lorry** (-)	
113	**'ROYAL MAIL' Van** (-)	
114	**'AMBULANCE'**, Grey (Wartime civilian) (-)	
114a	**'AMBULANCE'**, Khaki (Army) (-)	
115	**Sports Car** (-)	£100-200
116	**Coupé** (-)	£100-200
117	**'AMBULANCE'**, (Street, civilian) (-)	
119	**Racer** (AB)	
120	**Fire Engine** (AB)	
123	**Atlanta Touring Plane** (AB)	
124	**'AIR MAIL' Van** (AB)	
128	**Petrol Tanker** (-)	
129	**Breakdown Lorry** (-)	
137	**DH 'Comet' Aeroplane** (AB)	
138	**'AIR MAIL' Streamline Van** (-)	

139	**Saloon Car** (-)	
152	**Streamline Motor Coach** (-)	
163	**Streamline Fire Engine** (-)	
197	**Trolley Bus** (small) (AB)	£200-250
204	**Trolley Bus** (large) (AB)	£300-400
302	**Horse Drawn Covered Wagon** (-)	
304	**Sledge and Dogs** (FGT)	
306	**Aeroplane Set** (Comet, Atlanta and pilots) (FGT)	
307	**Fire Brigade Set** (-)	£300-400
310	**Rickshaw pulled by Chinese Coolie** (FGT)	
311	**Light Trailer Fire Pump in Action Set** (-)	
?	**Space Ship** (-)	
?	**Coronation Coach** (small) (AB)	
?	**State Landau Coach** (-)	
?	**Farmer's Gig** (FGT)	
?	**Farm Cart with Trotting Horse** (-)	
?	**Mobile Animal Trailer and Vet** (-)	
---	**Racing Car**, Red body with 'MG Magnette' cast into side, 110 mm. 'FGT & SONS'	
---	**Petrol Pumps**, Black/White with rubber hoses (T&B)	

Taylor and Barrett Auction Results

Sold by WALLIS & WALLIS, Lewes, Sussex. June 1999 Sale.

Two-seater boat-tail Sports Car (G) plus Fire Engine (F)	£100
Streamlined Fire Engine, white tyres (GC)	£130
Four-wheel Road Tanker (GC)	£95
Four-wheel Delivery Van (GC)	£125
Four-wheel Ambulance, paper roof labels (GC)	£160
Four-wheel Open-back Lorry (GC)	£125
Four-wheel Breakdown Lorry (GC)	£125

Sold by CHRISTIE'S

A rare **Taylor & Barrett 204 Trolley-Bus** (large size) 'Champion's Malt Vinegar' advertisement, destination 'Finchley', driver and conductor, in original box with illustrated label (G-E, boxes F-G)......................£690

Timpo Toys

Robert Newson has provided this history and listing of cast metal Timpo motor vehicles.

The name Timpo comes from 'Toy Importers Ltd'. It was only with the outbreak of war in 1939 that Timpo started to manufacture their own lines, when importing became impossible. A few vehicles were made in 1940-41, but the main Timpo range started in 1946. The models were cheap and sturdy, if somewhat crude, and many have survived. Relatively few suffer from metal deterioration. In 1949 Timpo advertised 'faithful replicas of famous delivery services' and introduced several vans with attractive advertising liveries. An AEC Monarch lorry in the livery of Vaux brewery was introduced around 1950, and this was a far better model than the earlier toys. Sadly it was not the first of a new range - the 1951-2 ban on the use of zinc meant that Timpo discontinued all their diecast vehicles. Some of the dies were subsequently sold to Benbros, including the AEC lorry. Timpo Toys are very rarely seen in mint condition, and prices are therefore quoted for good original condition. Dates given are the approximate year of introduction.

Colour pictures. See the colour section following page 160.

Year	Model name	Colours, features, dimensions	Market Price Range
1940	**MG Record Car**	Hollow-cast lead. Red, 'TIMPO TOYS' cast on side, 98 mm	£20-25
1940	**Streamlined Saloon**	Separate body and chassis. 'Timpo' in script underneath. 99 mm	£30-40
1940	**Pick-Up Truck**	Separate body and chassis. 'Timpo' in script underneath. Re-issued post-war with name blanked out. 97 mm	£30-40
1940	**Four-light Saloon**	Possibly re-issue of a Goody Toy. Details unknown	NGPP
1946	**MG Record Car**	Zinc diecast. 'TIMPO TOYS' cast at rear on offside. 97 mm	£10-15
1946	**'American Star' Racer**	Star transfer on each side, 101 mm	£10-15
1946	**'Timpo Saloon'**	Possibly a Morris 8. 93 mm	£10-15
1946	**Austin 16 Saloon**	Black. 'TIMPO TOYS' underneath. 96 mm	£30-40
		Re-issued by Betal in four versions:	
		1. No name on model, brass wheel hubs	£30-40
		2. 'A BETAL PRODUCT' under roof, tin base with friction motor, brass wheel hubs	£30-40
		3. As 2. but with plastic body rather than diecast	£20-25
		4. As 3. but with clockwork motor and solid metal wheels	£20-25
1946	**MG Midget**	Composition wheels. 82 mm	£15-20
1946	**Packard Saloon**	Fitted with aluminium baseplate and friction motor from 1948. 113 mm	£10-15
1946	**'Speed of the Wind' Record Car**	Similar to the Dinky Toy. 99 mm	£10-15
1947	**Alvis 14 Saloon**	A big four-light saloon. 106 mm	£15-20
1947	**Utility Van**	With aluminium baseplate and friction motor from 1948. (Early casting 102mm, later 104mm).	
		1. No transfers, numerous colours, without motor	£10-15
		2. Black, 'TYRESOLES SERVICE' transfers, no motor	£30-40
		3. 'HIS MASTER'S VOICE' transfers, pale Yellow, Orange-Yellow, pale Blue or Green, with or without motor.	£30-40
1947	**Articulated Petrol Tanker**	No transfers. Re-issued by Benbros. 149 mm	£10-15
1947	**Lincoln Convertible**	A very approximate model of the 1942 Lincoln. Aluminium baseplate and windscreen. Most models in single colours (many different). Late version in cream with blue seats. 115 mm	£15-20
1947	**Armstrong-Siddeley Hurricane**	A coupe with top up. 105 mm	£15-20
1947	**Streamlined Fire Engine**	Red, two Yellow aluminium ladders. With aluminium baseplate and friction motor from 1949. 105 mm	£25-30
1947	**Articulated Box Van**	Re-issued by Benbros. 146 mm	£25-30
		1. Green, Blue or Red trailer with 'TIMPO TOYS' transfers	£25-30
		2. Black cab and trailer with Grey roof, Red wheel hubs, 'PICKFORDS' transfers	£25-30
		3. Orange cab and trailer, Black roof, 'UNITED DAIRIES' transfers	£30-40
		4. Light Blue cab, Light Blue and Cream trailer, 'WALL'S ICE CREAM' transfers	£30-40
		5. Dark Blue cab and trailer with off-White roof, 'LYONS TEA' transfers	£30-40
		6. Pale Yellow cab and trailer, transfers with 'BISHOPS MOVE' logo and 'BISHOP & SONS DEPOSITORIES LTD. 10-12 BELGRAVE ROAD LONDON, S.W.1'	£30-40
		7. Pale Yellow cab and trailer, transfers with 'BISHOPS MOVE' logo and 'JOHN H. LUNN LTD. 6 HOPE CRESCENT EDINBURGH'	£30-40
1947	**London Taxi**	Cast in two parts. 94 mm	£20-25
1947	**Alvis 14 Police Car**	Police sign and loudspeakers at front of roof, wire aerial behind. Black. 106 mm	£20-25
1947	**Articulated Low Loader**	Re-issued by Benbros. 168 mm	£10-15
1947	**Buick Saloon**	A very crude model. Composition wheels. 99 mm	£10-15
1947	**Pick-Up Truck**	With eight cast-in barrels. 104 mm	£15-20
1947	**Forward Control Tipper Lorry**	Cream cab and chassis, Red tipper. 101 mm	£15-20
1947	**Forward Control Luton Van**	Same chassis as the tipper. 97 mm.	
		1. No transfers, Black lower half, Light Blue upper half	£15-20
		2. Dark Blue, 'SMITH'S CRISPS' transfers	£30-40
		3. Brown, 'W.D. & H.O. WILLS' transfers	£30-40
1949	**Forward Control Box Van**	Same chassis as above. Re-issued by Benbros. 96 mm. Dark Blue, 'CHIVERS JELLIES' transfers	£30-40
1949	**Normal Control Box Van**	Later models with aluminium baseplate and friction motor. 105 mm.	
		1. Dark Blue with White roof, 'EVER READY' transfers, with or without motor	£25-30
		2. Green, 'GOLDEN SHRED' transfers, with motor	£30-40
		3. Green, 'MELTONIAN SHOE CREAM' transfers, with motor	£30-40
1949	**Normal Control Petrol Tanker**	Red, paper labels reading 'MOTOR OIL ESSO PETROL'. Re-issued by Benbros. 116 mm	£30-40
1950	**AEC Monarch Brewery Lorry**	Red. 'VAUX' cast on headboard behind cab, 'SUNDERLAND' cast on cab sides. Brown hollow-cast barrels with 'VAUX' cast on ends. Re-issued by Benbros without the headboard and with other changes. 129 mm	£50-60
?	**Petrol Station No.2 Set**	Contains Saloon Car and Racing Car plus 3 Personnel and 5 Pumps. Pictorial box lid states: 'THE FAMOUS TIMPO CARS'	NGPP
1940s	**Bomber Station Set**	3 x twin-fuselage aircraft, 2 x twin-engined, single-fuselage aircraft and a single-engined fighter. Box has a pictorial label on its lift-off lid	NGPP

Timpo Auction Result

DREWEATTE NEATE AUCTIONS, Donnington, Newbury, Berkshire
June 1999 Auction Sale.
Timpo 'Pickfords' Pantechnecon, excellent condition, boxed, sold for £160

Tri-ang Minic Ships

Minic ships are accurately detailed waterline models made between 1958 and 1964 to a scale of 1:1,200 (1in to 100ft).
Six sales catalogues were published which nowadays are quite hard to find.
No single catalogue shows the full range.
Minic ships re-introduced in 1976 were fitted with wheels and have 'Hong Kong' on the base.

Ref.	Model name	Colours, features, dimensions	Market Price Range

Ocean Liners

Ref.	Model name	Colours, features, dimensions	Market Price Range
M701	RMS 'Caronia'	Green body, one plain Red/Black or detailed funnel, one mast, 178 mm. 'Painted in the correct Cunard green she is a most striking vessel'.	£35-45
M702	RMS 'Queen Elizabeth'	Black/White, 2 plain Red/Black or detailed funnels, 2 masts, 262 mm. 'The worlds largest ship and the pride of the Cunard fleet'.	£55-65
M703	RMS 'Queen Mary'	Black/White, plain Red/Black or detailed funnels, 2 masts, 259 mm. 'Her three funnels make her the most easily recognisable'.	£40-45
M704	SS 'United States'	Black/White body, two Red/White/Blue funnels, 252 mm. 'The present holder of the Blue Riband of the Atlantic'.	£35-45
M705	RMS 'Aquitania'	Black/White, four Red/Black funnels, two masts, 231 mm.	£80-100
M706	SS 'Nieuw Amsterdam'	Grey/White body, two Yellow funnels, two masts, 231 mm.	£45-55
M707	SS 'France'	Black/White, 2 Red/Black funnels, 5 masts, 262 mm. 'The longest ship in the world 1035ft being 4ft longer than Queen Elizabeth'.	£80-100
M708	RMS 'Saxonia'	Black/White body, one Red/Black or detailed funnel, nine masts, cargo handling gear on stern.	£35-40
M708/2	RMS 'Franconia'	Green body, one Red/Black funnel, nine Green masts, 155 mm, swimming pool on stern.480 made	£500-550
M709	RMS 'Ivernia'	Black/White or Green body, 155mm, cargo handling gear on stern.	£35-40
M709/2	RMS 'Carmania'	Green body, one Red/Black funnel, nine Green masts, 155 mm, swimming pool on stern.480 made	£500-550
M710	RMS 'Sylvania'	Black/White, one Red/Black funnel, nine masts, 155 mm.	£30-40
M711	RMS 'Carinthie'	Black/White, one Red/Black funnel, nine masts, 155 mm.	£35-40
M712	NS 'Savannah'	White, no funnels (nuclear powered), four masts, 149 mm.	£45-50
M713	SS 'Antilles'	Black/White, one Red/Black funnel, ten masts, 152 mm. All White body, one Red/Black funnel, ten masts	£45-60 / £65-70
M714	'Flandre'	Black/White, one Red/Black funnel, ten masts, 152 mm. All White body, one Red/Black funnel, ten masts	£35-45 / £45-55
M715	RMS 'Canberra'	White body, one Yellow funnel, three masts, 189 mm.	£55-65
M716	MS 'Port Brisbane'	Grey/White, one Red/Black funnel, eight masts, 140 mm.	£90-110
M717	SS 'Port Auckland'	Grey/White, one Red/Black funnel, seven masts, 140 mm.	£90-120
M718	RMS 'Amazon'	White, Yellow funnel, 19 masts, 10 lifeboats, 149 mm.	£115-130
M719	RMS 'Arlanza'	White, Yellow funnel, 19 masts, 149 mm.	£130-150
M720	RMS 'Aragon'	White, Yellow funnel, 19 masts, 149 mm.	£115-130
M721	RMS 'Britannia'	The Royal Yacht. Blue/White body, Yellow/Black funnel, 3 masts, 105 mm.	£15-18
M721/H	RMS 'Britannia'	Hospital Ship. White body, three masts, 105 mm.	£15-18

Smaller craft

CHANNEL ISLANDS STEAMERS (78mm long)

Ref.	Model name	Colours, features, dimensions	Price
M722	'Isle of Jersey'	Black/White, 2 Yellow/Black funnels, 2 masts	£18-24
M723	'Isle of Guernsey'	Black/White, 2 Yellow/Black funnels, 2 masts	£18-24
M724	'Isle of Sark'	Black/White body, 2 Yellow/Black funnels, 2 masts	£18-24
M726	'PILOTS' Boat	Black/White/Yellow, 45 mm.	£65-75
M727	Lifeboat	Blue body	£15-20

PADDLE STEAMERS (all are 78 mm long)

Ref.	Model name	Colours, features, dimensions	Price
M728	'Britannia'	Black/white, 2 funnels (black/blue, red/black or yellow/black), 2 masts	£20-25
M729	'Bristol Queen'	Black/white, 2 funnels (black/blue, red/black or yellow/black), 2 masts	£20-25
M730	'Cardiff Queen'	Black/White, 2 funnels (Black/Blue, Red/Black or Yellow/Black), 2 masts	£20-25

OIL TANKER

Ref.	Model name	Colours, features, dimensions	Price
M732	SS 'Varicella'	Black/White body, Black/Yellow funnel ('SHELL' logo), 2 masts, 169 mm.	£20-30

WHALE FACTORY SHIPS

Ref.	Model name	Colours, features, dimensions	Price
M733	TSS 'Vikingen'	Grey body, six masts, 125 mm.	£25-30
M734	Whale Chaser	Grey, Yellow/Black funnel, 39 mm.	£12-15

TUGBOATS (all except 'Turmoil' are 38mm long)

Ref.	Model name	Colours, features, dimensions	Price
M731	Tugboat	Black/Grey/Red, Red/Black funnel	£5-7
M731	Tugboat	Black/Grey/Red, Yellow/Black funnel	£5-7
M731	Tugboat	Black/Blue/Red, Yellow/Black funnel	£5-7
M731	Tugboat	Black/Grey/Yellow, Yellow/Black funnel	£5-7
M740	Barge	Intended to match M731, but not issued	NPP
M810	Navy Tug HMS 'Turmoil'	Black/Blue or Grey, Black funnel, 50 mm.	£5-8

LIGHTSHIPS (all are 33mm long)

Ref.	Model name	Colours, features, dimensions	Price
M735	'SUNK'	Red body, White logo/name	£7-10
M736	'SHAMBLES'	Red body, White logo/name	£7-10
M737	'CORK'	Red body, White logo/name	£7-10
M738	'VARNE'	Red body, White logo/name	£7-10
M739	'St GOWAN'	Red body, White logo/name, no number on base	£7-10

BATTLESHIP
M741 **HMS 'Vanguard'** .....Grey or Blue, two masts, 206 mm **£30-35**

AIRCRAFT CARRIERS
M751 **HMS 'Bulwark'** ......Grey or Blue, one mast, 186 mm **£20-25**
M752 **HMS 'Centaur'** ....Grey or Blue body with one mast **£20-25**
M753 **HMS 'Albion'** ....Grey or Blue body with one mast **£20-25**

COMMANDO SHIP
M754 **HMS 'Albion'** ....Grey ship with 12 Cream or Brown plastic
helicopters. 1000 models issued and given to H.M.S. 'Albion' crew
members (Capt. Adams in command) **£400-500**

CRUISERS
M761 **HMS 'Swiftsure'** ......Blue or Grey, one crane jib, 145 mm **£15-18**
M762 **HMS 'Superb'** ....Blue or Grey, one crane jib, 145 mm **£15-18**

DESTROYERS, FLEET ESCORT, 'DARING' CLASS
M771 **HMS 'Daring'** ....Blue or Grey, one mast, 98 mm **£5-8**
M772 **HMS 'Diana'** ....Blue or Grey, one mast, 98 mm **£5-8**
M773 **HMS 'Dainty'** ....Blue or Grey, one mast, 98 mm **£5-8**
M774 **HMS 'Decoy'** ....Blue or Grey, one mast, 98 mm **£5-8**

DESTROYERS, FLEET, 'BATTLE' CLASS
M779 **HMS 'Alamein'** ......Blue or Grey, one mast, 97 mm **£5-8**
M780 **HMS 'Jutland'** ....Blue or Grey, one mast, 97 mm **£5-8**
M781 **HMS 'Anzac'** ....Blue or Grey, one mast, 97 mm **£5-8**
M782 **HMS 'Tobruk'** ....Blue or Grey, one mast, 97 mm **£5-8**

DESTROYERS, GUIDED MISSILE, 'COUNTY' CLASS
M783 **HMS 'Hampshire'** ...Grey body with two masts, 136 mm **£20-25**

M784 **HMS 'Kent'** ....Grey body with two masts, 136 mm **£30-35**
M785 **HMS 'Devonshire'** ...Grey body with two masts, 136 mm **£20-25**
M786 **HMS 'London'** ....Grey body with two masts, 136 mm **£20-25**

FRIGATES, FAST ANTI-SUBMARINE, 'V' CLASS
M787 **HMS 'Vigilant'** ....Blue or Grey, one mast, 92 mm **£5-8**
M788 **HMS 'Venus'** ....Blue or Grey, one mast, 92 mm **£5-8**
M789 **HMS 'Virago'** ....Blue or Grey, one mast, 92 mm **£5-8**
M790 **HMS 'Volage'** ....Blue or Grey, one mast, 92 mm **£5-8**

FRIGATES, ANTI-SUBMARINE, 'WHITBY' CLASS
M791 **HMS 'Whitby'** ....Blue or Grey body, 94 mm **£5-7**
M792 **HMS 'Torquay'** ......Blue or Grey body, 94 mm **£5-7**
M793 **HMS 'Blackpool'** ....Blue or Grey body, 94 mm **£5-7**
M794 **HMS 'Tenby'** ....Blue or Grey body, 94 mm **£5-7**

MINESWEEPERS, 'TON' CLASS
M799 **HMS 'Repton'** ....Blue or Grey body **£5-7**
M800 **HMS 'Dufton'** ....Blue or Grey body **£5-7**
M801 **HMS 'Ashton'** ....Blue or Grey body **£5-7**
M802 **HMS 'Calton'** ....Blue or Grey body **£5-7**
M803 **HMS 'Picton'** ....Blue or Grey body **£5-7**
M804 **HMS 'Sefton'** ....Blue or Grey body **£5-7**
M805 **HMS 'Upton'** ....Blue or Grey body **£5-7**
M806 **HMS 'Weston'** ....Blue or Grey body **£5-7**

SUBMARINES, 'A' CLASS
M817 **Sub 'A' Class** ....Blue or Grey body, 61 mm **£5-7**
M818 **Sub Recon** ....Blue or Grey body, 61 mm **£7-10**

Accessories, Gift Sets, Hong Kong issues and Catalogues

DOCKSIDE ACCESSORIES

M827	**Breakwater Straights**, Grey	£3-4
M828/L	**Breakwater Angle**, Left, Grey	50p
M828/R	**Breakwater Angle**, Right, Grey	50p
M829	**Breakwater End**, Grey	50p
M836	**Quay Straights**, Tan	£3-4
M837	**Crane Units**, Tan, Brown or Green cargo	£3-4
M838	**Storage Tanks**, Grey/Silver and Red	£2-3
M839	**Customs Shed**, Green	£3-4
M840	**Warehouse**, Brown	£3-4
M841	**Ocean Terminal**, White with Black windows	£5-6
M842	**Swing Bridge**, Red, no description on base	£2-3
M843	**Terminal Extension**, White with Black windows	£5-6
M844	**Lock Gates** (pair), Brown	£1-2
M845	**Landing Stages**, Cream 'L' shaped, 1in long	£1-2
M846	**Lift Bridge**, Silver/Tan	£2-3
M847	**Pier centre section**, White	£2-3
M848	**Pier entrance section**, White	£2-3
M849	**Pier head**, White	£12-14
M850	**Pier Shelter**, Green, 35 mm	£5-6
M851	**Pier archways**	£2-3
M852	**Pier Building**, White/Blue/Green, Silver Cupola, 'RESTAURANT' plus 'DANCING TONIGHT'	£2-3
M853	**Factory Unit**, Pink and Buff, Black chimneys	£25-30
M854	**Tanker Wharf Straight**, Cream and Red	£65-75
M855	**Tanker Wharf Berth**, Red and Green or Cream and Green, Black plastic pipeline	£2-3
M857	**26in Sea**, Blue plastic	£14-18
M857	**52in Sea**, Blue plastic	£25-30
M861	**Lifeboat set**, Grey, Blue shed, one lifeboat	£35-40
M878	**Lighthouse**, White	£1-2
M880	**Whales**, White or plain Grey	£12-15
M882	**Beacon**, White/Red or Green	£1-2
M884	**Statue of Liberty**, Green/Grey	£15-20
M885	**Floating Dock**, Grey, 4 Black plastic cranes	£20-25
M -	**Helicopter**, Cream or Brown plastic	£20-25

GIFT SETS and SPECIAL PRESENTATION PACKS

M891	**'Queen Elizabeth'** Gift Set	£75-100
M892	**'United States'** Gift Set	£150-175
M893	**'Task Force'** Gift Set	£30-40
M894	**'Royal Yacht'** Gift Set	£80-100
M895	**'Nieuw Amsterdam'** Gift Set	£600-700
M702s	**'Queen Elizabeth'** Presentation Set	£80-100
M703s	**'Queen Mary'** Presentation Set	£100-120
M704s	**SS 'United States'** Presentation Set	£100-120
M705s	**RMS 'Aquitania'** Presentation Set	£125-150
M707s	**SS 'France'** Presentation Set	£125-150
M741s	**HMS 'Vanguard'** Presentation Set	£50-60

HONG KONG 'BLUE BOX' MODELS (1976-80)
'Queen Mary', 'Queen Elizabeth', 'United States', 'Canberra',
HMS 'Vanguard', HMS 'Bulwark', 'Missouri', 'Bismark',
'Scharnhorst', 'Yamato'. Each, boxed **£15-20**
RMS 'Canberra, boxed **£25-30**

HONG KONG SETS of MODELS

1	**Fleet Anchorage Set**	£25-30
2	**Quay Set**	£25-30
3a	**Ocean Terminal**, lid shows stern of RMS 'Queen Mary'	£45-50
3b	**Ocean Terminal**, lid shows bow of RMS 'Queen Mary'	£35-40
4	**Naval Task Force**, with HMS 'Bulwark' and 'Vanguard'	£35-40
5	**Naval Task Force**, with 'Bismark' and 'Scharnhorst'.	£50-55

MINIC CATALOGUES 1958-64

1	**Leaflet** .....with first Minic Ships listed	£75-100
2	**Booklet** ....with first Minic Ships listed	£25-30
3	**Booklet** ....with Ships and other Tri-ang products	£60-75
4	**Booklet** ....with Minic Ships only	£25-30
5	**Booklet** ....with Minic Ships only	£25-30
6	**Booklet** ....with Tri-ang range	£30-35
M862	**Leaflet** .....Minic illustrated leaflet	£10-15

Tri-ang
Spot-On models

Introduction

Spot-On Models were introduced in 1959 by Tri-ang Toys to gain a foothold in the diecast market dominated at the time by Dinky Toys and their recently established rivals Corgi Toys.

Tri-ang realised that they had to offer not only a range of features similar to those of their competitors' products but something more besides. They decided that collectors would appreciate models that were all made to the same precise scale right across the range.

The models would thus look right together and qualify as such rather than toys. Much of the Dinky and Corgi cars range was made to a scale of around 1:45 (with a few exceptions).

Tri-ang advertised the precise nature of their (larger) chosen scale as being 'spot-on' at 1:42.

A large modern factory was set up in Belfast, Northern Ireland to produce the models. A coloured picture of the real vehicle was included in the box of most early issues.

Well over a hundred different models were designed, the range being extended to include scale buildings and road signs. Production continued till the time that Tri-ang bought up Dinky Toys in 1967. After the cessation of UK production, some of the Spot-On dies went to New Zealand where some interesting versions were produced for a couple of years.

All Spot-On models are highly collectable today particularly commercial vehicles, buses and the Presentation and Gift Sets.

Market Price Range: Please note that the prices shown refer to pristine models and boxes.
Items failing to match this standard will sell for less.
Note also that boxes must contain all their original additional contents.

Spot-On model identification

Makers Name and Trade Mark are clearly marked on base of the model ('SPOT-ON' and 'Models by Tri-ang'). Some New Zealand produced versions have nothing at all on the base.

Model Name is shown on the base (except some New Zealand versions) while the **Model Number** is usually shown on box but not always on the model.

Baseplates can be any of a variety of colours: black, silver, grey - even green has been observed on the base of a maroon version of No. 155 Taxi !

Scale of models is 1:42 (with very few exceptions) and is usually (but not always) shown on the base.

Wheel hubs on cars are usually turned aluminium with a raised 'hub cap'. Truck models usually have diecast and more accurate representations of real hubs. **Tyres** are mostly black rubber (occasionally plastic) on all the vehicle models. Rear twin wheels have special 'double tyres'.

Number plates are represented on most Spot-On models with the exception of those having plastic chassis (such as 266 Bull Nose Morris and 279 MG Midget). A large range of

registration numbers were available to factory production staff and were applied randomly to most models. Different number plates are therefore to be expected on different examples of the same model and do not have any effect on the price.

Windscreens and windows are included in all vehicle models.

Other features include seats and steering wheel on most models, suspension on most cars, driver, other figures and lorry loads with some. Very few 'decals' or 'frills' is the norm.

Colours are all listed where known though different and previously unknown colours still come to light occasionally.

Prices shown in the 'Market Price Range' column are for mint models in pristine boxes. These models are rare, hence their high market prices. The condition of models generally encountered tends towards the average and consequently command lower prices. Similarly, rare colours or combinations of colours puts the price into the higher part of the range with common colours achieving a more moderate price level.

Colour pictures. See the colour section following page 64.

Spot-On Cars

Ref.No.	Year(s)	Model name	Colours, features, dimensions	Market Price Range
100	1959	**Ford Zodiac (without lights)**	Red / Cream or Blue / Cream body, 107 mm	£70-90
			Red body	£80-100
			Cream body	£70-90
			Yellow body	£110-140
			Light Blue, Salmon-Pink or Green body	£70-90
			Bluish-Grey and Brownish-Pink body	£75-100
			Grey/Blue body	£70-90
100sl	1959	**Ford Zodiac (with lights)**	Grey/Turquoise or Grey/Pink body	£75-100
			Grey/White, Grey/Light Blue, or Green/White body	£70-90
			Yellow/White, Grey/Green, or Two-tone Blue body	£70-90
101	1959	**Armstrong Siddeley 236 Sapphire**	Blue / Grey, Turquoise / Black, Blue / Black, Pink or Mauve body	£100-130
			Salmon body, Black roof	£180-220
			Mid-Green body, Dark Green roof	£220-250
			Light Blue body, Dark Blue roof	£170-200
			Metallic Green, Metallic Green / Black, or Bluish-Grey	£75-100
			Light Blue body	£80-100
			Light Blue / Black, Grey / Black	£95-125
			Pale Green / Metallic Charcoal, or Deep Lilac / Black roof	£80-100
			Cream / Metallic Charcoal or Metallic Blue / Black	£75-100
			Yellow body, Black roof	£150-175
102	1959	**Bentley Continental 4-door Sports**	Metallic Green / Silver, or Metallic Grey / Blue. 127 mm	£80-125
			Metallic Maroon / Silver	£175-200
			Two-tone Grey, Silver / Grey or Green / Grey	£95-125
			Silver / Light Blue or Grey / Light Blue body	£120-150
103	1959	**Rolls Royce Silver Wraith**	Metallic Silver and Maroon body, White seats, 131 mm	£250-400
			Metallic Silver and Metallic Light Blue (Cream seats), or	
			Metallic Silver and Metallic Green body	£120-200
104	1959	**M.G. 'MGA' Sports Car**	Beige body, 95 mm	£150-175
			Red body (Grey seats), Mid-blue or Pale Blue body (White seats)	£110-150
			Turquoise or Cream body (White seats)	£110-150
			Salmon Pink (Grey seats) or Bluish-Green (Lemon seats)	£150-200
			Greenish-Grey (Turquoise seats)	NGPP
			Deep Green body (White seats)	£150-200
105	1959	**Austin Healey 100/6**	Yellow (White or Grey seats), Grey (Red seats), Beige (Grey seats)	£140-200
			Red / Cream or Metallic Blue / Cream	£300-400
			Blue, Green, Cream, Turquoise, Metallic Blue, Metallic Green, or Pink	£130-170
			Light Blue body (Royal Blue seats) or Turquiose (Light Grey seats)	£150-180
107	1960	**Jaguar XK-SS**	Metallic Blue body, Lemon seats, Black folded hood	£150-200
			Cream, Beige, Red or Light Green body	£175-200
			Dark Olive (Light Grey seats / hood), or	
			Pale Blue (Pale Grey seats / hood)	£150-175
			Lilac body with Grey seats, Black folded hood	£175-225
			Light Blue with Dark Blue seats and folded hood	£150-200
			Light Grey body, Pale Blue seats and folded hood	£200-250
			Fawn body, cast hubs have 'stick-on' wheel trims that create a	
			spoked wheel and white-wall tyre effect	NGPP
108	1960	**Triumph TR3a Sports**	Light Blue with Dark Blue seats, 88 mm	£200-225
			Cream body with Dark Brown seats	£175-225
			Light Brown (White seats), Pale Green (Grey seats) or Apple Green (Cream seats)	£140-170
			Red or Sea Green body with Grey seats	£120-150
			Grey body (White seats), or Metallic Green (Lemon seats)	£125-175
			Pale Blue body with Pale Grey seats	£125-175
			Mid-Blue body with Mid-Grey seats	£125-175
			Note: Two baseplate castings are known with this model. One exposes	
			the axle ends near to the wheels, while the other completely hides the axles.	
112	1960	**Jensen 541**	Grey, Mauve, Pink, Maroon / Black or Metallic Green body, 106 mm	£100-125
			Light Blue or Pale Green or Metallic Blue body	£100-125
			Lemon body (Black roof), or Yellow body (Red seats)	£100-125
113	1960	**Aston Martin DB3 Saloon**	Light Blue, Grey, Red, Light Green, Dark Green, 104 mm	£125-150
			Maroon body	£200-250
			Very Pale Pink or Deep Pink body	£140-180
			Deep Lilac or Light Brown body	£130-170
			White or Metallic Dark Green body	£130-160
			Metallic Silver Blue body	£130-160
			Yellow body, Lemon interior, Red steering wheel	£175-225
114	1960	**Jaguar 3.4 Mark 1 Saloon**	Metallic Blue, Maroon, Mauve, Metallic Green, or Pink, 108 mm	£125-150
			Light Grey or Mid-Green body	£140-180
			Light Blue or Yellow body	£110-150
			White or Dark Red body	£150-180
			Very Pale Pink or Deep Pink body	£100-130

115	1960	**Bristol 406 Saloon**	Orange or Red body, 116 mm	£100-130
			Metallic Dark Steel body	£160-180
			Yellow or Metallic Green body	£100-160
			Grey body, Black roof, Cream seats	£100-130
118	1960	**BMW Isetta Bubble Car**	Pale Blue, Beige, Grey or Turquoise, 56 mm	£70-80
			Green or Metallic Green, Red, Pink or Yellow	£75-100
			Yellow body	£120-160
119	1960	**Meadows Frisky Sport**	Orange / Grey, Blue / Grey or Turquoise / Grey	£50-65
			Red / Light Grey, Red / Black, or Light Blue / White, 69 mm	£75-100
			Bluish-Green / Black or Red / White	£80-100
120	1960	**Fiat Multipla Estate**	Blue (Cream seats), or Mauve (Red seats), 85 mm	£70-80
			Pink, Light Blue, Yellow, Red, Dark Red, Sea Green or Pale Green	£100-125
			White (Off-White seats)	£100-125
131	1960	**Goggomobil Super Regent**	Grey / Black, Yellow / Black, Mauve / Black, Blue / Grey, Blue, Green, or Grey	£50-75
			Metallic Green, Beige, Light Grey, Pink, Deep Salmon Pink, Red or Turquoise	£50-75
			Light Blue / Black, Red / Black, Dark Blue / Black, Green / Black	£50-75
154	1961	**Austin A40 Farina Saloon**	Green, Grey, White, Light Blue/White or Grey/Blue	£50-70
			Light Grey, Metallic Blue, Beige, Light Blue, Navy or Turquoise body	£50-75
			Red / Black, Blue / Black, Green / Black, Lavender / Black	£60-80
	1966	**'MAGGI' Promotional**	Red body, Cream interior, 'MAGGI' in yellow on front doors. Housed in special red / yellow box with leaflet	£350-450
157	1963	**Rover 3-litre (without lights)**	Mid Blue, Mauve, Beige or Yellow	£70-90
			Mid-Grey, Dark Grey, Pale Grey, Sea Green, Dark Green, Light Blue or Deep Pink	£90-120
			Dark Blue body	£150-175
			White body	£95-125
157sl	1963	**Rover 3-litre with lights**	Mid Blue, Mauve, Beige, Red or Yellow	£90-120
			Grey, Pale Grey, Sea Green, Dark Green, Light Blue	£90-120
			Dark Blue or Dark Grey	£120-150
			White body	£95-125
165/1	1961	**Vauxhall PA Cresta Saloon**	Beige, Red, Maroon, Pink, Turquoise or Yellow, 115 mm	£80-100
			Blue, Light Blue, Grey or Light Grey	£90-120
			Plum Red or Sea Green body	£100-125
165/2	1961	**Vauxhall PA Cresta with roof rack**	Beige, Red, Maroon, Pink, Turquoise or Yellow, 115 mm	£80-100
			Blue, Light Blue, Grey or Light Grey	£90-120
			Plum Red or Sea green body	£110-150
166	1962	**Renault Floride Convertible**	Blue, Green or Grey body, 101 mm	£70-90
			Dark Red, White or Yellow body	£80-100
183	1963	**Humber Super Snipe Estate**	Beige / White, Blue / White, Green / White, Blue / Black, Beige, Blue, Metallic Bronze or two-tone Blue, with or without wing mirrors	£75-100
184	1963	**Austin A60 (with skis)**	Beige, Green or White body, 106 mm	£70-90
			Red, Light Blue or Light Grey (Grey rack)	£75-100
			Lime Green or Greyish-Blue (Black or Grey roof-rack)	£90-120
185	1963	**Fiat 500**	Light Blue, Green, Red or Grey body	£80-100
			Yellow or Dark Blue	£120-150
191	1963	**Sunbeam Alpine Convertible**	Beige, Mid-Blue, Green, Red, Mauve, Pink or Yellow, 95 mm	£70-90
			Turquoise or Grey (Cream seats), or Light Blue (White seats)	£90-120
			Deep Salmon Pink or White with Red seats	£100-130
191/1	1963	**Sunbeam Alpine Hardtop**	Red / White, Turquoise / White, Blue / Black, Blue / Cream, White / Black, Beige / White, Grey / Black body and hardtop, 95 mm	£70-90
			Dark Green (Red seats), or Metallic Green / Black	£100-130
			Pink (Cream seats)	£90-120
			Mauve (Cream seats), or Yellow body (Cream seats)	£120-150
			Light Blue, Light Blue/White, Pale Blue/White	£80-110
193	1963	**N.S.U. Prinz**	Turquoise, Beige, Pale Blue, Light or Dark Blue, Cream, Grey or Red	£50-70
			White body	£80-90
195	1963	**Volkswagen Rally Car**	Beige, Cream, Maroon, or Orange body, roof light, flags on bonnet, racing number '9' or '23', 110 mm	£150-175
			Red body, racing number '11', or Metallic Bronze	£200-300
			Light Blue ('6'), Turquoise ('9')	£150-175
210	1960	**Morris Mini Minor**	Shown in catalogue but not issued	NPP
211	1963	**Austin Seven (Mini)**	Light Blue, Grey, Red or Yellow body, 73 mm	£125-150
			Pink body	£200-250
			White body	£160-180
213	1963	**Ford Anglia Saloon**	Cream, Grey, Yellow or White body, 95 mm	£70-90
			Turquoise, Light Blue, Dark Blue, Red or Pink	£130-160
215	1961	**Daimler Dart SP250**	Beige, Green or Yellow body, 75 mm	£90-120
			White (Red seats), or Light Blue (Blue seats)	£140-160
			Turquoise (White seats), Red (Cream seats), Grey (Cream seats)	£100-125

216	1963	**Volvo 122s**	Red, Orange, Blue or Turquoise body, sliding roof, 110 mm	£80-100
			Grey, Bright Yellow, Dark Green or Lime Green	£100-125
217	1963	**Jaguar 'E' Type**	Beige, Cream, Light or Dark Green, Red, White or Yellow / Black	£90-120
			Mid-Blue or Light Grey body	£100-130
			Light Blue body	£200-250
218	1963	**Jaguar Mk.10**	Metallic Brown or Blue, 122 mm	£90-120
			Dark or Mid-Green, Bronze or White	£120-150
219	1963	**Austin-Healey Sprite Mk.III**	Red (White seats), Blue (Red seats), Beige (White seats); driver figure	£80-100
			Off-White or Light Blue body	£100-125
259	1963	**Ford Consul Classic**	White (Blue seats), Beige (White seats); or Blue, Light Blue, Red, Grey or Green body, 105 mm	£80-100
260	1963	**Royal Rolls-Royce Phantom V**	Maroon body, Blue interior, two flags on roof, Queen and Prince Philip in rear seats, driver and attendant in front. 143 mm	£300-400
261	1963	**Volvo P1800**	There are two versions of this model (with little or no price difference): 1: the bonnet and boot open and a spare wheel is supplied; 2: only the bonnet can be opened. Light Blue, Mid-Blue, Red, Turquoise, Grey or Metallic Bronze	£80-100
			Tan body	£100-130
262	1963	**Morris 1100**	Dark Blue or Red (Grey seats), Green or Beige (Red seats), 89 mm	£60-80
			Lime Green or Light Blue body	£70-90
263	1964	**Bentley 4½ Litre (Supercharged)**	Green body, Union Jack, racing number '27', '11' or '15', 108 mm	£60-75
266	1965	**'Bull Nose' Morris 1923**	Red / Black or Yellow / Black, Brown driver, (scale 1:48)	£45-60
267	1964	**M.G. 1100 Saloon**	White / Dark Green (Red seats), Red (Cream seats), or Green (Red seats), or Red / White or Beige / Cream, 88 mm	£60-75
			Royal Blue / White, Red interior	£350-450
268	1965	**Vauxhall PB Cresta**	Shown in catalogue but not issued under this number, see 280	NPP
270	1965	**Ford Zephyr 6 Mk.III**	Blue, Cream, Green, Greyish-Green or Grey (Red seats); or Red (Grey seats)	£70-90
274	1965	**Morris 1100 and Canoe**	Green, Grey, Light Blue, Dark Blue or Red car, Brown canoe on roof	£50-65
			Light Blue or Two-tone Blue (Red canoe) or Red (Red / White canoe)	£60-85
			Light Blue body with Blue / Red canoe, Orange paddle (Set 703)	GSP
276	1964	**Jaguar 'S' type**	Metallic Bronze body, 114 mm	£120-150
			Blue or Metallic Green body	£120-150
			Silver body	£180-220
278	1965	**Mercedes-Benz 230 SL**	Metallic Red, Cream, or Maroon body, 100 mm	£75-100
			Metallic Blue or Metallic Bronze	£90-120
279	1965	**M.G. PB Midget 1935**	Dark Blue or Red body, Black wings and seats, 79 mm	£50-65
280	1963	**Vauxhall PB Cresta**	Red / Beige, Dark Blue / Cream or Grey / Green body	£60-75
281	1966	**M.G. Midget Mk.II**	Blue or Red body, Driver with scarf, 83 mm	£75-100
286	1965	**Austin 1800**	Light or Dark Blue, Cream, Green or Beige (all with Red seats); or Red (Grey seats)	£60-75
287	1965	**Hillman Minx (with roof-rack and Luggage)**	Pale Green, Beige, Cream or Green (all with Red seats), Red (Grey seats) or Greyish-Green body, Two brown suitcases, 84 mm	£80-100
287/1	1965	**Hillman Minx (with roof rack)**	Same details as 287	£80-100
289	1963	**Morris Minor 1000**	Metallic Blue or Light Blue body	£120-150
			Red or Metallic Green body	£160-200
304	1967	**VW Variant Estate Car**	Mid-Blue body and plastic opening tailgate. See also 401/1	NGPP
306	1964	**Humber Super Snipe Estate**	Same casting as 183 but with roof-rack and two suitcases. Beige, Blue, Green or Red or Metallic Bronze body, 113 mm	£100-140
			Light Blue (White roof-rack) or Turquoise (White roof-rack)	£85-100
			White and Turquoise body, Grey roof-rack, 113 mm	£100-120
			Blue body, White roof	£80-95
307	1965	**Volkswagen Beetle 1200**	Metallic Blue or Metallic Dark Red body, 110 mm	£200-250
308	1965	**Land Rover and Trailer**	Green with Tan plastic canopy, trailer has Brown plastic body	£50-60
405	1966	**'BEA' Vauxhall Cresta**	Dark Grey body with Red 'BEA' logo	£70-90
407	1966	**Mercedes-Benz 230 SL**	Brown body, Red interior, boot rack and luggage, 103 mm	£50-60
408	1966	**Renault Caravelle**	Not issued	NPP
410	1966	**Austin 1800 and Rowboat**	Green, Blue, Beige or Red car with Red or Orange boat on roof	£60-70
401/1	1967	**VW Variant Estate Car**	Dark Blue body, White plastic opening tailgate	NGPP

Ref.No.	Year(s)	Model name	Colours, features, dimensions	Market Price Range
106a/0c	1960	**Austin Articulated Flatbed Lorry** **with MGA in Crate**	Light Blue, Dark Blue, Red or Orange cab, 234 mm	£250-400
106a/1	1959	**Austin Articulated Dropside Lorry**	Light Blue, Green or Orange cab and body, 234 mm	£150-200
106a/1c	1960	**Austin Articulated Flatbed Lorry** **with Crate Load**	Light Blue, Light Green or Orange cab, seven black plastic crates	£200-250
			Turquoise or Dark Blue body	£300-350
CB106	1961-62	**Four Wheel Trailer**	Turquoise or Red body, for use with ERF and AEC lorries	£90-110
109/2	1960	**E.R.F. 68g Flatbed Lorry**	Turquoise, Light Grey or Blue body, 210 mm	£160-190
			Maroon body	£350-400
109/2p	1960	**E.R.F. 68g Flatbed Lorry with Planks**	Turquoise (with or without Black cab roof), 210 mm	£200-250
			Yellow body	£400-450
109/3	1960	**E.R.F. 68g Dropside Lorry**	Dark Blue cab with Pale Blue or Silver truck body	£400-500
			Yellow body (Metallic Grey roof), Light Green body (Green roof), Blue body or Green body (Black roof)	£160-190
			Deep Blue body, Silver chassis	£250-350
			Orange-Red body, Light Grey chassis	£350-450
			Lemon, Pale Green or Turquoise body, Silver chassis	£190-225
109/3b	1960	**E.R.F. Dropside Lorry with Barrel load**	Turquoise, Light Blue or Red body (Silver truck bed on some), hinged tailboard, ten Brown plastic barrels	£200-350
110/2	1960	**A.E.C. Mammoth Major 8 Flatbed Lorry**	Red body (with or without Black roof), 210 mm	£170-200
			Maroon or Dark Blue body	£450-500
110/2b	1960	**A.E.C. Lorry 'London Brick Co Ltd'**	Red body, Black cab roof, 'brick' load, 'Phorpes Bricks'	£200-250
110/3	1960	**A.E.C. Lorry 'British Road Services'**	Red body, with or without Black cab roof	£200-250
110/3d	1962	**A.E.C. Lorry with Oil Drums Load**	Red body, Black cab roof	£225-300
110/4	1961	**A.E.C. Tanker 'SHELL-BP'**	Green cab, Red tank, Black chassis and catwalk	£300-400
			Yellow cab, White/Yellow tank, Silver chassis / catwalk	£500-750
111/30g	1962	**Ford Thames with Garage Kit**	Orange cab and truck body, Silver chassis, 219 mm	£300-350
			Light Blue cab and truck body, White garage	£250-300
111/a0t	1961	**Ford Thames Trader with Three Log Load**	Dark Blue or Red cab and truck body, 3 logs	£275-325
			Light Blue cab and truck body	£200-275
			Light Yellow cab and truck body	£325-375
111a/1	1959	**Ford Thames Trader 'British Railways'**	Maroon and White body, '4884 BGM', 'M 1741 GT6'	£225-300
111a/1	1960	**Ford Thames Trader 'R.Hall & Son'**	Green body, logo on door. Doubtful if model issued	NPP
111a/1s	1960	**Ford Thames with Sack Load**	Light Blue and Silver, twelve brown plastic sacks	£250-325
			Dark Green body	£300-350
			Two-tone Blue body	£500-700
			Strawberry and Cream body	£600-750
116	1959	**'CATERPILLAR' Tractor D9**	Brown / Silver body, Black rubber tracks, 'CAT D9'	£500-750
117	1963	**'JONES' Mobile Crane**	Cream cab and jib, Red body and wheels, Black chassis, Grey base	£150-200
			Dark Red cab / body, White jib, Light Grey chassis, Silver wheels	£300-400
122	1961	**'UNITED DAIRIES' Milk Float**	Red / White body, chains, 'Lada and New Yoghurt'	£75-100
123	1959	**Bamford Excavator**	Red / Yellow, 'J.C.B.'. Intended model but not issued	NPP
137	1962	**'MASSEY FERGUSON 65' Tractor**	Red / Grey body, Orange engine cover, yellow wheels	£350-500
158a/2	1961	**Bedford 'S' Type 2000 Gallon** **'SHELL-BP' Tanker**	Green cab, Red tank, Black chassis, 'P33A37' logo	£400-500
			Yellow cab, White tank, 'P33A37' logo, 202 mm	£700-1000
			Dark Metallic Green cab, Red tank, Black chassis	£500-600
158a/2C	1961	**Bedford Low Loader**	Red low-loader with cable drum load. Doubtful if issued	NPP
161	1961	**Land Rover (long wheel base)**	Grey / White, Light Grey / White or Blue / White	£65-80
210	1961	**Morris Mini Van**	Bright Yellow, seats / steering wheel, suspension	£90-120
210/1	1962	**Morris Mini Van 'Royal Mail'**	Red body, Post Office crest, 'E-II-R', suspension	£70-90
210/2	1962	**Mini Van 'P.O. Telephones'**	Olive-Green, Gold crown logo and 'TELEPHONE MANAGER'	£90-100
258	1963	**'R.A.C.' Land Rover**	Dark Blue body, 'RADIO RESCUE', 108 mm	£90-120
265	1964	**'TONIBELL' Ice Cream Van**	Blue body, thick Red flash, attendant, 'Tonibell' on doors	£90-135
271	1965	**'EXPRESS DAIRIES' Milk Float**	Blue / White, 3 wheels, driver, 'Drink Express Milk'	£100-125
273	1965	**Commer Van 'SECURITY EXPRESS'**	Green / Gold, driver and seated guard, coin slot in roof	£80-125
308	1965	**Land Rover and Trailer**	Green body, Beige hood, Brown trailer, 107 mm	£70-80
315	1965	**'GLASS & HOLMES' Commer Van**	Blue / Yellow, ladder, figures, 'Window Cleaning Co. Est 1891'	£80-120
402	1966	**Crash Service Land Rover**	Orange body, 'MOTORWAYS CRASH SERVICE' in Blue	£70-90
404	1966	**Morris Mini Van**	Yellow body, suspension, ladder, figure, 79 mm	£300-350
404/1	1966	**Morris Mini Van 'SHELL'**	As previous model but without ladder and figure	£400-500
404/2	1966	**Morris Mini Van 'AA'**	Shown in 1966 catalogue but never seen	NGPP

Spot-On Buses, Coaches and Taxis

145	1963	**Routemaster Bus**	Red 'London Transport' bus, route '284', 'Ovaltine - The Worlds Best Nightcap'.	
			1st type has chrome moulded radiator	£450-550
			2nd type has transfer print on plastic background	£400-500
155	1961	**Austin FX4 Taxi**	Maroon body, Cream steering wheel, Green base, tin-plate hubcaps	£400-500
			Black body, Red steering wheel, Grey base	£65-80
156	1961	**Mulliner Luxury Coach**	Pale Blue / Grey, Red flash, 'Tri-ang Tours', 213 mm	£250-400
			Yellow / White body, Brown side flash	£1500-1800
			Sea Green / Cream, Red flash	£800-1000
			Silver / Red / Dark Blue	£250-350
			Sky Blue / White body, Red flash	£600-800

Military models

415	1965	**R.A.F. Land Rover**	Blue/Grey, R.A.F. roundel, hose/pump/attendant, 111 mm	£80-100
416	1965	**Leyland Army Ambulance**	Olive Green body. Not issued	NPP
417	1965	**Military 'FIELD KITCHEN'**	Olive Green body, squadron markings, suspension, 108 mm	£100-125
418	1965	**Leyland Military Bus**	Olive Green body, 'Army Personnel'. Not issued	NPP
419	1965	**Land Rover and Missile Carrier**	Olive Green body, three White missiles.	£200-250

Emergency vehicles

207	1964	**Wadham Ambulance**	Cream body without Red crosses, with stretcher and patient	£200-300
			White body with Red crosses, with stretcher and patient	£350-500
256	1966	**Jaguar 3.4 'POLICE' Car**	White or Black. Very few exist with undamaged aerial or roof sign	£200-275
309	1965	**Police 'Z' Car**	Ford Zephyr police car from the BBC-TV series 'Z-Cars'.	
			1st type with aerial and 'POLICE' sign, White body	£100-130
			2nd type with no aerial or police sign. Black body	£600-700
			2nd type (no aerial or police sign), White body	£500-600
316	1966	**'FIRE DEPT' Land Rover**	Red body, suspension, two firemen, 112 mm	£80-100
402	1966	**Land Rover 'MOTORWAYS'**	Orange / Blue body, hook, Blue 'CRASH SERVICE' logo	£70-90
409	1966	**Leyland 'Black Maria'**	Blue body, 'Police', policeman and villain. Not issued	NPP

'Magicar' series

501	1965	**Jaguar Mk.10**	Blue or Green body	£70-90
502	1965	**Rolls-Royce Silver Cloud Mk.III**	Blue or Red body	£100-125
503	1965	**Bentley S3 Saloon**	Blue or Red body	£80-110
504		**Ferrari Superfast**	Blue or Red.	£80-110
505	1966	**Batmobile**	Black body with Batman and Robin figures	£150-175
?	?	**Tric-Trac car**	Plastic bodied racing car	£80-110
MG1	?	**Magicar**	no details	NGPP
MG2	?	**Magicar**	no details	NGPP
MG3	?	**Magicar**	no details	NGPP

Caravans, Boats, Motor Scooter

135	1961	**14ft Sailing Dinghy and Trailer**	Blue / Grey, Dark Blue / Red, Dark Blue / White, or Red / White boat (with or without cover), plastic trailer	£40-55
135	1964	**14ft GP Sailing Dinghy**	Brown or Yellow boat on trailer, 128 mm	£35-45
139	1960	**Eccles E.16 Caravan**	Blue body, White roof, 146 mm	NPP
229	1966	**Lambretta**	Blue body, Red or White rear casing	£175-225
264	1962	**Tourist Caravan**	Blue body, White roof, 152 mm	£90-120
			Yellow body, White roof	£70-90
			Tan body, White roof	£80-125

The 'Cotswold Village' series

The 'Cotswold Village' items are rare and it is suggested that larger buildings (church, shop, etc) are likely to be in the region of **£100 - £150**, while smaller items might be anything from **£10 - £50** depending on size, complexity, etc. These price levels can only be applied to pristine items in perfect original boxes.

1	School		3	'Cornerstones' Cottage		12	Post Office
2a	Haystack		4	'Fourways' Cottage		13	Church
			4b	'The Cot' Cottage		14	Forge
			5	Antique Shop		15	Memorial Stone
			6	General Store		16	Water Well
			7	Bourton Town Hall		16a	Stocks
			8	Barn		-	Set of Trees
			9	Public House		-	Bridge Sides
			10	Farm House			
			11	Manor House			

Garages and Equipment, Road Signs and Accessories

Garages and equipment

L146	'SHELL' lamp standard	£10-15
L147	'SHELL' sign	£10-15
L148	'SHELL' petrol pump	£10-15
L148	Trade pack, Blue card box of 6 of L148 pumps	£80-100
L149	Oil Dispenser Rack	£10-15
L159	'BP' Lamp Standard	£10-15
162	'BP' or 'SHELL' Filling Station	£35-45
162/1/2/3	Garages, each	£15-20
163	'BP' Petrol Pump	£10-15
164	'BP' Forecourt Sign	£10-15
172a	'SHELL' Garage Set	£50-75
172b	'BP' Garage Set	£50-75

Road signs and accessories

---	Road Traffic Signs: 20 different signs issued, each	£10-15
L1271/	Road Direction Signs: /1 Portsmouth, /2 Guildford, /3 Bristol, /4 Birmingham, /5 Biggar, /6 Dumfries	£10-15
	Bus Stops: No details available	£10-15
	Road sections: Straights, curves, T-junctions. Each	£6-8

Plastic Figures: In groups set on a card. Figures include: Garage Personnel, Newspaperman/Milkman/Postman, Doctor/Parson/Schoolmaster, 2 Policeman and an RAC Man, 3 Schoolboys, 2 Children and a Man (in country clothes), 3 Roadmen and Brazier or 3 Roadmen and Road Drill/Planks/Walls

Per card	£5-10
Retailer's sheet of any six cards of figures	£75-95

Spot-On Presentation and Gift Sets

Ref.	Year	Set name	Contents	Market Price Range

Colours of individual items are not listed. It is possible to find virtually any factory colour that was available at the time of manufacture in Spot-On Gift Sets. Early sets should contain Picture Cards, Fleet Owners leaflets and Magazine Club leaflets.

Ref.	Year	Set name	Contents	Market Price Range
A	1960	Presentation Set 'A'	102 Bentley, 108 Triumph TR3, 114 Jaguar 3.4, 118 BMW Isetta, 154 Austin A40	£350-450
No.0	1960	Presentation Set	106a/1 Austin Articulated Dropside Lorry, 100 Ford Zodiac, 103 Rolls-Royce Silver Wraith, 104 MGA and 113 Aston Martin	£500-600
No.1	1960	Presentation Set	100 Ford Zodiac, 101 Armstrong-Siddely, 103 Rolls-Royce and 104 MGA	£600-700
No.2	1960	Presentation Set	109/3 ERF Dropside Lorry, 101 Armstrong-Siddely, 102 Bentley Continental and 105 Austin-Healey 100/6	£600-700
No.3	1960	Presentation Set	Contains 111a/1 Ford Thames Trader, 101 Armstrong-Siddely, 104 MGA, 108 Triumph TR3a, 112 Jensen 541, 113 Aston Martin, 114 Jaguar 3.4	£600-750
No.4	1960	Presentation Set	106a/1 Austin Articulated Dropside Lorry, 109/3 ERF Dropside Lorry, 100 Ford Zodiac, 107 Jaguar XK-SS, 112 Jensen 541	£600-800
No.4a	1963	Presentation Set	104 MGA, 105 Austin-Healey, 107 Jaguar XK-SS and 108 Triumph TR3a	£400-500
No.5		Presentation Set	118 BMW Isetta, 119 Meadows Frisky Sport and 131 Goggomobil Super Regent	£250-300
No.6		'Miniature' Presentation Set	131 Goggomobil, 185 Fiat 500, 193 NSU Prinz and 211 Austin Seven	£300-400
			Variation with 210/1 'ROYAL MAIL' Van instead of 193 NSU Prinz	£300-400
No.6a		'Miniature' Presentation Set	131 Goggomobil, 185 Fiat 500, 119 Meadows Frisky and 211 Austin Seven	£400-500
No.7		Rally Presentation Set	Contains 166 Renault Floride, 191 Sunbeam Alpine, 211 Austin Seven, 213 Ford Anglia, 215 Daimler Dart, 217 Jaguar 'E'-type	£500-600
No.8		Presentation Set	157 Rover, 191 Sunbeam, 213 Ford Anglia, 216 Volvo, 258 RAC Land Rover	£500-600
No.9		Presentation Set	122 Milk Float, 145 Routemaster Bus, 193 NSU Prinz, 207 Wadham Ambulance, 211 Austin Seven, 256 Jaguar Police Car	NGPP
No.10		Presentation Set	122 Milk Float, 145 Routemaster Bus, 157 Rover 3 litre, 158a/2 Bedford Tanker, 185 Fiat 500, 165 Vauxhall Cresta, 166 Renault Floride, 211 Austin Seven, 215 Daimler Dart and 262 Morris 1100	£400-500
No.14		Presentation Set	211 Austin 7 Mini, 154 Austin A40, 156 Mulliner Coach, 191/1 Sunbeam (Hardtop), 122 'UNITED DAIRIES' Milk Float, 157sl Rover 3 Litre with lights	£500-600
173		Terrapin Building Set	A constructional set	£20-30
208/a		Road Construction Set	4 workmen, brazier, hut, poles, road sections and 18 other small items	£125-175
259		Garage Set	A constructional set	£20-30
701		'His, Her's, Junior's' Set	219 Austin-Healey Sprite, 267 MG 1100, 280 Vauxhall Cresta, in 'window' box	£200-250
702		Gift Set 702	270 Zephyr Six, 274 Morris 1100 and canoe, 286 Austin 1800 and 135 Dinghy	£200-250
702(a)		Gift Set 702	195 VW Rally, 217 Jaguar 'E' type, 261 Volvo P1800, 287 Hillman Minx	£300-350
212	1963	Car, Dinghy and Trailer Set	Contains 165 Vauxhall PA Cresta and 135 GP Dinghy	£125-150
269	1965	Ford Zephyr and Caravan	Contains 270 plus 264 Caravan	£125-175
308	1965	Land Rover and Trailer	Green bodywork, Fawn cover, 170 mm	£65-85
406	1966	Hillman Minx and Dinghy	Contains 287 Hillman Minx and 135 GP Dinghy and trailer	£70-95
MG1	1966	'Magicar Motoring' Set	501 Jaguar Mk.10 and 502 Rolls-Royce, roadway sections and traffic cones	NGPP
MG2		'Magicar Motoring' Set	503 Bentley S3 and 504 Ferrari Superfast, roadway sections and traffic cones	NGPP

'Tommy Spot' Gift Sets

All include a building kit and Tommy Spot figure.

801	'Home with Tommy Spot'	287 Hillman Minx (with Mr Spot), 270 Ford Zephyr Six with driver	£200-275
802	'Cops 'n' Robbers with Tommy Spot'	309 BBC-TV 'Z-Car' with driver and criminal, 276 Jaguar and driver	£275-350
803	'Superville Garage with Tommy Spot'	286 Austin 1800 with driver, 279 MG Midget, two garage workers	£200-275
804	'Sailing with Tommy Spot'	280 Vauxhall PB Cresta and sailing dinghy with Tommy and Mr Spot	£150-225
805	'Fire with Tommy Spot'	316 Fire Dept Land Rover and trailer, two firefighters	£195-260
806	'Royal Occasion with Tommy Spot'	260 Royal Rolls-Royce with chauffeur and royal passengers, 6 guardsmen	£450-650
807	'Pit stop with Tommy Spot'	Mercedes-Benz 230 SL and Jaguar 'S', two racing drivers	£300-400
808	'Motorway Rescue with Tommy Spot'	402 'Crash Service' Land Rover and mechanic, A.A. van and man	£400-500

Catalogues, Leaflets and Pictures

Ref.No.	Issued	Edition	Cover features and contents	Market Price Range
---	1959	**Early issue**	Red cover featuring a Target plus the dividers and diagram of Rolls Royce 'LTP 103'. Wording: '1/42' and 'SPOT-ON MODELS BY TRI-ANG'. Contains 8 pages.	£30-40
---	1959	**'1st Edition'**	Village scene with Spot-On buildings and models, 'Tri-ang' logo in bright red, '6d', 'dividers' mark, 'SCALE 1/42'. Thick numbered pages with superb pictures	£30-40
---	1960	**'2nd Edition'**	As 1st Edition but 'Tri-ang' logo in maroon and pages not numbered	£30-40
---	1961	**'3rd Edition'**	Same as 2nd Edition	£25-35
5a7383/DP	1963	**'4th Edition'**	Royal Rolls-Royce on cover, '3d', Page 19 shows the new Presentation Sets 5-10 and 14	£20-30
---	1964	**'5th Edition'**	Blue Austin 1800 (286) on cover, '2d', concertina type leaflet featuring new type of Black/Red window boxes for Gift Sets and single models	£20-£30
---	1965	**'6th Edition'**	Cover again features 286 Austin 1800 plus 289 Morris Minor, '2d', concertina type leaflet which includes 'Tommy Spot' and 'Magicar' listings and pictures	£20-30
---	1966	**'7th Edition'**	Booklet type featuring 407 Mercedes 230 SL and 287 Hillman Minx, '6d', 'Tommy Spot' featured with 'Royal Occasion' set and Car Spotters guide	£20-30

Leaflets and Model Pictures

The early 'blue boxes' for cars and small commercial vehicles and the early card boxes for the large commercial vehicles contained a model picture and a yellow / blue / white leaflet listing the models available. Prices of model picture cards can vary depending on the rarity of the model itself within a price range from **£5** to **£25**.
Spot-On 'Picture wallets' are to be found at **£15-20**.
It should be noted that no 'blue box' model or early large commercial boxed model is complete without the model picture.
Leaflets are not uncommon and may be obtained for **£2-3**.

Trade Display Material

---	---		Electric revolving Trade Display Unit	£300-400
---	---		Glass shop-sign with 'SPOT-ON MODELS' in red/black/yellow design, 25 inches long	£150-200

Spot-On New Zealand issues

When Tri-ang took over the production of Dinky Toys in 1967 they stopped production of Spot-On Models in the United Kingdom. Fourteen models were subsequently produced by the Tri-ang Pedigree company of New Zealand from the original dies sent out from the U.K.

New Zealand production lasted just two years and ceased in 1969 / 70. The New Zealand model reference numbers were different to their UK counterparts as listed in the Spot-On 7th Edition catalogue. Extras such as roof racks and luggage were not included with NZ issues and the models were housed in New Zealand yellow cellophane 'window' boxes. The following listing first appeared in 'Mini Cars' ('The News Sheet for Caledonian Autominologists'), dated September 1972 and was prepared by Eric Brockie in New Zealand. Thanks are due to James McLachlan (Club Secretary) for his kind permission to reproduce the listing.

PRICES OF NEW ZEALAND ISSUES: All are scarce - all NGPP.
NB Wallis & Wallis sold 401 VW Variant for £500 in 1993.

UK no.	NZ no.	Model name	Difference from UK version	NZ colour	Market Price Range
289	101	**Morris Minor 1000**	Not manufactured in New Zealand	-	NPP
219	102	**Austin-Healey Sprite**	Colour only	White body, Red seats	£200-300
281	103	**MG Midget**	No Policeman included	Dark Green or Red, White seats	£200-300
404	104	**Morris Mini Van**	No 'Shell' logo, ladder or mechanism	Yellow	£100-150
267	105	**MG 1100**	Single colour only	Green	£100-150
262	106	**Morris 1100**	Same as UK issue	Blue	£100-150
287/406	107	**Hillman Minx**	No roof rack or dinghy	Green	£100-150
280	108	**Vauxhall Cresta**	Single colour only	Blue	£100-150
276	109	**Jaguar 'S' type**	Same as UK issue	Blue	£200-300
286	110	**Austin 1800**	No lady driver or schoolboy	Light Brown	£100-150
270	111	**Ford Zephyr 6**	Same as UK issue	White	£100-150
308	112	**Land Rover**	No trailer included	Olive Green body, Pale Green tilt	£100-150
407	114	**Mercedes-Benz 230 SL**	Not manufactured in New Zealand	-	NPP
401	115	**Volkswagen Variant**	No roof rack or skis	Dark Blue, Red int., White hatchback	£200-300
279	116	**MG PB Midget**	Same as UK issue	Blue, Black	£150-200
265	117	**'TONIBELL' Ice Cream Van**	Same as UK issue	Turquoise	£200-300
402	118	**Crash Service Land Rover**	Same as UK issue	Orange, Blue	£100-150
316	119	**Fire Dept Land Rover**	No Firemen	Red	£100-150
415	120	**RAF Land Rover**	Not manufactured in New Zealand	-	NPP

Acknowledgements

The Editor would like to thank Ian Mair of ???????, David Kerr of Cambridge and Mr A. Paxton of Milton Keynes for their assistance with the Spot-On listings.

Spot-On Auction Results

For explanation of grading systems used by various auctioneers, see the Dinky Toys Auction Results section.

Wallis and Wallis

1998-99 RESULTS

A scarce **'A' Presentation Set**: vehicles VGC...........................£350
A rare **Presentation Set** of 4 Sports Cars. In early black, red presentation box, vehicles VGC to Mint. £530
A rare **Bedford 10 tonner with 2000 Gallons Tanker** No 158 A/Z in yellow, white and light. Boxed, minor wear, vehicle VGC to Mint. £400
A **Mulliner Coach,** No 156 in light metallic blue and silver. Boxed, vehicle VGC £220
Scarce **LT Routemaster bus,** No 145 in red livery, Ovaltine adverts, bus No 284. Boxed, vehicle VGC £190

Vectis Model Auctions

25TH NOVEMBER 1998

No.118 BMW Isetts Bubble Car - Dark Blue - A to A+ in B+ to A box with CC...£140
No. 183 Humber Super Snipe Estate - Turquoise/figures/roof rack and luggage/wing mirrors - A to A+ in B box with CC.....................£80
No. 195 VW Beetle Rally Car - White/Red Int/driver/roof light - A in good C box with leaflet and CC...............................£150
No. 210/2 Morris Mini Van "GPO" - A to A+ in A box with leaflet and CC £165
No. 229 Lambretta Scooter - Blue/White - B+ to A in good C box.........£180

WINDOW BOX ISSUES

No. 276 Jaguar S-Type - Met Blue/figures - A (a few minor paint chips obviously caused at the factory) - in A WB - inner card tray is A+ £110
No. 289 Morris Minor - Met Green/Red Int - A+ in B+ WB - inner card tray is A £160
No. 405 Vauxhall Cresta BEA Crew Car - superb A+ complete with figure in B+ WB - inner card tray is A+ £90

NEW ZEALAND ISSUES

N102 Austin Healey Sprite - White/Red Int/driver - in A to A+ WB £200
N104 Morris Mini Van - Yellow/Red Int - in A WB.......................£1,000
N105 MG 1100 - Grey-Green/Red Int - in A to A+ WB.......................£230
N108 Vauxhall Cresta - Blue/Red Int - some discolouration to paintwork where elastic band packaging has perished - in B+ WB £90
N109 Jaguar S-Type - Met Blue/Ivory Int/figures - in B+ WB £140
N112 Landrover - Olive Green/Fawn canopy/pressed tin seats/shaped spun wheels - in B+ to A WB £130
N115 VW Variant - Dark Blue/Red Int/White plastic tail gate, in A WB.£360
N116 MG PB Sports - Blue/Black chassis/Red seats and grille - in A to A+ WB £180

N117 Bedford "Tonibell" Ice Cream Van - in A to A+ WB..................£130
N118 Landrover Breakdown - Orange/Blue/pressed tin seats, good B.....£130
N119 Fire Dept Landrover - Red/Very Pale Green canopy/ pressed tin seats - in A to A+ WB £200

16TH DECEMBER 1998

No. 110/2B AEC Flatbed with Brick Load "London Brick Company" - Red/Black roof/Silver Grey chassis - B (missing plastic fuel tank) in good C box with leaflet and CC £130
No.158A/2 Bedford S-Type Articulated Tanker "Shell BP" - Sea Green cab/Black chassis/Red tank - cab is B to B+ - tank only B - adverts are A - in B box...£250
No.145 Routemaster Bus - Red/Cream Int/transfer print radiator - B to C (advrts are B+ in good B box with card packing..........................£180

NEW ZEALAND ISSUES

N107 Hillman Minx - Grey-Green/Red Int - A to A+ in A WB £80
N111 Ford Zephyr - Maroon/White Int/figure/dog - A to A+ in B WB £150
N119 Land Rover Fire Truck - Red/Fawn plastic canopy - A to A+ in A WB for N112 Land Rover Civilian version £105

10TH MARCH 1999, NEW ZEALAND ISSUES

N103 MG Midget - Red/Pale grey Int/driver - A to A+ in A to A+ WB ..£140
N111 Ford Zephyr - Maroon/Ivory Int/driver/dog - A to A+ in A+ WB - rare colour...£130
N1115 VW Variant - Dark Blue/White tail gate/Red Int - A to A+ in B+ WB (tear to perspex) £270

Lacy Scott and Knight

15TH MAY 1999

London Brick Company Ltd AEC lorry 'Phorpes Bricks' (110/2B) (BDNM) £150
Mulliner luxury coach (156) (BDNM)...................................£130
A Spot-On 801 At Home with Tommy Spot Gift Set in original box with Superville instructions (E-M, box E)..................................£220
806 Royal Occasion with Tommy Spot in original box with Superville instructions and Assembly instructions for Rolls-Royce Lighting Unit (E-M, box E)..£400
137 Massey-Harris Ferguson 65 Tractor, original box (E-M) £180
145 Routemaster Bus second type with transfer radiator grille, registration LBL100 (G-E, rear Barking Garage headboard transfer incomplete).........£130
'A' Presentation Set comprising pink Triumph TR3, pale grey BMW Isetta, turquoise Austin A40, pale grey and pale blue Bentley Saloon and apple green Aston Martin with Club slip, in original box (E, box G-E) £320

An illustration from the February 1959 Spot-On catalogue.

Collectable Modern Diecasts 1983 – 1999

Corgi Classics, Corgi 'Original Omnibus Company', Corgi Toys, E.F.E., Lledo 'Days-Gone' and 'Vanguards', Matchbox Collectibles, Matchbox Dinky 'The Collection', Oxford Die-Cast

Introduction

The diecast models in this section have mainly been produced for adult collectors. Consequently, they are very different from the traditional toy models aimed at the younger end of the market.

These modern issues are not toys which will ultimately become collectors items – they are high quality scale models that are produced as collectors items from birth.

The scarcity levels and prices of the older traditional toys are largely determined by factors such as how many have survived in good condition and their auction price track records. These factors are totally irrelevant in respect of modern diecasts, i.e., they will all be carefully stored or displayed and no auction price track records exist.

As a consequence, the scarcity levels and retail prices are simply determined by:

- the number of models making up a 'limited edition' production run
- the collectability of individual models
- manufacturers' suggested retail prices
- trade mail order prices
- the laws of supply and demand

As a result of these factors, the asking prices of popular short-run issues often escalate, and it may be two years before a reasonable Market Price Range can become established.

The Market Price Range information provided by the Catalogue has endeavoured to take into consideration all of the foregoing factors and reflect the market. The figures provided are in respect of RETAIL PRICES that a collector might reasonably expect to pay for a model as at September 1999. They do not represent an indication of the value of individual models and the information is solely given for guidance purposes only.

In conclusion, the Catalogue's position on collecting modern diecasts is that they should be collected for the enjoyment they provide. If, over a period of time, they should increase in value this is indeed a bonus.

New Catalogue Users Service - 'CollectorLink'
This service is aimed at bridging the gap between Catalogue editions and enables Catalogue users to keep in touch with market changes. Subscribers receive the quarterley 'CollectorLink' publication whic provides an interesting combination of updating information and articles. This information is particularly relevant in respect of market prices for both current and future short-run 'limited edition' issues. For full details, see the 'CollectorLink' Customer Service information page at the end of the Catalogue.

Corgi Classics and Corgi Toys

History
The models were introduced in 1987. Today the models are manufactured in China by Corgi Classics Ltd., which was formed in 1995 following a management buy-out from Mattel.

The model range
Corgi Classics have developed into a superb range of models by concentrating on 1/43rd and 1/50th scales for cars, coaches, buses and commercial vehicles; 1/76th scale for 'Original Omnibus Company' buses and coaches, and even 1/18 scale cars. Buses remain popular – so much so that the Corgi Collector Club now have a separate 'OOC' Club for bus devotees.

Basis of Market Price Range
The figures shown represent a guide to the retail price that a collector might reasonably expect to pay for a model at a Corgi Collector Centre. It must be stressed that the figures shown are RETAIL ASKING PRICES. They are NOT an indication of the value of models.

NB Subscribers to the Catalogue's CollectorLink Service receive regular updating price information on Corgi Classics models. See page 301 for details of how to subscribe.

The high retail prices of some models reflect low production runs, e.g., Premium Edition (PE) models where only 2,000 pieces have been manufactured.

The Editor would like to thank Susan Pownall of the Corgi Collector Club and Chris Brierley of the Corgi Heritage Centre for their valuable assistance in updating the listings.

Contents of Corgi Classics section

Contents of Corgi Toys section

Corgi Classics Commercials

Ref.	Intro	Model name, details	MPR

97084	91	'GRATTANS', mail order	**£12-15**
97085	91	'SLUMBERLAND BEDS'	**£15-20**
97086	92	'FREEBORNS'	**£15-20**
97087	92	'BARNARDO'S'	**£15-20**
97088	93	'WHITE & Co.', 'Portsmouth'	**£15-20**
97089	93	'JOHN MASON', Liverpool'	**£15-20**
97090	93	'RILEY'S BILLIARD	
		TABLES'	**£15-20**
97091	93	'G.H.LUCKING & SONS'	**£15-20**
---	95	'GOING FOR GOLD',	
		gold plated model	**£50-70**
97092	95	'CHIPPERFIELD'S'	**£30-35**
97093	94	'HAPPY BIRTHDAY'	**NGPP**
	94	Corgi Heritage Centre version	
		'1st Birthday' (250 issued)	**£30-35**
97195	92	'HOWELLS & SON'	**£15-20**

Bedford 'S' type Vehicles

19301	96	'LYON'S'	**£12-15**
19302	96	'WEETABIX'	**£12-15**
19303	96	'SPRATTS'	**£12-15**
19304	97	'WALL'S' box van	**£12-15**
19306	97	'EDDIE STOBART' box van	**£14-18**
19401	96	'KEN THOMAS Ltd'	**£12-15**
19601	96	'BASS', bottle truck	**£12-15**
19701	96	TETLEY'S, canvas back	**£12-15**
19801	97	'EDDIE STOBART' artic.	**£20-25**
19802	97	'J. W. RICHARDS' artic.	**£20-25**
19901	97	'BRS' covered artic.	**£12-15**
20001	97	'W. & J. RIDING' dropside	**£12-15**
20202	97	'MILK' tanker	**£12-15**
20401	97	'LAING' tipper, 1,000 issued	**£20-25**
31008	98	'WIMPEY' + Shovel	**GSP**

Bedford 'TK' and 'KM' Trucks

18801	98	'EDDIE STOBART' KM	**£30-35**
18901	98	'Soldier, Soldier' + figures	**£20-25**
22401	98	'BRITISH RAILWAYS' TK	**£30-35**
22502	98	'MACBRAYNES' TK artic.	**£25-30**
22503	99	'GUINNESS', artic. platform	**£45-55**
22601	98	'CADBURY' TK tanker	**£18-22**
22702	98	'EDDIE STOBART' TK box	**£20-25**
22704	99	'GUINNESS' TK box van	**£18-22**
22801	98	'SHELL-BP' TK tanker and	
		'SHELL' petrol pump	**£28-33**
23203	99	'EDDIE STOBART' TK	**£18-22**
22901	99	'TARMAC' TK	**£18-22**

Chipperfield's Circus

07202	97	Land Rover PA, clowns	**£18-22**
11201	97	ERF, Cage Lorry, animals	**£35-40**
14201	97	Foden S21, Hippo Tank	**£35-40**
17801	97	Scammell Cannon, Ringmaster	**£25-30**
31901	97	Mary Chipperfield's	
		Liberty Horses	**£18-22**
31902	97	Foden S21 Elephant Truck	
		and Trailer	**£35-40**
56901	96	Cameos Set of 10 vehicles in	
		'Chipperfields' livery	**£18-22**
96905	95	Bedford 'CA' Booking Office	**£30-35**
97022	95	AEC Regal Living Coach	**£35-40**
97092	95	Bedford 'OB' Pantechnicon	**£30-35**
97303	95	Bedford 'OB' Artic. Truck	**£80-100**
97885	95	Scammell, Pole Trailer	
		and Caravan	**£50-60**
97886	95	Scammell Crane Truck	**£35-40**
97887	95	Bedford 'O' Artic. Horsebox	**£35-40**
97888	95	Foden Pole Truck + Caravan	**£45-50**
97889	95	AEC Animal Truck + Trailer	**£35-45**
97896	95	AEC Pole Truck	**£30-35**
97915	95	Scammell and two Trailers	**£65-75**
97957	95	ERF Flatbed Lorry	**£45-50**
NB.		If traded as a collection (as one lot),	
		items 96905 - 97957 would be	
		expected to realise	**£500 - £600**

Diamond-T Vehicles

31007	97	'ANNIS' girder trailer + loco	**£45-55**
31009	98	'WYNN'S' trailer + boiler	**GSP**
55401	98	'PINDER' circus box trailer	**£50-60**
55501	98	'ELLIOT' low-loader	

		plus generator load	**£28-33**
55601	98	'USAF' wrecker	**£20-25**
55602	98	'De LORNE' fire wrecker	**£35-45**
55604	98	'BRS' wrecker	**£25-30**
55605	98	'BLACKPOOL' wrecker	**£18-22**
55607	99	'RENAULT' wrecker	**£25-30**
56301	98	'RICHFIELD' artic. with load	**£28-33**
56401	98	'SCHLITZ' beer delivery van	**£18-22**

ERF Trucks and Tankers

09601	99	'BRS', platform (PE)	**£50-60**
09701	96	'ERF Parts Dept.', flatbed	**£35-40**
09801	96	'JOHN SMITHS' flatbed	**£35-40**
09802	97	'CORGI CLASSICS', flatbed	**£20-25**
09901	96	'PAT COLLINS' circus	
		dodgem truck and trailer	**£30-35**
10101	97	'BRS' 8 wheel dropside	**£30-35**
10102	97	'GWYNNE BOWEN'	**£28-33**
10201	98	'BRS' grey 'V' tipper	**£25-30**
11001	97	'EDDIE STOBART'	**£35-40**
11101	97	'MOORHOUSE'S JAMS'	**£15-20**
11201	97	'CHIPPERFIELD'S', cage	**£35-40**
11301	97	'RUSSELL of BATHGATE'	**£35-25**
11401	97	'BLACK & WHITE' + trailer	**£22-28**
11501	98	'SHELL-BP' KV tanker and	
		'SHELL' petrol pump	**£28-33**
11601	98	'EDDIE STOBART' artic.	**£30-35**
11701	99	'BLOWERS' KV Tipper	**£30-35**
31011	98	'R. WALKER' KV low-loader	**£30-35**
59529	99	'GUINNESS', curtainside	**£14-16**
74901	99	'RUGBY CEMENT', tanker	**£40-45**
74902	99	'A. SMITH', powder tanker	**£40-45**
75101	99	'GULF' tanker	**£40-45**
75102	98	'SHELL' tanker	**£40-45**
75103	98	'BP' artic. tanker	**£40-45**
75104	98	'ESSO' artic. tanker	**£40-45**
75201	98	'EDDIE STOBART'	**£40-45**
75202	98	'BODDINGTONS' c/side	**£40-45**
75203	98	'RICHARD READ' c/side	**£40-45**
75204	98	'JACK RICHARDS' c/side	**£40-45**
75205	99	'POLLOCK' curtainside	**£40-45**
75206	97	'MASSEY WILCOX' c/side	**£40-45**
97319	96	'BASS' cyclindrical tanker	**£27-32**
97930	94	'BLUE CIRCLE', tanker	**£40-50**
97940	94	'EDDIE STOBART', flat	**£130-140**
97942	94	'FLOWERS', flatbed	**£28-32**
97957	95	'CHIPPERFIELD'S', flatbed	**£45-50**
97980	94	'ESSO', tanker	**£40-50**

Foden Trucks and Tankers

12101	98	'CADBURY'S FG tanker	**£25-30**
12301	97	'MOTOR PACKING', flatbed	**£28-32**
12302	99	'EASTWOODS' (PE)	**£55-65**
12401	96	'FREMLINS ALES', chains	**£25-30**
12501	96	'BLUE CIRCLE', flatbed	**£15-20**
12601	96	'SILCOCK'S', pole truck	**£25-30**
12801	97	'EDWARD BECK' artic.	**£28-32**
13501	97	'G. C. MUNTON' S21 artic.	**£28-32**
13601	97	'EDDIE STOBART' S21 van	**£35-40**
13602	97	'C.W.S.' box van	**£15-18**
13701	97	'ARROW' S21 tanker	**£25-30**
13901	97	'BASSETTS' S21 flatbed	**£25-30**
13902	98	'KNOWLES' S21 tank load	**£25-30**
13903	98	'BRITISH RAILWAYS' S21	**£28-33**
13904	99	'BLUE CIRCLE' S21	**£28-33**
14001	97	'BERESFORD', 6w dropside	**£25-30**
14101	97	'TUBY'S', S21 dodgem	
		truck and trailer	**£30-35**
14201	97	'CHIPPERFIELDS',hippo tank	**£35-40**
14401	98	'HOVERINGHAM' S21	**£28-32**
14501	98	'BLUE CIRCLE' S21	**£28-32**
31012	98	'MICKEY KIELY', FG Pole	
		Truck, Living Van, Boxing	
		Pavilion, figures, etc.	**£60-70**
31902	97	'CHIPPERFIELD'S'	
		Elephants Trailer	**£40-50**
97309	96	'BRS' flatbed with load, (Classic	
		Toys magazine promotional.	
		Limited Edition, 5,000)	**£45-55**
97317	96	'Scottish & Newcastle'	**£30-35**

97950	93	'GUINNESS',	
		with normal cab/tank gap	**£110-130**
		smaller cab/tank gap (500)	**£20-150**
97951	93	'MILK'	**£30-35**
97952	93	'HOVIS'	**£30-35**
97955	94	'GUINNESS', with chains	**£90-120**
97956	95	'PICKFORDS' flatbed	**£60-80**
97970	94	'REGENT', elliptical tanker	**£45-55**
97971	94	'ROBSONS', flatbed	**£40-45**

Ford Model 'T' Vans

C865	86	'LYONS TEA', white roof	**£10-15**
C865/1	87	'NEEDLERS'	**£10-15**
C865/2	86	'LYONS TEA', black roof	**£35-40**
C865/2	87	'DRUMMER DYES'	**£10-15**
C865/3	87	'KALAMAZOO'	**£10-15**
C865/4	87	'PEPSI COLA'	**£10-15**
C865/5	87	'TWININGS'	**£15-18**
D865/6	88	'AMBULANCE', see Set C88	**GSP**
D865/7	89	'KAYS'	**£10-15**
D865/8	89	'ROYAL LAUNDRY', Set C90	**GSP**
?	89	'SUNLIGHT', Set C90	**GSP**
C865/11	89	'STEIFF'	**£10-15**
D865/12	89	'A1 SAUCE', see Set D71/1	**GSP**
D865/13	89	'APS MEDICINES', Set D71/1	**GSP**
Q865/14	90	'NAAFI'	**£40-50**
Q865/15	90	'JOHN MENZIES'	**£10-15**
Q865/17	90	'WHITBREAD', see Set D94/1	**GSP**
C873	86	'ZEBRA GRATE POLISH'	**£10-15**
C874	87	'CORGI CLUB', 2nd anniv.	**£20-25**
C875	86	'SCHOKOLADE GOLD'	**£10-15**
C876	86	'DICKINS & JONES'	**£12-15**
C877	86	'ROYAL MAIL'	**£15-20**
C965	86	'FORD'S 75th', yellow letters	**£8-10**
C966	86	white lettering	**£8-10**
?	87	'SWAN VESTAS', see Set C69	**GSP**
?	87	'THE TIMES', see Set C49	**GSP**
?	87	'KAY & Co', see Set C68	**GSP**
?	87	T. C. BENNETT', see Set C50	**GSP**
?	87	'H. & C. MAILES', see Set C50	**GSP**
?	87	T. J. POUPART', see Set C50	**GSP**
08101	98	'BOURNVILLE'	**£18-22**
97464	92	'CADBURYS' (Woolworths)	**NGPP**
97469	95	'VICTROLA', USA	**£8-10**
97751/a	92	'BASS BREWERY', (Kay's)	**£8-12**
97753/a	92	'TERRY'S of YORK'	**£8-12**

Ford Model 'T' Tankers

C864	86	'PRATTS MOTOR SPIRIT'	**£8-10**
C864/1	87	'STALEY SALES CORP.'	**£10-12**
C864/2	87	'RIMMER BROS Ltd'	**£10-12**
C864/3	87	'SAN FRANCISCO'	**£8-10**
C864/4	87	'NATIONAL BENZOLE'	**£10-15**
C872	86	'DOMINION'	**£9-12**
C880	86	'BP MOTOR SPIRIT'	**£9-12**
C864/6	88	'OLYMPIC GASOLINE'	**£8-10**
D864/7	89	'TEXACO', see Set D71/1	**GSP**
D864/8	89	'SOMERLITE', see Set D71/1	**GSP**

Ford Popular (Fordson 8) Vans

D980/1	89	'S.A. PEACOCK'	**£12-15**
D980/2	89	'FULLERS'	**£12-15**
D980/3	89	'LUTON MOTOR Co'	**£12-15**
D980/4	89	'CORGI CLUB 89'	**£15-20**
D980/5	89	'SIGNSMITH', Set D23/1	**GSP**
D980/6	89	'FRASER COOK', Set D23/1	**GSP**
D980/7	89	'LEWIS EAST', Set D23/1	**GSP**
D980/8	89	'C. PEARSON'	**£12-15**
D980/9	89	'COLMANS', Kay's Set D72/1	**GSP**
D980/10	89	'BOWYERS', Kay's Set D72/1	**GSP**
D980/11	89	'PICKFORDS', Kay's Set D74/1	**GSP**
D980/12	89	'D. SHELDON'	**£12-15**
D980/13	90	'LIMA FURNITURE Ltd'	**£12-15**
D980/14	90	'CAMBRIAN FACTORY'	**£12-15**
D980/15	90	'ABBEYCOLOR'	**£12-15**
D980/16	90	'ROYAL MAIL' (99808)	**£12-15**
D980/17	90	'NCB', GUS Set D54/1	**GSP**
05901	97	'ROYAL MAIL'	**£12-15**
96860	91	'EASTBOURNE MOTORS'	**£12-15**
96862	91	'ROYAL MAIL'	**£12-15**
96863	93	'SUNLIGHT SOAP'	**£12-15**

96865 92 'BEEZER', 'Colonel Blink' **£12-15**
96866 94 'GAS' **£12-15**
98109 91 'ROYAL MAIL' **£12-15**
98755 91 'HOTSPUR', 'Willie Wallop' .. **£12-15**
99808 93 'ROYAL MAIL', (D980/16) **£12-15**

French 'Collection Heritage'

A series of models introduced in 1997 specifically for the French market. A very limited number were to be available in the UK but until quantities and demand are better known there can be no guide price at present (NGPP).

BERLIET TRUCKS and TANKERS
70001 97 'CHAMBOURCY' tanker **£35-40**
70101 97 'PINDER' circus elephants **£35-40**
70201 97 'PINDER' human cannon **£35-40**
70301 97 'PINDER' artic. horse-box **£35-45**
70401 97 'PINDER' heavy recovery **£35-40**
70402 99 'BOURGEY' heavy recovery .. **£25-30**
73001 97 'L'ALSACIENNE BISCUITS' **£35-40**
73002 97 'BANANIA' box van **£35-40**
73005 99 'ROQUEFORT' lorry **£30-35**
73101 97 'VINI-PRIX' beer lorry **£35-40**
73201 97 'SHELL' rigid tanker **£35-40**
73301 97 'PINDER' circus 'Luton' van .. **£35-40**
73401 97 'PINDER' box van and trailer.. **£50-60**
73501 98 GLR8 'COLMAR' fire ladder.. **£45-50**
73801 98 GLR8 military covered wagon. **£35-40**

BERNARD TRUCKS and VANS
72001 97 'DANONE' van **£35-40**
72002 97 'CALBERSON-FLAGEUL' **£35-40**
72003 97 'LUSTUCRU' egg van **£35-40**
72004 97 'PINDER' large box van **£35-40**
72008 99 'AIGUEBELLE' lorry **£35-40**

CITROEN type 55 TRUCKS
74001 98 Military, canvas back **£35-40**
74101 98 'La VACHE SERIEUSE' **£35-40**
74103 99 'CHAMBOURCY' **£35-40**
74201 98 'BOURGEY' low-loader **£30-35**
74401 98 'MULHOUSE' fire ladder **£45-50**
74402 99 Electro fire ventilator **£35-40**
74601 98 'DYNAVIA' Fruehauf tanker ... **£35-40**

DAIMLER DOUBLE-DECK BUS
35202 97 'PINDER' living quarters **£35-40**

DIAMOND-T
55401 98 'PINDER' circus box trailer **£60-65**
55602 98 'De LORNE' fire wrecker **£60-65**
55607 99 'RENAULT' wrecker **£60-65**

LAND ROVER PICK UP
07201 97 'PINDER' public address **£15-20**

RENAULT FAINEANT TRUCKS
71001 97 'MICHELIN' covered lorry **£20-25**
71004 99 'REGIE RENAULT' promo **£20-25**
71101 97 'DUMESNIL' lemonade lorry.. **£20-25**
71105 99 'VICHY ETAT' Renault promo NGPP
71201 97 'TOTAL' fuel tanker **£20-25**
71202 97 'PINDER' circus fuel tanker **£20-25**
71203 98 'VAR' fire service water tanker **£20-25**
71206 99 'SHELL' Renault promo ..... NGPP
71301 97 'PERRIER' box van **£20-25**
71401 97 'VALENTINE' box van **£20-25**
71402 97 'PINDER' mobile kitchen **£20-25**
71405 98 'SIC' soft drinks box van **£20-25**
71407 99 'RENAULT Services' promo .... NGPP

SAVIEM TRUCKS
71106 99 'PERRIER' drinks lorry **£20-25**
71408 99 'CIRAGE ABEILLE' lorry **£20-25**
71601 99 'RENAULT' farm lorry **£35-40**

SCAMMELL HIGHWAYMAN TRUCKS
16801 97 'PINDER' generator truck and animal trailers **£60-65**

Guy Invincible

29101 99 'BLUE CIRCLE', platform **£28-32**
29102 99 'WYNNS', platform **£28-32**
29103 99 'EDDIE STOBART', platform. **£28-32**
29301 99 'A. R. DUCKETT', tipper **£28-32**
29401 99 'DAWSONS FARGO', d/side .. **£28-32**

Guy Warrior

29001 99 'DEE VALLEY', 6-wheels **£28-32**
29201 99 'BRS', tractor / semi-trailer **£28-32**

Land-Rover

(see also French 'Collection Heritage')
07101 96 Corgi Club Land-Rover **£12-15**
07102 97 'MERSEY TUNNEL' **£10-12**
07103 97 Gold-plated Land-Rover **£18-22**
07104 98 'Daktari' + lion and chimp **£18-22**
07202 97 'CHIPPERFIELDS' PA **£18-22**
07301 97 'AFS' Line-layer **£12-15**
07302 98 British Army, olive green **£10-12**
07401 97 'ROYAL MAIL', closed **£10-12**
07402 97 'EDDIE STOBART', closed **£10-12**
07403 98 'A.A. ROAD SERVICE' **£10-12**
07407 98 'CITY of BATH' **£10-12**
07408 98 'BOAC' **£10-12**
07414 99 'RAC RADIO PATROL' **£10-12**
07410 99 'HAMPSHIRE' fire tender **£10-12**
07411 99 'CORNWALL' cliff rescue **£10-12**
07412 99 'ALPES MARITIMES' fire **£10-12**

Leyland Trucks and Tankers

(see also 'Modern Trucks' section)
20902 99 'GUINNESS', Ergo platform ... **£40-45**
22101 96 'BRS', Ergomatic / flatbed **£25-30**
23501 98 'CADBURY'S' tipper **£28-32**
24201 96 'McKELVIE & Co', tanker **£20-25**
24202 97 'POWER' tanker **£20-25**
24203 98 'SHELL-BP' tanker and 'BP Diesel' pump **£28-32**
24301 96 'Wm. YOUNGER', tanker **£28-32**
24302 96 'DOUBLE DIAMOND' tanker **£28-32**
24401 96 'CODONA'S', flatbed **£28-32**
24402 98 'EDDIE STOBART' flatbed **£28-32**
24901 99 'GUINNESS' tanks trailer **£45-50**
24501 96 'J & A SMITH', flatbed **£20-25**
24601 97 'BRS', Octopus + trailer **£30-35**
24701 96 'MICHELIN', articulated lorry **£25-30**
24801 96 'SILCOCK'S', dodgems truck + caravan **£35-40**
25101 96 'BRS', flatbed / container **£15-20**
25102 97 'EDDIE STOBART' Beaver **£18-22**
25201 97 'SMITH'S of ECCLES', artic. .. **£28-32**
25301 97 'HOLT LANE', Super Comet .. **£25-30**

Mack Trucks

(see also Fire Service Vehicles)
C906/1 87 'MACK PARTS' **£10-12**
C906/2 87 'SUNSHINE BISCUITS' **£10-12**
C906/3 87 'WHITE ROCK' **£10-12**
C906/4 87 'BUFFALO FIRE DEPT' **£10-12**
C906/5 87 'PEPSI COLA' **£10-12**
C906/6 88 'STANLEY TOOLS' **£10-12**
C906/7 88 'PEERLESS LIGHT' **£10-12**
C906/8 88 'BOVRIL' **£10-12**
C906/9 88 'CARNATION' **£10-12**
C906/10 88 'GULDENS MUSTARD' **£10-12**
50601 96 AC, 'M. K. T.' **£15-20**
50701 99 LJ, 'MERCHANTS', artic **£25-30**
50702 99 LJ, 'SCHAEFER', artic. **£25-30**
50901 99 LJ, 'MOBILGAS', tanker **£25-30**
51001 99 LJ, 'RICHFIELD', tanker **£25-30**
52301 96 B, 'GREAT NORTHERN' **£25-30**
52302 97 B, 'LIONEL CITY' **£25-30**
52303 97 B, 'SEMI-NICKEL PLATE ROAD' **£25-30**
52504 97 B, 'MILWAUKEE ROAD' **£25-30**
52501 96 B, 'NEW YORK CENTRAL' .. **£25-30**
52503 96 B, 'LIONEL CITY' **£25-30**
52801 96 B, 'RAILWAY EXPRESS' **£25-30**
52802 97 B, 'BURLINGTON ROUTE' .. **£25-30**
53202 98 B,'SINCLAIR' tanker **£25-30**
53601 98 B, 'A.N.D.' wrecker **£20-25**
98453 95 B, 'BREYER' **£15-20**
98454 95 B, 'WILTON FARM' **£15-20**
98481 95 'GOODYEAR', USA **£8-10**

Mini-Vans

06001 97 'P. O. TELEPHONES' **£10-12**
06002 98 'A.A. PATROL SERVICE' **£10-12**
06003 98 'BKS AIR TRANSPORT' **£10-12**
06004 99 'RAC ROAD SERVICE' **£10-12**
08002 97 'EXPRESS POST' (set of 2).... **£10-12**
96950 94 'ROYAL MAIL' **£10-12**
96951 94 'POLICE' **£10-12**
96952 94 'RAC Radio Rescue' **£10-12**
96953 94 'AA Road Service' **£10-12**
96955 94 'CORGI CLASSICS' Club **£10-12**
96956 94 'SURREY POLICE' **£10-12**
97337 95 'FAWLEY REFINERY' **£10-12**
97770 96 'HAMLEY'S' **£10-12**
97771 96 'CAVENDISH WOODHOUSE' **£10-12**
97772 95 'BURBERRY'S **£10-12**

'Modern Trucks'

LEYLAND-DAF TRUCKS
73501 98 'Q8' tanker **£40-45**
75302 99 'JET' fuel tanker **£40-45**
75401 98 'JAMES IRLAM' curtainside .. **£40-45**
75402 98 'TATE & LYLE' curtainside **£40-45**
75404 98 'HEINEKEN' curtainside **£40-45**
75405 99 'KNIGHTS of OLD' c/side **£40-45**
75406 99 'KEN THOMAS', curtainside .. **£40-45**
75407 99 'GUINNESS', curtainside **£40-45**
75501 98 'PARCELFORCE' box trailer .. **£40-45**
75502 98 'ROYAL MAIL' box trailer **£40-45**
75901 99 'KNOWLES', powder tanker ... **£40-45**
75902 99 'BLUE CIRCLE', tanker **£40-45**

M.A.N. TRUCKS
75701 99 'TNT', box trailer **£40-45**
75802 99 'CONTINENTAL', c/side **£40-45**
75804 99 'EDDIE STOBART', curtain ... **£40-45**
75803 99 'GALLACHERS', curtainside . **£40-45**
75805 99 'SAFEGARD', curtainside **£40-45**
76201 99 'ARAL', tanker **£40-45**

RENAULT ARTICULATED TRUCKS
75601 99 'EDDIE STOBART' c/side **£40-45**
75602 99 'MACFARLANE' c/side **£40-45**
75605 99 'NIGEL RICE' curtainside **£40-45**
75606 99 'JAMES IRLAM' curtainside .. **£40-45**

Miscellaneous

30901 99 'PREISTMAN' Luffing Shovel 1,000 only issued **£20-25**

Morris 'J' Vans

D983/1 90 'P. O. TELEPHONES' **£10-12**
D983/2 90 'ROYAL MAIL' **£10-12**
D983/3 91 'CORGI CLUB 91' **£10-12**
D983/4 90 'Metropolitan Police' ..... see 96883
D983/5 91 'WALLS Ice Cream' (98101)... **£10-12**
D983/6 90 'ELECTRICITY', Set D54/1 ..... GSP
D983/7 90 'BEANO', see Set D47/1 ..... GSP
D983/8 90 'BRITISH RAILWAYS', D46/1 ... GSP
06201 96 'CYDRAX' **£10-12**
06202 96 'OXO' **£10-12**
06203 97 'ROYAL MAIL' **£10-12**
06204 99 'RAC SIGN SERVICE' **£10-12**
96880 91 'PICKFORDS' (99802) **£15-20**
96882 91 'ROYAL MAIL' **£10-12**
96883 90 'Metropolitan Police' **£10-12**
96886 96 'FAMILY ASSURANCE' **£10-12**
96888 96 'SOUTHDOWN' **£10-12**
96887 92 'The TOPPER' **£10-12**
96891 93 'MORRIS SERVICE' **£10-12**
96892 93 'BOVRIL' **£15-20**
96894 94 'P. O. TELEPHONES' **£10-12**
96895 95 'BIRMINGHAM CITY', 'General Manager' **£10-12**
'Genetal Manager' **£20-25**
96896 94 'FAMILY ASSURANCE **£10-12**
98101 91 'WALLS Ice Cream' (D983/5). **£10-12**
98758 92 'WIZARD' **£10-12**
99140 93 'GPO Telephones' **£10-12**
99802 91 'PICKFORDS' (96880) **£15-20**
POV21 95 'ROYAL MAIL' **£15-20**

Morris Minor 1000 Pick-ups

06301	98	'DAN-AIR LONDON'	**£10-12**
96850	94	'WIMPEY'	**£10-12**
96851	95	'LONDON BRICK Co Ltd'	**£10-12**
96854	95	'MORRIS MOTORS' FB	**£10-12**
97344	95	'BLUE CIRCLE CEMENT'	**£15-20**
97346	95	'TARMAC'	**£15-20**

Morris Minor 1000 Vans

C957/1	87	'ROYAL MAIL',	
		with plastic base	**£18-20**
	87	with metal base	**£12-15**
C957/2	87	'GAS'	**£12-15**
C957/3	87	'CORGI Club 3rd Anniversary',	
		1st type wheels	**£15-20**
		2nd type wheels	**£15-20**
C957/4	88	'CASTROL'	**£15-20**
C957/5	89	'MICHELIN'	**£15-20**
C957/6	88	'FOYLES for BOOKS'	**£15-20**
C957/7	88	'MACFISHERIES'	**£15-20**
C957/8	89	'GRATTAN'S' Set C91	GSP
C957/9	89	'TELEGRAPH & ARGUS', C91	GSP
C957/10	89	'MITCHELL'S' Set C91	GSP
C957/11	89	'APPLEYARDS'	**£10-12**
D957/12	89	'D. MORGAN'	**£10-12**
D957/13	89	'KIMBERLEY CLARK'	**£10-12**
D957/15	89	'POLICE', see Set D13/1	GSP
D957/16	89	'FRY'S COCOA', Set D72/1	GSP
D957/17	89	'RINGTON'S TEA', Set D72/1	GSP
D957/18	89	'ROYAL MAIL', see Set D7/1	GSP
D957/19	89	'PICKFORDS', see Set D74/1	GSP
D957/20	89	'GUERNSEY POST'	**£10-15**
D957/21	89	'7 UP'	**£10-12**
D957/22	90	'BISHOPS'	as 96845
D957/23	90	'A. DUNN & SON'	as 96844
D957/24	90	'B.A.T.R.', (with cert)	**£70-80**
D957/25	90	'ROYAL AIR FORCE', D35/1	GSP
D957/26	90	'NAMAC 25' (Dutch),	
		'England' on base	**£30-35**
		'China' on base	**£15-20**
D957/27	90	'GPO TELEPHONES'	**£10-15**
C958/1	87	'POST OFFICE TELEPHONES',	
		with plastic base	**£20-25**
C958	87	same but with metal base	**£15-20**
D958/2	89	'GPO TELEPHONES', D15/1	GSP
C959	87	'SMITHS CRISPS',	
		black interior	**£15-20**
	87	brown interior	**£15-20**
06501	96	'SHELL / BP'	**£15-20**
06502	96	'NESTLES'	**£15-20**
06503	97	'ROYAL MAIL'	**£9-12**
06504	97	'TV LICENCE'	**£9-12**
06505	98	'BRITISH CALEDONIAN'	**£9-12**
06506	98	'COURTLINE'	**£9-12**
06507	99	'BRS PARCELS' (PE)	**£45-50**
06508	99	'RAC ROAD SERVICE'	**£9-12**
06601	96	'CARTERS STEAM FAIR'	**£15-20**
31006	97	'WYNN'S Thames Trader	
		and Morris 1000 Van	**£20-25**
31704	97	'EDDIE STOBART'	see Set 31704
96744	95	'LEICESTERSHIRE POLICE'	GSP
96837	91	'MAIDSTONE & DISTRICT'	**£10-12**
96839	95	'ROYAL MAIL', Xmas	**£10-12**
96840	91	'BRISTOL WATER'	**£10-12**
96842	91	'P.O. TELEPHONES'	**£10-12**
96844	91	'A.DUNN & SON'	**£10-12**
96845	91	'BISHOPS REMOVALS'	**£10-12**
96846	92	'TIGER', 'Roy of the Rovers'	**£10-12**
96847	93	'COLMANS'	**£10-12**
96848	93	'BIRDS CUSTARD'	**£10-12**
96849	94	'A.A. SERVICE'	**£10-12**
96852	94	'CORGI CLASSICS'	
		(3rd Gaydon Show)	**£15-20**
96855	55	'WILTSHIRE POLICE'	**£10-15**
97346	95	'TARMAC'	**£10-15**
97541	96	'P. O. ENGINEERING'	**£10-12**
98104	93	'ROYAL MAIL'	**£10-12**
98756	91	'The ROVER'	**£10-12**
POV22		'ROYAL MAIL' 'Engineers'	**£10-12**
POV23		'ROYAL MAIL' 'Epsom'	**£10-12**
POV24		'GPO' 'Bristol'	**£10-12**

Reliant Regal Vans

05201	99	'TROTTERS' ('dirty' version)	**£8-12**

Renault Trucks and Vans

(see also French 'Collection Heritage')
(see also 'Modern Trucks' section)

C823/1	85	'JULES COLARD' truck	**£7-9**
C824	?	'MARCEL GARDET' van	**£8-10**
C824/1	88	'HERLOIN' truck	**£8-10**
C824/3	88	'THE LIPTON' van	**£10-12**
D889/1	89	'STELLA ARTOIS' lorry	**£8-10**
C902	85	'ROYAL MAIL' van	**£25-45**
C917	86	'COURVOISIER' van	**£7-9**
C922	86	'GALERIES LAFAYETTE'	**£8-10**
C925	86	'GERVAIS DANONE' truck	**£10-12**
08705	99	'Printemps' Renault promo	NGPP
08706	99	'Au Bon Marché' Ren. promo	NGPP
08707	99	'BHV' Renault promo	NGPP
08708	99	'Samaritaime' Renault promo	NGPP
97000	91	'PERRIER WATER' van	**£7-9**

Scammell Trucks

(see also French 'Collection Heritage')

15901	66	'ANDERTON & ROWLANDS'	
		dodgem truck and trailers	**£30-35**
16001	97	'JAMESON'S', + trailer	**£28-32**
16101	96	'CROW'S', heavy recovery	**£20-25**
16201	97	'PENTUS BROWN', tanker	**£28-32**
16301	96	'GUINNESS', artic. tanker	**£55-65**
16302	96	'ESSO', articulated tanker	**£25-28**
16303	96	'EVER-READY', artic. tanker	**£25-28**
16304	97	'CROW CARRYING', tanker	**£28-32**
16306	98	'SHELL-BP' Highwayman	
		tanker and 'BP' petrol pump	**£28-32**
16401	96	'S.C. COOK Ltd', + trailer	**£25-30**
16501	96	'CARTERS' circus truck plus	
		pole trailer and caravan	**£30-35**
16502	96	'PAT COLLINS' + trailer and	
		caravan	**£30-35**
16601	97	'PICKFORDS' Scammell	
		Highwayman and Land-Rover	**£65-75**
16701	97	'WREKIN' artic. low-loader	**£25-30**
16901	97	'HALLETT, SILBERMANN'	
		Highwayman and low-loader	**£25-30**
17501	97	'S. C. COOK' Constructor	**£45-50**
17601	97	'HILL of BOTLEY'	
		Constructor and low loader	**£45-50**
17602	98	'SUNTER BROS' Constructor	
		and low-loader	**£45-50**
17701	97	'PICKFORDS' Constructors	
		and low-loader	NGPP
17801	97	'CHIPPERFIELD'S' Cannon	**£25-30**
17901	99	'BRS' wrecker (PE)	**£150-170**
17902	99	'SUNTER' Contractor	**£60-70**
17903	99	'WYNNS' Contractor	**£40-50**
18001	99	'ECONOFREIGHT', Contractor	
		and steam turbine	**£50-60**
18002	99	'PICKFORDS', two Contractors	
		and casting load	**£90-110**
31004	97	'WYNN'S' articulated low-loader	
		plus Bedford 'S' tractor unit	**£40-45**
31009	98	'WYNN'S' trailer + boiler	GSP
31010	98	'SHORT BROS' Highwayman	
		low-loader, Priestman Shovel	**£45-50**
31013	99	'A.L.E.' 2 Contractors, Nicholas	
		Bogies + pressure vessel	GSP
97637	96	'POINTER', tanker	**£25-30**
97638	96	'PICKFORDS', crane	**£45-55**
97840	95	'SHELL-MEX / BP', tanker	**£28-32**
97897	96	'BILLY SMARTS',	
		pole truck/trailer	**£50-55**
97920	94	'EDWARDS', + 2 trailers	**£50-60**

Scammell Scarab Trucks

15002	97	'ROYAL MAIL'	**£14-18**
15004	98	'BOURNVILLE'	**£18-22**
15005	99	'BRITISH RAILWAYS'	**£14-18**
15101	96	'EXPRESS DAIRY'	**£14-18**
15201	96	'M & B', with barrels	**£14-18**
15202	96	'BULMERS CIDER', barrels	**£14-18**
97318	95	'WEBSTERS', with barrels	**£14-18**
97335	96	'ESKIMO FROZEN FOODS'	**£15-20**
97910	93	'RAIL FREIGHT', yellow	**£35-40**
97911	93	'BRITISH RAILWAYS'	**£90-100**
97912	94	'ROYAL MAIL' limited ed.	**£15-20**
97913	94	'RAIL FREIGHT', grey	**£35-40**
97914	94	'BRS'	**£25-30**
97916	94	'CORGI CLUB' 10th Anniv.	**£15-20**
97917	95	'WATNEYS'	**£20-25**
POV29		'ROYAL MAIL' (G. Ward)	**£20-25**

Scania Trucks

59506	98	'EDDIE STOBART' c/side	**£10-12**
59531	99	'GUINNESS' + 4-w trailer	**£14-16**

Thames Trader Trucks

30101	99	'WIMPEY'	**£25-30**
30201	96	'R.A.KEMBERY & Sons'	**£12-15**
30202	97	'EDDIE STOBART' dropside	**£15-20**
30301	97	'SLUMBERLAND'	**£12-15**
30302	97	'EVER-READY'	**£12-15**
30303	96	'HEINZ'	**£12-15**
30304	97	'ROBSON'S of CARLISLE'	**£12-15**
30306	97	'LUCOZADE' box van	**£12-15**
30308	97	'FOX'S GLACIER MINTS'	**£12-15**
30309	99	'PICKFORDS'	**£12-15**
30401	97	'GULF OIL' tanker	**£12-15**
30501	98	'PICKFORDS' artic.	**£28-32**
31006	97	'WYNN'S + Morris 1000 Van	**£20-25**
31704	97	'EDDIE STOBART'	see Set 31704

Thorneycroft Box Vans

C821	85	'WAKEFIELD CASTROL'	**£12-15**
C821/1	88	'HEIDELBERGER'	**£12-15**
C828	85	'GAMLEYS'	**£12-15**
C830	85	'W & R JACOB'	**£30-40**
C831	85	'HUNTLEY & PALMERS'	**£12-15**
C832	85	'CORGI CLUB 1st Anniversary',	
		'Fforestfach Ind.Est.'	**£30-35**
		'Kingsway Ind.Est.'	**£30-35**
C833	85	'MACFARLANE LANG'	**£9-12**
C834	85	'LYONS SWISS ROLLS'	**£50-60**
C839	85	'NURDIN & PEACOCK'	
		with A4 certificate	**£35-40**
C840	85	'ALLENBURYS'	**£15-20**
C841	85	'PEEK FREANS'	
		with cab scuttle	**£12-15**
		no cab scuttle	**£50-60**
C842	85	'CARTER PATERSON'	**£12-15**
C843	85	'EDDERSHAWS'	**£12-15**
C845	85	'DUCKHAMS OIL',	
		spoked or disc wheels	**£12-15**
C846	85	'IND COOPE'	**£12-15**
C847	85	'KEILLERS'	**£12-15**
C848	85	'NEWS OF THE WORLD'	**£12-15**
C853	85	'M. A. RAPPORT'	**£12-15**
C854	85	'Lincolnshire Ambulance'	**£12-15**
C855	85	'Lincolnshire Fire'	**£12-15**
C856	85	'Lincolnshire Police'	**£12-15**
C859	86	'THORLEYS'	**£12-15**
C859/1	87	'SCOTTS EMPIRE BREAD'	**£12-15**
C859/2	87	'CHIVERS JAMS'	**£12-15**
C859/3	87	'ARNOTTS BISCUITS'	**£45-55**
C859/4	87	'GOODYEAR',	
		(USA), Tan scuttle	NGPP
		(UK), Grey scuttle	**£10-12**
C859/5	87	'GRATTANS 75th', no scuttle	**£25-30**
C859/6	87	'KAYS', see Set C68	GSP
C859/7	89	'LEDA SALT'	**£9-11**
C859/8	88	'VOLVOLUTUM'	**£9-11**
C859/9	88	'ASDA'	**£11-14**
C859/10	88	'BATCHELORS PEAS'	**£12-15**
C859/11	88	'LEA & PERRINS'	**£12-15**
D859/12	90	'SHELL OIL', see Set D9/1	GSP
C859/13	89	'McDOUGALLS'	**£20-25**
C859/16	90	'ASDA 25th Birthday'	**£11-14**
C907	86	'HP SAUCE'	**£14-18**
C910	86	'SMALL & PARKES'	**£14-18**
C911	86	'PERSIL'	**£12-15**
C913	86	'DEWARS WHISKY'	**£10-14**
C914	86	'LIPTONS TEA'	**£10-14**
C915	86	'OXO'	**£12-15**
C924	86	'SAFEWAY'	**£12-15**
C926	86	'DOUBLE DIAMOND'	**£18-22**

As seen on BBC 2 "Top Gear"

As seen on BBC 2 "Top Gear"

THE CORGI HERITAGE CENTRE
53 YORK STREET, HEYWOOD, NR. ROCHDALE, LANCS OL10 4NR
TEL: 01706 365812 FAX: 01706 627811
A CORGI CLASSICS VENTURE IN CO-OPERATION WITH CHRIS BRIERLEY MODELS

VISIT THE NEW CORGI HERITAGE CENTRE
The complete range of Corgi Classics
Selected obsolete Corgi Models
Worldwide Mail Order Service
Standing order facilities
Discounts for Corgi Collector Club members

Regular Corgi Collector Club presence,
facilities for joining the Club on the spot
& Club merchandise available
Free Admission

(Closed Tuesday and Sunday at present)

The Corgi Heritage Centre, 53 York Street,
Heywood, Nr Rochdale, Lancs. OL10 4NR.
Tel: 01706 365 812 Fax: 01706 627 811
email: corgi@zen.co.uk
http://www.zen.co.uk/home/page/corgi/

Disabled access. Free car park at rear.
Easy to get to by road and rail.

TRAFFORD MODEL CENTRE
Tel: 0161 202 9333 Fax: 0161 202 9444

The North West's Largest Corgi Collector Centre

Specialists in
Die-cast models, Plastic Kits, Model Railways, Scalextric,
Radio control Models, Britains Soldiers.

The Trafford Centre - A World Class City of Shopping,
Restaurants & Entertainment

**TRAFFORD MODEL CENTRE 56 & 57 FESTIVAL VILLAGE
THE TRAFFORD CENTRE MANCHESTER M17 8FS**

**Open 7 days per week, Opening hours: Mon - Fri 10am - 9pm,
Sat 9am - 7pm, Sun 12-noon - 6pm**

**AMPLE FREE PARKING 10,000 SPACES
WORLDWIDE MAIL ORDER A SPECIALITY**

 # CORGI *Classics*

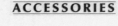

ACCESSORIES

26101 Albion Reiver 6 Wheel
Platform Lorry -
D.W. Ward of Stirling

26201 Albion Caledonian 8 Wheel
Platform Lorry with Sacks -
T.W. Davidson Jnr

31603 Ceramic Brick Load

31605 Ceramic Planks Load

31606 Ceramic Sack Load

31607 Ceramic Hessian
Sack Load

31604 Ceramic Pipes Load

36706 Fully Closed Tram -
Sheffield

35007 AEC Routemaster Bus -
RM1818 London Transport

36707 Fully Closed Tram -
Leeds

31804 Bus Depot Kit
(Figures and Models not Included)

35101 AEC Routemaster Open
Top Bus - RM94 London
Transport

Classics

80103 FOWLER B6 'SUPER LION' SHOWMANS ENGINE (KING CARNIVAL II)

80202 FODEN FLATBED STEAMER WITH 'LIFTVAN' - BISHOP & SONS

04303 James Bond
Aston Martin DB5 *1:36 Scale*

57402 Ford Torino with Figures -
Starsky & Hutch
1:36 Scale

01803 Jaguar MK II -
Inspector Morse
1:43 Scale

05301 Chitty Chitty Bang Bang
(Approx length 130mm)

04419 Mr Bean's Mini
1:36 Scale

57401 Ford Capri with Figures -
The Professionals
1:36 Scale

57403 Buick Regal with Figure -
Kojak
1:36 Scale

05506 Italian Job Mini Set
1:36 Scale

00101 Avengers Bentley
with John Steed Figure
1:43 Scale

C929	86	'GAMLEYS'	£15-20
C931	86	'STEPNEY TYRES'	£12-15
C932	86	'PURITAN SOAP'	£12-15
C933	86	'BUY PUNCH'	£20-25
C968	86	'RADIO STEINER'	£20-30
?	?	'SWANSEA BANKERS' (20)	NGPP
?	?	'MARCONI' (20)	NGPP
97150	92	'BUCKINGHAM PALACE'	£12-15
97151	92	'SANDRINGHAM'	£12-15
97152	92	'WINDSOR CASTLE'	£12-15
97153	92	'HOLLYROOD HOUSE'	£12-15
97154	92	'KENSINGTON PALACE'	£12-15
97155	92	'BALMORAL'	£12-15

Thorneycroft Brewery Lorries

C867	86	'THOMAS WETHERED'	£8-10
C867/1	87	'CHARLES WELLS'	£8-10
C867/2	87	'TOOHEYS PILSNER'	£8-10
C867/3	87	'SWAN LAGER'	£8-10
C867/4	88	'CARLSBERG'	£8-10
C867/5	90	'CHARRINGTONS', Set D52/1	GSP
C867/6	91	'GREENE KING', Set D51/1	GSP
C882	88	'ST. WINIFREDS'	£8-10
C883	88	'TAUNTON CIDER'	£8-10

Thorneycroft Trucks

C820/1	85	'EAST ANGLIAN FRUIT Co'	£5-8
C827	85	'G.W.R.'	£25-30
C836	85	'L.M.S.'	£25-30
C837	85	'SOUTHERN RAILWAY'	£25-30
C838	85	'L.N.E.R.'	£25-30
C923	86	'FIELD AMBULANCE'	£10-12
C923/2	86	'TROESCH', Swiss	£300-500
96970	?	'BOOTS'	£12-15

Volkswagen Vans

D985/1	90	blue, plain (no logo)	£10-15
06901	97	red / white, plain (no logo)	£10-15
07001	98	'LUFTHANSA' mini-bus	£10-15
98757	91	'SKIPPER'	£10-15

96960	91	'BOSCH ELECTRICAL'	£10-15
96961	92	'The LION', 'Captain Condor'	£10-15
96965	92	'CORGI CLUB'	£10-15
96965/b	92	'The EAGLE', 'Dan Dare'	£10-15

Volvo Trucks (1:64 scale)

59507	98	'EDDIE STOBART' c/side	£10-12
59530	99	'GUINNESS' artic. tanker	£12-15

White Trucks and Tankers

98449	95	'PETROL CORPORATION'	£15-20
98452	95	'VOLUNTEER' Fire tanker	£15-20
98455	95	'PENNSYLVANIA' truck	£15-20
98456	95	'SCHEIWE'S COAL', truck	£15-20
98457	95	'WHITE ROCK SODA'	£15-20
98458	95	'JACOB RUPPERT'S BEER'	£15-20
98459	95	'TRIPLE XXX' bottle truck	£15-20

'Vintage Glory' Steam Vehicles

Foden

80201	99	'TATE & LYLE', with tilt	£30-40
80202	99	'BISHOP & SONS' flatbed	£30-40
80204	99	'IND COOPE' tanker	£30-40
80205	99	'PICKFORDS' dropside	£30-40

Fowler

80101	99	'ANDERTON & ROWLANDS' 'The Lion'	£45-50
80102	99	'PICKFORDS' 'Talisman' plus cylinder load on trailer	£50-60
80103	99	'King Carnival II'	£40-50
80104	99	'NORMAN E. BOX' 'Atlas'	£35-40
80105	99	'Supreme'	£40-45
80106	99	'Titan'	£35-40

Sentinel

80001	99	'TATE & LYLE' dropside	£30-35
80002	99	'PAUL Bros.', with trailer	£35-40
80003	99	'SHEPHERD NEAME', tilt	£30-35
80005	99	'BLUE CIRCLE' platform	£30-35
80006	99	'McMULLEN' dropside	£30-35

Corgi Classics Fire Service Models

AEC

21801	99	'BLACKPOOL' pump esc.	£28-32
22001	97	'E. YORKSHIRE', turntable	£25-30
97352	93	'STOKE-on-TRENT' ladder	£25-30
97353	94	'DUBLIN' turntable	£25-30
97355	92	'DUBLIN' pumper	£25-30
97356	92	'NOTTINGHAM' pump esc.	£25-30
97357	93	'HERTS' pump escape	£25-30
97358	93	'CLEVELAND' pump escape	£25-30
97359	94	'DUBLIN' tender	£25-30
97360	95	'ROTHERHAM' pump esc.	£25-30
97361	96	'NEW ZEALAND' ladder	£25-30
97385	93	'CARDIFF' ladder	£25-30
97386	93	'BRISTOL' ladder	£25-30

Bedford

05604	97	'AFS' Personnel, ('CA')	£10-12
19201	96	'CAMBRIDGESHIRE' ('S')	£15-20
19701	97	'AFS', ('S')	£15-20
96906	95	'BLACKBURN' ('CA')	£15-20

Chevrolet (American)

51201	96	Fire Chief, 'Centerville'	£15-18
51301	96	Fire Chief, 'SAN DIEGO'	£15-18
51303	97	Fire Chief, 'NYPD'	£15-18
51304	97	Fire Chief, 'NASSAU'	£15-18
97389	94	Fire Chief, 'CHICAGO'	£15-18
97397	95	Fire Chief, 'PENSACOLA'	£15-18

Citroën type 55 (French)

74401	98	'MULHOUSE' fire ladder	£45-50
74402	99	Electro fire ventilator	£45-50

Diamond-T (French)

55602	98	'De LORNE' fire wrecker	£35-40

E-One Cyclone (American)

52201	97	Cyclone Rescue II, 'E-ONE'	£30-35
52202	97	'SCHAUMBURG'	£30-35
52204	97	'WASHINGTON DC'	£30-35
52903	97	'LONG LAKE'	£30-35
54701	98	'BOSTON Fire Dept.'	£30-35

54702	99	'FORT MONROE'	£30-35
54703	99	'NEWARK Fire Dept.'	£30-35
54801	98	'FISHER Fire Dept.'	£30-35
54901	99	Demo colours	£30-35
54903	99	'BARTLETT ILLINOIS'	£30-35

Ford Cortina

98165	95	'LONDON TRANSPORT'	£10-15

GMC Bus (American)

54506	98	GM5300, 'PEORIA'	£30-35

La France (American)

C1143/2	91	La France (97320)	£40-50
51501	97	'WESTMINSTER' pumper	£20-25
51701	97	'STATEN ISLAND' pumper	£20-25
51702	97	'BALTIMORE' pumper	£20-25
51801	97	'LIONEL CITY' ladder	£20-25
51901	96	'BOSTON' ladder	£20-25
97320	91	La France open cab	£40-50
97321	92	'CENTERVILLE'	£30-40
97322	93	'CHICAGO' pumper	£20-25
97323	93	'CARNEGIE' pumper	£20-25
97324	93	'ORLANDO' ladder	£30-40
97325	93	'DENVER' pumper	£20-25
97326	94	'ORLANDO' pumper	£20-25
97387	94	'DENVER' ladder	£20-25
97393	95	'WAYNE' pumper	£15-20
97395	95	'VERO BEACH' pumper	£15-20
97398	95	'JERSEY CITY' ladder	£30-35

Land-Rover

07102	97	'MERSEY TUNNEL'	£10-12
07301	97	'AFS' Line-layer	£10-12
07407	98	'CITY of BATH'	£10-12
07410	99	'HAMPSHIRE' tender	£10-12
07411	99	'CORNWALL' cliff rescue	£10-12
07412	99	'ALPES MARITIMES'	£10-12

Leyland

21901	96	'St. HELENS'	£25-30

Mack (American)

52001	96	'JERSEY CITY' CF pumper	£15-20
52002	96	'LIONEL CITY' CF pumper	£15-20
52003	97	'CITY of NAPA' CF pumper	£15-20
52004	98	'St MARY'S' CF pumper	£15-20
52005	97	'LODI' CF pumper	£12-15
52101	97	'LONG BEACH' ladder	£20-25
52401	97	'ELKRIDGE' B pumper	£15-20
52402	97	'LIONEL CITY' B pumper	£15-20
52403	99	'CORPUS CHRISTI' B pump	£15-20
52601	96	'MALVERN' B pumper	£15-20
52602	96	'GETTYSBURG' B pumper	£15-20
52603	97	'LAMPETER' B pumper	£15-20
52701	96	'CHICAGO' B ladder	£25-30
52702	97	'WILKES-BARRE' B ladder	£25-30
98450	95	'CHICAGO' B pumper	£15-20
98451	95	'BERWICK' CF pumper	£15-20
98484	94	'CHICAGO' CF pumper	£15-20
98485	95	'NEPTUNE' CF pumper	£15-20
98486	95	'PAXTONIA' B pumper	£15-20

Mini-Van

97337	95	'FAWLEY REFINERY'	£15-20

Morris 1000

96854	95	'MORRIS MOTORS' Pickup	£10-12

Simon Snorkel

32001	97	'CHESHIRE'	£25-30
97392	94	'WEST GLAMORGAN'	£25-30
97399	95	'CLEVELAND'	£25-30

Thames Trader

30307	97	Police Control Unit	£15-20

Volkswagen (American)

98475	95	Fire Marshall Van	£10-15

White

98452	95	Tanker, 'VOLUNTEER'	£15-20

AEC Regal half-cab Coaches

33201	96	'FINGLANDS', football fans	**£15-18**
97020	92	'WYE VALLEY'	**£15-20**
97021	95	'MacBRAYNES'	**£30-35**
97180	91	'GREY-GREEN'	**£15-20**
97181	91	'TIMPSONS'	**£15-20**
97184	91	'SHEFFIELD'	**£15-20**
97185	92	'WEST RIDING'	**£15-20**
97186	92	'GREY CARS'	**£15-20**
97187	92	'HANSON'	**£15-20**
97189	91	'OXFORD'	**£15-20**
97190	91	'LEDGARD'	**£15-20**
97191	91	'ROSSLYN MOTORS'	**£15-20**
97193	92	'CARNEYS'	**£15-20**
97194	92	'HARDINGS'	**£15-20**
97196	93	'STANLEY FIELD'	**£15-20**
97197	93	'WESTERN WELSH'	**£15-20**
98161	93	'EASTERN COUNTIES'	**£15-20**
98162	93	'WALLACE ARNOLD'	**£15-20**

AEC Regal IV Single-Deck Bus

97018	95	'DUNDEE'	**£12-15**

AEC Regent Double-Deck Buses

D41/1	90	'BARTONS' (see GS D41/1)	GSP
D47/1	90	'BEANO' (see GS D47/1)	GSP
C599	87	'T. S. B'	**£20-25**
C599/1	86	'WISK'	**£20-25**
D599/1	89	'WESTERN'	**£12-15**
C599/2	87	'WOODHAMS SCOOTERS'	**£15-20**
C599/3	87	'HUNTLEY & PALMERS'	**£15-20**
C599/4	88	'GLASGOW'	**£18-25**
C599/5	88	'RHONDDA'	**£15-20**
C599/6	89	'MORECAMBE'	**£15-20**
C599/7	89	'BRADFORD'	**£15-20**
C599/8	89	'HANTS & DORSET', (see Gift Set D4/1)	GSP
C599/9	90	'WESTERN'	**£12-15**
D599/10	90	'BRIGHTON & HOVE'	**£12-15**
D599/11	90	'DUBLIN'	**£8-10**
D599/12	90	'BATTLE OF BRITAIN'	**£10-12**
Q599/13	90	'HALIFAX'	**£10-12**
C634	86	'MAPLES'	**£10-12**
C643	86	'NEWCASTLE ALE'	**£10-12**
96980	91	'STEVENSONS'	**£10-12**
96983	91	'LIVERPOOL'	**£10-12**
?	91	'ROCHDALE'	**£10-12**
97001	93	'P.M.T.', 'Stoke'	**£10-12**
97002	93	'SHEFFIELD'	**£10-12**
97003	93	'WEST BRIDGEFORD'	**£10-12**
97062	91	'OXFORD'	**£10-12**
	93	'OXFORD' (re-run)	**£10-12**
?	93	'CORGI', club model	**£10-12**

AEC Reliance Buses

97130	95	'OXFORD'	**£10-12**
97900	95	'DEVON GENERAL'	**£10-12**

AEC Routemaster Buses

35001	96	RM 5 'LT', red	**£30-35**
35002	96	RM 664 'LT'	**£20-25**
35004	97	RM 1933 'LT'	**£20-25**
35003	96	'GEORGE SHILLIBEER'	**£20-25**
35006	97	'LIVERPOOL' ('Beatles')	**£20-25**
35007	98	RM 1818 'LT'	**£20-25**
35007H	98	'HAMLEYS'	**£30-35**
35101	97	RM 94 'LT SIGHTSEEING'	**£20-25**
36006	97	RM 254 'LT'	**£20-25**

American Buses (Modern)

GM 4502, 4507

54007	96	GM4502, 'LIONEL CITY'	**£25-30**
54103	96	GM4507, 'LIONEL CITY'	**£25-30**

GM 5301

54301	96	'NEW YORK'	**£25-30**
54302	96	'LIONEL CITY TRANSIT'	**£25-30**
54401	96	'LIONEL CITY BUS'	**£25-30**
54402	96	'GREYHOUND LINES'	**£25-30**
54404	97	'LIONEL CITY TRANSIT'	**£25-30**
54501	96	'SAN DIEGO'	**£25-30**

54502	96	'PENNSYLVANIA R-ROAD'	**£25-30**
54504	97	'SANTA MONICA'	**£25-30**
54601	96	'D. C. TRANSIT'	**£25-30**
54602	96	'CHICAGO TRANSIT'	**£25-30**
54605	97	'READING LINES'	**£25-30**

GM 5302

54303	98	'TRAILWAYS'	**£25-30**

GM 5303

54303	97	Greyhound 'NEW YORK WORLD FAIR'	**£25-30**

MCI buses

98421	95	MCI Demo Bus	**£25-30**
98422	95	'PETER PAN'	**£25-30**
98427	95	'BIRTHDAY BUS'	**£25-30**
98431	95	Bank version of 98427	**£50-75**
98432	95	Bank version of 98421	**£50-75**
98650	95	'CALIFORNIA'	**£25-30**
98651	95	'THRASHER Bros.' not issued	NPP
98652	95	'SEA WORLD'	**£25-30**
98653	95	Bank version of 98652	**£25-30**
98654	95	Bank version of 98651	**£25-30**
98655	95	Bank version of 98650	**£25-30**

American Buses (Vintage)

GM 4502 - 4515

54001	96	4506, 'SURFACE TRANSPORTATION'	**£20-25**
54002	96	4506, 'MADISON AVENUE'	**£20-25**
54003	96	4505, 'St. LOUIS'	**£20-25**
54004	96	4507, 'NEW YORK'	**£20-25**
54005	96	4502, 'PUBLIC SERVICE'	**£20-25**
54006	96	4507, 'WABASH RLY'	**£20-25**
54008	96	4502, 'SAN FRANCISCO'	**£20-25**
54009	97	4507, 'NEW ENGLAND'	**£20-25**
54010	97	4505, 'CHICAGO MC'	**£20-25**
54011	97	4507, 'LIONEL CITY'	**£20-25**
54101	96	4509, 'GREYHOUND'	**£20-25**
54102	95	4509, 'RED ARROW'	**£20-25**
54104	97	4509, 'PEERLESS'	**£20-25**
54106	97	4509, 'NEW HAVEN'	**£20-25**
54202	98	4515, 'SEATTLE'	**£20-25**
54401	97	'LIONEL' ('fishbowl' body)	**£20-25**

GM 5300

54506	98	'PEORIA' 'Hazardous'	**£28-32**

GM 5306

54507	98	'LIBERTY LINES'	**£28-32**

STREET CARS

55001	97	(PTC) 'PHILADELPHIA'	**£28-32**
55004	97	(PTC) 'LIONEL CITY'	**£28-32**
55005	98	(PCC) 'CINCINNATI'	**£28-32**
55007	98	(PCC) 'LOS ANGELES'	**£28-32**
55008	98	(PCC) 'BOSTON'	**£28-32**

TD 4502

97635	96	'LOS ANGELES'	**£28-32**
98600	96	'PACIFIC GREYHOUND'	**£28-32**
98601	96	'PACIFIC ELECTRIC'	**£28-32**

TD 4505, 4506 and 4507

98602	96	TD4505, 'GREYHOUND'	**£28-32**
98603	96	TD4506, 'DETROIT DSR'	**£28-32**
98604	96	TD4507, 'FIFTH AVE. Co.'	**£28-32**
98741	95	Greyhound, 'SAN FRANCISCO'	**£28-32**

YC 743, (YC = Yellow Coach)

53901	96	'UNION PACIFIC'	**£25-30**
53902	96	'LIONEL BUS LINES'	**£25-30**
53903	97	'EASTERN MICHIGAN'	**£25-30**
53904	96	'LIONEL CITY BUS LINES'	**£25-30**
53907	96	'BALTIMORE and OHIO'	**£25-30**
98460	94	Greyhound 'WORLDS FAIR'	**£25-30**
98461	94	Greyhound 'BATTLE of BRITAIN'	**£25-30**
98462	94	Greyhound 'CHICAGO'	**£25-30**
98462	94	Greyhound 'ATLANTA'	**£25-30**
98464	94	'BURLINGTON' 'whale-line'	**£25-30**
98465	94	'BURLINGTON' 'pin-stripe'	**£25-30**
98467	95	'NEW JERSEY'	**£25-30**
98468	94	'CHAMPLAIN'	**£25-30**
98469	95	Greyhound 'LOS ANGELES'	**£25-30**
98470	95	'SILVERSIDE'	**£25-30**

98471	95	'BATTLE of BRITAIN'	**£25-30**
98472	95	'W.A.C.'	**£25-30**
98473	95	'WAVES'	**£25-30**

Bedford 'OB' Coaches

C949/1	87	'NORFOLKS', small 'Ipswich'	**£50-60**
	87	large 'Ipswich'	**£40-50**
C949/2	78	'ROYAL BLUE', small 'Exeter'	**£80-90**
	87	large 'Exeter'	**£50-60**
C949/3	87	'ALEXANDER BLUEBIRD'	**£35-40**
C949/4	87	'GREY CARS'	**£20-25**
C949/5	87	'CROSVILLE'	**£25-30**
C949/6	87	'SOUTHDOWN'	**£100-125**
C949/7	87	'EASTERN COUNTIES'	**£20-25**
C949/8	88	'SOUTH MIDLAND'	**£25-35**
C949/9	88	'PREMIER', blue bonnet	**£25-30**
		without blue bonnet	**£50-75**
C949/10	88	'HIGHLAND'	GSP
949/11	88	'EAST YORKSHIRE'	**£20-25**
D949/12	89	'CLASSIC CARS'	**£20-25**
D949/13	89	'HANTS & SUSSEX'	**£25-30**
Q949/14	89	'WALLACE ARNOLD'	**£20-25**
D949/15	89	'MACBRAYNES'	**£40-45**
D949/16	89	'HANTS & DORSET', see Set D41/1	GSP
D949/17	90	'GREENSLADES'	**£10-15**
D949/18	90	'DEVON GENERAL'	**£15-20**
Q949/19	90	'SOUTHERN VECTIS'	**£15-20**
D949/20	90	'RAF COACH', see Set D35/1	GSP
Q949/22	90	'BOULTONS'	**£15-20**
D949/23	90	'HOWARDS TOURS'	**£15-20**
D949/24	90	'SOUTHERN NATIONAL'	**£15-20**
D949/25	90	'EASTERN NATIONAL'	**£15-20**
D949/26	90	'WEST YORKSHIRE'	**£15-20**
D949/27	90	'BRITISH Rlys', 'Melstead'	**£20-25**
Q949/28	90	'YORK FAIR', see Set Q55/1	GSP
D949/29	90	'BARTON'S', Set D41/1	GSP
Q949/30	90	'WESTERN NATIONAL'	**£18-20**
Q949/31	91	'BRITISH Rlys', 'Bristol'	**£18-20**
		CORGI ON THE MOVE', see Set D82/1	GSP
Q949/32	90	'STANDERWICK', Set Q57/1	GSP
Q949/33	90	'PEARCE & CRUMP' 'The Titfield Thunderbolt'	**£15-20**
33801	95		
33802	98	'MALTA', 'Melueha'	**£18-22**
33803	98	'BRITISH RAILWAYS'	**£22-25**
33804	99	'GUINNESS'	**£22-25**
97075	92	'SOUTH WALES'	GSP
97100	91	'ISLE of MAN TOURS'	**£12-15**
97101	91	'SCILLY ISLES'	**£12-15**
97102	91	'SKILLS of NOTTINGHAM'	**£10-15**
97104	91	'BRONTE'	**£15-20**
97105	92	'FELIX'	**£15-20**
97106	92	'BIBBYS'	**£15-20**
97107	92	'MURGATROYD'	**£15-20**
97108	92	'GRANVILLE TOURS'	**£15-20**
97109	93	'WHITTAKERS TOURS'	**£15-20**
97111	93	'MEREDITH'	**£15-20**
97113	93	'WARBURTONS'	**£15-20**
97115	95	'SEAGULL COACHES'	**£10-15**
97437	95	'MALTA'	**£30-35**
98163	93	'GREY-GREEN'	**£15-20**
98164	93	'EDINBURGH'	**£15-20**
no ref	92	'SMITH'S COACHES' (only 3 made)	NGPP

Bedford 'Val' Coach

35301	97	'YELLOWAYS'	**£22-25**
35302	97	'Magical Mystery Tour'	**£22-25**
35303	97	'SELNEC'	**£22-25**
35305	98	'WALLACE ARNOLD'	**£22-25**
36502	99	'The Italian Job'	see Gift Set 36502

Bristol 'K' type Bus

97853	95	'BRISTOL TRAMWAYS'	**£20-25**
97857	95	'LONDON TRANSPORT'	**£25-30**
97875	95	'CARDIFF 75th'	**£20-25**

Burlingham 'Seagull' Coach

34101	96	'RIBBLESDALE'	£15-20
97170	93	'WOODS'	£15-20
97171	93	'NEATH CARDIFF'	£20-25
97172	93	'STRATFORD BLUE''	£30-40
97173	93	'RIBBLE'	£30-35
97174	93	'YELLOWAY'	£30-35
97175	93	'DON EVERALL'	£15-20
97176	93	'KING ALFRED'	£15-20
97177	93	'NORTHERN ROADWAYS'	£15-20
97178	95	'COLISEUM COACHES'	£15-20
97179	95	'BANFIELD'S COACHES'	£15-20
97340	95	'TRENT'	£15-20
97342	95	'WEST COAST'	£15-20

Daimler 'CW' Bus
(see also French 'Collection Heritage')

36201	96	'GREEN LINE'	£18-22
97336	96	'GLASGOW'	£18-22
97820	94	'WEST BROMWICH'	£20-25
97822	94	'DERBY CORPORATION'	£20-25
97827	94	'SHEFFIELD'	£20-25
97829	95	'DOUGLAS'	£20-25

Daimler Duple Coach

97821	94	'SWAN'	£12-18
97823	94	'BLUE BUS SERVICES'	£12-18
97825	94	'BURWELL & DISTRICT'	£12-18
97830	95	'SCOUT'	£12-18

Daimler Fleetline Bus

97824	94	'BIRMINGHAM'	£25-30
97826	94	'MANCHESTER'	£25-30
97828	95	'ROCHDALE', 'Guernsey Tomatoes'	£25-30
	96	'Corgi Heritage Centre'	£40-50

Guy Arab Double-Deck Bus

34301	97	'SWINDON'	£20-25
97198	94	'SOUTHDOWN'	£30-40
97199	92	'BIRKENHEAD'	£20-25
97201	93	'BIRMINGHAM'	£30-35

97202	93	'MAIDSTONE'	£20-25
97203	93	'LONDON TRANSPORT'	£25-30
97204	93	'COVENTRY'	£20-25
97205	93	'BOURNEMOUTH'	£20-25
97206	93	'NORTHERN GENERAL'	£20-25
97208	93	'YORKSHIRE'	£20-25
97209	93	'WALSALL'	£20-25
97310	93	'SOUTHAMPTON'	£20-25
97311	94	'MIDLAND RED'	£20-25
97312	94	'WOLVERHAMPTON'	£20-25
97313	94	'PAISLEY & DISTRICT'	£20-25
97314	96	'OXFORD'	£20-25
97315	95	'LT' wartime livery	£20-25

Karrier 'W' type Trolley-Bus

34701	95	'NOTTINGHAM CITY'	£25-30
34703	97	'DERBY CORPORATION'	£25-30
97316	95	'IPSWICH'	£25-30
97870	94	'NEWCASTLE'	£25-30
97871	94	'BRADFORD''	£25-30

Leyland Atlantean Buses

33501	96	'GUIDE FRIDAY', open top	£25-30
97230	94	'RIBBLE', 'Gay Hostess'	£25-30
97231	94	'HULL'	£25-30
97232	95	'WALLASEY'	£25-30
97233	94	'DEVON GENERAL', open	£25-30
97341	95	'MAIDSTONE'	£25-30

Leyland Olympian Bus

34801	96	'WESTERN WELSH'	£12-15

Leyland Tiger Bus and Coach

34901	97	'MANCHESTER'	£20-25
97192	92	'RIBBLE'	£20-25
97210	93	'MAYPOLE'	£15-20
97211	93	'BARTON'S'	£15-20
97212	93	'ELLEN SMITH'	£15-20
97213	93	'RED & WHITE'	£15-20
97214	94	'SKILL'S 75th'	£15-20
97216	94	'THE DELAINE'	£15-20
97363	96	'EDINBURGH'	£15-20

97364	95	'NORTH WESTERN'	£15-20
97810	95	'LEICESTER'	£15-20

Sunbeam 'W' type Trolley-Bus

34702	96	'ASHTON under LYME'	£25-30
97800	94	'READING'	£25-30
9780?	95	'MAIDSTONE''	£25-30

Thorneycroft Double-Deck Bus
1st type: 4 top-rail supports
2nd type: 8 top-rail supports

C858	86	'SANDEMANS', 1st/2nd	£12-15
C858/1	87	'NATIONAL MOTOR MUSEUM', red/white 2nd type red cab canopy	£12-15 £20-25
C858/2	87	'CHARLIE CHAPLIN'	£12-15
C858/3	87	'PALM TOFFEE'	£12-15
C858/4	87	'IDRIS SODA WATER'	£12-15
C858/5	87	'The TIMES'	£12-15
C858/6	87	'L. & N.W.R.'	£12-15
C858/7	88	'OAKEYS KNIFE POLISH'	£12-15
C858/8	88	Military Bus, Kay's Set C88	GSP
C858/9	88	'BAXTERS', Kay's Set C89	GSP
C858/10	88	'SCHWEPPES', BP promo	£10-12
C858/11	88	'GREAT EASTERN Rly'	£20-25
C884	86	'BEER IS BEST', 1st type	£12-15
C885	86	'THOMAS TILLING', 1st same but 2nd type	£20-25 £15-20
C888	86	'GRANT'S', cert.,1st type 2nd type	£20-25 £20-25
C975	86	'ALLENBURYS'	£12-15
96985	92	'EAST SURREY'	£12-15
96986	93	'BRIGHTON & HOVE'	£12-15
96987	93	'SCHWEPPES'	£12-15
96988	93	'BEAMISH'	£12-15
96989	95	'GENERAL' (Corgi direct)	£10-12
96991	95	'SHEFFIELD' (Corgi direct)	£10-12
96992	95	'NORFOLK'S' (Corgi direct)	£10-12
96993	95	'YELLOWAYS' (Corgi direct)	£10-12
96994	95	'S. WALES' (Corgi direct)	£10-12

Corgi 'Tramlines' and 'Tramway Classics'

Corgi Tramlines were introduced in 1988 and were presented in 'window' display boxes with a printed diorama and a grey plastic road track base. These tram models were designed to fit 'OO' gauge model railway track, but note that since actual tram tracks are a narrower gauge than railway tracks, the scale of Tramlines models is not 1:76.

Double-Deck Trams
(closed top, closed platforms)

D37/1		'PENNY POST', special box	£15-20
D993/1	89	'PORTSMOUTH'	£15-20
D993/2	89	'DOVER'	£15-20
D993/3	91	'COVENTRY'	£15-20
36702	?	'DUNDEE'	£15-20
36704	99	'LONDON TRANSPORT'	£15-20
36705	99	'EDINBURGH CITY'	£15-20
36706	99	'SHEFFIELD'	£15-20
36707	99	'LEEDS'	£15-20
97262	93	'BLACKPOOL'	£15-20
97264	92	'CARDIFF'	£15-20
97265	92	'BELFAST'	£15-20
97273	94	'BLACKPOOL'	£15-20
97285	92	'LEICESTER'	£15-20
97286	92	'SUNDERLAND'	£15-20
97287	92	'NOTTINGHAM'	£15-20
97288	92	'SHEFFIELD'	£15-20
97293	92	'NEWCASTLE EVENING C'	£15-20
97294		'BIRMINGHAM'	£15-20
97296	92	'LIVERPOOL'	£15-20
98154	95	'DOVER'	£15-20

Double-Deck Trams
(closed-top, open platforms)

C992/1	88	'LEEDS CITY'	£15-20
C992/2	88	'GLASGOW'	£15-20
C992/3	88	'L.C.C.'	£15-20
C992/4	88	'BLACKPOOL'	GSP
C992/5	88	'BRADFORD'	£30-35
D992/6	89	'SOUTHAMPTON'	£15-20
D992/7	89	'BIRMINGHAM'	£40-45
D992/8	90	'LONDON TRANSPORT'	£15-20
D992/9	91	'SOUTH SHIELDS'	see 97261
36801	?	'GLASGOW'	£15-20
36802	?	'LEEDS'	£15-20
97260	91	'BIRKENHEAD'	£15-20
97261	91	'SOUTH SHIELDS'	£15-20
97267	94	'GRIMSBY'	£15-20
97268	94	'L.C.C.'	£15-20
97270	94	'BOLTON / ACDO'	£15-20
98152	93	'GLASGOW'	£15-20
98153	93	'LONDON'	£15-20
98154	93	'DOVER'	£15-20

Double-Deck Trams
(open-top, open platforms)

C991/1	88	'L.C.C.'	£30-35
D991/2	88	'BLACKPOOL'	£15-20
D991/3	89	'BATH ELECTRIC'	£15-20
D991/4	89	'BOURNEMOUTH'	£15-20
D991/5	89	'BURTON & ASHBY'	£15-20
D991/6	90	'CROYDON'	£15-20
Q991/7	90	'GARDEN FESTIVAL'	£15-20
D991/8	90	'LLANDUDNO'	see 97242
36601	96	'WALLASEY'	£15-20

36602	96	'LEICESTER'	£15-20
36603	96	'WEST HARTLEPOOL'	£15-20
36801	96	'GLASGOW'	£15-20
97240	91	'LOWESTOFT'	£15-20
97241	91	'SOUTH METROPOLITAN'	£15-20
97242	90	'LLANDUDNO'	£15-20
97265	95	'BELFAST'	£15-20
97266	95	'PAISLEY & DISTRICT'	£15-20
97268	95	'LONDON COUNTY'	£15-20
97269	95	'PLYMOUTH'	£15-20
97365	95	'BLACKPOOL TOWER'	£15-20
97290	92	'HULL'	£15-20
97291	92	'SOUTH SHIELDS'	£15-20
97365	96	'BLACKPOOL TOWER'	£15-20
98150	93	'LOWESTOFT'	£15-20
98151	93	'SOUTH METROPOLITAN'	£15-20

Single-Deck Trams (open platforms)

C990/1	88	'SOUTHAMPTON'	£18-22
C990/2	88	'SHEFFIELD'	£18-22
D990/3	89	'DERBY'	£18-22
D990/4	89	'WOLVERHAMPTON'	£18-22
D990/5	90	'MAIDSTONE'	£18-22
36901	96	'BLACKPOOL'	£18-22
97263	94	'ASHTON-UNDER-LYNE'	£15-20

Promotional Trams

?	93	'BRITISH TRAM CO.' newspaper	

promotionals: 'Nottingham', 'Newcastle', 'Leicester', 'Sunderland', 'Sheffield', 'South Shields', 'Hull', each ... £20-25

Corgi Classics Cars

Ref.	Intro	Model name, details	MPR

**Sections are listed alphabetically.
Models are listed numerically.**

Gift Set models are listed here individually
only if they have a different reference number
from the set that contains them. The Classics
Gift Sets listing includes additional details.
See also 'Corgi Classics TV and Film Vehicles'.

Austin-Healey
D733/1	90	hard-top, red/white	£10-15
D733/2	90	hard-top, Kay's Set D53/1	GSP
D734/1	90	open, blue, (99050)	£10-15
D735/1	90	soft-top, green/grey	£10-15
02401	96	soft-top, Primrose/black	£10-15
02501	96	open, Ivory/black	£10-15
96200	91	hard-top, turquoise/white	£10-15
96220	91	open, pale blue/cream	£10-15
96240	91	open, yellow	£10-15
99050	93	open, blue, (D734/1)	£10-15
99051	91	soft-top, dark green/grey	£10-15
?	96	open, chrome	£40-50
?	96	soft-top, chrome	£40-50

Chevrolet Bel-Air
(see also under 'Fire Service Vehicles')
C532	94	blue or black	£10-15
C582/2	89	pale blue	£10-15
	89	black / white	£10-15
96570	92	gold, 'Millionth'	£10-15
?	92	pale blue	£10-15
?	94	blue or gold	£10-15
97396	94	'HIGHWAY PATROL'	£10-15

The 'Donnington Collection'
97373	96	Hesketh 308, James Hunt	£10-12
97374	96	Surtees TS9, John Surtees	£10-12
97375	96	Shadow DN1, Jackie Oliver	£10-12
97376	96	Ferrari 312B, Mario Andretti	£10-12
97377	96	Lotus 74D, Emerson Fittipaldi	£10-12
97378	96	Surtees TS9B, Mike Hailwood	£10-12

Ferrari 250
D739/1	90	250 GTO Sport, red, '151'	£10-15
D740/1	90	250 GTO Road, red, (96320)	£10-15
02601	?	yellow	£10-15
96320	90	re-run of D740/1	£10-15
98124	93	250 GT Road, red	£10-15

Ford Cortina (and Lotus-Cortina)
D708/1	89	Lotus Cortina, white/green	£10-15
	89	Lotus Cortina, see Set D53/1	GSP
D708/2	89	Ford, maroon	£10-15
D708/3	89	Lotus, Monaco red	£10-15
D708/4	89	Lotus, aqua blue	£10-15
D708/5	89	Rally car, see Set D16/1	GSP
D708/6	90	'POLICE', white	£10-15
D708/7	90	Ford, black	£10-15
D708/8	90	Ford, spruce green	£10-15
01301	97	red	£10-15
01302	99	1966 RAC Rally, Jim Clark	£15-20
96500	92	'POLICE', (re-issued D708/6)	£10-15
96501	94	Ford, French blue	£10-15
96502	?	Rally car, 'Corgi Rally'	£10-15
96760	91	Rally car, 'J. Whitmore'	£10-15
96763	92	Rally car, 'Roger Clark'	£10-15
96764	92	Rally car, 'Jim Clark'	£10-15
98130	93	Lotus, white/green	£10-15
98165	95	'LT' 'Radio Control'	£10-15
98266	94	chrome-plated, plinth, certificate (1000)	£40-50

Ford Popular Saloon
C701/1	88	grey-blue	£10-15
C701/3	89	black	£10-15
C701/5	89	fawn	£10-15
D701/6	89	Rally car, see Set D16/1	GSP
D701/7	89	pale green	£10-15
D701/8	90	Newark grey	£10-15
D701/9	90	Winchester blue	£10-15
01401	97	white	£10-15
01402	98	black	£10-15
96481	94	sage green	£10-15
98132	93	black	£10-15
98132	93	re-run of C701/3	£10-15
98264	93	chrome-plated, plinth, certificate (1000)	£40-50

Ford Sierra Cosworth
59301	97	'SAFARI RALLY'	£8-10
96012	94	'SPENDER'	£10-12

Ford Thunderbird
C810/2	94	black	£10-12

Ford Zephyr Saloon
D710/1	89	black	£10-15
D710/2	89	blue	£10-15
D710/3	89	Monaco red	£10-15
D710/4	89	Regency grey	£10-15
D710/5	89	'POLICE', black	£10-15
D710/6	90	maroon	£10-15
D710/7	90	Pompadour blue	£10-15
?	?	Linden green	£10-15
96721	91	Rally car, 'Anne Hall'	£10-15
98133	?	re-run of D710/3	£10-15

Ford Zodiac Saloon
D709/1	89	maroon / grey	£10-15
D709/2	89	two-tone blue	£10-15
D709/3	89	yellow / white	£10-15
D709/4	89	red / white	£10-15
D709/5	89	Rally car, see Set D16/1	GSP
D709/6	90	black / blue	£10-15
D709/7	90	two-tone green	£10-15
D709/8	90	Ermine white / grey	£10-15
	90	grey / yellow (very few made)	NGPP
01601	97	turquoise / white	£10-15
01602	99	yellow / white	£10-15
98135	93	re-run of D709/3	£10-15
?	96	chrome-plated, certificate	£40-50

Jaguar 'E'-type
02701	96	open, dark green	£10-15
02702	98	open, Opalescent Maroon	£10-15
02801	96	soft-top, black	£10-15
96042	91	soft-top, cream / black	£10-15
96043	91	open, black, cream interior	£10-15
96080	92	open, red	£10-15
96081	92	open, primrose, red interior	£10-15
96082	92	soft-top, gold, 'K. Baker'	£10-15
98120	93	soft-top, British racing green	£10-15
98121	93	open, silver-blue	£10-15
?	96	open, chrome-plated	£40-50
?	96	soft-top, chrome-plated	£40-50

Jaguar Mk.II Saloon
C700/1	88	red	£10-15
C700/3	88	black, certificate (7,000)	£10-15
D700/4	89	Opalescent Golden Sand	£10-15
D700/5	89	green	£10-15
D700/6	89	metallic blue	£10-15
D700/7	89	metallic grey	£10-15
D700/8	89	silver-blue (96560)	£10-15
D700/9	90	willow green	£10-15
D700/11	90	Rally car, see Kay's Set D53/1	GSP
D706/1	88	'POLICE', black	£10-15
D706/2	89	Police car, Kay's Set D75/1	GSP
01801	97	'BUSTER', red	£10-15
01802	97	Opalescent Bronze	£10-15
01804	98	British Racing Green	£10-15
01805	99	'40th Anniversary' gold-plated	£20-25
96680	91	Rally car, 'Stirling Moss'	£10-15
96681	91	Rally car, 'John Coombes'	£10-15
96682	91	'Inspector Morse'	£90-100
96683	94	white	£10-15
96685	95	'Staffordshire Police'	£10-15
97702/a	92	dark red, plinth	GSP
98131	93	silver-blue (as in Set 97700/a)	£10-15
98263	93	chrome-plated, plinth, certificate (1,000)	£40-50

Jaguar XK120
02901	96	open, British Racing Green	£10-15
02902	98	open, Lavender Grey	£10-15
02903	98	'50th', gold-plated	£15-20
03001	96	soft-top, Gunmetal Grey	£10-15
96040	91	open, white	£10-15
96041	91	open, British Racing Green	£10-15
96044	91	soft-top, maroon, white top	£10-15
96060	91	open, black, white top	£10-15
98900	94	open, chrome-plated	£40-50

Mercedes-Benz 300sl
03401	96	open, pale green	£10-15
03501	96	soft-top, black	£10-15
96410	93	open, red, cream seats	£10-15
96411	93	open, dark grey, red seats	£10-15
96415	93	soft-top, ivory, black top	£10-15
96416	93	soft-top, silver, black top	£10-15

MGA
D730/1	90	hard-top, silver/black	£10-15
D730/2	90	hard-top, Kays Set D53/1	GSP
D731/1	90	open, British Racing Green	£10-15
D732/1	90	soft-top, red / black (99048)	£10-15
03101	98	Alamo Beige	£10-15
03201	96	soft-top, Iris blue	£10-15
03301	96	open, Orient red	£10-15
96140	91	hard-top, red, rack	£10-15
96160	91	open, black, rack	£10-15
96180	91	soft-top, white / grey, rack	£10-15
99046	93	hard-top, silver / black	£10-15
99048	93	soft-top, red / black (D732/1)	£10-15
?	96	open, chrome-plated	£40-50
?	96	soft-top, chrome-plated	£40-50

MGB 1:18 scale
45201	96	soft-top, Primrose Yellow	£20-25
95103	95	open, Tartan Red	£20-25
95104	95	open, Old English White	£20-25
95106	95	open, British Racing Green, limited edition 15,000	£25-30

MGF 1:18 scale
46601	96	open, Amaranth (purple)	£20-25
46602	99	open, British Racing Green	£20-25
46603	99	open, Signal Red	£20-25
46702	97	'JAPAN RACING'	£20-25
95100	96	Diamond White	£20-25
95101	95	hard-top, Flame Red	£20-25
95102	95	open, British Racing Green	£20-25
95105	95	open, Metallic Charcoal, plinth	£25-30
---	95	'Press Drive '95'. Gift to journalists	NGPP

Mini Saloons (Rally Minis) 1:36
04401	96	Rally car, 'VIKING TYRES'	£7-10
04402	96	Rally car, 'CORGI CLASSICS'	£7-10
04403	96	'Mr. BEAN' (see 96011)	£10-12
04404	96	Rally car, 'GISLAVED'	£7-10
04405	97	Rally car, 'CORGI 40th Anniv.'	£7-10
04406	97	'Tony Dron', 1966 Monte Carlo	£7-10
04407	97	'Crellin / Hopkirk' 1994 Monte Carlo Rally	£7-10
04408	97	'Dyson / Bird', 1966 Monte Carlo Rally	£7-10
04409	97	Mini Equinox	£7-10
04410	98	Union Jack Mini, red	£7-10
04411	97	'Kenya Safari' (with mud)	£12-15
04412	98	Charcoal and Chequers Mini	£7-10

04413	98	Union Jack Mini, BRG	£7-10
04414	97	Nurburgring Mini	£7-10
04415	97	Eddie Stobart Mini	£7-10
04416	98	Blue and Chequers Mini	£7-10
04417	98	'HSS 40th', 'Network Q'	£7-10
04418	98	'Monte Carlo Rally', '87'	£12-15
04419	98	'Mr BEAN'S Mini'	£7-10
04420	98	'Cadbury's Mini Egg'	£5-7
04421	97	'Safari Mini' (without mud)	£7-10
04422	98	'D.Paveley/A.Bull' '97 MCR'	£7-10
04423	98	'Geoff Taylor' 'Mighty Minis'	£7-10
04424	98	'British Gas' '94 RAC Rally'	£7-10
04425	99	'Horiba' '98 Spanish Rally'	£7-10
04426	99	'Mintex Rally'	£7-10
04427	99	'Plant Bros' '97 RAC Rally'	£7-10
04433	99	'Green Team' 'Network Q'	£7-10
04434	99	'Neil Burgess' 'Mighty Minis'	£7-10
04501	99	'40th', gold-plated	£20-25
04502	99	Dark Mulberry Red	£8-10
04503	99	Old English White	£8-10
04504	99	Island Blue	£8-10
05505	99	'Frizzell Insurance', 'CSMA'	GSP
94415	?	'NEON', Metallic Blue	£8-10
96011	?	'Mr. BEAN' (as 04403)	£10-12

Mini-Cooper 1:43 scale

36502	99	'The Italian Job'	see Set 36502
94140	92	red / white, 'Monte Carlo'	£10-12
94141	92	black / white, RN '7'	£8-10
98136	93	Almond green / white	£8-10
98137	93	black and 'wickerwork'	£8-10
98138	94	British Racing Green / white	£8-10
98139	94	red / white	£8-10
98141	95	'LIVERPOOL POLICE'	£8-10

Morris Minor 1000 Convertible

02001	97	Smoke Grey	£10-12
96750	94	Snowberry White, closed	£10-12
96751	94	Clipper Blue, open	£10-12
96752	94	Porcelain Green, closed	£10-12
96753	94	Frilford Grey, open	£10-12
96754	94	Highway Yellow, open	£10-12
96755	95	Rose Taupe, closed	£10-12
96757	95	dark blue, in 'Lovejoy' box	£10-12
96765	95	Almond Green, open	£10-12
96766	95	Turquoise, closed	£10-12
97345	?	black, open	£10-12
?	96	chrome-plated	£40-50

Morris Minor 1000 Saloon

C702/1	88	'BSM', black	£15-20
C702/2	88	dark blue	£10-12
D702/4	89	lilac, 'Millionth Minor'	£10-12
D702/5	89	maroon, grey grille surround	£10-12
	89	with maroon grille surround	£10-12
D702/6	90	Almond Green (see 98134)	£10-12
D702/7	90	Ivory	£10-12
D702/8	90	Clipper Blue	£10-12
D702/9	90	Sage Green (79137), not issued	NPP
C703/1	88	Police 'Panda' Car, separate or integral hubs, thin end of sign attached to roof, no mirror or wiper detail on windscreen, thick quarterlights	£15-20
	88	integral hubs, detailed windscreen, thick end of sign attached to roof, thin quarterlights	£15-20
01901	97	Rose Taupe	£10-12
01903	98	Almond Green	£10-12
02002	98	'50th', gold-plated	£15-20
96740	91	Rally car, 'Pat Moss', cream	£10-12
96741	92	'Himalayan Rally', dark blue	£10-12
96742	93	Rally car, 'London to Peking'	£10-12
96744	94	'Police', 'AMP 339H'	£10-12
	94	'Police', 'BDA 327H'	£10-12
96745	94	black, red stripe	£10-12
96746	94	Rally car, red, RN '323'	£10-12
96756	94	'Bristol Omnibus'	£10-12
96758	95	'Some Mothers Do 'Ave 'Em'	£10-12
96759	94	'Merthyr Tydfil Police'	£10-12
98134	93	Almond Green (D702/6)	£10-12
98262	93	chrome-plated, plinth, direct mail (1,000)	£40-50

Morris Minor 1000 Traveller

02201	97	Clipper Blue	£10-12
02202	99	Maroon	£10-12
96870	94	Almond Green	£10-12
96871	94	black	£10-12
96873	94	'Edinburgh Police'	£10-12
96874	94	Old English White	£10-12
97343	95	'Bomb Disposal'	£10-12
?	96	Corgi Collector Club	£10-12

Porsche 356

D741/1	90	hard-top, red / black	£10-12
D742/1	90	open, white / black	£10-12
D743/1	90	soft-top, black / red	£10-12
03701	96	soft-top, white	£10-12
03801	96	open, red	£10-12
96360	91	open, blue / black	£10-12
98122	93	soft-top, all black	£10-12
98123	93	open, silver / black	£10-12

Saab 96 Saloon

D711/1	90	dark red (99045)	£10-12
D711/2	90	light blue	£10-12
D712/1	90	Rally car, 'Erik Carlsson'	£10-12
01701	99	red	£10-12
96662	91	Rally car, 'Pat Moss'	£10-12
99045	93	dark red (D711/1)	£10-12

Triumph TR3a

D736/1	90	hard-top, red / black	£10-12
D737/1	90	open, pale blue (99053)	£10-12
D738/1	90	soft-top, cream/black (99054)	£10-12
03901	98	British Racing Green	£10-12
04001	96	soft-top, Sebring White	£10-12
04101	96	open, black	£10-12
96300	91	soft-top, red / black, rack	£10-12
99052	93	hard-top, red / black	£10-12
99053	90	open, pale bue (D737/1)	£10-12
99054	93	soft-top, cream/black (D738/1)	£10-12
?	96	open, chrome-plated	£40-50
?	96	soft-top, chrome	£40-50

VW Caravanettes and Campers

D984/1	90	Caravanette	see 96940
06701	98	Camper, red / white	£10-12
06801	97	Ochre / white	£10-12
06901	97	Red / white	£10-12
96940	92	Caravanette, red/grey	£10-12
96941	91	Caravanette, grey/white	£10-12
97040	91	Camper, green/white	£10-12

Corgi Classics 'TV and Film Favourites'

'Beatles' Collection

05401	97	'YELLOW SUBMARINE'	£25-30
05403	99	'YELLOW SUBMARINE' plus 54mm white-metal figures of the Fab Four	£30-35
05706	97	Bedford CA graffiti van	£15-20
22301	97	AEC advertising lorry	£20-25
35006	97	AEC Routemaster, 'LIVERPOOL'	£25-30
35302	97	Bedford coach, 'MAGICAL MYSTERY TOUR'	£20-25
58003	97	Taxi with Rita Meter Maid	£14-18

Bedford 'MK' Truck

18901	98	'Soldier, Soldier' + figures	£20-25

Chitty-Chitty-Bang-Bang

05301	99	Re-issue, driver figure only	£20-25
98751	90	Re-issue, all 4 figures	£100-120

Bentley

00101	99	'The AVENGERS', 1:43	£15-20

Buick Regal

57403	99	'KOJAK', 1:36	£14-18

Ford Capri

57401	99	'PROFESSIONALS', 1:36	£14-18

Ford Sierra Cosworth

96012	96	'SPENDER'	£9-12

Ford Torino

57402	99	'STARSKY & HUTCH', 1:36	£14-18

Ford Thunderbird

39901	99	'ELVIS', pink, 1:36, figure	£15-20

Jaguar Mk.II

01801	97	'BUSTER'	£10-12
01803	99	'INSPECTOR MORSE', 1:36	£14-18
96682	96	'INSPECTOR MORSE'	£90-100

Land-Rover

07104	98	'Daktari' + lion and chimp	£15-20

Mini and Mini-Cooper

04403	?	'Mr. BEAN' (see 96011)	£10-12
04419	99	'Mr. BEAN', 1:36	£10-12
05506	98	'The Italian Job'	see Set 05506
36502	99	'The Italian Job'	see Set 36502
96011	?	'Mr. BEAN' (as 04403)	£10-12

Morris 1000 Convertible

96757	95	dark blue, in 'Lovejoy' box	£9-12

Morris 1000 Saloon

96758	95	'Some Mothers Do 'Ave 'Em'	£9-12

Reliant Regal Van

05201	99	'TROTTERS' ('dirty' version)	£8-12

James Bond vehicles

ASTON-MARTIN DB5

04201	97	1:43, gold, with Oddjob. Films 'Goldfinger' / 'Thunderball'	£15-20
04202	99	1:43, gold-plated, 'Goldfinger' 35th anniversary	£18-22
04301	97	1:36, 'Goldeneye'	£10-12
04302	97	1:36, re-issue, silver	£10-12
04303	99	1:36, re-issue, black/red box	£10-12
96445	97	1:36, 30th Anniversary, gold plated	£90-100
96655	96	1:43, silver, replica box	£30-40
96656	96	1:43, gold plated	£50-60
96657	96	1:36, 'Goldeneye', silver	£10-12

CITROEN 2cv

65301	99	Yellow, 'For Your Eyes Only'	£15-20

FERRARI 355

92978	96	Red, in film 'Goldeneye'	£10-15

HELICOPTER

65501	99	'The Spy Who Loved Me'	£15-20

LOTUS ESPRIT

65001	97	'The Spy Who Loved Me'	£15-20

MOON BUGGY

65201	97	'Diamonds Are Forever'	£15-20

SPACE SHUTTLE

65401	99	'Moonraker'	£15-20

TOYOTA 2000GT

65101	97	'You Only Live Twice'	£15-20

Corgi Classics Military Models

Armoured Car
69901 98 Saladin ....see Set 69901

Bedford MK Truck
69902 99 Canvas back truck + 25lb gun..**£35-40**

Berliet Truck
73801 98 GLR8 military covered wagon.**£35-40**

Citroën 55 Truck
74001 98 Canvas back truck **£35-40**

Diamond-T
55601 98 'USAF' wrecker **£20-25**

Land-Rover
07302 98 British Army, olive green **£10-12**
57903 98 'Army' camouflage **£6-9**
07501 99 'British Army' LR with trailer.**£20-25**

Tanks
66501 98 Tiger Mk.I Tank.......................**£15-20**
66601 98 King Tiger Heavy Tank...........**£15-20**
69901 98 Centurion Tank ....see Set 69901

Thorneycroft
C858/8 88 Military Bus, Kay's Set C88 ....GSP

Corgi 'Aviation Archive'

Models and accessories in the 'Aviation Archive' range are made to a scale of 1:144.

Accessories and Kits
31805 99 Aircraft Hangar kit **£8-12**
31806 99 WWII Control Tower kit **£8-12**

Avro Lancaster
47301   98 'Battle of Britain Memorial' **£25-30**
47301A 98 500 only, sold on board a real
            Lancaster, signed by Sqd Ldr...**£40-50**
47302   98 'RAF Coastal Command' **£25-30**
47303   99 'Royal Canadian Air Force' **£25-30**
47401   98 'TRANS-CANADA' **£25-30**
49501   99 'Battle of Britain' ....see Set 49501

Avro Vulcan
48301 99 'RAF' '44 Squadron'...............**£25-30**
48302 99 'RAF' 'Dambusters Sqdn'........**£25-30**
48303 99 'RAF' 'First and Last'.............**£25-30**

Avro York
47202 98 'BOAC' **£25-30**
47203 98 'DAN-AIR LONDON'.............**£25-30**
47204 99 'RAF' 'King's Flight'..............**£25-30**

Boeing Flying Fortress
48201 99 'USAF' 'Bit o' Lace' **£25-30**
48203 99 'RAF' 'Coastal Command' **£25-30**
48204 99 'USAAF' 'Memphis Belle' **£25-30**
49502 99 'USAF' 'Sally-B' ....see Set 49502
?   99 'Sally-B Society' special ....NGPP

Boeing Stratocruiser
48102 99 'ILLINOIS AIR GUARD' HC.**£30-35**
48103 99 'DELAWARE AIR GUARD'...**£30-35**
48105 99 'BOAC' **£30-35**

De Havilland Comet
48501 99 'BEA'.......................................**£30-35**
48502 99 'DAN-AIR'...............................**£30-35**
48503 99 'RAF Transport Command'......**£30-35**

Douglas Dakota
47104 98 'BEA'.......................................**£20-25**
47105 98 'EASTERN AIRLINES' **£20-25**
47107 98 'AIR ATLANTIQUE'..............**£20-25**
47108 99 'KLM'......................................**£20-25**
47109 99 'LUFTHANSA' **£20-25**
47110 99 'AIR FRANCE' **£20-25**

Douglas Skytrain
47112 99 'USAF' 'Electronic Warfare' ...**£20-25**

Hurricane
49501 99 'Battle of Britain' ....see Set 49501

Lockheed Constellation
47501 98 'TWA' **£30-35**
47502 98 'QANTAS' 'Inaugural 50th' **£30-35**
47503 98 'AIR INDIA'.............................**£30-35**
47505 98 'BRANIFF AIRWAYS'...........**£30-35**
47506 98 'USAF' **£30-35**
47507 99 'EASTERN AIRLINES' **£30-35**
47508 99 'PAN AM' **£30-35**
47509 99 'MATS' **£30-35**
????? 98 'KLM' **£30-35**

Lockheed Hercules
48401 99 'RAF' air re-fueller **£30-35**
48402 99 'US Navy' 'Blue Angels' **£30-35**
48403 99 'RAF' 'Hephaeston' **£30-35**
48404 99 'U.S. COAST GUARD' **£30-35**

Mustang
49502 99 'Big Beautiful Doll' ......see Set 49502

Short Sunderland Flying Boat
48801 99 'RAF' 'Coastal Command' **£30-35**
48802 99 'BOAC' 'Hythe Class' **£30-35**
48803 99 'RAAF' **£30-35**

Spitfire
49501 99 'Battle of Britain' ....see Set 49501

Thunderbolt
49502 99 'No Guts, No Glory' .....see Set 49502

Vickers Viscount
47601 99 'BEA' **£25-30**
47602 99 'PARCELFORCE'....................**£25-30**
47603 99 'CONTINENTAL' **£25-30**
47604 99 'LUFTHANSA' **£25-30**
47606 99 'VIRGIN ATLANTIC' **£25-30**

'Aviation Archive' sets
49501 99 'Battle of Britain Memorial Flight':
           Avro Lancaster, Spitfire and
           Hurricane + badges..................**£45-50**
49502 99 B17g 'USAF', Mustang 'Big
           Beautiful Doll' and Thunderbolt
           'No Guts, No Glory'................**£45-50**

Corgi Collectors Club

Corgi Classics collectors are strongly recommended to join the above club which is led by Susan Pownall. Current membership is in excess of 10,000 worldwide. Members receive regular magazines, discounts on models and many other benefits such as special club models. Bus collectors have their own special 'Original Omnibus Company' magazine.
Full details on how to join are shown on the inside rear cover page.

Corgi Classics Gift Sets

Ref.	Year(s)	Set name	Contents, details	Market Price Range
D4/1	1989	'Transport of the Early 50s'	'HANTS & DORSET' OB Coach + Routemaster, dark green/cream, 4,800	£35-40
D7/1	1989	'ROYAL MAIL'	Bedford OB Box Van plus Morris Minor Van in Post Office Red, 4,600	£40-50
D9/1	1989	'SHELL 1910-1940'	Grattan's set: Thorneycroft Box Van and AEC Cabover Tanker, 4,400	£20-25
D13/1	1989	'Police Vans'	Two Morris Minor Vans: 'DOG SECTION' and 'GATESHEAD', 4,500	£40-50
D14/1	1989	'DANDY & BEANO'	Two Bedford CA Vans: 'DANDY' (yellow) and 'BEANO' (blue), 4,400	£35-45
D15/1	1989	'GPO Telephones'	AEC Cabover and Morris Minor vans in olive-green GPO livery, 4,400	£25-30
D16/1	1989	'RALLYING WITH FORD'	Zodiac (yellow/white, '21'), Zephyr (red, '29'), Popular ('139'), 3,400	£25-35
D17/1	1989	'SHELL 1950-1960'	Bedford OB Box Van and OB Pantechnicon, 5,000	£25-30
D19 /1	1989	'SHELL 1910-1940'	AEC Cabover Tanker and Thorneycroft Van	£20-25
D23/1	1989	Ford Popular Vans	Grattan's set. 3 vans: 'Fraser Cook', 'Lewis East' and 'Signsmith', 5,000	£30-35
D35/1	1990	'Battle of Britain'	Bedford OB Coach, Morris Minor Van, Ford Zephyr , 13,000	£25-30
D36/1	1990	'Racing Zephyrs'	Three Ford Zephyrs: white ('47'), yellow ('117'), black ('97'), 8,000	£20-25
D37/1	1990	'PENNY POST' Tram	Red/black fully closed tram, '150th Anniversary', 'Penny Black' design	£20-25
D41/1	1990	'BARTONS TRANSPORT'	Red Bedford OB Coach and red/cream AEC double-decker, 12,000	£20-25
D46/1	1990	'Vehicles of '50s & '60s'	Maroon/cream OB Box and Morris 'J' vans 'British Railways', 13,00	£20-25
D47/1	1990	'BEANO 1990'	AEC Bus 'Bash Street Kids' and Morris 'J' Van 'Minnie the Minx', 15,000	£15-20
C49	1986	'Transport of The 30s'	'The TIMES' Thorneycroft Bus and Ford Model 'T' Van, 8,900	£15-20
C50	1987	'Transport of The 30s'	'London Markets' set of three Ford Model 'T' Vans: 'Smithfield', 'Covent Garden' and 'Billingsgate', 5,000 (no cert.)	£15-20
D51/1	1991	'GREENE KING'	Kay's set: AEC Cabover Tanker and Thorneycroft Truck, 4,900	£20-25
D52/1	1990	'CHARRINGTONS'	Kay's set: AEC Cabover Tanker and Thorneycroft Truck, 5,000	£20-25
D53/1	1990	'Rally' Set	Kay's set: Jaguar Mk.II, Ford Cortina, Austin-Healey, MGA, 4,500	£25-30
D54/1	1990	'Utilities' Set (4 vans)	Kay's set: Bedford CA 'Gas', Ford Popular, Morris Minor, Morris 'J', 5,000	£30-35
Q55/1	1990	'YORK FAIR'	Bedford OB Coach and OB Pantechnicon, '225 Years', 5,300	£25-30
Q57/1	1990	'Northern Collection'	OB Coach 'Standerwick' and OB Pantechnicon 'Slumberland', 4,900	£25-30
C67/1	1991	'Systeme Rally'	Export set	£10-15
C67/2	1991	'Peugeot Rally'	Export set	£10-15
D67/1	1990	'UNITED DAIRIES'	AEC Cabover van (orange) and AEC Tanker (white), 7,500	£15-20
C68	1987	'Transport of The 30s'	Kay's mail-order set: Thorneycroft and Ford Model 'T' vans, 5,000	£30-35
C69	1987	'Transport of The 30s'	Mail-order set: Thorneycroft and Ford 'T' vans 'BRYANT & MAY', 10,000	£15-18
D71/1	1989	'Ford Model 'T' Set	Kay's mail-order set: 'SOMERLITE' and 'TEXACO' tankers with 'A1 SAUCE' and 'APS MEDICINES' vans, 2,500	£20-25
D72/1	1989	'Minor & Popular Vans'	Kay's vans Morris 'RINGTON'S TEA' and 'FRY'S COCOA' plus Ford Popular vans COLMAN'S MUSTARD' and BOWYER'S SAUSAGES', 3,400	£25-30
D74/1	1989	'PICKFORDS'	Kay's set: OB Pantechnicon, Ford Popular van and Morris Minor van, 3,500	£65-80
D75/1	1989	'Police Cars'	Kay's set: Jaguar Mk.II, 'PANDA' Morris Minor and Ford Zephyr, 3,100	£40-45
D82/1	1990	'CORGI ON THE MOVE'	OB Coach and Pantechnicon, Corgi club set, personal certificates	£20-25
C88	1988	'Military' Gift Set	Kay's set: Thorneycroft Bus and Ford Model 'T' Van, 6,000	£20-25
C89	1988	'60 Years Transport'	Kay's set: Thorneycroft Bus 'BAXTERS', OB Coach 'HIGHLAND' and Tram 'FORD for VALUE', 3,100	£140-160
C90	1988	'Ford Model T Utility' Set	Kay's set: Ford vans 'ROYAL LAUNDRY' and 'SUNLIGHT', 8,600	£10-12
C91	1989	'Morris Minor Vans'	Grattan's set: 'GRATTAN'S', 'MITCHELL'S', 'TELEGRAPH & ARGUS', 5,000	£45-55
D94/1	1990	'WHITBREAD'	Bedford OB Box Van and Ford Model 'T' Van, 5,800	£20-25
05506	1998	'The Italian Job'	Red, White and Blue Mini-Coopers in special packaging. See also Set 36502	£22-26
06203	1997	'EXPRESS POST'	Mini Vans set.	£9-12
08002	1997	'Royal Mail and Express Post'	Set of two Mini-Vans	£20-25
08004	1997	'HAMPSHIRE POLICE' Set	Bedford S.C.U. and Morris 1000 Van	£25-30
08005	1997	'STOCKPORT POLICE' Set	Mini-Van and Morris 1000 Saloon	£20-25
08006	1997	'STOCKPORT POLICE' Set	Mini-Van and Morris 1000 Saloon	£20-25
16601	1997	'PICKFORDS' Set	Scammell Highwayman ballast-tractor and Land-Rover LWB	£65-75
17701	1997	'PICKFORDS' Set	Two Scammell Constructors with a 24 wheel low-loader	£85-95
31001	1996	'SHAP FELL'	Leyland articulated flatbed and Atkinson flatbed in 'BRS' livery	£20-25
31002	1997	'NATIONAL BENZOLE' Set	Foden articulated tanker and Morris 'J' van	£35-40
31003	1997	'CHRIS MILLER Ltd'	AEC Ergomatic articulated low-loader with a Scammell Crane unit	£35-40
31004	1997	'WYNN'S'	Scammell articulated low-loader and Bedford 'S' tractor unit	£40-45
31005	1997	'SHELL-BP'	Bedford 'S' articulated tanker and a Land-Rover LWB	£35-40
31006	1997	'WYNN'S'	Ford Thames Trader dropside and Morris 1000 Van	£40-45
31008	1998	'WIMPEY'	Bedford 'S' Low-loader with Priestman Luffing Shovel, plus Thames Trader Tipper	£35-40
31009	1998	'WYNN'S' 'Oriana' Set	Two Diamond-T Tractors, girder trailer + 'Oriana' boiler + Scammell Tractor	£90-100
31013	1999	'A.L.E.' Set	Two Scammel Contractors, Nicholas bogie units and a gas pressure vessel	£80-90
31701	1996	'EDDIE STOBART'	Foden flatbed lorry and a Mini Van in Stobart livery	£25-35
31702	1996	'SADDLER'S'	ERF box van / trailer with VW van advertising 'Saddler's Famous Fun Fair'	£30-45
31703	1996	'CHIPPERFIELD'S BENGAL TIGERS'	Thames Trader van, Morris 1000 van, Land-Rover, AEC fire appliance	£50-65
31704	1997	'EDDIE STOBART'	Thames Trader articulated platform lorry and a Morris 1000 Van	£35-40
33001	1994	'Routemasters Around Britain'	Barrhead, Bournemouth, The Delaine, London Transport (route '30')	£20-25
36501	1997	'BARTONS'	Burlingham Seagull Coach and Morris Minor Traveller	£25-30
36502	1999	'The Italian Job'	Three 1:43 Mini Coopers plus a Bedford VAL Coach. See also Set 05506	£30-35
69901	1998	'Military' Set	Saladin Armoured Car and Centurion Tank	£35-40

91356	1994	**Eddie Stobart Gift Set**	Superhaulers (Transit Van, Box Van), Juniors plus figures	£15-20
93715	1992	**3-piece Mini Set**	Red, silver and green Minis sold only by Woolworths	£30-35
96445	1993	**'GOLDFINGER' Set**	30th anniversary of 'Goldfinger', James Bond's Aston-Martin	£90-100
96990	1992	**AEC Bus Set**	Yellow/dark blue AEC Bus and OB Coach, 'AEC' logos	£15-20
96995	1992	**'IAN ALLAN' Set**	Red AEC Bus and green/white Bedford CA Van	£15-18
97049	1994	**'YELLOWSTONE PARK'**	Ford Model 'T' tanker and a Ford Model 'T' car	£12-15
97050	1993	**'REGENT BUS' Set**	Two open-top buses, white/red and cream/blue	£16-18
97051	1993	**'INVICTAWAY' Set**	Dark blue Metrobus and cream/green Plaxton Coach	£16-18
97052	1994	**'DEVON GENERAL'**	Guy Arab and Leyland Atlantean double-deck buses	£35-40
97053	1994	**'YORK BROTHERS'**	AEC Regal and Burlingham Seagull coaches	£25-35
97061	1991	**'COVENTRY' Bus Set**	AEC double-decker 'VERNONS' and Bedford OB Coach in maroon	£15-20
97063	1991	**'YELLOWAYS' Set**	Yellow/orange Bedford OB Coach and AEC Regal Coach	£25-35
97064	1993	**'BLACKPOOL' Bus Set**	AEC 'Travel Card', Metrobus 'Roller Coaster', Plaxton 'Seagull'	£20-25
97065	1993	**'STAGECOACH' Set**	Routemaster, Metrobus 'Perth Panther' and Plaxton 'Bluebird'	£20-25
97066	1993	**'Routemasters In Exile'**	Scotland: Kelvin, Clydesdale, Perth, Strathtay	£20-25
97067	1993	**'Routemasters In Exile'**	Midlands: K & M Gagg, East Midlands, Confidence, United Counties	£20-25
97068	1994	**'Routemasters In Exile'**	North: Burnley/Pendle, Manchester, East Yorkshire, Carlisle	£20-25
97069	1993	**'WHITTLES'**	Burlingham Seagull and AEC Regal coaches, dark blue and red	£25-35
97070	1992	**'SILVER SERVICE'**	AEC Regal and Bedford OB coaches in silver and blue	£25-35
97071	1992	**'DEVON' Bus Set**	AEC double decker in red/white and AEC Regal coach in cream/green	£25-30
97072	1992	**'GOSPORT & FAREHAM'**	AEC double decker and AEC Regal coach, green 'Provincial' livery	£25-30
97074	1994	**'Routemasters In Exile'**	South: Southampton, Kentish, Capital, Southend	£20-25
97075	1992	**'SOUTH WALES'**	AEC Regal coach in maroon/red and OB coach in cream/red	£20-25
97076	1992	**'W. ALEXANDER'**	Red Guy Arab double decker and blue Leyland Tiger	£30-35
97077	1992	**'EAST LANCASHIRE'**	Guy Arab in red/black and Leyland Tiger in dark green	£30-35
97078	1993	**'CORKILLS'**	Two Bedford coaches, 'de Vanenburg', 'Hotel Kasteel', Dutch	£20-25
97079	1993	**'PREMIER'**	Premier's 70th Anniversary set (Tiger and OB)	£25-35
97200	1991	**'BRS' Set**	Kay's set: green/black Bedford OB Box and Morris 'J' Vans, 5,000	£20-25
97331	1992	**La France Set**	'SOUTH RIVER' (closed) and 'SCOTTDALE' (open) fire appliances	£30-35
97351	1992	**AEC Ladder Set**	AEC Ladder Truck and Bedford CA Van 'Bristol'. Not issued	NPP
97391	1992	**AEC Pumper Set**	AEC Fire Engine and Bedford CA Van 'Bristol'. Not issued	NPP
97541	1991	**'ROYAL MAIL VANS'**	Three Royal Mail Morris Minor vans	£25-30
97680	1991	**'30 Years of the 'E' type'**	Off-white open and red closed 'E'-type Jaguars	£15-20
97681	1991	**'STIRLING'S CHOICE'**	Austin-Healey (silver, '7') and Jaguar XK120 (green, open)	£15-20
97690	1991	**'FERRARI' Set**	Kay's set of 3: light green ('15'), dark blue ('5'), light grey ('10'), 5,000	£20-25
97695	1992	**'ABINGDON' Set**	Morris 'J' van 'BMC', MGA (white, '324'), MGA (red, '38')	£30-35
97697	1993	**'Leicestershire and Rutland Police'**	Morris 1000 Van and Jaguar Mk.II, both in white with 'POLICE' markings	£15-20
97698	1993	**'METROPOLITAN POLICE'**	Bedford OB Coach and Morris 1000 Saloon	£20-25
97700	1991	**'Jaguar Through the Years'**	'E'-type (black, '110'), XK120 (open, white), Jaguar Mk.II (light blue)	£30-35
?	1991	**'JAGUAR XK120'**	GUS set: cream ('65'), white ('166'), green ('64'), 5,000	£18-22
97701	1991	**'RACING 'E'-TYPES'**	Grey/black ('170'), red/black ('108'), 7,500	£15-20
97702	1992	**'JAGUAR COLLECTION'**	A maroon Mk.II, a green XK120, and a red 'E'-type, wooden plinth	£30-35
97703	1993	**'RAC RALLY'**	Three Jaguar XK120s: green ('64'), cream ('65'), white ('166')	£25-30
97706	1993	**'FIRST TIME OUT'**	Three Jaguar XK120s: blue ('6'), white ('7'), red ('8')	£25-30
97708	1993	**'TOUR de FRANCE'**	Jaguar Mk.II ('82'), Ferrari GTO ('165'), Mini-Cooper ('8')	£20-25
97709	1993	**'ALPINE RALLY'**	Ford Cortina ('29'), Austin-Healey ('95'), Mini-Cooper ('38')	£30-35
97712	1992	**'MONTE CARLO MINI'**	Three red/white Minis, racing numbers '32', '57', and '177'	£30-35
97713	1992	**'THE ITALIAN JOB'**	Three Minis from the film - red, white, blue	£30-35
97714	1994	**'D-DAY' Set**	Ford Popular, Bedford OB van, Morris 'J' van and an open-top Tram	£35-40
97721	1994	**'DURHAM POLICE'**	Mini-Cooper and Jaguar Mk.II police cars	£20-25
97722	1994	**'SOUTH GLAMORGAN POLICE'**	Morris 1000 Van and MGA hard-top in police livery	£20-25
97730	1992	**'AUSTIN-HEALEY' Set**	Three competition models: green ('18'), red ('76'), blue ('414')	£20-25
97735	1992	**'CUMBRIAN' Set**	Bedford OB Van plus Morris 'J' Van in red and white	£15-20
97740	1991	**'The TIMES' Gift Set**	Morris Minor Van and Bedford CA Van	£15-18
97741	1991	**'ISLAND TRANSPORT'**	Two Bedford OB Coaches in 'J.M.T.' and 'PIONEER' liveries	£15-20
97742	1991	**'JOHN SMITHS'**	Thorneycroft Beer Lorry and AEC Cabover Tanker	£18-22
97746	1991	**'TOYMASTER'**	Bedford CA van and 'Corgi' Morris 'J' van (Toymaster shops only)	£15-20
97747	1991	**'WEBSTERS'**	AEC Cabover Tanker and Thorneycroft Beer Lorry	£18-22
97749	1991	**'BRITISH RAIL'**	Ford Popular Van and Bedford CA Van in maroon/cream	£15-20
97750	1992	**'EAST KENT'**	Bedford OB Coach and AEC Regal Coach in dark red livery	£20-25
97751	1992	**'BASS' Brewery Set**	Kay's set: Thorneycroft Truck and Ford Model 'T' Van	£18-22
97752	1992	**'RUDDLES'**	Bedford OB Box Van and Thorneycroft Beer Lorry	£18-22
97753	1992	**'TERRYS of YORK'**	Thorneycroft Box Van and Ford Model 'T' Van	£18-22
97754	1993	**'LMS RAILWAY'**	AEC Cabover Van and Thorneycroft Van in 'LMS' livery	£25-30
97755	1992	**'WHITBREAD 250th'**	Anniversary set with AEC Cabover Tanker and Thorneycroft Beer Lorry	£12-15
97765	1993	**'STRATHBLAIR'**	Bedford OB Coach 'Wiles' and Morris 'J' Van 'Forbes'	£25-30
97781	1993	**'TATE & LYLE'**	Foden Tanker and Bedford OB Box Van	£40-50
97851	1996	**'CROSVILLE'**	Original Omnibus set containing a Bristol 'K' and a Bristol 'L'	£20-25
98759	1991	**'DANDY' Set**	Morris 'J' Van and Bedford CA Van	£20-25

98960	1992	'BEANO' Set	Morris 1000 Van 'Biffo' and Morris 'J' Van 'Beryl the Peril'	£20-25
98965	1993	'EAGLE' Set	Volkswagen Van and Bedford CA Van	£15-20
98970	1992	'X-MEN' Set	Bedford Van plus Morris 'J' Van	£15-20
98972	1992	'SPIDERMAN'	Morris 'J' Van and Morris 1000 Van	£20-25
98973	1992	'CAPTAIN AMERICA'	Volkswagen Van and Ford Popular Van	£15-20
99929	1992	MGA Set	Two chromed MGAs (1,000)	£45-55

032/A/96041   **'Classic British Sports Car Collection'** ...Eight cars on wood plinth: 96041, 96060, 96160, 96180, 96220, 96300, 99051, 99053.
Originally a Sunday magazine direct-mail offer, then through Corgi Club. £30-35

?	1993	'Premier Albanian' Set	Leyland Tiger and Bedford OB Coaches with 'Premier' logo	£15-20
?	?	'Connoisseur Collection'	2 'E'-type Jaguars, chrome, plinth, 5,000, direct mail	£45-55
05505	1998	'CSMA 75th Anniversary'	Civil Service Motoring Association set: Ford Capri, Jaguar XK120, 'Bullnose' Morris Van, Mini-Cooper Rally Car, plinth, certificate (5,000)	£35-40

New issues

Ref.	Intro	Model	MPR

'OOC' models are made to 'OO' scale (1:76).

Accessories and Kits
44901	97	Bus Station buildings kit	£7-10
44902	99	Victoria Coach Station kit	£8-10
95400	97	Bus Garage kit	£7-10

AEC 6641T Trolley Bus
43704	98	'CARDIFF'	£

AEC single-deck bus
97095	95	'MACBRAYNES'	Gift Set 97095
97096	95	'EDINBURGH'	see Gift Set 97096

AEC Regent II double-deck bus
40401	96	'KINGSTON upon HULL'	£10-12
40402	96	'NEWCASTLE'	£10-12
40403	96	'EASTBOURNE'	£10-12
40404	96	'BRIGHTON' bus ticket promotion	£100-150
40405	97	'GRIMSBY'	£10-12
40406	97	'CITY of OXFORD'	£10-12
40406	97	Same but with red roof	£40-50
40407	98	'KOWLOON MOTOR BUS'	NGPP
40408	98	'KOWLOON MOTOR BUS'	£30-40
40409	98	'ABERDEEN'	£10-12
97097	95	'TYNEMOUTH'	Gift Set 97097
97814	96	'LONDON TRANSPORT'	£12-15

AEC Regent V double-deck bus
41001	96	'ABERDEEN'	£10-12
41002	96	'HEBBLE'	£10-12
97943	96	'DOUGLAS'	£10-12

AEC Reliance
40202	96	'BEA'	£10-12
45002	96	'CITY of OXFORD'	Gift Set 45002
97130	94	'OXFORD'	£10-12
97902	96	'PMT'	£10-12
97904	96	'LEICESTER CITY'	£10-12

AEC Utility double-deck bus
43904	99	'LEICESTER'	£10-12

AEC Tower Wagons
41501	98	'MACBRAYNES'	£10-12
42101	96	'BRIGHTON'	£12-15
42102	97	'LT', green	£10-12
42103	98	'LT', red	£10-12

Bedford 'OB' coach
42501	96	'ROYAL BLUE'	£10-12
42501	96	'ROYAL BLUE', high seats	£18-20
42502	96	'TROSSACHS TRUNDLER'	£10-12
42502	96	Same but with high seats	£14-16
42503	97	'HANTS & DORSET'	£18-20
42504	97	'CROSVILLE'	£10-12
42505	97	'MALTA'	£10-12
42506	98	'VISTA COACHWAYS'	£10-12
42601	96	'MacBRAYNES'	£10-12
42601	96	'MacBRAYNES', high seats	£14-16
42602	96	'MOUNTAIN GOAT'	£10-12
42603	97	'Hants & Sussex' 60th	£10-12
42604	97	'GREY GREEN'	£10-12
42605	98	'SEAGULL COACHES'	£10-12
42606	98	'GUINNESS'	£11-13
42607	98	'SOUTHDOWN'	£11-13

Bedford VAL coach
35301	97	'YELLOW MOTOR'	£10-12

BET Federation bus
40203	97	'EAST KENT'	£10-12
97900	98	'DEVON GENERAL'	£10-12

Blackpool Balloon Tram
43501	97	1960s	£14-16

43502	97	Wartime	£14-16
43503	97	Pre-war	£14-16
43504	98	'ILLUMINATIONS', 701	£15-18
43505	98	1960s, second version	£14-16
43506	98	1934 version	£14-16
43507	98	'EMPIRE POOLS'	£14-16
43508	98	'WALL'S ICE CREAM'	£15-18
43509	98	'NORTH PIER', 1990s	£14-16
43510	98	'100 Years of Trams'	£18-22
43511	98	'St John's Tower Appeal'	£14-16
43512	99	'PONTINS'	£15-18
43513	99	1980s livery	£15-18
43514	99	'Pasje del Terror' / 'Ripleys'	£15-18

Blackpool Brush Tram/Railcoach
44001	98	Original livery	£14-16
44002	98	Current livery	£14-16
44003	98	'ALLINSON'	£14-16

Bristol 'K' double-deck bus
40701	96	'UNITED COUNTIES'	£10-12
40702	99	Plain green/cream (Tilling)	£10-12
43902	99	'SOUTHERN VECTIS'	£10-12
97851	96	'HANTS & DORSET'	£40-50
97854	96	'WESTERN NATIONAL'	£10-12
97856	96	'WEST YORKSHIRE'	£10-12
97857	96	'LONDON TRANSPORTER'	£10-12
97858	96	'CALEDONIAN'	£10-12
97859	96	'BRISTOL TRAMWAYS'	£10-12

Bristol 'L' single deck bus
40501	96	'LONDON TRANSPORT'	£10-12
40502	99	Plain red/cream (Tilling)	£10-12
97850	95	'MERTHYR TYDFIL'	£12-15
97852	95	'MAIDSTONE & DISTRICT'	£10-12
97855	94	'UNITED'	£10-12
97860	96	'BATH TRAMWAYS'	£10-12
97867	96	'NORTH WESTERN'	£10-12
97868	96	'EASTERN COUNTIES'	£10-12
97869	96	'LINCOLNSHIRE'	£10-12

Bristol Tower Wagon
42301	96	'MAIDSTONE & DISTRICT'	£12-15

Burlingham Seagull coach
40301	96	'WALLACE ARNOLD'	£12-15
40302	96	'PMT'	£10-12
40303	96	'SILVER STAR'	£10-12
40304	96	'BOULTON'S' bus ticket promotion	£50-60
40305	97	'YELLOWAY', 'Torquay'	£30-40
40305	97	'YELLOWAY', 'Rochdale'	£10-12
40306	97	'HAPPIWAYS TOURS'	£10-12
40307	98	'NEATH & CARDIFF'	£10-12
40308	97	'RIBBLE', 'Coventry'	£10-12
40309	98	'SEAGULL COACHES'	£10-12

BUT 9641T Trolleybus
43702	98	'BELFAST CORPORATION'	£

Dennis Dart
42801	97	'KINGFISHER'	£10-12
42802	97	'EASTERN NATIONAL'	£10-12
42803	97	'CITYSHUTTLE' (Hong Kong)	£10-12
42804	97	'STEVENSONS', 'Newport'	£10-12
42805	97	'PLYMOUTH CITYBUS'	£10-12
42806	97	'LONDON BUS LINES'	£10-12
42807	97	'THE BEE LINE', 'Heathrow'	£10-12
42808	98	'KOWLOON MOTOR BUS'	£10-12
42809	98	'VFM', 'South Shields'	£11-13
42810	98	'ORPINGTON BUSES'	£11-13
42811	98	'STAGECOACH BUSWAYS'	£11-13
42812	98	'BREWERS', 'RAF'	£11-13
42813	98	'ABERDEEN'	£11-13

Guy Arab double deck bus
43901	99	'OXFORD'	£12-15

43903	99	'LONDON TRANSPORT'	£12-15
43905	99	'LONDON GREENLINE'	NGPP
43906	99	'SOUTHDOWN', 'Brighton'	NGPP

Guy Tower Wagons
41601	96	'BOURNEMOUTH'	£10-12
41602	97	'SOUTHDOWN'	£18-20
42201	97	'BIRMINGHAM'	£10-12

Leyland Breakdown Wagon
41801	97	'RIBBLE', 'Stagecoach'	£10-12

Leyland Leopard
40201	96	'MIDLAND RED', black roof	£12-15
40205	97	'BALLYKISSANGEL'	£10-12
97835	96	'RIBBLE'	£10-12
97901	96	'MIDLAND RED', 'Gaydon'	£18-20
97903	94	'LOUGH SWILLY'	£10-12
97905	95	'SAFEWAY'	£10-12

Leyland Lynx Mk.I and Mk.II
43101	97	'WEST MIDLANDS', Mk.I	£12-15
43102	97	'WYCOMBE BUS', Mk.I	£10-12
43103	97	'CITYLINE', Mk.I	£10-12
43104	97	'NOTTINGHAM', Mk.II	£10-12
43105	97	'YORKSHIRE', Mk.I	£11-13
43106	98	'LONDON UNITED', Mk.I	£11-13
43107	98	'STAGECOACH', Mk.II	£11-13
43108	98	'BEELINE', Mk.I	£11-13
43109	98	'CROSVILLE CYMRU', Mk.I	£11-13
43110	98	'UNITED', 'Durham', Mk.II	£11-13
43111	98	'CARDIFF BUS', Mk.II	£11-13
43112	98	'RED & WHITE', (Mk.I)	£11-13
43113	98	'BRIGHTON & HOVE', Mk.I	£11-13
43114	98	'FISHWICK & SONS', Mk.II	£11-13
43115	98	'PMT INTER-URBAN'	£11-13
43116	98	'MAIDSTONE & DISTRICT'	£11-13
43117	99	'TRAVEL W. MIDLANDS'	£11-13

Leyland Olympian
43001	97	'WEAR BUSES', 'Go-Ahead'	£10-12
43002	97	'CROSVILLE'	£20-25
43003	97	'GATESHEAD', 'Go-Ahead'	£10-12
43004	97	'KEIGHLEY & DISTRICT'	£10-12
43005	97	'STAGECOACH'	£20-25
43006	97	'N. WESTERN BEE LINE'	£10-12
43007	98	'GO COASTLINE'	£11-13
43008	98	'BLACKPOOL TRANSPORT'	£11-13
43009	98	'UNITED COUNTIES'	£11-13
43010	98	'PMT'	£11-13
43201	97	'KOWLOON MB', standard	£65-75
43202	97	'KOWLOON RAILWAY' 10th Anniversary livery	£30-40
		'10th Anniversary' overprint	NGPP
43203	97	'KOWLOON', 'Handover'	£50-60
43204	97	'CITYBUS', 'Reunification'	£30-40
43205	97	'CITYBUS' (Standard)	£18-20
43206	97	'CHINA MB' (Standard)	£18-20
43207	97	'KOWLOON', 'Reunification'	£20-25
43208	98	'LONG WIN BUS Co.'	£20-25
43209	98	Promotional issue	NGPP
43210	98	'CHINA MB', 'Reunification'	£30-40
43211	98	'NEW WORLD'	£40-50
43212	98	'NEW WORLD'	£40-50
43213	98	'NEW WORLD'	£40-50
43214	98	'CAPITAL CITYBUS'	£18-20
43215	98	'YEAR of the TIGER'	NGPP
43216	98	'CHINA MB' Airport Bus	£30-40
43217	98	'STAGECOACH H.K.'	£18-20
43218	98	'KCRC' original livery	£30-35
43219	99	'SINGAPORE SUPERBUS'	NGPP
43220	99	'KMB' standard (new issue)	£30-40
43221	99	'YEAR of the RABBIT'	£30-40

Leyland PD1 and PD2
40801	96	'HANTS & DORSET', PD1	£10-12
40802	96	'CROSVILLE', PD1	£10-12
40901	96	'CHESTERFIELD', PD2	£10-12

40902	96	'A1 SERVICE', PD2	£10-12
40903	97	'LYTHAM St. ANNES', PD2	£12-15
41101	96	'MANCHESTER', PD2	£10-12
41102	97	'PORTSMOUTH', PD2	£10-12
41103	98	'BLACKPOOL', PD2	£11-13
41201	96	'CARDIFF', PD2a	£10-12
97837	96	'NORTH WESTERN', PD1	£10-12
97839	96	'EASTERN COUNTIES', PD1	£10-12
97941	96	'St. HELENS', PD2	£10-12
97944	96	'NEWCASTLE', PD2	£10-12
97945	96	'RIBBLE', PD2	£10-12

Leyland PS1 single-deck bus

40601	96	'WESTERN WELSH'	£10-12
40602	97	'ISLE of MAN'	£10-12
97836	96	'EAST YORKSHIRE'	£10-12
97838	96	'BIRCH BROTHERS'	£10-12

Neoplan Cityliner

| 44201 | 98 | 'PARRYS' | £14-17 |
| 44202 | 99 | 'HALLMARK' | £14-17 |

Optare Delta

42901	97	'GATESHEAD'	£10-12
42902	96	'NORTHUMBRIA'	£10-12
42903	97	'BLACKPOOL'	£18-20
42904	97	'TRENT'	£12-15
42905	97	'P. M. T.', 'Hanley'	£10-12
42906	97	'CROSVILLE', 'Barmouth'	£10-12
42907	98	'EDINBURGH'	£11-13
42908	98	'EAST LONDON'	£11-13
42909	98	'WESTLINK', 'Slough'	£11-13
42910	98	'BLACKPOOL FYLDE'	£12-15
42911	98	'BARTONS'	£12-15
42912	99	'SOUTH WEST TRAINS'	£12-15

Optare Solo

| 44101 | 99 | 'WILTS. & DORSET' | £10-12 |

Palatine II

43601	98	'BLACKPOOL', St Annes'	£11-13
43602	98	'CITY LINE', 'Centre'	£11-13
43603	98	'GREATER GLASGOW'	£11-13
43604	98	'UXBRIDGE BUSES'	£11-13
43605	98	'CAPITAL CITYBUS'	£18-20
43606	99	'ARRIVA NORTHUMBRIA'	£12-15
43607	99	'EAST YORKSHIRE'	£12-15
43608	99	'FIRST BADGERLINE'	£12-15
43610	99	'NORTHUMBRIA'	£12-15

Park Royal Trolley Bus

| 40102 | 96 | 'HASTINGS TRAMWAYS' | £10-12 |

Plaxton Beaver

43401	98	'EASTERN NATIONAL'	£10-12
43402	98	'STAGECOACH', 'Glossop'	£10-12
43403	98	'CORGI COLLECTOR CLUB'	NGPP
43404	98	'PMT'	£10-12
43405	98	'TRAVEL MERRY HILL'	£10-12
43406	98	'TRENT BUSES', 'Burton'	£10-12
43407	99	'ARRIVA MEDWAY'	£11-13
43408	99	'FIRST MIDLAND RED'	£11-13
43409	99	'TRENT BUSES'	£11-13
43410	99	'MIDLAND MAINLINE'	£11-13

Plaxton Excalibur

43801	98	'WALLACE ARNOLD', Team Coach	£12-15
43802	98	'ULSTERBUS TOURS'	£12-15
43803	98	'OXFORD CITYLINK'	£12-15
43804	98	'SHEARINGS HOLIDAYS'	£12-15
43805	99	'FLIGHTS COACH TRAVEL'	£12-15
43806	99	'VIRGIN RAIL'	£12-15

Plaxton Premiere

43301	98	'OXFORD CITYLINK'	£18-20
43302	98	'EXPRESS SHUTTLE'	£12-15
43303	98	'FLIGHTLINK', 'Heathrow'	£12-15
43304	98	'BUS EIRANN'	£12-15
43305	98	'STAGECOACH WESTERN'	£12-15
43306	98	'NATIONAL EXPRESS'	£12-15
43307	98	'EPSOM COACHES'	£12-15
43308	98	'SKILLS', 'Scenicruiser'	£12-15
43309	98	'BRIGHTON & HOVE'	£12-15
43310	98	'FIFE SCOTTISH'	£12-15
43311	98	'BASSETT COACHWAYS'	£12-15
43312	99	'SILVERDALE'	£12-15
43313	98	'PLYMOUTH CITYCOACH'	£12-15
43314	99	'SOUTHEND ARTERIAL'	£12-15
43315	99	'GNER', 'Railink'	£12-15

Trident 3-axle

44301	98	'KMB', gold/red stripes	NGPP
44302	98	'HONG KONG CITYBUS'	£20-25
44303	98	'KMB', gold (no stripes)	NGPP
44401	99	'NEW WORLD'	NGPP
44501	99	'CITYFLYER' A21	£30-35
44502	99	'CITYFLYER' A11 (UK)	£18-20
44502	99	'CITYFLYER' (Hong Kong)	NGPP

Q1 Trolley Bus

43701	98	'LT', 'Fulwell Depot'	£20-25
43702	98	'BELFAST'	£12-15
43703	98	'GLASGOW'	£12-15
43704	98	'CARDIFF'	£12-15
43705	98	'NEWCASTLE'	£12-15
43706	99	'CARDIFF'	£12-15
43707	99	'GLASGOW'	£12-15
43708	99	'LT', 'Kingston'	£12-15

Van Hool Alizee

42701	96	'SHEARINGS'	£18-20
42701	97	'SHEARINGS', seat variation	£50-60
42702	96	'NATIONAL EXPRESS'	£25-35
42703	97	'BUS EIRANN'	£12-15
42704	97	'WALLACE ARNOLD'	£20-25
42705	97	'OK TRAVEL', 'Go-Ahead'	£10-12
42706	97	'BAKERS DOLPHIN'	£10-12
42707	97	'CITYBUS', HK, (Standard)	£10-12
42707	97	with Chinese number plates	£30-40
42708	97	'BLUEBIRD', 'Aberdeen'	£30-35
42709	97	'EAVESWAY' ('football')	£10-12
42710	97	'RAILAIR', Heathrow	£10-12
42711	97	'SPEEDLINK', Heathrow	£10-12
42712	97	'SHEARINGS'	£10-12
42713	98	'CLARKES of LONDON'	£11-13
42714	98	'EUROLINES'	£11-13
42715	98	'SHEARINGS', '500th'	£11-13
42716	98	'SCOTTISH CITYLINK'	£11-13
42717	98	'LEGER TRAVEL'	£11-13
42718	98	'SEAGULL COACHES'	£11-13
42719	98	'EAST KENT'	£11-13
42720	98	'EAVESWAY', 'Everton FC'	£11-13
42721	98	'ROBINSONS HOLIDAYS'	£11-13
42722	98	'KINGS FERRY'	£12-15
42723	98	'SEAGULL COACHES'	£12-15
42724	98	'ELLEN SMITH'	£12-15
42725	99	'WESTERN NATIONAL'	£12-15

Weymann trolley buses

40101	96	'MAIDSTONE'	£10-12
40102	96	'HASTINGS TRAMWAYS'	£10-12
40103	97	'WALSALL CORPORATION'	£12-15
40104	97	'BRADFORD', 'Thornbury'	£10-12
40105	98	'BRADFORD', 'Coronation'	£10-12
40106	98	'MAIDSTONE & DISTRICT'	£11-13
97811	96	'NOTTS and DERBY'	£10-12
97813	96	'BRIGHTON'	£10-12

OOC GIFT SETS

45001	96	'DORSET DELIGHTS'	Weymann Trolleybus ('Bournemouth') and Bristol 'L' ('Wilts & Dorset') plus a bus terminus kit	£20-25
45002	96	'VARSITY'	AEC Reliance coach ('Oxford') and Burlingham Seagull coach ('Premier') plus a bus terminal kit	£20-25
45003	97	'STAGECOACH'	with figures	£20-25
45004	98	'CHINA MB OLYMPIAN STORY'		£50-60
97055	94	'THAMES VALLEY'	Bristol 'K' and a Bristol 'L'	£20-25
97056	94	'CROSVILLE'		£20-25
97057	95	'SOUTHDOWN'	Leyland PS1/ECW and Leyland Leopard	£25-30
97095	95	'LANCASHIRE HOLIDAY'	Leyland PD2 ('Bolton'), AEC Orion ('Macbraynes') and a kit	£20-25
97096	95	'CAPITAL & HIGHLANDS'	Leyland PD2 and AEC/MCW Orion ('Edinburgh'), terminus kit	£20-25
97097	95	'BRIDGES & SPIRES'	AEC Regent II and Bristol 'L' ('Tynemouth') and a terminus kit	£20-25

New issues

Corgi Toys Miscellaneous Modern Commercials Issues

Ford Escort 55 vans

Market Price Range £8-15

Type 1: Black plastic rear bumper (pre-'86)
Type 2: Metal rear bumper (mid-'86 to '89)
Type 3: New one-piece moulded body (without opening rear doors) from 1989.
Assume models to be Type 1 unless shown otherwise. The models feature a metal body with a plastic chassis and wheels. They have amber side and tail lights, opening rear doors (types 1 and 2) and beige (types 1,2,3) or black (2 & 3) interiors. White or brown interiors sometimes appear with type 1.
Model types shown in brackets.

Liveries issued:

C496 'ROYAL MAIL' (1, 2 & 3)......................
C496/2 'POLICE' (2 & 3).............................
C496/3 'BRITISH GAS' (2).........................
C496/4 'BRITISH AIRWAYS' (2)..................
C496/5 'NOTRUF' (2)..................................
C496/9 'BRITISH TELECOM' (2)..................

C496/15 'HOOVER' ....
C496/16 'B.B.C.' (2) ....
C496/17 'FORD' (2)............................
C496/18 'BRITISH GAS' (2 & 3) ....
C496/19 'BRITISH TELECOM' (3)............
C496/20 'UNIGATE' (3)........................
C496/24 'PTT TELECOM' (3).................
C497 'RADIO RENTALS' (2)................
C498 'BRITISH GAS' (1)....................
C499 'BRITISH TELECOM' (1)............
C503 'DUNLOP' (2).............................
C503/7 'TELEVERKET' (2)...................
C504 'JOHN LEWIS' (2)......................
C512 'BOLTON EVE. NEWS' (2) ....
C514 'CHUBB' ....
C514 'DIGBY'S' Light or Dark Blue .....
C515 'NEW' ....
C532 'RAC' ....
C534 'PIZZA SERVICE' ....
C537 'AA' ....
C543 'TELEVERKET'...........................

C549 'HOTPOINT' ....
C557 'FIRE SALVAGE'....................
C559 'JAGO AUTOMOTIVE' ....
C560 'WILTSHIRE FIRE' ....
C561 'WAITROSE' ....
C562 'GAMLEYS'............................
C563 'McVITIES' ....
C564 'TELEVERKET' ....
C577 'PLESSEY' ....
C578 'BEATTIES' ....
C584 'MANCHESTER Eve. News' .....
C621 'POLICE'................................
C626 'CHUBB FIRE'........................
C632 'KAYS' (2) ....
91610 'AA' (3)................................
91611 'RAC' (3)..............................
91612 'ROYAL MAIL' (3)..................
91620 'YORKSHIRE GAS' (3)............
91984 'AUTO FEDERATION' (3)........

Mercedes 207-D Vans issued 1984-89

Market Price Range £5-10

C516 'BMX SERVICE' ....
C535 'ATHLON' ....
C539 'GROUP 4' ....
C548 'SECURITAS' ....
C554 'ROYAL MAIL' ....
564 'PTT' ....

568 'B.F. GOODRICH' ....
576 'PEPSI' ....
C576/2 'PORSCHE RACING'....................
C576 'PARCELINE' ....
C576 'LEKER OG HOBBY' ....
C576 'OVERNITE TNT' ....

C576/10 'C.R. SMITH' ....
C588 'CURTIS HOLT' ....
C630 'KAYS'..
C631 'BLUE ARROW'...............................
C670 'PARCELFORCE' ....

Ford Transit Vans issued 1987-92

Market Price Range £5-10

656/1 'RAC' ....
656/3 'AMBULANCE' ....
656/4 'FORD'; 656/5 'AA' ....
656/7 'POSTBIL' ....
656/8 'POLISSI' ....
656/9 'POLIS'...
656/12 'KTAS'..
656/16 'BUNDESPOST' ....
656/18 'FALCK SERVICE' ....

C656/21 'LYNX' ....
C656/22 'POLICE'..............................
C656/28 'Nottingham Ambulance' .....
656/29 'CENTRE PARCS' ....
656/30 'CENTRE PARKS' ....
656/31 'UNICHEM' ....
656/33 'McDOUGALL ROSE' ....
656 'FIRE SERVICE' ....
656 'KAYS' ....

656 'AMBULANSE' (Norway) ....
656 'AMBULANSSI' (Finland)...........
91640 'SWALES POLICE' ....
91642 'FALKEN' (Denmark)............
91647 'POLITI' (Denmark)..............
91647 'POLIS' (Swiss)....................
91657 'BELGIAN RED CROSS' ....

Ford Cargo Box Vans

Issued 1985 - 1986
1190 'THORNTONS' £5-10
1190 'EVER READY' £5-10

1192 'LUCAS' £5-10
1228 'THE NEW LEWIS'S'.......£5-10
1249 'WHITES BAZAAR'..........£5-10

'ARNOTTS BISCUITS',
 Australian issue ....NGPP

Scania Box Vans

Scania Box Vans Issued 1983-88. Market Price Range **£5-10**
N.B. Seddon Atkinson and Vovlo Trucks are included in the Superhauler listings.

1123 'KOHLER' ....
1132 'SWEDISH POST'................
1132 'DANZAS'...........................
1133 Tipper Truck......................
1134 'LANTMANNEN' ....
1134 'CORGI'..............................

1146 'RYDER' ....
1148 'SECURICOR'......................
1150 'BRITISH SUGAR' ....
1151 'HONDA' ....
1182 'SUZUKI' ....
1183 'ADIDAS' ....

1183 'GLASSENHETER' ....
1183 'BROSSARD' ....
1238 'McCAIN' ....
1238 'CADBURY'S' ....
1238 'SECURICOR'......................
1251 'B.O.C' ....

1251/2 'ROLO' ....
1264 'ELF' Tanker ....

? 'BRS TRUCK RENTALS' ....

Corgi Truckers

A series of 1:76 scale models introduced in 1989; all **£8-12**

C1300/1   MAN Container 'YORKIE', Yellow/Blue ....
C1301/1   MAN Tanker 'BP', White, Yellow/Green design.....................
C1301/2   MAN Tanker 'MOBIL', Beige, Blue/Red logo....................
C1302/1   MAN Tipper, All Orange ....
C1303/1   Ford Cargo Container, 'SCHWEPPES' ....
C1302/2   Ford Cargo Container, '7 UP'......................................

C1304/1   Ford Cargo Tanker, 'DUCKHAMS OILS'...........................
C1304/2   Ford Cargo Tanker, 'SHELL'..............................
C1305/1   Ford Cargo Tipper, Grey/Green/Silver body ....
C1305/2   Ford Tipper, Red/Silver body ....

Corgi Super Juniors and Superhaulers

FORD D SERIES TRUCK issued 1970-75

2002	Car Transporter	
	White cab, Blue lower, Red deck	**£20-25**
	Red cab and chassis, White deck	**£40-50**
2003	Low Loader, Blue cab, trailer and chassis	**£20-25**
2004	'CORGI' Removals Van	
	Red cab and chassis, Silver trailer	**£40-50**
	Light Blue cab and chassis, Silver trailer	**£40-50**
2007	Low Loader	
	Red cab and chassis, Blue trailer	
	with Orange Junior digger load	**£25-35**
2012	Low Loader	
	Military Green with US vehicle	NGPP

FORD D SERIES TRUCK SETS 1970-76

3003	Car Transporter Set	
	White or Red cab plus 5 Juniors	**£40-50**
3011	Low Loader Set, Red cab plus 6 Juniors	**£50-60**
3024	Low Loader Set	
	Blue cab, Yellow trailer (1976), 6 Juniors	**£50-60**
3025	Car Transporter Set	
	Yellow cab, Orange deck (1976), 5 Juniors	**£30-35**

MACK TRUCKS issued 1971-75

2006	'ESSO' Tanker, White cab and tank	**£10-15**
2010	'EXXON' Tanker, White cab and tank	**£20-25**
2011	'US' Army Tanker, Military Green body	**£20-25**
2027	'RYDER RENTALS', Yellow cab and box trailer	**£10-15**

MERCEDES TRACTOR UNITS,
CAR TRANSPORTER issued 1976

2014/15	White cab and deck, Blue chassis	**£20-25**
2015	White cab, Yellow deck, Red chassis	**£20-25**

N.B. Car Transporter Sets 3023, 3015, 3105 ... **£30-35**

TANKERS issued 1983-84
Market Price Range - as shown otherwise **£10-15**. Liveries issued:

1130	'CORGI CHEMCO' Red or White cab	
1130	'SHELL' Yellow or White cab	
1166	'GUINNESS'	
1167	'DUCKHAMS'	
1167	'7 UP' **£20-30**	

BOX TRAILERS issued 1978-85
Market Price Range as shown otherwise **£10-15**. Liveries issued:

1111	'SAFEWAY'	**£15-20**
1129	'ASG SPEDITION'	
1129	'CORGI' Black or White cab	
1131	'CHRISTIAN SALVESON'	
1137	'SOUKS SUPERMARKET' (Saudi issue)	**£25-30**
1139	'HALLS FOOD'	
1144	'ROYAL MAIL PARCELS'	
1145	'YORKIE'	
1146	'DUNLOP'	
1166	'ARIA DAIRY'	
1175	'INTERNATIONAL Distributors Meeting'	**£70-80**
1175	'TI RALEIGH'	
1176	'ZANUSSI'	
1177	'WEETABIX'	
1178	'MAYNARDS'	
1202	'PICKFORDS HOMESPEED'	**£70-80**
2028	'GERVALS DANONE'	
2020	'BIRDS EYE'	
---	'BRITISH HOME STORES'	**£20-30**
---	'CARTERS LEMON DELINER'	**£25-35**

MERCEDES SETS

1200	'DUCKHAMS' & 'GUINNESS' Tanker plus 3 Scammells	**£40-50**
1403	'CORGI CHEMCO', plus Junior Van	**£25-30**
3128	'DUCKHAMS' & 'YORKIE', plus 10 Juniors	**£40-50**

SCAMMELL 4x2 LANDTRAIN TRACTOR UNITS
TANKERS issued 1985

1141	'SHELL' Yellow or Orange Cab	**£10-12**
1185	'DUCKHAMS'	**£10-12**

BOX TRAILERS issued 1984
Market Price Range as shown otherwise **£10-12**. Liveries issued:

1144	'ROYAL MAIL PARCELS'	

1145	'YORKIE' Yellow or Red cab	
1175	'ZANUSSI'	**£35-45**
1177	'WEETABIX'	
1186	'LUCAS CAV FILTERS'	**£15-20**
1186	'LUCAS GB TRUCK RACING'	**£15-20**
1186	McVITIES' Blue or Orange cab	
	'NORMANS SUPERMARKET'	**£20-25**
	'T.I. RALEIGH'	

SCAMMELL 4x2 SETS

1200	Contains: 1177 RALEIGH, 1177 WEETABIX	
	and 1186 McVITIES	**£23-45**

N.B. See also 'Corgitronic' Scammell issues.

SCAMMELL 6x4 LANDTRAIN TRACTOR UNIT

J3700	Car Transporter	
	'COCA COLA RACE TEAM' (US issue)	**£30-40**

BOX TRAILERS issued 1986-92
Market Price Range as shown otherwise **£8-15**. Liveries issued:

52/2	'CORNING'	
1246	'COCA COLA' (UK issue)	
	Grey shadow on wavyline.	
1246	'DR PEPPER'	
1246/1	'YORKIE'	
1246/6	'FRANCOIS AVRIL'	**£20-25**
1246/8	'FAO SCHWARTZ'	**£20-25**
1247	'BF GOODRICH'	
3300c	'COCA COLA' (US issue)	
	No Grey shadow on White wavy line on trailer	**£20-25**
71500	'7 UP'	
91320	'WEETABIX'	
	'HERSHEY'S CHOCOLATE', Purple or Dark Brown cab	

SCAMMELL 6x4 Sets

3004	'YORKIE' plus Volvo and 2 Juniors	**£20-25**
J3500/600	'COCA COLA' plus 3 Juniors	**£30-35**

FLATBED TRAILER issued 1986

1220/1	Red cab and flatbed with load (also 'BP' offer model)	**£7-10**

VOLVO F12 'Globetrotter' TRACTOR UNIT
Three cab types: Type 1: cast marker lights with or without airfoil; Type 2:
Cast air horns and marker lights; Type 3: cast marker lights, chrome air horns

CAR TRANSPORTERS issued 1984-92

1193	Red cab, White deck, Red chassis	**£7-10**
1222	Red, Blue or Yellow cab	**£7-10**
91380	Red or White cab	**£7-10**

CAR TRANSPORTER SETS 1984-92

Tractor units issued with Red, Blue, White or Yellow cabs ... **£10-15**

TANKERS issued 1986-92
Market Price Range as shown otherwise **£8-12**.
Liveries issued:

1250/2	'NOROL'	
1250/3	'POLO'	
1264	'BP' White cab	
1265	'BP' Green cab £15-20 (New Zealand issue)	
1265/4	'NESTE'	
91341	'BP' Green with White cab roof, 'BURMAH'	**£75-100**
91355	'TESCO'	
	'SHELL' Red or Yellow cab	
	'DUCKHAMS', Yellow or Blue cab	
	'GULF' White or Silver cab	
1250 & 1265/1/2	'TEXACO' Red or White cab Tanker Set	
	issued 1987/88 'TEXACO'	**£12-15**

BOX TRAILERS issued 1985-89
Market Price Range as shown otherwise **£8-12**.
Liveries issued:

V20	'COCA COLA' 1000 only, British Home Stores	**£30-40**
1188	'ROYAL MAIL PARCELS'	
1194	'LEE COOPER'	
1196	'HOTPOINT'	
1197	'ASG SPEDITION'	
1206	'HILLARDS' (2500 certificated)	**£40-50**
1211	'RILEYS'	

1212	'TNT OVERNITE'	£80-90
1212	'BRITISH HOME STORES'	
1217	'KAYS'	
1224	'CADBURY'S FLAKE'	
1225	'BILSPEDITION'	£20-25
1227	'BEEFEATER'	£25-35
1231	'WIMPY' Red or White cab	
1231	'LO COST'	
1231	'KAYS'	
1231	'MARS'	
1231	'MARS' Brown or Black cab	
1231	'McCAIN'	
1231	'ROYAL MAIL DATAPOST'	
1231	'ROYAL MAIL PARCELFORCE'	
1231	'SAFEWAY'	
1231/1	'WEETABIX'	
1231/5	'WOOLWORTHS'	
1231/6	'TESCO'	
1231/13	'GAMINO'	
1231/18	'GATEWAY'	
1231/19	'MARABOU CHOCOLATE'	
1231/23	'FRIZZY PAZZY'	
1231/22	'STEIFF'	
1231/29	'INTERMARCHE'	£20-25
1231/31	'FREIA CHOCOLATE'	
1231/37	'SAS CARGO'	£20-25
1232	'BOSCH PLATINUM'	£20-25
1233	'CADBURYS DAIRY MILK'	
1245	'FUJI FILM'	
1248	'CARTERS LEMONADE LINER'	£15-20
91300	'ORANGINA'	
91301	'SNICKERS'	£20-25
91310	'HULA HOOPS'	
91350/5	'EDDIE STOBART'	
	'YORKIE'	
	'BRITISH TELECOM'	
	'FEDERAL EXPRESS'	

VOLVO BOX TRAILER SETS
Each contains 2 Superhaulers plus matching Juniors.
Issued 1987-94. Market Price Range £6-9.

V37	'EDDIE STOBART' Superhauler plus Transit Van	
C43	'TOYMASTER' Superhauler plus 2 Juniors	£25-35
C43	'WEETABIX' Superhauler plus Routemaster & Junior	
J3167	'WIMPY' & 'WEETABIX'	
J3167/4	'WHITE ARROW'	
J3167/6	'KAYS'	
J3184	'ROYAL MAIL DESPATCH CENTRE'	
J3186	'ROYAL MAIL DATAPOST'	
J3189	'BRITISH TELECOM'	

CORGI CLASSICS - VOLVO BOX TRAILERS issued 1993-94
Market Price Range £7-10.

98100	'SWIFT SERVICE'
98101	'AMTRAK'
98102	'UNITED TRANSPORT'
98103	'P7O FERRYMASTERS'
98304	'CHRISTIAN SALVESON'
98305	'EXEL LOGISTICS'
98306	'DODDS TRANSPORT'
98307	'LYNX PARCELS'

SEDDON ATKINSON 400 SERIES TRACTOR UNITS
3171 Car Transporter

	'GLOBETROTTER' (Saudi Arabia issue)	£15-20

TANKERS issued 1987-92
Market Price Range as shown otherwise £8-12.

1251/1	'BOC CENTENARY'	
1251/2	'ROLO'	
1264/1	'CADBURYS'	£75-100
1264/1	'BP'	
1264/2	'ELF'	

BOX TRAILERS issued 1987-92
Market Price Range as shown otherwise £7-10.

SA4	'GATEWAY'	£35-40
1238	'ROYAL MAIL PARCELS'	

1238/1	'McCAIN'	
1238/2	'CADBURYS FLAKE'	
1238/3	'SECURICOR'	
1238/3	'SILENTNIGHT'	
1238/4	'RADIO 1 ROADSHOW'	
1238/6	'ROYAL MAIL DATAPOST'	
1238/7	'FEDERAL EXPRESS'	
1238/9	'CADBURYS CHOCOLATE'	
1238/10	'LYNX'	
1238/10	'MARS'	
1238/12	'WIMPY'	
1238/13	'CADBURYS WISPA'	
1238/14	'ROYAL MAIL PARCELFORCE' Red Shadowing	
91310	'SMARTIES'	
91420	'PERRIER'	
91422	'ROYAL MAIL PARCELFORCE' Grey shadowing	
91424	'ASDA'	
91430	'KIT-KAT'	

SEDDON ATKINSON SETS issued 1988-91
Market Price Range £15-20.

3087	'WIMPY' Superhauler plus 2 Juniors	
3167	'WIMPY' Superhauler plus 4 Juniors	
3184	'ROYAL MAIL DESPATCH CENTRE' Superhauler plus 4 Juniors	
92625	'ROYAL MAIL PARCELFORCE', Superhauler x 2 plus 2 Juniors	
	'SECURICOR' No details	NGPP

KENWORTH T600 & T800 AERODYNE TRACTOR UNITS issued 1993-94
Single models are certificated. Sold as Race Image Collectables in the USA.

91385	'VALVOLINE'	£10-15
81388	'QUAKER STATE'	£10-15
91389	'TEXACO HAVOLINE'	£25-30
91390	'PLASTIKOTE'	£25-30
91591	'LOTUS' RACE SET, Superhauler plus 2 Juniors etc	£15-20
93016	'FUJI FILM' RACE SET, Superhauler plus 4 Juniors etc	£20-25
98404	'RAYBESTOS'	NGPP
98405	'DUPONT'	NGPP
98511	'VALVOLINE'	NGPP
98516	'WESTERN AUTO' plus Drag car	
98518	'OLDSMOBILE'	NGPP
98519	'SUPER CLEAN'	NGPP
98521	'SLICK 50'	NGPP

FORD AEROMAX TRACTOR UNITS issued 1994
Single models certificated. Sold as Race Image collectables in the USA.

91391	'CITGO'	NGPP
98400	'MAXWELL HOUSE'	NGPP
98401	'MOTORCRAFT LAKE SPEED'	NGPP
98520	'MOTORCRAFT BOB GLIDDEN'	NGPP

CORGI/KIKO TOYS BRAZIL
Kiko Toys manufactured models for the South American market using Corgi Junior models in 1985/6.

KK1	Low Loader with Junior digger, White cab	£30-40
KK2	'ATLANTIC OIL', White/Blue Tanker	£30-40
KK3	'SATURNO' (ZANUSSI), Black cab/trailer	£30-40

RECOMMENDED READING

'CORGI SUPER JUNIOR and SUPERHAULER GUIDE' provides full details plus pictures of all the variations compiled by Andy and Pat Browning, 3 Waterside Terrace, Ninn Lane, Great Chart, Ashford, Kent, TN23 3DD. Tel: (01233) 643461.
NB All the profits from this publication go to a childrens charity.

Metrobus Mk.2 Double-Decker Bus issued 1988-96

Market Price Range as shown,
otherwise under £15

C675/1 'WEST MIDLANDS TIMESAVER' £15-20	Q675/14 'GM BUSES'	91859 'WY PTE' ....
C675/2 'READING TRANSPORT GOLDLINE' £15-20	Q675/15 'NATIONAL GARDEN FESTIVAL'	91860 'HUDDERSFIELD TRAMWAYS' ....
C675/3 'West MIDLANDS TRAVEL' £15-20	C676/16 'STRATHCLYDE'	91861 'TODMORDEN' ....
C675/4 'BEATTIES'	91702 'AIRBUS'	91862 'BRADFORD CENTENARY' ....
C675/5 'THE BEE LINE'	91848 'YORKSHIRE RIDER'	91863 'HUDDERSFIELD' ....
C675/6 'YORKSHIRE TRACTION'	91851 'READING'	91864 'GREY & GREEN' ....
C675/7 'WEST MIDLANDS'	91852 'STEVENSONS'	91865 'YORKS RIDER' ....
C675/9 'NEWCASTLE BUSWAYS'	91853 'BRADFORD'	97051 'INVICTAWAY' ....GSP
C675/10 'LONDON TRANSPORT'	91854 'HALIFAX'	97064 'ROLLER COASTER' ....GSP
Q675/12 'MAIDSTONE'	91855 'WEST YORKS'	97065 'STAGECOACH' ....GSP
Q675/13 'EAST KENT'	91856 'SUNDERLAND'	97802 'TRANSIT' (Sunbeam Models).............
	91857 'NEWCASTLE'	
	91858 'LEEDS'	

Plaxton Paramount Coaches issued 1985-96

Market Price Range as shown,
otherwise under £15

C769 'NATIONAL EXPRESS' £20-30	C774 'ALDER VALLEY'	91914 'SPEEDLINK' ....
C769 'CLUB CANTABRICA'...............£60-70	C775 'CITY LINK'	91915 'TELLUS' ....
C769/4 'SAS' £15-20	C776 'SKILLS SCENICRUISERS'.................	91916 'EAST YORKS' ....
C769/5 'GLOBAL' £15-20	C777 'TAYLORS TRAVEL' £25-30	91917 'HIGHWAYMAN' £20-25
C769/6 'POHJOLAN LIJKENNE' £50-75	C791 'SWISS PTT' £25-30	91918 'SOUTHEND' ....
C769/7 'SCOTTISH CITYLINK'	C792 'GATWICK FLIGHTLINE'...........£15-20	91919 'SHEARINGS' ....
C769/8 'BLUEBIRD EXPRESS'	C793/1 'INTASUN EXPRESS' £20-25	91920 'NOTTINGHAM' ....
C770 'HOLIDAY TOURS' £20-25	C1223 'PHILIPS'	97051 'INVICTAWAY' ....GSP
C771 'AIR FRANCE' £20-25	91908 'SAS'	97064 'SEAGULL' ....GSP
C771 'SAS'	91909 'FINNAIR'	97065 'STAGECOACH' ....GSP
C773 'GREEN LINE'	91911 'APPLEBY'	
C774 'RAILAIR LINK' £25-30	91913 'VOYAGER PLAXTON'	

Ford Transit Minibus issued 1988-89

Market Price Range £5-10

C676/1 'BLUEBIRD'	C676/5 'ROYAL MAIL'	C676/11 'POLIS' ....
C676/2 'SOUTH WALES TRANSPORT'	C676/6 'CHASERIDER'	C676/12 'OXFORD' ....
C676/3 'BADGERLINE'	C676/7 'BRITISH AIRWAYS'	701 'INTER-CITY' ....
C676/4 'FALCK SYGETRANSPORT'	C676/10 'AMBULANS'	

Major Models – Coaches

C1168	1983	'GREYHOUND' ....Red/White/Blue, 'Americruiser'		£15-20
C1168	1983	'MOTORWAY EXPRESS'.......White/Brown/Yellow/Red, Limited Edition		£10-15
C1168	1983	'EURO EXPRESS' ....White/Red/Blue, Limited Edition		£15-20
C1168	1983	'ROVER BUS' ....Blue, 'Chesham Toy and Model Fair', LE		£10-15
		As previous model but Cream body		£20-25
C1168	1983	SWISS 'PTT' ....Confirmation required - was this issued?		NGPP

In 1998, Corgi put together a range of 'budget' models (using stock castings and components) to encourage collecting by children. **Shop retail prices are shown.**

Aircraft
59701 98 Hughes 'POLICE' Helicopter **£4-99**
59901 98 'CONCORDE'............................**£4-99**

BMW 525
57801 98 'HAMPSHIRE POLICE' **£4-99**

ERF Curtainsider
59501 98 'CADBURY'S CRUNCHIE' **£9-99**
59502 98 'EDDIE STOBART'..................**£9-99**

Ford Cargo Box Van
59601 98 'EDDIE STOBART' **£6-99**

Ford Escort Van
58301 98 'PONY EXPRESS'..................**£4-99**
58302 98 'POWERGEN'........................**£4-99**
58303 98 'A.A.' Service Van **£4-99**
58304 98 'EDDIE STOBART' **£4-99**

Ford Transit
58103 98 'OMEGA EXPRESS' **£4-99**
58104 98 'NATIONAL POWER' **£4-99**
58105 98 'TARMAC'.............................**£4-99**
58106 98 'A.A.' Service Van **£4-99**
58108 98 'AUTOGLASS'......................**£4-99**
58109 98 'SECURICOR' **£4-99**
58111 98 'Cadbury's CURLYWURLY'...**£4-99**
58112 98 'EDDIE STOBART' Mini-Bus ..**£4-99**
58115 99 'GREEN FLAG' Service Van ...**£4-99**
58201 98 'BADGER BROS' Wrecker **£4-99**
58202 98 'A.A.' Wrecker **£4-99**
58701 98 'HIGHWAY SERVICES' tipper ..**£4-99**

Fork Lift Truck
56701 99 'City Forklift Services'............**£4-99**

James Bond vehicles (1:64)
99651 99 'Dr. No' Sunbeam Alpine...........**£3-50**
99652 99 'Thunderball' Aston-Martin **£3-50**
99653 99 'Goldfinger' Ford Mustang **£3-50**
99654 99 'You Only Live Twice' Toyota...**£3-50**
99655 99 'O.H.M.S.S.' Mercury Cougar ...**£3-50**
99657 99 'Spy Who Loved Me' Lotus **£3-50**

99658 99 'Living Daylights'Aston-Martin **£3-50**
99659 99 'Goldeneye' Aston-Martin **£3-50**
99660 99 'Dr. No' Aston-Martin...............**£3-50**
99661 99 'Goldfinger' Aston-Martin........**£3-50**
99662 99 'For Your Eyes Only' Lotus......**£3-50**
99725 99 'Diamonds are Forever' Mach I.**£3-50**

Land-Rover
57902 98 'ROYAL MAIL' Post Bus **£4-99**
57903 98 'Army' camouflage **£4-99**

Leyland Terrier
56502 99 'EDDIE STOBART' box van.....**£4-99**

Mazda vehicles
57201 99 'FIRE CHIEF' **£4-99**

Mercedes vehicles
58402 98 'EDDIE STOBART' 207D van..**£4-99**
58402 98 'LONDON ZOO' 207D van......**£4-99**
58501 98 'PIONEER' 6-w cement mixer ..**£4-99**

Mini
04420 98 'CADBURY'S MINI-EGGS'.....**£4-99**

Miscellaneous
58601 98 'City Cleansing' Refuse Truck...**£6-99**
58901 98 'Tripod Crest' Street Sweeper...**£6-99**
59001 98 'DoT' Snow Plough....................**£6-99**

Novelty Advertising Vehicles
57501 98 'CADBURY'S CREME EGG'....**£1-99**

Plaxton Coach
32601 98 'BLUEBIRD'.............................**£6-99**
32602 98 'NATIONAL EXPRESS' **£6-99**

Porsche 944
57701 98 'POLICE' **£4-99**

Range Rover
57601 98 'METROPOLITAN POLICE'....**£4-99**

Routemaster Bus
32301 98 'LT', 'London Standard' **£4-99**
32303 98 'Cadbury's
          DOUBLE-DECKER' **£4-99**
32402 98 'CITY TOUR' **£4-99**
32403 98 'LT', 'SIGHTSEEING' **£4-99**

Scania Trucks
59503 98 'EDDIE STOBART' c/side **£9-99**
60011 99 'EDDIE STOBART' 3-pc set...**£24-99**

'Steady Eddie'
59401 98 'Steady Eddie' **£2-99**
59402 98 'Oliver Overdrive' **£2-99**
59403 98 'Loretta Lorry' **£2-99**
59404 98 'Jock the Tartan Tanker'............**£2-99**
59406 98 'Steady Eddie' and story book ..**£5-99**
59407 98 'Steady Eddie', story book,
          Car Wash and Play Mat **£9-99**
59408 99 'Rich Van Rental' **£2-99**
59409 99 'Angie Ambulance' **£2-99**
59410 99 'Steady Eddie' with hard hat ..**£2-99**
59411 99 'Steady Eddie' with woolly hat..**£2-99**

Superhaulers
59504 98 'EDDIE STOBART' Volvo **£9-99**
59514 99 'CADBURY' Volvo tanker........**£9-99**
59515 99 'TATE & LYLE' ERF tanker....**£9-99**
56519 99 'Cadbury's Bike Boost' Volvo ..**£9-99**

Taxi
58002 98 'COMPUTER CAB' FX4 ....**£4-99**

Sets of toys
59101 98 Range Rover and Caravan........**£12-99**
60001 98 'Mounted Police' Set (Land-Rover,
          horsebox, mounted policeman.**£10-99**
60003 98 'LONDON' Set: Routemaster bus,
          Taxi and mounted policeman ..**£10-99**
60004 98 'ELLERDALE' Set (Land-Rover,
          Horsebox, horse.................**£10-99**
60006 98 'Kenya Safari Rally' (Land-Rover,
          Trailer with Mini '53')........**£19-99**
60007 98 3-piece 'Cadbury' set includes:
          'Freddo', 'Crunchie' and 'Buttons'
          Curtainside Trucks, plus a
          playmat **£24-99**
?   99 'Chad Valley' Motorway Play Set:
          a 'Woolworths' Superhauler, Plaxton
          Coach, Range Rover Police, 'AA'
          Wrecker, Porsche and BMW .....**NGPP**
?   99 'Toys 'R' Us Recovery' set: 'AA'
          Wrecker plus Mini Saloon.........**NGPP**

Corgi 'Motoring Memories'

A range of 'budget' models introduced in 1998 using mostly re-worked 'Cameos' castings. Note that some reference numbers refer to more than one model because those models came in a trade 'assortment pack'.

Austin A35 Saloon
67201 98 Black.......................................**£3-5**

Austin A35 Van
61209 98 'CADBURYS DAIRY MILK' **£3-5**
67301 98 'AUSTIN SERVICE' **£3-5**

Ford Capri Mk.I
67701 98 red/black **£3-5**

Ford Cortina Mk.III
67801 98 yellow/black............................**£3-5**

Ford Escort Mk.I
67001 98 light blue **£3-5**

Ford Escort Van
61209 98 'CADBURYS FLAKE' **£3-5**
61210 98 'A.A. ROAD SERVICE' **£3-5**
61212 98 'ROYAL MAIL' **£3-5**
61213 98 'FORD'...................................**£3-5**
67101 98 'FORD' **£3-5**

Ford model 'T' Van
?   98 'BRANNIGANS' on-pack offer...**£3-5**

Land-Rover
61209 98 'CADBURYS WHOLE NUT' **£3-5**
61210 98 'A.A. PATROL SERVICE'..........**£3-5**
61212 98 'ROYAL MAIL' **£3-5**

Mini
61211 98 'Mr BEAN' **£3-5**
68001 98 Racing green and white **£3-5**

Morris 1000 Van
61209 98 'CADBURYS FRUIT & NUT' **£3-5**
61210 98 'A.A. ROAD SERVICE' **£3-5**
61212 98 'ROYAL MAIL' **£3-5**

Volkswagen Beetle
67901 98 Yellow....................................**£3-5**

Assortments
'Cameos' castings loosely based on Ford Model 'T', Chevrolet, 'Bullnose' Morris and Leyland subjects in 'themed' packs of four.
61201 98 'ROYAL MAIL' **£3-5**
61203 98 'EDDIE STOBART'..................**£3-5**
61205 98 'CADBURY' 'Archive'..............**£3-5**
61206 98 'CADBURY' 'Modern'..............**£3-5**
61207 98 'PICKFORDS'...........................**£3-5**
61208 98 'GOLDEN OLDIES' **£3-5**

Corgi Cameos

A range of low cost models, which were first issued in 1990 as 'The Village Cameo Collection' and individually sold through retail outlets. In addition they were also used as promotional models.

In 1992 Corgi Direct became responsible for sales, and the models have been marketed in sets of ten via press and TV publicity campaigns and have been released in a wide variety of colour shades and promotional logos.

At this stage it is impossible to provide price guidance for either the individual models or the sets, some of which are limited editions of 10,000 pieces. The following provides a basic collectors' listing.

The Editor is indebted to George Hatt author of 'The Corgi Classics Collectors Guide' for providing much invaluable information. George's Guide contains a detailed listing of 'Corgi Cameo' models, colours and variations and collectors are strongly advised to obtain a copy. Send to:
Digby's Publications, 16 Horse Road, Hilperton, Trowbridge, Wiltshire, BA14 7PE. Tel: (01255) 768821.

Saloon Cars

(2nd colour indicates roof colour)

CITROEN 2cv
Cream/Brown ....
Blue/Grey, 'KELLOGGS' logo on some ....
Green/Grey ....
Dark Red/Black, 'CADBURYS' logo ....
Bright Red/Black ....
Yellow/Grey ....

MINI COOPER
Blue ....
Cream
    (2nd Corgi Convention promotional) ....

Grey ....
Dark Green (Cadbury 'Sixties' Set) ....
Light Green ....
Red/White, 'FINA PETROL' ....
All Red (no logo) ....
Purple/White, 'DRINKA PINTA MILK A
    DAY' (Cadburys 'Sixties' Set).......................
White ....
Yellow ....

MORRIS MINOR
Blue ....
Brown ....
Green, 'KELLOGGS' logo on some ....

Green (Cadburys 'Sixties' Set) ....
Pink ....
White ....

VOLKSWAGEN BEETLE
Beige ....
Blue ....
Maroon ....
Orange (Cadburys 'Sixties' Set) ....
Dark Orange ....
Off-White or Yellow with or without
    'KELLOGGS' logo ....

Commercial Vehicles

A.E.C. CABOVER VAN

'ANGLO PAK' - 'FINA' Set 3 ....
'BOUNTY' - Chocolate Set (10,000) ....
'CADBURY'S' - CO-OP Set ....
'CADBURY'S' - Set 97426 ....
'CADBURY'S DAIRY MILK' - Set 97436............

'CAMWALL' ....
'CARTER PATERSON' ....
'CHARRINGTONS' ....
'COLMANS MUSTARD' ....
'CRUNCHIE' - Set 97435 ....

'DRUMMER DYES' - 'FINA' Set............................
'DUNLOP TYRES' ....
'FYFFES' ....
'G.W.R. PARCELS' ....
'JOHN KNIGHT' - 'FINA' Set ....
'LIFEBUOY' - 'Unilever' Set (10,000) ....

'MARS' - Chocolate Set (10,000) ....
'MERRY CHRISTMAS' Set (20,000) ....
'METROPOLITAN RAILWAY'
    - Set 97833 ....

'OMO' - 'Unilever' Set (10,000) ....
'PEEK FREANS' - 'FINA' Set 2 ....
'PICKFORDS' ....

'ROYAL MAIL' Set.......................................
'SETH WILKINSON' - Set C26 ....
'STABILO SCHWAN',
    German promotional...................................

'THE HOLLY & THE IVY'
    - Christmas Set ....
'J. WARD' ....

'WHITBREAD TROPHY' Set.................................
'3rd DIVISION' - D-Day Set (10,000) ....
'12th CORPS' - D-Day Set (10,000)......................

BEDFORD BUS

'B.E.A.' ....
'B.O.A..C.' ....
'BLUEBIRD' ....
'BOURNEVILLE' - Set 97435 ....
'CLASSIC CARS' ....
'CROSVILLE' ....
'DEVON GENERAL' - 'FINA' Set 1 ....
'DOROTHY HOLBROOK' ....
'EASTERN NATIONAL' - 'FINA' Set 3
    with/without 3934 fleet No. ....
'FIRE DEPT' 3 - 'FINA' Set 2..........................
'GUARDS ARMOURED DIVISION'
    D-Day Set (10,000) ....
'HEINZ BEANS' ....
'KIT-KAT' - Chocolate Set (10,000).....................
'LUX' - Unilever Set (10,000) ....
'OSRAM LAMPS' ....
'QUALITY STREET' - Set (10,000) ....
'RAPID ROAD' ....
'RIVER VALLEY' ....
'SILENT NIGHT'
    - Christmas Set (20,000).............................
'SOUTHERN RAILWAY' - Set 97833 ....
'STELLA ARTOIS'
    - Whitbread Set (10,000) ....
'VIM' - Unilever Set (10,000)...........................
'WHITBREAD' Set (10,000) ....
'34th TANK BRIGADE'
    D-Day Set (10,000) ....

FORD Model 'T' VAN

'AERO' - Chocolate Set (10,000) ....
'BLACK MAGIC' Set (10,000) ....
'CADBURY'S ROSES' - Set 97436 ....
'CADBURY'S THE CHOCOLATE'
    - On Pack Offer ....
'COMMANDO BRIGADE'
    D-Day Set (10,000) ....

'CORGI' - Set 97426...................................
'CORGI' - Gaydon Show Special ....
'CHUPA CHIPS' ....
'CITY AND SUBURBAN' ....
'G. DAVID' - 'FINA' Set 3 ....
'DULUX PAINT' ....
'DONCASTER MUSEUM' ....
'FRESHBAKE' ....
'GRATTANS' - Set C26 ....
'HUDSONS SOAP'
    - Unilever Set (10,000)..............................
'JOHNNIE WALKER'
    (Gold or Maroon jacket)..............................
'KING OF THE ROAD' ....
'KLEENEZE' ....
'KELLOGGS' ....
'L.N.E.R.' - Set 97833 ....
'LANDBRO' - 'FINA' Set 3 ....
'L.M.S.' ....
'LONDON MAIL' ....
'LIPTONS TEA' ....
'MACKESON STOUT'
    - Whitbread Set (10,000) ....
'MURPHY'S IRISH STOUT'
    - Whitbread Set (10,000) ....
'NATIONAL GARDEN FESTIVAL' ....
'NOEL' - Christmas Set (20,000) ....
'PERSIL' - Unilever Set (10,000).........................
'PICKFORDS' Set ....
'PRINCES SPREAD' ....
'RIPLEY CO-OP' Set ....
'ROBERTSON' ....
'ROYAL MAIL' Set ....
'SEASONS GREETINGS'
    - Christmas Set (20,000).............................
'SMITHS CRISPS' - 'FINA' Set 2........................
'THE SKETCH' - 'FINA' Set 1 ....
'WEBSTERS' ....
'YULETIDE GREETINGS'
    - Christmas Set (20,000).............................
'ZEBRA POLISH' ....
'2ND ARMY' D-Day Set (10,000) ....

ROYAL FAMILY issues

H.R.H. The Queen ....
H.R.H. Prince Phillip ....
H.R.H. Prince Charles ....
H.R.H. Lady Diana ....

MORRIS TANKER

'W. BUTLER' - 'FINA' Set 3...
'CADBURY'S' - Set 97426 ....
'CADBURY'S' - Set 97436 ....
'CARLESS CAPEL' ....

'CHRISTMAS CHEER'
  - Christmas Set (20,000) ....
'CHRISTMAS WISHES'
  - Christmas Set (20,000)..

'CO-OP' - Ripley 'Co-op' Set ....
'CORNISH CREAM' ....
'DOUBLE DIAMOND' ....
'ELF PETROL' ....
'FINA PETROL' - 'FINA' Sets 1 or 2 ....

'FLOWERS FINE ALE'
  - Whitbread Set (10,000) ....
'FOSTERS LAGER' ....
'GALAXY' - Chocolate Set (10,000) ....
'HEINEKEN LAGER'
  - Whitbread Set (10,000) ....
'KNIGHTS CASTILE', Unilever Set (10,000).........
'MILKY WAY' - Chocolate Set (10,000) ....
'RINSO' - Unilever Set (10,000)...........................
'SHELL' ....
'SOMERLITE OIL' ....
'7TH or 79TH ARMOURED DIVISION'
  D-Day Set (10,000) ....

MORRIS PICK-UP TRUCK

'B.B' - 'FINA' Set 3 ....
'BEACH GROUPS' D-Day Set (10,000).................
'BODDINGTONS'
  - Whitbread Set (10,000) ....
'CADBURY'S DRINKING CHOCOLATE'
  - Ripley 'Co-op' Set ....
'CADBURY'S FRUIT & NUT'
  - Set 97435 ....

'CHARLES WELLS' ....
'FERROCRETE' - 'FINA' Set 2 ....
'GAYMERS CIDER' ....
'G.W.R.' - Set 97833 ....
'HARRY FIRTH' - Set C26 ....
'MILKY BAR' Chocolate Set (10,000) ....
'MORRIS COMMERCIALS' ....
'ROLO' - Chocolate Set (10,000) ....
'PEACE ON EARTH'
  - Christmas Set (20,000)..
'J. SMITH' ....
'SUNLIGHT SOAP'
  - Unilever Set (10,000) ....
'SURF' ....
'SUTTONS SEEDS' ....
''THORLEY'S - 'FINA' Set 1 ....
'WELSH BITTER'
  - Whitbread Set (10,000) ....

CHIPPERFIELDS CIRCUS SET

56901, (96) - Cameos Set of 10 vehicles in blue/red
'Chipperfields' livery...

Made between 1982 and 1987. Scale 1:36.

C801	1982	**1957 Ford Thunderbird**, White/Tan, Cream/Orange or Cream/Black, White-wall tyres, suspension	**£15-25**
C802	1982	**Mercedes 300 SL**, Burgundy or Silver body, with suspension, 126 mm	**£15-25**
		Red body, no suspension	**£15-25**
C803	1983	**1952 Jaguar XK120 Sports**, Red body/Black hood, suspension, spoked wheels, opening bonnet and boot	**£15-25**
C803/1	1983	**1952 Jaguar XK120 Rally**, Cream body, RN '56'	**£15-25**
		White body, rally number '56'	**£15-25**
C804	1983	**Jaguar 'Coupé des Alpes'**, Cream body, Grey/Black tonneau, rally plate and number '56' or '414'	**£15-25**
		As previous model but with rear wheel 'spats'	**£15-25**
C805	1983	**1956 Mercedes 300SC**, Black body, Tan hood	**£15-25**
	1984	Maroon body	**£15-25**
	1986	Beige body and hood	**£15-25**
	1987	Grey body, Black hood, export model	**£15-25**
C806	1983	**1956 Mercedes 300SL**, Black body, Grey/Black hood	**£15-25**
	1986	Black/Green body, Beige seats	**£15-25**
	1986	Red body, Cream interior, export model	**£15-25**
	1986	Blue body	**£15-25**
C810	1983	**1957 Ford Thunderbird**, White body, spare wheel	**£15-25**
	1984	Pink body	**£15-25**
	1987	Red body	**£15-25**
		Cream body, Orange roof	**£15-25**
		Black body, White flash, Red/White interior	**£15-25**
C811	1984	**1954 Mercedes SL**, Silver body, suspension	**£15-25**
	1986	Red body	**£15-25**
	1987	Grey body, export model	**£15-25**
C812	1985	**1953 MG TF**, Green body, Tan seats, spare wheel	**£15-25**
C813	1985	**1955 MG TF**, Red body, Black hood, spare wheel	**£15-25**
	1987	Cream body, Red mudguards, export model	**£15-25**
C814	1985	**1952 Rolls-Royce Silver Dawn**, Red/Black body	**£15-25**
	1986	White/Beige body	**£15-25**
	1986	Silver/Black body, export model	**£15-25**
C815	1985	**1954 Bentley 'R' type**, Black or Cream body	**£15-25**
	1986	Dark Blue and Light Blue body	**£15-25**
	1986	Cream/Brown body, export model	**£15-25**
		White body, Black roof	**£15-25**
C816	1985	**1956 Jaguar XK120**, Red body, Black tonneau, '56'	**£15-25**
		Red body, Cream hardtop	**£15-25**
C819	1985	**1949 Jaguar XK120**, White body, Black hood, '7'	**£15-25**
C825	1985	**1957 Chevrolet Bel Air**, Red body, White roof and flash, White-wall tyres	
	1987	Black body, White roof and flash, export model	**£15-25**
C869	1986	**MG TF Racing Car**, Royal Blue body, Beige seats, racing number '113', spare wheel, roll-bar	**£15-25**
C870	1986	**Jaguar XK120**, Green body, Yellow seats, racing number '6', export model	**£15-25**

Collectors notes

Exclusive First Editions

'Exclusive First Editions' were introduced in 1989 and are made to a scale of 1:76 ('00' gauge). Models enhanced by the addition of 'loads' or extra detail were marketed by EFE as 'Deluxe'. They have 'DL' appended to their reference number. If a model is listed separately but is only available in a set then 'GSP' (Gift Set Price) is shown and reference to the Gift Sets section will give the price for the set.
'L.T.' = 'London Transport'   'L.C.' = 'London Country'
Models are listed by vehicle type, in alphabetical order.

CONTENTS

Buses, Coaches, Trams

Ref.	Intro	Model	MPR

AEC Duple half-cab coach
25301	98	'EAST YORKSHIRE'	£10-12
25302	99	'GREY-GREEN'	£11-13

AEC Regal single-deck buses
20501	96	'HOWES of SPENNYMOOR'	£9-11
20502	96	'SOUTH WALES', 'Furnace'	£9-11
-- DL	98	'SOUTH WALES', 'Morfa'	£10-12
20503	98	'BRITISH RAILWAYS'	£10-12
20701	96	'TRENT', 'Nottingham'	£9-11
20702	96	'TIMPSON'S', 'Torquay'	£9-11
20703	96	'SOUTH WALES', 'Tour'	£10-12
20704	97	'S.U.T.', 'Switzerland'	£10-12

AEC Regent double-deck buses

'London Transport' fleetname
10101	89	'DURACELL', 'RT 981'	£12-15
10101	89	'DURACELL', 'RT 206', also in Gift Set 99901	£12-15
10104	90	'SCHWEPPES', red, also in Gift Set 99901	£18-20
10105	90	'TATE & LYLE', in GS 19901	GSP
10106	90	'RANK HOVIS', in GS 19902	GSP
-- DL	93	'RANK HOVIS'	£12-15
10107	90	'DULUX', red, 'RT 33'	£18-22
10109	90	'BIRDS', 'RT 4572'	£18-22
10110	91	'TAYLOR WOODROW' and in Gift Set 19904	£18-22 GSP
-- DL	94	'TAYLOR WOODROW'	£12-15
10111	91	'BARCLAYS', 'RT 4245'	£18-22
10112	91	'VERNONS', 'RT 2861'	£18-22
10115			not issued
10116	92	'AIR FRANCE', 'RT 3402'	£18-22
10121	95	'LT', green, part printed	£18-22
C -- a	95	'LT', green, 'ALLSORTS'	£18-22
C -- b	95	'LT', green, 'St ALBANS 95'	£18-22
C -- c	95	'LT', green, 'BAXTERS', (Kidney machine appeal bus)	£18-22
C -- d	96	'BROMLEY PAGEANT'	£15-17
C -- e	96	'AUSTRIAN ALPINE'	£10-15
C -- f	96	'RAMBLERS HOLIDAYS'	£15-18
C --x1	96	'Allsorts', 'Xmas', 'LLU613'	£18-20
C --x2	96	'Allsorts', 'Xmas', 'KYY877'	£12-15
10122	?	SRT, 'Woman's Own'	£20-25
10124	97	'SRT 29', 'Walthamstow'	£20-25
10127	95	'DULUX', green, 'RT 3148'	£12-15
16401	94	'NAT. SAVINGS', GS 99908	GSP
16402	94	'PREMIUM BONDS','RT602'	£20-25
c16402		'St ALBANS '94', 'RT 602'	£20-25
16403	94	'PEARL ASSURANCE', red	£15-20
16404	95	'VERNONS'	£20-25

'London Country' fleetname
10103	90	'BIRDS EYE', 'RT 4050', singly and in Gift Set 99901	£10-13
10123	97	'Hertford Bus Stn', 'RT3752'	£10-12
C -- a	97	'Ramblers Assoc', 'RT1095'	£14-17
C -- b	97	'Bromley Pageant', 'RT3752'	£15-18

C -- s	97	'Sutton Utd', 'RT1095'	£15-18

'Greenline' fleetname
10102	?	'BUXTED', 'RT 981'	£15-18
10117	92	'EFE CLUB 92', 'RT 3254'	£70-90
10125	?	'L. T.', 'Walthamstow'	GS 99914

Provincial operators
10108	90	'NORTHERN'	£18-22
10113	91	'DUNDEE'	£22-28
10113b	91	'DUNDEE', reversed blinds	£45-50
10114	92	'BRADFORD'	£12-15
10118	93	'St HELENS'	£12-15
10119	94	'HULL', route '25'	£9-11
10120	95	'ENSIGNBUS'	£9-11
19701	95	'SHEFFIELD', Regent III	£8-11
19702	95	'DEVON GENERAL', Reg.V	£20-25
19703	95	'ST HELENS', Regent II	£8-11
-- DL	96	'ST HELENS', subs. offer	£25-30
19704	95	'SOUTH WALES', Regent V	£8-11
19705	95	'SAMUEL LEDGARD', Reg.V	£8-11
19706	96	'HEBBLE', Regent V	£8-11
-- DL	96	'HEBBLE', 'Bradford', Reg.V	£10-12
19707	96	'WEST YORKSHIRE', Reg.V	£8-11
-- DL	97	'WEST YORKSHIRE'	£10-12
19708	96	'OXFORD', Regent V	£18-20
c19708		'OXFORD', 'Classic Bus'	£20-25

Commissioned models
C10101		'Austrian Airlines', 'RT981'	NGPP
C10101		'Austrian Airlines', 'RT206'	NGPP
C10101		'Austrian Airlines', 'RT981'	NGPP
C10101b		'Bromley Pageant '92', 'RT206'	NGPP
C10104		'Austrian Airlines'	NGPP
C10104b		'Bromley Pageant '92', 'RT858'	NGPP
C10111		'Austrian Airlines'	NGPP
C10110		'London Toy & Model Club'	£11-13
C10110/03		'PSV Circle '92'	Set of 3
C10001		'Pearl Assurance', 'RT3639'	£40-45
C101002a		'Birmingham', route '130'	£45-50
C101002b		'Birmingham', route '108'	NGPP
C101003a		Green (with yellow band), 'RT3254', route '50'	£480-500
C101003b		Green (no yellow band), 'RT3254', route '50'	£45-50
C101003c		Red, 'RT3254', route '50'	£55-60
C101003d		Green, 'Allsorts 10th'	£80-100
C101004a		'Star Group', LT legal lettering	NGPP
C101004b		'Star Group', no legal lettering	NGPP
C101004c		'Star Group', yellow band	£45-50
C101005		'Beatties', 'RT 1044'	£20-25
C101006		'Fisherman's Friend'	£20-25
C101007a		'Midland Red', 'Ev. Despatch'	£18-22
C101007b		'Midland Red', 'EFE 1'	£11-13
C101007c		'Midland Red', 'Fence Club'	£80-100
C101008		'Coventry'	£45-50
C101009		'Glasgow'	£35-40
C101010		'Devon General'	£75-100
C102001		'Devon General'	£75-100

AEC Regent open top buses
-	90	'EFE 2', 'Birmingham', with certificate	£12-15
-	90	'COLMANS', red, 'London'	£30-35
-	90	'See The Island', 'Southern Vectis'	£100-120
10201	89	'EASTBOURNE'	£11-13
10201	90	'EAST BOURNE'	£11-13
10202	89	'GREAT YARMOUTH', 'Caister'	£11-13
10203	90	'GREAT YARMOUTH', 'Coronation'	£18-22
10204	91	'LT', 'Typhoo'	£25-30
C102001		'SOUTHERN VECTIS'	NGPP
C102002		'LT', 'Coventry'	£30-35
C102003		'BIRMINGHAM', 'EFE 2'	£18-22
---		'LT', 'London Toy and Model Museum'	£30-35

AEC Reliance - see Harrington coaches

AEC RF buses
23201	98	'GREENLINE', in GS 99914	GSP
23202	98	'GREENLINE', 'Gravesend'	£20-25
23203	99	'L.C.', 'Staines'	£11-13
23301	97	'L.T. Country Service', 'Woldingham'	£15-18
c23301a		'L.T. Country Service', 'Ramblers Association'	NGPP
23302	97	'L.T.', 'Passingford Bridge'	£40-45
23303	97	'L.T.', 'East Grinstead'	£18-20
23304	97	'L.T.', 'Weybridge Station'	£18-20
23305	97	'GREENLINE', 'High Wycombe'	£20-25
23306	97	'BEA', 'Airside Coach'	£10-12
23307	97	'METROBUS', 'Tunbridge'	£10-12
23308	98	'L.T.', 'Golders Green Station'	£20-25
23309	98	'L.T.', 'Claygate'	£10-12
23310	98	'L.C.', 'Welwyn'	£10-12

AEC Routemaster buses

'London Transport' fleetname
15601a	93	'B.O.A.C.', 'RM 2110'	£11-13
15601b	93	'B.O.A.C.', 'RM 1910'	£11-13
15602a	93	'OVALTINE', 'RM 2103'	£11-13
15602b	93	'OVALTINE', 'RM 1818'	£11-13
15602c	93	'LT', 'RM 40', 'RM 966'	£30-35
c15602	93	'BEATTIES', 'RM 1818'	£15-18
c15602	93	'BRITISH DIECAST MODEL TOYS CATALOGUE'. Deluxe promotional only available with 5th Edition Catalogue. Red body, yellow posters	£15-18
c15602b	95	'BROMLEY PAGEANT', 'RM 2103'	£20-25
c15602c	98	'ASTON MANOR'	£20-25
15605a	93	'EVENING STANDARD', 'RM 1018', route '16'	£11-13

15605b	93	'RM 1277', route '73'	**£11-13**
c15605a	94	'I.A.P.H', 'RM 1277'	**£60-65**
c15605b	94	'BROMLEY PAGEANT', red, 'RM 1018'	**£20-25**
15605c	94	'Louis Dreyfus', 'RM 1277'	**£25-30**
c15605d	94	'Aston Manor', 'RM 158'	**£25-30**
15608a	93	'PICKFORDS', 'RM 1768'	**£18-20**
15608b	93	'PICKFORDS', 'RM 966'	**£65-75**
c15608hw		'TYPHOO', 1994 USA model, 'House of Windsor'	**£40-60**
15608dl	94	'TYPHOO', LT Museum	**£25-30**
c15608dl2		'Aston Manor', route '2b'	**£40-45**
15608e	?	'IAN ALLAN 500th'	**NGPP**
15608f	?	'LT', 'Manchester Museum'	**NGPP**
15610	94	'DALTONS', 'RM 1992'	**£11-13**
c15610	95	'BRITISH AIRWAYS', 'RM 1992'	**£30-35**
c15610s	?	'SUTTON Utd', 'RM 1992'	**£15-18**
15612	93	'FARES FAIR', GS 99908	**GSP**
15614	94	'BEA', 'RM 996'	**£11-13**
15614	94	'RM 40 YEARS'	**£15-20**
15616	95	'TRUMANS', 'RM 291'	**£11-13**
c15618a	?	'LT Red Buses 500th'	**£55-60**
15619	?	'LT Forest Ranger', GS 99911	**GSP**
15620	?	'South London', GS 99911	**GSP**
c15620a	98	'BROMLEY PAGEANT', route '146' (with '159')	**£65-75**
c15620b	98	'LT', route '146'	**£14-17**
15621	97	'BRITISH RAILWAYS'	**£12-15**
15622	97	'Forest Hill', with roundel	**£12-15**
15623	98	'LT', 'Victoria'	**£10-12**
25501	98	'LT', red, RML in GS 99917	**GSP**
25502	98	'LT', green, RML, GS 99917	**GSP**
25503	98	'Stoke Newington', (RML)	**£10-12**
c25503	98	'LT', 'Ramblers Association'	**£12-15**
25504	98	'LT', 'Metroline', (RML)	**£11-13**
25505	99	'East Ham', '15', (RML)	**£11-13**
25507	99	'Dartford', (RML)	**£11-13**

Provincial operators, etc.

15603	93	'BLACK PRINCE', 'X 51'	**£8-11**
15604	93	'SOUTHEND', route '29'	**£8-11**
15604dl	93	'SOUTHEND', route '1'	**£12-15**
15606	93	'EAST YORKSHIRE', no ads	**£8-11**
15606a	95	'E. YORKSHIRE', 'Beatties'	**£18-20**
15607	93	'CLYDESIDE', 'Scotsman'	**£8-11**
15607dl	94	'Model and Collectors Mart'	**£15-18**
15609	93	'MANSFIELD & DISTRICT'	**£8-11**
15609dl	94	'MANSFIELD', in Set 99910	**GSP**
15611	93	'BURNLEY & PENDLE', 180	**£8-11**
15611dl	94	Same, but in GS 99910, 186	**GSP**
15613	94	'BLACKPOOL', '527'	**£12-15**
15615dl	95	'UNITED COUNTIES', '704'	**£8-11**
15617	95	'EAST LONDON', 'RM1527'	**£8-11**
c15617a	95	'EAST LONDON', route '15'	**£20-25**
c15617b	95	'EAST LONDON', route '8'	**£20-25**
c15619a	98	'COBHAM', 'RM 2116'	**£25-30**
c15619b	98	'NORTH WEALD'	**£20-25**
15624	98	'G.M. BUSES', 'Piccadilly'	**£9-12**
15625	98	'HALIFAX', 'Hebden Bridge'	**£9-12**
25504	99	'METROLINE', (RML)	**£9-12**

AEC Routemaster open buses

17801	95	'LONDON COACHES'	**£8-11**
c17801	97	'North Weald Rally'	**£18-20**
17802	95	'LONDON PLUS'	**£8-11**
c17803		'THE BIG BUS Co.'	**£18-22**
17901	94	'LONDON', 'Sightseeing'	**£8-11**
17902	94	'LONDON', 'Metroline'	**£8-11**

AEC Routemaster RCL coach

25601	98	'GREENLINE', 'Forest Hill'	**£18-20**
c25601		'GREENLINE', 'Ramblers'	**£14-16**
25602	99	'LONDON COUNTRY'	**£11-13**
25603	99	'GREENLINE'	**NGPP**

Alexander buses

22701	96	'NORTH WESTERN'	**£10-12**
22702	97	'YORKSHIRE TRACTION'	**£10-12**
22703	97	'ROAD CAR', 'Louth'	**£10-12**
23501	97	'EDINBURGH', 'Oxgangs'	**£10-12**
23502	97	'BOURNEMOUTH'	**£18-20**

23503			not issued
23504	?	'HONG KONG CITYBUS'	**£20-25**
23701	97	'TRENT', 'Derby'	**£10-12**
23702	97	'EAST YORKSHIRE'	**£10-12**
23703	98	'BRADFORD', 'Leeds'	**£10-12**
23704	98	'HALIFAX', 'Mixenden'	**£10-12**
23705	99	'SELNEC', 'Jericho'	**£10-12**
23706	99	'BURY', 'Walmersley'	**£10-12**
23801	97	'GLASGOW', 'Maryhill'	**£10-12**
23802	99	'FISHWICK & SONS'	**£10-12**
24201	97	'MIDLAND RED', 'Colliery'	**£18-20**
24201sb		'MIDLAND RED', 'Duxford'	**£25-30**
24202	97	'E. YORKSHIRE', 'Circular'	**£10-12**
24401	98	'L.T.', 'Sightseeing Tour'	**£10-12**
24402	98	'YORKSHIRE WOOLLEN'	**£10-12**
24501	97	'NEWCASTLE', 'Station'	**£12-15**

Alexander 'Y'-type bus/coach

22501	97	'PREMIER'	**£10-12**
22502	97	'P. M. T.'	**£10-12**
22503	97	'S. M. T.'	**£30-35**
22504	97	'STRATFORD BLUE'	**£10-12**
22505	97	'VENTURE', 'Newcastle'	**£10-12**
22506	97	'MIDLAND RED', 'Hereford'	**£10-12**
22507	98	'WEST RIDING', 'Sheffield'	**£10-12**
22508	98	'CROSVILLE', 'Manchester'	**£10-12**
22509	98	'EAST YORKSHIRE'	**£10-12**
22510	98	'SHEFFIELD CITY', 'Leeds'	**£10-12**
22701	97	'NORTH WESTERN'	**£10-12**
22702	97	'YORKSHIRE TRACTION'	**£10-12**
22703	97	'ROAD CAR'	**£10-12**
22704	97	'HIGHLAND', 'Kyleakin'	**£10-12**
22705	98	'LOTHIAN', 'Juniper Green'	**£10-12**
22706	98	'LANCASTER', 'Morecambe'	**£10-12**
22707	98	'E. SCOTTISH', 'Edinburgh'	**£10-12**
22708	99	'ULSTERBUS', 'Express'	**£11-13**
22709	98	'NATIONAL', 'London'	**£10-12**
E22709	99	'MAIDSTONE'	**£10-12**

Bedford OB coaches

20101	95	'SOUTHERN VECTIS'	**£12-15**
20102	95	'ROYAL BLUE', 'Swanage'	**£8-11**
20103	95	'SOUTHDOWN', GS 99910	**GSP**
20104	95	'GREY CARS', 'Buckfast'	**£8-11**
20105	95	'EASTERN COUNTIES'	**£8-11**
20106	96	'PREMIER TRAVEL'	**£8-11**
20107	96	'PREMIER of WATFORD'	**£8-11**
20108	96	'SOUTH MIDLANDS'	**£8-11**
20109	96	'EAST YORKSHIRE'	**£8-11**
20110	96	'BERE REGIS', 'Relief'	**£8-11**
20111	96	'GREY-GREEN', 'Clacton'	**£8-11**
-- DL	96	'GREY-GREEN', Littlewoods	**£12-15**
20112	96	'WEST YORKSHIRE'	**£8-11**
20113	96	'SHEFFIELD UNITED'	**£8-11**
20114	96	'WILTS & DORSET', 'RAF Uphaven'	**£8-11**
-- DL	98	Pewsey'	**£9-12**
20115	96	'YELLOWAY', 'Bangor'	**£8-11**
20116	96	'BARTON'	**£8-11**
20117	96	'EAST KENT', 'Excursion'	**£18-20**
20118	96	'BRITISH RAILWAYS', 'FWO 615-1229W'	**£20-25**
20119	97	'BRITISH RAILWAYS', 'HWO 881-1203W'	**£10-12**
20120	97	'W. NATIONAL', 'Newquay'	**£18-20**
20121	98	'DEVON GENERAL'	**£18-20**
20121	99	'SKILL'S', 'Filey'	**£10-12**

Bedford SB coaches

18701	95	'ORANGE LUXURY'	**£8-11**
18702	95	'GORWOODS COACHES'	**£8-11**
18703	95	'GREY GREEN'	**£8-11**
18704	95	'SOUTHERN VECTIS'	**£8-11**
18705	95	'B.O.A.C.', 'London Airport'	**£11-13**
18706	95	'BARTON'	**£8-11**
-- DL	95	'BARTON', 'GS Littlewoods'	**£12-15**
18707	95	'STEVENSONS'	**£8-11**
18708	95	'McBRAYNES'	**£12-15**
18709	95	'PREMIER', 'Watford'	**£8-11**
18710	96	'BERE REGIS', 'Dorchester'	**£8-11**
18711	96	'BOLTON TRANSPORT'	**£8-11**
18712	99	'SKILL'S'	**£11-13**

B.E.T. style single-deck buses

24301	97	'PREMIER TRAVEL'	**£10-12**
24302	97	'MACBRAYNES', 'Inverness'	**£10-12**
24303	97	'DEVON GENERAL'	**£10-12**
24304	97	'VENTURE'	**£10-12**
24305	98	'SOUTHDOWN', GS 99915	**GSP**
24306	98	'MAIDSTONE & DISTRICT'	**£12-15**
24307	98	'NORTH WESTERN'	**£10-12**
24308	98	'HIGHLAND', 'Corpack'	**£10-12**
24309	98	'EAST YORKSHIRE'	**£10-12**
24310	98	'HALIFAX', 'Norton Tower'	**£10-12**
24311	98	'WESTERN WELSH'	**£10-12**
24312	98	'CROSVILLE', 'Northwich'	**£10-12**
24313	98	'CITY of MANCHESTER', 'Heywood Darn Hill'	**£10-12**
24314	98	'YORKSHIRE TRACTION'	**£10-12**

Bristol Lodekka buses

13901	92	'BRISTOL', 'Southmead'	**£18-20**
13902	92	'BRISTOL', 'BEATTIES'	**£18-20**
13903			not issued
13904			not issued
13905	94	'EASTERN COUNTIES'	**£8-11**
13906	94	'SOUTHERN VECTIS'	**£18-20**
13907	95	'CUMBERLAND', 'Ewanrigg'	**£8-11**
13908	95	'NOTTS & DERBY', 'Heanor'	**£8-11**
-- DL	95	'NOTTS & DERBY', 'B2'	**£9-12**
13909	95	'CAMBUS', 'Warrington'	**£8-11**
-- DL	96	'New Hospital', certificate	**£8-11**
13910	97	'WESTERN NATIONAL'	**£8-11**
13911	97	'CROSVILLE', 'Warrington'	**£10-12**
14001	92	'BRIGHTON'	**£8-11**
14002	93	'EASTERN NATIONAL'	**£8-11**
-- DL		'EASTERN NATIONAL'	**£18-20**
c14002		'PSV Circle'	**£18-20**
14003	93	'CROSVILLE', std and deluxe	**£8-11**
14004	93	'CHELTENHAM'	**£8-11**
c14004		same + 'Classic Bus H Trust'	**£25-30**
14005	93	'SOUTHDOWN', in Set 99907	**GSP**
14006	93	'LINCOLNSHIRE', 'TSB'	**£8-11**
-- DL	97	'BATH SERVICES'	**£45-50**
14007	93	'THAMES VALLEY'	**£8-11**
c14007		'BEATTIES'	**£20-25**
14008	96	'MORRIS BROS'	**£8-11**
14009	98	'HANTS & DORSET', 'Poole'	**£9-12**
14101	92	'UNITED', 'Darlington'	**£18-20**
14102	92	'UNITED', 'BEATTIES'	**£18-20**
14103	98	'BAXTER'S', 'Mull'	**£9-12**
14201	92	'ALEXANDER'	**£8-11**
c14201		'Scottish Bus Museum'	**£18-20**
c14201a		'Heart of the Pennines Run'	**£20-25**
14202	93	'MIDLAND GENERAL'	**£8-11**
--- DL	93	'MIDLAND GENERAL'	**£8-11**

Bristol LS single deck buses

16301	93	'UNITED'	**£18-20**
16302	93	'EASTERN NATIONAL'	**£18-20**
16303	94	'THAMES VALLEY'	**£8-11**
16304	94	'WESTERN NATIONAL'	**£12-15**
16305			not issued
16306			not issued
16307	94	'WILTS & DORSET'	**£8-11**
16308	94	'LINCOLNSHIRE', route '2a'	**£8-11**
16309	94	'GREENLINE', in Set 99909	**GSP**
16310	94	'EASTERN COUNTIES'	**£8-11**
16311	95	'BRISTOL', 'Cheltenham'	**£8-11**
-- DL	96	'BATH SERVICES', 'Devizes'	**£9-12**
16312	96	'WILTS & DORSET', 'Andover'	**£8-11**
-- DL	98	'Basingstoke'	**£8-11**
16313	96	'SOUTHERN NATIONAL'	**£8-11**
16314	96	'WEST YORKSHIRE', 'York'	**£8-11**
16315	97	'SOUTHERN VECTIS'	**£8-11**
16316	98	'EASTERN NATIONAL'	**£11-13**
16317	99	'PROVINCIAL'	**£11-13**
16318	99	'MIDLAND GENERAL'	**£9-12**

Bristol MW coaches

16201	93	'BRISTOL GREYHOUND'	**£18-20**
16202	93	'CROSVILLE', 'Private'	**£18-20**
16203	94	'ROYAL BLUE'	**£40-45**
16204	94	'SOUTH MIDLAND'	**£8-11**
16205	94	'WILTS & DORSET'	**£8-11**

16206 94 'LINCOLNSHIRE'......................**£8-11**
16207 95 'EASTERN COUNTIES'............**£8-11**
16208 95 'SOUTHERN VECTIS' (LS)......**£8-11**
16209 95 'UNITED', 'London', (LS) **£8-11**
16210 96 'ROYAL BLUE'......................**£25-30**
16211 96 'MORRIS BROS'......................**£8-11**
16212 99 'EASTERN SCOTTISH' **£10-12**

Bristol RE/LL single deck buses
25001 98 'SOUTHERN NATIONAL' **£10-12**
25002 99 'CUMBERLAND'......................**£10-12**
25003 99 'EASTERN NATIONAL'..........**£10-12**
25101 98 'UNITED', 'Sunderland'............**£10-12**
25201 98 'BADGERLINE', 'Weston'.........**£10-12**
25202 98 'TRENT', 'Matlock'.................**£10-12**
25203 98 'CROSVILLE'.........................**£10-12**
25204 98 'BRISTOL', 'Swindon' **£10-12**
25205 99 'WILTS. & DORSET'...............**£11-13**
25206 99 'WESTERN NATIONAL' **£11-13**

Bristol VR double-deck buses
18501 98 'SOUTHERN NATIONAL' **£10-12**
18502 98 'EASTERN COUNTIES'...........**£10-12**
18601 95 'SOUTH WALES'....................**£10-12**
18602 97 'WILTS & DORSET' **£18-20**
18603 97 'EAST YORKSHIRE'.............**£10-12**
18604 97 'CROSVILLE'.........................**£10-12**
20301 95 'EAST YORKSHIRE'.............**£10-12**
20302 96 'BRISTOL' **£10-12**
20303 96 'SOUTHDOWN', 'Solenteer' ...**£18-20**
20304 96 'MANCHESTER', 'Gatley'......**£10-12**
20305 96 'WEST YORKSHIRE'.............**£10-12**
-- DL 97 'YORK CITY & DISTRICT',
          'Ashley Park', numbered cert. ...**£12-15**
20306 99 'SELNEC CHESHIRE' **£11-13**
20401 96 'BADGERLINE', 'Bristol' **£18-20**
20402 96 'UNITED', 'Durham' **£10-12**
20403 96 'DEVON GENERAL' **£12-15**
20404 96 'EAST KENT', 'Singleton'......**£10-12**
20405 96 'NORTHERN', 'Newcastle'......**£10-12**
20406 96 'CAMBUS' **£8-11**
-- SB 96 'CAMBUS', Duxford special.....**£18-20**
20407 97 'CROSVILLE', 'Denbigh' **£10-12**
20408 97 'EASTERN COUNTIES' **£8-11**
20409 96 'SOUTHERN VECTIS' **£18-20**
20410 96 'SOUTHDOWN 75', set 99912.....GSP
20411 97 'WESTERN NATIONAL'..........**£10-12**
20412 98 'EASTERN NATIONAL' **£10-12**
20413 97 'GREAT YARMOUTH' **£10-12**
20414 98 'HEDINGHAM' **£10-12**
20415 98 'BLUE BUS', 'Gt Yarmouth'......**£10-12**
-- SB 98 'BLUE BUS', 'Showbus'...........**£12-15**
20416 98 'MAIDSTONE & DISTRICT' ...**£10-12**
20417 ....not issued
20418 98 'WALLACE ARNOLD'.............**£10-12**
20419 99 'ENSIGNBUS' **£11-13**

Bristol Windover coaches
20801 96 'THAMES VALLEY' **£8-11**
-- DL 98 'THAMES VALLEY' **£10-12**
20802 ? 'NORTH WESTERN' **£8-11**

Daimler CVG buses
19801 95 'MANCHESTER'.....................**£8-11**
-- DL 96 'MANCHESTER',
          Classic Bus magazine................**£20-25**
19802 95 'PMT'.................................**£8-11**
19803 95 'DUNDEE', std or deluxe **£8-11**
19804 95 'COVENTRY' **£8-11**
--- SB 95 'COVENTRY SHOWBUS' **£20-25**
19805 96 'WEST MIDLANDS' **£8-11**
-- DL 97 'WEST MIDLANDS',
          'Earlsdon', certificate **£9-12**
19806 97 'HALIFAX' **£10-12**
19807 98 'LANCASHIRE UNITED' **£10-12**
19808 98 'WEST BROMWICH' **£10-12**
c19808   'West Bromwich Classic Bus'....**£15-18**
19809 98 'SELNEC', 'Bolton' **£10-12**
19810 98 'LEEDS CITY', 'Halton' **£10-12**
19811 99 'DERBY', 'Shelton Lock'..........**£10-12**

Daimler DMS buses
25701 99 'L. T.', 'Edgware Station'....**£11-13**
25702 99 'ENSIGNBUS'.......................**£11-13**
25703 99 'S. YORKSHIRE'....................**£11-13**
25801 99 'WEST MIDLANDS'................**£11-13**
25802 99 'MIDLAND RED'....................**£11-13**

Daimler Fleetline buses
18001 94 'BIRMINGHAM'.....................**£18-20**
18002 95 'MANCHESTER', 'Chorlton'.....**£8-11**
18003 96 'BIRKENHEAD', 'Woodside'.....**£8-11**
18004 ? 'K.M.B.'....................................NGPP
18005 99 'DERBY, 'Henley Green'...........**£11-13**
18201 94 'LONDON COUNTRY'..............**£8-11**
18202 ? 'LT', in GS 99909 ....GSP
18203 ? 'LC', 'Blue Arrow' **£9-12**
25401 98 'BIRMINGHAM', 'Quinton' **£9-12**

Dennis Dart - see Plaxton Pointer

Guy Arab double deck buses
26201 99 'COVENTRY', 'Willenhall' **£10-12**
26301 99 'L.T.' utility bus, 'Wanstead' ...**£10-12**

Harrington Cavalier coaches
11901 ....not issued
11902 91 'YELLOWAYS' **£20-25**
11903 92 'GREY-GREEN'......................**£9-11**
12101 91 'SOUTHDOWN'.....................**£30-35**
12102 92 'EAST YORKS' **£11-13**
12103 92 'HEBBLE' **£11-13**
c12103 93 'PENNINE RALLY'..............**£15-18**
12104 92 'SURREY', in Gift Set 99906........GSP
12105 92 'NEATH & CARDIFF' **£8-11**
12106 93 'VALIANT' **£8-11**
-- DL 93 'VALIANT' **£8-11**
12107 93 'SOUTHDOWN', in GS 99907. ....GSP
12108 94 'RIBBLE' **£8-11**
12109 94 'ROBIN HOOD' **£8-11**
12110 96 'FLIGHTS TRAVEL Ltd' **£8-11**
12111 98 'CHARLIE'S CARS', 'West' **£10-12**
12112 99 'WALLACE ARNOLD' **£11-13**

Harrington Grenadier coaches
12201 91 'BLACK & WHITE'...............**£18-20**
12202 92 'PREMIER' **£8-11**
12203 92 'BARTONS', in Gift Set 99905 .....GSP
12204 92 'ORANGE LUXURY' **£8-11**
-- DL 92 'ORANGE LUXURY' **£18-20**
12301 91 'MAIDSTONE' **£25-30**
12302 92 'GREY CARS' **£8-11**
12303 92 'TIMPSONS', in Set 99906 ....GSP
12304 92 'SOUTHDOWN' **£11-13**
12305 93 'ELLEN SMITH', std and DL **£8-11**
c12305 93 'Ribble Road Safety'...........**£18-20**
12306 93 'B.O.A.C.', std and deluxe **£11-13**

Leeds Horsfield tram
13402 91 'TIZER'..............................**£12-15**
13402b 91 'TIZER', brown chassis.......**£45-50**
13403 92 'JACOBS'..............................**£12-15**
13404 99 Wartime finish **£10-12**
13405 99 'SAFETY FIRST' **£10-12**
13406 99 'MACKESONS' **£10-12**
14301 92 'YORKSHIRE POST'.............**£12-15**
14302 93 'WHITBREADS' **£20-25**
14303 94 'YORKS. EVENING POST'......**£12-15**
13404 95 'LEEDS', wartime livery **£10-12**
13405 97 'SAFETY FIRST' **£10-12**

Leyland Atlantean buses
see also Alexander and Daimler Fleetline

16501 94 'RIBBLE' **£25-30**
16502 94 'WALLASEY' **£25-30**
16503 94 'DEVON GENERAL' **£25-30**
16504 94 'MAIDSTONE', 'Hollington'.....**£25-30**
16505 94 'PLYMOUTH' **£8-11**
16506 94 'SHEFFIELD', 'Tetley' **£8-11**
16507 94 'GATESHEAD' **£8-11**
16508 94 'NORTHERN' **£8-11**
16509 95 'LEICESTER', route '26'............**£8-11**

16510 94 'BIRMINGHAM' **£8-11**
16511 95 'HULL', route '430'................**£8-11**
16512 ? 'LIVERPOOL', GS 19907 ....GSP
16513 95 'SALFORD', 'Walkden'.............**£8-11**
16514 95 'STEVENSONS', 'Uttoxeter' ...**£8-11**
-- DL 98 'STEVENSONS', 'Burton'.........**£10-12**
16515 95 'TRENT', 'Sileby'.....................**£8-11**
16516 95 'PORTSMOUTH', 'Eastney' **£8-11**
-- DL 96 'South Parade Pier'.................**£18-20**
16517 96 'GWR', 'Cornish Riviera'..........**£8-11**
16518 96 'LIVERPOOL', 'Speke' **£12-15**
16519 97 'SCOUT', 'Burnley'................**£10-12**
18101 94 'LT XA13', 'BOAC'................**£30-35**
18102 95 'LT XA9', 'Pimlico', '24' **£20-25**
--- DL 95 'LT XA9', route 'P3'..............NGPP
18103 96 'LEEDS CITY', 'Swinnow' **£8-11**
-- DL 98 'LEEDS CITY', 'Bramley'........**£10-12**
18104 97 'LONDON COUNTRY',
          'Reigate'...............................**£18-20**
18105 ? 'CHINA MOTOR BUS'.............**£20-25**
18106 ? 'CHINA MOTOR BUS'...............NGPP
18202 94 'LONDON XF2', in Set 99909......GSP
18203 97 'LONDON COUNTRY',
          'Chells'...............................**£10-12**
24701 98 'MANCHESTER','Piccadilly'....**£18-20**
24702 98 'DEVON GENERAL' **£18-20**
24703 98 'PLYMOUTH' **£10-12**
24704 98 'SELNEC', 'Reddish' **£10-12**
24705 98 'LANCASTER', 'University' **£10-12**

Leyland Duple coaches
26801 99 'SKILL'S', 'York' **£10-12**

Leyland National single deckers
14401 92 'GREENLINE' **£18-20**
14402 92 'MANCHESTER'.....................**£8-11**
14403 93 'UNITED', std and deluxe **£8-11**
14404 98 'LONDON UNITED'................**£11-13**
14601 94 'RIBBLE', short, Mk.I, red **£25-30**
14701 93 'McGILLS'..............................**£18-20**
14901 97 'YORK CITY RIDER'..............**£9-12**
15001 ? 'SOUTHDOWN', GS 99912 ....GSP
15101 92 'HANTS & DORSET' **£8-11**
c15101b 93 'Hants & Dorset', 'Beatties' **£25-30**
15102 93 'CROSVILLE', 'Woodside'........**£8-11**
c15102a 93 'CROSVILLE', Club model ...**£11-13**
c15102b 93 'CROSVILLE', 'Beatties' **£30-35**
15103 93 'NORTHERN', std and deluxe.....**£8-11**
15104 93 'BRISTOL', 'Temple Meads'.....**£20-25**
--- DL 93 'BRISTOL', 'Evening Post'.......**£18-20**
15105 99 'PROVINCIAL', 'Fareham' **£11-13**
-- DL 98 'Cheltenham Road'.................**£10-12**
16601 94 'L.T.', 'Kingston' **£18-20**
16602 94 'EASTBOURNE' **£8-11**
16603 95 'ENSIGNBUS' **£8-11**
16701 94 'LONDON LS 6'.....................**£18-20**
16901 93 'LONDON LS 487', GS 9908 ....GSP
17201 94 'TRENT', 'Mickleover' **£8-11**
17202 94 'THAMESWAY' **£8-11**
17203 95 'YORKSHIRE TERRIER' **£8-11**
-- DL 97 'YORKSHIRE TERRIER',
          'Bradway', certificate **£9-12**
17204 97 'WILTS & DORSET' **£9-12**
17205 97 'MAIDSTONE & DISTRICT' ...**£20-25**
17206 97 'MIDLAND RED', Ashby **£10-12**
17207 ....not issued
17208 98 'WESTERN NATIONAL' **£10-12**
17209 99 'J. FISHWICK & SONS'..........**£11-13**
17301 95 'READING', Volvo **£12-15**
17401 98 'BLUE BUS', 'Gt. Yarmouth'....**£10-12**

Leyland RTL double-deck buses
11101 90 'CONTRACTUS', Set 19903 ....**£11-13**
11102 90 'BOAT SHOW', Set 19903 ......**£11-13**
-- DL 90 'BOAT SHOW',
          (LT Museum only)....................**£28-30**
11103 90 'WILKINSON SWORD',
          singly and in Set 19903 ....**£11-13**
C11103a 92 'LT', 'PSV Circle'.................NGPP
C11103b 93 'LT', 'Bromley Pageant' ....NGPP
11104 90 'LOCKEYS', black, no ads.......**£18-20**
11105 91 'BRYLCREEM', 'RTL 2' **£25-30**

11106 91 'FISHERMANS FRIEND',
    'RTL 285', special box............**£18-22**
-- DL 93 'FISHERMANS FRIEND'........**£20-25**
11107 92 'BARTON', in Set 99905..............GSP
11108 92 'A1 SERVICE' **£12-15**
11109 95 'OK MOTOR SERVICES' **£9-11**
11110 96 'STEVENSONS', 'Uttoxeter' **£9-11**
-- DL 98 'STEVENSON'S', 'Anslow'......**£11-13**
11110 96 Same but with AEC grille ...**£175-200**
11111 ? 'WALSALL' **£11-13**
22801 ? 'LT', 'Guernsey Toms', 99913.......GSP
-- DL ? 'LT', 'Ireland by Rail' **£65-75**

Leyland STD double-deck buses
20201 94 'L.T.', 'Victoria' **£25-30**
20202 97 'L.T.', 'Typhoo', in Set 99913.......GSP
-- DL 97 'L.T.', 'Rail & Sea' ....NGPP

Leyland Tiger buses and coaches
18301 94 'YORKSHIRE WOOLLEN' **£12-15**
18302 94 'SUNDERLAND' **£8-11**
18303 95 'BARTON', route '26' **£12-15**
18304 95 'YORKSHIRE WOOLLEN',
    Wartime finish, + in GS 19906....**£8-11**
18305 95 'EAST MIDLAND', 'Retford'......**£8-11**
-- DL 97 'Clipstone' **£9-12**
18306 96 'WESTERN WELSH' **£8-11**
-- DL 96 'WESTERN WELSH' **£11-13**
18401 94 'WEST RIDING' **£8-11**
18402 95 'LANCASHIRE UNITED' **£8-11**
18403 95 'COUNTY MOTORS' **£8-11**
18404 95 'DONCASTER', '11 Arksey' **£8-11**
c18404 'DONCASTER', 'Ian Allan' **£8-11**
18405 95 'LINCOLNSHIRE', 'Grantham' ..**£8-11**
-- DL 97 'Mablethorpe' **£9-12**
18406 95 'O. K. MOTOR SERVICES' **£8-11**
c18406 'O. K. M. S.', 'Beatties' **£8-11**
18407 96 'YORKSHIRE TRACTION' **£8-11**

Leyland Titan PD1 Lowbridge
15801 94 'WIGAN CORPORATION' **£8-11**
15801 95 'WIGAN', Club Model..............**£12-15**
15802 93 'EAST KENT', red / white...........**£8-11**
15803 95 'EAST MIDLAND' **£8-11**
-- DL 96 'EAST MIDLAND', de-luxe **£10-12**
15804 96 'SCOUT', 'Preston'....................**£25-30**

Leyland Titan PD1 Highbridge
15901 93 'LEICESTER', std or deluxe........**£8-11**
15902 94 'RIBBLE', 'Dulux' **£20-25**
15903 94 'SAMUEL LEDGARD' **£8-11**
15904 94 'CITY COACHES' **£8-11**
15905 95 'SALFORD CITY' **£8-11**
15906 99 'LANCASHIRE UNITED' **£11-13**

Leyland Titan PD2 Lowbridge
16001 93 'TODMORDEN', 'LMS',
    with 'SUMMIT' side blind **£20-25**
    'TODMORDEN', 'BR'.................**£25-30**
16002 93 'TODMORDEN' **£15-20**
16003 94 'EAST KENT', 'Littlewoods' **£8-11**
16004 94 'DEVON GENERAL' **£8-11**
16005 94 'MIDLAND RED', 'Anstey'........**£8-11**
16006 94 'WEST RIDING' **£8-11**
16007 95 'NORTH WESTERN' **£8-11**
-- DL 96 'NORTH WESTERN', deluxe ...**£10-12**

Leyland Titan PD2 Highbridge
16101 93 'WIGAN CORPORATION' **£8-11**
c16101 95 'WIGAN', Club Model **£18-20**
16102 93 'LEICESTER CITY' **£8-11**
16103 94 'CROSVILLE', 'Beach' **£15-20**
16104 94 'LEEDS' **£8-11**
16105 94 'SHEFFIELD' **£8-11**
16106 94 'LIVERPOOL', in GS 19907 ....GSP
16107 95 'STRATFORD BLUE' **£8-11**
-- DL 99 'STRATFORD BLUE' **£11-13**
16108 ? 'SOUTHDOWN', GS 99910 ....GSP
16109 95 'PORTSMOUTH', 'Farlington' ...**£8-11**
-- DL 97 'PORTSMOUTH', 'Guildhall' ...**£18-20**
16110 96 'LIVERPOOL', 'Old Swan' **£8-11**
16111 96 'BIRMINGHAM' **£8-11**
c16111 96 'ASTON MANOR' **£18-20**

16112 97 'STOCKPORT', 'Piccadilly' **£8-11**
16113 97 'KING ALFRED' **£10-12**
16114 98 'NEWCASTLE' **£10-12**
16115 98 'GREAT YARMOUTH' **£10-12**
16116 98 'CITY of EXETER' **£10-12**
16117 99 'HALIFAX', 'Newlands' **£10-12**

Leyland Titan PD2/12
20001 95 'MAIDSTONE & DISTRICT' ...**£15-18**
20002 95 'RIBBLE'. **£8-11**
20003 96 'BOLTON TRANSPORT' **£8-11**
-- DL 96 'Belmont' **£9-11**
20004 96 'SUNDERLAND'
    'West Hartlepool'......................**£8-11**
-- DL 97 'SUNDERLAND', 'Durham'......**£8-11**
20005 96 'BIRKENHEAD' **£8-11**

Leyland TS8 single deck buses
18306
-- DL 99 'WESTERN WELSH' **£10-12**
18497 98 'YORKSHIRE TRACTION' **£10-12**

Leyland Windover coaches
20901 96 'YORKSHIRE TRACTION' **£10-12**
20902 97 'HEBBLE', 'Blackpool' **£10-12**
20903 ? 'SOUTHDOWN', set 99915 ....GSP

Mercedes-Benz Minibus
24801 98 'EASTERN NATIONAL'.........**£10-12**
24802 98 'WESTERN NATIONAL'.........**£10-12**
24803 98 'BADGERLINE', 'Ensleigh' **£10-12**
24804 98 'BRISTOL', 'Bradley Stoke' **£10-12**
24805 98 'MAIDSTONE & DISTRICT' ...**£10-12**
24806 98 'THAMESWAY' **£10-12**
24807 99 'SCARBOROUGH' **£10-12**
24901 98 'BREWERS', 'Neath' **£10-12**

Plaxton Panorama Elite coaches
15701 93 'SOUTH WEST NBC'................**£11-13**
15701dl and 15702dl:
    9? 'UNITED', (a pair of buses) **£35-45**
15702 93 'RIBBLE NBC', 'National'........**£11-13**
15703 93 'EAST KENT', std or deluxe......**£8-11**
15704 93 'ABBOTTS', std or deluxe.........**£8-11**
15705 93 'SHEFFIELD', std or deluxe......**£8-11**
15706 93 'BRISTOL', std or deluxe..........**£8-11**
15707 93 'GREY GREEN', std or deluxe ...**£8-11**
15708 94 'BARTONS' **£18-20**
15709 94 'SOUTHDOWN' **£45-50**
15710 98 'WALLACE ARNOLD' **£10-12**

Plaxton Pointer single-deck buses
20601 96 'METROLINE' **£14-16**
20602 96 'BADGERLINE' **£12-15**
20603 96 'THAMESWAY', 'Canvey' **£8-12**
-- DL 97 'THAMESWAY', 'Basildon' **£10-12**
20604 96 'YORKSHIRE TERRIER',
    'Darnall'.................................**£8-12**
-- DL 97 'Crystal Peaks' **£8-12**
20605 96 'YORKSHIRE TRACTION' **£8-12**
20606 96 'BREWERS', 'Bridgend' **£8-12**
20607 96 'BRIGHTON BUSES' **£18-20**
20608 96 'P.M.T.', 'Talke Pits' **£8-12**
20609 97 'PLYMOUTH' **£18-20**
20610 96 'MANCHESTER', 'Radcliffe' **£8-12**
20611 97 'WESTERN NATIONAL' **£8-12**
20612 97 'METROBUS' **£8-12**
20613 97 'EASTERN NATIONAL'...........**£8-12**
20614 97 'LEEDS CITYLINK' **£8-12**
20615 97 'THAMESDOWN' **£8-12**
20616 97 'DOCKLANDS TRANSIT' **£8-12**
20617 97 'GREY-GREEN' **£8-12**
20618 9? 'MACAU' **£18-20**
20619 9? 'MAINLINE' Volvo **£18-20**
20620 98 'MAIDSTONE & DISTRICT' **£8-12**
20621 98 'LEA VALLEY', 'Turnford' **£8-12**
20622 98 'ARRIVA' **£8-12**
20623 98 'BLUE BUS' **£8-12**

Reeves Burgess Beaver Mini-bus
25901 99 'BARTON' **£10-12**
25902 99 'NOTTINGHAM' **£10-12**

Original box types

Standard issues of single models were originally packed in rigid card window boxes coloured grey, with black and red printing. Special boxes were made for certain promotional models.

White boxes (with black printing) were used initially for the 'FISHERMANS FRIEND' issues that were part of an 'on-pack offer' promotion, and a subsequent RT bus promotion was presented in a pale blue box.

Certain of the models were designated 'De Luxe' and acquired additional detail or plastic 'loads' of various kinds. Each was packed in a 'double blister-pack' designed to hang on display stand pegs or stand (untidily) on a shelf. The first of the Gift Sets ('Tate & Lyle') was designed to look like a book (even having 'Volume One' printed on its blue card covering). The inner container was plain white expanded polystyrene. Subsequently the 'Rank Hovis' set (designated 'Volume Two') had an inner container of improved appearance with a flock base and clear plastic covering

Current box types

Standard issues are currently presented in black window boxes with light red printing. A similar box in royal blue is used for the De Luxe range, while standard commercial vehicles boxes are maroon. The Grocery Series have cream boxes, the Brewery Series have green boxes, and Gift Sets have special packaging appropriate to the contents.

New issues

AEC Ergomatic trucks
13801	97	'MIDLAND RED', tanker	£9-12
21501	96	'PHILLIPS', 8-wheel tipper	£8-11
21602	96	'SHORE PORTERS', flatbed	£8-11
21604	98	'FEDERATION BREWERY'	£9-12
21802	99	'TRUMAN'S', chain lorry	£8-11
22101	96	'EXPRESS DAIRY', artic	£8-11
22102	?	'TAYFORTH McKINNON'	£8-11
22601	96	'SPIERS of MELKSHAM'	£8-11
22602	97	'BRITISH ROAD SERVICES'	£9-12
23001	98	'BRS BRISTOL', box van	£9-12
23101	97	'WOODCOCK', brick lorry	£9-12
26001	98	'BRS LEEDS', 8-w flatbed	£9-12

AEC articulated trucks
19501	94	'HOOVER', artic. box van	£8-11
19502	95	'PICKFORDS', artic. box van	£8-11
19503	96	'HITCHMANS DAIRIES', box	£8-11
19601	95	'B.R.S.', artic. flatbed	£12-15

AEC 6-wheel box vans
10501	89	'LONDON CARRIERS'	£5-7
10501	89	'LONDON CARRIERS', darker green	£6-8
10501dl	91	'LONDON CARRIERS', in Set 99903	GSP
10502	89	'START-RITE'	£4-6
10503	90	'BRS', 'Huddersfield'	£6-8
10503dl	91	'BRS', deluxe, Set 99903.	GSP
--	91	'BRS', 'EFE Club 91'	£8-10
10504	90	'PEK PORK'	£5-7
10505	90	'OXYDOL'	£5-7
10506	91	'HOOVER'	£12-15
10507	93	'LORD RAYLEIGH'S'	£12-15
10905dl	92	'WELCHS TRANSPORT'	£8-10
c105001		'FISHERMANS FRIEND' `89	£8-10

AEC 8-wheel box vans
11001	89	'CROFT SHERRY'	£4-6
11002	89	'PICKFORDS'	£8-10
11002dl	91	'PICKFORDS', Set 99903.	GSP
11003	90	'TATE & LYLE' in Set 19901	GSP
11004	90	'RANK HOVIS', Set 19902.	GSP
11004dl	93	'RANK HOVIS', extra detail	£8-10
11005	90	'LACONS'	£8-10
11006	91	'ROSES LIME JUICE'	£8-10
11007	95	'BOUTS CARRIERS'	£9-11

AEC 6-wheel dropside wagons
10301	90	'FENLAND AGGREGATES'	£4-6
10301dl	91	Same but with plastic 'load'	£8-10
10302	90	'CYRIL RIDGEON'	£4-6
10302dl	91	Same but with plastic 'load'	£8-10
10303	90	'J. D. LOWN'	£4-6
10303dl	91	Same but with plastic 'load'	£8-10
c103001		'FISHERMANS FRIEND' `89	£35-40

AEC 8-wheel dropside wagons
10604dl	92	'MOBILOIL', with 'load'	£11-13
10801	89	'BRITISH STEEL'	£4-6
10801dl	92	Same but with plastic 'load'	£8-10
10802	89	'WHITBREAD'	£4-6
10802dl	91	Same but with plastic 'load'	£8-10
10803	90	'MARLEY TILES'	£11-13
10804	91	'MACREADYS'	£5-7
10804dl	92	Same but with plastic 'load'	£8-10
10805	91	'TAYLOR WOODROW' in GS 19904	
10805dl	93	Same but singly with 'load'	£8-10
- dl2	93	Model Collector offer version	£35-40
10806dl	93	'ROSES LIME'	£8-10
11005dl	92	'LACONS', with 'load'	£11-13
c108001	90	'FISHERMANS FRIEND'	£10-15

AEC 6-wheel flatbeds
10701	89	'FURLONG Bros.'	£4-6
10701dl	91	Same but with plastic 'load'	£8-10
10702	89	'BLUE CIRCLE'	£5-7
10702dl	91	Same but with plastic 'load'	£8-10
10703	90	'WIMPEY', yellow/black	£5-7
10703	90	'WIMPEY', orange / black	£5-7
10703dl	92	'WIMPEY', with plastic 'load'	£8-10
10503dl	92	'BRS', plastic 'load'	£18-20
10704dl	94	'J.D. LOWN'	£11-13
10904dl	93	'RANK HOVIS'	£11-13

AEC 8-wheel flatbeds
10401	89	'BATH & PORTLAND'	£4-6
10401dl	91	Same but with 'load'	£8-10
10402	89	'LONDON BRICK'	£6-7
10402dl	91	Same but with plastic 'load'	£8-10

AEC 6-wheel tankers
10901	89	'HEYGATES'	£4-6
10902	89	'LORD RAYLEIGHS'	£4-6
10903	90	'L.P.G.', white round tank	£4-6
10903dl	93	'L.P.G.', silver oval tank, and in Set 99904	£8-10
10904	90	'RANK HOVIS', in Set 99902	GSP
10905	90	'WELCHS TRANSPORT'	£5-7

AEC 8-wheel tankers
10601	89	'CENTURY OIL'	£4-6
10601dl	91	also in Set 99904	GSP
10602	89	'J. & H. BUNN'	£4-6
10603	90	'TATE & LYLE', in Set 19901	GSP
10604	90	'MOBILGAS'	£8-10
10604dl	91	'MOBILGAS', in Set 99904	GSP
10605	90	'REGENT'	£12-15
10606dl	93	'WHITBREAD', with ladder	£8-10

AEC 8-wheel tippers
12001	90	'WIMPEY', yellow / black	£8-10
12002	90	'TARMAC'	£8-10
12002dl	92	Same but with plastic 'load'	£15-18
12003	91	'TAYLOR WOODROW', in Set 19904	GSP
12003dl	92	Same but with 'load'	£8-10
12004	91	'KETTON'	£11-13

Albion Ergomatic trucks
21603	97	'BRS', rigid flatbed	£10-12
21801	96	'W.J. RICH & Sons'	£10-12
21802	?	'TRUMANS'	£11-13

Atkinson articulated trucks
13001	91	'TSL', car transporter	£11-13
13002	91	'SWIFTS', car transporter	£11-13
13003	92	'MIDLAND CAR', transporter	£11-13
13004	93	'CLASSIC', car transporter	£11-13
19301	95	'SUTTONS', red flatbed lorry	£8-11
19302	95	'BOWKERS', flatbed, 'load'	£8-11
19303	96	'PARKINSONS', covered load	£8-11
19401	95	'FLOWERS', box van	£8-11
19402	95	'TATE & LYLE', box van	£8-11
19403	96	'MONKS TRANSPORT'	£8-11
19404	97	'KRAFT', box van	£8-11
19405	99	'BRS Door to Door', box van	£11-13

Atkinson rigid trucks
12501	92	'WELLS DRINKS', box van	£18-22
12601	91	'McNICHOLAS', dropside	£6-8
12601dl	91	Same but with 'load'	£8-10
12701	91	'CHARRINGTONS', tanker	£12-15
12801	92	'McPHEES', flatbed truck	£35-40
12802	94	'SUTTONS', flatbed truck	£11-13
12803	96	'AARON HENSHALL' flat	£11-13
12901	91	'FYFFES', box van	£12-15
13101	96	'DENTS of SPENNYMOOR'	£8-11
13201	94	'SUTTONS', tanker	£8-11
13202	97	'M & B', beer tanker	£9-12
13203	97	'MACKESON' beer tanker	£9-12
13301	91	'St.ALBANS', tipping wagon	£8-11
13301dl	93	'St.ALBANS', extra detail	£8-11
13501	98	'PICKFORDS', oval tanker	£10-12
13701	92	'FINA', tanker	£25-30

Bedford TK articulated vehicles
22001	96	'SCHREIBER', artic box van	£10-12
22002	97	'WAVY LINE', artic box van	£10-12
22003	97	'V. G. FOODSTORES', box	£10-12
22004	97	'VLADIVAR VODKA', box	£10-12
22201	96	'BRITISH RAILWAYS'	£30-35
22202	96	'BRS'	£10-12
22203	97	'S. G. B.'	£10-12
22204	97	'BRITISH RAIL', flatbed	£10-12
22205	98	'BRITISH RAILWAYS', 'Door to Door', flatbed	£10-12

Bedford TK rigid trucks
21201	96	'BLOXWICH' dropside	£10-12
21202	96	'BRS'	£10-12
21202	96	'VP WINE' dropside	£10-12
21701	?	'BRS'	£10-12
21701dl	?	'BRS', Littlewoods	£12-15
21901	96	'BARTON' flatbed, load	£10-12
21902	98	'COURAGE', railside	£10-12
22901	97	'SOUTHERN BRS', box van	£10-12
22902	97	'SAINSBURY'S', box van	£10-12
22903			not issued
22904	97	'GOLDENLAY', box van	£10-12
22905	97	'BIRDS EYE', box van	£10-12
22906	97	'WAGON WHEELS', box van	£10-12
22907			not issued
22908	98	'ROADLINE', short box van	£10-12
22909	99	'BRS TRUCK RENTAL'	£10-12
23101	97	'GREY-GREEN', luton van	£10-12
23401	97	'WHITBREAD' beer lorry	£12-15
23601	98	'GREY-GREEN', luton van	£10-12
23602	98	'PICKFORDS', luton van	£18-20
23603	98	'PICKFORDS', all blue	£10-12
23604	99	'CROSVILLE', luton van	£10-12
24101	97	'S. A. BRAINS' dropside	£10-12
24102	98	'GREENE KING', dropside	£10-12
24103	99	'WATNEYS', dropside	£10-12

Bedford TK Rigid and Trailer
24001	97	'MYER'S BEDS', box trailer	£10-12
24002	98	'BRS PARCELS Ltd', box	£10-12

Leyland Ergomatic trucks
21601	96	'HOLT LANE TRANSPORT'	£10-12
21602	96	'SHORE PORTERS'	£10-12
22103	96	'R. WHITE'S DRINKS'	£10-12
22104	97	'TESCO', artic. box van	£10-12
22301	96	'MAJOR' tanker	£10-12
24601	98	'GUINNESS', malt carrier	£10-12

Open Touring Cars

These models were issued as pairs in a single box and it is to this 'twin-pack' that the price range refers.

1991	11401	Triumph Roadster (Red)	packed with	11601	Triumph Vitesse (White)	£12-15
1991	11402	Triumph Roadster (Black)	packed with	11602	Triumph Vitesse (Light Blue)	£5-8
1992	11403	Triumph Roadster (Blue)	packed with	11603	Triumph Vitesse (Red)	£12-15
1992	11404	Triumph Roadster (Dark Green)	packed with	11604	Triumph Vitesse (Dark Blue)	£5-8
1991	11501	MG MGB (Dark Green)	packed with	11701	Austin-Healey Sprite (Yellow)	£12-15
1991	11502	MG MGB (Red)	packed with	11702	Austin-Healey Sprite (White)	£5-8
1992	11503	MG MGB (Orange)	packed with	11703	Austin-Healey Sprite (Green)	£5-8
1992	11504	MG MGB (Black)	packed with	11704	Austin-Healey Sprite (Red)	£5-8

Gift Sets

19901	1990	'TATE & LYLE'	10105 AEC Bus, 11003 8-wheel Van, 10603 8-wheel Tanker	£30-35
19902	1990	'RANK HOVIS'	10106 AEC Bus, 11004 8-wheel Van, 10904 6-wheel Tanker	£20-25
19903	1990	'The RTL Story'	11101 'Boat Show', 11102 'Wilkinson', 11103 'Bott'	£25-30
19904	1991	'TAYLOR WOODROW'	10110 AEC Bus, 10806 8-wheel Dropside, 12003 8-wheel Tipper	£20-25
19905	1994	'Routemaster' Set	15609 and 15611 AEC Routemasters. 'Model Collector' magazine offer	£20-25
19906	1995	'World War II' Set	13404 Tram and 18304 Leyland Tiger	£20-25
19907	1995	'Liverpool' Set	16512 Atlantean and 16106 Leyland PD, only available from Ian Allan	£35-40
19908	1997	'RM' Set	15610 and 17802, only from Beatties	£25-30
99901	1990	'London Buses'	10101 'Duracell', 10103 'Birdseye', 10104 'Schweppes'	£35-40
99902	1990	'FISHERMANS FRIEND'	10108 AEC Bus, 10507 6-wheel Van, 6 or 8 wheel Dropside Wagon.	
		1st run	in separate boxes (smooth base RT Bus and 6 wheel Dropside Wagon)	£40-50
		2nd run	in separate boxes (textured base RT Bus and 8 wheel Dropside Wagon)	£20-25
		3rd run	in one box, (textured base RT Bus and 8 wheel Dropside Wagon)	£20-25
99903	1991	De Luxe 'Box Vans' Set	10501 'London Carriers', plus 10503 'B.R.S.' & 11002 'Pickfords'	£35-40
99904	1991	De Luxe 'Tankers' Set	'L.P.G.', 'CENTURY OIL', 'MOBILGAS'	£35-40
99905	1992	'BARTONS'	Leyland RTL and Harrington Grenadier	£16-20
99906	1992	'Harrington Coaches'	Cavalier 'Surrey' and Grenadier 'Timpsons' ('Model Collector' offer)	£25-30
c99906	1995	'Harrington Coaches'	Cavalier 'Surrey' ('Surrey United') and Grenadier 'Timpsons' ('Crystal Palace')	£25-30
99907	1993	'SOUTHDOWN' 1	Bristol Lodekka and Harrington Cavalier, ('Model Collector' offer)	£50-60
99908	1993	'London Transport Museum' 1	16401 Regent, plus 16901 Leyland and 15612 AEC, (LT Museum exclusive)	£45-50
99909	1994	'London Transport Museum' 2	18202 Leyland Atlantean plus 16310 Bristol LS coach, (LT Museum exclusive)	£65-75
99910	1997	'SOUTHDOWN' 2	Leyland PD, Bedford OB, ('Model Collector' offer)	£40-50
99911	1994	'London Transport Museum' 3	'RM Set' with two Routemasters, (LT Museum exclusive)	£40-50
99912	1997	'SOUTHDOWN' 3	Bristol VR and Leyland National, ('Model Collector' offer)	£40-50
99913	1994	'London Transport Museum' 4	'London Leylands': a standard Leyland + 'roof-box' RTL, (LT Museum exclusive)	£40-45
99914	199?	'London Transport Museum' 5	Two 'GREENLINE' buses, (LT Museum exclusive)	£55-75
99915	199?	'SOUTHDOWN' 4	EFE subscribers only	£25-30
	199?	'Littlewoods'	Littlewoods Gift Set (no details)	£25-30
99916				not issued
99915	199?	'London Transport Museum' 6	Two 'RML' buses, (LT Museum exclusive)	£35-40

Ships

10001	1999	RMS 'TITANIC'	The ill-fated liner	£18-22
?????	1999	'OLYMPIC'	?	£18-22
?????	1999	'BRITTANIA'	Hospital Ship	£18-22

EFE Collectors Association

Collectors wishing for further details of this range are recommended to read 'EFE – A Collectors Guide' by Ken Benham. This and other publications are available from the EFE Collectors Association, PO Box 24510, London E17 4TG. Subscription costs £4-00 per year and members receive a monthly Newsletter plus offers of special models.

Acknowledgement

The Editor wishes to thank Allsorts, the E.F.E. specialist model shopkeepers and mail order dealers of 12 Scots Hill, Croxley Green, Rickmansworth, Herts., WD3 3AD for all their help in updating the listings.

Lledo 'Days-Gone'

One of the founders of Matchbox Toys, Jack Odell OBE formed the Lledo toy company in 1982 and the first six models made their appearance at Easter 1983. The range was called 'Models-of Days-Gone'. Lledo introduced the 'Premier Collection' and the 'Military Collection' in 1991 to offer greater choice, more detailed finish and improved appearance of certain models. They have 'DG' numbers and their own attractive packaging. The standard range is now known simply as 'Days-Gone'. 'Vanguards' were introduced in 1993. The Editor wishes to thank Robert Barker, Lledo Products Manager, for his help with updating material, also Peter Lloyd for additional assistance.

Where no price is shown, the Market Price Range is below £6.
NGPP = no price grading possible at present GSP = Gift Set Price
SBX = special box, (C)LE = (certificated) limited edition, FB = Fire Brigade

Contents

Ref.	Intro.	Model	MPR

DG 1 Horse-Drawn Tram

Included with this model is a set of figures: two lady passengers, a male passenger, a girl and the driver.

Ref.	Intro.	Model	MPR
000a	83	'WESTMINSTER' Green chassis, Orange seats, Yellow crest	£15-25
000b	83	Green chassis, Orange seats, Cream crest	£10-15
000c	83	Green chassis, Orange seats, White crest	
		(a,b,c) with no strengtheners on end panel or shafts	£100-120
		(a,b,c) with strengtheners on shafts but not end panels	£20-30
000d	87	Green chassis, Red seats, White crest	
001a	84	'MAIN STREET', Green/Grey	
002a	84	Brown/Cream	
003		Not allocated	
004a	84	'CRICH'	
005a	84	'DOWNTOWN', Cream, Green seats	
005b	87	Cream chassis, Dark Green seats	
005c	88	Dark Green seats, no Gold in crest	
005d	92	Dark Green seats, reversed crest	
006a	90	'HERSHEY'	
	90	Model withdrawn, but re-run for DG1-005d and:	
007a	96	'DG Club' Summer Special	

DG 2 Horse-Drawn Milk Float

Includes a set of cream plastic figures: a woman, a man, the driver and a dog.

Ref.	Intro.	Model	MPR
000a	83	'EXPRESS DAIRY'	
001a	84	'CHAMBOURCY'	
002		Not allocated	
003a	84	'CLIFFORD DAIRY'	
004a	84	'CELTIC DAIRY'	
	90	Model withdrawn.	

DG 3 Horse-Drawn Van

Until 1985 a set of cream plastic figures was included - a woman, a boy and a driver.

Ref.	Intro.	Model	MPR
000a	83	'WINDMILL BAKERY', Yellow body,Cream shafts	
000b	84	Yellow body, Beige shafts	
001a	85	'COCA-COLA'	
002a	84	'FINE LADY BAKERIES'	
003a	84	'ROBERTSONS', Green/Yellow	
003a	87	re-run, darker green 'leaves'	
004a	84	'PEPPERIDGE FARM'	
005a	84	'STAFFS. COUNTY SHOW', Pale Green	
005b	84	Mint Green	£5-7
006a	84	'MATTHEW NORMAN'	
007a	84	'ROYAL MAIL', special box	
008a	84	'L.S.W.R.'	

Ref.	Intro.	Model	MPR
009a	84	'HAMLEY'S TOYS', SBX	
010a	85	'TRI-SUM POTATO CHIPS'	
011a	87	'LLEDO Worldwide CC'	£5-7
012a	88	'J. SPRATT', special box	
013a	90	'ROYAL MAIL', special box	
014a	92	'HARRODS', (Set HD1004)	GSP
015a	92	'GREAT EASTERN', (Set RSL4003)	GSP
016a	97	'DAYS GONE CLUB', 'Spring 97'	

1990: Model withdrawn from standard production but casting remained available for use in sets.

DG 4 Horse-Drawn Omnibus

Cream plastic figures included: two ladies, a man, the driver and conductor. (no. '4' moulded into the surround).

Ref.	Intro.	Model	MPR
000a	83	'VICTORIA-KINGS CROSS', Red body, Green seats, 'LIPTONS' on Off-White panel	£10-20
000b		As 000a but pure White panel.	
000c		As 000a but White logo, Green panel.	
000d	84	As 000c but Brown seats	
001a	84	'BOWERY to BROADWAY' Red body, Black wheels	
002a	84	'BOWERY to BROADWAY', Green body, Brown seats and wheels	
002b	84	Green body and seats, Brown wheels	
002c	84	Dark Green, Brown seats, Gold wheels	
002d	88	Mid-Green, Brown seats, Gold wheels	
003a	84	'PUTNEY'	
004a	85	'MASONS PANTRY'	
004b	85	with 'Mrs Beaton' on wrong sides	£18-22
005a	84	'PEARS', Red wheels	
005b	87	'PEARS', Black wheels	
006a	84	'MADAME TUSSAUDS' Red seats and wheels	
006b	87	Red seats, Black wheels	
007a	86	'HIGH CHAPARRAL'	
008a	84	'HAMLEYS TOYS', SBX	
009a	87	'BALMORAL TOURS', special box	
010a	88	'RADIO TIMES', 'A Million Copies' in special box	£100-125
010b	88	'RADIO TIMES', 'Thomas Tilling', SBX	
011a	88	'NEWS of the WORLD', special box	
012a	89	'COLMANS MUSTARD'	
013a	91	'STONES GINGER WINE'	
014a	92	'OXO'	
015a	93	'CO-OP TEA'	
016a	93	'FURNESS RAILWAY', (set RSL4003)	GSP
017a	94	'MADAME TUSSAUDS'	
018a	94	'HARRODS'	

DG 5 Shand-Mason Horse-Drawn Fire Engine

A set of three (dark blue) plastic firemen figures was included up to 1985 (and re-introduced in 1989 partially painted and affixed).

Ref.	Intro.	Model	MPR
000a	83	'LONDON', Red body, Black wheels	
000c	87	Gold wheels	£65-80
001a	83	'CHICAGO', Red body, Black wheels, Black horses	
001b	85	Gold wheels, Cream horses, (72 only)	£65-80
002a	83	'GUILDFORD', Green body, Gold wheels, Black boiler (288 made)	£100-150
002b	83	Green body, Gold boiler	
002c	84	Dark Green body, Gold boiler	
003a	84	'HONG KONG', White body, Red wheels, Red boiler (288 issued)	£100-150
003b	84	'HONG KONG', Gold boiler	
004a	84	'G.W.R.', Brown body, Brown wheels, Cream horses	
004b	85	Gold wheels, wood plinth, special box	£7-10
004c	85	Gold wheels, Black horses	
005a	85	'LAKE CITY', Yellow body, Red wheels	
005b	87	Yellow body, Black wheels	
006a	84	'PHILADELPHIA'	
007a	84	'BIFBAC 2'	
008a	88	'LONDON EAST HAM', special box	
009a	89	'CARROW WORKS'	
010a	94	'METROPOLITAN F.B.' (Set FB1003)	GSP
	91	Model withdrawn from standard production but re-run for DG 5-010a, and:	
---	94	'THORNEY', 24k gold-plated. Only 12 produced for the 1994 International Lledo Show	NGPP

DG 6 1920 Ford Model 'T' Van

Models 000-035 came with blue plastic figures: a policeman, man with starting-handle and dog, girl with teddy. There are 4 variations of baseplates: 1st (metal) 'DG6-DG', 2nd (metal) 'DG6-DG8', 3rd (metal 'DG6-8'), 4th (plastic) 'DG6-8-33'.

Ref.	Intro.	Model	MPR
000a	83	'OVALTINE', Orange body, with 1st baseplate	£8-10
		with 2nd or 3rd baseplate	
001a	83	'YORKSHIRE POST', (1st Lledo Code 1 Trade Special)	NGPP
002a	84	'COOKIE COACH Co', Yellow logo	
002b	84	'COOKIE COACH Co'	
003a	84	'BRITISH MEAT', Cream body, Brown chassis, Brown roof	£7-10

Ref.	Intro.	Model	MPR
003b	84	Black chassis and roof	£10-15
004a	84	'AEROPLANE JELLY'	
005a	84	'BRITISH MEAT'	
006	84	'MARCOL', with 'Red Dragon' on some	
007a	84	'POLICE AMBULANCE', CLE of 5000	£30-40
008a	84	'I.P.M.S.'	£7-10
009a	84	'LIVERPOOL GARDEN FESTIVAL'	
010a	84	'ILLINOIS TOYFAIR'	
011a	84	'STRETTON'	
012a	84	'YORKSHIRE EVENING POST'	
013a	84	'DAYS GONE CLUB', Black	£7-10
014a	84	'BRITISH BACON'	
015a	84	'HARRY RAMSDEN'	
016a	85	'OVALTINE 75th', Stone roof, special box	
016b	90	Tan roof, (000a re-run error)	
017a	84	'DAILY EXPRESS', (in CP1 Pack)	GSP
018a	85	'PERRIER JOUET'	
019a	85	'HOME ALES'	
020a	84	'COCA-COLA', 'At Soda Fountains'	
021a	84	'COCA-COLA', 'Every Bottle Sterilized'	
022a	84	'WONDERBREAD'	
023a	84	'RAILWAY EXPRESS', ('84 USA Pack)	GSP
024a	84	'KODAK'	
025a	84	'MARKS & SPENCER'	
026a	84	'MARCOL 2', Yellow body, printed rear door	
027a	84	'PHILADELPHIA', Cream/Black	
028a	84	Red/Black	
029a	84	'YORKSHIRE BISCUITS'	
030a	84	'AUTOMODEL EXCHANGE'	
031a	84	'ECHO 100'	
032a	85	'STRETTON', Green chassis and roof	£7-10
033a	85	'BARCLAYS', Light Blue body, Cream chassis, Blue headboard letters	£18-20
033b	85	Cream headboard letters	
033c	90	with Black chassis and roof	£300-500
034a	84	'MAGASIN du NORD', Dark Green, with White headboard lettering	£30-40
034b	84	Gold headboard lettering	
035a	84	'HAMLEYS' special box	
036	85	'AUSTRALIAN Collectors Club', Dark Beige body, Dark Brown chassis, Tan or Dk. Brown roof	£7-10
036c		Beige body, '85 Convention (36 only)	£750-1000
037a	84	'MURPHYS CRISPS'	
038a	85	'WELLS DRINKS'	
039a	85	'WOODWARDS'	
040a	85	'LINDT', Pale Blue body, Blue roof	
040b		Pale Blue roof	£30-40

041a 85 'EVENING CHRONICLE'.....
042a 86 'CWM DALE', White body,
        Blue chassis
042b   Red chassis **£7-10**
043a 85 'ROYAL MAIL', SBX ....
044a 85 'ALTON TOWERS', SBX .....
045a 85 'NORTHERN DAILY' ....
046a 86 'CADBURYS' ....
047a 86 'JOHN SMITHS' ....
048a 86 'BAY to BIRDWOOD RUN'..
049a 86 'HARDWARE JOURNAL',
        special box **£40-50**
050   **'TOY FAIR'.** Trade-only
        models, Red/Cream, in
        White promotional box:
050a 86 'TOY FAIR,
        '86, Harrogate' **£10-15**
050b 86 '86, Harrowgate',
        (with 'w') **£60-75**
050c 87 '87, Harrogate **£10-15**
050d 88 '88, Harrogate' **£10-15**
050e 89 '89, Harrogate' **£10-15**
051a 86 'CADBURYS', SBX ....
052   Not allocated
053a 86 'TIZER' ....
054a 86 'COCA-COLA', special box ...
055a 86 'HERSHEYS', special box......
056a 87 'HEDGES & BUTLER' ....
057a 86 'CANADIAN TRAVEL &
        GIFT', 500 ....**£60-75**
058a 86 'COCA-COLA', SBX,
        Red hubs, Chrome radiator ....
058b 87 Brass hubs and radiator ....
059a 86 'CRAFT & HOBBY',
        500, Canadian..............**£60-75**
060a 87 'BLACK VELVIT' ....
061a 87 'FAIRY SOAP' ....
062a 87 'ROSE & CROWN' ....
063a 87 'Royal Flying Corps' ....GSP
064a 88 'HAMLEYS' ....
065a 88 'BUDWEISER', SBX ....
066a 88 'LLEDO WORLDWIDE
        C.C.', Green/Black ....
067a   Not Allocated
068a 88 'GOLDEN SHRED' ....
069a 88 'CHARRINGTONS' ....
070a 88 'MILLBANK BOOKS' ....
071a 90 'H.M.V.' ....
072a 89 'SHELL PUMP SERVICE' .....
073a 89 'WALLS ICES' ....

074- 86 **Canadian models**, in 'maple
        leaf' boxes, as a set, ...**£40-45**
        later available singly:
074a 88 'ONTARIO' ....
075a 88 'YUKON' ....
076a 88 'N.W. TERRITORIES' ....
077a 88 'PRINCE EDWARD ISLE',
        wrong date ('1870') ....
077b 90 correct date ('1873') ..**£75-85**
078a 88 'NEWFOUNDLAND' ....
079a 88 'QUEBEC' ....
080a 88 'NOVA SCOTIA' ....
081a 88 'MANITOBA' ....
082a 88 'ALBERTA' ....
083a 88 'NEW BRUNSWICK' ....
084a 88 'BRITISH COLUMBIA' ....
085a 88 'SASKATCHEWAN' ....
086a 88 'CANADA' ....

087a 89 'SELFRIDGES',
        (in Set LS1004) ....GSP
088a 89 'AU BON MARCHE' ....
089a 89 'SCHNEIDERS' ....
090a 89 'WINCHESTER CLUB' ....
091a 89 'BRITANNIA FILM',
        (in 'Gold Set') ....GSP
092a 89 'NESTLES' ....
093a 89 'N.Y. MOORS', (in Set)...GSP
094a 89 'HAMLEYS '89', SBX ....
095a 90 '4711' ....
096a 90 'ROWNTREES COCOA' ....
097a 90 'JAEGER', Set LS2004 ...GSP
098a 90 'ROYAL MAIL' ....
099a 90 'HERSHEY', (USA) .....NGPP
100a 90 'DAYS GONE' Club Model,
        Burgundy and Black ....
101a 90 'ARNOTTS', ABL1003...GSP

102a 91 'DG Club', Blue/Green ....
103a 91 'JOSEPH LUCAS' ....
104a 91 'BLACKPOOL' ....
105a 91 'ZEBRA GRATE POLISH' .....
106a 92 'DAYS GONE' Club Model,
        Pale Metallic Green/Black .....
107a 92 'JAMESONS' ....
108a 92 'HOTEL COLUMBIA',
        (in Set HLL1003) ....
109a 93 'HUNTLEY & PALMERS' ....
110a 93 'MIDLAND' ....*
111a 93 'LANCS. & YORKS.' ....*
112a 93 'NORTH EASTERN' ....*
113a 93 'LMS' ....*
114a 93 'DAYS GONE' Club Model ...
115a 94 'Days Gone Club' 94 ....
116a 94 'FLORIS TOILETRIES' ....
117a 94 'LONDON NW' ....
118a 94 'LONDON SW' ....
119a 94 'CAMBRIAN' ....
120a 94 'SOMERSET & DORSET' ....
121a 94 'RUPERT BEAR' ....
122a 95 'PEPSI-COLA' ....
123a 94 'NORMAN ROCKWELL' ....
124a 94 'AUSTRALIAN POST'
        (Australia).....................NGPP
125a 95 'ANTON BERG' ....
126a 95 'Caledonian Railway' ....**
127a 95 'Great Eastern Railway' ......**
128a 95 'North British Railway' ......**
129a 95 'Great Western Railway' .....**
130a 95 'HUIS TEN BOSCH',
        Burgundy, Japan ....NGPP
131a 95 'HUIS TEN BOSCH',
        Dark Blue, Japan ....NGPP
132a 95 'HUIS TEN BOSCH',
        Green, Japan ....NGPP
133a 95 'DG CLUB 95', SBX ....
134a 95 'HUIS TEN BOSCH',
        Mid-Green, Japan.........NGPP
135a 95 'HUIS TEN BOSCH',
        Royal Blue, Japan ....NGPP
136a 95 'STOCKHOLM OLYMPICS'.
137a 95 'Dr. PEPPER' ....
138a 96 'LEA & PERRINS' ....
139a 96 'SHELL 100 Years', SBX ......
140a 96 'DAYS GONE CLUB 96' ....
146a 97 'DAYS GONE CLUB 97' ....
147a 97 'SMITH'S CRISPS' ....
148a 98 'COCKBURN'S PORT' ....
150a 98 'VAN HOUTEN' ....
---   96 'BRITISH OLYMPIC
        SQUAD', plinth ....NGPP
153   99 'McVITIE & PRICE' ....
154   99 'COURVOISIER' ....
155   99 'WILD TURKEY' ....
156   99 'GRANT'S' ....

DG 7   1934 Ford
Model 'A' Woody Wagon

Cream plastic figures of a woman with
3 poodles were discontinued after 005.
000a 84 'PATS POODLE PARLOUR'.
001a 84 'COCA-COLA' ....
002a 84 'FORD', (set GS1) ....GSP
002b 85 no headboard, special box ...
003a 84 'WEST POINT TOY SHOW'
004 84 'HAMLEYS', Chrome or
        Brass radiator, SBX ....
005a 84 'GODFREY DAVIS' ....
006a 86 'DELLA' ....
007a 86 'COMMONWEALTH
        GAMES' (in set) ....GSP
008a 88 'CASTROL OIL' ....
009a 90 'PASCALL SWEETS' ....
        90 New baseplate introduced
        ('7-9-13-14-37').
        1991: Model ceased production.

DG 8   1920 Ford
Model 'T' Tanker

The same blue plastic figures included
with DG 6 were provided with 000 to
004 inclusive.
000a 84 'ESSO', 'Inflamable'
        (only 1 'm') **£5-7**
000b 84 'Inflammable' (correct) .....
001a 84 'COCA-COLA' ....
002a 85 'CASTROL' ....
003a 84 'PHILADELPHIA', Red,
        Black roof ....
003b 85 White roof **£10-15**
004a 85 'PENNZOIL' ....
005a 85 'HOFMEISTER' ....
006a 86 'BLUE MOUNTAIN' ....
007a 87 'CROW CARRYING' ....
008a 86 'HERSHEYS', special box ....
009a 87 'WATER WORKS' ....
010a 87 'ZEROLENE'
        (dealer promo, 3,000)..**£10-15**
011a 87 'SHELL FUEL OIL' ....
012a 88 'HOMEPRIDE' ....
013a 88 'DUCKHAMS OILS'............
014a 89 'SHELL FRANCE' ....
015a 89 'BP MOTOR SPIRIT' ....
016a 89 'TEXACO' ....
017a 87 'ARMY WATER' ....GSP
018a 90 'PRATTS' ....
019a 91 'MOBILGAS' ....
020a 93 'RUSSIAN OIL' ....
023 99 'BP' ....

DG 9   1934 Ford
Model 'A' Car

White plastic figures (two villains and
seated policeman with gun) with 001a
and b. The same figures (but in black),
were with 001c and 002 to 004.
000a 84 'POLICE' Car,
        Mid Blue/Dark Blue....**£20-30**
000b 84 All Dark Blue, Cream seats....
000c 84 All Dark Blue, Black seats.....
001a 84 'NEW YORK - RIO' ....GSP
002a 84 'PHILADELPHIA FIRE' ....
003a 85 '15 MILLIONTH FORD' ....
        1991: Model ceased production.

DG 10   1935 Dennis Coach

Cream plastic figures included (1984-
85) were of: man leaning on bus-stop,
man and woman with boy, young
woman with dog.
000a 84 'BRIGHTON BELLE',
        Maroon body, Beige roof,
        Chrome radiator **£15-20**
000b   Beige roof, Brass radiator .....
000c   Cream roof, Brass radiator .....
001a 84 'TILLINGBOURNE' ....
002 87 'SILVER SERVICE',
        Silver or White 'Matlock' ......
003a 84 'SOUTHERN VECTIS',
        with Yellow logo ....
        with White logo..........**£12-15**
004a 84 'SCHOOL BUS',
        with Chrome radiator **£7-10**
004b 84 with Brass radiator ....
004c 87 'OAKRIDGE SCHOOL' ....
005a 84 'POTTERIES',
        with Cream roof ....
005b 86 with Red roof **£15-18**
006a 85 'GWR', special box,
        '150th Anniversary' **£8-12**
007a 85 'BARTON' ....
008 86 'LONDON COUNTRY',
        Brass or Chrome radiator ......
008c 88 with Black chassis ...**£150-200**
009a 84 'HAMLEYS', SBX **£5-8**
010   Not allocated
011   Not allocated
012a 85 'TARTAN' ....
013a 85 'TRAILWAYS' ....GSP
014a 85 'IMPERIAL AIRWAYS',
        with Blue roof......................

014b 87 with Red roof **£12-15**
015a 86 'REDBURNS' ....
016a 86 'COMMONWEALTH
        GAMES', (in set) ....GSP
017a 87 'HERSHEYS' ....
018a 88 'E.B. TAYLOR' ....
        1989: New baseplate text:
        'DG10-12-34-35'.
019a 89 'CITY of COVENTRY' ....
020a 90 'B.O.A.C.' ....
021a 91 'B.E.A.' ....
        1992: DG10 production ceased.

DG 11   Horse-Drawn
Removal Van

Cream plastic figures (up till 1985):
driver, woman with birdcage, girl with
hoop, boy with bag and bulldog. Driver
figure re-introduced in 1989, plus
change in design of horses.
000a 84 'TURNBULL & Co' ....
001a 85 'ABELS' ....
002a 85 'BIG TOP CIRCUS' ....
003a 85 'Staffs. COUNTY SHOW' .....
004a 85 'ROYAL MAIL', SBX ....
005a 85 'WILLIAMS GRIFFIN' ....
006a 86 'MacCOSHAMS' ....
007a 86 'COCA-COLA', (Hartoy) GSP
008a 88 'BUDWEISER', SBX ....
009a 89 'LLEDO WORLDWIDE' ....
010a 88 'R.P. COOPER' ....
011a   Not allocated
012a 89 'JAMES BROWN & SON' ....
013a 89 'ALBERT DALEY & Co' ....
014a 90 'MARKS & SPENCER',
        special box ....
015a 90 'ROYAL MAIL', SBX ....
016a 90 'ARNOTTS',(ABL1003) .GSP
017a 91 'ROBERT HEATON & SON'.
018a 91 'DG CLUB SUMMER '91' ......
019a 91 'SAINSBURYS' ....
020a 92 'HARRODS', (HD1002)..GSP
021a 92 'HAMLEYS',
        (in Set HAL1004) ....GSP
022a 93 'SCHWEPPES' ....
023a 93 'PEPSI-COLA', special box ...
024a 93 'GREAT NORTHERN',
        (Set RSL4003)...............GSP
025a 94 'OXO TRENCH HEATER' ....
026a 95 'RUPERT', special box ....

DG 12
1934 Dennis Fire Engine

Chassis, baseplate, wheels and radiator
as DG 10. Escape wheels fitted to
000a, 001a, 003a 3. Blue plastic firemen
included up to 1985.
000a 84 'LUCKHURST', Red/Green ....
000b 89 Red body and chassis ..**£10-15**
001a 85 'CARDIFF CITY' ....
002   Not allocated
003 85 'BERMUDA', Blue body,
        Cream or White floor ....
004a 86 'LCC' ....
005 86 'CHELMSFORD',
        Brass or Chrome radiator ....
006a 87 'AUXILIARY' ....
007a 87 'ESSEX COUNTY',
        Red/White ....
007b 90 with White 'ESSEX' **£40-50**
008a 87 'WARE FIRE SERVICE' ....
009a 87 'WINDSOR', special box ....
010a 88 'GLASGOW' ....
011a 88 'BOSTON' ....
012a 89 'BIRMINGHAM' ....
        1989: Baseplate with
        'DG10-12-34-35' introduced.
013a 90 'BRADFORD' ....
014a 90 'HERSHEY', special box ......
014b   'HERSHEY',
        new shape **£35-40**
015a 91 'MANCHESTER' ....
016a 92 'WEST HAM' ....
017a 93 'VALLETTA', (MG1003)..GSP
018a 94 'HAMLEYS 94' ....
019a 94 'LONDON FIRE BRIGADE'.

021a 98 'HULL POLICE F.B.' ....
023 99 'GUILDFORD' ....

DG 13
1934 Ford Model 'A' Van

Cream plastic figures up to 011: man reading paper, newsboy, deliveryman.
000a 86 'CAMP COFFEE', SBX ....
001a 84 'EVENING NEWS' ....
002a 85 'TUCHER BEERS', SBX ....
003a 86 'MITRE 10', SBX.......**£20-25**
004a 84 'HAMLEYS', SBX ....
005a 85 'MICHELIN', (also in Set) .....
006a 85 'JERSEY EVENING
    POST'.......................**£10-15**
007a 85 'MARY ANN' **£10-15**
008a 84 'ROYAL MAIL' ....
008b 92 'ROYAL MAIL',
    new longer body ....
009a 85 'COCA-COLA' ....
010a 85 'BASILDON BOND',
    with matt finish **£6-8**
010b 85 with gloss finish ....
011a 86 'RYDER' ....
012a 85 'COCA-COLA' ....
013a 85 'EVENING SENTINEL' ....
014a 85 'STROH'S' ....
015a 85 'ROYAL MAIL 350', SBX ....
016a 85 'FESTIVAL GARDENS' ....
017a 86 'ROBINSONS' ....
018a 88 'EVER READY' ....
019a 87 'H.P. SAUCE' ....
020a 86 'F.D.B.' (Danish).........**£20-25**
021a 86 'COCA-COLA',
    Black chassis ....
021b   Yellow chassis **£200-250**
022a 88 'J. LYONS' ....
023a 86 'HERSHEYS KISSES' ....
024a 86 'HERSHEYS' ....
025a   'ROYAL MAIL', SBX ....
026a 88 'HEINZ TOMATO SOUP' .....
027a 88 'CHARLES TATE' ....
028a 88 'EXCHANGE & MART' ....
029a 88 'ELIZABETH SHAW' ....
030a 89 'OXYDOL' ....
031a 89 'AQUASCUTUM',
    (in Set LS1004) ....GSP
032   Not allocated
033a 89 'ALLENBURYS' ....
034a 89 'EMPIRE', ('Gold Set')...GSP
035a 89 'KLEENEX' ....
036a 91 'AUSTIN REED',
    (in Set LS2004) ....GSP
037a 89 'B.B.C.' ....
038a 89 'ARMY RECRUITMENT',
    (in Set BA1003) ....GSP
039a 90 'PERSIL' ....
040a 90 'MADAME TUSSAUDS' ....
041a 90 'MARKS & SPENCER',
    special box ....
042a 90 'ROYAL MAIL' ....
043a 90 'HERSHEYS', Silver and
    Brown, (US issue) ....NGPP
044a 90 'N.Y. MOORS' (Set 2)....GSP
045a 90 'ARNOTTS',(ABL1003) .GSP
    1990: Baseplate with
    '7-9-13-14-37' introduced.
046a 91 'ROSELLA' ....
047a 91 'CASTROL' ....
    1991: Steering wheel and seats
    added to model.
048a 92 'HAMLEYS' ....
    1992: Longer body introduced.
049a 92 'RINSO' ....
050a 92 'SOUTHERN RAILWAY',
    (in Set RSL2003) ....GSP
051a 92 'HARRODS', (HD1004)..GSP
052a 92 'QANTAS', (QA1002)...GSP
053a 92 'GODE', (Germany) **£25-30**
054a 92 'RAMA', (Germany) **£20-25**
055a 92 'GOLDEN SHRED' ....
056a 93 'PEPSI-COLA', special box ....
057a 93 'MARKS & SPENCER',
    (in Set MS2004).............GSP
058a 93 'Grand Hotel Peking',
    (in Set HLL2003)............GSP

059a 94 'CARLSBERG' ....
060a 94 'KODAK' (Mexico).....**£30-40**
061a 94 'RUPERT BEAR' ....
062a 94 'Dr. PEPPER', special box.....
063a 94 'NORMAN ROCKWELL',
    special box ....
064a 95 'RITTER SCHOKOLADE' ....
065a 95 '7-UP' (USA, SBX) ......NGPP
066a 95 'DAILY HERALD',
    (Set VE 1003) ....GSP
067a 95 'LOS ANGELES
    OLYMPIC GAMES' ....
068a 96 'WATERMANS PENS' ....
072a 97 'CHERRY BLOSSOM' ....
073a 97 'DG CLUB', 'Summer 97'.....
074a 98 'ROYAL MAIL', 'Air Mail'....
075a 98 'HOLSTEN BIER' ....
076a 98 'TERRY'S' ....
--- 96 'BRITISH OLYMPIC
    SQUAD', plinth ....NGPP
077 99 'JEYES FLUID' ....

DG 14 1934 Ford
Model 'A' Car with Hood

Cream plastic figures (one US policeman and two firemen), were only issued with 000a/b and 001a.
000a 85 'SAN DIEGO',
    'Fire Chief' in Gold with
    Black surround **£150-200**
000b   'Fire Chief' not in Gold with
    Black surround ....
001a 85 'TAXI' ....
002a 85 'ACME CLEANERS' ....
003a 86 'HAMLEYS', special box .....
004 86 'GRAND HOTEL',
    Brown with Cream or Beige ..
005   Not allocated.
006a 87 'STATE PENITENTIARY' .....
007a 88 'SAN DIEGO',
    (US version) ....NGPP
    1990: Baseplate with
    '7-9-13-14-37' introduced.
008a 90 'RALEIGH CYCLES'............
    1991: DG14 production ceased.

DG 15 1932 AEC Regent
Double-Deck Bus

The first 'Days Gone' model without the plastic figures. Lower seats were absent till 1989.
000 85 'HALLS WINE', Red/Black,
    Chrome or Brass radiator ......
001a 85 'COCA-COLA' ....
002a 85 'CASTLEMAINE XXXX',
    (in 3-bus Set) ....GSP
003a 85 'HAMLEYS', special box .....
004a 85 'LIVERPOOL GARDENS' ....
005 85 'CINZANO',
    Chrome or Brass radiator ......
006a 86 'EVENING ARGUS' ....
007a 86 'HALLS WINE',
    Pale Brown body.......**£30-35**
007b 86 bare metal body.........**£15-20**
007 86 (a & b) in wooden
    display case with
    plated components...**£100-125**
008a 86 'ROYAL WEDDING'....**£10-15**
009 87 'MADAME TUSSAUDS',
    Chrome or Brass radiator ......
010 86 'SWAN VESTAS' ....
011a 86 'COMMONWEALTH
    GAMES', (in Set) ....GSP
011b 87 with Brass radiator ....
012a 87 'HEINZ' ....
013a 87 'STRATFORD BLUE', SBX ..
014a 87 'TV TIMES' ....
015a 88 'HAMLEYS' ....
016a 88 'BIRMINGHAM MAIL' ....
017a 88 'GOLDEN WONDER' ....
018a 88 'LLEDO CLUB' **£10-15**
019a 89 'MAPLES' ....
020a 89 'TERRY'S GYM' ....
021a 89 'St. IVEL CHEESE' ....
022a 89 'HAMLEYS', special box ....

023a 90 'PALMOLIVE' ....
024a 90 'R.A.C.' ....
025 90 'POST EARLY FOR XMAS',
    Red or Cream seats, SBX........
026a 90 'HERSHEYS', Beige and
    Brown, (US issue) ....NGPP
027a 90 'N.Y. MOORS', (Set 2)...GSP
028a 92 'HARRODS', (HD1002)..GSP
029a 93 'Mazawattee Tea' ....
030a 93 'Van HOUTENS COCOA' ....
031a 93 'D.G. CLUB' Autumn '93 ....
032a 94 'LIBBYS PINEAPPLE' ....
033a 94 'HAMLEYS', HA 2002...GSP
034a 94 'GODE', (Germany) **£15-20**
035a 95 'PEARS SOAP' ....
036a 94 'HARRODS', (HR 2004).GSP
037a 97 'SCHWEPPES' ....
038a 98 'NESTLES' ....
039a 98 'SPILLERS SHAPES' ....
040 99 'LUCOZADE' ....

DG 16
1934 Dennis Parcels Van

Seats and steering wheel did not appear until 1991. Separate wheel/tyre units or composite wheels can be found.
000a 85 'MAYFLOWER' ....
001a 85 'ROYAL MAIL', SBX ....
002a 85 'CROFT ORIGINAL'............
003a 86 'HAMLEYS', special box .....
004a 86 'TREBOR' ....
005a 86 'L.N.E.R.' ....
006a 86 'KIWI',
    Black hubs, Brass radiator......
006b 87 Cream hubs, Chrome radiator
007a 85 'BUSHELLS' ....
008   Not allocated
009a 87 'CADBURYS' ....
010a 87 'FYFFES' ....
011a 86 'COCA-COLA', special box ...
012a 86 'HERSHEYS GOODBAR',
    special box ....
013a 86 'HERSHEYS KRACKEL',
    Brass radiator, special box......
013b 87 Chrome radiator, special box..
014a 88 'PICKFORDS', Blue body .....
014b 89 Dark Blue body ....
015a 87 'LLEDO WORLDWIDE CC'.
016a 88 'HAMLEYS' ....
017a 89 'ABELS' ....
018a 90 'MADAME TUSSAUDS' ....
019a 89 'ALLIED' ....
020a 89 'COSMOS' ....
021a 89 'GOODYEAR' ....
021b 90 same but White 'Goodyear' ...
022a 89 'HAMLEYS' ....
023a 90 'OXO' ....
024a 90 'ROYAL MAIL' ....
025a 90 'N.Y. MOORS', (Set 3)....GSP
026a 91 'SCHWEPPES' ....
    1991: Steering wheel added.
027a 91 'ATORA FOR XMAS' ....
028a 91 'L.N.E.R.', (TPL1003)......GSP
029a 91 'L.N.E.R.', (RSL1003)......GSP
030a 91 'Y.M.C.A.', (HF1003) ......GSP
031a 92 'HUDSONS SOAP' ....
032a 93 'TUNNOCKS' ....
033a 93 'NAAFI', (Set DM1003)..GSP
034a 93 'RAF Runway Control',
    (Set DML1003)...............GSP
035a 94 'KODAK' ....
036a 94 'BOVRIL' ....
037a 94 'RUPERT BEAR' ....
038a 94 'D.G. CLUB' Autumn '94 ......
039a 95 'RUPERT BEAR', SBX ....

DG 17 1932 AEC Regal
Single Deck Bus

000a 85 'SOUTHEND',
    with filler cap casting.**£60-75**
000b   without filler cap casting.......
000c 86 with Red roof,
    (1,000 only)................**£25-35**
001a 85 'EUROTOURS',(in Set) ..GSP

002a 85 'CORPORATION'.................
003a 86 'HAMLEYS', SBX **£25-35**
004a 85 'LONDON TRANSPORT' .....
005a 86 'OXFORD (MORRELL'S)' ..
006a 86 'COMMONWEALTH
    GAMES', special box ....
007a 86 'STRATFORD BLUE',
    Chrome radiator.................
007b 87 Brass radiator **£6-9**
008a 87 'BURNLEY' ....
009a 86 'BIG TOP CIRCUS' ....
010a 87 'PENNINE' ....
011a 87 'RFC', (in Set)................GSP
012a 88 'HAMLEYS' ....
    1988: New roof (with 2
    hoardings) introduced.
013a 88 'HANTS & DORSET' ....
014a 88 'SUTTONS'.........................
015a 89 'ROYAL BLUE',
    Blue and Black ....
015b 89 Same but White background
    to headboard decal..............
016a 89 'COLCHESTER', Maroon ......
017a 88 'ROYAL NAVY',
    (in Set RN1003)............GSP
018a 89 'N.Y. MOORS', (Set).......GSP
019a 90 'RED & WHITE' ....
020a 91 'BUCKLAND OMNIBUS' .....
021a 92 'SOUTHERN VECTIS' ....
022a 92 'GREEN LINE' ....
022b 93 No fleet number on bonnet.....
022c 94 Silver print on side boards.....
023a 95 'SUNDERLAND' ....
024a 95 'US RED CROSS',
    (in Set VE 1003) ....GSP
026 99 'MACBRAYNES'.................

DG 18 1936 Packard Van

Steering wheel and seats did not appear on this model until 1991.
000 85 'AMBULANCE',
    Chrome or Brass radiator ......
001a 85 'AMERICAN
    AMBULANCE', as 000a
    but Red cross in circle ....
002a 86 'COMMONWEALTH
    GAMES', special box,
    with Chrome radiator **£6-8**
002b 87 Brass radiator, normal box .....
003a 86 'RAPID CASH' ....
004 86 'FIRESTONE',
    Chrome or Brass radiator ......
005   Not allocated
006 87 'WHITE STAR',
    Chrome or Brass radiator ......
007a 87 'COLMANS' ....
008a 87 'RFC', (in Set)................GSP
009a 88 'PERRONI BIRRA' ....
010a 88 'NATIONAL
    WESTMINSTER'.......**£10-15**
011 88 'FOTORAMA',
    Chrome or Brass radiator ......
012a 90 'St. IVEL' ....
013a 89 'FORTNUM & MASON',
    (in Set LS1004) ....GSP
014a 89 'B & C FILMS',
    (in 'Gold' Set)...............GSP
015a 88 'St. MARY'S HOSPITAL',
    (Canadian charity).......**£20-25**
016a 89 'LEYLAND PAINTS' ....
017a 89 'HAMLEYS', special box ....
018a 90 'ASPREY', (LS2004) ......GSP
019a 90 'DG CLUB', Autumn model...
020a 91 'McVITIE & PRICE' ....
021a 92 'CAMP COFFEE' ....
022a 92 'St.JOHN AMBULANCE',
    in Set MG1003...............GSP
023a 93 'FERODO' ....
024a 93 'IMPERIAL' (HLL2003).GSP
025a 94 'NORMAN ROCKWELL',
    special box ....
--- 86 'CAMPERDOWN' Australian
    hospital charity..........**£40-50**

DG 19 1931 Rolls-Royce Phantom II (Brewster)

Incorporates the DG 18 baseplate. It acquired a steering wheel in 1989.

000a 85 Burgundy ('TV Times')
001a 86 Yellow/Tan, Chrome radiator
001b 86 Yellow/Tan, Brass radiator
002a 86 'Basketweave', Beige/Cream, Grey tyres, Brass radiator
002b 87 Grey tyres, Chrome radiator
002c 87 Beige tyres, Brass radiator
003a 88 Metallic Grey/Black ... GSP
003b 88 Not mounted or drilled, (unofficial) ... **£7-10**
004a 87 Gold and White
005a 87 'Ruby Wedding', SBX
006a 89 Dark Green/Black/Beige
007a 88 'Minder', Gold/White
008a 89 'Lledo Worldwide CC', Silver/Black
009a 89 'Army Staff Car', in Set BA1003 ... GSP
010a 92 Black/Ivory, Chrome radiator
011a 92 Silver/Black, (for German market) ... **£20-25**
--- 85 All Cream, Chrome radiator, (108 only) ... **£30-35**
1993: Model withdrawn.

DG 20 1936 Ford Stake Truck

Steering wheel and seats from 1991.

000a 86 'EAGLE ALES'
001a 86 'COCA-COLA', special box
001b 87 same but with Red barrels
002 87 'STROH'S', Red/Black, Brass or Chrome radiator
003 86 'WHITBREAD', Brass or Chrome radiator
004a 86 'GOODRICH'
005a 88 'AULD SCOTCH GINGER'
006a 87 'UNIROYAL'
007a 88 'BUDWEISER', SBX
008a 88 'IND COOPE'
009a 89 'WATNEYS'
010a 89 'CALOR GAS'
011a 88 'ROYAL NAVY', (in Set RN1003) ... GSP
012a 90 'PIRELLI'
013a 90 'BRITISH OXYGEN'
014a 90 'HERSHEYS', US issue in special box ... NGPP
015a 90 'RAF', (in Set BB1003) ... GSP
016a 90 'WINN DIXIE'
017a 91 'DUNLOP TYRES'
93 'DUNLOP TYRES', 'Brooklands Collection'
018a 91 'GOODYEAR TYRES'
019a 93 'McDOUGALLS'
020a 94 'NESTLES MILK'
021a 94 'Dr. PEPPER', special box
022a 95 'PENNZOIL'

DG 21 1934 Chevrolet Van

Plastic roof may have front headboard, front and lengthways headboards or none. Seats and steering wheel added in 1991, baseplate updated in 1992.

000a 86 'SHARPS', Chrome radiator
000b 87 Yellow, Brass radiator
001a 86 'LLEDO WORLDWIDE CLUB', special box
001b 86 Maroon hubs, Black prototype logo
002a 86 'LEICESTER MERCURY'
003a 86 'HOSTESS CAKE'
004a 87 'Dr. PEPPER'
005a 86 'COCA-COLA', special box
006 Not allocated.
007a 88 'HAMLEYS'
008a 88 'BUDWEISER', SBX
009a 88 'BIRDS CUSTARD'
010a 88 'FARRAH'S TOFFEE'
011a 88 'VITA-WHEAT'
012a 89 'SIMPSONS', (LS1004) ... GSP
013a 89 'BENETTONS'
014a 89 'HERSHEYS KISSES'
015a 89 'CHERRY BLOSSOM'
016a 89 'MAJESTIC FILMS' ... GSP
017a 90 'TOYFAIR '90', ... **£9-12**
018a 90 'RECKITTS BLUE'
019a 90 'MARKS & SPENCER'
020a 90 'LIBERTY'S', (LS2004) ... GSP
021a 90 'CLUB SUMMER '90'
022a 90 'SCOTTISH BLUEBELL', in Set BM1004 ... GSP
023a 90 'BRYANT & MAY', in Set BM1004 ... GSP
024a 90 'SWAN VESTAS', in Set BM1004 ... GSP
025a 90 'ENGLANDS GLORY', in Set BM1004 ... GSP
026a 91 'HAMLEYS'
027a 91 'EXIDE'
028a 91 'FAIRY SOAP'
029a 91 'BUSHELLS COFFEE'
030a 91 'US MARINES', (in Set PH1003) ... GSP
031a 92 'ELLIMANS'
032a 92 'MAGGI'S SOUP'
033a 91 'SCRIBBANS', (Trade special) ... NGPP
034a 92 'LMS & LNER', in Set RSL2003 ... GSP
035a 92 'GRAND HOTEL', in Set HLL1003 ... GSP
036a 92 'LNER Country', in Set RSL3003 ... GSP
037a 92 'HAMLEYS', in Set HAL1004 ... GSP
038a 93 'PEPSI-COLA', special box
039a 94 'ROSES LIME JUICE'
040a 94 'SPRENGEL', (German market) ... **£20-25**
041a 94 'HENDERSON', (Set MCL 1003) ... GSP
042a 94 'USA WORLD CUP'
043a 94 'NORMAN ROCKWELL'
044a 95 'NIVEA CREME OL'
045a 95 'RUPERT BEAR', SBX
046a 95 'DG GOLD CLUB', special box ... NGPP
047a 95 'Dr. PEPPER', special box
048a 96 'La VACHE QUI RIT'
050a 97 'BRYLCREEM'
051a 98 'TEACHER'S WHISKY'
052a 98 'EVER READY'

DG 22 1933 Packard Town Van

000a 86 'STAG WHISKY'
001a 86 'LORD TED'
002 87 'FLORISTS'
003a 87 'WHITMANS'
004a 87 'LLEDO WORLDWIDE CLUB', special box ... **£6-8**
005a 88 'HAMLEYS'
006a 88 'PIZZA EXPRESS'
007a 88 'BUDWEISER', SBX
008a 88 'TESCO' ... **£20-25**
009a 89 'SOHO DAIRIES', Black
009b 90 Same but Dark Brown
010a 90 'HEINZ 57'
011a 91 'SHARPS TOFFEE'
012a 92 'PUNCH'
1993: Model withdrawn.

DG 23 1954 Scenicruiser

This was the first (and for many years, the only) 'Days Gone' model to feature window glazing.

000a 87 'GREYHOUND', Silver, pale windows, bare metal chassis ... **£10-15**
000b 87 dark windows, Silver chassis
000c 87 dark windows, Black chassis
001a 87 'GOLDEN WEST'
002a 87 'BUFFALO'
1991: DG23 withdrawn.

DG 24 Rolls-Royce Playboy (Brewster)

The radiator component is the same as on DG 19.

000a 87 Yellow body, ('TV Times')
001a 87 Lilac body
001b 87 Dark Lilac body
002a 88 Metallic Grey body ... GSP
002b 88 Not mounted or drilled, (unofficial) ... **£7-10**
003a 87 Red and White, special box
004a 88 Metallic Green body
005a 89 Dark Green body
--- 89 24k Gold plated, on plinth, (110 made) ... NGPP
1991: Model withdrawn.

DG 25 1925 Rolls-Royce Silver Ghost (Barker)

Seats and steering wheel are a single plastic moulding.

000a 87 Dk.Blue/Black, ('TV Times')
001a 87 Silver and Blue
002a 88 Metallic Grey ... GSP
002b 88 Not mounted or drilled, (unofficial) ... **£7-10**
003a 87 White / Black, (Cream seats)
003b 88 All White body, (White seats)
004a 89 Blue/Black/Tan
005a 89 Dark Green body
1991: DG25 production ceased.

DG 26 1934 Chevrolet Bottle Delivery Truck

Baseplate, chassis and radiator as DG 21. Steering wheel / seats from 1991.

000a 87 'SCHWEPPES', Lemon, Red chassis ... **£12-16**
000b 87 Yellow body, Red chassis
000c 88 with Black chassis ... **£150-200**
001a 87 'LLEDO WORLDWIDE CLUB.', White/Black
002 87 'COCA-COLA', Brass or Chrome radiator
003a 88 'BUDWEISER', SBX
004a 88 'BARR'S'
005a 88 'CORONA'
006a 88 'TIZER'
007a 89 'CANADA DRY', (illegible artwork)
007b 89 Legible rear, illegible side
007c 90 Legible rear and side
008a 90 'SCHWEPPES'
009a 91 'TENNENTS'
010a 92 'BASS'
011 92 'FYFFES', fleet no '6' at front or rear
012a 93 'PEPSI-COLA', special box
013a 93 'PERRIER'
014a 93 'BROOKE BOND'
015a 94 'Dr. PEPPER', special box
016a 95 'BECK'S BEER'
017a 95 '7-UP', special box
018a 96 'TUBORG LAGER'

DG 27 1934 Mack Breakdown Truck

The steering wheel appeared on this model in 1991.

000a 87 'A1 RECOVERY'
001a 88 'HANKS AUTO'
002 Not allocated
003a 88 'MOBILOIL' (UK issue)
004a 89 'MOBILOIL' (French) ... **£6-8**
005a 89 'ARTHUR DALEY'
006a 91 'U.S. ARMY', (US1003) ... GSP
007a 92 'LONDON CC'
93 'B.A.R.C.', (in 'Brooklands Collection')
1993: Model withdrawn.

DG 28 1934 Mack Canvas-back Truck

Chassis, plastic baseplate and radiator as DG 27. From 1991 the model was fitted with a steering wheel.

000 88 'TYPHOO'
001a 88 'TATE & LYLE'
002a 88 'LLEDO WORLDWIDE CLUB', special box
003 88 'HEINZ BEANS', Chrome or Brass radiator
004a 89 'DUNLOP'
005 Not allocated.
006a 89 'ROYAL NAVY', in Set RN1003 ... GSP
007a 90 'STROH'S'
008a 89 'N.Y. MOORS', (Set) ... GSP
009a 89 'COCA-COLA', (few released) ... **£400+**
010a 91 'GREENE KING'
011a 90 'RAF', (in RAF Set) ... GSP
012a 90 'WINN DIXIE', (US) ... **£20-25**
013a 91 'HAMLEYS', special box
014a 91 'L.N.E.R.', (TPL1003) ... GSP
015a 91 'L.M.S.', (RSL1003) ... GSP
016a 91 '8th ARMY', SBX
017a 91 'Quartermasters Corps', in Set USA1003 ... GSP
018a 91 'REVELL '91', US Trade special ... **£70-80**
019a 91 'Corps Truck', (PH1003) ... GSP
020a 92 'G.W.R.', (RSL2003) ... GSP
021a 92 'HAMLEYS', special box
022a 91 'Motor Torpedo', in Set PH1003 ... GSP
023a 92 'WINCARNIS'
024a 92 'D.G. Club 91-92'
025a 92 'TOYFAIR '92', Trade Fair model ... **£20-25**
026a 92 'ROYAL NAVY', in Set MG1003 ... GSP
027a 92 'US Marines',(GU1003) ... GSP
028a 92 'S.R. Express', in Set RSL3003 ... GSP
029a 93 'KAFFEE HAG'
030a 93 'RAF', Set DML1003 ... GSP
031a 93 'LLEDO SHOW' 1993
032a 94 'SAINSBURY'S LAMB'
033a 95 'PEPSI-COLA'
034a 94 'Dr. PEPPER', special box
035a 95 'PERSIL'
1995: DG28 withdrawn from standard production.

DG 29 1942 Dodge 4x4

000a 88 'US Field Ambulance'
001a 89 'RAF Aircrew'
002a 91 'TEXACO'
003a 91 'US Army Ambulance', in Set USAL1003 ... GSP
004a 92 'Bomb Disposal', SBX
005a 92 'Marines', (GU1003) ... GSP
006a 93 'Police Emergency'
007a 94 'SAN JOSE FIRE DEPT'
008a 94 'Canadian Army', (Set DDL 1003) ... GSP
009a 94 'US Army Signals', (Set DDU 1003) ... GSP
1994: DG29 withdrawn from standard production.

DG 30 1939 Chevrolet Panel Van

000a 88 'JOHN BULL TYRES'
001a 89 'FRY'S COCOA'
002a 89 'LIPTONS'
003a 89 'LLEDO WORLDWIDE CLUB', special box
004a 89 'HAMLEYS', SBX
005a 90 'SPRATTS'
006a 90 'BROOKE BOND'
007a 90 'HERSHEY', (US issue, special box) ... **£20-25**
008a 90 'RAF', Set BBL1004 ... GSP

009a 91 'NESTLES' ....
010a 91 'GOLDEN STREAM TEA' ....
011a 91 'Polish Army', SBX ....
012a 91 'Army Surgical Unit',
    in Set USA1003 ....GSP
013a 91 'US Navy', (PHL1003) ....GSP
014a 92 'STEPHENS INKS' ....
015a 93 'SHELL-BP' ....
016a 94 'RANSOMES
    LAWNMOWERS' ....
017a 94 'INDIAN', (MCL 1003) ..GSP
018a 95 '7-UP', special box ....
020a 97 'JACK DANIELS' ....

DG 31 Horse-Drawn Brewer's Dray

DG31 had DG 4/5/11 wheels, a dedicated driver figure and painted detail on the horses.
000a 88 'WHITBREAD' ....
001a 88 'EVERARDS', Red body,
    (Dealer Promotion) **£15-20**
002 89 'TAUNTON CIDER'..............
003 89 'GREENE KING',
    (reversed or correct tampo) ....
004a 89 'TRUMANS' ....
005a 91 'COURAGE ALES' ....
006a 92 'WORTHINGTON' ....
007a 93 'BASS' ....
008 94 'FULLERS ALES',
    (red or green bar), SBX ....

DG 32 1907 Rolls-Royce Silver Ghost

This model echoes the Odell design of the Lesney Y15-1 version of 1960 with its cast metal body, bonnet, chassis and windscreen.
000a 88 Silver body, Maroon seats ......
001a 89 Dark Green body, Beige seats .
002a 90 Metallic Green, Black seats ....
003a 90 'Gold-plate' effect ....NGPP
004a 91 Dark Red, Black seats ....
005a 92 Dark Blue, Black seats ....
006a 92 Bronze (Germany)........**£15-20**
007a 92 'Gold' (Germany)..........**£15-20**
008a 95 Gold-plated, (RPL 1003)..GSP
009a 96 Black ....

DG 33 1920 Ford Model 'T' Car

This model uses DG6 and 8 radiator, chassis, baseplate and wheels.
000a 89 Black body, chassis and roof ...
001a 89 'SINGER', Maroon seats ....
001b 89 'SINGER', Black seats ....
002 Not allocated
003a 90 'HERSHEYS', SBX,
    (US issue) ....NGPP
004a 91 'GRAND HOTEL' ....
005a 92 'HOTEL PARIS',
    in Set HLL1003..............GSP
006a Gold body ....NGPP
007a 93 'PFAFF' ....
008a 94 'EXCHANGE & MART' ......
009a 94 'HUIS TEN BOSCH',
    Maroon, Japan ....NGPP
010a 94 'HUIS TEN BOSCH',
    Green, Japan ....NGPP
011a 94 'HUIS TEN BOSCH',
    Blue, Japan ....NGPP
012a 94 'HUIS TEN BOSCH',
    Cream, Japan ....NGPP
013a 95 'HUIS TEN BOSCH',
    Bright Blue, Japan........NGPP
014a 96 'ROWNTREES' ....
015a 96 'DG CLUB', Summer '96 ....

DG 34 1932 Dennis Delivery Van

Modified DG 10 with a roof-rack and with reduced seating section.
000a 89 'HOVIS' ....
001a 89 'SMEDLEYS' ....

002a 89 'HAMLEYS' ....
003a 90 'CHEDDAR CHEESE' ....
004a 90 'RAF', Set BBL1003 ....GSP
005a 91 'DG CLUB, 'Spring' ....
006a 92 'Wartime Library' ....
007a 94 'HARRODS',(HR 2004)..GSP
008a 98 'JIF LEMON JUICE' ....
    1993: DG34 production ceased.
    Re-started in 1998.

DG 35 1932 Dennis Limousine

Another modification of DG 10, using the ladder component from DG 12 and a smaller roof-rack than DG 34.
000a 89 'EDINBURGH Fire Brigade' ..
001a 90 'POST OFFICE
    TELEPHONES' ....
002a 90 'RAF', Set BB1003.........GSP
003a 91 'SIGNALS HQ', SBX ....
004a 91 'N.F.S.', in Set HF1003....GSP
005a 92 'B.B.C. Wartime Outside
    Broadcasts' ....
    1994: withdrawn from DG range.

DG 36 1939 Chevrolet Pick-up

Based on DG30 Panel Van. Oil-drums load introduced in 1992.
000a 89 'BUCK & HICKMAN' ....
001a 90 'CAKEBREAD & ROBEY' ...
002a 91 'AVON TYRES' ....
003a 91 'US Army Explosives',
    Set USAL1003 ....GSP
004a 92 'DUCKHAMS'...................
005a 93 'REDEX' ....
    93 'CASTROL', ('Brooklands')...
006a 94 'GODE' (German) **£15-20**
007a 94 'PENNZOIL' ....
008a 94 Service Truck,
    (Set DDB 1003) ....GSP
009a 94 'Dr. PEPPER', special box ......

DG 37 1932 Ford Model 'A' Panel Van

The model has a modified DG 9 body plus a plastic van upper body and roof section.
000a 90 'CANADIAN CLUB' ....
001a 90 'Mr. THERM' ....
002a 91 'USA POLICE' ....
003a 92 'DAYS GONE CLUB '92'......
    1991: DG37 withdrawn from
    standard production.

DG 38 1925 Rolls-Royce Silver Ghost Saloon

Basically DG 25 + new roof moulding.
000a 89 Dark Green body, Gold lining .
    1990: DG38 withdrawn from
    standard production.

DG 39 1934 Mack Truck

Sack load. Steering wheel from 1991.
000a 90 'BLUE CIRCLE'...................
001a 91 'KETTON CEMENT' ....
002a 89 'GAS LIGHT & COKE' ....
003a 92 'PORTLAND CEMENT' ......
004a 92 Military Truck, SBX...............
    1993: DG39 withdrawn from
    standard production.

DG 40 1934 Mack Crane Truck

As DG 27 Breakdown Truck but with forward-facing crane.
000a 90 'TARMAC' ....
001a 91 'RICHARD COSTAIN' ....
002a 91 Ammunition Crane,
    in Set PH1003 ....GSP
003a 92 'US Navy', Set GU1003 ..GSP

004a 93 'RAF', in Set DM1003 ....GSP
    1992: DG40 withdrawn from
    standard production.

DG 41 1928 Karrier Trolley Bus

This Karrier 'E6' was the first model in the 'Premier Collection'.
000a 90 'ROBIN STARCH'.................
001a 90 'MARKS & SPENCER',
    special box ....
002a 91 'HAMLEYS', special box ......
003a 91 'BISTO' ....
004a 91 'BOVRIL' ....
005a 91 'N.Y. MOORS', in Set .....GSP
006a 92 'SAXA SALT' ....
007a 92 'SCHWEPPES' ....
008a 92 'HAMLEYS', HAL1004..GSP
009a 92 'SUNMAID RAISINS' ....
010a 94 'CROSSE & BLACKWELL' ..
011a 94 'ROWNTREE' ....
012a 94 'HUIS TEN BOSCH',
    (Japan) ....NGPP
013a 96 'COLMAN'S MUSTARD' ....
015a 98 'VENO'S' ....
016 99 'OXO' ....

DG 42 1934 Mack Tanker

DG 27 with a tank replacing the original crane. Steering wheel from 1991.
000a 90 'NATIONAL BENZOLE' ......
001a 90 'RAF', Set BB1003.........GSP
002a 91 'REGENT PETROL' ....
003a 91 'US Air Corps',
    in Set USAL1003 ....GSP
004a 91 'US Navy', (PHL1003) ....GSP
005a 92 Water Tank, (EAL1003)...GSP
006a 92 'SHELL FUEL OIL',
    (German market) ....NGPP
    'SHELL FUEL OIL'
    ('Brooklands') ....
007a 93 'PENNZOIL' ....
008a 94 'TEXACO' ....
    1995: DG42 withdrawn from
    standard production.

DG 43 1931 Morris Van

Another in the 'Premier Collection' range of models.
000a 90 'WEETABIX' ....
001a 90 'CHIVERS JAMS' ....
002a 91 'HAMLEYS', special box ......
003a 91 'D.G. CLUB Winter 90/91' .....
004a 91 'AC SPARK PLUGS' ....
005a 91 'LNER', (TPL1003).........GSP
006a 91 'METROPOLITAN Rly',
    (Set RSL1003).................GSP
007a 91 'BIRDS CUSTARD' ....
008a 91 '8th Army Ambulance', SBX..
009a 91 ''91 Toyfair', Dealer
    promo, special box **£8-12**
009b 91 no locations on door.....NGPP
010a 91 'Cornwall Home Guard',
    (Set HF1003).................GSP
011a 92 'HAMLEYS', special box ......
012a 92 'AMBROSIA' ....
013a 92 'ARNOTTS' ....
014a 92 'G.W.R.', (RSL3003) ....GSP

015a 92 'HARRODS', HD1004 ....GSP
016a 92 'SUNLIGHT SEIFE',
    (German market) ....NGPP
017a 93 'TATE SUGARS' ....
018a 94 'BRANDS' ....
019a 94 'RUPERT BEAR', SBX..........
020a 95 'BRASSO METAL POLISH' .
021a 95 'RUPERT', (RUL 1003) ..GSP
022a 96 'THREE in ONE OIL' ....
026a 97 'GOLDEN SHRED' ....
027a 98 'HORLICK'S' ....
028a 98 'EXPRESS DAIRY' ....
? 99 'BOOTS' ....

DG 44 1937 Scammell Six-wheeler

Realistic 'heavy-duty' wheels distinguish this model in the 'Premier Collection' range.
000a 90 'BISTO' ....
001a 90 'TOBLERONE' ....
002a 91 'MARMITE' ....
003a 91 'FOX's GLACIER MINTS' ....
004a 91 'N. Y. MOORS', in Set ....GSP
005a 92 'ROWNTREES' ....
006a 92 'McMULLEN' ....
007a 92 'D.G. CLUB Spring '92' ....
008a 92 'British Army',
    Set EAL1003.............GSP
009a 93 'BERLINER KINDL',
    German market ....NGPP
010a 93 'TETLEYS FINE ALES' ....
011a 94 'HEINZ PICKLES' ....
012a 94 'CARNATION' ....
013a 94 'Command Caravan',
    in Set DDB 1003.............GSP
014a 95 'KRONENBOURG' ....
015a 95 'RUPERT BEAR', SBX ....
016a 95 'VICTORY ALE',
    in VEL 1003 Set ....GSP
017a 95 'PEPSI-COLA', (US) ....NGPP
018a 96 'CASTLEMAINE XXXX' ....
019a 96 '7-UP' ....
020a 96 'BILLY SMART'S',
    in Circus Set CR 1003 ....GSP
022a 97 'QUALITY STREET' ....
023a 98 'BRILLO SOAP PADS' ....
024 99 'SHREDDED WHEAT' ....
025 99 'BELL'S' ....

DG 45 1908 Rolls-Royce Silver Ghost Coupé

000a 92 Metallic Green ....
001a 91 Crimson body, Black seats ......
002a 93 White body ....
003a 94 'DG Journal', 'gold' ......NGPP
    1993: DG45 withdrawn from
    standard production.

DG 46 1930 Bentley 4½ litre

Reminiscent of Lesney Y5-1 with separate wings and spare wheel.
000a 91 British Racing Green ....
001a 91 Dark Blue body, No. '1' ......
002a 91 'Gold-plate' effect **£20-30**
003a 92 British Racing Green, '2' ......
004a 92 Cream body, No. '18' ....
005a 93 Maroon body, No. '10'
    93 British Racing Green body,
    No. '85' ('Brooklands') ....
006a 93 Black ....
007a 95 Dark Green ....
008a 96 Blue, No. '3' ....

DG 47 1933 Austin Taxi

Introduced at the end of 1991 into the 'Premier Collection'.
000a 91 Dark Blue body ....
001a 92 Black body and wheels...........
002a 92 'HAMLEYS', (HA1002) .GSP
003a 92 'HAMLEYS',
    (in Set HAL1004) ....GSP
004a 93 Maroon body ....
005a 96 Dark Green ....
007a 97 Grey body and wheels ....
008a 98 'BOVRIL', Maroon / Black.....

DG 48 1939 Chevrolet

000a 91 Cream and Dark Green............
001a 91 'D.G. CLUB Autumn '91',
    Gold ....
002a 92 Cream and Maroon ....
003a 92 'British Army',
    in Set EAL1003..............GSP
004a 93 'YELLOW CABS' taxi ....

005a 93 'RAF', (Set DML1003)....GSP
006a 94 'HIGHWAY PATROL' ....
007a 94 'SHAEF', (DDL 1003) ...GSP
008a 94 'GHQ', (DDU 1003) ....GSP
009a 95 'BOOMERANG TAXIS'........
010a 96 'F.D.N.Y. Fire Chief' ....

DG 49   1931 AEC
Renown Double-Deck Bus

DG 15 and 17 radiator appear on this 6-wheeled bus in the 'Premier Collection'.
000a 91 'BOURN-VITA' ....
001a 91 'ROSES LIME JUICE' ....
002 92 'HAMLEYS',
    Black or Red chassis, SBX ....
003a 92 'MARTINI' ....
004a 92 'JANTZEN' ....
005a 92 'HAMLEYS', (HA1002) .GSP
006a 92 'D.G. CLUB 92' ....
007a 92 'HARRODS', (HD 1004) GSP
008a 92 'QANTAS', (QA1002) .....GSP
009a 93 'PEPSI-COLA', SBX ....
010a 93 'HAMLEYS', special box ....
011a 93 'LITTLEWOODS' ....
012a 93 'St. MICHAEL',
    in Set MS2004.................GSP
013a 94 'HEINZ SPAGHETTI' ......
014a 94 'SWAN VESTAS' ....
015a 94 'HUIS TEN BOSCH',
    (Japan) ....NGPP
016a 95 'SHREDDED WHEAT' ......
017a 95 'VICTORY-MARS',
    in Set VE 1003 ....GSP
018a 95 'CEAD MILE FAILTE',
    special box ....
019a 96 'MADAME TUSSAUDS' ......
020a 98 'GOLDEN SHRED' ....
021a 98 'JAFFA ORANGES' ....

DG 50   1926 'Bull-nose'
Morris Van

000a 92 'LYONS TEA' ....
001a 92 'BRYANT & MAY' ....
002a 93 'HAMLEYS' ....
003a 93 'H.M.V. - MILLERS' ....
004a 93 'DAYS GONE CLUB' ....
005a 93 'MARKS & SPENCER',
    in Set MS2004.................GSP
006a 93 'RAFFLES', (HLL2003)..GSP
007a 94 'KODAK' (Mexico).....**£30-40**
008a 94 'KIWI BOOT POLISH' ....
009a 94 'RUPERT BEAR' ....
010a 95 'PEPSI-COLA' ....
011a 94 'HARRODS', (HR 3002).GSP
012a 94 'NORMAN ROCKWELL',
    special box ....
013a 94 'AUSTRALIAN POST',
    (Australia)....................NGPP
014a 95 'SILVER KING' ....
015a 95 'GOLD CLUB' 3rd Ed.
    24k gold-plated.............NGPP
016a 96 'TOM SMITH'S' ....
019a 97 'LYLE'S GOLDEN SYRUP' ..
020a 98 'LIPTON'S TEA' ....
021a 98 'GLENMORANGIE' ....
023a 98 'BEEFEATER DRY GIN' ......
024 99 'HELLMAN'S' ....
025 99 'GLENFIDDICH' ....

DG 51
1934 Chevrolet Box Van

000a 92 'MADAME TUSSAUD'S' .....
001a 92 'STARTRITE' ....
002a 93 'HOVIS' ....
003a 93 'DAYS GONE CLUB' ....
004a 93 'MARKS & SPENCER',
    in Set MS2004.................GSP
005a 93 'BUSHELL'S TEA' ....
006a 94 'ERDAL', (Germany)....**£15-20**
007a 94 Army Wireless Truck,
    in Set DDB 1003............GSP
008a 94 'NORMAN ROCKWELL' ......
009a 95 'HAMLEYS' ....
010a 95 'RUPERT BEAR', SBX ....

011a 95 'Dr. PEPPER', SBX ....
012a 96 'JOHNSON'S WAX' ....
014a 97 'CHIVER'S JELLIES' ....
015 99 'BARR'S IRN-BRU' ....

DG 52
1935 Morris Parcels Van

Introduced in to the 'Premier Range' in October 1992.
000a 92 'ROYAL MAIL' ....
001a 92 'PICKFORDS' ....
002a 93 'PEPSI-COLA', SBX ....
003a 93 'LNER PARCELS' ....
004a 93 '43rd Division' ....
005a 93 'DAYS GONE CLUB' ....
006a 93 '1993 TOYFAIR' ....
007a 93 'RAF', in Set DM1003 ....GSP
008a 94 'NEW YORK TOY FAIR' .....
009a 94 'KODAK FILMS',
    (Mexico)....................**£30-40**
009b 94 (general release) ....
010a 95 'HARRODS' (HR 2002)..GSP
011a 95 'HAMLEYS' ....
012a 95 'SAROTTI SCHOKOLADE' .
013a 95 'RUPERT BEAR', SBX ....
014a 95 'A.R.P.', Set VEL 1003....GSP
015a 96 'P. O. TELEPHONES',
    in Set POL 1003..............GSP
018a 97 McVITIE & PRICES
    TOYLAND BISCUITS' ....
019a 98 'GUERNSEY P. O.' ....
020a 98 'BLUE BIRD LUXURY
    ASSORTMENT' ....

DG 53   1926 Rolls-Royce
Laudaulet

Introduced in 1992 as a Promotional. It was issued as a standard model in October of that year.
000a 92 'Days Gone Collector',
    'Gold-plate' effect ....
001a 93 'Gold-plate' effect,
    'Promotional' base ....NGPP
002a 95 Gold plated (RPL 1003)..GSP
    1995: DG53 withdrawn from standard production.

DG 54
1929 Rolls-Royce 'D' back

This version appeared first as a Promotional (in May 1992).
000a 93 Blue body, Tan roof ....
001a 94 'Days Gone Collector',
    Vol.4, 'Gold' effect ....
002a 95 Gold plated (RPL 1003)..GSP
003a 95 'Gold' effect, Germany .NGPP

DG 55
Horse-Drawn Tanker

Introduced in 1992 and given a Days Gone number, this model has only been used for Promotional purposes.

DG 56   1934 Ford Model
'A' Van (Raised Roof)

Introduced in 1992 for promotional use.
000a 94 'D. G. Club', Winter 94..........
001 99 'CHARRINGTONS' ....

DG 57   1939 Ford Tanker

000a 93 'SHELL-BP Aviation' ....
001a 94 'ESSO PETROLEUM' ....
003a 94 'USAF', Set DDU 1003 ...GSP
002a 95 'NAVY', DDL 1003 ....GSP
004a 95 'GULF GASOLINE' ....
005a 96 'CASTROL MOTOR OIL' .....

DG 58
1950 Morris 'Z' Van

The first in a new range of 1950s and 1960s model vehicles called 'Days Gone Vanguards'. It did not acquire cab window glazing until 1995.
000a 93 'P. O. TELEPHONES' ....
001a 93 'MALVERN WATER' ....
002 93 'MACKESONS STOUT' ....
003a 94 'ROYAL MAIL' ....
004a 94 'GILLETTE' ....
005a 94 'HAMLEYS' ....
006a 94 'PEPSI COLA' ....
007a 94 'D.G. CLUB', Spring 94 ....
008a 94 'D.G. GOLD CLUB',
    (Gold finish)..................NGPP
009a 95 'SINGER' ....
010a 95 'BRITISH RAILWAYS',
    in Set BRL 1003 ....GSP
011a not yet allocated.
012a 95 '7-UP' ....
013a 94 'HARRODS',(HR 2004)..GSP
014a 96 'A. A. Technical Service' ....
015a 97 'HEINZ BAKED BEANS' ......
017a 98 'NATIONAL BENZOLE' ....
018 99 'SMIRNOFF' ....

The second of the original 'Days Gone Vanguards'. Cab window glazing appeared in 1995.
000a 93 'BIRDS CUSTARD' ....
001a 93 'CANADA DRY' ....
002a 93 'DUNLOPILLO' ....
003a 94 'PEPSI-COLA XMAS', SBX ..
004a 94 'LUCOZADE' ....
005a 94 'BE-RO FLOUR' ....
006a 94 'HAMLEYS 94' ....
007a 94 'PEPSI-COLA' ....
008a 94 'WEET-BIX for HEALTH' ....
009a 94 '94 TOYFAIR' **£10-15**
010a 94 'NEW YORK TOYFAIR',
    USA **£100-125**
011a 95 'ARNOTTS BISCUITS' ....
012a 95 'OXYDOL' ....
013a 95 'BRITISH RAILWAYS',
    in Set BRL 1003 ....GSP
014a not yet allocated.
015a 95 'RUPERT', (RUL 1003)..GSP
016a 95 '7-UP', special box ....
017a 95 'D.G. CLUB', Autumn 95....
018a 95 'London Olympic Games',
    special box..................NGPP
019a 96 'SHELL 100 Years' ....
022 97 'CAMPBELLS' ....
026a 97 'B.S.A. MOTOR CYCLES' ....
027a 98 'FISHERMAN'S FRIEND' ....
028 99 'HEINZ' ....

The third model in the Days Gone 'Vanguards' range. It did not have cab window glazing until 1995.
000a 93 'ESSEX' ....
001a 93 'DERBYSHIRE' ....
002a 93 'WESTERN AREA - OBAN'.
003a 94 'WEST SUSSEX F. B.' ....
004a 94 'NEW ZEALAND F. B.' ....
005a 94 'LONDON', (FB 1003).....GSP
006a 94 'Special Fire Service',
    in Set HR 3002..............GSP
007a 95 'LONDON F. B.' ....
008a 95 'CIVIL DEFENCE CORPS' ...
009a 94 'MIDDLESEX F. B.' ....
011a 98 'CHESHIRE COUNTY' ....
012 99 'LANCASHIRE F. B.' ....
014 99 'SURREY' ....

DG 61
1953 Pontiac Delivery Van

The fourth model in the Days Gone 'Vanguards' range.
000a 93 'Dr. PEPPER' ....
001a 93 'DETROIT POLICE' ....
002a 93 'MILWAUKEE' Ambulance ...
003a 94 'T.W.A.' ....
004a 94 'PEPSI COLA', SBX ....

005a 94 'EXCELSIOR',
    in Set MCL 1003............GSP
006a 94 'Dr. PEPPER', SBX ....
007a 95 'AGFA FILMS' ....
008a 95 '7-UP', (US, SBX)............NGPP
    1995: DG61 withdrawn from standard production.

DG 62   1935 Ford
Articulated Tanker

Lledo's first articulated vehicle model.
000a 94 'REGENT PETROLEUM' ......
001a   not yet allocated.
002a 95 'FINA PETROL' ....

DG 63   1950 Bedford
30cwt Delivery Van

Another in the Days Gone 'Vanguards' range. Early 1994 issues had no cab window glazing.
000a 94 'SAINSBURYS' ....
001a 94 'PENGUIN BOOKS' ....
002a 94 'OXO' ....
003a 94 'D.G. Club', Summer 94 ......
004a 94 'HAMLEYS' ....
005a 95 'CEREBOS SALT' ....
006a 95 'WALL'S SAUSAGES' ....
007a   not yet allocated.
008a 95 'RUPERT', (RUL 1003) ..GSP
009a 95 'UK TRADE FAIR' **£10-15**
010a 95 'NEW YORK
    TRADE FAIR' **£100-125**
011a 95 'Dr. PEPPER', SBX ....
012a 96 'PERSIL' ....
016 97 'PEPSI-COLA' ....
017a 97 'RECKITT'S BLUE' ....
018a 98 'IMPERIAL LEATHER' ....
019 99 'TEACHER'S WHISKY' ....
020 99 'BLACK & WHITE' ....
021 99 'NEEDLERS' ....

DG 64
1950 Bedford Ambulance

Also in the Days Gone 'Vanguards' range. Some early 1994 issues did not have cab window glazing.
000a 94 'KENT COUNTY' ....
001a 94 'DURHAM COUNTY' ....
002a 95 'L.C.C. AMBULANCE' ....
003a 95 'FAMAGUSTA' ....
004a 95 'BRITISH RAILWAYS',
    in Set BRL 1003 ....GSP
005a 96 'P. O. TELEPHONES',
    Set POL 1003 ....GSP

DG 65   1960 Morris 1000
Traveller

The first car model in the original 'Vanguards' range and also the first Lledo model to be made to a quoted scale of 1:43. For further issues, please see number VA10 in the 'Vanguards' section.
000a 94 Green **£6-9**
001a 94 White **£6-9**
002a 95 Trafalgar Blue **£6-9**
003a 95 Smoke-Grey **£6-9**
004a 95 'Days Gone Journal',
    'Gold-plated' effect ......NGPP

DG 66
1926 Dennis Delivery Van

000a 94 'CASTROL MOTOR OIL' ......
001a 94 'AUSTRALIAN POST',
    (Australia)....................NGPP
002a 94 'PEPSI COLA XMAS',
    special box ....
003a 95 'CAMPBELL'S SOUPS' ....
004a 95 'HARRODS', (HR2004)..GSP
005a 95 'D.G. CLUB', Winter 94-95',
    special box ....

006a 95 'PARIS OLYMPIC
GAMES', special box ..NGPP
007a 95 'Dr. PEPPER', SBX ....
008a 96 'WHITBREAD'.......................
009a 96 'SHELL 100 Years' ....
012a 97 'IMPERIAL AIRWAYS' ....
014a 98 'B.P. MOTOR SPIRIT' ....
017a 98 'GROLSCH'..........................
018a 98 'ELIZABETH SHAW' ....
019 99 'CHIVERS & SONS Ltd'........

DG 67 1935 Ford Articulated Truck

000 94 'DUNLOP' ....
001a 94 'ROBERT BROS CIRCUS' ....
002a 95 'LYONS SWISS ROLLS' ....
003a 95 'D.G. CLUB' Summer '95,
special box ....
004a 95 'Dr. PEPPER', SBX ....
005a 96 'PEPSI COLA' ....
006a 96 'SMITHS CRISPS'.................
007a 96 'TOM ARNOLD'S
CIRCUS, Set CR 1003....GSP
010a 97 'SERVIS' ....
011a 98 'JEYES' FLUID' ....

DG 68 1932 AEC Open-top Bus

The lower section casting from DG 15
given a new open upper deck.
000a 94 'RAF DUXFORD',
(Lledo Show LE)............£6-8
001a 94 'D.G. CLUB', Summer '94....
002a 95 'SIGHTSEEING', SBX..........
003a 95 'CROSVILLE'.........................
004a 95 'Victory in Europe',
in Set VEL 1003 ....GSP
005a 96 'STRATFORD BLUE' ....
006a 96 '7-UP' ....

DG 69 1960 Morris 1000 Van

A popular subject in 1:43 scale.
000a 95 'EVER-READY' ....
001a 95 'CURRYS' ....
002a 95 'D.G. CLUB' Spring'95,
special box ....
1995: DG69 became VA 11.

DG 70 1939 Ford Canvas-back Truck

000a 95 'ANCHOR BEER' ....
001a 96 'N. C. B' ....
002a 96 'PEPSI COLA', SBX ....
003a 96 'SHELL 100 Years' ....
004a 96 'P. O. TELEPHONES',
in Set POL 1003..............GSP
005a 96 'DG CLUB', Autumn '96 ....

DG 71 1959 Morris LD150 Van

A 1:50 scale 'D-G Vanguards' model.
000a 95 'KODAK' ....
001a 95 'WORMWOOD SCRUBS'.......
002a 95 'H.P. SAUCE' ....
003a 95 'DUXFORD '95' ....
004a 95 'MELBOURNE OLYMPIC
GAMES',special box.............
005a 96 'ROYAL MAIL' ....
006a 96 '7-UP', special box ....
007a 96 'PEPSI COLA', SBX ....
008a 96 'D. G. CLUB', Winter '96 ......
009a 96 'Sir Robert Fossett's Circus',
in Set CR 1003 ....GSP
013a 97 'WHITBREAD'......................
014 97 '999', Limited Edition.............
015a 98 'MOBILGAS' ....
016a 98 'POST OFFICE
TELEGRAPH SERVICES' ....
017 99 'RAIL EXPRESS PARCELS'.

DG 72 1952 VW Beetle

'D-G Vanguards' VW in 1:43 scale.
000a 95 Blue...............................
001a 95 Pale Green ....
1995: DG72 became VA12.

DG 73 1955 VW Kombi Van

A 'D-G Vanguards' 1:50 scale model.
000a 95 'CINZANO'............................
001a 95 'BOSCH'..............................
002a 95 'PEPSI COLA', Xmas
special, Light Blue, SBX,
LE 5,000.....................NGPP
003a 95 'PEPSI COLA', Xmas
special, White, packed
in Pepsi 'can'....................NGPP
004a 96 'PEPSI COLA', SBX ....
005a 96 'GERMAN POST' ....
006a 96 'ESSO Paraffin' ....
007a 96 '7-UP', special box ....
008a 96 'UK TRADE FAIR 96'............
009a 96 'D. G. CLUB', Spring '96'......
013a 97 'MADAME TUSSAUD'S' .....
014a 98 'LAMBS NAVY RUM'...........
015 99 'ORANGINA'..........................
016 99 'MICHELIN' ....

DG 74 1959 Austin '7' Mini Saloon

A 1:43 'D-G Vanguards' model.
000a 95 Pale Blue.............................
001a 95 Red.....................................
002a 95 'POLICE', White....................
1995: DG74 withdrawn from
the 'Days Gone' range. See
the 'Vanguards' section for
subsequent issues as VA 13.

DG 75 1957 Bristol Lodekka Bus

A 'Days Gone Vanguards' model, in the
'HO' scale of 1:87.
000a 95 'DULUX'...............................
001a 95 'WESTONS'...........................
002a 95 'DG CLUB', Xmas '95 ....
003a 96 'TIZER', 'Fife' ....
005a 97 'POLO MINTS' ....
006 98 'TATE & LYLE' ....
008 99 'WHITE LABEL' ....

DG 76 Mercedes Bus

000a 96 'JAEGERMEISTER'.............
001a 96 'DG' Summer Special ....
002a 97 'SWISS POST' ....

DG 77 1937 Scammell Tanker

000a 96 'MOBILGAS - MOBILOIL' ...
001a 97 'I.C.I. CHEMICALS' ....
002 99 'NATIONAL BENZOLE' ....

DG 78 1939 Dodge Airflow

000a 96 'MOBILOIL' ....
001a 97 'TEXACO' ....

DG 79 1939 Ford Fire Engine

000a 96 'U.S.A.A.F.'...........................
001a 97 'CHICAGO FIRE Dept.' ....
002a 98 'US NAVY FIRE Dept.' ....

DG 80 1937 Scammell Tractor

000a 96 'PICKFORDS' ....
003a 97 'BRITISH RAIL' ....
004a 97 'ROYAL MAIL' ....
005 99 'E. W. RUDD' ....
006 99 'TATE & LYLE' ....

DG 81 1935 Sentinel S6 Steam Wagon

000 99 'TARMAC LIMITED' ....

DG 82 1930 Ford Model 'A' Coupé

000a 97 Two-tone Grey ....
001a 97 Brown and Beige ....

DG 83 Reo Van

000a 95 'ROME OLYMPIC GAMES' .

DG 84

DG 84 Not yet allocated

DG 85 1912 Renault Van

000a 97 'RENAULT' ....
001a 97 'MICHELIN' ....
002a 97 'ROYAL MAIL' ....
004a 98 'VAN HOUTEN'S COCOA' ...
006a 98 'BIRD'S GOLDEN
RAISING POWDER' ....

DG 86 1955 VW Camper

000a 97 'FLOWER POWER' ....
001a 97 Red and Black ....

DG 87 1957 M.A.N. Van

000a 97 'HOLSTEN BIER' ....
001 97 'De KUYPER' ....
003 99 'JOHNNIE WALKER' ....

DG 88 1931 Sentinel 4-wheel Steam Wagon

000a 97 'WATNEYS' ....
001a 97 'McMULLEN & SONS' ....
005a 98 'TATE & LYLE'S' ....
006a 98 'BASS & Co.' ....
008 99 'J. SAINSBURY' ....
009 99 'J. J. HATFIELD' ....
010 99 'MORRIS & Co.' ....

DG 89

DG 89 Not yet allocated

DG 90 1966 GMC Tanker

DG 90 1966 GMC TANKER
000a 98 'TEXACO' ....

DG 91 1930 Foden Steam Wagon

000a 98 'NEWQUAY STEAM
BITTER' ....
001a 98 'PICKFORDS'.........................
003 99 'FULLERS' ....
004 99 'WD' ....
005 99 'TATE & LYLE' ....

DG 92, 93, 94, 95, 96

DG 92 Not yet allocated
DG 93 Not yet allocated
DG 94 Not yet allocated
DG 95 Not yet allocated
DG 96 Not yet allocated

DG 97 1934 Sentinel S4 Steam Wagon

000 99 'TETLEY FINE ALES'..........
003 99 'GLENDRONACH' ....

DG 98

DG 98 Not yet allocated

DG 99 1931 Sentinel 4-wheel Steam Wagon

000 99 'McALPINE' ....

DG 100 1937 Fordson 7v Truck

000 99 'E. & K. BENTON' ....

DG 101 1931 Sentinel 6-wheel Steam Wagon

000 99 'McALPINE' ....

DG 102 Horse-Drawn Brewer's Dray

000 99 'Wm. YOUNGER' ....

New issues

287

'Days-Gone' Gift Sets

Individual models contained in these sets are listed separately in the 'Days Gone' listings. This list indicates the content of specific sets and prices where available.

Set 1 96 **'Assorted' Set**....Buses DG15-035, DG41-011 and DG75-000 ....**£10-12**
Set 1 97 **'Assorted' Set**....Vans DG26-018, DG44-018 and DG66-008......**£10-12**
Set 2 96 **'Assorted' Set**....Vans DG6-125, DG13-064 and DG52-012........**£10-12**
Set 2 97 **'Assorted' Set**....Buses DG49-019, DG68-005 and DG76-000....**£10-12**
Set 3 96 **'Assorted' Set**....Vans DG21-044, DG43-020 and DG66-003......**£10-12**
Set 3 97 **'Assorted' Set**....Tankers DG57-005, DG77-000, DG78-000.......**£10-12**
Set 4 96 **'Assorted' Set**....Tankers DG57-004 and DG67-000, plus VW Van DG73-001 ....**£10-12**
Set 4 97 **'Assorted' Set**....Vans DG6-138, DG21-048 and DG67-006........**£10-12**
Set 5 96 **'Assorted' Set**....Trucks DG26-016 and DG44-014, plus VW Van DG73-000 ....**£10-12**
Set 5 97 **'Assorted' Set**....Vans DG51-012 and DG63-012, plus Ford Model 'T' Car DG33-014....**£10-12**
Set 6 96 **'Assorted' Set**....Vans DG59-011 and DG67-002, plus Bristol Lodekka DG75-001 ....**£10-12**
Set 6 97 **'Assorted' Set**....Vans DG43-022, DG58-014 and DG73-006......**£10-12**

AB 1003 90 **Arnotts Biscuits Set** DG6-101a Ford T Van, DG11-016a Horse Drawn Removal Van, DG13-045a Ford Van....**£20-25**
BA 1003 89 **British Army Collection** DG8-017a Tanker, DG13-038a Ford Van 'Recruitment', DG19-009a Staff Car....**£20-25**
BB 1003 90 **RAF Ground Crew Support** DG20-015a Balloon Tender, DG35-002a RAF Riggers, DG42-001a Fuel Tanker....**£15-20**
BBL 1003 90 **RAF Personnel Transport** DG28-011a Truck, DG30-008a Ambulance, DG34 004a Office (12,500)....**£15-20**
BM 1004 90 **Bryant & May Set** Four DG21 vans: 022a 'Scottish Bluebell', 023a 'Bryant & May', 024a 'Swan Vestas', 025a 'Englands Glory'. (Limited Edition of 12,500)....**£20-25**
86 **Commonwealth Games Set** DG7-007a Woody Wagon, DG10-016a Coach, DG15-011a AEC Bus....**£10-12**
BPL 1003 96 **British Motoring Classics** 24k gold plated Ford Anglia 105E, Mini-Minor and Morris 1000 Traveller....NGPP
BRL 1003 95 **British Railways Set** DG58-010a, 59-013a, 64-004a....**£12-15**
CC 1003 86 **Coca-Cola Set** DG6-058a Ford T Van, DG11-007a Horse Drawn Van, DG13-021a Ford Van....**£25-35**
CC 2003 87 **Coca-Cola Set** DG6-054a Ford T Van, DG21-005a Chevrolet, DG26-002a Chevrolet....**£25-35**
CP 1 84 **Collector Pack** DG3-003a Robertsons, DG4-005a Pears Soap, DG6-017a Daily Express....**£10-15**
CR 1003 96 **Classic Circus Collection** DG44 'Billy Smart's', DG67 'Tom Arnold's', DG71 'Fossett's'....**£15-20**
DDB 1003 94 **British D-Day Set** DG36 Service Truck, DG51 Wireless Truck, and DG44 Command Caravan....**£12-15**
DDL 1003 94 **'D-DAY' Ltd. Ed. Set** DG29-008a, 48-007a, 57-002a....**£12-15**
DDU 1003 94 **American D-Day Set** DG29 Signals Truck, DG48 GHQ Staff Car, DG57 Flight Refueller....**£12-15**
DML 1003 93 **Dambusters Set** DG16-034a Control, DG28-030a RAF, DG48-005a RAF, (7,500)....**£12-15**
DM 1003 93 **Dambusters Set** DG16-033a NAAFI, DG40-004a RAF, DG52-007a RAF....**£12-15**
EAL 1003 92 **El Alamein Set** DG42-005a Water, DG44-008a Army, DG48-003a Army, (12,500)....**£12-15**
FB 1003 94 **London Fire Brigade** DG5-010a, 12-019a, 60-005a....**£12-15**
GS 1 84 **Gift Set** DG6-023a Railway Express, DG7-002a Ford Sales, DG9-001a NY-Rio....**£10-15**
GS 2 85 **Gift Set** DG6-033a Barclays, DG11-001a Abels, DG13-005a Michelin....**£15-20**
GS 3 85 **Bus Gift Set** DG10-013a Trailways, DG15-002a Castlemaine, DG17 001a Eurotour....**£10-15**
GS 4 86 **Coca-Cola Set** DG6-058a Ford T Van, DG11-007a Woody Wagon, DG13-021a Ford Van....**£20-25**
GS 5 86 **Hershey's Set** DG6-055a Ford T Van, DG13-023a Ford A Van, DG16-012a Dennis Van....**£20-25**
GS 1004 89 **Golden Days Of Film** Early Film Industry vans in 'gold-plate': DG6-091a Britannia, DG13-034a Empire, DG18-014a B & C Films, DG21-016a Majestic (10,000)....**£80-90**
GU 1003 92 **Guadalcanal Set** DG28-027a Marines, DG29-005a Marines, DG40-003a Navy....**£10-13**
84 **Hamleys Set** DG3-009a, DG4-008a, DG6-035a, DG7-004a, DG10-009a, DG13-004a....**£35-40**
HA 1002 92 **Hamleys London Set** DG47-002a Taxi and DG49-005a AEC Bus....**£8-12**
HA 2002 94 **Hamleys London Set** DG12-018a and DG15-033a....**£8-12**
HAL 1004 92 **Hamleys Limted Edition Set** DG11-021a, DG21-037a, DG41-008a, DG47-003a, (5,000)....**£15-20**
HD 1002 92 **Harrods Set** DG11-020a Van and DG15-028a AEC Bus....**£10-12**
HD 1004 92 **Harrods Set** DG3-014a, 13-051a, 43-015a, 49-007a....**£12-18**
HF 1003 91 **The Home Front Set** DG16-030a YMCA, DG35-004a NFS, DG43-010a Cornwall....**£12-15**
HFL 1002 97 **Henry Ford Set** 'Bronzed' finish DG9 and DG33, plinth, clear acrylic box 'FORD', 7,500....**£12-15**
HLL 1003 92 **Hotel Labels Set** DG6-108a 'Colombia', DG21-035a 'de Paix', DG33-005a 'de Paris', 12,500....**£12-15**
HLL 2003 93 **Hotel Labels Set** DG13-058a 'Grand', DG18-024a 'Imperial', DG50-006a 'Raffles', 7,500....**£12-15**
HR 2002 94 **Harrods Set** DG4-018a, DG52-010a....**£10-12**
HR 3002 94 **Harrods Set** DG50-011a, DG60-006a....**£10-12**
HR 2004 94 **Harrods Set** DG15-036a, 34-007a, 58-013a, 66-004a....**£15-20**
LOS 8002 95 **'Souvenir of London'** 'LCC' Fire Engine and Ambulance....**£8-12**
LOS10002 95 **'Souvenir of London'** Open top Bus 'See London' and Morris Z Van 'Royal Mail'....**£8-12**
LOS11002 95 **'Souvenir of London'** Taxi and 'Madame Tussaud's' Bus....**£8-12**
LP 1553 91 **Charles & Diana Set** Two Rolls-Royce models in special Purple box (not limited)....**£10-15**
LS 1004 89 **London Stores Set No.1** Four different vans: DG6-087a Selfridges, DG13-031a Aquascutum, DG18-013a Fortnum & Mason, DG21-012a DAKS Simpson....**£12-18**
LS 2004 90 **London Stores Set No.2** DG6-097a Jaeger, DG13-036a Austin Reed, DG18-018a Asprey, DG21-020a Liberty....**£12-18**
LSL 1005 98 **Land Speed Legends Set** 5 record breakers: LP 4903, LP 5267, LP 5268, LP 5269, LP 5270....**£20-30**
MCL 1003 94 **Motorcycle Vans Set** DG21-041a, 30-017a, 61-005a....**£12-15**
MG 1003 92 **Malta George Cross Set** DG12-017a Valletta, DG18-022a St John, DG28-026a Royal Navy....**£10-15**
MS 1004 90 **Marks & Spencer Set** DG11-014a, DG13-014a, DG21-019a, DG41-001a. (Also available singly)....**£10-15**
MS 2004 93 **Marks & Spencer Set** DG13-057a, DG49-012a, DG50-005a, DG51-004a....**£15-18**
NYMR1003 89 **North Yorks Moors Set 1** DG6-093a Cartage, DG17-018a NYM Railway, DG28-008a Parcels (7,500)....**£15-18**
NYMR2003 90 **North Yorks Moors Set 2** DG13-044a, DG15-027a, DG16-025a, (6,500)....**£15-18**
NYMR1002 91 **North Yorks Moors Set 3** DG41-005a Scarborough and DG44-004a NYMR, (6,500)....**£10-12**
PHL 1003 91 **Pearl Harbor Set 1** DG28-019a Corps, DG30-013a Navy, DG42-004a Navy, (12,500) .**£10-15**
PH 1003 91 **Pearl Harbor Set 2** DG21-030a Marines, DG28-022a Torpedo, DG40-002a Crane....**£10-15**
POL 1003 96 **Post Office Telephones Set** 52-015a, 64-005a, 70-004a....**£15-18**
QA 1002 92 **Qantas Set** DG13-052a Ford Van, and DG49-008a Bus....**£8-12**
? 87 **RFC / RAF Set** DG6-063a and DG28-011a '216 Squadron', DG18-008a Ambulance....**£45-55**
RN 1003 88 **Royal Navy Set** DG17-017a 'Britannia', DG20-011a 'Rooke', DG28-006a 'Devonport' (10,000)....**£35-45**
RPL 1003 95 **Gold Rolls-Royces Set** DG43-021a, 59-015a, 63-008a....**£15-20**
RR 1003 88 **Rolls Royce Set** 19-003a, 24-002a, 25-002a, plinth, 7,500..**£30-35**
RR 2003 97 **Rolls Royce Set** DG32, DG53 and DG54....**£10-12**
RSL 1003 91 **Railway Express Parcels 1** DG16-029a LNER, DG28-015a LMS, DG43-006a Metropolitan, (12,500)....**£10-15**
RSL 2003 91 **Railway Express Parcels 2** DG13-050a Southern, DG21-034a LMS/LNER and DG28-020a GWR, (10,000)...**£10-15**
RSL 3003 91 **Railway Express Parcels 3** DG21-036a LNER, DG28-028a Southern and DG43-014a GWR, (10,000)....**£10-15**
RSL 4003 93 **Railway Road Vehicles of the 1900s** DG3-015a GER, DG4-016a Furness and DG11-024a GtNorthern, (7,500)....**£15-18**
RUL 1003 95 **'RUPERT 75th' Set** DG43-021a, 59-015a, 63-008a....**£12-15**
TPL 1003 91 **LNER Parcels Vans** DG16-028a Dennis, DG28-014a Mack and DG43-005a Morris, (12,500)....**£12-15**
USA 1003 91 **US Army Set 1** DG27-006a, DG28-017a and DG30-012a ..**£12-15**
USAL1003 91 **US Army Set 2** DG29-003a Ambulance, DG36-003a Pick-Up, DG42-003a Air Corps, (12,500)....**£12-15**
VE 1003 95 **'VE-DAY' Set** DG13, DG17 and DG49....**£12-15**
VEL 1003 95 **'VE-DAY' Ltd. Ed. Set** DG44, DG52 and DG68....**£12-15**

Lledo Promotionals and 'View Vans'

Lledo Promotionals came into being in 1985. Using existing standard castings, they were originally produced in runs of as few as 500 and went direct to clients, not to normal retail outlets. Some earlier 'promotionals' were supplied with the 'Days Gone' logo on the baseplate (soon modified to read 'Lledo Promotional'). Runs of up to 1,000 units were finished with printed self-adhesive labels while runs of 1,000 or more warranted tampo printing. Many thousands of Promotionals have been produced and as a result it has proved impossible to provide meaningful price information for collectors.

View Vans and Souvenir Buses are a variation on the Promotional theme and include LP6, LP13, LP15, LP17 and LP21. They are printed with a standard 'camera' logo and supplied in a choice of three colours for each type. They are finished with photographic labels including stately homes, football teams, etc. The models are completed by a company independent of Lledo and are packed in distinctive 'dark gold' boxes. Values have yet to exceed the normal retail price of these souvenirs.

Vanguard Gift Sets

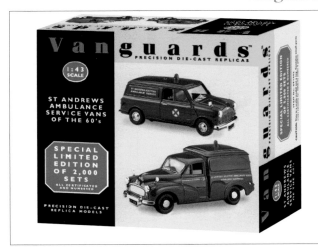

ST1002
St Andrews Ambulance
Service Set

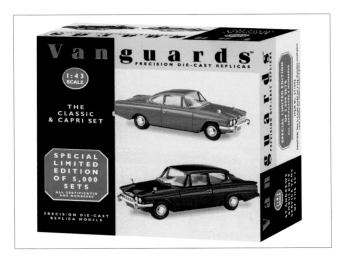

CL1002
Classic & Capri Set

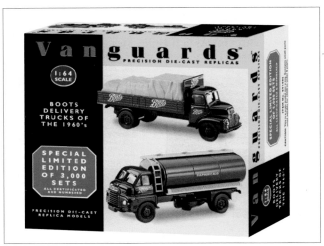

BO1002
Boots The Chemist Set

Pictures kindly supplied by Lledo PLC, & reproduced by their kind permission.

Lledo - Models of Days Gone

VA 33000
Ford 300E Van

VA 38000
Vauxhall Victor FA

VA 34000
Ford Capri 109E

DG 99000
1931 Sentinel Steam Wagon

E.F.E. Exclusive First Editions

16212 Bristol MW Coach
'EASTERN SCOTTISH'

26301 Guy Arab II Utility Bus
'LONDON TRANSPORT'

25507 RML Routemaster
'LONDON TRANSPORT'

23604 Bedford TK Luton
'CROSVILLE NBC'

Pictures supplied by E.F.E. and reproduced by their kind permission.

1906 Waterous

1907 Seagrave

1932 Ford Model AA

1912 Ford Model T

1937 GMC Van

1920 Mack AC Truck

1957 Chevy Pickup

1930 Ford Model A Pickup

Pictures supplied by Matchbox Collectibles and reproduced by their kind permission.

Matchbox Collectibles

1912 Benz

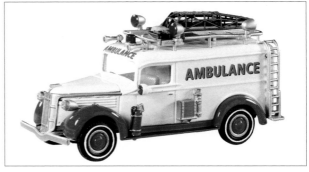

1937 GMC

1916 Ford Model T

1939 Bedford

1941 Chevrolet

1952 Land Rover

1954 Ford

1929 Fowler Crane

Pictures supplied by Matchbox Collectibles and reproduced by their kind permission.

Miscellaneous Lledo Series

'Fantastic Set-O-Wheels'

A series of models introduced in 1985 for the US toy market and distributed by Hartoy Inc. of Florida. They were blister-packed on card with the legend 'Made in England by Lledo (London) Ltd.' on most of the baseplates.

F1a	DG 6	'MALIBU OR BUST'	£10-15
F1b		same but 'Days Gone' baseplate	£10-15
F2a	DG 7	'TRI-STATE DEALER', Yellow wheels	£10-15
F2b		Black wheels, 'DG' baseplate	£10-15
F3a	DG15	'LIQUID BUBBLE'	£10-15
F4a	DG10	'OAKRIDGE SCHOOL'	£10-15
F5a	DG12	'BOSTON FIRE Dept'	£10-15
F5b		with 'Days Gone' baseplate	£10-15
F6a	DG13	'JOLLY TIME'	£10-15
F6b		with 'Days Gone' baseplate	£10-15
F7a	DG14	'POLICE' Car	£10-15
F7b		with 'Days Gone' baseplate	£10-15
F7c		As F7a but 20-spoke wheels	£10-15
F8a	DG14	'SAN-DIEGO FIRE'	£10-15
F8b		As F8a but Brass grille	£10-15

'Marathons'

Introduced in 1987. Some also used as promotionals. Range discontinued in 1988. **MPR is £5 or less.**

M1a	01a	87	**Leyland Olympian Bus**, 'LONDON PRIDE SIGHTSEEING', 'PINDISPORTS', Blue body
M1a	01b	87	same but 'PINDISPORTS' in Red
M1a	02a	87	'LONDON ZOO'
M1a	03a	87	'PAN AM'
M2a	01a	87	**Setra Coach**, 'PAN AM'
M2a	02a	87	'AIR CANADA'
M2a	03a	87	'GHANA AIRWAYS'
M3a	01a	87	**Neoplan Spaceliner**, 'ISLAND TOURS'
M3a	02a	87	'SPEEDLINK'
M3a	03a	87	'GATWICK FLIGHTLINE'
M4a	01a	88	**Leyland Rigid Truck**, 'FEDERAL EXPRESS'
M5a	01a	88	**Leyland Tipper**, 'LECCA ARC'
M6a	01a	88	**Leyland Tanker**, 'SHELL'

'Land Speed Legends'

This range of model Land Speed Record Cars employs an 'LP' reference system but are not considered to be 'promotionals'. See also Set number LSL 1005.

LP 4903	'THRUST SSC', Andy Green
LP 5267	'BLUEBIRD', Sir Malcolm Campbell
LP 5268	'THRUST 2', Richard Noble
LP 5269	'RAILTON MOBIL SPECIAL', John Cobb
LP 5270	'SONIC 1', Craig Breedlove

'London's Burning'

A small range of emergency vehicles based on the ITV drama series set in 'a London fire station'. Special packaging.

LP 5219	(DG5)	Shand-Mason Fire Engine
LP 5220	(DG12)	Dennis Fire Engine
LP 5221	(DG27)	Mack Breakdown Truck
LP 5222	(DG60)	Dennis F8 Fire Engine
LP 5223	(DG64)	Bedford Ambulance
LP 5224	(PM105)	Ford Transit

Edocar ('Old-Timer' Series)

Made in 1986 for Edor BV (Fred Beheer BV), in the Netherlands and sold there under the name 'EDOCAR'. The baseplates all have the wording 'EDOCAR - Made in England by Lledo' plus the model number. Some have original Days-Gone colours but have been left unprinted (without logos). All but A7 have only Black tyres. The 'double window' boxes were made and printed in Holland.

A1a	DG 8	Tanker (unprinted), Red/Black/Yellow	£10-15
A1b		'ESSO BLUE', Blue/White	£10-15
A2a	DG 12	Dennis Fire Engine, Red body, White floor	£10-15
A2b		Red body, Black floor	£10-15
A3	DG 14	Taxi, Yellow / Black	£10-15
A4a	DG 16	'HUMBROL', Chrome grille	£10-15
A4b		with Brass grille	£10-15
A5	DG 17	AEC Single Deck Bus, White, (box states 'AEC Double Decker Bus')	£10-15
A6a	DG 18	Packard 'Ambulance', Chrome grille	£10-15
A6b		Brass grille	£10-15
A7	DG 19	Rolls Royce Phantom, Silver/Black, Black or Cream tyres	£10-15
A8	DG 21	'EDOCAR'	£12-18

American '500' series

A range of six Days Gone models were marketed in the USA in plain colour finishes and with no printed logos or liveries. In each case the standard reference number carried the suffix '500'.

DG14	Ford Model 'A', Yellow / Black	£20-25
DG22	Packard Town Van, Black / Red	£20-25
DG30	Chevrolet Van, Red / Black	£20-25
DG33	Ford Model 'T', Black	£20-25
DG36	Chevy Pick-Up, Green	£20-25
DG37	Ford Model 'A' Van, Blue	£20-25

Lledo Display Cases

CC 0015	Wall Display Case. Wooden 'pigeon-hole' style case to contain 15 models	NGPP
CD 0002	Counter Display Case. Injection moulded and flock-covered, to contain 24 models, headboard	NGPP
WD 0001	Wall Display Case. Injection moulded and flock-covered, to contain 20 models, headboard	NGPP
WD 0002	'Queen' Display Case. Glass front, 8 glass shelves in addition to base, to contain 54 models	NGPP
WD 0003	'Standard' Display Case. Glass front, 3 glass shelves in addition to base, to contain 28 models	NGPP
WD 0004	'King' Display Case. Glass front, 11 glass shelves in addition to base, to contain 72 models	NGPP
WD 0017	Wall Display Case. Flock-covered plastic in green or black, to contain 20 models	NGPP
BG 2004	Perpetual Calendar. Holds one model plus reel of adhesive tape	NGPP

'The London Experience'

The musicals of Sir Andrew Lloyd-Webber feature in this range of London bus models based on the DG75 Bristol Lodekka casting. Special packaging.

LP 5142	'CATS'
LP 5143	'Phantom of the Opera'
LP 5144	'Starlight Express'
LP 5145	'Jesus Christ, Superstar'

The 'Grey' Series

Finished in neutral Grey and left unprinted for use as samples of promotionals (mainly in the USA). Only 144 sets of models were produced (in 1986) and all except DG7, DG11 and DG14 have 'Days Gone' baseplates. Beware fakes.

DG 2	86	Horse-Drawn Milk Float	£8-12
DG 3	86	Horse-Drawn Delivery Van	£8-12
DG 4	86	Horse-Drawn Omnibus	£8-12
DG 5	86	Horse-Drawn Fire Engine	£8-12
DG 6	86	Ford Model 'T' Van, White roof	£8-12
DG 7	86	Ford Woody Wagon, 'Lledo' and 'DG' baseplates	£8-12
DG 8	86	Ford 'T' Tanker, Green tank	£8-12
DG 10	86	Dennis Single Deck Bus	£8-12
DG 11	86	Horse-Drawn Large Van, Cream horses, Blue roof, 'Lledo' and 'DG' baseplates	£8-12
DG 12	86	Fire Engine	£8-12
DG 13	86	Ford Model 'A' Van	£8-12
DG 14	86	Ford Model 'A' Car, Cream wheels, roof and seats, 'Lledo' and 'DG' baseplates	£8-12
DG 15	86	AEC Double Deck Bus	£8-12
DG 16	86	Dennis Parcels Van	£8-12
DG 17	86	AEC Single Deck Bus	£8-12
DG 18	86	Packard Van	£8-12
DG 19	86	Rolls-Royce Phantom II	£8-12

'Cargo Carriers'

Introduced in 1999 to accompany the 'Cargo Kings' range. These versions of the 'Eurovan' have been introduced so far:

CC00 1000	'UPS' ('Universal Parcels Service')
CC00 1001	'PARCEL FORCE' ('Royal Mail')
CC00 1002	'TNT'
CC00 1003	'FEDEX' ('Federal Express')
CC00 1004	'LYNX'
CC00 1005	'SECURICOR EXPRESS'

'Cargo Kings'

Articulated truck models in 1:76 scale.

VOLVO ARTICULATED TRUCK

CK00 1000	98	'PARCEL FORCE'
CK00 1001	98	'P&O FERRYMASTERS'
CK00 1003	98	'CARLSBERG BEER'
CK00 1007	98	'THRUST SSC'
CK00 1008	98	'DUCATI 916 CORSE'
CK00 1009	98	'YORKIE'
CK00 1010	98	'SAINSBURY'S'
CK00 1011	99	'RNLI'
CK00 1016	99	'TNT'
CK00 1017	99	'BODDINGTONS'
CK00 1018	99	'TANGO'
CK00 1022	99	'REVE RACING'
CK00 1023	99	'GOODYEAR'
CK00 1024	99	'McCAINS'
CK00 1025	99	'GUINNESS'
CK00 1026	99	'JOHN SMITH'S'

KENWORTH ARTICULATED TRUCK

CK00 2005	98	'CARGO KINGS'
CK00 2006	98	'ICE WARRIORS'
CK00 2009	99	'PEPSI'
CK00 2010	99	'PEPSI'
CK00 2011	99	'7-UP'

'The Millennium Dome'

?	1999	Approximately 100mm in diameter, special 'Year 2000' packaging	NGPP

VA 1 FORD ANGLIA 105E
000	96	Navy Blue	£6-9
001	96	Pale Green	£6-9
002	96	White / Maroon	£6-9
008	97	Yellow	£6-9
010	97	Maroon / Grey	£6-9
011	96	Pale Blue	£6-9
012	98	'POST OFFICE SUPPLIES'	£7-10
014	99	White / Green	£7-10

VA 2 VOLKSWAGEN CABRIOLET
000	96	Red	£6-9
001	96	Pale Blue	£6-9
002	97	Black	£6-9

VA 3 AUSTIN A40 VAN
000	96	'RANSOMES LAWNMOWERS'	£6-9
001	96	'BRITISH RAILWAYS', see Set BR 1002	GSP
002	96	'A. A.'	£6-9
004	97	'H. M. V.'	£6-9
006	97	'CUSSONS IMPERIAL LEATHER'	£6-9
007	98	'BULMER'S CIDER'	£6-9
010	99	'HEINZ 57'	£7-10
011	99	'WHITBREAD CHANDY'	£7-10
012	99	'J. LYONS'	£7-10
013	99	'RALEIGH'	£7-10

VA 4 FORD ANGLIA VAN 305E
000	96	'ROYAL MAIL'	£6-9
001	96	'A. A.'	£6-9
002	96	'HOTPOINT'	£6-9
003	96	'P. O. TELEPHONES', see Set PO 1002	GSP
005	97	'R. A. C.'	£6-9
006	97	'BEA', 'Follow Me'	£6-9
007	97	'LONDON TRANSPORT'	£6-9
008	98	'ESSO AVIATION'	£6-9
009	99	'NATIONAL BENZOLE'	£7-10
010	99	'JORDANS'	£7-10

VA 5 TRIUMPH HERALD
000	96	Red	£6-9
001	96	'B.S.M.'	£6-9
002	96	Yellow	£6-9
003	96	Beige, Set HB 1002	GSP
005	96	Grey	£6-9
006	97	'THE MOTOR'	£6-9
007	97	Red / White	£6-9
008	98	White / Black	£6-9
010	99	Two-tone Green	£7-10

VA 6 FORD THAMES TRADER BOX VAN
000	96	'MARTINI'	£7-10
001	96	'BIRDS EYE'	£7-10
002	96	'PG TIPS'	£7-10
004	97	'LUCOZADE'	£7-10
005	97	'ATORA'	£7-10
006	97	'SAINSBURY'S', certificated LE	£7-10
008	99	'RALEIGH CYCLES', LE of 3,000	£7-10

VA 7 BEDFORD 'S' type TANKER
000	96	'REGENT'	£7-10
001	96	'SHELL-BP'	£7-10
003	97	'TOTAL'	£7-10
004	97	'COURAGE', 5,000	£7-10
005	98	'MOBILGAS', LE of 5,000	£7-10
009	99	'CEMENT MARKETING', LE of 3,000	£7-10

VA 8 BEDFORD 'S' type VAN
000	96	'HEINZ 57'	£7-10
001	96	'KODAK'	£7-10
002	97	'SURF', 5,000	£7-10
004	97	'SAINSBURY'S', certificated LE	£7-10

005	98	'MERRYDOWN CIDER', 5,000	£7-10
006	98	'POST OFFICE STORES', 5,000	£7-10
009	99	'POLICE', 3,000	£7-10
010	99	'SAINSBURY'S'	£7-10

VA9 FORD THAMES TRADER TANKER
000	96	'NORTH EASTERN GAS BOARD'	£7-10
001	96	'CASTROL'	£7-10
002	96	'CLEVELAND'	£7-10

VA 10 MORRIS MINOR TRAVELLER
000	96	Black	£6-9
001	96	Maroon	£6-9
002	97	Green	£6-9
003	97	'COASTGUARD'	£6-9
004	99	'RAF'	£7-10
005	99	Cream	£7-10
006	99	Red	£7-10

VA 11 MORRIS MINOR VAN
000	96	'A. A. PATROL'	£6-9
001	96	'BRITISH RAIL', see Set BR 1002	GSP
002	96	'OVALTINE'	£6-9
003	96	'P. O. TELEPHONES', see Set PO 1002	GSP
004	96	'SOUTHERN GAS'	£6-9
005	97	'R. A. C.'	£6-9
006	97	'ROYAL MAIL'	£6-9
007	98	'CAFFYNS'	£7-10
009	99	'SOUTHERN ELECTRICITY'	£7-10
010	99	'MAC FISHERIES'	£7-10
012	99	'BRS'	£7-10
013	99	'COALITE'	£7-10

VA 12 VOLKSWAGEN BEETLE
000	96	Beige	£6-9
001	96	Black	£6-9
002	96	'POLIZEI'	£6-9
003	97	'FEUERWEHR'	£6-9

VA 13 AUSTIN 7 MINI
000	96	Green	£6-9
001	96	White	£6-9
002	96	'POLICE'	£6-9
003	97	Grey	£6-9

VA 14 MINI-VAN
000	97	'R.A.C.'	£6-9
001	97	'ROYAL MAIL'	£6-9
002	97	'A.A. PATROL'	£6-9
004	98	'DEWHURST'	£7-10
007	99	'ROYAL NAVY'	£7-10
008	99	'CABLE & WIRELESS'	£7-10
009	99	'CASTROL'	£7-10
011	99	'SOUTHERN ELECTRICITY'	£7-10
012	99	'SOMERSET F.B.'	£7-10

VA 15 THAMES TRADER DROPSIDE LORRY
000	98	'MILK'	£7-10
001	98	'TRUMAN'S', 5,000	£7-10
002	99	'GUINNESS', 5,000	£7-10

VA 16 COMMER DROPSIDE LORRY
000	98	'CARLSBERG'	£7-10
002	98	'WESTON'S CIDER', 5,000	£7-10
004	99	'HOLTONS', 5,000	£7-10
007	99	'H-K ELECTRICAL'	£7-10
008	99	'JORDANS'	£7-10
009	99	'GUINNESS'	£7-10

VA 17 AUSTIN A35 VAN
000	97	'R.A.C.'	£6-9
002	98	'BARKERS'	£6-9
004	99	'SECURICOR'	£6-9

VA 18 LEYLAND COMET BOX VAN
000	97	'EVER-READY'	£7-10
002	98	'BASS', 5,000	£7-10
003	99	'TATE & LYLE', 5,000	£7-10
004	99	'LOVELL'S', 3,000	£7-10

VA 19 ROVER P4
000	97	Maroon	£6-9
001	97	Beige / Brown	£6-9
002	98	Black	£6-9
003	98	Green	£6-9
004	99	Blue / Grey	£7-10
005	99	Grey / Burgundy	£7-10
006	99	'POLICE'	£7-10
007	99	Two-tone Green	£7-10

VA 20 LEYLAND COMET TANKER
000	97	'POWER'	£7-10
001	97	'NATIONAL BENZOLE'	£7-10

VA 21 FORD POPULAR 100E
000	97	Yellow	£6-9
002	97	Green	£6-9
003	98	Blue	£6-9
004	99	Maroon	£7-10
005	98	Grey	£7-10
006	99	Sapphire Blue	£7-10

VA 22 RELIANT REGAL
000	98	'ROYAL MAIL'	£6-9
001	98	'A.A. PATROL'	£6-9
002	99	'NOTTINGHAM WATER'	£7-10
003	99	'Del Boy's' Reliant, grubby version, 14,860 only	£7-10
---	98	clean version, (LP4913)	£7-10

VA 23 AUSTIN A35
000	98	Green	£6-9
001	99	Grey	£6-9
002	99	Speedwell Blue	£7-10
003	99	Black	£7-10

VA 24 KARRIER BOX VAN
000	98	'RAIL EXPRESS PARCELS'	£7-10

VA 25 MINI-COOPER
000	98	Red/Black	£6-9
002	99	Green / White	£7-10
003	99	'Monte Carlo'	£7-10
004	99	'Monte Carlo'	£7-10
005	99	Cream	£7-10

VA 26 HILLMAN IMP
000	98	Red	£6-9
002	99	'COASTGUARD'	£7-10
003	99	'FRASER RACING'	£7-10
004	99	Green	£7-10

VA 27 ROVER 2000
000	99	Red	£7-10
001	99	White Police car	£7-10
002	99	Zircon Blue	£7-10
003	99	Willow Green	£7-10
004	99	'POLICE'	£7-10

VA 28 COMMER BOX VAN
000	98	'SHELL OIL'	£7-10
001	98	'GREEN SHIELD STAMPS', 5,000	£7-10

VA 29 LEYLAND COMET DROPSIDE LORRY
000	99	'BRS'	£7-10
002	99	'ARMSTRONG'	£7-10

VA 30 KARRIER BANTAM TANKER
000	99	'BUTLER FUELS'	£7-10

VA 31 KARRIER DROPSIDE LORRY
001	99	'CORONA'	£7-10

VA 33 FORD THAMES 300E VAN
000	99	'SINGER'	£7-10
001	99	'BRYLCREEM'	£7-10

VA 34 FORD CAPRI 109E
000	99	Turquoise / White	£7-10
002	99	Maroon / Grey	£7-10

VA 35 FORD CLASSIC 109E
000	99	Lime Green / White	£7-10
002	99	Yellow / White	£7-10

VA 36 COMMER FLATBED LORRY
000	99	'PICKFORDS'	£7-10
001	99	'JOHN SMITH'S'	£7-10

VA 37 LEYLAND COMET FLATBED
001	99	'JORDANS'	£7-10

VA 38 VAUXHALL VICTOR FA
000	99	Gypsy Red	£7-10
001	99	Primrose Yellow	£7-10
002	99	Black	£7-10

VA 39 THAMES TRADER FLATBED
000	99	'TATE & LYLE'	£7-10

VA ? SINGER CHAMOIS
000	99	Polar White	£7-10

Vanguards 'Gold'

Introduced in 1998. 3,000 of each.

VG0030
12s	Shelby Cobra 427s/c, silver	
51r	Shelby Cobra Daytona, red	
61r	Jaguar 'E'-type, red roadster	
62b	Jaguar 'E'-type, blue coupé	
73k	Lotus Europa Special, black	

VG0031
51g	Caterham Super Seven, green	
51k	Caterham Super Seven, black	

'Custom and Classic'

Though not intended for promotional use, this range of Volkswagen models employs an 'LP' reference system. Introduced in 1998.
See also DG 86 and VA 12.

VOLKSWAGEN BEETLE
LP 5255	99	Saloon, red / cream	
LP 5256	98	Saloon, blue / cream	
LP 5257	98	Cabriolet, yellow	
LP 5362	99	Saloon with oval rear window, lime green	
LP 5570	99	With oval window, 'Run to the Sun'	
LP 5573	99	Open, 'Run to the Sun'	

VOLKSWAGEN VAN and CAMPER
LP 5258	98	Van, black, 'Aircooled'	
LP 5259	98	Van, light blue with 'surfer' motif	
LP 5361	99	Van, 'LOTTERMANN'	
LP 5368	99	1955 Camper Van, lemon / white	
LP 5571	99	Van, 'Run to the Sun'	
LP 5572	99	Van, 'Run to the Sun'	

Vanguards Gift Sets

AU 1002 97 **'AUSTIN SALES / SERVICE'** VA3 Austin A40 Van
with VA17 Austin A35 Van, 5,000......................................**£12-15**

BA 1002 96 **'RACING ANGLIAS' Set** VA1-003 and VA1-004
'Broadspeed' Ford Anglias, numbers '6' and '7'.................**£12-15**

BO 1002 99 **'BOOTS the CHEMIST' Set** VA29 Leyland Comet
and VA7 Bedford 'S' Tanker, 3,000................................**£15-20**

BPL 1003 96 **'British Motoring Classics'** 24k gold plated Ford
Anglia 105E, Mini-Minor and Morris 1000 Traveller..........NGPP

BR 1002 96 **'BRITISH RAILWAYS' Set** VA3 Austin A40 Van
(Maroon), and VA11 Morris Minor Van (Yellow), 5,000.....**£12-15**

CL 1002 99 **'CLASSIC and CAPRI' Set** VA34 Ford Capri 109E and
VA35 Ford Classic 109E, 5,000..**£12-15**

HB 1002 96 **'HEARTBEAT COLLECTION'** Dr Kate Rowan's
Triumph Herald and the Ashfordley Police Anglia 105E.....**£12-15**

HB 2002 97 **'HEARTBEAT COLLECTION'** Ashfordley Police
Ford Anglia 100E and Mini-Van, 5,000............................**£12-15**

JOR 1002 99 **'JORDANS' Lorry Set** Commer Dropside VA 16008
and Leyland Comet Flatbed VA 37001..............................**£15-20**

KT 1002 98 **'KEN THOMAS'** 'Coronation Café' VA16 Commer
Dropside and VA8 Bedford 'S', 5,000..............................**£12-15**

MC 1002 99 **'MONTE CARLO MINIS'** VA25003 and VA25004
Monte Carlo Mini-Coopers **£12-15**

MS 1002 98 **'MACKESON DISPLAY SERVICE'** VA17 Austin
A35 Van and VA3 Austin A40 Van, 5,000..........................**£12-15**

PC 1002 97 **'POLICE PANDA CARS' Set** VA1 Ford Anglia and
VA13 Mini Minor Panda Cars in Blue/White, 5,000...........**£12-15**

PO 1002 96 **'P. O. TELEPHONES' Set** VA4 Ford Anglia Van and
VA11 Morris Minor Van, 5,000..**£15-20**

PO 2002 98 **'POST OFFICE TELEPHONES' Set** VA14 Minivan and
VA11 Morris 1000 Van, 5,000..**£12-15**

RP 1002 99 **'POLICE' Set** Featuring the two Rover Police
Cars VA19006 and VA 27004 ....**£12-15**

RS 1002 97 **'BRITISH ROAD SERVICES'** VA6 Thames Trader
Box Van and VA8 Bedford Box Van, 5,000.........................**£15-20**

ST 1002 99 **'St ANDREWS AMBULANCE'** VA14 Minivan and
VA11 Morris Minor Van, 2,000..**£15-20**

WV 1002 97 **'WHITBREAD SERVICE'** VA3 Austin A40 Van and
VA4 Ford Anglia 305E Van, 5,000 ....**£12-15**

'Special Licensed' series

Introduced in 1997 and presented in colourful boxes printed with 'brand' graphics appropriate to the model within.

SL 3 HORSE-DRAWN DELIVERY VAN
000 98 'COCA-COLA' ....
001 99 'PEPSI-COLA', '5c' ....

SL 6 FORD Model 'T' VAN
003 97 'COCA-COLA' ....
005 98 'GUINNESS' ....

SL 7 1930 FORD Model 'A' WOODY WAGON
000 98 'COCA-COLA' ....
001 99 'PEPSI' (SLO 7) ....

SL 8 1920 FORD Model 'T' TANKER
000 99 'GUINNESS' ....

SL 13 1930 FORD Model 'A' VAN
000 98 'COCA-COLA' ....
002 98 'CAMPBELL'S' ....
     99 'CAMPBELL'S' ....
003 99 'Ice-Cold PEPSI' ....

SL 17 1932 AEC REGAL BUS
002 99 '7-UP' ....

SL 18 1936 PACKARD VAN
000 98 'COCA-COLA' ....

SL 21 1928 CHEVROLET VAN
002 98 'COCA-COLA' ....
005 99 '7-UP' ....
006 99 'My GUINNESS' ....

SL 23 1954 SCENICRUISER
000 97 'ROUTE 66' ....
001 98 'COCA-COLA' ....

SL 26 1928 CHEVROLET DELIVERY VEHICLE
000 98 'COCA-COLA' ....
001 99 'PEPSI' ....

SL 30 1939 CHEVROLET PANEL VAN
000 98 'COCA-COLA In Bottles' .....

SL 32 1907 ROLLS-ROYCE SILVER GHOST 40/50HP
000 97 Silver body, Green seats,
          Grey tyres ....
001 97 Black body, Red seats,
          Black tyres ....
002 97 Red body, Silver bonnet,
          Black seats and tyres ....

SL 36 1938 CHEVROLET PICK-UP
000 98 'COCA-COLA' ....

SL 37 1937 FORD Model 'A' PANEL VAN
000 98 'COCA-COLA' ....

SL 43 1931 MORRIS VAN
000 97 'R. A. C.' ....
001 98 'CAMPBELL'S SOUPS'.......
002 99 'PEPSI-COLA' ....

SL 44 1937 6-wheel SCAMMELL
000 98 'COCA-COLA' ....
003 99 'GUINNESS' ....

SL 46 1930 4½ Litre BENTLEY
000 97 British Racing Green, '6' ....
001 97 Blue, '3' ....
002 97 Red, 8' ....
003 97 Yellow, 17' ....
004 98 Grey, 18' ....
005 99 Black, '1' ....

SL 48 1939 CHEVROLET CAR
000 97 'ROUTE 66' ....
001 98 'COCA-COLA' ....
002 99 'PEPSI-COLA' ....

SL 49 1931 AEC RENOWN BUS
000 98 'JOIN THE R.A.C.' ....
001 98 'GUINNESS as Usual' ....

SL 50 1926 MORRIS 'BULLNOSE' VAN
000 97 'JOIN THE R.A.C.' ....
002 99 '7-UP' ....

SL 51 1928 CHEVROLET VAN
000 98 'COCA-COLA' ....
002 98 'CAMPBELL'S SOUP' ....
     99 'CAMPBELL'S SOUP' ....
003 98 'My GUINNESS' ....

SL 53 1926 ROLLS-ROYCE LANDAULET
000 97 Mushroom/Maroon,
          Cream tyres...........................
002 98 Cream/Brown, Black tyres .....

SL 54 1929 ROLLS-ROYCE PHANTOM 'D'-BACK
000 97 White/Brown, Red wheels,
          Black tyres ....
001 97 Yellow and Black,
          Black wheels and tyres ....
005 98 Two-tone Green, Black tyres ..

SL 58 1950 MORRIS 'Z' VAN
001 99 '7-UP', 'Fresh Up'..................

SL 59 1950 BEDFORD 30cwt TRUCK
000 97 'PG TIPS', 'Geoff' ....
001 97 'MINNIE THE MINX',
          'BEANO' ....
005 98 'R.A.C.' ....
007 98 'GUINNESS' ....
009 99 'PEPSI' ....
?   99 'CAMPBELLS' ....

SL 63 1950 BEDFORD 30cwt VAN
000 97 'PG TIPS', 'Shirley' ....
001 97 'DENNIS THE MENACE',
          'BEANO' ....
002 97 'R.A.C.' ....
004 98 'COCA-COLA' ....
007 99 'My GUINNESS' ....

SL 66 1926 DENNIS VAN
001 98 'COCA-COLA' ....
003 99 '7-UP', 'Lemon Soda' ....
004 99 'GUINNESS' ....

SL 67 1935 FORD ARTICULATED TRUCK
000 97 'DESPERATE DAN',
          'DANDY' ....
002 98 'COCA-COLA' ....
005 99 '7-UP', 'Joyce Joliet' ....

SL 68 1932 AEC OPEN-TOP BUS
000 99 'PEPSI' (SLO 68) ....

SL 70 1939 FORD CANVAS-BACK TRUCK
000 97 'RAC ROAD SERVICE' ....
001 98 'COCA-COLA' ....
005 99 'PEPSI-COLA' ....
006 99 '7-UP In Cans' ....

SL 71 1959 MORRIS LD150 VAN
000 97 'PG TIPS', 'Kevin' ....
001 97 'BERYL THE PERIL',
          'DANDY' ....
004 98 'R.A.C.' ....
005 98 'GUINNESS TIME' ....
006 99 'PEPSI-COLA' ....

SL 73 1955 VOLKSWAGEN KOMBI VAN
000 97 'PG TIPS', 'Samantha' ....
001 98 'COCA-COLA' ....
005 99 'Had Your GUINNESS?' ....
?   99 'CAMPBELLS' ....

SL 78 1939 DODGE AIRFLOW
000 97 'ROUTE 66' ....

SL 79 1939 FORD FIRE ENGINE
000 97 'ROUTE 66', 'No. 4'.............

SL 85 1912 RENAULT VAN
000 98 'R.A.C. ROAD SERVICE' .....
001 98 'BEEFSTEAK SOUP' ....
002 99 'A GUINNESS a Day' ....
008 99 'JOSEPH LUCAS' ....

SL 88 1931 SENTINEL STEAM WAGON
000 97 'NEWTON & RIDLEY' ....
002 99 'DRAUGHT GUINNESS' .....

SL 89 1959 ROLLS-ROYCE SILVER CLOUD
000 98 Metallic Grey/Silver ....
001 98 Black ....
002 99 Gold/Black ....

SL 92 BENTLEY 'S' SERIES
000 98 Maroon/Silver ....
001 99 Green/Silver ....

SL 93 DODGE VAN
000 99 '7-UP'....................................

Matchbox Collectibles

In 1993 Matchbox Collectibles was launched to bring nostalgic die-cast models (many based on Yesteryears castings) direct to adult collectors. Current models are available direct from: **Matchbox Collectibles (Europe) Ltd, PO Box 35, Corporation Street, Rugby, Warwickshire, CV21 2DU.** It is also possible to obtain models via selected retail outlets known as 'Collectible Centres' some of whom also offer the models at toyfairs.

Thematic models based on 'Yesteryears' castings from 1993

'TASTE OF FRANCE' SERIES issued 1993
1947 Citroën Type 'H' Van
YTF01 'EVIAN MINERAL WATER' £12-15
YTF02 'MARTELL COGNAC' £12-15
YTF03 'YOPLAIT YOGHURT' £12-15
YTF04 'MARCILLAT BRIE' £12-15
YTF05 'TAITTINGER CHAMPAGNE' £12-15
YTF06 'POMMERY MUSTARD' £12-15
YTF501 Two models set on wooden plinth £24-27

'GREAT BEERS OF THE WORLD' SERIES
Iissued 1993/1994:
YGB01 Ford 'A' Van, 'CASTLEMAINE XXXX' (Australia)
    Red metal roof £16-18
    Red plastic roof £18-20
YGB02 Ford 'TT' Van, 'BECKS' (Germany)
    With body side window £16-18
    Without body side window £18-20
YGB03 Atkinson Steam, ''SWAN'' (Australia) £18-20
YGB04 Morris Van, 'FULLERS' (England) £16-18
YGB05 Ford 'AA' Van, 'CARLSBERG' (Denmark) £16-18
YGB06 Mercedes Truck, 'HOLSTEN' (Germany) £16-18
YGB07 Renault Van, 'KRONENBOURG' (France) £16-18
YGB08 GMC Van, 'STEINLAGER' (New Zealand) £16-18
YGB09 Mack AC, 'MOOSEHEAD' (Canada) £16-18
YGB10 Talbot Van, 'SOUTH PACIFIC' (New Guinea) £16-18
YGB11 Foden Steam Wagon, 'WHITBREAD' (England) £18-20
YGB12 Yorkshire Steam Wagon, 'LOWENBRAU' (Germany)...........£18-20

Issued in 1995:
YGB13 Ford 'TT' Van 'ANCHOR' (USA) £16-18
YGB14 Ford Model 'T' Van 'KIRIN' (Japan) £16-18
YGB15 Garrett Steam Wagon 'FLOWERS' (Eng.) £18-20
YGB16 Ford 'AA' Van 'CORONA' (Mexico) £16-18
YGB17 Mercedes-Benz 'HENNINGER' (Germany) £16-18
YGB18 Morris Van 'CASCADE' (Australia) £16-18
YGB19 Ford Model 'T' 'YUENGLING' (USA) £16-18
YGB20 Ford 'AA' Van 'STROHS' (USA) £16-18
YGB21 Mercedes-Benz 'DAB' (Germany) £16-18
YGB22 Atkinson Steam 'BEAMISH' (Ireland) £18-20
YGB23 Mack Truck 'TSING TAO' (China) £16-18
YGB24 Bedford Truck 'TOOHEYS' (Australia) £18-20

YBG501 Twin model issue on Plinth £25-28

HORSE DRAWN CARRIAGE SERIES issued 1993
YSH1 1900 Gypsy Caravan £35-40
YSH2 1886 London Omnibus £30-35
YSH3 1875 Wells Fargo Stage Coach £30-35

THE GRAND CLASSICS COLLECTION issued 1994
Y1-3 1936 SS Jaguar, Red with Black folded hood................£12-15
Y2-4 1930 Supercharged 4½ Litre Bentley, Dark Blue £12-15
Y4-4 1930 Duesenberg Town Car, Blue, Cream hood.............£12-15
Y34-1 1933 Cadillac 452 V16 Town Car, White/Black £12-15
Y36-1 1925 Rolls Royce Phantom 1, Red and Black £12-15
Y40-1 1931 Mercedes Benz 770, Grey body, Blue hood £12-15
Y45-1 1930 Bugatti Royale, Black/Royal Blue £12-15

'FIRE ENGINE' SERIES issued 1994/95.
YFE01 1920 Mack Fire Engine (YFE01 and YGB09 bases) (1995) £18-22
YFE02 1952 Land Rover Auxilliary and Trailer
   1: with Red wheels (1994) £40-45
   2: re-run with Silver wheels (1995) £18-22
YFE03 1933 Cadillac V16 Fire Wagon (1995)......................£18-22
YFE04 1939 Bedford KD Tanker Truck (1995) £18-22
YFE05 1932 Mercedes-Benz L5 Ladder Truck (1995) £18-22
YFE06 1932 Ford AA Fire Engine (1995) £18-22
YFE07 1938 Mercedes-Benz KS 15 Fire Truck (1996) £18-22
YFE08 1936 Leyland Cub FK7 (1995).................................£30-35

YFE09 1932 Ford 'AA' Open Cab (1996)...............................£18-22
YFE10 1937 GMC Rescue Squad 4th Precinct (1996)...............£18-22
YFE11 1923 Mack 'AC' Water Tanker (1996).........................£18-22
YFE12 1930 Ford 'A' Batallion Chief's Vehicle (1996) £18-22
YFE13 Citroën 'H' Van 'LONGUEVILLE' (1997) £18-22
YFE14 1953 Ford Pick-Up 'GARDEN CITY' (1997)..................£18-22
YFE15 1923 Mack 'AB' Water Tanker (1997)........................£18-22
YFE16 1948 Dodge 'Route' Canteen Support Truck (1997) £18-22
YFE17 1939 Bedford Pump Truck 'City of Manchester' (1997)...........£18-22
YFE18 1950 Ford E83W Van and Auxilliary Trailer (1997) £18-22
YFE19 1904 Merryweather, Fitchley Fire Brigade (1998) £28-32
YFE20 1912 Mercedes-Benz Motor Spritze Fire Engine (1998) £28-32
YFE21 1907 Seagrave AC53, VFD Fire Dept. (1998).............£28-32
YFE22 1916 Ford Model 'T' Fire Engine (1998)....................£28-32
YFE23 1906 Waterous SP Pumper, Radnor Fire Co. (1998).......£28-32
YFE24 1911 Mack Fire Pumper, UFALM Fire Dept. (1998).......£28-32
YSFE01 1930 Ahrens-Fox Quad, mounted on plinth (1994) £55-65
YSFE02 1936 Leyland Cub (YFE08) on wooden plinth (1995) £40-45
YSFE03-M Busch Fire Engine. White pipes, no figures (1996) £55-60
YSFE04-M Ahrens-Fox NS4, Lockheed, mounted on plinth (1997) £55-60
YSFE05-M 1880 Merryweather Horse-Drawn, on plinth (1997).........£55-60
YYM35193 1930 Ahrens-Fox, Coca-Cola, Xmas Holiday (1998) £55-65

YCC01 **'CHRISTMAS TREASURES' SET** issued 1994
Four 1938 Austin 7 models in Christmas '1994' liveries of
  Red, Metallic Green, White/Blue and Blue (5,000)...............£25-30
YCC02 1995 Set. Red, Gold, White, Metallic Green £25-30
'POWER OF THE PRESS' SERIES issued 1996
YPP01 Renault AG Van 'LE FIGARO' (France) £14-16
YPP02 Morris Courier 'THE TIMES' (Great Britain) £14-16
YPP03 Mercedes Truck 'MORGENPOST' (Germany) £14-16
YPP04 Dodge RT Van 'NEW YORK TIMES' (USA) £14-16
YPP05 Ford Truck 'LOS ANGELES TIMES' (USA) £14-16
YPP06 1923 AC Mack Truck 'PRAVDA' (Russia) £14-16
YPP07 GMC Van 'The AUSTRALIAN' (Australia) £14-16
YPP08 Ford 'A' Van 'WASHINGTON Post' (USA).....................£14-16

'STEAM POWERED VEHICLES' Collection, issued 1996/7.
YAS01 Stephenson's Rocket, (1996) £18-22
YAS02 Foden 'C' Steam Truck 'HULTON COALS', (1996)........£18-22
YAS03 Aveling & Porter Steam Roller 'COULSON', (1996) £18-22
YAS04 Yorkshire Wagon 'de SELBY QUARRIES', (1996)..........£18-22
YAS05 Fowler Showman's Engine 'JOHN HOADLEY', (1996).........£22-25
YAS06 Atkinson Logger 'J.B. KING Ltd', (1996)....................£18-22
YAS07 Fowler Crane Engine 'MARSTON'S', (1997).................£22-25
YAS08 Burrell Road Tracter 'WOODS MOORE', (1997)............£22-25
YAS09 Garrett Steam Lorry, 'RAINSFORD'S', (1997)..............£18-22
YAS10 Atkinson Steam Lorry, 'CITY of WESTMINSTER', (1997).......£18-22
YAS11 Yorkshire Steam Lorry, 'GWR', (1997) £18-22
YAS12 Foden 'C' Steam Lorry, 'R. BRETT', (1997) £18-22

'TROLLEYS, TRAMS & BUSES' Collection, issued 1996.
YET01 1920 Preston type Tram Car, Birmingham £16-18
YET02 1921 Leyland Titan Bus, Glasgow £16-18
YET03 1931 Diddler Trolley Bus, London United...................£16-18
YET04 1923 Scania Post Bus, Stockholm £16-18
YET05 1922 AEC Omnibus, Dublin £16-18
YET06 1910 Renault Motor Bus, Paris £16-18
'GRAND MARQUES' Collection, issued 1966.
YY014AC 1931 Stutz Bearcat, Red £18-20
YY017AD 1938 Hispano-Suiza, Dark Blue £18-20
YY018AC 1937 Cord, Cream £18-20
YY020AD 1935 Mercedes-Benz 500K, Black £18-20
YY024AD 1928 Bugatti T44, Black £18-20
YY064AC 1939 Lincoln Zephyr, Maroon £18-20

'The ANNIVERSARY COLLECTION', issued 1996.
All the models in this range have Gold coachlining.
YMS01 1911 Ford Model 'T', Black, Dark Brown seats £16-18
YMS02 1910 Benz Limousine, Blue, Black roof, Dark Brown seats ...£16-18
YMS03 1909 Opel Coupé, Yellow, Black hood, Black seats £16-18
YMS04 1911 Maxwell Roadster, Red, Black hood, Brown seats £16-18
YMS05 1911 Daimler, Maroon, Brown seats £16-18
YMS06 1912 Simplex, Red, Black hood, Black seats £16-18
YMS07 1914 Prince Henry Vauxhall, Dark Green/Silver, Brown seat £16-18
YMS08 1912 Packard Laundaulet, White, Black roof, Black seats £16-18

'FABULOUS FIFTIES - ROAD SERVICE COLLECTION'
Series 1, issued in 1996.
YRS01 1955 Chevy 3100 'AAA Towing and Service' £18-22
YRS02 1953 Ford F100 'Flying 'A' Tire Service' £18-22

YRS03 1956 Chevy 3100 'Mobil Battery Service' £18-22
YRS04 1954 Ford F100 'Sinclair' Snow Plough.................................£18-22
YRS05 1957 Chevy 3100 'Dixie Gas Parts and Service' £18-22
YRS06 1955 Ford F100 'Red Crown', 'Route US 66' on tilt £18-22
YRS06BM 1955 Ford F100 'Red Crown', 'Route US 83' on tilt.........£30-35
Series 2, issued in 1997.
YIS01M 1955 Chevy 55 'Harley Davidson'....................................£18-22
YIS02M 1955 Ford 55 'Caterpillar'...£18-22
YIS03M 1955 Chevy 55 'GM Parts' £18-22
YIS04M 1957 Chevy 55 'American Airlines' £18-22
YIS05M 1955 Ford 54 'Pennsylvania Rail Road' £18-22
YIS06M 1953 Ford 53 'Parts & Service' £18-22

'AMERICAN MUSCLE CARS'. Issued in 1996.
YMC01 1971 Chevelle SS454 ....£18-22
YMC02 1971 Plymouth 'Cuda 440 6-Pack £18-22
YMC03 1967 Pontiac GTO £18-22
YMC04 1970 Plymouth Road Runner Hemi £18-22
YMC05 1970 Ford Boss Mustang £18-22
YMC06 1968 Camaro SS396...£18-22
YMC07 1970 Plymouth Road Runner GTX £18-22
YMC08 1966 Chevelle SS396 ....£18-22
YMC09 1966 Ford Fairlane XL £18-22
YMC10 1969 Dodge Charger £18-22
YMC11 1970 Oldsmobile 442 ....£18-22
YMC12 ;971 Dodge Challenger £18-22

1996 XMAS SPECIALS
YSC01-M **Scania-Vabis Bus** White body, Xmas tree on roof.
5,000 total of which 1,236 shorter trees made in China...................£35-40
YSC02-M **Chevy 3100 Pickup.** Red body, Xmastree, sleigh,
reindeer, etc., in back. 7,500 worldwide £30-35
YSC03-M **Holiday Fire Engine.** Ford 'AA' Open Cab as
YFE09 model but with White chassis. Santa Claus and
sack of presents. 7,500 worldwide......................................£30-40
YY21A/SA-M **Ford Woody Wagon.** Blue/Cream, with
'Drink Pesi-Cola' and 'Smith's Apothecary'..................................£18-22
YY004/C-M **Duesenberg Town Car.** Brown body, Tan chassis
and seats, Black hood. 7,500 worldwide....................................£25-30
MB289/SA-M **Pontiac GTO** Purplish Black, 5,000 ....£15-20

The 'WHISKEY COLLECTION' Issued in 1997.
YWG01M 1930 Ford Model 'A' Van, 'BALLANTINES' £16-18
YWG02M 1930 Ford Model 'TT' Van, 'LONG JOHN' £16-18
YWG03M 1929 Morris Van, 'CUTTY SARK' £16-18
YWG04M 1937 GMC Van, 'LAPHROIG' £16-18
YWG05M 1912 Ford Model 'T' Van, 'SHEEP DIP' £16-18
YWG06M 1932 Ford Model 'AA' Truck, 'TEACHERS' £16-18

The 'COCA-COLA COLLECTION' Issued in 1998.
YPC01M 1957 Chevy Pick-up, 'Vending Service & Repair' £24-26
YPC02M 1937 GMC Van, 'Nine Million Drinks a Day' £24-26
YPC03M 1920 Mack AC Truck, 'Stoneleigh Pharmacy' £24-26
YPC04M 1912 Ford Model 'T' Van, 'Ice Cold Coca-Cola Sold Here' .£24-26
YPC05M 1930 Ford Model 'A' Pick-up, 'Parts & Maintenance' £24-26
YPC06M 1932 Ford Model 'A' Truck, 'Delicious and Refreshing' £24-26

'The 30's AND 40's Pick Up Collection'
YTC01 1998 1941 Chevrolet Model AK, Blue, Black chassis............£22-24
YTC02 1998 1946 Dodge Power Wagon WDX, Dark Green.............£22-24
YTC03 1998 1940 Ford De-luxe, Red, Black fenders £22-24
YTC04 1998 1939 Reo Speed Delivery Vehicle, White, Red stripe £22-24
YTC05 1998 1938 Studebaker Coupé Express, Yellow, Silver stripe .£22-24
YTC06 1998 1934 International Harvester C Series. Maroon/Black...£22-24

The Budweiser Vintage Dekivery Truck Collection
YYM35253 1999 1932 Diamond T Open Truck, Red/White/Brown .£22-24
YYM35254 1999 1937 Dodge Airflow Refrigerated Van................£22-24
YYM35255 1999 1926 Ford TT Delivery Van, Black/Red £22-24
YYM35256 1999 1955 Chevy 55 Pick Up Truck, Red/White..........£22-24
YYM35257 1999 1940 Ford Pick Up Truck, Red and Black £22-24
YYM35258 1999 1948 GMC Refrigerated Truck. Red/White..........£22-24

Special Limited Editions
YCH04M 1997 1929 Morris Van, RSPCA, Cream/Blue.......5000 £25-30
YHN01M 1997 1955 Holden FJ 2104 Panel Van, Grey 5000 £30-35
YHN02M 1997 1954 Holden FJ 2106 Pick-up, Black 5000 £30-35
YHN03M 1997 1951 Holden FX 2106 Pick-up, Fawn...........5000 £30-35
YRS05SA 1998 1957 Chevy 3100 Pick Up, The Classic
1957 Chevrolet 40th Ann. Coll. 5000 £28-30
YRS6SAM 1997 1955 Ford F100 Pick Up, Fire Marshall 9500 £50-55
YRS07SAM 1998 Ford F100 Pick Up. 50th Ann. Special Ed...9500 £36-38

YSC01M 1995 1922 Scania-Vabis Half Track Post Bus,
White, Xmas tree on roof 7000 **£140-160**
YSC02M 1996 1955 Chevy 3100 Pick Up, Red tree 7500 **£40 50**
YSC03M 1996 1932 Ford AA Fire Engine, Santa, presents.8000 **£34-36**
YSC04M 1997 1932 Ford AA Truck, Clayton Grain 9500 **£28-30**
YSC04M 1997 Ford Fire Engine, Santa and Mrs Claus 8000 **£34-36**

YY004CM 1996 1930 Duesenburg Town Car, Maroon/Tan 7500 **£28-30**
YY012SBM 1997 1912 Ford T Field Ambulance, UK Khaki ..5000 **£28-30**
YY013SAM 1998 1918 Crossley Truck, Sherwood Florists 9500 **£30-35**
YYI7ASAM 1997 1938 Hispano Suiza, Green and Tan 9500 **£28-30**
YY19BSCM 1997 Fowler Showmans Eng. 'Prince of Wales'...9500 **£30-35**
YY018ESA 1997 1918 Atkinson Steam Wagon, Conybeare 9500 **£40-50**
YY020SA 1997 1937 Mercedes 540K Special, Red 7500 **£35-40**
YY21ASAM 1996 1932 Ford A Woody Wagon, Pepsi 5000 **£18-20**
YY027SA 1995 1922 Foden C Type Steam Wagon. Fullers..7000 **£18-20**
YY027SC 1997 1922 Foden Steam Wagon, Maroon,
F. Parker & Co. Timber Importers 5000 **£20-140**
YY30ASAM 1997 1920 Mack AC Truck, Red, Allentown 5000 **£20-22**
YY30ASBM 1998 1920 Mack AC Truck, Fishermans Wharf ..9500 **£32-34**
YY032ASA 1997 1932 Mercedes Benz L5 Lorry, Green,
O'Neil Farm Produce 12500 **£28-30**
YY033SBM 1998 1957 BMW 507 Special, Cream, Black top.7500 **£24-26**
YY034SCM 1997 1937 GMC Ambulance, US Army Green 5000 **£28-30**
YY035 1997 1921 Scania Vabis Post Bus, Green,
Snow Mountain Ski Lodge.........................5000 **£70-80**
YY039SF 1997 1913 Ford TT Van.Jack Daniels................12500 **£28-30**
YY047SA 1995 1929 Morris Light Van, Fullers,
Green, Red roof, differences to YGR04.......7000 **£18-20**
YY052B 1998 Mack Truck, Matchbox Collectibles Club Model..**£28-30**
YY053SAM 1998 Mercedes 770K Special Ed., Red/Black 9500 **£24-26**
YYM36791 1998 Horse Drawn Wagon, Anheuser Busch........7500 **£38-40**
YYM36793 1998 Scania Vabis Post Bus, North Pole Mail......5000 **£28-30**
YYM36839 1999 Dodge Van. McDonalds Courtesy Wagon....9500 **£36-38**

Matchbox Collectibles Code 1 (Factory-produced)
privately commisioned Limited Edition models
Y5-5 1992 Leyland Titan Bus, 'Chester', MICA model, 5000 **£25-30**
Y19 1997 Fowler Showmans Engine, Billy Smarts......3500 **£30-35**
Y19 1997 Fowler Showmans Engine, Lesney 3000 **£30-35**
Y21 1997 Aveling & Porter Roller, Fred Dibnah 3500 **£30-35**
YY48 1998 Garrett Steam Wagon, Chester Plays 3000 **£30-35**
YCH01 1995 Ford T Van, 'Ronald McDonald House' 3000 **£90-100**
YCH02 1997 Collectors Set. Ford T Van, Ronald McDonald
Charities (Red with Yellow roof) and Ford
Model A Van, Camp Quality, Kids Support (Light
Blue with Dark Blue chassis and roof..........5000 **£50-60**
YCH02 1997 As above but with All-Red and All-Light
Blue models 500 **£200-250**
YCH06 1998 Mack Truck, Ronald McDonald, Perth 5000 **£25-30**
YCH07 1998 Ford A Van, Ronald McDonald, Tasmania ..5000 **£25-30**
YCH08 1998 Mercedes L5, Ronald McDonald, Brisbane.5000 **£25-30**
YCH09 1998 Morris Courier Van, R McDonald, Adelaide 5000 **£25-30**
YCH010 1998 Holden Van, Ronald McDonald, Sydney 5000 **£25-30**
YCH011 1998 Holden Van, Ronald McDonald, Melbourne 5000 **£25-30**
YFE04B 1995 Bedford KD Tanker, Belrose Bush Fire 3000 **£60-80**
YFE02B 1996 Land Rover & Trailer, Londonderry Fire.3000 **£100-120**
YFE05SA 1997 1932 Mercedes L5 Fire Engine, Solingen ..3500 **£30-35**
YFE07SA 1997 1938 Mercedes Fire Wagon, Oberndorf ...3500 **£30-35**
YFE10SA 1997 GMC Van, white/yellow, Cessnock Rescue.3500 **£30-35**
YHN01SA 1997 1955 Holden FJ Van, Auto One 3500 **£30-35**
YHN01SB 1997 Holden FJ 2104 Van, Temera Ambulance ..3500 **£30-35**
YHN01SC 1998 Holden FJ Van, Automodel Solingen 3500 **£30-35**
YPP02SA 1996 Morris Courier Van, Classic Toys 3000 **£35-40**
YPP02SB 1997 Morris Courier Van, Lesney Prodocts 3000 **£35-40**
YPP04SA 1996 1948 Dodge Express Van, Epress Delivery..3000 **£35-45**
YY012SA 1996 Ford T Van, Junior Collectors Club............. 3000 **£25-30**
Within the 3000 exist 36 with Blue roof
(normally Green)..................................36 **£300-400**
YY027B 1996 Foden Steam Wagon, MICA Club Model..3000 **£40-50**
YY034SA 1996 GMC Van, Chester Toy Museum 3000 **£35-40**
Within the 3000 exist 36 with 6 spoke Copper wheels
(normally Silver solid)................................36 **£300-400**
YY039SC 1997 Ford TT Van, Matchbox USA 20th Year ..3500 **£30-35**
YY048SA 1997 Garrett Steam Wagon, Pickfords 3500 **£30-35**
YY065SB 1996 1928 Austin 7 Van, 4th European Convention,
26nd October 1400 **£45-50**
YY065SC 1997 1928 Austin 7 Van, MICA 12th UK Conv. ..1400 **£45-50**
YY065SD 1997 Austin 7 Van, MICA 5th European Conv.....1400 **£45-50**

Thematic models based on 'The Dinky Collection' castings 1996 – 1998

'The Golden Age of British Sports Cars' (1996)

- 1969 **Triumph Stag**, Dark Blue, Tan seats £15-18
- 1967 **Jaguar 'E'-type**, Black body and top £15-18
- 1957 **Jaguar XK150**, Cream body, Red seats £15-18
- 1973 **MGB GT**, Red body...£15-18
- 1968 **Karmann-Ghia**, Red body, Tan seats...........................£15-18
- 1957 **Mercedes-Benz 300**, Blue body, Red seats £15-18

'Classic British Sports Cars' (1998)

DYB01	1959 **Triumph TR3a**, Green body, Brown top	£15-18
DYB02	1967 **Jaguar E-type**, Red body, Brown seats	£15-18
DYB03	1955 **Morgan 4+4**, Black body, Brown seats	£15-18
DYB04	1956 **Austin-Healey**, Cream body, Black seats	£15-18
DYB05	1967 **MGB**, Pale Yellow body, Black top and seats	£15-18
DYB06	1962 **Aston-Martin**, Silver body, Dark Red seats	£15-18
DYB07	1961 **Lotus Super Seven**, Red body, Brown seats	£15-18

American Classics, 'Stars of the Silver Screen'

These eight models were re-issued in 1995: DY 7c, 11c, 16c, 23a, 26b, 27c, 29b and 31b. They were presented in standard window boxes but had enhanced detail such as coloured rear lights, etc.

Market price range, each..£15-18

'Oldies But Goodies'

'Dinky' bases and standard closed boxes similar to those for 1996 Yesteryears.

1996 issues:

DYG 01	**Ford Mustang**, Dark Blue body, Red seats	£18-20
DYG 02	**Chevrolet Bel Air**, Red/White body, Red/Black seats	£18-20
DYG 03	**Studebaker Hawk**, Mid-Blue body, White flash and top	£18-20
DYG 04	**Buick Skylark**, Yellow body, Yellow and Brown seats	£18-20
DYG 05	**Cadillac Coupé de Ville**, Black body, Red seats	£18-20
DYG 06	**Chevrolet Corvette**, Black body, White flash, Gloss or Matt Black detachable top, Red seats	£18-20
DYG 07	**Tucker Torpedo**, Dark Green body, Cream seats	£18-20
DYG 08	**Ford Thunderbird**, Light Blue body, White top	£18-20

1997 issues:

DYG 09	**Chevrolet Impala**, White open body, Red seats	£18-20
DYG 10	**Chrysler Town & Country**, Fawn and 'wood' effect	£18-20
DYG 11	**Buick Special**, Metallic Dark Green, Silver flash	£18-20
DYG 12	**Ford Fairlane**, White body, Blue top	£18-20
DYG 12	**Cadillac Eldorado**, Black body, White top	£18-20
DYG 13	**1948 DeSoto**, Maroon body, Light Ivory seats	£18-20
DYG 14	**Nash Metropolitan**, Blue and White body and seats	£18-20
DYG 15	**Chevrolet Bel Air**, Red and Ivory body and seats	£18-20

'Classic European Economy Cars' (1998 issues)

VEM01	1949 **Volkswagen Beetle Cabrio**, Red/Black, Tan seats	£15-18
VEM02	1959 **Austin Mini-Minor**, Red body	£15-18
VEM03	1948 **Citroën 2cv**, Grey body, Black top	£15-18
VEM04	1954 **Messerschmitt KR200**, Yellow/Black	£15-18
VEM05	1961 **Wolseley Hornet**, Maroon / White, Brown seats	£15-18
VEM06	1960 **Fiat 500**, Lime Green, White top, Red seats	£15-18
VEM07	1962 **Renault R4L**, Blue body, Black top, Tan seats	£15-18

'Matchbox Collectibles' from 1998

From 1st November 1998, Mattel acquired both the **'Models of Yesteryear'** and the **'Dinky Toys'** names. They have 'rationalised' their intended future production along the following lines. All car models and some trucks (including 'Convoys') will carry the 'Dinky' name. All vintage commercial vehicle models will be branded 'Yesteryears'. A new, 8-digit numbering system has also been developed to cater for this new output. 'Coca-Cola Cruisers' and 'Cars of the Rich and Infamous' were first to appear under the new system.

'Coca-Cola Cruisers' (1:43 scale, all have 'Dinky' bases, 1998)

CCV06-B	1953 **Corvette**, open-top, multicolours	£20-22
DYG02-B	1957 **Chevrolet Bel Air**, open-top, multicolours	£20-22
DYG08-B	1955 **Ford Thunderbird**, hard-top, multicolours	£20-22
YMC03-B	1967 **Pontiac GTO**, soft-top, multicolours	£20-22
YMC05-B	1970 **Ford Boss Mustang**, hard-top, multicolours	£20-22
YMC06-B	1968 **Chevrolet Camaro**, hard-top, multicolours	£20-22

'Cars of the Rich and Infamous'

(based on previous Models of Yesteryear castings, 'Dinky' on base, 1998)

DYM35178	1937 **Cord**, Dark Blue, White roof	£20-22
DYM35179	1931 **Stutz Bearcat**, Yellow body, Black chassis	£20-22
DYM35180	1938 **Lincoln Zephyr**, Taupe body	£20-22
DYM35181	1933 **Cadillac V16**, Dark Green, Cream roof	£20-22
DYM35182	1930 **Duesenberg**, Dark Red body, White roof	£20-22
DYM35183	1931 **Mercedes 770**, Black body, Grey roof	£20-22

Special Limited Editions (Code-1, factory produced, 1:43)

DY002SAM	1997, **Chevrolet Bel Air**, Black and flame, 5,000	£55-60
DY016DM	1997, **Ford Mustang**, Red/White striped, 5,000	£25-30
DY011SAM	1998, **Tucker Torpedo**, Primrose, 9,500	£25-30
DY014SAM	1998, **Delahaye 145**, Two-tone Green, 7,500	£25-30
DYM37798	1999, **Buick Skylark**, Green and White, 7,500	£25-30
DYM36840	1999, **Citroën 2cv**, Yellow and Black, 5,000	£25-30

'Classic '57 Chevrolet 40th Anniversary Collection'

(Scale 1:43)

DYG02SAM	1998, **Chevrolet Bel Air**, Met. Lilac, White top, 5,000	£25-30
DY027SBM	1998, **Chevrolet Bel Air Conv.**, Bright Red, 5,000	£25-30
VCV01	1998, **Chevrolet Nomad**, Black, 5,000	£25-30
CCV03	1998, **Chevrolet Corvette**, Cream/Silver, 5,000	£25-30

Matchbox Collectibles Code-2 'Dinky Toys'

(Scale 1:43)

DY21	1991, **Mini-Cooper**, 'Classic Car Show', 1,000	£60-80
DY8	1991, **Commer Van**, 'Motorfair '91', 2,000	£25-30
DY28	1992, **Triumph Stag**, 'Classic Car Show', 2,000	£40-50
001	1994, **Mini-Cooper**, 'Police', Off-White, 2,000	£70-80
N01	1994, **Commer Van**, 'Classic Toys', 2,000	£70-80
003	1995, **Mini-Cooper**, 'No.13, Bathurst', 1,500	£50-60
DDS003	1995, **Ford E83W Van**, 'DDS', 300	£200-250
DY073	1995, **Cadillac**, 'Dinky Toy Club of America', 200	£60-80
002	1996, **Commer Van**, 'Bentalls', 1,500	£50-60
004	1996, **Austin A40 Van**, 'Major Print', 1,200	£40-50
DY033A	1996, **Mercedes**, 'Dinky Toy Club of America', 200	£60-80
DY15005	1996, **Austin A40 Van**, 'MICA 4th European', 1,000	£40-50
M2 Set	1996, DY15005 **A40 Van**, YY65 **Austin 7 Van**, 'MICA 4th European' 'The Dinky Collection', 250	£90-110
M4 Set	1997, DY4006 **Ford Van**, YY65 **Austin 7 Van**, 'MICA 5th European', 250	£90-110
DY4006	1997, **Ford E83W Van**, 'MICA 5th European', 1,000	£40-50
DY30	1997, **Austin-Healey**, 'DT Club of America, 150	£50-60
Gift Set	1997, **Mercedes 300SL** (Silver, Red/White seats) with 'The Dinky Collection' 87-page book, 600	£50-60
	Same but hardback version of the book and the model is Cream with Red logo, 24	£300-400
DY16DM	1998, **Ford Mustang**,, 'DT Club of America', 150	£60-80

The Canada Maple Leaf Club, Ford Thunderbird models

DY31	1996, Silver body, Red/White seats, 42 only	£300-400
DYG08M	1997, Turquoise body, Turquoise/White seats, 280	£60-80
DYG08M	1997, White body, Turquoise/White seats, 50	£300-400
DY31	1997, Black body, Red/White seats, 12 only	£400-500

Miscellaneous Matchbox Collectibles 'Dinky models'

DYM34577	1999, **Mack Articulated Rig**, 'McDonalds'	£55-60
DYM36838	1999, **Kenworth Tanker**, 'Gulf Oil', 9,500	£25-30

Colour pictures

The colour section following page 288 features models from the Fire Engine Series (see page 292) and the 'Coca-Cola' Collection (see page 293).

Matchbox Dinky - 'The Collection' 1988 – 1995

Manufactured by Matchbox International Ltd in Macau

DY 1	1988	**Jaguar 'E' type** (soft-top), Dark Green..................£10-12
DY 1b	1991	Yellow body, Black hood £10-12
DY 1c	1995	Black body, Black hood **£18-20**
DY 2	1989	**Chevrolet Bel Air**, Red body, White roof £10-12
DY 3	1989	**MGB GT**, Blue body, Black roof..........................£10-12
DY 3b	1992	Orange body £10-12
DY 4	1989	**Ford E83W 10 cwt Van**, 'HEINZ 57 VARIETIES',
		Yellow body, Black roof, riveted base **£8-10**
		Yellow body, Black roof, screwed base £25-30
DY 4b	1990	'RADIO TIMES', Olive-Green £14-16
DY 5	1989	**Ford V8 Pilot**, Black body..................£18-20
DY 5b	1992	Silver body £10-12
DY 5c	1993	Beige body..................£10-12
DY 6	1989	**Volkswagen Beetle**, Light Blue body, Grey top £20-25
DY 6b	1991	Black body with Grey top £14-16
DY 6c	1992	Red body with Grey top £14-16
DY 7	1989	**Cadillac Coupé de Ville**
		Metallic Deep Red body, White roof £10-12
DY 7b	1991	Pink body..................£14-16
DY 7c	1995	**Cadillac Torpedo**, Metallic Red £10-12
DY 8	1989	**Commer 8 cwt Van**
		'SHARPS TOFFEES', Red body.....................£10-12
DY 8b	1991	'HMV', Dark Blue £10-12
DY 9	1989	**Land Rover**, Green body, Tan tilt.....................£25-30
DY 9b	1991	'AA' Land Rover, Yellow/Black body.....................£10-12
DYS 10	1989	**Mercedes Konferenz Coach**, Cream/Dark Blue,
		'REISEBURO RUOFF', 'STUTTGART',
		special box, (1:50).....................£25-30
DY 11	1990	**Tucker Torpedo**, Metallic Red body £10-12
DY 11b	1991	Metallic Light Blue body £10-12
DY 11c	1995	Metallic Blue body, enhanced..........................£18-20
DY 12	1990	**Mercedes 300 SL**, Off-White body **£8-10**
DY 12b	1992	Black body, Silver trim..................£8-10
DY 13	1990	**Bentley Continental**, Metallic Light Blue,..........£10-12
DY 13b	1992	Dark Blue body..................£10-12
DY 14	1990	**Delahaye 145**, Dark Metallic Blue body.................£10-12
DY 14b	1992	Dark Red body..................£10-12
DY 15	1989	**Austin A40 Van**, 'BROOKE BOND TEA', Bright Red
		(Brooke Bond promo in plain box)................£10-12
DY 15	1990	Austin A40 Van, 'BROOKE BOND TEA', Bright Red
		(standard issue, normal box) £10-12
DY 15b	1991	'DINKY TOYS', Cream/Yellow.....................£10-12
DY 16	1990	**Ford Mustang Fastback**, Metallic Green body £10-12
DY 16b	1991	White body with Red seats.....................£10-12
DY 16c	1995	Lighter Metallic Green, enhanced..................**£18-20**
DYS17	1990	**Triumph Dolomite**, Red body, special box £10-12
DY 18	1988	**Jaguar 'E' type** (open), Red body..........................£10-12
DY 19	1990	**MGB GT V8**, Maroon body, Black seats £10-12
DY 19b	1990	Bright Red body **£18-20**
DY 20	1991	**Triumph TR4**, White body, Black seats..................£10-12
DY 21	1991	**Mini Cooper S**, Off-White body, Black roof..........£10-12
DY 22	1991	**Citroën 15cv**, Black body..................£10-12
DY 22b	1992	Off-White body £10-12
DY 23	1991	**Chevrolet Corvette**, Red body, White panels £14-16
DY 23b	1993	Metallic Copper body, Cream panels............£10-12
DY 23c	1995	Red body, White panels, enhanced **£18-20**
DY 24	1991	**Ferrari 246 Dino**, Red body £10-12
DY 25	1991	**Porsche 356a**, Silver body **£8-10**
DY 26	1991	**Studebaker Hawk**, Metallic Gold, White flash £18-20
DY 26b	1995	Darker Metallic Gold, White flash, enhanced .£18-20
DY 27	1991	**Chevrolet Bel Air Open Top**
		Light Blue/White body, White seats £18-20
		Light Blue/White body, Brown seats, 1,100....£75-85
DY 27b	1995	Pink body, Cream top, enhanced..................£18-20
DY 28	1992	**Triumph Stag**, White body..................£10-12
DY 28b	1995	Metallic Green body..................**£18-20**
DY 29	1992	**Buick Skylark**, Light Blue body..................**£18-20**
DY 29b	1995	Light Blue body, enhanced..................£18-20
DY 30	1992	**Austin Healey 100**, British Racing Green £18-20
DY 31	1993	**Ford Thunderbird**, Red body £18-20
DY 31b	1995	Red body, enhanced..................**£18-20**
DY 32	1993	**Citroën 2cv**, Grey body..................£10-12
DY 33a	1995	**Mercedes-Benz 300sl**, Dark Blue, Red seats...........£18-20
DY 35a	1995	**VW Karmann-Ghia**, Red, Black/Tan seats £18-20
DY 36a	1995	**Jaguar XK150**, Cream body,Black hood, Red seats,
		with or without 'DINKY' on base £18-20
DY902	1991	**Sports Cars Set 1**. Three models on wooden plinth,
		colours unique to set: DY 12 (Silver body),
		DY 24 (Metallic Blue), DY 25 (Red) £30-35
DY903	1992	**Sports Cars Set 2**. Three models on wooden plinth,
		colours unique to set: DY 30 (Metallic Blue),
		DY 20 (Red), DY 18 (Cream)........................£30-35
DY 921	1992	**Jaguar 'E' Type**, Cast in pewter, with 'DINKY' on
		wooden plinth, special box..............................£20-25

Collectors notes

Oxford Die-Cast

Designed primarily for promotional use, Oxford Die-Cast models were introduced in late 1993. Occupying the Swansea factory previously used by Corgi, the company has specialised in true Limited Edition production runs. Early in 1998, production moved to a new, purpose-built factory at Neath.

The company has formed the Oxford Die-Cast Club. Members get their own newsletter and catalogue, and a free club model produced to a limit equal to the number of club members at the time. 'Normal' production is available only via the club at £4-95 per model (£5-95 in the few cases of 'sporting' models where royalties are involved). The only other source of models is through the purchase of the product being promoted. There are also occasionally, special club models for members.

The Editor would like express his thanks to Dennis Bone of Oxford Die-Cast for his assistance in compiling this listing which usefully shows production quantities rather than prices. Club details from:
The Oxford Die-Cast Club, PO Box 195, Tring, Herts., HP23 4 JF, England.
Telephone (01442) 828422, or Fax: (01442) 822415.

Abbreviations

g after ref. no. = gold wheels   **h** after ref. no. = made for sale in Hamley's
t after ref. no. = Ford Model 'T'   **u** after ref no. = United States model
a after ref no. = Australian model
NC = not certificated   **NYP** = not yet produced
x or **y** after ref. no. = base plate colour changes

Morris ('Bullnose') Van

Ref.	Intro.	Model	Made
001	93	'CHESHAM Utd F.C.', winners of Diadora League Premier Division 92/93	2,000
001g	93	'CHESHAM Utd F.C.', 'Sportsman's Dinner'	500
002	94	'PRINCES SPREADABLES'	5,000
003	93	'LO-SALT'	10,000
003 g	94	'LO-SALT'	5,000
005	93	'OXFORD DIE-CAST', UK launch	5,000
005 g	93	'OXFORD DIE-CAST', UK launch	1,000
006 g	94	'OXFORD DIE-CAST', New York Premium Exhibition	7,500
007 g	94	'LION PEPPER'	7,500
007	94	'LION PEPPER'	4,000
008	94	'TREX'	12,000
008 g	94	'TREX'	12,000
008 x	94	'TREX', grey base	5,000
008 y	94	'TREX', blue base	5,000
009 g	94	'JORDANS'	50,000
009	94	'JORDANS'	1,000
009 x	94	'JORDANS', grey base	20,000
010 g	94	'BEDFORDSHIRE FESTIVAL'	10,000
011 g	93	'FOTORAMA'	10,000
012 g	94	'MACARONI' (Marshall's Foods)	5,000
013	94	'EVANS VANODINE 75th Anniversary'	1,250
		note: 400 out of the 1,250 were made with gold wheels.	
014 g	94	'OUTSPAN', offered with model 004	25,000
015	94	'PLASTI-KOTE', 2,300 were made with chrome wheels, 700 with black wheels	25,000
016	94	'CHEQUERS INN'	5,000
017	94	'TESCO MILK'	25,000
017 g	94	'TESCO MILK'	3,000
018 g	94	'LEYLAND AUTO	2,500
019 g	94	'SCOTTISH ISLAND LICQUER'	2,500
020 g	94	'OXFORD DIE-CAST', Club, Xmas '94	2,000
021	---		NYP
022	94	'WELSH TOURIST BOARD' 1994 Eisteddfod	4,000
022 g	94	1994 Eisteddfod	1,000
023 g	94	'MANCHESTER UNITED F.C.'	10,000
024	---		NYP
025	94	'ASTON VILLA'	7,500
026	94	'ZEB'S COOKIES' (US distribution)	2,500
027 g	94	'BLACKBURN ROVERS F.C.'	5,000
028 g	94	'BONE BROS', (Garden Centre)	2,000
029 g	94	'CHESHAM UNITED F.C.'	1,000
030 g	94	'GOLDEN SHRED'.	

Ref.	Intro.	Model	Made
		Robertson's intended promo via Kwik Save stores. First few NC	1,000
031	94	'QUEENS PARK RANGERS F.C.'	1,200
032	94	'DERBY COUNTY F.C.'	1,200
033	94	'BARNET F.C.'	1,200
034	94	'BRISTOL ROVERS	1,200
035 g	94	'ARSENAL F.C.'	2,000
036 g	94	PETERBOROUGH F.C.'	1,100
037 g	94	'BIRMINGHAM CITY F.C.'	1,200
038 g	94	'CITY LINK'	3,000
039	94	'RMS TITANIC', (World Exhibition)	2,000
040 g	95	'CUTTY SARK GREENWICH'. Sold on board the 'Cutty Sark'	2,000
041 g	94	'SKIPS'	1,100
042 g	95	'JOHN WEST'	60,000
043 g	94	'The LONDON GAS MUSEUM'	2,500
044 g	94	'GAS LIGHT & COKE COMPANY'	2,500
045 g	95	'BOSTIK'	5,000
046 g	95	'SODA CRYSTALS' (black roof and base, see 069G)	12,500
047 g	95	'STANLEY TOOLS'	2,500
048 g	95	'STOCKLEY'S SWEETS'	2,500
049	95	'SUNBLEST'. Double offer with 050G	35,000
050 g	95	'SUNBLEST', '50 Golden Years'. Double offer with 049	35,000
051 g	95	'IMPERIAL BITTER'. First 500 models not certificated	2,500
052 g	95	'KING HENRY Grammar School Coventry 45th Anniversary	1,000
053	95	'SHEFFIELD STEELERS' Wembley Basketball Champions 94/95	1,000
054 g	95	'STORK MARGARINE' 75th Anniversary	25,000
055 g	96	'BEN SHAWS' (soft drinks)	15,000
056 g	95	'PORKINSON BANGER'	7,500
057 g	95	'CHARTRIDGE PARK GOLF CLUB'. (Distributed at Pro-Am tournaments)	1,000
058	95	'NOTTINGHAM Parking Services'	2,000
059 g	95	'DOUWE EGBERTS'	2,500
059	95	'DOUWE EGBERTS'	1,000
061 g	95	'COLDSTREAM' (car care products)	2,000
062 g	96	'BULMERS'	2,000
063 g	95	'MELTONIAN' ('175 Years')	1,000
064 g	95	'MILLWALL F.C.'	1,250

Ref.	Intro.	Model	Made
065	95	'CHARLTON ATHLETICS F.C.'	1,250
066 g	95	'BUDGENS', (milk)	15,000
067 g	95	'RED LION', Little Missenden	5,000
068 g	95	'DUBLIN CRYSTAL'	10,000
069 g	95	'SODA CRYSTALS', (046g with red roof and base)	20,000
070 g	96	'DIAL-A-BEAR'. (St.Valentine's)	10,000
071	96	'FORCE WHEAT'	17,500
072 g	96	'ACDO'	18,000
073 g	95	'OXFORD DIE-CAST', Collectors Gazette	40,000
074 g	95	'CHESHAM BUILDING SOCIETY', 150th	15,000
075 g	96	'KILMEADEN CHEDDAR' (Eire)	7,000
076 g	96	'CO-OP '99' TEA	90,000
077 g	96	'CO-OPERATIVE TEA TIME BISCUITS', (Co-op '99' Tea)	90,000
078	96	'CO-OP TEA', 'English and Scottish'	90,000
079 g	96	'DUERR'S'	15,000
080	96	'GLIDER BISCUITS', (Co-op '99' Tea)	16,000
081	96	'BENSONS CRISPS' original logo	12,000
082	96	'BENSONS CRISPS', modern logo	12,000
083	96	'CARR-DAY-MARTIN', shoe care	4,500
084	96	'SWANSEA JACK' ('27 Lives Saved') special certificate and booklet	5,000
085 g	96	'VIMTO'	16,000
086	96	'ROYAL BUCKS LAUNDRY', (Chesham), special commemorative certificate	5,000
087	96	'KENNETH WOLSTEN-HOLME'	20,000
088 g	96	'BRYNMILL SCHOOL'	2,500
089 g	96	'STREAMLINE JAM'	25,000
090 g	96	'MANOR HOUSE HOSPITAL'	5,000
091 g	96	'SELLOTAPE'	5,500
092 g	96	'SPICERS' (Sellotape model)	2,500
093 g	96	'SELLOTAPE-VIKING 50th ANNIVERSARY' (Sellotape model)	2,500
094 g	96	'DUDLEY' (Sellotape model)	2,500
095 g	96	'HEART of BRITAIN' Royal Brompton Hospital / Daily Mirror	5,500
096gh	96	'HAMLEYS'	5,000
097 g	96	'SCO-FRO' / 'ICELAND', 2 sides	2,500
098gu	96	'THORSEN TOOLS', US model	2,500

Ref.	Intro.	Model	Made
099 g	96	'MACAW Kwiksave'	2,900
100	97	'KEN JONES & SON' builders	1,250
101 g	96	'PG TIPS', with certificate	10,000
		with product, no certificates	40,000
102 g	96	'WALLACE WHISKEY'	2,500
103 u	96	'AGH', (attorneys), US model	1,000
104	97	'HARRY RAMSDEN'S'	2,600
105 g	97	'SELLOTAPE'	5,000
106 g	97	'JOHN WEST'	38,000
107	97	'MINSTREL', (Eire only), with certificate	4,600
		uncertificated	8,000
108 g	97	'LUTON F.C.'	2,600
109	97	'COLCHESTER FC'	2,500
110 g	97	'TITANIC'	5,100
111	97	'SIMON TAYLOR', (furniture)	2,500
112	97	'CENTENARY Sunday School'	1,250
113 g	97	'BOOTHS Supermarket'	15,000
114	97	'HELP the AGED', ('Single Service')	40,000
115 g	97	'SCOPE', ('Single Service')	40,000
116	97	'PACE', ('Single Service')	5,000
117 g	97	'TULLAMORE'	15,000
118 g	97	'YORK CITY F.C.'	2,000
119 g	97	'PORTSMOUTH F. C.'	1,200
120 g	97	'AUTOMOBILIA'	1,200
121	97	'NAT. GRID'	1,750
122gu	97	'GRANTS FARM BREADS', (USA)	25,000
123 g	97	'BOOKER'	4,000
124 g	97	'SCOTCH WHISKEY CENTRE'	10,000
125 g	97	'The PUZZLER MAGAZINE'	10,000
126 g	97	'WALKERS NONSUCH TOFFEE'	8,000
127 g	97	'NEW ZEALAND LAMB', '75 Years'	6,000
128gu	97	'DAYS INN', (USA - 2nd in series)	10,000
129	97	'SAFFRON WALDEN LAUNDRY'	1,500
129 g	97	'SAFFRON WALDEN LAUNDRY'	1,100
130	98	'J. SAINSBURY'	28,000
131 g	98	'BOLTON EVENING NEWS'	2,500
132 g	98	'ELECTRICITY', ('SEEBOARD')	1,100
133	98	'The BUCKS EXAMINER'	2,500
134	97	'OXFORD DIE-CAST', Club, Xmas 97	10,000
135 g	98	'MICHAEL BUTLER', (leather goods)	2,500
136 g	98	'CHAMPION'	15,000

Morris ('Bullnose') Van
continued

137 g	98	'LYTHAM St ANNES EXPRESS'	1,500
138 g	98	'MICHELIN'	5,000
139 g	98	'DANEPAK'	45,000
140 g	98	'HORLICKS FARMS', (cheese)	20,000
141	98	'OSCARS'	2,500
142 g	98	'Mr BRAINS'	10,000
143 g	98	'Geo. ADAMS'	10,000
144ga	98	'JOHN WEST'	20,000
145 g	98	'HEART of MIDLOTHIAN'	5,000
146 g	98	'BOVRIL'	48,000
147 g	98	'O.D.C. NEATH'	2,600

Ford Model 'T' Tanker

013 t	96	'CO-OP COCOA', (Co-op '99' Tea)	90,000
028 tg	96	'VIMTO'	16,000
057 t	97	'BENZINE', '2nd Battalion', WW1	2,600

'Sporting Heroes'

'SPORTING HEROES' range models have certificate which is signed personally by the named celebrity. £5-95 each.

SH1g	95	John Emburey, testimonial	5,000
SH2g	98	Geoff Boycott, England	5,000
SH3g	97	Gordon Banks, Stoke City colours	5,000
SH4g	97	Geoff Boycott, Yorkshire	5,000
SH5	98	Stanley Matthews	4,000
SH6g	97	Gavin Hastings, Scotland colours	5,000
SH7g	97	Rob Andrew, England colours	5,000
SH8g	97	Ieuan Evans, Wales colours	5,000
SH9g	96	Nigel Winterburn, testimonial	1,100
SH10	97	Nick Popplewell	5,000

Novelty Advertising Vehicles

004	93	'OUTSPAN'	NC
004 a	96	'OUTSPAN GRAPEFRUIT'	NC

Renault Bus

B2	96	'PARIS FRANCE' 'Transport de Paris'	4,000

Ford Model 'T' Van

01 tg	95	'OXFORD DIE-CAST', launch model, gold base	2,500
02 tg	95	'WYCOMBE WANDERERS'	1,250
03 tg	95	'ARSENAL F.C.'	1,250
04 tg	95	'PURA OIL'	10,000
05 tg	95	'BUDGENS MILK TETRA PACK'	15,000
08 tg	95	'OXFORD DIE-CAST', Club Xmas '95	6,000
09 tg	96	'KINGSMILL'	27,500
011tg	96	'SIMPSON STRONG-TIE CONNECTORS' (USA promotional)	7,500
012tg	96	'PLASTI-KOTE'	18,000
016tg	96	'WD-40'	32,000
021 t	96	'CO-OP PELAW POLISH'	16,000
026tg	96	'CARR-DAY-MARTIN'	4,000
027tg	96	'VIMTO'	16,000
030tg	96	'COUNTRY LIFE'	60,000
032th	96	'HAMLEYS'	5,000
034tg	96	'EPICURE'	15,000
035tg	96	'THE GAZETTE', 'The Gazette: 9, Blackpool: 0'	2,500
036 t	96	'AMBULANCE', First World War model	2,600
038tg	96	'PG TIPS', cert. to the trade	40,000
039tg	96	'PG SCOTTISH BLEND', with cert.	4,500
		promotional	8,000
042tg	97	'WATERFORD CRYSTAL'	5,200
044tg	97	'MANOR HOUSE HOSPITAL'	6,100
045tg	97	'TITANIC'	5,100
047tgu	97	'NEW YORKER CHEESE', lhd	2,600
048tg	97	'E. H. BOOTH & Co.' (supermarkets)	15,000
049tgu	97	'DAYS INN'	15,000
050 t	97	'RNIB', ('Single Service' sugar)	40,000
051tg	97	'HEARING DOGS', ('Single Service')	40,000
053tg	97	'WIMPEY'	10,000
055tg	97	'HOLLAND'S Pies'	7,500
056 t	97	'SIEBE AUTOMOTIVE'	1,050
060tgu	97	'GEC MARCONI'	1,250
061 tg	97	'WALKERS NONSUCH TOFFEE'	8,000
067tg	98	'DAILY RECORD'	8,000
068tg	98	'SOREEN'	12,500
069tgu	98	'GRANT'S FARM'	20,000
070tgu	98	'COLONIAL'	15,000
071 t	98	'SHELDONS'	4,000

Chevrolet Pick-Up

C001	97	'OXFORD DIE-CAST' launch model	5,000
C002	98	'NORBERT DENTRESSANGLE'	6,000
C003u	98	'DAYS INN'	10,000
C004u	98	'U.S. NAVY'	3,000
C005	98	'FREMLINS'	10,000
C006	98	'TESCO'	12,000

Ford Model 'T' Pick-Up

05 tg	95	'BUDGENS', milk	15,000
06 tg	95	'SODA CRYSTALS'	20,000
07 tg	95	'LAGAN'	5,000
010 tg	96	'KINGSMILL'	27,500
014 tg	96	'CO-OP MILK', (Co-op '99' Tea)	90,000
015 t	96	'FEDERATION FLOUR', (Co-op '99' Tea)	90,000
017 t	---		NYP
018 t	96	'E. L. RHYS', coal	25,000
019 tg	96	'FRESH MILK', (Co-op '99' Tea milkman deliveries promo)	40,000
020 t	96	'WOODGATE DAIRIES'	2,000
022 t	96	'CO-OP COAL'	16,000
023 t	---		NYP
024 t	96	'CHIVERS', Canada	4,000
024 g	96	'CHIVERS', Canada	2,000
025 tg	96	'DUERRS', jam jar	15,000
029 tg	96	'OXFORD DIE-CAST', Club, Xmas '96	9,200
031 t	96	'COUNTRY LIFE'	8,000
033 th	96	'HAMLEYS'	5,000
037 tg	96	'BLACKFRIARS'	3,000
040 t	---		NYP
041 tg	97	'JOHN WEST'	328,000
043 t	97	'WATERFORD CRYSTAL'	5,200
046 t	97	'ARMY PROVISIONS', WW1, sacks	2,600
048 tg	97	'E. H. BOOTH & Co', (supermarkets)	15,000
052 t	97	'SINGLE SERVICE'	5,000
054 tg	97	'SODA CRYSTALS', (4th in series)	25,000
058 tg	97	'PERCY DALTON'	5,000
059tgu	97	'GRANTS FARM BREADS', USA	25,000
062 t	97	'B2', 'US', WW1, (members only)	2,600
063 t	98	'J. SAINSBURY'	28,000
064 t	98	'J. SAINSBURY'	28,000
065 t	98	'CHESHAM DAIRIES Ltd.'	2,500
066tg	98	'Mr BRAINS'	20,000
072 t	98	'AIRFIX'	6,000
073tgu	98	'SUPERFRESH'	15,000
074tu	98	'RAISIN BRAN'	28,000

Sets of models

1996
'BRONCHO BILLS CIRCUS' ..5,250
Six models in special box:
Morris Van, 'ALFREDO the HUMAN CANNON-BALL'
Morris Van, 'MADAME ZELDA, FORTUNE TELLER'
AEC Bus, 'ADVANCE BOOKING OFFICE'
Ford 'T' Van, 'PUBLICITY DEPT.'
Ford 'T' Pick-up, 'ANIMAL FEED'
Ford 'T' Water Tanker, 'ELEPHANT HERD'

'WORLD CUP SET' 20,000
Twelve Morris vans commemorating the 1966 World Cup winning team England vs Germany.

AEC Bus

B1	96	'OXFORD DIE-CAST', launch model	4,000
B3	96	'JOHN WEST'	50,000
B4	96	'KINGS HEAD', ODC Club model	7,500
B5	96	'NATIONAL MOTOR MUSEUM'	5,000
B6	96	'FOTORAMA'	8,000
B7	96	'CO-OP'	16,000
B8	96	'VIMTO'	16,000
B9	96	'SODA CRYSTAL'	19,000
B10	96	'OUTSPAN'	20,000
B11	96	'STREAMLINE'	25,000
B12	96	'HEART of BRITAIN', Royal Brompton Hospital / Daily Mirror	5,500
B14	96	'COUNTRY LIFE'	8,000
B15 h	96	'HAMLEYS'	10,000
B13	96	'OLE BILL' Bus	2,600
B16	97	'BEKONSCOT MODEL VILLAGE'	4,000
B17	96	'WALLACE WHISKEY LICQUER'	4,000
B18	97	'PG TIPS'	8,000 2
B19	97	'OAKEY'	4,200
B20	97	'WATERFORD CRYSTAL'	
B21nc	97	'INTERNATIONAL MEDICAL' Holland	2,600
B22	97	'ARSENAL F.C.'	2,500
B23	97	'E. H. BOOTH & Co', (supermarkets)	15,000
B24	97	'RNLI'	40,000
B25	97	'NSPCC'	40,000
BR26f	97	'HERALD TRIBUNE', (French issue)	2,500
B27	97	'NOTTINGHAM'S MARKETS'	2,500
B28	97	'MANOR HOUSE HOSPITAL' (3rd)	5,300
B29	97	'ELIZABETH II - PHILIP' (50 years)	5,000
B30	97	'BUDGENS Milk'	7,500
B31	98	'J. SAINSBURY'	28,000
B32	97	'DUBLIN CRYSTAL', (2nd), Eire	5,000
B33	97	'London Welcomes Our Boys Home'	3,200
B34	98	'BEAMISH'	5,000
B35	98	'TULLAMORE'	25,000
B36	98	'NOTTINGHAM FOREST F. C.'	5,000
B37	98	'BABBACOME Model Village'	2,600
B38	98	'BOVRIL'	48,000
B39	98	'SOREEN'	12,500
B40u	98	'DAYS INN'	10,000
B41	98	'BOLTON Evening News'	5,000
B42	98	'TESCO'	12,000

Display Cases

Wooden cabinets with 'Oxford Die-Cast' logo on front. Available in a variety of finishes.

OD1   24 x 16 in. , vertical, 7 shelves..........................
OD1a   24 x 16 in. , horizontal, 5 shelves..........................
OD2   32 x 22 in. , vertical, 11 shelves .
OD2a   32 x 22 in. , horizontal, 7 shelves..........................

Information required !

Many toys and models exist about which we know very little. The 1940s in particular saw a proliferation of small manufacturers (often only a one-man operation in a North London shed). In this post-wartime period the established manufacturers were engaged in an export drive that meant shortages of products at home. Not surprisingly, enterprising ex-servicemen and others turned their hands to toy production on a scale that they could manage. Their range was small (sometimes only one product) and they were often in business for only a year or two.

One outcome of this is that some toys and models discovered in attics or at swapmeets present us with a puzzle. Who made the item? When were they in production? Where was the maker's workshop? Very often there is no information at all on the product or simply a statement to the fact that it was 'Made in England'. Identification is sometimes diffcult – but is it impossible?

In a effort to bring as much information as possible to collectors of diecast, we seek your help. If you have, or know of any information that would help identify any of these oddities (from any period) please write to:

The Editor, Swapmeet Publications, PO Box 47, Felixstowe, Suffolk, IP11 7LP.

Here is list of small manufacturers from the 1930s, 1940s and 1950s. You may know of others.

Arbur	Condon	John Hill & Co.	Mafwo	Tal Developments
Baxtoys	W.H.Cornelius	Jolly Roger	Millbo	Teddy Toys
Betal	Denzil Skinner	Kenbo	Millbro	Industries
BMC	Eaglewall Plastics	Kenbro	Model Toys	Toby
Bren L Toys	Empro	Kemlow	Moultoys Ltd	Toy Products
Castle Art	Gaiety	Kitmaster	Salco	Trent Products
Cherilea	Goody Toys	Knight	Slikka	Wardie
City Toys	Johillco	Louis Marx	Sundaw	

ARBUR PRODUCTS   BREN L TOYS   TOBY   JOLLY ROGER

Official Company Acknowledgements

The names 'DINKY TOYS', 'SUPERTOYS', 'MATCHBOX', 'MODELS of YESTERYEAR', '1-75 SERIES', 'SKYBUSTERS', SUPER KINGS', 'BATTLE KINGS', 'SEA KINGS', 'The DINKY COLLECTION', 'TYCO-MATCHBOX' and 'MATCHBOX COLLECTIBLES' are trademarks of the Mattel Group of companies and are subject to extensive trade mark registrations (Marca Registrada) 1987 and 1988.
The names 'CORGI TOYS', 'CARS OF THE '50s', 'CORGITRONICS', 'CORGIMATICS', 'HUSKY', 'JUNIORS', 'ROCKETS' and 'CAMEOS' are all acknowledged as trademarks of Corgi Classics Ltd.
The names 'CORGI CLASSICS' and 'ORIGINAL OMNIBUS COMPANY' are acknowledged as trademarks of Corgi Classics Ltd.
The names 'LLEDO', 'MODELS OF DAYS-GONE', 'DAYS-GONE', 'VANGUARDS' and 'MARATHONS' are acknowledged as trademarks of the Hobbies, Collectables and Gifts Group.
'BRITAINS' is acknowledged as the trademark of Britains Ltd.

'EXCLUSIVE FIRST EDITIONS' is acknowledged as a trademark of Gilbow (Holdings) Ltd.
The name 'OXFORD DIE-CAST' is acknowledged as the trademark of Oxford Die-Cast Ltd., Aylesbury, Bucks.
The name 'TRI-ANG' is acknowledged as a trademark of Hornby Hobbies Ltd., Margate, Kent.
Meccano Magazines. With reference to the pages reproduced in the Catalogue, it is acknowledged that the trade name 'MECCANO' is the registered trademark of Meccano SA, of Calais, France.
Manufacturers and company trade names and logos
All the names of actual vehicles either listed or displayed as models in the Catalogue are the registered trademarks of the manufacturers of those products. Similarly, all company logos or trade advertisements displayed on model pictures or listed in the Catalogue are the registered trademarks of the respective companies.

Acknowledgements

The Editor would like to express his appreciation to these contributors for sending in new information:
SPOT-ON   Ian Mair, Maidstone, Bruce Sterling, New York City
BRITAINS   Hugo Marsh, Christie's South Kensington, London
TIMPO   Barry Potter of Barry Potter Auctions

MATCHBOX   R. Hoeksema, The Hague, Holland
               Eric Greenhalgh
               Jan Naessens, Moeskroen, Belgium
               R.G.B. Payne, Gaydon, Warwickshire
TAYLOR and BARRETT   Dave Jowett, D&J Fairs
MODERN DIECASTS   Mr G. Baker, Northampton

Abbreviations

A

A.E.C.	Associated Equipment Company
AA	Anti-aircraft
A.A.	Automobile Association
ABC	(ABC-TV) Associated British Cinemas (Television)
A.C.	Auto-Carriers
A.F.S.	Auxilliary Fire Service
AG	Amber glass
AMC	American Motor Corporation
APC	Armoured Personnel Carrier
ATV	Associated Television

B

BA	British Airways
BAC	British Airways Corporation
BB	Black base
BBC	British Broadcasting Corporation
BE	Black engine
BEA	British European Airways
BFPO	British Forces Post Office
BG	Blue glass
bhp	brake horsepower
BLMC	British Leyland Motor Corporation
BMC	British Motor Corporation
BMW	Bayrische Motoren-Werke
B.O.A.C.	British Overseas Airways
BP	British Petroleum
BPT	Black plastic tyres
BPW	Black plastic wheels
BR	British Railways
BRM	British Racing Motors
BRS	British Road Services
B.S.M.	British School of Motoring
BW	Black wheels

C

CA	A type of Bedford van
CE	Chrome engine
CF	A type of Bedford van
CG	Clear glass
CLE	Certificated Limited Edition
cv	chevaux-vapeur (a measure of power)
C.W.S.	Co-operative Wholesale Society
cwt.	hundred-weight

D

DG	(Lledo) Days Gone
DH	De Havilland
Dk.	Dark (shade of colour)
DTB	'Dinky Toys' on base
DUKW	An amphibious military vehicle developed by General Motors in WWII. The letters are not initials or an abbreviation but simply part of an early drawing office reference.

E

E	East
EEC	European Economic Community
E.F.E.	Exclusive First Editions
e.g.	exempli gratia (for example)
EMI	Electrical & Musical Industries Ltd

F

FB	Fire Brigade
Fiat	(or FIAT) Fabbrica Italiana Automobile Torino
fig(s)	figure(s)

G

GB	Green box, or Grey base
G.B.	Great Britain
GBT	Globe-Trotter
GER	Great Eastern Railway
GG	Green glass
GMC	General Motors Corporation
GP	Grand Prix
GPO	General Post Office
GPW	Grey plastic wheels
GR	Georgius Rex
GS	Gift Set
GSP	Gift Set price
GTO	Gran Turismo Omologato
GTV	Gran Turismo Veloce
GUS	Great Universal Stores
GWR	Great Western Railway

H

HM	His/Her Majesty
HMAC	His Majesty's Armoured Car
HMS	His/Her Majesty's Ship
H.M.V.	'His Masters Voice'
hp	horse-power
H.W.M.	Hersham & Walton Motors

I

IBM	International Business Machines
ICI	Imperial Chemical Industries
INTER	(or INTL) International
I.O.M.	Isle of Man

J

JB	James Bond
JCB	Joseph C. Bamford
J.M.T.	Jersey Motor Transport

K

K.D.F.	Kraft durch Freude
K.L.G.	Kenelm Lee Guinness
K.L.M.	Koninklijke Luchtvaart Maatschappij NV (Dutch airline)

L

L.A.P.D.	Los Angeles Police Department
LB	Lesney script box
LE	Limited Edition
LM	Le Mans
LMS	London Midland & Scottish Railway
LNER	London & North Eastern Railway
LNWR	London & North Western Railway
loco	locomotive
logo	lettering, trademark or advertising design
LP	Lledo Promotional
LT	London Transport
Lt.	Light (shade of colour)
Ltd.	Limited (Limited Liability Company)
LWB	Long wheel-base

M

MB	Matchbox
MB	Matchbox Series box
Met.	Metallic
MG	A make of car, derived from 'Morris Garages'
MGA, MGB, MGC	types of MG car
M.I.C.A.	Matchbox International Collectors Association
MK	Moko script box
mm.	millimetres
MOY	Models Of Yesteryear
MPR	Market Price Range
MW	Metal wheels

N

N	North
NAAFI	Navy, Army & Air Force Institutes
N.A.S.A.	National Aeronautics & Space Administration
NB	nota bene (mark well)
NCL	National Carriers Limited
NCO	Non-Commissioned Officer
NCP	National Car Parks
NEC	National Exhibition Centre
NGPP	No guide price at present
nhp	(or n.h.p.) nominal horsepower
No.	Number
NPP	No price possible
NRP	Normal retail price
NS	(or n/s) Nearside
NSPCC	National Society for the Prevention of Cruelty to Children
NW	Narrow wheels

O

OPO	On-pack offer
OG	Orange glass
OS	(or o/s) Offside

P

PB	Propeller blade(s)
PG	Purple glass
PLC	Public Limited Company (see also Ltd.)
P.M.G	Post Master General (Australia)
PO	Post Office
PRM	Promotional model
PSV	Public service vehicle
P.T.T.	Postes-Telephones-Telegraphes

R

RAC	(or R.A.C.) Royal Automobile Club
RAF	Royal Air Force
R.C.M.P.	Royal Canadian Mounted Police
RHD	Right-hand drive
RM	Routemaster (bus)
RN(s)	Racing or Rally number(s)
RNLI	Royal National Life-boat Institution

S

S	South
SB	Silver base
SBRW	Solid black rubber wheels
SBX	Special box
SE	Silver engine
S.F.F.D.	San Francisco Fire Department
S.F.P.D.	San Francisco Police Department
SPW	Silver plastic wheels
SR	Southern Railway, Southern Region
St.	Saint or Street
STP	Scientifically-Treated Petroleum
SWB	Short wheel-base
SWRW	Solid white rubber wheels

T

TC	Twin carburettors
TDF	Tour de France
TK	Type of Bedford truck
TP	Twin Pack
TS	'Touring Secours'
TT	Two-tone (or Tourist Trophy)
TV	Television
TWA	Trans-World Airlines

U

UB	Unboxed, or Unpainted base
UK	United Kingdom
UN	United Nations
US	United States (of America)
USA	United States of America
USAAF	United States Army Air Force
USAF	United States Air Force
USS	United Space Starship
UW	Unpainted wheels

V

VW	Volkswagen

W

W	West
WB	Window box, or White base
WR	Western Region
WW	Wide wheels

Y

YB	Yellow box, or Yellow base
YMCA	Young Mens Christian Association

ER

ER	Elizabetha Regina, (E II R, Queen Elizabeth II), or Eastern Region
ERA	English Racing Automobiles
ERF	Edwin Richard Foden
Est.	Established (or estimate/d)

Swapmeet Publications

The *PRICE GUIDE* for MODEL TRAIN COLLECTORS

1st EDITION

'British Model Trains Catalogue'

You can't afford to be without this unique book – it is just full of vital price and rarity information and it's all in one handy volume – 212 pages (32 in full colour). All you need to know to price obsolete 'OO' guage models. We'll refund your money in full if you disagree! Just look at the models listed and priced:

- **Hornby Dublo Trains 1938 – 1964** Locomotives, Rolling Stock and Train Sets
- **Wrenn Railways 1968 – 1992** Locomotives and Rolling Stock
- **Tri-ang and Tri-ang Hornby Railways 1958 – 1994** Locomotives and Rolling Stock

Plus Details of hundreds of actual Auction Results 1996 – 1997
Plus 'O' gauge and larger scale models – detailed Auction Results of the prices achieved by **Hornby Trains, Bassett-Lowke, Trix, Exley, Bing**, etc.

Price £15-95 plus p&p UK and EEC £2-00, Rest of World £6-00. Please ensure that cheques are made payable to Swapmeet Publications. Overseas cheques must be payable in Sterling on a UK bank. Eurocheques acceptable. Payment by credit card acceptable: Visa, Mastercard, Eurocard.

Swapmeet Publications, PO Box 47, Felixstowe, Suffolk, IP11 7LP
Telephone (01394) 670700   Fax (01394) 670730

The 2nd Edition will be available in the Autumn of 2000

'CollectorLink'

A New Service for Catalogue Users

The **CollectorLink Service** bridges the gap between Catalogue editions. Subscribers receive the quarterly **CollectorLink** publication which provides an interesting combination of articles and valuable updating information.

Unique CollectorLink subscriber's benefits include:

- **CollectorLink Model Sales Service** - sell your surplus models to other Catalogue users by using the very low-cost in-house magazine advertising opportunities.
- **Sales by Auction** - Specially discounted rates available to subscribers. Online auction sales also arranged!
- **Price Watch Features** - keeps you aware of potential price trends.
- **Auction Results Review** - a quarterly review of the key results.
- **Market Price Report** - a review of the results achieved by rarer issues.
- **BMCA - British Model Collectors Association** - Subscribers to **CollectorLink** gain free membership of the BMCA which offers special services such as Collection Insurance (UK only) and Valuation Reports.

'CollectorLink' Introductory Subscription Offer:

To: Swapmeet Publications, PO Box 47, Felixstowe, Suffolk, IP11 7LP.
I wish to subscribe to the **CollectorLink** *Service and enclose payment of* £_____ (UK £12-50, EEC £15, Rest of the World £17-50).
Please ensure that cheques are made payable to 'Swapmeet Publications'.
Overseas cheques must be payable in Sterling and drawn on a UK bank.
Eurocheques are acceptable.   Visa ☐   Mastercard ☐   Eurocard ☐
Credit Card No. | | | | | | — | | | | | | — | | | | | | — | | | | |

Expiry date _____ Signature _____
Name (BLOCK CAPITALS, please) _____
Address _____
_____

Post code: _____ Telephone _____

If you prefer not to cut your Catalogue page, a photocopy or even your details on a separate sheet of paper would be acceptable.

8th Edition
British Diecast Model Toys Catalogue

Users Survey

Whether you are a collector or a trader, we would greatly value your views on this new Edition and would ask you to kindly complete and return this questionnaire. (If you prefer not to cut your copy of the Catalogue, a photocopy of this page or just your comments on a separate sheet of paper would be equally welcome).

We hope to publish the results of this Survey, and for the three most helpful and constructive replies that we receive, we shall be giving **a year's free subscription** to the collecting magazine or newspaper of their choice.

1   What do you MOST like about the Catalogue? _____
_____
_____
_____

2   What do you LEAST like about the Catalogue? _____
_____
_____
_____

3   Do you like the new format? _____
_____

If you have model information not currently included in the Catalogue, do please send it to us – your costs will be fully refunded.

Name and Address (BLOCK CAPITALS, please) _____
_____
_____
_____
_____

Kindly send your comments to: Swapmeet Publications, PO Box 47, Felixstowe, Suffolk, IP11 7JU

Winners of the 7th Edition 'New Information' Competition:
Tim Walker, Grimsby for new Corgi Toys information
George Beevis, Lacy Scott and Knight Auctions for overall support
David Cooke, Norwich, for Dinky Toys information

Sale and Purchase Record

Date	Models bought or sold	Price

Guide to Advertisers

The Guide to Advertisers has been compiled as an extra service for Catalogue users. Whilst every care has been taken in compiling the listing, the publishers cannot accept responsibility for any errors or omissions. Similarly, the publishers cannot accept responsibility for errors in the advertisements or for unsolicited photographs or illustrations.

CORGI COLLECTOR CLUB APPLICATION FORM – NEW SUBSCRIPTIONS

PLEASE COMPLETE FORM CLEARLY IN INK USING BLOCK CAPITALS

☐ Please enrol me to the Corgi Collector Club

☐ Please enrol me to the Original Omnibus Collectors Club

☐ Please send me a joint subscription to both Clubs

1999 SUBSCRIPTION FEES	UK	Europe	Rest of the World
	£	£	£
Corgi Collector Club	15	17	20
Corgi Original Omnibus Collectors Club	8	9	10
Joint Membership of both Clubs	21	24	27

I enclose a cheque (drawn against a British bank / Postal Order / International Money Order / Eurocheque for £ _____
made out to **Corgi Collector Club**.

OR Debit my credit card (Visa / Mastercard / Switch) number:

| | | | | | | | | | | | | | | | | Expiry date __ /__

Issue Number _____ Signature _____

Name _____

Address _____

_____

_____

Postcode _____

Telephone _____   JR99

COMPLETED APPLICATION SHOULD BE SENT TO: **CORGI COLLECTOR CLUB, PO Box 323, Swansea, UK, SA1 1BJ**